Origins of Agriculture

World Anthropology

General Editor

SOL TAX

Patrons

CLAUDE LÉVI-STRAUSS
MARGARET MEAD
LAILA SHUKRY EL HAMAMSY
M. N. SRINIVAS

MOUTON PUBLISHERS · THE HAGUE · PARIS
DISTRIBUTED IN THE USA AND CANADA BY ALDINE, CHICAGO

Origins of Agriculture

Editor

CHARLES A. REED

MOUTON PUBLISHERS · THE HAGUE · PARIS

DISTRIBUTED IN THE USA AND CANADA BY ALDINE, CHICAGO

to

Robert and Linda Braidwood

General Editor's Preface

The growing threat to the planet and to humanity caused by the over-success of technology has generated severe doubts as to the entire notion of progress so popular in the Western world. But the idea, which seems to have been legitimate throughout our first three million years and which has become questionable only during the last fifty, has been one of species success in accumulating scientific knowledge and technology. And the largest of the giant steps forward, only 10,000 years ago, was the development of agriculture. To find out how that happened — to pull together what all the scientific disciplines have learned of the events and processes — was the object of the major conference reported so well in this book. The conference in turn was occasioned by an unusual congress which brought together scholars from every continent.

Like most contemporary sciences, anthropology is a product of the European tradition. Some argue that it is a product of colonialism, with one small and self-interested part of the species dominating the study of the whole. If we are to understand the species, our science needs substantial input from scholars who represent a variety of the world's cultures. It was a deliberate purpose of the IXth International Congress of Anthropological and Ethnological Sciences to provide impetus in this direction. The *World Anthropology* volumes, therefore, offer a first glimpse of a human science in which members from all societies have played an active role. Each of the books is designed to be self-contained; each is an attempt to update its particular sector of scientific knowledge and is written by specialists from all parts of the world. Each volume should be read and reviewed individually as a separate volume on its own given subject. The set as a whole will indicate what changes are in store for anthropology as scholars from the developing countries join in studying the species of which we are all a part.

The IXth Congress was planned from the beginning not only to include as many of the scholars from every part of the world as possible, but also with a view toward the eventual publication of the papers in high-quality volumes. At previous Congresses scholars were invited to bring papers which were then read out loud. They were necessarily limited in length; many were only summarized; there was little time for discussion; and the sparse discussion could only be in one language. The IXth Congress was an experiment aimed at changing this. Papers were written with the intention of exchanging them before the Congress, particularly in extensive pre-Congress sessions; they were not intended to be read aloud at the Congress, that time being devoted to discussions — discussions which were simultaneously and professionally translated into five languages. The method for eliciting the papers was structured to make as representative a sample as was allowable when scholarly creativity — hence self-selection — was critically important. Scholars were asked both to propose papers of their own and to suggest topics for sessions of the Congress which they might edit into volumes. All were then informed of the suggestions and encouraged to rethink their own papers and the topics. The process, therefore, was a continuous one of feedback and exchange and it has continued to be so even after the Congress. The some two thousand papers comprising *World Anthropology* certainly then offer a substantial sample of world anthropology. It has been said that anthropology is at a turning point; if this is so, these volumes will be the historical direction-markers.

As might have been foreseen in the first postcolonial generation, the large majority of the Congress papers (82 percent) are the work of scholars identified with the industrialized world which fathered our traditional discipline and the institution of the Congress itself: Eastern Europe (15 percent); Western Europe (16 percent); North America (47 percent); Japan, South Africa, Australia, and New Zealand (4 percent). Only 18 percent of the papers are from developing areas: Africa (4 percent); Asia-Oceania (9 percent); Latin America (5 percent). Aside from the substantial representation from the U.S.S.R. and the nations of Eastern Europe, a significant difference between this corpus of written material and that of other Congresses is the addition of the large proportion of contributions from Africa, Asia, and Latin America. "Only 18 percent" is two to four times as great a proportion as that of other Congresses; moreover, 18 percent of 2,000 papers is 360 papers, 10 times the number of "Third World" papers presented at previous Congresses. In fact, these 360 papers are more than the total of ALL papers published after the last International Congress of Anthropological and Ethnological Sciences which was held in the United States (Philadelphia, 1956).

The significance of the increase is not simply quantitative. The input of scholars from areas which have until recently been no more than subject matter for anthropology represents both feedback and also long-awaited theoretical contributions from the perspectives of very different cultural, social, and historical traditions. Many who attended the IXth Congress were convinced that anthropology would not be the same in the future. The fact that the next Congress (India, 1978) will be our first in the "Third World" may be symbolic of the change. Meanwhile, sober consideration of the present set of books will show how much, and just where and how, our discipline is being revolutionized.

As well as a volume on the origins of plant domestication in Africa (edited by J. R. Harlan, J. M. J. de Wet, and A. B. L. Stemler), readers of the present volume will find especially interesting at least twenty-five books in this series on culture theory, adaptation and evolution, and on the archaeology, history, and ethnology of several areas of Asia, Africa, Oceania, and the Americas.

Chicago, Illinois
September 7, 1976

SOL TAX

Preface

My decision to add a final chapter to this book, in an effort to pull together the data and thoughts of the individual authors of the several chapters, has delayed publication by at least a year, and I owe this note of apology to those authors, who will have waited for more than three years from the time of their writing to the day when they can see their articles in print. The only excuse for the delay is one which is true for any professor with a rather heavy load of teaching and advising, plus other academic duties: what he appears to be doing is only the tip of an iceberg; there is much to do and little time for the doing.

If this book serves to clarify the issues and present the problems of agricultural origins for botanists, zoologists, anthropologists, demographers, agricultural historians, and paleo-environmentalists in such a way that new students become fascinated with the challenges, it will have accomplished its purpose.

Many persons contributed to the success of the meeting held at the Woodstock Conference Center and to the subsequent work which went into the book that emerged rather slowly from the proceedings of that conference and from the chapters submitted by the individual authors. Ms. Judith Krysko was the efficient secretary for the conference and has continued her interest and active participation by typing and sometimes retyping many of the chapters and bibliographies during the intervening years. Others, too, have been called upon for typing and retyping; of these numerous helpers I signal out Ms. Elvira Bayod, graduate student in anthropology at the University of Illinois at Chicago Circle, for her particular industry. Ms. Adina Kabaker, who was a member of the conference and is also a graduate student in anthropology at Chicago Circle, spent more than one hundred hours doing proofreading, besides being helpful in many other ways. Ray Brod, cartographer for the Department of Geography, Chicago Circle, was the skillful artist who drew the figures for the last chapter. Karen Tkach, of Mouton's editorial office in The Hague, was responsible for patiently (and sometimes impatiently) pushing the often-inert editor toward finishing the last chapter.

Finally, a great debt of thanks — a debt hitherto unknown to all members of the conference other than myself — is owed to my wife, Lois Reed, for without her efforts no conference could have occurred. Conferences cost money: people must be transported from various parts of the world, housed, fed, entertained to some degree, and sent home again. All of my own efforts to find the several thousands of dollars necessary to have a conference were unavailing; I spent two summers trying, and failed. My wife then succeeded, by an appeal to a donor who wishes to remain anonymous.

Chicago, Illinois   CHARLES A. REED
July 19, 1976

Table of Contents

SECTION FIVE: CONCLUSIONS

SECTION SIX: APPENDIX

Introduction

CHARLES A. REED

This volume has resulted from a conference on the origins of agriculture held prior to and in conjunction with the IXth International Congress of Anthropological and Ethnological Sciences.

The conference has had its historical origins in my shared field experiences in the Near East with Robert and Linda Braidwood,[1] Bruce Howe, Herbert Wright, Hans Helbaek, Jack Harlan, Patty Jo Watson, Kent Flannery, Frank Hole, Charles Redman, and numerous others. One of the avowed purposes of the expeditions of the Prehistoric Project of the University of Chicago's Oriental Institute, expeditions organized and directed by R. Braidwood (1972), was the exploration, through field archaeology and studies in biology and environments, of the origin and early history of agriculture, with an emphasis on the Near East. At several informal meetings, mostly at the Braidwoods' pleasant country home in Indiana, numerous people interested in Near Eastern prehistory continued their discussions; these discussions, our field experiences, and our various stimuli from teaching and reading have broadened our horizons. My own interests, at first concentrated upon problems of domestication of animals, expanded to include the fascinating problems involved with the changing pace of cultural evolution, the origins of plant agriculture, and the changing pattern of the environment, not only for the Near East (where I am most knowledgeable) but for the whole world.

The path leading to this conference became more definite following a

[1] The Braidwoods, in their influence on their students and then both indirectly and directly upon their students' students, fit well the felicitous phrase, "The lengthened shadow of a man and his wife," used so admiringly by Needham (1946) in his short biography of John and Anna Comstock of Cornell University.

meeting at the Oriental Institute in October 1969, when several of us involved in the studies of the late prehistoric period in the Near East presented short public talks to an interested audience. My own unexpressed feeling that we were being quite superficial was, unknown to me at the time, shared by Wright, who subsequently circulated by mail a mimeographed outline (Wright 1970), in which he stressed his firm belief that, at least in the Near East at the end of the Pleistocene, cultural evolution in general and agricultural origins in particular were closely correlated with changes in environment and probably dependent on these. Such environmental determinism was not popular then, nor is it any more so now, but Wright has stuck to his thesis, as can be seen by his paper in this book.

At the time, Wright and I shared duties on a committee that met once or twice a year in Washington, D.C. As a result, we also shared waiting time and talking time in airports, and the idea for this conference was born directly from the resultant conversations.

Antecedent to the history outlined above was my experience as a farmboy. Hardly more than a toddler, I hunted for hen's eggs, rode the horses home from the field, slid on the hay in the barn, watched the rooting of pigs and helped with their feeding, played in the water of irrigation ditches, and pushed my way through fields of grain higher than my head. Later I harnessed the horses, plowed the furrows, planted and harvested the hay, dug the ditches to control the water, milked the cow, picked the fruit, butchered the pigs, fertilized the fields with the animals' manure, and prepared and tended the garden. The toil was long, hard, and financially unrewarding, but I became steeped in the knowledge and the emotion that comes to man with the growing of plants and animals, the annual cycle of the life of a farmer. When I reached the Near East I was once again with farmer folk, who functioned as they and their ancestors had for millennia, and as we excavated in the prehistoric villages — Jarmo, Sarab, Banahilk, Gerikihaciyan, Çayönü, and others — I felt kinship with the people of those villages; they too had lived the annual cycle of planting and reaping of plants, of births and deaths of animals, gaining their bread and their meat by the sweat of their brow.

A man is led to wonder, each of us at our conference has come by his own path to wonder: Why and how did man and his wife begin their farming? Why, after millions of years of hunting and gathering — with emphasis on the gathering — did man become a settled farmer? Why — the major question, why, why — did man in several parts of the world begin growing plants and domesticating animals at nearly the same time? After millions of years of hunting and gathering, the beginnings of domestication of plants and animals occurred within a period of only four thousand years in the Near East, southeastern Asia, northern China, south-central Mexico, and highland Peru (Table 1). Are these situations

Table 1. Chronology of earliest evidences of agriculture

Near East	?Domestic sheep, 10,750 B.P., Zawi Chemi Shanidar; cultivated emmer and einkorn from base of Çayönü, 9000 + B.P., domestic sheep by 9000 B.P.
Southeastern Asia	Taro and rice by 8000 B.P. (or earlier?)
Northern China	Millet and pigs, 6000 B.P. (or earlier?)
Middle America	Summer squash, possibly by 9790 B.P., certainly by 9300 B.P., at Guila Naquitz Cave, Oaxaca
Peru	Gourds, beans, and guinea pigs by 7000 B.P.?; major domestiaction of squashes and cotton soon after 5000 B.P.

Dogs are not included in this table as dogs were domesticated by hunters and gatherers, independently of the processes involved in the origins of agriculture. Dogs may well have become domestic in southwestern Asia by 12,000 B.P., but we do not know how widespread domestic dogs may have been at that time.

related or independent? If related directly by cultural diffusion (see the paper in this volume by Carter on "a single origin of agriculture"), how did man, with the primitive technology most of us think typical of nine or ten thousand years ago, cross Great Ocean, the fearsome wide and lashing sea, from one hemisphere to another? If independent phenomena, what were the factors, presumably similar factors, which separately led people of diverse races and cultures to the same principles of preparing the ground, planting, harvesting, storing the seed, preparing the ground, and planting again? Was there something mystic, preordained, the farming following inexorably when a particular (but hitherto unexplained) level of cultural complexity had been reached? Can we rely upon such an obvious explanation as the general warming and associated environmental transformation at the end of the Pleistocene, with new opportunities offering a challenge and certain cultures having the necessary complexity to effect a response — the response being toward agriculture? Is challenge-and-response a valid principle in prehistory? What were the responses to such environmental changes at the end of the Pleistocene of the people who did not become farmers?

Why farm at all? Farming by hand, or even with the help of domestic animals, has always been hard work, and mostly dull, whereas hunting-and-gathering — as numerous authors delight in telling us — provides the necessities of life with much less exertion, and, at least for the masculine hunters, is often exciting and also the stuff of which myth is made.

We find the contrast embedded in English mores and English literature; compare for instance:

Homeward plods the weary ploughman[2]

with the excitement of the hunter in pursuit of his quarry:

The stag of warrant, the runnable stag,
The runnable stag with his kingly crop,
Brow, bay and tray and three on top,
The royal and runnable stag.[3]

The farmer can only be exhorted to be steadfast, and plan his life with care:

Ye rigid ploughman bear in mind
    Your labour is for future hours:
Advance — spare not — nor look behind —
    Plough deep and straight with all your powers![4]

But the hunter ever exults in his skill:

An archer keen I was withal,
    As ever did lean on greenwood tree;
And I could make the fleetest roebuck fall,
    A good three hundred yards from me.[5]

The pattern continues; a recent author makes the contrast on opposite pages (Shepard 1973: 154–155):

Although it has long been fashionable to describe it so, the world of the hunting and gathering peoples is not a vale of constant demonic threat and untold fears. It is a life of risk gladly taken, of very few wants, leisurely and communal, intellectual in ways that are simultaneously practical and aesthetic. Most pertinent to our time, it is a life founded on the integrity of solitude and human sparseness, in which men do not become a disease on their environment but live in harmony with each other and with nature. The ways of the hunters are beginning to show us how we are failing as human beings and as organisms in a world beset by a "success" that hunters never wanted.

On the next page, the same author continues:

The capacity to learn to do brain surgery or play the piano may represent final touches added by our species. If so, the activity responsible for that final and delicate perfecting is probably the making and using of tools by early man for

[2] Thomas Gray, "Elegy Written in a Country Churchyard."
[3] John Davidson, "The Runnable Stag."
[4] Richard Henry Horne, "The Plough."
[5] Thomas Love Peacock, "Friar's Hunting Song."

killing, dissecting, and utilizing animals. Tools associated with the seasonal harvest of domestic grains and preparation of plant materials are gross by comparison. The "good hands" of the hunter is not a familiar image, yet he is the surgeon. Tuber grubbers and soil tillers have hands calloused, arthritic, swollen, and otherwise deformed by their work.

But for the man who thinks and writes thus, the mystique has indeed worked magic in his mind; no population dependent upon hunting and gathering ever produced a culture with brain surgeons or piano players. Only agriculture, with its pattern of population growth, urbanization, and economic surpluses has produced civilization. Our brain surgeons and our pianists come straight from generations of farmer folk, as did I myself, with my dissector's hands.

REFERENCES

BRAIDWOOD, ROBERT J.
  1972   Prehistoric investigations in southwestern Asia. *Proceedings of the American Philosophical Society* 116:310–320.
NEEDHAM, JAMES B.
  1946   The lengthened shadow of a man and his wife. *Scientific Monthly* 62: 140–150, 219–229.
SHEPARD, PAUL
  1973   *The tender carnivore and the sacred game.* New York: Charles Scribner's Sons.
WRIGHT, H. E., JR.
  1970   "Origin of agriculture in the Near East." Unpublished manuscript.

SECTION ONE

General Principles

The Origins of Agriculture: Prologue

CHARLES A. REED

The process of living involves the directed control of the acquisition and use of energy. In the long history of the cosmos, energy flows from centers of concentration to regions of diffusion, but in the process, as Homer Smith (1932) so succinctly said, life is a temporary eddy in the second law of thermodynamics, a temporary — but only a temporary — reversal of entropy.

Each protoplasmic entity must find its own energy or, as with a green plant, be placed in such a position that energy comes to it. Animals find energy by finding food; they eat (*sensu lato*). An amoeba surrounding and ingesting another protozoan, an octopus catching a crab, a cow grazing in a pasture, a fox eating mice, and a man picking and eating wild berries are all akin; they are using their individual protoplasm, their own private protoplasmic system, to provide themselves with the energy necessary for their life processes. Each is a "primary energy trap," not in any sense in relation to its position on the food web — that concept is not involved — but simply because it acquires energy via food by no other means than its own protoplasm. Also, to the degree that it maintains its own continuing individuality (escapes enemies, conserves energy) by using only its own protoplasm and its own cellular system, it functions as a primary energy trap.

Most organisms, whether prokaryote or eukaryote, plant or animal, unicellular or multicellular, are simply primary energy traps; the function without accessory nonprotoplasmic devices. Evolution is adaptive, obviously, and a considerable variety of complex structures has evolved which, while not strictly living, are still an integral part of the protoplasmic system. Bone, for instance, is internal, replaceable, repairable, porous, filled with tissue fluid and permeated by cells, and at the molecular level is a dynamic part of the biochemical system, even though the actual crystals and spicules of bone are extracellular. Bone — even the bone of an armadillo's "shell" — is a functioning part of the inner animal, and is thus part of the primary energy trap.

By contrast, a variety of noncellular structures or merely things, produced by the organisms or existing naturally in the environment, is utilized by animals for the acquiring or conserving of energy, and these can be called "secondary energy traps." (Tools, to be discussed later, are a special kind of secondary energy trap.)

A total catalog and discussion of secondary energy traps would fill a volume larger than this book, but some examples are: secreted, noncellular and nonliving external tests or shells, such as those of Foraminifera and Mollusca; natural cover, holes, crevices, etc., sought and utilized by animals for protection or by a predator for concealment, or similar structures (burrows) constructed by an animal for the same purposes; external secretions (mucus, silk, perspiration, body oils, a variety of toxins); tools, either objects naturally occurring in the environment and used without modification or those shaped and thus manufactured; social behavior, whereby the energy expended by the individuals of a group is pooled between them and benefits can accrue thereby which would be impossible for the lone operator (group hunting, food sharing, systems of communication, aid from kinfolk, economic networks, etc.).

Different animals accomplish the same ends differently, some with primary, some with secondary energy traps. A few such contrasts, as examples, are outlined in Table 1.

As typical of evolutionary sequences, a structure evolved in correlation with one function may be modified by secondary or tertiary adaptations as the result of subsequent natural selection. Thus, the silk produced by spiders, ancestrally used as guidelines and to line burrows, in most groups also became a food-catching device, and in some the web then also serves as a channel of communication by which a male may approach a female without being attacked; he must activate the web in a way that a struggling insect would not. Another species of animal, only distantly related, may use some part of the web as a secondary energy trap of its own, to become cross hairs in a transit; this same species takes the stuff of which cocoons are made, a secondary energy trap produced by an insect larva, and modifies that silk into its own secondary energy traps, to win a mate or buy an emperor's favor.

Modifications of behavior, as with the actions of the male spider mentioned above, are often part of such continuing evolution of secondary energy traps; they serve to continue the animal's energy system, which otherwise might be abruptly terminated. Thus, many animals secrete noxious substances to protect themselves from predators. Such poisons are obviously secondary energy traps, protecting the animal's own energy system from oblivion. Some animals, however, improve their efficiency by modifying both behavior and morphology; thus, the poison may be sprayed over an attacker (the bombardier beetles), or an appendage is used to wipe the poison on aggressors (one species of harvestman, or daddy longlegs; Eisner, et al. 1971). Many types of behavior, that of both solitary and social animals, are further examples of the principle that secondary energy traps are subject to natural selection; they have evolved and continue to do so.

From the viewpoint of reproduction, parents (and often other adults) are secondary energy traps, providing at the minimum some food in an egg, and often additional food and many services (protection, teaching) to the young. A nursing mother, to a baby, is a secondary energy trap. Many and complex are the secondary energy traps by which genetic (and in some cases cultural) endowments are passed from one generation to another.

These examples undoubtedly can be found in all phyla of animals — I can think of one such in the Protozoa, for instance — but mention of a few cases among the vertebrates will illustrate the principle. Among the primitive jawless fish, male lampreys prepare a depression ("nest") on the stream bottom in which the female spawns (Brigham 1973); salmon and many other bony fish do the same. This minor depression is some protection to the eggs and thus, to the hatching young, is a secondary energy trap. The eggs of many frogs are laid in a mass of noncellular jelly — a secretion of the female's reproductive system — which inhibits predation. The young of reptiles and birds are protected by an enveloping shell, and usually are deposited in nests, some extremely elaborate. Universally among mammals and almost universally among birds, the young are furnished food, and in many such animals are additionally given the time and effort of teaching. Among a few animals, humans for instance, the expenditure of energy by parents on the young continues long after the latter have reached reproductive age. Sometimes, one thinks, parents are little more than secondary energy traps for their offspring.

Tools, however defined, are all secondary energy traps. In dictionaries and in the numerous articles on tool using among animals, one finds lack of agreement on the precise meaning of the word "tool" (Alcock 1972). I do not intend here to pursue this semantic topic; van Lawick-Goodall (1970) has discussed the problem to some degree in her excellent summary

Table 1.   Some comparisons between primary energy traps and secondary energy traps

Animal	Action or function	Primary energy trap	Secondary energy trap
Most predators of ostrich eggs	Breaking of egg of ostrich	Use of body parts	
Man and Egyptian vulture[a]	Breaking of egg of ostrich		A rock, thrown at the egg
Whalebone whales	Filtering krill	Use of whalebone[b] and tongue	
Most filter feeders[c]	Filtering plankton	Use of part of body as filter	
Some filter feeders	Filtering plankton		Mucous traps as filters[d]
Robber fly	Catching insects	The robber fly is a direct predator	
Orb-weaving spider	Catching insects		Use of spider web as a trap
Trap-door spider	Catching insects		Prepared, silk-lined burrow with hinged door[e]
Polar bear	Protection against cold	Fur[f], fat, warm blood	Seeks or prepares shelter, particularly for sleeping
Man	Protection against cold	Fat, warm blood	Clothing, dwelling, fire[g]
Some insects	Protection between stages	Pupa case[h]	
Some insects	Protection between stages		Cocoon[h]
Most crabs	Protection against aggressors	Use of claws; escape	Threat, a direct communication
Hermit crab *Dardanus*	Protection against octopus		Sea anemone *Adamsia*, placed on adopted shell[i]
Hermit crab *Pagurus*	Protection against larger hermit crabs	Tolerance of commensal hydroids which live on some abandoned snail shells[j]	
Eolidoid nudibranchs	Protection against aggressors		Discharge of stinging cells (nematocysts) derived from consumed coelenterates[k]

[a]   J. van Lawick-Goodall and H. van Lawick (1966); see also Chisholm (1954) for reference to a similar practice of Australian buzzards in breaking emus' eggs.

of tool using among vertebrates. She regarded a tool as an object necessarily manipulated; thus, a rock thrown at or dropped on an egg is (in her opinion) a tool, whereas a rock against which an egg is thrown or upon which it is hammered is not a tool; knitting needles are tools, whereas yarn or the sweater produced by the knitting are not tools; a twig used by a chimpanzee to pull termites from a termite mound is a tool, but the nests the chimpanzees make — or that birds or other mammals make — are not tools.

Considering the problem from the viewpoint of secondary energy traps, the differences between these categories of tools and nontools (as used by

---

[b] In the mysticete whales, the filter (the so-called "whalebone") is an epidermal structure, and, thus, cellular and originally living tissue.

[c] The filter, whether antennae or mouthparts or other, is a part of the cellular structure of the animal's body.

[d] Mucus is a secreted, noncellular, nonliving substance. Even the mucus of pharyngeal filter feeders such as tunicates and *Branchiostoma* (= *Amphioxus*) amongst chordates is a secondary energy trap, since the whole of the digestive cavity of any metazoan is not INSIDE the animal but is merely a part of the external universe that is surrounded by the animal. The fanciest filter feeder that comes to mind is that of a marine pteropod (a particular kind of free-swimming, shell-less snail) which spreads a filmy net of mucus in seawater and then consumes it along with the trapped plankton (Gilmer 1972).

[e] The "home" of the trap-door spider is of course a secondary energy trap in that it hides and protects the spider, thus conserving its energy and continuing its being, but the "home" is more; as a camouflaged lair from which the spider can spring upon its prey, the "home" is a basic part of the feeding pattern, thus having a double function as a second energy trap.

[f] Hair, like whalebone, is composed of cells; these, once alive, are a part of the body, not a noncellular secretion from it.

[g] Fire was the first chemical reaction (oxidation) used as a secondary energy trap by man. Although man was the first to use fire, the slower oxidation of rotting vegetation has been used for millions of years by various other animals to control temperatures of domiciles (as with some ants) or nests of eggs. See Clark (1964) for a most interesting case among birds.

[h] A pupa case is a part of the animal's body, but a cocoon, like a spider's web, consists of a nonliving, noncellular secretion.

[i] Reilly and Stone (1971). The abandoned snail's shell which the hermit crab adopts is also, of course, a secondary energy trap for the crab using it, as it previously was for the snail.

[j] *Pagurus*, where in competition with populations of larger hermit crabs, may have his adopted snail shell taken from him by one of the larger hermits. If, however, an individual of *Pagurus* can find an empty snail's shell with hydroids growing on it, he can probably occupy it safely, as the populations belonging to *Pagurus* have evolved a natural immunity to the poison of the hydroids, an immunity lacking in the species of larger hermit crabs, which sometimes attempt to occupy such a shell with hydroids but are soon forced to leave (Wright 1973).

[k] The nudibranchs (shell-less, noncoiled, surface-creeping marine snails) feed on hydroids, jellyfishes, sea anemones, and corals; the delicately triggered nematocysts of these coelenterates are passed intact through the wall of the digestive tract and then through the tissues of the nudibranch, to be stored in special sacs in spurs on the back, discharging finally against aggressors attacking the nudibranch (Zeiller 1971).

van Lawick-Goodall and by Alcock) are not so important. All of the examples listed above are secondary energy traps in that the various objects provide means for utilization or conservation of energy which would not be available to a particular animal were it limited to the use of its own body without the additional help of the external object.

Unless one wishes the meaning of the word "tool" to include all secondary energy traps, a definition of the subcategory intended is obviously necessary, and probably the concept agreed upon by van Lawick-Goodall and Alcock is the easiest, even if to my own mind unduly restrictive. I myself have always automatically thought, in agreement with Lancaster (1968), that nests of birds in particular, but also those of such mammals as build nests (chimpanzees, for instance) are tools; they are built by the animal of objects manipulated to form a structure, and are used for a definite purpose. However, once one has crossed the line of the definition established so succinctly by Alcock — "Tool-using involves the manipulation of an inanimate object, not internally manufactured, with the effect of improving the animal's efficiency in altering the position or form of some separate object" — one would find difficulty, I can see, in locating another definitional boundary.

This digression into the use of the word "tool" is necessary in this introductory chapter because cultivated plants and domestic animals have sometimes been regarded as living tools of humans. By the above definition they would generally be excluded. A harness is a tool if used to pull a wagon which moves an object in a way that increases human efficiency; in this operation the wagon is also a tool, but the horse that wears the harness and pulls the wagon is not a tool. However, for the man involved, all three — horse, harness, and wagon — are secondary energy traps. Glue in a pot is not a tool (although presumably the pot is), but the same glue actually used in the process of manufacturing becomes a tool — or does it? Alcock stated that a tool must be an object, and perhaps glue is only a substance. A domestic animal would become a tool if one used a dead chicken to beat another chicken to death and then ate the second chicken. Such gentle chiding aside, the concept of tool use probably does have value in that manipulation of objects (and/or substances) producing changes which increase the user's efficiency would have selective value and thus may well be evolutionarily important. For the purposes of the discussion being presented here by me, the concept of secondary energy traps seems more fundamental.

With regard to feeding and food getting, an efficient technique for making energy available would be for the feeder to have control over the supply of food, whether that control be called husbandry, gardening, horticulture, herding, food production, or agriculture in general. Any action by the feeder which increases the yield of a food in a given area over the natural yield turns the particular plant or animal being fostered into a secondary energy trap for the feeder — the one who then utilizes the additional energy produced. The dominant population has, thus, evolved a mechanism for utilization by itself of a greater part of the energy available in a given environment than was available to its ancestors; the general trend that results is that the population increases over that of the ancestors.

Symbiosis and other kinds of mutualism are not rare in the living world; even such closely related intermutual benefits as the combination of an alga and a fungus to produce a lichen, or the combination of termite and intestinal flagellates to produce a wood-utilizing animal are not so rare. However, the propagation and protection of one species by another, to the benefit of both, ARE relatively rare in the biological world.

The leaf-cutting ants (genera *Acromyrmex* and *Atta*, of the tribe Attini) (Weber 1972) are the most specialized and the most successful of the "gardening" or agricultural ants. The ants cut leaves, blades of grass, or flowers, carry them to underground nests, clean them and chop them, force the pieces into prepared ground, and then transplant mycelia of a particular fungus onto the pieces so implanted. (In competition with human farmers, the ants are sometimes more successful, stripping fruit trees of their leaves.) The fungus grows luxuriantly on the rotting pieces of vegetation, and the ants thrive by eating the fungus. In parts of South America these ants plus the termites comprise the greater part of the animal biomass.

Other kinds of attine ants behave similarly, but use insect droppings or pieces of already-decayed vegetation upon which to grow their fungi. As termites are to flagellates, so are the attine ants to their fungi; neither insect can survive without its symbiotic organism. Each insect has its neural system programmed to maintain the symbiont; the termite, stripped of its necessary fauna by a molt, will beg and receive from a co-worker an anal drop teeming with the necessary protozoans, and the ants instinctively accomplish all of the necessary complex activities to maintain their gardens. The difference, and the reason we call the ants agricultural, is that they prepare the soil, maintain proper temperature and humidity, and plant their fungus. In neither instance can one of the partners survive without the other, but the ants — instinct bound as they seem to be — are not without some modicum of versatility; a population of ants in the laboratory, denied vegetation but furnished with nutrient agar, utilized the unaccustomed substance, planted their mycelia, and successfully reared both fungus and a new generation of ants. Another group, denied their own species of fungus, adopted another species which before had been grown only by another kind of ant.

Numerous other kinds of ants have domestic animals; none of these ants are also horticulturalists, nor do any of the fungus-growing attines keep livestock. Thus, no ant is a complete agriculturalist; only man has achieved that unique capability. All of the ants' livestock (aphids, leaf-hoppers, and scale insects, mealybugs and other coccids) belongs to suck-ing insects of the order Homoptera. Each homopteran inserts a hypo-dermic-like proboscis into the phloem sap of a plant, and sucks much more fluid than it can use. The excess, sweet and nutritious because of contained sugars, fats, and proteins, is normally ejected in jets or droplets from the hindgut. (Dried, this plant sap becomes the "manna" of Exodus, and is supposedly still gathered and eaten by the Bedouins of Sinai.) In both liquid and dried form this "honey-dew" is utilized by many kinds of insects, but certain ants have entered into productive symbiosis with certain homopterans. Most such ants are restricted to one species or a few related species of such sucking insects, but many and strange are the intermutual adaptations (Michener 1951; Sudd 1967; Wilson 1971).

In general, the ants tend, guard, defend, and sometimes transplant their livestock. In return, the aphids particularly, but some of the other homopterans as well, learn not to eject their liquid or kick it away with their hind feet (their typical solution of an obvious problem of sanita-tion), but instead to wait for a herder, and, being stroked by the ant's antennae, let a drop ooze out gradually, to be sucked up by the ant. Indeed, if the ant is disturbed at the feast, an aphid will pull the drop back in. (Cows, which function on a different principle, cannot do this.)

The ants drive off predators, and sometimes, from earth and plant debris, build protective sheds or tunnels for their charges. Greater care is given by ants which nest underground to aphids which feed on rootlets; here the ants care for the eggs of the livestock, as they would for their own, maintain optimal temperature and humidity, and when the aphids hatch, a cleared area is prepared around a rootlet and the aphid is carried to the spot. Indeed, these underground ants are reported sometimes to clip the wings of the sexual, migratory generation of aphids, thus keeping the eggs in the nest.

Certain ants keep scale insects instead of aphids; of these, those in Java move their livestock as desired on their own backs; at a given tactile signal the tiny coccids climb nimbly aboard. A new queen, leaving the nest to start a new colony, will be carrying one or more of the scale insects from the parent colony.

While several examples are known of Homoptera which have not been found except in ants' nests, only one case seemingly is known where both the ant and its domesticate are completely dependent upon each other (Flanders 1957). This population of ant, which lives in Colombia, keeps a particular scale insect; neither ant nor coccid is ever found separately. The nests, which are underground, are always small, and both sanitation and increases of population present potential problems; the ants have solved these problems by rotating the scale insects at the feeding stations (rootlets); typically only 30 percent of the livestock is allowed to feed at one time. When a new queen leaves, she carries a scale insect gently in her jaws as she flies; without the proper "cow" the new colony would be a failure.

Thus, we see that while some ants are agriculturalists, profound differences exist between such ants and men: the ants, although capable of some learning by experience (as tested in the laboratory, Sudd 1967), generally function at an instinctive level; only a few kinds of ants, of one tribe, are gardeners, but many kinds of several subfamilies keep livestock. By contrast, all men belong to but one species, and many if not most human farmers keep one or more kinds of domestic animals while at the same time cultivating plants. In that practice of mixed farming, man is unique in the animal kingdom. Ants are generally limited to the agricultural practices of their nearer ancestors, and must depend upon the slow mechanisms of evolution for any change, while man is culturally adaptable.

Aside from man and the relatively few kinds of attine ants, horticulture is unknown among animals (insofar as I am aware), with the possible exception of the curious case of a marine amphipod (Crustacea), *Dulicha rhabdoplastis*. This tiny animal, a small relative of the better known beach-hopper or sand flea, builds its own elongate, cylindrical, diminutive "farm" on the tip of a spine of the giant red sea urchin *Strongylocentrotus franciscanus*, living on the bottom of Puget Sound, Washington, United States (McCloskey 1971). The farm consists of the tiny amphipod's own feces, carefully placed and glued into position to make an elongate rod, from 2.5 centimeters to almost 4.0 centimeters long. In the summer this rod supports a luxuriant growth of diatoms, a form of unicellular plant, upon which the amphipod feeds, keeping the population spaced by the eating of the larger individuals. Other organisms, which could foul the surface, are carefully removed. The amphipod is not an obligate farmer, for during the winter and in part during the summer it is a filter feeder, ascending to the tip of its rod and spreading its two elongate, multisetaed antennae at right angles to the bottom current. Bits of plankton caught in the intermeshing setae are scraped off as each antenna is drawn through the mouth.

We do not know that *Dulicha rhabdoplastis* is a true horticulturalist, for the incomplete studies to date have not produced evidence that the amphipod plants the diatoms; instead the situation seems to be more similar to several examples known from ethnographic studies, where man weeded and might otherwise protect a patch of esteemed natural vegetation. The amphipod, however, has gone a step beyond this simple pre-agricultural situation, for he carefully prepares an environment which is not only his own home but is an optimum place for the growth of one of his favored foods.

Although man has used individuals of his own species as slaves, in agricultural work and otherwise, thus converting them to secondary energy traps on an economic and social level with domestic animals, slavery is not necessarily correlated with agriculture, either among humans or other animals. Some ants are slaveholders; they raid the nest of certain other species of ants, capture the inert pupae, and bring these back to their own nests. The ants that emerge from the captured pupae then become slaves, procuring food for their masters and feeding and otherwise caring for their larvae. The slaves are not themselves used for food, nor are they bred in captivity. The populations from which the slaves are captured are not dependent upon the slaveholders, but the slaveholders cannot survive without slaves. In this case, the slaves are obviously involuntary secondary energy traps for their masters, but the situation does not involve agriculture; instead it is more akin to the case of men in parts of southeastern Asia who train macaques to climb coconut trees and loosen and drop the nuts for the men to collect (Bertrand 1967). The master gets the coconuts, while the slave, belonging to another species, escapes punishment and is fed as the reward for his success. Agriculture may be but is not necessarily involved, nor are the macaques domestic. They are wild animals that are tamed and trained, as also are elephants who are caught and trained to work.

Agriculture, which includes in the broadest sense the domestication of either plants or animals (or both), is not a common phenomenon. Horticulture amongst the ants was probably innovative in the population ancestral to the tribe Attini, and the practice there has had its own adaptive radiation, coincident with that of the several genera and species of that tribe. The case of the diatom-feeding amphipod, *Dulicha rhabdoplastis*, shows a possible avenue toward true horticulture among non-human animals, particularly arthropods.

With men as with ants, a plant or animal which is protected, reared, and maintained (whether truly captive or not) is a secondary energy trap if it yields a return in energy. Insofar as men or ants furnish labor or protection or food or fertilizer for their charges, the dominant species serves in turn as a secondary energy trap for the domesticate! Man, however, is a canny beast; he will not long serve as a secondary energy trap for a domesticate if the return be less than the investment. Ants, of course, will not do so either, but the pattern is different; man would shift his ground, growing a different crop or quitting the soil for city life, but the ants (if obligate agriculturalists) simply starve to death, as do men sometimes in similar circumstances.

Domesticates which are totally dependent upon ants for survival undoubtedly have been changed genetically by the selective pressures of life under the restrictive conditions of the care by the ants. For similar reasons, plants and animals which have been domesticated by man have almost always been changed genetically — sometimes purposely, but often not; some (hexaploid wheats, maize, bulldogs) have undergone more change, and others (two-rowed barley and cats) less.

Domestication is not a clean-cut concept, and the word is difficult to define. I have become lost in this semantic bog before, and so avoid the morass now. The truth is that all situations are known to occur, from the free-living "wild" animals and plants, through such cases as animals of zoos and circuses (animals which often breed in captivity under conditions of controlled mating), to semidomestic or recently domestic species (white rats, "domestic" cats), to the typical domestic plants and animals (barleys, wheats, oats, rye, millets, etc.; sheep, goats, cattle (*sensu lato*), pigs, horses, guinea pigs, camels, llamas, etc.), to those forms which cannot survive without the assistance of man (maize, Ancon sheep, numerous toy dogs). These and any other categories, however, always have multiple exceptions. And additionally, one is always faced, at the one extreme, with the relative ease of taming some "wild" animals (American bighorn sheep, wolves, pigs), and at the other, with the ease with which many, but not all, of our well-established "domestic" animals (pigs, dogs, horses, water buffaloes) become successfully and even fiercely feral.

Each population of plant and animal that we call domestic — each of the many kinds involved in the topic agriculture — is a subject of its own. Yet agriculture is certainly a unit — the totality of the human practices involving those living secondary energy traps which man plants, breeds, nurtures, grows, guards, preserves, harvests, and prepares for his own use.

REFERENCES

ALCOCK, JOHN
  1972   The evolution of the use of tools by feeding animals. *Evolution* 26:
     464–473.
BERTRAND, MIREILLE
  1967   Training without reward: traditional training of macaques as coconut
     harvesters. *Science* 155:484–486.
BRIGHAM, WARREN U.
  1973   Nest construction of the lamprey, *Lampetra aegyptera*. *Copeia* 1973:
     135–136.
CHISHOLM, A. H.
  1954   The use by birds of "tools" or "instruments." *Ibis* 96:380–383.
CLARK, GEORGE A., JR.
  1964   Life histories and the evolution of Megapodes. *The Living Bird, Third
     Annual of the Cornell Laboratory of Ornithology*, 149–167.
EISNER, T., A. F. KLUGE, J. E. CARREL, J. MEINWALD
  1971   Defense of a phalangid: liquid repellent administered by leg dabbing.
     Science 173:650–652.
FLANDERS, STANLEY E.
  1957   The complete interdependence of an ant and a coccid. *Ecology* 38:
     535–536.
GILMER, RONALD W.
  1972   Free-floating mucus webs: a novel feeding adaptation for the open
     ocean. *Science* 176:1239–1240.
LANCASTER, J. B.
  1968   On the evolution of tool-using behavior. *American Anthropologist* 70:
     56–66.
MC CLOSKEY, LAWRENCE R.
  1971   A marine farmer: the rod-building amphipod. *Fauna, the Zoological
     Magazine* 1:20–25.
MICHENER, CHARLES D.
  1951   *American social insects*. Toronto: D. van Nostrand.
REILLY, C., JANE STONE
  1971   Protection of hermit crabs (*Dardanus* spp.) from octopus by com-
     mensal sea anemones (*Calliactis* spp.). *Nature* 230:401–403.
SMITH, HOMER W.
  1932   *Kamongo*. New York: Viking.
SUDD, JOHN H.
  1967   *An introduction to the behavior of ants*. London: Edward Arnold.
VAN LAWICK-GOODALL, JANE
  1970   Tool-using in primates and other vertebrates. *Advances in the Study of
     Behavior* 3:195–249.
VAN LAWICK-GOODALL, JANE, HUGO VAN LAWICK
  1966   Use of tools by the Egyptian vulture, *Neophron percnopterus*. *Nature*
     212:1468–1469.
WEBER, N. A.
  1972   Gardening ants, the attines. *Memoirs of the American Philosophical
     Society* 92:1–146.

WILSON, EDWARD O.
1971   *The insect societies.* Cambridge, Mass.: The Belknap Press of the Harvard University Press.

WRIGHT, H. O.
1973   Effect of commensal hydroids on hermit crab competition in the littoral zone of Texas. *Nature* 241:139–140.

ZEILLER, WARREN
1971   Naked gills and recycled stings. *Natural History* 80 (December):36–41.

The Earliest Farming:
Demography as Cause and Consequence

BENNET BRONSON

INTRODUCTION: DENSITY AND HUSBANDRY

I propose to discuss here the association between agriculture and population size in very early times in the millennia that separate the Palaeolithic from the first appearance of cities and states. That some such association exists, and that the association is in part causal, can hardly be doubted. But its precise nature remains elusive, the subject of many vexed and convoluted debates from Malthus' and Ricardo's time down to the present day.

Can the apparent explosion of population in the time of the early states be explained entirely by the Neolithic Revolution? Obviously not: the revolution precedes the explosion by several thousand years. Can the one partially explain the other, by saying that food production (i.e. agriculture) is a PRE-CONDITION though not a sufficient explanation for demographic expansion? Perhaps. Such explanations are a staple of elementary text-books in anthropology (and nowadays even history) and may well be limitedly valid. But they suffer from a number of practical defects. They are no longer as productive of important new hypotheses and stimulating research as they were in the 1930's and 1940's .Moreover, they are not so subtle as to inspire anyone with respectful surprise. Such defects may contribute to the relative eclipse of agriculture-as-cause formulations among modern theorists.

On the other hand, the idea that the causality is reversed, with expansion in population supplying the motive force behind agricultural progress, is presently enjoying a modest vogue. One of the principal proponents of this position is the agricultural economist Ester Boserup (1965), who has elaborated a typology of agricultural stages arranged in order of increasing intensity (by wnich she means increased frequency of land use) which evolve from one to another under the influence of the exogenous variable, population density. An attractive feature of the Boserup formulation is that it does not simply assume that more intensive farming appears because increasingly dense populations need it but instead provides a mechanism to explain the changeover. This mechanism depends on the reasonable assumptions that (1) the technology for some kind of agricultural intensification is readily available to most peoples, and (2) that the average farmer is inhibited from employing this technology by the fact that the more intensive systems are also the most labor demanding in terms of output per man-hour. Hence, all agricultural regimes, even if intrinsically quite intensifiable, will remain in the most extensive state possible until the farmers are forced to change through the pressure of population and an increasing scarcity of land.

This straightforward but novel view of agricultural evolution has been received by some (P. Smith and Young 1972; P. Smith 1972) with enthusiasm and has even been extended back into the prehistoric period (Cohen, this volume) on the grounds that hunting and gathering is still more economical of labor than the most extensive forms of true farming — thus, the very existence of agriculture is seen as a response to demographic factors. Others (Bronson 1972) have questioned the applicability of the Boserup model as originally presented, pointing out the lack of empirical evidence for the central proposition that extensiveness and labor efficiency are really correlated and suggesting that there are strong theoretical reasons for doubting that agriculture actually did evolve along a single track as Boserup proposes.

However, the details of this and similar models of agricultural change are not immediately germane. My concern here is to discuss the abstract issue of demographic explanations of subsistence systems, with reference not to recent alterations in farming methods but to the origins of farming itself. Can it be said that population pressure is a sufficient, or necessary, or even plausible precondition to the Neolithic Revolution? More importantly, is it an explanation? Do we gain anything in the way of theoretical rigor or predictive power by postulating a single demographic prime mover to explain all the manifold subsistence choices made by early man?

To answer these questions, I must redefine (or select among the definitions of) several concepts and reconstruct several models of subsistence economics and ancient demographics. Such concepts and models will be found to occupy the major portion of this paper.

DEFINITIONS AND RESTRICTIONS

Several terms in the following pages are likely to cause confusion unless the meanings assigned to them here are described. Among these are "efficiency," "intensiveness," and "permanence" as applied to subsistence regimes, and the more general terms, "agriculture," "cultivation," and "domestication."

"Efficiency" in this paper can be understood in two ways. When prefixed by the word, "labor," it refers to the success of a given subsistence method in minimizing the number of man-hours required for each unit of production. Prefixed by the word, "land," on the other hand, it refers to a related but sometimes opposed kind of success, the extent to which the subsistence method minimizes the quantity of land required for each unit of production. One could also evaluate efficiency according to other criteria (for instance, by social utility or effectiveness of capital utilization) but land- and labor-efficiency are what will mainly concern us here.

The concepts of "intensiveness" and "permanence" also have potential for causing misunderstanding. Both are applied to land use, but while the former is essentially a synonym of land-efficiency, the latter refers only to the relative frequency with which a plot of land is exploited. We know of subsistence regimes which are at once permanent and extensive (e.g. medieval plow farming — see Homans 1970 and Slicher van Bath 1963) and others which are intensive in spite of their impermanence (e.g. Ibo swiddening [Morgan 1955] which has a higher carrying capacity than many permanent regimes). The confusion between intensiveness and permanence is built into a good deal of the traditional terminology with which non-Western agriculture is described. Such terms as "shifting agriculture" have therefore been used sparingly here. They impute an excessive importance to simple permanence of field location, a datum which has only a limited relevance to demographic questions. We are far more interested in the land- and labor-efficiency of a regime than in whether its fields are in the same location from one year to the next.

"Agriculture" and "horticulture" are here treated as synonymous. Although some students of the subject have seen an evolutionary gap between *agris* and *hortus*, regarding one as an attribute of advanced societies and the other as intrinsically primitive, such an attitude is faintly ethnocentric. Many demographically successful modern peoples (e.g. the Javanese, Terra 1954) gain a major portion of their livelihoods from gardens, from plots of land too small and messy to be called, by our clean-cropping Western standards, "fields." Yet these plots may be centrally important from an economic point of view and, moreover, may be cultivated with a very high degree of skill, if not of hardware technology. My own feeling is that the owners of these plots are as much agriculturalists as any Ukrainian peasant or Nebraskan factory farmer. To treat horticulture as an essentially distinct system is misleading; it is equally misleading to talk as though horticulture is inferior from the standpoint of subsistence or necessarily early in an evolutionary sense. Some ancient farmers — wheat growers in the Near East, for example — undoubtedly possessed plots a Westerner would call a field as soon as they began to cultivate a staple crop. But others — root-croppers in South America and Africa, mixed farmers in eastern Asia — began with small gardenlike plots and have continued to depend on them down to the present day.

Agriculture is not, on the other hand, used synonymously with "cultivation," nor does either term necessarily mean "domestication." In the following pages, the term agriculture is reserved for contexts of substantial dependence on plants grown by humans, while cultivation denotes only that a useful species has been deliberately caused to reproduce by man. All agriculturalists are indeed cultivators, but a cultivator need not always be an agriculturalist; he may be just a gatherer (or a factory worker) who occasionally puts a seed or cutting into the ground with the expectation of using the result. This distinction is unorthodox but useful. One consequence of it is that cultivation is seen to be more elementary and perhaps older than agriculture, a theme which will be expanded in a later section.

"Domestication" is used here in the strictly biological rather than partly cultural sense, referring not to taming, growing or other patterns of regular human utilization but instead to the genetic effects that sometimes accompany that utilization. The term is arbitrarily restricted to effects produced specifically by human use. Even though one can easily conceive that plants might become adapted to, and undergo genotypic changes because of, preferential utilization by cows, and even though one might plausibly call a plant adapted for growth in a field favored by cow manure a "bovine domesticate," our present interest is focused on the causal interactions between the natural environment and man.

Even within this limited sphere, under other circumstances it might be necessary to make a still narrower restriction in the meaning of domestication, confining it to meaning the effects produced specifically by cultivation and thus excluding the inherited phenotypic changes that frequently have attended the adaptation of weeds to human, but not necessarily subsistence-connected, habitats. Luckily, distinguishing between weeds and useful domesticates is not necessary to what follows. All that matters is to establish a conceptual separation between cultivating and domesticating and to observe that neither can be assumed invariably to accompany the other. Cultivation (and even agriculture) without domestication is perfectly conceivable; there is no reason why even repeated cropping should necessarily always produce a phenotypically distinctive population. Likewise, a process much like domestication, and perhaps cytologically and morphologically indistinguishable from it, can be assumed to have occurred in numerous species of weed and perhaps in some selectively utilized wild species as well; hence, quasi domestication without cultivation is also possible.

The conceptual distinction thus has a practical consequence. If we have no evidence but remains of plants, we cannot demonstrate conclusively that cultivation did or did not exist. The plant remains can of course indicate probabilities. I myself am inclined to feel that the abundant presence of domesticated characteristics yields a fairly strong presumption of cultivation and that their absence is indecisive, indicating no more than that the site in question MAY have been inhabited by pure gatherers. But in either case, plant remains by themselves are insufficient. Acceptable proof or disproof of cultivation requires the use of several additional lines of evidence.

A last comment should be made relative to cultivation and agriculture. Here, both terms are confined to plant growing. Animal husbandry is indeed an integral part of many agricultural systems and the histories of the domestication of plants and animals in many areas are inextricably intertwined. Nonetheless, I have excluded animals from the following discussion. The reason is simple: I have not yet sorted out in my own mind how herding is related to population growth or whether, except insofar as traction power and manure are necessary to agriculture and scavengers to public health, it is related to population growth at all. Certainly, herding seems an inefficient way of getting protein and a most wasteful source of calories. In some environments it may be adaptive enough, but in others the idea of replacing the efficient wild fauna with domesticated animals seems demographic madness. If a causal relationship exists between population growth and herding, and if the adoption of herding is not due to quite different motives, that relationship is subtle and complex indeed.

With these distinctions and definitions in hand we can now return to the central subject, the association between population and agriculture. We must necessarily consider three sets of models before any conclusions are reached. The next three sections, accordingly, treat (1) the beginnings of cultivation, (2) the beginnings of staple agriculture, and (3) the history of population density.

BECOMING A CULTIVATOR

The proposition to be presented here is that the beginning of cultivation — that is, of the habit of deliberately growing useful plants — was neither a unique nor a revolutionary event. It probably happened repeatedly in different places, starting at a very early date. Its causes may have been comparatively trivial. And, for a period perhaps as long as ten or more millennia, it may have had few discernible social or genetic effects. The proposition is supported by the following arguments.

To begin with, cultivation is not in essence either a complex idea or one difficult to develop. True farming — committing one's resources to the establishment of an artificial ecosystem to yield a staple food supply — may be filled with subtle risks and calculations, but small-scale non-staple cultivating is elementary, so much so that it is not beyond the inventive reach of almost any human being. We can be quite sure that activities resembling cultivation go far back into the Palaeolithic. By the time a modest degree of intelligence had appeared in the human stock — certainly by the late Pleistocene if not before — extensive and in some cases massive interference with the habitat of certain selected species must have already begun. Even non-human predators (e.g. cows) are often observed to feed with discrimination, singling out a small number of species for special attention. But when the predators are intelligent and use fire, the potential for sustained, focused, and drastic selective pressure is clearly increased by several orders of magnitude. Through field fires lit by humans and intelligent concentration on selected food sources, numerous species must have been virtually exterminated long before the famous extinctions of big game during the terminal Pleistocene. Numerous others must have begun their adaptation to microhabitats influenced by humans such as refuse piles and fire clearings, and thus started to become quasi domesticates. It should be remembered that domestication as defined above is not necessarily a consequence of cultivation. Moreover a few species must have been deliberately favored by man. Many recent gatherers are reported to intervene extensively in the life cycles of wild species, going so far as to replant them (wild yams among the Andaman Islanders, wild rice among the Great Lakes Indians) or even to irrigate them (among the Paiute). Ancient gatherers surely were also given to this sort of intervention. One can easily imagine that a Neanderthaler had the foresight to spare a fruit tree growing near a regular camping spot, or that an Upper Palaeolithic *sapiens sapiens* had the intelligence to remove weeds from a bed of useful perennials.

It seems most realistic therefore to envision the process of human adaptation in the late Pleistocene as forming a continuum of selective exploitation, intervention, near-cultivation and quasi domestication. Somewhere in this continuum the first act of deliberate cultivation must have occurred, without fanfare, or important consequences, or awareness that anything new had been done. The contemporaries of the pioneer among all cultivators were surely as aware as he or she that seeds sprout and planted cuttings become new plants. Accidental planting and subsequent utilization must already have occurred numberless times. The only new aspect of the situation was the element of deliberation, the decision to plant a seed or cutting with the intention of using the result.

We may assume that this first of cultigens had the following characteristics: (1) it was of a kind necessary or strongly desirable in the eyes of a group with a rather simple lifestyle; (2) it was in short supply within collecting range of this group's usual camping places; (3) it was not a major staple — if it had been, then planting a few individual plants would not have solved the problem of scarcity while planting a whole field full would probably have seemed to the group a dubious investment of their labor; they could far more easily have moved to an entirely new area; and (4) the plant may have been perishable, or rare everywhere in the region, or distributed in what the ecologists call a "fine-grained" fashion: that is, spread evenly over the landscape rather than in widely separated but easily harvested patches. This last set of characteristics would make resupply difficult even if the group should resort to the strategy of detaching a large part of its labor force to concentrate on long range foraging expeditions. If the plant is hard enough to procure even under those conditions then its labor-cost will be unacceptably high. The group will have no choice but to do without or to learn to cultivate.

Under the assumptions that this protocrop was highly desirable, quantitatively unimportant in the everyday diet, locally scarce, and difficult to keep in adequate supply even when areas outside the local zone were exploited, one might venture an *a priori* description of the plant. It should be native to a fine-grained environment (like a tropical forest) or to an environment of low species and individual density (like a desert). It should have an annual habit and other traits that will make it likely to die off under careless exploitation (unlike a fruit tree or a grass). And it should contain some substance rarer than standard proteins, fats, sugars, and starches — perhaps an ester flavoring, an alkaloid stimulant, a glycoside poison, a fiber, or a dye. The theoretically ideal protocrop would be a non-staple plant with several important potential uses, such as flax, hemp, areca nut, turmeric, or the fruit banana. And empirically speaking, it is of interest that plants with these qualities are quite often found archaeologically in protoagricultural contexts — chile and agave in Mexico at Tamaulipas in the Infiernillo Phase (Mangelsdorf, MacNeish, and Willey 1964: 430) and at Tehuacàn during the El Riego phase (C. E. Smith 1967: 232); nuts of *Piper* and areca in the lowest levels at Spirit Cave, Thailand (Gorman 1973: 100); and cotton and *Lagenaria* in early South America (Pickersgill and Heiser, this volume).

But detailed speculative models of this kind are a luxury at this early stage of prehistoric research. What matters more at present is to produce general models, and such a model can be abstracted from the preceding paragraphs. The probability of an early hunting-and-gathering group becoming cultivators is seemingly controlled by only four sets of factors:
1.   Pre-existing technical knowledge — that is, familiarity with certain aspects of plant reproduction.
2.   Sufficient rationality to be capable of acting for the sake of remotely rather than immediately anticipated gains.
3.   A moderately strong locational constraint, which may be either positive or negative. It may be either (a) a focus of attraction, perhaps a natural resource that is difficult to transport and constantly used (e.g. a water source or a concentrated supply of a staple food) or a cultural resource with the same qualities (a defensible locale or, conceivably, a shrine); or (b) a circumscribing zone of negative attraction, rendered marginal by such factors as environmental poverty, climatic discomfort, military danger, or disease.
4.   A botanical commodity which is both highly desirable and scarce, scarcity being defined in terms of the labor cost of collection when the collecting group is under a locational constraint.

Seen through the glass of such a model, the probability of early cultivation in any area might seem quite high. Certainly knowledge and rationality can be assumed to exist in some degree even in remote pre-historic times, and the coincidence of locational constraint with scarcity must be a well-nigh universal condition. We might therefore conclude without further ado that the inception of cultivation should itself be a near-universal. But first a few comments on the role of population density are in order.

The main effect of the model in this regard is to reduce the role of demographic pressure to that of one among several factors producing scarcity. Perhaps the commodity in question has become scarce simply because the increase of population has outrun the ability of the local habitat to maintain the commodity in steady supply. In such a case, demography is one of two producers of scarcity, the other being the always-necessary factor of locational constraint — if no constraint exists, and the group is free to wander anywhere in search of what it needs then "scarcity" can hardly exist. But the commodity may be unobtainable for reasons other than straightforward population growth. Perhaps a small and non-increasing population has eaten all the commodity up over the years it has remained in a certain locality. Here, demographics remains a factor but in a rather less decisive way. Conceivably the commodity may never have existed in adequate quantities within foraging range of the place where the population is constrained to live. The population might have migrated to that place and brought their knowledge of the scarce plant with them, or might have acquired a taste for a previously unknown plant through chance discovery or trade. A case in point is the interest in and subsequent cultivation of tobacco among the Northwest Coast Indians during the eighteenth and nineteenth centuries. Tobacco can be said to have become scarce among the Kwakiutl as soon as they discovered its existence, but in "scarcity" of this kind demographics plays no role at all.

A last point to be considered is that resource scarcity (and for that matter, population pressure) is a highly subjective matter as far as causation in human societies is concerned. Whether a commodity has really become scarce and whether it really is necessary to survival are not entirely relevant when we seek to explain actual human decisions and actions. As modern specialists on agricultural development have begun to emphasize (e.g. Found 1971) what counts most in subsistence decisions is PERCEPTION. If a technique is perceived to be laborious then it will be resisted even if, from the standpoint of an outside observer, it is convenient and economical. And if a commodity is perceived to be scarce, even though it may in actuality be abundant enough, then appropriate action will be taken. Possibly the original cultivator decided to plant his crop because he wrongly evaluated the difficulty of finding the plant growing wild.

But if we ignore this problem of perception for the moment, we can arrive at four interim conclusions. First, cultivation of an elementary kind should be extremely old; there is no reason why it should not have come into being quite far back in the Pleistocene. Second, this rudimentary cultivation need not have had any decisive genetic effects on the plants involved. If only a few individuals were grown at once and especially if the parts of the plant utilized were not the flowers or the seeds, a proto-cultigen might be indistinguishable from its wild congeners. Third, early cultivation need not have had much effect on human populations. Perhaps it enabled a few groups to lead more comfortable lives and encouraged some to slow their wanderings, but it may not have contributed directly to any kind of archaeologically discernible increase in population. And fourth, increase in density of population need not have played a decisive causal role. Although a plant may have occasionally come into cultivation as a response to demographically induced scarcity, there are many alternative routes to that result.

All these conclusions are of course predicated on the notion that cultivation and agriculture, a substantial dependence on cultivated plants, are quite distinct institutions. As will be seen in the following sections, the interconnections between staple agriculture and demography are of a rather different kind.

BECOMING A FARMER

At this point we should inquire why the appearance of staple crop farming was delayed so long. Even if we reject the almost unprovable possibility of a Pleistocene origin for casual plant tending, we must still account for the fact that full-scale dependence on agriculture lags a surprising distance behind the known beginnings of cultivation. In Mexico, Peru and Southeast Asia, although perhaps not in the Near East, this time-lag seems to amount to at least several thousand years. What is the reason for such a long delay?

Several explanations can be invented. One of the most attractive is a hypothesis based on Boserup's model (see above) of agricultural development — that just as "extensive" agriculture is less labor demanding and therefore preferable to "intensive" agriculture, so gathering is still more economical of labor than agriculture itself. There is even some empirical evidence for such a hypothesis. Sahlins (1972: 1–39) has pointed out that many hunters and gatherers, contrary to what once was generally believed, are comparatively affluent. Both the Hadza (Woodburn 1968, 1972) and the !Kung Bushmen (Lee 1972a, 1972b) are said by their ethnographers to lead an easy life, devoting no more than a few hours a day to subsistence activities even (in the case of the !Kung) in distinctly marginal environments. Thus one can argue that the apparent reluctance of early gatherers and casual cultivators to convert to true farming may have been due to a simple lack of incentive. Before the appearance of the incentives of the later prehistoric period — denser populations, markets, perhaps government persuasion — remaining a gatherer may have been the economically rational course.

However, the labor-saving explanation is difficult to accept as a universally applicable rule. As I have argued elsewhere (Bronson 1972), a great many other factors enter into decisions concerning subsistence besides labor-efficiency: considerations of security, of prestige, of comfort, of health. For instance, nomadic gathering usually seems to exact a rather high price in natural and induced mortality among the very young and very old. It also limits substantially the possibilities of owning weatherproof dwellings, of developing non-subsistence technologies, and of storing food against times of scarcity. One is not convinced that the desire to do as little work as possible will invariably offset such considerations as these. It is far from certain, in fact, that gathering is always less work than some kinds of farming. Numerous food-production regimes, both shifting and permanent, require no more than a few hours' work each day in order to keep a family in food; most known hunter-gatherers (including the Hadza and !Kung) work at least this much, particularly when the labor cost of trekking from camp to camp is counted in. The labor-efficiency of gathering is indeed a factor to be considered, but it is not adequate as a full explanation for the apparent fact that substantial dependence on cultivation appeared so tardily.

An alternative explanation is that time was required for productive and trustworthy staple crops to evolve, and that the delay in the appearance of farming was thus due to a built-in lag in genetic possibility. But this explanation seems weak. Except for a few especially intractable species (perhaps maize), few staple crops can have needed more than a century or two of human attention to reach an adequate level of productivity.

A third explanation, which might be called the "naive-demographic" model, depends heavily on the idea that the development of farming was a straightforward adaptive response to the development of large, dense populations. Thus, it could be argued, true agriculture did not appear earlier simply because it was not needed until the time it did appear. But there are a number of serious objections to such a baldly eufunctional proposition, among them the fact that demographic development on a local scale is inherently too fast-moving to explain a series of events that extends over several millennia. As will be pointed out in a succeeding section, if demographic necessity were the only cause, agriculture would have appeared much more quickly than it did.

The fourth explanation that suggests itself has to do with the minimization of risk. When the casually cultivating hunter-gatherer turned to farming, he may not necessarily have had to work harder, and he may have obtained a number of benefits from the settled life that then was possible. But it is undeniable that he took a considerable gamble. He committed a substantial amount of labor to a course of action from which he could receive no immediate return. Indeed, in those days of pristine farming when no one had successful agriculturalist neighbors to observe, he could have reasonably doubted that he would receive any return at all. Even nowadays crops frequently fail, and still more frequently return no profit on the labor and capital expended, in spite of some nine or ten millennia of agronomic experience. Back in the days when farming began, the risk must have seemed and been very great indeed. While other factors may have contributed, simple caution is an almost adequate explanation for the reluctance of early cultivators to engage in full-scale farming.

The problem that remains is to find a model to explain why agriculture came to exist at all, why men everywhere, perhaps through judicious use of infanticide, war, and other fertility-controlling measures, did not remain casually cultivating hunter-gatherers down to the present day. The model that seems most useful is described below.

In its most generalized form, this model has a good deal of similarity to the one presented in the preceding section for the probability of becoming a cultivator. Again one must postulate a locational constraint and a scarcity of an important commodity. But here the commodity must be essential rather than simply desirable — that is, a staple food. And the question becomes more acute of why the proto-farmers stayed put when faced with this scarcity rather than just moving on. The risk they took by staying and attempting to grow the commodity was, as has already been pointed out, considerable. We must therefore assume that the locational constraint was very strong.

A number of more detailed submodels can be generated by considering the possible nature of this constraint.

The first submodel is a classically simple one — an island or otherwise circumscribed environment from which, for reasons of military danger, epidemiology, or sheer physical impossibility, the inhabitants cannot migrate. Within such an area it is plausible that population densities will increase quite quickly beyond the point where a hunting and gathering way of life can be sustained. In later times, such densely populated enclaves have been observed often to produce strikingly land-intensive agricultural systems, even in the midst of regions where most subsistence is of a very extensive kind. Numerous examples of what Clark and Haswell (1967: 50) call "societies under siege" occur in East and West Africa, Central and Southeast Asia, the Pacific, and the New World (see also Bronson 1972: 216). Since these isolated enclaves are often rather idio-syncratic in terms of the intensive farming technologies they use (e.g. the Haya — Allan 1965), one concludes that many of these technologies have evolved *in situ* in response to the fact that no one could migrate out when land grew scarce. But if constraints on out-migration can thus render inefficient farming systems efficient, then why could they not at an earlier date make a casual cultivator become a full-scale agriculturalist? Many of the same constraining forces were as operative in the early Neolithic as in recent times. It seems plausible that they could have had similar effects.

A rather more complex submodel is generated when the constraining forces are considered to be centripetal and positive: when, for instance, a population is drawn to a given place by the abundant presence of a second staple commodity different in kind from the one which is becoming scarce. A fishing lagoon on an otherwise unproductive coast would meet these requirements, as would a water source in a generally waterless region. The attractions of an abundant supply of protein or water might easily counterbalance the disadvantages of a shortage of a starchy staple in the eyes of a hunting-and-gathering group, causing them to attempt to raise that staple rather than move on to another place.

It will be observed that this two-staple model is a generalized version of two well-known theories of the origin of food production. The idea that the first agriculturalists may have been fishermen was originally suggested by Sauer (1952: 23) and has been subsequently taken up by several more recent authorities (e.g. Adams 1966: 40–41). The latter sources emphasize the importance of sedentarization as a factor in the decision to plant a staple crop; here, the conflict between two separate locationally fixed staples is assigned the central role. Sedentarization undoubtedly predisposes to agriculture but is not a necessary precondition in this model's terms. A conflict between the need for fish and the need for grain could result in the adoption of agriculture even in the absence of a settled life. The fishermen could use the vicinity of the lagoon only seasonally, planting a (necessarily pest-resistant) crop and then continuing on a gathering circuit for the remainder of the year.

The water-source-centered version of the model rather resembles the somewhat discredited "oasis theory" of agricultural origins, whereby the first domestication was assumed to have occurred within oases isolated by increasing regional desiccation. The main difference between this model and the oasis theory in its more highly elaborated form (e.g. Peake 1928) lies in the way the future farmers are assumed to get into the oasis in the first place. While Peake and Pumpelly postulated that the farmers had to be trapped there by a vast climatic change, here no catastrophe is necessary. Many nomadic pre-farming groups must have stayed within oases for long enough to consume most of the food supply inside the watered area and within the exploitable zone surrounding the oasis. That the group would always attempt to farm rather than move on to another oasis is of course unlikely. But, given a sufficient scarcity of water elsewhere and perhaps a reluctance to split the group into smaller units, it is entirely plausible that agriculture would sometimes have been the result.

A last submodel worth considering is the most diffuse and indeterminate of all. Let us assume that most of the conditions laid down previously do not always hold — that under some circumstances agriculture is less risky and easier than collecting, that no locational constraint exists, and that the desired staple commodity, although in short supply, is not necessary to survival. A wandering band of gatherers in an almost deserted rainforest will serve as an example. What is to keep them from cutting down a few trees and planting a moderately large crop of, say, manioc? The labor investment need not have been excessive. If they girdled the trees they would have had to do little cutting and if the forest was deserted, and hence primary, the undergrowth would have been minimal. A quarter hectare of cleared area might have needed no more than two weeks' work and could have produced, in the case of manioc, enough calories to live on for a year. Moreover, since manioc has few natural enemies, the members of the band would not have been obliged to wait around until harvest time; they could have gone off and gathered wild foods elsewhere in the forest while the crop took care of itself. The band thus took no risk, made little commitment, and enjoyed a greatly increased level of security — if the supply of other staples failed, it could always have fallen back on the manioc, which can be expected to remain in edible condition in the ground for several years. Whether such farming as this is theoretically significant — whether it would ordinarily lead to any kind of sociocultural or demographic progress — may seem questionable. But that it IS farming cannot be denied. Agriculture in some instances can have evolved for reasons which are both unrecoverable and trivial.

In summary, one can produce a number of quite disparate models of agricultural origins, varied according to the constraints and commodities assumed to be necessary. I myself see little to choose between them. Any could have happened. If we assume that agriculture was independently "invented" often enough, then all of these causal sequences should have unrolled at least once somewhere in the world.

As for the role of growth of population, this clearly varies from case to case. In the model of the population under siege, it is always present but not, as will be pointed out shortly, as a truly independent variable. In the two-staple model, increasing density may or may not be present, and demographic causation is entirely absent from the model of the part-time forest-farmers. But before demographic issues can be dealt with properly two observations on that subject must first be made.

THE NATURE OF POPULATION PRESSURE AND INCREASE

The two observations in question have to do with (1) the *a priori* probability of being able to project demographic growth curves into the past and so to make assumptions about the size of ancient populations, and (2) what does and does not constitute demographic pressure.

Increase Curves and Frame-Dependence

It is usual, when discussing the influence of demography on societal and economic development, to consider that long-term population growth is represented by the familiar exponential curve (Figure 1).

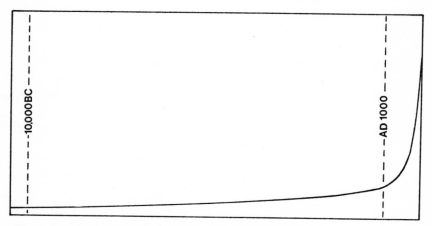

Figure 1.   Model of population increase on a worldwide scale

A curve much like Figure 1 would, with somewhat varying parameters, be accepted by most specialists as a fair model of worldwide demographic trends between the Palaeolithic and the present. It would be accepted validly; that international population growth has actually followed such a curve is not open to doubt. But its usefulness is quite another matter. There are reasons for questioning whether the exponential-curve model has any explanatory relevance to early socioeconomic evolution.

The main reason is that socioeconomic events do not (or did not until recently) happen on a worldwide scale. They take place instead within restricted blocks of area measuring at most a few hundred miles on a side, and have their roots in causes which operate within a similarly reduced frame. If we are interested in demographic causation then densities of continental populations are of no interest to us; such data are meaningless abstractions. And if we come to consider the probable history of populations within restricted regions and localities, the exponential-curve model becomes unsatisfactory as a predictor of demographic density.

Empirically speaking, it is difficult to find a single example of a regional or local population before the era of modern medicine known to have followed a steady pattern of exponential increase for longer than a few centuries. Virtually every population of this kind for which we have long-term documentary records can be shown to have undergone substantial fluctuations. If we consider only the period before A.D. 1800, taking the diffusion of the Jenner vaccine as the cut-off point for the beginning of demographically effective medicine, we find that the late eighteenth century rarely marks the known apogee of any regional population. Northern Europe may be an exception, but in most regions the premedical peak was reached long before 1800 and was followed by a considerable decline afterwards. Aztec Mexico, Byzantine Anatolia and Egypt, pre-Mongol Persia, and perhaps Sung China and Roman Italy and northern Africa are examples of such early peaks. And in areas smaller than regions and nations, the short-term fluctuations must completely overwhelm any secular trend toward gradual increase. Seen within a frame of this size, the exponential curve cannot be expected to resemble the actual histories of populations except in a small fraction of cases.

The theoretical explanation for the "frame-dependence" of demographic models is obvious and need not occupy much of our time. Human populations are capable of intrinsically high rates of increase — even under premedical conditions — of a doubling rate of less than fifty years. The inhabitants of a given locality should therefore be able to fill it solidly with human bodies within the space of one or two millennia. The probability that a population will actually sustain such an increase rate over a large area is of course vanishingly small, but as the spatial frame shrinks the probabilities change. If the frame is a region of 10,000 square kilometers, possibly this regional population has at some time in its history remained free from excessive mortality for long enough to produce a substantial population boom. And if the frame is a locality measuring only 500 square kilometers in size, the probability approaches certainty. Given a moderate reduction in mortality, the likelihood of in-migration, and the absence of controls over fertility that is almost universal among modern peoples, we may assume that almost all 500 square-kilometer local populations have undergone a number of extreme fluctuations during the last ten millennia. The actual population curve for a locality of such a size would probably resemble Figure 2 more closely than Figure 1.

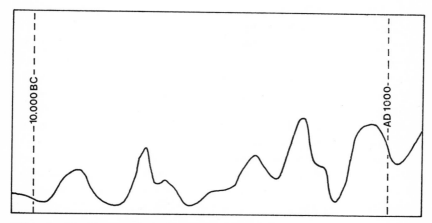

Figure 2.   Model of population increase on a local scale

One interest of this indeterminate population model is that it frees us of the need to find mechanisms by which low densities of continental populations can be assumed to exert significant pressures on resources of land and labor. There is no need, for instance, to postulate that pre-Neolithic gatherers were driven to adopt a major subsistence change because of crowding at high relative densities of several persons per hundred square kilometers. If high absolute local densities are needed for a hypothesis, then they can be assumed to have existed almost anywhere and at any date.

But this conclusion has a corollary, and the corollary is of equal interest and importance: high densities of population do not invariably lead to the adoption of agriculture. Density-induced resource scarcity must have occurred in numerous localities during the late Pleistocene; even though these densities must sometimes have been considerable, not once are they known to have resulted in the large-scale cultivation of staple crops. In the early Holocene, such densities must have occurred at numerous times and places again; yet in only five or ten small regions can they be shown to have led to farming. Demographic pressure is thus a most inefficient cause. When response follows the presumed stimulus only once in each ten thousand trials, one is justified in doubting the adequacy of that stimulus as an explanation.

Density versus Pseudo-Density

The second observation that should be made has to do with the nature of population density. From the standpoint of possible socioeconomic consequences, what does and does not constitute a "dense" population? No difficulties arise if we envision a classical situation of an increasing number of inhabitants, fixed renewable resources, an area finite in size, and a static exploitative technology; the population becomes dense and begins to experience scarcity at or rather below the point where the rate of consumption equals the rate of renewal of resources. A slight complication that also causes no real difficulties appears when consumers and resources are distributed unevenly within the area. A fine-grained distribution of resources can be expected to result in a lowered threshold of scarcity and population density. The same effect should follow if the consumers are distributed in a coarse-grained fashion. The maximum carrying capacity of a locality is reached only when resources are clustered into easily exploitable nodes, and when the exploiters are spread out as evenly as possible.

On the other hand, there are some sorts of complications which cause real difficulties for the concepts of density and scarcity. One is the probability that any resource which is not necessary for survival can be exhausted eventually by a bare handful of consumers, just as long as these consumers are sufficiently omnivorous, determined, and improvident. Into this category fall almost all individual species of plants and animals. The consumers can always fall back on other species once the preferred ones grow scarce or have been exterminated. The category also includes all non-staple species as a class; a few consumers can exterminate these without suffering any consequences except perhaps for a certain regret at the disappearance of a favored condiment. Hence, we cannot always glibly say that some sorts of scarcity are due to population pressures; they may be due to simple overconsumption. Population pressure is not a meaningful concept except when referred to a critical class of resources, so critical that increasing scarcity can be presumed to bring Malthusian demographic checks into operation.

Another serious complication arises when we consider more carefully the subject of population distribution within the local area. Let us imagine, for instance, an underpopulated valley inhabited by a number of house-holds which are relatively dispersed but focused around a single non-subsistence feature in the center, such as a shrine or defensible hilltop. The resulting settlement-pattern might resemble Figure 3. The issue here involves the problems of supply faced by households located at differing distances from the focal feature. The household marked B on Figure 3 is out at the edge of the settled area; its inhabitants may be far from the population focus but are otherwise in an advantageous position, closer to their fields, to wild resources, and to most other things necessary to the household economy. As a consequence, B's resupply costs, measured in time and effort of transportation, are relatively low. Household A, on the

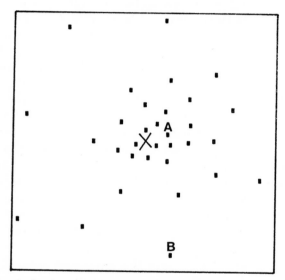

Figure 3.   Pseudo-density caused by locational factors

other hand, is in a high-cost location. It may gain some advantages from its proximity to the center, but few of these advantages are economic. It is further from most resources and must regularly expend more time and labor in obtaining them, in spite of the fact that the valley contains adequate land and that no resource is scarce in an absolute sense.

The model being constructed here is only a restatement of the familiar "Isolated State" model of Von Thünen (Chisolm 1967; Chayanov 1966), whereby locational considerations — factors of distance and ease of transportation — are said to be decisive in optimizing the choice of crops and farming techniques in a marketized regional economy. However, this particular version of the Von Thünen model is being used to point up a somewhat different conclusion: that even in an unmarketized pure subsistence economy, locational variations will still produce cost differentials and hence exert the same kind of economic pressure as does genuine scarcity. From an operational point of view, cost (in this case, labor cost) is the only meaningful measure of scarcity. That a given resource is actually common somewhere within the valley makes no difference to the inhabitants of Household A. For them, the resource is hard to get, and they are therefore under economic pressure, a kind of pressure which is most difficult to distinguish from the pressure caused by overpopulation.

Analogous forms of "pseudo-populational" pressure can be presumed to exist at some level in all societies for whom the choice of a place to live is not dictated by the location of a single food resource. If the location of the settlement, whether temporary or permanent, is chosen partly on the basis of defensibility, sociability, or the presence of a second critical resource, then some members of the society will be under appreciable pseudo-pressure. Depending on the keenness with which this pressure is felt, those members will be more or less receptive to the idea of new subsistence alternatives.

The last complication for the concept of population pressure has already been discussed, the fact that increased density must first pass through the filter of cultural perception before it is likely to have any socioeconomic effect. In human as distinguished from animal populations, pressure, scarcity, and stress are to a considerable extent states of mind. A group which feels itself in need of *Lebensraum* may take steps to solve the problem even though, by a more objective measure, the shortage of living space is largely imaginary. Likewise, the scarcity of a resource is not measured in actual labor cost but instead in terms of PERCEIVED labor, and this will clearly depend on a whole host of variables besides caloric expenditure and man-hours worked. In all probability such perceptual factors will usually tend to lower thresholds of pressure and scarcity rather than raise them. But how much these thresholds will be lowered in any particular case is impossible to predict. Thus it follows that an appreciable percentage of ancient subsistence changes will not be explainable by objective economic and demographic factors. Repugnant though it is to our nomothetic instincts, we must consider the possibility that some changes, including some instances of the inception of agriculture and cultivation, may have been caused by a perceptual mistake.

THE LIMITS OF DEMOGRAPHIC EXPLANATION

None of the foregoing is meant to deny the validity of some demographic explanations. Unquestionably population pressure has been significant and sometimes decisive in documented cases of recent alterations of subsistence patterns. The twentieth century intensification of farming by the Ibo (Netting 1969) is quite clearly a more or less direct effect of the recent population boom in Eastern Nigeria, and a whole series of historic shifts in English agriculture have been convincingly tied by Slicher van Bath (1963) to price fluctuations and, through this intermediary market mechanism, to long-term national demographic changes. But there are also numerous countervailing examples. Many of the pre-modern agricultural innovations in Tokugawa Japan (T. Smith 1968) seem to have been accomplished through administrative fiat, because of a concern for increased productivity on the part of landlords and tax collectors. Similar incentives to agronomic change are also known to have been present in eighteenth-century England and in Rome at the time of Virgil. Many modern changes of subsistence in Africa are better interpreted as responses to market development than to increase in population — witness the appearance of land-extensive commercial agriculture among the Gishu (Allan 1965) and Kofyar (Netting 1968). A twentieth-century farmer in New Jersey or Kent selects techniques and crops with regard only to input costs and output prices; he (and, one imagines, his counterparts on the outskirts of any ancient city) farms in a singularly labor- and land-intensive fashion because land is dear, transport to urban markets cheap, and prices for perishable produce high. Whether the total population within the city's hinterland is dense or sparse makes no difference to his choice of farm technology. If he is close to the city, even though that city may be in the midst of a fertile and uninhabited wasteland, he will be an intensive farmer.

Numerous other examples could be cited but there is no need. It is absurd to maintain that, in the modern and recent world, simple demographic density is invariably the prime mover of subsistence change. It may be important in many cases and decisive in some, but too many other factors affecting subsistence exist — market forces, administrative controls, limitations on information, differences in perception — for one to conclude that population pressure alone is an adequate explanation for the majority of ethnographically and historically known instances of the intensification of subsistence methods.

Perhaps it may seem that the early days of farming represent a more pristine and simpler pattern, when the primacy of population pressure should emerge more clearly. However, as the preceding pages have tried to show, this commonsense expectation encounters a number of theoretical difficulties.

The inception of cultivation (as distinguished from full-fledged farming) would seem to have a most tenuous *a priori* connection with increase in population. This follows directly from the postulate that the first cultivated plants need not have been staple crops. If they were not staples, or were not treated as staples, then they can hardly have begun to be grown because the growers were faced with imminent starvation. One of the archetypal instances of pre-agricultural cultivation is the El Riego phase at Tehuacán, where the ordinary diet, on the evidence of coprolites, is said by MacNeish (1972: 71) to have contained between 0 and 6 percent of cultivated plants. Now, this quantity of food may have made a considerable difference to the comfort and even nutrition of the ancient Tehuacanos. But it did not save anyone from starving to death. One cannot believe that the Tehuacanos began cultivating in order to obtain 6 percent more of a staple, or because they sensed that a decline of 6 percent in gathering output meant future disaster. Whyever they began, there was no perceptible wolf at their door.

The beginnings of agriculture, on the other hand, may have had a firmer relationship with demographic factors. If the knowledge of cultivation was already widespread, it is entirely plausible that a population crisis could have turned a group of hunter-gatherers into farmers almost overnight. But one can think of other equally plausible reasons for taking that drastic step — locationally generated pseudo-pressure, conflicts between positionally fixed resources, the social benefits of sedentism, perhaps even at times the increased ease and diminished risk of farming as against gathering. It is true that these other reasons may have had a demographic component, but then demographic causes themselves must always have been much diluted by other factors. The model of straight population pressure is inadequate as an explanation even of situations where a marked demographic increase can be shown to precede staple agriculture, for of necessity the increased population must be a purely local phenomenon which cannot exist without factors — called here, "locational constraints" — that keep the excess people from wandering off into the surrounding emptiness. And so which is the independent variable, the population increase or the constraint?

To my mind, such questions are both unanswerable and unnecessary. What we are dealing with is a complex, multifaceted adaptive system, and in human adaptive systems (as in real natural and human systems of any kind), single all-efficient "causes" cannot exist. True, it may be advantageous occasionally to construct models of such systems in which a single factor is given paramount status. But in the case of this particular system, the heuristic value of a simple model is most doubtful, perhaps especially when the paramount factor is to be demography. Population pressure is not the only possible explanation of farming. Nor does it invariably lead to farming. As pointed out earlier, high local densities must have occurred very early in man's history and with great frequency; only in a small percentage of post-Pleistocene cases can these have led to the adoption of large-scale food production. Thus, increase in population is neither necessary nor sufficient as an explanation. It is also among the most difficult of all data to recover archaeologically, depending as it does on excavations on a tremendous scale and on datings of an improbable accuracy. Even if it were true that in a given case a rapid increase in population had immediately preceded and thus presumably caused the appearance of true farming, that fact would be most difficult to demonstrate through any conceivable excavation. And, as I say, the farming may have many other explanations. The population-centered model of subsistence evolution may be pedagogically useful but it is of doubtful value as a research guide.

Much more satisfactory is the rather subliminal model that seems actually to guide much of the research on post-Pleistocene adaptations, whatever the explicit theoretical orientation of the individual researcher may be. The leading characteristics of this model are complexity, factor feedback, and instability. A great many agencies — sedentariness, epidemiology, genetics, environmental structure, technologies of subsistence and non-subsistence, political evolution, economic development, warfare, the density and distribution in space of populations — are recognized as potential influences, without seriously contending that any necessarily have priority. The relationship between each pair of these is visualized as one of feedback; the chicken-and-egg quality of interactions between adaptational factors has long been recognized by most specialists. And the rather Augustinian notion that all recent (i.e. post-Pleistocene) adaptive patterns are intrinsically unstable is gaining ground again after a brief setback during the heyday of functionalism. Change, driven by the sheer impossibility of keeping so many interacting factors out of disequilibrium, is a normal condition. What requires explaining is stability, not change.

Under the influence of this implicit model, a considerable quantity of significant work has been done. Indeed, in spite of the regrettable lack of detailed and overt consensus, the model has probably generated as much useful research as has the average paradigm of one of the Kuhnian "normal" sciences. It is too good a model to be replaced casually.

However, beyond question it will be replaced. The appearance of numerous proposals for new explicit models of socioeconomic evolution, together with a growing feeling that the field is on the edge (or over the edge) of a breakthrough, signals the old model's approaching demise. As yet the few comprehensive models that have been attempted have not been unqualified successes. But a number of partial models, focused on disentangling only a few strands of the web of factor relationships, have done quite well in terms of generating research hypotheses that are at once testable, non-trivial, and interesting. It would seem that studies of ancient demography could be aimed best at producing partial models like these, at clarifying the connections among a small number of precisely defined and quantified variables of which one is size of population. Such an aim may seem dishearteningly modest when compared with the dimensions of the overall problem of why the long Pleistocene stasis did slip over into a disequilibrating mode and produce the world as we now know it. But a sharply limited approach is the only one that is likely to be productive. Testable explanations for grand patterns are not necessary for research, nor are they practicable in the present state of the art.

REFERENCES

ADAMS, R. M.
  1966   *The evolution of urban society*. Chicago: Aldine.
ALLAN, W.
  1965   *The African husbandman*. Edinburgh: Oliver and Boyd.
BOSERUP, E.
  1965   *The conditions of agricultural growth*. Chicago: Aldine.
BRONSON, B.
  1972   "Farm labor and the evolution of food production," in *Population growth: anthropological implications*. Edited by Brian Spooner, 190–218. Cambridge, Massachusetts: M.I.T. Press.
CHAYANOV, A. V.
  1966   *The theory of peasant economy*. Homewood, Illinois: American Economic Association.
CHISOLM, N.
  1967   *Rural settlement and land use*. New York: John Wiley.
CLARK, C., M. HASWELL
  1967   *The economics of subsistence agriculture* (third edition). New York: St. Martin's Press.
FOUND, W. C.
  1971   *A theoretical approach to rural land-use patterns*. New York: St. Martin's Press.

GORMAN, C. F.
   1973   Excavations at Spirit Cave, north Thailand: some interim inter-
          pretations. *Asian Perspectives* 13:79–107.
HOMANS, G. C.
   1970   *English villagers of the thirteenth century.* New York: Harper and Row.
LEE, R. B.
   1972a "Population growth and the beginnings of sedentary life among the
          !Kung Bushmen," in *Population growth: anthropological implications.*
          Edited by Brian Spooner, 329–342. Cambridge, Massachusetts: M.I.T.
          Press.
   1972b "Work effort, group structure, and land-use in contemporary hunter-
          gatherers," in *Man, settlement and urbanism.* Edited by P. J. Ucko,
          R. Tringham, and G. W. Dimbleby, 177–186. Cambridge, Massachu-
          setts: Schenkman.
MAC ARTHUR, R. H., E. O. WILSON
   1967   *The theory of island biogeography.* Monographs in Population Biology
          1. Princeton, New Jersey: Princeton University Press.
MAC NEISH, R. S.
   1972   "The evolution of community patterns in the Tehuacan Valley of
          Mexico and speculations about the cultural processes," in *Man,
          settlement and urbanism.* Edited by P. J. Ucko, R. Tringham, and
          G. W. Dimbleby, 67–93. Cambridge, Massachusetts: Schenkman.
MANGELSDORF, P. C., R. S. MAC NEISH, G. R. WILLEY
   1964   "Origins of agriculture in Middle America,," in *Handbook of Middle
          American Indians,* volume one. Edited by R. C. West, 427–445. Austin:
          University of Texas Press.
MORGAN, W. B.
   1955   The change from shifting agriculture to fixed settlement in southern
          Nigeria. *Department of Geography Research Notes* 7. Ibadan, Nigeria:
          University College of Ibadan.
NETTING, R. M.
   1968   *Hill farmers of Nigeria.* Seattle: University of Washington Press.
   1969   Ecosystems in process: a comparative study of change in two West
          African societies. *National Museum of Canada Bulletin* 230:102–112.
PEAKE, H.
   1928   *The origins of agriculture.* London: E. Benn.
SAHLINS, M.
   1972   *Stone age economics.* Chicago: Aldine.
SAUER, C. O.
   1952   *Agricultural origins and dispersals.* New York: The American Geo-
          graphical Society.
SLICHER VAN BATH, B. H.
   1963   *The agrarian history of western Europe A.D. 500–1950.* London:
          Edward Arnold.
SMITH, C. E.
   1967   "Plant remains," in *The prehistory of the Tehuacan Valley,* volume one.
          Edited by Douglas S. Byers, 220–255. Austin: University of Texas
          Press.

SMITH, P. E. L.

1972 "Land use, settlement patterns, and subsistence agriculture: a demographic perspective," in *Man, settlement and urbanism*. Edited by P. J. Ucko, R. Tringham, and G. W. Dimbleby, 409–426. Cambridge, Massachusetts: Schenkman.

SMITH, P. E. L., T. C. YOUNG

1972 "The evolution of early agriculture and culture in Greater Mesopotamia: a trial model," in *Population growth: anthropological implications*. Edited by Brian Spooner, 1–59. Cambridge, Massachusetts: M.I.T. Press.

SMITH, T. C.

1968 *The agrarian origins of modern Japan*. Stanford: Stanford University Press.

TERRA, G. J. A.

1954 Mixed garden horticulture in Java. *Journal of Tropical Geography* 3: 34–43.

WOODBURN, J. C.

1968 "An introduction to Hadza ecology," in *Man the hunter*. Edited by R. B. Lee and I. DeVore, 49–55. Chicago: Aldine.

1972 "Ecology, nomadic movement, and composition of the local group among hunters and gatherers," in *Man, settelement and urbanism.* Edited by P. J. Ucko, R. Tringham, and G. W. Dimbleby, 193–206. Cambridge, Massachusetts: Schenkman.

The Concept of Environmental
Determinism in Cultural Evolution

PHILIP L. WAGNER

The natural environment undoubtedly exerts an all-pervasive influence on human life. Environment conditions every social, cultural, and economic situation. Abundant instances in history attest to nature's intervention in the fates of men and nations.

These generalities are not at issue here. Taking them as indisputable, we further may acknowledge that cultural evolution always must itself proceed under heavy influence and tight constraints imposed by the environment. This idea is central to, and quite inseparable from, what we mean by "evolution"; there would be no point, and indeed there would be error, in talking about cultural evolution without the core idea of change toward greater efficiency, for evolution is directional. Cultures may properly, if speculatively, be thought of as "adapting" by slow cumulative change to their particular environments. We may, according to our tastes, conceive of given environmental circumstances as either permitting, or favoring, or demanding, or evoking some particular direction of cultural development, and thus we may attribute change in culture to processes of "adaptation." Such reasoning is ecological and evolutionary, and is therefore much in vogue. It has a venerable history as well.

The history and substance of the various forms of environmental determinism have been discussed at length by many writers (Callot 1952: 275–360; Freeman 1961: 74–82; Fuchs 1966; Lowie 1937; Tatham 1951: 128–162; Thomas 1925), and it would be superfluous to recapitulate them here. Sorokin (1928: 99–103) and Hartshorne (1939) have contributed extensive critiques of the doctrine on logical and empirical grounds. The ensuing discussion, however, does not constitute an attempt to summarize those critiques. It seeks only to clarify some of the chief implications of the thesis of environmental determinism, and to assess its potential relevance to contemporary culture history. How useful is the concept in the explanation of cultural evolution? Can it lead to fruitful redirection of research? These questions will be foremost. We may begin with some approximations.

Environments, as well as cultures, are engaged in never-ending change. Evolution, then, can hardly be a static concept. Instead of seeking some advanced, perfected form of life, it could be interpreted in this light merely as a ceaseless striving to keep up with change. Yet this striving does appear to induce "progress" in a species, and perhaps in a society — that is, to lead to cumulative increase in their security and ecological efficiency. This fact implies, in turn, that changes in environment, at least over relatively great spans of time, follow a consistent trend; for otherwise, any momentary adaptation would probably prove fatal within a rather short span. Three notions are involved here: (1) consistent, cumulative change within societies; (2) similarly regular and incremental changes in their environments; and finally, (3) some kind of orderly relationship between the two developments.

We know empirically not only that a culture may reflect environmental states and changes, but also that all environments inhabited by man are prone to culturally guided transformations. This latter fact has major implications for our topic, but we must explicitly ignore it for the moment, and suppose that only natural environmental influence on man is relevant. In such a case, it is possible to conceive of an orderly relationship like the one mentioned above, which holds between ongoing environmental change, and coordinated with it or even subordinated to it, changes in society and culture. This conception is the central feature of environmental determinism.

The doctrine emphasizes order and not accident. Whereas human events and mankind's evolution must, by any reckoning, fall subject now and then to interferences of nature, it is not the exceptional, spectacular occurrence that impresses the environmental determinist, but the regular and gradual effects that he supposes are exerted by any environment upon any society. Accidents themselves, in fact, may hardly interest him. They are matters for historians. Determinism is a systematic and, in principle, predictive doctrine.

PHILOSOPHICAL DETERMINISM

The general concept of determinism holds that "for everything that ever happens there are conditions such that, given them, nothing else could happen" (Taylor 1967: 359). This concept has a lengthy history within philosophy and has found varied expression and application among philosophers. These can probably be fairly represented as falling into three categories. One group, embracing in modern times such leading thinkers as Leibniz, Hobbes, and most of the "logical positivists," would hold that all events and phenomena are determinately caused, or at least can best be explained by deterministic assumptions. A second group, typified by Kant and perhaps most existentialists, would regard determinism as a just hypothesis concerning certain classes of phenomena, but would reserve a place for the undetermined sphere of human freedom. The third viewpoint, perhaps best exemplified by thinkers like Hume and Wittgenstein, would eschew causality as an epistemological and ontological principle, and so reject determinism. There is no doubt at all that for a great many philosophers — analytic, existential, or other — deterministic explanation has become a losing game.

These philosophical differences, of course, go far beyond the special problem of environmental determinism. They relate to the question of whether or not ANY complete causal explanation of anything is possible. Furthermore, some of the most important perplexities in this regard revolve around whether or not anything whatever is possible, i.e. they affect the possibility of knowing discrete entities or particular events. If the flow of reality cannot be subdivided, how can anything be extricated as the effect of given "causes"? This notion translates into doubt that the character and delimitation of historical events may be important for the problems to which the environmental determinists address themselves. Such perplexities have entertained philosophers as far apart as Wittgenstein and Husserl.

The doctrine of determinism has a reciprocal predictive form, deriving known effects from known determinate circumstances. The proposition may be turned around so that successful prediction implies cause. Finding expression in contemporary probabilistic thinking, this idea permits an event predicted successfully, but NOT on the basis of strict (deterministic) causality, to be assigned *a posteriori* to a series of imputed causes. In effect this tends to make the "laws of nature" mostly retroactive! Such a rather fictive form of determinism may provide explanatory frames, if not the only rational account of things. Determinism and "destiny" display some common features here, as if myth and science had met. This viewpoint may or may not help in discovery procedures or experimental design.

The logic of explanation and prediction does not inherently depend upon deterministic assumptions. As Curry (1966) has argued, landscape change can be explained by chance events, operating cumulatively. Relations of possibility and likelihood, as well as necessity or certainty, can be subjected to successive transformations and summations; falsification serves as a criterion perhaps as good or better than confirmation for evaluating hypotheses (Popper 1962). There are manifestly full resources in philosophy to provide for logical analysis of problems of cultural evolution, even if deterministic doctrines now enjoy less currency.

As for the doctrine of environmental determinism, the decline of philosophical determinism may simply leave the controversy where it has been; for if nothing is determined, strictly speaking, then NEITHER environmental determinism nor any of its actual or potential rival theories can explain phenomena deterministically. As a doctrine concerning the tendency of evolution, even if not as a causal doctrine, environmental determinism may still attract adherents. It belongs to the wider tradition of determinism in history which, given mankind's unfortunate inability as yet to conquer circumstance, is likely to persist for a while.

DETERMINISTIC VIEWS OF HISTORY

Many peoples have regarded human history as dependent on the wills and whims of gods. Fatalism, an extreme determinism devoid of methods of prediction, has been widespread since ancient times, often in conjunction — as among the Aztecs or the Greeks — with some idea of either periodic cycles of creation, or successive and distinct epochs of development. Prescientific observation and interpretation of natural phenomena have given models for speculation about the course of human events, represented, for example, in the wide variety of concepts known collectively as totemism and animism. Astronomical, even more than biological exemplars, often having application to the notion of man's destiny, have figured prominently in the speculative determinisms of different peoples, from the Sumerians and probably the men of Stonehenge down to the mathematical macrocosmologists of the present day.

Astrology, unrivaled as a popular determinism, looks to astral controls on human life, and the deterministic view of history, first expressed in modern times by Vico, also rested in good measure on stargazing. For Vico, history manifested an overall direction of progress followed by decline. Like many subsequent conceptions, his bore a moral tone. That moral tone was even stronger in the doctrines that descended from theology. Christian eschatology continued to impart a teleological cast to views of history right down to at least the end of the nineteenth century in Europe. These Christian versions in their more predestinarian varieties presented nature and the human race as the abject executors of God's inexorable will and plan. Their dualistic struggle of the spirit with the flesh may echo Manichaean thought. Calvin brought this tendency in Christianity to its most categorical expression. The more or less self-conscious agents of the divine plan, the "saved," could be regarded as fulfilling ordained necessity — which, in Calvin's own time, operated through capitalist production and commerce.

Seldom have determinisms so specified their individual human agents; the "great man theory" of history is most commonly at odds with them. But one other great determinist system in which the roles of given individuals can be known is Marxism. According to Marxism, history is progressive and can be predicted through scientific laws. Class analysis permits progressive forces in society to be identified. Not nature, but the productive system of society itself, is for Marxism the locus of historical determination; cultural and social evolution is interpreted as man's progress in "the struggle with nature."

In all advanced modern societies, what is perhaps a more fundamental determinism inheres in practical decision and the public rationales of policy. It dates back at least to the physiocrats and English "classical" economists. The idea of progress, moral as well as material, is well bound up, in contemporary thinking, with what is often seen as a necessary order of development within technology. Popular thinking finds nothing astonishing in the conquest of the world by the industrial, commercial, urban order. Thus, all of history is sometimes seen as the growth of rational efficiency, full employment, and economies of scale. Strongly influenced by certain conceptions of the growth of science and by current scientific principles applied to social issues, this is a central tenet of both capitalist and socialist belief.

VARIETIES OF DETERMINISM IN ENVIRONMENTAL EVOLUTION

One rationalist view of history sees progress as the discovery and application of the laws of nature and society. Nature is constant, but knowledge of it grows; man does not evolve organically (for the time considered), but comes to know himself. Society does change, and culture — as the correct understanding and implementation of the principles of order in the universe — does grow and is dynamic. The modern temper finds congenial this particular materialism, sometimes expressed in what is loosely called a "cultural determinism" (cf. White 1949), in which nature takes a passive role, while shared, transmitted human knowledge (itself determinate, of course) evolves in its determined order, and in doing so transforms the world. The conception is a realist conception: the truth is "there," behind the principles we seek to grasp. The cosmic reality itself, if anything, is static; change does not proceed in consequence of a changing fundamental structure of reality, but occurs as human knowledge reaches ever deeper toward a comprehension of that fundamental structure, and becomes diffused increasingly among humanity. Environment, in turn, is changed as culture, and in this sense, evolves.

Cultural determinism on this realist basis has been vigorously challenged by such philosophers of history as Collingwood and Croce. Their idealist conceptions represent another kind of cultural outlook, in which no accessible underlying world structure compels recognition and obedience. Human evolution is for them a human creation-invention, rather than the product of discoveries. Implicitly, this outlook calls for a rejection of determinism in regard to human history. The most explicit opposition to deterministic philosophies of history has perhaps been that of Popper (1957), who has argued that the astronomically inspired model of a universe of order, on which these philosophies rest, itself is suspect. The apparent motions of the heavens are explained upon the basis of advance agreement on a model, then confirmed in observation. But no such agreed-upon model has developed for history. The appeal of Marxist thought, of course, must rest in large part precisely on possession of just such a model; but Popper impugns the model of that historical materialism on the epistemological ground that history can teach no lessons and reveal no order of its own, since fundamentally the very concepts of "event" and "tendency" and "cause" remain unclarifiable.

Another, rather odd, determinism is expressed in racial theories of history. Writers like Gobineau and Chamberlain have claimed innate superiority for certain groups, and attempted to explain most great historical achievements as the work of some single biological stock. Purity of race becomes for them the key to progress. Almost always chauvinistic, racial doctrines well exemplify the invidious way in which most determinisms single out particular social elements for a uniquely positive, progressive role.

The concept of inevitable developmental stages of historical development was widely prevalent in nineteenth-century European thought. It came to figure, through the influence of Lewis Morgan, in the stages of productive relationships adopted by Marx and Engels, as well as in the idea of inevitable stages of technological development so commonly still encountered among prehistorians and ethnologists (cf. Lowie 1937). A notion of this same sort is also inherent in the psychological determinism propagated by the school of Freud. Psychoanalysis interprets not only individual life histories in terms of unconscious motivations and images fixed in childhood, but history, also, as the enactment of the fundamental psychic dramas. Freudian concepts are vulgarized in visions of Oedipal confrontations that overthrow patriarchal systems, or of capitalism as an "anal" stage of social development. The symbols and encounters that make history, and all the underlying behavior, are, according to this viewpoint, just projections or realizations of the underlying psychic reality, obedient to its own "natural laws." Another immanence is apparent here, although its spelling out has remained only fragmentary.

The foregoing instances suffice to show the range of deterministic viewpoints in recent historical thought. All of these disparate doctrines emphasize the immanence of one or another supposedly immutable order: the divine plan, the laws of historical materialism, physical (and economic) law, the structure of the unconscious, or genetic inheritance. Each of them in its own way presents human cultures as dynamic applications of some fundamental principles that govern transformation of the world. Man, if not determinant, is agent and executor of underlying forces, and social evolution is PROGRESSIVE realization of those principles. For all these doctrines, man's evolutionary role is central; they are all more or less anthropocentric and some are also teleological.

GEOGRAPHICAL AND ENVIRONMENTAL DETERMINISM

Thoughtful men have always remarked not only differences in custom and appearance among the variously situated human populations, but deeper differences of character and temperament that seem to coincide with geographical location and, perhaps in consequence of these differences, great contrasts in the constitution of society and the political order. A plausible geography of character, as we should call it now, suggests itself to many discerning observers. Why should personal and national traits exhibit so much geographic regularity? Montesquieu and Buckle gave the classic expression to the idea that character and social forms agree with some environmental factors — an idea still vigorously advocated by some few writers today. Whatever cause may be adduced, it becomes but reasonable to investigate the geographic distribution of the causal factors indicated. Geographical determinism generally means "deterministic reasoning applied geographically," and an injunction to consider a phenomenon within its geographic context. Even in the absence of strict causal reasoning, and apart from any doctrinal position, this particular notion is unexceptionable.

One objection does arise, however, even at a most general level, to geographical determinism. For a dubious assumption may be hidden in this reasoning, to the effect that whichever causes (or, if "cause" is abdicated, then "associated circumstances") might account for the presence of a given phenomenon in a certain place, these causes will themselves be found in that place. It is unwarranted to assume that the geographical distributions of effects and "causes" must necessarily long remain congruent. Therefore, the simple comparison of distributions cannot ever lead to certainty concerning "cause."

Strictly speaking, environmental determinism ought probably to be distinguished as a special case of the more general geographical determinism just alluded to. The distinction does not, unfortunately, hold consistently in the literature, but it may help clarify some issues. The meaning of environmental determinism, as such, revolves around the common usage of the term "environment." In particular, it concerns itself with factors of the natural environment.

"Environment" is one of those words that seem to have an obvious intuitive meaning — until considered carefully. Let us examine some of its possibilities:

SPATIAL: Environment means the spatially contiguous surroundings — simply whatever exists in the vicinity of something. The spatial extent remains unspecified: how far away from a point is the perimeter of its environment?

SENSORY: Environment refers to the normal field of a subject's perception. The boundary of a person's environment lies at the limit of his sight, hearing, and so on. (The heavens make up, spatially, most of our environment. Or do they?)

DYNAMIC: Environment connotes the zone of interaction between a body and the forces impinging on it. Invisible microscopic pathogens infest it; distant nuclear explosions intrude themselves into it. Most restrictedly, "environment" in this sense stops at the surface of the skin and somewhere in the inner pulmonary sacs; most broadly, it includes whatever can touch or be touched, affect or be affected.

HABITUAL: Environment, as enduring and developing reality, includes the whole potential range in which an individual functions. It coincides with his daily round of places visited and occupied, or with seasonally various haunts. For mobile creatures, an environment cannot be (meaningfully) just a single point in space. (When is an "environment" a lifetime's range of wandering?)

CAUSAL: Environment signifies the physical (and perhaps symbolic) conditions associated necessarily with the presence or persistence of a given phenomenon. It is the characteristic situation in which a given phenomenon can occur. Yet other definitions, suitable for certain purposes, have been proposed. Clearly, "environment" can be conceived in many different ways. The causal viewpoint required by the idea of environmental determinism — some combination of immediate environmental conditions necessary and sufficient to produce a given phenomenon — in the present case becomes not merely a logical but also a geographical concept.

One of the implied premises of traditional environmental determinism holds that the environmental conditions presiding over human destiny or character are those conditions that are not man-made. Nature dominates mankind. Since physical rather than some kind of "mental" causality is almost always contemplated — even if supposedly it operates through physical effects upon mentalities — the relevant environment must be "physical." But more particularly, "physical environment" in this context emphatically does not include everything in the spatial, sensory, or dynamic fields that is physical; it carries the implication of the "natural" elements alone, and so in effect becomes the "natural environment" as against what I have called (Wagner 1960) the "artificial environment." Furthermore, according to this theory, even if the natural environment does at times allegedly affect mentalities, it operates primarily in a directly physical and not a symbolic fashion. Whatever environmental determinism offers, it is not a theory of perception.

The factors of the natural environment that have figured in the arguments of the environmental determinists include particularly spatial properties — e.g. contiguity; concentration or dispersion; climatic features, especially the seasonal march of temperature and rainfall; soil and mineral resources; and general surface configuration.

At its simplest, environmental determinism attempts to find an explanatory correlation between the areal patterns of physical and those of cultural geography. The relationships discovered have not always been envisaged as specific processes, which, as will be apparent, constitutes one of the fundamental weaknesses of this whole thesis. In more evolved form, the intimately related concepts of environmental influence and environmental adaptation, applied to historical developments in the context of environmental change, sometimes allegedly permit investigators to identify key processes. The concepts of environment evoked vary not only according to the several categories outlined just above, but also in their temporal reference. This permits four possible modes of relationship between society and (natural) environment: (1) gradual "adaptation" by society to constant environmental conditions; (2) continual adaptive "response" by society in consequence of continually varying environmental conditions; (3) fixed, unchanged "adjustment" to unchanged conditions; and (4) established "accommodation" of a society that serves to cope with considerable ongoing variation of environmental conditions.

VARIETIES OF ADAPTATION AND ADJUSTMENT

Every human society must somehow come to terms with its environment, and every such society must deal with some inconstancy in its surroundings. The amplitudes of variations in the social and environmental domains, as well as systematic correlations linking them, provide the basis for distinctions drawn above between what I shall call (using terms never well standardized in the geographic literature), "adaptation," "adjustment," "response," and "accommodation." The ideal of a society and its environment remaining constantly in close adjustment oversimplifies the case; however, we may assume that many a society becomes sufficiently accommodated that its normal functions adequately cope with modest amplitudes of environmental change. This situation in fact better represents a typical "adjusted" state than does an ideal thoroughly immobile, static case, wherein neither domain exhibits change. The relationship of society and environment, however, may become more or less stabilized, either when both remain comparatively constant or when both are changing but in phase with one another. Potential instability develops when environmental change occurs to which society is not accommodated, and the necessary response is long delayed; this may bring on cataclysm.

A balanced statement on adaptation and adjustment must make allusion to a formidable complication of the argument, to wit, the fact that when society "accommodates," "adapts," "adjusts," or "responds" to environmental influence, it does so, partly if not wholly, through transforming the environment itself. This is a salient universal characteristic of human societies. A view directed only toward the evolution of society and culture, therefore, may misread the history; alteration of the environment claims equal relevance.

A second complication that generally applies is the possibility of geographical mobility. A potent influence from the environment may fail to operate in the expected fashion because the society withdraws from that environment. This, too, is response. Such an eventuality gives rise to a special kind of environmental determinism — it has been contended that particular outbreaks of migration have ensued upon the occurrence of certain crucial changes in the environment. As developed especially by Huntington (1907, 1922, 1945), this has counted among the most striking and influential environmental determinist theses.

Having taken account of these reservations, we may consider both environmental and social or cultural change as capable of a varying degree of consistent directedness and continuity. The manifold number of possibilities expands: we can conceive now of societies possibly remaining altogether static in the face of either an unchanging environment, an environment of sporadic and disarticulated variability, or an environment that evolves progressively in some direction. Alternatively, we may entertain the corresponding possibilities of social systems undergoing articulated or chaotic change as a reflection of environmental influence of any one of these kinds.

MAN AND THE ICE AGE

A temporal coincidence between the reconstructed history of glaciation in the Pleistocene and what was known of mankind's record struck many people long ago. Although discoveries have demonstrated that the earlier episodes of human history took place outside the glaciated zones themselves, climatic, topographic, and biotic conditions differing substantially from the present ones presumably occurred in the intertropical and subtropical zones (apparently the scene of critical stages in mankind's development) concurrently with what was happening in higher latitudes. Hence a temptation arises to interpret mankind's cultural and physical development as "determined" by environmental changes during the Pleistocene.

If man "evolved" at all, as almost all authorities would nowadays acknowledge, it meant a process of becoming ever better fitted to survive and multiply within the conditions of environment prevailing at a given time. Consistent upward reassessments of the age of man imply that not only nonglacial but preglacial environments may have been of consequence for early man. The theme of human physical evolution lies outside our scope, but we ought to remark upon the seeming lack of a convincing correlation between certain critical periods in that development and the most impressive changes of environment of which we know. And when we come to the story of Neanderthal and diverse other mid-Paleolithic physical types, relationships with environmental change are somewhat puzzling, to say the least.

The actual environmental picture anywhere during Pleistocene time is still unclear enough that any close connections with man's cultural development are necessarily uncertain. Some broad outlines do suggest themselves, however. Simultaneous physical, social, cultural, and ecological distinctiveness among the recognizable ancestors of man began at the latest in the Lower Pleistocene and probably before, well outside the zones affected by the ice sheets. At least in Africa, several different environmental niches permitted, or encouraged, the development of divergent types of men. Climatic change may have exerted increasing selection pressure on the heavier, more vegetarian population of *Paranthropus* and ultimately brought about its extinction, while hunting bands evolved among its relatives, accentuating human sociability and encouraging some kind of culture.

The mastery of fire and possibly the invention of clothing may have given men the means of seizing ecological dominance themselves by the time of the Mindel glacial period, and may have allowed them to colonize and endure in much colder northern latitudes. Men did not, however, move toward a physical adaptation to cold environments in one zone, to warm wet or dry ones in another, and so on. The concomitant of climatic, vegetational, and faunal change seems not to have been physical specialization into very closely adjusted local stocks, leading toward new species, but rather development into a culturally accommodated, dominant stock, able, because of its versatility and artificial influence on environments, to survive virtually everywhere except on the ice caps. Nothing is perceptible physically, even in Neanderthal men, that is clearly and irretrievably cold-adapted; nor was their Mousterian cultural equipment obviously so adapted. Apparently man did not adjust to one or another environment as such, but to the very fact of secular climatic change with all its consequences. Finding nature's climates unreliable, he undertook to make his own.

Once the overthrow of the pressure of natural selection is accounted for, this interpretation of our evolution need not absolutely presuppose determinism. Insofar as man's physique was concerned, nothing henceforth needed to become a fixed commitment to a certain climate. Whereas until then mutation had been the source of evolutionary adaptation, after this point invention had to fill its place.

There remains the problem of the possible determination of inventions by environment. It is easy to admit selection pressure as applying equally to cultural innovations and to genetically induced novelties, once they have appeared. But whereas no one seems to question the virtual randomness of the process of genetic mutation in a living population — apart from some few mechanical, chemical, and radiational effects that bear on the frequency but not the character of mutants — random evolution of a culture is perhaps intuitively less acceptable. Culture, and emphatically its technical and organizational aspects, appears to show consistent growth and improvement (cf. Kroeber 1944, 1952), and to achieve them almost unerringly. It seems, to date at least, as if societies do not make as many blind mistakes as nature does in the course of producing and testing innovations. Hence we have to ask whether progressive culture change reflects particular determinate controls.

MENTAL ACTIVITY AND ENVIRONMENTALISM

Bodily adaptation and accommodation to the natural environment count for much less now than in the early Pleistocene, at least in the aggregate, despite the multiplicity of possible effects (e.g. of climate) enthusiastically alleged by Markham (1942), Huntington (1915), and others. The adaptation to natural conditions of man-modified environment itself, specifically technics, is of greater consequence. Technical systems of objects, in and of themselves, may well respond to advancing change in their surroundings, or they may accommodate over limited amplitudes to fluctuations therein, but they do not exactly "evolve." We should not think of artifacts as adapting or adjusting. Technology does not command its own development, nor has it, strictly speaking, any pattern of internal descent from form to form. Its continuities reside entirely in the concepts of observers.

But human populations, and their habitats, evolve by regular descent and truly cumulative change. Ideas, too, may well exhibit a genuine evolutionary pattern — one notion growing from another toward a given culmination. This evolution of ideas is what generates the changes or initiatives for change within the technological domain. Is it legitimate to see the application of ideas within technology as consequent on a genuinely evolutionary process external to technics? In what sense might this evolution be determined by environment?

Any idea evolves within an individual mentality. It can never be otherwise. Yet in order to belong to culture, and to contribute to the evolution thereof, we can agree that an idea must be diffused and therefore shared. Finally, if applied, it may enter into technics or some kind of group behavior. The evolution of culture involves a more complex process than simply a generation of ideas, but the character of culture must still depend on ideas, for the origin of which we may seek an explanation. Whereas a physicalist outlook, based upon the philosophical position that all physical phenomena can be explained by purely physical determinants or influences, suffices to account, say, for the effects of climate on the individual organism or on its living space and livelihood, the physicalist conception of mind is vague, and except for a rare minority of pathological subjects, is useless for explaining the genesis of a particular sort of idea.

What governs mental life? If chance alone determines it, we find an analogue to mutation in biology. But if it has a pattern that reflects some regular relationship with something else, that pattern possibly may prove intelligible. One potential source of mental patterns is the natural, and generally the physical environment. A conception of mankind as rational, even if incompletely so, entails the supposition that men learn — that is, that mind responds adaptively to environment. In recent years, many geographers — such as Lowenthal (1961, 1967), Brookfield (1969), and Saarinen (1969) — have reviewed the evidence for geographical perception as a factor in behavior. The concept of culture, more particularly, has emphasized learning as a sharing of experience and insight among men. As earlier proposed, cultural evolution means adaptive change; that position would imply that such change occurs in consequence of insights into man's environmental circumstances. By definition, adaptive evolutionary change reflects its environmental circumstances, and so our mentalism ought to be environmentalist as well.

Apart from physicalist climatic theories of environmental determinism which have to do with births and deaths and health (including mental health and vigor), the related doctrine of possibilism associated particularly with the French school of Vidal de la Blache, provided geographers with a view of man as rational within a world of intelligible possibilities — a view that is environmentalist, as Lewthwaite (1958) remarked, and also mentalist. For possibilism, cultural change is seen to follow upon discovery of inescapably obvious ideas through contemplation of the environment. Adaptation and adjustment through cultural means, in this view, require insight and the recognition of environmental possibilities or pressures. Reflection and deliberation are implied, and choice involves conjecture and prediction. The origin of such a technique as fire making, by this reasoning, might be explained by imaginative imitation of observed events in nature, or even by deliberate research in semiplayful contexts. A complex such as domestication likewise might have come about through some premeditated course of action, although not necessarily with practical intentions.

The possibilist conception of cultural evolutionary theory permits of various motivations in man's adaptation to environment. It need not presuppose a purely utilitarian intention. If men adapt to their environments by making more or less conscious and purposeful choices, their consciousness and purposes may well include symbolic, ritual, and ceremonial features. Cosmologies, as comprehensive explanations of human experience of environing reality, perhaps prescribe their own adjustments. The ritual origins of such evolutionary landmarks as animal domestication, urged by Hahn (1896), and urbanism, recently proposed by Wheatley (1971), command a certain plausibility. Methodologically, the importance of this version of possibilist environmentalism — in contrast to environmental determinism — lies in its indication of a source of explanation in the progress of cosmological speculation, for which, unfortunately, material evidence is often meager. The growth of cosmologies may often be slighted in the reconstruction of prehistory.

SITES AND ROUTES

Environments affect diffusion of ideas. Two kinds of influence apparently are relevant: those that confirm or refute, establish or extinguish, the idea itself, and those that favor or obstruct its physical communication. Consider first communication. The contacts among peoples play a major role in spreading new ideas, and so it must have been for ages past. A kind of environmentalism is inherent in the idea, so prominent in Ratzel's (1882, 1891) anthropogeography, that topographical configuration or proximity and distance must condition cultural development. Most of Ratzel's ideas — not nearly so mysteriously environmental-determinist as is sometimes alleged — lend themselves to statement as hypotheses about communication and its technical necessities, and in that guise call for no particular assumptions about controls of another order inherent in environments. Differences between Old and New World civilizations, or between Black Africa and the circum-Mediterranean world, are easiest explained with the help of such hypotheses. The known spatial patterns of the spread of many great inventions unmistakably attest to some necessities of spatial order. Little controversy need arise about the validity of these ideas of Ratzel, nor do they in themselves clarify the problem, strictly, of the origin of innovations. But nonetheless they have great logical bearing on the problem. Diffusion may figure as the alternative in a given place to independent local evolution or invention.

Historically, extreme differences of opinion have arisen among ethnologists, geographers, and prehistorians upon this issue. If true invention be regarded as a very rare event, and the geographic process of diffusion as a commonplace one, then most if not all cultural evolution anywhere can be explained, as Graebner (1911) and other *Kulturkreis* spokesmen would have it, by relatively simple stages in a universal process of diffusion of a small number of basic inventions. All of cultural evolution might constitute a series of emanations from one great dominating center of invention. For such theories, the original inventions could stand as utterly unique and probably inexplicable events, all importance then attaching to the routes, times, and means of their diffusion.

Demonstrable relationships preclude alternative hypotheses. A known diffusion obviates environmental deterministic explanation of local processes of cultural innovation. We should not forget that the immense majority of local cultural developments at any time empirically show obvious derivation from elsewhere, and close resemblance and connection with adjacent situations. Only rarely can an actual invention be even a possibility. Furthermore, the laborious quest for absolute beginnings may in fact be futile, yielding scant enlightenment about the course of cultural development, even if initial accidents or small determinate responses can be found. Their propagation is what counts.

The interesting cases, therefore, present themselves when very similar new traits arise in places isolated from each other and with little possibility of intercourse. As wandering and intermarriage militate against genetic isolation of the local human group, diffusion and related migratory movements intrude upon autonomous adjustment of local cultures to environment. Experience and ingenuity are shared. Trade equalizes resource allocation. Accordingly, one of the most fertile kinds of speculative explanation by determinists has focused on the predisposing circumstances for migration or diffusion. Much better arguments can be made for environmental limitations and incentives for communication and migration than for any environmental impulse toward invention. The crux of the question then becomes how conducive environmental conditions are to spatial propagation of the innovation.

POTENTIALS FOR DIFFUSION

Conditions for diffusion may serve to explain attested innovations introduced to given places, if not their ultimate beginnings. The category of conditions that impinge upon communication of a new idea, or actual movement of people, permits of probabilistic interpretation; conditions governing the establishment or extinction of the idea in any given spatial phase — and therefore continuity or interruption of the spatial process of its expansion — are capable of possibilistic assessment. In neither instance does a strict determinism seem to recommend itself.

Cultural evolution as exhibited by apportionment of great world areas at any period of history to culture regions reflects an unmistakable conformity to major geographical controls. Before the maritime age, the major boundaries ran through oceans, deserts, and high mountain ranges. Cultural communities conformed to topographic sectors like the valleys of great rivers. Connections now express the existing maritime and interurban networks of communications.

Thus, in regard to cultural evolution, the possibilities of diffusion should first be judiciously canvassed, and the relative ease and likelihood of intercourse, according to the transportation media peculiar to the time, should be considered. A certain net propensity to travel (and in consequence, communicate) applies in any situation where a group of human beings move about. On a probabilistic basis, the random spatial movements of all individuals within a given population, over a sufficient time, will tend to establish a pronounced pattern of circulation that describes the mean relative cost-distance values from all their points of origin.

Suppose, instead of delving into mentalistic theories, that we merely assume that innovative thoughts occur at stated rates, and that they spread according to "potentials" in a field of forces that reflects the cost in trouble, time, or resources, of crossing any given distance, topographically differentiated. Cost-distance governs the degree of interconnectivity. It is furthermore legitimate to suppose, in probabilistic terms, that cultural resemblance between any two selected points is *ceteris paribus* a function of the subsisting interconnections patterned by cost-distance. The problems of "inspiration" or "creativity" that bedevil mentalism are then obviated. We simply postulate that new ideas are very frequent and occur at approximately the same rate everywhere. Attention shifts to their dissemination. Such a viewpoint is reasonable, in the absence of any indication of geographically differential creativity, such as would arise from particular superiorities of climate, race, or other elements.

The peculiar sort of retrospective, pseudocausal reasoning mentioned earlier that reads back from a known result toward its initial conditions, can apply to the search for cultural initiatives. A known distribution in time and space, considered in the context of a differentiated spatial field (especially when we know it at several of its stages), will tend to reveal the sequence and direction of diffusion, and the points whence given movements came. The "naïve" space of ordinary distance does not serve such purposes, however, for the "distances" involved must register the complications and constraints produced by many other factors. Nor can the conclusions from such reasoning attain to certainty, for they must remain expressions of the probable and nothing more.

A good example of the application of distributional analysis to the reconstruction of a putative diffusion pattern, Sauer's study (1952) of agricultural origins and dispersals, has recently received from the research of Solheim and Gorman in southeastern Asia what may be independent confirmation of its startling claim for early planting cultures in that region. The thesis formerly had lacked all archaeological support (see Gorman's review elsewhere in this book). This instance demonstrates how altogether different lines of reasoning, employing quite distinct assumptions and a different sort of evidence, converge at times on certain problems and reinforce each other's results.

ENVIRONMENTAL SCREENING

An idea's viability, of course, depends not on the means of its communication alone. In the process of diffusion, described formally as a succession of temporal-spatial phases, the idea has to pass at each phase from the donors to the receptors accessible to them. We may calculate the probability of acceptance and further propagation of an idea on the part of the respective receptors — the transition probabilities — according to the compatibility of the idea with local cultural and natural circumstances and the dispositions of the receptors. If the innovative impulse is repeatedly presented to a representative variety of possible receptors, then this probability becomes fairly specific and reliable.

Although cost-distance may express a moderate diversity of variables, it shows an overall consistency. But factors that contribute to environmental screening take a great variety of forms. In formal terms, given an initial innovative impulse and the potential spatial field for its communication, what may be called the net environment for each point of reception (once cost-distance values are assigned) either rejects or accepts the impetus. Environment, in this case, includes personal and social as well as natural conditions. This concept of diffusion does not require complete, determinate articulation in each phase between the idea diffused and the circumstances of receptors. Some degree of latitude applies to possibilities for acceptance and incorporation of the new idea into the environment. Environmentally screened transitions decide what portion of the potentially accessible cost-distance field is attained in a given phase by the diffusing impulse.

The voluminous literature on diffusion surveyed by various geographers of late (Gould 1969; Brown and Moore 1969; Hägerstrand 1967; Hudson 1972) provides a wealth of formulations of the process, but no easy rule for coping with the problem of transitional probabilities. In fact, the same formidable issues that becloud environmental determinism might appear to arise here again. A combination of probabilistic and possibilistic reasoning avoids these pitfalls. The adoption of the innovation will presumably ensue, sooner or later, according to this approach, if environmental possibilities are such as somehow to allow it. Various recipients may be contacted in turn, and their several dispositions may affect the outcome, so that if one or more possibilities for it do exist, over some time random processes of introduction and attempted application of the new idea effectuate its establishment in one or a number of different versions in the new location. The propensity of human beings to travel, invoked above, insures repeated random exposures of potential receptors to the innovation, and guarantees in turn that once naturalized, the idea will henceforth undergo a further propagation at the hands of donors from the new area, again exhibiting the probable effects of random but repeated onward contacts and environmental screening. A random process operating in a field of possibilities thus explores and, given time, will actualize some of those possibilities, if not all of them.

Consider the examples furnished historically by the spread of grain crops. The diffusion of grain growing saw the introduction of the various wheats and barleys, from different but related origins, to peripheral regions, and at certain margins the gradual screening out of these in favor of some associated weeds like oats and rye, or conceivably certain millets. Sometimes climatic barriers intervened, but sometimes cultural preferences appear to have decided the election of a certain species or variety for planting. The possibilities were multiple, and active interchange involving numerous and various encounters prompted exploitation of them, until the middle latitudes of the Old World had acquired a well-diversified pattern of grain agriculture, sensitively adjusted to environments and cultures. Something similar must have happened, also, in the case of rice or maize in other areas, and in countless other cases of diffusion.

Environmental screening of diffusions carries with it another important effect, as the foregoing instance also shows. Innovations change en route. Ideas evolve while they move, and successive passages from one kind of environment to another may subject emerging variants to a powerful selection process leading to considerable differentiation as the impulse spreads. Slight random changes cumulate when shaped into a trend, and various environments eliminate some features altogether while preserving or intensifying others. Conjointly, the originally distinct diffusions of a number of ideas (or genetic lines of crops) may, under the pressures and incentives of particular environments, result in fusions and mutual modifications. Such a situation appears most clearly in the case of linguistic material, notably words that incorporate more than one remote influence. (The evolution of a language furnishes a wealth of suggestive indications concerning the possible course of cultural evolution in general.)

ENVIRONMENTAL PREDISPOSITIONS

The behavior that operates in the finding of compatible conditions for phenomena takes place within a realm of possibilities, some of them of natural provenance and some of them in whole or part man-made. If we know in advance (or retrospectively) the character and requirements of a given innovation as it moves, we may discern those situations where, once it arrives, it may become acclimatized. The prediction of this kind of fitness of a place to new ideas must depend upon the identification of minute particulars of both the innovation and the environments, but sometimes this procedure does prove feasible. More frequently than otherwise, the stipulated limiting conditions for the occurrence of phenomena provide a means of such prediction. Thus, a simulation of the spread of grains might be effected by compiling data on the geographic distribution of relevant factors, such as critical isotherms for the species concerned, crucial soil properties, or existing techniques of cultivation. The field of possible expansion for each crop appears quite clearly in such simulations where, of course, this geographic information has in fact assisted in determining the very limits here invoked; the reasoning is often circular, predicting what has already happened, on the basis of its having happened.

The probabilistic concepts introduced above allow for chance occurrence of ideas at equal rates at any point. They further postulate a fixed propensity to travel and exchange. Cost-distance sets controls on the diffusion of ideas in differentiated geographic fields, and continuity in diffusion rests upon the receptivity to the impulse of given environments reached by it. If a particular notion — quite hypothetically — has arisen here and there repeatedly throughout the time of man on earth, it necessarily has had to wait for certain propitious conditions in order to diffuse and become widely established. At first environmental barriers may have contained it; then environmental change facilitated its dissemination. Although the assumption that all ideas exist in embryo through all the ages, or arise repeatedly, may be unrealistic, this issue is irrelevant. What matters is the postulation that the spread of new ideas attests a changed environment.

Types of limiting (and facilitating) conditions vary. The crucial changes opening the way to new disseminations may involve: alterations in the mode of perception on the part of a people, consequent on cultural developments; modifications of technics, again a cultural acquisition; transformations of environment by man; variations in the natural conditions, either casual or secular — and of course, mutations in the idea that diffuses, or in the ways of implementing it. The foremost influence for receptivity to change, accordingly, appears to stem from previous diffusions that have modified the local culture, or through it, the environment. Only rarely, seemingly, would natural environmental change contain the key.

Environmental determinism, therefore, after having been watered down to such a minor theme as the foregoing one of favorable natural conditions opening the way for new ideas, remains a part of valid reasoning. Certain times occur in history when circumstances change in such a way as to favor rapid evolution. Progressive change takes place, we might infer, when natural conditions come about that favor the acceptance and establishment of new ideas — not necessarily of local origin — that institute a better adaptation of a culture to its environment. But redoubtable objections to a purely automatic supposition of this kind abound, as will be evident. Only rarely will environmental determinism offer an attractive explanation of events. Its fallacy lies in unwarranted metaphysical assumptions that induce a specious confidence in full foreknowledge or retrospective certainty.

With all due caution, we may embrace a functional interpretation of the growth and geographical adjustment of human cultures that almost (but only almost) demands the invocation of environmental determinism. The structural-functional anthropology that followed the pronouncements of Radcliffe-Brown (1948) was predisposed to this expedient, because it looked for close, or "best," adjustments of societies to habitats. Ideas emerge in abundance; only the impediments of nature (i.e. cost-distance) prevent their penetrating everywhere; where they reach, they are selected insofar as circumstance requires — not merely allows — them to be adopted. Whatever their inception, their vocation is assured and understandable.

Even the nonfunctionalist schools of anthropology regard some cultural features of a people as less successful than others, or less adaptive; some make a place for "irrational" behavior and beliefs. Such categories are a pale but true reflection of environmentalist ones: adaptation is their criterion and cue. Is it realistic to deny that house types, livelihood activities, or clothing tend to show conformity to climate, raw materials, and other geographic features? Hardly so! Culture does consult environment. The primary objection to the doctrine of environmental determinism rather cites the multiplicity of rational adjustments possible to given concrete habitat conditions. Ethnographic evidence profusely illustrates the multiplicity of viable adjustments to a given habitat. There are better and poorer adaptations, to be sure, but more than one of each can be conceived, and often demonstrated. As rationale, environmental determinism furnishes a useful literary tool, but as a method of exact prediction it deceives.

THE FEASIBILITY OF CHOICES

A negative determinism, in accord with limits known for given distributions, would arouse no controversy. An impulse spreads until it reaches limits. The possibilities for positive incorporation of a new idea within existing habitats are so diverse and numerous, however, that the stipulation of limits seldom proves convenient. Nor, given numerous conditions that distinguish a particular environment, can some uniquely suited innovation be foreseen. Always more than one solution to a problem may develop, more than one reaction may exploit an opportunity presented.

The defect of environmental determinist reasoning, even at its best, concerns its basic logic. A set of conditions necessary for the occurrence of a certain phenomenon may or may not also be sufficient for it. Furthermore, a condition that suffices to produce (or guarantee occurrence of) a phenomenon may or may not invariably co-occur with it, that is, count as a necessary condition for it. Environmental determinism never could attain to statements of the type "if and only if ...". Accordingly no test of constancy of co-occurrence of "effects" and "causes" could develop. Concretely, the doctrine could not assert empirically vulnerable (testable) claims of necessary implication such that a particular environmental conjuncture would hypothetically be accompanied, wherever and whenever it appeared, by some specific cultural result. The environmental determinists did not promise to discover what conditions would always insure the invention of agriculture, or the discovery of fire, or the preference for warm clothing, or human slavery. Nor did they ever describe in detail the processes supposedly sufficient to implement the influence they claimed.

In fact, the chief proponents of this thesis fell back on mentalism — either proposing that certain climatic conditions (for instance, frequent cyclonic storms) stimulate mental activity, to which they attributed all differential progress; or that particular conditions revealed themselves at crucial moments in a way that forced insight on men, and so led to inventions (such as the putative domestication of wild animals, confined along with men by the secular increase of regional dessication into rare oases).

From a logical standpoint, the possibility remains that for every situation (or rather, for every long chain of successive situations), one particular adaptation (or again, a chain of such ordained ones) will in the end prove to have served maximum advantage. But optimality is always relative. There exists no reason to suppose that long-run maximum advantage dictates always what the short-run largest gain demands, nor any indication that what happens in reality will correspond to either one. Evaluations of "success" will differ in accordance with the time span contemplated. The doctrine that whatever happens is determined by all that precedes it leaves us without much practical understanding, because we cannot know the infinite details of what has gone before. But even if we did, we have no reason to suppose that what preceded an event would always manifest the most efficient, economical determinants at every point most adequate to bring about the current state of things. So even a comprehensive and absolute environmental determinism, like any sort of strict determinism, might not enlighten us much, whether it be "true" or not.

The choices that become "inventions" may not figure as momentous in the minds of those who make them. A small idea succeeds in practice, spreads and still succeeds, and metamorphoses to some degree while spreading. At last it reaches limits set by some environment, or fails to find new pathways for diffusion. Entangled with a host of other novel notions, it does not impress receptors as exceptional, but somewhere it, or some associated new idea, becomes the key to a protean achievement like "toolmaking" or "agriculture" or "irrigation" or "the internal combustion engine." These entities may often not exist for their inventors. Nor, perhaps, do the moments of the vital transfers of ideas involved have any prominence as "historical events." All transpires in the flow of life and time.

The invention or discovery of anything important, then, must emerge out of small acts and happenings, reflecting very minor, often unobserved environmental changes. Recognition of importance in a new idea or artifact or method constitutes, itself, inventive insight. The small events concerned, however, fall increasingly within the sphere of culture; as human groups condition their surroundings more and more, ever greater influences issue from their handiwork to bear on further evolution of their culture and environment. The role of nature in the determination of their progress lessens as their own proficiency increases. But the cultural effects facilitate development in just as complicated and obscure a fashion as do the natural ones.

The crux is this: if every moment is determinate, its determinants are infinite. How can the course of history be known beforehand?

REFERENCES

BRIGHAM, A. P.
1915   Problems of geographic influences. *Annals of the Association of American Geographers* 5:1–25.

BROOKFIELD, H. C.
1969   "The environment as perceived," in *Progress in geography*, volume one. Edited by C. Board, R. J. Chorley, P. Haggett, and D. R. Stoddart, 51–84. London: E. Arnold.

BROWN, L., E. MOORE
1969   "Diffusion research in geography: a perspective," in *Progress in geography*, volume one. Edited by C. Board, R. J. Chorley, P. Haggett, and D. R. Stoddart, 119–157. London: E. Arnold.

CALLOT, E.
1952   *La société et son environnement. Essai sur les principes des sciences sociales*. Paris: Marcel Rivière.

CURRY, L.
1966   "Chance and landscape," in *Northern geographical essays in honour of G. H. J. Daysh*. Edited by J. W. House, 40–55. Newcastle-upon-Tyne: Oriel Press.

FREEMAN, T. W.
1961   *A hundred years of geography*. Chicago: Aldine.

FUCHS, G.
1966   *Der Wandel zum anthropogeographischen Denken in der amerikanischen Geographie. Strukturlinien in der geographischen Wissenschaftstheorie, dargestellt an den vorliegenden wissenschaftlichen Veröffentlichungen 1900–1930*. Marburg/Lahn: Selbstverlag des geographischen Institutes der Universität.

GOULD, P.
1969   *Spatial diffusion*. Association of American Geographers, Commission on College Geography, Resource Paper 4. Washington, D.C.

GRAEBNER, F.
1911   *Die methode der Ethnologie.* Heidelberg: C. Winter.
HÄGERSTRAND, T.
1967   *Innovation diffusion as a spatial process.* Chicago: University of Chicago Press. (Translation of *Innovationsforloppet ur korologisk synpunkt,* 1953. Lund.)
HAHN, E.
1896   *Die Haustiere und ihre Beziehungen zur Wirtschaft des Menschen.* Leipzig: Duncker und Humblot.
1909   *Die Entstehung der Pflugkultur (unseres Ackerbaues).* Heidelberg: C. Winter.
HARTSHORNE, R.
1939   The nature of geography. *Annals of the Association of American Geographers* 29:1–482.
HUDSON, J.
1972   *Geographical diffusion theory.* Evanston: Northwestern University Press.
HUNTINGTON, E.
1907   *The pulse of Asia.* Boston: Houghton-Mifflin.
1915   *Civilization and climate.* New Haven: Yale University Press.
1922   *Climatic changes.* New Haven: Yale University Press.
1945   *Mainsprings of civilization.* New York: John Wiley and Sons.
KROEBER, A. L.
1944   *Configurations of culture growth.* Berkeley: University of California Press.
1952   *The nature of culture.* Chicago: University of Chicago Press.
LEWTHWAITE, G.
1958   The nature of environmentalism. *Proceedings of the Second New Zealand Geographical Conference,* 1–8.
LOWENTHAL, D.
1961   Geography, experience, and imagination: towards a geographical epistemology. *Annals of the Association of American Geographers* 51: 241–260.
LOWENTHAL, D., editor
1967   *Environmental perception and behavior.* University of Chicago, Department of Geography Research Paper 109. Chicago.
LOWIE, R.
1937   *History of ethnographic theory.* New York: Rinehart.
MARKHAM, C.
1942   *Climate and the energy of nations.* London and New York: Oxford University Press.
POPPER, K.
1957   *The poverty of historicism,* two volumes. New York: Harper and Row.
1962   *Conjectures and refutations: the growth of scientific knowledge.* New York and London: Basic Books.
RADCLIFFE-BROWN, A. R.
1948   *A natural science of society.* Glencoe: Free Press.

RATZEL, F.
   1882   *Anthropogeographie*, volume one: *Zur Anwendung der Erdkunde auf die Geschichte*. Stuttgart: J. Engelhorns Nachfolger.
   1891   *Anthropogeographie*, volume two: *Die geographische Verbreitung der Menschheit*. Stuttgart: J. Engelhorns Nachfolger.

SAARINEN, T.
   1969   *Perception of environment*. Association of American Geographers, Commission on College Geography, Resource Paper 5.

SAUER, C. O.
   1952   *Agricultural origins and dispersals*. New York: American Geographical Society.

SCHMIDT, P. W.
   1937   *Handbuch der Methode der kulturhistorischen Ethnologie*. Münster: Aschendorff.

SEMPLE, E. C.
   1911   *Influences of geographic environment*. New York: Holt.

SOROKIN, P. A.
   1928   *Contemporary sociological theories*. New York: Harper and Row.

TATHAM, G.
   1951   "Environmentalism and possibilism," in *Geography in the twentieth century: a study of growth, fields, techniques, aims and trends*. Edited by Griffith Taylor, 128–162. New York and London: Philosophical Library.

TAYLOR, R.
   1967   "Determinism," in *Encyclopedia of philosophy*, volume two, 359–364. New York: Macmillan.

THOMAS, F.
   1925   *The environmental basis of society: a study in the history of sociological theory*. New York and London: Century.

WAGNER, P. L.
   1960   *The human use of the earth*. Glencoe: Free Press.

WHEATLEY, P. C.
   1971   *The pivot of the four quarters: a preliminary enquiry into the origins and character of the ancient Chinese city*. Chicago: Aldine.

WHITE, L.
   1949   *The science of culture: a study of man and civilization*. New York: Farrar, Straus.

SECTION TWO

Worldwide Concepts

Cultural Evolution in the Old World and the New, Leading to the Beginnings and Spread of Agriculture

JOSEPH R. CALDWELL

The problems approached in the present volume concern an important series of innovations: the domestication of certain plants and animals and the establishment of these domesticates in economic systems. This paper will begin with a discussion of some still earlier events for, in the present state of our knowledge, some of these earlier developments appear as preconditions for domestication. Such widespread events as the establishment of a degree of sedentary life and of hunting-gathering economies (as distinguished from more specialized hunting economies) may have helped set the stage for initial domestications at various times and places.

We shall, therefore, be interested in the kind of cultural milieu in which the first domestications would seem most likely to have taken place. While admitting that this is far from a complete explanation of the origins of agriculture, I shall offer some suggestions about general and special conditions facilitating or inhibiting agricultural innovation. In this connection I shall also reject some recent views attributing plant domestication to demographic or other kinds of stress.

Finally, one can argue that in our concern with the origins of agriculture, there has been some neglect of an equally important series of problems — the steps by which domestication of plants and animals became increasingly important in economic systems until, ultimately, they became the mainstay of the most successful systems. Probably archaeological, botanical, and zoological studies can provide more specific data on these matters than on the events leading to the initial domestications themselves.

CULTURE-HISTORICAL DEVELOPMENTS PERHAPS
LEADING TO AGRICULTURE

What in general do we know about developments prior to and possibly leading to food production? We know that from Middle through Upper Paleolithic times there was a notable increase in cultural complexity. This is evidenced by more specialized tool kits, by storage pits, discernible dwellings, and such large permanent settlements as are found in the eastern Gravettian-Pavlovian of Moravia and the Kostenki-Borshevo occupations in the Soviet Union (Klima 1962: 193–210; Klein 1969). We also find systematic burial practices, personal ornament, sophisticated art, and perhaps calendrical notation (Marshack 1972). In the long run, there was an increase in population.

We also know that prior to the warming trend that ended the Pleistocene there were in Europe and the Americas and, judging from tool types, perhaps in northeastern Asia and northeastern Africa, many societies that emphasized the hunting of large mobile game. I shall refer to these as specialized hunting societies. From various lines of evidence we believe that meat formed the greater part of their diet and that cooperative and sophisticated hunting techniques were used. Examples of these, in addition to the Pavlovian and Kostenki-Borshevo groups, are the Upper Paleolithic hunters of Western Europe and some of the Paleoindians of the Americas. There were other societies at this time whose hunting practices were not so well developed, or at least not so archaeologically recognizable as such. Some of the latter could probably be characterized as foraging or generalized hunting-gathering groups. We ought to make a special effort to look for these on all continents. They deserve more attention in the literature.

We also know that in Europe, northeastern Africa, eastern Asia and North America the age climaxed by specialized hunting societies was followed by warmer climates, changes in vegetation and sea level and a range of societies adapting to forest and waterside environments (Waterbolk 1968; Caldwell 1958; Treistman 1972).

The archaeology of these groups also reflects subsistence changes. There is now a greater emphasis on fishing, fowling, and the harvesting of shellfish and wild plants. The scene is set for societies which, while continuing to hunt rather smaller game, were also developing sophisticated food-collecting techniques. We find a whole series of devices which are not so characteristic of earlier times: traps, snares, boats, sleds, digging sticks, querns, and sickles. Some of these artifacts were later to be used in the technology of food production. Examples of such peoples are the mesolithic societies of Europe, the Natufians of the Levant, some contemporary peoples of Japan, and representatives of the Desert and Eastern Archaic cultures of North America. There were many others.

This is not to say that these major changes in subsistence necessarily meant the total disappearance of the old specialized hunting way of life. That way of life may only have become less characteristic. Specialized hunting under worsened conditions continued on the North American plains and I would be afraid to argue that the recently discovered permanent hunter's village of 8500 B.P. at Suberde (Perkins and Daly 1968) was a completely autochthonous development.

I find interesting the obvious conclusion that the broad sequence of economic adaptations noted above should have appeared on the major continents and, with the possible exception of Africa south of the Sahara, at roughly the same time. The widespread occurrence of the earlier specialized hunting societies is not difficult to accept, given the continuous Eurasiatic land mass and our present belief that a substantial number of the early immigrants to the Americas had arrived before the end of the Upper Paleolithic. Nor is it difficult to see how the Americas should happen to have turned, like Eurasia, to more diversified hunting-gathering economies including a similar emphasis on the use of shellfish where these were available. With many species of game moving northward or becoming extinct innovations of subsistence would have been toward diversification of resources of wild foods. Under such conditions the nutritious and readily available shellfish could hardly have been overlooked as a staple food supply.

With a world occupied by collectors who had developed an intensive and pragmatic interest in wild plants and their properties, I believe that, inevitably, some would have begun to develop the techniques of food production. We have, at least, nicely documented instances at Tamaulipas and Tehuacan (MacNeish 1958, 1964) of societies depending chiefly on wild plants and the slow appearance of cultigen after cultigen while wild plants continued to make up the bulk of diet. Jarmo, Deh Luran, and other sites in the Old World also show a combination of wild and domesticated plants of similar species, but these sites are evidently systadially more developed toward agriculture than the earlier levels of the Middle American sites.

Binford (1968) has proposed that food production originated under demographic stress. I cannot believe this. If I were hungry, I would not put seeds into the ground. Rather, I would eat them as many starving peoples have done. Nor would I experiment with the development of a complex technology. Rather would I turn to marginally nutritious wild foods, as in fact, some starving agriculturalists have also done. To suppose that agriculture could be developed under the stress of demographic pressure is to suppose, impossibly, that the first hesitant experiments with planting would have yielded an immediate and efficacious bounty. To the contrary, I rather think that the demographic stress would have been settled one way or another long before a primitive agriculture could have reached a point where it could provide any relief at all.

On the other hand, peoples ALREADY practicing a paleotechnic agriculture might turn more and more to planting as wild foods became increasingly inadequate. It is here that a theory of demographic stress would be more appropriate, and it is perhaps for this reason that the Near Eastern and Middle American regions of heavy dependence on domesticated plants are found in semiarid lands where wild foods were presumably far less abundant than in such areas as Western Europe and eastern North America. This would not have been the case with the tropical agricultures of southeastern Asia or South America, but in those areas there may well have been a longer and more substantial dependence on hunting and gathering.

I wonder if it might not be possible in the next few years to approach the origins of agriculture from another point of view in addition to those we have held in the past. We are dealing here, after all, with problems of innovation. If archaeology, botany, and zoology have not yet provided, or may never provide, all the answers we seek, perhaps the special insights of cultural anthropology may be of assistance. I am proposing here that we should make an effort to discover some systematic and ultimately testable propositions about innovation as a process. Such propositions might well provide some additional ways to interpret archaeological evidence bearing on the origins of agriculture. Moreover, more understanding of innovation as a process is a pressing need in anthropology today.

I propose that one general condition for innovation is an appropriate cultural milieu. This would include a cultural focus, in the sense of Herskovits (1951) — a strong concern with a particular kind of activity. Although the concept of cultural focus does not of itself entail receptivity to innovation — other conditions would have to be specified here — I do not think major innovations would be made when a cultural focus was absent. And, indeed, most students of the origins of agriculture look to a cultural context of ancient hunting-gathering societies showing great dependence on foods derived from wild plants.

Such societies, we suspect, would — like some recent hunter-gatherers — have an abiding and pragmatic interest in wild plants and their properties.

Another general condition is that innovations arising out of an activity should be congruent with other aspects of a society or culture in the sense of Radcliffe-Brown (1935). Innovations should not, at least in the beginning, require extensive rescheduling of other activities. They should not, at least in the beginning, be opposed to existing value systems. In either event they would not be readily accepted. We know of some recent hunting-and-gathering societies which either did not accept agriculture, or accepted it very slowly, and I think a very good case could be made that this was one of the reasons.

Finally, we might also think of a general condition in which innovations would be redundant. Little possibility exists of innovations being accepted when whatever benefit they might confer is already satisfied by another, better established, activity. Some years ago I argued that acceptance of agriculture in prehistoric eastern North America was slowed down because hunting-gathering activity had already been developed to such a degree of efficiency that the adoption of paleotechnic agriculture would have seemed irrelevant (Caldwell 1958).

In illustrating the propositions advanced above I am suggesting that some hunter-gatherers have accepted agricultural innovation while others have resisted it. This apparent contradiction could be understood in terms of these same propositions if we suggest the role of timing. A cultural focus on wild plants ought to facilitate innovations involving plants. On the other hand if there has been enough time to elaborate hunting-gathering efficiency to a point where domestication would seem redundant, then agricultural innovation would be resisted. We may note here that in southwestern Asia the first domestic plants may have appeared within two thousand years, or less, of the time when the wild progenitors of wheat and barley were available in the area (see Wright and also Reed, this volume). In eastern North America, where resistance seems to have been a factor, no less than eight thousand years elapsed between the appearance of hunting-gathering systems (e.g. the Modoc Rock Shelter in Illinois; see Fowler 1959) and the first domesticated plants (e.g. in Kentucky and Tennessee; see Yarnell, this volume).

In addition to these general propositions there are also others specifically relevant to agricultural innovation. A high degree of sedentary existence would also be a condition of the cultural contexts for the first domestications. Another special condition is the apparent propensity of wild plants to develop special characteristics as a result of interaction with man.

The exact processes of the first domestications may forever elude us, but I am partial to the view of Anderson (1952) that disturbance of habitats through human clearings may in some instances have caused inadvertently one of the processes which we would perform deliberately if we wished to domesticate a plant, i.e. take it out of competition with other species. I am equally partial to the suggestions of Kent Flannery and others that the collecting process itself will ultimately bring about certain selections in the direction of domestication. Nevertheless, I leave these matters to plant geneticists and others wiser than I.

The foregoing statements about general and special conditions of innovation say nothing about the efficient causes for the first domestications. I see these as necessary, but not sufficient, causes — as part but not all of the explanation for the origins of agriculture.

THE ESTABLISHMENT OF AGRICULTURE
IN ECONOMIC SYSTEMS

The developments leading to agriculture did not end with the planting of the first seed. The establishment of domestic plants and animals in various local economies probably proceeded slowly and at different rates. In southwestern Asia, for example, if such sites as Çayönü and Deh Luran show domesticated plants before 9000 B.P., there are certainly other sites that do not. In the Levant, Wright (1971) has regarded the early occurrence of domesticated grain at Beidha, marginal to the Mediterranean zone, as congruent with Binford's model, but it is in fact also congruent with a view of greater resistance to food production in the Mediterranean zone of greater natural resources. The spread of food production within southwestern Asia will have to be worked out site by site and region by region. But it is apparent that hunting-and-gathering had some persistence in southwestern Asia, and much ink has been spilled over Jericho by those who cannot believe that a substantial town could be built by collectors hearding a few goats. The seeds which may have been kept in the Jericho storage bins do not need to have been domesticated. Curiously, there have been fewer demands that the large permanent stone settlement of Khirokhitia on Cyprus be considered an agricultural community, and I understand that no grain has been found there either. I am less impressed by the cultigens and possibly domesticated cattle found at Çatal Hüyük (Mellart 1967) than by the amount of animal art and symbolism suggesting the importance of hunting. Indeed, hunting seems to have been the mainstay at the nearby contemporary site of Suberde (Perkins and Daly 1968).

Quite possibly we have erred in assimilating the Levant to south-western Asia instead of to the Mediterranean Basin of which it is a part. The "Perrot proposition" (Perrot 1968) and the revisions of western Mediterranean dates proposed by Renfrew (1971) are long steps in the recognition of the culture-historical importance of the Mediterranean Basin, which too long has been regarded as an almost passive recipient of Near Eastern diffusions. I think that additional studies would show the importance there of collecting societies with notable innovations being made by these collectors. In an even more speculative vein, one may wonder if the cultural precocity of Jericho, Çatal Hüyük and Khirokhitia may not derive from being in a position to receive diffusions from the nascent food producers of the Zagros and Syria and sophisticated collectors of the eastern Mediterranean and the Levant.

INNOVATIONS IN COLLECTING SOCIETIES

In the past we have been too prone to credit agricultural societies with innovations which may well have been made by collectors. Thus Brea (1956) has argued for a Near Eastern origin for early Mediter-ranean impressed pottery and shipping even though the former occurs most abundantly in the central Mediterranean and is being made by collectors whose domesticates may have included only sheep and goats.

The present emphasis in the Near East on the achievements of the early food producers *vis-à-vis* collectors reminds me a little of the situation which prevailed in eastern North America a few years ago when large mounds and other earthworks were regarded as evidence of a "social surplus" which could only be obtained through agriculture. Although we know that some cultigens were present in the Ohio and Tennessee Valleys (Yarnell, this volume) at this time and earlier, there can be little doubt that the bulk of foods came from hunting and gathering. The crucial point is not when cultigens first appear, but rather when they become an essential economic staple.

Outside of the "centers" of agricultural origins, collecting societies persisted for thousands of years and continued to make important innovations including substantial buildings, earthworks, elaborate tombs, some of the so-called Neolithic arts — pottery, weaving, the polishing of stone — and in North America, at least, even a kind of metallurgy.

There are several examples of cultural climaxes achieved by collectors in which a considerable surplus was obtained to be disposed of in curiously lavish ways. In addition to the Adena and Hopewellian societies of eastern North America (Caldwell 1958) we have such groups in central California and the American northwest coast, the prehistoric fishers of Lake Baikal in Siberia and others.

In a few instances we can trace the innovations through which collecting efficiency was achieved. People living at about 10,000 B.P. at the Modoc Rock Shelter in southern Illinois tapped all nearby sources of food (Fowler 1959). Later the site became a hunting station where parties of males came only to hunt deer. During this later period other sites in the region reflect similarly specialized activities. The Ferry site on the Wabash River shows thousands of charred acorn fragments, large burned areas where they were roasted, and dozens of querns for grinding the meal. Other sites in northern Kentucky were utilized for the collection of shellfish and still another for shellfish collecting and fishing (Fowler 1959). Thus we see the development of scheduling and procurement systems necessary to efficient collecting. Similarly, on the coast of Georgia at 8000 B.P. shell middens show no foods which could not be obtained in the nearby marshlands (DePratter n.d.). By late prehistoric times there was a much more diversified diet and historical accounts exist of whole communities moving in season into the woods to secure other kinds of foods.

In the overall view, collecting societies in one place or another achieved nearly all the things which we ordinarily attribute to agricultural peoples: permanent settlements, substantial architecture, craft excellence and sophisticated arts, and a notable amount of leisure time. We can further suppose that the systems of scheduling and procurement necessary for efficient collecting imposed a discipline not inferior to that necessary to early agriculturalists. With such accomplishments in mind, resistances to the diffusion of food production are not surprising. In eastern North America, for example, there was a thousand years between the appearance of the first cultigens in the Midwest and the use of maize as an economic staple. There are indications of similar resistances in prehistoric Europe and Manchuria. Other examples could be given. In hindsight, we know of only two cultural-historical disadvantages of the collecting way of life. There was usually a limit to population concentration, and above all there was a limit to cultural evolutionary potential. No collecting society has ever achieved a civilization in the sense of being a technologically complex society.

THE SPREAD OF FOOD PRODUCTION

I have mentioned some instances of resistance to spread of food production. There are other cases where the spread seems to have been rapid. In the first case we may suspect that diffusion is taking place. In the second case the first inference ought to be a migration or explosion of peoples already practicing agriculture. Examples of the latter would be the spread of the *Bandkeramik* peoples from central Europe to the Netherlands and the spread of Prepottery Neolithic B assemblages from Syria to Jericho and the Jordan Valley.

I have been a farmer and know that even paleotechnic agriculture was a complex thing. Complex technologies do not readily diffuse. Nor, may I repeat, could they be invented under demographic pressure. Here I will suggest additional reasons for agricultural resistances. It was not just that collectors were content with the good life and would have considered the introduction of agriculture unnecessary or irrelevant. There are also deep-seated cultural reasons militating against fundamental change in any society. One thing most anthropologists believe is that if we analyze cultures into parts, then we must conclude that all of these parts are related to a greater or lesser degree. In the words of Radcliffe-Brown (1935), who preferred the term society rather than culture, each part contributes to the maintenance of the whole. Fundamental innovations, if adopted, could not be confined to such a single part of culture as its techniques of subsistence, but would have immediate effects on the whole way of life. Therefore, fundamental innovations are adopted very slowly or not at all. Into the fabric of a culture are also woven its values. Hunters and warriors do not easily give up their statuses and personal *raisons d'être* to become agricultural laborers. Worse, they may regard this as women's work. I could give recent American examples. It does not surprise me, therefore, that sometimes the spread of agriculture has been so slow. Other things being equal, I would also expect most of the earlier agricultural innovations to have been made by women. Most primitive societies contain two economies: men's work and women's work. Women, collectors *par excellence*, could cultivate a few plants without disturbing either the fabric of society or their own self-esteem. Were it not for this, agricultural diffusion might in many cases have been impossible.

CONCLUSION

In looking over the above remarks, it appears to me that some of our thinking about the developments leading to the origin of agriculture could be characterized as the kind of catastrophism which prevailed in geology two centuries ago. In opposition to this I would suggest that the Pleistocene hunting societies did not invent collecting under the stress of changing environments. As do all modern hunting societies, they had been collecting all along. A long-term response to changing climate could be reasonably seen as a gradual augmentation of collecting activities with which they were already familiar. As collecting became more and more a cultural focus, we would expect collecting innovations to be made in terms of new sources of food, scheduling, food preparation and storage.

Similarly, I cannot believe that food production was invented under the stress of demographic pressure. It is just as complex a technology as food collecting. What may have happened in the Near East and Mesoamerica is that peoples already using some domesticated plants would turn more and more to these as sufficient supplies of wild foods became more and more difficult to procure.

In the foregoing pages are outlined some of the earlier cultural developments which may have served as preconditions for the origins of agriculture. I also attempted to specify certain conditions of innovation in general and agricultural innovation in particular. The establishment of domesticates in various local economic systems was identified as a problem amenable to archaeological solutions. In this, developments of food collecting in the eastern Mediterranean Basin might be of considerable concern. Some specific innovations and continued achievements of the later food-collecting societies were noted, and the spread of agriculture outward from its apparent centers was seen as a series of interactions between food producers and the later hunter-gatherers. I have suggested that these hunter-gatherers were probably responsible for some innovations usually credited to food producers, and, generally speaking, they do not usually accept agriculture without some degree of resistance.

REFERENCES

ANDERSON, EDGAR
1952   *Plants, life, and man.* New York: Harcourt, Brace.
BINFORD, LEWIS R.
1968   "Post-Pleistocene adaptations," in *New perspectives in archeology.* Edited by S. R. Binford and L. R. Binford, 313–341. Chicago: Aldine.
BREA, LUIGI BERNABO
1956   La Sicilia prehistórica y sus relaciones con Oriente y con la Península Ibérica. *Ampurias, Departamento de Barcelona del Instituto "Rodrigo Caro" de Arqueologia y Prehistoria* 14:138–213.
CALDWELL, JOSEPH R.
1958   *Trend and tradition in the prehistory of the eastern United States.* Memoirs of the American Anthropological Association 88.
DE PRATTER, CHESTER
n.d.   "Late Archaic subsistence and settlement on the Georgia coast." Manuscript in the files of the Department of Anthropology, University of Georgia, Athens, Georgia.
FOWLER, MELVIN L.
1959   *Summary report of Modoc Rock Shelter, 1952, '53, '54, and '56.* Illinois State Museum Report of Investigation 8.
HERSKOVITS, MELVILLE J.
1951   *Man and his works.* New York: Knopf.
KLEIN, RICHARD G.
1969   *Man and culture in the Pleistocene: a case study.* Chicago: Chandler.
KLIMA, BOHUSLAV
1962   *The first ground-plan of an Upper Paleolithic loess settlement in Middle Europe and its meaning.* Viking Fund Publications in Anthropology 32:193–210.
MAC NEISH, RICHARD S.
1958   Preliminary archaeological investigations in the Sierra de Tamaulipas, Mexico. *Transactions of the American Philosophical Society* 48(6):1–210.
1964   Ancient Mesoamerican civilization. *Science* 143:531–537.
MARSHACK, ALEXANDER
1972   *The roots of civilization.* New York: McGraw-Hill.
MELLAART, JAMES
1967   *Çatal Hüyük: a Neolithic town in Anatolia.* New York: McGraw-Hill.
PERKINS, DEXTER, JR., PATRICIA DALY
1968   A hunter's village in Neolithic Turkey. *Scientific American* 210 (5):96–106.
PERROT JEAN
1968   "La préhistoire palestinienne," in *Supplément au dictionnaire de la Bible,* volume eight, 286–446.

RADCLIFFE-BROWN, A. R.
    1935   On the concept of functionalism in the social sciences. *American Anthropologist* 37:394–402.
RENFREW, COLIN
    1971   Carbon-14 and the prehistory of Europe. *Scientific American* 225(4):63–72.
TREISTMAN, J. M.
    1972   *The prehistory of China.* New York: Natural History Press.
WATERBOLK, H. T.
    1968   Food production in prehistoric Europe. *Science* 162:1093–1102.
WEBB, WILLIAM S.
    1945   *The Adena people.* University of Kentucky Reports in Anthropology and Archaeology 6.
WRIGHT, GARY A.
    1971   Origins of food production in southwestern Asia: a survey of ideas. *Current Anthropology* 12:447–477.

A Hypothesis Suggesting a
Single Origin of Agriculture

GEORGE F. CARTER

> Nimble thoughts can jump
> both sea and land.
> WM. SHAKESPEARE

We can easily get stuck in a rut, going round and round, reinforcing our preconceived notions by the happy process of talking only to those who agree with us and avoiding any dangerous new thoughts that might expose us to critical comment. Surely this is one of the greatest blocks to the creative process that should infuse the scholarly world. But look, if you will, at the many conferences made up only of "accepted" scholars who blandly sweep over the most fundamental questions and plunge on with their "accepted" lines of inquiry. Note for instance the sweeping under the rug of any possibility of consideration of an overseas origin of the Olmec civilization in America. "There have been, over the past century, a number of arguments made for Old World germinating contacts, either by way of the Pacific or from Africa by way of the Atlantic. None of these OPINIONS in my judgment are to be seriously considered" (my emphasis). I will not identify the source since my purpose is not to ridicule anyone, but to exemplify a situation. How revealing that the carefully compiled evidence of real contact can be swept under the rug as mere opinion! Or, as an example of name calling, consider the coining of the term hyperdiffusionists for those who disagree with the independent inventionists on the extent of diffusion in culture history. And it is only a matter of extent. No one argues that diffusion does not occur. On the contrary, it is accepted that diffusion is immensely more frequent than invention. On the other hand, without invention there would be nothing to diffuse. There is little room for dogmatism, and great need for open-ended consideration of the evidence, and the many possible conclusions our tenuous evidence allows. Instead of this we find a dogmatic defense of the anthropological Monroe Doctrine: there were no ideas diffused to America, at least no important ideas, and anyway, American agriculture is utterly distinct. On a worldwide scale we find much the same thing. Independent agricultural origins are postulated not only for eight or more areas but also for the same genus of plant; e.g. *Phaseolus* is not only accepted without question as independently domesticated, but even as independently domesticated four or more times in the New World. These are extraordinary conclusions, for most of culture history shows that totally independent inventions are exceedingly rare. The gist of my argument will be that there is little reason or evidence to show that agriculture is different from other cultural systems, and that one might expect but one origin.

I am not really insistent on just one. Perhaps there were two: roots versus seeds. Or maybe there were four: two in the Old World and two in the New World. But, I will present a hypothesis suggesting a single origin. This will be one step beyond Carl Sauer's suggestion of a dual origin: root crops and then seed crops in both the Old and New Worlds, though with characteristic boldness he even suggested that the New World agriculture might stem from southeastern Asia (Sauer 1952: 40).

I would prefer to continue to mull over this idea of the single origin of agriculture for a few years and then someday present a book-length study of the problem complete with exhaustive botanical and historical arguments. At present it is still a hypothesis and one that is not at all developed to the degree that I would like it to be. It is presented now in hopes that it will forestall freezing of opinion too rapidly in the field of inquiry into the origins of the agricultures of the world, for it seems to me that we must keep our options open yet a while.

The gist of my thesis will be that the evidence is more in favor of an invention, dependent on individual genius, than on an inevitable process. Granted that genius functions in a particular cultural setting complete with antecedents and so forth, still there is a difference between emphasis on processes which will produce the end result by some inexorable functioning versus the flash of creative genius. Emphasis on process leads to an explanation favoring numerous cultures arriving at similar solutions, at various places at different times. Emphasis on invention leads, as with all fully documented inventions, to the expectation of single occurrences. So far as I know no one can actually prove a single case of absolutely separate multiple invention of anything. The zero, one of the perennial cases put forward, is certainly a poor one, for the idea of the zero far precedes the alleged Hindu invention, and appears in America in cultures which we have ample reason to believe were either Asiatic transplants or greatly influenced from Asia and the Mediterranean. Note for example the recent publication which called attention to a forty-year-old article suggesting a Chinese origin for the dot and bar mathematics that is the basis for Olmec-Mayan mathematics (Kraus 1971; I have been unable to get the original article). Needham (1959), however, shows a magic square where six is shown by such a system and illustrates bars used with the value of five in Chin and Han times. Let us return from this aside to the problem of time.

Man and his ancestors undoubtedly gained their daily sustenance by being primarily gatherers of vegetation — leaves, buds, bark, seeds, and fruit — for some thirty million years or more; the anthropoid primates — monkeys, apes, and man — had their evolutionary origins no later than the end of the Eocene, and the dentition of all of them indicates their predominantly herbivorous diet from that time to this. The essence of the act of gathering is aided by the grasping hand, which, in coordination with superb stereoscopic vision in color, allowed (and allows) complete discrimination in the process of gathering. As gatherers, the earliest hominids, man's more immediate ancestors, became bipedal on the ground fifteen or more million years ago. One of the major sources of food at that time for this population probably was the hard seeds of many glade- and plains-living plants, including the grasses (Jolly 1970).

Better known than the obscure hominid ancestors of fifteen million years ago are the gracile australopithecines, of which the earliest known fossil is now dated at five to five and a half million years (Howell 1972). In spite of much imagery expended on the supposed hunting prowess of those gracile australopithecines (Ardrey 1961), they more probably depended for food almost entirely upon gathered plants. If, as advocated by some anthropologists (Robinson 1972; Reed, personal communication), we include these gracile australopithecines in the genus *Homo*, as *H. africanus*, then we can state validly that the earliest representatives of our genus were primarily gatherers and — looking at their magnificent molars — we can guess that, as has been true of hominids before and since, at least some of their daily gathering (depending upon season) was of hard seeds. Present evidence indicates that not until the time of the differentiation of that population we call *Homo erectus*, not more than a million years ago, did humans become competent as hunters of medium- to large-sized game. Even so, as with many hunting populations of the present or documented past, the majority of the calories available to the people in tropic and temperate regions came from plants. On the long path of evolution, hunting is a relatively recent innovation; man has been basically plant oriented for almost all of his evolutionary history, and even when his style of life changed to that of the hunter, he (or, more importantly, she) remained a gatherer. The main truth to emerge from this brief evolutionary survey is to emphasize that man (*Homo*) was gathering roots and shoots and buds and leaves and fruits and seeds for millions of years before we detect, via the archaeological record, any change toward specialization in the use of plant foods.

In other papers Kraybill and I present the case for the metate (= grinding slab) as the earliest implement which we have that tells us that man was beginning to focus on grinding plant materials, and in this case on hard-seeded plants such as the grasses. An early origin for this tool and a worldwide diffusion seem indicated, though our data are miserably deficient due to archaeological ignoring of this highly significant piece of equipment. Rounded stones, possibly for reducing coarse foods, appear at the base of Olduvai Gorge, but fully developed grinding tools are late. Invention of the metate roughly about 100,000 years ago seems indicated. As shown in my paper on the metate, grinding is not the only way to make hard seeds edible. Indeed it is an illogical, laborious, nonobvious way to deal with hard grain. We only fail to see this because the complex of grain-flour-bread is part of our cultural heritage, and we, like all mankind, accept as natural the culture into which we are born.

If for our present concerns we accept such round numbers as fifteen million years for seed-gathering hominids, five to five and a half million years for the known history of *Homo*, 250,000 to 300,000 years for the appearance of *sapiens* men, 100,000 years for the appearance of the earliest specialized plant-food-processing tools (metates), and 10,000 years for the first appearance of agriculture, we are faced with a curious situation. The timing is incredibly long if we are to look for some ongoing process leading to domestication. What process is so slow as to require a million years to invent a seed-grinding tool, and 100,000 years to go from grinding wild seeds to domesticating the grasses that produce those seeds (see Table 1)?

If this is a general process, and if mankind is more or less genetically uniform, why did all men not go through this process? Almost all men were seed gatherers and were subject to environmental and population stress, and almost all men had the metate for at least tens of millennia. Yet at most, in only a few spots, and in terms of the time scales we are dealing with, AT ABOUT THE SAME TIME, men suddenly undertake the domestication of plants. Why if the need, opportunity and focus of interest had existed for millions of years, and the human ability (*Homo* with

Table 1. Time scale of domestication

Years B.P.		Years B.P.	
10,000 –	Agriculture	50,000 –	Neanderthals
	Domestic sheep	100,000 –	
20,000 –		200,000 –	
30,000 –		300,000 –	*Homo sapiens*
40,000 –	First grinding-slabs	400,000 –	"Peking Man"
	(metates) in Old World		
50,000 –		500,000 –	
60,000 –		600,000 –	
70,000 –		700,000 –	"Java Man"
80,000 –		800,000 –	
90,000 –		900,000 –	
100,000 –	?First metates	1,000,000 –	*Homo erectus*
	(grinding-slabs), New World		
		2,000,000 –	Base of Olduvai Gorge
		3,000,000 –	*Homo* from East Rudolf
		4,000,000 –	
		5,000,000 –	Australopithecine from Lothagam Hill
		6,000,000 –	
		7,000,000 –	
		8,000,000 –	
Logarithmic Scale		9,000,000 –	
			First hominid 15–18,000,000 years ago

brain capacities approaching ours) had existed for up to one million years should this rash of domestication have burst out all over the globe like an epidemic of measles? Was it, like measles, a communicable disease?

INVENTION, DIFFUSION, AND MAN-PLANT RELATIONS

Inventions are ideas and have a life of their own. In retrospect they are often obvious, and where the situation is subject to scrutiny the question is less "why did it occur?" than "why was it so long delayed?" The invention of evolution by Darwin is an appropriate case. Greek thought had speculated about the particulate nature of matter, and about combining of these particles to give rise to more and more complex forms and had included life forms. Finally in the century before Darwin the accumulating knowledge pressed men in the Western world ever closer to the idea, and it was in fact stated a number of times; Wallace working on this common body of observation, leapt to the conclusion, though one can hardly say totally independently since he and Darwin were both "reading the same textbook." Had a Hottentot and Darwin reached the same idea simultaneously, that would indeed have been an independent invention. Darwin's role was to crystallize and make explicit a concept that had been latent for at least 2000 years. Once he had done so the idea spread throughout the world revolutionizing thinking in many fields.

The parallel to agriculture is apt. Mankind had been intimately associated with plants. All conceivable pressures had been applied a sufficient number of times. Since man can double his population in a generation, population pressure must have arisen frequently. Natural pressures must also have been frequent. For instance Lowell Bean (personal communication) estimates that the gatherers of California experienced severe environmental stress about every twenty-five years. Each severe environmental stress must have reduced population, and the ensuing good period would see a distinctly underfit population in an improved environment. Such alterations of population and environmental stress followed by periods of underfit populations in underused environment (alternate push-pull stress if you will), must have occurred tens of thousands of times around the world during the immense time that men were in the gathering stage. If we assume all of mankind to be fundamentally alike, potentially useful plants to be ubiquitous, all of mankind to have been plant gatherers, all men to have tended to fill their ecological niche to where population pressure if not constant was frequently present, and all environments to be subject to sufficient change to induce stress, then all of mankind could be said to have been subject to stress an infinite number of times.

If stress, whether of population or environmental improvement (positive stress) or decline, could push men over the boundary between gathering and agriculture, then there should have been an infinite number of agricultural beginnings. Clearly there were not and the mechanistically causal, stress-and-strategy systems-analysis fails as a general explanation since the expectation to which it leads us does not fit the reality before us: agriculture arose rarely, not frequently.

Cases of mankind facing the need for an invention and failing to see it are commonplace. The Egyptians invented diacritical marks to clarify their pictographs. Presently it was possible to write in the simplified form, and the pictographic writing could have been discarded. The Egyptians nonetheless muddled along for two millennia with the two systems side by side. It was left to others to take the diacritical marks and use them as the basis for the alphabet, an invention that all literate societies had needed, and which was obvious once made, and trembled on the verge of discovery for millennia. We may suspect the presence of a Darwin in Sinai who did the obvious. There are many such cases with many variations including many failures. For example, the Chinese still cling to their ideographic writing, and the Japanese are paralleling the Egyptians in perpetuating a complex ideographic system alongside a simplified system.

The idea of agriculture does not seem to be obvious when the human record is examined. In Australia (Tindale, personal communication) women dig tubers exhorting the plant to be good, to be generous, to yield a big tuber. Once the tuber is out of the ground, no matter how large the tuber, custom decrees that the woman now complain and berate the plant: "Oh you worthless plant, you lazy thing, you stingy plant. Go back and do better." And so saying she cuts the top off the tuber and puts it back in the dug hole and urinates on it. Seemingly this is an ancient practice, and it so closely approaches agriculture as to leave one wondering how the step to deliberate propagation, the dividing of the tuber with separate sprouts separately planted and with at least minimal tending, could be missed. Yet, like the Egyptians with their writing or the Japanese with theirs, or the Europeans with the idea of evolution, or most recently the failure to see that the racemization of proteins, an idea known for more than a hundred years, could be used as a dating system, the Australians drifted along needing, stressed, pressed by drought and population — but not inventing. In passing, in Australia abortion and infanticide were widely practiced, and this surely measures perceived population pressure.

We must assume that all of these conditions endured for long periods of time. The concept that man only "settled into his environment" during the Archaic period following the Great Hunter period is an oddity of Americanist thought derived from a fixation on the late arrival of man in America with a specialized hunting culture. This is surely wrong as numerous C-14 dates for man in America make clear. Gordon Willey's admission (1971) of three distinct pre-Paleo-Indian lithic traditions epitomizes the belated recognition of the obvious presence of a long and complex Lower Paleolithic in America.

Man throughout the world was a gatherer. Only in some areas, belatedly, did he become a specialized hunter. Nor may it be objected, as some do, that the men of 20,000 and more years ago were not yet "settled into their environment" and sufficiently acquainted with their plant world to initiate a strategy of seasonal movements to collect varied harvests. Not only do Australians and Bushmen who never passed through a Great Hunter phase possess intimate knowledge of the plants and their seasonal productivity, but so do man's nearest relatives the chimpanzees and the gorillas, and even such more distant relatives as the baboons. These creatures follow seasonal rounds having worked out a "strategy" of plant harvesting. They had logistic and territorial problems and were subject to population and environmental pressures. Preman and earliest man surely had similar problems and even better knowledge and strategies of plant harvesting. Man has always been a gatherer, and the assumption that he belatedly came to an intimate knowledge of his environment is surely wrong. Mankind and the plant world have an association that extends for a practical infinity of time. Any explanation of the origin of agriculture must face the problem of the vast time available versus the belated, sudden worldwide appearance of agriculture, and consider whether invention and diffusion as defined above, or some other process best accounts for the observed facts.

ENVIRONMENTAL DETERMINISM

If neither human development nor worldwide focus on grass seeds led men in general to domestication, what was the cause? Currently one finds great emphasis on some form of environmental determinism. The end of the glacial period with its stressful climatic changes is invoked for initiating agriculture in the Near East. Any culture historian, especially a geographer, shudders at this return to a mode of explanation at once so seductive and so thoroughly examined and so justly discarded.

First, it should be noted that a positive correlation between two phenomena does not prove a causal connection. Second, in culture history all explanations using physical environment as a primary cause are suspect. Geographers in general, and the cultural historical geographers in particular, insist that the role of the physical environment is always secondary at best, and often less, in leading to invention, diffusion, and cultural change. To this should be appended that necessity is not the mother of invention. Except in modern times when we have a class of inventors, WHAT invention arose through necessity? Cows were not "invented" for milk, nor chickens for flesh or eggs, nor did the Eskimo invent clothes, oil lamps, and skin boats so he could live in the Arctic. Even in our time, the auto and airplane were not invented to fill needs. They were invented more in the spirit of play and the need FOLLOWED the invention.

These are general truths. The physical environment does not compel, suggest, hint, encourage — it is simply there. Men perceive their environment through cultural filters and behave accordingly. Man did not invent in response to needs. Neither did he invent in response to opportunity.

To argue that climatic change stimulated man to invent agriculture would be suspect from the beginning, for this places the initiative outside of man. But let us assume that this is an efficient operative; that man can indeed be stimulated by climatic change to initiate agricultural beginnings. If this is a sufficient cause, and if mankind is essentially uniform, and if all of mankind was plant oriented, then all men in zones of climatic change should be similarly stimulated. If we focus on areas comparable to the Near East, a dry-summer climate, verging on arid lands, with a mountain-foothill-plain situation, how many examples do we have? They are most of the perimeter of the Mediterranean basin, two areas in Australia, one area in Central Chile, and Southern California. We should include the borderlands of all the dry lands for along all of these climatic shifts would be frequent and often of large scale. Hence we would have the whole perimeter of the dry lands of northern and southern Africa, of Arabia, of northwestern India, or Inner Asia, the inner perimeter of all of Australia, immense borderlands in North and South America. This is a very large part of the world inhabited by early man.

In all of these areas there were wild grasses. Man specialized in gathering them and was equipped with specialized stone tools for milling the seeds. This situation had endured for an order of magnitude of 100,000 years. As an aside, my contention (Carter 1957) that 100,000 years is closer to the right order of magnitude for man's time in America than the long-maintained figure of 12,000 years is being supported by a drumfire of finds that have shattered the mythical barrier of 12,000 years.

In America man was present possibly by mid-Pleistocene times, and surely here by the time of the last interglacial period. Throughout the Americas he was a plant user and along all the lengthy arid-humid boundaries he was subjected to repeated climatic change. The deserts expanded and shrank, lakes filled and dried up, life zones marched north and south, and up and down mountains — in response not only to the long-range glacial-interglacial changes, but to the probably even more rapid fluctuations of the interstadials. And so it was around the world where man was present for immensely longer times than in America.

But do we find a frequent and similar response to the universal drive impinging on a physically uniform man living on a comparable stage of existence and sharing a focus on the harvesting of hard-seeded plants which he reduced to flour (a strange compulsion) by a grinding apparatus that all these men had in common? Most emphatically not! Despite all these uniformities, only in a few spots and very belatedly did men turn to domesticating plants. One must question a process of general explanation that operates so erratically in the presence of such uniformity — a process moreover that is never spelled out in specifics but only alluded to in vague generalities. The plain facts are that all men everywhere were plantsmen and "needed" domestic plants, were subjected to environmental stresses, and could have used domestic plants to great advantage; however, at most only a few men belatedly and all at about the same time (seen on a 100,000 year time scale, but in a geographic sequence on a 1000 year time scale) "invented" agriculture. The data fit a pattern of invention, NOT one of process, development, and inevitable conclusions.

Little if anything is gained when improving environment (expanding opportunity) is substituted for deteriorating environment, for all of the same arguments apply to the positive as to the negative argument. Man is neither driven by adverse physical environment, nor coaxed by good physical environments to make the fundamental inventions. Population pressures also fall into this generally mechanistic type of explanation. They were a normal part of man's existence, and climatic fluctuations increased this stress innumerable times for all men. If agriculture arose through the normal action of ubiquitous forces acting on uniform man in a single cultural stage (gathering) occupying all, or most, of the world then the product should be many agricultural beginnings randomly distributed through time and space, as at A in Figure 1. Instead agricultural origins are enormously compressed in time, as shown at B, and their distribution in time and space viewed simultaneously shows linear distributions suggesting origin from a center.

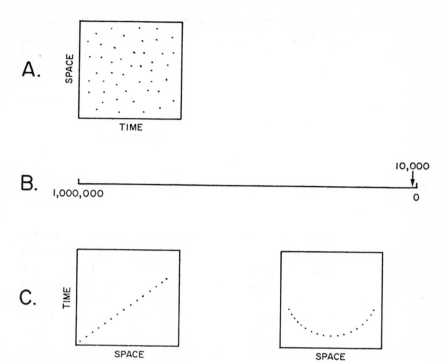

Figure 1.   Models of agricultural development

Theoretical and actual relationships of agricultural beginnings in space and time are shown in this figure. If agriculture arose through the action of ubiquitous forces acting on uniform man in a single cultural stage (gathering) then the expected occurrence of agricultural beginnings would be randomly distributed in time and space as shown at A. They would also be expected to have been frequent. Instead, all agricultural origins fall about 10,000 ± 2,000 years ago and this is diagrammed at B. Further, when plotted against space and time these beginnings form linear patterns radiating from a point of origin as suggested by Ekholm (Figure 1C, left), and Carter (Figure 1C, right). Also see Table 2 and Figure 2.

TIME OF ORIGIN OF AGRICULTURAL CENTERS

There is a most suggestive sequence for agricultural beginnings. It is currently accepted that the earliest known agriculture is in the Near East and the beginnings there go back to about 9000 B.P. While this dating may go back somewhat in time, it quite surely will not be moved more

Table 2. Approximate dates of the appearance of agriculture and pottery-making

Time B.C.	Mesopotamia	India	China	Americas
0				
1000				
				1500 B.C.
2000				
3000			3000 B.C.	
4000		4000 B.C.		
5000	5000 B.C.			

Source: Ekholm (1955).

recently. All other agricultural beginnings are not only later in time, but they are progressively later as one goes away from this hearth area. (The problem of a possible earlier center for southeastern Asia will be discussed below.) This was commented on long ago by Ekholm (1955), and I append his little diagram here (Table 2). His was a notable thought that seems to have been an idea born out of its time. The outmoded dates he used do not invalidate his thesis, for a diagram to show the current thought on the dating of the appearance of agriculture in the various agricultural centers of the world shows the same thing. It can clearly be seen that there is a progressively later appearance of agriculture as one proceeds outward from an assumed center in the Near East. The picture will be changed little if that center of origin is moved around a bit in southern Asia, or is moved backward in time. Indeed any movement backward in time will only increase the suggestion of progressively later appearances of agriculture elsewhere.

Note that while the dates today have moved back appreciably, American beginnings are still significantly later than those of the Old World. The material from Spirit Cave, Thailand, suggests that agricultural beginnings in southeastern Asia are likely to be moved back by comparable amounts. Ekholm's diagram is extended in Figure 2. It does not change the fundamental picture. Southern Asia remains primary in time, all other centers are later, and the farthest away are latest. At the moment the firmest data are in America and in the Near East, and the time sequence is supported by the botanical evidence. The Near Eastern center has a very great priority in time. The only possible challenge is in the Far Eastern center hypothesized by Sauer on philosophical grounds and possibly about to be supported by the finds in Thailand. We have almost no dates for Africa outside Egypt, and our east Asian dates are very insecure except for the list published by Ho (this volume). So far as current data go, the picture looks like a simple diffusion diagram with ideas radiating through space at a modest rate. The only possible change on the horizon is the movement of the Chinese center southward and backward in time. It could possibly change the model to fit Sauer's hypothesis, but if so it would not change the model from a diffusion model to a model of independent invention.

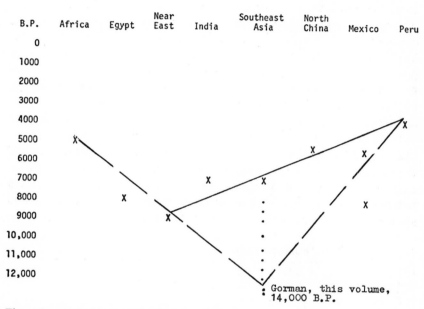

Figure 2. Agricultural origins in time and space

The dates are from various sources, including Ho (this volume) for China. The chronology is insecure outside Egypt, the Near East, China, and Mexico. For the Near East and Mexico we have the added data from plant development to tell us that we are near the real time of the initiation of agriculture. The dates from India are most insecure and those from Thailand need corroboration. However the great age of pottery in the Far East warns us that current dating may be off by millennia, and that southeastern Asia may yet prove to be the earliest agricultural center. (The degree to which our dating can be erroneous is shown in Africa by the shift of the beginning of the Later Stone Age from 6000 to 35,000 B.P.: a factor of six!) Still, the major picture holds: southern Asia has the precedence in time over Africa and the Americas, and, as the

trendlines show, moving the earliest agricultural center from the Near
East to the Southeast does not change the diagram essentially.

PLANT CENTERS AND NUMBERS OF PLANTS

If the major plant centers were to be assigned an antiquity in keeping
with the number of plants domesticated, on the assumption that the
older the center the more time for extensions of domestication, eastern
Asia would appear to be the most ancient, and the American centers,
despite tropical diversity of plant materials, would appear to be young.
Vavilov (1949–1950) commented on this as follows: of the 640 most important domestic plants, 500 are from the Old World, 400 of these from
Asia. The zone from India to China has produced two-thirds of all the
important plants, and this fits the suggestion of great antiquity for agriculture there. Only 50 are from Africa and 100 from all of America, and
only 50 of these latter fit Vavilov's category of most important plants
(Table 3). As Vavilov noted, Brazil with 40,000 species of plants is one of
the poorest regions as a source of domestic plants, and one must conclude that numbers of plants available is not an explanation for the
number of plants domesticated. Africa and America emerge as belated
starters, and the numbers suggest that Africa was later than America.

Table 3.   Number of plants per center

Center	Plants
China	136
India	117
Near East	83
Mexico	49
South America	45
Abyssinia	38

Source: Vavilov (1949-1950).

The Near East has an unexpectedly low number of domestics for an
ancient center. This is an unexpected finding if the Near East is the
earliest center of agricultural origins, but would fit a pattern of very
early beginnings in southeastern Asia coupled with preeminence in boat
culture. Perhaps this situation is due to a smaller wealth of plants in the
Near East as compared with humid tropical southeastern Asia, but it
may also be evidence of a younger center. For America, the poor showing
in comparison with either southeastern or southwestern Asia is probably
significant because tropical America was surely rich in available plants.

Rearrangement of centers is often done, but the overall picture, I believe changes little.

THE SUDANIC-ABYSSINIAN ZONE AS MODEL

Harlan (1971) has made a distinction between centers and noncenters and seemingly feels that agricultural beginnings go on under different conditions in these two types of situations. He did not delve deeply into the causes. He found despite changing views that the Near East remains THE center, with a clear priority in time and that this holds both for plant and animal domestication. The African center has few meaningful dates for the time of origin of agriculture there, but generally that time appears to be relatively late. In the vast zone from Cape Verde to Abyssinia there were, however, a considerable number of plants domesticated and some of them are major food plants, the sorghums, for example.

Harlan was impressed by the list of plants domesticated by Africans in Africa (Table 4). He listed twenty-seven principal plants: seven cereals including sorghum, three pulses, five tubers including the yam, five oil plants, and seven others. This last category includes okra, coffee, watermelon, and cotton. He notes that the high cultural levels of Nok, Ife, Benin, and the Sudanic Kingdoms were supported by an indigenous agriculture. What needs discussion is the origin of this agricultural impulse. Clearly, the plants are African. But was the idea African?

Here we come squarely up against invention, independent invention, diffusion, and stimulus diffusion. Invention means the breakthrough kind of thought epitomized by the wheel, arch, metallurgy, or in the world of complex ideas, by evolution, or the airplane. All of these can be shown to have single centers of origin. An independent invention is one where there is no connection of any kind between the two inventors. Simultaneous inventions of the telephone, telegraph, anesthetics, and calculus are not in this sense independent. The inventors or discoverers were within one cultural world, shared all of the necessary antecedents, read the same scholarly journals. The parallel between this situation in later time to the situation 10,000 years ago is probably not very close, though it needs discussion in depth. With all of mankind at the gathering stage, with everyone knowing intimately the plant world around him, and all people being subject to the pressures of physical environmental changes and of population pressures, are simultaneous inventions of agriculture expectable? This is what we are investigating. If we took as our model the simultaneous discoveries of anesthesia, calculus, and so forth we

Table 4.   African domestics: short list

		Near Eastern parallels

Cereals
Brachiara deflexa	a millet	
Digitaria exilis	fonio	
Eleusine coracana	finger millet	
Eragrostis tef	teff	} wheat and barley
Pennisetum americanum	pearl millet	
Sorghum bicolor	sorghum	
Digitaria iburua	black fonio	

Pulses
Kerstingiella geocarpa	a groundnut	} (This pair is of interest for their parallel
Vondzeia subterranea	a groundnut	in America, the peanut)
Vigna unguiculata	cowpea	peas and beans

Tubers
Dioscorea spp.	yams
Plectanthropus esculentus	kaffir potato
Sphenostylis stenocarpa	yam pea
Solenostemon rotundifolius	piasa

Oil-yielding
Balanites aegyptica	desert date
Butyrospermum paradoxum	karité
Elaeis guineensis	oil palm
Guizotia abyssinica	noog
Telfairia occidentalis	a gourd

Others
Abelmoschus esculentus	okra	
Adansonia digitata	boabab	
Caffea arabica	coffee	
Catha edulis	chat	
Colocynthis citrullus	watermelon	melons
Gossypium herbaceum	cotton	
Musa ensete	ensete	

Source: Harlan (1971).

would at most come to an expectation of dual invention and even then only under conditions of great similarity, really identity of cultural setting: antecedents, stage of development of a particular field, focus of interest, and so forth. Even then the role of the unusual individual, the chance observation, and the intuitive flash would emerge as paramount. Recall Fleming and penicillin, Daguerre and photography, Malus and the polarization of light, Smith and the invention of the propeller, Goodyear and the vulcanization of rubber as examples. Inventions that we can know in detail prove to be the work of extraordinary individuals capable of putting two and two together. Usually what they see is painfully obvious — once they have pointed it out. Often the connection has lain dormant for centuries, sometimes for millennia. For agriculture it can be said of the gathering stage that the idea of agriculture lay dormant for hundreds of millennia, for men had the most intimate relations with plants and were subject to every conceivable stress and still they failed to cross the border into agriculture.

Stimulus diffusion could be called the halfway house between independent invention and diffusion; but if no invention occurred no diffusion, direct or by stimulation, could follow. It is a truism that ideas can travel without migration. Ideas can also travel apart from specific objects or materials. The entire Old World jade complex best known to us from China was transferred in its entirety to Mesoamerica where the mineralogically different stones possessing most of the characteristics of the Old World jades were adopted. Better examples are to be found in Sequoya's and Doalu Bukere's invention of syllabaries in order to write their tribal languages (Cherokee and Vai respectively). While one must credit these men with creative genius, it is clear that they knew of writing and were stimulated by this knowledge to "invent" writing for their people. It is against this general background of known rarity of invention, of the truly exceptional nature of simultaneous invention, and the dominance of both direct and stimulus diffusion that we must look at the case of agricultural beginnings along the southern Sudanic zone.

First, note that no such agricultural beginnings occurred throughout the rest of Africa where the physical setting was similar: similar men, similar plants, similar landscapes, similar environmental and population stresses and pressures. What was lacking in eastern and southern Africa that was present in northern Africa?

A possible answer is found in cultural history. The Sahara was occupied by people possessing the idea of domestication at least as early as the fourth millennium B.C., and equally clearly they or their concepts *re* agriculture stemmed from the Near Eastern center. The Sudanic borderlands must have been attractive to them from the beginning, and with the deteriorating situation in the Sahara in the third millennium, these men (firmly within the world of ideas and practices of the agriculturists) must have been restricted more and more to the better watered Mediterranean borders, the oases, and the better watered southern border — the Sudan and Abyssinia.

If, as we may suppose, they began with Near Eastern crops, they could retain them in the oases where water could be controlled and on the Mediterranean border where the regime of winter rainfall would fit their crops. However, they would experience difficulty if they tried to move their crops into the areas of summer rainfall of the Sudan, and very great difficulty as they expanded into the rain forest areas of western Africa. Davies (1968) has also noted this as a possible explanation.

Man is innately conservative, and men do cling to their old crops. However, through time, given the idea of agriculture, the existence of fields, and the availability of domesticable plants, some changes and additions are to be expected. One route would be via weeds becoming domestics. Perhaps a more important one would be that of the "gathered plants" of the non-agricultural aboriginal peoples being taken into cultivation. Surely there was racial and cultural mingling and learning as the men with chariots and cattle so vividly portrayed in the rock paintings of the Sahara made extensive contact with the aborigines. If, as is the theme being advanced here, the IDEA of agriculture is the important thing, then the expectable result along the Sudanic contact zone would be the extension of the idea of propagation, which originated in the Near East, to the plants gathered by men in the Sudan over the past few million years — a practice that went on seemingly unchanging over the vast time, and which never changed over those parts of Africa not in an agricultural contact zone. For that in terms of cultural history is what the belt from Cape Verde to Abyssinia is: an ancient zone of contact of agricultural people with the non-agricultural peoples of Africa. This supplies a probable reason for this broad zone of agricultural beginnings and further analysis might carry this much further.

Seemingly this argument has become environmentally deterministic: the physical environment prevented man from carrying Near Eastern crops into tropical regions. Analysis will show that the primary decision is cultural: man elects to grow crops. Secondarily the causation is historical: his crops are long-day, cool-season plants from the Fertile Crescent. Thirdly, man elects (a human, cultural historical decision) to try to carry his agriculture into an area with short days and summer rain, and only then does the physical environment influence the decision-making process by changing some of the options. Nota bene: these men still had varied options. They could keep on with their old plants no matter how badly they did; adopt plants the gatherers used; wholly on their own and in keeping with their old traditions select new plants with which to work; some combination of all three; or abandon agriculture. Note that in cattle keeping men DID elect not to take local animals in hand, but in spite of tsetse flies and a change of fodder to tropical grasses they clung to their domestic animals of the mid-latitudes. Their motto could well be said to be: the environment be damned! This is all the more impressive when one considers that there were native disease-resistant animals that were similar to the exotic animals (cattle, sheep, goats) being introduced. Substitutions should have been obvious and profitable.

What kinds of plants would Near Eastern agriculturists find most attractive when they had the opportunity to shift from accustomed plants to local plants? Because they were oriented to the use of grass seeds, would one expect them to select preferentially from the broad spectrum of plants used by the plant gatherers and would not a selection of grass seeds then be expectable? Just such a weighted choice seems to have been made in western Africa. Note the presence of seven African cereal plants. This would seem to be the natural response. Men would expectably take up the plants that were in form and function like their familiar domestics. Table 4 above makes a beginning at showing the parallels. My unfamiliarity with the plants prevents my carrying it further. Extensive analysis might allow one to sort out the "parallel stimulus" and "extended stimulus." If stimulus diffusion began with plants alike in form and function, one would expect this use of "paralleled plants" to be "extended" to other plants. Would the melons of southwestern Asia set the pattern that led to the domestication of the watermelon in Africa?

Harlan's map (1971: 471) shows three nodes: far western Africa, the Niger, and Abyssinia. Each of these was a focal point of later contacts, and was perhaps equally important in earlier times. The Phoenician-Carthaginian voyages down the bulge of western Africa were persistent, and trading posts and colonies were founded. The trans-Saharan routes focused contact on the great bend of the Niger and on the area of Lake Chad, both focal points within Harlan's diffuse center. Abyssinia has had a long history of contacts with Egypt and Arabia, and via them with the Fertile Crescent. The details of the domestication of the sorghums would fit a picture of plural centers for there seems not to have been one center but a series of centers of sorghum domestication (deWet and Harlan 1971). The domestication pattern, even in its details, fits remarkably this well-known cultural pattern.

One could perhaps do more. The appearance of *Oryza glaberrima* (African rice) in the bend of the Niger is interesting. There have been persistent suggestions of direct Indonesian influences in western Africa. One of the most specific was made by Jones (1964) who showed that in minute details of manufacture, scales, tuning, and naming of notes the xylophones of western Africa duplicate the Indonesian instruments. Most hesitatingly he suggested the possibility of boat-borne influences rounding the cape of Africa to reach western Africa. Others have made similar suggestions based on bronzes, arts, and even races of man. Current work on the diffusion of domestic birds supports this theme (Ph. D. thesis in progress, by Glen Whitley).

If the idea of agriculture was being transferred to seed gatherers, one of whose major food sources was wild sorghums, just such a picture would be expectable. Varied species and races of sorghum would be gathered across the sub-Saharan zone, and under the influence of a wave of agricultural stimulation, domestication at several points would be expectable. Are these then independent domestications of sorghum? To so label them is to fail to make critical distinctions. If the idea is being diffused then they are part of a set of stimulus diffusion responses. They are not wholly independent since they all result from the same stimulus: the spread of Near Eastern agricultural ideas southwestward. They mark the beginning of agriculture in sub-Saharan agriculture, but they tell us little about the initial origin of agriculture. We may have similar cases in the American beans and cucurbits.

I will not press this further, for it should be obvious by now that we have hardly begun the task of examining the probable causes of the existence of a zone of agricultural beginnings in just that part of Africa where we have the longest and clearest record of ancient and long-sustained cultural contact. I propose the hypothesis that this situation resulted primarily from the contact of the agricultural ideas streaming from the Near East with the plant gatherers of the Sudanic-Abyssinian zone, with the resulting stimulation leading to the domestication of some of the staple food plants of the gatherers. It probably is best described as a case of stimulus diffusion.

Later, direct importation (*Oryza* perhaps, bananas surely, sweet potatoes probably) enriched the agriculture still further. These importations seem relatable to boat-borne cultures and are later in time than the agricultural stimulus of the fourth to third millennia in the Sudan, and their focus was more likely concentrated to the east. One should expect a focus of Indonesian influences in southeastern Africa opposite Madagascar. For this area there are linguistic data (Malayo-Polynesian speech), cultural items (outrigger canoes) and animal transfers (the chicken complete with an Indian name and southeastern Asian ritual usages and prohibitions). The cultural data (of which this is only a sample) suggest that these influences extended over a long period of time and stemmed from various sources.

The picture of plant diffusion must have been equally complex. While both stimulus and direct diffusion would be expectable, at some point in time these impulses must have begun to meet an already established agriculture. All the directions of selection would then change. Instead of native gatherers with their broad spectrum of plant uses, there would be native agriculturists with their narrowed, specialized plant uses. They would expectably have denser populations, hold the land more tenaciously and take new domesticates more selectively. Individual plants expectably would be accepted and perhaps the banana, sweet potato, and others fall in this category. But once agriculture was established there would be a greatly lessened probability of stimulus diffusion leading to the domestication of the plants once used by the gatherers.

SUMMARY

This examination of Harlan's African noncenter raises the question of why domestication occurred all along this long environmental front but not along all the similar frontage in the rest of Africa. The cultural history of Africa suggests an answer. This was the zone of earliest contact between the agriculturist impulse from the Near East with Africa. The plants, however, are not Near Eastern plants, and the question then becomes: did the Africans do this on their own initiative with no stimulus from prior agricultural centers? The location of these African agricultural beginnings both in time and space suggests that is probably not true. Despite literally millions of years of plant gathering by man over all of Africa domestication begins only at the time and place of demonstrable contact with cultures bearing agriculture. The replacement of the Near Eastern cereals by African plants can be accounted for on two bases: stimulus diffusion, aided perhaps by both cultural and environmental screening. The two factors are not totally independent, of course. The mid-latitude Near Eastern plants may have been less successful because of heat, drought, humidity, or problems of day length — to name a few. Africans may have preferred their sorghums, or they may have found them the cereal most readily converted from a gathered crop to a planted crop.

The initial agricultural impulse (or impulses, for across so wide a zone as the Sudanic-Abyssinian belt one could think of numerous stimuli) would be on people using a broad spectrum of wild plants. The expected result both culturally and environmentally would be the domestication of a number of these, with perhaps a skewing of the selection toward cereals because of the source of the stimulation: from the Near East. Once the African agriculture was established, all later introductions would face a much stronger cultural filter for they would now be in competition with already established plants. Without pressing the data further, this concept seems to contain the germ of a useful model to try elsewhere.

Reindeer Domestication as a Test Case

As a brief test of the applicability of this model consider the domestication of the reindeer. The center of primary domestication of animals seemingly was in the Near East. From this center the idea and the original domestic animals early spread out across Eurasia and northern Africa with additions on the edges: elephants and chickens to the east, donkeys to the southwest, horses to the north, and, belatedly, rabbits to the west. The examples are unimportant except to indicate something of the typical spread-with-additions. This created in Eurasia a broad belt of domestic animal keepers extending from the North Sea to Manchuria. They had developed quite varied animal usages: milking, riding, pulling (chariots, wagons, sleds, sleighs). Along this vast front contact was made with the people of the forest and tundra, who from Upper Paleolithic times on had been specialized hunters of reindeer. Along this zone there belatedly appeared an impulse to domesticate the reindeer. Horses, cows, sheep, and goats were not readily adapted to the taiga and tundra, especially when in the initial period they had to be fitted into a roving way of life. *Nota bene*, today with managed pastures, stored forage, good barns, and settled existence we can have dairies in the Arctic. Such was not the condition at the time the stimulus to domestication arrived in the Arctic. I do not wish to beat a dead horse, but I do find among some of my colleagues a strong tendency to leap to environmentally deterministic answers where cultural reasons abound.

Most interestingly, the reindeer keepers mirror the usages of the animal keepers to the south of them. Thus sleighs, toboggans, or riding are used in parallel to the near neighbors' customs. Of equal importance, in America, where the same physical environment contained virtually the identical animal and was peopled by virtually identical people (the similarity of the Paleo-Siberians to northern North American Indians has frequently been commented on) living similar ways of life, no domestication occurred. South of the Indians of the Northern Forest of America, there was no tradition of animal domestication to stimulate them, and despite all the other ingredients being present — man, animal, environment, need, challenge — there was no response. The failure of the Amerinds to domesticate the sheep (Carr, this volume) is another example. Despite the presence of a suitable animal in varied environments and with several cultural settings (gatherers, hunters, sedentary agriculturists) no one undertook the domestication of this easily tamed and potentially valuable animal. Everything was present except the idea of animal husbandry. It does give one cause to pause and reflect on this mysterious process that somehow just leads men with some fatalistic inevitability to re-create solutions to life's problems. Most of mankind only seems to have solved its problems with the aid of some help from the audience.

The Far East

The Far East is exceedingly difficult to discuss in terms of centers, times and diffusions. We have almost no dates, and a proportionately large number of fixed and often conflicting ideas. Chang (1970) has reviewed the situation with a very careful statement of the degree of uncertainty. Perhaps the greatest uncertainty concerns time. The Western orientation of research has given us a near fixation on the Near East as the Garden of Eden from which all ideas flowed. The utter unbelief with which the dates for pottery from Japan were received a few years ago measures our naïveté. Although these pottery dates should have prepared us for startling findings in Asia, the recently reported finds from Thailand suggesting agricultural beginnings there as early as between 8000 and 12,000 B.P. (hereafter rounded off at 10,000 B.P.) are being treated now just as the pottery dates were then. Chang has cited Tsukada's evidence of massive vegetational disturbance with much evidence of frequent fire beginning around 12,000 years ago as suggestive of the beginning of slash-and-burn agriculture on Taiwan. These would be pottery-making agriculturists equipped with boat cultures, a most significant way of life to find poised on the western side of the Pacific at so early a date. By 6200 B.P. there is clear evidence of Lungshanoid cereal growers. Possibly both root crops and cereals were boat-borne in the Pacific prior to the beginning of agriculture in America. At Spirit Cave, Thailand, the earliest of these agricultures had *Lagenaria* and beans, which are amongst the earliest domestic plants in America. It is time to look at American agricultural origins.

American Agricultural Origins

American agricultural origins are generally held to be quite separate from those of the Old World. This idea clearly rests on two main assumptions. First, man could not possibly have crossed the world's oceans and brought ideas to America sufficiently early. Second, the totally different plants of the New World show that the first dictum is probably correct. There are many variants on this: that an occasional drift-voyager would have no effect on cultures; that any late and belated voyagers who did arrive would have had slight effect, if any; that possible belated transfers of a plant or two such as sweet potatoes to Polynesia and coconuts to America were insignificant, if true; that there is no evidence at a time level sufficiently early to have any significance for American Indian agricultural origins. All of these objections seem to be subject to challenge (Carter 1950a, 1950b, 1953, 1963, 1971).

Without trying to dodge responsibility for the ideas put forward here, still I should note that they have occurred to others. One of the most notable of these was Robert Heine-Geldern and I digress at this time to include a short review of his *Kulturpflanzengeographie und das Problem vorkolumbischer Kulturbeziehungen zwischen Alter und Neuer Welt* (1958). This was little noted in America, one assumes because it was published in German. His *Die asiatische Herkunft der südamerikanischen Metalltechnik* (1954) also has considerable value still. (And as an old-fashioned scholar I watch sadly the dropping from Ph.D. programs of all foreign language requirements. True, too many men passed their examinations and never translated another line, but the wholesale abandonment of the ancient scholarly requirements is closing too many intellectual doors.)

Heine-Geldern observed that contacts with transfers of culture but without transfers of domestic plants are commonplace. He cited centuries of contact with Australia with strong transfers of intellectual and material culture, but without agriculture being initiated. (Tindale, in personal conversation in 1973, told me of very extensive evidence of Polynesian contact, even in South Australia, still with negligible evidence of transfers of material culture.) It is a negative model worthy of much attention. For Australia the answer, in part, was the kind of men making the contact: fishermen, carrying a supply of rice adequate for their stay, and hence not practicing agriculture there. Were this the case for America, says Heine-Geldern, we might find similar results, and he suggests that seekers of gold and gems about the eighth century B.C. were the first Asiatics in Mesoamerica. Twenty-five years later, we know that colonies of Asians were arriving by 5500 B.P. Heine-Geldern pointed to the following as evidence of Asiatics in America: patolli-pachisi, betel-coca, metal techniques and designs, weaving, dyeing, art motifs, cosmologies, time counts by permutation, lucky and unlucky days and associated prophecies, governmental structures and principles, court ceremonial and marks of dignity, etc. In retrospect it is surprising that he did not suggest that colonization was indicated. Instead he assumed that only special groups, gold seekers, metal workers, merchants, artists, and artisans came from Asia to America. He pointed to the parallel to events in Asia: trading journeys from China to Indonesia as early as 3000 B.P., followed in time by merchants, artists, and missionaries from India; these were small groups, rapidly assimilated into the local population but who exerted a powerful influence as a result of their more advanced cultural level. He pointed out that in southeastern Asia this was an ongoing process lasting for millennia and suggested that the American scene was to be seen as similar. His argument was that the nature of the contact with America was such that transfers of plants were not expectable.

One hundred and sixty years ago Alexander von Humboldt (1814) had already said much the same: art, architecture, governmental forms, everything except linguistics indicated an Asiatic origin of the civilizations of the American Indians. And in 1971 Eric Reed almost plaintively commented that he did not see why an African castaway arriving in America with the idea of agriculture might not have started the Amerind agricultural revolution.

Boats and Time

The suggestion that an agricultural impulse spread to America raises several questions. Were there boat cultures so early that they were capable of such voyages? If such voyages were made did they come via the Pacific or the Atlantic or both?

First, the question of boat-borne ideas. It has frequently been pointed out that most culture historians are deskbound theorists rather than boatmen. Two culture-historical geographers who have focused on boats, Doran (1971) and Edwards (1960, 1971) are both accomplished sailors and builders of boats. Significantly, both of these men know the history of boats and see no practical limit on man's ability to cross the sea in early times. Heyerdahl (1950, 1952, 1971) with his surprising feats showed first that the ancient sailing log raft with its sophisticated equipment of fore and aft rig sails and dagger boards could cross the world's greatest ocean, and then demonstrated that boats of lashed bundles of reeds could cross the Atlantic from east to west at its narrow waist in the trade wind belt. The sailing log raft is well within the technological range of Upper Paleolithic man and the boat of reed bundles within the range of the abilities of Lower Paleolithic man. (In panel discussion at the IXth International Congress of Americanists it was pointed out that the resemblances of artifacts on the two sides of the Straits of Gibraltar imply contact in Acheulean time, presumably by watercraft.)

While this last statement might be considered mere opinion there is supporting evidence. Man must cross water barriers (Wallace's line) to reach Australia. He had already arrived there before 32,000 B.P. (Barbetti and Allen 1972), and probably was there much earlier. (Tindale, personal communication 1973, has estimated the time of arrival of man in Australia at 100,000 years ago.) His boating equipment was the reed bundle (or bark bundle) boat. The Tasmanians, cultural (although not physical) examples of Lower Paleolithic survivals, also were limited to bark bundle boats. I do not argue that men equipped with boats of reed bundles crossed either the Atlantic or the Pacific to America, though I do not consider it an impossibility. However, for men with sailing rafts, reaching America was a virtual certainty. Storm-driven rafts would reach America automatically and with greater safety than the disabled Chinese junks that arrived so regularly during the nineteenth century. The probability of storm-driven and/or disabled watercraft reaching America repeatedly, beginning at least as early as the Upper Paleolithic, seems quite high.

We may move on then to consider what the nature of contacts within "agricultural time" may have been, and what evidence we might expect to find.

CASTAWAYS   First, we must deal with the notion that a shipwrecked mariner could have no influence on the people among whom he landed. It seems most arbitrary simply to assume the negative. I will not attempt a catalogue of cases here although I have noted many over the years. One can find both successes and failures and plenty of them. Jett (1971) for instance cites the case of seventeen Negroes shipwrecked in Ecuador in the early sixteenth century who gained political control over an entire province, and the Palauans who in historic times invited individual sailors to remain as innovators. During the period of exploration in the sixteenth century the world's sea coasts were sprinkled with shipwrecked or lost Spanish, Portugese, Englishmen, and others. Many married native women and settled into the local communities where later expeditions often found them to be of great value for their knowledge of the local language, customs, and geography. No one seems to have catalogued this body of knowledge and examined it for evidence of transfers of knowledge, and I will limit myself to brief mention of one earlier example.

The northwestern coast of America is loaded with Asiatic traits: Japanese raincoats, rod and slat armor, whaling with aconite poisoning associated with complex tabus, and many more. Most of these are traceable to Japan, and Japanese fishermen were found among these people at the time they were discovered by Europeans. Too much has been made of the slave status of these Japanese, and too little notice paid to the overwhelming evidence of cultural transfers. There are probably several more areas of such transfers but this extremely clear example should suffice. In passing, the art of the Northwest Coast is typical of the Old Pacific art style, and an age of about 5000 B.P. is thus indicated for massive overseas influences on the American Northwest Coast.

VOYAGING AND COLONIZATION   Massive cultural influence, however, is not expectable from castaways. This suggests colonization at least of the magnitude and perhaps of the type exemplified by the influence from India on Indonesia about the time of Christ. I have presented models (Carter 1963) showing that transfers of even minor agricultural plants normally required colonization. The sweet potato and its naming (see below), the presence of a particular blood group (the Diego factor) in southern Mesoamerica and known elsewhere only in China, and most probably also the presence of a mass of monosyllabic tonal languages in Mexico in the center of Mesoamerica and associated with such traits as burden bearing on a carrying pole, all suggest colonization. Races of Asiatic chickens used in America in Asiatic fashion (ritual uses only) and known by two or more Asiatic names (Carter 1971) are simply further indications that the contacts began early, continued through time, and had varied origins in Asia.

Twenty years ago, the idea that Asiatics had influenced American Indian cultural growth in any way at any time was utterly unthinkable, and I was chastised by my friends for saying that the presence of art in America typical of that of the Shang dynasty suggested important Asiatic contacts as early as 4500 B.P. Now there is growing acceptance of Asiatic influences as early as 5000 to 6000 B.P. including the beginning of pottery in America due to influences from Asia arriving by sea onto the coast of Ecuador (Meggers, Evans, and Estrada 1965). While the precise origin of this pottery is challenged by some (Lathrap 1967) most scholars acknowledge a probable Asiatic source not only because of specific resemblances but also because of the long developmental history for pottery in Asia as opposed to the sudden appearance of a fully developed pottery in America. In terms of the history of shipping as now known, one would expect the voyages that initiated the extensive influences brought from Asia at that time to have been accomplished with sailing rafts.

However we now have the startling situation that C-14 dated culture bearers are arriving in America surprisingly close to the beginning of agriculture in America: potters on the coast of Ecuador at 4000 to 6000 B.P.; agriculture at Tehuacan about 7000 B.P. (7200–5400 B.P.). Nor, as the lines of reasoning developed above indicate, is there any reason to think that these are the first boat-borne men to reach America. The Asiatic potter-fishermen who so greatly affected American cultural growth may have been the first colonists to arrive, or they may only be the earliest we have yet detected. As of this moment our knowledge of important direct diffusion begins with them. We think of them as settled fisherfolk who built coastal villages to fixed plan and who made pottery (cf. Ford 1969). Did they know of agriculture? Did they bring agricultural plants?

POTTERS AND PLANTERS   While the first attempts at localizing the Asiatic source of the Valdivian potters of Ecuador pointed to Japan, this may not be the exact area of origin. The real source may be Taiwan or the mainland of southern China. These areas all shared a basic pottery tradition, and some of the difficulties with precise comparisons between Valdivia and Jomon may be that the wrong areas are being compared. Should the source of the early potter-fishermen who reached America so early be shifted southward and to the mainland the odds that they already knew of agriculture would be enormously increased, for, as we have seen, planters and potters were on Taiwan by 6200 B.P. surely, and planters possibly as early as 14,000 B.P.

For the moment we are left with people from Asia, arriving in America by sea, bearing sizable amounts of cultural baggage and coming from one of the centers of earliest agricultural beginnings.

We have at the moment no comparable evidence for early trans-Atlantic influences and this is surprising since winds, currents, and distances all suggest that the earliest influences could most easily come that way. We do have suggestions of pre-Columbian inputs from the Mediterranean although at slightly later times. There are Rowe's interesting list (1966), Sorenson's enormous list (1971), and Beirne's very specific study (1971) of types of axes that document contact with or diffusion from the eastern Mediterranean, and even a specific Egyptian ax-type (also noted by Rowe). The times suggested by most of these traits are relatively late, seldom pointing earlier than 3500 B.P. However, *Lagenaria*, cotton, and perhaps a stimulus diffusion leading to domestication of peanuts in parallel to African *Geocarpa* may be straws in the wind hinting that we may have much yet to learn. There is no reason to think that these early attempts to come to grips with the evidence from trans-Atlantic influences have plumbed the depths.

Kinds of Plant Evidence Expectable   If there were overseas influences on the beginning of Amerind agriculture it could take many forms. Specific plants might be carried: direct diffusion. Plants might not be carried, but the idea of domestication might: stimulus diffusion. There could be a combination of these two: one or two plants carried plus the idea of agriculture.

The application of the idea of agriculture in the new plant world of the Western Hemisphere could follow one or more courses and their blends. The men with the knowledge of agriculture could look for plants comparable in form and/or function to those they had known. They could pick up from the gatherers in this new land the plants already in use and apply the idea of domestication to them. Most expectably, they would do a bit of both.

They would be assisted in their efforts by the fact that to some extent familiar forms would already be in use, even if not cultivated. The users of metates would be hard-seed specialists, mostly grass users, and as I have reasoned elsewhere, could already have developed through a near symbiotic relation grasses adjusted to man and his harvesting methods (Carter 1964). Could it be otherwise? Could men have gathered grass seeds annually for up to 100,000 years without modifying the grasses? Would not the grass with the larger seed, attractive to man and which held its seed until men with seed-beaters harvested the plant, be assured a better dispersal of its seeds and thus be subject to selection for larger seeds and a less brittle rachis? All of this would be unconscious, of course. This was the nature of the relationship of man to grasses in the area of California and the Great Basin, a relationship that endured for tens of thousands of years.

Where was the process that should have led these people to agriculture? Man, plant, climatic change, wide ranges of ecology in short distances were all similar here to the situation in the Near East: need, necessity, opportunity, challenge (but no response), climatic change (but no cultural change). What is this mysterious process that is assumed to lead by some unexplained inevitability to agriculture?

And we have hardly begun. Suppose that the oceanic drifters or voyagers came now from one area and now from another. One would focus on seed plants; another on root crops; and still another on tree crops. What is the situation in America? If we have not looked at our data with such questions in mind, perhaps we have missed something.

Is the early agriculture of the eastern United States due to the arrival of the Early Formative Cultures (Ford 1969), clearly with Asiatic roots? In addition to the purely local domestics and ruderals discussed by Yarnell (this volume) *Lagenaria* is early; cucurbits and beans are added later and only belatedly does maize appear. *Lagenaria* is an Old World plant and present in the Hoabinihian agriculture of southeastern Asia, along with beans. The American beans and cucurbits are in form and function like *Lagenaria* and the Old World beans. Nor should it be overlooked that Asia even had the same genus, of beans, *Phaseolus*, in domestication as the Americas. Indeed, one could view the American pulses as an impoverished duplication of the Old World wealth of species of these kinds of plants.

Is the root crops' hearth in North Atlantic-facing South America a reflection of people oriented toward root crops reaching America? It is the appropriate area for arrivals by sea from tropical Africa. Would early influences from Africa be oriented towards root crops? Would yam growers cast away in America turn to sweet potatoes? Is it significant that in Africa there are two plants with the same strange growth habit as the peanut and that in an area otherwise of little importance for agricultural origins (Brazil) the peanut was domesticated early? Were there Negros in America before Columbus? The Spaniards emphatically said yes and Von Wuthenau (1969) has presented us with the portraits in clay of Africans in America done by American Indians. Studies of human proteins frequently show American Indian-Negro relationships but the data have little time dimension on them, and I will cease to explore this idea with the comment that repeated arrivals of men from various places would expectably lead to multiple agricultural initiations. These would expectably stress the type of plant used in the homeland: seeds, or roots, or fruits. The idea deserves investigation, and there is much there to be investigated. The field would be a fertile one for perception-behavior study. How would a castaway from a root-crop culture see the particular American world that he reached? Africans would most probably have arrived in northeastern South America. Europeans would arrive in the Caribbean and the southeastern United States. Asiatics would arrive on the Northwest Coast and also, but to the surprise of those who do not know the history of watercraft, all along the Pacific Coast of America. What would they find? What plants might strike a responsive chord?

Plant Evidence   We have bits of direct plant evidence and more indirect evidence. I will deal with a few cases as examples, and apologetically, not in depth. While my paper sounds argumentative, and is lamentably thin in spots, it is really meant to raise questions indicating areas needing investigation.

The most curious case, and perhaps the most important, is the bottle gourd *Lagenaria siceraria*. This plant has long been known to be both an Old World plant and to have been in America at an astonishingly early time.

The bottle gourd is an Old World plant, of African origin but very early also found in Asia, a dispersal problem that I will not discuss here. It is ubiquitous in American archaeology (Cutler and Whitaker 1961, general source for this section). It is found in Mexico in the Ocampo Caves by 9000 B.P., at Tehuacan around 7500 B.P., and at Huaca Prieta in Peru at 5000 B.P. Native cucurbitas also appear at these sites, seemingly domesticated by 7200 B.P. at Tehuacan and by 7000 B.P. at Ocampo. Whitaker and Cutler consider that domestication had occurred prior to these dates (but Mangelsdorf, et al. [1964] favor domestication only by 7000 B.P.). One could allow a quite generous amount of time and *Lagenaria* would still be earlier than any American domestic. Earlier the same authors (Cutler and Whitaker 1961) had stated that squashes and gourds may have been the earliest domestic plants in the New World for they are consistently found with beans but before maize.

We should also note, if *Lagenaria* is an import and marks the arrival of the idea of agriculture, that Tehuacan, an interior arid location, is more likely an example of good preservation than of earliest beginnings. If boat-borne people brought *Lagenaria*, it must first have been grown in coastal sites, and if the time was as early as 9000 B.P. these will be difficult to document for the sea was still six meters below its present level at that time. However, zones of coastal uplift such as mark the Ecuadorian sites of early pottery indicate that the problem is not hopeless.

This curious situation has not been adequately discussed. Whitaker and Carter (1954) demonstrated that *Lagenaria* could float to America and arrive with viable seeds, and also promptly noted that this did not prove that it did. First, so far as we know, *Lagenaria* did not get to America until early post-Pleistocene time, although natural dispersal must have been a possibility for a million years or more. If natural means was the answer, why did the plant wait so long? Why indeed wait until the era of human boating ability? To this one must add: so far as our evidence now goes. However, we have excellent reasons for man to carry *Lagenaria*. Not only was it a most useful plant for all kinds of culinary purposes, but it was also early and widely used as a net-float. In this form it would contain seeds and be carried by fishermen, the likely candidates for earliest seaborne arrivals in America. Seamen with domestic gourds are carriers of a domestic plant, hence the idea of domestication. The presence of *Lagenaria* in America so early is of crucial importance. If man brought it, then we can date important agricultural transfers to at least 9000 B.P., and the most important transfer may have been the idea of agriculture. This discussion leaves all kinds of loose ends flapping in the breeze. Gourd-floats need not have been domestic gourds, yet the evidence from

Asia suggests that this gourd was domesticated early, appearing (as it does) in the Hoabinhian. It does seem as if *Lagenaria* is likely to be a key plant indicator for agricultural dispersals for, despite Whitaker's and Carter's demonstration of its potential for oceanic dispersal, Carter agrees with the critics that think it is more likely dispersed by man. The plant worried Mangelsdorf, et al. (1964) also for they accepted Sauer's dictum that even if the gourd floated to America it would require an agriculturist to take it off the beach and plant and tend it.

Sweet Potato Ipomoea batatas   The sweet potato got swept under the academic rug by Donald Brand (1971). He has provided us with an unexcelled review of the whole question marred by a pair of errors. First he overemphasized the mistakes made by scholars less dilligent than he in using the early chroniclers. Brand correctly distinguished between early and late usage of names and showed that attribution of the word *kumar* to the Quechua was incorrect. From that, however, he proceeded to discard *kumar* entirely as a South American name for sweet potato. But this is to throw the baby out with the bathwater. *Kumar* was indeed the name for the sweet potato on the coast of Colombia. Brand's claim that no one had used that name on that coast overlooked the fact that the Cuna, now in Panama, originally lived on the Colombian coast. Their name for the sweet potato is *kumar*. Also it has repeatedly been pointed out by others, as I in turn have reported more than once, that *kumar* is a Sanskrit word.

Its parallel is "corn" as a name for *Zea mays*. This name clearly records the arrival of a colonizing group that placed their own name on a domestic plant that they found in native hands but adopted for their own use. Corn in Old English means grain or in wider usage any small hard round thing, thus a pepper corn, a corn on your foot, powder corns, and so forth. Such usage is a sign of antiquity for a word in a language. Narrow usage is a sign of recency. *Kumar* has extremely wide meaning in India just as corn does in England. In America *kumar* has only one meaning and only in a restricted area, exactly as corn does in America. In the case of corn we know that this resulted from British colonization, and the suggestion is very strong that *kumar* in Ecuador points to colonization from southeastern Asia. For the coast of Ecuador we have galaxies of evidence of Asiatic arrivals and colonization: see Beirne (1971) on axes, Meggers, Evans, and Estrada (1965) for archaeological evidence, consult the folklore of the region with its very specific accounts of plural arrivals of groups of people from overseas, and take special note of the existence of the Asiatic sailing raft with an Asiatic name (*balsa*) on that very coast (see Doran 1971).

The sweet potato is not evidence of earliest agricultural influences. It is, however, too important a piece of evidence to be lightly discarded. It shows that names could be transferred, that plants could be carried both ways, and that it was plants that fitted the cultural pattern of the contacting group that were carried. Whoever carried the sweet potato out of America was from a culture oriented toward root crops. If maize was carried, it would have been by a people oriented toward cereals.

The sweet potato tells us that on this time level plant carriage was selective and that the selective factor was cultural. This cultural factor would also be important in acceptance of plants or ideas about plants. Either colonists or castaways would be entering a world already peopled. They would be subject to strong pressures to conform, and there would be both cultural and natural pressures. The native population with whom admixture can be assumed and with whom exchange of ideas would be certain would influence the newcomers toward the adoption of native plants. Simultaneously, some of any domestic plants or ideas about domestic plants carried by the newcomers could be expected to be out of step with the environment of the new homeland, and others might not fit into the way of life of the native people.

The European settlement of the United States provides instructive models. The settlers adopted maize, beans, and squash, partially because they had considerable difficulty adapting their own small grains to the new environment. They virtually abandoned the European bean in favor of the American bean (*Vicia faba* replaced by *Phaseolus vulgaris*), but they enriched the American agriculture with the pea. The changes were complex and selective, but predictable given hindsight. Properly used, the body of data available from the colonial period, worldwide, could teach us much, for it allows of almost limitless comparisons: like or unlike climates, like or unlike cultures (agricultural to agricultural, agricultural to nonagricultural, seed users to root-croppers, etc.), dense or sparsely settled lands. What happened in these many cases? Would not our theorizing be bolstered with some factual data if we developed some classic cases? All of these cases, however, would illustrate how agriculture spreads or fails to spread, and what kind of selective factors operated, and what kinds of additions to agriculture arose under the stimulus of this new idea. Such studies, however, would tell us little about the ultimate origins, the first invention, of agriculture.

Plant Pairs: Old World-New World   No one has compiled a good list of plant pairs between the Old World and the New World. To do it well will require long and thoughtful consideration. Direct transfers will have to be screened out: coconuts, sweet potatoes, peanuts, *Lagenaria*, and others. However, even these direct transfers have value for, as we have seen, *Lagenaria*, if it was transferred by man, establishes a startlingly early time level for the initiation of such exchanges. There are others at surprisingly early levels: the Brazilian domestic, the peanut, may have appeared in China in Lungshanoid times (about 5000 B.P.) as Chang (1968) has repeatedly noted. If this transfer is validated, it establishes a two-way exchange of plants across the Pacific at the very time level that Asiatic potters appear on the coast of South America, and this in turn tends to reinforce the suggestion that the early potters were indeed also planters.

A student at Texas A. and M. University in 1971 made a comparison of DeCandolle's list of Old World and New World plants and found the following to be common to both: *Diospyros* [persimmon], *Fragaria* [strawberry], Cucurbitaceae [pumpkins and squashes], Solanaceae [potato, tomato, eggplant], *Phaseolus* [beans in China and America], *Gossypium* [cotton]. The list is of historic interest. It is curious that an overlap of 16.7 percent of New World domestics with those of the Old World seems to have caused no surprise when DeCandolle published. The same student compared Vavilov's lists and found a pairing of 21.9 percent. However, this list is marred by the inclusion of such problematic cases as *Zea mays* which, if it was in Asia in pre-Columbian time (as seems probable), was carried there by man. However, for the record the list is: *Amaranthus, Canavalia, Crataegus,* Cucurbitaceae, *Diospyros, Eugenia, Gossypium, Ipomoea, Lepidium, Lupinus, Pachyrrhizus, Phaseolus, Salvia, Solanum,* and *Zea.* It is a mixed bag, but one is faced with the interesting question of just why a plant should be taken into domestication, even once, much less twice. Are the wild ancestors of our domestic plants such obvious choices? Wild tepary beans (*Phaseolus acutifolius*) are the size of the head of a pin. Wild cotton's lint is not an obvious source for fiber. The American cucurbits have obvious fruits but astringent flesh. Some *Phaseolus*, e.g. *lunatus* can be deadly poisonous, and some species of *Solanum* are known as "deadly nightshade." True, the ancient gatherers knew all of these matters and also knew how to utilize for food a surprising number of bitter, astringent, and even poisonous plants. Nevertheless we would be rather hasty if we said that certain plants were such obvious candidates for domestication that they would be repeatedly domesticated. The list might also be expanded for I note in Chang (1970) that *Nasturtium* and *Oxalis* were used in China and paralleled in the highland agriculture of South America, and that *Setaria*, an early grain in Mexico, is also the earliest grain in northern China.

However, these lists seem to me probably to tell far less than half the story. *Lagenaria* produces a large, obvious, round-bodied fruit that grows on a vine. In the Old World it served both as a vegetable and a vessel, with a general division into African inedible forms but with Asia having some edible forms. As noted, it is the earliest candidate for a domestic plant in the New World. The earliest additions are: the American cucurbitas (I follow Liberty Hyde Bailey in his use of "cucurbits" to refer to the whole tribe, Cucurbitaceae, and of "cucurbitas" for the American representatives of the group.) that look gourdlike and can be used in the same way as *Lagenaria*. Is this an accident, just natural, or are we looking at stimulus diffusion? To the gourd growers and potters reaching America, would not the most obvious candidate in this strange botanical world be the most gourdlike plant, hence the cucurbitas? The suggestion has been made that the earliest use of the cucurbitas was for their seeds. If the gatherers of America were already using those plants in this way, the newcomers who had grown *Lagenaria* in their own homeland could have stimulated the use of cucurbitas in parallel to the Asiatic pattern. The Asiatic *Lagenaria*, interestingly, includes edible forms while the African one does not.

The gourd growers and potters would also have been acquainted with beans. Is it mere coincidence that beans too are early? Belatedly, maize is cultivated. Is this due to an extension of the idea of agriculture to an important cereal anciently gathered and now belatedly domesticated, was this due to native extensions of the idea of agriculture, or was it due to renewed impulses from overseas with the grain-growing ideas beginning to reach America?

If it be argued that it was perfectly natural for Amerinds to domesticate plants, due to some process unexplained, why did they wait to begin agriculture until just the time when Asiatic potters and farmers were afloat on the western side of the Pacific? Why when they began their agricultural careers did they start with an Old World plant to which they added New World equivalents (cucurbits) and then added still another plant (*Phaseolus*) of a genus known to the Asiatics familiar with gourds and pottery? Surely, we should pause to consider these questions, and many more, before we proclaim the plural origins of agriculture, and especially the utter separateness of American agricultural beginnings.

THE AMERICAS AS A NONCENTER FOR AGRICULTURAL ORIGINS

As we have seen, Harlan's interesting case of Africa as a dispersed zone of agricultural beginnings may best be explained as a probable case of diffusion. The Americas may possibly be viewed in much the same way. They are sufficiently late in time, both to be stimulated from prior centers and to fall within the era of boat-borne transoceanic stimulation. In the Mexican beginnings (Table 5) the plants at the earliest level suggest direct inputs from the Old World, with extension in the levels immediately following of the idea of agriculture to the plants that in form and function are like Asiatic forms. Table 5 presents the curious picture that the earliest agriculture presently known in the New World gives enormous precedence in time to two Old World plants, and then adds plants that either duplicate the genera of Old World domestics, or in form and function are like an Old World plant. Even *Capsicum* recalls the southeastern Asian passion for spices. Callen (1967a, 1967b) has suggested from the study of coprolites at Tehuacan that *Setaria* was the first domesticated cereal, but was abandoned when maize was domesticated. (Is it significant that *Setaria italica*, foxtail millet, is also listed as the earliest Chinese domestic cereal?)

Table 5.   Mexican agricultural origins

Years B.P.	
9000	
Lagenaria	The Old World bottle gourd
Setaria	Foxtail grass, also is cultivated in China. Abandoned in America after maize was domesticated.
7000–5000	
Amaranthus	
Phaseolus	Genera also cultivated in Old World
Gossypium	
Cucurbitas	Form and function like *Lagenaria*
Capsicum	A spice; parallel to Asian spices?

Source: Mangelsdorf, et al. (1964).

Thereafter we come to such truly American forms as maize. But even here we tread on parallels of form and function. Maize is very much like some Asiatic plants e.g. sugar cane and Job's tears, and even more like the African sorghums. This I admit to be a dangerous game to play, for one could extend form and function pretty far. It is nevertheless the kind of comparison that should be investigated rather than avoided, though the need for restraint is apparent.

Nevertheless we must ask questions. Is the beginning of agriculture in Mexico due to Asiatic inputs, and is the belated turning of attention to the sorghum-like maize an African input? It would fit a form-and-function, stimulus-diffusion pattern. The fit does not prove the case, but it does suggest that we might pause to consider the situation.

Since we have hardly begun to investigate this matter, it is hard to judge just where such a line of inquiry will lead. The eggplant of Indo-china is a *Solanum*. In America the Solanaceae give us the tomato. The eggplant could be called a tomato that requires cooking. In China the tomato is known as the foreigner's eggplant; this assures us that the eggplant predates the tomato and simultaneously tells us that the Chinese recognized the botanical affinity of these none-too-obvious relatives. Is then the tomato too an example of stimulus diffusion? In America there are also such intertwined puzzles as fish-poisoning and fish-poisons. This has been discussed at great length by Heizer (1953), who concluded that it was a case of multiple reinvention, and by Quigley (1956) who by contrast decided that it was more likely a case of diffusion. Among the poisons used are those derived from *Lonchocarpus* and *Derris*. Higbee (1948) has noted that these plants are so close botanically that one botanist considers them to be generically identical. This makes it a bit difficult to decide whether we are looking at a direct diffusion or a stimulus diffusion. The case is of some importance either way.

Is it possible that potatoes, beans, and cucurbits are the most likely plants for domestication? That is not very likely. Further, outside the areas where we have good reason to suspect direct and stimulus diffusion, such plants were not domesticated. Examples abound. Wild potatoes extend far beyond the areas where they were domesticated. They were gathered but not domesticated. Tobacco also was available and gathered and used far beyond the center of domestication. Cucurbits extend far beyond the zones where they were domesticated. If they are so obvious and desirable, why were they domesticated only where we have a suggestion of early arrivals from overseas?

The cucurbits also may serve to test and perhaps ultimately to clarify the idea of independent domestication. In America cucurbits were domesticated in separate areas, and in each area there were suitable species to serve as wild ancestors: *C. pepo* in northern Mexico, *C. mixta* and *C. moschata* in central and southern Mexico, *C. maxima* in South America. These are surely separate domestications, but are they wholly independent? Are we looking at seed gatherers who were utilizing these large, obvious, wild fruits throughout America, perhaps initially for their seeds, and who then quite independently domesticated these plants and developed them as a "sweet fleshy vegetable"? It was no obvious thing to do for many wild cucurbits have astringent flesh. Further, in areas marginal to agricultural origins the wild cucurbits were not domesticated: in the United States, for instance, where there are wild cucurbits from the Southwest to Florida. Then there is the time element. Man had been in America for tens of thousands of years, but all domestic cucurbits appear about 7000 (+2000?) years ago, or about one or two thousand years after the appearance of the Old World *Lagenaria*, which the cucurbits parallel in form and function. If we are looking at the spread of the idea of agriculture, and if in various parts of America this idea was applied to the local cucurbits because of their resemblance either to *Lagenaria* or to the Old World melons then we are looking at stimulus diffusion rather than at totally independent domestication. There are other possibilities, of course. Agricultural impulses may have reached America at various points at various times but all of them contained knowledge of the potential utility of gourds and melons.

An interesting test case or example is found in tobacco. This "useless" plant was fully domesticated in South America, semicultivated in the southeastern United States, aided in its growth to the northwest, and finally simply gathered wild on the northern borders of its cultural use. At least five species were used. Few, I believe, would argue that the use of tobacco was just natural, and surely neither population nor environmental pressures are easily invoked to account for its domestication. It seems to be a strange idea, an invention which spread from a South American center. In the course of its spread local species of *Nicotiana* were taken in hand: now fully domesticated, now semidomesticated, now tended but not planted, and finally fully wild but used. In time, with the spread of agriculture in some of these areas and its intensifications in others, the probable end product would have been five or more domestic species of tobacco. Yet, underlying this would be the spread of an idea, and the case would be better described as a stimulus diffusion than as independent domestications. Possibly the beans (*Phaseolus vulgaris, lunatus, acutifolius,* and *multifloris*) fit the same pattern. The suggestion of double domestication of some beans, e.g. *P. lunatus,* the lima bean in Peru and sieva in Mexico, would fit either a category like tobacco, or a hypothesis of multiple contacts leading to multiple centers with like domesticates because of like stimuli.

The principle even applies to domestic animals. All the American domestics are in the magic central zone. Turkeys ranged from Panama to New England but only in Mesoamerica were they domesticated. The Pueblos under heavy Mexican influence had domesticated them. The

Indians of the southeastern part of the United States did not. There were plenty of sheep, Rocky Mountain "goats," cows (bison are Eurasiatic "cattle" which were immigrant into North America only in the late Pleistocene), horses, camels, elephants, ducks, and geese in the American landscape but the Amerinds did not perceive them as potential domesticates, except in the very areas of demonstrable strong overseas influences.

The chicken (Carter 1971) was surely a direct introduction, and the domestication of the turkey may perhaps be a case of stimulus diffusion. Throughout the Americas the Amerinds have (had) Asiatic races of chickens. They laid eggs with brown (or blue) shells, and recognizable Chinese, Malay, and Indian races of chickens were widespread. Many American Indians would eat neither the flesh nor the eggs of their chickens. Instead they were used for sacrifice, divination, and curing ceremonies. Neither the Asiatic races of chickens nor these prohibitions and usages were known to fifteenth-century Spaniards who ate chickens freely. Spanish chickens laid white-shelled eggs and were in body, build, feathering, combs, and personalities at least as different from Asiatic chickens as Spaniards are from Chinese. Most interestingly, the Tarahumara name for chicken is *totori*, and this duplicates the Japanese name for domestic fowl. The Aztec for turkey is *cihuatotolin*, or *huexolotl* [cock and hen]. *Totolin* differs from *totori* only in the substitution of *l* for *r*, a linguistic simplicity. *Olotl* seems to be only a slightly larger shift. If, as this suggests, the Aztecs were calling turkeys chickens, then the turkey too may have been an example of a stimulus diffusion. Nor does the case end here. The name for the chicken amongst the Arawak of the Amazon is some variant of *karaka*. In India the name for the melanotic silky chicken is *karaknath*. Melanotic silkies are widespread in South America. We have here then evidence for plural introductions of an Old World biological item into widely separated areas of the New World. Chickens had reached the northern frontier of agriculture in the southwestern part of the United States in pre-Spanish time, a long way from their probable points of introduction, and this situation suggests moderately early introduction in pre-Columbian time.

At the opening of this paper I stated that this is a premature presentation. I would like to see a Ph.D. study of *Seteria*, and another on *Hibiscus* (see Carter 1954) and so on. However, time, energy, and graduate students are all in short supply, and questions and suggestions will have to suffice.

For full development of this study we need much more evidence of the plant uses of the preagricultural Amerinds. Fortunately the rapidly developing study of coprolites will provide us with a great deal of invaluable data on this. It would be most interesting to know if beans and cucurbits were especially important prior to the time of arrival of *Lagenaria*. If not, why should they suddenly become the first domesticates unless there was a model, or pattern, or perception that arrived with *Lagenaria*?

Evidence of Oceanic Routes

Meanwhile our knowledge of times and sources of early arrivals in America via the sea lanes of the world is rapidly widening and deepening. That Norse, Irish, Semites, Canaanites, various Mediterraneans, Africans, and even people from the Indian Ocean reached America via the Atlantic can be assumed to be proven, probable, or possible. We already have suggestive data for their impacts in varied cultural fields, and as the peanut suggests, there may also be agricultural influences that we have failed to perceive.

The Pacific side is startlingly far in advance of the Atlantic in time and influence: Jomon potters by 5000 to 6000 B.P.; the Old Pacific art styles at the base of American civilizational beginnings; Shang and Chou art between 4000 and 2200 B.P.; Asiatic negritos in the Olmec culture complete with a numerical notation pointing to China. The small, dark people of southern China had folk memories and the taller, yellow folk of northern China had written records of a great land across the eastern sea and both knew it by the same name: *fusang*. The little, dark folk said that the red-flowered hibiscus came from the remote eastern land beyond the sea; this hibiscus has a flower designed for pollination by hummingbirds, but hummingbirds are strictly American! This Asiatic priority is probably due to their being the earliest men to possess sophisticated deep-sea craft: unsinkable rafts with dagger boards and fore-and-aft rig-sails. This combination gave them the ability to move not just WITH the wind and current, but to travel very easily across the wind, and even to tack and thus to sail INTO the wind.

CONCLUSION

The evidence already before us shows that only after an Old World plant appears in America do we have agricultural beginnings. Thereafter an unexpected set of plants (cucurbits and beans) are domesticated over a broad area from northern Mexico to Argentina in a manner fitting the stimulus-diffusion model of the African noncenter. Thereafter there is increasing evidence of the extension of the idea of agriculture to other American plants and the exchange of plants (sweet potatoes, coconuts) and even the transport of such animals as chickens to America.

It seems probable that we must view Africa and possible that we must view the Americas as late and peripheral cases of stimulus diffusion. At this time we seemingly do not know with any real degree of certainty where in southern Asia the earliest agricultural beginning is: southwestern Asia or southeastern Asia. Should a clear priority in time be established for one, then the possibility that the other was a case of stimulus diffusion would have to be considered. As of the moment, the early dates from Spirit Cave and from Taiwan, combined with the great predominance of numbers of plants domesticated, together suggest that southeastern Asia may be the earliest center. If, as Sauer and Chang hypothesize, these were fisherfolk, then a rapid dispersal of agricultural ideas around the Indo-Pacific realm would be expectable.

Quite clearly we do not have all the answers as to time, motivation, dispersal, marks of direct and stimulus diffusion, and equally clearly the waters have been enormously muddied by preconceived notions about boats, water barriers, and the inventiveness of man. We have tended to treat the process of plant IMPROVEMENT as if that was an explanation for the ORIGIN of the idea of domestication. The gist of this study is that it is the idea of domestication that is important. I suspect that it may have arisen but once, and I have both advanced some reasons for this suspicion and pointed to several lines of inquiry that should be pursued before we harden our opinionated arteries and proclaim a dogma of plural origins of Amerind agriculture in particular.

Neither a single origin nor several separate origins can be demonstrated. We should, therefore, treat the question as open and advance numerous working hypotheses. For too long we have blandly assumed the reality of multiple centers of origin for agriculture. Perhaps we overemphasized the centers, writing as if all cucurbits in America stemmed from one valley. We should guard against the opposite extreme; there is no connection in the world of ideas between the domestication of one cucurbit and its neighbor. We need to achieve a felicitous combination of culture historical processes and botanical knowledge.

REFERENCES

ARDREY, ROBERT
1961   *African genesis.* New York: Atheneum.
BARBETTI, M., H. ALLEN
1972   Prehistoric man at Lake Mungo, Australia, by 32,000 B.P. *Nature* 240:46–48.
BEIRNE, D. RANDALL
1971   "Cultural patterning as revealed by a study of pre-Columbian ax and adze hafting in the Old and New Worlds," in *Man across the sea.* Edited by C. L. Riley, J. Charles Kelly, C. W. Pennington, and R. L. Rands, 139–177. Austin: University of Texas Press.
BRAND, DONALD D.
1971   "The sweet potato: an exercise in methodology," in *Man across the sea.* Edited by C. L. Riley, J. Charles Kelly, C. W. Pennington, and R. L. Rands, 343–365. Austin: University of Texas Press.
CALLEN, E. O.
1967a   "Analysis of the Tehuacan coprolites," in *The prehistory of Tehuacan Valley,* volume one: *Environment and subsistence.* Edited by D. S. Byers, 261–289. Austin: University of Texas Press.
1967b   The first New World cereal. *American Antiquity* 32:535–538.
CARTER G. F.
1950a   Plant evidence for early contacts with America. *Southwestern Journal of Anthropology* 6:161–182.
1950b   Ecology-geography-ethnobotany. *Scientific Monthly* 70:73–80.
1953   Plants across the Pacific. *American Antiquity* Memoirs 18 (3,2):62–71.
1954   Disharmony between Asiatic flower-birds and American bird-flowers. *American Antiquity* 20:179–187.
1957   *Pleistocene man at San Diego.* Baltimore: Johns Hopkins Press.
1963   "Movement of people and ideas across the Pacific," in *Plants and the migration of Pacific peoples: a symposium.* Edited by Jacques Barrau, 7–22. Honolulu: Bishop Museum Press.
1964   *Man and the land.* New York: Holt, Rinehart and Winston.
1971   "Pre-Columbian chickens in America," in *Man across the sea.* Edited by C. L. Riley, J. Charles Kelly, C. W. Pennington, and R. L. Rands, 178–218. Austin: University of Texas Press.
CHANG, KWANG-CHIH
1968   *The archaeology of ancient China* (second edition). New Haven, Conn.: Yale University Press.
1970   The beginnings of agriculture in the Far East. *Antiquity* 44:175–185.
CUTLER, H. C., T. W. WHITAKER
1961   History and distribution of the cultivated cucurbits in the Americas. *American Antiquity* 26:469–485.
DAVIES, OLIVER
1968   The origins of agriculture in West Africa. *Current Anthropology* 9:1–5.
DE WET, J. M. J., J. R. HARLAN
1971   The origin and domestication of *Sorghum bicolor. Economic Botany* 25:128–135.

DORAN, E. D.
1971 "The sailing raft as a great tradition," in *Man across the sea*. Edited by C. L. Riley, J. Charles Kelly, C. W. Pennington, and R. L. Rands, 115–128. Austin: University of Texas Press.

EDWARDS, CLINTON
1960 Sailing rafts of Sechura: history and problems of origin. *Southwestern Journal of Anthropology* 16:368–391.
1971 "Commentary," in *Man across the sea*. Edited by C. L. Riley, J. Charles Kelly, C. W. Pennington, and R. L. Rands, 293–305. Austin: University of Texas Press.

EKHOLM, GORDON
1955 "The new orientation toward problems of Asiatic-American relationships," in *New interpretations of aboriginal American culture history*, 95–109. Seventy-fifth anniversary volume. Washington, D.C.: Anthropological Society of Washington.

FORD, JAMES
1969 *A comparison of formative cultures in the Americas: diffusion or the psychic unity of man*. Smithsonian Contributions to Anthropology 11.

HARLAN, JACK R.
1971 Agricultural origins: centers and noncenters. *Science* 174: 468–474.

HEINE-GELDERN, ROBERT
1954 Die asiatische Herkunft der südamerikanischen Metalltechnik. *Paideuma* 5:347–423.
1958 Kulturpflanzengeographie und das Problem vorkolumbischer Kulturbeziehungen zwischen Alter und Neuer Welt. *Anthropos* 53:361–402.

HEIZER, R. F.
1953 Aboriginal fish poisons. *Bureau of American Ethnology Bulletin* 151: 225–283.

HEYERDAHL, THOR
1950 The voyage of the raft Kon Tiki. *Geographical Journal* 115:20–41.
1952 *American Indians in the Pacific*. London: George Allen and Unwin.
1971 *The Ra expeditions*. Garden City, N.Y.: Doubleday.

HIGBEE, E. C.
1948 *Lonchocarpus, Derris* and *Pyrethrum*. United States Department of Agriculture Miscellaneous Publications 650.

HOWELL, F. CLARK
1972 "Pliocene/Pleistocene Hominidae in eastern Africa: absolute and relatives ages," in *Calibration of hominoid evolution: recent advances in isotopic and other dating methods applicable to the origin of man*. Edited by W. W. Bishop and J. A. Miller, 331–368. Edinburgh: Scottish Academic Press.

IRVINE, F. R.
1956 The edible cultivated and semi-cultivated leaves of West Africa. *Materiae Vegetabiles* 2:35–42.

JETT, STEPHEN C.
1971 "Diffusion versus independent development: the bases of controversy," in *Man across the sea*. Edited by C. L. Riley, J. Charles Kelly, C. W. Pennington, and R. L. Rands, 5–53. Austin: University of Texas Press.

JETT, STEPHEN C., GEORGE F. CARTER
  1966   A comment on Rowe's "Diffusionism and archaeology." *American Antiquity* 31: 867–870.
JOLLY, CLIFFORD J.
  1970   The seed-eaters: a new model of hominid differentiation based on a baboon analogy. *Man*, n.s. 5:1–26.
JONES, A. M.
  1964   *Africa and Indonesia: the evidence of the xylophone and other musical and cultural factors.* Leiden: E. J. Brill.
KAPLAN, L., THOMAS F. LYNCH, C. E. SMITH, JR.
  1973   Early cultivated beans (*Phaseolus vulgaris*) from an intermontane Peruvian valley. *Science* 179:76–77.
KRAUS, GERHARD
  1971   Who started American civilization? *The New Diffusionist* 2:59–61. (Refers to "Resemblances between the Maya civilization and that of China," by Kiang Kang Hu [Transactions of the Royal Society of Canada, Ottawa, 1933] who allegedly stated that in Chinese numerals of Soochow the numeration is by dots and bars as in the Olmec-Maya system.)
LATHRAP, DONALD
  1967   Review of *Early formative period of coastal Ecuador* by B. J. Meggers, C. Evans, and E. Estrada. *American Anthropologist* 69:96–98.
MANGELSDORF, P. C., R. S. MAC NEISH, G. R. WILLEY
  1964   "Origin of agriculture in Middle America," in *Handbook of Middle American Indians*, volume one: *Natural environment and early cultures.* Edited by R. C. West, 427–445. Austin: University of Texas Press.
MEGGERS, B. J., CLIFFORD EVANS, EMILIO ESTRADA
  1965   *Early formative period of coastal Ecuador.* Smithsonian Contributions to Anthropology 1.
NEEDHAM, J.
  1959   *Science and civilization in China*, volume three: *Mathematics and the sciences of the heaven and the earth.* Cambridge: Cambridge University Press.
QUIGLEY, CARROLL
  1956   Aboriginal fish poisons and the diffusion problem. *American Anthropologist* 58:508–526.
REED, ERIC
  1971   "Comment," in *Man across the sea.* Edited by C. L. Riley, J. Charles Kelly, C. W. Pennington, and R. L. Rands, 106–111. Austin: University of Texas Press.
ROBINSON, JOHN T.
  1972   *Early hominid posture and locomotion.* Chicago: University of Chicago Press.
ROWE, JOHN H.
  1966   Diffusionism and archaeology. *American Antiquity* 31:334–337.
SAUER, C. O.
  1952   *Agricultural origins and dispersals.* New York: American Geographical Society.

SORENSON, JOHN L.

1971 "The significance of an apparent relationship between the ancient Near East and Mesoamerica," in *Man across the sea*. Edited by C. L. Riley, J. Charles Kelly, C. W. Pennington and R. L. Rands, 219–241. Austin: University of Texas Press.

VAVILOV, N. I.

1949–1950 The origin, variation, immunity and breeding of cultivated plants. *Chronica Botanica* 13:1–364.

VON HUMBOLDT, ALEXANDER

1814 *Researches concerning the institutions and monuments of the ancient inhabitants of Mexico*, volume one, part thirty. London.

VON WUTHENAU, ALEXANDER

1969 *Terra cotta pottery in pre-Columbian Central and South America*. New York: Graystone Press.

WHITAKER, T. W.

1948 *Lagenaria:* A pre-Columbian cultivated plant in the Americas. *Southwestern Journal of Anthropology* 4:49–68.

WHITAKER, T. W., G. F. CARTER

1954 Oceanic drift of gourds: experimental observations. *American Journal of Botany* 41:697–700.

WILLEY, GORDON

1971 *Archaeology of South America*. Englewood Cliffs, N.J.: Prentice-Hall.

Population Pressure and the Origins of Agriculture: An Archaeological Example from the Coast of Peru

MARK N. COHEN

Since the time of Morgan's comprehensive statement (1877) on the nature of cultural evolution in which he embodied themes of considerable antiquity, two main ideas contained in his work have dominated our ideas about the development of cultural systems: first, that the process of cultural change is primarily an accumulation of technological capabilities and that the level of technological development is the primary determinant of the culture system as a whole; and second, that cultural evolution consists of a succession of well-defined and relatively static stages separated by abrupt revolutionary transitions. The combination of these two themes has led anthropology toward a one-sided view of the relationship between technology and population growth. Technology is considered an independent variable; technological changes modify the carrying capacity of the environment; population simply adjusts to the new limits in a Malthusian sense and is not seen as having any significant effect on technological change; as a result, the history of population growth is assumed to have a stepped pattern in which periods of stable equilibrium alternate with periods of rapid population growth.

Perhaps the most explicit modern expression of these two themes and the resulting model of population growth is in the work of Childe (1951) who discussed the development of European civilization in terms of a series of technological revolutions (for example the "Neolithic" or food-producing revolution) involving relatively short term massive reorganizations of technology which resulted in periods of rapid population growth and reorganization of social institutions.

Recently, however, the assumptions about the revolutionary nature of technological changes and culture growth have been questioned. For example, Adams (1966) has questioned the applicability of the revolution concept in explaining the development of urban society in Mesopotamia or Mexico which he describes as a gradual (although not necessarily continuous or homogeneous) process. As another example, local sequences worked out for the Tamaulipas, Tehuacán and Oaxaca regions of Mexico (MacNeish 1958, 1967; Flannery 1968) have all demonstrated quite convincingly that the transition from hunting and gathering to agriculture was extremely gradual rather than revolutionary.

The assumption of technological determinism and the related assumption of the dependent, responsive nature of population growth, has had a much more pervasive influence, however, and still persists as a major, if tacit, assumption in much work on cultural development. The assumption is so pervasive for example that it has survived even the introduction of systems-models in the analysis of cultural change. The systems approach (not necessarily to be confused with the more recent explicit use of systems-theory terminology) has the advantage of viewing cultural change (for example, the evolution of domestication) not simply as a sequence of isolated historical events, but rather as a series of shifts in the balance between a number of interrelated variables. This approach allows us to consider multiple dimensions of feedback between variables instead of making simple cause-effect or independent–dependent variable statements. As a result, the potential for accurate analysis of the processes of cultural evolution is greatly enhanced. However, the full potential of this method is lost since we are tending to retain our traditional assumptions about causal relationships and tending simply to translate our old assumption into the new language. Flannery (1968), for example, described the evolution of agriculture in Oaxaca, not as a series of discoveries, but as a series of quantitative shifts in the balance between alternative strategies of getting food. However, pressed for an explanation of these shifts, Flannery has argued that the original nexus of change in the system is a mutation of the maize-plant which increases its productivity and therefore increases the efficiency of one part of the human economic cycle, and that on this basis there was a shift in human economic strategy toward domestication. Here Flannery has made two assumptions which reflect old biases of traditional anthropology and which produce a logically impossible result. First, he has presumed that human population simply remains in (or actively seeks) one equilibrium level until that equilibrium is upset by an outside event. And second, he has assumed something which is implicit in technological determinism — that the critical event which triggers the adjustment must be an increase in the AVAILABILITY of food-resources (increased productive CAPACITY).

He has assumed that new productive potential is the key to change and that the other elements in his system simply respond to this altered productivity in maize. Here he betrayed his intellectual ancestry, but he was also forced into a logical error. Mutations are recurrent aspects of the environment which occur with statistical regularity. The mutations which increased the productivity of maize would have been regularly available to primitive hunter-gatherers dealing with wild populations of maize, and they cannot logically therefore account for a shift in their exploitative system. We must instead look for the reason behind the altered human response to this aspect of the environment. Why did the hunter-gatherers choose to make use of a mutation which they had previously ignored? The way out of this problem lies in a slightly more complex model in which we view human population not simply as an equilibrium-seeking system responding to altered productive potential but rather as a system with inherent growth, actively redetermining the nature of its relationship with the environment. Such a model can be constructed if we consider population growth (or population pressure defined in terms of the degradation of existing resources whether or not accompanied by actual increase of population) as an inherent feature of the human adaptive system and not simply as a response to environmental or technological changes. Such an approach would solve Flannery's dilemma. We could simply assume that his population began to make use of the potential of the mutated maize-plant when the population was too large to manage easily with its traditional strategies.

There is, of course, a certain basic logic in considering population growth as a contributing factor in culture change. We know that human populations have enormous growth potential (Polgar 1972: 205; Birdsell 1957: 193) and we know that population growth is one of the most noticeable trends of human history. Moreover, a model emphasizing population growth would correspond well with the newly discovered gradual nature of the major features of cultural evolution.

A number of recent studies have attempted to demonstrate the importance of growth and pressure of populations in contributing to the process of cultural growth rather than simply resulting from technological change (e.g. Dumond 1965; Boserup 1965; Harner 1970; Spooner 1972). The basic discussion of the role of population growth as a determinant of technological change is that provided by Boserup (1965) who argued that agricultural technology is largely a function of population density and that the various known technologies represent a continuous series of more or less elastic responses to growing population. Despite these studies, and despite what I consider to be the cogency of Boserup's logic (if not always of her supporting data) this approach is not widely recognized. It is explicitly dismissed in a number of recent studies (Polgar 1972; Sheffer 1971) and it is ignored (see e.g. Flannery 1968) where it might provide useful insights.

I believe that such dismissal is unfortunate. I intend to argue that population growth and population pressure are in fact contributing factors in the origins and growth of an agricultural economy and, incidentally, I intend to suggest that the model of human cultural systems as equilibrium-seeking and-maintaining systems must be replaced with a model stressing their inherent growth through expanding population. I do not intend simply to replace technological determinism with a new population determinism or assume that population grows independent of other factors. I do intend to argue that population growth is an inherent factor in the adaptive histories of many, if not most, human populations and that such growth can be used to explain aspects of the development of agriculture which are otherwise inexplicable.

THE THEORY OF POPULATION GROWTH AND AGRICULTURAL ORIGINS

In order to get around the legacy of technological determinism and look at population growth as a factor in the origins of agriculture, we must deal with a number of myths concerning agriculture and its origin. The first myth is that agriculture is a difficult concept, whose discovery was a major obstacle in human progress. There are a number of lines of evidence which refute this assumption and suggest in fact that the concept of agriculture was probably readily available to evolving human populations. First, it is becoming increasingly apparent that agriculture was in fact discovered independently a number of times. A recent review of agricultural origins by Harlan (1971) indicated that the origins of our major domesticates must be traced over an extremely broad area of the New and Old Worlds and that defined centers of domestication are recognizable only in certain cases. He pointed out in addition that there are a large number of genera of plants in which two or more species were domesticated at different times and in different places. The evidence of interregional contacts of great antiquity is sufficient to suggest that many of these regions learned the idea from others. However, to account for all of these several origins by assuming that the concept of agriculture spread from one or a few hearths is not supportable in terms of known patterns of diffusion: the indigenous crops occur earlier than the imports in too many regions. Hence, we can assume that there were at least several independent discoveries of agriculture. Moreover, our knowledge of the ecology of hunter-gatherer groups suggests that the independent discovery of the concept of domestication by several of these groups is not only possible, it is highly probable, and I maintain that lack of insight into the process of domestication would rarely have offered an obstacle to the progress of any group. The techniques of agriculture are self-evident to any hunter-gatherer group. We know, for example, that even nonhuman primates regularly accumulate around their home-ranges gardens of their favorite produce grown from seeds or vegetative parts dropped in the course of eating or in feces (Jolly 1972: 59). We know that human hunter-gatherers also tend to collect gardens of their favorite foods near their houses quite independent of any attempts at domestication (Schwanitz 1966: 12). And we know that these people often unintentionally propagate their food plants by accidentally re-sowing parts of their crops in the process of harvesting (Schwanitz 1966: 12). We know that pre-agricultural man created new open habitats for plants in the form of dumps, pathways, and recently burned areas (Anderson 1969: 144) and that many of man's cultivated plants originated as species which enjoyed these disturbed habitats (Anderson 1969: 144; Sauer 1952: 71). We know that most hunting and gathering groups have a very thorough knowledge of the characteristics and ecological needs of the species of their preferred food and that they even know how to assist them in their survival (Stewart 1956: 120). We know that hunters and gatherers are aware, for example, of the value of a fire in promoting the growth of preferred species (Stewart 1956: 120; Sauer 1952: 11; Isaac 1970: 18–19). We know also that desirable morphological changes such as gigantism of edible parts and early maturity have occurred in plants growing in the vicinity of human settlement although without direct human participation (Isaac 1970: 18).

All this suggests that the break between gathering and agriculture is not very sharp and, therefore, that the conceptual break was not very difficult. In fact, I maintain no such break occurred. There is rather a continuum in degrees of assistance offered to the plants on which one depends. This sort of continuum is reflected in Anderson's (1969: 131ff) description of primitive gardens with their haphazard organization of crop plants and the graded distinction from weeds which are discouraged, through tolerated weeds, through unplanned but cultivated plants to purposefully planted domesticates. With these considerations in mind, the view that the bulk of humanity was seriously blocked from the discovery of agriculture for any period of time is untenable. Local inequities in the type of plants available might have hindered individual populations, but given the range of plants which have been cultivated at various times and places, this cannot have been a widespread limitation. In addition, I must stress that even people of those regions which learned about agriculture from others or imported their cultigens from other areas probably would not have been delayed for lack of access to agricultural techniques. We are finding increasingly that cultural contacts between regions are of great antiquity (see for example Lanning 1967a and MacNeish 1969, 1970 concerning the distribution of early artifact styles in Peru). The suggestion, therefore, is that even those regions lacking suitable cultigens had access to agricultural knowledge and to suitable cultigens long before they were needed or utilized as is true in the case to be discussed. What this suggests is that we must look for some reason other than ignorance why some people have remained hunters, and conversely, some reason other than discovery why some became farmers.

The second myth concerns the benefits which result from the transition to an agricultural economy. Recent studies of the diet of hunters and gatherers by Lee (1968, 1969), by Woodburn (1968) and by Neel (1970) indicate that modern hunters and gatherers are commonly well nourished and healthy. Their diets are found to be sufficient in total caloric intake, and also in protein and necessary elements. This is true despite the fact that modern hunters and gatherers (for example Lee's Bushmen in the Kalahari desert) have been pushed by political pressure into marginal environments which are presumably less productive than the environments of their prehistoric counterparts. It is questionable, therefore, whether agriculture would have brought any significant dietary improvement to hunting and gathering peoples. There is even indication that the quality of the diet will decline with agriculture since agriculture presumes concentration on a relatively small number of food-sources. By reducing the dietary variety inherent in a gathering economy, agriculture may actually reduce the balance of the diet. (As Lee points out, hunter-gatherers may be better nourished than their agricultural neighbors.) Agriculture may also reduce rather than increase the reliability of the food sources. The natural plant-community is buffered against ecological disaster by its very complexity. The number of species represented in the wild community means that some edible parts will be available at most seasons and, more important, assures that some foods will survive droughts, fires and other natural disasters, especially since the plants represented have already undergone a long process of selection for tolerance to these particular conditions. The replacement of the natural community by an artificial plant community of fewer members means that the food-supply will be more seasonal (geared to the cycles of the few crop plants) and much more susceptible to ecological breakdown. Lee also suggested (1969: 73) that the Bushmen suffered less from a drought experienced prior to his visit than had their agricultural or pastoral neighbors.

The work of Lee and Woodburn also destroys one other misconception about the benefits of agriculture, the assumption that agriculture makes food-getting easier (i.e. less costly in terms of labor). Lee's statistics and Woodburn's description indicate that hunters and gatherers, again in marginal, difficult environments, put in very little time in the food quest. Lee indicated, for example, that the bulk of the food for the Bushmen is gathered by a fraction of those we would consider able-bodied adults working only a very few hours per week. This is not surprising when we realize that their labor is generally equivalent only to the harvesting portion of an agricultural cycle. Sufficient figures are not available to demonstrate conclusively the greater ease of hunting and gathering, especially since it is difficult to compare labor figures cross-culturally. However, Lee's figures are sufficiently striking to suggest that leisure time does not appear for the first time with agriculture and that labor-saving is hardly likely to have been an incentive for technological change. Once these myths are destroyed, we arrive at a new problem about the origins of agriculture. If agriculture provides neither better diet, nor greater dietary reliability, nor greater ease, but conversely appears to provide a poorer diet, less reliably, with greater labor costs, why does anyone become a farmer? (Lee's Bushmen who know all about planting seeds argue that this would be silly since it is much easier to harvest wild foods.) What does agriculture actually accomplish? It provides only one economic benefit: the ability to grow and harvest more food from a unit of space in a unit of time. In other words, agriculture permits denser food-growth supporting, denser population and hence larger social units, but at the cost of lower dietary quality, less reliability, and more work per unit of food. If I am correct then that agriculture is not a difficult concept, but something readily available to hunting and gathering groups, and if I am correct then that its only advantage is in the greater density of food available, then it follows that agriculture will occur primarily in response to a situation of need resulting either from population growth or from resource degradation. The hunter-gatherers in Oaxaca (Flannery 1968) shifted their ecological response to favor maize-agriculture when the need arose, not because the mutation became available. I will argue further that while resource degradation (or even political incentive to greater production) may have played a part under certain circumstances, the predominant historical motivation for agriculture has been growth of population.

To understand the latter position, a third major misconception that underlies prevailing assumptions about the technology/population inter-action must be considered: the uncritical use of models of carrying capacity in the study of human society based on the assumption that human population historically has simply responded to fixed population ceilings established by available resources. Many, but by no means all, populations of non-human animals tend to reach stable levels balanced at, or near, the optimum level which the environment can support without resource degradation. Working with modern hunter-gatherers, anthropol-ogists like Birdsell (1957) have demonstrated that human populations also achieve relatively stable optimum levels balanced with their resources. The failure here is the failure to realize that these studies of modern hunter-gatherers are studies on populations which are anomalous pre-cisely because their populations have remained small. I would argue that the concept of carrying capacity as a fixed ceiling to which population responds, although applicable to specific populations under particular conditions, has little general validity for human history. Human popula-tions, aware of agricultural potential, know that they can expand their resources by intensifying their labor-inputs if it should become necessary. Such a population has a choice whether to stabilize at a given level of population and a given productivity or to expand its population and work harder. We do not need to consider a stable population growing to a new stable ceiling whenever technology permits, although such may, of course, happen in some historical events. We can rather visualize a popu-lation growing and pushing its technology with it. Human populations have grown historically. The remaining populations of hunters and gather-ers are anomalous groups which either by cultural choice or by reason of unidentified biological factors have remained small and survived. Let us consider for a moment the model of a hunting and gathering popula-tion and consider its alternatives. If the Kalahari Bushmen are in any way typical, we can assume that such a population obtained an adequate and nutritious diet with a minimum of work by exploiting the wild resources within a loosely defined radius of its camp. Typically, such exploitative systems appear to support less than one person per square mile (Lee and DeVore 1968: 11), so that the size of the group is limited by the distance people are willing to walk to obtain food. Among modern hunter-gatherers an exploitative radius of a few miles seems typical. A radius of 6 miles brings 100 square miles within the area of exploitation so that it is again typical of such groups that the population of a single camp is rarely more than 100 people and typically closer to one-half or one-quarter of that figure (Lee and DeVore 1968: 11). Depending on local conditions, the group may be required to move once or more during the year to exploit new areas.

The high quality of diet and the low labor costs involved can be maintained as long as population is constant, but this nice balance is threatened if population tends to grow beyond these limited figures, and my contention is that for many, if not most, human populations, this tendency had constantly to be dealt with. Increased population threatened the group with a decline in the quality and quantity of food available, an increased work load, or both, and I think we must assume that the people involved were capable of realizing as a practical matter, if not theoretically, that the more mouths there were to feed, the harder the gathering process would be. The group then had several alternative solutions to its dilemma. First, it could limit population either by infanticide, which is obviously available to all human populations, or by techniques of abortion or contraception which are also almost universal (Birdsell 1968; Devereux 1967: 98). This is the solution most in keeping with retaining both the quality of diet and low labor costs, but it is not the only solution. The alternatives are to increase the radius exploited (which implies increased labor-costs in travel); to search harder for the less readily available food sources within the area exploited (again implying increased labor-costs); to move from camp to camp more often (increased labor-costs); or to settle for less desired and less nutritious foods. We can be sure that some combination of these alternatives entered into the response of any particular population. But, these responses are limited in their adjustive capacity. An increase in the radius of exploitation leads eventually to the budding off of new village units by persons who feel that they are forced to walk too far from new resource-areas to old villages, or who realize that they can get food for less work by starting a new smaller social group. This is, I suspect, the process by which hunter-gatherers populated the world. But, eventually this sort of territorial expansion abuts against natural barriers to migration or against the ranges of competing groups. Similarly, working harder on finding wild foods within the same area or settling for lesser foods are only temporary solutions to growing populations. Again, the decision may be made belatedly to limit population and stabilize labor-costs at the new higher level. For those who do not take this option, and continue to allow population to grow, the only other alternative is to begin artificially to increase the density of desirable crops within their gathering radius by the use of one of a number of techniques which must have been known to them: removing the competing plants (weeding); protecting from other animals; improving the physical environment (hoeing etc.); placing the plants in areas where they did not formerly grow (planting); selecting and selectively aiding the most productive plants. These techniques add up to agriculture, but it is important to stress that the techniques probably accumulate *de facto* and piecemeal as responses to the need for more food, long before the concept of agriculture was developed. Also important to note is that these changes which we call agriculture only occurred when the people decided that the labor involved in these practices was the least of evils. Each technique represented higher labor-costs and would only have been added when the costs were outweighed by the costs of retaining old methods.

All of this, of course, allowed for a wide range of latitude in group decision. Were there good rational reasons for wanting or needing a larger population despite the costs? Were there cultural norms favoring the prestige of large families or preventing the use of techniques of population control? Did the joys of parenthood outweigh the additional labor-cost? Was it considered harder to walk farther to collect food, to move the village more often, or to weed the plants close to home? Are there biological reasons why some populations grow and some do not?

Clearly, given these alternatives, populations have an enormous number of possible strategies. Some in fact chose to limit population at the hunter-gatherer level. Some just as clearly did not. These variables however are ultimately regulated by the one overwhelming factor of competition. If we assume that various groups of hunter-gatherers made different decisions in these situations and some limited population while some did not, how do we explain the scarcity of hunter-gatherers? The simple answer is that those who for one reason or another chose to allow populations to grow and responded to the need by putting extra labor into agriculture were able to compete successfully for space with those groups that chose to remain small (or who for biological reasons did not grow). Thus, even if only a relatively few populations allowed population growth and compensated with agriculture, they would over a period of time replace hunter-gatherers in all but the most marginal environments. (Moreover, the awareness of such competition may very well have been one factor involved in the original choices). (Also to be noted: it is not population growth *per se* which is the critical variable, but demand for production outstripping the wild resources of a given region for whatever reasons. A similar result will occur with a stable population if it stabilized above the carrying capacity of the land for a given technology and therefore progressively degraded resources. Such results would also occur if climatic change eliminated resources or if social factors required new production standards.)

In sum, I am suggesting a model in which expanding population (along with environmental changes or altered sociopolitical conditions) may cause a more or less continuous modification of adaptive strategy. The population has a choice of several adaptive strategies at any point in time, but only one choice, the intensification of resources by application of agricultural techniques, is viable for most populations in the long run. The other choices either provide only temporary solutions which delay but do not eliminate the beginnings of agriculture, or they lead to evolutionary dead ends since such populations cannot ultimately compete with those utilizing agriculture. (One other alternative, that of exploiting other agriculturalists, is, of course, available but only to a few populations.) The point is that although the intent at all times is to retain a balance between population and resources, the system is not simply designed to maintain stable equilibrium. The continual tendency for population to grow, and the ready availability of techniques for intensifying resources (agriculture) mean that new equilibria are constantly being redefined. This does not, however, imply that population growth is an independent variable in any simple sense. Clearly rates of population growth are subject to cultural choice. Moreover, nothing in this model precludes feedback from technological or social changes to the rate of population growth. The achievement of a certain level of agricultural competence (for example, the development of sedentary life) may subsequently alter either biological factors or cultural values concerning population growth.

This model helps to account for the apparently gradual nature of much major technological change, since it implies that technological change does not occur solely by its own momentum but in large part occurs only as necessitated by the demand for new resources. The model also implies that population growth historically may be smoother and more gradual than is commonly assumed, and that it may approximate a ramplike model or a stepped ramp, rather than the simple stepped model which is commonly applied in anthropology (e.g. Deevey 1960: 198; Polgar 1972: 204). (There is, of course, no need to assume that population growth is totally gradual since I do not assume that it is an independent variable.)

This in turn requires us to explore one more myth in anthropological thinking concerning the reconstruction of prehistoric population curves. The archaeological record is commonly read in such a way as to support the assumption that population is constant before agriculture and that rapid revolutionary population growth follows the discovery of agriculture suggesting a Malthusian model. (See, for example, Braidwood and Reed 1957.) Such a conclusion may, however, represent a misreading of the evidence. In the first place, archaeological techniques for reconstruction of populations invariably rely on counting the number of units of some parameter representing population which are in use at the same time, for example the number of archaeological sites of a given period, the number of houses, the number of square meters of floor space, the number of grindstones. While this method has inaccuracies in dealing with populations of sedentary peoples, it is totally inadequate to deal with mobile populations. Moreover, the nature of temporary campsites suggests that they will be underrepresented in the archaeological record. They are harder to find and identify and more easily obliterated than permanent villages. Since the inception of agriculture is roughly associated with the beginnings of sedentary villages it is hardly surprising that the archaeological record shows a marked increase in the number of settlement units at this time. The apparent enormous expansion of population after the beginning of agriculture may simply reflect the inaccuracy of archaeological samples and the growth curve of the historical population may have been somewhat smoother than a direct reading of the evidence suggests.

Ultimately, of course, the issue of the role of population-growth in culture change needs to be settled empirically by the study of culture systems in transition. Ethnographic examples of the transition to agriculture are hard to come by. Reconstruction from archaeological evidence is difficult because all of the important variables (population, resources, agricultural techniques etc.) can be reconstructed only from indirect evidence which is prone to sampling errors of many kinds. For these reasons, I do not think that it is possible to prove my case archaeologically. However, I do believe that it is possible to present archaeological sequences which are best interpreted according to the model I have suggested.

The Peru Coast, where I have done my fieldwork, provides what is in many ways an ideal area for testing. The dry climate results in excellent preservation of organic remains so that the status of agriculture can be readily assessed. The desert conditions also mean that archaeological sites are readily amenable to surface description and survey (although there are important limitations which weaken the argument). In addition, the long history of sophisticated, anthropologically oriented archaeological work in Peru, particularly the emphasis on settlement pattern analysis, means that there is a well-defined prehistoric context in which to work.

Finally, the nature of the coast provides well-bounded ecological units of study.

My example from the Ancón-Chillón Region of the Peru Coast is not a perfect model of agricultural origins since the evidence suggests that the people of this region imported their first cultigens from other regions rather than developing native food resources as domesticates. The value of the evidence from this region is fourfold. First, the data indicate that the hunting and gathering population of the region was growing (if slowly); that it was degrading its resources; and that it was being forced to modify its collecting strategy prior to the beginnings of agriculture in the region. Second, the data indicate that the people of the region had access to agricultural techniques and resources at least several hundred years before they were used as evidenced by established diffusion-contacts with agricultural regions. (In particular I will show that the Ancón-Chillón region lags at least several hundred years behind the Ayacucho region of the Peruvian highlands in the development of agriculture and the domestication of major crops despite the fact that more direct diffusion-contacts between the two regions can be demonstrated.) Third, the data suggest that agricultural technology, when it does appear in the region, does so in a period of ecological crisis following the progressive exhaustion of the wild resources of the region. Fourth, the data suggest that even after the beginning of agriculture in the region, new domestic crops and animals and new technologies appear slowly and gradually in response to need rather than in correspondence to known diffusion patterns.

THE ANCÓN-CHILLÓN REGION OF THE PERU COAST

Between 1961 and 1971, Edward P. Lanning of Columbia University, Thomas C. Patterson, now of Temple University, M. E. Moseley of Harvard and their students engaged in a systematic study of the archaeology of the lower portion of the Chillón Valley and the adjoining Ancón region of the Central Coast of Peru. (See Figure 1.) As a result of their studies, a complete archaeological sequence for the last 12,000 years has been worked out. The distribution of archaeological sites and environmental zones can be determined or inferred for each prehistorical period; and organic collections from site excavations are available for each of the main time periods (Lanning 1967a, b; Patterson 1966a, b, 1971a, b; Patterson and Moseley 1968; Moseley 1968, 1972). In 1969–1971, working under the guidance of Dr. Margaret Towle of Harvard University, I undertook a study of the botanical remains from the region. My intention

A   Ancón-Chillón region
B   Ayacucho
C   Callejón de Huaylas (Ancash)
D   Huarmey

Figure 1. Peru (showing the location of the Ancón-Chillón region and other regions referred to)

was to describe economic changes through time and to relate these changes to population growth and settlement patterns.

The region studied includes the delta of the Chillón River and an area of the coastal desert to the north covering a total of approximately 360 square kilometers (see Figure 2). The area measures 29 kilometers north to south with an east to west distance which varies between 9 kilometers and 16 kilometers because of the irregularity of the coastline. The zone is located just to the northwest of Lima (11° 58′ to 11° 40′ South latitude by 77° 13′ to 77° 03′ West longitude). The area is predominantly an extremely dry desert due to the cold offshore ocean currents, and over much of the land no natural biological communities exist. Within the area there are, however, three major communities utilized as resource-zones by pre-

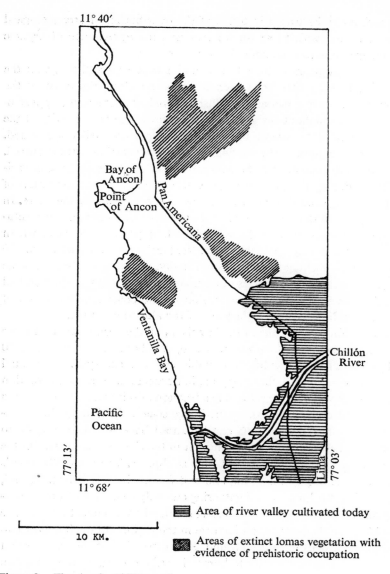

Figure 2.   The Ancón-Chillón region

historic populations: the ocean itself with its rich marine fauna; the river's valley with its riverine fauna and its naturally irrigated forest later replaced by cultivated fields and extended by artificial irrigation; and patches of *lomas* vegetation or vegetation supported by the moisture of fogs on the upper slopes of hills facing the sea. The history of human occupation can be traced in terms of the distribution of archaeological sites associated with these three zones and the appearance of organic refuse pertaining to each zone found in the sites.

The ocean appears to have been a major food source throughout the sequence. Fishing sites have been recorded all along the coast of the survey zone. Marine fish and shellfish, as well as shore-birds, appear in abundance throughout the sequence. Changes in the productivity of the oceans are hard to assess, but certain changes are well documented. First, slight changes in the configuration of the coastline have occurred. These seem to have altered the composition of available shellfish at various times during the prehistoric sequence by causing an alternation of molluscs using sand or rock as substrates at locations along the shore. In addition, late in the sequence, changes in the coastal configuration actually seem to have eliminated shellfishing along portions of the coast. In particular, the drying up of the bay at Ventanilla sometime after A.D. 600 eliminated shellfishing in this region. Finally, at approximately the same date, some of the major species of marine mammals that were hunted had probably disappeared from this region of the coast either because of over-exploitation by man or because of the altered coastline.

The Chillón River is one of the few rivers on the Peru Coast that flows throughout the year. At present, it supports between 6,000 and 7,000 hectares under annual cultivation within the zone surveyed. The annual temperature permits double cropping, but because of seasonal fluctuation in the flow of water in the river only a fraction of this area can be irrigated for a second crop during the year. Large scale irrigation reaching substantially to its modern limits can be traced back for at least 1,000 to 1,500 years before the Spanish conquest in the sixteenth century, but the history of irrigation prior to that time is obscure. The use of the river's valley for farming of the floodplain and for small scale irrigation, and, prior to that, for hunting and gathering can only be inferred from archaeological site-distribution and refuse-content. There is almost no evidence of *pukio* or sunken-garden agriculture in the region although one or two such fossil gardens have been found. Reconstruction of the environment of the 'wild' river valley prior to human interference is a problem. Ramón Ferreyra of the *Museo de Historia Natural*, Lima (personal communication), has cited evidence in the form of modern remnants of primary forest and fossilized seeds which suggests that the river may once have supported a forest in a band several kilometers in width. In this case, the primary forest would have been substantially equal in area to that of the modern cultivated zone, and as such the valley would have been a rich source of varied fauna and flora for early man.

The vegetation of the *lomas* is the most problematic of the three zones. The vegetation is dependent on moisture from fogs and as such only occurs today in locations (hillsides near the sea above 300 meters) and at seasons (mid-winter) when the fog is densest. During this period, a highly visible green patch occurs on isolated hillsides in the region. The vegetation of the *lomas* is a loosely knit community of herbaceous annual plants plus a number of tuber-, bulb- and rhizome-bearing plants, some species of which could have provided food for early inhabitants in the region, as well as supporting grazing fauna which could be exploited (Weberbauer 1932: 16ff.). At present these regions are used for grazing domestic herds but there is no evidence in this region at least that the areas of *lomas* have ever been farmed or contributed any species which have become domesticated.

In 1970, during my visit, the vegetation of the *lomas* consisted only of tiny patches in one or two restricted locations in the survey zone. These patches contained tubers of the edible species *Solanum tuberiferum* in great abundance. I estimated ten such tubers (not to be confused with true potatoes) per square meter (or a total of about 150,000 tubers in one patch) which along with other edible species of plants and small fauna even today would have provided rich resources for exploitation by a small human population. These resources would be available not only in the winter season when the *lomas* blooms, but throughout the year since the tubers would remain available for harvest long after the superficial parts of the plants which provide the *lomas* with its temporary bright green color had disappeared.

The extent of this vegetation at various times in the past, however, is in dispute. There is abundant historical evidence that the distribution of the vegetation of the *lomas* responds markedly to the alternation of wet and dry years (Goodspeed and Stork 1955) and there is extensive evidence of fossil plants and snails covering a much larger area of the survey-zone of the *lomas* than that which supported active vegetation in 1970 (Figure 2). Lanning (1967a, b) has argued that the expanse of fossil vegetation represents a period of generally wetter conditions in the areas of the *lomas*, corresponding to a period of warmer climate between 8000 and 4500 B.P., and he has argued that the vegetation of the *lomas* was extensively utilized by man only during this period. He has been criticized by Parsons (1970), who has claimed that the fossil *lomas* vegetation is nothing more than the remains of occasional wet years which do not correspond to any particular time period. The carbon-14 dates and the artifactual content of Lanning's sites, however, are so consistent (Cohen 1971) that there is no question that these sites in the *lomas* represent individual industries and exploitation of particular portions of the vegetation corresponding to particular time-periods. Lanning's climatic hypothesis, however, is questionable. Judging by the position and content of the various sites in the *lomas* apparently there was a trend in the use of the vegetation (see below) that suggests that the pattern of its use and subsequent abandonment owe more to human population pressure than to climate. In short, clearly the vegetation of the *lomas* was exploited primarily during one prehistoric era (just prior to the advent of agriculture). It is not clear that this use pattern necessarily reflects climatic change, and for reasons which will be discussed below I prefer a model that emphasizes population pressure as a cause of their decline. In either case, I intend to show that the origins of agriculture in the region are bound up with the declining productivity of the vegetation of the *lomas*.

Lanning and Patterson (Lanning 1967a; Patterson 1966a; Patterson and Moseley 1968) have divided the prehistory of the region into six preceramic and six ceramic periods (Table 1), following the standard Peruvian chronology. They recognized approximately forty separate phases with finer discriminations still being worked out. Three hundred archaeological sites have been mapped from the area so that settlement patterns for all periods are known (Figures 3 and 4). Occupation of the region appears to have been continuous from about 14,000 B.P. to the Spanish conquest in the 16th century with only one possible break. The gradual nature of the changes which occur in the artifact content, site-distribution and refuse suggest that we are dealing with a continuous process of cultural development *in loco*. Outside influences are felt but there is no evidence of wholesale replacement of population or culture with the possible exception of the one gap in the sequence. Approximately 50,000 floral specimens have been analyzed by the author from 105 excavation units at ten sites representing the entire sequence with only one or two gaps. The plant material represents a total of thirty-nine taxa. The taxa identified are listed in Table 2, and are broken down into three groups: those definitely or very probably wild species indigenous to the area; those of unresolved origins; and those which are clearly domestic imports into the region. The latter category, it will be noted, includes almost all of the significant food plants. Some of the wild plants and plants of unknown origin are now grown under conditions of domestication, but in these cases there are insufficient data available to distinguish domestic and wild types from the archaeological record. I also undertook a crude sorting of the faunal material, sorting out the domestic groups, llamas and guinea pigs, marine mammals, nondomestic terrestrial mammals such as deer, fish and various types of shellfish. These data are

Table 1. Chronological table of prehistoric periods for Peru and approximate chronology of archaeological assemblages in the Ancón-Chillón Region

Prehistoric period		*Ancón-Chillón*	
Late Horizon	A.D. 1534 A.D. 1476	(Late Horizon)	
Late Intermediate Period	1000 B.P.	(Late Intermediate)	
Middle Horizon	1400 B.P.	(Middle Horizon)	
Early Intermediate Period	2200 B.P.	Lima (8 phases) Miramar (4 phases)	
Early Horizon	2900 B.P.	8–10 unnamed phases	
Initial Period	3800- 3500 B.P.	Colinas Thick Brown Ware Thin Brown Ware	3350–2900 B.P. 3650–3350 B.P. 3750–3650 B.P.
Preceramic 6	4500 B.P.	Gaviota Conchas Playa Hermosa Pampa	3900–3750 B.P. 4100–3900 B.P. 4300–4100 B.P. 4500–4300 B.P.
Preceramic 5	6200 B.P.	Encanto Corbina	5600–4500 B.P. 6200–5600 B.P.
Preceramic 4	8000 B.P.	Canario Luz Arenal	7000–6200 B.P. 7500–7000 B.P. 8000–7500 B.P.
Preceramic 3	10,000 B.P.	(Hiatus in occupation?)	
Preceramic 2	11,500 B.P.	Chivateros II Chivateros I	10,500–10,000 B.P. 11,500–10,500 B.P.
Preceramic 1		Oquendo Red Zone	12,500–11,500 B.P. 14,000–12,500 B.P.

supplemented by descriptions of organic remains of sites in the region provided by Lanning (1967a, b; Patterson and Moseley 1968; Moseley 1968).

A summary of the major changes in settlement-patterns and organic refuse follows.

Table 2. Botanical remains identified from archaeological samples in the Ancón-Chillón Region

Taxa considered to be definitely or probably wild species indigenous to the region	
Inga feuillei	*Asclepias* sp. (Milkweed)
Sapindus saponaria	*Typha* sp. (Cattails)
Caesalpinia sp.	*Cyperaceae* spp. (Sedges)
Prosopis	*Equisetum* spp. (Horsetails)
Schinus molle	*Tillandsia latifolia*
Galactia striata	*Gramineae* sp. (Grasses)
Jusseia peruviana	*Hymenocallis amencaes*

Taxa of undefined origin	
Psidium guajava (Guavas)	*Cucurbita ecuadorensis* (Squash)
Lagenaria siceraria (Gourds)	

Domestic plants imported into the region	
Zea mays (Maize)	*Solanum* spp. (Potatoes)
Cucurbita ficifolia (Squash)	*Oxalis tuberosa* (Oca)
C. moschata (Squash)	*Polymnia* sp.
C. maxima (Squash)	*Bunchosia armeniaca*
Phaseolus lunatus (Lima beans)	*Campomanesia lineatifolia*
P. vulgaris (Common beans)	*Lucuma bifera* (Lucumas)
Canavalia sp. (Jack beans)	*Persea americana* (Avocados)
Arachis hypogaea (Peanuts)	*Capsicum baccatum* (Peppers)
Erythrina sp.	*Erythroxylon* sp. (Coca)
Ipomoea batatas (Sweet potatoes)	*Gossypium barbadense* (Cotton)
Manihot esculenta (Manioc)	
Canna sp. (Achira)	

THE ARCHAEOLOGICAL SEQUENCE TO 4500 B.P.

The sites of the first five periods (Preceramic Periods 1–5, 14,000 to 4500 B.P.) represent a period of nomadic or transhumant hunting and gathering prior to the introduction of domestic crops or animals. They are without exception thin superficial surface sites with no permanent structures or other indication that habitation was other than temporary, and their organic refuse, with one exception late in the sequence, consists entirely of remains of wild plants and animals. However, although a hunting and gathering economy is retained throughout this portion of the sequence, the content and distribution of the sites demonstrate economic trends leading to, and helping to account for, the origins of agriculture and settled life.

The sites of the earliest assemblages are all quarry-sites located on the top of a hilly massif within the valley near the mouth of the Chillón River. The actual camp-sites, presumably on the valley floor, are unknown since sites on the valley floor have regularly been covered or destroyed by

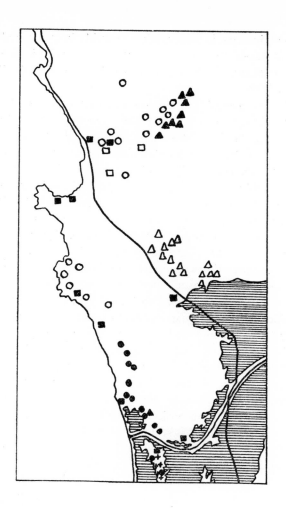

▽ Red Zone Complex   ○ Canaric Complex
+ Oquendo Complex   ⊡ Corbina Complex
● Chivateros Complex   ▲ Encanto Complex
△ Arenal and Luz Complexes   ▨ Preceramic Period 6

Figure 3.   Preceramic sites in the Ancón-Chillón region

4,000 years or more of subsequent cultivation. But since there is a
dearth of usable stone throughout the survey area and no evidence of
contemporary sites outside this limited area, clearly the quarries indicate
the approximate position of the camp-sites. The quarry sites are almost

totally lacking in organic preservation, possibly because food was rarely consumed at those locations. Nevertheless, certain inferences about exploitative patterns can be made on the basis of site distribution and content.

The Red Zone assemblage (Figure 3) dated 14,000 to 12,500 B.P. is represented only by a single site, a quarry at the mouth of the Chillón River (Patterson 1966b). The industry consists entirely of chipped stone. It is characterized by small tabular pieces of quartzite and flakes with steep edge retouch. The tools identified include spokeshaves, perforators, and scrapers and burins, but the assemblages lack projectile points. Little of a positive nature can be said about the economy of the site based on its artifacts. However, the site-location within the river valley and close to the coast indicates, despite the lack of refuse, that it was situated to permit simultaneous exploitation of the wild resources of these two zones. This interpretation is supported by Lanning's suggestion (1967b: 11) that the assemblage was adapted for woodworking.

The Oquendo complex (12,500 to 11,500 B.P.) is represented by seven small superficial sites, all quarries, again on the top of the hills at the mouth of the river. Again they lack refuse, but again they are situated so as to be able to exploit coast and valley simultaneously. The industry resembles that of the Red Zone, retaining burins, scrapers, perforators and spokeshaves as well as the technique of edge retouch, but it displays minor differences both in technique and in tool-kit which mark it as a separate assemblage. Again projectile points are lacking, suggesting that the hunting of large animals is still not a significant part of the economy. The industry is again characterized by Lanning (1967b: 12) as being a woodworking assemblage.

The sites of the Chivateros complex (11,500 to 10,000 B.P.) are again quarries without refuse except some shells of marine molluscs. The sites again focus at the mouth of the river, but now they expand out of the river's valley along the coast (Figure 3). Six sites occur on the hilly region at the foot of the Chillón River; nine sites occur just outside the valley on the coast and nine more occur slightly to the north of the valley on the south shore of Ventanilla Bay. Site distribution again indicates exploitation of a combination of coast and valley, but for the first time there is evidence that the area of exploitation has expanded beyond the valley's margins, presumably because a larger area was needed to feed a growing population or because the population had begun to exhaust the food available at the mouth of the river. The industry, as described by Lanning (1967b: 13), consists of bifaces, long thin spear points, denticulates, spokeshaves, flakes and scrapers. Again Lanning considered this a woodworking assemblage, but he noted the existence of spear points as the first evidence of specialized tools for hunting of big game.

Period 3 represents the one apparent hiatus in the occupation of the area. The area possibly was unoccupied at this time. However, if quarrying activities on the hilltops were abandoned as is true of subsequent periods, but no other shift in economy and site-distribution had occurred (i.e. if the economy of this period, as might be expected, was at an intermediate stage of development between that of the preceding and following periods), we would expect to find no evidence of sites of this period because of destruction of sites even if the valley was occupied. Such a pattern is, I think, the best explanation of the hiatus, but whether the apparent hiatus in the occupation sequence is real or is merely a result of destruction of sites does not affect the major logic of the analysis although it would affect the time sequences involved.

The sites of Periods 4 and 5 are almost all located outside the river's valley in areas of extinct *lomas* (Figure 3). Only an occasional site related to these complexes is found in the valley, but the presence of such occasional sites, the existence of culturally related sites in other river-valleys along the Central Coast, and the content of the sites in the *lomas* (which include the refuse of plants from the valley) indicate strongly that we are dealing with people who are exploiting and probably camping both in the valley and on the *lomas*. The abandonment of quarrying activities of the type described above and the history of subsequent cultivation on the floor of the valley account for the scarcity of preserved valley-sites. Since the vegetation of the *lomas* blooms in winter, the season of reduced flow of water in the river, possibly we may be dealing with seasonal transhumance between valley and *lomas*. On the other hand, since much of the produce of the *lomas* is available year-round, there is no reason to assume that this pattern represents strictly seasonal movement.

The earliest of the known *lomas* complexes are the Arenal and Luz complexes dated between 8000 and 7000 B.P. These sites are small superficial patches of refuse or huge coalescences of such patches in areas of extinct *lomas* vegetation. The twenty-three sites occur in a single cluster nine kilometers from the river but averaging only three kilometers from the modern valley margin, and they are about six kilometers from the coast. The refuse of the sites regularly consists of twenty to thirty centimeters of sand and ash with fragments of wood and wood charcoal in addition to culms of grass (*Gramineae* spp.), fragments of *Tillandsia* (*T. latifolia*), a desert dwelling plant usable only for fuel (and often charred), and fragments of gourd-rinds (*Lagenaria siceraria*). In addition the shells of marine molluscs occur along with the bones of fish, large birds, and land-mammals. These sites have a relatively high content of mammalian bone and a small content of shell. Although the sites, by their location, are primarily for exploitation of the *lomas*, the presence of gourd (a plant requiring much water and thus clearly unsuited to growth in the *lomas*) and of marine molluscs indicates that the river's valley and the coast were part of the exploitative pattern. The tool-kit demonstrates two new techniques, pressure flaking and pecking. Scrapers, core tools and cobble flakes (which Lanning (1967b: 19) considered to have been used as sickles) were found in addition to projectile points. Most important, rare grinding tools including milling stones and manos occur. The Arenal and Luz assemblages are related by typological similarities in the manufacture of projectile points to the Jaywa complex of the Ayacucho region of the Peruvian highlands (MacNeish 1970: 37), indicating some degree of cultural contact between the two regions even at this date, before agriculture is known in either region.

The twenty-two sites of the following Canario complex (7000–6200 B.P.) occur in two clusters, one in the hills north of the town of Ancón, the second just north of the Bay of Ventanilla, both clusters substantially farther from the river than those of the preceding complexes. Again the sites consist of shell and ash and again they appear to represent non-permanent seasonal or temporary camps of people utilizing resources of valley and coast as well as those of the *lomas*. The refuse of the sites on the *lomas* (Lanning 1967b: 19) differed from that of earlier complexes in having a higher content of seeds but less wood, more shell and fewer remains of vertebrates. Compared to the previous assemblages, the stone-industry characterizing the Canario sites displays an increase in the frequency of cobble flakes (sickles?) and grinding equipment (milling stones, manos, mortars and pestles) suggesting an increased reliance on the harvesting and grinding of seeds. However, there is no evidence of domestication (Lanning 1967b: 19). In this light the tool assemblage, culturally related to the Piki complex in Ayacucho in the Peruvian highlands where agriculture with squash is well attested (MacNeish 1970: 38; 1969: 38), is of extreme interest. Agriculture may be found in the Canario complex on the coast when river valley sites, as opposed to sites on the *lomas*, are found and excavated. I consider this highly unlikely, however, for two reasons. First, the *lomas* sites consistently contain produce from the valley so we would expect cultigens to be represented if they were being utilized in the valley. Second, a site of the Canario complex has been excavated by Patterson in the Lurín Valley immediately to the south of the survey area. I have had a chance to study the refuse from the site and it too is devoid of cultigens. All this strongly suggests that the absence of cultivated plants in the Canario complex is historically significant and not just a function of lack of preservation.

After the Canario complex, two further complexes associated with the *lomas* are identified: the poorly defined Corbina complex (6200 to 5600 B.P.) and the Encanto complex (5600 to 4500 B.P.). Corbina is identified at only three sites at the northern end of the Canario cluster. No collections of refuse have been made and little need be said. The fifteen Encanto sites occur in a single cluster at the northern end of the surveyed area over 20 km. from the river and appear to represent seasonal or temporary camps forming part of an exploitative pattern of people utilizing resources of coast and valley as well as those of the *lomas*. One site, a quarry, was actually preserved from this period in the river's valley. The industry consists primarily of milling stones, manos and small projectile points. Lanning (1967b), Patterson and Moseley (1968), and Moseley (1968) have all done test-excavations of Encanto sites. The refuse has produced shellfish (in great abundance), crayfish, fishbone, and mammalian bone (deer in very small quantities) in addition to *Tillandsia*, sedge (*Cyperaceae* spp.) gourd, fragments of bulbs (*Hymenocallis amencaes*?), fragments of pods of unidentified wild legumes, fragments of the river-valley fruit *Jusseia peruviana*, and a variety of the vegetative portions of unidentified wild plants. In addition, two items of particular importance have been found. Lanning found seeds of grass (*Gramineae* spp.) in enormous concentrations, clearly representing a pattern of harvest and (temporary?) storage, which along with the incidence of milling stones indicates the importance of seed-grinding in the economy. In addition, squash seeds were found in both Moseley's and Patterson's excavations. The seeds, twenty-six in all, are clearly domestic on the basis of the size criteria published by Cutler and Whitaker (1961: 478) and are tentatively identified as *Cucurbita ficifolia*.

In summary, the sites of these earliest assemblages all represent quarries or temporary camps of nomadic hunter-gatherers who utilized wild resources from the coast, the river's valley and, somewhat later, of the vegetation of the *lomas*. For most of the period the only possible domestic crop is the gourd whose status in this regard cannot be assessed. At the end of this period squash appeared, the size of the seeds indicating that it was imported fully domesticated. The squash was at first utilized as part of the old economy, occurring in *lomas*-camps of a type essentially similar to those of earlier periods.

Analysis of the sites of these hunting and gathering periods provides a number of clues about the circumstances surrounding the inception of agriculture in the region. The earliest quarry sites occur only at the mouth of the river suggesting (since there was no limit to potential quarry areas *per se*) that the pattern of exploitation of the group was limited to resources of the coast and valley and to the small area at the mouth of the river where these resources occur together. Subsequently the sites occur at the mouth of the river as well as extending along the coast outside the valley, suggesting an expanded radius of exploitation. The exploited area continued to expand in subsequent periods. Sites of the following periods occur primarily in the areas of *lomas*, but their content (gourd, squash, *Jusseia peruviana*, and sedge, as well as crayfish, bones of fish, and shells of molluscs) along with occasional preserved river-valley sites indicates that these sites on the *lomas* are a preserved remnant of an exploitative pattern utilizing coast, valley and *lomas* together. As such it is of great interest that the sites on the *lomas* get progressively further from the valley with time, again indicating an enlarging area of exploitation.

I suggest that the picture presented is that of a hunting and gathering population needing to travel progressively farther afield to obtain food, because its population was expanding and because resources closer to home were being exhausted. This interpretation is supported by three other types of evidence. First, the refuse of the sites on the *lomas* shows a progressive decline in the hunting of land-mammals and increased reliance on shellfish as a source of protein, suggesting increased pressure of population on land-resources (Harner 1970: 71) and suggesting also, perhaps, the degradation of the environment of the *lomas*. Second, there is a progressive decrease of wood in the sites on the *lomas* and an increase in remains of herbaceous plants, again suggesting a degrading of resources. Third, there is a progressive increase in the importance of grinding tools in the assemblages which, along with the large quantities of grass-seed in the Encanto sites, suggests progressive emergence of more and more intensive patterns of utilization of wild resources. The implication of the distribution and content of the sites is, therefore, that population pressure on resources was increasing. The population was being required to move farther to obtain food and was utilizing resources requiring more intensive preparation. The appearance of domestic squash in sites of the Encanto group appears to have been a response to the increased difficulty of a hunting and gathering economy and as such, the use of agriculture seems at first to have been intended as a minor dietary supplement in order to preserve the old way of life.

There are, then, two lines of evidence from this sequence contributing to the assumption that agriculture responds to need rather than to the availability of new technology. The first is the evidence outlined above which suggests that, prior to the beginnings of agriculture, hunting and gathering were becoming increasingly difficult and probably were resulting (in combination with climatic change?) in degradation of the wild resources of the area. The second is the date of arrival of agriculture itself. Agriculture is first attested in this region sometime after 5600 B.P., at least 700 years and possibly as much as 2,000 years after its appearance in the highland region of Ayacucho. This time-gap is significant only because there is evidence of repeated culture contact between the two regions well before this date and evidence that styles in the manufacture of projectile points were shared by diffusion between the regions much more rapidly. The beginnings of agriculture in the Ancón-Chillón region thus do not seem to correspond to known diffusion horizons as might be expected if agricultural technology were inherently desirable.

I believe that, clearly, imbalance between population and resources resulted in the beginning of agriculture, but the separation of the roles played by population growth *per se* from the decline of the vegetation on the *lomas* by reason of changing climate is not easy. The evidence for climatic change, as it affects the vegetation of the *lomas*, is largely speculative and cannot be considered here except to point out that degradation of resources by climate alone would not be expected to produce the steady pattern of movement of *lomas* vegetation and archaeological sites away from the river. It would instead result in remnant patches of vegetation in climatically favored locations with the result that the archaeological sites of the various periods would be mixed. The consistent outward movement of the exploitation of the sites on the *lomas* argues for the role of human populations in the degradation of the environment. However, we are still faced with the difficulty of assessing the actual growth of population. Analyzing such growth in the pre-agricultural period is difficult since, as indicated above, good parameters for estimating population are lacking. There is evidence that part of the occupation of each period is not preserved. Quarry sites give no indication of population and the superficial *lomas* sites are mostly large, poorly defined scatters, often of great extent, with no definition of individual camping areas. Determining how many sites are strictly contemporaneous is impossible. Lanning (1967a: 50) found a cluster of seventeen milling stones at one Encanto site which he takes to represent a population of fifty to seventy-five people. But there is no way of determining what fraction of the total population this represents. We can, however, get a crude estimate by working back from the population of the first agricultural settlement. I have estimated on the basis of the extent of preserved village space that there were at least 200 to 300 persons living in the survey zone in the first permanent villages just after the beginning of agriculture (Cohen 1971: 193).[1]

If we take these figures as the ceiling for the preagricultural population, then we can visualize the expansion of population in the survey zone from a minimum of perhaps twenty-five to fifty individuals (roughly standard size among hunter-gatherer groups) at about 12,000 B.P. to a maximum of 200 to 300 by 4500 B.P. This represents an increase of population of at least 400 percent and possibly as much as 1200 percent. Stated in terms of populational growth rates, however, this averages out to only about .01 percent per year or less, indicative of very slow average growth. (There is, however, no way to determine the extent to which population growth was balanced by out-migration, and a possible interpretation is that a growing population at once shunted off excess population by migration and gradually expanded its exploitation of wild resources, finally turning to agriculture when neither recourse remained possible.)

GROWTH OF POPULATION AND AGRICULTURAL DEVELOPMENT AFTER 4500 B.P.

In the period following the inception of agriculture, Preceramic Period 6, there is a marked change in economy and settlement patterns, resulting from the progessive exhaustion of the resources of the *lomas* and of land mammals as sources of food, plus the availability of the new agricultural produce. Permanent villages were then located on the coast and in the river's valley. Most of the known sites (Figure 4) in fact are found on the coast outside the valley and outside the areas of potential cultivation, but the rich agricultural refuse of these coastal sites leaves no doubt that they were part of a cooperative economic pattern involving agricultural sites in the valley which have been destroyed by subsequent cultivation. The areas of vegetation on the *lomas* were at the time almost entirely abandoned. Cotton (*Gossypium barbadense*) is found in refuse of sites of this period, and with the exception of the earliest of the coastal sites, the sites of this period are characterized by twined cotton textiles and cotton fish nets and lines along with other fishing equipment. Pottery is not yet encountered and chipped stone tools and grinding tools of the previous periods gradually disappear (Moseley 1968).

[1]   Patterson (1971b) has more conservatively estimated only a hundred persons for the same period of time, but his estimate fails to account for the population in the valley's bottom, for which no sites are preserved but which is attested by the quantity of agricultural produce in preserved coastal sites which are outside the agricultural areas.

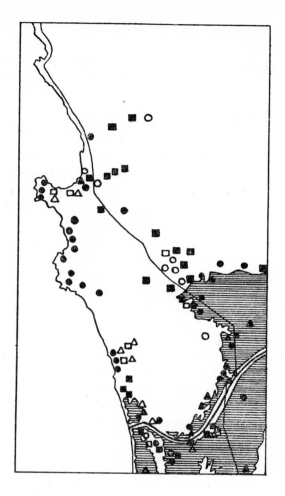

□ Initial Period   ▲ Middle Horizon
△ Early Horizon   ▣ Late Intermediate Period
● Early Intermediate Period   ○ Late Horizon

Figure 4. Ceramic sites in the Ancón-Chillón region

Two major trends are observable in the sites of this period, both presumably related to agriculture and sedentary living. First, there is evidence
suggesting a very high rate of growth of population. The existence of
permanently bounded habitation sites whose extent can be measured and
whose duration of occupation is known allows us to assess the total area
of sites occupied (i.e. the total area of village space) at various points in
time. By assuming that the density of population of villages is at least

roughly constant we can determine the relative size of population at various times, by determining the relative site-areas occupied. The method is crude, first because the population density of villages, of course, is not strictly constant and second, because only a portion of the sites of each period are preserved. But the method does provide at least a crude estimate of change in population. At the beginning of Preceramic Period 6 there was only a single small coastal village, and allowing for at least an equivalent population of the valley, of which the evidence has been destroyed, we can estimate that total occupied villages covered no more than perhaps two to four hectares. By the end of this period the total site-space occupied, including a preserved valley site, was at least on the order of fifty to sixty hectares, suggesting that population may have increased on the order of 2000 to 3000 percent. I have estimated (Cohen 1971: 193) a population of 200 to 300 persons for the survey region at the beginning of this period and of 3000 to 6000 at the end. Over a span of 750 years this represents an average growth-rate of between .4 and .7 percent per year, so obviously the rate of growth has responded markedly to the combination of sedentary living and agriculture. In addition, by the end of this period we encounter the first evidence of centralized political and economic organization for the area and possibly the first evidence of social stratification.

The first phase of this period is represented at a single coastal site, the Pampa site (4500–4300 B.P.), the earliest permanent village in the region. The lower levels of the site contain, in addition to quantities of shell and other marine refuse, an enormous quantity of remains of squash including seeds, rinds and peduncles of three separate species, two domesticates, *Cucurbita ficifolia* and *C. moschata* (Patterson and Moseley 1968: 117) and a wild form, *C. ecuadorensis* (Cutler and Whitaker 1969). I have identified a number of other minor plants occurring for the first time in the area in the refuse of this site including *pacae* (*Inga feuillei*), achira (*Canna* sp.), guavas (*Psidium guajava*), milkweed (*Asclepias* sp.) and a small-seeded legume (*Galactia striata*). In addition, Patterson and Moseley (1968: 116) reported jack beans (*Canavalia* sp.) from a portion of the refuse I have not had an opportunity to study. These are accompanied by gourd, a number of unidentified tubers and rhizomes, plus the usual assortment of *Tillandsia*, cattails, sedges, grasses and twigs. The fauna includes abundant remains of shellfish, shorebirds and sea-mammals, particularly sea lion. Bones of land-mammals are extremely scarce, and from this time on, until the introduction of domestic mammals sometime after 2200 B.P., land-mammals played only a very minimal part in the economy of the region.

In the subsequent Playa Hermosa and Conchas phases of Preceramic Period 6, the overall pattern does not change significantly. Again, we appear to have had small permanent coastal villages gradually increasing in size and number on the coast outside the river's valley, but these coastal sites are filled with vegetable produce indicating that additional sites in the valley existed but have been destroyed. The subsistence pattern remained largely unchanged except that squash declined as a major staple.

During the Playa Hermosa phase (4300–4100 B.P.) only one new cultigen, peppers (*Capsicum baccatum*), occurred. In the refuse of the Conchas phase (4100–3900 B.P.) lima beans (*Phaseolus lunatus*), lucumas (*Lucuma bifera*), and sapindus seeds (*Sapindus saponaria*) all occur for the first time. Bones of land-mammals are again very rare and protein was provided primarily by fish, shellfish, shorebirds and sea-mammals. The persistence of large numbers of unidentified tubers and rhizomes along with milkweed, cattails, sedge, grasses, and twigs indicate that a proportion of the diet was still obtained from wild vegetables.

In the Gaviota phase of Preceramic Period 6 (3900–3750 B.P.) in addition to the coastal villages, we actually encounter three sites preserved in the river's valley, the most important of which is Chuquitanta, a large site with stone ruins located at the foot of the Chillón River on the same hilly massif as the quarry sites of earlier periods. The site itself is located near a wide expanse of river, and Patterson and Moseley (1968: 125) suggested that the site represents floodplain farming. For this reason it is important that Patterson (1971a: 197) has recorded the existence of populations farther up in the valley, outside the survey zone, at this time, which because of their location far from a cultivable flood plain must have been using small-scale irrigation. The Chuquitanta site is a large town or small city, whose population I have estimated at 3,000 to 4,000 people (Cohen 1971: 179). Moreover, the symmetry of its stone construction involved a large well-organized labor force and suggests political centralization and possibly social stratification, and it is interesting that this large population and highly evolved society occurred in the apparent absence of either irrigation or maize, which are often considered the *sine qua non* of New World civilization. Engel (1967), who excavated the site, reported cotton, gourds, *achira*, lima beans, guavas, *lucumas*, *pacae* and *jicama* (*Pachyrrhizus tuberosus*), the latter being the only new cultigen mentioned. In addition, my own studies of the refuse from the Gaviota phase from coastal sites added peanuts (*Arachis hypogaea*), and possibly sweet potatoes (*Ipomoea batatas*), to the list of cultigens.

Beginning with the Initial Period (3750 to 2900 B.C.) and extending through the Early Intermediate Period (2200 to 1400 B.P.) we witness a gradual expansion of the valley's population accompanied by a progressive increase in the number of occupied sites. The growth of population during this span, however, was markedly less than that of Preceramic Period 6. Judging by the number and size of sites occupied, the peak population in the prehistoric valley was reached by about the third quarter of the Early Intermediate Period (1800 to 1600 B.P.).

The peak population of the area is estimated at 25,000 to 50,000, roughly ten times that of the end of Preceramic Period 6, representing an average annual rate of population-growth between 3750 B.P. and 1600 B.P. of only about .1 percent, a much slower growth rate than during Preceramic Period 6 (Cohen 1971: 196). This expansion of population was accompanied by a gradual change in location of sites outward from the banks of the river to the modern margins of the river valley; growth of a valley-wide system of irrigation and the gradual accumulation of new and significant crop plants are suggested.

In the Initial Period (defined by the arrival of pottery in the area) there is no direct evidence of irrigation in the survey region. Moseley (1972: 41) suggested that the abandonment of Chuquitanta implies a shift from floodplain farming to irrigation agriculture, but the few sites known in the valley are still near its bottom, suggesting that floodplain agriculture still predominated (Figure 4). The refuse from the early part of the Initial Period is very similar to that of the preceding periods. The only new cultigen in the early part of the period is coca (*Erythroxylon* sp.), identified from chewed quids complete with well-defined tooth rows. Late in the Initial Period, however, three significant new cultigens were added: potatoes (*Solanum tuberosum*), polymnia tubers (*Polymnia* sp.) and maize (*Zea mays*). The appearance of maize can be dated by careful pottery seriation to a very late phase of the Initial Period, about 3200 B.P., long after maize is known elsewhere in Peru (see below). The cobs are large; the broken fragments are fifty to sixty millimeters long and the diameters range from thirteen to eighteen millimeters which, on size alone, makes these cobs comparable to all subsequent prehistoric maize from the region. There is clearly no evidence of wild, or even of primitive maize in the region.

During the Early Horizon (2900–2200 B.P.) nine sites occur in the river's valley (in addition to those along the coast) and most still cluster close to the river, indicating again a predominance of floodplain agriculture (Figure 4). However, two sites occur on the margins of modern cultivation where the valley is narrow, and appear to suggest small-scale irrigation. The only additions to the organic refuse during this period are avocados (*Persea americana*), ciruelas (*Bunchosia armeniaca*), campo-manesia (*C. lineatifolia*), manioc (*Manihot esculenta*), and the common bean (*P. vulgaris*). The latter occurs first in levels dated to about 2900 B.P., again long after its first appearance in other regions of Peru. Middens of this period also mark the last time when large sea-mammals are encounter-ed in this region, suggesting that from this point on this source of protein was either no longer available or no longer utilized.

During the Early Intermediate Period (2200 to 1400 B.P.) we witness the sudden blossoming of archaeological sites along the modern margins of the river valley. The size and quantity of these sites occupied at any one time during this period appear to indicate that the maximum prehistoric population of the area had now been achieved, and from this time on, with the exception of a decline in the Middle Horizon, the population, as measured from the size and number of habitation-sites, appears to have remained approximately constant until the Spanish conquest. The loca-tion of these sites at the edge of the valley indicates that by this period the valley's irrigation system had been developed to its fullest prehistoric extent, which is equivalent, as far as can be determined, with the present-day extent of the valley's irrigation. During this period the whole of the coast appears to have been utilized very intensively, judging by the num-ber of sites found here, and a few sites even occur in areas of *lomas*-vegetation, indicating continued but small-scale use of the products of the *lomas*. No new cultigens appear in the middens of this period, although the fauna of the period show some significant changes. Bones of sea-mammals are notably absent from the refuse for the first time and, as indicated, these animals are never again encountered along this region of the coast. At the same time, bones, pelts and coprolites of llamas and guinea pigs provide the first evidence of domestic animals in the region (at a remarkably late date).

After the end of the Early Intermediate Period there were only minor economic changes. One species of squash (*Cucurbita maxima*) and a num-ber of inedible or minor legumes (*Caesalpinia* sp., *Erythrina* sp. and *Prosopis* sp.) are found for the first time in the Late Intermediate Period (A.D. 1000 to 1476) and *oca* (*Oxalis tuberosa*) is tentatively identified in my samples from the Late Horizon (A.D. 1476–1534). In addition, Towle (1961) lists a number of taxa identified by various workers from mummy-bundles at the Ancón Necropolis in the Late Intermediate or Late Hori-zon, of which only *quinoa* (*Chenopodium quinoa*) and *cherimoyas* (*Annona cherimolia*) are of particular significance.

The distribution of the main archaeological sites remains basically the same after the end of the Early Intermediate Period, although two new related patterns become evident. First, certain areas of the coast utilized for fishing in the Early Intermediate Period were abandoned. Since the sites of the Early Intermediate Period are now stranded well behind the modern coastline, apparently abandonment of the region was due to modification of the coastline which eliminated the region as a source of fish and shellfish. Possibly by way of compensation, in the Late Intermediate Period and Late Horizon, a number of superficial archaeological sites occur in the regions of *lomas*-vegetation, often including rectangular stone corrals which appear to suggest the use of this vegetation for grazing domestic flocks. In short, while no major shifts in the vegetable portion of the diet occurred after the Early Intermediate Period, apparently declining coastal resources were gradually replaced by domestic flocks as sources of protein.

Analysis of the Ancón-Chillón Sequence and Conclusions

The general patterns of changes in the subsistence-economy of the region may be summarized as follows:

In the sites of Preceramic Periods 1 to 4, the diet appears to have been composed entirely of wild foods. Wild plants, game, fish and shellfish are all represented in the refuse. During this period, however, four important trends are apparent. First, the sites show a progressive increase in the relative importance of shellfish over land-mammals as sources of protein; second, they demonstrate an increasingly intensive use of harvested wild grass seeds as a vegetable staple; third, they demonstrate a gradual replacement of woody by herbaceous plants; and fourth, the area exploited grows increasingly larger. As indicated above, all of the trends suggest increased pressure of population on wild resources, and I have suggested that population growth during this span of time was on the order of 400 to 1200 percent.

In the sites of the Encanto complex (Preceramic Period 5) these trends continued, so that shellfish dominated the protein sources in the almost total absence of evidence of land-based hunting, and remains of grass grain occur in great abundance. At this time the first domesticated plant food (squash) occurred but appears to have been only a minor portion of the diet. Agriculture appears to have occurred out of the need to supplement the old economy, and at first it appears to have had little influence on that economy.

In Preceramic Period 6, however, there was a shift in the location of known sites from the areas of vegetation on the *lomas* to the seacoast, prompted by the exhaustion of that vegetation and of land-animals to be hunted, plus the availability of agricultural produce. The economy shifted to a mixture of agriculture and coastal gathering. At the beginning of the period, squash was the major item in the diet, but this was gradually replaced by a series of other cultigens. The settlements of the period were permanent villages which increased in size and number throughout the period, suggesting a period of rapid growth of population. By the end of the period there is some evidence of the emergence of a complex society involving centralized political authority and possibly social stratification. What evidence there is, however, suggests that agriculture was still of a relatively simple floodplain type although irrigation is attested in nearby regions. Evidence for the crops which later become the staples of Peruvian agriculture, maize and common beans, has not yet been found, although lima beans, peanuts, jack beans, sweet potatoes, *achira*, *lucumas*, peppers, guavas and the squashes do occur.

From the Initial Period through the Early Intermediate Period there is evidence of a slower expansion of population, accompanied by a gradual extension of irrigation in the valley and a gradual accumulation of new cultivated plants. Maize, potatoes and *polymnia* occur late in the Initial Period; common beans, manioc and avocados occur in the Early Horizon. By the early Intermediate Period the maximum prehistoric population of the area occurred; irrigation reached its modern limits, and the main domestic animals (llamas and guinea pigs) were present for the first time, correlated apparently with the decline in sea-mammals in the area.

After the Early Intermediate Period, except for a decline and resurgence during the Middle Horizon and the Late Intermediate Period, population growth ceases. Since the leveling off of such growth is coincident with the expansion of irrigation to its modern limits, we may have had for the first time in the region a truly Malthusian situation in which population was limited by the capacity of the technology to expand agricultural production. During the next 800 years, until the Spanish conquest, the main agricultural patterns appear to have remained unchanged, although a new pattern of grazing domestic herds did appear in the later periods.

If we analyze the patterns of the archaeological sequence, a number of points emerge. First, the Ancón-Chillón region clearly received all of its major cultigens from other regions, since none of these are traceable to local origins. Moreover, there is no evidence of any independent experimentation with the domestication of lesser local crops, since the first plausible cultigen (squash) was clearly an import. The most striking pattern, however, is the absence of correlation between the arrivals of new cultivated plants (and animals) in this region and the dates at which they appeared in nearby, culturally related areas. Table 3 summarizes the arrival of new crops by period, and Table 4 lists the first arrivals of the major cultigens in the area in comparison with their known occurrences elsewhere in Peru. The time-gap in the two dates is often striking, especially since cultural contact of a much more direct nature can often be attested between the two regions in question. For example, domestic squash, which in the Ancón-Chillón region represented the beginning of agriculture, did not occur here until the Encanto Complex (5700–4500 B.P.), whereas it is definitely known in the Piki Complex in the Ayacucho region of the Peruvian highlands between 7500 and 6300 B.P. (MacNeish 1969: 38). Significantly, the Piki complex shows definite cultural affiliations in artifact forms with the earlier Canario complex of the Ancón-Chillón region (MacNeish 1970: 38). Similarly, maize did not appear in the Ancón-Chillón region until the Initial Period (about 3200 B.P.), whereas it is known in Ayacucho in the Chihua complex, 6300–4800 B.P. (MacNeish 1970: 38), a complex which again had earlier and more direct cultural ties with the Encanto phase of the Ancón-Chillón region (Mac-Neish 1969: 42). Moreover, maize is known from another region of the Peruvian Coast (Huarmey), which again shows cultural affiliations by about 3800 B.P. (Kelley and Bonavia 1963). Similar delays can be observed in the case of other cultigens including many of the important ones. Common beans (*P. vulgaris*) occurred in the region during the Early Horizon between 2900 and 2600 B.P. although they are known in Ayacucho in the Chihua or Cachi complexes between 6300 and 3700 B.P. (MacNeish 1969, 1970) and have been found in the Callejón de Huaylas, Ancash, Peru between 10,500 and 7500 B.P. (Kaplan et al. 1973). Lima beans (*Phaseolus lunatus*) occurred at Ancón as early as the Conchas complex, 4100 to 3900 B.P. but are also known in the Callejón de Huaylas by 10,500 to 7500 B.P. (Kaplan et al. 1973). Moreover, the technique of irrigation is not evident here at least until the Initial Period and probably not until the Early Horizon although it is in evidence elsewhere in adjoining areas as early as Preceramic Period 6.

Although the dates of first occurrence of cultigens in the region do not correspond well with those of other regions, they do show correlations with growth of population and ecological crises in the survey-zone. In the case of squash in particular, a case has been made to the effect that this cultigen and the whole concept of agriculture appeared in the region at a time of critically diminished wild resources. Agriculture, in other words, appears to have been adopted not when first exposure might have occurred, but rather at the point when the absence of wild resources necessitated cultivation. Domestic crops first appeared in a hunting and gathering context where they supplemented and supported the old economy in a time of increasing shortage. Only later did any revolutionary effects emerge in the form of stable settlement and accelerated growth of population. A similar, though more speculative case, can be made for maize and common beans and for irrigation. Perhaps these three late arrivals were related, and maize and beans were only utilized here in conjunction with irrigation. What is more important is that all three occurred in the area AFTER the period of rapid growth of population was completed, and during a period of more gradual growth. I suggest that the rapid expansion of population in Preceramic Period 6 represented the relatively easy expansion of pre-maize floodplain agriculture, which reached its limits by 3750 B.P. or shortly thereafter. Maize, beans and irrigation arrived when the potential of this relatively easy agriculture in the valley's bottom had been exhausted, and when continued growth of population began to necessitate the more tedious expansion of farmland by artificial irrigation and experimentation with more productive crops.

The evidence for domestic animals shows similar patterns. Llamas and guinea pigs appeared here, at least in quantity, only in the Early Intermediate Period (2200 to 1400 B.P.) although the former was found elsewhere on the Coast in the Initial Period (3750 B.C. to 2900 B.P.) (Lanning 1967a: 82) and the latter occurred on the coast by the end of Preceramic Period 6 (2500 to 3750 B.P.) (Lanning 1967a: 63), while both have been reported in Ayacucho in the Piki Complex between 7500 and 6300 B.P. (MacNeish 1969: 38). Here again they appeared in the survey zone when sources of wild protein appear to have been diminishing, as evidenced by the disappearance of sea-mammals from the middens, and later, by the decline of coastal sites as related to eustatic or tectonic modification of the coastline.

In general, the history of technology and of growth of population in the region is totally in keeping with the assumption that the technology of domestication developed in response to the pressure of population. Technological change is slow — late, compared to nearby regions — and closely associated with population pressure on resources. This evidence suggests that attempts to deal with technological change as an independent variable must be questioned. For example, attempts to trace the spread of cultigens as a pattern of simple diffusion does not work. We cannot hope to isolate simple patterns of symmetrical diffusion of crops or technology from hearths of domestication. Instead we are forced to consider the ecological requirements of various localities in understanding the appearance of economic changes. In particular, apparently economic conservatism is the rule, to be broken in a region only when pressure on existing resources necessitates change.

Table 3.   First occurrence of the main economic plants in the Ancón-Chillón region by period or complex

Late Horizon:	*Oxalis tuberosa* (?), (*Chenopodium quinoa*)
Late Intermediate Period:	*Cucurbita maxima, Caesalpinia* sp., *Erythrina* sp., *Prosopis* sp.
Middle Horizon:	No sample
Early Intermediate Period:	(domestic camelids and guinea pig)
Early Horizon:	
Late	No sample
Early	*Phaseolus vulgaris, Bunchosia armeniaca, Manihot esculenta, Campomanesia lineatifolia, Persea americana*
Initial Period:	
Late	*Zea mays, Solanum* spp. (?), *Polymnia* sp. (?)
Middle	None
Early	*Erythroxylon* sp.
Preceramic Period 6:	
Gaviota	*Arachis hypogaea, Lucuma bifera, Ipomoea batatas* (?), *Pachyrrhizus tuberosus*
Conchas	*Phaseolus lunatus, Lucuma bifera* (?), *Sapindus saponaria*
Playa Hermosa	*Capsicum baccatum*
Pampa	*Cucurbita moschata, Cucurbita ecuadorensis, Inga feuillei, Galactia striata, Canna* sp., *Psidium guajava, Asclepias* sp., *Gossypium barbadense, Canavalia* sp.
Preceramic Period 5:	
Encanto	*Cucurbita ficifolia*
Corbina	No Sample
Preceramic Period 4:	
Canario	None
Arenal-Luz	*Lagenaria siceraria*

Table 4.   First occurrence of the main economic plants in the Ancón-Chillón region by cultigen

Cultigen	Date of appearance Ancón-Chillón region	First appearance in Peru
Zea mays	Late Initial Period 3200 B.P.	Huarmey 3800 B.P.[a] Chihua Complex, Ayacucho[b] 6300–4800 B.P.
Cucurbita ficifolia	Encanto Complex 3600–4500 B.P.	(*Cucurbita* sp. Piki Complex, Ayacucho 7500–6300 B.P.)[b]
C. maxima	Late Intermediate Period A.D. 1000–1476	Ica Valley, 1400 B.P.[c]

Cultigen	Date of appearance Ancón-Chillón region	First appearance in Peru
C. moschata	Pampa Complex 4500–4300 B.P.	*Cucurbita* sp. Piki Complex, Ayacucho 7500–6300 B.P.)[b]
Phaseolus lunatus	Conchas Complex 4100–3900 B.P.	Chilca Valley 5800 B.P. (?)[d] Ancash 7500–10,500 B.P.[f]
P. vulgaris	Early Horizon 2900–2600 B.P.	Chihua or Cachi Complexes[b] Ayacucho, 6300–3700 B.P. Ancash 7500–10,500 B.P.[f]
Canavalia sp.	Pampa Complex 4500–4300 B.P.	Cachi Complex, Ayacucho[b] 4800–3700 B.P.
Arachis hypogaea	Gaviota Complex 3900–3750 B.P.	
Erythrina sp.	Late Intermediate Period A.D. 1000–1476	
Ipomoea batatas	Gaviota Complex (?) 3900–3750 B.P.	
Manihot esculenta	Early Horizon 2900–2600 B.P.	
Solanum tuberosum	Late Initial Period 3200 B.P.	
Polymnia sp.	Late Initial Period 3200 B.P.	
Bunchosia armeniaca	Early Horizon 2900–2600 B.P.	Huaca Prieta (Chicama)[e] (3900 B.P.)
Campomanesia lineatifolia	Early Horizon 2900–2600 B.P.	Huaca Prieta (Chicama)[e] (3900 B.P.)
Lucuma bifera	Conchas Complex 4100–3100 B.P.	Chihua Complex, Ayacucho[b] 6300–4800 B.P.
Persea americana	Early Horizon 2900–2600 B.P.	Early Horizon on coast
Capsicum baccatum	Playa Hermosa Complex 4300–4100 B.P.	
Erythroxylon sp.	Early Initial Period 3700–3600 B.P.	
Gossypium barbadense	Pampa Complex 4500–4300 B.P.	Chihua Complex, Ayacucho[b] 6300–4800 B.P.
Inga feuillei	Pampa Complex 4500–4300 B.P.	
Canna sp.	Pampa Complex 4500–4300 B.P.	
Psidium guajava	Pampa Complex 4500–4300 B.P.	
Lagenaria siceraria	Arenal and Luz Complexes 8000–7000 B.P.	Jaywa Complex, Ayacucho[b] 8600–7500 B.P.

[a] Kelley and Bonavia (1963)
[b] MacNeish (1969, 1970)
[c] Cutler and Whitaker (1961)
[d] Engel (1964)
[e] Towle (1961)
[f] Kaplan et al. (1973)

Conversely, population growth in the region clearly was not constant but responded markedly to technological changes. Population growth was slow in the pre-agricultural period, rapid immediately after the beginning of agriculture when the floodplain was being farmed, slower when the cultivated area was being expanded by irrigation, and finally limited in a Malthusian sense when irrigation reached its practical limits. This in turn suggests that we cannot consider population growth an independent variable and should not expect smooth, regular population curves.

Much of this analysis is, of course, tenuous. Interpreting sequences of cause and effect or the interaction of various factors of change from archaeological evidence requires indirect interpretations of such evidence. Moreover, the existing archaeological evidence in this region, as in other well-studied areas, is still no more than a (fairly minor) sample of the potential evidence. The interpretation, therefore, is subject to modification as further evidence accumulates. This discussion is not offered as a final statement on the nature of population and technological growth in the region, or as proof of a population-oriented hypothesis about culture change. The population-growth hypothesis is, I believe, worthy of further consideration on logical grounds alone. The result of the study of the archaeological sequence from the Peruvian coast is an attempt, first, to suggest that this hypothesis can and should be considered in the evaluation of sequences of cultural growth; second, to suggest that archaeological evidence can be used, albeit crudely, in the analysis of patterns of change and, therefore, should be applied to the consideration of large theoretical issues in anthropology; and third, to suggest avenues of approach to theory in anthropology necessitating refinement of archaeological techniques and necessitating new approaches to the interpretations of archaeological sequences.

REFERENCES

ADAMS, R. M.
  1966   *The evolution of urban society*. Chicago: Aldine.
ANDERSON, EDGAR
  1969   *Plants, man, and life*. Berkeley: University of California Press.
BIRDSELL, JOSEPH
  1957   On population structure in generalized hunting and collecting populations. *Evolution* 12:189–205.
  1968   "Some predictions for the Pleistocene based on equilibrium systems among recent hunter-gatherers," in *Man the hunter*. Edited by R. B. Lee and Irven DeVore, 229–240. Chicago: Aldine.

BOSERUP, ESTER
1965 *The conditions of agricultural growth.* Chicago: Aldine
BRAIDWOOD, R. J., C. A. REED
1957 The achievement and early consequences of food production: a consideration of the archaeological and natural-historical evidence. *Cold Spring Harbor Symposia in Quantitative Biology* 22:19–31.
CHILDE, V. G.
1951 *Man makes himself.* New York: New American Library.
COHEN, M. N.
1971 "Population growth, subsistence and settlement in the Ancón-Chillón region of the central coast of Peru." Unpublished doctoral dissertation, Columbia University, New York.
CRAIG, A., N. P. PSUTY
1968 *The Paracas papers: studies in marine and desert ecology 1, reconaissance report.* Occasional Publications of the Department of Geography, Florida Atlantic University 1.
CUTLER, H. C., T. W. WHITAKER
1961 History and distribution of the cultivated cucurbits in the Americas. *American Antiquity* 26:469–485.
1969 A new species of *Cucurbita* from Equador. *Annals of the Missouri Botanical Garden* 55:392–396.
DEEVEY, EDWARD
1960 The human population. *Scientific American* 203(3):194–204.
DEVEREUX, G.
1967 "A typological study of abortion in 350 primitive, ancient and pre-industrial societies," in *Abortion in America.* Edited by H. Rosen, 97–152. Boston: Beacon Press.
DUMOND, D. E.
1965 Population growth and cultural change. *Southwestern Journal of Anthropology* 21:302–325.
ENGEL, F.
1964 El preceramico sin algodon en la costa del Peru. *Actas y Memorias del XXXV Congreso Internacional de Americanistas.* Mexico. 3:141–152.
1967 Le complexe précéramique d'El Paraiso (Pérou). *Journal de la Société des Américanistes,* n.s., LV–1:43–95.
FLANNERY, K. V.
1968 "Archaeological systems theory and early Mesoamerica," in *Anthropological archaeology in the Americas.* Edited by Betty Meggers, 67–87. Washington: Anthropological Society of Washington.
GOODSPEED, T. H., H. E. STORK
1955 The University of California Botanical Garden Expedition to the Andes, 1935–1952. *University of California Publications in Botany* 28(8):97–142.
HARLAN, JACK
1971 Agricultural origins: centers and non-centers. *Science* 174:468–474.
HARNER, MICHAEL
1970 Population pressure and the social evolution of agriculturalists. *Southwestern Journal of Anthropology* 26:67–86.

ISAAC, ERICH
    1970   *Geography of domestication.* Englewood Cliffs: Prentice-Hall.
JOLLY, A. J.
    1972   *The evolution of primate behavior.* New York: Macmillan.
KAPLAN, LAWRENCE, T. F. LYNCH, K. A. R. KENNEDY
    1973   Early cultivated beans *(Phaseolus vulgaris)* from an intermontane
            Peruvian valley. *Science* 179:76–77.
KELLEY, DAVID, DUCCIO BONAVIA
    1963   New evidence for pre-ceramic maize on the coast of Peru. *Nawpa
            Pacha* 1:39–41.
LANNING, EDWARD
    1967a   *Peru before the Incas.* Englewood Cliffs: Prentice-Hall.
    1967b   "Preceramic archaeology of the Ancón-Chillón region, central coast
            of Peru." Report to NSF on research carried out under grant GS869,
            1965–1966.
LEE, RICHARD
    1968   "What hunters do for a living or how to make out on scarce re-
            sources," in *Man the Hunter.* Edited by Richard Lee and Irven De-
            Vore, 30–43. Chicago: Aldine.
    1969   "!Kung Bushman subsistence: an input-output analysis," in *Eco-
            logical studies in cultural anthropology.* Edited by A. P. Vayda, 47–79.
            New York: Natural History Press.
LEE, RICHARD, IRVEN DE VORE
    1968   "Problems in the study of hunters and gatherers," in *Man the hunter.*
            Edited by R. Lee and I. DeVore, 3–20. Chicago: Aldine.
MAC NEISH, RICHARD S.
    1958   Preliminary archaeological investigations in the Sierra de Tamaulipas,
            Mexico. *Transactions of the American Philosophical Society* 48(6):1–
            210.
    1967   "A summary of subsistence," in *The prehistory of the Tehuacan Valley.*
            Edited by D. S. Byers, 290–319. Austin: University of Texas Press.
    1969   *First annual report of the Ayacucho Archaeological-Botanical Project.*
            Andover, Massachusetts: Robert S. Peabody Foundation for Archaeo-
            logy.
    1970   *Second annual report of the Ayacucho Archaeological-Botanical Project.*
            Andover, Massachusetts: Robert S. Peabody Foundation for Archaeo-
            logy.
MORGAN. LEWIS HENRY
    1877   *Ancient society.* New York: Henry Holt.
MOSELEY, M. E.
    1968   *Changing subsistence patterns: late preceramic archaeology of the
            central Peruvian coast.* Unpublished doctoral dissertation, Harvard
            University.
    1972   Subsistence and demography: an example of interaction from pre-
            historic Peru. *Southwestern Journal of Anthropology* 28:25–49.
NEEL, J. V.
    1970   Lessons from a primitive people. *Science* 170:815-822.

PARSONS, M. H.
  1970   Preceramic subsistence on the Peruvian coast. *American Antiquity* 35:292–304
PATTERSON, THOMAS
  1966a Pattern and process in the Early Intermediate Period pottery of the central coast of Peru. *University of California Publication in Anthropology* 3:I–IX, 1–180.
  1966b Early cultural remains on the central coast of Peru. *Nawpa Pacha* 4:145–153.
  1971a "The emergence of food production in central Peru," in *Prehistoric agriculture*. Edited by S. Streuver, 181–208. Garden City: Natural History Press.
  1971b Population and economy in central Peru. *Archaeology* 24:316–321.
PATTERSON, THOMAS, M. E. MOSELEY
  1968   Late preceramic and early ceramic culture of the central coast of Peru. *Nawpa Pacha* 6:115–133.
POLGAR, STEVEN
  1972   Population history and population policies from an anthropological perspective. *Current Anthropology* 13:203–209.
SAUER, CARL
  1952   *Agricultural origins and dispersals*. New York: American Geographical Society.
SCHWANITZ, FRANZ
  1966   *The origin of cultivated plants*. Cambridge: Harvard University Press.
SHEFFER, CHARLES
  1971   Review of Boserup: *The conditions of agricultural growth. American Antiquity* 36:377–389.
SPOONER, BRIAN, *editor*
  1972   *Population growth: anthropological implications*. Cambridge: MIT Press.
STEWART, OMER C.
  1956   "Fire as the first great force employed by man," in *Man's role in changing the face of the earth*. Edited by William L. Thomas, 115–133. Chicago: University of Chicago Press.
TOWLE, MARGARET
  1961   *Ethnobotany of precolumbian Peru*. Chicago: Aldine.
WEBERBAUER, A.
  1932   "Phytogeography of the Peruvian Andes," in *Flora of Peru* (volume one). Edited by J. F. MacBride, 18–31. Chicago: Field Museum of Natural History.
WOODBURN, J. C.
  1968   "An introduction to Hadza ecology," in *Man the hunter*. Edited by R. B. Lee and I. DeVore, 49–55. Chicago: Aldine.

Alternative Pathways Toward Agriculture

DAVID R. HARRIS

During the last decade ethnographic studies of present-day hunter-gatherers[1] have demonstrated that, contrary to earlier assumptions, the size of their populations is not limited directly by the availability of food supplies. Far from eking out a precarious living searching unremittingly for food, such hunter-gatherers as the !Kung Bushmen (Lee 1969), the Hadza (Woodburn 1968), and the Mbuti (Turnbull 1968) in Africa, and various aboriginal groups in northern Australia (Gould 1969; McCarthy and McArthur 1960; McCarthy 1957), devote less time to the food quest — on an average two to five hours per person per day — and enjoy more leisure than do shifting cultivators and other agricultural groups practicing forms of paleotechnic cultivation. Such hunter-gatherers obtain abundant and varied supplies of food with relative ease and appear to live well within the capacity of the physical environment to sustain them.

In reassessing hunter-gatherer life Sahlins has gone so far as to characterize it as "the original affluent society" (1968: 85, 1972: 1–39), but this reassessment is based on studies of contemporary hunter-gatherers surviving in tropical desert, semidesert, and rain-forest environments. It

I wish to thank my colleagues Robert Frenkel and Richard Munton for their constructive comments on the first draft of this paper. I have benefited too from discussion of the paper at seminars given during 1973 at University College London, the University of Michigan, and Syracuse University, and during 1974 at the Australian National University and the University of New England, as well as from the exchange of views with other participants in the conference on "The Origins of Agriculture" at Woodstock, Illinois, for which the paper was originally prepared. I thank Margaret Thomas of the University College Cartographic Unit for drawing the figures in final form.

[1] This traditional term is used in preference to "non-" or "preagricultural," but its use should not obscure the fact that "hunter-gatherer" economies varied greatly.

remains uncertain whether hunter-gatherer groups in temperate and polar environments, most of whom now either have been eliminated or have abandoned their traditional ways of life, also lived at population levels below maximum carrying capacity. Although population increase may justifiably be regarded as the "normal" condition of mankind (Kunstadter 1972: 348), it is probable that they did so, as malnutrition or actual starvation leading to reductions in population appears to be exceptional among hunter-gatherers in all but arctic and subarctic environments (Dunn 1968: 223). There is also abundant evidence of population densities being maintained by such controls on natality and mortality as sexual abstinence, contraception, homosexuality, abortion, infanticide, and senilicide, below levels at which the food resources of the local environment are overexploited (Benedict 1972; Hayden 1972; Turnbull 1972).

In this paper the assumption therefore will be made that past and present hunter-gatherer populations have normally stabilized at levels below the maximum carrying capacity of the environment exploited at a given level of technology. If they did not do so we must presume that, as population progressively increased, groups — in situations where surplus population could not be hived off by emigration — would have striven to intensify methods of food procurement. Some groups did so, but the prehistoric and ethnographic record of hunter-gatherer populations fails to indicate any such overall trend towards intensification. Indeed, if it had occurred it seems probable that agriculture would have emerged much earlier as a widespread subsistence strategy than it apparently did.

The assumption that hunter-gatherers normally maintain equilibrium with their local environments by limiting population to levels below maximum carrying capacity does not imply a lack of correlation between population density and available food resources. Hunter-gatherer populations do vary in size and density in relation to habitat differences, although band size usually appears to fall within the range of twenty-five to fifty individuals, and population density rarely exceeds one person per square mile (Lee and DeVore 1968: 11). The salient point is that regardless of habitat differences populations stabilize at levels well below carrying capacity, and there is therefore little apparent incentive for hunter-gatherers to develop and adopt technological innovations that intensify food procurement. Seen in this perspective, the problem of why and how agriculture originated needs to be recast. We are not so much concerned to pose the familiar question of why agriculture did not emerge earlier in time and more widely in space, as to wonder why the hunter-gatherer life-style ever gave way to food production. Or, as Binford has expressed it: "The question to be asked is not why agriculture and food-storage techniques were not developed everywhere, but why they were developed at all" (1968: 327).

The aim of this paper is to explore that question deductively in three stages: first, by examining what "stress" factors might have induced hunter-gatherers to develop new subsistence strategies incorporating techniques of food production; second, by proposing a general model for the transition to food production; and third, by analyzing specialized systems of resource exploitation which might have served as alternative pathways toward agriculture. This framework is based on the premise that a transition from foraging to food production requires three necessary conditions to be met: (1) the operation of one or more stress factors of sufficient magnitude and duration to disturb the equilibrium of a hunter-gatherer subsistence system to such an extent that new techniques are developed; (2) a physical environment or ecological setting which is suited to cultivation and affords the possibility of plant and/or animal domestication; and (3) techniques of exploitation appropriate to the new subsistence strategy. Analysis of non- and preagricultural communities in terms of these three conditions should contribute significantly to a general explanation of the circumstances in which agriculture originated.

FACTORS CAPABLE OF INDUCING SUBSISTENCE STRESS AMONG HUNTER-GATHERERS

Before discussing possible stress factors that might have induced hunter-gatherers to develop techniques of food production, we should comment on alternative hypotheses that do not assume stress. The most influential of these are represented in the work of Braidwood and of Carl Sauer. Braidwood offers an explanation which implies that it was inherent in human nature for man to domesticate, cultivate, and rear useful plants and animals as soon as he had become thoroughly familiar with the biota of a particular environment (1960: 134). This hypothesis of "settling in" is attractive, but it does not specify at all precisely the processes involved and it is consequently not amenable to being tested. A similar stricture applies to all general constructs which, like the stage theories of human development that dominated late nineteenth-century cultural evolutionism (see, for example, Kramer 1967), regard the emergence of agriculture as an inevitable step in human progress, whether it is attributed to the progressive development of man's mental powers or to some other immanent human quality.

Sauer based his hypothesis of agricultural origins on a number of premises, one of which was that "Agriculture did not originate from a growing or chronic shortage of food" and that "needy and miserable societies are not inventive, for they lack the leisure for reflection, experimentation, and discussion" (1952: 20–21). This view regards the absence of subsistence stress as a necessary condition for the emergence of agriculture, but it does not provide any testable hypothesis that might explain why hunter-gatherers ever embarked on the "experimentation" that led to domestication and agriculture. The implication is that if leisure time is available experimentation will follow, but this is difficult to reconcile with the empirical data which indicate that most hunter-gatherers enjoy abundant "spare" time. The logical extension of this line of reasoning would be to expect domestication and cultivation to arise as a matter of course among a majority of hunter-gatherer groups, but available evidence does not bear out this proposition, nor did Sauer himself advocate it.

Changes in the Physical Environment Independent of Man

Among the stress factors that can be deduced as possible causes of a shift toward food production, physical environmental change has most often been proposed as the fundamental stimulus. The type of alteration most commonly envisaged is climatic change toward conditions less well suited to plant growth. Childe was the foremost proponent of the view that the development of food production in the Near East was the result of "desiccation" following the retreat of the ice sheets of the last glacial. He envisaged the enforced concentration of human, animal, and plant populations in river valleys and around oases as leading to domestication and the adoption of a food-producing economy (1941: 66–79), but he did not suggest what precise processes of adaptation might have been involved in the establishment of this new mode of subsistence. His vigorous advocacy of postglacial climatic change as the primary cause of the Neolithic Revolution did, however, have a lasting impact on the thinking of many scholars and until recently it was accepted as an explanation of the shift to food production (for example by Clark 1961: 80).

Childe's hypothesis was challenged by Braidwood and his coworkers on the grounds that there was no evidence either of major postglacial climatic changes in the ancient Near East or of earlier developments of food production following previous Pleistocene glaciations (Braidwood and Howe 1960: 142; Braidwood 1961: 103). More recent interpretations of Near Eastern prehistory have continued to reject "the facile explanation of ... environmental change" both because "for much of South-west Asia we have no evidence to suggest that late Pleistocene or post-Pleistocene environmental changes forced any of the significant subsistence shifts seen in the archaeological record" and because reliance on "the *deus ex machina* of climatic change" is theoretically unsatisfactory (Flannery 1969: 75–76).

The fundamental objection to explanations that regard climatic change as a primary stress factor is that they fail to demonstrate precisely how a secular change in climate affects hunter-gatherer subsistence patterns. They rest on the assumption that climatic change induces adjustments in the distribution and density of the plant and animal communities on which forager populations depend, but they usually fail to specify the nature of those adjustments with sufficient precision that a hypothesis may be tested against empirical evidence. They also suffer from the inadequacy and ambiguity of the evidence itself, as the uncertainties surrounding the interpretation of the Near Eastern palynological record clearly demonstrate (van Zeist 1969; Wright 1968, and this volume; Wright, Andrews, and van Zeist 1967).

Nevertheless climatic change continues to find favor as an explanatory hypothesis in certain regions currently under investigation, notably in Africa along the southern fringes of the Sahara, where it is suggested that progressive desiccation following the so-called Saharan "sub-pluvial" period was a major factor in the adoption of food-producing strategies by hunter-gatherer populations in the present Sahelian and Sudanic zones of Africa (Butzer 1972: 581–594; Clark 1976; Munson 1976). This approach contrasts with a current disinclination to seek climatic "explanations" in other regions where the emergence of food production is being investigated, such as Mesoamerica (Flannery 1968; MacNeish 1967), Peru (Lynch 1971; Moseley 1972; Patterson 1971), eastern North America (Munson, Parmalee, and Yarnell 1971), and southeastern Asia (Gorman 1971; Solheim 1972).

Natural changes in the physical environment independent of climatic variation have received little attention as possible factors favoring the emergence of food production. Prehistoric changes in plant and animal communities, insofar as they can be elucidated, are usually regarded as a result either of climatic change or of human activity. And, although nonclimatic changes in disease distribution, geomorphological processes, and other physical environmental factors can be envisaged, any hypothesis based upon them is likely to be difficult to test. The same applies to explanations of the origins of agriculture in terms of broad changes in postglacial environments involving climatic, eustatic, and biotic adjustments, despite the fact that a persuasive case can be made for the generally synchronous occurrence of the beginnings of agriculture and of the major environmental changes associated with deglaciation, as has been done, for example, by Chang (1970) and C. Sauer (1948).

However, our response to explanations couched in terms of physical environmental changes should not be a fashionable rejection of "environmental determinism" but a demand that the processes by which such changes might have functioned as stress factors inducing a shift towards food production be explicitly hypothesized in a form capable of being tested against archaeological and/or ethnographic data. It is also necessary whenever possible to hypothesize rates of environmental change, as cultural responses will vary accordingly. Thus it might be argued that secular changes tend not to disrupt equilibria, that short-term catastrophic changes frequently lead to migratory responses, and that changes of intermediate duration and magnitude are most likely to induce major shifts in subsistence strategy.

Changes in the Physical Environment Induced by Man

Environmental changes which result from man's activities present problems of interpretation similar to those associated with natural changes. But, insofar as natural changes are regarded as the "norm," cultural changes raise additional difficulties of definition. This is seen clearly in the controversies that surround such questions as the causes of the extinction of Pleistocene megafauna and the relative importance of natural fires and aboriginal burning in the ecology of forest and grassland. However, against the problem of distinguishing between naturally and culturally induced changes may be set the positive advantage that the student of environmental changes attributable to man is necessarily examining interaction between cultural and natural processes; his interest is focused directly on the subsistence-environment relationship.

Hunter-gatherers are usually thought of as having only a limited capacity to change their physical environment. This assumption stems from their characteristically low population densities and their simple technical equipment, but it tends to underestimate the potential for environmental alteration of one universal trait of hunter-gatherer populations: their use of fire. Much has been written about the varied uses to which primitive man put his ability to light and control fire (Eiseley 1954; C. Sauer 1952: 12–18; Stewart 1956), but changes in the physical environment that result from burning have seldom been considered as trigger or stress factors directly related to the emergence of agriculture. When this possibility has been envisaged it has usually been in terms of the creation of more open habitats around settlement sites as a prelude to the domestication of plants with weedy tendencies (Harris 1969: 9; Hawkes 1969: 18–20).

In a recent paper Lewis (1972) has framed a broader hypothesis on the role of fire in plant and animal domestication, with specific reference to southwestern Asia. His exploration of the relationships between fire-induced changes in the relative extent of Near Eastern woodland and steppe communities, the increase of hard-grained grasses and of ruminants, and the domestication of wheat, barley, sheep, and goats, is the most explicit statement to date of the possible role of fire as a stress factor. A deliberate search for evidence of similar fire adaptations and environmental changes in other areas can be expected to refine understanding of the processes leading to agriculture. For example, evidence of extensive fire along the Nile valley in Upper Egypt in the thirteenth millennium B.P. (Wendorf and Schild 1976: 8) may relate to early intensive utilization of grain collected from stands of wild grass selectively favored by accidental or deliberate burning.

No other categories of environmental change induced by man appear to have potential significance as stress factors equivalent to the effects of burning vegetation. Changes in the structure and nutrient status of soils and in the distribution of plants brought about by gathering, independently of the use of fire, were probably too small-scale and local in their effects to have triggered off major shifts in subsistence strategy. But the specialized hunting of large game animals with slow natural reproduction rates may have been practiced sufficiently widely and persistently in some regions as to have induced changes in patterns of food procurement.

Many authors have suggested both that hunters contributed significantly to the widespread extinction of large mammals toward the end of the Pleistocene in temperate and subtropical areas of both the Old and the New World (Martin and Wright 1967; Reed 1970: 284–285) and that the disappearance of big game was causally related to the increased utilization of small game, vegetal foods, and aquatic resources observed in the archaeological record. One can argue that this was an essential step toward development of the less specialized, more omnivorous patterns of food procurement that preceded the emergence of food production, but it is difficult to demonstrate any direct relationship between megafaunal extinction and agricultural origins because of the extended time intervals that apparently separate these phenomena, at least in Eurasia and North America (Braidwood and Willey 1962: 331–333; Flannery 1969: 78). The situation in northern Africa is less clear because in both the Sahara and the Maghreb the hunting of large mammals of the Ethiopian fauna persisted well into post-Pleistocene time in association with both intensified seed collection and the exploitation of aquatic fauna (Clark 1976: 6–9). We might, therefore, postulate that there the progressive elimination of the more vulnerable, slow-breeding big game animals did contribute directly to the establishment of pastoralism and, in more restricted areas, of cultivation.

Competition for Scarce Resources

If nonenvironmental explanations are sought for the emergence of food production a number of stress factors can be envisaged which are essentially socioeconomic in character and which involve in one way or another competition for scarce resources. They manifest themselves both in intragroup competition, which implies some degree of social stratification, and in intergroup competition, including trade and warfare.

Although it may be imagined that competition for food and other resources within and among hunter-gatherer groups occupying the same or contiguous habitats might lead to intensification of techniques of food procurement and ultimately to food production, this postulate runs counter to what is known of hunter-gatherer life-styles and is also exceedingly difficult to incorporate into any hypothesis that may be tested archaeologically. The fact that bands of hunter-gatherers appear to be essentially egalitarian or "familistic" in their social organization and to minimize differences of wealth among individuals (Lee and DeVore 1968: 12; Service 1966) suggests that intragroup competition is most unlikely to function as a stress factor in the earliest stages of a shift toward food production.

Only when some degree of ranking or stratification has evolved in larger-scale societies, based on differential access to resources, is intragroup competition likely to emerge as a factor capable of promoting further intensification of production. It may then act as a powerful influence if an elite is established capable of extracting surpluses from a dependent population, but this phenomenon is more likely to be related causally to the emergence of specialized systems of agriculture, and to the origins of urbanism (Wheatley 1971: 268–305) than to the beginnings of food production.

Intergroup competition also appears to be incompatible with hunter-gatherer society. If Lee and DeVore (1968: 12) are correct in ascribing to hunter-gatherers a general absence of exclusive rights, coupled with the techniques of resolving conflicts by fission, then intergroup competition cannot be regarded as a stress factor capable of initiating a shift to food production. Indeed, hypotheses that incorporate warfare, trade, or other forms of intergroup competition as explanatory variables are usually concerned with the emergence of civilizations or states rather than with shifts from foraging to food production. At the higher level of socio-economic integration a heterogeneous pattern of communities in a region may well be detectable in the archaeological and/or historical record and the idea of competition for scarce resources within a circumscribed region can be used as an explanatory postulate, as has been done recently by Carneiro (1970) for Peru and by Renfrew (1972) for the Aegean.

Population Pressure

In the last few years increasing attention has been paid to the possibility that changes in the ratios of population to resources may be capable of initiating major shifts in subsistence among both hunter-gatherers and primitive agriculturalists (Spooner 1972). The growth of interest in pre-historic demographic change and its consequences has recently been examined by Smith (1972: 5), who points out that, whereas changes in population were previously regarded as the consequence of technological developments and/or of access to more abundant resources, the tendency now is to treat demographic change, in some circumstances at least, as an independent explanatory variable.

This approach was first applied explicitly to the transition from foraging to food production by Binford (1968), whose model of hunter-gatherer equilibrium systems subject to disturbance by population increase was effectively applied to the Near East by Flannery (1969). In his original exposition Binford argued that changes in the demographic structure of a region which result in the impingement of one group on the territory of another would act as stress factors favoring intensification of subsistence procedures. He suggested specifically that increase of population in "donor systems" occupying optimal habitats would lead to emigration which in turn would raise the population density of neighboring "recipient systems" in more marginal habitats sufficiently close to maximum carrying capacity to favor the development of more intensive subsistence strategies such as food production. It is, of course, possible to envisage population pressure leading to intensification within as well as between group territories in areas where emigration cannot or does not occur, but regardless of whether internal or external pressure is postulated this formulation still begs the question of how the process of population increase gets started in the donor system in the first place.

In the articles mentioned neither Binford nor Flannery address themselves directly to this question, but if the assumption made earlier is correct — that hunter-gatherers normally limit their populations below maximum carrying capacity — then it is necessary to postulate some process whereby the cultural regulation of births and deaths is relaxed sufficiently to allow population pressure to build up. The most obvious suggestion is that control of population is not always effective and that certain hunter-gatherer groups who failed to adjust their populations to the carrying capacity of their habitat sought means of intensifying food procurement. This is quite possible, but it is too general an explanation of growth of population to be empirically useful. A more specific hypothesis is needed, and one can be developed if population pressure is related to the last stress factor to be considered here, namely reduction in mobility.

Reduction in Mobility

The significance of this variable was discussed briefly by Binford in his original paper (1968: 332) and he has since examined, in an as yet unpublished monograph, the demographic consequences of a recent change from mobility to sedentism among the Nunamiut Eskimo of Alaska. From this work, and from Lee's research among Bushmen groups undergoing sedentarization (Lee 1972), a causal relationship between reductions in mobility and increases in population clearly emerges.

The population of the Eskimo group studied by Binford doubled in the decade from 1950 to 1960, during which the people became sedentary. This increase resulted partly from a decrease in the incidence of miscarriages, but chiefly from the closer spacing of births which was itself related both to reduced female mobility and to less prolonged male absence on hunting trips. Binford makes a useful distinction between residential and logistic mobility and demonstrates that a shift in subsistence from a narrow to a broader pattern of resource exploitation, as occurred among the Nunamiut after 1898 following a major reduction in the numbers of caribou, tends to result in increased residential but decreased logistic mobility. In the case of the Nunamiut the shift was away from dependence on long-distance hunting of caribou to the more local exploitation of a wider variety of game and fish, which demanded more frequent residential moves as well as greater expenditure of time on the food quest by the group as a whole. As a result of decreased logistic mobility among the former caribou hunters, nuclear families remained together for longer periods and so the birthrate went up, thus providing for the greater labor needs of the new, broader-spectrum pattern of subsistence (Binford 1972: personal communication).

The conclusions to be drawn from the studies of Binford and Lee have immediate relevance to the transition to food production as they provide a clue to the problem of how population pressure may initially be generated. If changes in the availability of a staple resource of wild food, such as caribou, are capable of triggering compensating adjustments in mobility, which in turn lead to an increase in population, then a spiral of population increase and intensified procurement of wild food may be inaugurated. This positive feedback or deviation-amplifying process will not necessarily result in a shift to food production, but we may postulate that the trend that it incorporates toward increasingly intensive use of particular resources may, if the necessary environmental and technological conditions are fulfilled, lead ultimately to agriculture. Systems C and D in Figure 1 represent two such self-amplifying systems in which the stress or trigger factors which initially disrupt the "normal" state of equilibrium of a hunter-gatherer group are assumed to be either immigration or naturally and/or culturally induced changes of intermediate duration and magnitude in the physical environment.

A STRESS MODEL FOR THE TRANSITION TO FOOD PRODUCTION

Figure 1 summarizes in diagrammatic form four possible types of subsistence system differentiated in terms of their response to varying rates of change in the physical environment and to changes in mobility. In System A demographic equilibrium is maintained by cultural controls on population, in relation to an ecologically stable physical environment or resource base subject only to slow, secular change. Migration into or out of the subsistence territory may occur, but it is assumed not to disrupt the equilibrium. This is postulated as the "normal" pattern of non-food-producing subsistence, which manifests itself in a variety of hunter-gatherer systems, both generalized and specialized in their patterns of procurement of wild foods.

In System B demographic equilibrium is reestablished following perturbations in the physical environment of intermediate duration and

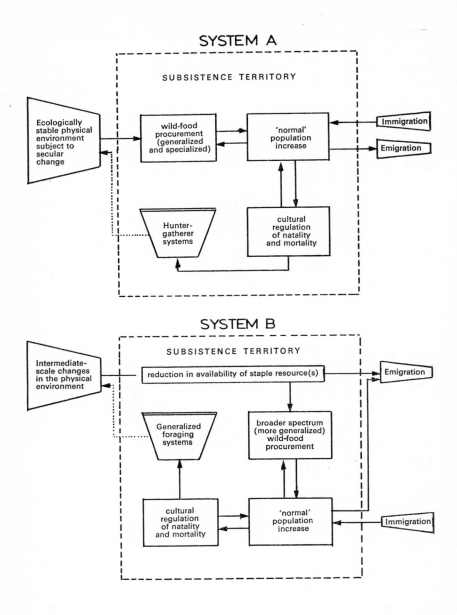

Figure 1.   A stress model for the transition to food production, showing four types of subsistence system

SYSTEM C

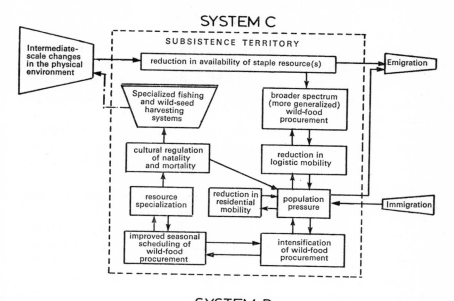

SYSTEM D

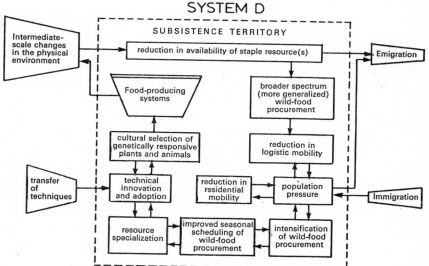

magnitude, which reduce the availability of one or more staple resources. The response of a hunter-gatherer group to this stress may be emigration out of the subsistence territory or, alternatively, a shift toward a more generalized, somewhat broader-spectrum pattern of procurement of wild foods. Such a shift, it is assumed, does not entail significant reductions in mobility and consequent "abnormal" increases in population. As in System A, emigration or immigration may occur, but it is assumed that cultural regulation of natality and mortality reestablishes demographic equilibrium at the level of generalized foraging. In Systems A and B the feedback effects of procurement of wild foods on the physical environment are assumed to be relatively weak.

Systems C and D resemble System B in that they are subject to intermediate-scale changes in the physical environment which reduce the availability of staple resources. But, more significantly, they differ from both A and B in the assumption that a shift to a broader-spectrum pattern of procurement of wild foods leads to reductions in logistic and/or residential mobility. These in turn trigger "abnormal" increases in population which cultural controls fail to regulate. A situation of population pressure on resources is thus created, which results in an intensification of labor input into the food quest and leads, via improved seasonal scheduling of procurement of wild foods, to increasingly specialized exploitation of particular resources.

At this stage in the processual model Systems C and D diverge. System C postulates the reestablishment of demographic equilibrium at the level of specialized food procurement such as intensive fishing and harvesting of wild seeds, whereas in System D resource specialization leads on to food production, via internally generated or externally introduced changes in techniques of exploitation and the cultural selection of genetically responsive populations of plants and animals. Migration into and out of the subsistence territory may occur in Systems C and D, and immigration can be postulated as the initial stress factor inducing population pressure and leading to resource specialization, rather than change in the physical environment. If this alternative is assumed, then the first four stages in Systems C and D can be omitted, but this does not alter the end results. Finally, a progressive increase in the effects of feedback on the physical environment is envisaged in the model, with systems of Type C having greater effects than those of Types A and B, and food-producing systems of Type D having the greatest capacity to modify the habitats they occupy.

In Figure 1 processes and resultant states have not been diagrammatically separated. This blending of cause and effect is logically unsatisfactory, but the diagram is presented in this form in the belief that this disadvantage is outweighed by the conceptual and visual advantages of simplification. To prevent misunderstanding of the model, I must also stress that the variables shown are deliberately reduced to the minimum necessary to make the systems work. Many other factors can be conceived as theoretically relevant to the emergence of food production but I have thought it more useful to present a working model, which is at least partially capable of being tested, than a more comprehensive and theoretically satisfactory one. Thus the all-important variable of social organization does not appear in the diagrams, although transformations in social organization were undoubtedly of central significance in the transition from foraging to food production. Likewise, many feedback relationships of possible relevance are not indicated in Figure 1.

In singling out the factors of environmental, demographic, and technological change as key variables I have tried to develop a testable working model which is only a first approximation to an "explanation" of how agriculture may have originated. Despite the importance it accords to demographic change, it is not a single-factor model of the type that Bronson (this volume) rightly deplores, but an attempt to specify some of the processes, responses, and feedback relationships that are amenable to archaeological investigation and likely to have conditioned shifts in subsistence from hunting and gathering to food production.

Thus, if the processes and relationships outlined in the four systems of Figure 1 are to have more than hypothetical value they must be tested against paleoenvironmental, archaeological, and ethnographic data. The categories of environmental and demographic change postulated are in part at least open to investigation — as, for example, by inferring changes in population and mobility from the size, spacing, and duration of occupation of settlement sites — and the model needs to be tested in a wide variety of ecological and cultural settings. No general validation of it is attempted here, but some of its salient features are briefly exemplified in the context of late and post-Pleistocene Eurasia and North America, before the processes leading to the emergence of five systems of specialized resource exploitation are examined in more detail in the third and last part of the paper.

If the model is applied to late and post-Pleistocene Eurasia and North America a change in the physical environment which might have initiated a self-amplifying process of subsistence change is reduction in the larger mammals, which were a staple resource of late Pleistocene hunters. But, as has already been pointed out, apparently many millennia separated the phenomenon of late Pleistocene megafaunal extinction from the emergence of the broader-spectrum patterns of subsistence that characterized the early post-Pleistocene or "Mesolithic" period. Closer examination of evidence for changes in hunting patterns through the late Pleistocene and into the post-Pleistocene may, however, indicate that disappearance of the megafauna was followed first by greater dependence on ungulates such as caribou, reindeer, and red deer, which migrate seasonally over considerable distances, and subsequently by a shift toward broader patterns of exploitation incorporating smaller terrestrial animals, fish and other aquatic fauna, and wild vegetal foods. If such trends can be demonstrated from the archaeological record then we have a situation of positive feedback in which, as dependence on the strongly migratory ungulates decreases, logistic mobility is reduced and population pressure results.

Such trends are discernible in the archaeological record of Europe north of the Alps, where the late Pleistocene hunting of ungulates, especially reindeer, gave way in the early post-Pleistocene — as sea level rose and forest vegetation became reestablished — to broader-spectrum patterns of exploitation of smaller terrestrial animals, birds, fish, sea mammals, invertebrates, and plant foods such as hazelnuts (Waterbolk 1968). Broadly comparable trends are observable in eastern North America (Caldwell 1962: 288–296) and in the Near East (Flannery 1969: 77–79).

The model next postulates an intensification of labor input into the procurement of wild foods in response to population pressure which leads to specialization in the use of particular resources within the broad-spectrum pattern. This may or may not involve reductions in residential mobility, i.e. increased sedentism, but if it does, then a positive feedback loop is activated which results in further population growth and thus reinforces trends toward intensification and specialization.

Evidence suggestive of this processual sequence is abundant in the archaeological record of Eurasia and North America and may be illustrated with four examples: first, the specialized exploitation of fish and mollusks, which characterizes coastal and riparian cultures in "Mesolithic" Europe and which is associated with long-term occupation of settlement sites (Waterbolk 1968: 1096); second, the use of nuts as a staple resource in the post-Pleistocene forests of "Archaic" eastern North America, which situation is also associated with a relatively high degree of sedentism (Munson, et al. 1971; Struever 1968: 303–311; Winters 1969: 117); third, the harvesting of the seeds of wild grasses, such as wheat and barley, in the "early Neolithic" Near East (Harlan and Zohary 1966; Harlan 1967; van Loon 1966; Zohary 1969) and the harvesting of setaria and maize-teosinte in "Archaic" southern Mexico (Callen 1967: 287–288; de Wet and Harlan 1972; Wilkes 1972), which in the latter area was associated with considerable seasonal mobility (MacNeish 1972: 71–73); and fourth, the exploitation of wild or partly domesticated sheep and goats in "early Neolithic" Iraq (Perkins 1964; Reed 1969: 371–372) and in "Neolithic" northern Italy (Jarman 1971: 261–263), which may have involved a transhumant pattern of herding.

Although the postulated trend toward intensification and specialization in response to reductions in mobility and concomitant population pressure receives some confirmation from the archaeological record, the examples cited do not in themselves indicate what selective processes operated to bring this about. Flannery's (1968) examination of the interplay of seasonality and scheduling in early Mexican systems of food procurement does, however, provide an illuminating interpretation of how specialization and intensification of resources may have developed.

By suggesting that in a broad-spectrum situation of multiple, seasonally scheduled systems of food procurement, a system, such as that of procurement of wild grasses, that was capable of responding to exploitation with increased yield would tend to expand at the expense of other systems, Flannery provided a testable hypothesis of general applicability. He argued that it was the genetic responsiveness of certain gathered food plants, such as maize and beans, that provided the initial stimulus for change in equilibrium between procurement systems, but he did not demonstrate why such change should be incorporated into and reinforced by the cultural system as a whole. In discussing the establishment of the cultivation of maize as eventually "the most profitable single subsistence activity in Mesoamerica" he did suggest that increased yield led to higher population and hence to more intensive cultivation (Flannery 1968: 80), but he did not set the initial expansion of the system of procurement of wild grasses and its cultural acceptance in a general context of population pressure. If one does so, then the explanatory power of Flannery's model is increased and it can be integrated usefully into the general stress model proposed here (Systems C and D in Figure 1).

With increasing dependence on the higher-yielding systems of food procurement within a broad-spectrum pattern of food collecting, the stage appears to be set for the emergence of agriculture. But, as has already been indicated for System C, the expectation theoretically is that hunter-gatherers may reestablish demographic equilibrium at the level of specialized utilization of resources. Unless both technological and physical environmental conditions are appropriate to food production it will not emerge as a dominant subsistence strategy. Figures 2 through 6

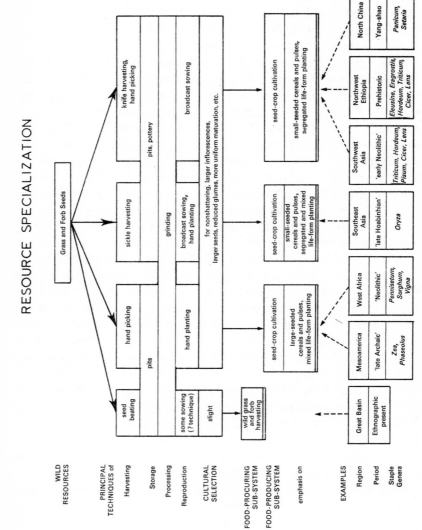

Figure 2.   Grass- and forb-seed-harvesting subsystems

elaborate the processual sequence from resource specialization onwards as postulated in systems C and D of Figure 1, in terms of five specialized systems of food procurement, three of which represent pathways to food production. All five systems are exemplified by reference to ethnographic as well as archaeological data in the belief that the insights which ethnographic comparisons afford outweigh the hazards of analogy.

SYSTEMS OF SPECIALIZED RESOURCE EXPLOITATION

Harvesting of Grass and Forb Seeds

In the first specialized system to be considered (Figure 2) food procurement focuses on the harvesting of seeds of wild grasses and of other herbaceous plants (forbs). This system appears to have functioned as a pathway to agriculture in some areas where it was practiced but not in others. This difference is in part at least explicable in terms of technological variables.

The Indians of the Great Basin of western North America are among the best-known ethnographic examples of specialized harvesters of grass seeds. Although they did sow as well as harvest wild grasses they failed to domesticate any of them — in the sense of establishing a phenotypically differentiated reproducing population — and they did not develop agriculture. Wilke, et al. (1972) have suggested that this failure is attributable to the harvesting methods employed. Because grasses were harvested by beating the ripened seeds into baskets there was no cultural selection in favor of plants with poorly shattering inflorescences, as occurs when harvesting is carried out by handpicking or with a sickle. Consequently, sowing and harvesting could continue indefinitely without producing "domesticated" forms with nonshattering inflorescences and, equally significantly, without improving yield per unit of area or labor by increasing the proportion of plants that retain their inflorescences intact until harvest. Therefore this procurement subsystem, which did not respond to exploitation with increased productivity, failed to expand at the expense of other procurement subsystems and a transition to food production never occurred.

If among the Indians of the Great Basin and other groups, the technique of harvesting acted as a deterrent to domestication of the wild grasses of which the people made intensive use, other harvesting methods may have functioned as stimuli to cereal domestication. As Wilke, et al. (1972) pointed out, harvesting by sickle or by hand combined with reseeding favors the selection of plants with poor self-dispersal of seed, and increases yields. Harlan, et al. (1973:11) have suggested that "Mutants toward nonshattering probably occur in all large populations of wild grasses," and if so, then the continued exploitation of populations of wild grasses by a combination of harvesting by hand or by sickle, followed by reseeding, will automatically result in "domestication," at least insofar as establishment of the trait of nonshattering is regarded as a criterion of domestication. Other changes advantageous to the cultivator, such as the suppression of lateral seed-bearing branches, increases in the size of inflorescences and of seeds, and more uniform maturation (Harlan, et al. 1973:12–15) also would follow from sustained harvesting and reseeding, so that the combined effect is to enhance yields and favor the rise to dominance of cereal cultivation over other subsystems of food procurement.

The cultivation of cereals and other plants with hard seeds which have relatively low moisture content and long viability probably also was favored by the suitability of the seeds for storage. The development of storage facilities such as pottery vessels, underground pits and silos, and drying racks, stacks, and barns, amplifies the role of seed cultivation within the overall subsistence system and at the same time accentuates tendencies towards sedentism. Similarly, the use of grindstones for processing seed contributes another positive feedback effect to an emergent system of seed agriculture.

If the techniques of harvesting, storage, processing, and sowing of grains were compared systematically for a large sample of hunter-gatherers and agriculturalists exploiting annual seed plants probably many of the observed differences in subsistence procedures could be explained in terms of these technological variables. For example, such an analysis might help to explain the differential importance of seed harvesting and reseeding among nonagricultural and early agricultural groups specializing in the procurement of wild grasses and forbs. This type of study might throw interesting light on the varying importance among non- and early agricultural populations of some of the more obscure exploited genera, such as *Amaranthus* (J. Sauer 1950, 1967, 1969), *Brachiaria* (Munson 1976: 9–13; Portères 1951), *Cenchrus* (Munson 1976: 8–11), *Chenopodium* (Gade 1970; Godwin 1956: 168–169; Pennington 1969: 89; Simmonds 1965), *Setaria* (Callen 1967; Ho 1969: 15–18), and *Zizania* (Dore 1969), as well as on the failure of some grass harvesters, such as many African and Australian aboriginal groups, to develop agriculture.

That such technological variables can be investigated in an archaeological context is clear from recent work in southern Egypt, which has yielded evidence of intensive utilization of seeds at various sites dated to between 8000 and 14,500 B.P. (Clark 1971; Hobler and Hester 1969; Wendorf and Schild 1976), The appearance of numerous grindstones at sites along the Nile upstream of Luxor from about 14,500 B.P. indicates that "the exploitation of ground grain as a source of food became an important economic activity" (Wendorf and Schild 1976). This contrasts with the extreme rarity of grindstones at an equivalent time in the archaeological record of Europe and the Near East and shows that at least one technological prerequisite for intensive seed exploitation was available in "late Paleolithic" Egypt (see also Kraybill, this volume; Reed, this volume 543–568).

Still more interesting is the question of what harvesting techniques were used at this time. At some of the sites, such as those at Tushka and Isna in the Nile valley, lustrous-edged microlithic flakes were recovered in association with grindstones. Some of the flakes had traces of adhesive on them and this fact, together with their form, sheen, and pattern of wear, suggests that they were probably mounted in a shaft to make a composite cutting tool of sickle type. Whether such tools were used principally to harvest wild grasses or to cut other materials cannot be determined yet, but the recovery of gramineous pollen grains, cell structures, and spores from associated deposits strengthens the presumption that the harvesting of wild grasses had become an important subsistence activity. Some of the pollen grains have been tentatively identified as from barley, suggesting that the late Pleistocene range of this grass may have extended from the Near East into northeastern Africa (Wendorf and Schild 1976, but there is no indication that any of the grasses exploited were domesticated forms.

Not all the sites in the northern Nile valley yielded lustrous-edged flakes as well as grindstones, and some yielded neither. At Gebel Silsila near Kom Ombo numerous grindstones were recovered but no "sickles," and at the Affian sites near Isna neither type of artifact was found. If these variations are compared with settlement size it becomes apparent that the Isnian sites are the smallest and most compact, that the sites at Gebel Silsila are larger, and that the Isnian sites other than the Affian ones are several times larger still (Wendorf and Schild 1976). We are tempted, therefore, to suggest that here we have evidence of a late-Pleistocene self-amplifying system involving reductions in mobility, population pressure, and intensification of one subsistence strategy at the expense of others, which accords closely with the model proposed in Systems C and D of Figure 1.

As there is also evidence at some sites that sickles may have been used to harvest grass seeds, conceivably seed cultivation of cereals had been initiated or possibly at least the "domestication" of local grasses had begun to occur in "late Paleolithic" times. Of extreme interest is the possibility that further work on materials from these sites will produce positive evidence for cultivation and/or domestication. If so, we need not be surprised that the process occurred so early, but it would pose the intriguing question as to what factors checked the rise to dominance of seed agriculture in the particular subsistence system. Perhaps the presence or absence of pottery vessels or other facilities for the storage of grain might prove to be a crucial variable in this context.

Differences in techniques of harvesting and reseeding wild grasses and forbs may also help to explain contrasts between the patterns of domestication and cultivation of seed crops that developed in disparate parts of the world. Perhaps the most striking contrast is between southwestern Asia, where cultural selection evidently favored grasses, legumes, and other annuals (such as species of *Triticum, Hordeum, Pisum, Lens, Cicer,* and *Linum*), which bore many small seeds or fruits per plant, and Mesoamerica, where selection of larger-seeded and larger-fruited forms (especially of *Zea, Phaseolus,* and *Cucurbita*) occurred. Traditional seed agriculture in these two regions also contrasts strongly in terms of patterns of crop planting. Whereas in southwestern Asia cereals tend to be segregated, either in mixed or in relatively pure stands, from crops of different life form, in Mesoamerica seed crops of varied life form, such as the familiar triad of maize, beans, and squash, are traditionally planted together, often in the same hole or mound.

An explanation of these contrasts may lie in differences in the techniques of harvesting and sowing. Harvesting by sickles and sowing by shallow broadcast are traditional to southwestern Asia, and both are relatively indiscriminant methods which do not encourage the sower or reaper to focus his attention on variations in the size, form, and color of seeds. Selection for such variations is therefore less likely to have occurred there than in Mesoamerica, where the handpicking and hand planting of seed crops is traditional. If most seeds are individually handled at the time of harvest, and/or when planted, selection for variant forms is likely to be more intensive and discriminating. Moreover, in Mesoamerica with its tradition of "holing and hilling," seeds tend to be planted more deeply than in southwestern Asia so that selection in favor of larger-seeded, more competitive variants would have been likely to occur automatically.

The joint planting of crops that complement each other ecologically and nutritionally, as do maize, beans, and squash, and so maximize the effective use of sunlight, air, moisture, and nutrients above and below ground, is also more probable in a tradition of attention to individual seeds and plants in which broadcast sowing and harvesting by sickle are not practiced. In particular the use of sickles would reinforce tendencies toward the cultivation of crop complexes of relatively uniform morphology, such as cereals and their associated weeds, and would discourage the cultivation of mixed assemblages of crops of varied life form. In this technological contrast between southwestern Asia and Mesoamerica we may, therefore, have a clue which helps to explain the otherwise puzzling fact that the Mesoamerican complex of seed plant domesticates is more diverse biotically, especially in terms of life forms, than is that of the southwestern Asian complex. If broadcast sowing and sickle harvesting had become established in Mesoamerica, would a pattern of seed cultivation much more similar to that of southwestern Asia have evolved, perhaps with small-seeded cultivars of *Zea, Setaria, Phaseolus*, and other genera emerging as the dominant crops?

Similar contrasts in traditional techniques of harvesting and reseeding may also help to explain the pathways towards the cultivation of seed crops followed in other parts of the world, such as the interior western Africa, highland northwestern Ethiopia, the Huang-ho valley of northern China, and the mainland of southeastern Asia (Figure 2). In the zone of the long dry season in the interior of western Africa, traditional agriculture focuses upon grasses and pulses indigenous to Africa, such as sorghum, pearl millet, cowpea, and Bambara groundnut (Harris 1976). Most of the cultivated forms have large seeds and inflorescences and they are normally hand planted in holes made with a dibble. Planting in mounds is common and crops of different life form are often raised together in the same field. Sometimes seeds are first germinated in a seed-bed and later transplanted. Harvesting is by handpicking or cutting of individual heads or pods, or a whole plant may be cut or uprooted prior to hand-picking of the fruit. Sickles are not traditionally used, nor are they definitely reported archaeologically from western Africa. Trapezoids with a gloss near the cutting edge have been found in the forest zone of Nigeria, but they appear to belong to an early microlithic industry and probably do not indicate food production (Shaw 1969: 369–370). The parallel between western Africa and Mesoamerica thus appears close, with a tradition of attention to individual plants leading in both areas to domestication of larger-seeded and larger-fruited forms and the cultivation of mixed plant assemblages.

In highland northwestern Ethiopia and in the Huang-ho valley of northern China the pathway toward cultivation of seed crops appears to have approximated more closely the pattern of southwestern Asia. Traditionally, agriculture in both regions has depended on cereals with relatively small seeds and inflorescences, particularly teff, finger millet, barley, and wheat in highland Ethiopia (Simoons 1960: 85), and in northern China foxtail and common millet, rice, wheat, barley, and the kao-liang sorghum which de Wet and Harlan (1971: 130–131) include among the sorghums of the Race Nervosum. These cereals are cultivated principally by dry-farming methods, which include broadcast sowing and sickle harvesting, and indeed Simoons (1960: 67) describes the preference for broadcast sowing in northwestern Ethiopia as "overwhelming" and comments that "Though some planting of seeds in holes is done, it is generally limited to certain of the garden plants." The traditional crop assemblage of northwestern Ethiopia also includes several small-seeded pulses such as lentils and chick peas. Lentils are harvested by pulling the whole plants from the ground prior to drying and threshing (Simoons 1960: 109–110), which contrasts with the more selective practice of hand-picking of pods that is associated with the larger-seeded legumes of Mesoamerica and western Africa. Leguminous crops are, however (with the exception of soybean), conspicuously absent from traditional northern Chinese seed agriculture. In both northwestern Ethiopia and northern China cereals and other crops of similar life form tend to be segregated in fields, and cropping of mixed life forms is usually restricted to small garden plots close to houses or streams.

If the assemblages of seed crops of the two regions are examined in relation to archaeological evidence and probable areas of origin of specific domesticates, the early importance of small-seeded and small-fruited forms is confirmed. Archaeological evidence from Ethiopia is lacking as yet, but teff appears to be an ancient indigenous domesticate, and barley, emmer (tetraploid) wheat, chick pea, and lentil, which were probably initially introduced from southwestern Asia, exist there in great varietal diversity (Harlan 1969; Simoons 1960: 99–110), thus suggesting a long history of cultivation and continuing selection.

In northern China archaeological investigation of the "Neolithic" Yang-shao culture indicates that the earliest staple crops were foxtail millet and probably common millet, to which were added later in pre-historic and early historic times rice, wheat, and barley (Chang 1970: 181–184; Ho 1969: 15–27, and this volume). Kao-liang sorghum has been reported from one Yang-shao site (Ho 1969: 18, and this volume), but the identification is uncertain and it is probable that sorghum was not widely cultivated until after the Mongol conquests of the late thirteenth century A.D. (Hagerty 1940). Unlike sorghum, the soybean probably is of northern Chinese origin, but it is unlikely to have emerged as a domesticated crop much before the eleventh century B.C. (Ho 1969: 28–29; Hymowitz 1970). Wheat and barley are thought to have been introduced during the second millennium B.C. (Ho 1969: 27), and remains of rice found in northern China in a Lungshanoid context, which may date to the fourth millennium B.C., are thought by Chang to indicate the intrusion of rice from the south into an area of already established cultivation of millet (Chang 1968: 138, 1970: 183–184).

Among the artifacts found at Yang-shao sites are semilunar stone sickle blades (Chang 1968: 90) which presumably were used, among other purposes, for harvesting millet. Broadcasting was probably the normal method of sowing millet and other cereals. Indeed, as Ho has pointed out (1969: 26), rice was evidently sown broadcast rather than transplanted until about the beginning of the Christian era. Also of interest is the relation of Yang-shao settlement sites to cemeteries; the inference has been made that the growth of population was sufficient to cause, by the end of the period, the fissioning of residential villages and the establishment of smaller peripheral settlements in cultivable areas (Chang 1968: 102–103; Wheatley 1971: 24–25). Perhaps this is an expression of the kind of change postulated earlier in the relative importance of logistic and residential mobility which would lead to population pressure. And in any case it probably implies continuing selective pressure in favor of the procurement of grass seeds which, through the agency of sickle harvesting and other technical innovations, was leading toward the dominance of the cultivation of seed crops in the subsistence system.

In mainland southeastern Asia seed agriculture appears to have developed in a direction broadly similar to that inferred for southwestern Asia, northwestern Ethiopia, and northern China, but distinctive trends can be discerned. Rice is the dominant staple in the traditional seed agriculture of most of southeastern Asia. It is cultivated in several different ways and in association with a variety of other crops. The technique of dry-rice cultivation involving the hand planting of seeds in holes dibbled with digging sticks is practiced over the greatest area, commonly within systems of shifting or swidden cultivation (Hanks 1972: 25 and 28; Spencer 1966: 150). There are two principal modes of the cultivation of wet rice: one depends on the natural flooding of undiked land and the other on diking and irrigation. The former is associated with broadcast sowing onto fields still dry, and the latter with the transplanting of seedlings from seedbeds to fields already flooded (Hanks 1972: 34–39). Techniques of harvesting rice also vary from the hand plucking of individual seed heads to the use of specialized harvesting knives, which are often employed where rice is raised as a staple crop in relatively pure stands; sickles also are used, although not as commonly as in India and China (Spencer 1966: 143–150).

Field crops which are cultivated with rice vary from small-seeded millets and pulses, to larger-seeded grains and beans such as Job's tears (*Coix lachryma-jobi*) and broad bean (*Vicia faba*), to vegetatively reproduced taros and yams. The raising of rice in mixed life-form assemblages is most characteristic of rain-fed swidden systems where dibbling and hand plucking are the norm, whereas wet-rice cultivation is associated with fixed fields, knife harvesting, and either with more uniform combinations of small-seeded annuals or with rice grown alone. In the domestication of rice there does not appear to have been sustained cultural selection of forms with large inflorescences and seeds, but selection for differences in color, gluten content, and hardness of seeds, etc., has resulted in great varietal diversity. This pattern may imply the early development of wet-rice cultivation by broadcast sowing, natural flooding, and knife harvesting which, by relying on shallow sowing and relatively indiscriminate harvesting, would have tended to retain the small inflorescences and seeds of wild rice. With the development of specialized techniques of paddy irrigation and transplanting, shallow sowing in the fields would persist but more attention would be paid to choosing seed prior to planting in the seed bed; cultural selection for varietal diversity would thus be favored.

If this interpretation is correct, I would postulate that cultivation of rice began in southeastern Asia as a simple technique by which seasonally flooded land was exploited by reseeding, as has been suggested for the initial cultivation of African rice (*Oryza glaberrima*) in the area of the "inland delta" of the Niger (Harris 1972: 31–33). The development of dry-rice cultivation and the incorporation of "upland" varieties into mixed-crop swidden systems probably occurred later. Evidently this did not lead to the selection of varieties with larger seeds and inflorescences, perhaps because rice was insufficiently responsive genetically or because deep planting and hand plucking were not dominant techniques in those parts of southeastern Asia where dry-rice cultivation first became established. That some large-seeded forms of cultivated grains were selected in southeastern Asia is clear from the widespread occurrence of Job's tears as a traditional crop but it is possible that its domestication first occurred in the context of the deep tillage of root crops such as yams and taro.

Archaeological evidence bearing on the origins of cultivation of seed crops in southeastern Asia remains scanty, despite recent impressive discoveries at Spirit Cave and other sites in northern Thailand. At the upland site of Spirit Cave, Gorman (1969, 1970, 1971) has recovered in "Hoabinhian" levels the remains of twelve genera of exploited, seed-reproduced plants which have been radiocarbon dated to between 10,000 and 8000 B.P. Although both pea (*Pisum*) and bean (*Vicia* or *Phaseolus*) are reported from the site, the plant assemblage as a whole suggests the harvesting of wild or semidomesticated species for food, condiments and stimulants, oil, and domestic utensils, rather than the systematic cultivation of staple crops. A degree of resource specialization is implied by this assemblage, such as might have occurred if broad-spectrum gathering began to give way, under pressure of increase of population, to the more intensive harvesting of familiar and favored plants.

No remains of rice or other cereals are reported from Spirit Cave, but a complex of stone tools and pottery dated to 8800 B.P. includes bifacially ground slate fragments which Gorman (1971: 314) interprets as rice-harvesting knives. Evidence of rice in the form of pottery tempered with rice chaff has also been found at the lowland village site of Non Nok Tha (Bayard 1973: 135; Higham 1972: 465; Solheim 1972: 34–35). Most of the tempered sherds date to between 5000 and 3000 B.P., but one pot with rice chaff was recovered from the lowest level which is thought to predate 5500 B.P. (Bayard 1973: 135). The evidence from Non Nok Tha suggests that by the later third or early fourth millennium B.C. specialization on rice as a staple crop suited to cultivation in the lowlands had progressed sufficiently to support permanent villages. Whether rice was first cultivated on a small scale in seasonally flooded habitats in the uplands or the lowlands remains uncertain. The intervening piedmont zone may have been the locale of the earliest rice cultivation (Gorman, this volume; Harris 1974) and it may be helpful to envisage population pressure among relatively sedentary upland and piedmont communities stimulating migration to the lowlands, which, by reducing access to upland resources, would have intensified dependence on the cultivation of rice and other domesticates transferred to the new environment. The selection of domesticated forms would also tend to be accentuated if, as may have been the case with rice, such transference increased their isolation from related wild species.

So far the question of how technological innovations arise which lead toward agriculture within systems of seed-plant exploitation has not been considered. A full discussion of this theme is beyond the scope of this paper, but clearly innovations either may arise internally within a developing subsistence system as a response to a recognized need, or they may be adopted as a result of the transfer of a technique from one socio-economic context to another (Figure 1, System D). In the pathways from the harvesting of wild grasses and forbs to seed agriculture the transference of techniques developed for other purposes is likely to have been critically important. Specifically, the technique of grinding seeds to remove or pulverize the hard, indigestible exosperm and produce flour or other "fines," which was a necessary step for the rise to dominance of seed agriculture, probably originated as a byproduct of previously developed techniques of grinding ochre and other substances to obtain pigment. Certainly grindstones found in "preagricultural" contexts, as well as in association with seed gathering or cultivation, frequently show traces of pigment, as for example in the sites of the "late Paleolithic" in the Nile valley previously discussed (Wendorf and Schild 1976).

The development of sickle harvesting may represent another case of technical innovation resulting from transference. Composite cutting tools of saw or sickle type made by setting microliths in a wood or bone handle may have originated as devices for gathering fibrous wild plants such as reeds, sedges, and grasses for thatch, basketry, and cordage (C. Sauer 1958), and only later been used to harvest wild grain, thus giving "accidental" impetus to the process of cereal domestication.

Harvesting of Tree Nuts

The harvesting of nuts from wild trees (Figure 3) represents a second system of food procurement in which seeds are the focus of the specialization of resources. However, in contrast to the harvesting of the seeds of grasses and forbs, this system does not appear to have functioned as a pathway toward domestication and food production. The gathering of nuts for food is widely practiced by hunter-gatherers in tropical and temperate environments, but specialized dependence on this resource is best attested ethnographically in subtropical and temperate woodlands and forests. This fact relates primarily to the lower diversity in tree species of such areas by comparison with tropical forests. In a plant community of relatively low diversity index, with a high ratio of individuals to species, there is a greater likelihood that a nut-bearing tree will, if it is a natural dominant, become a focus of wild food procurement because it offers a high and seasonally predictable yield in relation to the energy expended in harvest.

Such was evidently the case, for example, in aboriginal central California where acorns (*Quercus* spp.) and buckeye (*Aesculus californica*) were heavily exploited, and in parts of the eastern woodland of North America, where hickory (*Carya* = *Hicoria* spp.) and walnut (*Juglans* spp.)

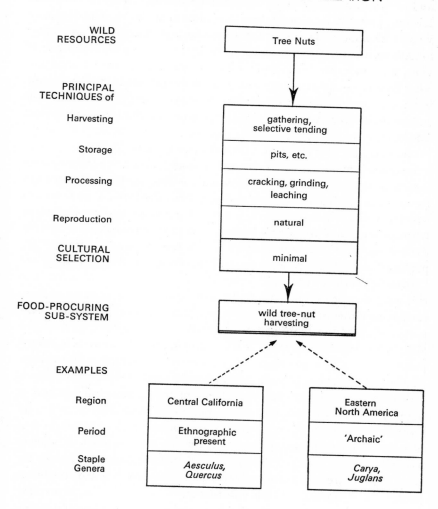

Figure 3.   Wild tree-nut-harvesting system

were staples. Not only were these seeds abundant per unit area of woodland or forest, but their calorific food value was high. Their exploitation did not, however, lead to cultivation and domestication. The ease with which tree nuts could be gathered by hand, stored in pits and other containers, and processed by cracking and grinding — and, in the case of acorn and buckeye, by leaching with hot water to remove tannin and other toxins — helps to explain why such tree seeds became staple resources. But the failure of the harvesters of nuts to develop arboriculture probably relates more directly to biological than to technological factors.

The time taken for a tree to reach nut-bearing maturity compared with more quickly maturing herbs and shrubs would have discouraged planting, particularly in the context of seasonally shifting settlements in relation to resource availability which characterized Californian and eastern woodland Indian groups. But the fact that trees tend to be cross-pollinated whereas herbs tend to be self-pollinated may also have helped to prevent the emergence of nut tree cultivation as a food-producing strategy. By maximizing genetic mixing, cross-pollination reduces the probability of "domestic" varieties becoming segregated from wild forms as a result of cultural selection, even if the pattern of exploitation were to include reseeding. Varieties can more easily be selected and perpetuated if techniques of vegetative reproduction are used — as with many tropical and some subtropical tree crops — but there is no indication that ethnographically known specialized nut harvesters attempted to raise their staple trees either by seed planting or by vegetative reproduction.

Seasonal gathering of wild nuts thus remained a more efficient procedure in relation to both the overall pattern of food procurement and group mobility, and the reproductive system and rate of maturation of the trees. It is not surprising, therefore, that such archaeological evidence as we have of specialized dependence on tree-nut harvesting, as in the example of "Archaic" eastern North America already cited, relates to predominantly nonagricultural subsistence. As a system of food procurement tree-nut harvesting is an efficient use of available wild resources, but in terms of the development of food production it is a cul-de-sac.

Harvesting of Roots and Tubers[2]

The harvesting of roots and tubers (Figure 4) constitutes a third special-

[2]   The phrase "root and tuber" as used in this paper includes all forms of underground food-storage organs, whether they are enlarged roots, root or stem tubers, rhizomes, or

ized system of procurement of plant food and, like the harvesting of seeds of wild grasses and forbs, it has served as a pathway toward food production. Tuberous plants with underground organs for food storage are adapted to survive dry or cold seasons and to grow quickly to maturity once the rains return or the ground warms up again. They achieve this by accumulating starch in their roots or stems during the growth period, and many of these bulk foods are relished and sought by man and animals. Such plants occur wild in temperate as well as tropical seasonal environments and are used for food by most hunter-gatherers. But they are particularly characteristic of the intermediate tropical zone between the equatorial evergreen rain forests and the perennial deserts (Harris 1972: 186–187 and Figure 2), and it is among tropical hunter-gatherers that specialized dependence on this resource of wild food is most evident. Ethnographic examples of groups who depend heavily for food on wild yams and other carbohydrate-rich roots and tubers are known from the American, African, Asian, and Australian tropics, and in all but the last area utilization of this food source has led to the development of systems of cultivation of root crops.

These systems are most widespread and diversified in northern lowland South America and in southeastern Asia, where they are based on vegetatively reproduced indigenous cultigens, principally manioc, taro, and yams, together with many lesser-known cultigens (Barrau 1965, 1970; Harris 1969: 10, 1971; C. Sauer 1950: 507–513). In Africa cultivation of root crops appears to have developed as a major system of food production only in tropical western Africa, where it depended primarily on the locally domesticated Guinea yams (*Dioscorea cayenensis* and *D. rotundata*) (Coursey 1976; Harris 1976: 21–31). Cultivation of root crops has also developed in certain tropical highlands, most notably in the central Andes, where the white potato and several minor tuberous cultigens are adapted to low temperatures as well as to seasonal drought (Hawkes 1967; C. Sauer 1950: 513–519; Ugent 1970). In tropical Australia, however, the cultivation of root crops never emerged as a system of food production, despite the fact that aboriginal groups in Arnhem Land, the Cape York Peninsula, and elsewhere made quite intensive use of wild yams and other tuberous plants (Coursey and Coursey 1971: 470–471; Golson 1971; White 1971).

The question therefore arises as to what factors may have precipitated

---

corms. The adjective "tuberous" is used in a similarly comprehensive sense, and "rootcrop cultivation" indicates any system of cultivation in which plants are raised for their underground storage organs.

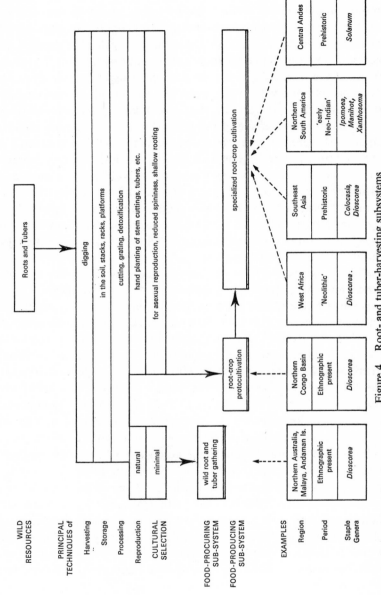

Figure 4.   Root- and tuber-harvesting subsystems

a shift in particular tropical areas from the intensive gathering of wild roots and tubers to established systems of cultivation of root crops. If ethnographically described techniques of harvesting, storing, and processing tuberous plants are examined an impression of relative uniformity emerges. Digging sticks of simple design are most commonly used to unearth the root or tuber, although sometimes hoes or, as in the Andes, "foot plows" are used for this purpose (Donkin 1970). The simplest technique of storage is to leave the root in the ground and to dig it out when required for consumption or exchange. This obviates the difficulty of rapid decay in tropical climates, particularly in the more humid areas, although it may increase the risk of damage from pests and predators.

Differences in the capacities of tuberous plants to persist underground prior to harvest may help to explain why particular taxa were domesticated and not others. Many species have evolved protective adaptations such as toxins, spiny roots and tubers, and deep burial in the soil, to decrease their attraction as food for animals. Such adaptations are highly developed, for example, in manioc (Renvoize 1970, 1972) and yams (Coursey 1967). Cultural selection has tended to discriminate against these adaptations, but in the case of bitter manioc retention of toxicity appears to have been culturally advantageous because the tubers are "stored" underground and only harvested when required. If methods of storage above the ground are practiced, as, for example, they are for yams in stacks and on racks and platforms in western Africa, southeastern Asia, and the Pacific (Coursey 1967: 174–177), then any cultural advantage there may be in selecting toxic forms to discourage uprooting by predators will be reduced and selection of nontoxic varieties will be more likely to occur. Toxicity can confer other advantages, especially if it is present in the parts of the plant above the ground, for example, by reducing vulnerability to attack by insects (Janzen 1970), but such advantage may be outweighed by the need to detoxify the product prior to consumption.

The relationship between toxicity and storage can be illustrated by a closer comparison of bitter manioc with the principal cultivated yams of southeastern Asia and western Africa. Once they have been harvested, manioc tubers decay very rapidly as a result of enzymic action induced by drying, and it is therefore essential that they be processed as soon as possible after being dug; they can, however, be left in the ground for up to three years without deterioration (Renvoize 1970: 53). Underground storage is therefore advantageous, but as long as the tubers remain in the soil they are vulnerable to nonhuman predators. Thus retention of toxicity in the manioc tuber is important to the cultivator to protect his stored product, but this in its turn requires that the tuber be detoxified before it can safely be eaten.

Aboriginal techniques for removing the hydrocyanic acid that is the active poison in manioc vary according to whether sweet or bitter varieties are involved. In sweet manioc the poison is concentrated in the skin and outer cortical layer, and the tuber is eaten after being boiled or roasted whole and then peeled. In bitter manioc the poison is more evenly distributed through the tubers and detoxification is a much more elaborate procedure which involves peeling, grating, extraction of the poisonous juice by squeezing the grated pulp in elastic basketry cylinders (Harris 1972: Figure 7), and heating the squeezed pulp over a fire to produce either meal or flat cakes of cassava "bread" (Renvoize 1970: 56–70). Both meal and cakes are relatively resistant to decay, a fact which, together with the fact that bitter manioc yields more and purer starch than do the sweet varieties, helps to account for the predominant importance of bitter manioc as a staple crop among the Amerindians of tropical lowland South America.

In the selection of cultivars of manioc the greatest possible advantage to man apparently lay in retaining some toxicity to protect tubers "stored" underground, and to obtain better yields at the cost of an elaboration of detoxifying procedures. With yams, however, the relationship between toxicity and storage is not a positive one. Most of the species of yams gathered for human food, such as wild forms of *Dioscorea dumetorum* in tropical Africa and of *D. hispida* in eastern Asia, contain toxic, water-soluble alkaloids (Coursey 1967: 147–149). But, because yam tubers can — if protected from heat and adequately ventilated — be stored above ground for considerable periods without deterioration, retention of toxicity in domesticated forms confers no advantage unless underground storage is in fact practiced. Techniques for storage above ground are well developed in the major Asian and African areas of yam cultivation, and it is not surprising, therefore, that the principal cultivars domesticated there — the greater yam (*Dioscorea alata*) in southeastern Asia and the Guinea yams in western Africa — belong to the *Enantiophyllum* section of the genus, the wild forms of which are deep-rooting and usually spinous rather than poisonous (Coursey and Coursey 1971: 475).

Close examination of toxicity and techniques of storage for other tuberous crops might reveal comparable relationships and help to explain the processes of cultural selection operating on them, but this would not necessarily enhance understanding of how gathering gave way to the cultivation of root crops. The toxins present in such plants are valued by many aboriginal peoples in the tropics as poisons for use in hunting and fishing. For example, in Asia and Africa poisons from wild yams are mixed with bait or released in streams to stupefy monkeys, birds, and fish, and they are also used as arrow poisons (Coursey 1967: 149). Similarly, in South America reports occur of manioc being used in the stupefaction of fish, and a traditional Brazilian method of preparing manioc meal involves partial detoxification by soaking the peeled tubers in streams (Renvoize 1970: 56, 108). This suggests a possible reason for the adoption of toxic tubers as food sources, developing from earlier uses of them as stupefacients and poisons. This possibility was envisaged by C. Sauer (1948: 75) for southeastern Asia, where he pointed to the remarkable number of poisonous and acrid aroids which have become important sources of starch food, such as species of *Alocasia, Colocasia,* and *Amorphophallus.* He also suggested (1948: 74) that the use of toxic plants for stupefaction of fish may have developed out of the macerating of stems and roots to obtain plant fibers, a process that might have contributed to the domestication of certain yams and other tuberous plants, the fibrous stems of which are used for cordage.

The diverse uses of tuberous plants for fibers, poisons, and food help to explain their importance to tropical gatherers, but without the development of techniques of vegetative reproduction by planting stem cuttings, tubers, and other parts of the parent plant, this pathway would not have led to cultivation. We may assume that empirical understanding of the ability of many plants to reproduce vegetatively was widespread if not universal among tropical gatherers. The techniques of harvesting with simple digging sticks and knives would commonly result in plant fragments being left at or near the gathering ground or settlement site, and the ability of some of these to regenerate would readily be observed. The step from this observation to the deliberate replanting of such fragments is a simple one, which was no doubt taken repeatedly. Indeed the collection of wild yams, followed by the replanting near settlements of tubers not immediately needed, has been observed by Chevalier among recent African hunter-gatherers (Coursey 1976: 23).

Although the capacity of many vegetatively reproduced cultigens to produce viable seed has been greatly reduced or even eliminated by cultural selection, the wild ancestors of early domesticated forms would have reproduced sexually, and the question therefore arises as to why vegetative planting was generally preferred to seed sowing in the development of root-crop cultivation. The simplest answer is that the part of the plant that was the focus of human interest — in this case the root or stem — was replanted, just as seeds were the objects gathered and resown in areas of emerging seed agriculture. But this is not in itself an adequate

explanation. More important may have been the observation that, although the tuberous plants would grow from seed, they formed the desired
starchy roots more rapidly if propagated from cuttings or tubers. Thus, if
harvesting and planting are done at the same time — as with manioc,
which, where climatic conditions permit, is often replanted at harvest
time with stem cuttings taken from the plants that have just been dug
up — then growth above ground can be seen to be continuous. A further
factor reinforcing the practice of vegetative reproduction must have been
its ability to segregate clones of near-identical genetic makeup and thus
to isolate and perpetuate diverse forms of particular value to the cultivators.

In general, differences in techniques of harvesting, storing, processing,
and propagating vegetatively reproduced tuberous plants appear less
varied than those applied to seed plants. They do not in themselves yield
a hypothesis comparable to that developed for herbaceous seed plants,
which might explain why the cultivation of root crops emerged in particular areas of the tropics. However, if consideration is given to the
nutritional value of the tuberous cultigens as plants yielding abundant
carbohydrates for relatively little input of human energy and thus com-
plementing fishing-and-hunting activities which provide chiefly protein
and fat, then the emergence of the cultivation of root crops is less surprising. The ecological and nutritional complementarity of fishing and
cultivation of root crops in tropical forest environments is well known and
we may postulate that, given the operation of a stress factor such as
population pressure, a forager group already exploiting tuberous plants
and aquatic resources would tend to invest more time and energy in their
procurement at the expense of other subsistence activities. The result
might well be a self-amplifying system of increasing dependence on
fishing and cultivation of root crops, associated with riparian settlements
that gave access both to areas for good fishing and hunting and to more
fertile alluvial soils for cultivation. If, as is likely, this led to decreased
residential mobility then further increase in population and resource-
specialization would tend to occur.

Quite possibly, a self-amplifying process of this kind led to the early
establishment of cultivation of root crops, with bitter manioc as the
principal crop, along the relatively restricted alluvial floodplains of the
Amazon and Orinoco basins. Lathrap (1970, 1973, and this volume)
makes a persuasive case for the early emergence and spread of manioc-
based agriculture in the lowlands of northern South America, but there is
no empirical evidence to suggest that such cultivation of root crops
became established throughout the tropical areas to which it was well

adapted, and, as I have argued elsewhere, it is, by comparison with cultivation of seed crops, inherently an ecologically stable mode of production not liable to expand into new territory unless spread by populations migrating for other reasons (Harris 1972, 1973). We are therefore still faced with the need to explain the emergence of the cultivation of root crops as a specialized indigenous system in specific areas — for example, western Africa — and its absence in others, for example, the Congo basin, to which it is ecologically suited.

One approach to this problem is to examine the role of ritual sanctions in relation to tuberous plants. Coursey and Coursey (1971) have demonstrated that the New Yam Festival of West Africa serves an important biological need by protecting the growing yam plants from premature removal of the tubers, and Barrau (1970) has stressed the significance of ritual protection in the process of domestication of many cultigens in southeastern Asia and the Pacific. It is quite possible that ritual sanctions played an important role in the cultural selection of particular taxa, but, because they are widely reported among hunter-gatherers who did not develop food production — as, for example, among collectors of wild yams in India, Ceylon, the Andaman Islands, Malaya, and Australia (Coursey and Coursey 1971:470–473) — it is less convincing to argue that the development of ritualism might explain the emergence of cultivation of root crops in certain areas and its absence in others. However, until detailed comparative study is undertaken of ritualism in relation to a wide range of tropical food plants this possibility remains open.

An alternative approach is to appeal to external factors to explain the establishment of root-crop cultivation in particular parts of the tropics. If, as has already been suggested, the principle of vegetative propagation was widely understood by tropical hunter-gatherers, then we should perhaps look upon root-crop cultivation as a minor subsistence activity practiced by many hunter-gatherer groups in the tropics, but which tended to develop into a specialized mode of production only when particular groups came under demographic or environmental pressure as a result of cultural contact. Cultural interaction has been suggested for the origins of yam cultivation in southeastern Asia, western Africa, and tropical America (Alexander and Coursey 1969:412–423), but there the assumption is that pressure was exerted by grain cultivators upon hunter-gatherers using wild yams. I suggest rather, that the small-scale propagation or "protocultivation" of tuberous plants by vegetative techniques may be an ancient and widespread practice among tropical hunter-gatherers which complemented the strategies of fishing and hunting, but which usually remained of minor importance except where population pressure or other stress resulting from cultural contact induced specialized cultivation of these plants for food (Figure 4). Such small-scale propagation is envisaged as part of a long phase of protocultivation by ecosystem manipulation which preceded the emergence of specialized agricultural systems in the tropics (Harris 1973). And if, as has been argued on ecological and nutritional grounds, seed-crop systems of swidden cultivation are inherently more expansive than vegecultural systems (Harris 1972: 188, 1973), then the contact needed to induce a shift to specialized root-crop cultivation often may have taken the form of interaction between expanding seed-crop shifting cultivators and more stable fisher-hunter-vegeculturalists.

I do not mean to imply that external stress factors were responsible for the emergence of all specialized systems of cultivation of root crops. The above speculations need to be tested against archaeological data before an acceptable explanation is reached of how the gathering of tuberous plants functioned as a pathway to food production. That it did so at least in tropical southeastern Asia, western Africa, and northern South America is evident from the importance of indigenous vegetatively reproduced cultigens in the aboriginal systems of cultivation of those areas; but as yet there is little archaeological evidence to indicate the extent and antiquity of cultivation of root crops in the tropics. Such evidence as there is is indirect and, as it has recently been reviewed (Harris 1972:188–193, 1973), it will not be examined here. It is possible that contact between expanding systems of cultivation of seed crops and localized vegecultural systems of protocultivation was associated with a shift to specialized cultivation of root crops in western Africa (Harris 1976) and perhaps in southeastern Asia as well, whereas in northern South America dependence on specialized root-crop cultivation may be an essentially indigenous phenomenon which developed independently of externally generated stress factors, as Lathrap (1970: 63–67; and in this volume) has postulated. In the central Andes too (Kaplan, Lynch, and Smith 1973; MacNeish 1969, and this volume; MacNeish, et al. 1970) an autonomous pathway was probably followed towards specialized dependence on the white potato and minor tuberous cultigens in association with the hunting and herding of llamas and the local cultivation of seed crops.

Fishing, and Hunting of Aquatic Mammals

A fourth specialized system of food procurement is the exploitation of

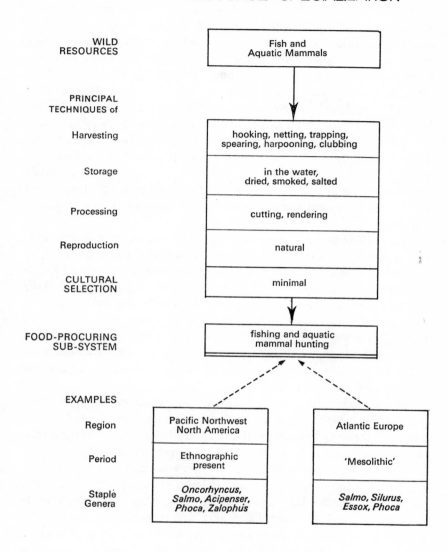

Figure 5.   Fishing and aquatic-mammal-hunting system

aquatic resources by fishing and by hunting marine and riverine mammals (Figure 5). As with specialized dependence on tree nuts, this mode of subsistence did not apparently serve as a pathway toward food production. Although many hunter-gatherers in tropical and temperate environments exploit aquatic resources, relatively few ethnographically known groups depend primarily upon them. In Lee's sample of fifty-eight nonagricultural societies drawn from Murdock (1967), only eighteen were found to depend primarily on fishing (Lee 1968: 41–48). The sample excluded both fishers who practice some agriculture, such as tropical fisher-vegeculturalists, and archaeologically known groups who depended heavily on aquatic resources, but it demonstrated that most specialized fishing groups occupied temperate mid- to high-latitude environments: only one of the eighteen groups was within the tropics and fourteen of them occupied coasts and valleys poleward of 44 degrees of latitude.

Some of these groups, such as the Ingalik in Alaska, the Kutchin in the Yukon, the Alacaluf and Yaghan in sourthernmost Chile, and the Gilyak in Sakhalin Island, occupied environments climatically unsuited to agriculture, but the remainder occupied areas with a sufficiently long growing season to allow cultivation. The fact that apparently they did not develop or adopt techniques of cultivation or domestication is explicable both in terms of seasonal variations in the availability of wild foods of high calorific value in the habitats they occupied and in terms of discordance between the biology of the wild species that were staple foods and the methods used to exploit them.

The specialized fishers of the northwestern coast of North America attained much higher levels of poulation, fuller sedentism, and greater cultural complexity than other ethnographically known hunter-gatherers, and we commonly assume that this was made possible by the local abundance of wild foods, especially salmon and other anadromous fish, together with the efficiency of the techniques of food procurement used. However, as Suttles has shown (1960, 1968), this view greatly oversimplifies a complex subsistence pattern and in particular obscures the significance of seasonal variations in the availability of staple foods. The fluvial and marine ecosystems of the Pacific Northwest have low diversity indices in the sense that there are relatively few species of fish, each of which is present in relatively large numbers. The dominant species, such as salmon and sturgeon, as well as aquatic mammals such as the seal, sea lion, and whale, are large and offer man bulk food in compact units of high caloric value. If, furthermore, the locational and seasonal availability of these foods can be predicted, as can be done with considerable accuracy for the anadromous fish, then it is to be expected that food procurement will focus upon them, just as it does on the nut harvest in temperate forests dominated by trees bearing edible nuts.

The elaboration of techniques for procuring, processing, and storing fish and marine mammals that is such a well-known feature of the material culture of the Pacific Northwest is thus not in itself surprising, particularly if it is assumed that the development of sedentism was accompanied by population growth. But this does not adequately explain the failure of the Indians of the Northwest Coast to move toward the cultivation and domestication of locally gathered food plants. They did weed and protect small patches of useful wild plants and the Tlingit and Haida actually cultivated a tobacco-like plant as a masticatory (Drucker 1963: 105), but these activities never attained more than minor significance in the subsistence economy. The cultivation of starch-rich plants might be expected on nutritional grounds because the Indians' diet, although rich in proteins and fats, notably lacked carbohydrates. Gathered roots and tubers provided carbohydrates in small quantities, but there is no evidence that the cultivation and/or propagation of such plants ever became established as a procedure providing a dietary counterpoint to aquatic protein and fat, as it evidently did in the tropics.

The answer to this apparent anomaly probably lies in the greater seasonal variation in the availability of fish and other staples in the Pacific Northwest as compared with the tropics. Suttles (1960: 302, 1968) has emphasized the seasonal and interannual variation in availability of the wild foods on which the Indians of the Northwest Coast depended, and has demonstrated how population movements, methods of food storage, and patterns of exchange acted to maximize the advantages and minimize the disadvantages of this variation. The development of resource specialization in the Pacific Northwest may therefore be looked upon as an example of seasonal scheduling for the procurement of wild food in which the fish — the availability of which was relatively predictable — were the resource which responded best to intensified exploitation by increased productivity. If population growth continued, the procurement and processing of fish could be expected eventually to dominate the subsistence system as a whole, and, because of the priority accorded to it, to prevent the rise of other subsystems of food procurement such as exploitation of roots and tubers which might compete with it in terms of energy expenditure. In the tropics, on the other hand, where variations in the availability of aquatic resources are much less pronounced, scheduling conflicts between fishing and gathering of roots and tubers can be avoided and the dietary advantages of both activities are likely to be realized in the form of a subsistence system which combines fishing with the protocultivation of tuberous plants, as was suggested in the previous section.

We may also ask why specialized fishing and hunting of aquatic mammals did not lead toward "aquaculture" and the "domestication" of salmon and other species. The Indians of the Northwest Coast did not develop any technique comparable to the raising of fish in ponds such as is often associated with wet-paddy cultivation in southern and eastern Asia. Methods of procurement focused upon the capture of full-grown fish migrating upstream to breed and there was generally no attempt to intervene positively in the breeding system itself. The Nootka did try to regularize the salmon supply by restocking depleted streams with spawn obtained elsewhere (Forde 1949:78) but the fact that the staple species of fish and aquatic mammal are strongly migratory would effectively have prevented any development of fish culture, even if the sheer richness of natural supplies and the demands on time and energy made by processing and storing seasonally abundant wild foods did not in itself do so.

Thus exploitation of the rich but variable aquatic resources of temperate coasts and rivers, like the seasonal gathering of wilds nuts in temperate forests, appears not to have functioned as an evolutionary pathway toward agriculture. And this expectation is supported by the fact that both ethnographic and archaeological evidence of specialized fishers in temperate areas other than the Pacific Northwest, such as the Ainu of Hokkaido (Watanabe 1968), is confined to essentially non-agricultural contexts.

Exploitation of Social Ungulates

The last specialized system of food procurement to be considered is the exploitation of social ungulates (Figure 6). As with the harvesting of the seeds of wild grasses and forbs, this activity apparently led to domestication and food production in some but by no means all of the areas in which it was practiced. Comparative examination of man–ungulate relationships suggests a variety of factors that help to explain how the exploitation of wild ungulates gave way in certain areas to the management of domesticated herd animals.

Reed (1969:364–367) has shown that anatomical and physiological adaptation to diets high in cellulose and low in protein is a common denominator of the mammalian taxa from which the domesticates have been derived. In such animals ingested cellulose is broken down to simpler,

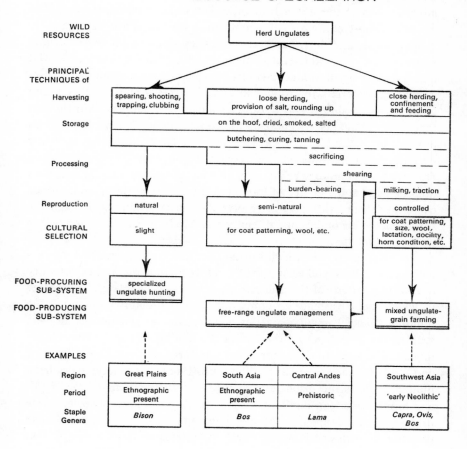

RESOURCE SPECIALIZATION

Figure 6. Herd-ungulate-exploitation subsystems

digestible molecules by bacteria present in fermentation vats, which are modifications of the stomach or other parts of the digestive tract. This process is most efficient in the ruminants, which include cattle, sheep, goats, camels, and deer, but it also operates — although less efficiently — in horses, pigs, rabbits, and many rodents. Thus utilization of wild ruminants opens an indirect channel by which man can exploit cellulose-rich plant materials for food, particularly grasses and the leaves and young twigs of shrubs and trees. This advantage, coupled with the fact that wild ruminants which tend tot congregate in herds offer to man bulk units of food rich in protein and fat, largely accounts for their importance in the subsistence economies of many hunter-gatherers. However, the migratory behavior of ruminants and other social ungulates does demand some degree of mobility on the part of the human groups exploiting them, who have to resolve the inherent conflict between the subsistence value of the animals and the demands their exploitation makes on group mobility.

The varying ways in which this conflict has been resolved by hunter-gatherers, herders, and early agriculturalists provide the first explanatory clue to the pattern of the domestication of social ungulates. The degree to which the subsistence economies of hunter-gatherers focus upon the hunting of social ungulates varies greatly. Among generalized foragers such as the Bushmen and the Hadza the hunting of antelope and other ungulates is a relatively minor activity in terms both of time expended and food obtained (Lee 1969; Woodburn 1968), but among specialized hunters such as the bison- and guanaco-hunting Indians of the North and South American mid-latitude grasslands, economy and society were intimately bound up with the ungulates on which they depended. The presence in such specialized natural ecosystems of large herds of wild ungulates offered hunting groups abundant food, provided they maintained a highly mobile lifestyle. Probably, as I have previously suggested (Harris 1969:8), the demands of frequent movement imposed by dependence on a strongly migratory staple resource acted as a constraint on the domestication of social ungulates in these environments; certainly there is no ethnological evidence to suggest that the historically known bison- and guanaco-hunters of the American grasslands ever bred the animals on which they depended for food, clothing, and shelter.

It must be assumed, however, that they and other specialized hunters did alter the breeding systems of wild ungulates through the selective effects of different hunting methods. Higgs and Jarman (1969:35–36) have criticized the view that hunting was random in its effects and have rejected the assumption that domestication can be inferred from a high percentage of bones of young animals in an archaeological site. Quite conceivably other types of relationships approximating nomadic herding developed among mobile, nonagricultural groups who specialized in the exploitation of particular ungulates. The Chukchi reindeer herders of northeastern Siberia are a well-known ethnographic example of a group whose animals were only semidomesticated (Forde 1949:363–364; Leeds 1965), and the herding of wild or semidomesticated deer and gazelle by pre- and early agricultural populations in Europe and Palestine has been postulated by Jarman (1972) and Legge (1972).

Regardless of the extent to which selective hunting or the herding of semidomesticated animals affects the breeding systems of ungulates, it does not in itself constitute "domestication." If one accepts the definition of a population of domesticated animals as one which reproduces under direct human control and is phenotypically distinct from the wild population, it follows that, in seeking an explanation for the development of food production based on domesticated social ungulates, we need to examine processes that resulted in man establishing such control, either inadvertently or deliberately, and maintaining it sufficiently long to produce phenotypically differentiated breeds. As has already been implied, this development demands at least partial sedentism and is unlikely to occur among highly mobile hunters.

Full or partial sedentism can be regarded as a necessary condition for domestication of social ungulates, but that it is not a sufficient condition is clear from the absence of such domestication among many semi-sedentary and sedentary hunter-gatherers and primitive agriculturalists who nevertheless exploited wild ungulates quite intensively; the failure of such hunters and farmers in North America and tropical Africa to domesticate any of the native species of ungulate which they exploited supports this generalization. Indeed one of the most striking features of the domestication of social ungulates is its rarity in relation to the ubiquity of their hunting. This is apparent in the almost complete restriction of such domestication prehistorically to Eurasia and northern Africa, the only definite occurrence outside that area prior to A.D. 1500 being the domestication of llama and alpaca in the central Andes (Murra 1965).

We should, therefore, ask what processes resulted in early semi-sedentary and sedentary hunting, herding, and farming communities in Eurasia establishing close and sustained control over the breeding systems of some but not all of the social ungulates they exploited. The southwestern Asian upland and adjacent regions, including southeastern Europe, appear to have been the area in which most of the domestic social animals were first domesticated and present evidence suggests

(Protsch and Berger 1973; Reed 1969:371–375) that sheep and goats may have been the earliest of the social ungulates to attain this status. Bones of Caprini have been recovered from most of the early "Neolithic" sites excavated in the Near East and southeastern Europe, and, although the archaeological contexts in which they were found vary considerably, they indicate in general that the human populations were practicing cereal cultivation and living in at least semipermanent settlements, although hunting and gathering still contributed substantially to the food supply.

One process that may have contributed to the domestication of sheep and goats, while other hunted ungulates apparently remained wild, is the alteration of Near Eastern ecosystems by fire. This possibility has been suggested by Lewis (1972:215–217) who has argued that extension of grassland at the expense of woodland as a result of persistent burning could have been accompanied or followed by an increase in the numbers and range of sheep and goats. He has suggested that gazelle and wild cattle, which were the dominant ruminants of the steppe grassland, also would have increased in number, but they would not have extended their habitat range, as did the sheep, which presumably would have spread from the upland oak-pistachio woodland, which they already dominated, into the expanding areas of grassland. Sheep and goats were the best adapted of the ungulates to the seasonal pattern of transhumant hunting, gathering, and cultivation in both upland and lowland zones which early "Neolithic" populations are thought to have followed because these caprines could, more readily than deer or cattle, be hunted or herded as semidomesticates throughout the range of habitats exploited seasonally from permanent or semipermanent settlements.

This hypothesis is more persuasive in relation to sheep, which are primarily grazers, than to goats, which are by preference browsers, and it requires testing against much fuller evidence of ecological changes than is at present available, but it does go some way towards explaining the early focus on caprine exploitation that is apparent at many southwestern Asian sites. The hypothesis does not, however, postulate the actual processes by which breeding populations of caprines were established under direct human control. It is commonly supposed that domestication was initiated by the capture and rearing of infant young rather than by the confinement of sexually mature animals (see Reed, this volume), and there are reports in ethnographic literature of hunters occasionally bringing back to camp live infant animals to be reared. It appears from modern experiments in the domestication of ungulates, such as those carried out with musk ox, elk, and eland (Jewell 1969; Wilkinson 1972a, 1972b), that, if the calves are young when taken, and feeding is regular, the animals quickly become tame and continue to associate with their human providers even when mature and unconfined. Breeding populations of musk ox, elk, and eland have also been established without difficulty, but phenotypic differentiation from the wild forms is thought unlikely to arise in these and other ungulates unless deliberate selective breeding towards a predetermined end is practiced (Jarman and Wilkinson 1972; Wilkinson 1972b).

When viewed in this perspective the question of what processes resulted in the domestication of sheep, goats, and other social ungulates has again to be refined. If the initial steps toward establishing a breeding population of tamed animals are easily taken and do not pose technological difficulties we should expect them to have been taken more widely and frequently in the past than is commonly supposed. Perhaps, as Higgs (1972) and his coworkers suggest, they were: many animals may have gone in and out of a state of semidomestication, some possibly several times, but the fact remains — and demands explanation — that relatively few became fully domesticated staple resources in food-producing economies, and, of those that did, the majority are social ungulates. We should, therefore, explore the question of what selective factors operated to bring into a state of full domestication certain herd animals only, out of a wider spectrum of ungulates exploited by varied techniques of hunting and herding.

In the context of "Neolithic" southwestern Asia I would first postulate an extended phase during which sedentary and semisedentary communities with mixed food-procuring and food-producing economies brought a variety of social ungulates into a state of semidomestication by establishing loose control over their breeding systems. This may have taken a form comparable to the free-range management of feral livestock, which is known historically from the West Indies (Harris 1965:110–112) and elsewhere, whereby the animals breed in the wild and are rounded up as required.

A particularly useful ethnographic model of such a pattern of loose control is provided by Simoons's study (1968) of the mithan (*Bos frontalis*) of northeastern India and northern Burma. This animal is domestic in the sense that it is phenotypically distinct from its wild relative and probable ancestor, the gaur (*Bos gaurus*), but it is not confined, and little or no attempt is made to control its breeding. It is valued primarily as a ritual and sacrificial animal, as a measure of prestige, and as an important element in systems of exchange. Its use for milk and for traction is minimal and apparently recent. The mithan-keeping peoples are dominantly swidden cultivators and the mithan, which is a browser rather than a grazer, is well adapted both to the forested environment and to the system of cultivation. Mithan herds browse unattended in the secondary forests that regenerate on abandoned swidden land and the frequency with which they come into contact with their human owners varies from voluntary and regular return to a village every evening to occasional encounters after weeks or months in the forest. Some tribal groups mark the earlobes of their mithan as an aid to identification, but the actual control of the animals is effected through the provision of salt. Even when mithan return nightly to a village, their owners do not feed them but only provide salt and sometimes shelter. Contact is maintained with mithan in the forest by providing them with salt, and in some cases they will respond to calls from their owners. There are also accounts of wild or feral mithan being gradually tamed by the scattering of balls of salt in the forest and by mingling with domestic stock until a man is able to approach and caress the wild animals (Simoons 1968:19–20).

Although ideas derived from ethnographic knowledge of mithan keeping should not be transposed uncritically to "Neolithic" southwestern Asia, they do suggest how a system of loose control over semi-domesticated social ungulates may have arisen prior to the full domestication of a small number of species. The ethnographic analogy is presumably closest between mithan and common cattle, and Simoons (1968:234–258) fully explored its relevance to the domestication of cattle in southwestern Asia. But the use of salt in binding animals to man may well have extended beyond the bovines to other social ungulates, many of which share the bovine craving for salt. For example, wild mountain goats and sheep in North America regularly concentrate about salt licks and Geist (1971:41–45) has reported that the mountain sheep easily can be tamed through the provision of salt. As he says, "It is hard to imagine a wild animal more readily tamed than a mountain sheep. They habituate readily to man if not hunted and will accept him as a two-legged salt lick if he so wishes" (Geist 1971:41).

We can therefore envisage free-range techniques of ungulate management developing through the provision of salt, and I would further postulate that, as the cultivation of seed crops by swidden methods developed and spread in southwestern Asia, it reinforced this process of herd ungulate "domestication," particularly in relation to cattle. Wild and feral cattle and other browsers show a strong preference for the nutritious buds and twigs of young, second-growth woodlands and forests. They are attracted to regenerating, abandoned clearings as well as to the crops in cultivated swidden plots and to the salt-rich ash of recently burned clearings. Such ecologically disturbed habitats would have oeen natural foci for interaction between man and browsing ungulates, in the context of which semidomestication and free-range management could well have developed. Perhaps this hypothesis has relevance to the discovery in Thailand of remains of *Bos* in early archaeological contexts (Higham and Leach 1971). Higham (this volume) regards the bovines found at the site of Non Nok Tha as probably domestic, and possibly their early close association with man developed in the context of intensifying systems of exploitation of rice, including swidden cultivation.

If these interrelationships between man, ungulates, salt, and swidden enable us to hypothesize more clearly some of the processes leading to the domestication of social ungulates, they do not in themselves help to resolve the question of why some species and not others became fully domesticated and incorporated as staple resources into food-producing economies. This is too large a question to consider fully here, but as the exploitation of social ungulates did function as a pathway to food production it demands some discussion. Factors that may have contributed to the establishment of selective breeding and full domestication include intensification of agricultural production and reduction of wild habitats, the transfer of semidomesticated ungulates across major ecological boundaries, and the development of specialized uses such as sacrifice, milking, and traction.

A generalized explanation of this process could be sought in the gradual development and spread of agriculture in and around the periphery of the southwestern Asian upland, accompanied by increases in population and sedentary settlement and by the progressive degradation of the forests, woodlands, and grasslands in which wild and semidomesticated ungulates browsed and grazed. Certainly as cultivation came more and more to dominate subsistence activities the incentive to protect fields and crops from free-ranging, semidomesticated ungulates would have increased. The intensifying conflict between crops and ungulates could be resolved either by eliminating the animals or by establishing closer control over them through confinement. Which course was followed would depend upon the place particular animals held in the value system of the people involved. The association with man of animals that were only marginally valued would gradually weaken and they would either be eliminated or revert to a wild state, but for animals that fulfilled important economic and social roles efforts would be made to retain a breeding population under human control. The clue to understanding why certain species were fully domesticated may therefore lie in an evaluation of the socioeconomic roles of ungulates within the general southwestern Asian context of intensifying agriculture, sedentism, and the degradation of wild habitats.

A particular process that may have accentuated a tendency for breeding populations to be retained under control is their transfer to new habitats. If groups already exploiting semidomesticated ungulates migrated across major ecological boundaries and established long-term settlements in new habitats, or if trading or tribute links resulted in the transfer of animals across such boundaries, closer control likely would be exerted over the transferred animals, and opportunities for interbreeding with wild populations would be reduced. In these circumstances natural and cultural selection would tend to evolve races which were both adapted to the changed environmental conditions and more directly under human control. Thus a closer dependence of ungulate on man would become established, involving selective control of reproduction and leading to the emergence of phenotypically distinct, fully domesticated breeds. Such a process, associated in particular with the spread of agricultural settlement onto the alluvial lowlands of Mesopotamia, may help to explain the full domestication of several types of social ungulates in southwestern Asia, as was suggested for woolly sheep by Flannery (1965: Figure 4), but it does not bring us appreciably closer to understanding why particular ungulates only were fully domesticated and incorporated into the developing socioeconomic systems of southwestern Asia.

Direct evidence bearing on the economic and social roles of social ungulates in "Neolithic" southwestern Asia is extremely meager so that it is impossible to establish with any confidence when the use of particular species for such special purposes as sacrifice, milking, traction, and fiber production first became established. One commonly assumes that ungulates were first valued for their meat (Herre 1969:267), and to a lesser extent for their hides and hair. Such interest may account for the semidomestication of many ungulates, particularly if, as I have suggested, semidomestication was more the result of changing ecological relationships than of deliberate choice of man. But, the work of Simoons (1968) on the mithan demonstrates that free-ranging cattle can be tended for their social value as sacrificial and prestige-conferring objects rather than for their economic value as producers of meat, milk, hair, and hides. This possibility is seldom considered in the context of southwestern Asia, but conceivably some of the early relationships that developed there between man and ungulate rested primarily on the significance that certain animals acquired as objects of sacrifice and symbols of fertility and prestige.

A case for the ritual domestication of common cattle from the wild aurochs in the Near East was first made by Hahn (1896). More recently, the idea has been reexamined and modified by Isaac (1962) and by Simoons (1968:234–264), and its protagonists find support in the discovery of abundant evidence of a cattle cult at the site of Çatal Hüyük in Anatolia, dating to the seventh millennium B.C. (Mellaart 1967:77–177). This hypothesis will not be examined here, but it does point to the possible importance of noneconomic factors in the domestication of cattle. What, if any, role ritual may have played in the domestication of other ungulates remains unknown, but it may be significant, as Isaac has argued (1970:105–109), that the three main genera of ungulates domesticated early in the Near East — cattle, sheep, and goats — all have crescent- or scimitar-shaped horns, which are symbolically associated with the lunar goddess, whose cult was widespread in the ancient Near East. The ritual roles of ungulates may have more relevance to the question of why certain species crossed the threshold from partial to full domestication than is generally supposed, and this topic certainly deserves more scholarly attention than it has so far received.

Another factor that may have contributed to the full domestication of particular ungulates is an increasing interest in them as providers of milk. It is a striking fact that all the domestic herd animals associated with southwestern Asia are or have been valued for their milk and that traditionally milking was confined to Eurasia and Africa (C. Sauer 1952: 86–87 and Plate IV). Even within those continents milking was not practiced in eastern and southeastern Asia or in central Africa, where milk was either unknown as a food or strongly rejected (Simoons 1954, 1970a; Wheatley 1965). Nor is there evidence of milking in the Americas, where the only indigenous domesticated ungulates, the Andean llama and alpaca, are thought never to have been used as a source of milk for human food (Gade 1969). The fact that milking is, except for the pig, a use common to all the domestic ungulates associated with southwestern Asia, which differentiates their usage from that of all wild ungulates and of the domesticated Andean camelids, strengthens the supposition that selection for artificially increased and prolonged lactation contributed to their full domestication. In the wild state lactation is restricted to the period of suckling, and a variety of techniques are known ethnographically whereby the milk-ejection reflex is stimulated artificially to allow ungulates to be milked by humans (Amoroso and Jewell 1963). Milking probably began with animals in a state of semidomestication and may have originated as a means of relieving adult females whose suckling young had been killed, but the time required to select milk-yielding breeds with enlarged udders and prolonged lactation implies closer and more sustained control over reproduction than free-range management allows.

Evidence for the antiquity of milking is elusive and often ambiguous, but there is conclusive proof of it in Mesopotamia by around 2900 B.C., in Egypt by around 3100 B.C., and in the Sahara between 6000 and 5000 B.C., although it was probably practiced considerably earlier in all three areas (Simoons 1971). In Europe and India the earliest definite proof of milking derives from 1500 B.C. onwards in Minoan, Greek, and Vedic records, but again there are indirect indications of its greater antiquity (Simoons 1970b:703–705). Confirmation of the traditional distribution of milking and nonmilking peoples is also emerging from studies of primary lactose intolerance among present-day human populations, and the evidence that differences in lactose tolerance are mainly inherited and have been subject to genetic selection over many generations supports arguments for the antiquity of milking in Eurasia and northern Africa (Simoons 1969, 1970b).

The inference that the development of milking played an important part in the full domestication of the social animals associated with southwestern Asia is thus strengthened by much circumstantial evidence. However, milking is unlikely to have been equally important in the domestication of all of them. Most of the early evidence of milking relates to cattle and it is from them, together with goats (Harris 1962), that selective breeding in ancient times produced the most numerous and specialized milk-yielding varieties. By comparison, although sheep, ass, horse, Bactrian camel, and dromedary (Mikesell 1955:245) have all traditionally been milked, none has been intensively bred for milk yield and the development of other uses, such as production of meat and fibers, burden bearing, and/or riding, may largely account for their emergence as fully domesticated animals in prehistoric western Eurasia and northern Africa.

The use of social animals for traction, and in particular their use in pulling plows, is often regarded as a contributory reason for their domestication, along with their exploitation for meat and milk. However the earliest definite evidence of the use of animals for draft purposes — Mesopotamian representations of cattle harnessed to sledges and wagons in religious processions and pulling plows attended by priests (Isaac 1962:198) — dates from the latter half of the fourth millennium B.C., over two millennia later than the dates attributed to "domestic" cattle at sites in eastern Europe and the Near East. As with the development of milch cows, it must be presumed that the emergence of relatively docile breeds of draft cattle was the outcome of selective breeding sustained over long periods of time. One critical step in this process may have been the discovery that castration of bulls produced more tractable animals with meat of superior texture. Isaac (1962) has argued that the involvement of the ox in agriculture, particularly its use to pull plows, grew out of the earlier ritual role of cattle in Near Eastern fertility cults, and a similar argument can be made for the ritual origins of milking (Simoons 1968:259–263).

In sum, therefore, I would postulate first a prolonged phase in southwestern Asia and adjacent regions, during which sheep, goats, cattle, and possibly other ungulates became semidomesticated as free-ranging animals breeding in the wild but loosely controlled by man, mainly through the provision of salt (Figure 6). The spread of swidden cultivation in forests and woodlands probably reinforced this developing man–ungulate relationship, and it is possible that cattle and perhaps other ungulates were valued as much for their social significance as sacrificial objects and symbols of fertility and prestige as economically for their meat, hides, and hair. I presume that specialized uses such as milking, wool production, traction, and riding were dependent on selective breeding and only developed later in the context of full domestication.

Secondly, a shift from free-range management to confinement is postulated (Figure 6) in relation to the gradual intensification of agriculture and sedentism that accompanied population growth and caused the progressive degradation of forests and other wild habitats. Confinement necessitates feeding, and the process of ungulate domestication is likely to have been further reinforced by extending the provision of fodder to include uprooted wild or cultivated cereals as well as the harvested leaves of, for example, oak and pistachio (Bohrer 1972). Certain ungulates that had probably become semidomesticated, for example gazelle in Palestine, failed to become established as staple domesticated resources. Cattle, sheep, and goats did so because they already fulfilled such important socioeconomic needs that efforts were made to establish populations breeding in confinement. The most adequate explanation at present of why cattle were fully domesticated derives from their symbolic significance rather than just from their subsistence value. Sacrificial and other ritual uses may have been of paramount importance in leading to deliberate attempts at selective breeding. Later, as cattle cults declined and special breeds were developed, mundane uses of cattle for milk production and agricultural traction replaced formerly sacred ones and the fully domesticated animals became integrated into fixed-field systems of mixed farming.

Whether goats and perhaps sheep followed a similar pathway to full domestication is quite uncertain, but the possibility that their attainment of the status of cult animals in association with cattle resulted in their shifting from partial to full domestication deserves study. The same possibility might be envisaged for the other ungulates domesticated in the Old World, but the equids and camels, notably hornless, appear to have had less symbolic significance and to have been fully domesticated later than the horned Bovini and Caprini. Horses and camels were probably domesticated in areas peripheral to the southwestern Asian upland, and their economic uses for meat, milk, burden bearing, and riding may largely account for their domestication, particularly if it is assumed to have taken place after bovine and caprine domestication was already established. Reindeer likewise appear not to have become cult animals and in any case they never became as fully domesticated as the other Old World domestic ungulates, remaining unconfined and dependent on wild foods.

The hypothesis developed here goes some way to explain why specialization in the exploitation of social ungulates led to the full domestication of several genera in Eurasia and northern Africa but failed to do so in almost all other parts of the world where ungulates were hunted. The exception of the domestication of the llama and alpaca in the central Andes appears anomalous, but like reindeer, these ungulates remained unconfined and dependent on wild foods, although tended by herdsmen. They were valued for meat, wool, burden bearing and sacrifice, and particular shrines had their own herds (Murra 1965: 201–202), but the failure of llama and alpaca to become completely domesticated may be explicable in terms of the maintenance of a relatively mobile pattern of transhumant herding and the fact that they were never integrated into a system of fixed-field mixed agriculture as consumers of fodder and providers of manure, as were cattle and to a lesser extent sheep and goats in prehistoric Eurasia.

In this exploration of the problem of the origins of agriculture I have deliberately adopted a broad perspective in the belief that a comparative approach is a necessary complement to the work of regional and subject specialists. By adopting a systemic framework and proposing a general model for the transition from foraging to food production I hope to raise questions of general significance that field investigation may seek to resolve. The model itself represents a greatly simplified, partial view of the complex, real-world situations that led to the emergence of agriculture, but it does so because I have sought to frame it in a form that is both internally consistent and susceptible to testing against archaeological and ethnographic data. For that reason I have not attempted to integrate into the model relevant nonmaterial variables, such as the ritual significance and regulation of populations of plants and animals and other aspects of information exchange in social systems, although in the text I have discussed some nonmaterial variables where they seem most relevant.

Given the present state of knowledge of hunter-gatherer and early food-producing societies, a more elaborate model would, although more satisfactory theoretically, suffer in practice from redundancy because many of the relationships posited would remain untestable. To students of higher levels of socioeconomic integration than early food production more data are available on nonmaterial variables, and their models, appropriately, incorporate these more fully, as is well illustrated for example in recent work by Flannery (1972) and Renfrew (1972). However, "back in the Neolithic," we still need to formulate and test more rudimentary hypotheses that relate to modes of subsistence, levels of population, and patterns of settlement. This paper represents one such attempt, and in writing it I have sought to demonstrate that it is necessary and fruitful to examine developmental pathways that did not lead to agriculture within the same framework as those that did.

REFERENCES

ALEXANDER, J., D. G. COURSEY
  1969 "The origins of yam cultivation," in *The domestication and exploitation of plants and animals*. Edited by Peter J. Ucko and G. W. Dimbleby, 405–425. London: Duckworth.
AMOROSO, E. C., P. A. JEWELL
  1963 The exploitation of the milk-ejection reflex by primitive peoples. *Occasional Papers of the Royal Anthropological Institute* 18:126–137.
BARRAU, JACQUES
  1965 L'humide et le sec: an essay on ethnobiological adaptation to contrastive environments in the Indo-Pacific area. *Journal of the Polynesian Society* 74:329–346.
  1970 La région indo-pacifique comme centre de mise en culture et de domestication des végétaux. *Journal d'Agriculture Tropicale et de Botanique Appliquée* 17:487–504.
BAYARD, DONN T.
  1973 Excavations at Non Nok Tha, northeastern Thailand. *Asian Perspectives* 13:109–143.
BENEDICT, BURTON
  1972 "Social regulation of fertility," in *The structure of human populations*. Edited by G. A. Harrison and A. J. Boyce, 73–89. Oxford: Clarendon Press.

BINFORD, LEWIS R.
1968 "Post-Pleistocene adaptations," in *New perspectives in archeoiogy.* Edited by Sally R. Binford and Lewis R. Binford, 313–341. Chicago: Aldine.

BOHRER, VORSILA L.
1972 On the relation of harvest methods to early agriculture in the Near East. *Economic Botany* 26:145–155.

BRAIDWOOD, ROBERT J.
1960 The agricultural revolution. *Scientific American* 203(3):130–148.
1961 *Prehistoric men* (fifth edition). Chicago Natural History Museum Popular Series, Anthropology, 37.

BRAIDWOOD, ROBERT J., BRUCE HOWE
1960 *Prehistoric investigations in Iraqi Kurdistan.* Oriental Institute Studies in Ancient Oriental Civilization 31. Chicago: University of Chicago Press.

BRAIDWOOD, ROBERT J., GORDON R. WILLEY
1962 "Conclusions and afterthoughts," in *Courses toward urban life.* Edited by Robert J. Braidwood and Gordon R. Willey, 330–359. Chicago: Aldine.

BUTZER, KARL W.
1972 *Environment and archeology: an ecological approach to prehistory* (second edition). London: Methuen.

CALDWELL, JOSEPH R.
1962 "Eastern North America," in *Courses toward urban life.* Edited by Robert J. Braidwood and Gordon R. Willey, 288–308. Chicago: Aldine.

CALLEN, E. O.
1967 The first New World cereal. *American Antiquity* 32:535–538.

CARNEIRO, ROBERT L.
1970 A theory of the origin of the state. *Science* 169:733–738.

CHANG, KWANG-CHIH
1968 *The archaeology of ancient China* (second edition). New Haven and London: Yale University Press.
1970 The beginnings of agriculture in the Far East. *Antiquity* 44:175–185.

CHILDE, V. GORDON
1941 *Man makes himself.* London: Watts.

CLARK, GRAHAME
1961 *World prehistory: an outline.* Cambridge: Cambridge University Press.

CLARK, J. D.
1971 A re-examination of the evidence for agricultural origins in the Nile valley. *Proceedings of the Prehistoric Society* 37:34–79.
1976 "Prehistoric populations and pressures favouring plant domestication in Africa," *Origins of African plant domestication.* Edited by Jack R. Harlan, Jan. M. J. de Wet, and Ann B. L. Stemler, 67–105. World Anthropology. The Hague: Mouton.

COURSEY, D. G.
1967 *Yams.* London: Longmans, Green.
1976 "The origins and domestication of yams in Africa," in *Origins of African plant domestication.* Edited by Jack R. Harlan, Jan M. J. de

Wet, and Ann B.L. Stemler, 383–408. World Anthropology. The Hague: Mouton.

COURSEY, D. G., C. K. COURSEY
1971 The New Yam festivals of West Africa. *Anthropos* 66:444–484.

DE WET, J. M. J., J. R. HARLAN
1971 The origin and domestication of *Sorghum bicolor. Economic Botany* 25:128–135.
1972 Origin of maize: the tripartite hypothesis. *Euphytica* 21:271–279.

DONKIN, R. A.
1970 Pre-Columbian field implements and their distribution in the highlands of Middle and South America. *Anthropos* 65:505–529.

DORE, WILLIAM G.
1969 *Wild-rice.* Research Branch, Canada Department of Agriculture, Publication 1393. Ottawa.

DRUCKER, PHILLIP
1963 *Indians of the Northwest coast.* Garden City, New York: Natural History Press.

DUNN, FREDERICK L.
1968 "Epidemiological factors: health and disease in hunter-gatherers," in *Man the hunter.* Edited by Richard B. Lee and Irven DeVore, 221–228. Chicago: Aldine.

EISELEY, LOREN C.
1954 Man the fire-maker. *Scientific American* 191(3):52–57.

FLANNERY, KENT V.
1965 The ecology of early food production in Mesopotamia. *Science* 147: 1247–1256.
1968 "Archeological systems theory and early Mesoamerica," in *Anthropological archeology in the Americas.* Edited by Betty J. Meggers, 67–87. Washington, D.C.: Anthropological Society of Washington.
1969 "Origins and ecological effects of early domestication in Iran and the Near East," in *The domestication and exploitation of plants and animals.* Edited by Peter J. Ucko and G. W. Dimbleby, 73–100. London: Duckworth.
1972 The cultural evolution of civilizations. *Annual Review of Ecology and Systematics* 3: 399–426.

FORDE, C. DARYLL
1949 *Habitat, economy and society* (seventh edition). London: Methuen.

GADE, DANIEL W.
1969 The llama, alpaca and vicuña: fact vs. fiction. *Journal of Geography* 68: 339–343.
1970 Ethnobotany of cañihau (*Chenopodium pallidicaule*), rustic seed crop of the Altiplano. *Economic Botany* 24: 55–61.

GEIST, VALERIUS
1971 *Mountain sheep: a study in behaviour and evolution.* Chicago and London: University of Chicago Press.

GODWIN, H.
1956 *The history of the British flora.* Cambridge: Cambridge University Press.

GOLSON, JACK
1971 "Australian aboriginal food plants: some ecological and culture-historical implications," in *Aboriginal man and environment in Australia*. Edited by D. J. Mulvaney and J. Golson, 196–238. Canberra: Australian National University Press.

GORMAN, CHESTER F.
1969 Hoabinhian: a pebble-tool complex with early plant associations in Southeast Asia. *Science* 163:671–673.
1971 The Hoabinhian and after: subsistence patterns in Southeast Asia during the late Pleistocene and early Recent periods. *World Archaeology* 2: 300–320.
1973 Excavations at Spirit Cave, North Thailand: some interim interpretations. *Asian Perspectives* 13:79–107.

GOULD, RICHARD A.
1969 *Yiwara: foragers of the Australian desert*. New York: Scribner.

HAGERTY, MICHAEL J.
1940 Comments on writings concerning Chinese sorghums. *Harvard Journal of Asiatic Studies* 5: 234–263.

HAHN, EDUARD
1896 *Die Haustiere und ihre Beziehungen zur Wirtschaft des Menschen*. Leipzig: Duncker and Humblot.

HANKS, LUCIEN M.
1972 *Rice and man: agricultural ecology in Southeast Asia*. Chicago: Aldine-Atherton.

HARLAN, JACK R.
1967 A wild-wheat harvest in Turkey. *Archaeology* 20: 197–201.
1969 Ethiopia: a center of diversity. *Economic Botany* 23: 309–314.

HARLAN, JACK R., J. M. J. DE WET., E. GLEN PRICE
1973 Comparative evolution of cereals. *Evolution* 27: 311–325.

HARLAN, JACK R., DANIEL ZOHARY
1966 Distribution of wild wheats and barley. *Science* 153:1074–1080.

HARRIS, DAVID R.
1962 The distribution and ancestry of the domestic goat. *Proceedings of the Linnean Society of London* 173:79–91.
1965 *Plants, animals, and man in the outer Leeward Islands, West Indies: an ecological study of Antigua, Barbuda, and Anguilla*. University of California Publications in Geography 18. Berkeley and Los Angeles: University of California Press.
1969 "Agricultural systems, ecosystems and the origins of agriculture," in *The domestication and exploitation of plants and animals*. Edited by Peter J. Ucko and G. W. Dimbleby, 3–15. London: Duckworth.
1971 The ecology of swidden cultivation in the upper Orinoco rain forest, Venezuela. *Geographical Review* 61: 475–495.
1972 The origins of agriculture in the tropics. *American Scientist* 60:180–193.
1973 "The prehistory of tropical agriculture: an ethnoecological model," in *The explanation of culture change: models in prehistory*. Edited by Colin Renfrew. London: Duckworth.
1974 Rice and man in Southeast Asia. *Geographical Review* 64: 140–142.

1976 "Traditional systems of plant food production and the origins of agriculture in West Africa," in *Origins of African plant domestication.* Edited by Jack R. Harlan, Jan M.J. de Wet, and Ann B.L. Stemler, 311–356. World Anthropology. The Hague: Mouton

HAWKES, J. G.
  1967 The history of the potato, Part I. *Journal of the Royal Horticultural Society* 92:207–224.
  1969 "The ecological background of plant domestication," in *The domestication and exploitation of plants and animals.* Edited by Peter J. Ucko and G. W. Dimbleby, 17–29. London: Duckworth.

HAYDEN, BRIAN
  1972 Population control among hunter/gatherers. *World Archaeology* 4: 205–221.

HERRE, WOLF
  1969 "The science and history of domestic animals," in *Science in archaeology* (second edition), 257–272. London: Thames and Hudson.

HIGGS, E. S., *editor*
  1972 *Papers in economic prehistory.* Cambridge: Cambridge University Press.

HIGGS, E. S., M. R. JARMAN
  1969 The origins of agriculture: a reconsideration. *Antiquity* 43:31–41.

HIGHAM, C. F. W.
  1972 "Initial model formulation *in terra incognita*," in *Models in archaeology.* Edited by David L. Clarke, 453–476. London: Methuen.

HIGHAM, C. F. W., B. F. LEACH
  1971 An early center of bovine husbandry in Southeast Asia. *Science* 172: 54–56.

HO, PING-TI
  1969 The loess and the origin of Chinese agriculture. *American Historical Review* 75:1–36.

HOBLER, PHILIP M., JAMES J. HESTER
  1969 Prehistory and environment in the Libyan desert. *South African Archaeological Journal* 23:119–130.

HYMOWITZ, T.
  1970 On the domestication of the soybean. *Economic Botany* 24:408–421.

ISAAC, ERICH
  1962 On the domestication of cattle. *Science* 137:195–204.
  1970 *Geography of domestication.* Englewood Cliffs, N.J.: Prentice-Hall.

JANZEN, DANIEL H.
  1970 The unexploited tropics. *Bulletin of the Ecological Society of America* 51:4–7.

JARMAN, MICHAEL R.
  1971 Culture and economy in the north Italian Neolithic. *World Archaeology* 2:255–265.
  1972 "European deer economies and the advent of the Neolithic," in *Papers in economic prehistory.* Edited by E. S. Higgs, 125–147. Cambridge: Cambridge University Press.

JARMAN, MICHAEL R., P. F. WILKINSON
  1972 "Criteria of animal domestication," in *Papers in economic prehistory.*

Edited by E. S. Higgs, 83–96. Cambridge: Cambridge University Press.

JEWELL, P. A.
1969 "Wild mammals and their potential for new domestication," in *The domestication and exploitation of plants and animals.* Edited by Peter J. Ucko and G. W. Dimbleby, 101–109. London: Duckworth.

KAPLAN, L., THOMAS F. LYNCH, C. E. SMITH, JR.
1973 Early cultivated beans (*Phaseolus vulgaris*) from an intermontane Peruvian valley. *Science* 179:76–77.

KRAMER, FRITZ L.
1967 Eduard Hahn and the end of the "three stages of man." *Geographical Review* 62: 73–89.

KUNSTADTER, PETER
1972 "Demography, ecology, social structure, and settlement patterns," in *The structure of human populations.* Edited by G. A. Harrison and A. J. Boyce, 313–351. Oxford: Clarendon Press.

LATHRAP, DONALD W.
1970 *The Upper Amazon.* London: Thames and Hudson.
1973 "Gifts of the Cayman: some thoughts on the subsistence basis of Chavín," in *Variation in anthropology.* Edited by D. W. Lathrap and J. Douglas, 91–105. Urbana, Ill.: Illinois Archaeological Survey.

LEE, RICHARD B.
1968 "What hunters do for a living, or how to make out on scarce resources," in *Man the hunter.* Edited by Richard B. Lee and Irven DeVore, 30–48. Chicago: Aldine.
1969 "!Kung Bushman subsistence: an input-output analysis," in *Environment and cultural behaviour.* Edited by Andrew P. Vayda, 47–79. Garden City, N.Y.: Natural History Press.
1972 "Population growth and the beginnings of sedentary life among the !Kung bushmen," in *Population growth: anthropological implications.* Edited by Brian Spooner, 329–342. Cambridge, Mass.: M.I.T. Press.

LEE, RICHARD B., IRVEN DE VORE
1968 "Problems in the study of hunters and gatherers," in *Man the hunter.* Edited by Richard B. Lee and Irven DeVore, 3–12. Chicago: Aldine.

LEEDS, ANTHONY
1965 "Reindeer herding and Chukchi social institutions," in *Man, culture, and animals.* Edited by Anthony Leeds and Andrew P. Vayda, 87–128. American Association for the Advancement of Science Publication 78. Washington, D.C.

LEGGE, A. J.
1972 "Prehistoric exploitation of the gazelle in Palestine," in *Papers in economic prehistory.* Edited by E. S. Higgs, 119–124. Cambridge: Cambridge University Press.

LEWIS, HENRY T.
1972 The role of fire in the domestication of plants and animals in southwest Asia: a hypothesis. *Man* 7:195–222.

LYNCH, THOMAS F.
1971 Preceramic transhumance in the Callejón de Huaylas, Peru. *American Antiquity* 36:139–148.

MC CARTHY, FREDERICK D.
1957   Habitat, economy and equipment of the Australian Aborigines. *Australian Journal of Science* 19:88–97.

MC CARTHY, FREDERICK D., MARGARET MC ARTHUR
1960   "The food quest and the time factor in aboriginal economic life," in *Records of the American-Australian scientific expedition to Arnhem Land*, volume two: *Anthropology and nutrition*. Edited by Charles P. Mountford, 145–194. Melbourne: Melbourne University Press.

MAC NEISH, RICHARD S.
1967   "A summary of the subsistence," in *The prehistory of the Tehuacan valley*, volume one: *Environment and subsistence*. Edited by Douglas S. Byers, 290–309. Austin and London: University of Texas Press.
1969   *First annual report of the Ayacucho archaeological-botanical project.* Andover, Mass.: R. S. Peabody Foundation.
1972   "The evolution of community patterns in the Tehuacán Valley of Mexico and speculations about the cultural processes," in *Man, settlement and urbanism*. Edited by Peter J. Ucko, Ruth Tringham, and G. W. Dimbleby, 67–93. London: Duckworth.

MAC NEISH, RICHARD S., A. NELKEN-TERNER, ANGEL G. COOK
1970   *Second annual report of the Ayacucho archaeological-botanical project.* Andover, Mass.: R. S. Peabody Foundation.

MARTIN, P. S., H. E. WRIGHT, JR., editors
1967   *Pleistocene extinctions: the search for a cause.* New Haven: Yale University Press.

MELLAART, JAMES
1967   *Çatal Hüyük: a Neolithic town in Anatolia.* London: Thames and Hudson.

MIKESELL, MARVIN W.
1955   Notes on the dispersal of the dromedary. *Southwestern Journal of Anthropology* 11:231–245.

MOSELEY, M. EDWARD
1972   Subsistence and demography: an example of interaction from pre-historic Peru. *Southwestern Journal of Anthropology* 28:25–49.

MUNSON, PATRICK J.
1976   "Archaeological data on the origins of cultivation in the southwestern Sahara and their implications for West Africa," in *Origins of African plant domestication*. Edited by Jack R. Harlan, Jan M. J. de Wet, and Ann B. L. Stemler, 187–209. World Anthropology. The Hague: Mouton.

MUNSON, PATRICK J., PAUL W. PARMALEE, RICHARD A. YARNELL
1971   Subsistence ecology of Scovill, a terminal Middle Woodland village. *American Antiquity* 36:410–431.

MURDOCK, G. P.
1967   *Ethnographic atlas: a summary.* Pittsburgh: University of Pittsburgh Press.

MURRA, JOHN V.
1965   "Herds and herders in the Inca state," in *Man, culture, and animals*. Edited by Anthony Leeds and Andrew P. Vayda, 185–215. American

Association for the Advancement of Science Publication 78. Washington, D.C.

PATTERSON, THOMAS C.
1971   "The emergence of food production in central Peru," in *Prehistoric agriculture*. Edited by Stuart Struever, 181–207. Garden City, N.Y.: Natural History Press.

PENNINGTON, WINIFRED
1969   *The history of British vegetation*. London: English Universities Press.

PERKINS, DEXTER
1964   The prehistoric fauna from Shanidar, Iraq. *Science* 144:1565–1566.

PORTÈRES, ROLAND
1951   Une céréale mineure cultivée dans l'Ouest Afrique (*Brachiaria deflexa* C. E. Hubbard, var. *sativa* nov. var.). *L'Agronomie Tropicale* 6:38–42.

PROTSCH, REINER, RAINER BERGER
1973   Earliest radiocarbon dates for domesticated animals. *Science* 179: 235–239.

REED, CHARLES A.
1969   "The pattern of animal domestication in the prehistoric Near East," in *The domestication and exploitation of plants and animals*. Edited by Peter J. Ucko and G. W. Dimbleby, 361–380. London: Duckworth.
1970   Extinction of mammalian megafauna in the Old World Late Quaternary. *BioScience* 20:284–288.

RENFREW, COLIN
1972   *The emergence of civilisation: the Cyclades and the Aegean in the third millennium B.C.* London: Methuen.

RENVOIZE, BARBARA S.
1970   "Manioc (*Manihot esculenta* Crantz) and its role in the Amerindian agriculture of tropical America." Unpublished thesis submitted for the degree of M.Phil. in the University of London.
1972   The area of origin of *Manihot esculenta* as a crop plant — a review of the evidence. *Economic Botany* 26:352–360.

SAHLINS, MARSHALL D.
1968   "Notes on the original affluent society," in *Man the hunter*. Edited by Richard B. Lee and Irven DeVore, 85–89. Chicago: Aldine.
1972   *Stone age economics*. Chicago and New York: Aldine-Atherton.

SAUER, CARL O.
1948   Environment and culture during the last deglaciation. *Proceedings of the American Philosophical Society* 92:65–77.
1950   "Cultivated plants of South and Central America," in *Handbook of South American Indians*, volume six. Edited by Julian H. Steward, 487–543. Washington: Smithsonian Institution, Bureau of American Ethnology.
1952   *Agricultural origins and dispersals*. New York: American Geographical Society.
1958   Jericho and composite sickles. *Antiquity* 32: 187–189.

SAUER, JONATHAN D.
1950   The grain amaranths: a survey of their history and classification. *Annals of the Missouri Botanical Garden* 37: 561–632.
1967   The grain amaranths and their relatives: a revised taxonomic and

geographic survey. *Annals of the Missouri Botanical Garden* 54: 103–137.

1969 Identity of archaeologic grain amaranths from the valley of Tehuacán, Puebla, Mexico. *American Antiquity* 34:80–81.

SERVICE, ELMAN R.
1966 *The hunters.* Englewood Cliffs, N.J.: Prentice-Hall.

SHAW, THURSTON
1969 The late stone age in the Nigerian forest. *Études et documents tchadiens, Mémoires* 1:364–373.

SIMMONDS, N. W.
1965 The grain chenopods of the tropical American highlands. *Economic Botany* 19:223–235.

SIMOONS, FREDERICK J.
1954 The non-milking area of Africa. *Anthropos* 49:58–66.
1960 *Northwest Ethiopia: peoples and economy.* Madison: University of Wisconsin Press.
1968 *A ceremonial ox of India: the mithan in nature, culture, and history.* Madison: University of Wisconsin Press.
1969 Primary adult lactose intolerance and the milking habit: a problem in biological and cultural interrelations, I: Review of the medical research. *American Journal of Digestive Diseases,* new series 14: 819–836.
1970a The traditional limits of milking and milk use in southern Asia. *Anthropos* 65:547–593.
1970b Primary adult lactose intolerance and the milking habit: a problem in biologic and cultural interrelations, II: A culture historical hypothesis. *American Journal of Digestive Diseases,* new series 15:695–710.
1971 The antiquity of dairying in Asia and Africa. *Geographical Review* 61: 431–439.

SMITH, PHILIP E. L.
1972 Changes in population pressure in archaeological explanation. *World Archaeology* 4:5–18.

SOLHEIM, WILHELM G., II
1972 An earlier agricultural revolution. *Scientific American* 226(4):34–41.

SPENCER, J. E.
1966 *Shifting cultivation in southeastern Asia.* University of California Publications in Geography 19. Berkeley and Los Angeles: University of California Press.

SPOONER, BRIAN, *editor*
1972 *Population growth: anthropological implications.* Cambridge, Mass.: M.I.T. Press.

STEWART, OMER C.
1956 "Fire as the first great force employed by man," in *Man's role in changing the face of the earth.* Edited by William L. Thomas, Jr., 115–133. Chicago: University of Chicago Press.

STRUEVER, STUART
1968 "Woodland subsistence-settlement systems in the lower Illinois valley," in *New perspectives in archeology.* Edited by Sally R. Binford and Lewis R. Binford, 285–312. Chicago: Aldine.

SUTTLES, WAYNE
  1960   Affinal ties, subsistence, and prestige among the Coast Salish. *American Anthropologist* 62:296–305.
  1968   "Coping with abundance: subsistence on the Northwest Coast," in *Man the hunter*. Edited by Richard B. Lee and Irven DeVore, 56–68. Chicago: Aldine.
TURNBULL, COLIN M.
  1968   "The importance of flux in two hunting societies," in *Man the hunter*. Edited by Richard B. Lee and Irven DeVore, 132–137. Chicago: Aldine.
  1972   "Demography of small-scale societies," in *The structure of human populations*. Edited by G. A. Harrison and A. J. Boyce, 283–312. Oxford: Clarendon Press.
UGENT, DONALD
  1970   The potato. *Science* 170:1161–1166.
VAN LOON, MAURITS
  1966   Mureybat: an early village in inland Syria. *Archaeology* 19:215–216.
VAN ZEIST, W.
  1969   "Reflections on prehistoric environments in the Near East," in *The domestication and exploitation of plants and animals*. Edited by Peter J. Ucko and G. W. Dimbleby, 35–46. London: Duckworth.
WATANABE, HITOSHI
  1968   "Subsistence and ecology of northern food gatherers with special reference to the Ainu," in *Man the hunter*. Edited by Richard B. Lee and Irven DeVore, 69–77. Chicago: Aldine.
WATERBOLK, H. T.
  1968   Food production in prehistoric Europe. *Science* 162:1093–1102.
WENDORF, FRED, ROMUALD SCHILD
  1976   "The use of ground grain during the Late Paleolithic of the lower Nile valley, Egypt," in *Origins of African plant domestication*. Edited by Jack R. Harlan, Jan M. J. de Wet, and Ann B. L. Stemler, 269–288. World Anthropology. The Hague: Mouton.
WHEATLEY, PAUL
  1965   A note on the extension of milking practices into Southeast Asia during the first millennium A.D. *Anthropos* 60:577–590.
  1971   *The pivot of the four quarters: a preliminary enquiry into the origins and character of the ancient Chinese city*. Edinburgh: Edinburgh University Press.
WHITE, J. PETER
  1971   "New Guinea and Australian prehistory: the 'Neolithic problem'," in *Aboriginal man and environment in Australia*. Edited by D. J. Mulvaney and J. Golson, 182–195. Canberra: Australian National University Press.
WILKE, PHILIP J., ROBERT BETTINGER, THOMAS F. KING, JAMES F. O'CONNELL
  1972   Harvest selection and domestication in seed plants. *Antiquity* 46:203–209.
WILKES, H. GARRISON
  1972   Maize and its wild relatives. *Science* 177:1071–1077.

WILKINSON, PAUL F.
  1972a Oomingmak: a model for man–animal relationships in prehistory. *Current Anthropology* 13:23–44.
  1972b "Current experimental domestication and its relevance to prehistory," in *Papers in economic prehistory*. Edited by E. S. Higgs, 107–118. Cambridge: Cambridge University Press.
WINTERS, HOWARD D.
  1969 *The Riverton culture: a second millenium occupation of the central Wabash valley*. Springfield, Ill.: Illinois State Museum and Illinois Archaeological Survey.
WOODBURN, JAMES
  1968 "An introduction to Hadza ecology," in *Man the hunter*. Edited by Richard B. Lee and Irven DeVore, 49–55. Chicago: Aldine.
WRIGHT, H. E., JR.
  1968 Natural environment of early food production north of Mesopotamia. *Science* 161:334–339.
WRIGHT, H. E., JR., J. H. ANDREWS, W. VAN ZEIST
  1967 Modern pollen rain in western Iran and its application to plant geography and Quaternary vegetational history. *Journal of Ecology* 55:415–443.
ZOHARY, DANIEL
  1969 "The progenitors of wheat and barley in relation to domestication and agricultural dispersal in the Old World," in *The domestication and exploitation of plants and animals*. Edited by Peter J. Ucko and G. W. Dimbleby, 47–66. London: Duckworth.

Zoological Considerations on the Origins of Farming and Domestication

WOLF HERRE and MANFRED RÖHRS

Agriculture and animal husbandry belong to the important economic foundations of human civilization. As economic profit is obtained from biological objects, biologists are called upon to take part in discussions on the evolution of farming. If zoologists are asked to make a point on the beginning of animal husbandry, they will be most useful if they define the zoological view more clearly in order to stress the difference between their point of view and that of the more economico-historical pattern of interpretation of the archaeologist. This contrasting will also contribute to a better understanding of the opportunities and limits of the zoologists' cooperation.

Zoologists investigate the variability of animal species and their adaptations to certain environmental conditions and changes, and they try to study the evolution of these differentiations and their causes in the course of history. Zoologists study domestic animals as these are derived from wild species because, compared to their wild ancestral stock, they show differences which are often quite remarkable, which may appear in a similar way in species rather different from each other, and which often are of primary importance to economic efficiency. Although these traits are mostly quite unusual for wild species, zoologists consider them as models for many events which occurred during natural evolution (Herre and Röhrs 1973), especially since Darwin (1868) aroused people's interest in domestic animals. Man's influence is viewed from a context of nature, while the domestic response of animals is interpreted biologally. Hence, from the biological angle, domestication does not count as a special phenomenon. The zoologist asks questions concerning the origins of, the duration of, and the events during the domestication, and the answers elucidate some general problem areas of zoology. Two questions have always interested the zoologist: why did only five of seventeen recent animal orders furnish ancestors of domestic animals, and why is the number of species which developed into "classical" domestic animals so small in comparison to the multitude of forms within each of the respective orders? Do these facts have to be attributed to the qualities of the biological material or is it a result of artificial selection? With these questions the relationship to other fields of research dealing with the history of civilization becomes evident.

The methods of zoological research are not sufficient to answer all questions on the origins of, and the events in, the course of domestication. Cooperation with other disciplines, especially with the study of prehistory, is an absolute necessity. Primary evidence for domestic animals is found in excavations of prehistoric dwellings. The zoologist's task is to examine the bones; in most cases only fragments are available. We have frequently stated (Herre 1966; Herre and Röhrs 1971, 1973) that zoological data alone cannot ensure complete information on the origins of animal husbandry; additional evidence which provides details on the general way of life of these early human societies is indispensable. However, the details of such evidence, if taken by themselves, cannot furnish a complete description.

Modern zoo-archaeologists strongly advocate the belief that very early human groups developed more or less regular relationships between humans and other animals in order to facilitate their food supply (Higgs and Jarman 1972). Paleoanthropologists assume that relationships of this kind date back very far, probably well into the Paleolithic. While scavenging may have been a factor in the life of the earliest hominids (Bayanov and Bourtsev 1974), there is no doubt that hunting was the first dependable means of providing meat for mammals. The hunting of many different species of animals developed gradually into a strong link between a few species and some human groups and, this relationship led to a more regular, dependable food supply for the humans. But such associations brought not only advantages; even primitive stages of keeping livestock require regular care to some extent and, with an increasing yield, man's efforts had to be increased, too. This required the development of a special mentality in man, who until that time had been accustomed to the freedom of a hunter's life. The new attitude developed slowly, and not in all human populations. Such developments in mentality and spirit cannot be explained by zoology alone, although many indicators can be obtained from biological observations.

Generally speaking, the development of farming can be considered a kind of process of acquaintanceship with biological objects, a knowledge which had to be more comprehensive than that of hunters and food gatherers. We may assume that in the course of the domestication of wild animals, man experimented with many different species before he found suitable ones. Jarman (1972) and Legge (1972) have given us comprehensive reports on these events. Obviously those first attempts only served the purpose of procuring a better and more dependable meat supply. Man developed further and more differentiated needs, and these were satisfied by transforming some species of wild animals into "classical" domestic animals which enabled people to improve agriculture considerably. The importance of "genuine" or "classical" domestic animals should be emphasized.

Animal husbandry, which led to a regular production of animals' products and productivities, required first of all manipulation of the natural environment of which better breeding may be a byproduct. Animals do not react in a uniform way to changes of the ecological structure. Only some species, perhaps just certain strains of species, could be developed into agriculturally usable livestock. The animals which became adapted to new living conditions changed in an unpredictable way in the course of domestication; the recognition of new opportunities and their further development became extremely important for human civilizations. Wool, which is not present in wild species except as an undercoat, may be taken as an example here: Spöttel and Taenzer (1923), Taenzer (1926), and Frölich, Spöttel, and Taenzer (1933), with their classic, comprehensive investigations, have given a complete survey of the biological qualities of wool; Ryder (1962, 1969) has confirmed their results, primarily by the microscopic study of dated parchments. The study of the history of civilization by humanists' methods alone is insufficient to explain the mutual influences between species of animals and an environment created and manipulated by man; for that reason cooperative study is a primary need in this field. As in many types of cooperation, difficulties may arise, among which is the fact that progress in the various fields of knowledge and its theoretical foundations is frequently not appreciated and adopted quickly enough by the neighboring disciplines. This is why we think it proper to make some general remarks from the zoological angle.

The zoologist's task is to identify nonhuman bones, which in prehistoric excavations are generally found as fragments only. For several reasons these determinations sometimes have to be indefinite, especially when only single pieces exist. Previously such difficulties were less known, since the system of classification was based on a more static, morphological species-concept. The development of a "new systematics" suggested by Kleinschmidt (1900), Rensch (1929), and others led to a recognition of the concept of the biological species, based mainly on the publications of Huxley (1948) and Mayr (1963). These studies have promoted the realization that species are not constant units but rather undergo changes both in space and time. Recent species are subdivided into subspecies which are related to geographical conditions. Subspecies also often differ in some characteristics of their skeletons. Since the geographical conditions underwent considerable changes since the beginning of domestication, division into subspecies and sometimes even the distribution of species have not remained constant, particularly as environmental conditions were changed by increasing agriculture. Man often considered the wild ancestral species of his domestic animals to be unwanted ecological competitors; hence the wild species were driven out or eradicated (Herre 1949a, 1949b; Eequate 1962; Nobis 1971; and others). Because of these practices, knowledge concerning the ancestors of domestic animals and their variability is often insufficient, and it is sometimes difficult to determine the formation of subspecies and the differentiation of domestic animals. In some cases the modification of the area of distribution implies a splitting into isolated populations. Normally some useful indications concerning the general distribution at the time of the beginning of agriculture are available. A good method consists of studying the recent distribution of species in the light of knowledge of the changes in the world's history. When identifying bones of animals from prehistoric settlements, one must always take into consideration the remarkable plasticity of biological material and its dependence on abiotic and biotic factors such as population density (Klein and Strandgaard 1972). These facts indicate, too, that a search, in the attempt to discover their places of origin, for recent subspecies of wild ancestral species which resemble domestic animals in some aspects is not necessarily sensible. All subspecies can change very quickly, and certain environmental conditions of the domestic state may influence bodily characteristics in a way similar to the influence of natural factors. In any quest for subspecies similar to domestic animals, there will be some difficulty in avoiding errors, especially if similarities are not sufficiently analyzed by biological methods, e.g. allometric ones.

Another difficulty concerning the identification of bones lies in the fact that sufficient collections for comparative purposes which could prove the natural variability are usually still lacking. In some cases bones found in excavations do not show any specific characteristics. For that reason not all bones of sheep and goats can be identified, in spite of all endeavors to do so (Radulesco and Samson 1962; Boessneck, et al. 1964; Tiessen 1970). Even more difficult is the process of determining whether a bone belonged to a wild species or to a domestic one. Domestication is a gradual process, not a sudden event. Only after a certain number of generations (sometimes about fifty), preliminary changes which can be detected are known (Koch 1951; Shakelford 1949; Belyaev 1969; Sossinka 1970), but neither species nor populations show any uniformity. Moreover, such changes mostly concern single characteristics only. For instance, the investigations of Bückner (1971) have shown that the widths of epiphyses of canid limb bones change in relation to their size, while their lengths change independently from size. Hence decisions on wild or domestic species are often difficult, especially where fragments are concerned. Thieme (in litt.) has found proximal fragments of metatarsal bones of cattle showing a width normally specified as typical for *Bos primigenius*; some complete metatarsal bones, however, with the same width of epiphysis, were so short that a determination as *Bos primigenius* is quite uncertain. Thus mistakes in the determination of wild species as well as of domestic animals occur quite frequently, and the importance of additional finds becomes evident.

There are many different methods which have been used to find more criteria for determining early domestic animals. Some conclusions on the first patterns of maintaining and using animals have been determined from the study of osteological remains retrieved from archaeological sites. If the relative numbers of one or more species changed from earlier to later levels in a site, the increase in numbers probably indicates increased economic utilization, and thus possibly change toward domestication. Within a species, evidence of change in age groups within a population pointing to greater utilization of (i.e. killing of) younger animals is usually considered evidence of increase in control over that population and thus for its domestication. Evidence of an increase in the relative numbers of adult females of a species in a site or culture over time is usually considered to indicate considerable control over the prehistoric population of animals, and such data provide evidence for domestication. New field studies on the prey of predators have confirmed the existence of a correlation between the biology of the prey animals and the quantity and kind of prey. In the case of herd animals, there are normally some males which acquire and defend larger families which are strictly organized and, because of this, also well protected. The rest of the males make up loose associations in which the individuals are easier prey; this situation explains why a given collection of bones may contain greater numbers of bones of young males. To date, in our study of material left by prehistoric hunters, we have not been able to perceive whether the hunters used biological conditions in a way similar to that of other predators.

One should not overlook the fact that excavations of prehistoric settlements dating back to the time of the beginning of farming and animal husbandry are still rare. Hence statements on the beginning of animal husbandry deduced from single finds may not be of general significance. Indeed, in some communities, hunting as a means of providing food continued for a long time; this applies to the central part of Europe, too, even into the Middle Ages. Considering the problem of the origins of animal husbandry, these are quite important discoveries since they teach us that an absence of game may give rise to the keeping of livestock — but that hunting may well be preferred to animal husbandry. This conclusion may be drawn from quite different data; zoology also contributes to a resolution of the question of the origins of animal husbandry. Before tackling this latter study, we have to raise the important question of what we understand by the terms "domestic animal" and "domestication" and determine what the conditions were for the development of wild species into domestic animals.

Difficulties impeding a recognition of the first stages of animal husbandry led in the past to the attempt to find partial solutions by means of partial determinations. In principle, it is quite justifiable to advance by partial solutions — but it is dangerous if old concepts are filled with new meanings, as, for instance, Wilkinson (1972) did by giving an archaeological definition for the term "domestication." A similar attitude, it seems, is also held by Jarman and Wilkinson (1972), who have emphasized the difficulties in finding general criteria for domestication. In spite of all problems, the term "domestication" should be used universally in order to avoid confusion and mock solutions. Certainly man has conducted natural experiments to facilitate his access to a supply of animal products, but not all of these experiments led to the development of "classical" domestic animals (Jarman 1972; Legge 1972). Possibly breeding was often unsuccessful or undesirable, and people were satisfied with new captures from different regions. These captured animals may have been assembled to form herds near the settlements in order to ensure a regular supply. Certainly these facts merit some interest, but the development of those domestic animals which attained universal significance for farming has been achieved with only a very few species.

According to Wilkinson (1972), domestication means "to change the seasonal subsistence cycle of the species involved to coincide with the requirements of human groups." We do not hold the opinion that this definition contains the more important facts relating to the origins of true farming. We shall not, however, give any further comment on this matter. Wilkinson himself expressed doubts over the general value of his definition. (He described particularly a new case of using a wild animal as a model for animal husbandry.) Higgs and Jarman (1972) expressed the opinion that it is suitable to limit the term "domestication" to stages of a more developed kind of farming. We do not intend to add another definition but rather to try to find facts which facilitate an understanding of the origins and development of classical domestic animals. Ethnological findings teach that primitive societies raise and tame individuals from quite different wild species. In spite of that practice, domestication does not often occur. We can only call a process domestication when people isolate small populations from wild species in order to make use of them, and when they breed the animals in sufficiently large numbers to ensure a regular supply for certain human groups. There are higher civilizations where people regularly tame and train animals — such as the Indian elephant and the cormorant — to use them for various purposes, but these animals cannot be regarded as domestic animals as they are not usually bred in captivity. There are cases, too, of wild animals being maintained in captivity and reproducing under these conditions, for example in enclosures or in zoological gardens. In all of these cases there exists a regular man–animal relationship, and it is functional, in a way. The line between the beginning of animal husbandry and captivity in enclosures or zoological gardens is difficult to draw. In the latter case, however, the primary motive is not the fulfillment of vital needs but the expression of a higher standard of living. We do not consider it necessary to refer to such cases in order to explain the development of animal husbandry. This statement is meant as a critical comment on the opinions of Jarman and Wilkinson (1972). We do not deny, however, that changes may occur as a result of captivity which tend to be in the same direction as are some changes achieved under domestication (Herre and Röhrs 1973). However, the subject of distinguishing domestic animals from those which are maintained in captivity and merely used for various purposes has been discussed often in zoological publications since the beginning of this century (Keller 1905; Hilzheimer 1926; Antonius 1922; Klatt 1927; Herre and Röhrs 1973), so we will not pursue it further here.

Probably a selection had already occurred by the time of the first efforts to maintain livestock, which led to the development of domestic animals and favored animals which could be controlled more easily and which were less wild. Social species are preadapted in this respect since the individuals conform more easily to the conditions of captivity.

According to new investigations, however, hereditary reductions of the size of the brain and of individual brain areas coincide with the development of domestic animals (Herre and Röhrs 1973; Kruska 1973).

We assume that these selection results produce an effect on behavior, too. Hence it is highly improbable that crossing first stocks of domestic animals with the wild species played a considerable part in the process, although, of course, we can be sure that such hybridization occurred now and then.

The isolated stocks had to be bred and increased to such proportions that a regular and sufficient supply was ensured. Probably the increase of the herds and their regular use was secured by some special protection, something like a taboo or another link to religious ideas. In the past, there has been a lot of discussion on the hypothesis that religious beliefs provided the motivation for keeping animals, but we do not think this has been sufficiently proved and consider it improbable. Those links with religion which have been proved in some cases might have developed later.

Related to the isolation and breeding of the first domestic livestock was observation of and care for the animals; man had to fulfill certain requirements and new duties. The animals had to grow and stay healthy on the available food and within the space allotted to them, and they had to reproduce and to rear their offspring. Probably man did not collect spare fodder at the early stages of maintaining his first herds and raising the stocks of young animals. The first domestic animals probably had to find their food themselves, as is still the case with primitive livestock (Herre 1955, 1958). For the animals these conditions meant a narrowing of the free choice of food and a change of nourishment, and in most cases an abandonment of some rare food plants which some animals not only prefer but need for their health. For each species, only certain individuals with a low degree of food specialization could be successfully developed into domestic animals; some indications for this fact can be found in Klein's investigations (1970). Within these species, smaller animals with a smaller absolute food requirement would more often survive and reproduce. The decrease of body size, which is often mentioned as confirmation of the first stages of animal husbandry, may thus be explained. Modifications caused by the environment and the selection of suitable animals may have brought about something like the Waddington effect and have produced the decrease in body size.

The strange fact that only very few wild species have developed into domestic animals may have been caused by a further phenomenon. For early domesticators, it was breeding and not repeated new captures from wild livestock which represented a condition for the beginnings of farming. It is fairly well known today that there are animals with long reproductive cycles and others with rigid refractory periods. Cases have been studied in which only those individuals from related species with long reproductive cycles developed into domestic animals (Lofts and Murton 1968; Herre and Röhrs 1973). This characteristic might have possessed a preadaptive value for domestication.

These indications are intended to show that the development of farm animals is more than just taming, using, or maintaining animals in captivity. This opinion has already been substantiated in early zoological publications on domestic animals; it has been, however, and often is still overlooked. The number of hunted species was large, that of domestic animals stayed small. The old statement that domestic animals belong to species with social dispositions is certainly important, but there are many social mammalian species which have not been developed into domestic animals. The violence of fights for dominance within a group of animals and the strength of the natural weapons of aggressive animals can be an obstacle to domestication. Thus aurochs, wild rams, and male goats can be considered to have been dangerous enemies of man. Many questions as to why some of the wild species accepted domestication and others did not will have to stay unanswered. We have to stress these problems as some speculations on the origins of domestication use insufficient or false arguments. Thus the achievement of the peoples who accomplished domestication is partly concealed.

There is no doubt that problems of food were of considerable importance in early farming. Zoological investigations teach that early farm animals were herbivorous or omnivorous. The dog, taxonomically a carnivore, has quite a wide food range, too. Of these, all of the ungulates (but particularly the ruminants) are able to make use of natural food sources, rich in cellulose but poor in protein content, to transform them into animal protein needed by man, and to store it. Dogs, as well as pigs, are able to feed on human waste products. As Reed (1969) has emphasized, such animals are in this respect preadapted for domestication. Many animals, however, fulfill the same requirements without having been developed into domestic animals. This fact may also be considered an indication of an artificial selection marked by experience and observation — but what were the first motives for the beginning of animal husbandry?

In order to be able to answer these questions we must remember that the earliest farm animals, even horses and dogs, were primarily used for their meat (Degerbøl 1962; Geyvall 1969; Coy 1973). As an exception, possibly the guanaco was used as a pack animal at a very early time and perhaps was the first such. However, meat supply alone does not mean farming, and this is why the beginning of other ways of using animals must not be neglected if we wish to appreciate the development of human intelligence which expressed itself in the creation of economic foundations. Many special qualities for which domestic animals are bred developed slowly in the course of domestication; as an example, we can again refer to the wool of sheep and alpaca. Such achievements were completely unexpected. For the origins of animal husbandry this means that the attempt to procure a dependable meat supply must have been the one of major importance.

If we accept the fact that, in general, hunting is the preferred method of procuring meat, the opinion that a decrease in number of the hunted animals in comparison to the size of the human population occurred may be strongly supported. Whether climatic change or the increasing population was of decisive importance for the disturbance of the former balance is a question that cannot be answered. Klein (1972) has clearly demonstrated how quickly populations of wild animals decrease if the human population grows and hunting is continued as a means for supplying animal protein.

Even more important for an explanation of the reasons for domestication is another early observation of zoologists who studied problems of domestic animals. Centers of domestication are not evenly distributed over the world. Regions abounding in game or those with a low population density like Australia and huge areas in North and South America as well as in Africa have not produced any domestic animals.

In Eurasia, too, the centers from which domestication originated were limited to relatively small regions within the total area of distribution of the ancestral stocks of classical domestic animals. There is no doubt that wild species suitable for domestication are found in all continents (Talbot, et al. 1965; Jewell 1969). We should mention here the African eland, *Taurotragus oryx*, which proves this fact in our time (Roth, et al. 1970–1972). Hence we may conclude that in huge areas of the earth, men could easily continue to procure their supply of meat by hunting, so long as the human population stayed small in comparison with that of the game. Therefore there was initially no need for domestic animals, and later they could be imported from other regions. This supports the hypothesis that the desire for a regular supply of animal protein became the primary motive for domestication. Population changes destroying the balance between man and animal are a more probable cause of domestication than are climatic changes. The problem of the selection of species, however, has not been solved; it is another indication of the remarkable achievements of the human groups which domesticated animals.

There is no doubt that wild animals could only be domesticated within their natural areas of distribution. This is why observations of animal geography can provide useful information: it is possible to develop concepts of the areas of distribution of the wild ancestral species at the time of early farming as, for example, in the case of the autochthonous American domestic animals.

The domestication of native American animals was a relatively recent series of events which were achieved in areas which were already primarily agricultural. The domestic animals of America have to be considered as independent domesticates (Nachtigall 1965). There are few controversies now on the subject of their wild ancestral species and their areas of distribution. The domestic mammals of America are the llama, the alpaca, and the guinea pig; the dog was probably introduced from abroad. According to the criteria of "modern systematics," it is obvious that the llama and the alpaca have been derived from the guanaco, *Lama guanaco* (Herre 1952, 1953, 1958, 1964, 1968; Herre and Röhrs 1973). The wild ancestral species of the domestic guinea pig is *Cavia aperea* (Hückinghaus 1961). Domestic fowl evolved from the turkey, *Meleagris gallopavo*, and from the moscovy duck, *Cairina moschata*. When the areas of distribution of the wild species are compared, it is evident that while they are not identical (Herre 1961, 1968), some overlapping areas can be found. The areas of distribution of the guanaco and the guinea pig overlap in the High Andes and those of *Meleagris* and *Cairina* overlap in what is now Mexico. We know that in these areas high cultures with a high population density developed, and we may well assume that the domestic animals were also evolved there. Worth noting is the fact that the area of distribution for each of the wild ancestral species is large, whereas the area where domestication took place is quite small: this fact indicates special activities of single human groups. The human population in other regions of the distribution area could cover their protein requirements by other means, e.g. hunting, fishing, and food gathering.

According to recent archaeological findings, the sheep has to be considered the oldest domestic animal. Domestication of other wild species which became important for farming took place in succession, separated by remarkable intervals. This fact gives rise to the question of whether the idea of domesticating animals had been passed on or if it had been accomplished anew with other animals — or if the matter was so much more complicated that it cannot yet be interpreted in detail. The distribution of sheep as a domestic animal took place in a very short time. Inasmuch as the use of sheeps' wool was already known at a time when other animals were not yet domesticated, we must assume that peoples of that period knew that animal products could be used for purposes other than food. This fact should not be overlooked, and any consideration of food production as the only motive for domestication seems one-sided; this does not of course exclude the fact that the meat was also used. Thus we cannot agree with Butzer's statement (1971) that food production was the unique aim of domestication. From the biological angle, and perhaps also in the view of the history of civilization, "late" domestic animals present considerable problems. Butzer himself has pointed out that the development of agriculture is manifold, that some developments took place independently of others, and that many details cannot yet be understood completely.

In terms of modern zoology, all domestic sheep are descendants of one wild species, *Ovis ammon* L., 1758. The area of distribution of this wild species reached from western Europe to eastern Asia. The species is split into several subspecies (Kesper 1954; Herre and Röhrs 1955; Ellermann and Morrison-Scott 1951; Haltenorth 1963) which may be combined into groups (Map 1). According to available data, the first animal husbandry must have occurred soon after 11,000 B.P. (Perkins 1964; Drew, Perkins and Daly 1971; Higgs and Jarman 1972). From this evidence we may conclude that the first domestic sheep were derived from the *orientalis* group, and this is confirmed by anatomical data. The wild species was not domesticated in the whole of the area of distribution. It is remarkable how quickly domestic sheep became widely distributed and were introduced into regions where the wild species had never occurred. Presumably domestic sheep were already being kept in Libya around 8000 B.P. (Higgs 1962a); at about 7000 B.P. they could be found in India as well as in southeastern Asia and in the Danubian region (Butzer 1971); and they reached the northern part of middle Europe between 5000 and 6000 B.P. This is evidence for the movement of human populations or the exchange of products between different cultures. We should mention here, however, that the hypothesis of a close association between particular human groups and certain breeds of domestic animals has not proved to be correct (Epstein 1971). Breeds of domestic animals show an extreme variability when exposed to new environmental conditions (Herre and Röhrs 1973). That domestic sheep were quite important even outside their natural area of distribution at a time when the domestication of the aurochs was just beginning may be inferred from recent archaeological data.

The area of distribution of the wild goat — which still belongs to a natural reproductive community in spite of considerable phenotypic differences — is large (Map 2). Morphologic differences are so pro-

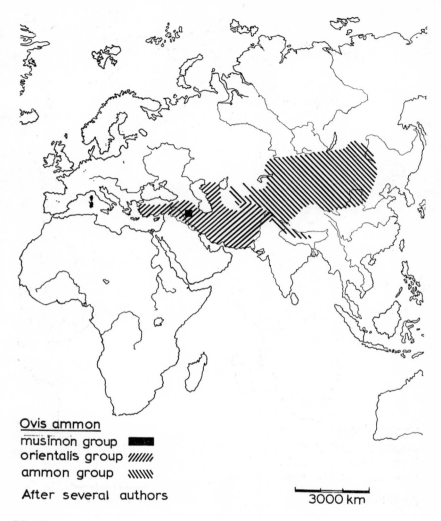

Ovis ammon
musimon group ▨
orientalis group ⫰⫰⫰
ammon group ⫰⫰⫰

After several authors

3000 km

Map 1.

nounced that we can talk of a super-species. The phenotypic groups are ibex and the true goats of the species *falconeri* and *aegagrus*. The earliest domestic goats, as a recent summary by Higgs and Jarman (1972) stated, were found in Iran at Alikosh; they date back to about 9500 B.P. Hence we may be sure that populations of *Capra aegagrus* were the first to be domesticated, a theory confirmed by morphological analyses (Herre and Röhrs 1973). The domestic goat, according to Clutton-Brock (1971) and Higgs and Jarman (1972), spread quickly beyond the area of distribution

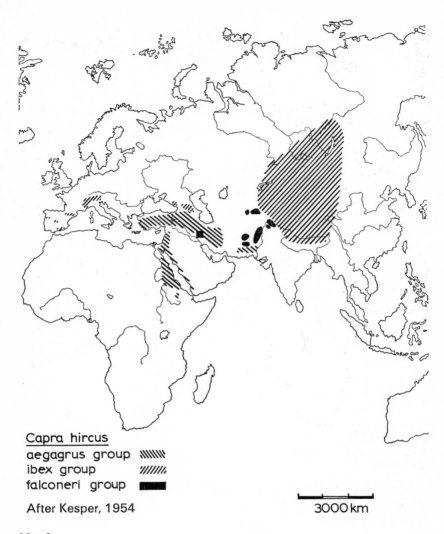

Capra hircus
aegagrus group \\\\\\
ibex group ////////
falconeri group ▄▄▄▄

After Kesper, 1954

3000 km

Map 2.

of its wild ancestral species. In this respect a question arises as to why
two species of small ruminants were domesticated in neighboring
areas. The fact that the number of mammalian species suitable for
domestication was definitely small is important, as quite probably early
domesticators experimented with all easily manageable animals which
reproduce in captivity. In addition, there is another factor which may be
related to the habitat of the domesticators: goats feed mainly on leaves
and for this reason they can also live in hilly and bushy regions; sheep,

however, prefer short grasses and their preferred habitat is that of wide pastures. Thus both species supplement each other in making use of the plant reserves. The fact that both species were kept at the same time — which is obvious in many prehistoric sites — may have contributed markedly to the increase of food production. The proximity of the domestication centers of sheep and goats should be stressed, a fact which is confirmed by the overlapping areas of distribution where these species supplement each other ecologically to a considerable extent.

The wild pig *Sus scrofa* is omnivorous and lives mainly, but not entirely, in forests. It was widely distributed over western Europe and northern Africa, and continued into eastern Asia (Map 3). In this large area numerous subspecies can be distinguished. Kelm (1939) gave us a complete analysis of these subspecies, and further information is to be found in the publications of Ellermann and Morrison-Scott (1951) and Haltenorth (1963). We may assume that at the time of domestication the wild species lived in the same regions as it does today, but that the distribution of subspecies was slightly different (Herre 1949b). A further difference lies in the fact that the European subspecies possess long, rectangular lacrimal bones while in the subspecies of southeastern Asia this bone is more square. This characteristic has not proved modifiable by environmental conditions. Many details about the first domestications of wild pigs are still unclear, and quite a few findings indicate that wild pigs have been domesticated at a number of different places. Formerly the Crimea was considered the first center of domestication, but more recently, however, Higgs and Jarman (1972) have joined Tringham (1969) in maintaining that the finds on the Crimea are remains of wild animals, for cultural documents which could prove domestication are still lacking. The earliest domestic pigs have been recorded as existing at Çayönü, Turkey, around 9000 B.P. (Braidwood, et al. 1971, 1974). The evidence further indicates that the first finds of domestic pigs were limited to a small region within the total area of distribution, but that the domestic pig was distributed quickly over a large area. It is not usually known whether the distribution took place in a direct way or whether only the idea of domestication was passed on. Watson's article (1969) on early domestic animals in China is therefore of particular interest. According to him, pigs and dogs were the only known domestic animals in the earliest period of agriculture in China. This conclusion is corroborated by additional evidence from Ho (this volume). In southeastern Asia domestic pigs with square lacrimal bones, typical of the wild populations there, are known; this proves that these subspecies have also been domesticated. As far as we know, precise information on the date of this

3000 km

Sus scrofa

1 castilianus	8 attila	15 leucomystax	22 nicobaricus
2 barbarus	9 libycus	16 moupinensis	23 jubatus
3 meridionalis	10 sennaarensis[1]	17 chirodontus	24 vittatus
4 majori	11 nigripes	18 riukiuanus	25 floresianus
5 reiseri	12 raddeanus	19 taivanus	26 timorensis
6 scrofa	13 ussuricus	20 cristatus	27 papuensis[1]
7 falzfeini	14 coreanus	21 adamanensis	

[1] Probably reverted to a wild state   After several authors

Map 3.

domestication is still lacking. Sauer (1952) postulated a separate development of agriculture in the region of southeastern Asia; Butzer (1971) and
Gorman (this volume) have enlarged on this subject.

With reference to the areas of distribution of domesticated cattle it
should be pointed out that at about 5000 B.P. new species of wild oxen
were domesticated in southeastern Asia. This evidence leads to the conjecture that wild hogs of that region were domesticated at the same time.
More precise data on the time range and the intervals between the

domestication of populations of wild hogs would be useful in order to discover if domestication was the invention of the indigenous people or merely an imitation. Here again the variability of the early farming activities and developments becomes obvious.

In an examination of the domestication of the dog, one fact can be considered certain: the wolf, *Canis lupus*, is the only ancestral species (Herre and Röhrs 1973). The area of distribution of the wolf extends over most of Eurasia and North America (Map 4). The species has been split into many subspecies. In Eurasia as well as in North America populations of both large and small wolves occur. Current opinion holds that the domestication of the wolf occurred first in northern Europe (Starr Carr) around 9500 B.P. (Higgs and Jarman 1972). The more recent suggestion of Turnbull and Reed (1974), that a part of the mandible of a dog dated at 12,000 B.P. or earlier was recovered from the archaeological site of Palegawra in northern Iraq, seems based on insufficient evidence considering the great variability in wolves.

For northern Europe, evidence indicates that the first domestic dogs were bred for their meat (Degerbøl 1962). Domestic dogs from Neolithic strata of the Aegean region also seem to have been used for food (Geyvall 1969; Coy 1973). At a very early time, man discovered that the dog could be utilized in other ways, but many questions concerning this problem in the history of culture have remained unanswered. The domestic dog spread quickly over a large area. Reed (1969) has withdrawn his initial objections about the presence of the dog as an early domestic animal in the Near East, and indeed domestic dogs have been identified at Cayönü for the time around 9000 B.P. (Braidwood, et al. 1974). Lawrence (1967, 1968) has claimed that in North America (Idaho), dogs were kept as early as 10,300 B.P. Higgs and Jarman (1972) have expressed their doubts as to the validity of this information, and we have pointed out that the criteria used for the determination of the specimens as domestic dogs are not precise enough. The geographical factors, too, do not corroborate Lawrence's claim.

Domestic cattle likewise produce several interesting problems concerning the origins of agriculture. The fact that the domestic cattle of the world belong to zoologically different species should not be overlooked. Both wild and domestic cattle are widely distributed in the form of the so-called "taurine" cattle. These evolved from the aurochs or urus, *Bos primigenius* (Herre and Röhrs 1973). Aurochs survived into the seventeenth century but were eventually eradicated. We have certain knowledge of the distribution of aurochs in Europe in the evidence of fossils and that of written documents. Information on distribution in Asia is far less

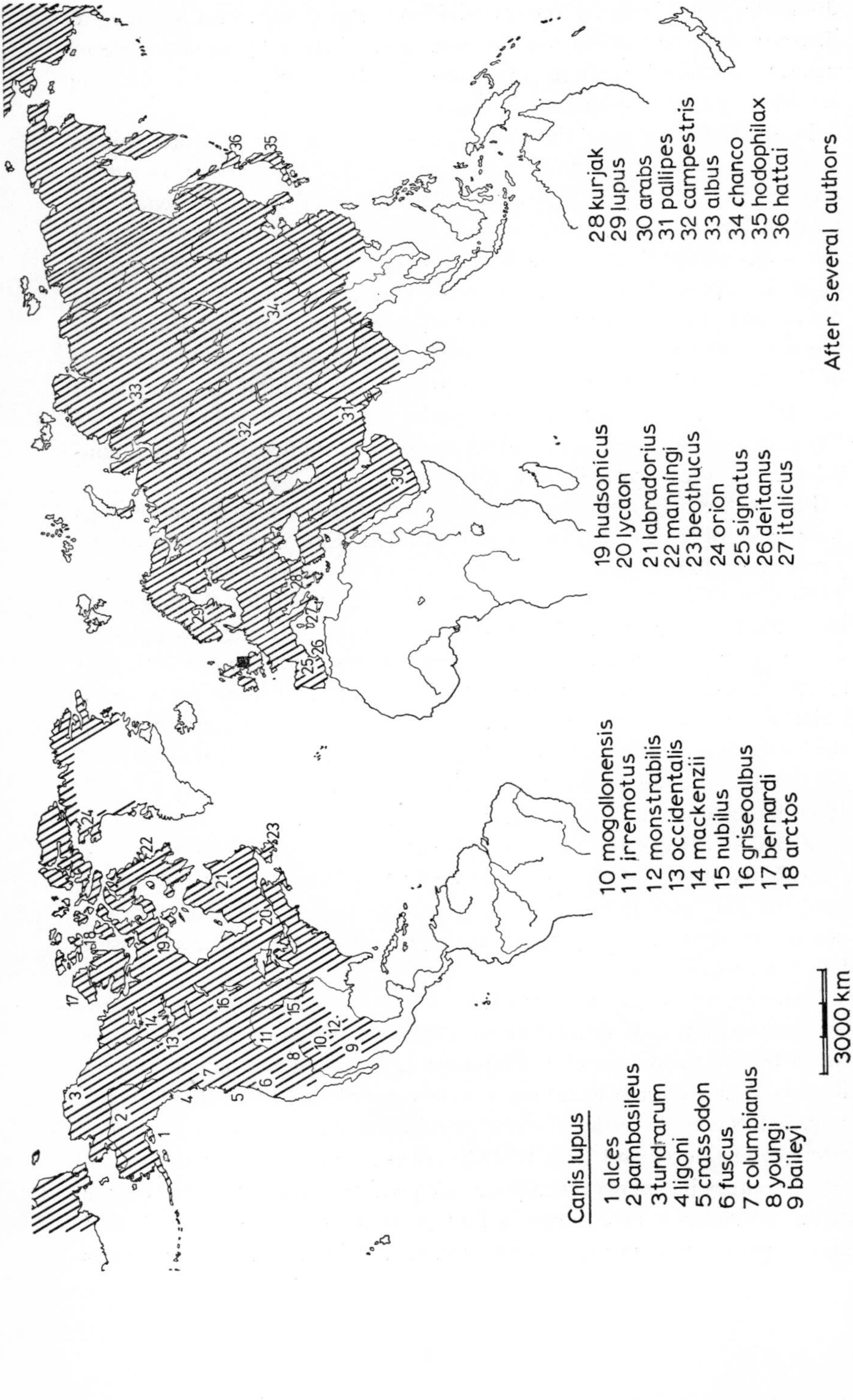

Canis lupus

1 alces
2 pambasileus
3 tundrarum
4 ligoni
5 crassodon
6 fuscus
7 columbianus
8 youngi
9 baileyi

10 mogollonensis
11 irremotus
12 monstrabilis
13 occidentalis
14 mackenzii
15 nubilus
16 griseoalbus
17 bernardi
18 arctos

19 hudsonicus
20 lycaon
21 labradorius
22 manningi
23 beothucus
24 orion
25 signatus
26 deitanus
27 italicus

28 kurjak
29 lupus
30 arabs
31 pallipes
32 campestris
33 albus
34 chanco
35 hodophilax
36 hattai

After several authors

3000 km

Map 4.

Bos primigenius

Interrupted hatching indicates areas·
insufficiently known.

▲ Evidence in western Siberia and Kasachstan

After several authors   3000 km

Map 5.

complete, but the general outline may be traced (Requate 1962; Degerbøl
1970; Jarman 1969; Bohlken 1964; and others) (Map 5). The auroch
probably lived in open park-like areas. Available data suggest that the
first domestication of aurochs was probably accomplished around 8500
B.P. in southeastern Europe; little less than 1,000 years later domestic
cattle were also used in Asia Minor. Domestication of aurochs occurred
more than 2,000 years later than that of sheep, and likewise later than
domestication of goats (Higgs and Jarman 1972). Domestic cattle spread

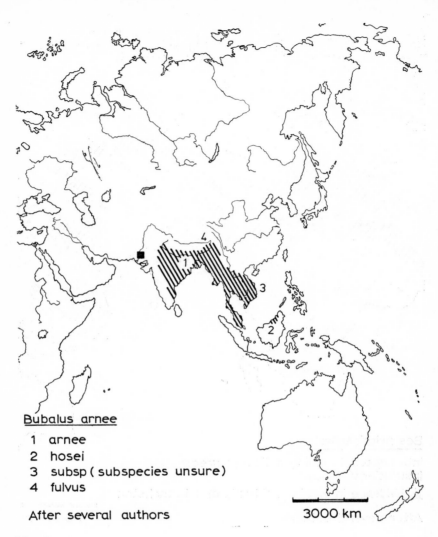

Bubalus arnee

1 arnee
2 hosei
3 subsp (subspecies unsure)
4 fulvus

After several authors   3000 km

Map 6.

quickly and gained considerable importance as domestic animals. This fact probably played a part in the early eradication of the ancestral species, which were considered food competitors. It has been suggested that aurochs were domesticated at different places within their natural distribution area (*Palestine*: Clutton-Brock 1971; *Asia Minor*: Röhrs and Herre 1961; Perkins 1969; *Hungary*: Bökönyi 1971; *eastern Germany*: Nobis 1954; *northern Germany*: Herre 1949a; and others). Tringham (1969) has stated that in the Bug and Don districts of the southeastern

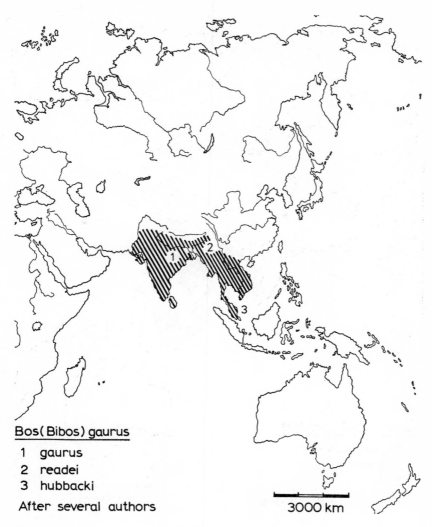

Bos(Bibos) gaurus

1 gaurus
2 readei
3 hubbacki

After several authors   3000 km

Map 7.

U.S.S.R., animal husbandry started with cattle breeding. This fact indicates the development of different kinds of farming. More precise analyses of the temporal range of local domestications of aurochs will lead to a better understanding of many problems.

In contrast to the aurochs, other species of wild Bovini live in high mountains or in subtropical regions: the buffalo, *Bubalis arnee* (Map 6), lives mainly on the Indian subcontinent; the distribution of the gar, *Bos (Bibos) gaurus* (Map 7), and the banteng, *Bos (Bibos) javanicus* (Map 8), is

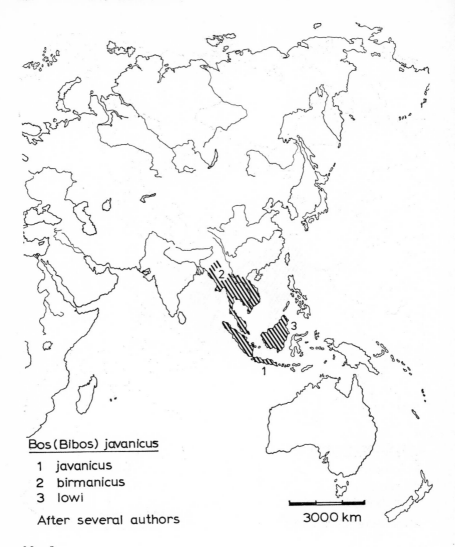

Bos (Bibos) javanicus

1   javanicus
2   birmanicus
3   lowi

After several authors   3000 km

Map 8.

in southeastern Asia and on the neighboring islands. These wild oxen were domesticated, too, but about 3,000 years later than the aurochs. The first evidences of these species of cattle as domestic animals date from around 5000 B.P. As the number of excavations in this part of the world is still small, decisive knowledge on the origins of domestication of those animals is still lacking. It is worth noting that three different species from two different genera developed into domestic cattle in southeastern Asia. This indicates the existence of special tendencies which can only be

Bos (Poëphagus) mutus

After several authors

3000 km

Map 9.

explained by the history of civilization. We have already mentioned that the wild pigs of these regions might possibly have been independently domesticated, too.

Human populations also settled in the severe climates of high mountain areas. This led to new forms of farming which included the domestication of another species of wild oxen. The wild yak, *Bos (Pöephagus) mutus*, is well adapted to the cold climate of high mountains (see Map 9). Yaks are still valued today as domestic cattle; the few available data

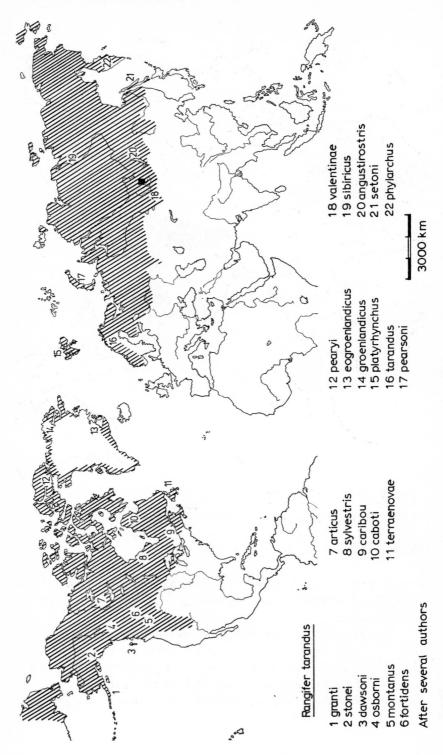

Rangifer tarandus

1 granti
2 stonei
3 dawsoni
4 osborni
5 montanus
6 fortidens

7 articus
8 sylvestris
9 caribou
10 caboti
11 terraenovae

12 pearyi
13 eogroenlandicus
14 groenlandicus
15 platyrhynchus
16 tarandus
17 pearsoni

18 valentinae
19 sibiricus
20 angustirostris
21 setoni
22 phylarchus

3000 km

After several authors

Map 10.

indicate that this species was domesticated around 3500 to 3000 B.P. This is an example of secondary domestication, i.e. imitation. Undoubtedly these specific environmental conditions led to special forms of farming, and man learned how to develop domestic animals suitable for such living conditions. In this respect our view differs from that of Butzer (1971).

The phenomenon described above applies also to the reindeer, *Rangifer tarandus* (Map 10), which is the ancestor of an important domestic animal. The domestic reindeer facilitates a regular and dependable food supply in regions which normally seem uninhabitable for man. The wild species is able to live under more extreme conditions than most other mammals and is widely distributed in the north of Eurasia and America. The domestication of the reindeer originated in a very limited region within the total distribution area, probably the region of Sajan (see Map 10), around 3000 B.P. In northern Eurasia, human populations were thus able to penetrate into previously uninhabitable regions; these populations were nomadic, and they still are (Herre 1955). This is another argument for the assumption that domestication has only been achieved by small human groups.

Two domestic species were derived from the Perissodactyla; they were domesticated comparatively late — according to available data around 5000 B.P. These are the horse, *Equus przewalskii*, and the wild ass, *Equus africanus*. The hypothesis that an additional species, the onager, *Equus hemionus*, was domesticated cannot be supported either by natural science (Herre and Röhrs 1971) or by an examination of the history of civilization (Brentjes 1971). In terms of animal geography, the domestication of the Perissodactyla presents considerable problems, as the areas of distribution are extremely far from each other. The wild horse, *Equus przewalskii*, the ancestor of all domestic horses (Herre and Röhrs 1973), lived in a region north of the Caucasus. Its distribution extended from western Europe to eastern Asia (Map 11). The wild horse lived mainly in grasslands but also penetrated into forested regions. Three subspecies have been distinguished (Heptner, et al. 1966; Herre 1967). The first domestic horses have been recorded as inhabiting southern Russia around 5000 B.P., but further times and places of domestication are conceivable (Hancar 1955; Nobis 1971). According to available evidence, horses were first bred for their meat; in some parts of Europe this habit has continued to the present day. At about 4000 B.P. domestic horses were introduced into regions outside of the natural area of the wild species. In Asia Minor horses were used for the first time for drawing chariots: this was one of the reasons for the special position of the horse compared to those of other domestic animals, and another was the use of horses as mounts by warriors in Asia.

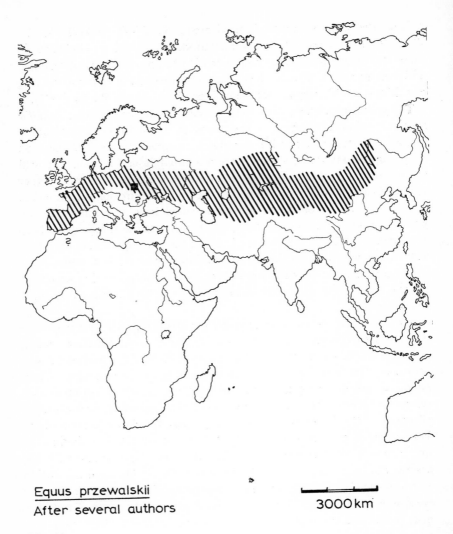

Equus przewalskii

After several authors

3000 km

Map 11.

The natural distribution area of the wild ass is northern Africa (Map 12). Domestic donkeys have been recorded in northeastern Africa from about 3000 B.C. and later. They spread from Africa over Asia Minor to many parts of the world. While there are no reliable documents on the first use of the domestic donkey, we can say that it became man's pack animal at a very early time and is still used as such.

We have already mentioned the independent domestications of the South American domestic animals: llama, alpaca, and guinea pig. The

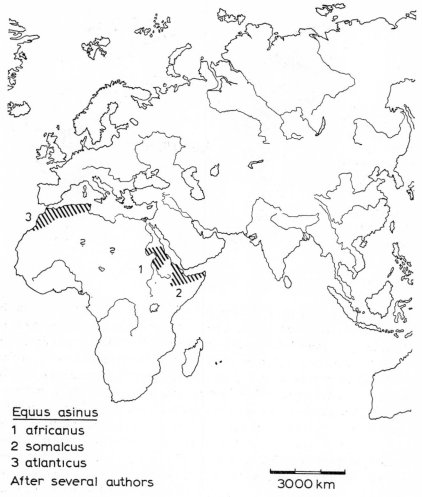

Equus asinus
1 africanus
2 somalcus
3 atlanticus
After several authors

3000 km

Map 12.

ancestral species of llama and alpaca is the guanaco, distributed from the southern pampas regions up to the High Andes beyond the Titicaca Basin (Map 13). The area of distribution of the wild guinea pig lies in the northern part of the subcontinent, excluding the tropical jungle of the Amazonian region (Map 14). This is another example of the phenomenon in which domestication of an animal developed only in a limited part of its range. The same human group probably domesticated both animals around 3000 B.P.

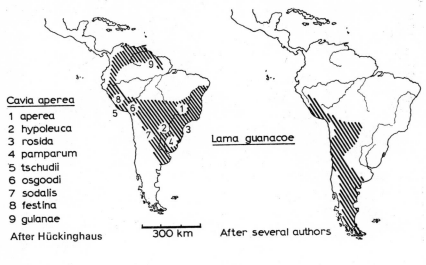

Cavia aperea

1 aperea
2 hypoleuca
3 rosida
4 pamparum
5 tschudii
6 osgoodi
7 sodalis
8 festina
9 guianae

After Hückinghaus

300 km

Lama guanacoe

After several authors

Map 13.   Map 14.

Speaking as zoologists, we have indicated the various difficulties which have to be considered before a better understanding of the origins of farming and animal husbandry is possible. We have emphasized the importance of tracing the areas of distribution of the wild ancestral species of domestic animals. Animal geography teaches that all domestic animals cannot have developed within the same area. If we use available archaeological data on the origins of animal husbandry as a basis for our investigations, it is difficult to believe that the different domestications were achieved at the same time; rather, they must have been separated by considerable intervals. From the study of animal geography we may draw certain conclusions, such as the assumption that domestication must be attributed to the initiative of small human groups. Biological data on wild species suggest that the different domestic species were introduced to different forms of agriculture. This gives rise to another question: can we speak of a uniform origin of agriculture? To answer this, we have to examine whether the different domestications occurred independently, and to examine what kinds of correlations exist. In this respect, however, zoologists can only bring forward suggestions; they cannot elucidate any ot these problems without the help of other disciplines.

REFERENCES

ANTONIUS, O.

1922   *Grundzüge einer Stammesgeschichte der Haustiere.* Jena: Gustav Fischer.

BAYANOV, D., I. BOURTSEV

1974   The Troglodytidae and the Hominidae in the taxonomy and evolution of higher primates — Reply. *Current Anthropology* 15: 452–456.

BELYAEV, D. W.

1969   Domestication of animals. *Science Journal* 5 (1): 47–52.

BOESSNECK, J., H.-H. MÜLLER, M. TEICHERT

1964   Osteologische Unterscheidungsmerkmale zwischen Schaf (*Ovis aries* L.) und Ziege (*Capra hircus* L.). *Kühn-Archiv* 78: 1–129.

BOHLKEN, H.

1964   Vergleichende Untersuchungen an den Schädeln wilder und domestizierter Rinder. *Zeitschrift für Wissenschaftliche Zoologie* 170: 323–418.

BÖKÖNYI, S.

1971   The development and history of domestic animals in Hungary: the Neolithic through the Middle Ages. *American Anthropologist* 73: 640–674.

BRAIDWOOD, R. J., H. ÇAMBEL, C. L. REDMAN, P. J. WATSON

1971   Beginnings of village-farming communities in southeastern Turkey. *Proceedings of the National Academy of Sciences, USA* 68: 1236–1240.

BRAIDWOOD, R. J., H. ÇAMBEL, B. LAWRENCE, C. L. REDMAN, R. B. STEWART

1974   Beginnings of village-farming communities in southeastern Turkey — 1972. *Proceedings of the National Academy of Sciences, USA* 71: 568–572.

BRENTJES, B.

1971   "Onager und Esel im alten Orient," in *Beiträge zur Geschichte, Kultur und Religion des alten Orient.* Edited by M. Lurker, 131–145. Baden-Baden: Valentin Körner.

BÜCKNER, H.-J.

1971   Allometrische Untersuchungen an den Vorderextremitäten adulter Caniden. *Zoologischer Anzeiger* 186: 11–46.

BUTZER, K. W.

1971   *Environment and archeology: an ecological approach to prehistory* (second edition). London: Methuen.

CLUTTON-BROCK, J.

1971   The primary food animals of the Jericho Tell from the proto-Neolithic to the Byzantine period. *Levant* 3: 41–45.

COY, J. P.

1973   "Bronze Age domestic animals from Keos, Greece," in *Domestikationsforschung und Geschichte der Haustiere.* Edited by J. Matolcsi, 239–243. Budapest: Akadémiai Kiadó.

DARWIN, C.

1868   *Variation of animals and plants under domestication.* London: John Murray.

DEGERBØL, M.
1962   Der Hund, das älteste Haustier Dänemarks. *Zeitschrift für Tier-züchtung und Züchtungsbiologie* 72: 334–341.

DEGERBØL, M., B. FREDSKILD
1970   The Urus (*Bos primigenius* Bojanus) and Neolithic domesticated cattle (*Bos taurus domesticus* Linné) in Denmark with a revision of *Bos*-remains from kitchen-middens. *Det Konigelige Danske Videnskabernes Selskab Biologiske Skrifter* 17:1–234.

DREW, I. M., D. PERKINS, P. DALY
1971   Prehistoric domestication of animals: effects on bone structure. *Science* 171: 280–282.

ELLERMANN, J. R., T. C. S. MORRISON-SCOTT
1951   *Checklist of Palaeartic and Indian mammals.* London: British Museum (Natural History).

EPSTEIN, H.
1971   *The origin of the domestic animals of Africa,* two volumes. New York: Africana.

FRÖLICH, G., W. SPÖTTEL, E. TAENZER
1929   *Wollkunde. Bildung und Eigenschaften der Wolle.* Technologie der Textilfaser, Band 8, Teil 1. Berlin: Springer.
1933   *Haare und Borsten der Säugetiere. Die Rohstoffe des Tierreiches,* Band 1. Edited by F. Pax. Berlin: Bornträger.

GEYVALL, N. G.
1969   *Lerna, a preclassical site in the Argolid.* Princeton, N.J.: American School of Classical Studies at Athens.

HALTENORTH, T.
1963   "Artiodactyla," in *Handbuch der Zoologie,* Band 8, Lieferung 32. Edited by Helmcke, Lengerken, Starck, and Wermuth. Berlin: De Gruyter.

HANCAR, F.
1955   *Das Pferd in praehistorischer und frühhistorischer Zeit.* Wiener Beiträge zur Kulturgeschichte und Linguistik 11: 1–650.

HEPTNER, V. G., A. A. NASSIMOVIC, A. G. BANNIKOW
1966   *Die Säugetiere der Sowjetunion,* Band I: *Paarhufer und Unpaarhufer.* Jena: Gustav Fischer.

HERRE, W.
1949a   Zur Abstammung und Entwicklung der Haustiere I. Über das bisher älteste primigene Hausrind Nordeuropas. *Verhandlungen der Deutschen Zoologischen Gesellschaft zu Kiel 1948,* 312–324. Leipzig: Akademische Verlagsgesellschaft.
1949b   Zur Abstammung und Entwicklung der Haustiere II. Betrachtungen über vorgeschichtliche Wildschweine Mitteleuropas. *Verhandlungen der Deutschen Zoologischen Gesellschaft zu Kiel 1948,* 324–333. Leipzig: Akademische Verlagsgesellschaft.
1952   Studien über die wilden und domestizierten Tylopoden Südamerikas. *Der Zoologische Garten* (N.F.) 19: 70–98.
1953   Die Herkunft des Alpaka. *Säugetierkundliche Mitteilungen* 1: 176–177.
1955   *Das Ren als Haustier. Eine zoologische Monographie.* Leipzig: Akademische Verlagsgesellschaft.

1958 Züchtungsbiologische Betrachtungen an primitiven Tierzuchten. *Zeitschrift für Tierzüchtung und Züchtungsbiologie* 71: 252–272.
1961 Tiergeographische Betrachtungen an vorkolumbianischen Haussäugetieren Südamerikas. *Schriften des Geographischen Instituts der Universität Kiel* 20: 289–304.
1964 Zum Abstammungsproblem von Amphibien und Tylopoden sowie über Parallelbildungen und zur Polyphyliefrage. *Zoologischer Anzeiger* 173: 66–91.
1966 Zoologische Betrachtungen zu Aussagen über den Domestikationsbeginn. *Palaeohistoria* 12: 283–285.
1967 Gedanken zur Erhaltung des Wildpferdes *Equus przewalskii* Poljakow 1881. *Equus* 1: 304–325.
1968 "Zur Geschichte der vorkolumbianischen Haustiere Amerikas," in *Das Mexiko-Projekt der Deutschen Forschungsgemeinschaft. I. Berichte über begonnene und geplante Arbeiten.* Edited by Z. von Veselowsky and H. Dathe, 90–97. Wiesbaden: Franz Steiner.

HERRE, W., M. RÖHRS
1955 Über die Formenmannigfaltigkeit des Gehörns der Caprini Simpson. *Der Zoologische Garten* (N.F.) 22: 85–110.
1968 Die Tierreste aus den Hethitergräbern von Osman Kayasi. *Wissenschaftliche Veröffentlichung der deutschen Orient-Gesellschaft* 71: 60–80.
1971 "Domestikation und Stammesgeschichte," in *Die Evolution der Organismen.* Edited by G. Herber, Band II/2, pages 29–174. Stuttgart: Gustav Fischer.
1973 *Haustiere — zoologisch gesehen.* Stuttgart: Gustav Fischer.

HIGGS, E. S.
1962a "Early domesticated animals in Libya," in *Background to evolution in Africa.* Edited by W. W. Bishop and J. D. Clark, 165–173. Chicago: University of Chicago Press.
1962b The fauna of the early Neolithic site at Nea Nikomedaia. *Proceedings of the Prehistoric Society* 28: 271–274.

HIGGS, E. S., M. R. JARMAN
1969 The origin of agriculture: a reconsideration. *Antiquity* 43: 31–41.
1972 "The origins of animal and plant husbandry," in *Papers in economic prehistory: studies by members and associates of the British Academy Major Research Project in the Early History of Agriculture.* Edited by E. S. Higgs, 3–13. Cambridge: Cambridge University Press.

HILZHEIMER, M.
1926 *Natürliche Rassengeschichte der Haussäugetiere.* Berlin: De Gruyter.

HÜCKINGHAUS, F.
1961 Zur Nomenklatur und Abstammung des Hausmeerschweinchens. *Zeitschrift für Säugetierkunde* 26: 108–111.

HUXLEY, J.
1948 *Evolution, the modern synthesis* (fifth edition). London: George Allen and Unwin.

JARMAN, M. R.
1969 The prehistory of Upper Pleistocene and Recent cattle, part I: East Mediterranean with reference to North-West Europe. *Proceedings*

of the Prehistoric Society 35: 230–266.

1972   "European deer economies and the advent of the Neolithic," in *Papers in economic prehistory: studies by members and associates of the British Academy Major Research Project in the Early History of Agriculture.* Edited by E. S. Higgs, 125–147. Cambridge: Cambridge University Press.

JARMAN, M. R., P. F. WILKINSON

1972   "Criteria of animal domestication," in *Papers in economic prehistory: studies by members and associates of the British Academy Major Research Project in the Early History of Agriculture.* Edited by E. S. Higgs, 83–96. Cambridge: Cambridge University Press.

JEWELL, P. A.

1969   "Wild animals and their potential for new domestication," in *The domestication and exploitation of plants and animals.* Edited by P. J. Ucko and G. W. Dimbleby, 101–109. London: Gerald Duckworth.

KELLER, C.

1905   *Naturgeschichte der Haustiere.* Berlin: Paul Parey.

KELM, H.

1939   Zur Systematik der Wildschweine. *Zeitschrift für Tierzüchtung und Züchtungsbiologie* 43: 362–369.

KESPER, K.-D.

1954   "Phylogenetische und entwicklungsgeschichtliche Studien an den Gattungen *Capra* und *Ovis.*" Dissertation Mathematisch-Naturwissenschaftliche Fakultät der Universität Kiel.

KLATT, B.

1927   "Entstehung der Haustiere," in *Handbuch der Vererbungswissenschaft,* Band 3. Edited by E. Baur and M. Hartmann, 1–107. Berlin: Bornträger.

KLEIN, D. R.

1970   Food selection by North-American deer and their response to over-utilisation of preferred plant species. *British Ecological Society Symposium* 10: 25–46.

1972   Problems in conservation of mammals in the North. *Biological Conservation* 4: 97–101.

KLEIN, D. R., H. STRANDGAARD

1972   Factors affecting growth and body size of roe deer. *The Journal of Wildlife Management* 36: 64–79.

KLEINSCHMIDT, O.

1900   Arten oder Formenkreise. *Journal für Ornithologie* 48: 134–139.

KOCH, W.

1951   Das erste Auftreten von Mutationen bei neu domestizierten Tieren. *Züchtungskunde* 23: 1–5.

KRUSKA, D.

1973   "Domestikationsbedingte Grössenänderungen verschiedener Hirnstrukturen bei Schweinen," in *Domestikationsforschung und Geschichte der Haustiere.* Edited by J. Matolcsi, 135–140. Budapest: Adadémiai Kaidó.

LAWRENCE, B.

1967   Early domestic dogs. *Zeitschrift für Säugetierkunde* 32: 44–59.

1968 Antiquity of large dogs in North America. *Tebiwa, Journal of the Idaho State University Museum* 11: 43–49.

LEGGE, A. J.

1972 "Prehistoric exploitation of the gazelle in Palestine," in *Papers in economic prehistory: studies by members and associates of the British Academy Major Research Project in the Early History of Agriculture.* Edited by E. S. Higgs, 119–124. Cambridge: Cambridge University Press.

LOFTS, B., R. K. MURTON

1968 Photoperiodic and physiological adaptations regulating avian breeding cycles and their ecological significance. *Journal of Zoology* (London) 155: 327–394.

MAYR, E.

1963 *Animal species and evolution.* Cambridge, Mass.: The Belknap Press of Harvard University Press.

NACHTIGALL, H.

1965 Probleme des indianischen Grossviehzüchtertums. *Anthropos* 60: 177–197.

NOBIS, G.

1954 Zur Kenntnis der ur- und frühgeschichtlichen Rinder Nord- und Mitteldeutschlands. *Zeitschrift für Tierzüchtung und Züchtungsbiologie* 64: 155–194.

1971 *Vom Wildpferd zum Hauspferd. Studien zur Phylogenie pleistozäner Equiden Eurasiens und das Domestikationsproblem unserer Hauspferde.* Fundamenta. Monographien zur Urgeschichte, Reihe B, Band 6. Cologne and Vienna: Böhlau.

PERKINS, D.

1964 Prehistoric fauna from Shanidar, Iraq. *Science* 144: 1565–1566.

1969 Fauna of Catal Hüyük: evidence for early cattle domestication in Anatolia. *Science* 164: 177–179.

RADULESCO, C., P. SAMSON

1962 Sur un centre de domestication du mouton dans le mésolithique de la grotte "La Adam" en Dobrogea. *Zeitschrift für Tierzüchtung und Züchtungsbiologie* 76: 282–320.

REED, C. A.

1960 "A review of the archeological evidence on animal domestication in the prehistoric Near East," in *Prehistoric investigations in Iraqi Kurdistan.* Edited by R. J. Braidwood and B. Howe, 119–145. Studies in Ancient Oriental Civilization 31.

1969 "The pattern of animal domestication in the prehistoric Near East," in *The domestication and exploitation of plants and animals.* Edited by P. J. Ucko and G. W. Dimbleby, 361–380. London: Gerald Duckworth.

RENSCH, B.

1929 *Das Prinzip geographischer Rassenkreise und das Problem der Artbildung.* Berlin: Bautträger.

1934 *Kurze Anweisung für zoologisch-systematische Studien.* Leipzig: Akademische Verlagsgesellschaft.

REQUATE, H.
1962   Über nacheiszeitliche Säugetiere und die Geschichte der Haustiere Schleswig-Holsteins. *Zeitschrift für Tierzüchtung und Züchtungsbiologie* 77: 242–254.

RÖHRS, M.
1958   Ökologische Betrachtungen an wildlebenden Tylopoden Südamerikas. *Verhandlungen der Deutschen Zoologischen Gesellschaft in Graz 1957*, 538–554.

RÖHRS, M., W. HERRE
1961   Zur Frühentwicklung der Haustiere. *Zeitschrift für Tierzüchtung und Züchtungsbiologie* 75: 57–78.

ROTH, H. H., M. A. KERR, J. POSSELT
1970–1972   Studies on the agricultural utilization of semi-domesticated eland (*Taurotragus oryx*) in Rhodesia. Part I: *Rhodesian Journal of Agricultural Research* 8: 67–70. Part V: *Zeitschrift für Tierzüchtung und Züchtungsbiologie* 89: 69–83.

RYDER, M. L.
1962   The histological examination of skin in the study of domestication of sheep. *Zeitschrift für Tierzüchtung und Züchtungsbiologie* 77: 168–171.
1969   "Changes in the fleece of sheep following domestication (with a note on the coat of cattle)," in *The domestication and exploitation of plants and animals*. Edited by P. J. Ucko and G. W. Dimbleby, 495–521. London: Gerald Duckworth.

SAUER, C. O.
1952   *Agricultural origins and dispersals*. New York: The American Geographical Society.

SHAKELFORD, R. M.
1949   Mutations affecting coat color in ranch-bred mink and foxes. Congress of Genetics, Stockholm. *Hereditas*.

SOSSINKA, R.
1970   Domestikationserscheinungen beim Zebrafinken *Taeniopygia guttata castanotis*. *Zoologische Jahrbücher, Abteilung Systematik* 97: 445–521.

SPÖTTEL, W., E. TAENZER
1923   Rassenanalytische Untersuchungen an Schafen unter besonderer Berücksichtigung von Haut und Haar. *Archiv für Naturgeschichte* 89, Heft 6.

TAENZER, E.
1926   Haut und Haar beim Karakul im rassenanalytischen Vergleich. *Kühn-Archiv* 18: 151–297.

TALBOT, L. W., W. J. H. PAYNE, H. P. LEDGER, L. D. VERDVOURT, M. H. TALBOT
1965   *The meat-production potential of wild animals in Africa*. Bucks, England: Commonwealth Agricultural Bureaux.

TIESSEN, M.
1970   "Die Tierknochenfunde von Haithabu und Elisenhof. Ein Vergleich zweier frühmittelalterlicher Siedlungen in Schleswig-Holstein." Dissertation Mathematisch-Naturwissenschaftliche Fakultät der Unversität Kiel.

TRINGHAM, R.
 1969   "Animal domestication in the Neolithic cultures of the south-west
        part of European U.S.S.R.," in *The domestication and exploitation of
        plants ana animals.* Edited by P. J. Ucko   and G. W. Dimbleby,
        381–392. London: Gerald Duckworth.
TURNBULL, P., C. A. REED
 1974   The fauna from the terminal Pleistocene of Palegawra Cave, a Zarzian
        occupation site in northeastern Iraq. *Fieldiana: Anthropology* 63: 81–
        146.
VITA-FINZI, C., E. S. HIGGS
 1970   Prehistoric economy in the Mount Carmel area of Palestine: site
        catchment analysis. *Proceedings of the Prehistoric Society* 34: 1–34.
WATSON, W.
 1969   "Early animal domestication in China," in *The domestication and
        exploitation of plants and animals.* Edited by P. J. Ucko and G. W.
        Dimbleby, 393–395. London: Gerald Duckworth.
WILKINSON, P. F.
 1972   Oominmak: a model for man/animal relationship in prehistory.
        Current Anthropology 13: 23–44.

Environmental Change and the Origin of Agriculture in the Old and New Worlds

HERBERT E. WRIGHT, JR.

More than forty years have passed since V. Gordon Childe presented his unified theory of environmental determinism in cultural history, in particular with respect to the origin of agriculture (Childe 1929). Childe's theory was based on the presumption that climatic change in Western Europe, as inferred from the glacial and pollen sequence, was matched in the Near East by a change from a moist-temperate phase, corresponding to the glacial period, to the semiarid climate of today, forcing animals, plants, and man to congregate at oases, where domestication was born.

In those forty years, archaeological investigations have confirmed in some detail that agriculture was indeed first developed in southwestern Asia, but paleoecological studies have shown that the climate in this region went from dry to moist rather than the reverse, thus vitiating the essence of Childe's hypothesis. On the other hand, the new technique of radiocarbon dating has shown that the cultural and climatic changes here were nearly synchronous, as Childe supposed, so the problem of climatic determinism remains.

This review first examines the paleoecological evidence for environmental change in the Mediterranean area during the critical time span, to set the stage for considering the influence of this change on the cultural history of man.

Emphasis is placed on the pollen record of vegetational history, because vegetation is generally sensitive to climatic change, and because the chronology of vegetational change is easily established by radiocarbon dating of pollen-bearing sediments. Several pollen diagrams are presented in a form extracted and redrawn from the originals, which are generally very difficult to follow because of crowding and excessive reduction. Only the major pollen types that show significant stratigraphic changes are included in these simplified versions.

Briefly, the pollen studies across the lands of the northern Mediterranean provide evidence that the climatic change at the end of the Pleistocene caused the semiarid *Artemisia* steppe to withdraw to southern Asia, to be replaced by the distinctive vegetation of the dry-summer Mediterranean climate. The hypothesis is presented that the wild cereal grains, which are adapted to a dry-summer climate, immigrated at this time to the hill-lands and plateaus northeast of the Mediterranean, setting the stage for their domestication.

Other centers of agricultural origin may have developed independently elsewhere at later dates, with different crops and different animals, so the same problem of environmental determinism arises. Of these other areas, the situation for the New World is reviewed. Here the evidence for climatic control is weak, and the case for domestication may instead rest with cultural factors.

MEDITERRANEAN REGION

Vegetational Change

In the northern Mediterranean region (Figure 1) evidence is now extensive for the existence of a cool, dry steppe for the period from before 35,000 years ago to about 11,000 years ago. Pollen studies in Iran, Syria, Greece, Italy, and Spain all show the same trends.

In Iran, the pollen study for Lake Zeribar in the Zagros Mountains (van Zeist and Wright 1963; van Zeist 1967, 1969) is supplemented by studies of plant remains (Wasylikowa 1967) and lacustrine microcrustacea (Megard 1967) and is also supported by analyses of pollen surface samples collected in transects from the Mesopotamian desert lowland across the oak-covered mountains to the interior plateaus, to determine the pollen assemblage produced today from known vegetation types (Wright, et al. 1967). The results (Figure 2) indicate that before about 11,000 years ago the vegetation was a steppe dominated by *Artemisia* [sagebrush], with a climate cooler and drier than today, perhaps like that of the higher parts of the Anatolian and Iranian Plateaus to the north. Subsequent to 11,000 years ago, oak invaded the area, leading to the open oak woodland of today.

The severity of the environmental change is reflected not only in the

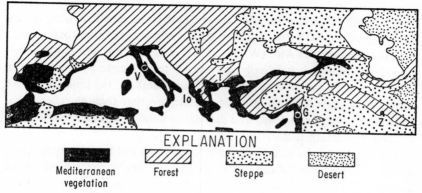

Figure 1. Map of Mediterranean region to show present distribution of Mediterranean vegetation (black) and other types of vegetation, as well as the location of the following pollen sites described in the text:

G – Ghab, Syria
Io – Ioannina, Greece
T – Tenagi Philippon, Greece
V – Vico, Italy
Z – Lake Zeribar, Iran

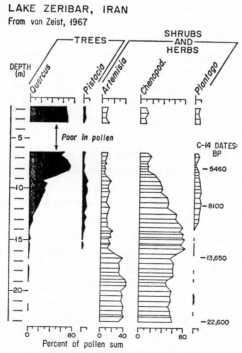

Figure 2. Selected pollen curves for Lake Zeribar, western Iran (redrawn from van Zeist 1967)

vegetational differences but also in the fact that the snowline in the mountains was depressed 1,200–1,800 meters, as much as or more than was the case in the European Alps (Wright 1961). Although this amount of snowline depression was originally attributed to a Pleistocene increase in precipitation as well as a decrease in air temperature, the pollen evidence seems to indicate a decrease of precipitation rather than an increase, at least in the interior plateau. The glaciation must owe its severity instead to the temperature factor.

The climate of the glacial period in this region did not simply result in downward migration of the oak forest, which presumably existed in the area prior to glaciation, for a supplemental pollen site at the base of the modern tree belt indicates that before 11,000 years ago trees were absent from that area as well. The conclusion must be drawn that the entire Zagros Mountains, as well as the Iranian Plateau and the Mesopotamian piedmont, were essentially treeless during the glacial period, and that the oak woodland withdrew to moister refuges close to the Mediterranean.

Farther west, in the Levant, the nature of the climatic change at the end of the Pleistocene is somewhat in dispute. A profile from the Ghab depression (Figure 3) just inside the coastal mountain range in northwestern Syria shows a dominance of herb pollen (*Artemisia* and chenopods) before 11,000 years ago, just as in the Zagros Mountains, implying steppe vegetation. Oak was usually present in minor amounts, and cedar, juniper, and pine occurred at certain times (Niklewski and van Zeist 1970). In this area today the coastal mountains are completely covered with forest, and the second range (east of the Ghab depression) has a much-altered steppe forest. The pollen rain in the depression itself has been dominated throughout Holocene time by oak, pistachio, olive, ironwood, and pine, indicating relatively moist conditions compared to the Pleistocene. The conclusion is clear that the climate of the late Pleistocene in this area was drier than that of today.

Only 200 kilometers farther south, however, in the Jordan Valley of Palestine, pollen profiles from Lake Huleh are interpreted by Horowitz (1971) as representing a cool and humid pluvial interval 16,000 to 11,500 years ago, followed by a "warm, humid" postpluvial period. These findings are taken to support the traditional view in Palestine that the last glacial period of Europe was matched by a pluvial interval in the Mediterranean region, for which a variety of geomorphic, paleolimnologic, paleontologic, and sedimentologic evidence of variable quality has been adduced (Farrand 1971). Study of the pollen diagram from Huleh, however, reveals that each of the two pollen zones in question is based on only a single analysis. In fact, the entire 120 meters of core, representing perhaps more

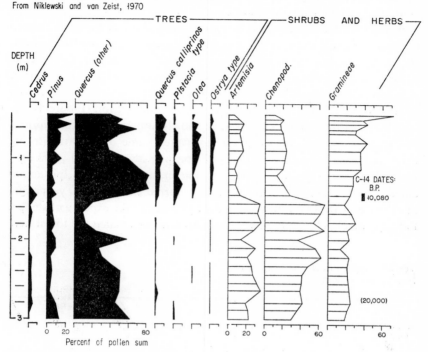

Figure 3.   Selected pollen curves for Ghab Marsh, northwestern Syria (redrawn from Niklewski and van Zeist 1970)

than 60,000 years, is subdivided into eight pollen zones on the basis of only fourteen analyses. The paleoecological significance of the various zigzagging pollen curves is not at all clear, because the pollen sums used in the percentage calculation do not readily permit a vegetational interpretation, and because nothing is known about what kind of pollen rain is produced today by the modern vegetation in the region. The Huleh study suffers severely in these respects in comparison with that of Ghab described above, which uses much more substantial evidence (e.g. more than 100 pollen types in 75 stratigraphic levels) to yield the opposite climatic interpretation for the same time range.

On the other hand, it is conceivable that in Pleistocene time the Palestinian area occupied a different climatic zone not affected by the expansion of the Asiatic high-pressure air mass and its attendant dry climate. Today, however, this region has the dry-summer climate characteristic of both the northern and southern Mediterranean, and it is not easy to visualize a major climatic and vegetational boundary between the

Syrian and Palestinian segments of the Levantine coast. The subject needs continued critical study to resolve the anomaly.

West of the Levant, the next two pollen sites of interest are in northern Greece, in Tenagi Philippon (near Salonika), where the published pollen sequence for thirty meters of sediment covers at least the last 70,000 years, as extrapolated from twelve finite radiocarbons dates in the upper part of the core (Wijmstra 1969; van der Hammen, Wijmstra and Zagwijn 1971). The vegetation for most of the Pleistocene portion (Figure 4) was characterized by a steppe of *Artemisia* and chenopods, with interruptions before 50,000 years ago when forest covered some of the area during brief intervals. The situation changed abruptly about 13,500 years ago, when the modern types of trees (oak, linden, hazel, ash, elm, pistachio) entered the area. A temporary reversal occurred about 10,500 years ago, but thereafter the oak forest gradually expanded at the expense of steppe. Pine, fir, beech, elm, and other deciduous trees diversified the forest here

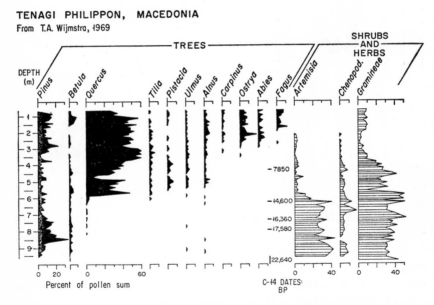

Figure 4.   Selected pollen curves for Tenagi Philippon, northeastern Greece (redrawn from Wijmstra 1969)

more than in the Iranian mountains, for the site is close to the ecotone between temperate and Mediterranean vegetation. But apparently during the last glacial period both areas were characterized by essentially treeless vegetation, as was the intervening area of Levantine Syria described above.

For the mountains of northern Greece, located farther to the west, Bottema (1967) presents a preliminary pollen diagram for a marsh site near Ioannina (Figure 5). As in the lowland Macedonian site, the interval before 11,000 years ago, corresponding to the time of the last glaciation, was marked by steppe with *Artemisia*, chenopods, and grasses, back to

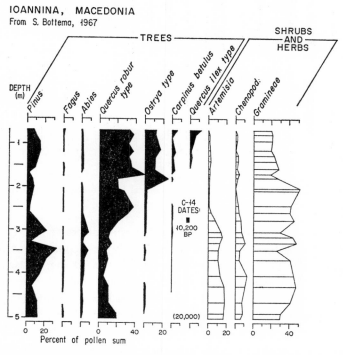

Figure 5. Pollen diagram for Ioannina, northern Greece (from Bottema 1967)

about 35,000 years ago, locally with oak and beech trees on mountain slopes. In early Holocene time an oak forest with grassy openings was followed by the complete forest cover of today, which is dominated by oak but contains pine and fir as well as hornbeam, beech, and other deciduous trees. Again the interpretation calls for a cool, dry climate for the late Pleistocene.

In central Italy, the dominance of *Artemisia* steppe during the glacial period, and thus a dry climate compared to the Holocene, was first documented by Bonatti (1966, 1970) at Lago de Monterosi near Rome.

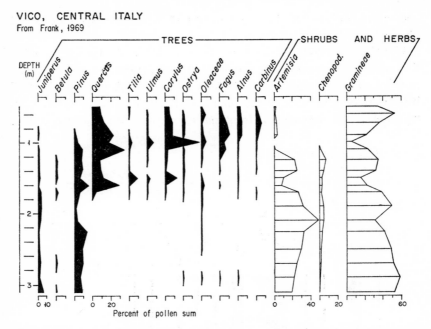

Figure 6.   Selected pollen curves for Vico, central Italy (redrawn from Frank 1969)

A more detailed but undated diagram for another crater lake (Vico) in central Italy amplifies this picture (Frank 1969): a steppe with *Artemisia* and grass, with few trees except juniper, dominated the landscape for thousands of years before the invasion of pine and a whole suite of temperate deciduous trees at the beginning of Holocene time (Figure 6).

Finally, both northern and southern Spain were apparently marked by *Artemisia* steppe during the last glacial period, according to well-dated profiles published by Menendez Amor and Florschütz (1963). Oak and other deciduous trees contribute most of the pollen in these regions today.

Thus the entire area of the northern Mediterranean from Iran to Spain was characterized during the last glaciation by an *Artemisia* steppe, in which grasses or chenopods were generally common. Trees were sparse, being represented primarily by oak, and in the Iranian sector not even oak was present. The steppe apparently extended northward into the Alps (Grüger 1968) and merged with the Pleistocene "tundra" of the rest of Europe, perhaps in the way the warm steppe of the Zagros foothills in southern Iran today merges with the relatively cool steppe of the Iranian Plateau at the point where the depauperate oak woodland that separates them farther west pinches out eastward because of the increasing aridity.

The entire picture points to aridity throughout Eurasia during the glacial maximum, extending to the Mediterranean shores, with a simple temperature gradient from north to south.

Climatic Change

Aridity characterizes much of the region of the eastern Mediterranean today, especially the treeless Anatolian and Iranian plateaus and of course the deserts east of the Levant. The entire area is marked by the dry-summer Mediterranean climate (Figure 7), and the plant cover includes species of

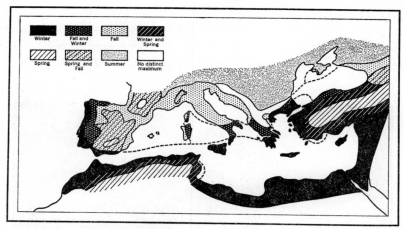

Figure 7. Present distribution and intensity of Mediterranean-type climate in the Mediterranean region (from Trewartha 1968)

Artemisia and chenopods. One might propose that a simple westward extension of this vegetation type to Greece, Italy, and Spain could account for the Pleistocene *Artemisia*-chenopod pollen assemblage in these areas, rather than a southwestern expansion of the Soviet steppe, which is characterized by summer as well as winter rainfall. Three points may be raised against this hypothesis:
1.   The transect of pollen surface samples from the Mesopotamian desert steppe to the Iranian plateau indicates that the relatively cool steppe of the plateau carries higher pollen percentages of *Artemisia* and chenopods than does the warm steppe of the lowlands, which are marked instead by high pollen percentages of plantain (*Plantago*). The pollen profiles of

Lake Zeribar in western Iran show that plantain was not present in significant quantities until after 11,000 years ago. On this basis the Pleistocene *Artemisia*-chenopod assemblage in Iran is correlated with a cool steppe with northern affinities rather than a warm steppe related to the Mesopotamian lowland.

2. For the pollen study at Tenagi Philippon near Salonika in northern Greece, Smit and Wijmstra (1970) examined by electron microscopy the fine-structure of two fossil chenopod pollen types, comparing them with reference pollen of ten species of chenopods. The fossil material best resembles pollen of two genera that are confined to the cool, arid steppes of the Pamir and other parts of southern Asia, which lack the summer droughts of the Mediterranean climate. One may conclude from these results that the Asiatic steppe climate in the Pleistocene extended at least to Macedonia.

3. Pollen studies for northern Greece (Tenagi Philippon) and Levantine Syria (Ghab) show that the pollen type for the evergreen oaks of the central and eastern Mediterranean region (*Quercus ilex, Q. coccifera,*

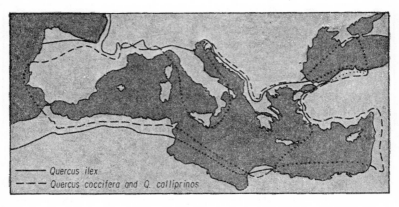

Figure 8.   Present ranges of three evergreen oaks that produce the distinctive *Quercus ilex-coccifera-calliprinos* pollen type (after Rikli 1943)

Q. calliprinos; range map on Figure 8) do not appear until the beginning of the Holocene. Pistachio, which is a common and characteristic tree or shrub of the Mediterranean region (although it also occurs farther east and also in Mexico), is confined to the Holocene sediments at Tenagi Philippon and Ghab. Olive, also almost entirely a Mediterranean genus, at least as far as the cultivated form is concerned (Figure 9), is a definite Holocene newcomer at Ghab.

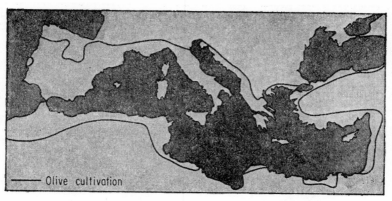

Figure 9.   Present area of olive cultivation in the Mediterranean region (from Pansiot and Rebour 1961)

These three points support the hypothesis that the Mediterranean climate, with summer drought, is a Holocene innovation in the region, and that the late Pleistocene climate was characterized instead by year-round precipitation at levels too low to support growth of trees, along with relatively low temperatures, including frequent frost, as in southern Russia. Such a climatic regime is consistent with the indication of deep snowline depression in the Mediterranean mountains (Wright 1961), which points to a decrease in mean annual temperature of at least 8° Centigrade — perhaps more if the total precipitation were reduced (as postulated) and shifted in part from winter snow to summer rain. (On the other hand, increase in summer cloudiness might decrease summer melting of snowfields.) Such a postulated temperature change is in fact comparable to the current temperature difference between, say, the Aegean coast and the Russian steppe north of the Caspian Sea.

The Mediterranean type of climate occupies a distinctly transitional belt between the temperate zone of prevailing westerly winds and the subtropical dry belt. Such a climatic belt occurs on the western sides of all continents at this latitude, in both northern and southern hemispheres, but it is well developed only around the Mediterranean Sea (Figure 10). In the winter, in that region, the westerly storm tracks move south, and the Mediterranean Sea provides not only a broad lowland but a continued warm source of moisture for deep eastward penetration of storms. In the summer, the subtropical Azores High expands, and the air dries as it subsides and spreads over the Mediterranean area.

A more normal development of the Mediterranean type of climate is found in southern California and Chile, where the mountain barriers

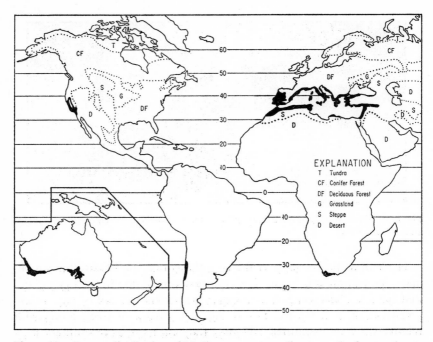

Figure 10.   Present distribution of Mediterranean-type climate on the five continents in which it occurs; note its restriction to narrow coastal areas everywhere except around the Mediterranean Sea; other major vegetation areas are shown by letter in the northern hemisphere only (from Trewartha 1968)

limit the eastward extension of winter storms, and where the narrowness of the land mass permits moist Atlantic air to spread westward in the summer and develop convective storms.

The traditional paleoclimatic reconstruction, utilized by Childe (1929), Zeuner (1952), and many others, supposes for the Pleistocene a shift of summer storm tracks to the south of the Alps, bringing precipitation and thus a pluvial interval to the Mediterranean region. The concept was popularized by the presentation of a map of Pleistocene vegetation belts by Büdel (1949), which has since been entrenched in textbooks (Flint 1971; Woldstedt 1954), showing temperate deciduous forest along both north and south sides of the Mediterranean Sea.

The picture now developing still involves a southward shift of summer storm tracks, bringing summer rains to the Mediterranean area. But the winter picture is different. Europe during the Pleistocene was cold, as manifested by the development of glaciers and tundra vegetation. Even the Mediterranean region was cold. Winter storm tracks, which today occupy a diffuse belt from Scandinavia to the Mediterranean Sea, were displaced to the south, probably to northwest Africa. They no longer travelled the easy, self-nourishing course over the length of the Mediterranean Sea, whose northern shores therefore received less winter rain than today.

Thus instead of the interglacial temperate forest migrating into the Mediterranean region, the Asiatic steppe spread southwest to the very shores of the Mediterranean, grading north to the tundra that covered the rest of Europe. Both the coniferous and the deciduous forests, which today occupy such a broad latitudinal range, disintegrated to isolated stands in favorable localities, perhaps in the Balkan peninsula and elsewhere in the Mediterranean mountains (Beug 1968), from which they could rapidly immigrate to Europe at the beginning of the Holocene — an immigration that is documented in great detail by dozens of pollen diagrams north of the Alps. The isolated stands were generally too small to leave a significant pollen record, although the consistent presence of beech pollen in the Ioannina profile is an example of the situation that might be postulated.

Positive field evidence for such a southward displacement and severe restriction of the Mediterranean climatic belt is sparse and poorly dated, especially concerning vegetational relations. East Africa was apparently drier in the late Pleistocene than in the Holocene, although glaciers were lower on the mountains (Livingstone 1967; Butzer, et al. 1972). Sub-Saharan Africa (Lake Chad area: Faure 1969) was also drier. These results are provocative, to say the least. Although they may imply that the traditional glacial/pluvial correlation is no longer valid for tropical latitudes, a substitute paleoclimatic picture is far from being established. But somewhere in the northern part of Africa there must have been the refuge for Mediterranean plant species. The pollen studies show that at earlier interglacial times in the Pleistocene the Mediterranean plant types were as common at the same localities as today.

In conclusion, it may be emphasized that the Pleistocene/Holocene boundary about 11,000 years ago was marked by a profound and relatively abrupt climatic and vegetational change throughout the northern Mediterranean, as it was in many other parts of the world. The late Pleistocene steppe of this region, merging northward with tundra, reflected a semiarid climate that included summer as well as winter rains and was cold enough to bring glaciers and frost soils at least 1,200 meters down the mountains. The aridity was less in the mountains, which locally provided refuges for north-temperate trees such as beech and deciduous oaks. The combination of summer rains and relatively low temperatures was apparently the reason why the typical Mediterranean species of trees and shrubs of today, such as evergreen oak, pistachio, and olive, were not present. Their abrupt expansion 11,000 years ago signaled the return of the inter-glacial-style Mediterranean climate to the Mediterranean region.

Such a major geographical shift in the range of these species of plants over a period of a very few thousand years may be a surprise to the geneticist and taxonomist unaccustomed to the effects of rapid climatic change. Such shifts are well established for temperate parts of both Europe and North America, however. Because of the great distance of the eastern Mediterranean region from the Scandinavian ice sheet, many have thought that the climatic effects were diffuse and had relatively little influence on the main distribution of plant species. The present thesis, independently developed from both botanical and glacial evidence, implies that climatic and environmental changes in the Mediterranean area were fully as severe as those in Western Europe — presumably because they represented fundamental global changes in the general cir-culation of the atmosphere rather than periglacial effects of the ice sheet.

Domestication of Plants

Vavilov (1926) argued that the domestication of wheat, barley, and the other seed plants occurred in the region of their primary natural ranges in southwestern Asia, especially in the mountains, where the diversity of habitats permitted maximum genetic variations. The essence of this thesis has stood the test of subsequent botanical and genetic research, and the archaeological excavations accomplished by Braidwood and others in Iraq, Iran, and Turkey specifically to test the hypothesis in the field do in fact support it, for there the earliest fossils of domesticated plants and animals have been recovered. The thesis, however, involves the tacit assumption that the modern distribution of the wild forms approximates their natural distribution at the time of domestication.

The principal plants involved at the beginning are einkorn wheat (*Triticum boeoticum*), emmer wheat (*T. dicoccoides*), and barley (*Hordeum spontaneum*), all of which have their main distribution today in oak wood-land and associated steppes of the Taurus-Zagros Mountains and the Anatolian-Iranian Plateaus adjacent to the north (Figure 11), with some occurrence westward to the Balkan Peninsula or southward to the Pales-tinian plateaus (Zohary 1969).

With some minor exceptions, the entire range of these three wild cereal grains is within the region of summer-dry Mediterranean climate, and indeed their methods of seed dispersal and germination are highly adapted

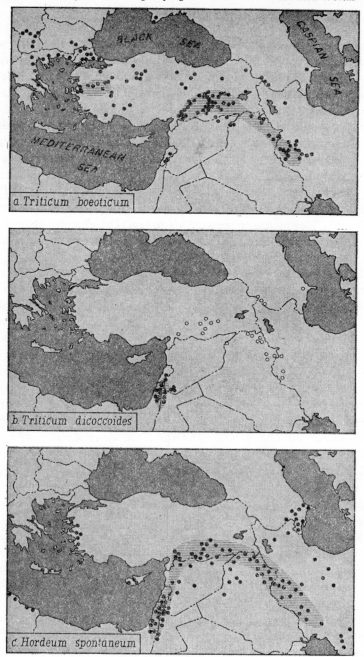

Figure 11. Present distribution of wild einkorn wheats and barley in the eastern Mediterranean (from Zohary 1969)
a. Distribution of wild einkorn (shaded pattern shows primary habitats)
b. Distribution of wild emmer (shaded pattern shows area of common occurrence; open circles include some stands of related tetraploid wheats, as well as *T. dicoccoides*)
c. Distribution of wild barley (shaded pattern shows primary habitats)

to this type of environment (Zohary 1969). Specifically, the mature seeds break freely from the brittle rachis soon after the end of the winter rains, and they are adapted to become inserted into the dry ground deeply enough to be protected during the long hot summer. Also, their large size provides the food storage by which they germinate and grow rapidly as soon as the rains come the following winter. The paleoclimatic evidence presented above points to a Pleistocene displacement and perhaps a severe diminution of the Mediterranean climatic zone, so that it occupied only a small area on the west and north of Africa, like its small extent today in the west of North America. The wild cereal grains, if tied to a Mediterranean climate, may therefore have had quite a different distribution in the Pleistocene, compared to today. The climatic change that introduced the Holocene may thus have brought the cereal grains to the area where Vavilov first plotted them.

Although this account of history suggests an instability in the plant distributions not incorporated in Vavilov's theory, it does not in fact vitiate the theory. Indeed it may strengthen it, because the distant migration of the plants is an indication of the vigor and adaptability of their populations, and thus of variability and diversity that are the essence of Vavilov's theory. Immigration of the wild cereal grains into the mountains and plateaus northeast of the Mediterranean Sea may have permitted hybridization with other grasses that had been common there during the Pleistocene. Development of polyploidy (*T. dicoccoides* is a tetraploid wheat) may also have been stimulated by the environmental stress resulting from climatic change and migration. The diversification associated with hybridization and polyploidy may have set the stage for domestication.

The proposed sequence of events makes a strong pitch for environmental influence in plant domestication. The general idea was tentatively put forward earlier (Wright 1968, 1970) only with respect to the Iranian scene, and without the benefit of the new pollen diagrams from Syria, Greece, and Italy. The rest of the hypothesis, involving largely human factors, remains speculative, but the propitious combination of climatic, geologic, geomorphic, vegetational, and human factors at that point in time may have made the whole thing work.

Certainly the wild cereal grains existed in the late Pleistocene, somewhere. Why were they not domesticated then? Perhaps their distribution (Africa?) was in an area where human populations were small or lacked diversity, or had not reached a cultural stage of a nature appropriate to take the necessary steps to domestication. The size of a population devoted to hunting and gathering depends in part on the abundance and diversity of the food resource, which in turn may depend on physical factors of the environment, such as the topography and thus the geology. These factors may all have been unfavorable in the area of the late-Pleistocene refuge.

In contrast, in the foothills of the Zagros Mountains and in parts of adjacent areas, all factors were favorable after the end-Pleistocene climatic change. The following points can be made:

1. The Zagros-Taurus Mountains consist largely of folded limestones marked by long ridges and valleys, sharp canyons, broad gravel terraces, and other diverse geomorphic features that provide a wide variety of habitat for wild game and edible plants. Numerous caves and rock shelters have served as temporary or year round homes for man.

2. Archaeological surveys indicate that a great many of these caves and shelters were occupied by late-Paleolithic man, who utilized a variety of animals as a food resource, according to the bones collected at the sites. Plants presumably were used as well, but there are no indications of domestication of either plants or animals at that time.

3. The late-Pleistocene climate was colder and drier than today, and the vegetation was treeless. Winters must have been inhospitable for man, but the caves gave shelter. The diversity of topography provided sufficient cover for the same group of mammals that occurred there in Holocene times, even though the climate and the vegetation were different.

4. With the end-Pleistocene climatic change about 11,000 years ago, a new suite of plants immigrated into the region, including the wild cereal grains. These and other wild plants were added to the diet of man.

5. The warmer climate made living conditions more equable in the mountains, and the hunter-gatherers could move out of the caves to establish year-round living sites in the open.

This integrated hypothesis may contain an important link in the challenging problem of agricultural origin — the environmental link that explains the localization of the great event in time and space. After thousands and even tens of thousands of years of hunting and gathering, with slowly differentiating cultural patterns amidst relatively stable Pleistocene environments, a great change occurred in nature — the end of the ice age — and this set in motion a series of events that triggered a cultural change in the one area in which the organisms were most easily adapted to human manipulation — the Near East.

All other areas may have been secondary centers of origin, at later times, for it cannot be disproven that once the idea of domestication was established it was transmitted through the movements of man, even though the crops and animals involved were different. Even in those days most parts of the world were accessible to man, and it is conceivable that cultural connections may have existed between the Near East and the most distant lands.

One may also look in these other areas for environmental controls on the development of agriculture, whether this development be primary or secondary. In most of the other areas, such as China or southeastern Asia, the nature and chronology of environmental change are not well enough known at the present time to justify the kind of analysis possible for the Mediterranean region. In the following section the situation is examined for the New World, which perhaps has the greatest chance of being a completely independent primary area of domestication, because it is relatively inaccessible for cultural communication with the Near East.

THE NEW WORLD

Introduction

The New World has as many and as varied physiographic regions as the Old, and the cultural history, although of much shorter duration, has complexity and diversification that certainly reflect environmental factors. As in the Old World, the question that must be posed is whether changes in these environmental factors have had important effects on human exploitation of resources, and more specifically whether the development of agriculture can be related in any way to environmental change.

The chronology is critical. Whereas in the Near East plants can be demonstrated to have been first domesticated soon after the end-Pleistocene climatic change about 11,000 years ago, and animals at about the same time, in the New World the first very tentative steps toward farming are not demonstrable until 9,000 years ago or later. But these steps were indeed tentative and prolonged, and not until thousands of years later did domestic plants constitute a major proportion of a diet that otherwise involved a great variety of wild plants and animals. What can be stated, however, is that gradual shifts in resource utilization did occur during these early times.

For example, the replacement of "big-game hunters" about 9,000 years ago is usually attributed to the extinction of big mammals about this time, whether as a result of climatic change or of overexploitation by man himself (Martin and Wright 1967). Although opinions differ on the details of the readaptation to the changed animal resource (Flannery

1966), the paleontological and archaeological evidence is now abundant enough and dated well enough to state with some assurance that a major shift in fauna occurred throughout the New World, and that the human populations adapted to the shift more by changing their patterns of collecting food than by domesticating available plants and animals. On the other hand, one might say that the loss of big game led to more thorough use of other food resources, which in turn led to domestication in some groups, and in this respect the chain of events starting with the faunal shift ultimately resulted in New World agriculture. Thus we may still think of an agricultural revolution in Middle America, in which the first domestication may have occurred 9,000 years ago, leading gradually to village farming 5,500 years ago and the great city states 1,500 years ago. Certainly the pace of the revolution was slow compared to that of the Near East, where comparable stages can be identified at 11,000 years ago, 9,000 years ago and 6,000 years ago — a total range of much less time. But the pace of change was faster than it had been during the long interval of big-game hunting that preceded, and in this respect it qualifies as a cultural "revolution."

Although the impetus for some of the cultural changes in parts of the New World may have been the extinction of the big mammals, the story of domestication here is a story of plants rather than of animals. Only the guinea pig, the turkey, the llama, and the dog were domesticated; their development was generally later than that of domesticated plants. Many of the New World plants that came into widespread cultivation — e.g. maize, common bean, squash, amaranth — were seed-plants apparently first domesticated in the semiarid valleys of Mexico (Pickersgill and Heiser, this volume), although domesticated common bean and lima bean have recently been reported from the Peruvian highlands that may be older (Kaplan, et al. 1973). Other plants were developed later from wild types in other natural habitats — e.g. potatoes from the Peruvian highlands, sweet potatoes, peanuts, and probably manioc from the tropical lowlands of South America.

Although the principal species of plants and animals involved in domestication in the New World were completely different from those in the Old World, the geographic settings of the two areas have some similarity. The highlands north of Mesopotamia in the Old World and the intermontane valleys of southern Mexico and highland Peru both have the topographic diversity and the varied vegetational types that provide the habitats for a diverse flora and fauna — a condition particularly favorable for the kind of unconscious human manipulation of food resources that can easily lead to domestication (Harris 1972). They also are both characterized by limestone caves that provided year-round living sites for the hunters and gatherers. In the Old World the primary spread of agricul- ure from the nuclear area was to the west and northwest into more temperate latitudes, where the seed crops and domestic animals could flourish, and where the main problems involved forest clearance. Migra- tion to the south, on the other hand, was inhibited by the great deserts of northern Africa, Arabia, and the Persian Gulf. In the New World migra- tion to the south from the nuclear area was possible because the Central American mountains and the Andes provided the topographic range for several life zones, and at the same time they furnished additional plant types susceptible to domestication — the root crops and other vegetative cultigens so common in the diverse flora of the tropics (Harris 1972).

Because Mexico was the principal focus of New World domestication, a review of the environmental history of Middle America should be presented first. Vegetation is the most sensitive key to climatic change in most areas, but unfortunately the vegetational history of Middle America is poorly known, partly because of the paucity of small lakes suitable for stratigraphic pollen analysis. One substitute approach is to examine the situation for North America, and then to evaluate a southward extra- polation of the climatic sequence to Mexico, on the principle that major climatic changes are continental, if not global. The review that follows for North America will start with the end-Pleistocene climatic change, for we must consider the equally relevant question of why domestication in the New World did not occur coincidently with the major climatic change, as it did in the Near East, rather than later.

North America

The climatic change terminating the Pleistocene in North America has left its best record in glaciated areas, where glacial features indicate the course of ice retreat, and where abundant lakes and bogs provide material for reconstruction of vegetation history since the ice retreat. The main ice sheet reached its maximum about 18,000–20,000 years ago in the region of the Great Lakes and then commenced a fluctuating retreat, which accelerated after about 11,000 years ago. The contemporaneous vegeta- tion close to the ice margin was tundra only in the northern part of the Great Lakes region and in New England. Elsewhere in the glaciated area spruce forests prevailed — even on debris-covered stagnant ice itself (Wright 1971a). The boreal coniferous forest extended southward at least to Kansas and southern Illinois, and down the Atlantic coastal plain and the

Appalachian Mountains to northern Georgia, where spruce as the dominant conifer gave way to jack pine, also a tree whose distribution today indicates a cool-temperate climate (Watts 1970).

The transformation to temperate deciduous forest similar to that of today occurred rapidly through a series of successional stages, and in most of the area it was essentially completed by 9,000 years ago, with relatively minor changes since then in the proportion of the principal forest components (oak, hemlock, beech, hickory, and, in the more northerly areas, pine). In the prairie-border region of Minnesota, however, the trend to warmer, drier climate that brought about this transformation continued until about 7,000 years ago, causing expansion of prairie into the area previously occupied by deciduous forest, which in turn invaded the coniferous area. The climatic trend then reversed, and the situation today resembles that of 9,000 years ago, with important differences in vegetation that may be related to the progressive leaching of soils, development of bogs on filled lake basins, and delayed westward migration of certain major tree species, such as hemlock and white pine.

Thus we have in the prairie-border region of Minnesota the evidence for a significant environmental shift in mid-postglacial time. Such a shift is not clearly manifested in the heart of the forest mosaic of areas to the east. The climatic and vegetational shift certainly must have involved concomitant changes in animal populations and in their human predators, for the faunas of prairie and forest are different. The paucity of archaeological sites for the region in the relevant time range does not permit any confirmation of the hypothetical effects of the environmental changes on human cultures. In any case, a geographic shift of life zones of only about 100 kilometers was involved.

There is evidence that the prairie itself was a little drier in mid-postglacial time. Lakes and water holes in South Dakota, for example, apparently dried up more frequently than they do today, according to the stratigraphic record, and this situation must certainly have affected the abundance of game and thus of early man. But at this stage of cultural development in central North America there was no glimmer of agricultural origin, and by the time the first farmers practiced in the area, about 3,000 years ago, the epoch of significant environmental change in the midwest had long passed. A vigorous effort was made by Bryson and Baerreis (1968) to relate cultural change to environmental change in northwestern Iowa about 700 B.P. (1250 A.D.), but other interpretations are possible (Wright 1974).

In the region of the Rocky Mountains and the American Southwest, much the same paleoclimatic picture emerges. Glaciers retreated at an accelerated rate after about 11,000 years ago, pluvial lakes dried up, and vegetation belts that had been depressed in the mountains during the glacial interval rose rapidly, although they may have changed their composition and broadened or narrowed their elevation ranges (Wright, et al. 1973). A postglacial altithermal interval can be recognized in the pollen sequence for the area of Yellowstone Park, centering about 6,000 years ago (Waddington and Wright 1973), and the glacial and geomorphic record for subsequent time in many parts of the West and Southwest gives evidence for regrowth of glaciers and other evidences for cooler climate (Porter and Denton 1967). Again, however, field evidence for significant effects of these minor environmental changes on human cultures is sparse, although attempts have been made to make the connection (Baumhoff and Heizer 1965). In the Southwest, the pollen record gives no satisfactory evidence of an altithermal interval (Martin 1963).

If the north-temperate conifer forests were forced south in central and eastern North America during the glacial period, logic calls for spread of temperate deciduous forest in the south and southeast. Pollen sites to test the hypothesis have not been found in southcentral United States. In Florida and southern Georgia the expectable sequence has not materialized, and in fact much of the terrain at least as far as 27° North Latitude was apparently characterized by treeless openings before 8,000 years ago, presumably because the climate was too dry to support continuous forest. Many of the lakes were apparently dry during this time, although this phenomenon may be a reflection of a lowered water table in response to the lowered sea level of glacial times. It is difficult to reconstruct the meteorological conditions necessary to produce a climate in peninsular Florida that is too dry for complete forest growth, but the evidence is strong. These findings bring to mind the situation for the northern Mediterranean area of the Old World, in which a climate drier than today's is inferred for this time range. At any rate, the greater extent of grazing habitat in Florida must have had a profound effect on animal distributions and thus on the hunting cultures that characterized the area. Again, however, agriculture was not involved.

Thus for North America we have abundant evidence for profound environmental change at the time of glacial retreat about 11,000 years ago, but no concomitant domestication of plants and animals. In most of North America the habitats both before and after the change were not the natural habitats for those plants and animals that were ultimately domesticated in Middle America, and subsequently imported to North America, so perhaps the best explanation for the continuance of hunting and gathering as a way of life is simply that the materials appropriate for domestication were not at hand. In this respect the situation is the same as that for Western Europe, in which the evidence for pronounced environmental change about 11,000 years ago is abundant, yet hunting and gathering persisted, although with a greatly changed resource, until agriculture was introduced from southwestern Asia thousands of years later.

Middle America

The unexpected nature of the paleoclimatic inferences for Florida makes the situation for Mexico more critical, for it is here that we have the earliest archaeological evidence for agriculture and where we must therefore examine in particular the environmental sequence. Unfortunately the story for all of Mexico is poorly documented. The oft-quoted pollen sequence for Lake Texcoco (20° North Latitude) near Mexico City (Sears and Clisby 1955) has a speculative interpretation and correlation that are not based on pollen-surface-sample analyses from the surrounding areas nor on radiocarbon dates. The pollen and diatom study for the sediments of Lake Patzcuaro suffers from similar deficiencies (Hutchinson, et al. 1956). A stratigraphic diatom study for the sediments of Lake Texcoco, however, permits an interpretation of climatically controlled changing lake levels: the time interval of North American glaciation is marked by a dry climate compared to today (Bradbury 1971). This conclusion is consistent with that derived from a study of mammal bones from a cave farther southeast (18° North Latitude), in which species now found only in drier regions are represented in levels dating 9,000–12,000 years ago (Flannery 1967). The same conclusion is also consistent with the evidence for dry climate for this time interval in peninsular Florida (27° North Latitude), as recounted above. Study of a series of strategically located continuous stratigraphic sections of pollen-bearing deposits covering the time range since 20,000 years ago in various parts of Mexico would go far toward answering some very general questions about Pleistocene climatic shifts in low latitudes.

The paleoclimatic record in Mexico for post-Pleistocene time, during the critical period of agricultural origins, is so deficient as to make discussion of environmental relations fruitless. In view of the lack of similarity of the sequence in Florida with that farther north, any postulated southward extrapolation of a mid-postglacial climatic fluctuation from the Middle West or the Rocky Mountains would be folly indeed, although such extrapolation is commonly made. Willey (1966: 83), for example, has stated:

With the increasing heat and dryness of the Altithermal climatic era, after 5,000 B.C., this casual, minimal cultivation seems to have been taken more seriously. It may have been that as the natural wild plant cover retreated before the increasing aridity, man became anxious about and conscious of plant growth and sought to aid, protect, and encourage it in whatever small favored localities were available.... Then, with the return to the cooler and more moist conditions of the Medithermal, after 2500 B.C., plant cultivation apparently "exploded."

Rather than accept such extrapolations from distant climatic provinces, it would be better to await the discovery of proper pollen-bearing deposits within Mexico itself, not necessarily associated with early agricultural sites, but at least in the same climatic province and closely cross-dated by radiocarbon analysis.

Extension of the Florida paleoclimatic anomaly might be sought better in the Yucatan Peninsula rather than in upland Mexico, because it is closer and is characterized by forest vegetation. Although limestone lakes exist in the area, no one has yet succeeded in raising a core that covers any of Pleistocene time, to say nothing of revealing a pollen sequence that unequivocally indicates environmental changes preceding or coincident with the development of agriculture.

Perhaps the most interesting site in the Yucatan Peninsula is Lake Petenxil in lowland Guatemala (17° North Latitude), only 40 kilometers from the big Mayan development of Tikal. The pollen sequence reveals a strong stratigraphy, which is interpreted by Tsukada (1966) as recording extensive agricultural land clearance by slash and burn, correlated with Mayan settlement on the basis of carbon dates, and followed by reforestation after the decrease of population in post-Classic time. Evidence for agriculture rests in the presence of maize pollen and the abundance of charcoal fragments. Otherwise, one might be able to make a case for a climatic influence to reduce tree growth and allow the spread of such herbs as ragweed and chenopods. The cultural explanation seems to be much more reasonable, however, and it has the interesting implication that the vast lowland rain forest of today is a secondary product of Mayan occupation. Such a conclusion needs confirmation through the discovery of a pollen sequence that covers the entire Holocene, so that the nature of the preagricultural vegetation is revealed.

Elsewhere in Guatemala and adjacent El Salvador, Tsukada and Deevey (1967) investigated four sites (14–15° North Latitude) in the highlands and the adjacent lowland rain forest. The localities are all close to archaeological sites, and the cores all cover less than the last 3,000 years, coincident with Classic and later occupancy of the area. Evidence for slash-and-burn agriculture at all sites is provided in the cores by the frequent occurrence of maize pollen, the intermittently high pollen values for ragweed and other indicators of vegetational disturbance, the irregularities in the curves for certain types of tree pollen, and the abundance of charcoal fragments.

The only pollen study in Middle America that covers the late Pleistocene is from highland Costa Rica, at an elevation of 2,400 meters (10° North Latitude) in temperate forest (Martin 1964). The dominance of grass and other herbaceous pollen types before about 12,000 years ago implies a lowering of the alpine grassland zone (paramo) by 650 meters. The stratigraphy, chronology, and interpretation are convincing enough to support the contention that Pleistocene climatic cooling in this region was comparable in magnitude and timing to that in the Rocky Mountains of western North America. The subsequent pollen sequence at this site, however, provides no basis for inferring significant environmental changes during the Holocene in this area, which has little archaeological evidence for early agriculture in any case.

South America

COLOMBIA In the Andean Highlands of Colombia the several pollen studies of van der Hammen and associates provide substantial evidence for environmental changes during the late Quaternary, as long as a magnifying lens is available for examination of the published pollen diagrams. In the eastern Cordillera several areas have been studied. The principal locality is on the plain of Bogotá (elevation 2,580 meters, 5° North Latitude), where a 200 meter core shows a pollen sequence believed to record several major cold phases of the Pleistocene (van der Hammen, et al. 1971). The hills beside the plain are now marked by *Weinmannia* and other forest trees. The higher elevations, in the heavily clouded areas, are dominated by oak forest, above which is the grassland of the paramo (van der Hammen and Gonzalez 1960a).

In a detailed diagram for the upper few meters of the core, the pollen maximum of grass and *Acaena* (a genus of the paramo) at the base of the section are believed to indicate that the tree line was depressed to the level of the Bogotá plain, with pollen of *Quercus* (oak), *Podocarpus*, *Hedyosmum*, *Alnus* (alder), and *Myrica* being blown up to the site from forested slopes at lower elevations (Figure 12).

This section of inferred colder climate terminates about 24,000 years ago, according to a C-14 date, although the authors indicate that the date should rather be 16,000 years ago, in order to correlate with the beginning

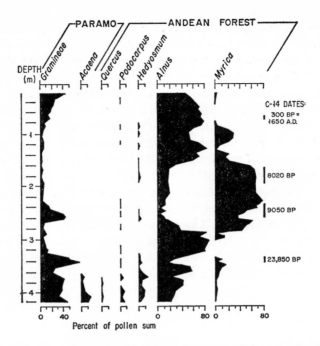

Figure 12. Selected pollen curves for Sabana de Bogota, Colombia, elevation 2,580 meters, in the Andean forest (redrawn from van der Hammen and Gonzalez 1960a)

of ice recession in Europe. The remainder of the diagram is marked by only three major pollen types — grass, alder, and *Myrica*. Other pollen types are represented by extremely small quantities. The authors use the fluctuations for detailed correlation with the standard European late-glacial and postglacial pollen zones — Alleröd, Younger Dryas, Pre-boreal, etc. — and they construct detailed paleoclimatic curves for the region.

This type of detailed paleoclimatic reconstruction, however, cannot be justified on the basis of the evidence presented. Not only is the end of the *Acaena* pollen zone much older than expected, but it corresponds with a stratigraphic change from lake sediment to alluvial clay. The grass maximum that follows, as well as two later grass maxima, is coincident with layers of "humic clay," implying some local control. The alder maximum that comes next represents local spread of alder over the wet soils of the alluvial plain. Only then, about 15,000 years ago according to the C-14 dates, does *Myrica* first appear in quantity, representing the *Weinmannia* forest. Subsequent alternations of grass, *Myrica*, and alder may be controlled by flooding of the plain, which in turn may be affected by tectonic instead of climatic conditions. If climatic conditions are the sole cause, however, the broad maximum of *Myrica* between 15,000 and 6,000 years ago would point to absence of flooding of the plain and thus relatively dry conditions during this long interval, compared to subsequent time.

This more conservative interpretation of the much-quoted pollen sequence of the Sabana de Bogotá recognizes a basic vegetational and climatic change about 15,000 years ago (rather than 24,000, corrected without basis to 16,000 years ago). At this time climatic warming raised the Pleistocene oak cloud forest and perhaps the paramo of the Bogotá region several hundred meters up to their present limits higher in the cordillera. Beyond this, however, the timing and details of vegetational changes are sufficiently equivocal to reserve judgment on climatic fluctuations, and certainly on intercontinental correlations. Clarification could be provided not only by additional C-14 dates but by a more comprehensive transect of pollen samples from the various existing vegetation belts in the mountains and the plain, to sort out regional and local influences on the pollen rain. Tropical forests have a notorious pattern of under- and overrepresentation of pollen types, because many trees dominant in tropical forests produce and disperse very little pollen, whereas a few trees and shrubs that are not dominant in the forest deliver most of the pollen to the open plains.

In any case, the pollen sequence for the Bogotá plain does not help us in our quest for relations between environmental change and the origin of agriculture, because this was not the heartland of early agriculture. The rise of grass pollen near the top of the section, attributed to agricultural land clearance, carries a C-14 date of 1650 A.D. and thus postdates the Spanish conquest.

A second area in Colombia is the Paramo de Palacio, on the northwestern rim of the Bogotá plain, at an elevation of 3,500 meters, or 250 meters above the tree line (van der Hammen and Gonzalez 1960b). Here a pollen assemblage of grasses and other herbs of the paramo (Figure 13) changes upward abruptly to one dominated not only by grasses but by *Weinmannia, Miconia*, Urticaceae, and other types derived from elements of the Andean forest, implying a rise of tree line to approximately its present position just below the site. The change is dated by radiocarbon at 8130 B.P., but it is correlated by the authors with the Alleröd of northwestern Europe (11,300 B.P.) without comment.

Subsequent minor trends in the Palacio pollen sequence involve the identification of a series of zones that are correlated with those of the Bogotá plain as well as with those of northwestern Europe. Without more support from pollen surface samples taken from different modern veg-

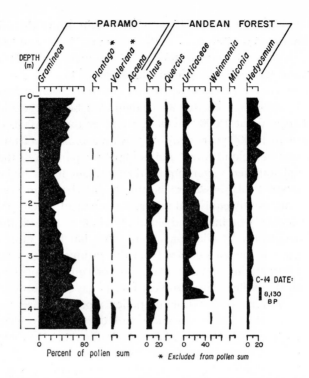

Figure 13.   Selected pollen curves for Paramo de Palacio, Colombia, elevation 3,500 meters (redrawn from van der Hammen and Gonzalez 1960b)

etation types and without more information about the occurrence and ecological significance of the plants represented by some of the major pollen types (e.g. Urticaceae), the paleoclimatic interpretation of these trends must remain tentative.

A third area of pollen studies in the Eastern Andes is in the Sierra Nevada del Cucoy (elevation 3,880 meters, 6° North Latitude) 150 kilometers north of the Bogotá plain (Gonzalez, et al. 1965). Here are moraines and lakes that date from the last glaciation, according to a whole series of radiocarbon dates. The pollen profiles show a conspicuous change about 11,500 years ago from a pollen assemblage of grass plus tree pollen to one dominated by grass alone, which extends up to modern time (Figure 14). This sequence carries the interpretation, anomalous at first glance, that the abundance of tree pollen before 11,500 years ago means that the tree line was farther below the locality rather than closer. The rationale, however, is that when the tree line is depressed the pollen site is higher in the paramo, in fact in the "superparamo,"

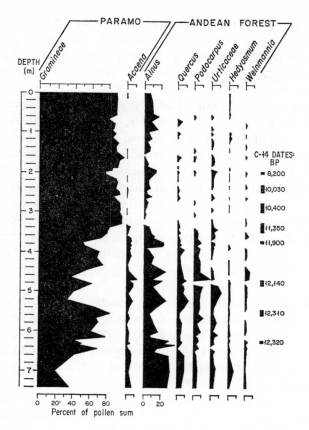

Figure 14. Selected pollen curves for Sierra Nevada del Cucoy, Colombia, elevation 3,880 meters, in the paramo (redrawn from Gonzalez, et al. 1965)

where pollen production from scattered local grasses and other herbs is less than in the warmer areas of the paramo proper closer to the tree line, so that tree pollen carried up from the forest below have a higher representation in the percentage diagrams. Such an assumption has been validated for other alpine areas (Maher 1963) but not thoroughly for the Andes. The only alternative explanation is that the tree line fell rather than rose 11,500 years ago, an explanation that is not consistent with the evidence for contemporaneous retreat of glaciers in the area.

Slight changes in the grass-pollen percentages prior to 11,500 years ago are interpreted as recording glacial and climatic fluctuation correlated with the Alleröd interstadial of Europe and the "Mankato" and "Valders" stadials of the Great Lakes region, and the authors express surprise at the lack of a record of the Cochrane moraine of the area of Hudson Bay. Because even some of the North American fluctuations of ice margins have doubtful regional climatic significance (Wright 1971b; Mercer 1969), it is double jeopardy to attempt correlation between temperate and tropical latitudes in such detail.

The caution is equally important in the case of the Holocene pollen profiles for the Cucoy area. For example, very slight fluctuations in the curves for types like pollen of Urticaceae (nettle family) and spores of *Lycopodium* (club moss) are made the basis of the pollen zones. Yet these plants are of unknown importance in ecological reconstruction without further information concerning their life-zone distribution, and some of the fluctuations are of doubtful statistical significance with counts of less than 200. The matter is of some concern in the problem at hand, because here is positive claim for climatic change in the Andean highlands that should also have affected parts of adjacent highland Peru, where agriculture was practiced at an early date.

PERU   The Andean highlands in Peru recently have been the scene of extensive archaeological studies that have led to the discovery of cave sites (13° South Latitude) dating back to 19,000 years ago, indicating occupation by early hunters who utilized horse, ground sloth, and other large mammals until about 9,500 years ago (MacNeish 1971). As in North America, extinction of the large mammals apparently occurred at or soon after the time of major environmental change, although the chronology of change there has not yet been documented by carbon determinations keyed to pollen profiles or the history of deglaciation. MacNeish's attempt to use the pH of poorly dated cave layers as indicators of types of soil and vegetation in the region has little credibility, especially when a case is attempted for detailed negative climatic correlation of the layers with the glacial sequence of the Great Lakes region of North America. The conspicuous array of glacial features in the Peruvian highlands, along with the abundance of glacial lakes containing pollen-bearing sediments suitable for carbon dating, provides the opportunity to work out the environmental history in detail, and the abundance of archaeological sites in the intermontane plains of the highlands means that integrated paleoecological studies will be profitable. The potato and the llama were first domesticated in this region, but the timing and relation to environmental events are uncertain. A recent report of domesticated bean possibly as old as 10,000 years ago (Kaplan, et al. 1973) adds new significance to the problem.

CHILE The only other major pollen study in South America is that in southern Chile (41°30′ South Latitude) by Heusser (1966a), apart from the earlier work still farther south in Fuego-Patagonia by Auer (e.g. 1958). The principal sites investigated are glacial lakes and bogs only 100 meters above sea level. The area is climatically and physiographically analogous to southeastern Alaska (Heusser 1966b).

The pollen sequence is closely repeated in the several sites examined and therefore provides primarily a record of the regional vegetation. The climatic interpretation is based on existing botanical knowledge of the elevational and latitudinal ranges and climatic characteristics of the various forest types, but no pollen surface samples were collected from these forests to document the necessary step between the modern pollen rain and the known vegetation.

The pollen sequence shows strong stratigraphic changes that are interpreted by Heusser as indicating altitudinal shifts in the various dominant forest types as controlled primarily by changes in the summer temperature. Changes in certain pollen types are attributed to drying of bogs and thus to long-range variations in rainfall. Numerous radiocarbon determinations lead to the detailed correlation of the various pollen zones and inferred climatic events with the late-glacial and postglacial sequence of northwestern Europe, as well as with Alaska.

The sequence starts as long as 16,000 years ago, marking the retreat of glaciers from the area. The transition from late-glacial to postglacial is placed at 10,000 years ago, but the pollen changes at this horizon are not so striking as one might expect. The postglacial sequence involves primarily the changing ratios of two pollen types, which are believed to represent two forest trees that have somewhat different but overlapping ranges in elevation (*Nothofagus dombeyi* below and *Weinmannia* above). The trends in the ratios, along with evidence at one site for desiccation of the bog surface, are taken to indicate a climatic interval of maximum warmth and dryness centering about 7,000 years ago.

One may conclude from the study that the climatic sequence is at least grossly similar to that at similar latitudes in the northern hemisphere — with a Pleistocene/Holocene warming correlated with retreat of glaciers, and a mid-postglacial interval of maximum warmth. No direct relations with the archaeological sequence can be inferred for this mountainous region, particularly with respect to questions about early agriculture.

Conclusions

The evidence from studies of Andean glacial and vegetational history in both tropical and temperate latitudes is that a major climatic warming occurred about 16,000–10,000 years ago, roughly contemporaneous with well-documented North American changes of the same type. Glaciers retreated, and the alpine grassland (paramo) and various forest belts migrated up the mountain slopes. This event was only one of several major climatic shifts that marked the Quaternary history of South America and had profound effects on the flora and fauna, particularly of the Andean cordillera (Vuilleumier 1971).

Man occupied portions of South America during this last major interval of climatic change, and the association of bones and artifacts gives evidence of a hunting culture that exploited horse, ground sloth, and other large mammals, which soon thereafter became extinct. As in North America, data are insufficient to determine whether these mammalian extinctions are solely the result of environmental change or in part an effect of overkill by man himself. Whatever the cause, human populations adapted to the changed resource, and they gradually developed greater dependence on wild plants and finally on cultivated plants, some of which were locally developed. As in Middle America the chain of cultural events leading to agriculture may be said to have started with the end-Pleistocene climatic change, but the relation between the climatic change and the development of agriculture in this region is so tenuous as to be inconsequential.

CONCLUDING REMARKS

Comparisons between the presumably independent origins of agriculture in the Old and New Worlds are really not very close. Different plants and animals are involved, the times of occurrence are different, and the rate of adoption of agricultural economies is different. These contrasts depend in part on the nature of the people involved, but certainly many of the differences go back basically to the nature of the environment — the terrain, the climate, and the biota available for domestication.

Pronounced environmental change occurred in both areas at the end of the Pleistocene. In Europe north of the Alps, tundra succeeded to forest, and Paleolithic big-game hunters were followed by Mesolithic hunter-gatherers. Agriculture was introduced from the southeast thousands of years later, with no strong influence from environmental change.

In the Mediterranean area, the semiarid steppe, dominated by *Artemisia*, which prevailed throughout the late Pleistocene, gave way largely to dry-summer Mediterranean forest and shrubland, which had previously been confined to some much more restricted area of Mediterranean-type climate, perhaps in northwestern Africa. In the somewhat drier areas of the Mediterranean climatic belt, from Macedonia and Palestine to Iran, the early Holocene forest graded to oak woodland and grassland. Important components of this dry-summer grassland were the wild wheats and barley that soon thereafter were domesticated to mark the real beginning of agriculture. This reconstruction of events thus ties plant domestication directly to environmental change.

In the New World, the climatic and vegetational changes at the end of the Pleistocene were just as pronounced as in the Old World, from the front of the North American ice sheet to the forests and grasslands of the Andean highlands. Concurrently the fauna of large herbivores was greatly decimated, resulting in major cultural adaptations of early man. Domestication of plants came later, and much more slowly than in the Old World, probably starting principally in central Mexico. The pollen record for this nuclear area is grossly deficient and no strong case can be made at present for climatic influence on changing cultural patterns. In the secondary areas of agricultural development, such as the Andean highlands or America north of Mexico, the case for climatic influence is poor indeed.

Progress toward understanding the relations between environmental and cultural change has been rapid indeed during the last decade, with new and more critical archaeological techniques of excavation and analysis, along with independent paleoecological studies in critical areas. The complete upset of the environmental sequence for the north Mediterranean region is only ten years old. Hopefully some paleoecological sites can be found in northern and northwestern Africa to test critically the hypothesis presented here that the Mediterranean climate and vegetation during the Pleistocene were displaced southward and severely restricted.

For the New World, the nature of low-latitude climatic changes is very poorly known, especially for central Mexico, the heartland of the origin of agriculture. Perhaps here also future research can test more closely the relations between environmental and cultural change.

Recent research has resulted in new anthropological insights in the relative population stabilities of hunting and agricultural societies, the morphology and genetics of domesticated plants and animals and their wild progenitors, and the chronology of domestication. Arguments identifying environmental influences on cultural change, such as those presented here, can only be tested by more detailed paleoecological investigations in critical areas.

REFERENCES

AUER, V.
1958   The Pleistocene of Fuego-Patagonia, Part II: The history of the flora and vegetation. *Annales Academiae Scientiarum Fennicae*, Series A III. *Geologica-Geographica* 50:1–239.

BAUMHOFF, M. A., R. F. HEIZER
1965   "Postglacial climate and archaeology in the Desert West," in *The Quaternary of the United States*. Edited by H. E. Wright, Jr. and D. G. Frey, 679–707. Princeton: Princeton University Press.

BEUG, H.-J.
1968   Probleme der Vegetationsgeschichte in Südeuropa. *Deutsche Botanische Gesellschaft, Jg. 1967, Berichte* 80:682–689.

BONATTI, E.
1966   North Mediterranean climate during the last Würm glaciation. *Nature* 209:984–985.
1970   "Pollen sequence in the lake sediments," in *Ianula: an account of the history and development of the Lago di Monterosi, Latium, Italy*. Edited by G. E. Hutchinson, 26–31. Transactions of the American Philosophical Society 60(4).

BOTTEMA, S.
1967   A Late Quaternary pollen diagram from Ioannina, northwestern Greece. *Proceedings of the Prehistoric Society for 1967*, n.s. 33:26–29.

BRADBURY, J. P.
1971   Paleolimnology of Lake Texcoco, Mexico: evidence from diatoms. *Limnology and Oceanography* 16:180–200.

BRYSON, R. A., D. A. BAERREIS
1968   "Introduction and project summary," in *Climatic changes and the Mill Creek culture of Iowa*. Edited by D. R. Henning, 1–34. *Iowa Archeological Society Journal* 15.

BÜDEL, J.
1949   Die räumliche und zeitliche Gliederung des Eiszeitklimas, III. *Naturwissenschaften* 36:105–112.

BUTZER, K. W., G. LL. ISAAC, J. L. RICHARDSON, CELIA WASHBOURN-KAMAU
1972   Radiocarbon dating of East African lake levels. *Science* 175:1069–1076.

CHILDE, V. G.
1929   *The most ancient East*. London: Routledge and Kegan Paul.

FARRAND, W. R.
1971   "Late Quaternary paleoclimates of the eastern Mediterranean," in *The late Cenozoic glacial ages*. Edited by K. K. Turekian, 529–564. New Haven: Yale University Press.

FAURE, H.
1969 Lacs quaternaires du Sahara. *Internationale Vereinigung für Theoretische und Angewandte Limnologie, Mitteilungen* 171:134–146.

FLANNERY, K. V.
1966 The postglacial "readaptation" as viewed from Mesoamerica. *American Antiquity* 31:800–805.
1967 "Vertebrate fauna and hunting patterns," in *The prehistory of the Tehuacan Valley*, volume one: *Environment and subsistence*. Edited by D. S. Byers, 140–145. Austin: University of Texas Press.

FLINT, R. A.
1971 *Glacial and Quaternary geology*. New York: Wiley.

FRANK, A. H. E.
1969 Pollen stratigraphy of the Lake of Vico (central Italy). *Palaeogeography. Palaeoclimatology, Palaeoecology* 6:67–85.

GONZALEZ, E., T. VAN DER HAMMEN, R. F. FLINT
1965 Late Quaternary glacial and vegetational sequence in Valle de Lagunillas, Sierra Nevada del Cucoy, Colombia. *Leidse Geologische Mededelingen* 32:157–182.

GRÜGER, J.
1968 Untersuchungen zur spätglazialen und frühpostglazialen Vegetationsentwicklung der Südalpen im Umkreis des Gardasees. *Botanisches Jahrbuch* 88:163–199.

HARRIS, D. R.
1972 The origins of agriculture in the tropics. *American Scientist* 60:180–193.

HEUSSER, C. J.
1966a Late-Pleistocene pollen diagrams from the Province of Llanquihue, southern Chile. *American Philosophical Society Proceedings* 110:270–305.
1966b "Polar hemispheric correlation: palynological evidence from Chile and the Pacific Northwest of America," in *World climate from 8000 to 0* B.C. Edited by J. S. Sawyer, 124–141. London: Royal Meteorological Society.

HOROWITZ, A.
1971 Climatic and vegetational developments in northwestern Israel during Upper Pleistocene-Holocene times. *Pollen et Spores* 13:255–278.

HUTCHINSON, G. E., R. PATRICK, E. S. DEEVEY
1956 Sediments of Lake Patzcuaro, Michoacan, Mexico. *Geological Society of America Bulletin* 67:1491–1504.

KAPLAN, L., T. F. LYNCH, C. E. SMITH, JR.
1973 Early cultivated beans (*Phaseolus vulgaris*) from an intermontane Peruvian valley. *Science* 179:76–77.

LIVINGSTONE, D. A.
1967 Postglacial vegetation of the Ruwenzori Mountains in Equatorial Africa. *Ecological Monographs* 37:25–52.

MAC NEISH, R. S.
1971 Early man in the Andes. *Scientific American* 224(4):36–55.

MAHER, L. J., JR.
1963 Pollen analyses of surface materials from the southern San Juan

Mountains, Colorado. *Geological Society of America Bulletin* 74: 1485–1503.

MARTIN, P. S.
1963   *The last 10,000 years: a fossil pollen record of the American Southwest.* Tucson: University of Arizona Press.
1964   Paleoclimatology and a tropical pollen profile. *International Quaternary Association VI Congress (Warsaw, 1961), Report* 2:319–323.

MARTIN, P. S., H. E. WRIGHT, JR., editors
1967   *Pleistocene extinctions: the search for a cause.* New Haven: Yale University Press.

MEGARD, R. O.
1967   Late Quaternary Cladocera of Lake Zeribar, western Iran. *Ecology* 47:179–189.

MENENDEZ AMOR, J., F. FLORSCHÜTZ
1963   Sur les éléments steppiques dans la végétation quaternaire de l'Espagne. *Boletin Real Sociedad Española de Historia Natural* (G) 61:121–133.

MERCER, J. H.
1969   The Alleröd Oscillation: a European climatic anomaly? *Arctic and Alpine Research* 1:227–234.

MESSERLI, B.
1967   Die eiszeitliche und die gegenwärtige Vergletscherung im Mittelmeerraum. *Geographica Helvetica* 22:105–228.

NIKLEWSKI, J., W. VAN ZEIST
1970   A late Quaternary pollen diagram from northwestern Syria. *Acta Botanica Neerlandica* 19:737–754.

PANSIOT, F. P., H. REBOUR
1961   *Improvement in olive cultivation.* Food and Agricultural Organization of the United Nations, FAO Agricultural Studies 50.

PORTER, S. C., G. H. DENTON
1967   Chronology of neoglaciation in the North American Cordillera. *American Journal of Science* 265:177–210.

RIKLI, M.
1943   *Das Pflanzenkleid der Mittelmeerländer.* Bern: Hans Huber.

SEARS, P. B., KATHRYN H. CLISBY
1955   Pleistocene climate in Mexico. *Geological Society of America Bulletin* 66:521–530.

SMIT, A., T. A. WIJMSTRA
1970   Application of transmission electron microscope analysis on the reconstruction of former vegetation. *Acta Botanica Neerlandica* 19:867–876.

TREWARTHA, G. T.
1968   *An introduction to climate* (fourth edition). New York: McGraw-Hill.

TSUKADA, MATSUO
1966   "The pollen sequence," in *The history of Laguna de Petenxil, a small lake in northern Guatemala.* Edited by Ursula M. Cowgill, 63–66. Connecticut Academy of Arts and Sciences, Memoir 17.

TSUKADA, MATSUO, E. S. DEEVEY
1967   "Pollen analyses from four lakes in the southern Maya area of Guatemala and El Salvador," in *Quaternary paleoecology.* Edited by

E. J. Cushing and H. E. Wright, Jr., 303–331. New Haven: Yale University Press.

VAN DER HAMMEN, T., E. GONZALEZ

1960a Upper Pleistocene and Holocene climate and vegetation of the "Sabana de Bogota" (Colombia, South America). *Leidse Geologische Mededelingen* 25:262–315.

1960b Holocene and late glacial climate and vegetation of Paramo de Palacio (Eastern Cordillera, Colombia, South America). *Geologie en Mijnbouw*, n.s. 22:737–746.

VAN DER HAMMEN, T., T. A. WIJMSTRA, W. H. ZAGWIJN

1971 "The floral record of the late Cenozoic of Europe," in *The Late Cenozoic glacial ages*. Edited by K. K. Turekian, 391–424. New Haven: Yale University Press.

VAN ZEIST, W.

1967 Late Quaternary vegetation history of western Iran. *Review of Palaeobotany and Palynology* 2:301–311.

1969 "Reflections on prehistoric environments in the Near East," in *The domestication and exploitation of plants and animals*. Edited by P. J. Ucko and G. W. Dimbleby, 35–46. London: Duckworth.

VAN ZEIST, W., H. E. WRIGHT, JR.

1963 Preliminary pollen studies at Lake Zeribar, Zagros Mountains, southwestern Iran. *Science* 140:65–67.

VAVILOV, N. I.

1926 *Studies on the origins of cultivated plants*. Leningrad: Institut de Botanique Appliquée et d'Amélioration des Plantes.

VUILLEUMIER, BERYL S.

1971 Pleistocene changes in the fauna and flora of South America. *Science* 173:771–780.

WADDINGTON, JEAN C. B., H. E. WRIGHT, JR.

1973 Late Quaternary vegetational changes on the east side of Yellowstone Park, Wyoming. *Quaternary Research* 4:175–184.

WASYLIKOWA, K.

1967 Late Quaternary plant macrofossils from Lake Zeribar, western Iran. *Review of Palaeobotany and Palynology* 2:313–318.

WATTS, W. A.

1970 The full-glacial vegetation of northwestern Georgia. *Ecology* 51:17–33.

WIJMSTRA, T. A.

1969 Palynology of the first 30 metres of a 120 m deep section in northern Greece. *Acta Botanica Neerlandica* 18:511–527.

WILLEY, G. R.

1966 *An introduction to American archaeology*, volume one: *North and Middle America*. Englewood Cliffs, N.J.: Prentice-Hall.

WOLDSTEDT, P.

1954 *Das Eiszeitalter. Grundlinien einer Geologie des Quartärs*. Stuttgart: Enke.

WRIGHT, H. E., JR.

1961 Pleistocene glaciation in Kurdistan. *Eiszeitalter und Gegenwart* 12:131–164.

1968   Natural environment of early food production north of Mesopotamia. *Science* 161:334–339.

1970   Environmental changes and the origin of agriculture in the Near East. *Bioscience* 20:210–213.

1971a   "Late Quaternary vegetational history of North America," in *The Late Cenozoic glacial ages*. Edited by K. K. Turekian, 425–464. New Haven: Yale University Press.

1971b   Retreat of the Laurentide ice sheet from 14,000 to 9,000 years ago. *Quaternary Research* 1:316–330.

1974   "The environment of Early Man in the Great Lakes region," in *Aspects of upper Great Lakes anthropology*. Edited by Elden Johnson, 8–14. *Minnesota Historical Society, Minnesota Prehistoric Archaeology Series* 11.

WRIGHT, H. E., JR., ANNE M. BENT, BARBARA S. HANSEN, L. J. MAHER, JR.

1973   Past and present vegetation of the Chuska Mountains, northwestern New Mexico. *Geological Society of America Bulletin* 84:1155–1180.

WRIGHT, H. E., JR., J. H. MC ANDREWS, W. VAN ZEIST

1967   Modern pollen rain in western Iran, and its relation to plant geography and Quaternary vegetational history. *Journal of Ecology* 55:415–443.

ZEUNER, F. E.

1952   *Dating the past. An introduction to geochronology*. London: Methuen.

ZOHARY, D.

1969   "The progenitors of wheat and barley in relation to domestication and agricultural dispersal in the Old World," in *The domestication and exploitation of plants and animals*. Edited by P. J. Ucko and G. W. Dimbleby, 47–66. Chicago: Aldine.

SECTION THREE

*The Beginnings of Agriculture
in the Old World*

A Priori *Models and Thai Prehistory:* *A Reconsideration of the Beginnings of* *Agriculture in Southeastern Asia*

CHESTER GORMAN

1. INTRODUCTION

At present, consideration of the transformation from hunting and gathering to the early domestication of plants and animals in southeastern Asia is hampered by the interference of beliefs and ideas on the nature of such changes in other areas of the world. The extent of this influence in structuring thinking on the subject becomes most evident when one attempts to design a field strategy for the archaeological investigation of this shift in subsistence patterns. Two of the most limiting, yet generally accepted, propositions with which the prehistorian in southeastern Asia has had to contend are:
1. The postulated Sinocentric origin of southeastern Asian cereal agriculture, and
2. The generally accepted belief in an earlier stage of precereal, root crop horticulture in southeastern Asia.
Separately and in combination, these two tenets have for many years influenced both general discussion and fieldwork concerned with the beginnings of domestication in southeastern Asia.

This paper reevaluates the data supporting these two reconstructions and proceeds from there to construct a new model based on southeastern Asian data; this model is then presented as a working hypothesis for the examination of this stage in southeastern Asian prehistory. The pertinent data are appropriately reorganized and the implications of the model discussed. With the data thus reorganized, the southeastern Asian shift from hunting and gathering to early domestication is viewed from a new quarter, that is, in terms of the Asian humid tropics themselves.

2. THE POSTULATED SINOCENTRIC ORIGINS OF SOUTHEASTERN ASIAN AGRICULTURE

Recent Statements of the Position

While many scholars specializing in the study of southeastern Asia are willing to acknowledge an early and indigenous root crop horticultural development in southeastern Asia (see Section 3 below), most of them view southeastern Asian cereal agriculture as an introduction from northern China. Ho* (1969: 34), in a review of the origins of agriculture in China, concluded that "so far as grain-centered agriculture of the Far East is concerned, our aggregate evidence clearly indicates that it made its debut in the southeastern part of the loess highlands of China." Ho (1969: 19) discussed the importance of this "nuclear area of northern China" as an early center of agriculture and drew on the earlier work of Andersson (1934) in conjunction with his own philological studies (Ho 1969: 20–26) to support his later conclusion that "our combined archaeological and historical data seem reasonably to have established China as one of the original homes of rice and as the first area in the world where rice was cultivated" (Ho 1969: 24).

Kwang-chih Chang, the foremost synthesizer of mainland Chinese prehistory for non-Chinese speakers, has supported this position in several recent works (Chang 1968a, 1968b, 1974). Chang has considered the cultivation of cereal plants to be a secondary derivation in the Asian humid tropics (1974) and has continued to support the argument that the cultivation of rice was introduced into southeastern China and thence to

---

* The following discussion by Gorman, in opposition to the hypothesis that cultivation of rice may have originated in northern China and from there spread southward, ignores the fact that during our conference Ho modified his earlier views on this point, as expressed in his own chapter in this volume (p. 442), "While existing comparative data" (on the topic of the place of the earliest cultivation of rice) "are in favor of China, I share the views of the majority of the participants of this conference on the origins of agriculture that the geographical distribution of pre-domesticated rice was much wider than has hitherto been believed, and that rice most probably was independently domesticated in the southern half of China, the southeastern Asian mainland, and the Indian subcontinent." Gorman is, in part thus, arguing against a pre-conference point of view, but has failed to change his argument although given the opportunity to do so. — *Editor.*

southeastern Asia by "Lungshanoid farmers" (see Chang 1968a: 523; 1968b: 184; 1974).

Both Ho and Chang face one major problem: for rice (*Oryza sativa*) the botanical data at least appear to bespeak a more southerly origin. Ho (1969: 2) has stated: "The aggregate archaeological, botanical, historical, and philological evidence indicates that the SOUTHERN HALF OF CHINA, as much as India and Southeast Asia, is one of the original homes of rice" (emphasis added). Chang (1968b: 138; 1970: 183), recognizing this, has regarded rice, at least in one instance — namely, its earliest appearance in northern China in Yang Shao contexts — as probably representing an intrusive element "(apparently from the south) into the millet area." Thus, while both Ho and Chang acknowledge rice as a more southerly domes-ticate, they nonetheless continue to tie its first cultivation to the nuclear area of northern China (Chang 1968b: 85) and see its emergence in southeastern Asia (and here I include in southeastern Asia, China south of the Yangtze, as does Chang [1968a: 523]) as a result of the spread of "Lungshanoid pioneer farmers" (Chang 1968b: 444).

While Chang has regarded the earliest evidence of rice in the nuclear area as intrusive from the south, Ho and Chang have agreed that the remains of rice found at sites (grouped together under the general term Ch'u-chia-ling) in the lower Hanshui Valley (Chang 1968b: 137; Ho 1969: 19) document the earliest Chinese subsistence patterns clearly based on rice agriculture. Chang (1968b: 137) has considered Ch'u-chia-ling to be a "Lungshanoid culture" and would date it to around 4500 B.P. (1968b: 445, Table 16). Ho (1969: 19) dates Ch'u-chia-ling "somewhere around 5000 B.P." and places the earliest cultivated rice in the area at around 6000 B.P. While there seems little doubt that the Ch'u-chia-ling sites present evidence of a subsistence economy based on domesticated rice, there is considerable doubt about their dates.

In spite of their recognition of an ultimate southern origin for rice agriculture, both Ho and Chang continue to assert, as shown in their most recent works, that cereal (INCLUDING RICE) agriculture was intro-duced into southeastern Asia from a center of development somewhere in NORTHERN China.

Conflicting Data

At this point I should note that a considerable body of data conflicts with the assumption that rice agriculture is a development that spread from northern China. These data are drawn from (1) botanical, (2) archaeo-logical, and (3) linguistic sources.

BOTANICAL DATA   Botanical sources indicate that rice is indeed a native of an "Indo-Oceanic tropical zone" (after Barrau 1965a: 71) and was introduced from that region northward into China (see, for example, Barrau 1965b: 342, n.d. as quoted in Chang 1970: 183; Vavilov 1949/ 1950; Zukovskij 1962: 9). Li (1966, as translated and quoted in Chang 1970) himself lists the origins of rice as being in his southern Asian zone (i.e. Burma, Thailand, and old Indochina).

Northern China, north of the Tsinling line, has evidently never been an important center of rice production (Tregear 1965: 63, 116 [Figure 34], 125 [Figure 36h]). Shen (1951: 134–138), discussing the agricultural resources of China, thought that all major rice-producing regions lay in areas from the Yangtze Valley south; he stated that north of the Tsinling Mountains the climate was unfavorable for rice cultivation and that rice was rarely planted, except in certain localities provided with irrigation facilities (1951: 197). Given that the nuclear area of northern China as delineated by Chang lies in this northern zone, and that even now, with modern techniques, the region is inhospitable to rice cultivation, it seems surprising that this area should even be considered as the earliest center of rice domestication. Ho (1969: 25) has stated that recent experiments show higher yields of rice per acre in Shensi (in the nuclear area) than in the southern provinces; however, he did not mention whether these plants were recent hybrid varieties and whether or not they were in irrigated fields. Ho argued, on the same page (1969: 25), that the technique of irrigation is a very late introduction (about sixth century B.C.).

The cultural geographers Tregear (1965: 63) and Wiens (1954: 65) both emphasized that the domestication of rice was developed by T'ai-speaking inhabitants of southern China. In any event, from a botanical point of view, the consensus of opinion clearly favors a tropical Asian origin for early rice domestication.

ARCHAEOLOGICAL DATA   Chang (1968b: 138) and Ho (1969: 19) both considered the remains of rice from Ch'u-chia-ling the best and possibly earliest (see Chang 1968b: 138) evidence for intensive rice cultivation in China. There is little doubt that the sites at Ch'u-chia-ling represent early rice agriculturalists; the question is, just how early? If the sites at Ch'u-chia-ling do in fact date from around 4500 to 5000 years B.P., then the Hanshui/Yangtze valleys might indeed have been tied to early centers of rice domestication. However, Treistman (1968) has recently presented a detailed discussion of the sites at Ch'u-chia-ling, focusing specifically on the evidence for their stratigraphic and chronological placement and treating only those sites whose stratigraphic relationships are securely demonstrated (Treistman 1968: 71). Her quite convincing analysis indicates at least a threefold cultural/stratigraphic succession: (1) early cultural material comparable to the Yang Shao material of the Shensi Pan-p'o/Miao-ti-kou sequence; (2) an intermediate Ch'u-chia-ling component; and overlying this (3) a "Lungshan" component (Treistman 1968: 88). In Treistman's analysis (1968: 88):

The "Lungshan" component is probably entirely historic, showing late Shang-Chou stylistic affinities. The intermediary Ch'u-chia-ling is basically historic in time, although there may be continuity with late persisting local neolithic cultures.... The fact that the painted Ch'u-chia-ling pottery is all wheel-produced, the appearance of geometric stamped decoration at the type site, at I-chia-shan and Yang-chia-wan, and the presence of bronze implements or apparent imitations of bronze vessels all argue for late dating, at least post-1000 B.C.

From her revised chronology for the sites at Ch'u-chia-ling, Treistman has suggested that sometime in the first millennium B.C. rice replaced millet as the principal local domesticate; after its establishment there, it spread rapidly over the Yangtze delta and along the coast of southeastern China (Treistman 1968: 90).

Chang and Ho agree with Treistman that the Ch'u-chia-ling sites present evidence of the earliest appearance of rice as a subsistence crop (Treistman 1968: 69; Chang 1968b: 138); however, their datings of these sites do not agree. Consideration of Treistman's more detailed summary of the relevant stratigraphy of these sites and Chang's acknowledgment (1968b: 393) of the association of Ch'u-chia-ling/Lungshan pottery with early bronze in the Hanshui/Yangtze site of P'an-lung-ch'eng argues strongly in favor of Treistman's revised chronology. If this is correct, the earliest archaeologically recovered rice from southern China is much too late to be the source of rice domestication in either India or southeastern Asia.

While the denouement of the northern Chinese prehistoric sequence awaits the application of radiocarbon analysis to well-excavated and stratified material, the first radiocarbon results from China (An Syrz Min 1972: 55) presumably give some indication of what is to come. Three of these dates are relevant to this argument: the Kansu Yang-Shao assemblage of Ma-Chia-Yao has been dated by radiocarbon to 4135 ± 100 B.P. (ZK-21); two other dates, 3675 ± 95 B.P. (ZK-15) and 3645 ± 95 B.P. (ZK-23), on Kansu Ch'i-Chia material and one further date of 4015 ± 100 B.P. (ZK-25) on Kansu Pan-Shan material together lend credence to Chang's ordering (1968a: 443) of the sequence in eastern Kansu. While Chang (1968a: 89) has argued that these assemblages from eastern Kansu are considerably later than their counterparts of the nuclear area, their radiocarbon dates, clustering as they do just prior to 4000 B.P., raise serious doubts to ascriptions of a much greater antiquity to the Shensi/ Honan Yang-Shao material.

Turning now to India and southeastern Asia, we find that both areas have yielded direct evidence of rice from radiocarbon-dated contexts. In India the earliest dated remains of rice occur in period III B of the Narbada Valley site of Navadatoli (Vishnu-Mittre 1962; Allchin and Allchin 1968: 264). Two radiocarbon determinations from period III B, 3608 ±131 B.P. (P-202) and 4249 ± 72 B.P. (P-476), indicate the presence of rice there around 4000 B.P. Singh (1971), on the basis of his palynological investigations, suggests that scrub burnings and the accompanying rise in cerealia-type pollens indicate an even earlier development of cereal agriculture in Rajasthan beginning possibly around 9000 B.P.

The earliest dated occurrence of rice (*Oryza sativa*) from anywhere in eastern Asia, however, is derived from Bayard's excavations at Non Nok Tha in northeastern Thailand (Bayard 1971, 1973). Bayard's dates and the relevant material from Non Nok Tha are discussed below in Section 5. What is important at this juncture is that both Navadatoli and Non Nok Tha contain evidence for the cultivation of rice much earlier than that encountered in the Yangtze Valley, itself considered a part of prehistoric southeastern Asia.

LINGUISTIC DATA   Although Ho (1969: 17–18) has stated, "It is true that in the study of the origin of cultivated plants philological evidence alone is seldom decisive," he and others (see Chang 1968b) place considerable emphasis on ancient Chinese literature in arguing for a Chinese derivation of eastern Asian cultivation of rice. If rice agriculture in China dates from the appearance of the Ch'u-chia-ling assemblages and if their revised chronology is accepted, these written sources might well be relevant to the beginnings of rice agriculture in China. However, literary records, such as *The book of odes* (about 600 B.C. [see Ho 1969: 10]) or later Chinese classics from the Former Han period onward, would seem to have little relevance to the BEGINNINGS of Asian cultivation of rice which we know to have been present in southeastern Asia at about 6000 B.P., that is, more than 3,000 years before these works were written.

While the historical records are too late to illuminate the cultural dynamics of initial domestication of rice, studies in historical linguistics may have more to offer. Both Solheim (1973: 156–157) and I (Gorman 1969) have called attention to Benedict's recent Austro-Thai studies (1966, 1967) and specifically to his examination of early Austro-Thai/ Chinese lexicons concerned with just such cultural complexes as rice agriculture, metallurgy, etc. Benedict (1967: 203) reconstructed an Austro-Thai language family that "includes Indonesian and the Austronesian languages in general, together with Thai, Kadai, and certain 'para-Thai' languages (Kam-Sui, Ong-Be)." He then examined a group of Austro-Thai roots that show correspondences with forms from Archaic Chinese and analyzed these relationships. To summarize this analysis, Benedict (1967: 323) stated:

> The linguistic evidence as a whole points conclusively to an extensive cultural contact between the early Chinese and AT [Austro-Thai] peoples ... the process was essentially unidirectional, with the Chinese as the recipients rather than the donors. It would appear that the bulk of these loans were from an obsolete AT language, here labelled AT-x, not ancestral to any modern AT speech.

Examining the content of Austro-Thai loan words in Chinese, Benedict (1967: 316–317) noted:

> [They] constitute the outlines of a substantial material culture: [they include] the higher numerals (above 100); the fowl and egg (and perhaps the duck); horse, saddle, and riding; elephant and ivory; the pig and rabbit (but not the dog); cattle and goat/sheep; the bee (curiously prominent in this material) and perhaps honey; garden and manure; plough; mortar and hull grain with pestle; seed, sow and winnow; rice (various, including cooked rice) and sugarcane (whence sugar); banana and coconut; ginger and mustard; the dipper (made of a coconut or gourd), ladle, and vessel (container); salt; smoking (meat) and steaming (rice); bait (meat) and net; metals (gold, copper, iron, tin/lead); the ox; ladder/stairs; boat, rafts and oars; washing (metals and rice); hunting (but not the bow or arrow); crossbow (but precise origin unknown); fireplace, kiln, and pottery; weaving and plaiting (twisting rope); the needle and embroidery; basket and bag; indigo; cowry (= money); market, price, and sell.

I would draw special attention here to those roots forming a lexicon reflecting a rice complex association, e.g. plow, mortar and hull grain, pestle, seed, sow, winnow, rice (in all its forms), and steaming (of rice). Benedict (1967: 203) suggested an origin in southern China for the Austro-Thai language family, and this fits well with the work of the cultural geographers Wiens (1954: 65) and Tregear (1965: 63), both of whom derive early rice agriculture in China from early T'ai speakers of the Yangtze Valley.

A Suggested Reevaluation

At present, the beginnings of rice agriculture in southeastern Asia should probably be considered an indigenous development. Most likely, rice was first domesticated by T'ai peoples living somewhere south of the Yangtze River, and from this southern area it later diffused both north and east. If Treistman's updating of the Ch'u-chia-ling assemblages is correct, this and the much earlier dates for rice from India and northeastern Thailand argue for even more southerly origins. The botanical, archaeological, and (at least tentatively) linguistic data all argue against a more northern center of initial domestication of rice, although the "North China Nuclear Area" postulated by Chang may well have been a center of early millet agriculture and later a focus of historic development in China. Bayard (1971: 19–27) has argued convincingly for a center in the Yangtze Valley for Lungshanoid expansion and has suggested that these Lungshanoid farmers spoke languages within Benedict's Austro-Thai family. Again, however, if Treistman's updating of Ch'u-chia-ling is correct, the Lungshanoid assemblages are even later, much too late to represent the center of dispersion of rice cultivation in any direction.

Chang (1970: 183) has himself discussed the possibility that early southeastern Asian horticulturalists first domesticated rice:

The only problem is that if the modern Pacific situation is any guide, the taro and yam would not only have yielded a much greater harvest than rice within identical acreage but must have also played important roles in the social and religious life of their growers. If indeed some taro and yam growers adopted rice as their staple food early in their history, the changeover could not have taken place without the strongest possible stimulus.

Chang then suggested that this strong stimulus might in fact have been the migration of Lungshanoid farmers into subtropical southeastern Asia (Chang 1970: 183–184).

This strong stimulus, however, is required ONLY IF the early Asian farmers were cultivating only the root crops normally assigned to them. In Section 3 below I argue that root crops and rice are not mutually exclusive crops but were probably "sister domesticates"; that there was no precereal, exclusively root-cropping stage of plant domestication in southeastern Asia; and that Pacific populations represent early southeastern Asian "mixed farmers" who, under the "strong stimulus" of dispersion into island ecosystems, switched to the tuberous component of an originally mixed Indo-Oceanian complex that included both rice and taro.

Rice is today the most important staple in eastern Asia, and its initial domestication must have had a marked effect on patterns of both subsistence and settlement. The cultivation of rice appears to have been a southerly development, probably centering somewhere in Barrau's Indo-

Oceanian zone. It apparently was introduced into China from the south, reaching the Yangtze Valley sometime around 1000 B.C. and from there spreading north to the limits of its range. We can no longer maintain the view that southeastern Asia was the recipient of rice agriculture from the north. As Bayard (1971: 26) so succinctly phrased it, southeastern Asia can no longer be regarded as "dominated for millennia by the unwavering influence of the Huang Ho Valley."

3. THE POSTULATED STAGE OF EARLY ROOT CROP HORTICULTURE IN SOUTHEASTERN ASIA

Recent Statements of the Position

For the past several decades the idea has existed, in either explicit or implicit form, that plant domestication in southeastern Asia was a "two-stage" affair. Rice agriculture in southeastern Asia is generally seen as a more recent subsistence pattern; a more ancient pattern, based on root crops and other vegetatively reproducing plants, is postulated as an earlier development. The two stages then refer to (1) a stage of root crop horticulture, followed by (2) a stage of cereal (primarily rice) agriculture (see, for example, Yen 1971: 4).

To the prehistorian of southeastern Asia, this sequence and its implications are of great importance. After accepting this reconstruction for so many years, perhaps we should examine its factual basis.

The argument that cereal agriculture was preceded by a stage of domestication of vegetatively reproducing plants has a rather complex history and seems to have developed from a number of rather tenuously linked ideas. Botanists primarily interested in the process of domestication have suggested that the cultivation of vegetatively reproducing plants is less specialized and simpler than the cultivation of graminaceous crops. Anderson (1960: 72) employed this suggestion in arguing against the acceptance of SOUTHWESTERN Asia as an indigenous center of domestication; Ames (1939: 128–129) earlier argued that horticultural practices most likely bridged the gap between subsistence based on hunting and gathering and the beginnings of agriculture. Ames's distinction (1939: 32) between horticulture and agriculture, the former based on the cultivation of individual plants and the latter based on cultivation practices in which the individuality of the plant "becomes completely submerged in the vastness of the enterprise," is still useful and corresponds to a more recent definition by Barrau (1965a: 56): "Horticulture is a system of land utilization where each plant is multiplied, cared for, and individually harvested, whereas agriculture is a collective, a mass system" (translation mine).

The view of the course of plant domestication as a progression from noncereal to cereal, from horticulture to agriculture, was incorporated into similar reconstructions offered by early cultural geographers. This view in conjunction with studies in the geography of plant utilization can be seen in Sauer's reconstruction (1952) and earlier in Pelzer's work (1945: 7). Sauer's contention (1952: 24) that southeastern Asia was one of the most important cradles of early agriculture is based both on an assumed early domestication of asexually reproducing plants and on a (subsequent) dispersal of these plants into adjacent areas (Sauer 1952: 24–39 and Plate I). In distinguishing between "grain and grainless culture," Pelzer (1945: 6–7) argued that in southeastern Asia at least "grainless agriculture preceded the cultivation of cereals." He goes on to state:

Still further substantiation [for this sequence] is found in Polynesia, where the inhabitants cultivated no cereals when they were first visited by westerners. This may be explained by the assumption that the ancestors of the Polynesians migrated from Southeastern Asia to the islands of the Pacific before cereals had replaced root crops as dominant plants (1945: 67).

More recently, botanists have shown interest in the prehistory of plant use in the Indo-Oceanic/Pacific area and specifically in the ways in which the record of plant distribution might call forth more general prehistoric reconstructions. Barrau (1965a: 57) has suggested that horticulture might well have been an ancient development in the humid tropical regions of southeastern Asia or western Indo-Oceania. He would base this development on the domestication of perennial plants, especially those with edible tubers that can be propagated vegetatively. Discussing the development of Oceanic agriculture, Yen (1971: 4) cited Burkill (1951) and Spencer (1963) in proposing at least a two-phase sequence of agricultural diffusion into Oceania. He advanced a model for the course of plant domestication within southeastern Asia much in line with the above views, viz. a sequence from hunting and gathering to horticulture (taro and yam) to rice cultivation (Yen 1971: 5; see also Harris 1969).

This work by botanists and cultural geographers has not escaped the attention of prehistorians working in southeastern Asia or the adjacent Oceanic area, most of whom have accepted this two-stage model (e.g. Chang 1967, 1968b, 1970, 1974; Golson 1971b; Green 1967; Solheim 1969,

1973; etc.). A recent archaeological statement of the position might best be drawn from Chang (1970: 180): "There is almost general agreement that in southeast Asia root, tuber, and fruit plants were cultivated much earlier than cereal plants." Chang (1970: 182) later emphasized that there was a considerable time lag between the cultivation of roots, tubers, and fruits and the cultivation of cereal. With similar conviction Golson (1971b) has stated:

An ancient Southeast Asian agriculture, based on the tubers and fruits that were diffused into the South Pacific, must have antedated the cultivation of the cereals, rice and millet, which never reached New Guinea or Oceania at large in pre-European times.

Although I could quote many other authors on the same point, these two quotations do, I believe, reflect a widely accepted position.

The data used to reconstruct the early, precereal, root-cropping stage are, interestingly enough, based primarily on two nonarchaeological constructs. The first is the rather philosophical and awkward contention that early farmers would have been quicker to notice the reproductive process when dealing with vegetatively reproducing plants and consequently would have focused on these. Yen (1971: 4) cited Ames (1939) in referring to this "principle" and to the possibility of its application to his prehistoric reconstructions. The second, rather less tenuous basis is the widespread distribution of a basically southeastern Asian root-crop complex extending out into the Pacific.

Considering the rapid advances now being made in the field of southeastern Asian prehistory (see, for example, Solheim 1967, 1969, 1973) and the need for new alternatives, I believe that a reexamination of the foundations for the acceptance of this hypothesized root crop stage in southeastern Asia is now in order.

Pioneer Settlement in the Pacific: The Southeastern Asian Affinities

There seems little doubt that the pioneer settlers (Golson 1971a: 75) of the southwestern Pacific who later moved out into the wider expanse of the eastern islands ultimately originated on the southeastern Asian mainland (see, for example, Capell 1962; Duff 1970; Grace 1964; Green 1967; Pawley n.d.; Poulsen 1968; Solheim 1964; Yen 1971). Prehistorians of the Pacific Islands have focused, for the most part, on centers of secondary dispersion and/or local, archipelago-specific adaptations (see, for example, Yawata and Sinoto 1968; Green and Kelly 1971). For the prehistorian of southeastern Asia, the more important questions concern the cultural complex(es) carried by the early settlers entering Oceania and the approximate date of that entrance. Reviewing the concordance of traits carried by the earliest Austronesian settlers in the southwestern Pacific (see Golson 1968; Green 1967), we are confronted with a widespread, though basically homogeneous, assemblage, including:

1.   A basically Austronesian language (see Groube 1971: 18).
2.   A general Southeast Asian assemblage enumerated by Green (1967).
3.   Adzes fitting within Duff's (1970) Type 2 category (although quite variable in cross section, they are uniform in the lack of modifications of the butt).
4.   A pottery complex showing considerable variability and generally called "Lapita" (Golson 1971a; Groube 1971).
5.   A complex of domesticated animals and/or tended plants that derive primarily from the mainland of southeastern Asia.

Green (1967) examined the southeastern Asiatic mainland in an attempt to locate the area from which this particular assemblage could have been derived. He tied the technological assemblage to the coast of southern China (i.e. a Lungshanoid assemblage); however, there it occurs in the context of an agricultural system based on the cultivation of rice and millet (Green 1967: 56). Green was then faced with the problem of transferring this assemblage (associated with rice and millet in southern China) into association with the postulated southeastern Asian root crop complex, because he contended that they spread together into the farther Pacific islands. As Green stated, "Clearly, it seems necessary to show how, in some fashion, a South Chinese Lungshanoid technology with pigs, chickens, and dogs, but without a millet and rice economy, became associated with a South-east Asian food complex [and then moved out into the Pacific]." Attempting to resolve this dilemma, Green suggested that an early settlement of Taiwan by southeastern Asian horticulturists and a subsequent settlement on that island by Lungshanoid cereal agriculturists "would provide the basis for further expansion of Neolithic speakers of Malayo-Polynesian languages throughout the Pacific island world" (Green 1967: 60).

Although Green did not specifically discuss the movement of a ceramic complex (Lapita) out into the Pacific, others (Solheim 1964; Shutler and Shutler 1968; Golson 1971a; Groube 1971) have done so, and each has tied this early Lapita pottery complex of the Pacific Islands to the Sahuynh complex (Solheim 1961, 1964, 1967), with which most Lungshanoid material is also classed. At this point Green's linguistic argument (1967:

54) that the early Pacific settlers were not familiar with rice cultivation seems rather suspect, for both the Lungshanoid technological assemblage and the Lungshanoid/Sa-huynh pottery complex are commonly held to be associated with rice cultivation (Chang 1968b; Treistman 1968). If we now examine the date at which this set of traits associated with Lapita (and thus with the earliest settlement of the far southwestern Pacific) spreads out into the Pacific (Golson 1971a; Groube 1971), we find that it is much later than similar appearances on the mainland of southeastern Asia (Gorman 1971; Bayard 1973). As Golson (1968: 8–9) has stated:

Lapita ware characterizes the earliest settlement [of the far western Pacific]. ... There can be little doubt about the general relationship of the Lapita style of the southwest Pacific to the Sa-huynh tradition defined for Southeast Asia and its archipelagos.

From this I conclude that the subsistence technology of the early settlers of the Pacific does not represent a stage of precereal, root crop horti-culture from mainland southeastern Asia and that those traits associated with the earliest settlement of the southwestern Pacific area can be most easily derived from rice agriculture contexts of mainland southeastern Asia.

While a number of the islands of the far western Pacific, especially those islands from the eastern end of New Guinea west to Wallace's line, were undoubtedly settled quite early (White, Crook, and Ruxton 1970; White 1971), the dispersal of those traits associated with the settlement of the farther islands (i.e. western Polynesia) occurred much later. By perhaps 3500 B.P. the Lapita complex reached New Caledonia. Both linguistic data (Pawley n.d.: 31) and archaeological data (Shutler 1971; Golson 1971a; Groube 1971: 21) strongly suggest the initial settlement of eastern Melanesia and western Polynesia (i.e. Fiji, Tonga, etc.) shortly thereafter. This initial settlement probably derived from what is now western Melanesia, somewhere in the New Hebrides/New Caledonia.

The "Polynesian Problem" (Groube 1971) is really not important to the present discussion; it seems apparent that Polynesians "became" Poly-nesian within the island ecosystem, some time about 3000 B.P., if Pawley (n.d.) is correct, and somewhere in the vicinity of the Fiji-Tonga island groups (Groube 1971: 28). What is important is the technological com-plex carried by their earlier western forebears as they moved along the coast of New Guinea and into the areas of New Caledonia/New Hebrides. This complex consisted of a fairly characteristic southeastern Asian assemblage. The ULTIMATE southeastern Asian origin of this assemblage seems, at the present time at least, a certainty. This assemblage — the adze kit, the ceramic complex, and the other associated traits character-istic of the early Austronesian settlement of the Pacific (Green 1967: 56) — is best known from original Lungshanoid contexts on the mainland of China (Chang 1968b: 121–160) or from Lungshanoid-related contexts in Taiwan (Chang 1969; Green 1967).

The late date for the entrance of this assemblage into the Pacific and the increasingly early dates for rice subsistence on the mainland of south-eastern Asia (Bayard 1973) suggest a reexamination of the argument that the horticultural patterns of subsistence of the Pacific Islands reflect a similar precereal stage of subsistence on the Asiatic mainland. Probably, at the beginning of their dispersal into the Pacific area, these early Aus-tronesian settlers were acquainted with the cultivation of both rice and root crops, and subsequently cereal cultivation proved to be nonadaptive (as did pottery at a later date). Both Yen (1971: 5) and Barrau (1965a: 74), interestingly enough, have suggested this possibility on purely botan-ical grounds.

4. AN INDIGENOUS MODEL FOR THE ORDERING OF THE DATA FROM SOUTHEASTERN ASIA

Introduction

In Sections 2 and 3 above I have reexamined both of the generally accepted reconstructions with a view to constructing alternative hypoth-eses. Initially these two lines of argument were questioned on empirical rather than theoretical grounds. That this is so can best be shown by a review of a presently accepted, generalized model for prehistoric develop-ment in southeastern Asia.

Archaeological remains lacking evidence of cereals (?precereal, but presumably geologically recent) from southeastern Asia have generally been ascribed to an "archaeological culture" termed Hoabinhian (Colani 1927, 1939; Matthews 1968). In 1969 I presented a redefinition of the Hoabinhian (Gorman 1969: 5–6) based on several newly excavated Hoabinhian sites (Gua Kechil, Sai Yok, Laang Spean, Padah Lin, and Spirit Cave). I suggested that the wide distribution of Hoabinhian traits reflects an early southeastern Asian techno-complex, widely diffused and evidencing common ecological adaptations to the southeastern Asian tropics. This techno-complex first appeared during the late Pleistocene (by at least 17,000 B.P.) and continued as a recognizable complex until about 8500 to 7000 B.P. (and even later in some areas). In time the Hoabinhian complex underwent modification and gained new cultural elements, including early domestication of plants, edge grinding of tools, and various ceramic styles.

Recent excavations of post-Hoabinhian sites (Solheim, Parker, and Bayard 1966; Watson and Loofs 1967; Sørensen and Hatting 1967) have presented us with a corpus of new data associated with the development of early rice agriculture in southeastern Asia. Presumably, this is a new techno-complex, quite different from the Hoabinhian and clearly associated early with piedmont settlement and later with lowland plains settlement and generally with a subsistence pattern based on rice agriculture.

Returning for a moment to the Hoabinhian sites, we should note that where their layers of terminal occupation form an interface with later cultural remains, these later remains — primarily pottery and adzes — are characteristic of the later rice-associated material. At Spirit Cave, small slate knives, whose closest relationships seem to be with rice-harvesting knives reported by ethnologists in southeastern Asia, further support the idea that these terminal, intrusive materials are from contexts with rice agriculture (Gorman 1971: 314).

It is the character of these terminal alterations of Hoabinhian deposits that first called into question the postulated precereal, root crop stage. I shall now diagram an indigenous model (Figure 1) based on the theory of a two-phase domestication and shall return to these problems following its discussion.

Model and Discussion

The model presented in Figure 1 seems to be a relatively accurate representation of a combination of available archaeological data and theoretical reconstructions. I have previously summarized the spatial and chronological aspects of Hoabinhian patterns (Gorman 1971: 301); several dated sequences indicate that those patterns actually continued until relatively recent periods (about 4800–4000 B.P.) in more remote areas.

Stage II in the diagram, the phase of root crop horticulture, is at present only a postulated reconstruction. If it did exist as an initial phase of domestication, the time placement shown below would seem fairly accurate. Stage II would continue until the initial forms of rice cultivation were sufficiently successful to allow a replacement of root crop horticulture by rice agriculture, rice then becoming the primary subsistence crop. If the complex of artifacts entering the area of Spirit Cave at about

Stages   Techno-environmental Adaptations   Dates (Approx.)
                                                              B.P.

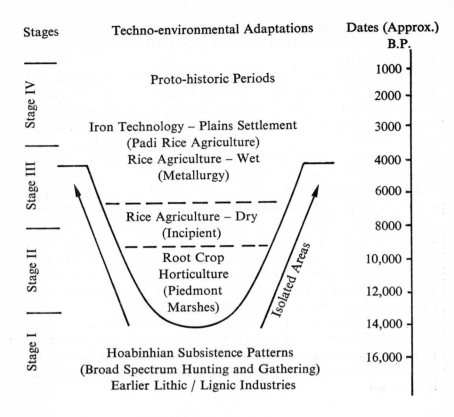

Figure 1.   Model of the development of rice agriculture

9000 B.P. does in fact indicate rice agriculture (and this is certainly con-
jectural at this point), it would suggest that cultivation of rice is somewhat
earlier than is presently suspected. For some time near the transition
between Stage II and Stage III, we have good evidence for a complex
including rice subsistence, domestic cattle (Higham and Leach 1971), and
bronze metallurgy.

Bayard (1971) has recently discussed the early metallurgy of southeastern Asia; his data strongly suggest the working of native ores of
copper in association with early patterns of rice subsistence before the
appearance of bronze. Data now available suggest that initial cultivation
of rice was an adaptation of the lower piedmont, with the settlement of
the more central plains taking place only after the introduction and
development of iron technology (Bronson and Dales 1973; Bayard 1971;

Chin 1969; Gorman 1973; Higham and Parker 1970:15). Surveys and test excavations undertaken on the northeastern plateau of Thailand in 1969–1970 by the Fine Arts Department, Thailand, and the University of Otago, New Zealand, support this reconstruction of late settlement on the plains. At Don Tha Pan, one of the sites excavated in the area of Roi-Et, the lower levels, radiocarbon dated to the beginning of the Christian era, about 25 B.C. to A.D. 20 (Higham and Parker 1970: 23–24, and personal communication) contain rice-chaff tempered pottery. Whatever triggered the movement onto the central areas of at least the Thailand plains, the occupation of those areas seems concomitant with the first appearance of an iron technology.

Settlement of the centers of either the higher plains (the northeastern plateau averages 180 to 200 meters above sea level) or the lower alluvial plains might almost be viewed as a "gamble" in subsistence strategies. Initial clearance of the natural vegetation combined with the relative inaccessibility of the varying biota of the vertically stratified mountainous zones would soon result in extreme pressures for a successful adaptation to padi rice. Initial steps in rice domestication probably occurred in piedmont areas where the subsistence patterns could still include the exploitation of the nearby vertically stratified ecozones. I have previously noted at two early sites on the piedmont a continuation of at least partial dependence on hunting patterns present during the earlier Hoabinhian stage. While I am tempted to speculate on these relationships, I will simply state that only in the most general terms do stage reconstructions have some permanence; none is considered intransmutable.

Problems and Alternatives

The above model (Figure 1) is based on prehistoric data and reconstructions now available. We are faced, however, with one dilemma — what is the significance of the intrusive elements appearing in the terminal layers of Hoabinhian sequences? These have been enumerated above; what seems most important is the cultural apposition between Hoabinhian assemblages, on the one hand, and assemblages associated with early rice agriculture, on the other — in terms of the above model, an apposition between assemblages of stage I and stage III. In other words, at all sites containing evidence of prehistoric cultural contact, this contact was between people carrying an earlier, well-established, Hoabinhian assemblage and people introducing into those areas an assemblage characteristic of later rice agriculturists.

The first and most obvious question is, where are the remains of the stage II occupation? Are there no archaeologically recoverable data reflecting a stage I/stage II subsistence shift? This same question holds for the shift from stage II to stage III. There are, of course, several possible answers, the most obvious being that we just have not yet found the relevant transitional sites. A second alternative might be to suggest cultivation of root crops within the Hoabinhian; however, we know that when these root crops entered the area of the farther Pacific, they were associated with a stage III technology similar to items recovered from early rice contexts on the mainland. A third alternative, which I discuss below, is that there was no separate stage of root crop horticulture in the development of southeastern Asian plant domestication. This alternative views rice and root crops (primarily taro and yams) as "sister domesticates," with their joint initial domestication beginning prior to 9000 B.P., probably in palustrian zones somewhere in piedmont areas of mainland southeastern Asia. This view is diagramed (Figure 2) and discussed below.

In general, the correlations suggested for the first model are applicable to the second; the primary difference between the two is that in the second, the phase of root crop horticulture has been deleted. The second model advances in three stages: (1) an initial Hoabinhian stage, whose beginnings are dated from several sites to roughly 16,000 to 14,000 B.P.; (2) a period of initial domestication of palustrian species (taro and rice) probably centered in a piedmont zone; and (3) the spread of rice agriculture out onto the central areas of the lower-lying plains.

The Hoabinhian stage may well include the beginning of cultivation or tending of a rather broad spectrum of plant species, reflected, for example, by the botanical remains from Spirit Cave (Gorman 1969; Yen 1971). The next posited development is the domestication of palustrian species, including the two basic food crops — taro and rice. The fact that both plants are hydrophytes occupying similar microenvironmental niches supports a reconstruction favoring their joint exploitation and subsequent domestication. Numerous writers (Haudricourt 1962; Barrau 1965a, 1965b; etc.) have drawn attention to this ecological parallel; however, many scholars still contend that a dry-rice, swidden complex represents the initial stages of rice domestication (van Heekeren and Knuth 1967: 116; Higham 1972; Pelzer 1945: 6; Yen 1971: 5). An opposite view is advanced here. It seems more probable that the initial domestication of either of these palustrian species would combine attempts at expanding the natural habitat of the plant with artificial pressures for an increase in yield.

The first question here concerns the wild progenitors. While we have as yet no DEFINITE wild progenitors, Barrau (1965b: 331; 1965a: 64) has suggested that the wild taro may have been similar to the wild variety *aquatilis* of *Colocasia esculenta*, first described from swampy areas in Indonesia. *Oryza perennis* is generally accepted as the wild progenitor of *Oryza sativa*; however, rice is so widely distributed, with between twelve and twenty-three recognizable species, that several different species may have contributed to *Oryza sativa*. The fact remains, however, that for both taro and rice the wild progenitors are hydrophytes; the extension of their original natural habitats would probably have been the extension of marshy/seasonally inundated areas.

At this point distinctions should be made among systems of wet-rice cultivation as they can be seen in operation today. Geertz (1963) has discussed the differences between wet-rice systems (padi, sawah, etc.) and swidden or dry-rice systems. He has further distinguished between what he calls "rainfall farms, swampy-plots, or stream-bank" systems of wet rice cultivation and what he considers more developed "true irrigation systems" (Geertz 1963: 34). The former systems are referred to here as inundation systems, the latter as irrigation systems. Inundation systems like those mentioned by Geertz seem to involve a more limited modification of natural conditions; such technological adaptations as the building of canals and ditches, and the movement of water over long distances are not necessarily required. The extension of natural palustrian habitats most likely was initially based on inundation systems; piedmont zones, especially in the vicinity of streams or rivers, would have provided excellent natural preconditions for such modifications.

Stage II in Figure 2 begins with inundation systems as an initial stage of rice domestication. If the adzes, ceramics, and slate knives entering the Spirit Cave sequence are associated with an early rice complex, the beginning of this stage would be somewhat earlier than 9000 B.P. Between 1,000 and 2,000 years have been tentatively allowed for the florescence of technological developments represented by these elements. Geertz (1963: 32) has suggested that early inundation systems had the capacity to respond to the subsistence demands of rising populations; the data from southeastern Asia would seem to support this suggestion. From about 6000 B.P. we have evidence at both Ban Chiang (Chin 1969: 83) and Non Nok Tha (Bayard 1971, 1973) of at least two distinct ceramic assemblages from northeastern Thailand; there is no reason to believe these are isolated groups. Bayard's data (1971: 8) suggest trade in raw materials over a wide area among groups separated by several hundred kilometers during the early period of Non Nok Tha.

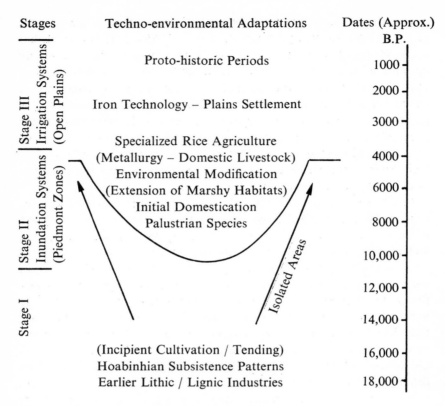

Figure 2. Revised model of the development of rice agriculture

Developments associated with stage III of the second model (Figure 2) parallel those cited for the corresponding stage (IV) of the first (Figure 1); the primary distinction is a shift from inundation to irrigation systems. Movement onto the central portions of both the more northern, higher, broad alluvial valleys and the lowland alluvial plains requires irrigation systems for the flooding and the draining of rice fields. This change presumably reflects an increase in population and a social organization capable of directing these more complex environmental modifications.

In both models, dry rice is viewed as a later adaptation, dependent upon the initial domestication of rice as a "wet" crop. At what point, in terms of either time or the process of cultivation, this secondary adaptation to swiddening began remains unknown. The entrance of adzes and ceramics into upland Hoabinhian sequences may well represent the upland spread of this adaptation.

While the second model allows a more economical ordering of the presently available data, BOTH models are quite speculative. Paleoenvironmental archaeology is only just beginning in southeastern Asia; environmental data are available from only a handful of sites. The models are put forward here primarily to order what is known about overall developments in southeastern Asia and, from there, to generate more specific problems for further research. In the section below, the findings of recent southeastern Asian researchers are organized in terms of the stage divisions of the second model.

5. SOUTHEASTERN ASIAN ARCHAEOLOGICAL DATA: MORE RECENT RESULTS

Stage I: The Hoabinhian Material

In section 4 above, I have presented a very short statement toward a redefinition of the Hoabinhian. Matthews (1968: 94) stated that for old Indochina at least, the excavations to date have

... sketched the outlines of a distinctive culture, based on a hunting and food-gathering economy, with flaked stone artifacts made primarily of pebbles. It was a mesolithic culture in that it exhibited no evidence of agriculture. The rather inadequate faunal data would seem to indicate a post-Pleistocene date. It is commonly called the Hoabinhian.

In a recent paper (Gorman 1971), I examined Hoabinhian patterns of subsistence and discussed the characteristic exploitations of plants and animals. These patterns can best be described as broad-spectrum hunting, fishing, and gathering of flora and fauna that indicate the exploitation of a number of vertically stratified ecozones. I tabulated the faunal remains from twenty-four Hoabinhian sites (or site areas) (Gorman 1971: Table 2) and explored the particular species recovered. In general, the list includes elephant, rhinoceros, bovines, goat antelopes, hog deer, elk deer, barking deer, sambar deer, suids, primates, bears, tigers, miscellaneous small carnivores, porcupine, squirrels, murids, and bats. Turtles, other reptiles, and birds are represented, and freshwater species include snails, bivalves, crustacea, and fish. In addition to many of the above, Hoabinhian coastal sites yielded marine species, including dugong, snails, bivalves, crustacea, and various fish. Exploitation of plants is evidenced by many botanical macrofossils recovered from Spirit Cave. I enumerated these elsewhere (Gorman 1969, 1971) and commented on their possible role as early domesticates.

Hoabinhian lithic material has not been amenable to typological analysis (van Heekeren and Knuth 1967; Matthews 1964, 1968). Unifacially worked stream pebbles and pebble-grinding stones may prove to reflect some type of metal template of the Hoabinhian manufacturers; however, most lithic objects recovered fall into a utilized-flake category. These seem more amenable to statistical techniques based on microscopically identified edge-damage patterns (see Gorman 1971: 312 and Plate 2). Hoabinhian sites are generally small rock shelters located in mountainous karst regions, although several coastal sites have been noted from Malaya, Sumatra and the Democratic Republic of Vietnam (see Gorman 1971: 302, Figure 11). To date, no Hoabinhian sites have been reported from plains regions.

At the time of Matthews' synthesis (1968) of the "Indo-Chinese" material, no Hoabinhian site had produced a stratified radiocarbon sequence. Since that writing, several sites have allowed radiocarbon determinations, the most secure sequence coming from Spirit Cave (Gorman 1971: 303). The earliest dates so far recorded for Hoabinhian sites are from Padah-lin in Burma — 13,400 ± 200 B.P. (R-2547/5-B) (U Aung Thaw, personal communication); from Spirit Cave — 9260 ± 560 B.P. (FSU 315); and from the Ongba Cave site in Thailand — 11,180 ± 180 B.P. (Chin 1969: 12). If we can assume that low-latitude climatic changes were relatively synchronous, the data from Connolly (1967), Frerichs (1968), and Tsukada (1966) supply a median figure of about 10,000 B.P. as a reasonable approximation of the Pleistocene/Recent boundary, a boundary that the basal layers of the three Hoabinhian sites above most certainly antedate. Hoabinhian patterns of stage I are then clearly visible during the terminal Pleistocene and undoubtedly date back for some considerable time. The latest date for unmodified Hoabinhian materials is derived from Gua Kechil, where the Hoabinhian sequence ends at about 4700 ± 800 B.P. (Dunn 1966). Hoabinhian orientations from available data can then be said to span at least 8,000 years. During most of this time the relevant assemblages seem to reflect a relatively stable ecological adaptation.

HOABINHIAN TERMINAL ALTERATIONS   Certain technological items characteristically appear, although at various times, in the terminal layers of most Hoabinhian sites (Gorman 1971: 313–314). These items — ground adzes and ceramics — are characteristic of the earliest sites of rice agriculture, and their appearance is considered tentatively as representing stage II horizon markers. At Gua Kechil, Dunn (1964) distinguished his third level, Gua Kechil III, by the appearance of ceramics and ground-stone tools and a decrease in faunal remains. He interpreted this as indirect evidence for the introduction of agriculture. At Spirit Cave, level II is similarly marked by the appearance of quadrangular adzes, ceramics, and small bifacially ground knives (Gorman 1971: 303). The knives from level II at Spirit Cave are archaeologically unique; their closest affinity lies with rice-harvesting knives reported by ethnologists in Java and other parts of southeastern Asia (Colani 1939; Gorman 1971: 314). I have tentatively dated the beginning of stage II to the first appearance of these new technological items. Although there is no botanical evidence for agriculture at this level in Spirit Cave, these items (ceramics and adzes) do appear in the earliest agricultural contexts for which botanical evidence of *Oryza sativa* is available, namely, the earliest levels at Non Nok Tha. What can be stated generally is that in all cases, irrespective of the particular date, where Hoabinhian material is overlaid with non-Hoabinhian material, the overlying non-Hoabinhian material is characteristic of later archaeological assemblages deriving from piedmont sites with rice agriculture. At present, almost no data are available for the elucidation of processes in the transition of subsistence orientations between stage I and stage II. The general discussion of the second model, Section 4 above, presents a hypothetical reconstruction only; this remains to be tested through actual field research.

Stage II: The Beginnings of Early Village Farming on the Southeastern Asian Piedmont

David Harris (1969: 8–9) stated, "If gatherer-hunter-fishers are the most likely progenitors of plant domestication we may next ask which habitats offered the best opportunities within the generalized ecosystem that they occupied." He suggested that the answer is "the marginal transitional zones or ecozones between major ecosystems, especially forest- and woodland-edge situations."

This seems to be the best area in which to look for the beginnings of domestication in southeastern Asia. Evidence cited below suggests that the low alluvial plains were settled very late, and all sites out on these plains argue for settlement after the introduction of iron technology. Whatever the original contexts of the late introductions at Spirit Cave, they appear to have been located neither in the nearby highlands nor on the lower terraces or alluvial plains. This negative distribution may indicate an origin on the piedmont, which is given some support by more general surveys in northern and northeastern Thailand. Also in this piedmont zone are the most probable natural environments favoring initial rice domestication, i.e. the points where intermontane valley streams emerge into lowland marshy areas.

Although the beginnings of stage II patterns are still obscure, we have good evidence shortly thereafter for settlement farther out, though not yet on the midmost areas or on the plains. Two sites in northeastern Thailand — Non Nok Tha and Ban Chiang — date to about 7000–6500 B.P. and probably both (but certainly the former) reflect a base of rice subsistence. The sequence at Non Nok Tha (Bayard 1971, 1973) begins prior to about 6500 B.P. and from the early period exhibits a complex of elaborately incised and cord-marked pottery, low-profile rectangular stone adzes, rice agriculture, domestic cattle, and probably domesticated pig (Bayard 1971). The sequence at Non Nok Tha continues with what Bayard (1971) considered an early indigenous metallurgical development about 5000–4500 B.P. Occupation at Non Nok Tha continued through to the historic periods; the strata of the late period of the site contained tanged iron blades, porcelain, and celadon shards attributable to the beginnings of the historic periods in Thailand. Bayard (1971) presented a detailed chronology for Non Nok Tha, and there seems little doubt that the site was occupied prior to 6000 B.P.

The spectacular red-on-white painted ware from Ban Chiang has parallels with red-on-white painted ceramics from late early-period/early middle-period material from Non Nok Tha. This Ban Chiang pottery has been dated by thermoluminescence to 6580 ± 52 B.P. (Chin 1969: 83). As Bayard noted (1971: 12), this date supports the early dating of Non Nok Tha and both sites strongly suggest the presence of rice farming in the northeastern Thai plateau prior to 6500 B.P. In a more recent article, Chin (1971: 44) synthesized these data and considered wet rice farming to date from about 5500 B.P. No evidence suggests marshy habitats near either Non Nok Tha or Ban Chiang, and these settlements probably represent environmental modifications reflecting inundation systems of rice cultivation similar to those known from the area today.

Moving from Ban Chiang-Non Nok Tha forward in time, we find the next dated sequence at the Thai-Danish excavation of Ban Kao, a late rice agriculture/early Iron Age site in western central Thailand (Sørensen and Hatting 1967; Sørensen 1967; Parker 1968). Sørensen and Hatting considered the material from Ban Kao to be Neolithic; however, to date, only the studies of the human skeletons and associated grave goods have been published (Sørensen and Hatting 1967; Sangvichien 1969). In a review of Sørensen and Hatting's major report on the burials, Parker (1968) suggested a revision of the chronology, arguing for an early Iron Age date for the burials and related materials. In his reconsideration of the evidence from Ban Kao, Parker suggested a date of about 2500 B.P. as the earliest possible for the middle period of the Ban Kao interments — those with the carinated bowls of burnished black ware. Results from the thermoluminescence dating of similar black burnished ware from Ban Kao (Chin 1969: 27) produced a date of 2290 ± 255 B.P., thus arguing strongly for Parker's revised chronology.

While the temporal status of the remains published in the report on the burial material is thus questionable, there is little doubt that Ban Kao is indeed an early agricultural site into which the intrusive Iron Age burials were dug. The radiocarbon determinations available from Ban Kao in conjunction with the initial cultural reconstructions (Sørensen and Hatting 1967; Sørensen 1967) indicate that the "Neolithic" settlement of Ban Kao was from its beginning, about 4000 B.P., an agricultural settlement with domesticated pig and possibly domesticated fowl (chicken) and cattle (Sørensen 1967: 13). The presence of stone and shell sickles and of querns probably reflects cereal agriculture. However, Sørensen (1967: 12) suggested that a swidden technique — evidenced by the "thousands of pieces of burned clay" — was used; as I find it rather difficult to imagine the early agriculturists at Ban Kao swiddening either their village or their cemetery, I would search for some alternative explanation for the burned clay and leave open the exact nature of the agricultural system. The dates for metalworking at Non Nok Tha indicate that Ban Kao is "Neolithic" only insofar as no metal was recovered from the site itself.

The evidence for stage II exploitations derive, then, primarily from three sites — Ban Chiang, Non Nok Tha, and Ban Kao — all in what is now Thailand. As Loofs (1970: 177) noted, Thailand recently has been the subject of much prehistoric research; the location of these sites within Thailand may represent either its prehistoric importance or the fact that it is one of the few countries on the mainland of southeastern Asia where the political situation allows both Thai and foreign scholars to undertake extensive prehistoric research.

Stage III: Iron Technology and the Settlement of the Southeastern Asian Alluvial Plains

During the past ten years, a number of archaeological surveys have been carried out in Thailand (van Heekeren and Knuth 1967; Sørensen and Hatting 1967; Solheim and Gorman 1966; Watson and Loofs 1967; Watson 1968; Loofs 1970; Gorman 1969; Bronson and Dales 1973; Higham and Parker 1970; etc.). These results have been published by foreign researchers. However, the Fine Arts Department of Thailand maintains regional officers throughout Thailand who conduct regional surveys and excavations; their reports are available in their archives in Bangkok and, for those literate in Thai, in their journal *Silapākǫn* as well as in their monograph series. In the light of this not inconsiderable amount of surveying, the fact that no pre-metal-age sites have been located on the central areas of the lowland alluvial plains — areas that are today the most densely settled, the most intensively cultivated and hence the most productive zones in the kingdom — seems most curious indeed. Some 800 years of historic settlement might account for the paucity of earlier sites, the latter perhaps destroyed by earlier alluviation or later intensive settlement. However, the assumption that some earlier sites would have survived this presumed obliteration seems reasonable. The failure of surveys to date to locate such sites has led Higham (1972) to suggest that for the area of Roi-Et at least, the initial settlement of the hitherto unoccupied tracts was triggered by the introduction of iron, the tractive power of the water buffalo, and wet-rice farming.

During 1965–1966, several stream-laced Quaternary alluvial plains lying in the eastern section of northern Thailand were surveyed; all remains from the central areas of these plains appeared to reflect early Iron Age/late historic settlement (Gorman 1973). Surveys along the piedmont fringes of the plains yielded a wealth of data, primarily in the form of ground-stone adzes and cord-marked ceramics — generally the property of village antiquarians who had recovered them during the cultivation of nearby fields. Although this is still certainly speculative, apparently the early agriculturists initially occupied the piedmont margin of the Thai plains; the midmost areas of these plains seem to have been settled more recently — possibly only after the advent of iron technology and irrigation systems, and then perhaps as a consequence of increasing population density.

While questions concerning the movement of people out onto the lowland plains and the processes involved must remain open, on the basis of excavated material we can make some comments on the introduction of iron technology, initial Iron Age settlements, and what appears to be a subsequent increase in population. The sequences at Non Nok Tha and Ban Kao, as outlined above, continue through to the introduction of iron implements. Research in other areas — Lopburi (Chin 1969: 103), Chansen (Bronson and Dales 1973), Phu Wiang (Higham and Parker 1970), and Roi-Et (Higham and Parker 1970) — has provided sites whose basal layers represent initial Iron Age settlements. Of these, the Lopburi Artillery Site is the earliest and thus, chronologically, the most interesting.

The Lopburi Artillery Site was first excavated in 1964 by Nai Vidja Intakosai, curator at the National Museum, Bangkok (Chin 1965, 1969). It is a burial site containing artifacts of stone, bronze, and iron, and earthenware ceramics; Chinese ceramics of the Ming period occurred in upper layers. Subsequent excavations in 1965 yielded another thirty burials containing earthenware ceramics, bronze bracelets and rings, stone and clay bracelets, and more iron and stone implements. While the detailed report on this site is not yet available, Chin (1969: 103) has reported one thermoluminescence date of 2700 ± 166 B.P. derived from a Lopburi earthenware shard.

Chansen is the remains of a moated city excavated during 1968 and 1969 by Bronson, then at the University of Pennsylvania (Bronson and Dales 1973). Their preliminary report indicates that Chansen was occupied from about 2200 B.P. to A.D. 1000. The initial phase represents an apparently indigenous Iron Age settlement sharing some, but not many, general traits with the Lopburi Artillery Site (Bronson and Dales). This phase I can be dated on typological grounds to about 2200 B.P. or perhaps earlier. The material of phase I is typologically unrelated to that of phase II, which initiates a sequence showing cultural continuity through to the last main occupation phase (IV), dating from about A.D. 800 to 1050 and described by Bronson as Late Dvaravarti. During the second and third phases of Chansen, there is an increase in the area occupied; by phase V at least, the inhabitants had fortified their settlement by the construction of a moat enclosing an area of about 700 by 70 meters. Nearby contemporaneous sites, fortified by both moats and earthen walls were also found. The expanding settlement at Chansen, the moat, and the presence of other moated and walled sites in the area seemingly indicate a rising population density from about A.D. 200 to 800.

In 1970 an intensive survey of approximately ten square miles in the area of Roi-Et on the central portion of the northeastern plateau of Thailand yielded a number of sites which have been described by Higham and Parker (1970). The sites comprise large mounds and give a general impression of intensive occupation during the late prehistoric period. Three sites (Ban Tha Nen, Don Tha Pan, and Bo Phan Khan) were excavated. Preliminary analysis (Higham and Parker 1970) indicated that rice cultivation was practiced from the earliest levels in all three, and deer, domesticated cattle, and probably domesticated pig have been identified from the earliest levels of Ban Tha Nen. The radiocarbon determinations now available (Higham 1972) indicate that the initial settlement of the area occurred around the beginning of the Christian era. Higham (1972) tied the initial settlement to the availability of iron, the tractive power of the water buffalo, and wet-rice farming.

After their work in Roi-Et, Higham and Parker (1970: Section VI) carried out a survey and excavations in the interior of Phu Wiang, a large monadnock near the site of Non Nok Tha. The most interesting site tested was Non Nong Chik, a cemetery which, from a comparison of pottery styles with the neighboring Non Nok Tha, can be said to have been in use from the late bronze period of the latter through to the introduction of iron. Radiocarbon determinations from Non Nong Chik indicate that iron entered the area shortly after about 2500 B.P. — iron slag present in these layers indicates the local smelting of iron ore.

There are other Thai sites that have yielded evidence of an early iron technology; the ones mentioned above suffice to set the introduction of iron somewhere within the first thousand years B.C. We have no evidence for the settlement of the central areas of either the lowland rolling plains or the flat alluvial plains earlier than this. We have several sites (the Roi-Et group) showing a movement onto more central plains after this; inferential evidence in the form of moats, earthen fortifications, and the expansion of settlement areas argues for a concomitant increase in population density. Radiocarbon determinations indicate that this process began about 3000 B.P. and ended, at least as a prehistoric phenomenon, with the Khmer expansion into what is now northeastern Thailand and the development of early historic Thai kingdoms in central Thailand. Historic records are available for Thailand from shortly after A.D. 1000, and the area can be said to have entered its own historic period.

6. CONCLUSIONS

Reevaluation of the *a priori* allegations of a Sinocentric origin for southeastern Asian cereal agriculture and of the existence of an earlier, indigenous stage of root crop horticulture suggests that both these reconstructions lack empirical foundations and in fact run contrary to the aggregation of prehistoric data.

Reorganization of the southeastern Asian data along lines of the second model presented above suggests that by about 16,000–14,000 B.P., groups of people carrying Hoabinhian assemblages were spread over much of mainland southeastern Asia. A lowered sea level during this period indicates the possibility that riparian habitats along the now submerged stream systems on the floor of the Sunda shelf were similarly occupied. By 9000 B.P., technological developments that may well reflect the initial domestication of rice or a similar early cereal crop had occurred in or around southeastern Asia. This date is roughly contemporary with the appearance of domestication in other areas of the world, viz. southwestern Asia and Mesoamerica.

This widely separated yet synchronous development of domestication has led prehistorians to seek nomothetic explanations of worldwide application for the courses toward this development. The presumed climatic amelioration associated with the end of the Pleistocene has often been advanced as a possible triggering factor. The southeastern Asian climatic regimen, however, seems to have been only slightly affected; a more serious environmental change — keyed to the terminal Pleistocene/early Recent eustatic rise in sea level — was the reduction of the land mass of southeastern Asia to approximately one-half of its late Pleistocene size. Effects of this reduction upon human population densities and accompanying modifications in cultural adaptive systems remain to be researched; what can be said is that southeastern Asia was the only area in the world to undergo such inundation.

If, as Boserup contends (1965: 11), population growth should be viewed as the independent variable — and agricultural growth as the dependent variable — then a 50 percent reduction in land area might well have radically increased population densities, simulating overall growth and thus providing a strong, idiographic factor in the development of domestication. The present lack of developmental sequences for the complex of adzes, knives, ceramics, and cereal cultivation may indicate that domestication developed in riparian habitats on what is now the submerged floor of the Sunda shelf. Several working hypotheses could be generated to guide field research into these problems; perhaps most important is investigation of the process of southeastern Asian domestication in terms of regionally meaningful variables.

By 7000–6500 B.P. the presence of rice agriculturists is attested by artifactual remains from sites along the piedmont margins of the plains of southeastern Asia. Distribution of archaeological remains suggests the intensive, early agricultural use of this piedmont zone to the exclusion of other areas (coastal areas, previously important, have yet to be surveyed for early agricultural settlement). Between 3500 and 3000 B.P. iron technology and increasing population density impelled the settlement of the more open plains. Once the technological adaptation to settlement on the open plains had been made, evidence — the expansion of habitation areas and the construction of fortified and moated settlements — suggests even more rapidly increasing populations.

Examining the course of domestication from about 9000 B.P. to the beginning of the Christian era, I think it useful to posit two adaptive thresholds. The crossing of the first marked the initial domestication of certain key palustrian species (e.g. taro and rice) and caused a shift in settlement from upland areas to piedmont zones where more agriculturally productive habitats could be expanded artificially with minimal effort. A second threshold, traversed much later (about 3500–3000 B.P.), seems to have depended on the emergence of iron technology and increased population pressure; this second threshold immediately preceded the beginnings of true irrigation systems and laid the foundation for the extensive settlement of the lower alluvial plains. Without such a two-stage developmental model, the ubiquitous rise about A.D. 500 to 1200 of populous kingdoms on the southeastern Asian plains, which were apparently uninhabited only a few thousand years earlier, is difficult to explain.

Since southeastern Asia incorporates China south of the Yangtze River, it is important to recognize the existence of rice agriculture in the lower Yangtze Valley by the end of the fourth millennium B.C. (Ho, this volume). This date is similar to those obtained for Ban Chiang by the Nara University of Education, Tokyo, and is close to Bayard's estimates for the early occupation of Non Nok Tha (Bayard 1971). Obviously economic changes of some magnitude were in progress in southeastern Asia by at least 6500 to 7000 B.P.

The relationships between such developments and those incorporating Yang Shao cultivation of millet and pig-husbandry in the loess lands of the Chinese nuclear area are at present difficult to define, but diffusion south as far as Thailand is hard to accept on the basis of archaeological evidence currently available.

REFERENCES

ALLCHIN, BRIDGET, RAYMOND ALLCHIN
  1968   *The birth of Indian civilization.* Harmondsworth: Penguin.
AMES, OAKES
  1939   *Economic annuals and human cultures.* Cambridge, Mass.: Botanical Museum of Harvard University.
ANDERSON, EDGAR
  1960   "The evolution of domestication," in *Evolution after Darwin*, volume two. Edited by Sol Tax, 67–84. Chicago: University of Chicago Press.
ANDERSSON, J. G.
  1934   *Children of the yellow earth.* London: Kegan Paul, Trench, Trubner.
  1947   Prehistoric sites in Honan. *Bulletin of the Museum of Far Eastern Antiquities* 19:1–24.
AN SYRZ MIN
  1972   Discussing the era of our prehistoric culture. *K'ao-ku* (1):52–56.

BARRAU, JACQUES

1965a Histoire et préhistoire horticoles de l'Océanie tropicale. *Journal de la Société des Océanistes* 21:55–78.

1965b L'humide et le sec. *Journal of the Polynesian Society* 74:329–346.

BAYARD, DONN T.

1971 "An early indigenous bronze technology in north-east Thailand: its implications for the prehistory of east Asia." Paper presented at the Twenty-eighth International Congress of Orientalists, Canberra, January, 1971.

1973 Excavations at Non Nok Tha, northeastern Thailand. *Asian Perspectives* 13:109–143.

BENEDICT, PAUL K.

1966 Austro-Thai. *Behavior Science Notes* 1:227–261.

1967 Austro-Thai studies, 3: Austro-Thai and Chinese. *Behavior Science Notes* 2:275–336.

BOSERUP, ESTER

1965 *The conditions of agricultural growth.* London: George Allen and Unwin.

BRONSON, B., G. F. DALES

1973 Excavations at Chansen, Thailand, 1968 and 1969: a preliminary report. *Asian Perspectives* 113:15–46.

BURKILL, I. H.

1951 The rise and decline of the greater yam in the service of man. *Advancement of Science* 7:443–448.

CAPELL, A.

1962 Oceanic linguistics today. *Current Anthropology* 3:371–428.

CHANG, KWANG-CHIH

1967 The Yale expedition to Taiwan and the Southeast Asian horticultural evolution. *Discovery, Yale Paebody Museum* 2(2):3–10.

1968a Archaeology of ancient China. *Science* 162:519–526.

1968b *The archaeology of ancient China* (revised and enlarged edition). New Haven: Yale University Press.

1969 *Fengpitou, Tapenkeng and the prehistory of Taiwan.* Yale University Publications in Anthropology 73.

1970 The beginnings of agriculture in the Far East. *Antiquity* 44:175–185.

1974 "Ancient farmers in the Asian tropics: major problems for archaeological and palaeoenvironmental investigations of southeast Asia at the earliest Neolithic level," in *Perspectives in paleo-anthropology: a Festschrift in honor of D. Sen.* Edited by A. K. Ghosh, 273–286. Calcutta: F. K. L. Mukhopadyay.

CHIN YOU-DI

1965 *Prehistory and prehistoric excavations in Lopburi Province* (in Thai). Bangkok: Fine Arts Department, National Museum.

1969 *Prehistoric man in Thailand* (in Thai). Bangkok: Fine Arts Department, National Museum.

1971 Archaeological evidence for rice in Thailand (in Thai). *Silpākǫn* 15:39–44.

COLANI, MADELEINE
  1927   *L'Age de la pierre dans la province de Hoa-Binh, Tonkin.* Hanoi.
  1939   La civilization hoabinhienne extrême-orientale. *Bulletin de la Société Préhistorique Française* 36:170–174.

CONOLLY, JOHN R.
  1967   Postglacial-glacial change in climate in the Indian Ocean. *Nature* 214: 873–875.

DUFF, ROGER
  1970   *Stone adzes of southeast Asia.* Canterbury Museum, Christchurch, New Zealand, Bulletin 3.

DUNN, FREDERICK L.
  1964   Excavations at Gua Kechil, Pahang. *Journal of the Malayan Branch of the Royal Asiatic Society* 38:87–124.
  1966   Radiocarbon dating of the Malayan Neolithic. *Proceedings of the Prehistoric Society* 32:352–353.
  1970   Cultural evolution in the late Pleistocene and Holocene of Southeast Asia. *American Anthropologist* 72:1041–1054.

FRERICHS, WILLIAM E.
  1968   Pleistocene-Recent boundary and Wisconsin glacial biostratigraphy in the northern Indian Ocean. *Science* 159:1456–1458.

GEERTZ, CLIFFORD
  1963   *Agricultural involution: the process of ecological change in Indonesia.* Berkeley and Los Angeles: University of California Press.

GOLSON, JACK
  1968   "Archaeological prospects for Melanesia," in *Prehistoric culture in Oceania: a symposium.* Edited by I. Yawata and Y. H. Sinoto, 3–14. Honolulu: Bishop Museum Press.
  1971a "Lapita ware and its transformations," in *Studies in Oceanic culture history,* volume two. Edited by R. C. Green and M. Kelly. Pacific Anthropological Records 12. Honolulu: Bishop Museum Press.
  1971b Both sides of the Wallace line: Australia, New Guinea, and Asian prehistory. *Archaeology and Physical Anthropology in Oceania* 6:124–144.

GORMAN, C. F.
  1969   Hoabinhian: a pebble-tool complex with early plant associations in southeast Asia. *Science* 163:671–673.
  1971   The Hoabinhian and after: subsistence patterns in Southeast Asia during the late Pleistocene and early Recent periods. *World Archaeology* 2:300–320.
  1973   Excavations at Spirit Cave, north Thailand: some interim interpretations. *Asian Perspectives* 13:79–107.

GRACE, GEORGE W.
  1964   Movement of the Malayo-Polynesians: 1500 B.C. to A.D. 500. The linguistic evidence. *Current Anthropology* 5:361–368.

GREEN, R. C.
  1967   "Chinese-Pacific relations (in the Neolithic)," in *China and its place in the world.* Edited by N. Tarling, 43–63. Auckland: B. and J. Paul.

GREEN, R. C., M. KELLY, *editors*
  1971   *Studies in Oceanic culture history,* volume two. Pacific Anthropological Records 12. Honolulu: Bishop Museum Press.

GROUBE, L. M.
  1971 Tonga, Lapita pottery and Polynesian origins. *Journal of the Polynesian Society* 80:278–316.

H ARRIS, DAVID R.
  1962 New light on plant domestication and the origins of agriculture: a review. *Geographical Review* 57:90–107.
  1969 "Agricultural systems, ecosystems and the origins of agriculture," in *The domestication and exploitation of plants and animals.* Edited by P. J. Ucko and G. W. Dimbleby, 3–15. London: Gerald Duckworth.

HAUDRICOURT, A.
  1962 Domestication des animaux, culture des plantes et traitement d'autrui. *L'Homme* 2.

HIGHAM, C. F. W.
  1972 "Initial model formulation in *Terra Incognita,*" in *Models in archaeology.* Edited by D. L. Clarke, 453–476. London: Methuen.

HIGHAM, C. F. W., B. FOSS LEACH
  1971 An early center of bovine husbandry in Southeast Asia. *Science* 172: 54–56.

HIGHAM, C. F. W., R. H. PARKER
  1970 *Prehistoric investigations in N.E. Thailand 1969–70: preliminary report.* Dunedin: Department of Anthropology, University of Otago.

HO, PING-TI
  1969 The loess and the origin of Chinese agriculture. *American Historical Review* 75:1–36.

LOOFS, HELMUT H. E.
  1970 A brief account of the Thai-British archaeological expedition. *Archaeology and Physical Anthropology in Oceania* 5:177–183.

MATTHEWS, JOHN M.
  1964 "The Hoabinhian in Southeast Asia and elsewhere." Unpublished Ph.D. dissertation, Australian National University, Canberra.
  1968 A review of the "Hoabinhian" in Indo-China. *Asian Perspectives* 9: 86–95.

PARKER, R. H.
  1968 Review of: *Archaeological excavations in Thailand,* volume two: *Ban Kao Part I: The archaeological material from the burials,* by Per Sørensen and Tove Hatting (1967, Copenhagen: Munksgaard). *Journal of the Polynesian Society* 77:307–313.

PAWLEY, ANDREW
  n.d. "Austronesian languages." Working papers in linguistics, University of Auckland. Mimeographed manuscript.

PELZER, KARL J.
  1945 "From hunting and gathering to agriculture," in *Pioneer settlement in the Asiatic tropics.* American Geographical Society, Special Publication 29.

POULSEN, JENS
  1968 "Archaeological excavations on Tongatapu," in *Prehistoric culture in Oceania: a symposium.* Edited by I. Yawata and Y. H. Sinoto, 85–92. Honolulu: Bishop Museum Press.

SANGVICHIEN, SOOD
1969   *Archaeological excavations in Thailand*, volume three: *Ban Kao Part 2: The prehistoric Thai skeletons*. Copenhagen: Munksgaard.

SAUER, C. O.
1952   *Agricultural origins and dispersals*. New York: American Geographical Society.

SHEN, T. H.
1951   *Agricultural resources of China*. New York: Cornell University Press.

SHUTLER, M. E., RICHARD SHUTLER, JR.
1968   A preliminary report of archaeological explorations in the southern New Hebrides. *Asian Perspectives* 9:157–166.

SHUTLER, RICHARD, JR.
1971   "Pacific Island radiocarbon dates, an overview," in *Studies in Oceanic culture history*, volume two. Edited by R. C. Green and M. Kelly. Pacific Anthropological Records 12. Honolulu: Bishop Museum Press.

SINGH, GURDIP
1971   The Indus Valley culture (seen in the context of post-glacial climate and ecological studies in northwest India). *Archaeology and Physical Anthropology in Oceania* 6:177–189.

SOLHEIM, W. G., II
1961   Sa-huynh related pottery in southeast Asia. *Asian Perspectives* 3:177–188.
1964   Pottery and the Malayo-Polynesians. *Current Anthropology* 5:360, 376–384, 400–403.
1967   Southeast Asia and the West. *Science* 157:896–902.
1969   Reworking Southeast Asian prehistory. *Paideuma* 15:125–139.
1973   Northern Thailand, Southeast Asia, and world prehistory. *Asian Perspectives* 13:145–162.

SOLHEIM, W. G., II, CHESTER GORMAN
1966   Archaeological salvage program: northeastern Thailand; first season. *Journal of the Siam Society* 54:111–210.

SOLHEIM, W. G., II, R. H. PARKER, DONN T. BAYARD
1966   *Preliminary reports on excavations at Ban Nadi, Ban Sao Lao, Pimai No. 1*. Honolulu: Social Science Research Institute, University of Hawaii. (Mimeographed.)

SØRENSEN, PER
1967   "The Neolithic cultures of Thailand (and north Malaya) and their Lungshanoid relationship." Paper presented at the symposium "Early Chinese art and its possible influence in the Pacific Basin," Columbia University, New York, 1967.

SØRENSEN, PER, TOVE HATTING
1967   *Archaeological excavations in Thailand*, volume two: *Ban Kao Part I: The archaeological material from the burials*. Copenhagen: Munksgaard.

SPENCER, J. E.
1963   "The migration of rice from mainland Southeast Asia into Indonesia," in *Plants and the migration of Pacific peoples*. Edited by Jacques Barrau, 83–89. Honolulu: Bishop Museum Press.

1966   *Shifting cultivation in southeastern Asia.* University of California Publications in Geography 19.

TREGEAR, T. R.
1965   *A geography of China.* London: University of London Press.

TREISTMAN, JUDITH
1968   Ch'ü-chia-ling and the early cultures of the Hanshui Valley, China. *Asian Perspectives* 11:69–92.

TSUKADA, MATSUO
1966   Late Pleistocene vegetation and climate in Taiwan (Formosa). *Proceedings of the National Academy of Sciences* 55:543–548.

U AUNG THAW
1969   The "Neolithic" culture of the Padah-Lin caves. *Journal of the Burma Research Society* 52:9–23.

VAN HEEKEREN, H. R., EIGIL KNUTH
1967   *Archaeological excavations in Thailand,* volume one: *Sai-Yok.* Copenhagen: Munksgaard.

VAVILOV, N. I.
1949–1950   The origin, variation, immunity and breeding of cultivated plants. (Selected writings of N. I. Vavilov.) *Chronica Botanica* 13: 1–364.

VISHNU-MITTRE
1962   *Plant economy in ancient Navadatoli-Maheshwar.* Lucknow: Birbal Sahni Institute of Palaeobotany.

WATSON, WILLIAM
1968   The Thai-British archaeological expedition. *Antiquity* 42:302–306.

WATSON, WILLIAM, HELMUT E. LOOFS
1967   The Thai-British archaeological expedition: a preliminary report on the work of the first season, 1965–1966. *Journal of the Siam Society* 55:237–272.

WHITE, PETER
1971   "New Guinea: the first phase in Oceanic settlement," in *Studies in Oceanic culture history,* volume two. Edited by R. C. Green and M. Kelly. Pacific Anthropological Records 12. Honolulu: Bishop Museum Press.

WHITE, PETER, K. A. W. CROOK, B. P. RUXTON
1970   Kosipe: a late Pleistocene site in the Papuan highlands. *Proceedings of the Prehistoric Society* 36:152–170.

WIENS, HEROLD J.
1954   *China's march toward the tropics.* Hamden, Conn.: Shoe String Press.

YAWATA, I., Y. H. SINOTO, *editors*
1968   *Prehistoric culture in Oceania: a symposium.* Honolulu: Bishop Museum Press.

YEN, DOUGLAS E.
1971   "The development of agriculture in Oceania," in *Studies in Oceanic culture history,* volume two. Edited by R. C. Green and M. Kelly. Pacific Anthropological Records 12. Honolulu: Bishop Museum Press.

ZUKOVSKIJ, P. M.
1962   *Cultivated plants and their wild relatives.* Abridged translation by P. S. Hudson. Bucks, England: Commonwealth Agricultural Bureaux.

The Origins of Cereal Agriculture in the Old World

JACK R. HARLAN

Three major and several minor cereal agricultures evolved in the Old World. The major ones are: (1) the Near Eastern complex, eventually dominated by wheat, which became the staff of life for hundreds of millions of people, (2) rice-based agriculture, also nourishing hundreds of millions, in southern and eastern Asia, and (3) the African savanna complex, whose major contributions were sorghum and pearl millet. More than half the people on earth are fed on wheat and rice. The world's greatest single source of protein, far exceeding all animal proteins in the human diet, is wheat, and the greatest caloric intake comes from rice. Many millions of people in Africa and Asia are supported by sorghum and pearl millet. These are the great cereal agricultures of the Old World.

Lesser cereal agricultures are or were at some time extremely important locally, yet they never achieved the status of wheat, rice, and sorghum cultures. I shall deal briefly in this paper with these in order to balance the perspective. The lesser cultures include: (1) African cereals — teff, finger millet, African rice, fonio, black fonio, and guinea millet; (2) warm season Eurasian millets — foxtail millet and panic millet; and (3) southern and eastern Asian cereals — Job's tears, slender millet, koda millet, and Japanese millet.

Cereals, of course, were not domesticated alone or out of context. Wherever agriculture emerged, it was based on a complex of plant domesticates. Other species such as grain legumes, vegetables, fruits, and tuber crops are often as important as the cereals themselves in helping to provide balanced nutrition and variety in the diets. Cereals must be considered in proper context, and the complexes must be viewed as agricultural systems.

A few brief remarks concerning the genetic affinities between cultivated cereals and their nearest wild relatives may be in order. The taxonomy of cultivated plants has long been in a state of disorder, if not outright chaos. The methods of formal taxonomy have been completely inadequate to deal with the vast variation found in cultivated plants. As a result, far too many names have been applied. An appropriate use of Latin names is a problem for those who deal with crops professionally and an italic jungle for the uninitiated. If a few simple facts are kept in mind, however, the confusion can be reduced, perhaps, to a tolerable state. These include the following:

1. All true cereals belong to the grass family (Gramineae).

2. Domestication can be carried to various degrees. Some cultivated races closely resemble their wild progenitors, while others are strikingly different from their nearest wild relatives.

3. However great the morphological differences between wild and cultivated races may appear to be, domestication almost never leads to the evolution of new species in a biological sense. Morphological changes in the process may be spectacular, but the genetic differences accumulated tend to be relatively modest.

4. All forms, races, or varieties that can be hybridized readily and that yield fertile offspring belong to the same biological species, whatever the morphological differences among them.

5. With very few exceptions, a biological species that includes a crop will also include wild and weed races. The wild races are adapted to fairly primary (little-disturbed) habitats; the weed races are adapted to disturbed habitats, such as along paths, roads, ditches, edges of fields, or in cultivated fields themselves. Highly selected cultivated races are restricted to cultivated fields and cannot survive without the aid of man.

6. Wild, weed, and cultivated races can often be distinguished morphologically and consequently are likely to receive different Latin epithets from botanists who feel compelled to name everything recognizable. This compounds the confusion, but because the literature is full of such names, we cannot avoid them; we can only try to understand what they mean.

7. Table 1 lists some of the more common epithets for the cereals discussed in this paper. A single epithet for each crop would have been more correct from a genetic point of view and would have emphasized the close genetic affinities among wild, weed, and cultivated races of each crop.

The processes of plant domestication and crop evolution are not yet well understood. Many theoretical models have been proposed, usually without foundation in experimental research and too often based on

Table 1. Cereals domesticated in the Old World

Crop	2n chromo-some number	Cultivated races	Wild races	Weed races
NEAR EASTERN COMPLEX				
BARLEY	14	*Hordeum vulgare*	*H. spontaneum*	*H. spontaneum*
WHEATS				
Einkorn Wheat	14	*Triticum monococcum*	*T. boeoticum*	*T. boeoticum*
Emmer Wheat	28	*T. dicoccum*	*T. dicoccoides*	—
Timopheevi Wheat	28	*T. timopheevi*	*T. araraticum*	*T. timopheevi*
Bread Wheat	42	*T. X aestivum*	—	—
RYE	14	*Secale cereale*	*S. cereale*	*S. cereale*
OATS				
Sand Oat	14	*Avena strigosa*	⎰*A. hirtula* ⎱*A. wiestii*	*A. strigosa*
Ethiopian Oat	28	⎰*A. abyssinica* ⎱*A. vaviloviana*	*A. barbata*	*A. barbata*
Cereal Oat	42	*A. sativa* *A. byzantina*	*A. sterilis*	*A. sterilis*
SOUTHERN AND EASTERN ASIAN COMPLEX				
RICE (Asian Rice)	24	*Oryza sativa*	*O. rufipogon*	*O. rufipogon*
JOB'S TEARS	20	*Coix lachryma-jobi*	*C. lachryma-jobi*	*C. lachryma-jobi*
MILLETS				
Japanese Millet	54	*Echinochloa frumentacea*	*E. crus-galli*	*E. crus-galli*
Slender Millet	36	*Panicum miliare*	*P. psilopodium*	*P. miliare*
Kodo Millet	40	*Paspalum scrobiculatum*	*P. scrobiculatum*	*P. scrobiculatum*
EURASIAN MILLETS				
Foxtail Millet	18	*Setaria italica*	*S. viridis*	*S. viridis*
Panic Millet	36	*Panicum miliaceum*	*P. miliaceum*	*P. miliaceum*
AFRICAN COMPLEX				
SORGHUM	20	*Sorghum bicolor*	ssp. *arundinaceum*	*S. drummondi*
RICE (African Rice)	24	*Oryza glaberrima*	*O. barthii*	*O. stapfii*
TEFF	40	*Eragrostis tef*	*E. pilosa*	*E. pilosa*
FONIO				
Common Fonio	54	*Digitaria exilis*	*D. exilis*	*D. exilis*
Black Fonio	(?)	*D. iburua*	*D. iburua*	*D. iburua*
MILLETS				
Pearl Millet	14	*Pennisetum americanum*	*P. violaceum*	*P. americanum*
Finger Millet	36	*Eleusine coracana*	*E. africana*	*E. africana*
Guinea Millet	(?)	*Brachiaria deflexa*	*B. deflexa*	*B. deflexa*

armchair fantasies without adequate field experience. If we have learned anything in the last decade or two, it is that we should be extremely cautious about universal generalizations. A model that has some utility for a particular crop or for a particular case of the emergence of agriculture from a nonagricultural economy can be devised, but models with general or even very wide application are likely to be deceiving.

With this caveat in mind, I shall try to summarize our present understanding of the emergence of cereal agriculture in the Old World. We may begin with the *fait accompli*. Wheat, rice, sorghum, and millets did indeed become the staffs of life for some two billion or more people. The story of how this came about is beginning to unfold. Evidence is slowly coming from painstaking archaeological, genetic, anthropological, and historical research. We have much yet to learn, but our understanding has improved markedly in the last two decades, and greater clarification can be expected in the near future.

THE NEAR EASTERN COMPLEX

The three initial cereal domesticates of the Near East were barley, emmer wheat, and einkorn wheat, essentially in that order of importance. From the beginnings of plant domestication in that region until early historic times, barley was the primary cereal. Einkorn apparently was always a minor crop. Emmer was important in Egypt until Hellenistic times and was a major crop to ancient Romans, but it gave place to the derived hexaploid bread wheats by classic times.

Presumably, domesticated cereals were derived from wild progenitors. In the cases of barley, einkorn, and emmer, the wild races are now fairly well known. Their geographic distributions have been plotted reasonably well and their ecological habitats have been described. Figures 1–3 show the geographic distributions of the wild races of these cereals (after Harlan and Zohary 1966; and Zohary, Harlan, and Vardi 1969). Einkorn is the most tolerant of cold, reaching elevations of 2,000 meters or more and extending into the Balkans. Wild barley is the most tolerant of heat and drought, with races extending into the Negev-Sinai and the hot steppes of southern Afghanistan. Both have weed races that thrive under the disturbance of grazing and cultivation. Emmer, on the other hand, has a rather limited distribution, is not weedy, and is rather exacting in its requirements for growth.

All three cereals show disjunct distributions of their wild races. Presumably, the ranges were continuous in each case at one time. This would require a shift southward from their present distributions. If the wild barley of Cyrenaica were once continuous with that of Sinai, wild barley must have been present in the Nile delta, if not further upstream. Indeed, if the zone of winter rainfall had extended at one time into the Sahara,

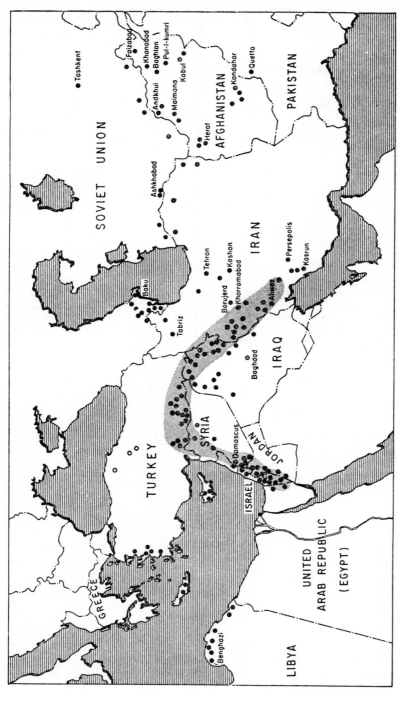

Figure 1.   Distribution of known and reasonably certain sites of wild and weed barley. Massive stands in fairly primary habitats may occur within the shaded area. Elsewhere, spontaneous barley is mostly a weed confined to highly disturbed habitats (from Harlan and Zohary 1966)

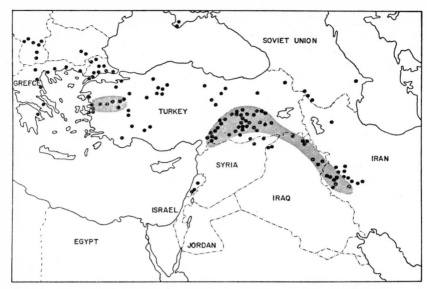

Figure 2.   Distribution of known and reasonably certain sites of wild and weed einkorn. Stands may occur in fairly primary habitats within the shaded areas. Elsewhere, spontaneous einkorn is mostly a weed (from Zohary, Harlan, and Vardi 1969)

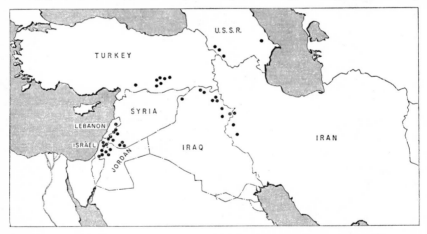

Figure 3.   Distribution of known and reasonably certain sites of wild emmer (from Harlan and Zohary 1966)

the range of wild barley might have been very large. These are conjectures at the present time, but there is tenuous evidence from Africa that these conditions may have prevailed during one or more of the Sahara "pluvials." The point is that present distributions do not necessarily reflect faithfully the distributions at the time of initial domestication.

The time and place of domestication can best be given by direct archaeobotanical evidence, whenever this is available. Evidence for the Near East has been accumulating for some two decades and is now adequate to sketch an outline. Many details remain to be filled in, but the general picture that has emerged appears to be reasonably reliable. Future research probably will not provide many surprises, but a far more precise geography and chronology of plant domestication in the Near East may emerge in the future.

Evidence of the earliest stages of plant manipulation is understandably tenuous. What sort of evidence could be expected? We find grindstones here and there in the Near East and along terraces of the Nile, dating to perhaps the fifteenth millennium B.P. We find sickle blades with a sheen that is thought to be produced in the course of cutting cereal stalks, wild or tame. We find boulder mortars and reasonably nontransportable equipment for reducing (plant?) materials from perhaps the twelfth millennium B.P. onward. Nothing is very conclusive. The plant remains elude us at this time range. Grinding equipment is used in nonagricultural societies today. Mortars and blades are generalized tools and can be used for many purposes.

The first extensive culture with some discernible cohesion that might have seriously harvested wild cereals appears to be the Natufian of Palestine, mostly of the eleventh millennium B.P. Some dozens of sites are now known. The tool kits are reasonably diagnostic and include grinding stones, stone mortars (both movable and those dug into bedrock), and not only sickle blades with sheen, but actual sickles with grooved hafts. Again, the plant remains elude us to date, but the artifacts strongly suggest an economy oriented toward the harvest of wild cereals. The distribution of Natufian sites is within the present range of wild barley, and most sites are within the present range of wild emmer.

The actual remains of wild cereal grains begin to appear in such sites as Mureybit (about 10,000 B.P.), Jericho (the Prepottery Neolithic), and Ali Kosh, perhaps dating to the mid-tenth millennium B.P. At Mureybit we find large quantities of wild einkorn and wild barley (van Zeist 1969). The wild einkorn does not occur in the region today and the nearest stands are some 100 to 150 kilometers to the north. Mureybit is in the present zone of wild barley. Early Ali Kosh provides cultivated emmer, wild and tame einkorn, and wild barley. Prepottery Neolithic Jericho gives us cultivated einkorn, emmer, and barley, as well as peas, lentils, and vetch. Çayönü, founded perhaps a little before 9000 B.P., was an agricultural village from the start. Emmer, einkorn, lentil, pea, vetch, and flax were grown. No barley has been identified, although wild barley grows on the site today.

A sample of early village sites of the Near East is plotted in Figure 4, and the archaeobotanical remains for some of them are shown in Table 2 (Renfrew 1969). The area of concern would appear to be fairly well bracketed by the Near Eastern nuclear arc in which races of barley may occur in reasonably primary habitats (see Figure 1). As far as the evidence now shows, this arc appears to be the arena of domestication of barley, emmer, einkorn, pea, lentil, flax, chick-pea, broad bean, bitter vetch, and other vetches, as well as sheep, goat, and pig. Cattle probably were first domesticated within this arc or close to it.

The time range of these activities is not so easy to assess, because we do not know when the process began. Domesticated races of most, if not all, of these species seem to have appeared by 9000 B.P., and we can presume that domestication took place during the tenth millennium B.P.

By 9000 B.P. the initial job was done, but certain innovations and improvements can be traced. For example, wild barley and the earliest cultivated races have two rows (Figure 5). Three spikelets are produced at each node of the rachis, but only the center one produces a seed. The lateral spikelets may produce pollen or may be entirely sterile, the flower parts being reduced to rudimentary organs. In six-rowed barley, the lateral as well as the central spikelets produce seed (Figure 5). This character is found only in cultivated barley and does not occur in any other species of *Hordeum*. The six-rowed character can be detected in well-preserved archaeological materials and appeared at Ali Kosh before 8000 B.P. A single recessive mutation is sufficient to change a two-rowed barley into a six-rowed one. Another gene frees the grain from the lemma and palea, producing "naked barley." Barleys of this kind have been reported from the early eighth millennium B.P. at Tell-es-Sawwan, Çatal Hüyük, and Hacilar.

The wild and cultivated races of both emmer and einkorn are "glume wheats" in that the seeds are firmly enclosed by the glumes and rather severe processing is required to free them (see Figure 6). The processing can be done in a mortar; this is well documented in Egyptian tomb models and is described by Pliny. In the free-threshing wheats, the glumes are softer and deciduous, so that the seeds fall free upon threshing. These occur at both the tetraploid (2n = 28) and hexaploid (2n = 42) levels. Free-threshing wheats are known from Çatal Hüyük about 7750 B.P. and from Tepe Sabz, Tell-es-Sawwan, and Hacilar by about 7500 B.P. We do not know the ploidy level of these wheats, although they have been reported as "bread wheat" (Helbaek 1966). Club wheat is a hexaploid bread wheat carrying a gene that shortens the internodes, producing very compact heads and plump seeds. Because shapes of seeds can be greatly

Table 2. Finds of domesticated plants and related species from the Near East and Europe before 5000 B.P.

Sites	Dates B.P.	Wild einkorn	Einkorn	Wild emmer	Emmer	Bread wheat	Wild two-rowed barley	Hulled two-rowed barley	Naked two-rowed barley	Hulled six-rowed barley	Naked six-rowed barley	Oat	Millet	Pea	Lentil	Vetch	Flax
Ali Kosh																	
Bus Mordeh phase	9500–8750	×	×	–	×	–	×	–	x?	–	–	–	–	–	–	–	–
Ali Kosh phase	8750–8000	–	–	–	×	–	–	×	–	×	–	Wd	–	–	–	–	–
Mohammad Jaffar phase	8000–7600	–	–	–	×	–	–	×	–	–	–	Wd	–	–	–	×	–
Çayönü	9500–8500	×	×	×	×	–	–	–	–	×	–	–	–	×	×	×	×
Tepe Sabz (Sabz)	7500–7000	–	–	–	–	×	×	×	–	–	–	–	–	–	×	×	×
Tepe Guran	8200–7500	–	–	–	–	–	–	×	–	–	–	–	–	–	–	–	–
Tell-es-Sawwan	7800–7600	–	×	–	×	×	×	×	–	×	×	–	–	×	–	–	×
Tell Mureybit	10,050–9542	×	–	–	–	–	×	–	–	–	–	–	–	–	×	×	×
Jericho, Prepottery Neolithic	circa 9000	–	×	–	×	–	×	–	–	×	–	–	–	×	–	×	–
Beidha, Prepottery Neolithic, B	circa 9000	–	–	–	×	–	×	–	–	–	–	–	–	–	×	×	–
Jarmo	circa 8750	×	×	×	×	–	×	×	–	–	–	Wd	–	×	×	×	–
Tell Ramad	circa 8500	×	×	–	×	C	–	×	–	–	–	–	–	×	×	×	–
Matarrah	circa 7500	–	–	–	×	–	×	B	–	–	–	–	–	×	×	–	–
Amouq A	circa 7750	–	–	–	–	–	–	–	–	–	–	–	–	–	–	–	–
Mersin, Early Neolithic	circa 7750	–	×	×	×	×	×	–	×	×	×	–	–	×	×	×	–
Çatal Hüyük, VI-II	7850–7600	×	–	–	×	–	–	×	–	×	×	Wd	–	×	×	×	–
Aceramic Hacilar	circa 9000	–	×	–	×	×	–	–	–	×	×	–	–	×	×	–	–
Ceramic Hacilar	7800–7000	–	–	–	W	–	–	B	–	×	×	×	–	×	×	×	–
Can Hasan, Late Neolithic	circa 7250	–	–	–	×	×	–	×	×	–	–	–	–	×	–	–	–
Knossos, Stratum X	circa 8100	×	×	–	W	×	–	×	–	–	–	–	–	×	×	×	–
Aceramic Ghediki	circa 8000–7000	–	–	–	×	–	–	B	–	–	–	–	–	–	–	–	–
Aceramic Sesklo	circa 8000–7000	–	×	–	×	–	–	×	×	×	×	–	×	×	×	×	–
Aceramic Argissa	circa 8000–7000	×	–	–	×	–	–	×	–	×	×	–	–	×	×	×	–
Aceramic Achilleion	circa 8000–7000	×	×	–	×	–	–	×	–	×	×	–	–	×	×	×	–
Nea Nikomedeia	circa 8200	–	–	–	W	–	–	B	–	–	–	–	–	–	–	–	–
Karanovo I	circa 7000	×	×	–	×	–	–	–	–	–	–	–	–	–	×	×	–
Azmaska Moghila, Early Neolithic	circa 7000	×	×	–	×	–	–	–	–	–	–	–	–	–	×	–	–

W = Wheat unspecified; B = Barley unspecified; Wd = Wild form; C = Club wheat. After Renfrew (1969) with additions.

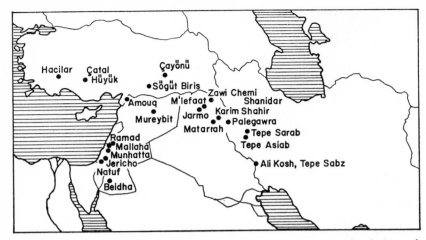

Figure 4.   A sample of archaeological sites bracketing the time range of early domestication of plants and animals in the Near East

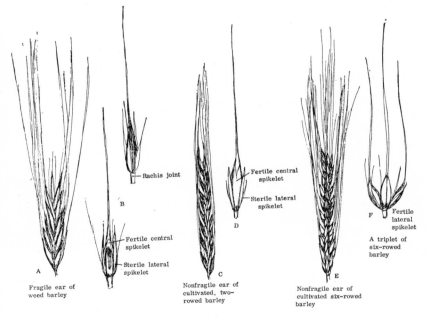

Figure 5.   Sketches of barley ears.   A. Portion of fragile ear of weed barley. B. Two rachis joints with spikelets attached, disarticulated from ear of weed barley. C. Ear of two-rowed cultivated barley. D. A detached triplet from two-rowed cultivated barley showing fertile central spikelet and reduced lateral spikelets. E. Ear of cultivated six-rowed barley. F. A detached triplet from six-rowed cultivated barley showing all three spikelets fertile

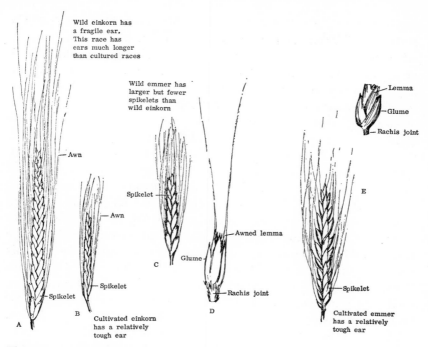

Wild einkorn has
a fragile ear.
This race has
ears much longer
than cultured races

Wild emmer has
larger but fewer
spikelets than
wild einkorn

Lemma

Glume

Rachis joint

Awn

Awn

Spikelet

Spikelet

E

Awned lemma

Glume

C

Spikelet

Spikelet

Spikelet

Rachis joint

B

A

D

Cultivated einkorn
has a relatively
tough ear

Cultivated emmer
has a relatively
tough ear

Figure 6. Primitive glume wheats. A. Ear of wild einkorn of the two-rowed race from southeastern Turkey. B. Ear of cultivated einkorn from Turkish Thrace. (Note that the ear from the wild race is actually larger than the domesticated one.) C. Ear of wild emmer from southeastern Turkey. D. Ear of domesticated emmer from Yugoslavia. E. Spikelet of cultivated emmer from Fayum granary, about 6300 B.P. (The seeds are still enclosed in the glumes and additional processing is required to free them)

altered in the process of carbonization, the identification of club wheats in early contexts should be viewed with caution. We do not yet know when hexaploid wheat was added to the complex. There is some botanical evidence that it originated in the Transcaucasian-Caspian area (Zohary, Harlan, and Vardi 1969).

The system filtered down from the uplands onto the alluvium, where irrigation became necessary for sustained production. Tepe Sabz, founded about 8000 B.P., was a village that practiced irrigation. The mounds became quite large. Pottery became widespread, and the base for Mesopotamian civilizations began to take form.

The agricultural system spread across Anatolia, reaching Greece perhaps a little before 8000 B.P., thence slowly through the Balkans and up the Danube and down the Rhine, reaching the Netherlands about 6000 B.P. (J. G. D. Clark 1965; Tringham 1971). Farmers had reached Spain somewhat before that and they settled in France and much of the rest of Europe during the sixth millennium B.P. (see Murray 1970). The Near Eastern agricultural complex had also spread along the coasts of Africa to Morocco. It is known from the Fayum in Egypt by mid-seventh millennium B.P. but may well have arrived in the delta before that. Farming villages can be traced across Turkmenistan, Iran, and eventually to the Indus valley, where the agricultural complex arrived before the Mohenjo Daro and Harappan cultures developed (Allchin 1969). Wheat and barley were probably grown in Pakistan by 5000 B.P. The complex did not reach China until about 3500 B.P. (Ho 1969). The system also spread southward across Arabia to the Yemen, and, at some as yet unknown time, was introduced to the high plateau of Ethiopia.

Oats and rye were added to the complex as secondary crops. The concept of a secondary crop was devised by N. I. Vavilov and refers to the domestication of weeds that infest fields of earlier or primary crops. Rye is both wild and weedy in Anatolia and Transcaucasia and probably spread northward as a weed of emmer as agriculture was carried into Europe. Where or when it achieved the status of a domesticated plant, we do not know, but ecologically it is one of the hardiest of cereals and became particularly important in northern Europe and the Soviet Union.

The picture of oats is very complex. There are three different levels of ploidy and at least three independent domestications, that is, if Ethiopian oats can be called domesticated (see Table 1). The diploid oats, *Avena strigosa*, were probably domesticated in the Mediterranean region and are now used primarily for fodder. The tetraploid oats, *Avena abyssinica*, are derived from the Mediterranean weed *Avena barbata*, which infested Neolithic fields of emmer and cultivated barley. When the Near Eastern complex reached the plateaus of Ethiopia, the weed oats and several other Mediterranean weeds came along. In Ethiopia the weed oats developed nonshattering races that are harvested along with the emmer and barley. Ethiopians do not grow oats as a crop but accept the oat contamination of the primary crops and do not try to get rid of the oats.

The hexaploid oats, *Avena sativa*, were probably derived from weed races of *Avena sterilis*, common and widespread in the Mediterranean Basin and the Near East. The weed oats have been found by archaeologists at Ali Kosh, Beidha, and Amouq, and cultivated sorts are reported from Greece by the late eighth millennium B.P. They do not appear to be important as a crop, however, until much later, and then in northern Europe. Presumably, the history was much the same as for rye, with the weed races moving northward with agriculture and becoming domesticated well beyond the range of the original wild races.

Written history is much too late to help us with respect to the origins of the Near Eastern agricultural complex, but it does reveal which cereals were most important and the significance attached to them by ancient people. At the dawn of written history, in Sumer, barley was the most important cereal. It was the most abundant, the most productive, the food of the masses, the ration of the slaves and serfs. After 2500 B.C. it became even more important as wheat almost disappeared from southern Mesopotamia. This disappearance is attributed to salting up of the irrigated lands (Jacobsen and Adams 1958). Barley is much more salt tolerant than wheat, and a near monoculture of barley developed in the south.

An ancient word for a bearded grain, still used in Hebrew, was *bar*. In northern Europe, the word was used as an adjective (e.g. barlic corn, which became barlie corn, and finally barley) and also as a noun (barb, beard, barber, beer, brew, brewing,brewery, and similar derivatives). South of the Alps the people spoke more softly and the word was *far*, Latin for emmer. Emmer was the holy cereal of the Romans, called *far adoreum*, and eventually simply *adoreum*. The root *far* was used in the word *farnacalia*, the harvest ceremonies of ancient Rome; the Roman marriage vows were *confarati*, derived from the same word; and the term lingers on in farina and farinaceous (starchy). The word for bread, *panis*, survives in modern English, e.g. company (those who eat bread together) and companion (with whom one breaks bread). Wheat has been woven into the spiritual and religious life of the cultures based on the Near East. The cereal is, for example, featured in the Passover rituals and Holy Communion.

ASIAN RICE AGRICULTURE

Our information on the origin of rice agriculture in Asia is tenuous and unsatisfactory. The distribution of the wild races is not as well known as those of the wheats and barley, nor even the African cereals. The archaeological picture is scanty, to say the least, and the time range is extremely tenuous. Until the Orient is studied far more intensively than it has been to date, we cannot expect to have more than a sketchy history of the rise of rice-based agriculture.

Wild races of *Oryza sativa (Oryza rufipogon)* are found south of the line shown in Figure 7. Details are very spotty. We have excellent information for the distribution of wild rice in Thailand and in parts of India, but much of the rest of southeastern Asia and China is little known in this respect. *Oryza rufipogon*, in Asia, has both annual and perennial

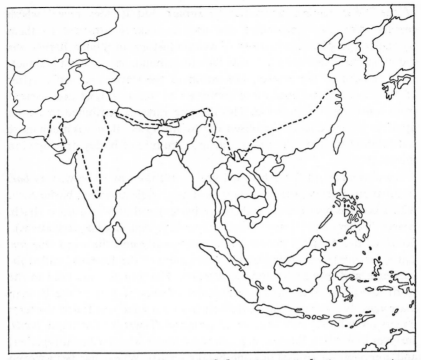

Figure 7.   Distribution of wild races of rice in Asia. Dotted line indicates approximate northern limits

races, which intercross rather freely with one another and with cultivated races as well. Collections of wild or spontaneous annuals often segregate for cultivated characters. Cultivated characteristics are often transferred to spontaneous races by natural means. The situation is genetically messy and the interactions are so extensive that the nature of the original wild race is difficult to untangle.

In preagricultural times, the deltas of the great rivers of southeastern Asia were probably vast seas of wild rice. The mouths of the Ganges in Bangladesh, the delta of the Irrawady in Burma, the Chao Phraya in Thailand, the Mekong in Vietnam, and other lesser deltas were probably once covered with rice of a floating type adapted to deep water and the rapid rise and fall of the rivers during the monsoon season. During high water, seed heads probably covered huge areas, sticking up above the water. When the water receded, tangled masses of stems must have covered the ground. These floating rices were mostly perennial but were not as strongly rhizomatous as the related African perennial rice. The stems elongate very rapidly as water rises, and when the water recedes, the tangled mass tends to root at the nodes.

While this kind of rice was probably abundant and undoubtedly harvested to some extent from canoes or rafts by hunting-gathering people, the floating rices are generally poor seeders and the environment almost impossible for the initiation of agriculture. Without control of water, no planting or selection is really possible. These areas eventually became the rice bowls of Asia, but not until dikes and canals could be built. The environment of the delta is not the place to begin domestication of rice.

Far more likely are shallow depressions and water holes in the savanna zones that fill with water during the rains and dry out during the dry season. Such habitats are suited for annual races. At least, that is exactly the situation in Africa, and it seems most likely that something analogous occurred in monsoon or even warm temperate Asia.

The annuals are better seeders than the perennials, and the habitat could be exploited with a minimum of equipment and investment of labor. Where and when and by whom rice was domesticated, in this vast area from India to China, remains to be determined.

We are not without archaeobotanical remains of rice. This cereal has been reported from very early Lungshanoid sites and is characteristic of most Lung-shan sites. Ho (1969) has assembled evidence indicating that wild rice was used as food for the poor in historical times and perhaps had a wider distribution formerly than it does at present.

Carbon-14 dates have recently become available for three Chinese sites in which rice has been found (Anonymous 1972a, 1972b). At the site of Ch'ien-shan-yang in Wu-hsing District, Chekiang Province, carbonized rice was so abundant that it was used for the carbon-14 determination, which gave a date of about 4700 B.P. Other sites are Sung-tse (about 5400 B.P.), near Shanghai and Huang-lien-shu (about 4200 B.P.) in Hsi-ch'uan, Honan Province. Probably several more dates will soon be available for China.

Rice turns up in late Harappan sites in western India dated to approximately 4000 B.P. (Allchin 1969), but the Harappans basically were growers of wheat and barley, and in northwestern India rice may have moved slowly in competition with the Near Eastern complex. One indication of this is the lack of reference to rice in the earliest Vedas. We have no excavated sites with remains of rice from eastern India, Assam, or Burma. Solheim (1971) has reported rice at Non Nok Tha in Thailand from about 5000 B.P. or earlier, but it is not known whether this rice was wild or tame. Wild rice is abundant throughout Thailand today.

So far we have no evidence for extreme antiquity of rice. We do have ample historical evidence that wet rice as the staple of hundreds of millions is a rather late development. In Yang-shao China it was certainly later than foxtail millet and probably later than panic millet. In Harappan India, it was later than wheat and barley. In the wet tropics of southeastern Asia, it was later than the original agricultural system, founded on taro, yams, banana, coix, and other crops. Both upland and swamp rice invaded the southeastern monsoon belt and to a large extent replaced the agriculture based on roots and trees.

Taro was apparently a wet-field crop long before rice appeared in the area. Small but well-constructed terraces were built and flooded by water led to them by canals. Such systems occur today in New Guinea, for example, in regions where rice has not yet penetrated. It has been suggested that rice was domesticated from a weedy race infesting wet-field taro plantations. We have no evidence for or against this theory at the present time, but if this process took place, it was probably in addition to the domestication of rice in the savanna zones.

Rice became woven into the religious ceremonies, rites, and worship practices of rice-eating people. Many Hindus consider wild rice a more appropriate cereal offering at the temple than cultivated rice. Rice cakes, rice balls, rice wine, rice flour, and whole-grain rice are all used as thanks offerings.

THE AFRICAN SAVANNA COMPLEX

Direct archaeobotanical evidence for domestication of sorghum and pearl millet is essentially lacking. Munson (1968, 1976) has evidence for the culture of pearl millet in Mauritania at about 1100 B.C., but the crop had arrived in India by that time. The sequence elaborated in Mauritania implies a switch from harvesting wild seeds of a sandbur, *Cenchrus biflorus*, to the cultivation of pearl millet, rather than the domestication of the crop. The conversion took place in the space of about two centuries and suggests that the people were taking up a new practice.

Many remains of sorghum are reported from eastern and southern Africa, and a great amount has been found at Daima in Nigeria, but all of these are from A.D. 500 or later and tell us little about the initial domestication of the crop.

Evidence from the wild races is subject to correction because of changes in climate in the last few millennia B.C. Evidence for changes in the Near East is somewhat subtle, but this is certainly not the case in Africa. Both more arid and more humid conditions existed in the past. Stabilized dunes are recognizable well within the broad-leafed savanna on both sides of the equatorial forest. On the other hand, Lake Chad was once ten times its present size and Lake Rudolph overflowed into the Nile watershed. The Nile itself was at times a much larger river than at present.

The patterns of change are very complex and cannot be dealt with here in any detail. The earliest period that might be significant appears to be the Sahaba aggradation of the Nile ranging from approximately 14,500 to 10,500 B.P. The Nile was relatively high at that time and during the flood filled hollows and depressions of the flood plain with ephemeral lakes that dried up before the next flood. A number of village or semipermanent camp sites have been found in association with these temporary lakes. Included in the standard Upper Paleolithic tool kit are numerous grinding stones and flint blades with sickle sheen. No remains of plants have yet been found, but there is a suggestion that the people were harvesting wild grass seeds as a part of their diet (Wendorf and Schild 1976).

After this phase, the evidence becomes very sketchy for some millennia, but by 8000 B.P. or so rather similar sites and artifacts are found again, not only along the Nile, but also scattered widely across the Sahara. The earlier Sahara "Neolithic" sites suggest that people camped near shallow lakes (which were rather abundant and widely distributed at that time), fished, and hunted hippopotamuses and other types of a rather typical African fauna. If we can so interpret the grindstones and sickle(?) blades, they also ate ground grain of some sort (J. D. Clark 1970, 1971).

By about 7000 B.P. the "Neolithic" sites show signs of the herding of cattle, sheep, and goats. The people continued to camp by shallow lakes, to fish, and to hunt, and had grinding equipment and blades with sheen. Domestic animals are evidenced not only by their bones, but also by their frequent appearance in rock art scattered widely over what is now desert. There is no evidence that plants were actually domesticated, but wild grass seeds are still important to many Africans, especially those who live in the desert or desert margins. Jardin (1967) lists more than sixty species of grass harvested in recent years in Africa.

About 2500 B.C. a progressive desiccation had reached the point where populations began to decline and people started to move out. The trend accelerated sharply about 2000 B.C. and desert conditions began to descend across northern Africa. The sequence studied by Munson in southeastern Mauritania indicated a considerable population density until well into the third millennium B.P. The people there herded cattle, sheep, and goats; hunted and fished from lakes now dried up; and toward the close of the fourth millennium B.P., took up the growing of pearl millet. Archaeology does not tell us much more than this at present.

Some information can be extracted from the plants. Wild sorghum is widespread in Africa (Figure 8). However, the wild race of western Africa is adapted to the forest and not to the savanna. Cultivated sorghum is decidedly a plant of the savanna and does very poorly in the forest. For this reason, sorghum was unlikely to have been domesticated in western Africa. Archaeological chronology would suggest equally strongly that the crop was domesticated north of the equator. In their argument for the origin of sorghum, Harlan and Stemler (1976) outlined the area containing the most massive stands of wild sorghum adapted to the savanna zones of eastern Africa north of the equator, and they suggested that this was the nuclear area of sorghum domestication. If the climate had been different at the time of the initial domestication of sorghum the area may have been somewhat north or south of the region indicated, but it probably was not in western Africa (see Figure 9).

Figure 8.   Distribution of wild races of sorghum in Africa. Dotted line indicates approximate limit of the tropical forest

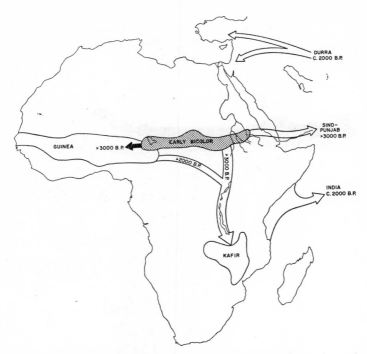

Figure 9. An attempt at reconstructing the early evolutionary history of sorghum. The earliest race to be domesticated is thought to be "early bicolor," which later gave rise to the guinea race in western Africa, the kafir race in southern Africa, and the durra race, perhaps in India (after Harlan and Stemler 1976)

Pearl millet is much more drought resistant than sorghum and is adapted to the desert margins. The presumed progenitor is *Pennisetum violaceum,* and the present known distribution of this species is shown in Figure 10. The picture is spotty in detail, but the distribution and use of the crop suggest domestication in a zone from Darfur in Sudan to Mauritania-Senegal in the dry savanna. This zone may well have shifted to the south during the desiccation of the second and first millennia B.C. and may well have had a wide range across the Sahara when the region was populated by "Neolithic" cultures. Munson suggests that pearl millet was domesticated in the Sahara at that time.

Before this theory can be supported, the distribution of the winter rainfall belt and tropical monsoon climates needs to be worked out for the fifth and sixth millennia B.P. Our present ignorance is such that we cannot state where or when the indigenous African crops were domesticated. We can only suggest (Figures 8–12) the most likely regions based on the current evidence of the cultivated, wild, and weedy races.

Figure 10.   Distribution of known sites of wild pearl millet. Dark shading indicates
the northern pearl millet belt; light shading indicates the zone in which pearl millet is
grown but sorghum is the dominant crop. Areas of culture in eastern and southern
Africa are more diffuse and are not shown

In Arabic *'aish* means life. In the pearl millet belt of Sudan, that
cereal is called *'aish*, a source of nourishment, the staff of life. To the
south, in the sorghum belt of Sudan, sorghum is called *'aish*. The two
cereals are complementary and should be considered together. Pearl
millet is much more drought resistant than sorghum and can be grown
at the extreme limits of agriculture, around the fringes of the Sahara,
Indian, and Kalahari deserts. Sorghum requires more rainfall and is
adapted primarily to savanna zones with an ample rainy season and a
pronounced dry season. These cereals, too, have entered into the religious
life of those who depend on them for nurture. Both are a part of ceremonies, sacrifice, and ritual in many cultures of Africa.

MINOR CEREAL AGRICULTURES OF AFRICA

In general these cultures are considered minor only because they did not

Figure 11.   Known sites of wild African rice, *Oryza barthii*. The wild progenitor of the cultivated *glaberrima* rice is an annual with a short ligule adapted to the savanna zones

spread extensively. To the people who depend on them, they are major. Rice is just as important to the rice-eating tribes of western Africa as it is to any tribe or culture in Asia. To be sure, most of the rice grown in western Africa today is Asian rice, which has largely replaced the ancient traditional African rice. The progenitor of African rice is *Oryza barthii*, a savanna plant (Figure 11). It is an annual, an excellent seeder, and is adapted to ephemeral water holes that dry up in the dry season. Not uncommonly it is found in association with its perennial relative *Oryza longistaminata*, but the latter requires a more secure water supply. Both are harvested in the wild today, although *Oryza longistaminata* is a poor seeder and does not contribute very much.

African rice, probably first domesticated in or about the central delta of the Niger, spread along the Senegal River and southward to Casamance and Guinea. Upland types were developed and rice became the staple for the tribes from the Bandama River in the central Ivory Coast westward through Liberia, Sierra Leone, Guinea, and Senegal.

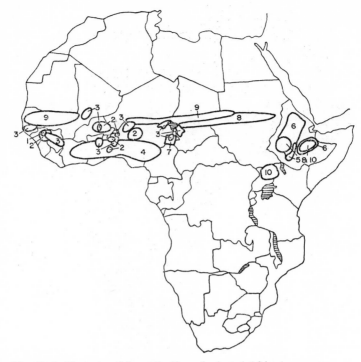

Figure 12. Probable areas of domestication of selected African crops

1. *Brachiaria deflexa*
2. *Digitaria exilis* and *D. iburua*
3. *Oryza glaberrima*
4. *Dioscorea rotundata*
5. *Ensete ventricosum* and *Guizotia abyssinica*

6. *Eragrostis tef*
7. *Voandzeia* and *Kerstingiella*
8. *Sorghum bicolor*
9. *Pennisetum americanum*
10. *Eleusine coracana*

The culture of African rice also spread eastward across the savanna of Ghana, Togo, Dahomey, and Nigeria to the Lagone region of Chad. African rice was not a major crop in the wet forests east of the Bandama River of the Ivory Coast because the staff of life there was indigenous African yams, and rice was never especially important to the yam-eating tribes.

Teff is the staff of life for some millions of Ethiopians. It is a royal, if not actually sacred, grain and is planted on more acreage than any other crop in Ethiopia. As a lovegrass *(Eragrostis)*, the seeds are very small and special techniques are required to establish stands. The seedbed must be very fine and the last operation in preparing the soil may be stamping with the human foot. Weeds are meticulously removed; other crops may be permitted to become weedy, but teff may not.

The grain is ground whole; the flour is fermented and the dough baked into a remarkably palatable and nutritious flat bread called *ingera*. To Ethiopians this is basic to life; it is not used elsewhere to any appreciable extent. The progenitor of the cereal is thought to be *Eragrostis pilosa*, but the crop has been little studied, and we have no evidence concerning the time of domestication.

Another important cereal of eastern Africa is finger millet, *Eleusine coracana*. We do not know where it was domesticated, but the area was most likely to have been in Ethiopia or Uganda. Today the cereal is used primarily for the production of beer, but it was at one time much more important for bread, gruel, and other human foods. The crop has spread to western Africa as a minor cereal and was taken to India by about 3000 B.P. It is fairly important in the foothills of the Himalayas and the Nilgiris of southern India. It is a tetraploid and is derived from the wild-weedy *E. africana* (also a tetraploid), with which it crosses readily and spontaneously.

Fonio, *Digitaria exilis*, is an important crop to only a few people of western Africa but a prestige crop to many more. The crop has been called hungry rice, but this is a serious misnomer. Frequently it is grown, not because it will alleviate hunger, but because it will produce the best couscous or the finest breads and dumplings. In many tribes this is a luxury item or a chief's food. The origin of the crop is treated in some detail by Portères (1955). As with other endemic cereals, we know more or less where it was domesticated but have no direct information about when the process began or ended (Figure 12).

Black fonio, *Digitaria iburua*, and Guinea millet, *Brachiaria deflexa*, are two very minor cereals of western Africa. They may have been more important at one time but do not qualify now as basic cereal agricultures.

WARM-SEASON EURASIAN MILLETS

Foxtail millet, *Setaria italica*, and panic millet, *Panicum miliaceum*, are thought to have been the staff of life for the Yang-shao people of China. Remains of the foxtail millet, at least, were found in enormous quantities in some Yang-shao sites, and the panic millet became basic to the agriculture of northern China a little later. The classic Yang-shao site of Pan-p'o now has four carbon 14 dates indicating that the village was established about 6,000 years ago (Anonymous 1972b). Both cereals are thought by some to have been domesticated in the Chinese center, yet both are found in a sprinkling of Neolithic village sites over Europe through the sixth millennium B.P. They were seldom important components of the plant's remains. They were reported only from Niederwil among the Swiss lake dwellers, for example, but they occurred in enough sites that there can be little doubt of the presence of both millets in Europe of the sixth millennium B.P. (Murray 1970). *Panicum* has also been reported from Jemdet Nasr, Mesopotamia, at 5000 B.P. and possibly Argissa, Greece, about 7500 B.P. (Table 2). The only European culture that grew *Panicum miliaceum* really extensively was the Tripolye of the Ukraine. The culture flourished from 5800 to 3900 B.P., and panic millet was one of the major crops.

Neither foxtail nor panic millet has been studied intensively, and the archaeology of the vast Eurasian steppe between China and the Ukraine is not yet sufficiently advanced for us to choose among possible alternatives. The possibilities are: (1) the millets were domesticated in China and were dispersed to Europe before 6000 B.P.; (2) they were domesticated in the West and were dispersed to China before Yang-shao times; or (3) they were domesticated more than once. The presumed progenitor of *Setaria italica* is *S. viridis*, a weed ubiquitous from Japan to England and now widespread in North America and elsewhere. The frequent statement that the progenitor of *Panicum miliaceum* is not known is probably erroneous, for the *Flora of the USSR* reports it as weedy, naturalized or escaped, and common from European Russia to eastern Siberia. Without very careful analysis, the separation of wild from weedy races is often difficult.

At any rate, both millets are adapted to the belt of summer rainfall of temperate Eurasia. They were well known to the Greeks and Romans and to the Indians of ancient times. It may be important, however, that a number of Indian names for panic (e.g. Sanskrit: *cinaka* [Chinese]; Hindi: *chena, cheen*; Bengali: *cheena*; Gujarati: *chino*) suggest that it came to India from China. The Persian word is essentially the same as the Chinese, *shu-shu*.

There are no other known crops with such a distribution in that time range. Wide dispersals in the seventh millennium B.P. are certainly possible, but if this were in fact the explanation, more than two millets might be expected. The rather slow spread of agriculture across Europe at that time suggests that early farmers were having enough trouble just crossing Europe without attempting a trip to China. In our present state of ignorance, independent domestications appear to be the most likely answer, but new information could easily lead to other conclusions.

THE MINOR CEREALS OF ASIA

Slender millet, *Panicum miliare*, and kodo millet, *Paspalum scrobiculatum*, are grown on a minor scale in the wetter parts of India. They are not important enough to be considered as components of cereal agriculture, but *Paspalum scrobiculatum* is interesting in illustrating the process of domestication of a secondary crop. The species is very widespread and abundant in the wetter and warmer parts of the Old World. It is found from Japan to Indonesia and across the wet tropics to the Congo Basin and West Africa. It is a weed along paths and ditches, is found in low, wet spots, and frequently invades rice fields. It is actually cultivated as a cereal in southern India but is harvested for food over a much wider area. It infests some African rice fields so abundantly that an appreciable amount is harvested along with the rice crop, processed, and eaten. The species illustrates how easy multiple domestications would be for such a widespread, weedy grass with relatively large seeds.

Coix (Job's tears) was at one time a fairly important cereal of the wet tropics of southeastern Asia and the islands of the South Pacific. It is still cultivated as a cereal in the Philippines and New Guinea and by the hill tribes of Vietnam, Cambodia, and Laos. Because it has spread to areas where rice culture has not yet penetrated, it is thought to be an older domesticate than rice. At present it is a rather minor cereal, having been replaced to a large extent by rice.

Japanese millet is a domesticated form of a common weedy grass often called "barnyard grass." The weed is common and widespread in Eurasia and now in North America and other temperate regions with summer rainfall. The cultivated forms are raised on a considerable scale in China, Japan, and Korea but are minor crops elsewhere. We know little about the time of domestication, but most likely this is a secondary crop, being derived from weed races that began to thrive after agriculture was established. Despite its common name, it is probably Chinese in origin.

SUMMARY AND CONCLUSIONS

Seeds of grasses evidently were an important source of food for pre-agricultural societies. Of the sixty or more species known to have been harvested in Africa, eight were developed into domesticated cereals. We have less information on the harvesting of wild grass seed in Eurasia, but certainly more species were harvested than were domesticated, and the Eurasian domesticates number about fifteen. (The exact number depends on definitions.) Thus, at least twenty-three members of the grass family were taken into the domestic fold in the Old World because their seeds were important in the human diet.

There were probably other domesticated cereals that were once grown and later abandoned. A number of those mentioned here once were much more important to human nutrition and were more widely grown than they are now. The less efficient cereals have been largely replaced by those that yield more for a given investment in labor and capital. The efficient cereals are competitive with other food crops and tend to expand geographically and in economic and nutritional importance. The dominant Old World cereals are wheat, rice, and sorghum. Together they provide far more than half of the food that presently sustains the human race.

Archaeological evidence suggests that wheat was domesticated in the Near East before 9000 B.P., and rice was grown in China more than 7,000 years ago. We do not yet know the antiquity of sorghum, but it is an African domesticate.

REFERENCES

ALLCHIN, F. R.
  1969   "Early cultivated plants in India and Pakistan," in *The domestication and exploitation of plants and animals*. Edited by P. J. Ucko and G. W. Dimbleby, 323–329. Chicago: Aldine.
ANONYMOUS
  1972a Report on radiocarbon-determined dates I. *K'ao-ku* [Archaeology] (1):52–56.
  1972b Report on radiocarbon-determined dates II. *K'ao-ku* [Archaeology] (5):56–58.
CHANG KWANG-CHIH
  1970   The beginnings of agriculture in the Far East. *Antiquity* 44:175–185.
CLARK, J. D.
  1970   *The prehistory of Africa*. Southampton: Thames and Hudson.
  1971   A re-examination of the evidence for agricultural origins in the Nile Valley. *Proceedings of the Prehistoric Society* 37:34–79.
CLARK, J. G. D.
  1965   Radiocarbon dating and the spread of farming economy. *Antiquity* 39:45–48.
HARLAN, J. R.
  1971   Agricultural origins: centers and noncenters. *Science* 174:468–474.
HARLAN, J. R., ANN STEMLER
  1976   "The races of sorghum in Africa," in *Origins of African plant domestication*. Edited by Jack R. Harlan, Jan M. J. de Wet, and Ann B. L. Stemler, 465–478. World Anthropology. The Hague: Mouton.
HARLAN, J. R., D. ZOHARY
  1966   Distribution of wild wheats and barley. *Science* 153:1074–1080.

HELBAEK, H.
1966 Commentary on the phylogenesis of *Triticum* and *Hordeum*. *Economic Botany* 20:350–360.

HO, PING-TI
1969 The loess and the origin of Chinese agriculture. *American Historical Review* 75:1–36.

JACOBSEN, T., R. MC C. ADAMS
1958 Salt and silt in ancient Mesopotamian agriculture. *Science* 128:1251–1258.

JARDIN, C.
1967 *List of foods used in Africa*. Rome: United Nations Food and Agriculture Organization.

MUNSON, P. J.
1968 Recent archaeological research in the Dhar Tichitt region of south central Mauritania. *West African Newsletter* 10:6–13.
1976 "Archaeological data on the origins of cultivation in the southwestern Sahara and their implications for West Africa", in *Origins of African plant domestication*. Edited by Jack R. Harlan, Jan M. J. de Wet, and Ann B. L. Stemler, 187–209. World Anthropology. The Hague: Mouton.

MURRAY, JAQUELINE
1970 *The first European agriculture*. Edinburgh: Edinburgh University Press.

PORTÈRES, R.
1955 Les céréales mineures du genre *Digitaria* en Afrique et en Europe. *Journal d'Agriculture Tropicale et de Botanique Appliquée* 2:349–675.

RENFREW, J. M.
1969 "The archaeological evidence for the domestication of plants: methods and problems," in *The domestication and exploitation of plants and animals*. Edited by P. J. Ucko and G. W. Dimbleby, 149–172. Chicago: Aldine.

SOLHEIM, W. G., II
1971 New light on a forgotten past. *National Geographic Magazine* 139:330–339.

TRINGHAM, RUTH
1971 *Hunters, fishers, and farmers of Eastern Europe 6000–3000 B.C.* London: Hutchinson University Library.

VAN ZEIST, W.
1969 "Reflections on prehistoric environments in the Near East," in *The domestication and exploitation of plants and animals*. Edited by P. J. Ucko and G. W. Dimbleby, 35–46. Chicago: Aldine.

WENDORF, F., R. SCHILD
1976 "The use of ground grain during the late Paleolithic of the lower Nile Valley, Egypt," in *Origins of African plant domestication*. Edited by Jack R. Harlan, Jan M. J. de Wet, and Ann B. L. Stemler, 269–288. World Anthropology. The Hague: Mouton.

ZOHARY, D., J. R. HARLAN, A. VARDI
1969 The wild diploid progenitors of wheat and their breeding value. *Euphytica* 18:58–65.

Economic Change
in Prehistoric Thailand

CHARLES F. W. HIGHAM

The traditional interpretation of later Thai prehistory is that a scattered, Hoabinhian population of hunter-gatherers was succeeded by intrusive rice farmers emanating ultimately from China and arriving in Thailand by about 3800 B.P. (Clark 1969; Sørensen 1967). Bronze technology was introduced at about 2700 B.P., again from an eastern source, and use of iron, together with new religious concepts, resulted from Indian influence commencing about two thousand years ago, from which grew the Khmer and Dvāravatī states. Excavations undertaken during the past decade, however, have provided data for a different synthesis (Solheim 1969; Bayard 1971; Gorman 1971; Higham 1972).

Viewed within the context of the major environmental zones of Thailand (Figure 1), it is apparent that the limestone uplands were indeed occupied by Hoabinhian groups from at least 14,000 B.P. until the mid-sixth millennium B.C. The Hoabinhian technocomplex, which was initially recognized half a century ago in Vietnam, has recently been

I acknowledge with gratitude the financial support of the Wenner-Gren Foundation, National Science Foundation Grant NSF-GS-29133, and the New Zealand University Grants Committee.

Professor W. G. Solheim II, through his vision and encouragement, first made possible my participation in southeastern Asian prehistory. I am indebted to Dr. C. F. Gorman for inviting me to collaborate with him in his fieldwork in Thailand, and to Dr. D. T. Bayard for asking me to study the faunal remains from Non Nok Tha. Mr. B. F. Leach masterminded the statistical studies involved, and Mr. Mark Jurisich assisted in bone sorting and analysis. I am grateful for the interest and assistance given me during the period of my research at the British Museum by all the staff of the Sub-department of Osteology.

My thanks are no recompense for all the willing assistance and advice I have received.

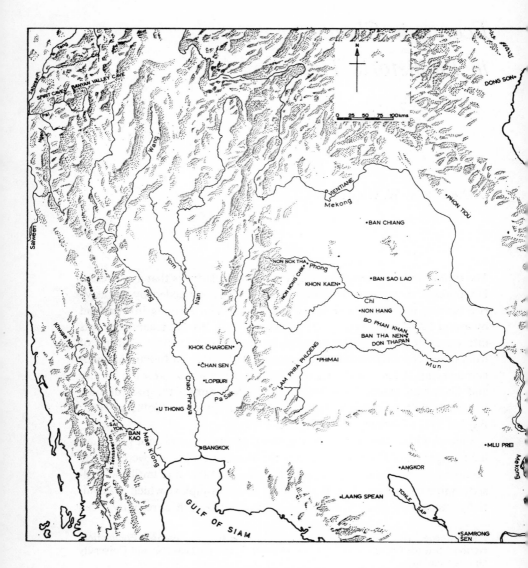

Figure 1.   Map showing the major environmental areas and relevant prehistoric sites in Thailand, Cambodia, and Vietnam

described by Gorman (1971) as a broad-spectrum hunting-and-gathering society with a lithic technology characterized by unifacially worked discoid implements. Upper layers in the excavated caves indicate continuation of this Hoabinhian lithic technology, in association with pottery, polished quadrangular adzes, and bifacial slate knives. This new assemblage appeared by around 8000 B.P. at Spirit Cave. No Hoabinhian sites have been found on the flat lowlands of the Khorat Plateau or the Central (Chao Phraya) Valley, although many will almost certainly have been destroyed with the drowning of the Sunda shelf.

Most of our knowledge of the nature of prehistoric occupation in the piedmont ecotone between the uplands and the Khorat Plateau, is based on Bayard's excavations at Non Nok Tha (Bayard 1971). Apart from one gap in the occupation between A.D. 200 and A.D. 1000, the seventeen cultural layers at this village and its associated cemetery cover the period, according to the excavator, from at least 5,500 B.P. to the nineteenth century A.D. The period of abandonment at Non Nok Tha between A.D. 200 and 1000 is represented at the nearby sites of Don Sawan and Non Nong Chik (Higham and Parker 1970). Recent thermoluminescence dates suggest that the heavy soils of the Central Plain were settled by the end of the second millennium B.C. at Chansen (Bronson and Dales 1973), while the poor, sandy soils of the Khorat Plateau did not attract settlement until around 2500 B.P. (Higham and Parker 1970). The control of water would have been a prerequisite of rice agriculture in both areas, and iron was in use from the earliest occupation of the sites in question.

Major trade contacts with India from about A.D. 0 led to pervasive cultural changes in parts of southeastern Asia. The religious and artistic manifestations of this influence are clearly apparent in the remains of the Khmer and Dvāravatī (Central Thai) civilizations.

The present paper accepts that the chronological framework for Thai prehistory set out in Figure 2 is an acceptable hypothesis and will examine the available evidence for changes in the utilization of faunal resources during the 11,000 year period in question. Such changes will be considered in the light of shifts in settlement and other associated economic developments.

There are seven Thai sites and one Cambodian site with reasonably sized faunal samples. Of these, Spirit and Banyan Valley caves are situated in a high range of limestone hills on the Thai-Burmese border. Both have yielded cultural layers with Hoabinhian occupation material. The fauna from Sai Yok (Kanchanaburi Province) has been published by Hooijer (1967). Some preliminary remarks on the Cambodian cave of Laang Spean have been made by Mourer and Mourer (1970).

The period between about 5500 B.P. and the initial settlement of the Khorat Plateau is represented only by Non Nok Tha, although other

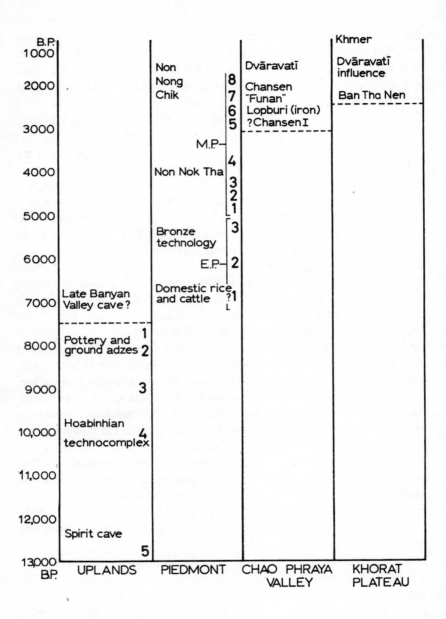

Figure 2.   Tentative scheme of cultural developments in four different areas of Thailand

sites, such as Ban Chiang, have faunal remains from insecure stratigraphic contexts. Chansen in the Central Valley (Weatherill 1973) and
Ban Tha Nen on the Khorat Plateau have provided some faunal remains
but, in general, remains of animals from these two areas are disappoint-
ingly rare.

THE HOABINHIAN

The occupation of Spirit Cave covered the period from at least 12,000 to
7500 B.P. Five general layers have been identified. The lowest (5) consists
of limestone detritus but the upper four include faunal remains. Layers 4,
3, and 2 may be conveniently grouped as Hoabinhian. Gorman (1971)
has recognized an important technological discontinuity within the
Hoabinhian context between layers 2 and 1, with the advent of ground
quadrangular adzes, pottery, and slate knives. He has argued that these
implements might well indicate contact with people already conversant
with agriculture. During the course of his excavations at Spirit Cave,
Gorman recovered remains of species of plants from early levels similar
to those used in northern Thailand for consumption and for stimulants.
Although Yen's proposition (1969) that some of these plants may have
been tended requires further study, the possibility is posed that during
the occupation of Spirit Cave, Hoabinhian hunter-gatherers became
acquainted with either horticulture or agriculture or perhaps both. This
makes a study of the associated faunal remains more than usually interesting.

During May and December 1972, Gorman excavated a Hoabinhian
occupation site in the Banyan Valley, only fifteen miles from Spirit Cave.
At the time of writing, it is known that carbonized rice grains were
recovered, but the type of rice and the site's chronology are still under
investigation. The pottery from the Banyan Valley Cave is, if anything,
typologically later than that at Spirit Cave, which would indicate occupation after 7500 B.P.

The identification of the Hoabinhian faunal remains was undertaken
with reference to collections in the British Museum (Natural History).
In the case of the murids, bats, and squirrels, specific identification
was ruled out because of the fragmentary nature of the prehistoric
specimens, the absence of diagnostic crania, the considerable range of
indigenous species and in certain cases, the lack of available comparative
material. Thus, of the twenty-one species of the genus *Rhinolophus*, eleven
occur or may have occurred within the study area during the prehistoric

period. All the eight species of *Callosciurus* are indigenous to Thailand. There are at least a dozen indigenous species of Thai rat. The incisor and metapodials ascribed to *Bibos* are not sufficiently diagnostic to permit the distinction between gaur, banteng and kouprey. The identification of fragmentary ribs and vertebrae was not attempted because so many of the comparative specimens available retain these bones in articulation.

As may be seen in Table 2, the faunal spectra of the two sites are com-

Table 1.   Species present at only one of the caves

Absent from Spirit Cave	Absent from Banyan Valley Cave
Bibos	*Nycticebus coucang*
Muntiacus muntjak	*Hemigalus derbyanus*
Tragulus napu	*Felis viverrina*
Nemorhaedus/Capricornis	*Felis bengalensis*
Rhinoceros sondaicus	*Martes flavigula*
Didermocerus sumatrensis	*Cannomys badius*
Selenarctos thibetanus	(very little) fish

Table 2.   Species found at the caves

Species		Spirit Cave				Banyan Valley Cave
		1	2	3	4	1ᵃ
Artiodactyla						
1 *Sus scrofa jubatus*	Pig	*	*	*	−	*
2 *Bibos gaurus*	Gaur	−	−	−	−	*
3 *Bibos javanicus*	Banteng					
4 *Muntiacus muntjak*	Muntjac	−	−	−	−	*
5 *Axis porcinus*	Pig deer	−	−	*	*	*
6 *Tragulus napu*	Mouse deer	−	−	−	−	*
7 *Capricornis sumatrensis* or	Serow ⎫	−	−	−	−	*
8 *Nemorhaedus goral*	Goral ⎭					
9 *Cervus unicolor*	Sambar deer	*	*	*	*	*
Perissodactyla						
10 *Didermocerus sumatrensis*	Rhinoceros	−	−	−	−	*
11 *Rhinoceros sondaicus*	Rhinoceros	−	−	−	−	*
Primate						
12 *Homo sapiens*	Man	−	−	−	−	*
13 *Presbytis* sp.	Langur	*	*	*	*	*
14 *Macaca* sp.	Macaque	*	*	*	*	*
15 *Macaca assamensis*	Assam macaque	−	−	*	−	*
16 *Presbytis obscura*	Dusky langur	*	*	−	−	−
17 *Presbytis cristata*	Crested langur	*	−	−	−	*
18 *Hylobates* sp.	Gibbon	*	*	*	*	*
19 *Nycticebus coucang*	Slow loris	−	−	−	*	−
Carnivora						
20 *Paradoxurus hermaphroditus*	Common palm civet	*	*	*	*	*
21 *Hemigalus derbyanus*	Banded palm civet	−	*	−	−	−

Table 2 (continued)

Species		Spirit Cave	Banyan Valley Cave
		1 2 3 4	1[a]
22 *Felis viverrina*	Fishing cat	– – * –	–
23 *Felis bengalensis*	Leopard cat	* – – –	–
24 *Selenarctos thibetanus*	Bear	– – – –	*
25 *Arctonyx collaris*	Hog badger	* * * *	*
26 *Lutra* sp.	Otter	– – * –	*
27 *Martes flavigula*	Marten	– * – *	–
28 *Cuon alpinus*	Red dog	– – – –	*
Rodentia			
29 *Petaurista petaurista*	Flying squirrel	– – * –	*
30 *Cannomys badius*	Lesser bamboo rat	* – – –	–
31 *Rhyzomys sumatrensis*	Hoary bamboo rat	– * – *	*
32 *Hystryx* sp.	Porcupine	– * * –	*
33 *Rattus* sp.	Rat	* * * *	*
34 *Callosciurus* sp.	Squirrel	* – – –	*
Chiroptera			
35 *Hipposideros* sp.	Bat	* * * *	–
36 *Rhinolophus* sp.	Bat	– – – –	*
37 *Megaderma* sp.	Bat	– – – –	*
Cyprinidae			
38 *Acrossocheilus* sp.	Carp	* * * *	*
39 *Barbius* sp.	Carp	– – – –	*
40 *Varanus salvator*	Monitor lizard	– – – –	*
41 *Agamidae*	Lizard	* – – *	–
42 *Emydidae*	Turtle	* * * –	*
43 *Potamonidae*	Crab	* * * *	*

[a] The layer correlations for Banyan Valley Cave are at present unavailable.

plex. At the most basic level, mammals, birds, reptiles, fish, shellfish, and crustaceans may be added to the plants already identified as part of the Hoabinhian complex of food resources. Such variability in Hoabinhian sites has been noted by Gorman (1971), who aptly described it as broad-spectrum hunting-and-gathering. The environment during the late Pleistocene and early Holocene was probably dominated by the deciduous monsoon forest which favors a large number of arboreal species but a relatively low biomass. Also worth recalling is the fact that, although there are some indigenous terrestrial ungulates such as the sambar deer and gaur, the heavily wooded environment would have vitiated their exploitation unless fire was widely used (Wharton 1966).

The mammalian species present at the two caves may be conveniently subdivided into at least four groups. The first, and most significant in terms of food potential, comprises the bovines, pig, deer, serow, goral, and rhinoceros. Larger samples would permit an estimation of their relative abundance, but the present sample sizes are sufficient only for a consideration of their presence or absence. Small arboreal mammals include the primates, martens, civets, and squirrels. Smaller terrestrial mammals include the porcupine, bamboo-rat, smaller rats, otter and badger. The cave resource zone itself is represented by the bat.

Table 1 sets out the qualitative differences between the two faunal spectra. Spirit Cave has produced considerably more bones of fish (carp), but several of the larger mammalian species found at Banyan Valley Cave are absent. Banyan Valley Cave, on the other hand, lacks several small carnivores, the slow loris and the bamboo rat.

It may well be that each cave was the focus of slightly different hunting strategies. Such a situation may be documented in terms of different assemblages of artifacts, although the perishable nature of wooden implements would make it difficult to consider this hypothesis closely. The possibility that differences in faunal spectra reflect seasonal activities needs further investigation. Large rockfalls at Spirit Cave make difficult any estimation of the size of the original area occupied, but the cave itself is situated toward the top of a limestone ridge, a sharp half-hour's climb from the Khong stream valley. It commands an excellent view, but shortage of water makes it difficult to envisage the cave being occupied for extended periods. The Banyan Valley caverns, however, are much larger than Spirit Cave and have a plentiful water supply.

More assemblages from this area are required before patterns of different faunal spectra can be recognized and explained, but the differences between the species found at these two sites are not surprising. Thus, although the abundance of fish at a site with a water shortage may seem unusual, the Khong stream is large enough to support the carp, whereas the Banyan Valley stream is not. The absence of bones from large species at Spirit Cave may be due to its being used for trapping expeditions. Banyan Valley Cave, on the other hand, seems more likely to have been a base camp.

Most of the species likely to have been present in Thailand during the Hoabinhian period of occupation have been listed in the appendix. I must stress that the collections of comparative material at the British Museum (Natural History) are large, but not exhaustive, and that some of the prehistoric bones must, by a process of elimination, come from species not available for comparison.

Many of the smaller species, such as the cat, civet, marten, and otter, may have been valued for their pelts. With the exception of the smaller rodents and bats, however, the bones have been subjected to persistent and heavy battering, and some bones of all species, including teeth and terminal phalanges, have been burnt. There is no doubt that the bones were subjected to intense direct heat after they were smashed, because the burning extends over broken surfaces. Probably, therefore, the game recovered was processed and subsequently cooked within the cave itself. This would tend to favor the survival of small, compact bones of the extremities, such as the calcanea, metapodials and phalanges and it is, indeed, this class of anatomical bones which predominates. An overwhelming proportion by weight of all bone recovered, however, may be ascribed to the smashed long bones of large species. No evidence exists that only selected portions of the dead animals were returned to the caves. The presence of so many comminuted fragments of bone indicates the use of a heavy, probably stone, tool in the caves themselves.

Were a larger sample available, it would be possible to confirm the impression that an unusually high proportion of primates represented come from either young or old animals. The range of species of *Macaca* and *Presbytis* native to Thailand, allied to their size variation and the fragmentary nature of the prehistoric specimens, rules out specific identification in nearly all cases.

Two of the genera (*Bibos* and *Sus*) in question were subsequently found as domesticates in Thailand, but neither the bovines nor suids were common at either site. The jackal is completely absent, and *Cuon* very rare. There is no evidence, either zoological or cultural, that cattle and pigs were treated differently at either site than the other species identified.

The inhabitants of the two sites were wide ranging in their quest for food. They obtained fish, shellfish, and turtles from the riverine habitat, and bats[1] from the caves themselves; they exploited the forest for small arboreal species and the forest floor for the deer and rhinoceros. The serow and goral prefer limestone outcrops and wooded slopes, and the gaur is usually confined to grassy clearings and well-grassed forest margins or banks of rivers (Medway 1969).

The faunal report for the cave of Sai Yok (Hooijer 1967) suffers from the lack of a stratigraphic context for the species identified. If the bones came from the Hoabinhian occupation layers, it is remarkable that all represent large species. It may be that the techniques of excavation employed did not permit the recovery of fragments of small bones.

Laang Spean, on the other hand, has produced faunal remains from the Hoabinhian levels which appear broadly similar to those from the

---

[1]   Most of the bones of bats are probably those of individuals which died naturally in the cave. A few of the bones are charred, however, and may represent animals which were eaten.

two northern Thai sites excavated by Gorman (Mourer and Mourer 1970).

NON NOK THA

Excavations at Non Nok Tha have provided important data for an understanding of later Thai prehistory. The excavator has recognized an Early Period (EP) with three phases, a Middle Period (MP) with eight, and a Late Period (LP) with six. The site comprises a low mound built up over approximately 5,500 years through use as a cemetery and for occupation. There is evidence of early bronze metallurgy (from Early Period 1) and for rice cultivation from the site's initial occupation (Bayard 1971, 1972). The mound is situated on the eastern edge of a large sandstone monadnock and has easy access to flat land suitable for wet-rice farming and the lower hillslopes of monadnock itself where swidden agriculture is practicable. Both the hillside and plain would have been suitable for hunting.

The inhumation burials and occupation deposits have produced sufficient bones to permit a tentative review of certain economic factors. As has been seen, Hoabinhian sites in Thailand have provided evidence for the hunting of bovids and pigs, both species being important as domestic animals in Thailand at present. The intensification of the utilization of these species, in a word domestication, has yet to be analyzed. The well-known relationship between harnessing the tractive powers of water buffalo and wet-rice agriculture makes it important to trace the history of the former in dated archaeological contexts. Finally, the extent to which settled agriculture and stock raising replaced or integrated with an earlier economy of hunting, gathering and plant tending evidenced at Spirit Cave between the eleventh and sixth millennia may be reviewed.

The nonhuman bones from Non Nok Tha were analyzed in the Anthropology Department of the University of Otago (Table 3). Most specimens were associated with inhumation burials dating from the initial occupation to Middle Period 6 (Figure 2). The conjunction of human and nonhuman bones ceased with the subsequent adoption of cremation.

Acquisition of modern comparative material was greatly facilitated by the loan of bones of water buffalo (*Bubalus bubalis*), gaur (*Bibos gaurus*), zebu (*Bos taurus indicus*), sambar (*Cervus unicolor*) and hog deer (*Axis porcinus*) by the American Museum of Natural History. During December 1969, the author obtained bones of water buffalo and zebu from the Bangkok Municipal Abattoir. All specimens came from female animals,

Table 3. Non Nok Tha: the faunal spectrum from burials (B) and occupation (O) contexts (figures refer to the minimum number of individuals)

	Bos		Sus		Canis		Cervus unicolor		Axis porcinus		Muntiacus muntjak		Bubalus bubalis		Small felid		Crab		Felis tigris		Murid	
	B	O	B	O	B	O	B	O	B	O	B	O	B	O	B	O	B	O	B	O	B	O
L.P. 6		1		1																		
5																						
4				4		2	1		1		1		1									
3																						
2				2		1			1		1											
1				1		1					1											
M.P. 8	1			2		1	1		1		1										1	
7				2		1	1				1											
6	5			4	2																	
5	3		1		1	3	1		1										1			
4	7			2	8	2	1		2	1	1											1
3	1				1	1					1			1								
2	3			1	6	1			1		1		1									
1	9	3	14	3	1	1	1				1											
E.P. 3	5			6	1													1				
2	1			4											1							
1	5		2		10	1	1				1						1					

due to legal sanctions against killing males. Animals were inspected in the stockyards before killing to ensure both that there were no males present and that the cattle were of zebu type. All animals were reared on the central plain north of Bangkok.

Due to the butchering practices involved, extensive data could be obtained only on the metapodials and phalanges. The bones were disarticulated and measured by the author. Phalanges were retained for subsequent study in New Zealand, but metapodials were taken by contractors after measuring was completed. A number of carpals particularly the magnum, were also obtained, and measurements from large limb bones were taken when no disruption to the killing line was involved.

From a zoological and archaeological point of view, consideration of the natur of the bovine and suid remains from Non Nok Tha is desirable. The origins of the domestic fauna of southeastern Asia are unknown, due to the lack of adequate data and the reliance on hypotheses of invasions to account for the introduction of domesticates from other, better-known areas (Sørensen 1967). There are three principal methods for approaching this question. One is broadly cultural, relying on the context in which the bones are found, allied to the age structure of the animals represented. Thus a high proportion of mature bones in a cave deposit associated with stone implements used in hunting would be said to derive from wild animals, but an assemblage comprising a high ratio of young animals in a large village complex in an area where the species in question is exotic would be considered to be evidence for domestication.

By itself, however, cultural context is not a convincing method. Higgs and Jarman (1969) have examined it in relation to late Pleistocene European sites, concluding that the concept of herd followers rather than a rigid distinction between pastoralists and/or hunters is worthy of consideration. Moreover, faunal spectra from Swiss Neolithic sites include both wild and domestic bovines and suids (Higham 1968).

Consequently, zoological examination of the bones themselves, both for morphological characteristics which distinguish between genera, species, and even sexes, and for statistically valid metrical differences between the prehistoric and modern samples, is necessary. In most cases there are insufficient prehistoric specimens from the same layer to provide an acceptably sized sample. This is certainly the case for Non Nok Tha. Nevertheless, the superimposed levels of Non Nok Tha have produced a considerable number of complete phalanges and magna, compact bones which combine the two characteristics most desirable in the present analysis. The former are sexually dimorphic and the latter have important morphological differences between *Bibos* on the one hand, and *Bubalus* on the other (Plate 1).

The investigator faced with the problem of small sample size at Non Nok Tha has two principal alternatives. The first is to suspend analyses until further investigations increase the number of specimens available. The second is to combine the specimens from superimposed layers into a pooled "sample," and build into his conclusions *caveats* to take account of its shortcomings. In the following review of bovine phalanges from Non Nok Tha, the latter course is preferred.

This problem does not apply to a morphological examination of magna. As may be seen in Plate 1 the magnum of *Bubalus bubalis* is distinguished from that of *Bibos* both by its greater ratio of length to width, and by the configuration of the lateral interior fossa (Figure 3). An examination of the magna from Non Nok Tha suggests that all but one are from *Bibos*, the sole exception being from Late Period 4. As may be seen in Figure 4, there is a clear distinction between female cattle of the zebu breed and female Thai water buffalo on the basis of the size and shape of the first phalanx of the anterior limb. I must stress however, that were male phalanges from water buffalo and zebu, as well as those from both sexes of gaur, kouprey, and banteng available, the scatter diagram would probably reveal considerable overlap of the several groups.

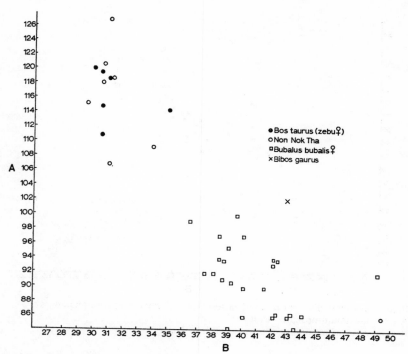

Figure 3. Scatter diagram of southeastern Asian bovine magna
A axis: ratio of breadth to length
B axis: maximum breadth

Nevertheless, a preliminary analysis of the status of the animals in question may be made by means of multivariate techniques.

The principal problem with a multivariate analysis of phalangeal dimensions is the rarity of the necessary modern comparative samples. The kouprey (*Bos sauveli*) for example, is close to extinction, and comparative material is almost nonexistent. Both gaur and banteng are rare. Three male gaur phalanges have been measured and are used in the canonical analysis described below. The remaining comparative data come from thirty-eight female adult *Bubalus bubalis* reared in the Central Valley of Thailand, eighteen female adult *Bos taurus* of zebu breed raised in the Central Valley, forty female adults of Aberdeen Angus breed, thirty-eight adults of Red Danish breed, and forty male adults of Aberdeen Angus breed. The three dimensions employed are maximum length, proximal width, and distal width. Ten specimens from Non Nok Tha are involved, all coming from inhumation burials and three being from the earliest level encountered (Plate 2).

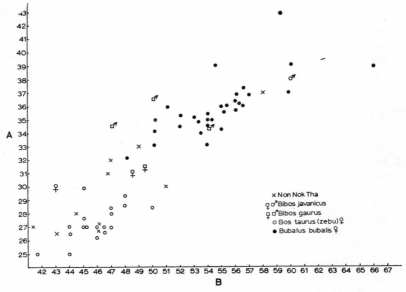

Figure 4. Scatter diagram of southeastern Asian bovine first fore phalanges
A axis: maximum proximal width
B axis: ratio of maximum proximal width to lenth

In the first stage of the statistical analysis, linear discriminant functions based on the generalized Mahalanobis D^2 statistic were calculated for the five samples of modern specimens. A reapplication of these functions to the individual members of these modern groups demonstrated, in general, considerable group divergence. When applied to the Non Nok Tha specimens, the functions located six of the ten bones into the sample of *Bos taurus* (zebu breed), demonstrating their similarity with this group. Significances were uniformly greater than 0.5, and three were as high as 0.999.

Caution should be exercised in accepting these significance levels too literally, because this method is relatively crude, and both allocation and significance are markedly affected by changes in the size of the universe under consideration (Rao 1952). Nevertheless, with small samples this method has several advantages over others.

Of the four remaining bones, three are most similar to Red Danish cows and one to Aberdeen Angus cows. Probably because of their higher plane of nutrition, these breeds have more robust phalanges than the zebu, and close analysis of the four prehistoric specimens suggests strongly that at least three may come from male animals equivalent to the females whose affinities lie with *Bos taurus* (zebu).

In terms of a canonical analysis, the Non Nok Tha group with or without the putative male specimens, is closer to female *Bos taurus* than any other comparative group. On theoretical grounds the argument could be made that a direct application of the D^2 statistic to those data might prove the most reliable, and therefore this application was undertaken with use of the generalized form of $D^2/_3$. This is a small number of variables, but the canonical variates were highly significant, a fact which demonstrates the discriminative power of the three dimensions in question. The results show that the specimens from Non Nok Tha could be confused at varying levels of significance with all other groups (Table 5). Once again, however, the sample from *Bos taurus* (zebu breed) is the most similar. Each of the three analyses reinforces the other insofar as they all point to an extremely close morphological similarity between the phalanges of *Bos taurus* (zebu) and those from Non Nok Tha.

Table 4.   The dimensions of bovine first fore phalanges from Non Nok Tha

		Length	Proximal breadth	Distal width
	1	65.0	31.2	28.0
	2	60.1	27.5	28.5
	3	61.2	28.5	28.5
	4	58.0	28.2	26.8
	5	56.2	28.0	23.5
	6	59.0	28.6	27.0
	7	60.5	27.0	26.5
	8	58.0	26.5	24.8
	9	65.0	31.2	28.0
	10	66.0	37.0	33.0
Bubalus bubalis ♀ ($\overline{X}$)	32	66.1	35.8	35.9
Bos taurus ♀ ($\overline{X}$)	18	59.7	27.4	28.5

The question remains of the relationship between the bovine bones from Non Nok Tha and those from the female gaur and banteng. As might be anticipated, sexual dimorphism is clearly apparent in the skeletal dimensions. In the following review, the bovine bones from each burial listed will be considered in turn.

The phalanges from the forelimb in Burial 125 match those from female banteng and gaur in terms of length, but in no case are the prehistoric specimens as broad. The rear phalanges are slightly shorter and considerably narrower than in the wild species.

Burial 30 contained the remains of an immature bovine whose astragalus and metatarsal were still growing at death. The adult dentition, however, indicates that the animal was smaller than the female gaur and banteng.

400 CHARLES F. W. HIGHAM

Table 5.

Samples	Statistic value	2	3	4	5	6
1 *Bubalus bubalis*	D^2	5.4	10.5	12.1	15.5	3.7
	F	20.0	27.1	69.7	89.0	20.7
	P.L.	0.025	0.025	0.005	0.005	0.025
2 *Bos taurus* (zebu breed)	D^2		1.4	18.1	7.6	4.2
	F		3.0	72.3	30.2	16.3
	P.L.		0.25	0.005	0.025	0.025
3 Non Nok Tha	D^2			3.9	2.6	1.9
	F			10.7	7.1	5.1
	P.L.			0.1	0.1	0.25
4 Aberdeen Angus (male)	D^2				3.0	2.1
	F				19.7	13.3
	P.L.				0.025	0.1
5 Aberdeen Angus (female)	D^2					1.6
	F					10.0
	P.L.					0.1
6 Red Danish (female)						

Note:

Values of D^2, F, and associated significance levels (P.L.) on comparing six samples of bovine phalanges: D^2, value of the Mahalanobis D^2 statistic in question; F, variance ratio obtained in order to test the significance of the value of D^2; P.L., the level of probability at which F is significant (for full explanation of these terms, see Rao [1952]).

The rear limb bones and cranium in Burial 6 are very similar in size to those of the female banteng and gaur.

As a group, the bovines from EP1 indicate the presence at Non Nok Tha of animals smaller than the female bantengs and gaurs available for study. One animal, however, was similar in size to females of the wild species.

The bovine bones in Burial 42 (EP2) are too immature to permit conclusions on the species in question. If the phalanges were to thicken with further growth, the animal in question could have attained the size of a female gaur.

The metacarpal from Burial 79 (EP3) is too short to be considered a banteng or gaur. Its slender proportions indicate a female. The radius is likewise smaller than are those from the wild specimens available. Although the breadth of the fore-phalanx in Burial 12 exceeds that of the female banteng, it is considerably shorter. Both bovines from EP3 fall outside the size-range of banteng and gaur.

The tibia and astragalus from Burial 25 (MP1) are particularly large, the former slightly exceeding in size the corresponding bones from the

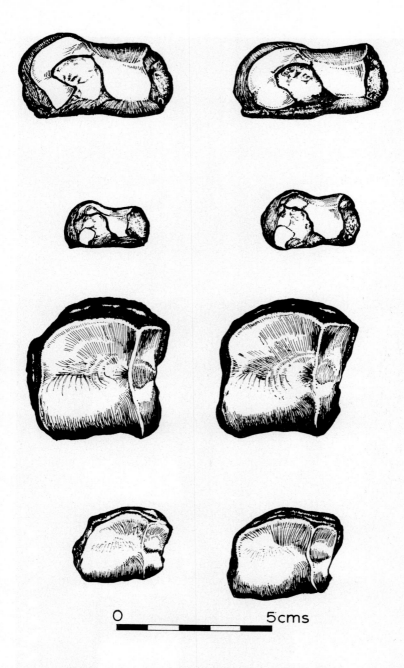

Plate 1.   Modern and prehistoric bovine magna. First and third rows from top: (left)
Bubalus bubalis. Second and fourth rows: (left) *Bos taurus* (zebu). All specimens on the
right are from Non Nok Tha

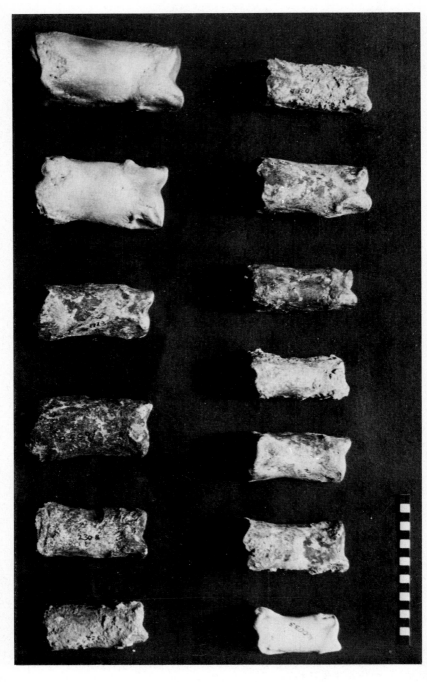

Plate 2. Non Nok Tha and modern bovine phalanges. Top row (left to right): E.P.1, M.P.5, E.P.1, M.P.2–5, M.P.2, E.P.1, *Bos taurus* (zebu). Bottom row: *Bubalus bubalis*, *Bibos gaurus*, M.P.5, M.P.6, L.P.2 or 3, M.P.6 (scale in centimeters)

bull banteng. The same holds for the metacarpal and femur from the mound of the same burial. All the limb bones from burials 8 and 20, however, come from an animal much smaller than the banteng or gaur.

There are two assemblages of bovine limb bones from MP2, both of which come from an animal smaller than the female banteng. The same situation obtains for Burials 85, 63, 27 and 56 from MP4.

Burial 57 (MP5) has yielded a first phalanx from the anterior limb comparable in breadth with that of a bull gaur or banteng. The mandible from Burial 68 is also as large as in the male gaur. The humerus from Burial 1 and the astragalus from Burial 56, on the other hand, are particularly small.

The overlap in size of bovine bones from the burials is paralleled in those from the occupation deposits from EP1 to LP4.

It is known that the robustness of phalanges and metacarpals is influenced by the level of nutrition and by sex. Zalkin (1962) has outlined the effect of castration on the shape of the latter bone, and the clear sexual dimorphism which exists in the case of phalanges has been considered by Dottrens (1947) and Higham (1969). If one assumes that all bovines reared at Non Nok Tha had a similar plane of nutrition, then one should be able to discuss the sex of the animals represented. The assumption is not entirely unreasonable. Two principal food sources are currently available in the area: the natural forest and rice stubble. While the former would have been more extensive during the prehistoric period, both were present from the initial occupation of the site.

The relevant data are set out in Table 4. Of the prehistoric specimens, number 10 stands out because of its particularly great breadth relative to the width. Numbers 1 and 8 are long specimens, but lack the relative breadth of number 10. Axial lengthening of this nature is a characteristic of bones coming from bovines castrated at an early age, due to the resultant delays in epiphysial closure. If all the specimens came from the same herd it would be reasonable to conclude that the ten bones come from seven cows, two steers and one bull. On the other hand, the two particularly long specimens could come from female wild *Bibos banteng*.

The results of the three methods for considering the status of prehistoric bovines may now be reviewed. The morphology of the magna indicates an overwhelming preponderance of *Bibos* over *Bubalus*. The metrical characteristics of phalanges and metapodia suggest the presence of a bovine statistically closely akin to modern female *Bos taurus* of the zebu or humped breed.

A comparison between the dimensions of the Non Nok Tha bovine bones and those of modern banteng and gaur of known sex has revealed an overlap in size throughout the site's occupation. A precisely similar situation was found to occur in prehistoric sites on the Alpine foreland of Switzerland except that the prehistoric specimens in the latter case overlapped those of *Bos primigenius* and *Bison bonasus* (Higham 1968).

Unlike the Swiss sites, however, the sample size from Non Nok Tha does not allow a judicious ordering of the alternative hypotheses in terms of plausibility. Nevertheless one can conclude that the majority of the bovine bones from the burials at Non Nok Tha are smaller than the specimens of female gaur and banteng available for comparison and appear themselves to come from cows. The larger bones may come from the female banteng or gaur, male banteng or gaur, or bulls or steers of the same breed as the small females. These alternatives are not mutually exclusive. The value of cows approaching breeding age to a cattle-breeding society hardly needs emphasis. All the animals represented could, of course, have died from natural causes. Had this been the case, a greater incidence of older, nonfemale animals could reasonably be expected. A larger sample, allied to specimens from culturally related sites, could support or reject the hypothesis that young females were specifically culled for mortuary use. Confirmation would strengthen the present conclusion that some, if not all, of the Non Nok Tha bovines were domesticated. The simplest origin for domestic bovines in this area is in the indigenous species, *Bibos banteng* and/or *Bibos gaurus*.

The suid bones from Non Nok Tha may derive from *Sus scrofa jubatus*, *Sus barbatus*, or a domestic form of either.[2] The former has a much wider range and is still found in the vicinity of Non Nok Tha. The latter is considerably more restricted, and is not found in northeastern Thailand at present. It is said to be the larger of the two. The British Museum has a series of skulls from both species.

Histograms of the lengths of the first and third molars respectively are shown in Figure 5, together with the same dimensions taken from the specimens from Non Nok Tha. With one exception, the latter fall within the size range of the modern, wild teeth. There are insufficient prehistoric specimens to make a statistical comparison meaningful and I conclude that, until more data are available, I cannot decide whether the Non Nok Tha prehistoric suids were domesticated.

The canid remains from Non Nok Tha could presumably come from the golden jackal (*Canis aureus*), a domestic dog, or possibly the red dog (*Cuon alpinus*). The lack of a third molar in *Cuon* rules out its presence at Non Nok Tha.

---

[2]   I have followed Medway (1969) in listing these pigs. However, not all systematists agree on the taxonomy of the wild pigs of southeastern Asia and other possibilities exist. See, for example, Herre and Röhrs (this volume).

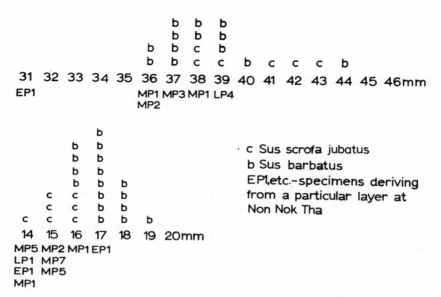

Figure 5. Scatter diagram of (top) length of M_3, (bottom) length of M_1 in modern and prehistoric suids

The dimensions of the canid skeleton in Burial 8 (EP1) fall, in all cases, within the range of comparable measurements from *Canis aureus*. The assignment of the bones to a domestic dog under these circumstances would be unreasonable, and the prehistory of the domestic dog at Non Nok Tha remains open.

THE KHORAT PLATEAU AND CENTRAL PLAIN

Fieldwork undertaken in the Khorat Plateau and Central Plain has yet to reveal sites culturally similar to Non Nok Tha. It seems at present that the initial occupation of these areas, which are now densely settled, represents a significant stage in Thai prehistory.

Hole, Flannery, and Neely (1969) have cited environmental barriers to the settlement of the Tigris-Euphrates lowlands. A similar situation obtains in the case of the Khorat Plateau, where many soils are too pervious, and rainfall too low, to permit a predictable rice crop to be grown unless soils are carefully chosen and control of water practiced.

There are two principal technological factors which, taken in conjunction with social and economic needs such as population pressure, would favor the settlement of the Khorat Plateau. One is the possession of iron tools to facilitate clearing of the forest and the construction of paddi embankments, and the second is the water buffalo. Although cattle can plough a wet paddy field, the buffalo is more adept at this onerous work. Weatherill (1973) has tentatively identified bones of buffalo at Chansen by A.D. 0–25 in its second occupation phase. Iron was available on the margins of the Khorat Plateau by at least 2200 B.P. It is within the contexts of these finds that the fauna from Ban Tha Nen is considered.

The few specimens recovered reveal that swine and cattle predominated. The bovine bones were, with one notable exception, considerably smaller than those of the banteng or gaur and are considered to be domestic. It is not possible to be as specific in the case of the suid remains, because the dimensions in question are close to those available for *Sus barbatus* and *Sus scrofa jubatus*. There is no firm evidence for the presence of water buffalo.

SUMMARY AND CONCLUSION

The faunal remains considered above permit some preliminary conclusions on the relationship between man and the indigenous fauna of southeastern Asia from the end of the Pleistocene to the establishment of the historic kingdoms.

Banyan Cave, Spirit Cave, and Laang Spean have yielded similar remains in a Hoabinhian cultural context. The local Hoabinhian culture was itself undergoing basic changes during the period from 8000 B.P. to around 7500 B.P. The surface of level 2 at Spirit Cave bore impressed pot sherds and polished quadrangular adzes. Yen has suggested that the occupants of Spirit Cave may have been plant tenders. Certainly the remains of the bean, water chestnut, peas, and cucumber have been identified there. Even more startling evidence for economic change comes from Banyan Valley Cave in the form of carbonized rice, in association with pottery.

The faunal remains from both sites suggest a wide-ranging food quest involving trapping, hunting, and collecting. The fauna of the deciduous tropical forest in the vicinity of Spirit Cave and Banyan Valley Cave is related to that described for Sundaland by Medway (1969). It has a relatively low biomass, rich in species but low in animal density. Most species in question are arboreal and of the major ground-dwellers, few are large and regularly gregarious. There is no equivalent to the reindeer of late Pleistocene Europe, or bison of early America, as a food source.

This situation is reflected in the faunal spectrum of Banyan Cave, which has over twenty species but no dominance by any one. While all the principal ground-dwellers, except pig, were represented, many small arboreal species are also present, for example the monkey, squirrel and civet. The evidence for economic innovation in plant exploitation is not at present matched by domestication of animals. I must stress, however, that small cave sites are not likely to produce evidence for animal domestication if they were used as bases for hunting expeditions. A precise parallel is provided in the same area today, where people either growing rice or with access to rice will take a supply with them when hunting. Many open Hoabinhian sites are now known in northern Thailand through surface scatters of stone artifacts and waste flakes. These sites might yield a different type of faunal spectrum from the more specialized caves.

A major contrast exists between the nonhuman bones associated with the late Hoabinhian caves and those from Non Nok Tha. Both the burials and occupation deposits indicate specialization on bovines and suids. The sites have also provided a number of clearly wild species, particularly cervids. The hillslopes of Phu Wiang are visited by hunters to this day, the principal quarry being deer, monkey, and pig. Even from the earlier burials some bovine bones appear to be too small to be either wild banteng or gaur. Indeed, a multivariate statistical analysis has shown that the bovine phalanges from Non Nok Tha closely resemble those of modern female Thai cattle.

The presence of rice at Banyan Cave and pottery with stone adzes at Spirit Cave well before the occupation at Non Nok Tha, however, must make the links between the Hoabinhian and the initial farmer occupation of the Piedmont zone a topic for future research. There is at present an interval of about 2,000 years between the end of the occupation of Spirit Cave and presumed occupation of Banyan Valley Cave on the one hand, and the earliest reasonable date for settlement at Non Nok Tha. There are, however, no sites yet which fill the void.

The nature of the faunal spectrum for EP1 at Non Nok Tha set a pattern which remained virtually unaltered until the beginning of the Christian era. The cattle, which could have been descended from the banteng or gaur, continued to fall within the size range for the modern Thai breed of zebu. Pigs were associated with cattle in burials and occupation deposits, although it is not possible on osteological evidence to conclude that they were domestic. The same pattern of species, and problems over defining their status, were observed at Ban Kao by Hatting (1967). Hunting of deer certainly continued at Non Nok Tha, but the range of small species so characteristic of Hoabinhian sites is no longer evident.

The hiatus in occupation at Non Nok Tha covers part of the period when water buffalo could reasonably be expected to be present. The only osteological evidence for the buffalo comes from the fourteenth century A.D. This species was present in Thailand considerably earlier than that date at Chansen in the Central Valley. Chansen was initially occupied by at least 2500 B.P., and a similar date is reasonable for the first settlement at Ban Tha Nen (Roi Et Province) and Phimai on the Khorat Plateau. There are insufficient faunal remains from Ban Tha Nen to allow definitive conclusions on the economy practiced there. Cattle and swine were present, but there is no evidence yet for the water buffalo. The hypothesis that the tractive power of this species was a prerequisite to wet rice agriculture on the Plateau must await further data before it can be tested.

The early dates obtained for cultivation of rice, domestication of cattle, and bronze technology in Thailand, together with the sharp break in economy between the terminal Hoabinhian and the early levels of Non Nok Tha, make it necessary to reconsider the possibility that these changes resulted from ethnic movement into Thailand. This hypothesis has been proposed by Sørensen to account for the presumed intrusive features at Ban Kao at a much later date (around 3800 B.P.). If the possibility of migration is admitted it is surely more logical to seek the sources of such impulses in the seats of advanced culture to the west and/or to the north rather than in Sundaland or the further island chain of southeastern Asia.

Singh (1971) has pointed out recently that the large cereal-type pollen grains which occur from the start of his Phase III in Rajasthan (9500–5000 B.P.) may well indicate early agriculture in India. As yet, no firm archaeological remains have been correlated with the pollen data. Indeed the earliest evidence for agriculture and stock rearing in the Indian subcontinent is still in the lowest levels of Kili Ghul Mohammed near Quetta, where the top stratum of layer 1 has two radiocarbon dates in the region of 5700 B.P. The layer in question contained the remains of presumably domesticated sheep, goats, and cattle (Allchin and Allchin 1968).

That sophisticated agricultural practices, including draught animals, were present at an early date in the western part of the subcontinent is demonstrated by the remarkable plow marks recently uncovered by Lal (1971) at Kalibangan in a clear pre-Harappan context.

There are, however, over two thousand miles between the Indus Valley and Thailand. Central Indian Neolithic culture is little known, although the rice grains in the early levels of Chirand (Verma 1971) provide an intriguing hint of agriculture in the Ganges Valley by 2500 B.C. The bovine bones from Chirand have not been studied in detail and it is therefore not known whether they represent wild or domestic animals.

If it is agreed that the long chronology for Non Nok Tha and Ban Chiang is valid, there is no evidence at present in favor of an intrusion of agriculturalists into southeastern Asia from the West.

Precisely the same situation obtains for China where Treistman's (1972) recently proposed date for the Chu-Chia-Ling rice cultivation is far too late to be relevant to southeastern Asian prehistory. Parker (1968) has convincingly argued against Lungshanoid influence in the Thai early Neolithic, and Watson (1972) has stressed the ambiguity of evidence for early animal domestication even in the Huang Ho Valley. Further research will show whether or not the present picture of economic innovation in prehistoric Thailand is justified.

APPENDIX 1

Checklist of major species in northern Thailand, their availability in reference collections, and presence in Hoabinhian faunal spectra from northern Thailand.

		Comparative skeleton examined	Present in Thai Hoabinhian
Artiodactyla			
Sus scrofa jubatus	Crested pig	√	√
Sus barbatus	Bearded pig	√	–
Bibos gaurus	Gaur	√	√
Bibos javanicus	Banteng	√	
Bos sauveli	Kouprey	–	–
Bubalus bubalis	Water buffalo	√	–
Capricornis sumatrensis	Serow	√	√
Nemorhaedus goral	Goral	√	√
Cervus unicolor	Sambar	√	√
Cervus eldi	Eld's deer	√	–
Cervus schomburgki	Schomburg's deer	√	–
Muntiacus muntjak	Muntjac	√	√
Tragulus napu	Large mouse deer	√	√
Tragulus javanicus	Lesser mouse deer	√	–
Axis porcinus	Pig deer	√	√
Perissodactyla			
Didermocerus sumatrensis	Sumatran rhinoceros	√	√
Rhinoceros sondaicus	Javan rhinoceros	√	√
Tapirus indicus	Tapir	√	–
Proboscidea			
Elephas maximus	Elephant	√	–

		Comparative skeleton examined	Present in Thai Hoabinhian
Primates			
Homo sapiens	Man	√	√
Nycticebus coucang	Slow loris	√	√
Tupaia glis	Tree shrew	√	–
Presbytis obscura	Dusky leaf monkey	√	
Presbytis cristata	Silvered-leaf monkey	√	√
Presbytis melalophos	Banded-leaf monkey	√	
Presbytis phayrei	Phayre's leaf monkey	√	
Macaca fascicularis	Crab-eating macaque	√	
Macaca nemestrina	Pig-tailed macaque	√	√
Macaca speciosa	Stump-tailed macaque	√	
Macaca assamensis	Assamese macaque	√	
Hylobates lar	Lar gibbon	√	√
Pholidota			
Manis javanica	Pangolin	√	–
Carnivora			
Cuon alpinus	Red dog	√	√
Canis aureus	Golden jackal	√	–
Helarctos malayanus	Malayan sun bear	√	–
Selenarctos thibetanus	Bear	√	√
Arctonyx collaris	Hog badger	√	√
Melogale personata	Badger	√	–
Martes flavigula	Yellow-throated marten	√	√
Amblonyx cinerea	Oriental small-clawed otter	–	–
Lutra sumatrana	Sumatran otter	–	–
Lutra lutra	Common otter	√	√
Lutra perspicillata	Smooth otter	√	
Viverra zibetha	Large Indian civet	√	–
Viverra megaspila	Large spotted civet	–	–
Viverricula malaccensis	Little civet	–	–
Prionodon linsang	Banded linsang	√	–
Paradoxurus hermaphroditus	Common palm civet	√	√
Paguma larvata	Masked palm civet	√	–
Arctictis binturong	Binturong	√	–
Arctogalidia trivirgata[a]	Small-toothed palm civet	√	–
Hemigalus derbyanus	Banded palm civet	√	√
Herpestes brachyurus	Short-tailed mongoose	√	–
Herpestes auropunctatus	Small Indian Mongoose	√	–
Herpestes javanicus	Javan mongoose	–	–
Felis tigris	Tiger	√	–
Felis pardus	Leopard	√	–
Neofelis nebulosa	Clouded leopard	√	–
Felis bengalensis	Leopard cat	√	–
Felis temmincki	Golden cat	√	–
Felis chaus	Jungle cat	√	–
Felis viverrina	Fishing cat	√	√
Felis marmorata	Marbled cat	√	–
Ailurus fulgens	Cat bear	√	–

		Comparative skeleton examined	Present in Thai Hoabinhian
Dermoptera			
Cynocephalus variegatus	Flying lemur	√	–
Lagomorpha			
Lepus peguensis	Burmese hare	√	–
Insectivora			
Talpa micrura	Mole	√	–
Echinosorex gymnurus	Gymnure	√	–
Hylomys suillus	Lesser gymnure	√	–
Chiroptera			
Pteropodidae	Fruit bats	√	–
Emballonuridae	Tomb bats	√	–
Megadermatidae	False vampires	√	√
Rhinolophidae	Horseshoe bats	√	√
Vespertilionidae	Common bats	√	–
Molossidae	Free-tailed bats	√	–
Rodentia			
Sciuridae	Squirrels	√	√
Hystricidae	Porcupines	√	√
Muridae	Rats and mice	√	√
Rhyzomyidae	Bamboo rats	√	√

[a] The British Museum (Natural History) has only one skull of this species, so comparative study of the whole skeleton was not possible.

REFERENCES

ALLCHIN, B., R. ALLCHIN
1968 *Birth of Indian civilisation*. London: Penguin.
BAYARD, D. T.
1971 "Non Nok Tha: the 1968 excavation. Procedure, stratigraphy and a summary of the evidence," in *Studies in prehistoric anthropology*, volume four. Dunedin: University of Otago.
1972 Early Thai bronze: analysis and new dates. *Science* 176:1411–1412.
BRONSON, B., G. F. DALES
1973 Excavations at Chansen, Thailand, 1968 and 1969: a preliminary report. *Asian Perspectives* 15:15–46.
BRONSON, B., M. HAN
1972 A thermoluminescence series from Thailand. *Antiquity* 46:322–326.
CLARK, J. G. D.
1969 *World archaeology* (second edition). London: Cambridge University Press.
DOTTRENS, E.
1947 "Les ossements de *Bos taurus brachyceros* Rütim. et de *Bos primigenius* Boj. *Revue Suisse de Zoologie* 54:459–544.

GORMAN, C. F.
  1971   The Hoabinhian and after: subsistence patterns in southeast Asia during the late Pleistocene and early Recent periods. *World Archaeology* 2:300–320.
HATTING, T.
  1967   "Ban Kao," part I, in *Archaeological excavations in Thailand*, volume two. Edited by P. Sørensen. Copenhagen: Munksgaard.
HIGGS, E. S., M. JARMAN
  1969   The origins of agriculture: a reconsideration. *Antiquity* 43:31–41.
HIGHAM, C. F. W.
  1968   Patterns of prehistoric economic exploitation on the Alpine Foreland. *Vierteljahrsschrift der Naturforschenden Gesellschaft in Zürich* 113: 235–286.
  1969   The metrical attributes of two samples of modern bovine limb bones. *Journal of the Zoological Society* 157:63–74.
  1972   "Initial model formulation *in terra incognita*," in *Models in archaeology*. Edited by D. L. Clarke, 453–476. London: Methuen.
HIGHAM, C. F. W., R. H. PARKER
  1970   *Prehistoric investigations in N.E. Thailand 1969–1970: preliminary report.* Dunedin: Department of Anthropology, University of Otago.
HOLE, F., K. V. FLANNERY, J. A. NEELY
  1969   *Prehistory and human ecology of the Deh Luran Plain.* Memoirs of the Museum of Anthropology, University of Michigan. 1.
HOOIJER, D. A.
  1967   "The faunal remains," in *Archaeological excavations in Thailand, I: Sai-Yok*. Edited by H. R. van Heekeren and Count Eigil Knuth. Copenhagen: Munksgaard.
LAL, B. B.
  1971   Perhaps the earliest ploughed field so far excavated anywhere in the world. *Bulletin of the Indian Archaeological Society* 4:1–4.
MEDWAY, LORD
  1969   *The wild mammals of Malaya.* Kuala Lumpur: Oxford University Press.
MOURER, C., R. MOURER
  1970   The prehistoric industry of Laang Spean, Province of Battambang, Cambodia. *Archaeology and Physical Anthropology in Oceania* 5:128–145.
PARKER, R. H.
  1968   A review of evidence from the Thai-Danish expedition at Ban Kao. *Journal of the Polynesian Society* 77(3):307–313.
RAO, C. R.
  1952   *Advanced statistical methods in biometric research.* New York: Wiley.
SINGH, G.
  1971   The Indus Valley culture (seen in the context of post-glacial climate and ecological studies in north-west India). *Archaeology and Physical Anthropology in Oceania* 6:177–189.
SOLHEIM, W. G.
  1969   Reworking southeast Asian prehistory. *Paideuma* 15:125–139.

SØRENSEN, P.
1967 *Archaeological excavations in Thailand,* volume two: *Ban Kao Part I.* Copenhagen: Munksgaard.
TREISTMAN, J. M.
1972 *The prehistory of China.* Newton Abbott: David and Charles.
VERMA, B. S.
1971 Excavations at Chirand: new light on the Indian Neolithic culture complex. *Bulletin of the Indian Archaeological Society* 4:19–24.
WATSON, W.
1972 "Neolithic settlement in East Asia," in *Man, settlement and urbanism.* Edited by Peter Ucko, Ruth Tringham, and C. W. Dimbleby, 329–341. London: Duckworth.
WEATHERILL, E.
1973 "A preliminary report on the faunal remains from Chansen." Appendix to "Excavations at Chansen, Thailand, 1968 and 1969: a preliminary report" (Bronson and Dales). *Asian Perspectives* 15:44–45.
WHARTON, C. H.
1966 Man, fire and wild cattle in north Cambodia. *Proceedings of the 8th Annual Tall Timbers Fire Ecology Conference,* 23–65.
YEN, D.
1969 "The development of agriculture in Oceania" in *Studies in Oceanic culture history,* volume two. Edited by R. C. Green and M. Kelly. Pacific Anthropological Records 12. Honolulu: Bishop Museum Press.
ZALKIN, V.
1962 *Livestock raising and hunting in the woodland strip of Eastern Europe.* Moscow: Nauka.

ADDENDUM

The following relevant information has been obtained since this article went to press.

The occupation of Banyan Valley Cave and the newly discovered Steep Cliff Cave covers the period from *circa* 7500 B.P. to 3000 B.P. The Hoabinhian occupation of Mae Hongson thus ovelaps that of Non Nok Tha and Ban Chiang. The faunal remains from Steep Cliff Cave, which are at present being studied, are dominated by the bones of large ungulates, a striking contrast to the other two Hoabinhian caves mentioned above. The sambar, *Cervus univolor,* and either gaur or banteng, *Bibos,* are the most common animals represented. The latter correspond in size to modern southeastern Asian wild mammals.

A very small metatarsal from *Bubalus bubalis* is present in the earliest occupation horizon at Non Nok Tha, and a reexamination of the suid jaws from this site together with those from late Pleistocene caves in southern China suggests strongly that the occupants of Non Nok Tha maintained domesticated animals. The excavations of 1974 at Ban Chiang by Chester Gorman and Pisit Charoenwongsa have revealed the presence there of a burial rite similar to that of Non Nok Tha in that extended human inhumations were accompanied by nonhuman bones.

Finally, reference to the late occupation of the Khorat Plateau in the text above is concerned with the dry southern part; the wetter northern sector was the seat of the early Ban Chiang culture of which Non Nok Tha was an outlier.

The Indigenous Origins of Chinese Agriculture

PING-TI HO

1. CHRONOLOGY

Numerous archaeological finds since 1949 indicate that field agriculture and animal domestication began in China with the emergence of the first full-fledged Chinese Neolithic culture, named after the Yang-shao village in western Honan, where in 1921 the Swedish geologist J. G. Andersson discovered painted pottery and other Neolithic artifacts. In 1928 at the village of Ch'eng-tzu-yai near the capital city of Chi-nan, in Shantung Province, members of the Institute of History and Philology of the Academia Sinica discovered another Neolithic culture, characterized by black pottery and oracle bones and named after the nearest township Lung-shan. Although Yang-shao, Lung-shan, and Shang dynasty cultural remains were subsequently found in temporal succession in several northern Honan sites, the time span separating these two Neolithic cultures and their interrelationship remained matters of conjecture and debate throughout the 1930's and 1940's. The relative chronologies suggested and revised by Andersson were probably the only ones widely known in the West until 1949, but they were little more than educated and sometimes self-contradictory guesswork.

Not until the discovery in the 1950's of a series of important local and regional Neolithic cultures throughout China were archaeologists able to reclassify China's major Neolithic cultures with more systematic data. It is now reasonably clear that the newly discovered Neolithic cultures — including the Miao-ti-kou II culture of western Honan, eastern Shensi, and southern Shansi; the Ta-wen-k'ou culture of Shantung; the Ch'ing-lien-kang culture of the Huai River region and southern Kiangsu; the

Liang-chu culture of northern Chekiang; and the Ch'ü-chia-ling culture of the lower Han River valley in Hupei and southwesternmost Honan — represent a fairly long period of cultural transition from the Yang-shao to the Lung-shan stage. We now know that such Neolithic cultures as Ma-chia-yao, Pan-shan, and Ma-ch'ang, discovered by Andersson in the northwestern province of Kansu, are also transitional, both culturally and stratigraphically. The Ch'i-chia culture in Kansu, which Andersson in his revised chronology regarded as earlier than the Yang-shao culture, has now proved to be later than all the other major Neolithic cultures mentioned above.

By using the method of developmental classification, K. C. Chang, an anthropologist from Yale University, has given these newly discovered local and regional Neolithic cultures the generic name of Lungshanoid and has made the following generalization (1968:132):

Largely speaking these phases [that is, the newly discovered Miao-ti-kou II culture, and so forth] are all characterized by painted pottery but differ substantially from the Yang-shao, and the features on which they differ from the Yang-shao are similar to those of the Lung-shan. In time they were without exception demonstrably earlier than the Lung-shan cultures wherever they occurred with these cultures, but at the same time they were later than the Yang-shao within the area in which the latter occurred.

While the generic name of Lungshanoid has generally been ignored by archaeologists specializing on China, I have found it very convenient and will use it throughout this paper in the sense that Chang has defined it.

Not until after the beginning of 1972, when the Institute of Archaeology of the Academia Sinica in Peking resumed the publication of its official organ, K'ao-ku [Archaeology], did the scholarly world belatedly learn that the institute had already carried out its first series of radiocarbon age determinations in the winter of 1965–1966 and that the announcement of the results had been delayed by the Cultural Revolution. By the summer of 1973, twenty-nine radiocarbon dates had become available, of which the twenty given in Table 1 deal with China's prehistory.

While a systematic chronology for China's prehistory must await more comprehensive series of radiocarbon age determinations from Peking, the available data already yield solid information for a fresh review of the chronology and main phases of the Yang-shao culture — the first full-fledged Neolithic culture in China — and for a better understanding of the sequence in which some major regional Lungshanoid cultures emerged.

By far the most comprehensive series of radiocarbon dates is that related to the Pan-p'o phase of the Yang-shao culture. The Pan-p'o phase is of

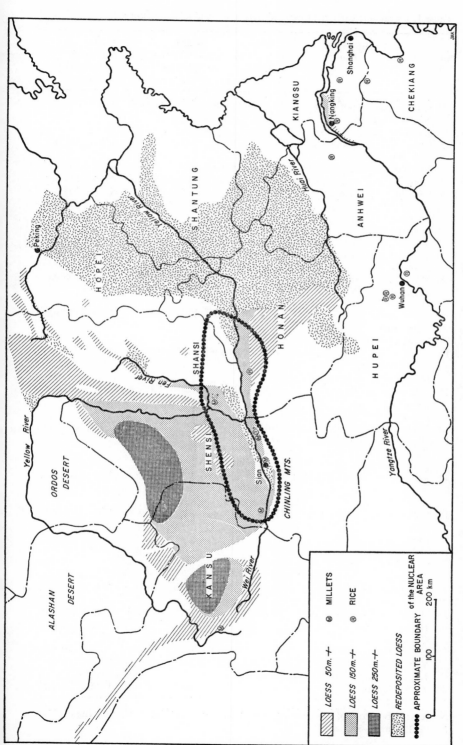

Figure 1. Map of northern China showing the nuclear area of early agriculture. Adapted from Ho (1969) by the Cartographic Laboratory, Department of Geography, University of Illinois at Chicago Circle

Table 1.   Available carbon-14 determinations for China's prehistory

Site	Culture	Carbon-14 determinations (half-life = 5,570 years)	Carbon-14 determinations (half-life = 5,730 years)	Bristlecone-pine dates (calculated by author)
1. Huang-shan-hsi, Tzu-yang, Szechwan	not clear	7275 ± 130 B.P.	7485 ± 130 B.P.	?
2. Pan-p'o, Sian, Shensi	Yang-shao	5895 ± 110 B.P.	6065 ± 110 B.P.	4865 ± 110 B.C.
3. Pan-p'o	Yang-shao	5740 ± 105 B.P.	5905 ± 105 B.P.	4555 ± 105 B.C.
4. Pan-p'o	Yang-shao	5676 ± 105 B.P.	5840 ± 105 B.P.	4490 ± 105 B.C.
5. Pan-p'o	Yang-shao	5429 ± 105 B.P.	5585 ± 105 B.P.	4235 ± 105 B.C.
6. Hou-kang, An-yang, Honan	Yang-shao	5331 ± 105 B.P.	5485 ± 105 B.P.	4135 ± 105 B.C.
7. Sung-tse, Ch'ing-p'u, Shanghai	Ch'ing-lien-kang	5195 ± 105 B.P.	5345 ± 105 B.P.	3995 ± 105 B.C.
8. Miao-ti-kou, Shan-hsien, Honan	Yang-shao	5084 ± 100 B.P.	5230 ± 100 B.P.	3880 ± 100 B.C.
9. Ch'ien-shan-yang, Wu-hsing, Chekiang	Liang-chu	4568 ± 100 B.P.	4700 ± 100 B.P.	3300 ± 100 B.C.
10. Ts'ao-chia-tsui, Lan-chou, Kansu	Ma-chia-yao	4398 ± 100 B.P.	4525 ± 100 B.P.	3125 ± 100 B.C.
11. P'ao-ma-ling, Hsiu-shui, Kiangsi	Neolithic	4165 ± 95 B.P.	4285 ± 95 B.P.	2785 ± 95 B.C.
12. Miao-ti-kou	Lungshanoid	4141 ± 95 B.P.	4260 ± 95 B.P.	2760 ± 95 B.C.
13. Huang-lien-shu, Hsi-ch'uan, Honan	Ch'ü-chia-ling	4102 ± 95 B.P.	4220 ± 95 B.P.	2720 ± 95 B.C.
14. Ma-chia-wan-ts'un, Yung-ching, Kansu	Ma-chia-yao	4019 ± 95 B.P.	4135 ± 95 B.P.	2635 ± 100 B.C.
15. Ch'ing-kang-ch'a, Lan-chou, Kansu	Pan-shan	3903 ± 95 B.P.	4015 ± 95 B P.	2415 ± 100 B.C.
16. Shuang-t'o-tzu, Lü-ta, Liaoning	Lung-shan	3898 ± 95 B.P.	4010 ± 95 B.P.	2410 ± 95 B.C.
17. Wang-wan, Lo-yang, Honan	Honan Lung-shan	3893 ± 95 B.P.	3950 ± 95 B.P.	2350 ± 95 B.C.
18. T'a-li-t'a-li-ha, No-mu-hung, Chinghai	not clear	3669 ± 90 B.P.	3775 ± 90 B.P.	2175 ± 90 B.C.
19. Ta-ho-chuang, Yung-ching, Kansu	Ch'i-chia	3572 ± 95 B.P.	3675 ± 95 B.P.	2075 ± 95 B.C.
20. Ta-ho-chuang	Ch'i-chia	3543 ± 95 B.P.	3645 ± 95 B.P.	1945 ± 95 B.C.

Sources: Laboratory of the Institute of Archaeology, Academia Sinica, Peking (1972a: 52–56, 1972b:56–58).

utmost importance for an understanding of the beginnings of Chinese civilization because it represents the earliest proven phase of field agriculture based largely on millets, of animal domestication centered mainly on pigs, of settled village communities with well-patterned grave-yards, of painted pottery, and of the archetypal Chinese script and numerals (Ho 1975). A series of four radiocarbon dates and my converted bristlecone-pine dates show that this site was occupied almost continuously for 600 years during the fifth millennium B.C.

The emergence of the mature Pan-p'o phase, however, cannot be equated with the birth of the Yang-shao culture. As will be further ex-plained in Section 3, the earliest known phase of the Yang-shao culture is that exemplified by the Li-chia-ts'un site in Hsi-hsiang County in Shensi, barely south of the natural demarcation of the Ch'in-ling Moun-tains. Although no remains of grains have so far been found in this and similar cultural sites north of the Ch'in-ling, the presence of cord-marked pottery and especially of stone spades and millstones would indicate some form of sedentary life and protoagriculture. We can be reasonably safe in assuming that the Li-chia-ts'un phase of the Yang-shao culture must have emerged some time during the sixth millennium B.C.

Almost vying with Pan-p'o in cultural importance was the type of Yang-shao culture represented by the site of Miao-ti-kou in western Honan. This type was characterized chiefly by the unique dynamic floral spiral motifs of its painted pottery and was geographically dis-tributed over westernmost Honan, southern Shansi and the lower Wei River valley east of Sian in Shensi. The temporal and historical relation-ship between the Pan-p'o and the Miao-ti-kou types has been a subject of considerable debate since the late 1950's. Not until radiocarbon dates were available did we learn that the Miao-ti-kou type was considerably later. In fact, it was even slightly later than the Hou-kang type, in northern Honan, which revealed strong Pan-p'o influence but also had distinct local characteristics. The latest data also show that the Pan-p'o type spread more widely than the Miao-ti-kou type, reaching as far as northern Honan and southern and western Hopei (Ho 1975: Chapter 1, Section 1).

As to the various regional cultures that were later than Yang-shao and that have been called "Lungshanoid" for convenience by Chang, recent radiocarbon datings show that they were chronologically dis-parate rather than roughly contemporaneous. Long before the Yang-shao culture had run its course, the Ch'ing-lien-kang culture had already emerged in eastern China. On the basis of published reports as well as new data not yet released by the Nanking Museum, Wu Shan-ching has arrived at the following generalizations about the Ch'ing-lien-kang culture (Wu 1973). First, of some four score of Ch'ing-lien-kang cultural sites so far discovered, sixty-five are within the boundaries of Kiangsu Province. From Kiangsu this culture spread westward to parts of Anhwei, northward to southern and central Shantung, and southward to northern Chekiang, where it later merged with the Liang-chu culture. The total area within the orbit of the Ch'ing-lien-kang culture is approximately 100,000 square kilometers. Second, the Ch'ing-lien-kang culture can be divided into the northern and southern types. The northern type consisted of four phases and the southern type consisted of three phases. Stratigraphically and culturally the three phases of the southern type can be synchronized with the first three phases of the northern type. Third, the early phase of the northern type, exemplified by the lowest cultural stratum of the Ta-tun-tzu site in P'ei-hsien, northern Kiangsu, has recently been radiocarbon dated at 5625 ± 105 B.P. The bristlecone-pine date should be 4450 ± 105 B.C. No radiocarbon age determination has been carried out for the lowest cultural stratum of the Ma-chia-pin site in Chia-hsing, northeastern Chekiang, which best typifies the early phase of the southern type. The only available radiocarbon date for the likely late stage of the early phase of the southern type, represented by the lowest cultural stratum of the Sung-tse site near Shanghai, is 5185 ± 105 B.P. (bristlecone-pine date: 3995 ± 105 B.C.). In Wu's opinion, a difference of 455 years provided by these two dates is more likely to represent the approximate duration of the early phase of both the northern and southern types rather than to indicate the earlier emergence of the northern types.

Equally unexpected is the early emergence of the Liang-chu culture in northern Chekiang around 3000 B.C. (bristlecone-pine date), a culture which was generally believed to have appeared considerably later than those more northerly regional Lungshanoid cultures. As will be discussed in following sections, the Ch'ing-lien-kang and Liang-chu dates are important in establishing the beginnings of rice culture and in providing clues for early domestication of cattle and water buffalo in eastern-central China.

The other regional Lungshanoid and Lung-shan cultures arose between the late fourth and the late third millennium B.C. The two dates for the Aeneolithic Ch'i-chia culture in Kansu are fairly close to the beginning of the Shang dynasty, the first authenticated historical period in Chinese history. The results of my recent critique of the methodology for determining the Shang and Chou chronologies incline me to believe that the Shang dynasty began around 1600 B.C. and that the Western Chou period definitely began in 1027 B.C. (Ho 1975). While we will need many more series of radiocarbon determinations to date the various phases and types of the Lungshanoid and Lung-shan cultures, we can at least begin our study of the origins of Chinese agriculture from 7000 B.P.

2. PALEOENVIRONMENT

The homeland of the proto-Chinese of the Yang-shao period was the southeastern part of the loess highlands, which consists of the entire Wei River valley in central Shensi, southern Shansi, and western Honan. From the geological point of view, this Yang-shao nuclear area may be regarded as a "classic" loess area. Here, not only are the loess deposits unusually thick, but the fine particles that make up the loessic soil are exceptionally homogeneous in texture. This exceptional textural homogeneity can be explained only by the high probability that wind, rather than any other natural agent, transported the loess material from far and near and deposited it during long periods of desiccation that characterized the Pleistocene climate of northern China (Liu Tung-sheng, et al. 1965). Indeed, recurrent deposition of loess by the wind on various parts of northern China is well attested by 3,000 years of Chinese historical records (Wang Chia-yin 1965:1–8).

During the past 1,000,000 years there have been four periods of desiccation interrupted by three periods of relative abundance of rain. During the comparatively rainy periods erosion on a large scale took place; as a result, the loess material was carried by water from higher grounds to the low plains of northern China. Although the causes of the formation of the loess of the low plains are highly complex, much of the soil of this area is of alluvial and diluvial origin. In many localities in the low plains the soil contains a mixture of pebbles, gravels, and conglomerates. In contrast, the loess of the highland area, which is largely of aeolian origin, is texturally uniform, fine, friable, and porous, and hence offered much less resistance to primitive wooden digging sticks. This may have been one of the reasons why, in spite of more arid climatic conditions, the highland area of loess was the cradle of Chinese Neolithic culture.

The climate of northern China is severe, noted for its icy winters, hot summers, and frequent spring sandstorms. The average rainfall of the loess highlands is between 250 and 500 millimeters (slightly less than 10 and 20 inches). The average rainfall of the low plains is between 400 and 750 millimeters. The 750-millimeter rainfall line generally marks the southern and eastern boundaries of the redeposited loess. An annual rainfall of between 10 and 20 inches, if evenly distributed over the four seasons, should meet the minimal requirements of ordinary dry-land farming. But in the loess area much of the rain is concentrated in the summer, when the temperature and the rate of evaporation are both very high. While the concentration of the rain in summer is favorable to the growth of certain drought-resistant cereal plants like millet, it made other types of farming very difficult, at least in prehistoric times. Besides, because much of northern China lies on the margins of the two main rain-producing systems of warm-season monsoons and cool-season cyclonic storms, the loess area is a semiarid region.

During the past few decades there has been considerable controversy about the paleoclimate of northern China. The latest opinion on the subject, based on many-sided scientific investigations of the Chinese loess, is that, despite the alternations between very dry and relatively wet periods during the entire Pleistocene, the long-range climatic tendency has been one of periodic and probably progressive desiccation (Lee 1939: 371; Liu Tung-sheng, et al. 1965).

The arid conditions in which the loess was formed are best reflected in the physical and chemical properties of the soil. As is well known, soils of humid regions are well weathered, leached, and acidic, whereas soils of dry belts are little weathered, unleached, and alkaline. The loess of the highland area of China has undergone little weathering, has retained much of its original mineral content, and is almost invariably alkaline. After meticulous comparison with the loess of several European countries, Chinese geologists concluded that the Chinese loess was formed under climatic conditions more arid than those prevailing during the formation of the loess in Europe (Liu Tung-sheng, et al. 1965:141–227).

For the sake of studying climatic changes in northern China during the Pleistocene, Chinese geologists in recent years have paid much attention to the various layers of reddish soil buried in the thick loess deposits. The buried soil is of considerable scientific interest, because only under conditions of above-normal warmth and humidity could the loess be weathered into reddish soil. Yet a systematic analysis of various samples of the reddish soil taken from the loess profile of Li-shih County, Shansi Province, shows pH values ranging from 7.5 to 8.8 (Liu and Chang 1962:2, Table 1). In other words, the buried soil is still moderately or fairly strongly alkaline. What is even more revealing is the composition of the pollen found in the uppermost layer of the buried soil in a loess profile of Wu-ch'eng County, Shansi. This particular layer lies between 10.6 and 12.9 meters under the surface, a stratum that should represent a "humid" subperiod of a rather recent geological age. Of forty-seven grains of pollen found in the stratum, only four are arboreal (one *Abies*, three *Pinus*); the remaining forty-three are accounted for by the single genus of *Artemisia* (Liu and Chang 1962:6, Table 2), one of the best botanical indicators of an arid or semiarid environment. In discussions of the paleoclimate of northern China, therefore, the word "pluvial" must be used with caution and only in a relative sense.

Of all the scientific factors relating to the paleoenvironment of northern China, the most puzzling is the faunal assemblage, which runs the whole gamut from animals of tundral and subarctic habitats, such as the woolly rhinoceros (*Coelodonta antiquitatis*) and the mammoth (*Mammuthus primigenius*), to animals of warm habitats, such as the elephant (*Eelephas maximus*) and the ordinary rhinoceros (*Rhinoceros* sp.). Some scholars today would still use the presence of remains of the elephant and the rhinoceros as evidence with which to argue that the paleoenvironment of northern China must have been warm and humid at certain times in the past. This argument can be offset easily by an equally partial listing of woolly rhinoceroses and mammoths, normally of subarctic habitats, or of camels and ostriches, now confined almost exclusively to desert and semidesert areas. Besides, many fossils of elephants and rhinoceroses found in northern China during the early decades of this century were not accompanied by detailed stratigraphic reports, with the result that they were wrongly attributed to various strata of loess. A recent systematic reexamination of the relevant verified paleontological data shows that fossils of elephants and rhinoceroses almost always came from lacustrine beds, which were formed during periods of erosion and which are as a rule unconformably overlain by deposits of loess. After considering all aspects of the faunal data, a leading synthesist of the Chinese loess concludes that ever since the mid-Pleistocene the faunal assemblage of the loess area has been dominated by species of rodents, especially *Myospalax* sp., a clear indication of a semiarid steppe environment (Liu, et al. 1965:115–132).

Probably the most remarkable recent advance in the study of the paleoenvironment of the loess region lies in the field of palynology. To my knowledge, there are at least ten pollen studies relating to northern China (for a complete listing see Ho 1969a:7, note 12). The one study that deals with the pollen composition of the P'u-lan-tien site in the Liaotung Peninsula obviously reflects ancient maritime climatic conditions, but the remaining nine studies all throw important light on the paleoenvironments of both the loess highland and the low plain areas of northern China. By far the most useful study is the one that deals with the pollen composition of an entire loess profile of Liu-shu-kou, Wu-ch'eng County, Shansi. This is because few localities can offer a more complete loess profile than Wu-ch'eng, a name that in recent years has been used by Chinese geologists to exemplify all strata of the loess deposited during the early Pleistocene. Unlike other studies of the pollen of northern China, which deal with certain specific periods of the Pleistocene epoch, the Wu-ch'eng study covers the past 1,000,000 years. The entire Wu-ch'eng profile of 121 meters is divided, for palynological study, into as many as 106 strata, so that vegetational and implied climatic changes can be studied in minute detail. Because this paper is concerned mainly with the vegetation and climate of the geological period nearest to the dawning of Chinese agriculture, I have tabulated separately the pollen of the loess profile of the upper twenty meters (Table 2).

Table 2.   Analysis of the pollen of the loess profile of Wu-ch'eng

Plant	Total number of pollen grains (1–20 meters)	Total number of pollen grains (20–121 meters)	Total number of pollen grains (entire profile, 1–121 meters)
A. Arboreal			
Abies	2	0	2
Pinus	15	13	28
Cupressaceae	3	0	3
Juglans	0	3	3
Carpinus	0	3	3
Quercus	2	6	8
Ulmus	0	1	1
Morus	2	0	2
Acer	0	1	1
Ephadra	0	2	2
Salix	7	12	19
Corylus	2	0	2
Total (Arboreal)	33	41	74
B. Nonarboreal			
Typha	1	1	2
Gramineae	56	118	174
Cyperaceae	3	3	6
Humulus	3	16	19
Chenopodiaceae	18	58	76
Caryophyllaceae	1	1	2
Clematis	48	5	53
Convolvulus	14	0	14
Compositae	32	45	77
Dicotyledoneae	72	1	73
Artemisia	722	330	1,052
Total (Nonarboreal)	970	578	1,548
Total (A and B)	1,003	619	1,622

Note: In the original table *Filicales* and *Bryales* constituted a small separate category. Because this category was not counted in the original table, I omit these two genera entirely from the summary. Source: Liu and Chang (1962).

Table 2 reveals several important aspects of the paleoenvironment of the loess highland. First, the fact that trees and shrubs account for merely 74 of the 1,622 grains of pollen testifies that this area was, much as it is today, rather meager in forest resources. The relative significance of *Pinus* (pines) and *Salix* (willows), which account for 47 of a total of 74 arboreal pollen grains, should be briefly discussed. Pine pollen, with its two air sacks, can travel a long distance from its mountainous habitat, and willows generally grow along edges of water. In other words, the overall meager forest resources and the likely special habitats of the two numerically significant groups of trees would indicate that the level areas of the semiarid steppe were little, if at all, forested.

Second, the most striking phenomenon in the pollen profile is the overwhelming predominance of herbaceous plants, which account for 1,548 grains of pollen, or 95.4 percent of the total. There can be little doubt that the loess highland area, except for mountains, hills, slopes, and places near watercourses, has always been a nonwooded steppe. The fact that *Artemisia* alone accounts for as much as 64.8 percent of the pollen emphatically reflects the ecology of a semiarid steppe.

Third, whereas *Artemisia* represents 53.3 percent of the pollen found deeper than twenty meters, it represents 71.8 percent of the pollen found in the upper twenty meters. This sharp increase in the percentage of *Artemisia* indicates that the climate in the late Pleistocene epoch was becoming cooler and drier.

Fourth, next to *Artemisia* the most significant groups of herbaceous plants are the family of Gramineae, which consists of many kinds of weeds later domesticated by men as food crops, and the family of Chenopodiaceae, which consists of a large number of spinachlike plants sometimes used as vegetables and often grown by primitive men for their seeds (Hedrick 1919:160–161). Gramineae account for 10.7 percent of the pollen total and are fairly well distributed chronologically throughout the past million years. In the light of archaeological and literary evidence concerning the earliest Chinese crops, the prevalence of Gramineae cannot be interpreted as an indication that a wide range of potential food plants has existed since the early Pleistocene; on the contrary, it indicates the existence of rather few kinds of potential cereal plants which, in spite of the prolonged and relentless struggle against such xerophytic plants as *Artemisia* and Chenopodiaceae, had survived in a semiarid area in sufficient quantities to be utilized eventually by the Yang-shao farmers.

The main characteristics of the paleoenvironment revealed in Table 2 are corroborated not only by studies of pollen profiles gathered from other localities in northern China (except the one in the Liaotung Peninsula) but also by the botanical records preserved in ancient Chinese literary works. Of all the literary works, *The book of odes (Shih-ching)* contains by far the most extensive botanical records. Sinologists the world over agree on the authenticity and textual excellence of this ancient work, which illuminates the life of the Chinese from the late eleventh to the middle of the sixth century B.C. While this anthology of 305 songs and odes collected from the Chou royal domain and the feudal states mentions fewer than 150 plants, a number that is infinitesimal compared with the number of species known to botanists today, in contrast to the Bible and the works of the ancient Egyptians, Homer, and Herodotus — in which respectively only 83, 55, 60, and 63 plants were known and mentioned (Kanngiesser 1912:81) — *The book of odes* is really a mine of information for historians and botanists. For a majority of cases, moreover, *The book of odes* (Karlgren 1950b) states the type of topography in which a plant grows — mountain, plain, wet lowland near water, marsh, pond, or river. The geographic areas covered by the 305 songs and odes are Shensi, Shansi, and Honan provinces, the Han River valley down to the middle Yangtze valley, western and central Shantung, northwestern Anhwei, and southern Hopei. It is fortunate that this ancient work's botanical records on the southeastern part of the loess highland are especially comprehensive.

Using archaic Chinese written records to check recent scientific findings on the loess area, I have identified, analyzed, and tabulated all the arboreal and nonarboreal plants in *The book of odes* except the aquatic plants and cereals, as my concern is the ancient "natural" vegetation. I have supplemented the botanical data of *The book of odes* with information culled from various classics — historical, geographical, and philosophical works written or compiled mostly before and during the Former Han period (206 B.C.–8 A.D.) — and from *Wen-hsüan* — the earliest extant comprehensive literary anthology, compiled during the first half of the sixth century A.D. By comparing literary records with modern scientific findings, I have reached the following conclusions (Ho 1969a: 35–84, especially Table 3 [42–55] and Table 4 [57–64]).

First, there has been little, if any, truly significant change in the composition of northern China's forest since the late Pleistocene epoch, and deciduous trees have always outnumbered the conifers.

Second, an examination of the habitats of trees and shrubs mentioned in *The book of odes* reveals that these plants were virtually confined to mountains, hills, slopes, and places near watercourses. In other words, apart from the uneven seasonal distribution of rain and the high evaporation in summer, the level loess areas of northern China do not seem to have been able to retain enough water for the growth of trees and shrubs. The statements made by the late V. K. Ting, founder of the China Geological Survey, in his famous review of Marcel Granet's *La civilisation chinoise*, which depicts the loess highland as a dense woodland dotted with marshes, are largely valid and still worth citing as a corrective to some recent writings on China's paleoenvironment:

Now all geologists agree that in the loess there has never been any forestation. ... The water table is so low that even today trees planted in the loess need to be watered in their young stages until the roots become sufficiently deep. ... It is not denied that forests existed on mountain slopes, but the loess area has always been a semi-steppe. Marshes exist even today in the alluvial plains, but most of Professor Granet's marshes lay in loess-land (Ting 1931).

My only revision of Ting's view is that the Wei River basin in Shensi even today has marshes, caused by poor drainage owing to special physiographic factors (Kuan 1965). In spite of climatic conditions that cannot be regarded as humid, the poorly drained areas in the low plains abounded in marshes and peat bogs, some of which are known to have been formed during late prehistoric and early historic times.

Third, it is by no means coincidental that *The book of odes* provides an eloquent testimonial to the predominance of *Artemisia* on the loess plains; this can be gauged from the number of its varietal names and from its frequency of occurrence. The single genus of *Artemisia*, with ten varietal names, leads all the plants recorded in this ancient work, arboreal and nonarboreal, by a wide margin. In terms of the number of times various plants appear in the songs and odes, *Artemisia* is barely exceeded by mulberry, at a ratio of nineteen to twenty, and followed by the *shu* and *chi* subspecies of millet (*Panicum miliaceum*), which appear in fifteen and twelve odes, respectively. Because *P. miliaceum* was the most important source of food for the ancient Chinese and because mulberry was so vital to sericulture and was extensively grown in many parts of northern China in Shang-Chou times, the fact that weeds of the genus *Artemisia* receive such prominent mention in *The book of odes* is an unmistakable indication that the loess area was a semiarid steppe.

Fourth, while *The book of odes* mentions Chenopodiaceae only twice, the combined evidence of other ancient works shows their prevalence on the loess plains. Unless weeds of the family of Chenopodiaceae were truly endemic, it would be hard for modern scholars to explain why in Chou times, if not still earlier, the fallow land was generally called *lai* [Chenopodiaceae] and virgin soil *ts'ao-lai* [literally 'grasses and Chenopodiaceae'] (Ho 1969a:80–85). The accuracy of the aggregate ancient literary records concerning the prevalence of Chenopodiaceae is borne out by a recent analysis of a pollen profile gathered from the famous Yang-shao cultural site of Pan-p'o. Of a total of 278 pollen grains found in a Yang-shao cultural stratum 2.8 meters deep, arboreal pollen grains account for only 40, but Chenopodiaceae and *Artemisia* account for 141 and 38 respectively (Chou K'un-shu 1963).

The main characteristics of the ancient vegetation of the loess plains revealed in archaic Chinese literature, therefore, concur remarkably well with those of recent palynological studies. If we take into account such major factors as the climatic conditions under which the loess was deposited, the physical and chemical properties of the loessial soil, the predominance of typical steppe animals in the faunal assemblage, the relative sparsity of arboreal plants, and the preponderance of such xerophytic and halophytic plants as *Artemisia* and Chenopodiaceae in both geological and early historical times, it is difficult not to arrive at the conclusion that the natural environment of the loess highland, in ancient and modern times, has always been one of a semiarid steppe.

It is important for scholars interested in the origins of Chinese agriculture to keep in mind that, although the natural environment of the loess highland has been unquestionably harsh, it nevertheless has had certain advantages. Precisely because of its aeolian origin and the prolonged arid and semiarid conditions in which the loess was formed, the soil is unusually homogeneous in texture, friable, and porous, and was amenable to primitive wooden digging sticks. There is reason to believe that the grass cover of the loess highland has never been as dense as that usually found in other major steppe and forest-steppe belts of Eurasia. Significantly, while "the most current surface rocks [of the forest-steppe zone of the Soviet Union] are loess and loesslike formations," the characteristic soils of this belt are blackish "meadow-chernozem" and those of Russia's "steppe zone" are the classic dark chernozem, an indication of a much denser cover of grass (Rode 1962:364). William McNeill, a leading synthesist of world history, is certainly right in pointing out that agriculture in the Old World first appeared, as a rule, on wooded slopes and foothills because "natural grassland offered stubborn resistance to the wooden digging sticks" (1963:16). That the only major exception in the Old World is Yang-shao China is substantially explained by the peculiar property of the loess and its relatively sparse cover of grass. Because the loess is little weathered, it has retained most of its minerals and is therefore very fertile. In spite of a limited annual rainfall of less than twenty inches, its concentration in summer enabled the Yang-shao farmers to grow successfully the few kinds of cereals that survived the prolonged process of natural selection in a semiarid environment. Besides, loess generally has excellent water-holding and water-yielding capacity; good growth can be expected with less rainfall than on other soils. All in all, therefore, the natural environment of the nuclear area in which Chinese agriculture and Neolithic culture occurred definitely imposed certain restrictions on its early inhabitants, but a limited range of opportunities peculiar probably only to China's loess highland partially compensated for these restrictions.

In addition to the peculiarities of the natural environment of the loess highland, which had so much to do with setting the pattern of Yang-shao agriculture, the earliest Chinese agricultural system was also characterized by its freedom from the influence of the great flood plain of the lower Yellow River and, as a corollary, by the absence of primitive irrigation.

In the early decades of this century, little was known about China's prehistory. Scholars generally believed that the cradle of Chinese civilization was probably the great flood plain of the Yellow River because, among other things, since the turn of the nineteenth century tens of thousands of oracle bones had been unearthed in An-yang, a locality in northernmost Honan that lies within the area of the low plains. In the West this view was systematically expounded by the late Henri Maspero (1927:20–26) and has gained currency among Western scholars through Arnold Toynbee's monumental synthesis of history (1934:318–321). During the past twenty years, so many Neolithic sites have been discovered and excavated and so much more about the general sequence of major Chinese Neolithic cultures has become known that there can be no doubt that the cradle of Chinese civilization is the southeastern portion of the loess highland, an area that has little in common with the great flood plain of the lower Yellow River.

From generalized and specific descriptions given in numerous archaeological reports on northern Chinese sites that belong to the Yang-shao, Lungshanoid, Lung-shan, and other prehistoric cultures, the following facts have clearly emerged. Most of such sites, in the loess highland as well as the low plains, are loess terraces or mounds along various tributaries of the Yellow River rather than along the great river itself. A closer examination of these sites shows that most are clustered along numerous small rivers and streams that often do not appear even on detailed general maps of China and are known only locally. This is important testimony confirming that the birth of China owed little to the Yellow River itself, although in theory these numerous small rivers and streams are within the drainage of the Yellow River (Ho 1969a:107–117).

There are, to be sure, a few score prehistoric sites in Kansu, north-western and southwestern Shansi, and western Honan that are along the upper and middle course of the Yellow River itself. Topographically, however, these sites are exactly like all the rest: loess terraces or mounds of varying altitudes ranging from fifteen or twenty to hundreds of feet above riverbeds. All prehistoric sites of northern China are, in other words, close to water, but they are also sufficiently high to be safe from floods. The elevated terraces and mounds provide the best argument against the possibility of irrigation before the invention of sophisticated water wheels and water pumps.

Although the generalized descriptions of the environments of more than a thousand Neolithic sites already imply the impossibility of irrigation in very early times, I shall present positive evidence that irrigation arrived late in China. It is true that ditches and trenches have been discovered at the Yang-shao site of Pan-p'o near Sian and also at Hsiao-t'un in An-yang, the last Shang capital, but the supervising Chinese archaeologists believe that the main trench of the Pan-p'o site was dug for defense, and the smaller ditches (which all pass through the residential area) cannot possibly have been used for irrigation (*Hsi-an Pan-p'o* 1963:52). The more elaborate network of ditches of Hsiao-t'un, which cuts through much of the ensemble of royal palaces, royal ancestral halls, residences, and workshops, is clearly for drainage (Shih Chang-ju 1959:268). Indeed, in an extensive study of relevant inscriptions on Shang oracle bones, Yü Hsing-wu, a Chinese paleographer, was struck by the Shang people's fear of floodwater and general ignorance of diking, water conservancy, and irrigation (1957b:103–104).

The first account of the construction of ditches in the fields, probably for irrigation, is given in the *Tso-chuan* [Chronicles of the Feudal States]. It declares that some time after Tzu-ssu's appointment as the chief minister of the Cheng state in north-central Honan in 571 B.C., "in laying out the ditches through the fields, [he] had occasioned the loss of fields" to five aristocratic clans; consequently Tzu-ssu was assassinated in 563 B.C. by a band of "ruffians" instigated by the five clans. While the exact year of construction of these ditches is not given, it is likely to be nearer 563 B.C. than 571 B.C. This abortive irrigation project was resumed some twenty years later by Tzu-ch'an, the most famous Cheng statesman. In so doing, he first incurred the wrath of the people, but three years later he won their high praises when the benefits of irrigation became known. Unless irrigation had been novel and little known, these two high officials would not have encountered such initial resistance. The *Tso-chuan* further states that in 548 B.C. the powerful Ch'u state of the central Yangtze began "enumerating the boundaries of flooded districts [and] raising small banks on the plains between dykes" (Legge 1873: 447–448, 558, 517).

The late beginnings of irrigation are further reflected in the scale of the first famous irrigation network, completed by the Wei state between 424 and 296 B.C. in the Chang River area in northern Honan. From the meticulous description in the *Shui-ching-chu* [Commentaries on the Classics of Waterways] of the fifth century A.D., we learn that this whole irrigation system was only twenty *li* in length, a little more than five miles (Yu Yü 1959). Not until the third century B.C. did large irrigation networks appear in the Wei River basin in Shensi and in the Red Basin in Szechwan.

Clearly, the rise of Chinese agriculture and civilization bore no direct relationship whatever to the flood plain of the Yellow River, and of all the ancient peoples who gave birth to higher civilizations in the Old and the New World, the Chinese were the last to know irrigation. As MacNeish (1967) showed in a comprehensive survey of the origins of agriculture in the New World, irrigation began in Mesoamerica around 2750 B.P., nearly 4,000 years later than irrigation in Mesopotamia, yet still slightly earlier than irrigation in China. Insofar as ancient China is concerned, Karl A. Wittfogel's theory (1957) of an "hydraulic" genesis of culture or of "despotism," which for years has had an irresistible appeal to the intellectually unwary, is completely without foundation. Chinese civilization arose in the semiarid loess highland, where the Yang-shao farmers practiced dry-land farming.

3. FIELD AGRICULTURE

Prior to an analysis of the main characteristics of the Yang-shao agricultural system, it seems pertinent to discuss and speculate briefly on the ethnic and geographic origins of the Yang-shao people. That the Yang-shao people were proto-Chinese is seldom disputed, but little is known about whence they came. So far only two British scholars, Roxby (1938) and Smalley (1968), have explicitly speculated on the geographic origin of the Yang-shao people. They both believed that during the postglacial period, the Yang-shao people moved into the southeastern part of the loess highland from the north. They suggested that the main reason was that, in the millennia immediately preceding the appearance of the Yang-shao people in the loess highland, much of the southern half of China was covered by glaciers. They proposed that the sudden burst of the Yang-shao culture resulted primarily because "people moving in from the north were presented with a challenge offered by the loess deposit; they responded to their challenging opportunity by settling and developing a civilization" (Smalley 1968).

The hypothesis of northern origins of the Yang-shao people would be partially validated if existing scientific data could prove that glaciation was confined to the southern half of China and that it was of such "continental" type as to make human habitation in the south extremely difficult. But available scientific data indicate rather that glaciation in China was not of the continental type, that it was confined mostly to mountains, and that mountain glaciers occurred in both northern and southern China (Sun and Yang 1961). Of the 1,120 localities where glaciers and vestiges of glaciers have been found in China in recent decades, more than 30 percent are located in the upper half of China north of the Ch'in-ling mountain range (Liu, et al. 1964).

There are other basic scientific facts that indicate the repeated occurrences of mountain glaciers but the absence of continental ice sheets in China during the Pleistocene. In many localities in northern and southern China are soils that have been developed from rocks of the Cretaceous (140,000,000 to 65,000,000 years ago) and Tertiary (65,000,000 to 1,800,000 years ago). Because polyglaciation was strictly a recent geological phenomenon confined to the last million years, the existence in many places in China of soils that were developed long before the onset of the great Ice Age is important evidence that glaciers in China were limited largely to mountains and that the country as a whole was never covered by continental ice sheets (Chou and Liu 1956).

Phytogeographic evidence testifies even more strongly against the view that the southern half of China was several times sealed in ice during the Pleistocene. A Chinese botanist has summarized the main phytographic characteristic of the southern half of China:

The extraordinary richness of the ligneous flora of eastern Asia is a well-known fact. In China alone no less than 959 genera of woody plants were reported in 1935. This exceeds in number of genera of all the rest of the North Temperate Zone [in the world] and is more than three times the number [313] found in North America, floristically a closely related region. Recent discoveries may possibly bring the total to nearly a thousand. ... The richness of the flora of eastern Asia, especially China, is due to its great diversity in topographic, climatic, and ecologic conditions. Historically, the absence of extensive glaciation during the Pleistocene permits the preservation of a large number of genera formerly extensively distributed but which later became extinct in other parts of the world (Li 1953).

Because of the occurrences of continental ice sheets in the temperate zones of other continents in the northern hemisphere and their absence in China, a number of so-called relict plants have survived only in China, having become extinct elsewhere. *Ginkgo biloba*, the lone survivor of an entire order of gymnosperms, and *Metasequoia*, the unique primeval relict conifer, are but the most famous of the "living fossils" that testify to the absence of continental ice sheets in China (Li 1948, 1964).

The above scientific data provide reason to believe that during the last glacial epoch the valleys, basins, and lowlands south of the Ch'in-ling are likely to have been more genial to the early men than were the northerly areas, in terms of climate and especially of available natural resources for human sustenance.

Our view that the Yang-shao people may have entered the loess highland from somewhere south of the Ch'in-ling is supported in the main by evidence from physical anthropology. In recent years a significant number of human skeletons unearthed from Yang-shao cultural sites at Pan-p'o, Pao-chi, and Hua-hsien in the Wei River valley in Shensi have been studied (Yen, et al. 1960a, 1960b, 1962). When their physical features are compared with those of other divisions of the Mongoloids, the Yang-shao people are seen to resemble most closely the modern Chinese of the southern half of China and the modern Indo-Chinese, and then the modern Chinese of northern China. They have physical features markedly different from those of the Eskimos of Alaska, the Tungus of Manchuria, the Tibetans, and the Mongoloids of the Lake Baikal area. According to the Soviet anthropological terminology adopted by mainland Chinese scholars, the Yang-shao Chinese are classified under the "Pacific branch of the Mongoloids" or under the "Southern Mongoloid race" and are distinguished from the prehistoric Mongoloid peoples of the Lake Baikal area and the proto-Tungus of Manchuria, who are classified under the "Northern Mongoloid" group. This basic physical anthropological fact concurs well with linguistic evidence that from time immemorial the Chinese language has been fundamentally different from the agglutinative tongues spoken by various "Northern Mongoloid" ethnic groups who belong to the Altaic language family. Both anthropological and linguistic evidence point to the "southern" affiliations of the Yang-shao people.

An equally strong type of evidence for these "southern" affiliations is artifactual and cultural. V. Y. Larichev, one of the very few Soviet scholars at home with both northeastern Asian and Chinese archaeology, has discussed the characteristics of Yang-shao artifacts in the context of Asian prehistory:

The most striking trait of the stone artifacts of the Yangshao culture, apart from their typological uniqueness, is the prevalence of polished tools. The people of this culture did not know the techniques of flaking and chipping. In manufacturing axes, spear points, and arrowheads, and ploughs, sickles, and punch awls, they used the grinding method. This demonstrates the specific cultural traditions and sources of the Yangshao culture, which are not related to the north where the percussion technique was prevalent but to the south and the eastern maritime regions of China (Larichev 1964).

While crude chipping techniques were known to the Yang-shao Chinese, Larichev's comparative typological statement remains generally true.

By far the most definite evidence on the southern cultural affiliations of the Yang-shao people is the cultural sequence recently established by Chinese archaeologists in which the earliest phase of the Yang-shao culture is exemplified by the artifactual complex of the Li-chia-ts'un site in Hsi-hsiang County, Shensi, on the southern side of the Ch'in-ling Mountains. At Li-chia-ts'un many of the pottery shapes are similar to those of other Yang-shao sites, but there are two important differences, namely, the prevalence of the cord-marked pottery and the absence of the painted pottery. In a number of Yang-shao cultural sites in the Wei River basin north of the Ch'in-ling and in western Honan, the stratum containing the Li-chia-ts'un type of pottery lies immediately beneath the strata containing the characteristic Yang-shao painted pottery (Hsia 1964; Su 1965).

Because the earliest pottery along the Pacific coast of eastern and southeastern Asia and in many parts of the southern half of China is invariably cord marked, and because Li-chia-ts'un is on the southern side of the Ch'in-ling demarcation and on the upper Han River, which links Shensi with the central Yangtze, the certain southern cultural heritage of the Yang-shao people can no longer be much doubted. While this probable southern cultural heritage does not detract from the important fact that the Yang-shao culture as a whole was unquestionably a product of the loess highland, it does help to explain why the Yang-shao culture had so little in common with Microlithic cultures that flourished from Manchuria through the Inner Mongolian steppe to westernmost Kansu and Sinkiang from pre-Yang-shao times to the early historical periods.

Because the vast areas south of the Ch'in-ling are archaeologically much less extensively surveyed than is the loess highland, the cultural evolution of the Yang-shao people prior to the full flowering of the Pan-p'o phase is little known. The artifacts of the Li-chia-ts'un site include cord-marked pottery, stone axes, adzes, spades, chisels, sinkers, and millstones. Stone axes, adzes, and chisels suggest wood cutting and wood dressing; stone sinkers suggest deepwater fishing; spades and millstones suggest some protohorticultural or protoagricultural activity, the exact mode of which is impossible to tell. The use of pottery also suggests that the people enjoyed a certain degree of "settled" life. Conceivably, certain areas south of the Ch'in-ling but adjacent to the Yang-shao heartland in the Wei River basin — southern Shensi, northern Szechwan, and the middle course of the Han River — may someday yield important clues to the phase of increasingly efficient food collection that preceded the appearance of field agriculture in the loess highland from the Pan-p'o phase onward.

If we know so little about the positive attributes of the prior cultural evolution of the Yang-shao people, we can at least offer some basic reasons why the areas south of the Ch'in-ling were much less conducive to the rise of field agriculture and full-fledged settled village community than was the loess area immediately to their north. It is true that much richer flora and fauna south of the Ch'in-ling encouraged more intensive food gathering and food collecting. However, these areas presented the early men with two great difficulties, namely, forests that covered hills and mountains and the heavy clay soils of the southern plains that were covered by forests and sometimes by luxuriant grass. While many primitive peoples could clear forest by barking and burning, one peculiar trait of prehistoric and early historic Chinese was their unwillingness to destroy forestry by such a simple and wanton method (Ho 1969a: 85–106). Obviously, the heavy clay soils of various southern plains also offered much greater resistance to primitive agricultural implements. The difficulties that confronted prehistoric Chinese in developing field agriculture in areas south of the Ch'in-ling can be better understood in the light of knowledge of other primitive agricultures. Jack R. Harlan (personal communication) has pointed out: "In Africa where hoe agriculture is practiced, the heavy soils are avoided altogether or may be worked by burning the grass and transplanting seedlings at the end of the rainy season." His broader generalization is even more helpful: "Contrary to some popular ideas, agriculture in the wet tropics and subtropics is difficult and as far as we know rather late in development."

In our long-range historical perspective, the foundation of the world's most persistently self-sustaining agricultural system, which has had so much to do with the enduring character of Chinese civilization, was laid in the Yang-shao nuclear area from 5000 B.C. onward. This remarkably self-sustaining agriculture was an outcome of the response of the Yang-shao people to a natural environment that was in some ways restrictive but in one peculiar way uniquely favorable. The environment was restrictive in terms of extremities of climate, light rainfall, relative scarcity of plant resources, and rather dissected land forms. The susceptibility of the loess to erosion and its capacity to form vertical walls have accounted for the prevalence in the Wei River basin and elsewhere in the loess highland of deep and often ramified gullies and ravines, with small flat areas between them. What the natives of this region since at least early Chou times have called the *yüan* "plains" are but small and comparatively level areas of land bounded by gullies, ravines, riverside terraces, and mounds. The Yang-shao farmers made their debut on such numerous riverside terraces and mounds. Not only does the topography where Yang-shao cultivation began differ from those where other ancient agricultural systems of the Old World arose, but also the highly dissected land forms were hardly conducive to the practice of the classic type of "slash-and-burn," "swidden," or "shifting" agriculture characteristic of the tropics.

The single most important natural endowment of this area, which on balance more than offsets its natural disadvantages, is the loess. With a sense of history rare among pioneering investigators of the loess, Raphael Pumpelly, an American geologist who led an archaeological expedition to Russian Turkestan in 1904, pointed out the important role played by the loess soil in the history of man, with special reference to the loess of China:

Its fertility seems to be inexhaustible, a quality it owes partly, as [Ferdinand von] Richthofen remarks, to its depth and texture, partly to the salts brought to the surface after rains by capillary attraction acting through the tubular channels left after the decay of successive generations of the grass stems enclosed during its accumulation, and partly to the increment of fresh dust that is still brought by winds from the interior. Its self-fertilizing ability is shown by the fact that crops have been raised continuously, through several thousands of years, on its immense areas in China, and practically without fertilizing additions. It is on these lands that dense populations accumulate and grow up to the limit of its great life-supporting capacity (Pumpelly 1908, 1:7).

Because the "slash-and-burn" system of the tropics is dictated primarily by the incapacity of the soil to restore its fertility without long fallow, and because the loess of China is famous for its self-fertilizing capacity, the Yang-shao agricultural system was not "slash-and-burn" in the conventional sense, even during its initial stage.

Yang-shao farmers probably first cleared the grass by burning. They broke up the virgin sod with stone hoes and spades and probably they also used wooden digging sticks (*Hsi-an Pan-p'o* 1963:59–75). Without prior experience in field agriculture, they almost certainly would have planted millet soon after the sod was turned over. They would soon have learned that the yield of the first year was meager but the yields of the second and third years were much better. This is because during the first year most nitrogen in the soil is consumed by the various micro-organisms that are the main agents in decomposing plant residues. By the second year, when plant residues have already been decomposed, the various microorganisms, instead of continually tying up the nitrogen in the soil, release it to nourish the seed plants. This phenomenon of differential yields naturally would have led the Yang-shao farmers to the discovery that freshly broken lands should be rested for a year and millet grown from the second year onward.

We may also assume that without prior experience the Yang-shao farmers initially might have grown millet continually on the same plots of land. For types of loess soil that have superior moisture-holding capacity, consecutive planting of millet for a number of years might not have been difficult. For types of loess soil that do not hold moisture too well, consecutive planting would have resulted in diminishing returns or even crop failure, especially in years of subnormal rainfall or serious drought, not because of the deterioration of soil fertility, but because of insufficient moisture. Plots of land that showed signs of diminishing returns or failed to yield a crop naturally would have been rested tem-porarily. Yang-shao farmers could not have failed to realize that if they did not keep the surface of the temporarily rested land clear of weeds, all their previous labor would be lost. Depending on the type of the loess soil, such cleared and rested land would have conserved enough moisture in a year or two to make planting again feasible. There was nothing about the necessity of periodically resting the land that Yang-shao farmers could not have learned empirically. Thus their primitive fallow system came into being.

Unlike the classic "slash-and-burn" system, which requires a very long fallow to restore the fertility of the land, the Yang-shao system seems to have required only a short fallow to restore moisture in the land. The Yang-shao system of short fallow that we have reconstructed from basic principles of agronomy accords almost exactly with the fallow system in the Shensi area described in *The book of odes* and *The book of documents*. The three key terms for agricultural land in early Chou works are: *tzu* 菑 , *hsin* 新 , and *yü* 畬 . The character *tzu* consists of three components — the upper part is the radical for grass, the middle part is the archaic form of the character that means "to bring calamity to" or "to kill," and the lower part means the field. From commentaries of various ancient Chinese etymologists we learn that *tzu* has two essential meaning: first, the process by which the "grass [residue] is returned to the soil" after the sod has been turned, and second, the first-year land that is not yet ready for planting. *Tzu* is therefore the newly broken sod that has to wait a year for actual planting because of the time interval necessary for plant residues in the soil to decompose. Because the term *tzu* appears in two authentic chapters in *The book of documents* composed at the beginning of the Chou dynasty (Legge 1865:372–373, 417), this system of initial land preparation is undoubtedly of much greater antiquity than 1000 B.C.

The term *hsin* means the land in its second year of preparedness, ready for planting. The character *hsin* literally means "new," because it is the new land to be actually planted. The term *yü* means the well-treated land in its third year of preparedness, ideal for planting. Concerning these two terms there was never any disagreement among traditional Chinese etymologists. Ode 275, definitely one of the earliest in *The book of odes*, describing land cultivation in the Chou royal domain in the Wei River basin in Shensi, says:

Ah! Ah! ministers and officers,
Reverently attend to your public duties.
The king has given you perfect rules; —
Consult about them and consider them.
Ah! Ah! ye assistants,
It is now the end of spring;
And what have ye to seek for?
[Only] how to manage the new fields (*hsin*) and those of the third year (*yü*).
How beautiful are the wheat and barley,
Whose bright produce we shall receive!
(Legge 1872:582)

The fact that in this ancient ode crops are grown only on the second-year and third-year lands further proves the correctness of the explanation by ancient Chinese etymologists for the character *tzu* — the first-year land not yet ready for actual planting.

The three-year cycle within which lands were rested and cultivated is reflected in the generalized description of the system of land allotment in the *Chou-li* [Rituals of Chou]. Owing to their inclusion of valuable authentic early Chou materials as well as Han interpolations of Chou institutions and administrative rituals, the various chapters and passages in the *Chou-li* have uneven values as sources of historical information. Each passage must therefore be evaluated separately against relevant information that can be culled from other Chou sources. Concerning the principle of land allotment in Chou times, the *Chou-li* states: "In case of the non-changing land, each [peasant] household be allotted 100 *mou*; in case of the once-changing land, each household be allotted 200 *mou*; and in case of the twice-changing land, each household be allotted 300 *mou*" (*Chou-li chu-shu*: Chapter 10, 9a).

This general principle is most likely to have been true for Chou times because various Chou works testify to the unit of 100 *mou* as the standard allotment for a peasant household and because the fallow system implied in this *Chou-li* passage accords well with the three-year cycle of land use described in *The book of odes*. Even the *Chou-li*'s reference to the "non-changing land," that is, land that was planted continually without fallow, should not surprise agronomists familiar with the nature of the loess soil, nor should it strike the orientalists as exceptional because some best-quality land in the prehistoric Near East could grow crops consecutively.

In summary, it was primarily nature, more specifically the loess, that gave the agriculture of northern China from Yang-shao times onward its self-sustaining character. In contrast, it was almost entirely human efforts, largely over the past two thousand years, that made the southern Chinese agricultural system self-perpetuating and highly productive (Ho 1975). In our long-range historical perspective, the most striking and important characteristic of Chinese agriculture has been its endurance, and the roots of this enduring agriculture must be traced back to Yang-shao times.

We should now turn our attention to the prehistoric and early historic cropping system of China. The origins of cultivated plants have long been a favorite topic of botanical scientists and geographers. There is a considerable Western literature on the subject, but it usually does not treat systematically those cereal plants that are indigenous to China and were first extensively cultivated by the Chinese. The language and disciplinary barriers are so great that the vast body of Chinese literature on food plants has been little known to Western scientists and seldom systematically utilized by Chinese botanists. Because of the relative abundance of recent archaeological finds concerning ancient cereal grains and the rich archaic Chinese literature, we can discuss the origin of each of the major indigenous and introduced food plants and can suggest possibilities of revising certain Western views that do not seem to stand the test of the aggregate Chinese evidence. These food and industrial plants — millets, rice, wheat, barley, soybeans, hemp, and mulberry — will be discussed in turn.

Chinese millets are domesticated and wild plants that belong to the genera *Setaria* and *Panicum*. The former is chiefly represented by the species *Setaria italica*, which the Chinese call *su*. The latter is mainly represented by two subspecies of *P. miliaceum*, which the Chinese call *shu* and *chi*. This taxonomic division was of course not always understood by ancient and later Chinese etymologists and herbalists. There is reason to believe that some confusion in nomenclature of Chinese millets has persisted from the beginning of China's recorded history. Neolithic millets are reported to have been largely *S. italica*, but Shang oracle-bone inscriptions and *The book of odes* both indicate an overwhelming importance of *shu* and *chi* as a source of food. Yet in the works written and compiled during the fourth and third centuries B.C., *Setaria* regains its dominant position (Ho 1969a: 123–135). This seemingly sharp vicissitude of the relative importance of *Setaria* and *Panicum* can be accounted for only by certain confusion in nomenclature.

What we do know clearly is that *S. italica* was extensively grown in the loess highland during Yang-shao times. The most important archaeological proof is the discovery in several storage places at the typical early Yang-shao site of Pan-p'o of bushels of husks of *S. italica*. The quantity of the stored millet, along with the abundance of agricultural implements and the whole complex layout of the village, establishes beyond doubt that *S. italica* was a crop cultivated and harvested by men (*Hsi-an Pan-p'o* 1963:223). Husks of *S. italica* have also been found in three other Yang-shao sites in Shensi and southern Shansi and in a site at Ta-ho-chuang, Yung-ching County, Kansu, that belongs to the Ch'i-chia culture. While most of the millets are *Setaria*, those found at Ching-ts'un, southern Shansi, are reported to contain *P. miliaceum* (Bishop 1938:369). According to the chronology given in Table 1, millet farming began at Pan-p'o shortly after 5000 B.C. (bristleconepine date).

Two independent experiments carried out by American botanists show that among common cereal plants, *S. italica* has the highest "efficiency of transpiration," that is, is best suited to dry conditions (King 1966: 180, Table 4). While no similar field experiment has ever been done for *P. miliaceum*, its capacity to resist drought is well known. *The book of odes* mentions the existence of black, red, white, early-ripening, late-ripening, nonsticky, and glutinous millets, an indication of their varietal richness. Even today wild species of millets can be found in the loess area. All this, together with the extreme antiquity of their cultivation, should establish *Setaria* and *Panicum* millets as indigenous plants.

Although two pioneering investigators of the origins of cultivated plants, Alphonse DeCandolle and N. I. Vavilov, both regarded *Setaria* and *Panicum* as native Chinese plants, there is still considerable confusion about their original habitats. The 1936 edition of *A. Engler's Syllabus der Pflanzenfamilien*, for example, attributes the original home of *P. miliaceum* to India. A leading Indian expert on millets, Krishna-swamy (1951), thinks that millets in general are native to tropical and subtropical areas rather than to China. Hermann von Wissmann, a geographer known for his studies of the dry belts, states without giving any evidence that millets originated in northwestern India (von Wissmann, 1956:285). All this, and much else, calls for a reexamination of millets in the context of world history.

In the Old World, *P. miliaceum* has been found in a prehistoric Near Eastern site at Argissa, Greece, which is dated between 7950 and 6950 B.P. (Renfrew 1969:168). In the New World, *Setaria* of the foxtail variety "was eaten in quantity" in Tamaulipas, Mexico, between 5950 and 5450 B.P., before maize was introduced into this area (Callen 1967: 535–538). But in these areas millets were soon abandoned in favor of superior crops. Millets in the Near East and in Mesoamerica never played an important role, as they did in Yang-shao China.

Indeed, as Vavilov suggested, there are millets other than *Setaria* and *Panicum* that are likely to have originated in Ethiopia. These species are *Eleusine coracana* and *Pannisetum spicatum* (Vavilov 1949–1950:38). Recent archaeological research on Africa suggests that these African millets may have been cultivated by the people belonging to the "Stone Bowl" culture sometime during the second millennium B.C. (Clark 1962:19–21) Of course the difference in species and the late chronology make these African millets totally irrelevant to our study of the origin of millet farming in China.

The view that *Panicum* is indigenous to India does not withstand close scrutiny. For one thing, Indian botanists admit that no wild species are known to exist in the subcontinent of India (Government of India 1966: s.v. "Panicum"). For another, in India no *Panicum* has ever been discovered in cultural strata that contain India's most ancient cereal grains — wheat and barley. What is more, the philological evidence is overwhelmingly against India as a country of origin. The Sanskrit name for *P. miliaceum* is *cīnaka* 'Chinese' (Laufer 1919:595). The Hindu names *chena* and *cheen*, the Bengali name *cheena*, and the Gujarati name *chino* all sound suspiciously close to "China" (Government of India 1966). The variant Bengali name *bhutta* clearly indicates Bhutan, the Himalaya foothill country, as a stepping-stone in the long route of its introduction from China (Edward C. Dimock 1969: personal communication). Furthermore, also, the Sanskrit names for a number of cultivated plants introduced from China are known to reflect faithfully their origin, for example, *cīnanī* 'Chinese fruit' for peach and *cīnarājaputra* 'crown prince of China' for pear (Laufer 1919:540, 567). The Persian name of *šušu* for *P. miliaceum*, which is undoubtedly derived from the Chinese *shu-shu* *(P. miliaceum glutinosa)*, is additional philological evidence that this food plant was introduced into western Asia from China (Laufer 1919: 565).

It is true that in the study of the origins of cultivated plants, philological evidence alone is seldom decisive. But our evidence is at once archaeological, botanical, historical, and philological; there is also geological and palynological evidence. In the light of various types of evidence already presented in this and preceding sections, the significant position held by the family of Gramineae in the pollen profile of Wuch'eng, Shansi, which chronologically covers the past million years, can have been substantially accounted for only by *Setaria* and *Panicum*. Indeed, since the beginning of agriculture the life of the inhabitants of the loess highland had been so dependent on millets that even the name of Hou Chi, the legendary ancestor of the Chou tribe, literally means the "Lord of Millet."

Of the various Neolithic artifacts discovered in 1921 at the Yang-shao village and taken to Sweden by J. G. Andersson for further study, no single finding can be more significant than the identification by two Swedish botanists of the imprints of cultivated rice (*Oryza sativa*) on fragments of a pottery jar (Edman and Söderberg 1929). "This discovery was," in the words of Andersson, "in a high degree sensational not only because it sets back the history of rice an immense distance in time, but also because it points, not to dry central Asia, but to the rainy southern Asia, which is the homeland of rice" (Andersson 1934:336). As we now know, although the name for the first full-fledged Neolithic culture in China is derived from the village of Yang-shao, the whole cultural assemblage discovered at this village is of a considerably later type than that of Pan-p'o.

Finds of prehistoric rice in China after 1949 are exceptionally plentiful. While the rice discovered in 1921 at the Yang-shao village in western Honan has remained the only verified case of rice culture within the southeastern portion of the loess highlands, prehistoric rice has been found in more than ten localities in the area south of the Huai River and in the lower and central Yangtze regions, which lie outside the Neolithic nuclear area. As is shown in Table 1, the cultural site of Ch'ing-lien-kang at Sung-tse, Ch'ing-p'u County, now within the enlarged municipality of Shanghai, where rice remains were found, is radiocarbon-dated at 5195 ± 105 B.P. — approximately 4000 B.C. when converted to bristlecone-pine dendrochronology. The Sung-tse rice has been morphologically identified as the *hsien (Oryza sativa indica)* subspecies — the early-ripening "tropical" subspecies with long grains. The remains of carbonized rice from the Liang-chu cultural site of Ch'ien-shan-yang, Wu-hsing County, on the southern fringe of the T'ai-hu Lake in northern

Chekiang, are radiocarbon-dated at 4568 ± 100 B.P. (bristlecone-pine date: 3300 ± 100 B.C.). Not only do these two finds of rice chronologically strengthen each other, but the latter finds are extremely important scientifically and historically in that they contain both the *hsien* and the *keng* (late-ripening rice with round grains, i.e. the subspecies *japonica*). The combined evidence further confirms the conclusion of an early study of my own, based exclusively on literary and local-historic records, that, although most of the varieties of rice grown in China up to about A.D. 1000 were heavy-yielding and late-ripening (subspecies *japonica*), a number of *hsien* varieties had been native to the southern half of China (Ho 1956).

Of additional importance is the fact that, in the lower Yangtze delta, remains of rice have been found from the lowest cultural stratum of the site of Ts'ao-hsieh-shan in Wu-hsien and that of Hsien-li-tun in Wu-hsi, which stratigraphically corresponds to the Ma-chia-pin phase — the earliest phase of the southern type of the Ch'ing-lien-kang culture. Since, as has been pointed out in our introductory discussion on chronology, the two available radiocarbon dates for the Ch'ing-lien-kang culture (5785 ± 105 B.P. and 5345 ± 105 B.P.) probably represent the approximate upper and lower chronological boundaries of its early phase, there is reason to expect that future radiocarbon age determinations of pre-historic finds of rice of the lower Yangtze area may yield dates a few centuries earlier than that of the rice remains of Sung-tse. The beginnings of rice culture in the lower Yangtze area may well fall within the latter half of the fifth millennium B.C., according to bristlecone-pine dendro-chronology.

Outside of the lower Yangtze, unusually large quantities of rice husks have been found in the baked red clay in several sites in Hupei that belonged to the Ch'ü-chia-ling culture. The quantities of rice husks would indicate the cultivation of rice on a considerable scale, but these sites probably can be dated back only to the early half of the third millennium B.C.

The quality and quantity of these archaeological finds raise serious doubt about the general view so far held by botanical scientists that rice is indigenous only to southern and southeastern Asia and that rice was introduced from India to China. The opinion of Vavilov, which has been widely accepted, is worth citing:

Even though tropical India may stand second to China in the number of species [of cultivated plants], its RICE, which was introduced into China, where it has been the staple food plant for the past thousand years, makes India even more important in world agriculture. That India is the native home of rice is borne out by the presence there of a number of wild rice species, as well as common rice, growing wild, as weeds, and possessing a character common to wild grasses, namely, shedding of the grain at maturity, which insures self-sowing. Here are also found intermediate forms connecting wild and cultivated rice. The varietal diversity of the cultivated rice of India is the richest in the world, the coarse-grained primitive varieties being especially typical. India differs from China and other secondary regions of cultivation in Asia by the prevalence of dominant genes in its rice varieties (Vavilov 1949–1950:29).

The scientific reasons given by so eminent a botanist as Vavilov for regarding tropical India as the original home of rice merit respect. But scientists and historians must further investigate whether rice was indeed introduced from India to China; whether China, at least the area south of the demarcation of the Ch'in-ling and Huai River, may not have been one of the original homes of rice, especially of the subspecies *japonica* of the temperate zone of eastern Asia; and whether there is sufficiently strong botanical and historical evidence for the existence of wild species of rice in China.

When the problem of rice culture is studied in the context of world history, the available radiocarbon dates as well as the quality and quantity of prehistoric finds of rice all seem to indicate the southern half of China as one of the original habitats of rice and as the region where rice was first domesticated. Mortimer Wheeler's discussion of early archaeological evidence of rice in India, being radiocarbon dated at around 3750 B.P., is already out of date (Wheeler 1966). The latest radiocarbon date for the earliest occurrence of rice in India, as reported by a leading Indian paleobotanist, Vishnu-Mittre, is around 5000 B.P. It is to his credit that he frankly admits the impossibility of determining whether the rice was wild or domesticated (Vishnu-Mittre, this volume). The available evidence of prehistoric rice in northern Thailand is indirect, being based on rice imprint on pottery, which is dated by the technique of thermoluminescence at about 5450 B.P. (Gorman, this volume). While existing comparative data are in favor of China, I share the views of the majority of the participants of this conference on the origins of agriculture that the geographical distribution of predomesticated rice was much wider than has hitherto been believed and that rice probably was independently domesticated in the southern half of China, the southeastern Asian mainland, and the Indian subcontinent.

Twenty-three species of the swampy grasses of *Oryza* have been recognized taxonomically by scientists, and only two of the twenty-three have been domesticated. Of the domesticated species, *Oryza glaberrima* is strictly a regional crop confined to western Africa, and only *O. sativa* has worldwide significance. The regions known to Western scientists where species of rice have been discovered are India, Indochina, Indonesia, Taiwan, western Africa, Madagascar, Central and South America, and Australia (Government of India 1966: s.v. "Oryza"). Because the geographic distribution of wild species of rice is truly worldwide and because the southern half of China, the world's largest single rice-producing area, has much in common climatically and phytogeographically with the rest of monsoon Asia, no generalization about the original homelands of rice is convincing without a thorough search of the historical and modern records of wild species of rice in China.

Not only is the nomenclature of Chinese rice highly complex, but Chinese historical records on rice are the richest in the world. In addition to references to cultivated rice, records of Shang oracles significantly mention a wild species called *ni* (Yü 1957a:101). *Shuo-wen chieh-tzu*, the earliest systematic Chinese lexicon, compiled shortly after A.D. 100, explains: "The kind of rice that ripens this year and will grow all by itself again next year is called *ni*." *Ni* is almost certainly the common *Oryza perennis*, which is believed by an increasing number of experts on rice to have been the probable progenitor of cultivated rice (Government of India 1966).

The Chinese vocabulary was rapidly expanding from Shang to Han times. Because of different pronunciations in different regional dialects and because of the inevitable process of corruption of the original usage, by Han times four homonyms of *lü* and a character *li* had been derived from the original character *ni* (Ho 1969b:21, 34–36). *Huai-nan-tzu*, an eclectic work of the second century B.C. compiled by scholars employed by the prince of Huai-nan, contains an important entry about the *li* wild rice: "*Li* ripens somewhat earlier than [cultivated] rice, but farmers treat it as a weed for fear that whatever small crop it might yield would be more than offset by the harm it might do to the main harvest [of cultivated rice]" (Ho 1969b:21, note 66). Kao Yu, who made systematic commentaries on this work around A.D. 205, explained that "the *li* [wild rice] usually grows alongside the [cultivated] rice." This passage from *Huai-nan-tzu* provides not only the rationale for destroying the wild perennial rice but also the best explanation of why the species of wild rice in ancient China had been reduced through conscious elimination.

The term *li* in ancient times might well have been peculiar only to the dialect of the area immediately south of the Huai River. From Han times onward the common term for wild rice was *lü* in four variant forms. Though used at first as a noun to mean wild rice exclusively, *lü* acquired so many new meanings that it was soon employed as a general term for all kinds of wild cereal plants and also as an adjective or adverb describing the naturally wild state of any food plant. Because of the ever broadening meaning of *lü*, I have excluded some fifteen entries culled from various dynastic histories in which the character *lü* was used in a general sense without a specific association with rice. However, some of these excluded entries might well have actually referred to the occurrence of wild rice, especially when the recorded habitats of such *lü-sheng* 'wildly grown' grains were marshes and edges of rivers and lakes south of the Huai River. For prudence I have eliminated all entries that are not precisely phrased and checked through various post-Han dynastic histories, so that none of the entries presented in Table 3 can be construed as escapes

Table 3. Post-Han records on wild species of rice

Year (A.D.)	Place (modern name)	Essential description
231	Chia-hsing (Chekiang)	Wild rice ripened naturally.
446	Chia-hsing	"Wild rice ripened naturally, being of more than thirty varieties."
537	Kiangsu (south of Huai)	In the ninth lunar month, "wild rice had grown over an area of 200,000 *mou* [about 30,000 acres]."
537	Wu-hsing (Chekiang)	Wild rice ripened, much to the benefit of the local poor and hungry.
731	Yang-chou (Kiangsu)	In early spring, wild rice ripened in an area of 21,000 *mou*, and perennial wild rice ripened in an area of 180,000 *mou*.
852	Kao-yu and T'ai-hsien (Kiangsu)	Poor people of the two counties procured "strange rice" by straining its grains in public rivers; they called it "divine rice."
874	Ts'ang-chou (Hopei)	Wild rice ripened in an area of more than 200,000 *mou*, much to the benefit of the poor of local and neighboring counties.
979	Su-hsien (Anhwei)	In the eighth lunar month, wild rice ripened in lakes; harvest was gathered by the poor, who called it "divine rice."
1010	Kung-an (Hupei)	In the second lunar month, wild rice ripened, and people procured a harvest of 400 bushels.
1013	Four counties of T'ai-chou (Kiangsu)	In the second lunar month, "divine rice" ripened in various places in the four counties.
1023	Soochow (Kiangsu) and Chia-hsing (Chekiang)	"Divine rice" ripened in the sixth month in the lakes of these areas; harvests were gathered by the poor.

Source: Ho (1969a:137–139).

from cultivation resulting from temporary abandonment of fields caused by wars or natural calamities.

The entries in Table 3 probably represent only a very small fraction of the reports submitted to the imperial government by various provincial and local authorities. Concerning the report on the appearance of wild rice in early Sung times, Ma Tuan-lin, the great encyclopedist of the late thirteenth century, said that they were so numerous that he could choose only a few for inclusion in his encyclopedia in the chapter on unusual plants (*Wen-hsien t'ung-k'ao*, Chapter 299). The founder of the Ming dynasty, who reigned from 1368 to 1398, ordered that only natural calamities, but not auspicious natural phenomena, be regularly reported to the throne (*Ta-Ming hui-tien* 1587, Chapter 103:3b–4a). This regulation, which was observed by later rules of the Ming and Ch'ing periods, caused the virtual disappearance of the mention of wild rice from all central-government records. The continual dissemination of early-ripening and relatively drought-resistant rice since the beginning of the eleventh century, the endless process of breeding better strains of rice, and an increasingly labor-intensive system of rice culture during the past millennium have all contributed to a drastic decline in the incidence of wild rice in China (Ho 1956). Despite all this, the late E. D. Merrill found in the 1910's some wild species of rice in Kwangtung, and Chinese botanists have recently discovered more in Kwangtung, Kwangsi, and Yunnan (Hsia 1962).

The entries of wild rice tabulated above deserve further analysis. The extents of the areas in which wild rice grew and ripened were so large as to rule out the possibility of accidental ascape from cultivation. The places in which wild rice appeared — public and untitled lakes, rivers, marshes — further show that the rice must have been truly growing wild. Those kinds of wild rice that ripened in early spring were obviously different from the cultivated rice that usually ripened in late summer and early fall. It is most interesting that the vulgar name of "divine rice" suggests not only its wild origin but also the likelihood that it might be *Oryza fatua*, a weed that some rice experts believe to have been the progenitor of cultivated rice. I. H. Burkill, an authority on the flora of southern and southeastern Asia, has described the peculiarities of *O. fatua* (1935, 2:1539):

In the fields of south-western and western India, it [*O. fatua*] is exactly like the annual *O. sativa* in every respect except that it shatters at maturity. In the Gangetic plains it is seen in a different form, but still is just like *O. sativa* except for shattering. The poor do not ignore it, but tying the awns together before maturity save the grain for themselves, or they collect the fallen grain, which is made an easier process by the length of the awns.

Had it not been for the shattering of the "divine rice" at maturity, the

Chinese poor would not have had to collect the grains by straining through river and lake water. The records on wild species of rice in 3,000 years of Chinese literature are truly impressive.

Of particular interest to plant geneticists is that most of the varieties of rice recorded in Chinese literature prior to A.D. 1000 are of the *keng* subspecies, or *O. sativa japonica*. The *keng* varieties are usually confined to the temperate zone of eastern Asia and are characterized by their heavy yields and by their shorter and more rounded grains, as compared with the tropical *O. sativa indica*, which the Chinese call *hsien*. Some geneticists believe that "the two groups differ in morphological and several physiological features including response to temperature and day length" (Government of India 1966). A preliminary morphological study of the prehistoric and ancient rice husks found in northern China and the middle Yangtze valley shows that they were of the *keng* subspecies. Ting Ying, a leading Chinese expert on rice, concludes that "the *keng* varieties of [some Ch'ü-chia-ling Neolithic sites in] Hupei may have a certain pedigree relationship with those found in Han tombs of Lo-yang and the Yellow River valley, as well as with those discovered at the Yang-shao sites" (1959).

It is also worth noting historically that the *Ch'i-min yao-shu*, the earliest systematic Chinese agricultural treatise extant, compiled in the early half of the sixth century A.D., prefaces its chapter on rice with a selective listing of unusual varieties, some of which are of the subspecies *indica*. For reasons unexplained, however, the limited number of varieties of *indica* had not acquired any true economic significance since early times. Not until the introduction of early-ripening and relatively drought-resistant varieties of *indica* from Champa in Indochina at the beginning of the eleventh century A.D. did the Chinese begin to develop more and better strains of *indica* by which to extend the frontier of rice culture from southern deltas, basins, and low valleys to terraced hills and mountains, a process that went on apace during much of the past millennium (Ho 1956). The finds of rice from the Neolithic cultural site of Liang-chu at Ch'ien-shan-yang, which contain both subspecies, *japonica* and *indica*, confirm the reliability of Chinese historical and agricultural works, since the radiocarbon date of 4568 B.P. (3300 B.C. bristlecone-pine date) for this site was derived from its carbonized rice.

In spite of the latest opinion of students of southeastern Asia that "wet rice farming" in the northern Thai plateau is likely to have begun "from ca. 5500 years B.P." (Gorman this volume), our combined archaeological and historical data seem to have firmly established China as one of the original homes of rice and certainly as the first in the world where rice of the *japonica* subspecies was cultivated. Because rice is the main food for more than half of humanity and because the temperate zone of eastern Asia accounts for some two-thirds of the world's output, with China as the largest single producer, the contribution that China has made to world agriculture should be recognized as much greater than Vavilov and other botanical scientists realized. Whereas wheat has assumed an eminent position in the agriculture of the Western world only during the last 150 years, rice has supported a larger portion of the human race during the past millennium. China's contribution to world agriculture is therefore even greater than that of Mesopotamia, which first supplied the world with wheat and barley.

Two problems about rice remain to be solved in the discussion on the origins of Chinese agriculture. First, while rice is generally a tropical and subtropical plant, archaeological evidence and archaic literary records show that it was cultivated in the semiarid loess highland. As I pointed out in my discussion on environment, there have been marshes in both the highlands and the low plains of northern China, largely for physiographical reasons. Besides water, the rice plant requires a range of fairly high temperatures and long exposure to sunlight for growth and maturation. Because of the continental type of climate, the loess provinces have average temperatures of 24° to 26° Centigrade, or 75° to 79° Fahrenheit, in July and August; the average is actually considerably higher than the minimal average temperature of 20.5° Centigrade required to bear a normal crop of rice in the temperate zone of eastern Asia. Solar radiation is considerably stronger in northern China than in the areas south of the Yangtze. Experiments in recent years show that the highest yield of rice per acre in China is found not in the southern provinces but in Shensi, the Neolithic nuclear area (Chu 1964). Our knowledge of the summer climatic conditions of northern China shows that there is actually nothing strange about the growing of rice in the marshes of northern China in prehistoric and ancient times.

The second problem is whether rice culture in prehistoric times does not necessarily imply some form of irrigation. Indeed, some Chinese paleographers are so sure of the absence of irrigation before the sixth century B.C. and also of the dependence of rice on irrigation that they are reluctant to identify the character for rice in the inscriptions on Shang oracle bones. The truth is that primitive rice culture does not depend on irrigation, as two Western experts testify concerning southeastern Asia:

A dry-land crop like wheat requires some sort of tool for working the ground, though it be only a digging stick. For lowland rice no such tool is required. Even today there are localities [in southeastern Asia] where the rice field is neither plowed, spaded, or hoed. The soil may be thoroughly puddled and all the weeds destroyed merely by driving a carabao around in the flooded field, or the farmer and his family may accomplish the same purpose by splashing around in bare feet (Wichizer and Bennet 1941:14–15).

Chou Ch'ü-fei, a twelfth-century scholar-official, described primitive rice culture in southernmost China:

Of all the boundless land that lies beyond what human eyes can reach, not 1 percent of such land has been brought under cultivation. In preparing the fields for rice planting, the peasants choose only the kind of land that is evenly submerged under water all year round. If the land is a bit too high [to be submerged constantly], they would reject it. Even when they do cultivate, they would barely break up the ground without deep plowing or hoeing. They simply broadcast the [rice] seeds, never transplant the shoots. After the seeds are broadcast, they do not water the fields during drought; nor do they drain off [the surplus] water after excessive rain. Caring nothing about manuring, deep plowing, and weeding, they leave everything to heaven (*Ling-wai tai-ta*: 36).

Chou's description of primitive rice culture in the backward southernmost part of China during the twelfth century A.D. must have been generally true for the prehistoric method of growing rice. That rice seeds were broadcast in prehistoric time is almost certain, for not until after the time of Christ did the Chinese character *yang* [young rice shoots] begin to appear in the lexicon *Shuo-wen*, and not until the second century A.D. was the method of transplanting young rice shoots from nursery beds to the main paddies described in a short agricultural treatise (Shih 1965). The technique of transplantation, which contributes so much to the increase of yield per acre, was undoubtedly a Chinese invention, because even today in many parts of India transplantation of rice shoots is not practiced.

After millets and rice the next crops in chronological order are wheat and barley. Shang oracle inscriptions contain two names for wheat but none for barley. Because wheat was considered an "aristocratic" cereal while barley was not, the absence of the character for barley in oracle-bone inscriptions is not a sure indication that barley was not known to the commoners of late Shang times. Besides paleographic evidence, there has not been a single verified prehistoric find of wheat or barley in China. It is true that nearly a kilogram of carbonized wheat grains is reported to have been found in a Lung-shan cultural site in northern Anhwei along the Huai River, but because the grains are contained in a Chou-type pottery jar, some prudent Chinese archaeologists reject the wheat find as prehistoric (Ho 1969a:160–161).

The quantity and quality of Western scientific and archaeological studies of wheat and barley, especially some recent ones, make it unnecessary for historians of Chinese agriculture to examine the original habitats of these two food plants (Harlan and Zohary 1966). Northern China must be excluded from the homelands of wheat and barley because these cereals are indigenous to areas of winter rain in southwestern Asia, and northern China offers a climate and a pattern of rainfall exactly opposite to that of southwestern Asia and the eastern Mediterranean. Even today the growing of wheat in many localities in northern China is difficult because of uneven distribution of rainfall and especially because of frequent spring droughts (Chu K'e-chen 1964).

In sharp contrast to the Chinese characters for other cereal plants, which invariably have the radical *ho* [cereal plant], the characters for wheat, *lai* and *mai*, and barley, *mou*, are all derived philologically from the character *lai* 'come', which is used in these three characters as a radical. Whereas the native origins of millets are vividly reflected in many ancient odes, those few odes that mention wheat and barley never fail to point out that these cereals were bestowed on the people by God on High. Knowing that they were not native to northern China but not knowing exactly where they had originated, the men of genius who created new logographs could only regard them as coming from God, hence the radical 'come'. Because the characters for wheat are already found in the Shang oracle-bone inscriptions of the post-1300 B.C. period, and because barley is very likely to have been introduced into the north along with wheat, it is reasonably safe to say that these cereals came to China some time during the second millennium B.C.

For over a millennium after their introduction, wheat and barley do not seem to have made rapid progress in northern China. Various late Chou and Han works testify to their better adaptability to the low plains, where the rainfall is considerably heavier than that of the loess highland. The difficulty with which wheat and barley were adapted to the semiarid loess highland is fully reflected in a memorial by Tung Chung-shu, a leading scholar and philosopher of the second century B.C., who, in addition to urging the emperor to exhort the people of the loess highland to grow more wheat, testified that people of this area had hitherto been rather reluctant to grow wheat (*Han-shu*, Chapter 24A).

We should note that until the time of Christ, wheat and barley were always grown as dry-land crops in northern China. The dry-land culture had been made possible only by the discovery through trial and error of certain special devices for saving soil moisture. Fragments of the *Fan-sheng-chih shu*, a famous agricultural treatise of the first century

B.C., give interesting information on the peculiarly Sinitic method of growing wheat:

If at the time of wheat planting the weather has been rainless and dry for some time, one is advised first to soak the wheat seeds in a thin starchy congee which, slightly acidic [through fermentation], should be mixed with discharges of silkworms. [Wheat seeds] should be soaked at midnight and must be sown shortly before dawn, so that the congee and the ground dew will all go down into the soil.

Amidst the autumn drought, [wheat] should be watered menially at the time when the mulberry sheds its leaves.

In winter after the snow comes to an end, one should use a tool to press the snow into the ground and then have it duly covered, so that the snow will not be blown away by the wind. This process should be repeated after each snow (Shih 1956:20).

In the light of modern scientific knowledge, most of these pre-Christian Chinese devices are ingenious. Especially resourceful was the utilization of the heavy predawn dew, whose importance to farming in arid and semiarid areas was almost entirely unsuspected in the West until recently. As the findings of an Israeli scientist, Shmuel Duvdevani, show, in many arid and semiarid areas the early morning dew "could equal as much as 10 inches of annual rainfall" (Leopold 1961:102).

The *Fan-sheng-chih shu* mentions for the first time the existence of the *hsüan-mai*, spring wheat. Because spring wheat had been grown in the cooler foothill country of ancient Greece (Jasny 1944:70–71), if not earlier elsewhere in southwestern Asia and the eastern Mediterranean, and because the Former Han Empire did have diplomatic and military contacts with the Greco-Bactrian states in central Asia, spring wheat was almost certainly introduced into China not much earlier than the time of Christ.

Like rice, wheat was a luxury food in ancient China, consumed mainly by members of the ruling class on ceremonial occasions. What is really significant about wheat and barley in ancient China is that, despite their southwestern Asian origin and late introduction, they were not grown on irrigated fields as they had been in Mesopotamia since about the middle of the fifth millennium B.C.; instead they were adapted to the typically northern Sinitic system of dry-land farming. Whereas the indigenous origins of millets and rice, so well proven by our aggregate evidence, clearly show the fundamental difference between the cropping systems of the ancient East and West, the above sketch of the early history of wheat and barley in China further helps to sharpen our perception that ancient Chinese agriculture had its distinctive regional traits and characteristics, developed independently of Mesopotamia.

An additional significant difference between the earliest Chinese and other ancient agricultural systems in the Old World is the conspicuous absence in the former of leguminous plants rich in protein. No trace of legumes has been found in any Neolithic site in northern China or in the records of Shang oracles. Not until after the Chou conquest of the Shang in 1027 B.C. did the soybean appear in bronze inscriptions and *The book of odes.*

There is little doubt, however, that the soybean (*Glycine max* L. Merrill) is indigenous to China, for many varieties of its wild ancestor (*Glycine ussuriensis* Regal et Maack) exist in China today (Skvortzow 1927; Hermann 1962). The typical habitats of wild soybeans are wet lowlands and edges of rivers and lakes where soybeans grow together with reeds. While extensive field observations by two Chinese botanists show that wild varieties of soybeans exist in many parts of China, including the loess highland, these wild varieties are concentrated mostly in the eastern provinces north of the Yangtze (Sun and Keng 1959).

Despite the existence of wild soybeans in parts of the loess highland in modern times, we do not definitely know whether they have been native to that area since prehistoric times. Modern experiments do show that the soybean requires three times as much water as does *Setaria italica* to produce the same amount of solid matter (excluding root) and that its "efficiency of transpiration" is the lowest among common food plants (King 1966). Botanists are well aware that the soybean can be adapted to only a comparatively narrow range of environmental conditions and usually requires a long growing season with a plentiful water supply. The natural environment of the loess highland does not seem to have been congenial to this plant, at least not before suitable strains were developed by men. The absence of Leguminosae in the pollen profiles gathered from Wu-ch'eng and Li-shih in Shansi and from the Yang-shao site at Pan-p'o, though significant, may not be conclusive evidence that wild soybeans did not exist in the loess highland in prehistoric times. On the other hand, pollen profiles gathered near Peking, whether of the middle and late Pleistocene or of late prehistoric and early historic times, invariably contain Leguminosae (Ho 1975, Chapter 1, note 25).

Because soybeans are most likely to have been domesticated in early historic times, Chou literary works are extremely valuable in pinning down almost exactly the area where soybeans were first domesticated. The *I Chou-shu* [Lost History of the Chou], a late Chou compilation, contains a chapter describing the tributes brought to the Chou royal court by various peoples shortly after the Chou conquest of the Shang. It mentions that the Shan-Jung [Mountain Jung], a proto-Tungusic people who by the eighth and seventh centuries B.C. at the latest had expanded toward northeastern Hopei, offered the *Jung-shu* 'the beans of the Jung' [soybeans] as their special tribute (*I Chou-shu*, Chapter 7:10b). In some songs and odes in *The book of odes* soybeans are referred to either as *shu* or as *jen-shu*; Han classical commentators were certainly right in interpreting *jen* as a phonetic variation of *Jung*, the name of a proto-Tungusic tribe.

The special significance of the *I Chou-shu* account is its precision about the geographic and ethnic origins of the domesticated soybean. Admittedly this work was compiled in late Chou times, but this particular account is well corroborated by other independent late Chou works. The *Kuo-yü* [Discourses of the Feudal States] contains a saying of Confucius to the effect that shortly after the Chou conquest of the Shang, various peoples — including the Mountain Jung and the Su-shen, another proto-Tungusic people in Manchuria — came to the court of the Chou king to pay tributes (*Kuo-yü*, Chapter 5: 11b). The *Kuan-tzu*, an eclectic work of political and economic philosophy and strategy attributed to the famous statesman Kuan Chung of the Ch'i state in Shantung in the early seventh century B.C., contains valuable Chou records (although its compilation was not completed until Han times) and throws further light on the subject. It states that Lord Huan of the Ch'i state led an army to punish the Mountain Jung, who had been a serious menace to its immediate southern Chinese neighbors, and brought back "winter onions and soybeans [*Jung-shu*] for dissemination throughout the various states" (*Kuan-tzu*, Chapter 10: 4a). Other late Chou works indicate that this event took place in 664 B.C. The Ku-liang commentaries of the *Ch'un-ch'iu* [Spring and Autumn Annals] contain an entry for the year 663 B.C. in which the lord of Ch'i sent some newly acquired soybeans to the lord of the neighboring Lu state as a personal present (cited in Li Ch'ang-nien 1958:33). All these accounts concur in showing that, although soybeans were known to the Chou royal court shortly before 1000 B.C., they did not become widely disseminated in northern China until after 664 B.C. These facts explain satisfactorily why in various works of the fourth and third centuries B.C., soybean and millet were almost unanimously regarded as the two most important food crops.

Although the best Western study on the domestication of the soybean suggests that it may have occurred first in China between 35° and 45° north latitude (Hymowitz 1970), the combined accounts given in various Chou works clearly indicate the Manchurian plains as the area of greatest concentration of wild species of soybeans. The area inhabited by the

Mountain Jung was hilly and on the southwestern fringe of the area of concentration. Probably because their land was not ideal for the natural propagation of wild soybeans, the Mountain Jung had to resort to domestication, in which they succeeded after prolonged trial and error. The original area of greatest concentration of wild species of soybeans and the area in which domestication took place seem to have been within 40° and 45° north latitude. To be more precise, the area stretches from the central Manchurian plains southwestward to the present eastern section of the Great Wall barely north of Peking. In spite of the remarkably specific accounts given by Chou works, we cannot rule out the possibility that the soybean may have been domesticated by Tungusic tribes other than the Mountain Jung in the Manchurian plains centuries before the Chou conquest of the Shang.

In any case, the soybean was undoubtedly an important contribution to Sinitic agriculture by proto-Tungusic peoples. In light of the dominant position held by the soybean in present-day American agriculture and of the soybean's ever increasing importance in world trade, China's contributions to world agriculture, chiefly through rice and the soybean, have been far greater than Vavilov and other botanical writers have assessed.

Once the soybean was known to the Chou people, the peculiar nitrogen-bearing nodules of the root of this plant apparently were well observed by both peasants and those learned men who enlarged the Chinese vocabulary. Unlike the early Chinese logographs for other cereal plants, which emphasize the stem and leaves, the new character *shu* for the soybean emphasized the nodules of its root. Because the numeral three symbolizes many, the three elongated dots at the lower half of the character pictographically represent the root's bulging nodules caused by rhizobium (Hu 1963; see also Figure 2).

Figure 2. Examples of characters representing soybeans

The effect of the domestication and dissemination of the soybean on Chinese agriculture and on the nutrition of the ancient Chinese cannot be exaggerated. At long last, the Chou Chinese had found a food plant that, instead of exhausting the soil, actually helped to preserve and enhance the fertility of the soil. The soybean supplied all classes of the population with cheaper and more abundant protein and also with an important source of oil, although at first the art of oil extraction was unknown. Not until the soybean was domesticated and widely distributed did the ancient Chinese cropping system become well balanced. Within three centuries of the beginnings of wider dissemination in 664 B.C., the soybean and millet reigned supreme in areas north of the Huai River. The unusually long interval between the first domestication of millets and that of the soybean is yet another indication that the maturation of the ancient Chinese agricultural system was an outcome of prolonged trial and error, not only by the proto-Sinitic people themselves, but also by some other ancient peoples living in a world that in later centuries of Sinitic expansion was called China.

Two industrial crops — hemp and mulberry — are the final plants to be discussed. Several imprints of textiles have been discovered on Yang-shao pottery, but the fibers of such textiles cannot be easily identified from imprints. J. G. Andersson (1923) suggested, probably quite rightly, that the fiber may be hemp (*Cannabis sativa* L.). With his broad knowledge of phytogeography, Vavilov (1949–1950) thought that northern China might have been one of the original homes of hemp. Modern research indicates that no fiber plant other than hemp could have grown in northern China in Yang-shao times, for the cotton shrub was introduced into China well after 1000 A.D. and ramie is native to more southerly parts of China. The character for hemp is missing from both Shang oracle bones and Chou bronze inscriptions, but in *The book of odes* hemp appears seven times. It is well known that the ancient Chinese not only used hemp for its fiber but also ate its seeds as auxiliary food.

More is known about mulberry (*Morus alba*) and several kinds of "wild mountain mulberries," one of which has been identified as *Broussonetia papyrifera* Vent (Ho 1969a: Table 3). Several pollen profiles gathered from the loess highland and the low plains contain mulberry. In 1927 a Chinese archaeologist made a sensational find at the Yang-shao site of Hsi-yin-ts'un, in southern Shansi, of one-half of a silk cocoon that had been artifically cut (Li Chi 1927). Although the attribution of the artificially cut cocoon to Yang-shao times has been seriously challenged recently (Hsia 1972), remnants of textiles on some Shang bronzes have been identified as fine silk (Sylwan 1937). Shang oracle texts contain characters for mulberry, silk, and kinds of silk fabrics. If the two varieties of *Panicum miliaceum*, *shu* and *chi*, are counted separately, then mulberry leads all the plants of *The book of odes*, with twenty occurrences. The areas represented by the odes in which mulberry is mentioned show that mulberry was much more widely distributed in northern China in ancient times than it is now. Unlike hemp, which was essentially the fiber for the common people, mulberry was grown extensively for the production of silk for the ruling class.

From our detailed discussion of the origins and early history of the major food and fiber crops, it is obvious that the early Chinese crops are botanically different from those of the ancient West. This distinctively different cropping system, the peculiarities of the natural environment of the loess highland, the freedom from the influence of great flood plains, and the absence of irrigation all testify to the indigenous origins of Chinese field agriculture.

4. DOMESTICATION OF ANIMALS

For scholars familiar with the archaeology and history of Western agriculture, animal husbandry constitutes as vital a part of agriculture as does grain production. For most Chinese scholars, however, agriculture means essentially, if not exclusively, field agriculture based on cereal grains, because insofar as is traceable, the Chinese agricultural system has always been lopsided in favor of grain production at the expense of animal husbandry. This section traces the beginnings of animal domestication in China, analyzes the characteristics of animal husbandry in prehistoric and early historic China, and explains the subordinate role played by animal husbandry in the Chinese agricultural system.

For our study of the origins and early history of domestication of animals in China, the existing data are inferior in quality and quantity to those available for the study of field agriculture. For one thing, since 1949 Chinese archaeology has shared the bias of conventional Near Eastern archaeology of the past in stressing the importance of artifacts and in overlooking natural remains, plant and animal. On balance, remains of animals have been more neglected than those of plants. Most Chinese archaeological reports barely mention the presence in certain cultural sites of nonhuman bones and do not identify them. Many reports mention only those bones that are recognized by fieldworkers, who are not zoologists. Some mention only the remains of the numerically important animals. So far only five site reports have contained a detailed zoologist's or paleontologist's appendix, and a few more, although without a special appendix, have stated that the osteological remains have been identified by qualified scientists. Moreover, even when the taxonomic identification is meticulously done, it is still difficult to tell whether certain animals were domesticated, a difficulty that is by no means confined to Chinese archaeology. Besides, while osteoarchaeology of the Near East and parts of Europe has recently shown new vigor and is based on relatively ample series of radiocarbon dates, only a few radiocarbon dates have become available very recently for the study of the origins and early history of animal domestication in China. Last but not least, while ancient Chinese literary records often throw important light on food plants, they rarely yield specific information on domesticated animals. Given the circumstances, the best we can hope is that a sketchy historical outline may emerge from the following data, which for convenience will be arranged partly chronologically and partly geographically (Table 4).

Table 4.   Animal remains from Yang-shao cultural sites (w = wild)

Site	Pig	Dog	Cattle	Sheep	Goat	Horse	Chicken
Pan-p'o, Shensi	x	x	x(w)?	x(w)?		x(w)?	
Chiang-chai, Shensi	x	x					
Ching-ts'un, Shansi	x	x		x			x(w)?
Kao-tui, Honan	x		x			x	
Miao-ti-kou I, Honan	x	x					
San-li-ch'iao I, Honan	x	x					
Ch'ih-k'ou-chai, Honan	x	x	x				
Chung-chou-lu, Lo-yang, Honan	x						

Sources: For Pan-p'o, *Hsi-an Pan-p'o* (1963: Appendix II, 255–269); for Chiang-chai in Lin-t'ung, which was culturally closely related to Pan-p'o, *K'ao-ku* (1973b); for Ching-ts'un, T'ung Chu-ch'en, *K'ao-ku hsüeh-pao* (1957); for Kao-tui, *Wen-wu* (1956: 53–56); for Miao-ti-kou I and San-li-ch'iao I, *Miao-ti-kou yü San-li-ch'iao* (1959: 63, 92); for Ch'ih-k'ou-chai, Andersson (1943:43); for Chung-chou-lu of Lo-yang, *Lo-yang Chung-chou-lu* (1959:18).

The indentification of the pig as a domesticate in Table 4 is based mainly on two factors: the prevalence of pig bones in practically every ash pit and the unusually high proportion of yearlings and young adults among the pig population. A fragment of a dog's skull, some broken jaw bones and whole teeth are all noticeably smaller than, and show other marked differences from, those of the wolf (*Canis lupus*), hence its identification as the dog (*Canis familiaris*).

Very few fragments of bones of sheep (*Ovis* sp.) are found in the entire Pan-p'o site. Some teeth bear a certain resemblance to those of the sheep found at the last Shang capital city near An-yang; the sheep of An-yang (*Ovis "shangi"* Teilhard and Young — a name which is not taxonomically valid) indicates "a form domesticated during a sufficiently long time" (Teilhard and Young 1936:42). But the extreme scarcity of remains of sheep makes the two paleontologists Li Yu-heng and Han Te-fen, who prepared the special appendix for the Pan-p'o site report, hesitant to say whether the sheep was indeed domesticated. For the same reason they regard the cattle and the horse, along with the sheep, as "domesticable" but not necessarily "domesticated." There is further uncertainty as to whether the cattle was *Bos* or water buffalo (*Bubalus*). The horse is similar to the wild horse indigenous to northern China (*Equus przewalskii* Poliakof).

Quantitatively, the bones of water deer (*Hydropotes inermis*) at the Pan-p'o site only rank below those of pigs; indeed the aggregate remains of various wild animals, ranging from deer (*Pseudaxis hortularum*), lagomorphs (*Lepus* sp. and *Ochotona* sp.), and gazelle to several kinds of small felines and the fox (*Vulpes* sp.), seem to outnumber those of domestic and domesticable animals. This, together with the prevalence of various types of hunting and fishing tools unearthed from this site, suggests that in this early Yang-shao state (fifth millennium B.C.) hunting and fishing were probably still more important than incipient animal husbandry based almost exclusively on pigs.

Not much about the artifactual assemblages of the Kao-tui and Ch'ih-k'ou-chai sites can be learned from Andersson's article (1943), but, from their geographic locations and that of the Chung-chou-lu site in Lo-yang, they probably fall within the cultural orbit of the Miao-ti-kou type, hence comparatively late. These sites may in fact be later than some early Ch'ing-lien-kang "Lungshanoid" sites. There has not been a full site report on Ching-ts'un in southern Shansi. Of the eight Yang-shao cultural sites, therefore, Pan-p'o and Chiang-chai are the earliest but Pan-p'o yields by far the most detailed report on osteological remains, carefully prepared by the two paleontologists, Li Yu-heng and Han Te-fen.

The Yang-shao cultural site of Ching-ts'un in southern Shansi, which was discovered in 1930, is one of unusual interest. It was the first Yang-shao site where millets, *Setaria italica* and *Panicum miliaceum*, were found. Unfortunately, there has been no systematic report on this important site, partly because of the long interruption of the Sino-Japanese War; its artifacts and natural remains have been mentioned only briefly in archaeological articles. Although pigs, dogs, and cattle from Ching-ts'un are generally presumed to be domestic and the chicken is regarded as wild, the validity of these identifications cannot be checked.

The detailed report on the twin sites of Miao-ti-kou and San-li-ch'iao in Shan-hsien, western Honan, has no appendix on remains of animals and merely states that the Yang-shao strata contain bones of pigs and dogs. The detailed report on the site of Chung-chou-lu, Lo-yang, western Honan, states that in a Yang-shao ash pit as many as 120 bone fragments belonging to three yearling pigs were found and that "domesticated pigs may have supplied a major source of meat" for its dwellers. The Yang-shao site at Ch'ih-k'ou-chai in Kuang-wu County, north-central Honan, was discovered by Andersson and its animal remains were later identified by a professional zoologist, Elias Dahr. Pigs, dogs, and cattle are all "well represented" and considered to have been "domesticated." We are now reasonably certain that these Yang-shao sites are chronologically later than Pan-p'o.

Because of the sparsity of scientific information, there is reason to abide by the cautious generalization of the Institute of Archaeology of the Academia Sinica in Peking that the proto-Chinese of the Yang-shao period probably domesticated only pigs and dogs and that hunting and fishing still played a relatively important role as compared with millet farming and incipient animal husbandry based mainly on pigs (*Hsin-Chung-kuo ti k'ao-ku shou-huo* 1962:12).

Of the fourteen sites listed in Table 5, only Ch'eng-tzu-yai in Shantung is a typical Lung-shan site. The other sites are all what Chang calls Lungshanoid, which chronologically fall between the Yang-shao and the classic Lung-shan cultures. The full reports on the K'e-hsing-chuang and Ch'eng-tzu-yai sites contain osteological appendices, which treat all the common animals as domesticates. The remains of animals of all four Lungshanoid sites from Shantung are yet to be systematically identified. The site of Tzu-ching-shan in P'eng-lai County contains remains of pigs and sheep. The predominance of pigs is consistently striking in Pao-t'ou in Ning-yang County, Kang-shang in T'eng-hsien, and Ch'ü-fu County. In nearly every grave unearthed at Pao-t'ou and Kang-shang there are a number of teeth and bones of pigs that were used as funerary gifts. At the Ch'ü-fu site a clay pig figurine looks so fat, short-legged, and short-tailed that it was based unmistakably on pigs that were domesticated. The nonhuman bones of the site of Ta-ch'eng-shan in Hopei were identified by the well-known paleontologist P'ei Wen-chung, although there is no detailed report on whether the pigs, dogs, cattle, and sheep were domesticated.

Table 5. Animal remains from Lungshanoid and Lung-Shan sites

Site	Pig	Dog	Cattle*	Sheep	Goat	Horse	Chicken
K'e-hsing-chuang II, Shensi	x	x	x^a	x			
Miao-ti-kou II, Honan	x	x	x		x		x
San-li-ch'iao II, Honan	x	x	x	x			
Pao-t'ou, Shantung	x						
Kang-shang, Shantung	x						
Ch'ü-fu, Shantung	x						
Tzu-ching-shan, Shantung	x			x			
Ch'eng-tzu-yai, Shantung	x	x	x	x		x	
Ta-ch'eng-shan, Hopei	x	x	x	x			
Ch'ü-chia-ling, Hupei	x	x		x			x
Liu-lin, Kiangsu	x	x	x	x			
Ta-tun-tzu, Kiangsu	x	x	x				
Mei-yen, Kiangsu			x^a				
Ma-chia-pin, Chekiang			x^a				

* x = Water buffalo only (*Bubalus* sp.); x^a = Both common cattle (*Bos* sp.) and water buffalo.
Sources: For K'e-hsing-chuang II, *Feng-hsi fa-chüeh pao-kao* (1962: Appendix I, 156–159); for Miao-ti-kou II and San-li-ch'iao II, *Miao-ti-kou yü San-li-ch'iao* (1959: 82, 112–113); for Pao-t'ou, Yang (1959:61–64); for Kang-shang, *K'ao-ku* (1963a: 351–361); for Ch'ü-fu, *K'ao-ku* (1963b:362–368); for Tzu-ching-shan, *K'ao-ku* (1973a: 11–15); for Ch'eng-tzu-yai, *Ch'eng-tzu-yai* (1934:90–91); for Ta-ch'eng-shan, *K'ao-ku hsüeh-pao* (1959:33); for Ch'ü-chia-ling, *Ching-shan Ch'ü-chia-ling* (1965:23, 41, 74); for Liu-lin, *K'ao-ku* (1965:26); for Ta-tun-tzu, *K'ao-ku hsüeh-pao* (1964:18, 49); for Mei-yen in Kiangsu and Ma-chia-pin in Chekiang, Wu Shan-ching (1973:57).

The site of Ch'ü-chia-ling in Hupei represents an important Lungshanoid culture of the central Yangtze. So far only one radiocarbon date, based on carbonized materials of the Huang-lien-shu site in southwestern Honan, is available for this culture. If this radiocarbon date of 4199 B.P. (bristlecone-pine date of 2720 B.C.) is representative of the Ch'ü-chia-ling culture as a whole, then this culture is likely to have come into being during the early half of the third millennium B.C. The inhabitants were proto-Ching-Man, who until late Chou or even post-Chou times were still considered by the Chinese of early-developed northern China as "southern barbarians." From Ch'ü-chia-ling and several neighboring sites large amounts of rice husks were excavated, along with numerous nonhuman bones, of which only those of pigs and dogs were identified by fieldworkers. The most interesting finds are artifactual — clay figurines of sheep and chickens, presumptive evidence of their domestication.

Since the chicken is still believed by many southeastern Asian experts to have originated only in southern and southeastern Asia, the relevant Chinese data should be discussed in the context of world history. In the 1950's wild ancestral forms of domestic fowl were found in Yunnan

(Hsia 1962). Remains of wild fowls (*Gallus*) were found in the early 1960's in the "Spirit Cave" in Wan-nien County in Kiangsi, a very primitive cultural site that is probably of a rather early age (*K'ao-ku hsüeh-pao* 1963). These recent finds would indicate that the southern half of China, like India, Burma, and southeastern Asia, must have been one of the original homes of wild fowls. The presence of chicken bones in the Lungshanoid stratum of the Miao-ti-kou site in western Honan (radio-carbon date of 4141 ± 95 B.P.) and in a Ma-chia-yao cultural site in Lan-chou, Kansu (radiocarbon date of 4398 ± 100 B.P.), in the extreme northwest of China proper (see Table 6), suggests that the prehistoric distribution of wild fowls may not have been confined strictly to the southern half of China. That one of the favorite hunting places of late Shang kings, on the southern foothill of the T'ai-hang Mountain in western Honan north of the Yellow River, was named Chi 'chicken' is yet another strong argument for the prevalence of wild fowls in parts of northern China in ancient times (Li Hsüeh-ch'in 1959:21). Some anthropologists, geographers, and other scientists have believed that India was the original home of wild fowls and the first area to domesticate the chicken chiefly because some clay figurines of domestic chicken have been found in some Mohenjo-daro cultural sites in the Indus Valley (Zeuner 1963:443–444). But these sites range only from 3850 to 3550 B.P. according to recent radiocarbon dating (Allchin and Allchin 1968:337). Our combined evidence shows that the domestication of the chicken in China antedated that of the culture of Harappa and Mohenjo-daro by centuries.

The twin sites of Liu-lin and Ta-tun-tzu in northern Kiangsu represent an early phase of the Ch'ing-lien-kang culture of the Huai River area and southern Kiangsu. Ta-tun-tzu has recently been radiocarbon dated at 5785 ± 105 B.C., or 4435 B.C., when converted to bristlecone-pine dates. Liu-lin was later. The report on the finds at Liu-lin is quantitatively interesting in that the site yields a total of 652 fragments of bone (excluding shells of tortoises), of which pigs, dogs, cattle, sheep, and wild deer respectively account for 171, 12, 30, 8, and 59. The majority of the pigs of the Ta-tun-tzu site were about two years old.

Although the report on the twin sites of Miao-ti-kou and San-li-ch'iao in western Honan is detailed on artifacts, its brief mention of remains of animals without a zoologist's appendix and without scientific names presents a taxonomic and very likely also a textual problem. From the Miao-ti-kou site the report mentions the presence in the Lungshanoid ash pits of bones of pigs, dogs, cattle, and goats (*Miao-ti-kou yü San-li-ch'iao* 1959:82). In the nearby San-li-ch'iao site, however, the fauna of the Lungshanoid stratum consists of pigs, dogs, cattle, and sheep, but not goats. While the English abstract of the entire site report faithfully translates the goats, the final conclusion in Chinese does not mention the goat, which is replaced by the sheep (*Miao-ti-kou yü San-li-ch'iao* 1959: 102, 127, 113). Aside from the common difficulty in distinguishing the bones of the goat (*Capra hircus*) from those of the sheep (*Ovis aries*), especially in the absence of horn cores (Reed 1959), the lone mention of the goat in the Lungshanoid stratum of Miao-ti-kou could conceivably be a typographical error. This typographical error could happen in Chinese more easily than in English because the difference between the sheep (*yang*) and the goat (*shan-yang* 'mountain sheep') is only a prefix. Significantly, in summarizing the faunal finds of various Yang-shao, Lungshanoid, and Lung-shan cultures of northern China the Institute of Archaeology has never mentioned the goat (*Hsin-Chung-kuo ti k'ao-ku shou-huo* 1962). The goat in the Lungshanoid stratum of Miao-ti-kou is therefore highly suspect.

The site report for Miao-ti-kou nevertheless yields interesting information on the early history of animal domestication. Although this site contains only 26 ash pits belonging to the Lungshanoid stratum as compared with 168 ash pits belonging to the Yang-shao stratum, the remains of domestic animals from the Lungshanoid stratum far exceed in quantity those from the Yang-shao ash pits. The aggregate evidence from various Lungshanoid and Lung-shan sites presented above also

Table 6. Animal remains from prehistoric and early historic sites in Inner Mongolia and Kansu (w = wild)

Site	Pig	Dog	Cattle	Sheep	Goat	Horse	Chicken
A. *Inner Mongolia*							
Sha-wa-tzu			x	x		x	
Hung-shan-hou	x(w?)	x	x	x			
Ta-pei-kou			x	x			
Yo-wang-miao	x						
Hsia-chia-tien	x						
Chuan-lung-tsang	x	x	x	x			
B. *Kansu*							
Ma-chia-yao	x	x	x(w?)				
Hsi-p'o-wa	x	x	x	x			
Ch'i-chia-p'ing	x	x	x	x	x		
Lo-han-t'ang	x	x	x	x	x		
Ta-ho-chuang	x		x	x			

Sources: Lü (1960); Hamada and Mizuno (1938); Lü (1958); T'ung (1960); *K'ao-ku* (1961:77–81); *Hsin-Chung-kuo ti k'ao-ku shou-huo* (1962:38); Andersson (1943); Bylin-Althin (1946); *K'ao-ku* (1960b: 1–4, 1960a:11).

indicates an increase in quantity and range of animals domesticated since Yang-shao times.

For the study of the possibility of the spread of animal domestication from the ancient hearth of Mesopotamia to northern China, two crucial areas are Inner Mongolia and Kansu. If animals first domesticated in the Near East were introduced into northern China, such introduction must have left some traces in these areas immediately north and northwest of the loess highland and the low plains of northern China (Table 6).

Existing knowledge does not enable us to suggest relative chronologies for the prehistoric cultures of Inner Mongolia north of the Great Wall. On this northern steppe, microlithic cultures based on hunting and fishing, which show Yang-shao and/or Lungshanoid influence, persisted until northern China proper had entered well into early dynastic periods. The determination of approximate dates of beginnings of animal domestication in Inner Mongolia is therefore extremely difficult.

At the site of Sha-wa-tzu, Lin-hsi County, eastern Inner Mongolia, formerly the province of Jehol, bones and teeth of cattle, sheep, and horses have been identified. As these remains of animals are found at the bottom of surface sandpits, they probably belonged to a period rather close to the beginnings of the historic age in northern China. The same observation may apply to the animal remains of Chuan-lung-tsang, near Pao-t'ou, in western Inner Mongolia.

The most thoroughly explored site in Inner Mongolia is Hung-shan-hou, Ch'ih-feng County, in central Jehol. It was first discovered by a Japanese archaeologist and was investigated by Japanese scholars in 1930 and 1935 and by an archaeological team of Peking University in 1956. In the microlithic-Neolithic stratum of this site only antlers of wild deer are found. Bones and teeth of pigs, dogs, cattle, and sheep are present only in the cultural stratum that is synchronized with the late Bronze Age in northern China, i.e. the first half of the first millennium B.C. (Lü 1958). The Japanese paleontologist Naora Nobuo has identified the dog as domesticated and has described the pig as small, like the prehistoric pig found at the vicinity of Port Arthur, "and clearly not identified with the present Chinese pig, *Sus vittatus*. ... They [the pigs] were probably tamed, but under wild conditions" (Hamada and Mizuno 1938: Appendix 2). Both the cattle (*Bos taurus*) and the sheep (*Ovis aries*) are regarded as domestic.

Japanese and Chinese scholars who have investigated this Hung-shan-hou site agree that its cultural complex shows that the inhabitants were primarily farmers but were also engaged in hunting and stockbreeding. That *Setaria italica* is reported to have been found in the vicinity supports this conclusion (An 1949:33). The dates for the remains of cattle and sheep from the Ta-pei-kou site, also in Ch'ih-feng, have never been ascertained, but the oracle bones made of pig scapulae unearthed from the Yo-wang-miao and Hsia-chia-tien sites of Ch'ih-feng all come from an upper cultural stratum that chronologically corresponds to the Chou dynasty (*K'ao-ku* 1961:77–81). The aggregate ascertainable data indicate that animal domestication in Inner Mongolia was later than in northern China proper and that the pattern was one of greater reliance on cattle and sheep.

The animal remains of the sites Ma-chia-yao, Ch'i-chia-p'ing, and Lo-han-t'ang in Kansu in the extreme northwest of China proper were collected by J. G. Andersson and subsequently identified by Elias Dahr, a Swedish zoologist. The stratigraphic conditions at Ch'i-chia-p'ing were so disturbed that "some mandibles of goats and sheep ... still possess a distinct smell of fat. However, after the elimination of some specimens, the material from Ch'i-chia-p'ing shows the same state of preservation as collections from other prehistoric sites" (Bylin-Althin 1946:457–458). The presence at the site of Ch'i-chia-p'ing of significant numbers of bones of pigs, sheep, goats, and cattle is confirmed by the animal remains from the undisturbed site of Lo-han-t'ang. Additionally, a pair of goat's horns (ibex) was found in 1945 by Hsia Nai, now director of the Institute of Archaeology in Peking, from a grave belonging to a later local culture called Ssu-wa, which is generally synchronized with the Chou dynasty in northern China proper (Hsia 1949:104). Our problem is not one of identification but one of chronology.

Because of Kansu's crucial position in the investigation of possible prehistoric cultural exchange and especially because of Andersson's revised opinion that the Ch'i-chia culture, exemplified by the artifacts of the Ch'i-chia-p'ing site, was the earliest Neolithic culture in Kansu, Chinese archaeologists, particularly Hsia Nai, have done a great deal of excavation during the past quarter of a century in order to determine the stratigraphical sequence of the Neolithic and early historic cultures of this province. According to the correct stratigraphical sequence as firmly established by Hsia Nai and other Chinese archaeologists, in the entire highland area of loess the earliest Neolithic was the Yang-shao culture, followed by the Ma-chia-yao and such kindred cultures as the Pan-shan and Ma-ch'ang, and then followed by the Ch'i-chia culture. This has been confirmed by recent radiocarbon determinations. The two radiocarbon dates for the Ma-chia-yao culture are 4400 ± 100 B.P. and 4019 ± 100 B.P. and the two available dates for the Ch'i-chia culture are 3572 ± 95 B.P. and 3543 ± 95 B.P.

Having presented data on faunal remains chronologically and regionally, I would like to make a few observations on the origins and early history of the domestication of animals in China, including the special significance of the material from Kansu.

First, a prerequisite for the study of the origins of domestication of animals is a systematic knowledge of the geographic distribution of the wild ancestors of domestic animals. With regard to pigs, all domestic pigs are derived from the wild *Sus scrofa*, which formerly had a wide distribution throughout northern Africa and most of Eurasia. While these pigs have been divided into numerous subspecies (see Map 3 in the article by Herre and Röhrs, this volume), no conclusive evidence exists that all domestic pigs have been derived from a single wild population. Domestication has undoubtedly occurred at different times and different places, involving different subspecies. Wild piglets, if fed and given good care, are not difficult to tame, and can then be bred in captivity (Reed 1960:139).

No evidence known to me exists which would deny the logical supposition that the early domestic pigs of northern China were derived directly from local wild pigs. The discussion by Herre and Röhrs (this volume) on the domestication of pigs in southeastern Asia from local wild pigs of the same region, as based upon the similarity of the squarish lacrimal bones in both populations, is interesting but is not pertinent at the present time to the history of domestication of pigs in northern China. Until evidence is produced on the shape of the lacrimal — if this character is the decisive one — of prehistoric wild and domestic pigs of the drainage of the Hwang-Ho, we may continue with our logical belief that early domesticated pigs in northern China were derived from local wild ones. Only if the lacrimal bones are different between these wild and domestic pigs of northern China need we look beyond the local populations for the ancestors of the earliest pigs of the area.

The wild prototypes of most other common domestic animals are also known to have existed in prehistoric China. Wild cattle of the species *Bos nomadicus* had already reached China and Siberia in the Holocene from their supposedly original habitat in India (Zeuner 1963:203). The Chinese buffalo (*Bubalus mephistopheles*), far from being a southern animal in prehistoric and early historic times, accounted for an astoundingly large portion of the entire osteological remains of An-yang; this has led two well-known Chinese scientists to believe that the animal was native to both southern and parts of northern China (Yang and Liu 1949). The Mongolian wild horse (*Equus przewalskii*) is native to northern China and the Mongolian steppe (Zeuner 1963:302–03).

The situation regarding sheep is more complex: a nearly continuous series of populations of wild *Ovis* (thirty-six by latest count; Nadler, et al. 1973:119) occupies most of the hills and mountains of southwestern and central Asia, continuing into Mongolia and southern Siberia and moving northeastward into Manchuria. Their prehistoric distribution may have been even wider because remains of wild sheep have also been found in Wan-nien County in the province of Kiangsi in the central drainage of the Yangtze (*K'ao-ku hsüeh-pao* 1963: Appendix 2). Another population, of "snow-sheep," occurs in the far northern and northeastern parts of Siberia, but these do not concern us here as no one has suggested any of this latter group as an ancestor of domestic sheep. The thirty-six (or more or fewer) populations found from Cyprus and Anatolia to Manchuria have been variously classified, from the recognition of seventeen distinct species to one all-inclusive species, *Ovis ammon* (as is done by Herre and Röhrs, this volume). Nadler, et al. (1973), using recent knowledge of differences in chromosome numbers and the correlated differences of distribution of gene frequencies of transferrins (Lay, et al. 1971), as well as the older data on horns, heads, fleece, and size, separate this group of Asiatic sheep (not including the snow-sheep) into three species (*Ovis musimon*, *O. vignei*, and *O. ammon*). Only one of these three corresponds with one of the named "groups" of populations, the *ammon* group, presented in this volume by Herre and Röhrs. Agreement thus continues to be lacking on the proper classification of Eurasiatic wild sheep, and anyone writing or reading on the subject has to be able to pick his way carefully through the various usages.

Regardless of the classification, several populations of wild sheep are to be found today in northern and western China, and undoubtedly occurred there also in the post-Pleistocene prehistoric period. Presumably they could have been domesticated there during the time when northern Chinese, by all available evidence, were experimenting with the domestication of dogs, pigs, chickens, and other animals. However, all domestic sheep examined to date for karyotypes and gene frequencies of transferrins show a definite relation to the wild sheep of Anatolia and the adjacent parts of Iran and Iraq (Asiatic representatives of *Ovis musimon* in the terminology of Nadler, et al. 1973), suggesting that wild populations further east were rarely, if ever, domesticated. Such testing has not, however, been extended to any of the breeds of Chinese sheep, of which there are several (Epstein 1969), and so the question of indigenous versus introduced domestic sheep in prehistoric China cannot be settled as yet. In any case, domestication of sheep in China was later than pig husbandry and the problem of sheep has, therefore, no bearing on the origins of animal husbandry on the mainland of eastern Asia.

Although the wolf has only recently been firmly established as the ancestor of the dog, its wide distribution in the northern hemisphere in prehistoric times has never been disputed and it is generally believed to have been one of the first animals domesticated by man. While more precise details about the origins of animal domestication must await more intensive study, evidence exists that before the dawning of the Neolithic age all the wild prototypes of the above-mentioned animals (cattle, buffalo, horse, sheep, dog) were available in China. The only conspicuous absence in prehistoric China was the wild ancestor of the domestic goat (*Capra hircus*), whose significance will be discussed later.

Second, as far as can be ascertained, the sequence in which animals were domesticated in China was somewhat different from that in the ancient Near East. In the Near East the order was first dogs, then sheep, then goats and pigs and, after a considerable time interval, cattle. In Yang-shao and Lungshanoid China the pig was first and foremost. The scarcity of remains of cattle and sheep from Yang-shao sites makes it impossible to say whether they were already domesticated; even if they were domesticated, they were certainly quantitatively insignificant. Not until Lungshanoid times do we have reasons to believe that they were domesticated. It is no exaggeration to say that animal domestication in Neolithic China was very largely pig husbandry. This contrasts with recent osteological findings in the ancient Near East, where "pigs, prior to the period of Sumerian cities, were found at numerous sites but rarely represented more than 5 percent of the bones of food animals; they were however more numerous (25 percent) at Matarrah" (Reed 1969:371). In terms of both the sequence and the relative importance of the various animals domesticated, prehistoric China differed from the ancient Near East.

Third, by far the most significant fact is that animal domestication, much like field agriculture, first occurred in the Neolithic nuclear area and then radiated northwestward to Kansu, eastward to the low plains of northern China and further south, and northward to Inner Mongolia. This pattern of centrifugal spread is probably the strongest argument against earlier views held by some Western scholars that animal domestication, like many other major cultural elements, came to China from Mesopotamia (Bishop 1940).

Finally, the only sure indication of foreign cultural loan is the presence of the domestic goat in the osteological remains of Ch'i-chia-p'ing and Lo-han-t'ang sites in Kansu. There can be little doubt that the goat was first domesticated in the Near East and that its wild prototype was not native to northern China proper. The concrete osteological evidence has been found exactly in an area where modern scholars would expect to find a cultural linkage between China and southwestern Asia. The case of the goat, however, has limited significance to our study of the origins of animal domestication in China. For one thing, the Ch'i-chia culture was much later than the Yang-shao, which gave rise to field agriculture and pig husbandry. For another, although the two available radio-carbon dates for Ch'i-chia, as adjusted for the bristlecone-pine correction, indicate a time in the the neighborhood of 2000 B.C., in eastern Kansu the Ch'i-chia cultural stratum is usually overlain by the Chou cultural stratum. In other words, the Ch'i-chia goat could be as early as 2000 B.C. or as late as the eleventh century B.C. The reticence of the Institute of Archaeology in Peking concerning goats in prehistoric Kansu and also the extreme rarity of goat horns and the great value placed on them by people belonging to the still later Ssu-wa culture provide reasons to believe that the goat probably arrived relatively late in the second millennium B.C. In any case, the arrival of the goat was much too late to have had any effect on the beginnings of animal domestication in China. Moreover, although the goat was first domesticated in the Near East by 9000 B.P. at the latest, five thousand years elapsed before the goat finally reached northwesternmost China, and then it appeared only in insignificant numbers. The presence of the goat in some Ch'i-chia sites does not necessarily mean direct cultural contact between the inhabitants of Kansu and Mesopotamia. In view of the extraordinarily long interval between the goat's first domestication and its arrival in Kansu, it is much safer to assume that the goat was brought to northwestern China by one of the many intermediary bands of herdsmen of central Asia than to assume a direct import from the highly civilized Near East.

Our aggregate data on animal domestication, like those on field agriculture, indicate independent Chinese origins.

The independent origins of animal domestication in China will be better understood when we investigate further the reasons why animal husbandry in China, in sharp contrast to animal husbandry in prehistoric and historic Europe and the Near East, seems to have played always a subordinate role in the entire agricultural system. Let us first speculate on the likely limiting effect of the peculiar land form of the Yang-shao nuclear area on the growth of animal husbandry. Dissected by numerous gullies and ravines, this area lacks large open pasture, a requisite for the development of large-scale raising of stock. The majority of the known Yang-shao cultural sites are found within a narrow strip of fertile land lying south of the Wei River and north of the Ch'in-ling foothills. Within this narrow strip where dozens of Yang-shao sites congregate, the various tributary rivers and streams are only between twenty and fifty kilometers in length, and the maximum distances between them vary from five to twenty kilometers. Granted that not all of these discovered Yang-shao sites were contemporary, it is still obvious enough that after the amount of land necessary for residence, actual annual cultivation, and fallow was deducted, the land available to each village community for pasture was limited. This topographic factor substantially accounted for the invariable numerical predominance of the omnivorous pig, not the herbivorous cattle and sheep, as a domestic animal. Moreover, from what we can learn from the paleoenvironment of this area, the grass cover is not likely to have been dense or ideal for pasturing because of the predominance of *Artemisia* and Chenopodiaceae. Under these circumstances, animal husbandry could not compete effectively against field agriculture for limited amounts of land; long-range growth of population made even more necessary the assignment of priority to millet farming.

The geographic sphere of agriculture in prehistoric China was greatly expanded from the beginning of the fourth millennium B.C., consequent upon the spread of the Yang-shao culture and the rise of a number of regional Lungshanoid cultures both within and outside of the loess highland. The Lungshanoid cultures outside the loess highland flourished under diverse natural environments. The low plains of northern China and the regions north and south of the Huai River are a vast expanse of open flat lands, in contrast to the dissected land forms of the loess highland. The original vegetation of the low plains is likely to have been taller and denser grass, more suitable for large-scale pasturing. The alluvial plains of central and lower Yangtze, where the Ch'ü-chia-ling, Ch'ing-lien-kang, and Liang-chu cultures arose, have rich plant resources and, except for the swampy areas that are likely to have been covered by luxuriant grass, were forested in prehistoric and early historic times. Probably there was little about the environments of easterly and southerly Lungshanoid regions that would have naturally prevented the agricultural systems from achieving better balance between grain production and animal husbandry. The importance of meat production relative to grain production in post-Yang-shao times cannot be gauged without more systematic quantitative data from future archaeological research. Indeed, within a relatively short time span soon after the Yang-shao and in certain localities, animal husbandry may have assumed considerable importance as compared with field agriculture. But throughout the long recorded history of China, we can be reasonably sure that the agricultural systems, in spite of increasing regional differences, have always been lopsided in favor of grain production, for the most persistent emphasis in Chinese agriculture has been to produce as many calories as possible from each unit of land for the sustenance of the maximum possible local population.

Throughout the ages the inability or reluctance of Chinese farmers fully to develop animal husbandry may also have been due to the lingering influence of some very early traits. Among the relevant early cultural traits, the most noticeable was the lack of sufficient knowledge on the part of Chinese farmers to make and utilize dairy products. Because the land form of the Yang-shao nuclear area was hardly conducive to large-scale raising of stock, and because cattle and sheep may not even have been domesticated on any significant scale in Yang-shao times, the ignorance of the earliest farmers about dairy products is not surprising. Although we do not definitely know whether Lungshanoid and Lung-shan farmers knew much about milking cows and ewes, the Chinese throughout the historic periods certainly regarded as comparative novelties the various dairy products brought in occasionally by tribesmen of the northern steppe and by Indian Buddhists (Wang 1958:107–14).

Indeed, early in the present century, Laufer (1914) noted what was to him, an anthropologist with unusual philological tools, the cultural peculiarity of the avoidance of milk by Chinese, and assumed that other nonusers of milk and milk products in eastern Asia (Koreans, Japanese, Indo-Chinese, and Malayans) were under such strong influence from Chinese culture that they persisted in their nonuse of milk even though generally having available bovids.

As compared with other ancient agricultural systems of the Old World, the Chinese system had yet another peculiar trait, namely, the unusually late beginnings and persistent underutilization of draft animals for cultivation. The character *li* 犁 , which in its late connotation means plow and which contains the radical *niu* 牛 [ox], appears in Shang oracle texts. This has led some unwary modern Chinese paleographers to believe that the cattle-drawn plow already existed in Shang times. However, the more careful etymologists, both ancient and modern, interpret *li* as a cow or a bull with dappled skin (Li Hsiao-ting 1965, 2:327–330). Some traditional and modern Chinese scholars believe that the cattle-drawn plow must have come into use during the lifetime of Confucius (551–479 B.C.) because of the combination of the character *keng* 耕 [cultivation] and *niu* [cattle] in the personal and pen names of two disciples of Confucius. However, a leading Ch'ing etymologist, Wang Yin-chih (1766–1834), conclusively proved that the character *keng* in both personal names is actually a synonym and homonym of *k'eng* 脛 [the shin bone of a cow or bull] (Hsü 1930:57). The negative etymological conclusions on the cattle-drawn plow are undoubtedly correct because archaeological evidence indicates that the simple plow did not come into use until the fifth century B.C. and literary records testify that the cattle-drawn plow was introduced around the end of the reign of the Former Han Emperor Wu (140–87 B.C.) (*Han-shu*, Chapter 24A:17a–18a). While we cannot rule out the possibility that the cattle-drawn plow may have first occurred some time before it was recorded, there can be no doubt about the unusually late beginnings of the plow, cattle-drawn plow, and the use of draft animals for cultivation in ancient China.

In Mesopotamia the first proof of the use of a rather complex cattle-drawn plow "is probably that found on an archaic Sumerian seal of about 3500 B.C., from the Royal Cemetery at Ur" (Bishop 1938). During the second millennium B.C., possibly considerably earlier, a "seeder" was sometimes attached to the traction plow so that seeds could be dropped into the furrows mechanically (Oppenheim 1964:314). In comparison, early Chinese agriculture was characterized by its simpler and cruder implements and especially by its exceptional lateness in using draft animals. This trait, together with many others already discussed, not only reflects the secondary role played by animal husbandry but also confirms our perception that the entire early Chinese system of field agriculture and animal husbandry, being so basically different from that of the Near East, could only have been born independently.

5.   RECAPITULATION AND PERSPECTIVE

The southeastern portion of the loess highland is an area of yellow earth *par excellence*. The many-sided scientific findings and ancient Chinese literary records concur remarkably well in indicating that the homeland of the Yang-shao Chinese has always been a semiarid steppe, at least since the late Pleistocene. This semiarid steppe environment surely imposed certain restrictions on its early inhabitants, but it also offered them a narrow range of peculiar opportunities: the classic loessial soil of fine homogeneous texture, which was not only very fertile but also amenable to primitive agricultural implements; the availability of a few kinds of exceptionally drought-resistant potential cereal plants that, selected by a million years of relentless struggle for survival, would have been fairly easy for primitive men of ingenuity to domesticate; and the concentration of limited annual rainfall in summer, which was practically all that was needed by these few hardy food plants for growth and maturation. The Yang-shao Chinese made full use of these opportunities to lay the foundation of what may justifiably be called a typically Sinitic agricultural system.

This system was typically Sinitic because during the first four thousand years of its history it knew no irrigation. It is true that field agriculture began around 9000 B.P. on the hilly flanks of the "Fertile Crescent." But from about the middle of the fifth millennium B.C. it moved down to the great flood plain of the Tigris and Euphrates. The early Sinitic agricultural system was therefore fundamentally different from the major agricultural systems of Mesopotamia, Egypt, and the Indus Valley, which were all based on the triad of flood plains, primitive irrigation, and a cropping system focused on wheat and barley.

The autochthonous character of Chinese field agriculture becomes even more obvious after our detailed study of the origin of each of its major food and fiber crops — the millets (*Setaria* and *Panicum*), rice, soybean, hemp, and mulberry. With these indigenous plants the Chinese from Yang-shao times onward created and enriched their agriculture. Major exceptions are, of course, wheat and barley, which are likely to have been introduced into northern China relatively late in the second millennium B.C. But the introduction of these food plants indirectly from southwestern Asia was too late to have had any significant impact on the well-established pattern of the Sinitic system of dry-land farming. No proof of the strength and stubbornness of the Sinitic system of farming can be more eloquent than the refusal of the ancient Chinese to adopt slavishly the entire southwestern Asian complex of wheat and barley culture based on flood plains and irrigation, and their resolute insistence on growing these cereals as dry-land crops.

We have also discussed the origins of animal domestication in China and the persistently subordinate role played by animal husbandry in the ancient (and later) Chinese agricultural system. That the Chinese agricultural system was so lopsided in favor of grain production constituted another fundamental difference from the agricultural systems of the ancient West. But if we look beyond Mesopotamia and review our problem in the context of world history, we find that the grain-dependent agricultural system of China is not actually unique. It appears unusual to those familiar only with the long tradition of Western agriculture which can be traced back to the prehistoric Near East and prehistoric Europe and which culminated technologically in the Norfolk system of eighteenth-century England. From the vantage point of the Norfolk system, in which stock raising and grain production reached a perfect equilibrium and became virtually convertible, the Chinese system does appear to have been one-sided. In reality, the early Chinese agricultural system was somewhat less one-sided than the ancient agriculture of the New World, which began almost exclusively with plant domestication and developed relatively few domestic animals (see Wing in this volume). Even today, the agriculture of some African tribes is based totally on grains and other plants. Nevertheless, the grain-centered agricultural system of China, with its persistent underdevelopment in farming implements and animal husbandry and its unusually late beginnings and underutilization of draft animals, further reflects its distinctive regional trait complex and native origins.

From our long-range historical perspective, the Chinese agricultural system has had its peculiar strengths as well as weaknesses. Despite certain shortcomings as compared with traditional Western agriculture at its best, Chinese agriculture has been singularly successful in terms of its power to sustain and rejuvenate itself. By virtue of its ability to endure, Chinese agriculture, together with the Chinese script, certain values, and institutions, has made the Chinese civilization the most enduring in the annals of man. Whereas "progressive changes in soil salinity and sedimentation contributed to the breakup of past civilizations" in Mesopotamia (Jacobsen and Adams 1958), and whereas "the destruction of the local ecological patterns and the consequent failure of food resources" contributed to the decline and fall of the ancient Harappan civilization in the Indus Valley (Fairservis 1967), Chinese agriculture after seven thousand years can still manage to support more than one-fifth of humanity out of a cultivated area nearly 25 percent smaller than that of the United States. Of all the inherent characteristics of the Chinese agricultural system, therefore, nothing can be more striking than its self-sustaining quality; and this self-sustaining quality has now been traced to its very beginnings in Yang-shao times.

My overall conclusion of indigenous origins for Chinese agriculture would have raised the eyebrows of most archaeologists, ancient historians, and sinologists, serious and cavalier, of past generations, who practically took for granted that anything worthy of the name of agriculture or civilization in the Old World must have originated in the single oldest hearth of southwestern Asia. Even some leading botanical scientists a generation ago, wary of theoretical speculation and concerned with concrete regional scientific evidence, were inclined to believe that, while agriculture in the New World is unquestionably of independent origins, the limits of prehistoric diffusion of agricultural crops and knowledge could only have been hemispherical (Merrill 1936). As archaeology benefited increasingly from the natural sciences, a few archaeologists more than a decade ago began to become less certain of the monogenetic theory of Old World agriculture and civilization. What Robert J. Braidwood said in 1960 was prophetic:

The first successful experiment in food production took place in southwestern Asia, on the hilly flank of the "fertile crescent." Later experiments in agriculture occurred [possibly independently] in China and [certainly independently] in the New World. The multiple occurrence of the agricultural revolution suggests that it was a highly probable outcome of the prior cultural evolution of mankind and a peculiar combination of environmental circumstances. It is in the record of culture, therefore, that the origin of agriculture must be sought.

While it is impossible at this stage to know much about "the record of culture" of China prior to Yang-shao times, this paper has at least studied the "peculiar combination of environmental circumstances" as a prelude to more detailed analysis of the main characteristics of ancient Sinitic agriculture.

The outcome of the recent intensive multidisciplinary study of Meso-american archaeology clearly indicates "the multiple origins of agri-culture in Mesoamerica," a finding that "may signal a revolution in our thinking about the development of culture and the rise of civilization everywhere" (MacNeish 1967). Insofar as the new "thinking about the development of culture and the rise of civilization" is concerned, China now appears to hold a position perhaps even more crucial than that of Mesoamerica, because China is not separated from the Old World by oceans but rather is an integral part of it.

For the reference of scholars and scientists of various disciplines, I can hardly refrain from making a broad final remark based on a five-year examination of the archaeological and literary records relating to Neo-lithic and early historic China and also on an intensive search for evidence on ancient China's cultural imports. Because the trait complex of each of the major Chinese cultural elements, whether belonging to the realm of technology or ideas, reveals at once a regionally distinctive Sinitic character and a pattern of centrifugal geographic spread from the Yang-shao nuclear area, it is only logical to conclude that the totality of the trait complexes of the major cultural elements that belatedly coalesced and articulated in the Shang civilization must have been indigenous (Ho 1975). The conclusion of my larger study have therefore reaffirmed and reinforced those given in this paper.

6. THE GOAT AND THE EARLY EAST–WEST TRADE ROUTE

In July, 1974, I had an opportunity to present the main findings of *The cradle of the East* to the faculty and students of the Department of History of National Peking University and some members of the Institute of Archaeology and the Institute of History of Academia Sinica. One of the questions I brought up during my presentation was whether the mention of the remains of the goat in the Miao-ti-kou II cultural stratum might not be due to a typological error in the report on the important twin sites of Miao-ti-kou and San-li-ch'iao. Professor An Chih-min, a senior member of the Institute of Archaeology and also a leader of the team that had excavated the twin sites, answered my query by affirming the presence of the goat in the Miao-ti-kou II cultural stratum. I also learned from him that all the remains of nonhuman animals of these twin sites were identified by paleontologists.

The Miao-ti-kou II stratum has been radiocarbon-dated at 4260 ± 95 B.P. ($= 2310 \pm 95$ B.C., or 2760 ± 95 B.C. of bristlecone-pine chronology). The remains of goats unearthed from this stratum represent by far the earliest evidence of intercultural exchange between China and the Eurasian steppe. They also rule out the possibility that the goat arrived first in some Ch'i-chia cultural sites in the northwestern province of Kansu, which are at least 700 years later than the Miao-ti-kou II culture. Since the Miao-ti-kou II goat arrived two thousand years later than the earliest record of pig husbandry in the Pan-p'o nuclear area, it could not have had anything to do with the origins of animal domestication in China. But the arrival of the goat in Honan during the first half of the third millennium B.C. does serve as a reminder that wheat and barley might have been brought into the low plains of northern China centuries before they were recorded in Shang oracle texts and Western Chou literary works and bronze inscriptions.

Like bronze weapons and tools of Seima motif and the horse chariot, which were introduced into China after 1300 B.C., the goat, wheat, and barley must have been brought into the low plains of northern China through the intermediary of a number of Neolithic, proto-Turcic, and possibly also some proto-Tungusic peoples who inhabited the area south and east of Lake Baikal. Detailed Soviet archaeological data show that from Lake Baikal westward to Soviet Europe prehistoric trade took place in the steppe zone, north of the 50th parallel, where a water supply was not a serious problem. The location of the earliest finds of goats in China further strengthens my belief that the "silk route," which traverses the world's largest dry belt between the Kansu corridor and the Aral and

Caspian Seas, cannot have been a thoroughfare for intercultural exchange in prehistoric times, at least not until man had mastered the art of horse riding and succeeded in using camels for caravan trade.

7. POSTCRIPT

This paper has drawn freely from my previous studies on the origins of Chinese agriculture (Ho 1969a, 1969b) and from the first three chapters of a recent book (Ho 1975).

The one significant difference in my treatment of Chinese agricultural crops between 1969 and the present is the entire omission in this paper of a discussion on the "Chinese sorghum." Jack R. Harlan's scientific opinion on the origin of sorghum and my revised opinion on the early history of sorghum in China have been given in Appendix 2 of Ho (1975).

The view we now jointly hold is that sorghum is not indigenous to northern China, that it seems to have been introduced into China more than once throughout the historical period, and that its economic significance did not become widely known until about the time of the Mongol conquest in the thirteenth century A.D.

Although in one of my publications of 1969 I made a preliminary and tentative comment on certain new claims about agricultural origins and remarks about ancient Chinese agriculture by some southeastern Asianists, I have decided not to discuss southeastern Asia in this paper. Those who are interested in the prehistoric agricultural interrelationship between China and southeastern Asia, or the lack thereof, are advised to consult Appendix 1 of Ho (1975).

REFERENCES

This reference list is minimal. For a full listing of primary archaic Chinese works, modern monographs and articles, and archaeological and scientific journals, interested readers are advised to consult the bibliography in Ho (1969a). Although the portions of the bibliography in Ho (1975) relating to chronology, paleoenvironment, field agriculture, animal domestication, the problem of the "Chinese sorghum," and the relationship between China and southeastern Asian "agriculture" and bronze, are slightly less comprehensive in some ways than the bibliography in Ho (1969a), which is in Chinese, the more recent work contains English translations of the titles for nearly all the Chinese works, ancient and modern, and hence is more useful to Western scholars.

Most of the Chinese archaeological books and articles published since 1949 give not the authors' names, but only the names of the numerous archaeological organizations and excavation teams; I have not provided transliterations and translations of the latter because they would be too cumbersome and would serve no useful purpose. I have given here only my translations into English of the titles. Since 1949 Chinese scholarly journals have tended to have, instead of volume numbers, merely the number of the issue and the year. Furthermore, nearly all archaic Chinese literary sources cannot be dated precisely to the year, and the names of authors and compilers, even when accurately known, make no sense to Western scientists. I have decided simply to give only the transliterated titles without other specifics. To save the trouble of reproducing Chinese characters, I have decided to omit glossaries for Chinese place names that have archaeological significance and for ancient Chinese names of crops and plants. For interested botanical scientists, a glossary of Chinese food plants (and others) is available in Ho (1969b:34–36).

Chinese and Japanese Works

Titles of traditional Chinese works are transliterated only; titles of modern books and monographs are both transliterated and translated (except those archaeological site reports whose transliterated titles are self-explanatory); titles of modern articles are given only in English translation.

AN CHIH-MIN
    1949   Prehistoric Chinese agriculture. *Yen-ching she-hui k'e-hsüeh* 2.
Ch'eng-tzu-yai
    1934   *Ch'eng-tzu-yai*. Nanking: Academia Sinica.
Ching-shan Ch'ü-chia-ling
    1965   *Ching-shan Ch'ü-chia-ling*. Peking.
CHOU CH'Ü-FEI
    n.d.   *Ling-wai tai-ta*. (*Ts'ung-shu-chi-ch'eng* edition.)
CHOU K'UN-SHU
    1963   Analysis of the pollen gathered at the Pan-p'o Neolithic site near Sian. *K'ao-ku* (9):520–522.
Chou-li chu-shu
    n.d.   *Chou-li chu-shu*. (*Ssu-pu pei-yao* edition.)
CHOU T'ING-JU, LIU P'EI-T'UNG
    1956   *Chung-kuo ti ti-hsing yü t'u-jang kai-shu* [An outline of China's physiography and soils]. Peking.
CHU K'E-CHEN
    1964   On the relationship between China's climatic characteristics and food production. *Ti-li hsüeh-pao* 30 (1).
Feng-hsi fa-chüeh pao-kao
    1962   *Feng-hsi fa-chüeh pao-kao* [Report on excavations in the vicinity of Sian, Shensi]. Peking.
HAMADA SOSAKU, MIZUNO SEIICHI
    1938   *Ch'ih-feng: Hung-shan-hou* [Report on excavations at the Hung-shan-hou site in Ch'ih-feng, Inner Mongolia]. Tokyo.

Han-shu
 n.d.   *Han-shu*. Taipei reprint of the edition with Wang Hsien-ch'ien syn-
        cretic commentaries.
HO PING-TI
 1969   *Hiang-t'u yü Chung-kuo nung-yeh ti ch'i-yüen* [The loess and the
        origins of Chinese agriculture]. Hong Kong: Chinese University of
        Hong Kong.
 1973   A critique of the methodology for determining the year of the Chou
        conquest of the Shang. *Journal of the Chinese University of Hong
        Kong* 1 (1).
Hsi-an Pan-p'o
 1963   *Hsi-an Pan-p'o*. Peking.
HSIA NAI
 1949   Report on the excavation at Ssu-wa-shan, Lin-t'ao (Kansu). *Chung-
        kuo k'ao-ku hsüeh-pao* 4.
 1962   Problems concerning the archaeology of the Yangtze regions. *K'ao-ku*
        (2).
 1964   China's archaeological accomplishments during the past five years.
        K'ao-ku (10).
 1972   Silkworms, mulberry and silk fabrics of ancient China. *K'ao-ku* (2).
Hsin-Chung-kuo ti k'ao-ku shou-huo
 1962   *Hsin-Chung-kuo ti k'ao-ku shou-huo* [New China's archaeological
        accomplishments]. Peking.
HSÜ CHUNG-SHU
 1930   On ancient Chinese agricultural implements. *Bulletin of the Institute
        of History and Philology* 2 (1).
HU TAO-CHING
 1963   An etymological study of the character *shu* [soybean]. *Chung-hua
        wen-shih lun-ts'ung*, third series. Peking.
Huai-nan-tzu
 n.d.   *Huai-nan-tzu*. (*Ssu-pu pei-yao* edition.)
I Chou-shu
 n.d.   *I Chou-shu*. (*Ssu-pu pei-yao* edition.)
K'ao-ku [Archaeology]
 1960a A brief report on the excavation of the two Ch'i-chia cultural sites
        of Ta-ho-chuang and Ch'in-wei-chia, Lin-hsi County. *K'ao-ku* (3).
 1960b A brief report on the exploratory excavation at Hsi-p'o-wa, Lan-chou,
        Kansu. *K'ao-ku* (9).
 1961   A brief report on the exploratory excavation at Yo-wang-miao and
        Hsia-chia-tien, Ch'ih-feng, Inner Mongolia. *K'ao-ku* (2).
 1963a A report on the initial excavation of Neolithic graves at Kang-shang
        Village, T'eng-hsien, Shantung. *K'ao-ku* (7): 351–361.
 1963b A survey of Neolithic sites in Ch'ü-fu, Shantung. *K'ao-ku* (7): 362–368
 1965   A report on the second excavation of Neolithic sites at Liu-lin, P'ei-
        hsien, Kiangsu. *K'ao-ku* (2).
 1973a A brief report on the excavation at Tzu-ching-shan, Peng-lai, Shan-
        tung. *K'ao-ku* (1): 11–15.
 1973b A brief report on the excavation at Chiang-chai, Lin-t'ung, in the
        spring of 1972. *K'ao-ku* (3): 134–145.

K'ao-ku hsüeh-pao [Archaeological Review]

1957   *K'ao-ku hsüeh-pao* (2): 9.

1959   A report on the excavation at Ta-ch'eng-shan, Municipality of T'ang-shan, Hopei. *K'ao-ku hsüeh-pao* (3).

1963   An exploratory excavation at the Spirit Cave of Ta-yüan Township, Wan-nien, Kiangsi. *K'ao-ku hsüeh-pao* (1).

1964   A report on exploratory excavations of archaeological sites at Ta-tun-tzu, Ssu-hu Township, P'ei-hsien, Kiangsu. *K'ao-ku hsüeh-pao* (2).

KUAN EN-WEI

1965   A discussion of problems relating to the history of physiography of the Wei River valley. *Chung-kuo ti-ssu-chi yen-chiu* [*Quaternaria Sinica*] 4 (1).

Kuan-tzu

n.d.   *Kuan-tzu.* (*Ssu-pu pei-yao* edition.)

Kuo-yü

n.d.   *Kuo-yü.* (*Ssu-pu pei-yao* edition.)

LABORATORY OF THE INSTITUTE OF ARCHAEOLOGY, ACADEMIA SINICA, PEKING

1972a   Report of radiocarbon-determined dates (I). *K'ao-ku* (1).

1972b   Report of radiocarbon-determined dates (II). *K'ao-ku* (5).

LI CH'ANG-NIEN, *editor*

1958   *Tou-lei* [Selected sources relating to the history of legumes in China]. Shanghai.

LI CHI

1927   *Hsi-yin-ts'un shih-ch'ien ti i-ts'un* [The prehistoric remains from the Hsi-yin-ts'un site (in southern Shansi)]. Peking.

LI HSIAO-TING

1965   *Chia-ku wen-tzu chi-shih* [Selected studies of the characters in the Shang oracle-bone inscriptions], 16 *ts'e*. Taipei: Academia Sinica.

LI HSÜEH-CH'IN

1959   *Yin-tai ti-li chien-lun* [A brief study of the geography of Shang China]. Peking.

LIU TUNG-SHENG, CHANG TSUNG-YU

1962   The loess of China. *Ti-chih hsüeh-pao* [*Acta Geologia Sinica*] (March).

LIU TUNG-SHENG, *et al.*

1964   An investigation of the characteristics of the regional distribution of deposits in China during the Quaternary. *Ti-ssu-chi ti-chih wen-t'i* [Symposium on geological problems of the Quaternary]. Peking.

1965   *Chung-kuo ti huang-t'u tui-chi* [The loess deposits of China]. Peking. *Lo-yang Chung-chou-lu*

1959   *Lo-yang Chung-chou-lu* [Report on the archaeological finds from the Chung-chou-lu site in Lo-yang]. Peking.

LÜ TSUN-EH

1958   Report on the archaeological investigation of the Hung-shan-hou site in Ch'ih-feng, Inner Mongolia. *K'ao-ku hsüeh-pa* (3).

1960   Archaeological investigation of the Lin-hsi area in Inner Mongolia. *K'ao-ku hsüeh-pao* (1).

Miao-ti-kou yü San-li-ch'iao

1959   *Miao-ti-kou yü San-li-ch'iao.* Peking.

SHIH CHANG-JU
1959   *Hsiao-t'un*, I: *Yin-hsü chien-chu i-ts'un* [Hsiao-t'un, I: The architectural remains of the Shang palace area]. Taipei: Academia Sinica.

SHIH SHENG-HAN, editor
1956   *Fan-sheng-chih shu chin-shih* [Commentaries on *Fan-sheng-chih shu* in the light of modern knowledge]. Peking.
1957–1958   *Ch'i-min yao-shu chin-shin* [*Ch'i-min yao-shu:* textual emendation with commentaries], four volumes. Peking.
1965   *Ssu-min yüeh-ling chiao-chu* [*Ssu-min yüeh-ling:* textual emendation with commentaries]. Peking.

SUN HSING-TUNG, KENG CH'ING-HAN
1959   A taxonomic study of soybeans. *Chih-wu fen-lei hsüeh-pao* [*Acta Phytotaxonomica Sinica*] 2 (1).

SUN TIEN-CH'ING, YANG HUAI-JEN
1961   The great Ice Age glaciation in China. *Acta Geologia Sinica* 41 (3–4).

SU PING-CH'I
1965   Some problems concerning the Yang-shao culture. *K'ao-ku* (1):52–56.

Ta-Ming hui-tien
1587   *Ta-Ming hui-tien*, Chapter 103:36–4a.

TING YIN
1959   An investigation of the Neolithic rice husks unearthed from the central Yangtze and lower Han River region. *K'ao-ku hsüeh-pao* (4).

T'ING CHU-CH'EN
1957   The distribution and periodization of the Neolithic cultures of central and lower Yellow River and Yangtze regions. *K'ao-ku hsüeh-pao* (2).
1960   Some characteristics of the late prehistoric society of China. *K'ao-ku* (5).

WANG CHIA-YIN
1965   The problem of the loess seen from historical records. *Quaternaria Sinica* 4 (1).

WANG YÜ-HU
1958   *Chung-kuo hsü-mu-shih tzu-liao* [Selected sources on the history of animal husbandry in China]. Peking.

Wen-hsien t'ung-k'ao
Commercial Press edition.

Wen-wu
1956   A preliminary survey of the cultural remains of early men in five southern Shansi counties. *Wen-wu* (9).

WU SHAN-CHING
1973   A brief discussion of the Ch'ing-lien-kang culture. *Wen-wu* (6).

YANG CHUNG-CHIEN, LIU TUNG-SHENG
1949   A supplement to the mammalian remains of the Shang capital near Anyang. *Chung-kuo k'ao-ku hsüeh-pao* (4).

YANG TZU-FAN
1959   A preliminary report on the archaeological finds from Pao-t'ou, Ning-yang, Shantung. *Wen-wu* (10).

YEN YIN, *et al.*
1960a   A report on the investigation of the Neolithic human skeletons unearthed from Pao-chi [Shensi]. *Ku-chi-tsui-tung-wu yü ku-jen-lei* [*Paleovertebrata et Paleoanthropologia*] 2 (1).

1960b An investigation of the Neolithic human skeletons unearthed from Pan-p'o. *K'ao-ku* (9).

1962   An investigation of the Neolithic human skeletons unearthed from Hua-hsien [Shensi]. *K'ao-ku hsüeh-pao* (2).

YÜ HSING-WU

1957a On the food crops of Shang times. *Tung-pei-jen-min-ta-hsüeh jen-wen-k'e-hsüeh hsüeh-pao* (1).

1957b Some characteristics of the Shang society seen from oracle-bone inscriptions. *Tung-pei-jen-min-ta-hsüeh jen-wen-k'e-hsüeh hsüeh-pao* (2–3).

YU YÜ

1959   A study of the chapter on hydraulic engineering in the *Kuan-tzu*. *Nung-shih yen-chiu chi-k'an* [Bulletin of Studies on Agricultural History] 1 (2).

Works in Western Languages

ALLCHIN, BRIDGET, RAYMOND ALLCHIN

1968   *The birth of Indian civilization: India and Pakistan before 500 B.C.* Baltimore: Penguin.

ANDERSSON, J. G.

1923   An early Chinese culture. *Bulletin of the Geological Survey of China* 5 (1).

1934   *Children of the yellow earth.* London: Kegan Paul, Trench, Trubner.

1943   Researches into the prehistory of the Chinese. *Bulletin of the Museum of Far Eastern Antiquities* 15.

BISHOP, CARL W.

1938   Origin and diffusion of the traction plow. *Annual Report of the Board of Regents of the Smithsonian Institution for 1937*: 531–547.

1940   Beginnings of civilizations in eastern Asia. *Antiquity* 14: 301–316.

BRAIDWOOD, ROBERT J.

1960   The agricultural revolution. *Scientific American* 203 (3): 130–148.

BRAIDWOOD, ROBERT J., HALET ÇAMBEL, CHARLES L. REDMAN, PATTY JO WATSON

1971   Beginnings of village-farming communities in southeastern Turkey. *Proceedings of the National Academy of Sciences U.S.A.* 68: 1236–1240.

BURKILL, I. H.

1935   *A dictionary of economic plants of the Malay Peninsula*, two volumes. London: Published on Behalf of the Governments of the Straits Settlements and the Federated Malay States by the Crown Agents for the Colonies.

BYLIN-ALTHIN, MARGIT

1946   The sites of Ch'i Chia P'ing and Lo Han T'ang in Kansu. *Bulletin of the Museum of Far Eastern Antiquities* 18.

CALLEN, ERIC O.

1967   The first New World cereal. *American Antiquity* 32: 535–538.

CHANG, KWANG-CHIH
1968   *The archaeology of ancient China* (second edition). New Haven, Conn.: Yale University Press.

CLARK, J. DESMOND
1962   *Africa south of the Sahara.* Viking Fund Publications in Anthropology 32:1–33.

EDMAN, G., E. SÖDERBERG
1929   Auffindung von Reis in einer Tonscherbe aus einer etwa fünftausend-jährigen chinesischen Siedlung. *Bulletin of the Geological Society of China* 8 (4).

ENGLER, A.
1936   *A. Engler's Syllabus der Pflanzenfamilien* (eleventh edition). Berlin: Gebrüder Brntraeger.

EPSTEIN, H.
1969   *Domestic animals of China.* Farnham Royal, Bucks., England: Commonwealth Agricultural Bureaux.

FAIRSERVIS, WALTER A., JR.
1967   *The origin, character, and decline of an early civilization.* American Museum Novitates 2302.

GOVERNMENT OF INDIA
1966   *The wealth of India: a dictionary of Indian raw materials and industrial products,* volume seven. New Delhi.

HARLAN, JACK R., DANIEL ZOHARY
1966   Distribution of wild wheats and barleys. *Science* 153:1074–1080.

HEDRICK, U. P., *editor*
1919   *Sturtevant's notes on edible plants.* Albany, N.Y.: J. B. Lyon.

HERMANN, F. J.
1962   *A revision of the genus* Glycine *and its immediate allies.* United States Department of Agriculture Technical Bulletin 1268.

HIGGS, E. S., M. R. JARMAN
1969   The origins of agriculture: a reconsideration. *Antiquity* 43:31–41.

HO, PING-TI
1956   The early-ripening rice in Chinese history. *Economic History Review,* second series, 9.
1969   The loess and the origin of Chinese agriculture. *American Historical Review* 75:1–36.
1975   *The cradle of the East: an inquiry into the indigenous origins of techniques and ideas of Neolithic and early historic China, 5000–1000 B.C.* Hong Kong and Chicago: Chinese University of Hong Kong and University ofChicago Press.

HYMOWITZ, THEODORE
1970   On the domestication of the soybean. *Economic Botany* 24:408–421.

JACOBSEN, THORKILD, ROBERT M. ADAMS
1958   Salt and silt in ancient Mesopotamian agriculture. *Science* 128:1251–1258.

JASNY, NAUM
1944   *The wheat of classical antiquity.* Baltimore: Johns Hopkins Press.

KANNGIESSER, F.
  1912   Die Flora des Herodot. *Archiv für Geschichte der Naturwissenschaften und der Technik* 3.

KARLGREN, BERNHARD, *translator*
  1950a   *The book of documents.* Stockholm Museum of Far Eastern Antiquities.
  1950b   *The book of odes.* Stockholm Museum of Far Eastern Antiquities.

KING, LAWRENCE J.
  1966   *Weeds of the world: biology and control.* London: C. Hill.

KRISHNASWAMY, N.
  1951   Origin and distribution of cultivated plants of South Asia: millets. *Indian Journal of Genetics and Plant Breeding* 2:67–74.

LARICHEV, V. Y.
  1964   "Ancient cultures of North China," in *The archaeology and geomorphology of northeastern Asia: selected works.* Edited by Henry N. Michael, 232–248. Toronto: University of Toronto Press.

LAUFER, BERTHOLD
  1914   Some fundamental ideas of Chinese culture. *Journal of Race Development* 5.
  1919   *Sino-Iranica: Chinese contributions to the history of civilization in ancient Iran with special reference to the history of cultivated plants and products.* Chicago: Field Museum of Natural History. *and products.* Chicago.

LAY, DOUGLAS M., CHARLES F. NADLER, JERRY D. HASSINGER
  1971   The transferrins and hemoglobins of wild Iranian sheep. *Comparative Biochemical Physiology* 40B:521–529.

LEE, J. S. (LI, SSU-KUANG)
  1939   *The geology of China.* London: T. Murby.

LEGGE, JAMES, *translator*
  1865   *The Chinese classics,* volume three: *The Shoo king.* Hong Kong.
  1872   *The Chinese classics,* volume four: *The She king.* Hong Kong.
  1873   *The Chinese classics,* volume five: *The Ch'un Ts'ew with the Tso Chuen.* Hong Kong.

LEOPOLD, A. STARKER
  1961   *The desert.* Life Nature Library. New York: Time-Life Books.

LI, HUI-LIN
  1948   Floristic significance and problems of eastern Asia. *Taiwania* 1.
  1953   Endemism and ligneous flora of eastern Asia. *Proceedings of the Seventh Pacific Science Congress* 5.
  1964   *Metasequoia,* a living fossil. *American Scientist* 52:93–109.

MACDONNEL, A. A., A. B. KEITH
  1912   *Vedix index of names and subjects.* London: J. Murray.

MAC NEISH, RICHARD S.
  1967   "Mesoamerican archaeology," in *Biennial review of anthropology.* Edited by Bernard J. Siegal and Alan B. Beals, 306–331. Stanford, Calif.: Stanford University Press.

MASPERO, HENRI
  1927   *La Chine antique.* Paris: E. de Boccard.

MC NEILL, WILLIAM H.
1963 *The rise of the west: a history of the human community.* Chicago: University of Chicago Press.

MERRILL, E. D.
1936 Plants and civilizations. *Scientific Monthly*: 43:430–439.

NADLER, C. F., K. V. KOROBITSINA, R. S. HOFFMAN, N. N. VORONTSOV
1973 Cytogenetic differentiation, geographic distribution, and domestication in Palearctic sheep (*Ovis*). *Zeitschrift für Säugetierkunde* 38: 109–125.

OPPENHEIM, A. LEO
1964 *Ancient Mesopotamia: a portrait of a dead civilization.* Chicago: University of Chicago Press.

PUMPELLY, RAPHAEL
1908 *Explorations in Turkestan: prehistoric civilizations of Anau,* two volumes. Publications of the Carnegie Institute of Washington 73.

REED, CHARLES A.
1959 Animal domestication in the prehistoric Near East. *Science* 130: 1629–39.
1960 A review of the archeological evidence on animal domestication in the prehistoric Near East. *Studies in Ancient Oriental Civilization* 31: 119–145.
1969 "The pattern of animal domestication in the prehistoric Near East," in *The domestication and exploitation of plants and animals.* Edited by Peter J. Ucko and G. W. Dimbleby, 361–80. Chicago: Aldine.

RENFREW, J. M.
1969 "The archaeological evidence for the domestication of plants: methods and problems," in *The domestication and exploitation of plants and animals.* Edited by Peter J. Ucko and G. W. Dimbleby, 149–72. Chicago: Aldine.

RODE, A. A.
1962 *Soil science.* Washington, D.C.: Published for the National Science Foundation, Washington, D.C., by the Israel Program for Scientific Translations; available from the Office of Technical Services, U.S. Department of Commerce.

ROXBY, P. M.
1938 The terrain of early Chinese civilization. *Geography* 23:225–236.

SKVORTZOW, B. M.
1927 The soybean — wild and cultivated in eastern Asia. *Manchurian Research Society Publications, Natural Science Section,* series A, 2.

SMALLEY, IAN J.
1968 The loess deposits and Neolithic culture of north China. *Man: Journal of the Royal Anthropological Institute* 3:224–41.

SYLWAN, VIVI
1937 Silk from the Yin Dynasty. *Bulletin of the Museum of Far Eastern Antiquities* 9.

TEILHARD DE CHARDIN, PIERRE, C. C. YOUNG
1936 On the mammalian remains from the archaeological site of Anyang. *Paleontologia Sinica,* series C, 12 (1).

TING, V. K.
  1931   Professor Granet's *La civilisation chinoise*. *Chinese Social and Political Science Review* 15.

TOYNBEE, ARNOLD J.
  1934   *A study of history*, volume one. London: Oxford University Press.

VAVILOV, N. I.
  1949–1950   The origin, variation, immunity, and breeding of cultivated plants. *Chronica Botanica* 13:1–364.

VON WISSMANN, HERMANN
  1956   "On the role of nature and man in changing the face of the dry belt of Asia," in *Man's role in changing the face of the earth*. Edited by William L. Thomas, 278–303. Chicago: University of Chicago Press.

WHEELER, MORTIMER
  1966   *Civilizations of the Indus Valley and beyond*. London: Thames and Hudson.

WICHIZER, V. D., M. K. BENNET
  1941   *The rice economy of monsoon Asia*. Stanford, Calif.: Food Research Institute, Stanford University.

WITTFOGEL, KARL A.
  1957   *Oriental despotism: a comparative study of total power*. New Haven, Conn.: Yale University Press.

ZEUNER, FREDERICK E.
  1963   *A history of domesticated animals*. New York: Hutchinson.

Pre-Agricultural Tools for the Preparation of Foods in the Old World

NANCY KRAYBILL

The philology of words concerned with milling is too broad for this discussion. However, examples of common ancestry of such words are numerous. The Sanskrit root *mar* means 'to grind'. The related Latin word *mola* was applied to all mills and gave rise to the late Latin word *molina*. Other words that mean mill are *Mühle* in German, *muileann* in Gaelic and *melin* in Welsh (Curwen 1941: 32). The Latin word *pistor* 'baker' means "one who pounds emmer" (Curwen 1937: 133; Moritz 1958: 26).

The presence of pottery, mortars, and querns is no longer definitive of settled agricultural life. The idea that man utilized and processed seeds and other plant-foods prior to settled village life enjoys wide acceptance, but investigations related to such processes remain few. Although there have been, in recent years, a number of analyses directed toward understanding man's relation to the environment and those changes which may have led to the beginnings of agriculture, interest in the "pre-adaptive" techniques of processing plant-food prior to agriculture has been almost entirely confined to the Natufian in the Near East. As a result, serious attention is rarely devoted to tools for processing plants in assemblages antedating the Natufian.

Some of the existing studies of mortars and querns and grinding stones have been carried out by some who were not archaeologists (Bennet and Elton 1898; Moritz 1958; Storck and Teague 1952) and a few by specialists (Curwen 1937, 1941; Farmer 1960; McCarthy 1941a; and R. L. Solecki 1969). While pottery has been subject to exhaustive description and analysis, mortars and grinding stones, when reported, are usually given cursory enumeration and description; not only the measurements of dimension and weight, but even the distinction between upper and lower stones, is frequently neglected. Those workers who have reported such details are conspicuously few in number.

Food-processing tools offer a unique opportunity for the study of man's actual utilization of plant-foods in a given environment. While palynology, paleobotany, and botanical surveys of present environments can aid in the reconstruction of past environments, they cannot tell us what part of the plant community was utilized. Exploitative behavior is known to be selective so that the array and availability of resources are no reflection of actual utilization (Freeman 1968: 263). Tools used for the processing of plants offer a valuable means of determining what part of the reconstructed plant community was utilized in specific environments, both in time and space.

Equipment for plant processing in the form of mortars, pestles, querns, and mullers has been associated with settled agricultural communities and communities where intensive collection was practiced both in the Old and New Worlds. The recovery of the same equipment from sites of greater antiquity and antecedent in evolutionary "grade" of economic and technological activity created problems in both their classification and the understanding of their functional relationships. Creating more "types" and "levels" to accommodate the new material would result, not in the understanding of their "evolution," but in "taxonomy" (Freeman 1968: 263). Persistence in associating equipment for plant processing with a "level" of cultural evolution, while seemingly extending that level further back in time, can only succeed in obscuring the operations involved in the use of plant-processing tools and the functional relations of those tools to sets of activities and the relationship of those sets of activities to settlement types and systems.

Understanding of the functional relationship of tools to site is dependent upon the understanding of the function of the tools themselves. Not only is the taxonomy of plant-processing tools in a confused state, but the understanding of the relations of morphology to function and the operations of milling are confused as well. Much of the confusion surrounding the typology, taxonomy, and functional interpretations of equipment for processing plants is a result of misunderstanding of the operations carried out in the milling process.

Semenov has noted the value of ethnographic material in the study of function and manufacture of prehistoric tools (1964:2). The lack of useful reports on material culture in the ethnographic literature has sent some archaeologists into the field to study material culture of existing technologically simple societies. The results of those investigations are just beginning to be published; consequently the majority of ethnographic information comes from reports by nineteenth-century non-specialists. The quality of the material, sometimes surprisingly detailed, is uneven but remains the major source of information for contemporary study. Of all the elements of material culture, the most poorly reported and described in the early literature are the mundane details of techniques for processing plants, which lack the masculine appeal of hunting. That bias persists in the contemporary literature where information on hunting outstrips that on plant utilization.

NOMENCLATURE

The present state of confusion in the nomenclature has been noted by others (Hole, Flannery, and Neely 1969: 170; Carter, this volume) and will not be belabored here. In an effort to avoid complicating further an already seriously confused nomenclature, tools used for the operation of pounding will be termed mortars and pestles, even where their morphology differs from the traditional. The suggestion (Carter, this volume) that mano and metate be adopted for all grinding tools is well taken; however, the terms "grinding slab" and "handstone" have been adopted by me for the present discussion as they are already part of the synonymy in the Old World (Hole, Flannery, and Neeley 1969). Where the distinction is known, the lower grinding stone will be termed "grinding slab" and the upper stone, "handstone"; where the distinction is not made in the literature cited, "grinding stone" will be used. The terminology used here will follow the operations involved without regard for morphology. Because some tools are used for both pounding and grinding, the term "grinder/pestle" has been retained for its descriptive value. The morphology of any tool used for processing plants is directly related to its use, which not only results in the gradual reduction in size but also in morphological changes as a tool "develops" during its lifetime; thus typological distinctions between "flat," "basined," and "troughed" will be used as adjectives here except where citing previously published materials.

Where terms in the literature cited differ, they will follow the terminology adopted here *en paren.* Synonymy for pounding tools is given in Table 1 and for grinding tools in Table 2. Neither table is exhaustive but each reflects some of the misunderstanding and confusion of the interpretation of the function of the tools themselves. McCarthy (1946: 57) has commented on percussion tools from Australia:

The percussion implements form a puzzling group to classify. There is little precise information about them, and in only a few instances is there any published record of first-hand observation of their use by aborigines. A great deal of misconception has also arisen because of the incorrect application to them of such names as hammer, anvil, husking, pestles and pounding stones by which they are commonly known. These terms are suitable in some instances, but they have been taken over from our own tools of similar function and applied to aboriginal implements in a manner that has made the implement fit the term rather than the reverse.

Table 1.   Names for pounding tools

Lower stone	Upper stone
mortar	pestle
mortar	pounder
mortar	percussion muller
anvil	rounded hammer-anvil
anvil	"pitted" anvil stone

Table 2.   Names for grinding tools

Lower stone	Upper stone
grain-rubber	rubber
grinding stone	grinder
grinding slab	handstone
mealing stone	mealing stone
quern	muller
grinding dish	grinder
saddle-quern	muller
milling stone	hand millstone

FOOD-PROCESSING EQUIPMENT IN THE ETHNOGRAPHIC PRESENT

The humble nature of plant processing has resulted in the neglect of information gathering about tools used for these activities in contemporary, technologically simple societies. Semenov has noted that the material on hand still retains a great deal of value despite its inadequacy and sporadic nature (1964: 2).

In Australia plants are processed both by pounding and grinding. Fruits, roots, bulbs, rhizomes, nuts, and seeds are first reduced by pounding on "anvils," mortars, or in "seed-pounding pits." During the pounding process they are shelled, hulled, and pulverized. If further reduction is desirable, the pounded pieces are then ground on grinding slabs.

"Seed-pounding pits" are holes in rock outcrops and have been reported in northern, northwestern, western, and central Australia (McCarthy 1962: 7; 1970: 60, 83). Portable mortars and "anvils" are either water-worn pebbles or roughly shaped stone slabs (Howchin 1934: 71; McCarthy 1941a: 329; 1946: 66). The lengths of mortars and "anvils" range from seven to twenty-six centimeters, but have been reported up to forty-five centimeters (McCarthy 1946: 66; Howchin 1934: 71). The pestles used with the mortars and "anvils" are either round pebbles or elongate-shaped stones. Sizes of the round pestles range from five to 12.5 centimeters in diameter and the oblong pestles range up to 17.5 centimeters in length (McCarthy 1941a: 331). Some of these tools are specialized and bear special names such as the *kulki*, which is a cylindrical stone with flattened sides and rounded edges (McCarthy 1946: 57). Mortars, "anvils," and pestles frequently bear one or more pits in the center called "anvil pits" in the literature. "Anvil pits" are known to occur when aborigines have been observed pounding nuts with tough, woody cases (McCarthy and Setzler 1960: 247).

In Africa grains are pounded in wooden mortars using wooden pestles prior to grinding (Stefaniszyn 1964: 42; Barnes 1948: 12; White 1948: 10). Ground beans are shelled and crushed by pounding, as well as ground-nuts and seeds of pumpkin which are roasted prior to pounding (Stafaniszyn 1964: 45). Green vegetables, herbs, tobacco, and nuts are still pounded on stone (Frosbrooke 1952: 15; Boshier 1965: 131). The "anvils" used for pounding marula nuts may weigh up to fifty pounds while the "hammers" used with them range from one-half to four pounds (Boshier 1965: 131).

Australian lower grinding stones are quarried from rock outcrops. Quarries have been reported near Mt. William, Mt. Slavety, near Lake Eyre, and near Wilcannia (McCarthy 1970: 21, 29, 46). Because suitable stone is unevely distributed in Australia, grinding stones were an important item of trade. Quarried grindstones are either flat or basined, sometimes carefully pecked but usually roughly shaped, as the qualities of smoothness and hardness are selected for rather than shape (McCarthy 1941a: 330–331; Thomson 1964; Gould, et al. 1971: 164). Grinding stones range from twenty to ninety centimeters in length and include special types like *morah* stones, which are incised transversely and longitudinally for the release of poisonous juices of some plants (McCarthy 1941a: 331; 1946: 62). Grinding depressions may consist of one large, wide depression, or up to four narrower depressions. A groove for sharpening an ax may be on one surface (McCarthy 1946: 62). The upper grinding stones, mullers, are either round or oval. The oval stones measure from seven to twenty-one centimeters in length (McCarthy 1946: 62).

In Australia foods which are not eaten raw, or simply roasted in a fire, are processed, at least in part, with the few simple tools described above. The kinds of plant-foods include many varieties of fruit and some varieties of bulbs, roots, and rhizomes, all of which during their preparation may require pounding. Some nuts and all seeds are ground as well.

Roasting, soaking, and the addition of water are sometimes necessary additional steps in the processing of plant-foods. In Africa water is sometimes added to grain as it is pounded (Stefaniszyn 1964: 43; Gast 1968). In Australia some plants require roasting prior to pounding: gum scrub root; belillah root; and rhizomes of the bracken fern (Eyre 1845: 249, 269; Mitchell 1955: 132). Some yams must be soaked to remove poisons, and are then dried, after which they are sometimes pounded. Nuts of cycad are pounded, then roasted and leached to remove poisons (Berndt and Berndt 1964: 98; McCarthy and Setzler 1960: 247). Winnowing of seeds usually follows pounding and is followed by grinding (Barnes 1948: 12; Gould 1969: 261; Stefaniszyn 1964: 433).

In addition to grinding foods, some grinding stones in Australia are used to grind ochre (Gould 1968: 120; McCarthy and Setzler 1960: 218; McCarthy 1946: 57). Handstones are also brought into use for smoothing wooden implements and odd pieces of stone are often used for sharpening ax blades (McCarthy 1941a: 333). The same tool may be used as a handstone for grinding one time and as a pestle for pounding another time. Kulki are frequently used as both handstones and pestles (McCarthy 1946: 57). Mortars, pestles, handstones, and grinding slabs are very generalized tools which have as their major function the processing of food, but which function, at times, in other maintenance tasks. McCarthy (1946: 57) has commented on the eclectic nature of these tools in Australia:

... the same percussion stone may be used by the aborigines on its margins and upper and lower surfaces for a variety of purposes, including knapping and trimming, for pounding ochre, nuts, bones and seeds, for breaking open and striking off shells, and for shredding bark.

Equipment that is associated with pounding and grinding plants includes mats, baskets, trays, and small round stones used to sharpen or roughen grinding stones. Called kgekgetos in South Africa, they are also known in East Africa (Boshier 1965: 133; Frosbrooke 1952: 15; Jeffreys 1966: 58). Stones used for the purpose of "sharpening" upper and lower grindstones are selected for toughness rather than hardness. Sources of the desired stone are scarce enough that "quern rougheners" are items of trade (Boshier 1965: 133–135). "Quern rougheners" differ from spheroid stones used to pound and grind plant-foods in that they do not have the smoother texture of the pounders and grinders (Frosbrooke 1952: 15).

Although pounding and grinding equipment, except "seed-pounding pits," is portable, in Australia it is not transported from camp to camp but left for use on a return visit or for others who might occupy the camp (Gould 1968: 112; McCarthy 1941a: 331; Gould, et al. 1971: 164). Pounding and grinding equipment may be the only material equipment remaining in the camp when it is deserted; grinding stones can be found in most deserted camps, and near wells and water holes in Western Australia (Thomson 1964: 403). In South Africa stones used for pounding marula nuts are usually left in place beneath the trees where they were used (Boshier 1965: 131). Stones used for sharpening grinding slabs and spheroids used for pounding and grinding tobacco, vegetables, and herbs by some tribes of eastern Africa are also left behind when the site is abandoned (Frosbrooke 1952: 15).

The tools used by contemporary technologically simple societies are most often portable, except holes *in situ* in rocks, but are rarely transported from camp to camp. Pounding stones are either water-worn pebbles or roughly shaped stone slabs. Grinding stones are quarried, roughly shaped, but carefully pecked on occasion and are either flat or basined oval slabs. The hand-held pestles are round or elongate and shaped. The equipment, except for specialized *morah* stones, is used casually with the most appropriate stones at hand used for the task without regard for their morphology, specificity to the task, or their previous use. Therefore, the equipment often demonstrates wear both from pounding and grinding. The use of pounders and grinders is not confined to their major function of processing plants but they are also used for a variety of maintenance tasks not confined to either sex. When a tool is so worn that it can no longer function to pound or grind, the crescent-shaped section may be used as a skinning knife (McCarthy 1941a: 331). The morphology of the tools results from the processes involved in their use, which is determined by the task and the convenience of the processor, and not by an ideal "type" residing in the mind of the processor.

Milling as a Process

Milling as a process involves two major operations when carried out by hand on non-rotary equipment: pounding and grinding. Pounding and grinding are separate operations and either one, or both, may be used. The literature on the subject is not abundant but can be found in Bennet and Elton (1898), Curwen (1937), Moritz (1958), Harlan (1967), Gast (1968), Gast and Adrian (1965), and Helbaek (1969). There is ethnographic evidence in both Africa and Australia for the separateness of the two operations (Barnes 1948: 10; Stefaniszyn 1964: 43; McCarthy 1941a: 332; Specht 1958: 482; Spencer 1914: 394; Thomson 1964: 402). Failure to distinguish between pounding and grinding in the milling process has been responsible for the major part of the confusion in the nomenclature. The operations of pounding and grinding of an edible plant-part depend on a number of factors which result in the selection of the operation or operations most appropriate to the reduction of an item: the material to be processed; the physical properties of the item to be processed; and the physical and chemical characteristics desirable in the end product.

Stone is usually available to societies although the kind may be restricted. All known grinding in technologically simple societies in the ethnographic present is carried out using stone implements. The choice of wood in preference to stone seems to be related to the characteristics desired in the end product rather than the physical properties of the plant-part, as most plant-parts which are pounded in wooden mortars are also, or can be, pounded in mortars of stone. Wooden mortars were used in classical times so that grain would not be grated too much or broken prematurely, thus severely crushing and mashing the inner seed material as the hull was "cracked" (Harlan 1967: 199; Moritz 1958: 25).

The pounding operation is used to crush vegetables and fruits and to hull and pulverize nuts and seeds. The physical properties of the plant-part, notably seeds, may need processing prior to pounding in the form of soaking, drying, or roasting. The hulls of wild einkorn, emmer, and especially barley are tightly held to the seeds, making them difficult to thresh (Harlan 1967: 199; Helbaek 1969: 409). Drying and roasting facilitate the separation of the grain from the tightly held husks (Harlan 1967: 199–200). Leaching to remove poisonous juices from some vegetables and nuts takes place before or after pounding. Water is frequently added during pounding to aid in the removal of bran (Bennet and Elton 1898; Gast 1968). More complete removal of the indigestible bran results in a nutritionally superior product according to some investigators (Gast and Adrian 1965).

Pounding in a mortar not only "cracks" nuts and seeds, separating them from their hulls, but reduces them mechanically to a rough texture suitable for "sauces" or porridge. Pounding grain in a mortar prior to grinding persisted after the adoption of the technique of baking. In Pliny's time Roman bakers pounded grain in a mortar before grinding (Bennet and Elton 1898: 125; Moritz 1958: 25) and the practice is still in existence today in Ethiopia, Italy, Yugoslavia, Turkey, and India (Harlan 1967: 199).

Winnowing is sometimes carried out before pounding, for example by the Ambo of Northern Rhodesia, Africa, when processing millet (Stefaniszyn 1964: 43) or takes place before and after pounding; for example, some Australian aborigines when threshing certain seeds tread them with their feet (McCarthy 1941a: 332). Or it follows poundings as when the Ngoni of Africa process maize (Barnes 1948: 12) or Australians process wild rice (Specht 1958: 484).

Seeds are ground more easily and quickly if they are first dried. Water is sometimes added to hulled seeds before grinding (Storck and Teague 1952: 52). Grinding and mixing dough may take place at the same time on a tilted grinding stone where the meal is moistened and kneaded into cakes as it is ground (McCarthy 1941a: 333). In ancient Mesopotamia hulled barley was soaked in water until it had sprouted, after which it was either preserved in that state or ground. Not only did the process produce a sweet taste but both the nutritional and preservative properties of the barley were enhanced (Hartman and Oppenheim 1950: 13).

Grinding tools exhibit grinding facets and are often polished. As a tool is worn by long use it becomes polished and smooth, necessitating sharpening or roughening if grinding is to be efficient. Grinding is predominately in a back-and-forth manner but some tasks such as the preparation of seed-paste from sun-dried *kampurarpa*, a tomato native to Australia, are done with a motion using both hands "pushing and rotating vertically in a 30° arc from back to front at the same time" (Gould, et al. 1971: 164). Over time a grinding slab which begins flat will become "basined"; after long and repeated use it may be deeply troughed.

Pounding is a percussion operation and tools used for pounding show traces of crushing, bruising, and battering. Wear is sometimes specific to a certain foodstuff processed such as the "anvil pits" produced by the tough, hard cases of the Australian *tay tay* nuts (McCarthy and Setzler 1960: 247). When an operator misses the mark and strikes the mortar or anvil, chipping occurs which eventually leads to a smooth, rounded or spherical shape (Boshier 1965: 132; Frosbrooke 1952: 15). Hence a pestle which begins as a quadrangular stone may develop into a spherical stone after repeated and long use.

PLANT-PROCESSING TOOLS SOUTH OF THE SAHARA

Although the milling properties of wild seeds are imperfectly known and most information is confined to varieties which later became cultigens, ethnographic evidence from the Old World for treatment of seeds by pounding prior to grinding suggests that the pounding operation was antecedent to grinding for many wild seeds. Tools used for pounding seeds and other foods by some technologically simple societies of the Old World include tools which have been described in the literature as spheroids, stone balls, subspheroids, cuboids, and polyhedrons. Their presence in the archaeological record has a long history in Africa where they occur as early as 1.8 million years ago at DK, an occupation floor in lower Bed I at Olduvai Gorge, and as late as the Later Stone Age, thought to have commenced around 35,000 B.P. (Leakey 1971; Curtis and Hay 1972: 293; Vogel and Beaumont 1972: 50).

Polyhedrons are not a common type of tool at Olduvai. Spheroids and subspheroids form an important element in the assemblages in both Bed I and Bed II, where they occur at all sites except those at FLK. They are scarcer in Bed I but increase in importance in Bed II where they are never less than 20 percent of the total tools (Leakey 1971: 266). Average mean diameters of spheroids range from 5.6 to 6.3 centimeters and from 5.3 to 6.3 centimeters for subspheroids (Leakey 1971: 31, 79, 104, 112, 153, 189). The range in weight was plotted for 17 specimens from HWK East, levels 3, 4 and 5 (lower part of Middle Bed II); 159 specimens from the Main Site at MNK (Middle Bed II); and 199 specimens from BK (Upper Bed II). The most common weight at the earlier sites was from 116 grams to 464 grams, while most specimens from the later site, BK, were less than 116 grams (Leakey 1971: 266–267). Spheroids and subspheroids are both faceted, but the projecting ridges are battered and partly reduced (Leakey 1971: 266, and Plates 16, 19, and 24). The spheroids and subspheroids were present on most occupation floors, except FLK NN, and also were absent from both kill and butchering sites: FLK North, Upper Bed I and Lower Bed II (Leakey 1971: 65, 86).

One spheroid and two cuboids have been recovered from the Sterkfontein Extension site in Transvaal (Mason 1962a: 110, 114, and Figure 3, Number 2; and Figure 4, Number 4). The 286 tools recovered were not concentrated in any one area but scattered randomly (Robinson 1962: 103). Although Mason designated both Sterkfontein and Klipplaatdrif tools, which do not include spheroids, as Early Acheulean, the similarity to the developed Oldowan tools in Bed II has been recognized (Mason 1962b: 149; Leakey 1971: 273). Maguire has described both "pounders" and spheroids from the Phase 2 breccia at Makapansgat but they were a small part of the assemblage, 1.5 percent and .9 percent respectively (Maguire 1965: 124). Partridge has reported three cuboids from Phase 1 grey breccia at the same site (1965: 113).

Spheroids are widely distributed in Africa, having been recovered from sites in north, west, central, east, and south Africa but being the most common at Middle Stone Age sites in south Africa (Lagercrantz 1950: 164; van Riet Lowe 1950: 72). These spherical objects are pecked and battered over their surface and have been classed as bolas by some workers, missiles by others, and stone balls by still other investigators. Kleindienst has expanded the category of stone balls to include not only spheroids but all "more-or-less deliberately shaped, more-or-less spheroid forms": polyhedrals, subspheroids, missiles, and bolas (1959: 68). The analysis by Kleindienst of several Late Acheulean assemblages from eastern Africa reveals the disparate importance of stone balls in different Late Acheulean sites: Kariandusi, .7 percent; Isimila, 1.7 percent; Kalambo Falls, .3 percent; and Broken Hill, 26.6 percent (1959: 151, 181, 225, 267). The difference between the frequencies of stone balls at the northern sites and at Broken Hill in the south has suggested to Kleindienst (1959: 282) that heavy duty tools, which include stone balls, may have been more important in the south. The frequency of stone balls, 10 percent, in the Late Acheulean assemblage at Cave of Hearths in the Transvaal (Mason 1962b: 282) would seem to bear her out.

The earliest stones with evidence of grinding were recovered at Florisbad, Orange Free State, South Africa, beneath Peat I (sample GrN-4208) dated at 48,900 B.P. (Vogel and Beaumont 1972: 51). The smaller of the two stones showing grinding wear measured 68.5 centimeters long and 35.6 centimeters wide, indicating by the large size that it was a grinding slab (measurements taken from Meiring 1956: Plate V, Number 4). "Pounders" were recovered which ranged in size from "small to large" and were sometimes pitted. Forty-six spheroids, 21.5 percent of the assemblage, were recovered and bore signs of bruising and battering (Meiring 1956: 227).

Grinding stones, some discolored by pigment, have been recovered from the Bushman Rock Shelter in eastern Transvaal (Louw 1969: 47) from levels dated from a charcoal sample (GrN-4855) at 42,950 to 46,950 B.P. (Vogel 1969: 56). The stones were not described as either upper or lower stones in the preliminary report.

At Cave of Hearths, grindstones, both upper and lower, are present, beginning in levels dated at $15,000 \pm 730$ B.P.; however, the determination is probably affected by contamination (Mason 1962b: 244). Mason described the handstones as similar to Iron Age types except that specimens from the earlier levels frequently had pecked-out cavities in the middle of each face (Mason 1962b: 258 and Figure 140, Number 1). Cuboids and spheroids were also present. Some of the spheroids show traces of battering while others bear traces of grinding (Mason 1962b: 257). No information was presented as to the level at which spheroids of Middle Stone Age begin to show traces of grinding.

Olieboomspoort Cave in the Transvaal yielded five grindstones, eighty-five cuboids and three spheroids, as well as sixty-four pieces of haematite and ochre from levels dated from a carbon sample at 33,000 B.P. (Mason 1962b: 259, 273). One grindstone was encrusted with pigment (Mason 1962b: 259 and Figure 142).

At Kalambo Falls grinding stones have been recovered from Rubbles 1a and 1b. The grinding stone from 1a is Magosian and described as a "rubber" (Clark 1969: 167). The handstones in 1b are with a collection of mixed upper and lower Lumpemban artifacts; however Magosian tools are included (Clark 1969: 168). An age of 26,950 to 28,950 B.P. has been suggested for the levels from which the handstones were recovered (Clark 1962: 197).

The function of stone balls has been a subject of debate. Louis Leakey and Revil Mason, among others, favored an interpretation as hunting bolas used in slings (Leakey 1971:266; Mason 1962b:167). Other suggestions include use as missiles, stone club-heads, quern rougheners, and vegetable pounders (Meiring 1956: 227; Lagercrantz 1950: 165; Boshier 1965: 136; Jeffreys 1966: 58; Pyddoke 1950: 144; Frosbrooke 1952: 15; Dart 1965: 144).

Ethnographically, the most frequently cited examples are for plant pounding and two instances of food grinding. Only one instance of stone balls used as bolas was known to Lagercrantz and that is among the Dogon in Africa where they are used by children for killing birds (1950: 165). The interpretation as bolas is weakened by the absence of stone balls at kill sites at Olduvai Gorge and from open sites in South Africa where they are more frequent in workshops and on living floors (van Riet Lowe 1950: 72). While they are 10 percent of 2,150 specimens in Bed 3 at Cave of Hearths, they are less than 1 percent at Blaubank, also in the Transvaal, which has led Mason to remark: "The higher proportion of spheroids in the cave industry is surprising, as this class would be expected at an open site presumably devoted to hunting but we have seen spheroids to be similarly absent at the Wonderboom site" (1962b: 216).

The use of stone balls as "quern rougheners" without evidence of the grinding slabs themselves is not very convincing. The earliest stones used for grinding slabs are at Florisbad, where there are forty-nine stone balls, yet only two grinding slabs.

The distribution of handstones and grinding slabs in the Transvaal demonstrates a more frequent occurrence at cave sites during the Middle

Stone Age and at 15,000 B.P. The grindstones are not always associated with pigment: grindstones at Mwulu Cave are associated with pigment at one level and not associated with pigment at another level. Of interest is the long period of time between the oldest reported grinding slab at Florisbad at 49,000 B.P. and the next reported grinding slab at Cave of Hearths at 15,000 B.P. For the interim period only handstones are reported, beginning at 33,000 B.P. at Olieboomspoort. The yet undescribed specimens from Bushman Rock Shelter, 42,000 to 47,000 B.P., may yield more information.

Grindstones and Pestles from Europe

In the literature of the last century "rubbers" and grinders recovered from caves in France were reported by Lartet and others. The similarity among the specimens from the French caves, stones used in Siberia for pounding acorns and nuts, and stones used by Australians for crushing roots was noted by Bennet and Elton (1898: 16). Since the turn of the century, reports of grinding stones recovered from European sites are rare despite the increase of both professional care and the number of sites excavated. The absence of grinding stones, one suspects, is more in the reporting than in the ground.

Tools described as grinders/pestles have been recovered at Molodova on the Dniester River in the Ukraine. Molodova I has yielded a number of the grinders/pestles from the Mousterian levels dated by charcoal sample (GrN-3659) as older than 44,000 B.P. (Vogel and Waterbolk 1967: 119). Horizons 3 and 5 have each yielded three and Horizon 4 yielded forty-one of the grinders/pestles, in addition to twenty-six handstones (Klein 1966: 47–54). In general, the grinders/pestles are mostly sandstone pebbles, sometimes spherical and sometimes flattened ovals. Measurements taken from Klein's figures of nine of the grinders/pestles indicate that they range from eight to ten centimeters in length and from seven to eight centimeters in width (1966: 52, Figure 6, Numbers 21–30). The grinders/pestles show traces of use as hammerstones and as handstones for grinding (Klein 1966: 47).

Chernysh has recovered a similar grinder/pestle from layer XIb at Molodova V located 1.2 kilometers from Molodova I (1961: 82). The grinder/pestle is 5.8 by 7 by 3.2 centimeters (Chernysh 1961: 82, Figure 37, Number 12). The tool is a sandstone pebble which has traces of use as a handstone (Klein 1966: 33). Mousterian layers at Molodova V have been dated by charcoal sample (GrN-4017) at older than 40,000 B.P.

(Vogel and Waterbolk 1967: 119). At Molodova V there are many grinders/pestles in the Late Paleolithic levels (Chernysh 1961: 82). The presence of grinders/pestles has suggested to Sulimirski that the occupants must have supplemented their diet by gathering roots and seeds of wild grasses (1970: 12).

In France a side-chopper made on a piece of grindstone was recovered from Mousterian level F.I.1. at Abri Olha, Basses Pyrénées, France (Freeman 1964: 134 and Figure 47). The reworked grindstone measured 17.5 centimeters in length and 10.8 centimeters wide (measurements taken from a photograph). At a cave site, Cueva del Castillo, Cueva Morin, Spain, large grindstones were reported from Mousterian levels. One large chopper made from a grindstone recovered from level Alpha measured 17.8 centimeters and 16.5 centimeters (measurements taken from a photograph). The Alpha and Beta levels at Cueva del Castillo also yielded polyhedrals, bolas, and hammerstones (Freeman 1964: 90, 99, Tables 25 and 27). The grindstones are often quite large, leading Freeman to attribute the grinding to the processing of foods (1966: 231).

At another cave site in Spain, Cueva del Conde, grindstones have been reported from Aurignacian Levels 1 and 2. Freeman has commented on one large grindstone: "This is larger than pieces usually associated with color-grinding processes, at least in the New World. It is testimony I believe, of either meat or vegetable food-grinding" (Freeman 1964: 55).

Archaeological Evidence from Nubia, Northeastern Africa

Grinding slabs have been recovered in Nubia from levels dated as early as 14,000 B.P. During Vignard's excavations in Nubia, he collected grinding stones from Sebilian 1 levels. One basined grinding slab measured 43 by 30 by 4 centimeters (1923: Plate XIV *bis*). More recently, grindstones have been recovered from Kom Ombo on the east bank of the Nile in Upper Egypt (Reed 1966: 22; Smith 1968: 392), from the southern part of Egyptian Nubia (Wendorf 1968: 880–940), and as far as the second cataract from levels tentatively assigned to the lower Tshitolian (Marks 1968: 527).

Smith has recovered grinding stones from surface finds in the region of Sebil and subsurface finds at Gebel Silsila, both on the Kom Ombo plain some fifty-five kilometers north of Aswan (1967: 146–147). Small occupation sites disturbed by erosion and deflation to some extent, yielded grinding stones at Khor-el-Sil, another site in the southern part of the Kom Ombo plain. A sample of shell of fresh-water clams (I-1297) at Khor-el-Sil III was dated at 17,000 ± 600 B.P.

The Yale expedition to Nubia recovered basined grinding slabs and handstones stratigraphically *in situ* from a level at Gebel Silsila 2B, of which the artifacts would be categorized as Sebilian III in Vignard's terminology; this terminology, however, is being reevaluated with the present study of this assemblage by James Phillips. This level has been dated from shell of fresh-water clam (Y-1447) and charcoal (Y-1375) at $13,000 \pm 120$ and $13,070 \pm 160$ B.P. (Reed 1965: 101; Reed, et al. 1967: 151–152). There were numerous whole and fragmentary handstones but pieces of grinding slabs were rare (Reed et al. 1967: 152). Numerous pieces of ochre were reported. Of interest was the absence of grinding slabs and handstones in levels dated from a charcoal sample (Y-1376) at 15,310 ± 200 B.P. and containing tools of a microlithic industry at Gebel Silsila 2B (Reed, et al. 1967: 152; Stuiver 1969: 642).

In the southern part of Egyptian Nubia, at site 8905 (Tushka), along the shore and around the ponds between dunes, members of the Combined Prehistoric Expedition to Nubia in 1962 to 1964 recovered numerous grinding slabs and handstones from the surface and from beneath silt and cemented inter-dune deposits between 14,000 and 15,000 B.P. (Wendorf 1968: 865, 940).

The twenty-four handstones, all made from local sandstones, were circular and ovate, pecked to shape and measuring 10.1 to 15.2 centimeters in length and 8.5 and 15 centimeters in width, with thicknesses between 1.8 and 8.5 centimeters (Wendorf 1968: 880, 885, 893, 906). Grinding surfaces were convex transversely and flat longitudinally, or convex in both dimensions, on one surface or two (Wendorf 1968: 880, 906, and Figure 63 A–B). Two pitted handstones were recovered.

Numerous grinding slabs were collected from the surface and single sandstone specimens were recovered stratigraphically from each of three localities. One grinding slab was roughly rectangular with a concave grinding surface and measured 34 by 33 by 9 centimeters. Wear was "free, but not circular" (Wendorf 1968: 893, and Figure 63D). Another specimen was fragmentary with an oval grinding surface which was flat with wear from "free motion and back and forth." The third specimen was an unshaped slab with a flat to slightly convex grinding surface worn from a back-and-forth motion and measuring 36 by 28 by 9 centimeters (Wendorf 1968: 927, and Figures 84 and 91). A carbon sample from charcoal (WSU-315) has yielded a date of $14,500 \pm 490$ B.P. (Wendorf 1968: 940).

The Near East

Spheroids and semi-spherical balls were reported in Middle Pleistocene levels at 'Ubeidiya in the central Jordan Valley (Stekelis, et al. 1960: 182 and Plate 1, Figure 1). At Latamne, in northern Syria, Clark has recovered spheroids thought to be associated with anvils on an occupation floor of the Middle Pleistocene (1966: 217). A mortar and two pestles were recovered from an Upper Paleolithic deposit at Ein Guev, Israel, dated (GrN-5576) at $15,700 \pm 415$ B.P. (Vogel and Waterbolk 1972: 49). The basalt mortar is 28.5 centimeters high with a superior rim of 28 centimeters (Stekelis and Bar-Yosef 1965: 182 and Figure 4, Number 3). Two pestles accompanied the mortar, one broken but the other intact and measuring 30 centimeters long (Stekelis and Bar-Yosef 1965: 182 and Figure 4, Number 4). In the Negev, bedrock mortars have been reported for levels thought to be Late Paleolithic: two bedrock mortars at Rosh Horsha and twelve deep bedrock mortars associated with a few well-made handstones at 'En-Avat (Marks, et al. 1971: 21; 1972: 80).

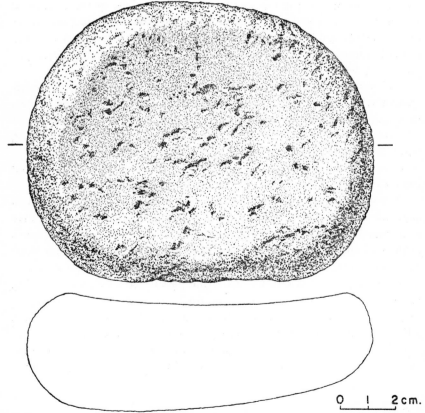

Figure 1.   Grinding slab from Ein Aqev, central Negev, Palestine. The dimensions are 12x10x4 cm. (Drawing courtesy of Marks, et al. 1975)

Mortars have been reported at the Natufian sites Mugharet-el-Wad, Erg-el-Ahmar, Kebara, Ain Mallaha, and Hayonim Cave in Israel (Garrod 1957: 217; Perrot 1966: 466; Bar-Yosef and Goren 1973: 63). The only Natufian dates available are from Jericho, taken from levels thought to be coincident with other Natufian sites in Palestine and yielding the dates (Gl-69) 9850 ± 240 B.P. and (P-376) $11,166 \pm 107$ B.P. (Perrot 1968: 367). Mortars have also been recovered at Mureybit, Syria (van Loon 1968: 279), Zawi Chemi Shanidar, Iraq (R. L. Solecki 1969: 990), and Ganj Dareh Tepe, Iran (Smith 1970). Mortars at Mugharet-el-Wad and from Ganj Dareh Tepe, dated at $10,400 \pm 150$ B.P. (Lawn 1970: 579), were limestone and irregular or roughly shaped slabs (Garrod 1957: 217; R. L. Solecki 1969: 990). Mortars at Erg-el-Ahmar were made from stones taken from the wadi bed (Garrod 1957: 217). Mortars at Kebara and Ain Mallaha (see Harlan, this volume) were basalt, beaker-shaped, with rim often ornamented, and occasionally footed. Sizes vary from "small to large"; the smallest at Kebara was ten centimeters high (Garrod 1957: 217). Mortars from Ain Mallaha described as similar to those from Kebara measure from thirteen centimeters high and twelve centimeters at the rim to a large specimen sixty centimeters high with a rim diameter of forty-five centimeters (measurements taken from Perrot 1966: Figure 16, Number 1 and Figure 15, Number 14). Of interest at Ain Mallaha is a deep basin excavated in a stone block near a hearth in shelter Number 26 and described as a mortar which was similar to basins found dug in the rocks fifty meters from the site (Perrot 1966: 450, 458, 482).

Shaped, cylindrical basalt pestles, some decorated with three incised rings, some fluted and one shaped like the hoof of a gazelle accompanied Natufian mortars (Garrod 1957: 217 and Plate 1). Cylindrical basalt pestles from Ain Mallaha measure from twelve to thirty centimeters long and from three to eight centimeters in diameter (measurements taken from Perrot 1966: Figure 17, Numbers 1, 8, 10, 14). Pestles have been reported at Beidha (Kirkbride 1968: 268; see map for this and following sites in Harlan, this volume), at Mureybit where they were made of cylindrical river pebbles (van Loon 1968: 279), in the Bl levels at Shanidar Cave (R. S. Solecki 1957: 25), and at Zawi Chemi Shanidar where the pestles (pounders) were either unmodified stones or shaped by pecking; one measured twenty-two centimeters long (R. L. Solecki 1969:990).

The oldest reported basined grinding slabs (Figure 1) in the Old World, dated between 18,000 and 17,000 B.P., have been recovered from an Upper Paleolithic terrace at the site of Ein Aqev, located in the central Negev, Israel (Marks, et al. 1975:69). Grinding slabs have been reported at Beidha in levels dated at 10,450 B.P. (R. S. Solecki 1957:25), at Ain

Mallaha (Perrot 1966:466), Ganj Dareh Tepe, and Zawi Chemi Shanidar, dated at 10,870 B.P. (R. L. Solecki 1969:989–994). Detailed descriptions are lacking but two grinding slabs from Ain Mallaha, one a basined fragment, the other flat and twenty-four centimeters lang and seventeen centimeters wide are illustrated in Perrot (1966, measurements taken from Figure 19, Number 9). Rose Solecki has provided descriptions and a classification for specimens from Zawi Chemi which she has divided into three types: flat querns, troughed querns, and quern-mortars (1969: 989). Of twenty-one grinding slabs recovered, flat slabs (querns) were the least numerous and generally smaller than the troughed slabs (querns) which were up to fifty-eight centimeters in length and thirty-three centimeters wide. Four of the grinding slabs (querns-mortars) were deeply troughed with the following dimensions: 28.5 to 30 centimeters long by 17 to 19 centimeters wide with troughs 5 to 12 centimeters deep (R. L. Solecki 1969:989).

Handstones accompanied grinding slabs at all sites except Mureybit (van Loon 1968: 279). Rose Solecki divided the 250 handstones at Zawi Chemi Shanidar into four types. Circular or ovate single- and double-faced mullers are distinguished by the number of working surfaces and may be bi-flat, plano-convex, bi-convex or concavo-convex in section (R. L. Solecki 1969: 989). Circular or ovate single- and double-pitted mullers are distinguished by the presence of pits on one, or two, surfaces which are otherwise unmodified. Sizes range from 7 by 8.4 by 4.5 centimeters to 12 by 12.6 by 6 centimeters (R. L. Solecki 1969: 989–990). Some of the specimens were polished.

Grinding slabs, handstones, and mortars and pestles are widely distributed in the Near East but kinds and proportions of tools represented differ from site to site. Mortars are numerous at Mureybit where handstones are absent but one stone ball and many pitted flint balls are present (van Loon 1968: 268). At Ganj Dareh most of the reported grinding slabs were mortars with many handstones (rubbers) and pestles (R. L. Solecki 1969: 990). At Beidha mortars were rare but handstones (grinders) and grinding slabs (querns) were numerous. Mortars and pestles are characteristic of most Natufian sites but grinding slabs and handstones occur at Ain Mallaha (Perrot 1966: Figure 19) and handstones but no grinding stones occur at Hayonim Cave (Bar-Yosef and Goren 1973: 63). In contrast, only one mortar was recovered at Zawi Chemi. Most of the grinding slabs at Zawi Chemi are deeply troughed (quern-mortars) while B1 levels at Shanidar Cave coincident in time with the occupation of the nearby site of Zawi Chemi yielded a higher percentage of flat slabs (R. L. Solecki 1969: 990).

Mongolia, Manchuria, and Chinese Turkestan

American and Swedish expeditions in central Asia from 1922 to 1935 recovered a wealth of artifacts, including food-processing tools, from numerous sites within Inner and Outer Mongolia. The richest localities were around extinct lakes Ulan-nor, Tsagan-nor, and Orok-nor situated in valleys between dunes (Cheng 1966: 38–39). The economy of the Gobi Desert dune-dwellers was based on hunting and collecting; ostrich eggs were especially important to them (Chang 1968: 68). Grinding slabs (mealing stones), handstones, and mortars and pestles were an important element in the microlithic industry (Cheng 1966: 54, 56). The microlithic industry of the Gobi extended eastward into Manchuria and westward into the region of Sinkiang, Chinese Turkestan. Teilhard de Chardin collected a pebble at Djalai-nor which had been used as a hammer and pestle (Cheng 1966: 42 and Figure 14, Number 2). In Sinkiang, handstones and pestles were collected at Aksu and handstones and grinding slabs were collected at the Singer site (Cheng 1966: 61–62).

The microlithic culture of the Gobi might be linked to the western microlithic industry, indicating a distribution from the Eurasian and Afrasian steppe to the desert zone (Cheng 1957: 132; 1966: 40). However, most of the sites are surface finds, or where present, disturbance of the stratigraphy or wrong identification has complicated the establishment of relations of the material to the rest of the Old World (Cheng 1966: 40). In China, proper grinding slabs are associated with food cultivation and are thought to be younger than the more northern sites, which are presumed to have been terminal Pleistocene.

Australian Equipment for Food Processing

The oldest Australian grinding stones said to be food-processing equipment were recovered from the sites of Malangangeer and Nawamoyn in northwestern Arnhem Land, from levels dated by carbon-14 at 22,000 and 18,000 B.P. (White 1967: 151). In addition to handstones (grinders) White recovered mortars (anvils) and pestles (pounders) which she suggests were used for processing vegetable foods (White 1971: 153). Both Malangangeer and Nawamoyn are situated on plains where the flora at present includes eucalyptus, cypress pines, annual grasses, and herbs. Wild rice and sedge occur on estuarine flats of the coastal plain (White and Peterson 1969: 49).

Other early food-processing tools have been reported by Mulvaney and

Joyce at the Mt. Moffatt Station, Queensland. The site was occupied from 17,000 B.P. intermittently until around 5000 B.P., with most intensive occupations occuring between 17,000 and 15,000 B.P. and again around 5000 B.P. (Mulvaney and Joyce 1965: 167). A large oval stone bearing a pronounced depression was recovered from a level dated at $10,000 \pm 180$ B.P. The stone measured thirty-one by eleven centimeters and has been described as a mortar (Mulvaney and Joyce 1965: 192).

The site of Lake Mungo in western New South Wales, occupied 26,000 to 18,000 years ago, has yielded no grinding stones, which are common in nearby sites. These sites are undated but probably of Pleistocene age according to the investigators (Bowler, et al. 1970: 56). The presence of emu eggs, which are ordinarily available in the region in late winter, and a fresh-water bivalve *Velesunio ambiguus*, normally palatable during winter at present in the region, have led the investigators to suggest seasonal occupation at Lake Mungo. The local environment at the time of occupation is thought to have differed markedly from the present. If occupation was indeed seasonal, then the absence of grinding stones at Lake Mungo may be an artifact of seasonality, as the dependence on seeds and nuts is known to vary seasonally among contemporary aborigines (Thomson 1939; Meggitt 1962; Gould 1968).

Two kinds of mortars are known in Australia: bedrock mortars (seed pounding "pits"); and mortars made from water-worn pebbles or blocks of quarried stone (McCarthy 1962: 7; 1970: 60). Pestles are rounded or elongate natural pebbles up to 17.8 centimeters long (McCarthy 1941a: 328; 1946: 66). Both mortars and "anvils" are made from either pebbles or quarried stones ranging in size from seven to twenty-six centimeters and from five to ten centimeters thick. Each is roughly shaped to an oval form by removal of large flakes. Mortars and "anvils" may have one, two, or three depressions, or pits, on one or more surfaces, and often have marks of percussion on their sides. McCarthy and Setzler collected two sets of mortars in Arnhem Land, northern Australia, from aborigines who had been using them. One specimen was rectangular, measuring 12.7 by 7.6 by 12.7 centimeters with one pit in both upper and lower surfaces. There were three pestles used with the mortar: one round, one quadrangular, and one triangular. The pestles were roughly the same size, ranging from 7.6 by 5 by 5 centimeters with the round pebble being eight centimeters in diameter. The other mortar was triangular with one wide pit on one surface and two small pits on the other surface (McCarthy and Setzler 1960: 247). The mortars were used for pounding nuts; each nut was placed separately on the mortar and flattened with a blow from the pestle. The investigators observed that after several dozen *tay tay* nuts, which have a hard woody case, were opened the pounding process produced a pit in the surface (McCarthy and Setzler 1960: 247).

The distinction between anvil and mortar would seem more apparent than real. Both implements are used for the same operation and tasks in the ethnographic present (McCarthy 1941a: 330; 1946: 57; McCarthy and Setzler 1960). As evidenced from their descriptions and various photographs of their use, what appear to be two types of tool may be sequences in the development of an implement through use.

Stones which show evidence of grinding on their surface include anvils, mortars, and grinding slabs (millstones). Grinding slabs are oval, ellipsoid or pear shaped, may be flat or "basined" with one to four depressions parallel to one another and several centimeters deep (Gould 1968: 106; McCarthy 1946: 62). Stone slabs are generally roughly shaped but are carefully shaped and trimmed in western Queensland. Sizes of the stones range from twenty to ninety centimeters in length. Occasionally a groove for axe sharpening is on one surface. A distinctive type of grinding stone, the *morah*, is found in northwestern Queensland, characterized by transverse and longitudinal grooves on the grinding surface; the grooves function to drain off poisonous juices of some plants (McCarthy 1941a: 331). The larger grinding stones are used primarily for grinding nuts, dried fruits, and seeds which sometimes are associated with larger grinding slabs characteristic to the variety, such as *nardoo* seeds.

Handstones are generally round or oval in shape with grinding facets on one or both surfaces, or several on one surface. They range from seven to twenty-one centimeters long (McCarthy 1946: 62). Handstones are several centimeters thick but are used until they are quite thin and worn into thin slabs, or crescents, after which they are reported to be used as knives (McCarthy 1941a: 331). Pestles are sometimes used as handstones (McCarthy 1941a: 332; 1946: 57).

While some grinding slabs are small and easily portable, others weigh up to fifty pounds. As a result they are left behind when the aborigines leave camp and can be found in most deserted camps, near wells and rock-holes where fruits, nuts, and seeds were processed (Gould 1968: 112; Gould, et al. 1971: 164; McCarthy and Setzler 1960: 247).

The confusion in the distinction between mortars, anvils, and grinding slabs stems from the fact that the aborigines fail to make the same distinctions as the archaeologists. Mortars have been reported to be used for grinding nuts, pigments, and gum (McCarthy and Setzler 1960: 218). Anvils have been reported with evidence of grinding wear (Howchin 1934: 74). The latter may be the same as Gould's "hand-held" grinding stones (1968: 111). Although large grinding slabs appear to be used more consistently for nuts, seeds, and dried fruits, smaller, flat-surfaced stones seem to be used for any grinding job at hand: the aborigine grinds nuts, fruits, seeds, ochre, or an ax, or may repair a digging stick on a mortar, anvil, or grinding slab with no selectivity or consideration save convenience.

THE STUDY OF MORTARS AND GRINDSTONES

The range of dependence of prehistoric or surviving non-agricultural peoples on plant resources has yet to be established but has been estimated as high as 80 percent for the !Kung Bushman and Hadza (Lee 1968; Woodburn 1968). Contemporary hunting and gathering adaptations are diverse (Freeman 1968) but there is little reason to believe that they were less diverse in the past or that dependence on plant-foods did not comprise the greater part of the diet, as with some contemporary groups (Clark 1971: 1212).

While utilization of plant-foods is assumed, most analyses rarely go beyond the enumeration of various components of species available, which leads to the construction of localized and narrow niches (Peterson 1971: 245). Societies are selective in their utilization of their surroundings (Freeman 1968) and there are suggestions that both contemporary and extinct societies utilize and utilized a number of microenvironments (Schrire 1972; Flannery 1968). The range of utilization of resources in extinct populations can be aided by the study of the preserved material produced by activities, preserved in the archaeological record, of exploitation and utilization of the environment.

The suggestion has been made that the activities of technologically simple societies can be categorized by two classes: extractive and maintenance (Binford and Binford 1966). Extractive activities are centered around the direct procurement of subsistence items and raw materials for manufacture of artifacts. Maintenance activities involve the preparation and distribution of subsistence items and the production tools. Equipment for processing plants would be used for maintenance activity and would be expected at sites related to maintenance activity such as base and transient camps but not at kill sites or quarries. While many of the tools used to process plant resources may have been of skin, bone, and wood, almost always poorly preserved in the archaeological record, the remaining stone tools could prove valuable in the analysis of activities because they were in direct contact with the plants utilized and less removed from the subsistence items than tools used to make other tools. In a settlement system where the presence or absence of tools is dependent upon the activities specific to the site, the distribution of tools associated with a set of activities could lead to the understanding of that set of activities as well as the sites characteristic of those activities (Clark 1971: 1212).

Freeman has made some suggestions for the functional definition of activities: detailed examination of formal characteristics which indicate techniques of manufacture and the motor habits involved; macroscopic and microscopic analysis and study of variation of wear; analysis of the distribution of associated materials to discover ranges of variation of characteristics (1968: 266). Tools for processing plants are suitable for the study of plant-processing activity, because wear is a product of both the materials processed and the motor habits involved in the processing. Wear characteristics can be established by microscopic and macroscopic study, and the variations can be established. If reporting and description are adequate, distributions and ranges of variation can be discovered.

Wear Patterns and What They Reveal

Laboratory study of wear pattern similar to Semenov's investigations (1964) has not been applied to grinding slabs and handstones although Semenov did include some observations on mortars and pestles used to grind and pound colorants. Reports of wear patterns on pre-Neolithic grinding slabs and handstones are rare (Wendorf 1968; McCarthy and Setzler 1960) and field observations of processing techniques are equally rare (Gould, et al. 1971; McCarthy and Setzler 1960).

In a description and analysis of plant-processing tools from a site in California, Riddell and Pritchard (1971) have devised a classification of manos and metates based on wear patterns. They contend that wear patterns can be utilized to deduce processes and from the processes infer the kinds of food milled, and have distinguished two types of metates: block and basined. Block metates are simple slabs of stone with no depressions but which have the worn, flattened area extended to the edges of the stone. Basined metates are square to rectangular blocks with shallow depressions that are quite concave and generally oval in outline.

Riddell and Pritchard have used classificatory terms for manos based on wear patterns:

U.   Uniface (one facet only)
B.   Biface (two facets opposite each other)
Q.   Quadraface (four or more facets, randomly placed)
M.   Multifaced (two or more facets, randomly faced)

O. Ovoid
R. Rectangular
I. Irregular
E. Elongate

S. Shaped (sides and/or ends pecked and ground to desired form)
C. Cobble (natural form, cortex generally showing)
   r. Right-angle grinding to the long axis
   l. Lateral grinding
   t. Transverse grinding
D. Diminutive size

Using a typology based on the above characteristics, Riddell and Pritchard have associated different manos at the California site with the processing of different foodstuffs. The suggestion is made that fragile grass seeds could not have tolerated a heavy pulverizing process, so that the most suitable tool would be held in one hand, probably controlled by the fingers rather than the palm of the hand and moved in a back-and-forth motion across a flat or shallow basined metate, producing flat facets at right angles to the long axis. For hulling, shelling and grinding fragile seeds, the investigators suggest mano types UICr and BICr which have flat facets and are associated with flat block metates (Riddell and Pritchard 1971: 76). Flat facets have been observed to develop on Australian handstones used to grind seeds of *kalpari* (*Chenopodium rhodinostachyum*) and of some other plants using a back-and-forth motion on a flat grinding slab (Gould, et al. 1971: 164).

Types BOSr and BECr are similar to the common "loaf"-shaped mano with deeply convex facets, sometimes sharpened by pecking, and pecked and battered ends. The suggestion was made that such manos served to grind coarser materials requiring the heavy pressure of both hands, and were probably used with a rocking motion on basined metates. Riddell has observed a variation of that motion which involved a "snappy wrist action" used by a Paiute woman (Riddell and Pritchard 1971: 73, 76).

Manos used to process chokecherries by smashing and then straining through a basket sieve, leaving the seeds behind, have polished rather than striated facets according to observations among the Paiute (Riddell and Pritchard 1971: 73). In contrast, in Australia the preparation of seed-paste from dried *kampurarpa*, a native tomato, involves a "pushing and vertical rotation in a 30° arc from back to front" with a handstone held in both hands resulting in a smooth and convex surface on the handstone after repeated use (Gould, et al. 1971: 164).

Riddell and Pritchard recovered five diminutive manos, types BOCr[d] and UECr[d], which were stained with ochre and sometimes show battering wear (1971: 74). Semenov noted irregular facets and the absence of polishing and battering and evidence of friction on Russian specimens (Semenov 1964: 137). With the exception of Frosbrooke's and Boshier's observations in Africa on the rounding effect of pounding nuts and vegetables with pestles and the "pitting" produced by pounding Australian *tay tay* nuts, observations of the wear produced by pounding plant-foods are few (Frosbrooke 1952; Boshier 1965; McCarthy and Setzler 1960).

The availability of stone is known to affect the size of handstones; in the Australian Western Desert, handstones are large, up to 1105.64 grams where stone is plentiful, but are worn to very small size (206.45 grams in the smallest) where stone is scarce (Gould, et al. 1971: 164). Many observations are needed on the effects of pounding and grinding of various plant-foods to establish differences in wear; in Australia different seeds are said to require different techniques but these remain unrecorded (Gould, et al. 1971). The work done thus far is barely suggestive.

Exploitation and Seasonality

Seasonality of exploitation is well known for contemporary hunters and gatherers. Subsistence activity is regulated by the quantity of available water, too much being perhaps as inhibitory as too little, as much as the presence of food (Lee 1968; Meggitt 1962: 4; Thomson 1939; McCarthy 1941b; Schrire 1972). Where lack of water is a factor, subsistence is organized around its availability (Lee 1968) and where its abundance seasonally inhibits travel, life is organized around the presence of foods on drier ground (Schrire 1972: 658), or can be organized to avoid difficult travel through dense grass, or even to escape the attacks of mosquitoes (Thomson 1939: 219).

There would be more grinding activity during some seasons than others. In the Western Desert of Australia, where utilization of seeds is important, exploitation is seasonal: *yawalyuru* and *kalpari* in April; *kalpari* and *wangunu* in May and June; and *wangunu* through July. During other months fruits, berries, and nuts provide more than 50 percent of the subsistence (Gould, et al. 1971: 164). Wear patterns specific to processing certain foods (Gould, et al. 1971: 164) should be noticeable on tools used in seasonal camps, particularly if those camps were revisited on a regular basis. Although resources may be available in a particular region during a season, they may not be available near a specific camp. Resources are distributed differently within an area of exploitation: cypress pines and

wild figs on granite hills; bean-tree, coolibahs, and river red-gums along
water courses; bloodwood, blue mallee and ghost-gum in drier localities;
and desert plum, plumbush, *mulgu*, and wichetty-bush in sandy loam
(Meggitt 1962: 4).

Plant-foods used in one region may not be utilized in another. There is
low botanical correspondence between Arnhem Land and central Australia, where the exploitation of seeds is high (Golson 1971: 204, 205;
McCarthy 1941b: 303). Two-thirds of the plant-foods available in Arnhem Land are absent in central Australia but over half of the genera of
central Australia are present in Arnhem Land but are not utilized (Golson
1971: 205). Of forty species of grasses common at the generic level to both
regions, none was used in Arnhem Land, which circumstance may be a
reflection of the importance in that region of wild rice, a plant not found
in central Australia, and the lesser importance of seeds in the diet in
central Australia.

Nearly all contemporary hunting and gathering groups live in marginal
subsistence areas; where they do not, as in Arnhem Land, subsistence
strategies are based more on comfort and convenience than availability of
food. During the wet season (*karp*), in late December to early March,
groups withdraw to higher ground, hunting becomes more important, and
berries and fruit are the major plants exploited (Schrire 1972: 658;
Thomson 1939: 218–219). During the beginning of the dry season (*ontjin*),
the seashore, swamps, and lower ground are exploited and molluscs and
crabs become important as well as a variety of yams, lily tubers, roots, and
seeds (Schrire 1972: 658; Thomson 1939: 219). During *ontjin*, camp locations which avoid mosquitoes are sought. At the height of the dry season
(*kaiyim*) most vegetables and seeds are less abundant and more mature;
only yams are abundant. The seasonal transhumance of contemporary
inhabitants of Arnhem Land was probably true of extinct populations
living there. Distributions and frequencies of tools differed between sites
of the coasts, plains, and plateaus (White 1971; White and Peterson 1969:
61). In Arnhem Land only five species of seeds are used during the wet
season, and only thirteen species of seeds during the dry season. (Golson
1971: Table 15, 3).

Because exploitation is selective, the problem of identifying the resource
utilized out of the number available is acute. Sickles can be useful in
determining exploitation of grasses, as grasses leave a characteristic band
of sheen on sickle blades after repeated use. Sickle blades with sheen are
characteristic of Natufian sites. Fragments of bone hafts, some with sickle
blades still in place, have been reported at Mugharet-el-Wad, Um ez-Zuet-
ina, and Nahal Oren; and two complete sickle hafts with curved animal

heads were recovered at Kebara (Garrod 1957: 215–216; Perrot 1957: 104). Sickle blades are reported at Mureybit and in B1 levels at Shanidar Cave but are absent at Zawi Chemi Shanidar (van Loon 1968: 290; R. S. Solecki 1957: 26; R. L. Solecki 1964: 409). Wendorf has reported lunates with thick retouched edges bearing sickle sheen at Tushka (1968: 942). The edges were set in a slot at a slight angle and held in place with an adhesive which is still preserved on one specimen (Wendorf 1968: Figure 92E). Experiments carried out by Harlan indicate that large amounts of grain can be harvested quickly with these sickles (1967).

Frequently grasses are exploited without sickles. Grass may be uprooted and the seeds beaten or stripped off. Bohrer has reported the practice of uprooting as rare but widespread in the Middle East and Europe (1972: 145). She suggests that dense stands of grain and grains growing in soils that form heavy clods around roots are more easily harvested by sickle but grains with poorly developed roots growing in poor or dry soil may be easily uprooted (1972: 145). In Australia grass is uprooted and beaten with digging sticks (McCarthy 1941a: 332).

Distribution and frequencies of plant-processing tools bearing wear patterns specific to processing certain plants should differ at different sites used during the subsistence cycle. The absence of grinding stones at Lake Mungo might have a seasonal basis. Factors outside of plant exploitation itself are important. A group of aborigines was observed in central Australia maintaining their camp near some desert oaks which provided their winter fuel supply. By maintaining their camp near a good fuel supply, they were forced to subsist on a diet of *jala* yams which resulted in swelling and protruding bellies (Stehlow 1965: 124).

CONCLUSIONS

Curwen remarked on grinding stones in 1937: "We are, happily, emerging from that state of blissful ignorance of the subject." His optimism was premature. Our understanding of Pleistocene grinding and pounding stones will remain in the state of "blissful ignorance" until mortars, anvils, pounders, hammerstones, rubbers, spheroids, subspheroids, cuboids, and grinders are subject to the same recovery, reporting, description, measuring, and analysis as are cleavers and choppers. So long as these tools continue to be lumped into categories "other," "secondary classes," or "miscellaneous" their relationship to subsistence cannot be understood. The study of anvils, spheroids, subspheroids and cuboids is needed, if only to eliminate them as plant-processing tools. Even though vegetable foods are suggested to have comprised the greater part of extinct diets in tropical and semitropical populations (Clark 1971: 1211) nearly all the inferences of functions of tools associate them with activities related to meat exploitation (Clark 1971: 1212).

Spheroids and semispherical balls were reported in Middle Pleistocene levels at 'Ubeidiya, Israel (Stekelis, et al. 1960) and spheroids, which were possibly associated with anvils, on an occupation floor at Latamne in northern Syria (Clark 1966). The spheroids and subspheroids from Olduvai Gorge compare well in size with the rounded pebbles used at present to pound vegetables and fruits in Australia: 5 to 12.5 centimeters at Olduvai and 8.7 centimeters in diameter for the specimen collected from aborigines in Arnhem Land. The "nether" stones may have been anvils. Anvils bearing "pits" at Olduvai (Leakey 1971: Plate 17) are strikingly similar to Australian mortars and anvils (McCarthy and Setzler 1960: Plate 5, Numbers 2 and 5) used for pounding nuts with hard, woody cases.

Bedrock mortars are reported in the Near East and Australia. Flat mortars and anvils, often "pitted," are reported from Early Pleistocene levels in Africa, Middle Pleistocene levels in Africa and the Near East, and in contemporary Australia. Their size remains small, 8.6 to 12 centimeters at Olduvai (DK and FLK North) and 7.6 to 12.26 in Australia (Arnhem Land). At present they are used to process a wide variety of foods, sometimes to repair and manufacture tools or to pound pigments. Pestles are spherical, oval, cuboid, triangular, and quadrangular. They are usually rounded pebbles from 5 to 12.7 centimeters in diameter in Australia, except along the eastern coast where they are elongate, up to 22.8 centimeters long and 15.4 centimeters wide, which is comparable to an elongate "pounder" 18.5 centimeters long and 7 centimeters wide recovered at Florisbad, South Africa. At the close of the Pleistocene, elongate, incised pestles appeared in the Near Eastern sites, the earliest at Ein Guev, Israel, in association with an assemblage otherwise typical of the Upper Pleistocene. What is of particular interest is the unspecialized nature of the use of these tools among Australian aborigines.

The earliest lower stones used for grinding have been recovered from Florisbad, South Africa, from levels dated at 49,000 B.P. Handstones occur in Mousterian undated levels in Spain and France and in dated levels in Russia as early as 44,000 B.P. and at 33,000 B.P. at Oliebooms-poort Cave, South Africa. Grinding stones, not yet described as upper or lower, were reported at Bushman Rock Shelter at 46,000 B.P. Early grinding equipment has both pounding and grinding wear; tools were not yet specialized for either activity. Of interest is the appearance of grinding behavior first in regions of steppe and grassland. That tools were unspecialized for either activity is not surprising since the same behavior obtains in Australia at present.

The earliest "basined" grinding stones have been recovered from Upper Paleolithic levels at Ein Aqev in the central Negev, Israel. Basining might indicate an increased dependency on foods which require grinding or use for longer periods of time, continuous or intermittent (Riddell and Pritchard 1971: 78).

The distribution of mortars, pestles, grinding slabs, and handstones in the Near East may have seasonal significance, reflect dietary preferences, or reflect the physical properties of the resources exploited. The frequency of mortars is higher at Mureybit, Ganj Dareh Tepe, and Natufian sites but the frequency of grinding slabs is higher at Zawi Chemi, B1 levels at Shanidar Cave, and at Beidha. The fact that each kind of tool (excepting handstones at Mureybit and grinding slabs at most Natufian sites) was present at each site indicates at least occasional use, but the greater frequency of each kind at different sites suggests that some kind of selectivity was operating. At Zawi Chemi deeply troughed grinding slabs showed evidence of pounding and use as mortars (R. L. Solecki 1969), a phenomenon observed also by Riddell and Pritchard (1971) in California. Rose Solecki has suggested that the outdoor site of Zawi Chemi was occupied during the warmer months when grain was harvested, which would indicate threshing activity, while the nearby Shanidar Cave was occupied during the winter months which would indicate storage of grain and intermittent grinding, reflected in the higher frequency of flat and shallow basined slabs (1969: 993). Seasonal camps of the Natufians which are located in the peripheral zone generally lack grinding equipment (Bar-Yosef and Tchernov 1970: 149).

When too worn to use for pounding and grinding, grinding slabs continue in use as building material at Beidha and Nahal Oren (Kirkbride 1968: 271; R. L. Solecki 1969: 993). Grinding slabs and handstones may have been part of the equipment used in burial rites. A broken, troughed slab and a handstone stained with ochre were placed beneath the feet of one skeleton, probably a young adult female, in B1 level at Shanidar Cave (R. S. Solecki 1957: 29).

Pleistocene grinding equipment is assumed to have been used to grind pigment, yet not all the grinding stones from the Bushman Rock Shelter had ochre stains (Louw 1969: 47), nor did all the handstones and slabs from the Cave of Hearths (Mason 1962b: 257); the grinder/pestle from Molodova V had traces of ochre but none of those from Molodova I had any traces reported (Klein 1966: 33). The lack of ochre on some of the handstones and grinding slabs would suggest that they were not used for that activity alone, nor does the ethnographic evidence support such an assumption.

The pre-adaptive phase of intensive collection of grains prior to the cultivation of grains evident in both the Old and New World has led specialists to several assumptions: that man knew and exploited seeds of grasses prior to cultivation; that grinding slabs and handstones were invented in response to a subsistence based on seeds intensively collected; and that man was familiar with the processing of plants prior to that period. The suggestion is made here that pounding behavior, including the pounding of plants, began at least as early as Makapansgat, thought by Howell to be 2,000,000 years old (Howell 1967) and preceded grinding behavior, which has been part of man's repertoire of activities at least since 49,000 B.P. and included the grinding of seeds. The use of "basined" grinding slabs was not the beginning of a new activity but merely reflects a shift in emphasis from foods that were processed by pounding to seeds that were also ground. Only careful reporting and description of tools which were possibly equipment for food processing will establish the antiquity and duration of the pre-adaptive phase of seed utilization.

Mortars, pestles, grinding slabs, and handstones offer the opportunity to study tools that were in direct contact with the resources utilized, some of which are known to leave wear patterns specific to certain foods. The use of these tools is still observable in the field and they are amenable to laboratory study both macroscopic and microscopic. The motor habits involved in pounding and grinding are observable in the field, can be reproduced in the laboratory, and are not likely to have differed in the past. Intensive study can aid in the clarification of the distribution of the tools, their association with activities of plant utilization, and the relations of those activities to particular sites.

REFERENCES

BARNES, J. A.
  1948 *The material culture of the Fort Jameson Ngoni.* Occasional Papers of the Rhodes Livingstone Museum 1.
BAR-YOSEF, O., N. GOREN
  1973 Natufian remains in Hayonim Cave. *Paleorient* 1:49–67.
BAR-YOSEF, O., E. TCHERNOV
  1970 The Natufian bone industry of Hayonim Cave. *Israel Exploration Journal* 20:141–150.

BENNET, RICHARD, JOHN ELTON
1898　*History of corn milling,* volume one: *Handstones, slave and cattle mills.* London: Simpkin, Marshall.

BERNDT, R., C. H. BERNDT
1964　*The world of the first Australians.* Chicago: University of Chicago Press.

BINFORD, L., SALLY BINFORD
1966　A preliminary analysis of functional variability in the Mousterian of Levallois facies. *American Anthropologist* 68 (2, 2):238–295.

BOHRER, VORSILA
1972　On the relation of harvest methods to early agriculture in the Near East. *Economic Botany* 26:145–155.

BOSHIER, ADRIAN
1965　Effects of pounding by Africans of northwest Transvaal on hard and soft stones. *South African Archaeological Bulletin* 20:131–136.

BOWLER, J. M., RHYS JONES, HARRY ALLEN, A. G. THORNE
1970　Pleistocene human remains from Australia: a living site and human cremation from Lake Mungo, western New South Wales. *World Archaeology* 2:39–60.

CHANG, KWANG-CHIH
1968　*The archaeology of ancient China* (second edition). New Haven: Yale University Press.

CHENG, TE-K'UN
1957　*Archaeological studies in Szechwan.* Cambridge: Cambridge University Press.
1966　*Prehistoric China,* volume one. Cambridge: Cambridge University Press.

CHERNYSH, A. P.
1961　Mousterskie sloi stoyankii Molodova V. *Kratkie Soobshchenya Instituta Arkaeologie* (Moscow) 82:77–84.

CLARK, J. D.
1962　*The Kalambo Falls* pre-historical site: an interim report. *Actes du IV Congrès Africain de Préhistoire et de l'Étude du Quaternaire,* 195–200.
1966　Acheulean occupation sites in the Middle East and Africa: a study in cultural variability. *American Anthropologist* 68 (2,2): 202–229.
1969　*The Kalambo Falls prehistoric site,* volume one. Cambridge: Cambridge University Press.
1971　Human behavioral differences in southern Africa during the later Pleistocene. *American Anthropologist* 73:1211–1236.

CURTIS, G., R. L. HAY
1972　"Recent studies in isotopes and other dating methods applicable to the origins of man" in *Calibration of hominoid evolution.* Edited by W. W. Bishop and T. A. Miller, 289–301. Toronto: University of Toronto Press.

CURWEN, CECIL
1937　Querns. *Antiquity* 11:131–151.
1941　More on querns. *Antiquity* 15:15–32.

DART, RAYMOND
1965   Pounding as a process and the producer of other artefacts. *South African Archaeological Bulletin* 20:141–147.

EYRE, EDWARD
1845   *Journals of expeditions of discovery into Central Australia and overland from Adelaide to King George Sound, in the years 1840–1841; sent by the colonists of South Australia, with the sanction and support of the government: including an account of the manners and customs of the aborigines and the state of the relations with Europeans.* London: T. and W. Bonner.

FARMER, MALCOLM
1960   A note on the distribution of the metate and muller. *Tebiwa* 3:31–38.

FLANNERY, KENT
1968   "Archaeological systems theory and early Meso-america," in *Anthropological archaeology in the Americas.* Edited by Betty Meggars, 67–87. Washington: Anthropological Society of Washington.

FREEMAN, L.
1964   "Mousterian developments in Cantabrian Spain." Unpublished Ph.D. thesis, University of Chicago.
1966   The nature of the Mousterian facies in Cantabrian Spain. *American Anthropologist* 68:230–237.
1968   "A theoretical framework for interpreting archaeological materials," in *Man the Hunter.* Edited by R. Lee and I. DeVore, 262–267. Chicago: Aldine.

FROSBROOKE, H. A.
1952   Quasi bola stones. *Man: Journal of the Royal Anthropological Institute* 52:15.

GARROD, DOROTHY
1957   The Natufian culture: the life and economy of a Mesolithic people in the Near East. *Proceedings of the British Academy* 43:211–227.

GAST, MARCEAU
1968   *Alimentation des populations de l'Ahaggar.* Mémoire du Centre de Recherches Anthropologiques, Préhistoriques et Ethnographiques 8.

GAST, MARCEAU, JEAN ADRIAN
1965   *Mils et sorgho en Ahaggar: étude ethnographique et nutritionnelle.* Mémoire du Centre de Recherches Anthropologiques, Préhistoriques et Ethnographiques 4.

GOLSON, J.
1971   "Australian aboriginal food plants: some ecological and culture-historical implications," in *Aboriginal man and environment in Australia.* Edited by D. J. Mulvaney and J. Golson, 197–238. Canberra: Australian National University Press.

GOULD, RICHARD
1968   Living archaeology: the Ngatajara of Western Australia. *Southwestern Journal of Anthropology* 24:101–122.
1969   Subsistence behavior among the Western Desert aborigines. *Oceania* 39:253–274.

GOULD, RICHARD, D. A. KOSTER, A. H. SONTZ
1971   The lithic assemblage of the Western Desert aborigines of Australia.

American Antiquity 36:149–169.

HARLAN, J.
1967   A wild wheat harvest in Turkey. *Archaeology* 20:197–201.

HARTMAN, L. F., A. L. OPPENHEIM
1950   On beer brewing techniques in ancient Mesopotamia according to the XXIIIrd tablet of the series Har.ra=*hubullû*. Supplement to *Journal of the American Oriental Society* 10.

HELBAEK, H.
1969   Plant collecting, dry-farming and irrigation agriculture in prehistoric Deh Luran. *Memoirs of the Museum of Anthropology, University of Michigan* 1:383–426.

HOLE, FRANK, KENT FLANNERY, J. A. NEELY
1969   *Prehistory and human ecology of the Deh Luran Plain: an early village sequence from Khuzistan, Iran.* Memoirs of the Museum of Anthropology, University of Michigan 1. Ann Arbor: University of Michigan Press.

HOWCHIN, WALTER
1934   *The stone implements of the Adelaide tribe of aborigines.* Adelaide: Gillingham.

HOWELL, F. CLARK
1967   Review of "Man-apes or Ape-men?," by Wilfred E. Le Gros Clark. *American Journal of Physical Anthropology* 27:95–101.

JEFFREYS, M. D. W.
1966   Pounding implements. *South African Archaeological Bulletin* 21:57–58.

KIRKBRIDE, DIANA
1968   Beidha: early Neolithic village life south of the Dead Sea. *Antiquity* 42:263–274.

KLEIN, RICHARD
1966   "The Mousterian of European Russia." Unpublished Ph.D. thesis, University of Chicago.

KLEINDIENST, MAXINE
1959   "Composition and significance of a Late Acheulean assemblage based on an analysis of East African occupation sites." Unpublished Ph.D. thesis, University of Chicago.

LAGERCRANTZ, S.
1950   *Contributions to the ethnography of Africa*, volume one. Studia Ethnographia Upslaiensia.

LAWN, BARBARA
1970   University of Pennsylvania radiocarbon dates XIII. *Radiocarbon* 12:577–589.

LEAKEY, M. D.
1971   *Olduvai Gorge*, volume three: *Excavations in Beds I and II, 1960–1963.* Cambridge: Cambridge University Press.

LEE, RICHARD
1968   "What hunters do for a living, or how to make out on scarce resources," in *Man the Hunter.* Edited by R. Lee and I. DeVore, 30–48. Chicago: Aldine.

LOUW, A. W.
   1969   Bushman Rock Shelter, Ohrigstad, eastern Transvaal: a preliminary
          investigation. *South African Archaeological Bulletin* 24:39–55.
MAGUIRE, BRIAN
   1965   Foreign pebble pounding artefacts in the breccia and the overlying
          vegetation soil at Makapansgat limeworks. *South African Archaeo-*
          logical Bulletin 20:117–130.
MARKS, ANTHONY
   1968   "The Sebilian industry of the second cataract," in *The prehistory of*
          Nubia, volume one. Edited by Fred Wendorf, 461–531. Dallas:
          Southern Methodist University Press.
MARKS, A. E., H. CREW, R. FERRING, J. PHILLIPS
   1972   Prehistoric sites near Har Harif. *Israel Exploration Journal* 22:73–85.
MARKS, A. E., C. R. FERRING, F. MUNDAY, P. JESCHOFNING, N. SINGLETON
   1975   Prehistoric sites near 'En-'Aqev, in the central Negev. *Israel Explora-*
          tion Journal 25:65–76.
MARKS, A. E., J. PHILLIPS, H. CREW, R. FERRING
   1971   Prehistoric sites near 'En-Avat in the Negev. *Israel Exploration*
          Journal 21:13–24.
MASON, REVIL
   1962a The Sterkfontein artefacts and their maker. *South African Archaeo-*
          logical Bulletin 17:109–126.
   1962b *Prehistory in the Transvaal: a record of human activity.* Johannesburg:
          Witwatersrand University Press.
MC CARTHY, FREDERICK A.
   1941a Aboriginal grindstones and mortars. *Australian Museum Magazine* 7:
          329–333.
   1941b The food supply of the aborigines. *Australian Museum Magazine* 7:
          300–305.
   1946   *The stone implements of Australia.* Australian Museum Memoir 9.
   1962   *The rock engravings of Port Hedland, northwestern Australia.* Kroeber
          Anthropological Society Papers 26.
   1970   *Aboriginal antiquities in Australia.* Australian Institute of Aboriginal
          Studes 22.
MC CARTHY, F., FRANK SETZLER
   1960   "The archaeology of Arnhem Land," in *Records of the American-*
          Australian Scientific Expedition to Arnhem Land, volume two: *Anthro-*
          pology and nutrition. Edited by C. Mountford, 215-295. Melbourne:
          Melbourne University Press.
MEGGITT, M. J.
   1962   *The desert people: a study of the Walbiri aborigines of central Australia.*
          Chicago: University of Chicago Press.
MEIRING, A. J. D.
   1956   *The macrolithic culture of Florisbad*, volume one, part nine, 205–238.
          Bloemfield: Researches of the Museum.
MITCHELL, S. R.
   1955   Comparison of the stone tools of the Tasmanians and Australian
          aborigines. *Man: Journal of the Royal Anthropological Institute* 55:
          131–139.

MORITZ, L. A.
1958   *The grain-mills and flour in classical antiquity.* Oxford: Clarendon.
MULVANEY, D. J., E. B. JOYCE
1965   Archaeological and geomorphological investigations on Mt. Moffat Station, Queensland, Australia. *Proceedings of the Prehistoric Society* 31:147–212.
PARTRIDGE, P. C.
1965   A statistical analysis of the limeworks lithic assemblage. *South African Archaeological Bulletin* 20:112–116.
PERROT, JEAN
1957   Le Mésolithic de Palestine et les récentes découvertes à Eynan (Ain Mallaha). *Antiquity and Survival* 2:91–110.
1960   Excavation at Eynan (Ain Mallaha): preliminary report on the 1958 season. *Israel Exploration Journal* 10:14–22.
1966   Le gisement Natoufien de Mallaha (Eynan) Israël. *L'Anthropologie* 70:437–484.
1968   La préhistoire palestinienne. *Supplément au Dictionnaire de la Bible* 8: 286–446.
PETERSON, N.
1971   "Open sites and the ethnographic approach to the archaeology of hunters-gatherers," in *Aboriginal man and environment in Australia.* Edited by D. J. Mulvaney and J. Golson, 239–248. Canberra: Australian National University Press.
PYDDOKE, EDWARD
1950   False bolas stones. *Man: Journal of the Royal Anthropological Institute* 50:144.
REED, CHARLES A.
1965   A human frontal bone from the Late Pleistocene of the Kom Ombo plain, Upper Egypt. *Man: Journal of the Royal Anthropological Institute* 65:101–104.
1966   The Yale University Prehistoric Expedition to Nubia, 1962–1965. *Discovery, Yale Peabody Museum* 1(2):16–23.
REED, CHARLES A., MARTIN A. BAUMHOFF, KARL W. BUTZER, HEINZ WALTER, DAVID S. BOLOYAN
1967   "Preliminary report on the archaeological aspects of the research of the Yale University Prehistoric Expedition to Nubia, 1962–1963," in *Fouilles en Nubie (1961–1963),* 145–156. Cairo: Antiquities Department of Egypt.
RIDDELL, F. A., W. PRITCHARD
1971   Archaeology of the Rainbow Point Site (4-Plu-S94), Bucks Lake, Plumas County, California. *University of Oregon Anthropological Papers* 1:59–102.
ROBINSON, J. T.
1962   Sterkfontein stratigraphy and the significance of the Extension Site. *South African Archaeological Bulletin* 17:87–107.
SCHRIRE, C.
1972   "Ethno-archaeological models and subsistence behavior in Arnhem Land," in *Models in archaeology.* Edited by David Clark, 653–670. London: Methuen.

SEMENOV, S. A.
1964   *Prehistoric technology.* Translated by M. W. Thompson. London: Barnes and Noble.

SMITH, P. E. L.
1967   New investigations in the late Pleistocene archaeology of the Kom Ombo plain (Upper Egypt). *Quaternaria* 9:141–152.
1968   "A revised view of the later Paleolithic of Egypt," in *La préhistoire: problèmes et tendances*, 391–399. Paris: Centre Nationale de la Recherche Scientifique.
1970   Ganj Dareh Tepe. *Iran* 8:174–176.

SOLECKI, RALPH S.
1957   The 1956–1957 season at Shanidar, Iraq: a preliminary statement. *Quaternaria* 4:23–30.

SOLECKI, ROSE L.
1964   Zawi Chemi Shanidar, a post-Pleistocene village site in northern Iraq. *Report of the VIth International Congress on the Quaternary* 4:405–412.
1969   "Milling tools and the Epi-paleolithic in the Near East," in *Etudes sur le Quaternaire dans le monde*, 989–994. Paris: VIII Congrès Union Internationale pour l'Etude du Quaternaire.

SPECHT, R. L.
1958   "An introduction to the ethnobotany of Arnhem Land," in *Records of the American-Australian Scientific Expedition to Arnhem Land*, volume three: *Botany and plant ecology.* Edited by R. Specht and C. R. Mountford, 479–503. Melbourne: Melbourne University Press.

SPENCER, BALDWIN
1914   *Native tribes of the northern territory of Australia.* London: Macmillan.

STEFANISZYN, B.
1964   *The material culture of the Ambo of northern Rhodesia.* Occasional Papers of the Rhodes Livingstone Museum 16.

STEHLOW, T. G. H.
1965   "Culture, social structure and environment in aboriginal central Australia," in *Aboriginal man in Australia.* Edited by R. Berndt and C. H. Berndt. London: Angus and Robertson.

STEKELIS, M., O. BAR-YOSEF
1965   Un habitat du Paléolithique Supérieur à Ein Guev (Israël): Note préliminaire. *L'Anthropologie* 69:176–183.

STEKELIS, M., L. PICARD, N. SCHUMAN, G. HAAS
1960   Villafranchian deposits near 'Ubeidiya in the central Jordan Valley (preliminary report). *Bulletin of the Research Council of Israel* 90:175–183.

STORCK, JOHN, W. D. TEAGUE
1952   *Flour for man's bread.* Minneapolis: University of Minnesota Press.

STUIVER, MINZE
1969   Yale natural radiocarbon measurements IX. *Radiocarbon* 11(2):545–648.

SULIMIRSKI, TADEUSZ
1970   *Prehistoric Russia: an outline.* London: John Baker.

THOMSON, D.
1939 The seasonal factor in human culture: illustrated from the life of a contemporary nomadic group. *Proceedings of the Prehistoric Society* 5:209–221.
1964 Some wood and stone implements of the Bindibu tribe of central Western Australia. *Proceedings of the Prehistoric Society* 30:400–422.

VAN LOON, MAURITS
1968 The Oriental Institute excavations at Mureybit, Syria: Preliminary report on 1965 campaign, Part 1: Architecture and general finds. *Journal of Near Eastern Studies* 27:265–282.

VAN RIET LOWE, C.
1950 The bolas of South Africa. *Man: Journal of the Royal Anthropological Institute* 50:71–72.

VIGNARD, M. EDWARD
1923 Une nouvelle industrie lithique, le "Sebilien." *Bulletin de l'Institut Français d'Archéologie (Le Caire)* 22:1–76.

VOGEL, J. C.
1969 Radiocarbon dating of Bushman Rock Shelter, Ohrigstad District. *South African Archaeological Bulletin* 24:56.

VOGEL, J. C., P. B. BEAUMONT
1972 Revised radiocarbon chronology for the Stone Age in South Africa. *Nature* 237:50–51.

VOGEL, J. C., H. T. WATERBOLK
1967 Groningen radiocarbon dates VII. *Radiocarbon* 9:107–155.
1972 Groningen radiocarbon dates X. *Radiocarbon* 14:6–110.

WENDORF, FRED
1968 "Late Paleolithic sites in Egyptian Nubia," in *The prehistory of Nubia*, volume two. Edited by Fred Wendorf, 791–954. Dallas: Southern Methodist University Press.

WHITE, CARMEL
1967 Early stone axes in Arnhem Land. *Antiquity* 41:149–152.
1971 "Man and environment in northwest Arnhem Land," in *Aboriginal man and environment in Australia*. Edited by D. J. Mulvaney and J. Golson, 141–157. Canberra: Australian National University Press.

WHITE, CARMEL, N. PETERSON
1969 Ethnographic interpretations of the prehistory of western Arnhem Land. *Southwestern Journal of Anthropology* 25:45–67.

WHITE, CHARLES
1948 *The material culture of the Lunda-Lovale.* Occasional Papers of the Rhodes Livingstone Museum 3.

WOODBURN, JAMES
1968 "An introduction to Hadza ecology," in *Man the hunter*. Edited by R. Lee and I. DeVore, 49–55. Chicago: Aldine.

Man, Domestication, and Culture in Southwestern Asia

CHARLES L. REDMAN

One of the major goals of prehistoric archaeological research is to learn how and why men adopted agriculture. My article, like the other contributions in this volume, seeks to describe for one region of the world the conditions and temporal sequence of when prehistoric men became food producers. I approach this problem in five sections, beginning with a discussion of important definitions. There follows the presentation of an analytical model which helps orient future research, and an examination of the major forces associated with the introduction of agriculture. Next, a brief outline of the archaeological evidence from two areas of southwestern Asia is presented. I conclude with a discussion of the chronological order of major inventions in southwestern Asia.

DEFINITIONS AND THE "WHY?" QUESTION

In an agricultural community there are three basic sets of activities that are necessary components of a food-producing subsistence system. First is propagation — the selective sowing of seeds or breeding of animals. Second is husbandry — the activities associated with the care of plants or

My views on the origins of agriculture have been derived from a combination of sources. I have been stimulated by many of the scholars who contributed to this volume. My field experience relevant to early farming and much of my academic training was under the direction of Robert J. Braidwood. I have benefited immeasurably from my work with him and other scholars who participated in the Joint Prehistoric Project in Turkey. However, I alone am responsible for the opinions expressed in this article. As in all of my work, my wife, Linda, has been of assistance at many tasks.

animals while they are growing. Third is harvesting — the collection of the food resources that have been fostered by the first two sets of activities. When I use the terms "agriculture" or "domestication," all three sets of activities are involved. Domestication or agriculture also implies that a symbiotic relationship has developed between the plants and animals on the one hand and the people tending them on the other.

I define "gatherers" as prehistoric people who only harvested the food resources by reaping or hunting, and did not purposefully propagate or tend the growing organisms. If, through an intimate knowledge of the potential resources of an area, the community utilized a wide variety of food resources, then I refer to them as "intensive hunters and gatherers." If, in addition to gathering the resources, the prehistoric people also cared for the plants or animals, I use the term "husbandry" (this term was suggested by R. Yarnell during the conference which led to this book). Hence, there is a series of different relationships which man has adopted in order to increase his food supply. The successful differentiation of these subsistence patterns in the archaeological record will aid in understanding the process of domestication.

Despite Gordon Childe's reference to an agricultural revolution, the adoption of agriculture does not seem to have been a rapid process. Although current data are not exhaustive, apparently a long period elapsed between the time when plants and animals were first domesticated in an area and when the communities in that area came to rely heavily upon them for food. This lag varied in different localities, but seems to have been no shorter than several generations and may have been as long as several millennia. I reserve the term "agriculturists" or "agricultural community" for groups which relied on domesticated plants and animals for at least 25 percent of their diet. This is an arbitrary figure, and perhaps it would be more important to know how crucial the domesticated resources were during times of critical food shortage in order to estimate their true importance to the community.

The three different sets of activities which comprise agriculture and the incremental manner in which agriculture was usually adopted lead to the question of whether one is dealing with an "invention" at all. To the contrary, several scholars have suggested that the growth and reproduction of plants and animals were adequately understood by hunters and gatherers, who depended on the wild progenitors of the early domesticates. It is also uncertain whether early agriculture was an improvement, either in time required or food produced, over successful intensive hunting and gathering. If we regard the introduction of agriculture as an incremental process in which the advantages are not readily apparent, then the question of why agriculture was adopted in any region of the world becomes a more complex issue. It is clearly a combination of interrelated factors, and these factors may vary from region to region.

Because one of the major goals of this volume is to answer, or at least to illuminate, the "why?" question of the origin of agriculture, it is important to examine in detail what is meant by this query. There are two aspects to my examination of the problem. First, how does one answer a "why?" question about any broad topic? Second, how can the general theories on the origins of agriculture be made operational in order to make them capable of being tested against available archaeological evidence, and to help direct future field investigations in collecting relevant information? I suggest that in order to arrive at a sufficient answer to a "why?" question one must have an understanding of the process and the preconditions sufficient to be able to predict its occurrence. This is an assertion of the general parity between explanation and prediction (Watson, LeBlanc, and Redman 1971: 5). Hence, if one is able to outline in detail the necessary situation (preconditions for agriculture), the stimuli for change, and the predictable result (agriculture), then the process is adequately understood. This can be formally stated as follows: given conditions A, if B occurs, then C will occur. In determining the pre-conditions and stimuli toward agriculture, one must be careful to delineate not only the products of the process, but also the relationships of the variables involved. It is these relationships that comprise the process itself. Hence, it is the understanding of the interrelationships of the various preconditions and stimuli which led to agriculture that will yield the explanation of its origins.

AN ANALYTICAL MODEL FOR INVESTIGATING THE ORIGIN OF AGRICULTURE

Converting these definitions and goals into a workable research strategy is not a simple matter. The primary step discussed in this article is the formulation of a systems model of the alternative subsistence-settlement states for prehistoric communities. This helps to clarify the areas which require further research and makes explicit the exact nature of the data to be collected (Figure 1 and Table 1). The first stage of this procedure is to define the various phenomena under study, as has been done above for the forms of manipulation of plants and animals. Then, an attempt should be made to delineate the various characteristics associated with early farming and prefarming communities, and to distinguish those which should logically affect this transition. Attempts should be made to define the transitional factors objectively so that they are recognizable archaeologically. Generalities included in present theories, such as "population pressure," or "adequate level of technology," should be broken down into more concrete analytical factors whose direct effects can be evaluated. The ultimate goal is to assemble the characteristics that are both necessary for the transition to food production and sufficient to stimulate this transition.

These characteristics are clearly not going to be independent, nor of equal importance in every situation. Some of the factors are mutually reinforcing, while other innovations may act to impede particular changes or other factors. An example of such interdependence is that the settling down to permanent occupation sites facilitated the utilization of heavy, nonportable, food-processing equipment (e.g. mortars and milling stones). This valuable, yet nonportable, cultural equipment in turn tended to discourage a transition back to a more mobile settlement system. In this way, some factors can be considered as positive influences on certain transitions, while others may exert a negative or impeding influence on some transitions in patterns of subsistence-settlement.

There were also threshold levels in the changing systems of subsistence-settlement in the late prehistoric Near East. Sedentism can be thought of as a threshold that was difficult to attain. However, once it was accomplished, it facilitated other developments that would have been less likely to occur without sedentism, such as population growth. Another series of thresholds may have been involved in the form of social organization required for managing a large community of individuals. Shifting from groups that probably ranged from twenty-five to fifty people to communities of one to two hundred people may have necessitated basic changes in social interrelationships, such as the introduction of a ranked society. This innovation, which some scholars have characterized as tribal organization, was undoubtedly of fundamental importance in many of the changing attitudes and organization patterns that facilitated later adoption of agriculture and its eventual success.

The following is an attempt to treat the introduction of agriculture in an analytical manner by breaking down various processes into component parts and defining them objectively. I am not suggesting that there was only one path to agriculture and that all groups, even within the same region, followed the same steps or responded to the same stimuli. This type of conclusion is to be proved or disproved by the archaeological evidence and not to be assumed *a priori*. Although I recognize that every cultural occurrence is a unique event and there will be particulars that distinguish each site and each group of sites, I believe that there are regularities shared by many sites in different regions. I consider that the most important goals of our inquiry into the origins of agriculture are the discovery of the regularities in relationships of development and the understanding of the differences that are observed.

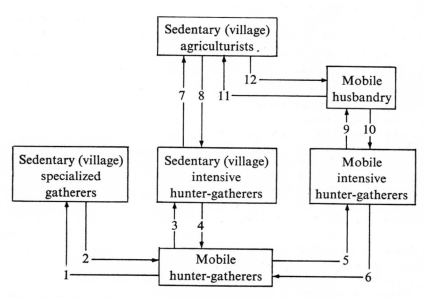

Figure 1.   Alternative subsistence-settlement states for southwestern Asian prehistoric communities

The model shown in Figure 1 and the accompanying information in Table 1 are a very modest attempt at an analytical approach to the origins of agriculture. I have constructed the diagram of the alternative states for subsistence-settlements on the basis of archaeological evidence from southwestern Asia. This diagram is an exposition of the possible community forms which the late prehistoric populations could have assumed. The numbered arrows represent the potential transitions between alternative states. Hunters and gatherers can become agriculturists in some situations, but under other conditions agriculturists may return to a hunting and gathering strategy. Of crucial importance are the factors that favor

Table 1.   The effect of each factor on the alternative state transitions

Description of factors	1	2	3	4	5	6	7	8	9	10	11	12
I. Understanding of environmental potential	+		pr		+		pr		pr		pr	
II. Ability to organize scheduling of activities for group			pr		pr		pr		pr		pr	
III. Availability of potential domesticates			+				+		+		+	
IV. Climatic change: improved conditions for potentially domestic plants			+				+				+	
V. Climatic change: worse conditions for potentially domestic plants				+				+		+		+
VI. Climatic change: more temperate conditions for human occupation	+		+				+				+	
VII. Climatic change: increased frequency or duration of bad seasons		+		+		+		+		+		+
VIII. Culturally altered environment								+		+		
IX. Ecological uniformity in vicinity	+				+				+			
X. Ecological diversity in vicinity			+				+				+	
XI. Dependence on migratory herd animals						+		+				
XII. Dependence on nonmigratory animals	+		+				+					
XIII. Dependence on tree nuts	+		+				+					
XIV. Dependence on cereal grasses			+				+					
XV. Dependence on a combination of plants and animals			+				+				+	
XVI. Inventory of specialized harvesting tools or techniques	+		+		+		pr		pr		pr	
XVII. Inventory of heavy equipment for food preparation	+		+*		−		+*		−		+*	
XVIII. Storage facilities (e.g. silos)	+		+*		−		+*		−		+*	
XIX. Substantial architecture (nonportable)	+		+*		−		+*		−		+*	
XX. Microlithic composite tools			+		+							
XXI. Local exchange or redistribution	+		+				+					
XXII. Long-distance trade					+				+			
XXIII. Interpersonal stress within large groups		+		+					+			+
XXIV. Tribal or ranked organization							+		+		+	
XXV. Spatial impingement by other groups				+			+			+	+	
XXVI. Competition from hostile groups		+		+			+					+

Key: pr means factor is a prerequisite for transition
   +   means factor exerts a favorable influence on transition
   −   means factor impedes transition
   *   means that transition favors factor (feedback)

transitions leading to agricultural communities and inhibit transitions back to hunting and gathering.

This model shows two possible pathways (trajectories) that mobile hunters and gatherers can follow to become sedentary agriculturists. One possible set of transitions ("state trajectory") would be from mobile hunters and gatherers to sedentary, intensive hunter-gatherers (transition 3), and on to sedentary agriculturists (transition 7). This seems to be the pattern followed in some areas of the Levant. An alternative state trajectory hypothesized for the Near East is from mobile hunter-gatherers to mobile intensive hunter-gatherers (transition 5), to mobile husbandry (transition 9), and on to sedentary agriculturists (transition 11). One can argue that this pattern of development is characteristic of what took place in the Zagros-Khuzistan area. I have also included a transition from mobile hunter-gatherers to sedentary specialized gatherers and back (transitions 1 and 2). By "specialized gatherers" I mean groups that depend almost entirely on one resource that can be readily gathered, such as the fishermen on the northwest coast of North America, or several acorn-gathering tribes of California. I am not certain that this extreme specialization ever occurred in the Near East or that it could ultimately lead to agriculture, so I have not included transitions from sedentary specialized gatherers to sedentary agriculturists. The possibility of such a transition could be included, however, without substantially changing the remainder of the model.

Table 1 is a tentative attempt to define explicitly all of the factors associated with the transition to food production, and what their influence would be on each of the potential transitions of the model in Figure 1. Some factors listed in Table 1 are still too general and too nebulous to be recognized archaeologically or to be useful analytically (e.g. "understanding of environmental potential"). One of the first steps in this approach should be to refine these general factor definitions further.

Four different symbols (pr, +, −, *) are used to represent the influence of each factor on each transition. Certain factors are prerequisites (pr) for particular transitions; it might appear oversimplistic to include these obvious requirements, but it is important to do so because these factors do not exert an equally strong influence on all transitions. The term "favorable influence" (+) covers a wide range of possible effects; one of the first requirements in using this approach is to try to measure the magnitude of the various positive factors. Some factors, on the other hand, impede, or exert a negative influence (−) on particular transitions. Finally, it is possible that certain transitions, when they occur, encourage the development of certain factors (*); I have referred to this as feedback between the factors and the transitions. Another type of relation which, due to its complexity, is not represented in Table 1, is the positive influence of one factor upon another. Some factors seem to occur together and to facilitate one another. These linkages are of fundamental importance and should be included in a final model.

The factors I have listed in Table 1 are not exhaustive, and could be added to and made more objective. There are four basic categories of factors: environmental (I–X), subsistence (XI–XV), technological (XVI–XX), and organizational (XXI–XXVI). Using this model, the initial stage of analysis is to record values for each factor for each of the relevant sites in a particular region. The sites could then be arranged according to the transitions suggested in Figure 1. The empirical values and changes known from the archaeological evidence could be compared to the theoretically hypothesized influences put forth in Table 1. Disagreements between the model and the empirical reality could be examined more closely to determine the cause of the discrepancies. Relative values for the influences might be obtained from an evaluation of the occurrence of these factors in numerous situations. This comparison would then focus later inquiry on anomalous categories, and methods of obtaining values for the postulated influences and for objectively defining the factors and their interrelationships.

THE "PRIMARY" FORCE IN THE ORIGIN OF AGRICULTURE

A more general approach to the development of agriculture in southwestern Asia than is offered in Table 1 is to discuss the major forces associated with this change. In trying to understand any important changes in the human career one should attempt to determine whether the observed changes were largely due to stimuli from the biophysical environment, the cultural milieu, or the contemporary social institutions. Factors associated with these three realms are often interrelated and do not act in isolation. Nevertheless, it is fundamental to an adequate explanation to be able to delineate which of these factors is the primary mover and which reacts secondarily or remains static.

The environmental situation has often been suggested as the crucial element in many fundamental developments of the past. Wright (this volume) and Wagner (this volume) present cogent arguments concerning the importance of the appropriate environmental situation for the introduction of agriculture. What are the crucial elements in the environment and did the environment play a passive or active role? Climatic change has been proposed as the primary force in the introduction of agriculture by

Childe (1936), Wright (this volume), and others. From the evidence of pollen cores taken in several locations of the Near East, Wright has suggested that at approximately 11,000 years B.P. there was a change from a colder, drier climate to a wetter, warmer climate in the Near East. There was an advance of forests into new territories, perhaps accompanied by potential domesticates of cereal plants. The warmer weather also encouraged people to move from predominantly cave dwellings into open-air communities. There is considerable controversy as to whether or not this was just a local phenomenon that varied from locality to locality. How important this effect was on the inhabitants of each area is hard to evaluate, because what the evidence portrays is the relative proportions of some of the important plant species growing in a locality, but not necessarily the plants that men were collecting. Also, we must be very careful not to think that people utilized only plants that were available directly around their community. From what we know of both ethnographic and archaeological evidence, groups often travelled great distances to gather some resources. In situations of vertical relief, several climatic and biotic zones are available within a modest distance. Hence, it is important to determine what constitutes a relevant climatic change in terms of the prehistoric people's subsistence patterns and life styles. This is a more difficult task, and to ascertain the real effect of the climatic change requires that a complete matrix of climatic information from surrounding regions be compared with the plants and animals that the ancient communities utilized.

If climatic change or other environmental variables are basic causal factors in the origin of agriculture, are they determinant? (Cf. Wagner, this volume.) This question pervades all inquiries into human adaptations and cultural developments. The critical test is the detailed examination of areas in which agriculture did not develop, which seem to share the same crucial environmental factors. Explanations for the different courses of development should also be sought. If these negative instances and the alternative paths could be convincingly related to certain environmental variables, then the case for environmental determinism would be considerably strengthened.

The second major group of forces which could have been responsible for the introduction of agriculture is cultural. I define as cultural things that are learned and transmitted by men. This includes technological items and techniques, as well as knowledge and ideas. It has been suggested that a sufficient level of technology and an intimate knowledge of the potential domesticates are key elements in the origin of agriculture in the Near East (Braidwood 1967). Although this is a difficult concept to define objectively, clearly certain implements for harvesting and preparing food are necessary for agriculture to succeed. Inventions such as storage facilities make the farming of storable grains a more worthwhile undertaking. There are two types of technological inventions that are important in both the introduction and establishment of agriculture. One type of innovation helps to increase production — for example, more efficient harvesting equipment, or fish nets, or other devices that afford man more free time. The second type of invention is one that increases the usefulness of the yield. This includes innovations concerned with the selection and breeding of more productive plants and animals, and implements that facilitate their preparation. The major question is whether these inventions came first and allowed agriculture to emerge, or whether the inventions were a response to a more fundamental stimulus. Population growth and density have often been cited as a factor in the rate of cultural innovation. With an increasing population there is additional pressure on the existing resources which may tend to stimulate innovation. Some scholars have countered by suggesting that under these conditions of stress it is not so much that new technologies are developed, as that old ones are intensified. Another observation, made by some geographers, is that in the early history of America the most important inventions were made along the agricultural frontier. Given a potentially rich environment and insufficient labor to exploit it, men will attempt to create mechanisms for collecting the resources more efficiently. Whether it was population pressure or sparsity of population that triggered the innovations is a question that can be answered archaeologically, once sufficient data have been collected using appropriate methods.

The third major force, social organization, is often discussed but infrequently tested archaeologically. In many ways it may be the changes in human organization that are crucial to the adoption of agriculture. Integrating larger community sizes, organizing the scheduling of activities, and developing a radically new ethic are probably the most revolutionary aspects of early agricultural society. We may consider the developing social institutions in two categories; those associated with subsistence pursuits, and those asscociated with prolonged sedentism.

Subsistence-related developments which may have been either causes of agriculture or results of it include the specialization and division of labor required for efficiency in farming pursuits, the greater concentrations of people in one place permitted by the increasing food supply, and the useful participation by youth and the elderly in the subsistence activities. These factors would encourage the removal of population restraints by people who were successful in farming. Even with these positive factors, however, population growth would not continue unrestrained. New limitations on resources, problems of diseases, and limits on social interrelationships would inhibit growth beyond certain levels. Agricultural subsistence would also necessitate new forms of redistribution to be developed by the community. The permanent herds and fields of the agriculturist demand different redistributive mechanisms than those used by hunters dividing their occasional kills of big game. Trade and exchange on the inter-community level also developed during this period, and may have made early farming a more profitable pursuit. The trend toward specialization and exchange started in this era, and it is one of the fundamental processes that have continued up to this day.

Other developments in the realm of social institutions and values are more directly associated with the increasing degree of sedentism. The primary change that came with sedentism was larger community size. Mobile groups were probably limited to a maximum of twenty-five to fifty people during part of the year, while early sedentary villages ranged between one and two hundred people. Organizing the interrelationships and scheduling the activities of groups of this larger size necessitated major changes in the social structure of the community. Probably, ranked society became more prevalent, and tribal organization (Service 1971) was common. Remaining in one location for long periods of time would encourage groups to make more nonportable items, or would at least remove restrictions on their fabrication. Milling stones, mortars, pottery, and elaborate architecture would be more worthwhile for people who stayed in one location for many years, for they would get more use out of their investment in fabricating these items. With the increase in the quantity of the nonportable cultural inventory and with substantial houses, there might be a tendency for notions of personal property to develop. The success of early farming was connected with the willingness and ability of people to store sufficient resources to use as seed for the following year and to get them through periods of poor or bad years. It is unlikely that the first attempts at farming or the yield of early domesticates were very impressive. It is only with the ability to store large quantities of goods that the sedentary farmer is able to survive in situations which even the mobile hunter and gatherer would find difficult. One further step in the social organization of the community would be to have people not only store supplies for themselves, but to produce and store a surplus to be used for community projects. The institutions and value systems required to convince people to work harder and to produce more than they themselves will use, are other fundamental innovations on which we still depend in contemporary society.

OUTLINE OF TWO DEVELOPMENTAL SEQUENCES
IN SOUTHWESTERN ASIA

Here, in brief, is the current state of archaeological evidence in two areas within southwestern Asia, the Levant and the Zagros-Khuzistan area. Although developments are roughly contemporaneous and similar in these two areas, the details of the subsistence-settlement patterns and the resources utilized are different. Perhaps the association of causal factors that gave rise to these two subtly distinctive cultural patterns will shed light on the crucial elements in the introduction of agriculture in the Near East.

From the nature of the available evidence, archaeologists generally assume that the people of the Upper Paleolithic in southwestern Asia depended predominantly on a few species of large animals, such as the gazelle, aurochs, deer, and wild goat. Small mammals and vegetable material may have been collected, but there are few primary remains of these and little artifactual evidence. With the advent of the cultures at the end of the Pleistocene, fundamental shifts in resources and artifacts occurred which seem to have been the precursors of agricultural life. In the Levant the sites which exhibit this transformation are referred to as Kebaran. The Kebaran is generally dated 17,000 to 13,000 B.P., and is characterized by microlithic tools. Kebaran sites are more numerous than are those of the previous phase of the Upper Paleolithic period. Probably during the Kebaran, people were already experimenting with the plants and animals around them, but it is during the succeeding Natufian period that this becomes clear.

The Natufian culture, which is dated 13,000 to 10,000 B.P., is characterized by microlithic implements, and for the first time in the Levant, large quantities of food-preparation equipment made of ground stone and large structures with stone foundations are found. The most important site for our understanding of the Natufian is Ain Mallaha in the Huleh basin of northern Israel (Perrot 1966). This site is composed of large, round, semi-subterranean structures, and may have had a total population of 150 people. The Natufians of Ain Mallaha utilized a variety of animals, plants, and aquatic resources for their food, and can be considered sedentary intensive (broad spectrum) hunter-gatherers. Ain Mallaha is the largest Natufian site yet excavated, although more extensive ones have been discovered recently. From the evidence at Ain Mallaha and the other Natufian sites, located on terraces in front of caves and in open areas, it is clear that the locus of habitation had shifted from the more cave-oriented locations of the Upper Paleolithic.

There are several sites which seem to share many characteristics with the earlier Natufian material. Mureybit in northern Syria on the eastern bank of the Euphrates is a large open-air community with circular structures that was inhabited between 10,000 and 9000 B.P. (van Loon 1968). Although the archaeological evidence implies that the people at Mureybit were intensive hunter-gatherers, probably they were also experimenting with plants and animals. In the Levant the Natufian is followed by an inventory referred to as prepottery Neolithic A (PPNA). This inventory was first defined from the excavations at Jericho (Kenyon 1957), where it is associated with rather spectacular architectural remains. The buildings are circular and similar to their Natufian predecessors. Hunting wild animals was still a major activity. However, it is possible that the barley and emmer harvested by the inhabitants of Jericho were in the initial stages of being domesticated or at least husbanded.

From about 9000 to 8000 B.P. the sites in the Levant are characterized by an inventory known as prepottery Neolithic B (PPNB). Several large villages have been excavated with rectangular structures, plastered floors, well-made projectile points, and evidence for domesticated plants and animals. The sites of Jericho (Kenyon 1957), Beidha (Kirkbride 1966), Munhatta (Perrot 1968), and Ramad (de Conteson 1971) are well known. The number and average size of sites during the PPNB seem to increase compared to what we know from the PPNA.

In addition to the development of ground stone and chipped stone industries, there is increased attention paid to the dead, in the form of decapitation and skull plastering. Long-distance trade seems to be on the increase; most of the PPNB sites contain at least a few pieces of Anatolian obsidian as part of their chipped stone assemblage. Clay figurines are also more common, predominantly in the form of animals.

The contemporary developments in the Zagros mountains and the adjacent Khuzistan plain are substantially different from those of the Levant. From a base of Upper Paleolithic people who, like the coeval peoples of the Levant, also seemed to rely on large game and to live for the most part in caves, an assemblage known as the Zarzian developed, as the terminal Pleistocene adaptation. The Zarzian is roughly equivalent to the Kebaran of the Levant, although not as well known archaeologically. Following the Zarzian is a period of time which is recognized in three sites — Karim Shahir (Braidwood and Howe 1960), Zawi Chemi Shanidar (Solecki 1964), and Asiab (Braidwood, Howe, and Reed 1961). The best known is Zawi Chemi, a relatively large community with some traces of circular architecture. In the lowest levels there is no evidence for domestication, but by the upper levels of the site there is a selective bias in the age and sex of the animals slaughtered. This has been interpreted (Perkins 1964) as a statistical demonstration that the people were herding animals ("husbandry" in my definition).

Only traces of architecture are found at Karim Shahir and Asiab, and both communities seem to have been relatively small. One possibility is that these two communities were completely sedentary, year-round communities. An alternative view is that at this stage of development people were herding animals and following them in their seasonal migrations. Hence, these could have been base camps for one or another season, located at different elevations.

The basal layers of two other sites reach back to almost this same time period — Ganj Dareh (Smith 1972) in the Kermanshah valley of western Iran (near Asiab), and Ali Kosh (Hole, Flannery, and Neely 1969), in the lowland plain of Khuzistan in southwestern Iran. The earliest deposits from Ganj Dareh are approximately 10,000 B.P., and the lowest level from Ali Kosh, known as the Bus Mordeh phase, is dated to approximately 9500 B.P. Both communities are small and were probably not full-year occupation sites.

Both Ganj Dareh and Ali Kosh developed into more substantial communities which were most likely year-round sedentary villages. These two, and other well-known contemporary sites in the Zagros area, such as Jarmo (Braidwood and Howe 1960) and Tepe Guran (Mortenson, Meldgaard, and Thrane 1964), offer a good outline of the life-styles of the period between 9000 and 8000 B.P. in the region of the Zagros mountains. There is evidence for domestic (morphologically distinct) animals and cereal grain at sites of this period, and seemingly farming was becoming well established in the area.

We know of no very large sites during this time range in the Zagros similar to Jericho or Besamun in the Levant. The heavy reliance on herded animals, which might require part of the community to move with them during different times of the year, probably kept the maximum community size down to one to two hundred people. The architecture at these sites is of mud and mud bricks, made into rectangular multi-roomed structures. The ground stone industry becomes increasingly diverse, and finely worked stone bowls are common. Poorly fired clay objects, such as figurines of both zoomorphic and anthropomorphic form, are also common. Clay-lined bins are found at several sites, which were probably used to store grain. Early coarse pottery is found at both Ganj Dareh and Tepe Guran.

For a period of time early villages continued to "experiment" with agriculture while they maintained some of their hunting and collecting

pursuits. As the plants and animals were selectively bred for more productive strains, as tools and techniques became more efficient, and as man
altered the landscape to provide for agriculture, the possibility and
motivation for returning to hunting and gathering ways diminished and
ultimately disappeared. The introduction of agriculture was not always a
successful transition at the outset, and probably many communities
experimented with it but did not adopt it fully. However, after some period
of time due to the alteration of the environment by men, the process
became more irreversible, and there was less chance for agriculturists to
give up their sedentary ways.

THE CHRONOLOGICAL ORDER OF IMPORTANT INNOVATIONS

In regarding the sweep of human history it is striking how after a seemingly long period of human existence with little noticeable innovation, there
is a veritable technological explosion at approximately the time agriculture is introduced. Is this a result of the fundamental change in life-style
brought about by agriculture, or is agriculture just one aspect of a much
broader range of innovations which took place during a relatively short
period of creativity from 12,000 to 7000 B.P.? I will attempt to classify in
three categories the major developments as they occurred in southwestern
Asia — those that took place before agriculture, those that accompanied
agriculture, and those that immediately followed early agriculture. This
will help in the analysis of these inventions, and will shed light on whether
they were causal elements in the introduction of agriculture or effects of an
already accomplished transition.

Before agriculture, fully sedentary villages were established in at least
some parts of the Near East. This is a fundamental development and
facilitated a number of the other inventions. Sedentism seems to have
been more prevalent in the Levant than in the Zagros-Khuzistan area,
where communities remained small and perhaps not fully sedentary until
after agriculture had been established. One suggested explanation is that
the greater importance of plants and aquatic resources in the Levant
would encourage sedentism, while the greater reliance on animals in the
Zagros-Khuzistan area kept at least part of the community on the move.
One of the first innovations found in sedentary and semisedentary villages
is storage facilities (often used in the archaeological definition of senden-
tary villate). Storage is the key to the success of agriculture, and ultimately
it made farming a more reliable and productive form of subsistence than

hunting and gathering. In this way early agriculturists were able to store energy for lean periods and unpredictably bad years. Grinding slabs, handstones, mortars, and pestles have now been found in a variety of pre-agricultural communities. These specialized implements for preparing food and making it more edible are important innovations. They make the utilization of grass seeds (cereal among them) more efficient and more competitive with other food sources in terms of the time required to collect and prepare an equivalent amount of nutrients.

Another important preagricultural invention was specialized harvesting tools, such as sickle blades and composite sickles with hafted blades. These allowed for more efficient collection of cereal grain, which became the basic element of the domesticated-plant complex in southwestern Asia. The widespread introduction of microlithic tools in terminal Pleistocene times seems to be closely tied to an alteration in the subsistence systems of the makers of these tools. It is not the size of the microliths which is the important invention. The fundamental innovation of microlithic technology is the idea that the stone artifact is only one element to be combined into specialized composite tools of a variety of shapes and functions.

Various kinds of containers were in use before agriculture. In addition to stationary storage silos and basins, there were stone bowls and probably baskets. The more durable containers, made of materials that have been preserved archaeologically, are found only in rough form in pre-agricultural times. Less durable items made of perishable materials, such as basketry and skin containers, probably had been in use for a long period of time.

One of the most striking developments in southwestern Asia during immediately pre-agricultural times is the improvement in substantial architecture. The circular structures of Natufian Ain Mallaha are very impressive, as is the masonry of the PPNA levels of Jericho. This effort at building structures and creating heavy, nonportable, ground stone implements shows a commitment to sedentism which in its own way discouraged any shift away from sedentism, and in addition made it more worthwhile to stay in one place.

There are several inventions which seem to appear along with the first distinctive evidence of agriculture. Long-distance trade, as evidenced by Anatolian obsidian and marine shells found hundreds of kilometers from their sources, is a common occurrence in early farming villages. Although it is likely that men travelled the seas long before this, the first unequivocal evidence of seafaring dates from the period of the first farming villages (obsidian traded among the Aegean islands). The working of metal in the form of native copper also seems to accompany agriculture.

Architecture develops considerably with the widespread use of rectangular multiroomed structures. Mud bricks are widely used and there is good evidence for buildings of more than one story. As an important shift, the change from circular to rectangular structures is more fundamental than it might seem. A circular structure is the most efficient shape for insulating against outside weather, but it is very difficult to make additions to it. Rectangular structures are simple to build as many-roomed buildings and to increase in size. This encourages architecturally distributed specialization and small additions which might serve as storage space, food-processing areas, or workshops. This seems to have occurred in several early farming villages, whereas in the preagricultural structures it would appear that all activities took place in a single structure.

Soon after the introduction of agriculture there were several important innovations which are often mistakenly attributed to the earliest farmers. In most localities in southwestern Asia, pottery seems to appear only after agriculture has been established. There may have been earlier experiments with clay containers, but well-fired material occurs later. Pottery is an important tool for storage, preparation, and exchange. In addition to its utilitarian purposes, the technology of making a pot must have been a major stimulus toward other inventions. The ability to change one compound into another compound by firing must have promoted later experiments with metallurgy and glass manufacture, as well as the preparation of foods. Smelting of metals came soon after agriculture, enabling man to create more durable and useful tools. Other important agricultural tools (most important among them being the plow) were developed after a longer period of time. Irrigation, which increased the productivity of many marginal areas, developed early in the Near East. It was the combination of these post-agricultural innovations — improved strains of plants and more adaptable animals, combined with irrigation and more efficient tools — which allowed agriculturists to move into and colonize areas that had been beyond the boundaries of potentially farmable land. One of these regions, lowland Mesopotamia, was colonized by early farmers and soon became the center of innovation for southwestern Asia.

After the establishment of agriculture, architecture began to change. Increasingly, sites came to be composed of large, contiguous, walled buildings. The shift from free-standing buildings to structures that shared walls and passageways must be a reflection of a major shift in the organizational framework of the community. It is likely that after the establishment of agriculture there came to be a more centralized control of society, and that the ranked structure of society continued to increase. Some community organizations at this time may even have extended beyond the boundaries of a single community, and it would not be unreasonable to expect what Service has referred to as a chiefdom organization among many established agricultural societies (1971).

Specific conclusions are difficult to reach from this brief discussion of the priorities of innovations in conjunction with the introduction of agriculture in southwestern Asia. The general pattern that emerges is that the major changes before agriculture were innovations in technology that enabled men to become farmers. The major innovations that followed agriculture were primarily designed to allow men to expand into new areas and to colonize zones that were previously unfarmable. The changes that seem to occur at each stage of development and that may be most fundamental in the introduction of agriculture are in the realm of social organization. The modification of the life-style and ethics of hunters and gatherers that allowed them to live together in far larger communities under a significantly different form of subsistence is truly a revolution.

In this article I have attempted to outline briefly the developmental sequences in southwestern Asia and to suggest productive lines of model building and research. Clearly it is necessary for us to do more thinking, and to attempt to formulate more interesting and compelling theories. It is also imperative for us to continue to collect more information from a greater variety of archaeological situations. I would suggest that in addition to these two widely accepted courses of action, it would be of great benefit if we would spend some time trying to make both our current theories and the data that have been collected already more usable. Theories and models should be refined, and should be formulated in terms of objectively observable archaeological entities. The key variables to be measured should be determined, and the available evidence should be reanalyzed accordingly, to obtain the desired information. Given this type of background work and a more coordinated field effort, I am convinced that an understanding of the origins of agriculture in southwestern Asia is within our reach.

REFERENCES

BRAIDWOOD, R. J.
  1967 *Prehistoric men* (seventh edition). Glenview, Illinois: Scott, Foresman.
BRAIDWOOD, R. J., B. HOWE
  1960 *Prehistoric investigations in Iraqi Kurdistan.* Studies in Ancient Oriental Civilizations 31. Chicago: University of Chicago Press.

BRAIDWOOD, R. J., B. HOWE, C. A. REED
   1961   The Iranian Prehistoric Project. *Science* 133:2008–2010.
CHILDE, V. G.
   1936   *Man makes himself.* London: C. A. Watts.
DE CONTESON, H.
   1971   Tell Ramad, a village of Syria of the seventh and sixth millennia B.C. *Archaeology* 24:278–285.
HOLE, F., K. V. FLANNERY, J. A. NEELY
   1969   *Prehistory and human ecology of the Deh Luran Plain: an early village sequence from Khuzistan, Iran.* Memoirs of the Museum of Anthropology, University of Michigan 1. Ann Arbor: University of Michigan Press.
KENYON, K.
   1957   *Digging up Jericho.* London: Ernest Benn.
KIRKBRIDE, D.
   1966   Five seasons at the pre-pottery Neolithic village of Beidha in Jordan. *Palestine Exploration Quarterly* 1966:8–72.
MORTENSON, P., J. MELDGAARD, H. THRANE
   1964   Excavations at Tepe Guran, Luristan. *Acta Archaeologica* 39:110–121.
PERKINS, DEXTER, JR.
   1964   Prehistoric fauna from Shanidar, Iraq. *Science* 144:1565–1566.
PERROT, J.
   1966   Le gisement Natufien de Mallaha (Eynan), Israël. *L'Anthropologie* 70:437–484.
   1968   La préhistoire palestinienne. *Supplément au dictionnaire de la Bible* 8:286–446.
SERVICE, E.
   1971   *Primitive social organization: an evolutionary perspective* (second edition). New York: Random House.
SMITH, P. E. L.
   1972   Ganj Dareh Tepe. *Iran* 10:165–168.
SOLECKI, R. L.
   1964   Zawi Chemi Shanidar, a post-Pleistocene village site in northern Iraq. *Report of the VIth International Congress of Quaternary Studies, Warsaw,* 4:405–412.
VAN LOON, M.
   1968   The Oriental Institute excavations at Mureybit. *Journal of Near Eastern Studies* 27:265–290.
WATSON, P. J., S. A. LEBLANC, C. L. REDMAN
   1971   *Explanation in archeology: an explicitly scientific approach.* New York: Columbia University Press.

A Model for the Origin of Agriculture in the Near East

CHARLES A. REED

This essay is frankly speculative, and the ideas presented are not necessarily limited to the kinds of data that are at present testable by archaeological research. Prehistoric peoples obviously had many aspects of their behavior, such as communication, ritual, and dance, which left no archaeologic record, and we have even less chance of knowing their thoughts or restrictions on their thoughts. Anyone who has had archaeological experience and also lived in a village lacking evidence of literacy must have pondered on the vast gulf between the life of the village and what would be reconstructed at present if the long-abandoned remnants of that village were to be excavated with present techniques. As archaeologists we do our best within the limits of time, money, and our individual abilities, but beyond the data emerging from our best is room for surmise. This essay is surmise, but I hope controlled surmise.

A major cultural innovation, such as that of an agricultural beginning, necessitated the prior existence of certain environmental and cultural prerequisites, followed by a distinctive sequence of events; these prerequisites and that sequence need not necessarily have been identical in different areas IF agriculture originated several times independently; Carter (this volume) has become so impressed with the seeming complexity of the process that he strongly recommends that we give serious consideration to the possibility that agriculture originated only once, and diffused thereafter from that original center by transport of ideas at least, if not always of actual cultigens and domesticates.

A considerable literature of surmise already exists on the possible cultural pathways by which hunter-gatherers might have become settled agriculturists. Most such articles subsequently have been negatively treated by various critics, sometimes on the basis that the ideas advanced were not "archaeologically testable." As mentioned above, we cannot reasonably limit ourselves to ideas that are archaeologically testable. If, however, an infinite number of concepts by a like number of authors were sincerely to be advanced regarding the pattern of the cultural shift to agriculture, one of them would necessarily be correct. Obviously, each one of the infinite number of sincere authors would believe his contribution to offer the solution.

I am one of that number; in this case the argument is limited to the Near East. That region for my present purposes includes the northern (lower) valley of the Nile below the second cataract, and southwestern Asia west of the central deserts of Persia. I am making the assumption that agriculture DID originate in this area, independently of possible origins elsewhere; if I am wrong in my assumption, as Carter believes possible, then obviously this essay will be found to have been unnecessary.

Most of southwestern Asia during the later Pleistocene was, according to the conclusions of Wright (this volume) an area dominated by a continental climate which resulted in a generally treeless and dry steppe with a predominance of *Artemisia* [sagebrush]. This climatic pattern may have varied locally, particularly southward in the Levant, as Anthony Marks (personal communication) has found palynological evidence for oak and pistachio trees in the central Negev at around 17,000 B.P., and Horowitz (1971) found that, beginning about 15,000 B.P. and continuing for several millennia thereafter, 75 percent or more of the arboreal pollen in a core from the center of Lake Hula, northern Jordan drainage, was of oak. This same core for the same period shows a low percentage of *Artemisia*. Wright has suggested (personal communication) that the oak-pollen recorded from deposits of the late Pleistocene at Lake Hula may have been from deciduous species of *Quercus* and not from the non-deciduous kinds typical of the Mediterranean climate with dry summers. The archaeological record indicates continuous human occupation in the Nile Valley, along the Levantine coast, and on the inner side and in some of the inner valleys of the Zagros Mountains. Some other parts of the Zagros, as indicated by the sequence at Shanidar Cave on the southwestern side of the Zagros, may have been vacated by man between approximately 28,000–12,000 B.P. (R. S. Solecki 1955) and much of Iranian Azerbaijan may also have been largely unoccupied during the late Pleistocene and early Recent (R. S. Solecki 1969). For some other parts of the Near East we do not yet have evidence sufficient to state continuous or non-continuous occupation. Where palynological evidence is available for a Near Eastern continental climate (parts of Syria and western Iran) grasses were seemingly reduced in numbers and perhaps limited as to areas and numbers of species. The oak-pistachio forest, typical of the hills and mountains before the historical period of deforestation, was completely or almost completely absent from Europe and most of the Near East until approximately 12,000 years ago. Wright thinks that the Mediterranean-type, dry-summer forest was at the time limited to northwestern Africa, but this is perhaps too distant and too restricted a range, particularly considering the evidence from Palestine. By contrast, A. Horowitz (personal communication) believes that the continental-type steppe dominated by *Artemisia* may well have extended southward on the highlands of Palestine, but that both the coast and the Jordan Valley, being at lower altitudes, were each more modern in their floral assemblage. In any case, deeply dissected, protected coastal spots of the Levant and southern Turkey may have had copses of residual forest. Wright believes further that the wild ancestral cereal grains (einkorn and emmer wheats and two-rowed barley), often if not typically found in association with the oak woodlands, were rare in, or quite possibly absent from, southwestern Asia.

TOOLS FOR REAPING AND GRINDING IN THE NEAR EAST DURING THE LATE PLEISTOCENE

All of the considerable archaeological evidence from the Nile Valley north of the Second Cataract indicates continuous human occupation from at least the Middle Paleolithic to the present. Evidence of use of tools for preparation of foods is absent from much of this record, but grinding slabs and handstones appear in sites around 15,000 B.P., and are generally found thereafter; mortars are absent. I conclude that, in addition to continuing dependence upon hunted game (these ancient Egyptians had a taste for hartebeest) and other foods that had been gathered previously, they were turning in part to large-seeded grasses for nutrition, and that these seeds were being ground. We have no evidence, unfortunately, as to storage of grain, nor do we have much if any evidence as to the duration of occupancy each year of any of the various sites which have been excavated. The seeds of grasses presumably ripened in the late spring, as they do now, and would have been harvested then.

In addition to grinding slabs and handstones, three Egyptian sites, but only three, also yielded sickle blades. One site was at Tushka (around 14,450–12,450 B.P.) in Egyptian Nubia (Wendorf 1968; Wendorf and Schild 1976), and another was at Esna (around 12,700–12,000 B.P.) in

Upper Egypt south of Luxor (Wendorf, personal communication; Wendorf and Schild 1976). A third site with sickle blades and the milling stones is near El-Kilh, and is small, late in the Pleistocene (11,560±180 B.P.), and relatively unimportant except as indicating to us that reaping continued to be practiced. Other sites, some earlier than these, some at the same approximate periods, and some even in the Holocene, have grinding slabs and handstones, but no sickle blades; presumably most grain was gathered by stripping, plucking, or having the seed from the heads beaten into a container.

The site at Esna is particularly informative as pollen there has been identified by two palynologists as being almost certainly that of barley;[1] of the total pollen, 15 percent was of this barley. However, barley is not now native to Egypt; the climate is too hot and dry. The sickle blades comprised 14 percent of the total flaked stone, and Wendorf and Schild have concluded from the totality of the evidence that a major increase in population occurred in the area at the time.

The importance of the human activities in the valley of the lower Nile during the late Pleistocene has only recently been realized. Specifically, with regard to the history of agriculture we can state at present: (1) the earliest known appearance of the complex of sickle blades, grinding slabs, and handstones was in the Nile Valley in Egypt, beginning about 15,000 B.P. or soon after; (2) this complex may have been, and probably was, locally important in the economy of the people using it, but most of the population, while having grinding slabs and handstones in considerable numbers, did not use sickles; (3) the combination of grinding slabs, handstones, and sickles continued in Egypt until the end of the Pleistocene, and later; data are incomplete but the tradition probably persisted in diminished expression until it became important again with the introduction of cultivated grains in the pre-Dynastic period; (4) no evidence is known which suggests that any grains were cultivated in northeastern Africa (or elsewhere on that continent) during the late Pleistocene or for several millennia thereafter.

In southwestern Asia during this same period of the terminal Pleistocene, tools used for pounding or grinding foods or reaping grasses were seemingly few, and probably have often not been well reported when found. Both the pounding combination of mortar-and-pestle and the grinding combination of handstone and grinding slab are known (see

[1] At the conference (Aug. 28–Sept. 1, 1973) on the Origin of Agriculture for which this paper was prepared, three individuals with palynological experience (Vishnu-Mittre, Harlan, and Wright) expressed doubt that the pollen of barley could be distinguished from that of some other grasses.

Kraybill, this volume). From a functional point of view, mortars may have been used not only for pounding but also for grinding, by a rapid circular rubbing but non-rotatory motion of the pestle within the mortar (Jean Perrot, personal communication). Additionally, a compound tool, consisting of a grinding slab, with a small mortar built into one end, has been reported and illustrated by R. L. Solecki (1969), from Zawi Chemi Shanidar in the hills of northern Iraq. The date was ca. 10,750 B.P., barely post-Pleistocene. A tool as complex as this compound one indicates a long prior experience with pounding and grinding, yet the archaeological evidence for that experience in the Zagros-Tauros arc has, if existing, not been found as yet.

By contrast, in Palestine some such partial history does exist; mortars and pestles were becoming increasingly common throughout the latter part of the late Pleistocene (see Kraybill, this volume). Additionally, a grinding stone and a handstone, with clear signs of red ochre, have been recovered from a stratum with a late Paleolithic assemblage in Kafzeh Cave, Galilee (O. Bar-Yosef, personal communication). No absolute date is available for the particular layer, but it is thought by Bar-Yosef to have been older than the occupation at Ein Aqev in the central Negev, where Marks et al. (1975) have recovered a handstone and a grinding slab (Kraybill, this volume: Figure 1) from a stratum which has been carbon-dated at no less than 17,000 B.P. This date is more than two millennia earlier than that known for any grinding slabs in adjacent northeastern Africa, but the Egyptian association between sickle blades and grinding slabs and handstones remains earlier. The absence of sickle blades from southwestern Asia until those found in Natufian assemblages after 13,000 B.P. is noteworthy. Were these a cultural import from Africa, an independent invention, or are they present but simply not reported from late Paleolithic sites in southwestern Asia? The latter possibility is unlikely, as every archaeologist working in the area has been looking for evidence of reaping in late Paleolithic and transitional-Mesolithic sites. The diffusion of the use of sickle blades from Egypt would seem most reasonable; new knowledge of late Paleolithic and Natufian sites in Sinai (J. Phillips, et al. i.p.) indicates that this bridge between Asia and Africa could have served as a cultural channel but certainly was no environmental barrier, as some have suggested in the past (see Reed 1969: Note 59). A mystery at present, thus, is why the artifacts of chipped stone of the late Paleolithic in the Nile Valley and those of the Levant remain so distinctively different. An obvious need is much intensive field work in Sinai. In the meantime we can conjecture that possibly one behavior pattern with its necessary tool — the reaping of large-seeded grasses with a sickle — did cross from Egypt into Asia by way of Sinai. Perhaps the transfer of the cultural association between reaping and the sickle accompanied a natural movement of the large-seeded grasses (barley and wheats?) northward into Asia in the latest Pleistocene? The data to answer this question are not now known, but they can be sought.

CULTURAL CHANGE IN SOUTHWESTERN ASIA AT THE END OF THE PLEISTOCENE

Reaping and grinding of grain in southwestern Asia became important at the end of the Pleistocene, and certainly was the behavioral and economic basis in that area for the later emergence of the cultivation of the cereal grains. The conditions in southwestern Asia may indeed have been unique to that part of the world, although I suspect that parallels will be found with northern China at the time of the emergence of agriculture there.

For our consideration of cultural change leading to agriculture, let us think of an analogy with microbiology. The bacteriologist has various nutrient media which he can put in his petri dishes and he has a variety of strains of bacteria as inoculants; some of these latter will grow well in one dish, others will die, but some of these latter strains may thrive in another dish. The bacteriologist can also change the environment — temperature and humidity. Utilizing all of these variables, he may find under one limiting set of conditions that only one of his introduced strains grows profusely, and some of its particular mutations may also grow well in an environment which was previously unusable by any of the strains, with a new adaptive niche thus being opened.

So it was with the Near East toward the end of the Pleistocene. The environment was still cold and dry; the landscape was generally a treeless steppe. That environment, however, was changing toward one with a Mediterranean climate with warmer and wetter winters; trees were beginning to colonize, moving in from the south and out of their refugia; presumably grasses were increasing in number and kinds, and some of these grasses presumably would have been barley, and einkorn and emmer wheats.

The cultural substrate, analogous to the bacteriologist's nutrient media, was the Kebaran in the Levant and the Zarzian further to the north and northeast. Why the way of life of the peoples of the Kebaran and Zarzian traditions provided such splendid cultural nutrition is at present unclear, but it may be somehow associated with a strong emphasis, new to south-western Asia, on the use of microliths in both traditions.

Into this cultural substrate, at a time of rather rapid environmental change (a change, remember, that may well have included the introduction of wild wheats and barley), the cultural inoculum of the reaping and milling complex — grinding slabs, handstones, and sickles — was introduced. This innovative complex of human behavior and associated tools may have accompanied the northward movement of the cereals out of Africa, although at present no evidence is known that supports this suggestion.

Aside from the few milling stones already mentioned for the Levant, these tools had been practically unknown in southwestern Asia during the Pleistocene, although found in southern Africa as early as 49,000 B.P. (Kraybill, this volume); for all of non-Levantine southwestern Asia prior to 11,000 B.P., I believe that passing mention (Braidwood and Howe 1960: 58) of a "quern fragment" at the Zarzian site of Palegawra (14,000–12,000 B.P.) in northern Iraq is the only reference to a true milling stone in all of the literature on the Paleolithic of southwestern Asia other than the Levant. (At Palegawra, however, contamination of the quern-bearing layer from higher and later [Uruk] strata cannot be excluded.) By contrast, mortars and pestles, which are typically used for pounding a variety of hard or tough foods, were fairly widespread in southwestern Asia by the end of the Pleistocene; an early and well-made example was found at Ein Gev I (Stekelis and Bar-Yosef 1965) in the northern Jordan Valley; the site has since been dated at 15,700±415 B.P. Mortars and pestles were in wide use by the end of the Pleistocene, and continued in use thereafter (R. L. Solecki 1969).

With the exception of a reference to a few blades with lustrous edges excavated at Ein Gev I, nothing resembling sickles or sickle blades has been reported for the late Paleolithic of southwestern Asia, during a time when sickles were already in use in Egypt. However, they are reported at almost every site of the Natufian culture, beginning approximately 13,000 years ago in the Levant; mortars and pestles are typically common, too, but by contrast, grinding slabs and handstones are rare in Natufian sites (see Kraybill, this volume). Obviously the reaping and preparation of grain was important to the Natufians, although undoubtedly a wide variety of other plants also continued to be gathered, and hunting persisted.

The Natufian was certainly a time of cultural enrichment. The sites are relatively numerous in the Levant, and a wide variety of large and small animals were utilized for food (the "wide spectrum utilization" of Flannery, or "the settling into the environment" of Braidwood and Howe), trade inland in seashells became fairly common, and the stone walls forming the bases of dwellings are often found (see Perrot 1968a for the most complete review).

Several matters of importance to our thesis emerge from consideration of the period of the immediate post-Pleistocene in southwestern Asia: (1) no evidence for cultivation of plants or the domestication of food-producing animals; (2) the associated presence of milling slabs, hand-stones, and sickles in the Natufian of the Levant; (3) presence of grinding slabs and handstones (but not of sickles) elsewhere, as at Shanidar and Zawi Chemi Shanidar (R. L. Solecki 1969); (4) storage by the Natufians, probably of dried grain and possibly of other dried foodstuffs, if the use of the "silos" ascribed to them by Perrot is correct; (5) evidence of a more intense utilization of a wider variety of foodstuffs than was seemingly true of earlier hunter-gatherers in the area; (6) stone-based walls for houses, and houses clustered into villages, the population of one of which (Mallaha) has been estimated at 100–200 (Perrot 1968b).

From these archaeological data, I conclude: (a) people were not only reaping and milling grain at the time of its ripening, but they were thresh-ing and storing it for later use; (b) the population was increasing, and each group had less area from which to support itself; (c) the storage of grain led to a more sedentary life (Reed 1969: 377).

I believe that this introduction of sedentism was an important link in the chain of events leading to agriculture.

SEDENTISM AS A DISRUPTIVE PATTERN

Harris (this volume) has argued with considerable logic that for a people to be changed from hunter-gatherers to agriculturalists would require a major cultural disruption, during which period they would probably modify or lose their accepted techniques for control of the size of their population. A considerable body of data has been accumulated (reviewed by Hayden 1972, and by Divale 1972) on the mechanisms by which hunter-gatherers stabilize (and have stabilized) their populations below carrying capacity of the environment and thus escape the Malthusian fate of geometric increase and ultimate starvation. Although a variety of techniques are employed, the most frequent is infanticide, more often of daughters, the deed being done directly by the mother soon after giving birth. She is the one who is faced with the necessity, in a mobile group, of carrying whichever children cannot walk or cannot keep up with the group. Feuding, in such pre-agricultural societies, also reduced populations.

Divale (1972) thought that at least by 70,000 years ago the habitable lands of the Old World would have become filled insofar as the technological capacity of the hunter-gatherers allowed, and after that time dissident groups in an increasing population would have had no empty land to acquire. Under such conditions, local warfare might have become another factor in reducing populations, particularly of young males.

With sedentary life, such as the Natufian peoples and possibly some others in the Near East were settling into, the practical reasons for infanticide as associated with the need for mobility would disappear; no longer faced with the problem of carrying another babe, a woman would more often put it to her breast. Other techniques for control of population — that of abortion and those resulting in non-fertilization — may well have lost their importance also. Population would have increased, even if feuding and local warfare did continue. We have no archaeological evidence for such feuding or local warfare at the time; only with the erection of the first wall around the early Neolithic settlement at Jericho, nearly two millennia later, do we have evidence that warfare was a part of Near Eastern life. One factor in the favor of the Natufians and other peoples of the period in the Near East may have been that, with the climate continuing to change from the continental to the Mediterranean type until 5500 B.P. (van Zeist and Wright 1963), some lands may have been continually available for a group fissioning off of a parent population; particularly on the edges of settled areas would this have been true.

The main point is that population seemingly did increase, although extremely slowly by modern standards. However, for much of the Old World for much of the later Paleolithic, population must have been static, and any increase thus signalled a different pattern of living. That pattern, for the Natufians, was the adoption of a sedentary way of life, in villages supported by hunting and gathering. The earliest villages seem to have been permanent establishments, with permanent houses; even so, we have no evidence that all the villages were occupied the year around, although they may well have been. The important change was that to the sedentary life, where at least for the greater part of the year the greater part of the population lived together in increasing numbers on one spot. Whereas the optimum size for a band of hunter-gatherers has usually been estimated to be about twenty-five, Mallaha, by the side of Lake Hula in the upper Jordan Valley, may well have had some 150 people.

Any estimate of size of population or change of rate of growth of a population for prehistoric peoples can be no more than an educated guess, based on fragmentary data and questionable comparisons with historical data, yet obviously we must do the best with what we have. An

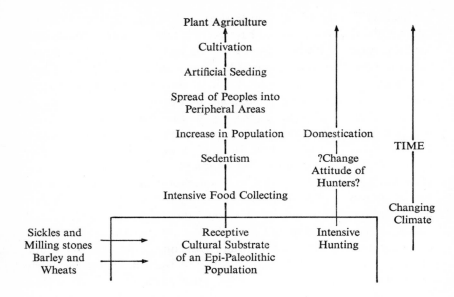

Figure 1.   Diagram of a suggested pattern whereby some human populations of South-western Asia made the initial changes from hunters-and-gatherers to agriculturalists

attempt to estimate the population of the former British mandate of Palestine, an area occupied spottily by the Natufians,[2] can be made by using the concept of the "site-catchment area" (Vita-Finzi and Higgs 1970; Higgs and Vita-Finzi 1972).[3] The "site-catchment area" is the land around a settlement which the inhabitants use and upon which, essentially, they depend for their livelihood. For sedentary peoples the land beyond 10 km. (6.2 miles) from the village is little used for daily supplies, and the bulk of gathering, at least, occurs within 5 km. of the settlement. If we estimate the population of Mallaha to have been 150 persons, a site-catchment area with a radius of 10 km. would have had 314 sq. km.; one with a radius of 5 km. would have been only 78.5 sq. km. On the basis of an independent survey of Natufian sites in the area of Mount Carmel, a Natufian "territory" was estimated to have occupied between 300 and

[2]   The Natufians occupied areas beyond Palestine proper, in Jordan at Beidha, into Sinai on the south, in Lebanon north to the Beqa'a, and in Syria at least to the Euphrates River northeast.
[3]   I was indebted to Fekri Hassan (1972) for the idea of using the area of the site-catchment in a study of paleo-populations until I recollected that I had used the same technique, although not with the same name, in an attempt to calculate the population of England and Wales at the time of the occupation of Star Carr (Braidwood and Reed 1957).

400 sq. km. (O. Bar-Yosef, personal communication). My figure of 314 sq. km. falls within, but toward the lower end of, this range of 300 to 400, so is assumed thereby to have some degree of accuracy; thus a Natufian site-catchment area with a radius of only 5 km. will not here again be considered.

If we think of all of the 27,000 sq. km. (10,429 sq. miles) of Palestine during the early Natufian period as having been neatly dotted with contiguous areas of 314 sq. km., each holding 150 people, we would have had a human population of 12,900. To think thus, however, is obviously an error; the Negev undoubtedly then, as now, was less densely occupied and the central hills of Palestine probably were likewise somewhat sparsely populated. Many parts of Palestine, thus, probably had no central settlements at the time and their people were not yet becoming sedentary. Taking these various factors into consideration, I suggest[4] a population of 10,000 people for Palestine near the end of the Pleistocene, 11,000 B.P. This figure seems reasonable, although even this would probably be too high if Carneiro and Hilse (1966) were even close to actuality in their estimate of no more than 100,000 for the whole of the Near East (which they define essentially as I do) at 10,000 B.P.

If, however, we accept this figure of 10,000 for Palestine at 11,000 B.P., and accept the annual rate of increase of 0.001 (0.1 percent) which Carneiro and Hilse ascribed to the Neolithic of the Near East for the later period of 10,000–6000 B.P., we find an increase to 27,000 people by 10,000 B.P. and 74,000 by 9000 B.P., approximately the time of the first appearance of plant agriculture in the Near East. The truth probably lies somewhere between these extremes of 10,000 people in Palestine at 11,000 B.P. and 74,000 at 9000 B.P., and indeed the latter figure is probably too high. However, even with the extremly low rate of increase of 0.1 percent per annum the population would have expanded rapidly ("rapidly" for a prehistoric period), out of logical bounds. One could halve the assumed rate, and even halve the assumed original population and still, in two millennia, get a respectable growth.

My point in the above discussion of populations and rates of increase is to show that even a low rate of such increase, with a doubling time measured in centuries instead of generations, will produce quite dramatic increases in population.

In the Near East, by 9000 B.P., we find villages not only in Palestine but at Mureybit on the Euphrates in eastern Syria (earliest date of 10,200 B.P.), at Çayönü in southeastern Turkey (base of the village dated at

[4] Paleo-demography is not an exact science.

9400 B.P.), at Ganj Dareh on the "inner" (northern) side of the Zagros Mountains in western Iran (earliest date at 10,400 B.P.), and the simple villages of the Bus Mordeh phase on the Deh Luran plain, southwestern Iran (beginning around 9500 B.P.). Numerous others, not yet discovered, must surely have existed. We could perhaps include here the site of Zawi Chemi Shanidar, in northern Iraq, dated at 10,850 B.P., but the evidence that it was a permanently occupied village, or even a settlement of any long duration, is not secure.

If village life is to be correlated with an increase in population, as I believe we must accept, then the arc of hills from western Iran through northern Iraq and southeastern Turkey down through Palestine and western Jordan almost to the Red Sea was sprouting villages. A few (Mureybit and those of the Bus Mordeh phase) were out on the plains, away from the hills. In all of these villages, and probably in dozens if not hundreds we have not found and may never find, the population was slowly but surely increasing; in each such village, rarely but consistently, a group would depart and found a new village.

THE ORIGINS OF CULTIVATION

By 9500 B.P. husbandry, even if not yet full-blooming agriculture, had certainly arrived. Since by this time people in various parts of the Near East had shown that, given intensive hunting and collecting and probably considerably storage of grass seeds, villages could be maintained on a hunting and gathering basis, why or how did purposeful seeding and cultivation begin? We can, on the basis of archaeological evidence and radiocarbon datings, state where and when we get the first evidence of that beginning, but the how and why as yet elude us, and the only reasonable answer continues to be the original suggestion of Harlan and Zohary (1966), discussed since by several authors, that as people moved away from centers of dense natural growth of the cereal grains (mostly barley, einkorn and emmer wheats) they found their supply of cereal foods diminishing. Since man by this time certainly knew the relationship between a seed in the ground one year and a plant growing at that spot the next, someone or many people may have had the idea of helping the natural crop by adding seeds. Since all of these people used sickles, perhaps an effort was being made to have the stalks grow more closely, so that the sickle would continue to be an efficient secondary energy trap. These kinds of decisions and actions do not leave traces in the archaeological record, but even so our thoughts turn back the ten or more millennia to those hunters and gatherers of the Near East, that we may live with them in thought and try to understand their problems and their solutions.

As long as people gathered the natural wild grain, by reaping or otherwise, and never replaced any seed in the ground, they may have changed the gene pools of the wild wheats and barleys very little. However, modern studies of human influences on the evolution of plants (Baker 1972) have shown numerous and subtle ways in which the gene pools of wild plants are changed by human influences without conscious effort or intent by man. The same types of forces were surely operating ten thousand years ago, even if not so intensively as at present, but without experimental data these are difficult to evaluate. For instance, George Carter (personal communication) has suggested that the use of seed beaters would lead to dispersal of, and thus selection for, those seeds which ripened early on a brittle rachis; over a long period this selection might well produce a physiological race with a high proportion of seed heads which ripened earlier and more uniformly, at the same time. Would hand stripping or reaping with hand-held blade or sickle induce different selective forces?

The wild grains, as Wright (this volume) has outlined, are well adapted to re-seeding and surviving for growth the next year. Enough seed was lost during the harvest, due to the natural shattering of the riper heads, to guarantee a return crop of the same kind, with a majority of the heads being of the shatterable type — i.e. each with a brittle rachis. Under these circumstances, the heads that had the relatively rare genetic character for non-shattering would be continuously removed from the gene pool.

When people began planting, however, they planted seeds they had reaped successfully the harvest before. Such harvested seeds would have the genes for the character of non-shattering (tough rachis) represented in a slightly higher proportion in the reaped grain than in the wild, and these seeds would then — planting by planting — be returned to the soil in increasing quantities. This situation is a case of natural selection, with the factors for selection changed unknowingly by man. The result was that the people on the peripheries, those who were planting each year, began to get in their fields increasing numbers of non-shattering heads on the stalks, which would stand intact in the fields for days longer than would the natural wild grasses of the same kind. Perhaps, for this reason, the cultivated grains began to displace the wild grains even in areas of optimum habitat of the latter, as people in the latter areas borrowed such seeds for planting.

Whatever the factors, plant agriculture did arrive in the Near East, and with such a rush and such a rapid spread that we are amazed. And indeed, if we think of the Levant as central by reason of the early complexity of the Natufian there and because of the possible derivation together from Egypt of the cereal grains and the sickling part of the tool complex for reaping and milling those grains, then the sites for which we know first of what we call cultivated grains — "cultivated" by reasons of the morphological characters which the experts tell us mark cultivated grains — are all peripheral.

The earliest dates we have, both well before 9000 B.P., are at Çayönü in southeastern Turkey and from the Bus Mordeh phase of the cultural sequence on the Deh Luran plain, Khuzistan, southwestern Iran (Hole, Flannery, and Neely 1969). I have worked at Çayönü and so will mention it first; my information comes from my own experience, from the major publication on the site (Braidwood, et al. 1971, 1974), from personal communications with Braidwood, and from personal communication with Barbara Lawrence, who is in charge of the faunal analysis at Çayönü.

The site was first occupied around 9400 B.P., at a time when the effects of the continental type of climate typical of the late Pleistocene must have still been dominant. Yet winter rains must have occurred, to allow the germination of the einkorn and emmer wheats, both presumably of cultivated strains, which are found there at the time of the origin of the site and for some seven centuries thereafter. Sickle blades, grinding slabs, and handstones also occur through the various levels of the site; when the site was founded, plant-agriculture was already well established in the area. The people grew no barley, and indeed probably knew neither wild nor domestic barley of any kind; the assumption is that this grain had not at the time penetrated so far north.

No domestic ungulates were reared by the people who first settled Çayönü; of domestic animals they had only dogs, and seemingly few of them. To get meat the people hunted successfully for wild cattle, deer, and pigs mostly, but in the latter part of the seven centuries of the first occupancy they had added domestic pigs and domestic sheep, and perhaps goats, and dependence on wild game had decreased markedly.

On the Deh Luran plain of Khuzistan, in what is now southwestern Iran, people who built small villages of simple mud slabs began settling by or before 9500 B.P. (Hole, Flannery, and Neely 1969). The assemblage they left has been named the Bus Mordeh Phase, and it continued until approximately 8700 B.P., some 800 years. The environment was a steppe adjacent to marshlands which were fed by freshwater streams from the mountains, so that the people exploited a variety of ecological zones for food, but in large part they depended upon a wide variety of small seeds of native grasses and legumes, none of which seemingly were cultivated.

One might think, considering the early date, the simplicity of the mud slab houses, and the wide-spectrum use of the environment that we had here a pre-agricultural society. However, cultivated varieties of both emmer wheat and two-rowed hulled barley (neither now native to the area) were also utilized; presumably these grasses were sown in prepared ground.

The situation is further complicated by the fact that at present the wild ancestor of emmer wheat is limited to the Levant (Harlan and Zohary 1966); where that variety was growing 9500 years ago is not known, but one would not expect it to have been present near Khuzistan, which area and its environs would presumably still have had a near-continental climate. From whence, then, did the people originally import emmer wheat, either wild or cultivated? For this question I have no answer.

No evidence of dogs appears in the remains of villages of the Bus Mordeh Phase, but the people did have two domestic, hoofed, food animals: more numerous goats and relatively few sheep. Goats in particular would not be native to the environment of the steppe, although the mountains from which they must have been derived are not far away, and indeed the herds of goats and sheep may well have been driven into the mountains for summer grazing. Additional evidence of domestication for the goats is the preponderance of bones of young and subadult animals, and such evidence for sheep is the hornless condition of one specimen.

Grinding slabs and handstones were present but never common in some of the remains of the Bus Mordeh Phase; sickle blades were also present but rare. Much of the seed must have been gathered by stripping or beating, and prepared thereafter by means other than grinding.

The people occupying the Khuzistan plain during the Bus Mordeh Phase were clearly agriculturalists, with two kinds of grains and two kinds of domestic ungulates. However, they continued as hunters and gatherers for a major quantity and variety of their food and seemingly utilized the reaping and milling complex to a minimum. One might think Khuzistan to be too far removed from our expected "center," the Levant, of original utilization of the reaping and milling complex to have been influenced by it, but long-distance trade is indicated by the presence of Turkish obsidian, and other geographically intermediate sites, such as Karim Shahir and M'lefaat in northern Iraq, are known with milling stones but without evidence of agriculture, so probably the milling complex and possibly the distribution of domestic sheep and/or goats may have been more widespread than we now know.

The earliest record of true agriculture in the Levant or its environs is also somewhat peripheral; this is the village of Beidha (Kirkbride 1966), which lies in Jordan high on the eastern side of the graben running south from the Dead Sea to the Gulf of Aqaba. Looking at a political map, one would think the site to be in the middle of a desert, but it is actually situated high enough on the great fault of the Wadi Arabi to catch the winter winds with their rain clouds. A date of around 8800 B.P. for the base of the village indicates that settlement here, in what is certainly a peripheral area for agriculture, was later than that at Çayönü and in Khuzistan, but yet early for the Near Eastern agricultural period.

Barley was cultivated at Beidha, the earliest record for this grain to my knowledge; presumably we catch the situation immediately at the beginning of cultivation, for the plants which Helbaek (1966) ascertained as being cultivated had been so treated for so few generations that few of the differentiating morphological characters by which "domestic" two-rowed barley has become separated from wild had appeared; the "natural selection" which follows early cultivation had not yet had time to act. Helbaek (1966) introduced the term "cultivated wild barley" for this particular situation. Cultivated emmer wheat was also present, and this in the absence of any evidence of wild emmer in the area at the time indicates that the original seeds of the cultivated emmer must have been introduced from elsewhere.

Of domestic animals the people at Beidha seemingly had only goats (Perkins 1966). The presence in the same samples of remains of hunted wild ibex made studies on the goats difficult, as postcranial parts of the closely related goats and ibexes are not separable.

One could proceed further with this concept that sites actually having evidence of really early agriculture are all peripheral to the supposedly "central" area of the Levant, but the purpose of this essay is more to introduce ideas than to try to pound them home.

THE DOMESTICATION OF ANIMALS

During the past fifteen years much research on free-living wild animals has shown that many if not most of them can be approached, even as adults, if one is willing to take the time to learn the ways of the animals and let them become accustomed to the human intruder. Bringing up young animals is even easier, as numerous people have now proved with wolves (Banks, et al. 1967; Hellmuth 1964) and as Adamson (1960) has shown with lions. Jarman and Wilkinson (1972) have mentioned similar behavior for young European elk, red deer, eland, and musk oxen separated from their parents and hand-reared by man; Wilkinson (1972a,

1972b) has described the case of the musk oxen in greater detail, and I have seen this same principle illustrated in northern Iraq, where the tame and fearless young of wild goats and gazelles are kept in and around police posts or in compounds within homes of the wealthy. Geist (1971a, 1971b) discovered that adult wild North American mountain sheep, once they had learned he was a source of salt, would actually come to him and climb upon him. Unknown to most Americans, the European elk (called "moose" in North America) was early broken to harness and to riding in northern Europe (Zeuner 1963: 425–429), and presumably the North American population could be domesticated as successfully. The natural tameness of "wild" deer in North America is known to some, but is best typified by the situation at Wateron, Alberta, Canada, where the local mule deer, not being hunted or even chased, stroll through town, feed on the lawns, and on windy days find shelter lying under peoples' front porches (Geist 1971b). At the Wankwar Ranger Post, Murchison Falls Park, Uganda, a similar but more dramatic situation occurs; the grasses of the mowed lawn around the post provide more palatable grazing than do the natural coarse grasses of the area, and a number of old male Cape buffalo (*Syncerus caffer*) use the lawn for grazing. Not having been disturbed, they have become so tame — in contrast to the idea generally held that old males are particularly aggressive individuals — that the local children clamber on their backs and ride them (Parker and Graham 1971). This is the species widely proclaimed to be the world's most dangerous game animal! Another of the world's "most dangerous animals," a killer whale, has been tamed by a man in Galveston. The great apes, too, will accept humans in their midst, as Jane van Lawick-Goodall (1971) has proved with chimpanzees and Dian Fossey (1970, 1971) with gorillas. (But have you read the horrendous tales of ferocious terror about gorillas recounted in bone-breaking detail by African explorers of the nineteenth century?)

We of the Western world at least have been too long "educated" on a mixture of misinformation stemming from a combination of old peasant's lore (Grimm's fairy tales, etc.) and the equally fallacious tales of hunters, who could not achieve their ego-building if they let it be known, to themselves or others, that the animals they were pursuing with such murderous intent might well, if left alone, be sniffing curiously at the end of the gun's barrel. We suffer overmuch from too many hunter's tales, embellished in "sportmen's" magazines, and from the mystique of the self-hypnosis of those who make a cult of killing.

The truth is that taming most large mammals, particularly ungulates, offers no great difficulty, and once tamed they can be kept and bred in captivity, as shown recently by the "domestication" of musk oxen and eland. Of such tamed populations undergoing domestication, those of each generation which are born to be wilder, due to genetic characteristics which are expressed behaviorally via neurological and endocrinological mechanisms, either escape or are killed, and so their genes are removed from the population, which thus becomes tamer and more "domestic" with each generation. Prehistoric hunters knew a great deal about the behavior of the animals they hunted, but quite naturally they acquired and used that knowledge to help themselves in the hunt. To keep animals, to feed them, rear them, and allow them to breed requires a difference in attitude.

This matter of change of attitude has not hitherto been stressed in studies on the origins of domestications. Instead, various other patterns of events have been suggested as leading to ever-closer association between man and potential domesticates, and so eventually to full domestication. One such suggestion of a possible path toward domestication of the smaller bovids, particularly sheep and goats, has been that hunters followed them throughout their annual movements in the hills and mountains, gradually becoming so familiar with them, and they with the hunters, that the closer association resulted somehow in domestication. The details of this supposed sequence have not been worked out, nor indeed is the idea workable, as long as one population is that of the hunter and the other is the hunted. The hunters will do their utmost to kill, the hunted to escape being killed; no social bond can become established. Even superbly efficient hunters who also have successful records of purposeful maintenance of the prey population, as with the northern Cree and the American population of moose, *Alces alces* (Feit 1973), have no tendency toward domestication of such animals, although these large deer are undoubtedly domesticable; at least the European population (European elk) of *Alces alces* can be and has been so domesticated (Zeuner 1963: 425–429).

The case of the reindeer as a migratory animal first followed and then domesticated by man does not apply to the earlier domestication of sheep and goats, as reindeer had been hunted for tens of thousands of years, from the mid-Paleolithic into the Recent, without the hunters having domesticated them. Only after hunters of reindeer came into contact with people who had domestic cattle and horses did the hunters borrow the idea and apply it to the animal best known to them and the one naturally adapted to the environment of the far north (Carter, this volume). In this case, as with other domestication, the attitude of the hunter was the factor which changed.

I hold that the relation between hunter and hunted, a relation which will not result in domestication, applies also to the "crop-robber" concept (Zeuner 1963: 56) of the behavior of ungulates. The idea was that fields of cultivated plants would be attractive to grazers and browsers (quite true, too), and also that such ungulates would feed on the stubble of the fields after the harvest. In some way never specified this closer association between agricultural man and social ungulates was supposed to have led to the domestication of some of the latter. Aside from the fact that we now believe that early domestication of ungulates (as with sheep at Zawi Chemi) can and did occur prior to any plant husbandry, the further fact exists that any grower of crops, seeing wild ungulates eating in his fields, would certainly have chased the animals out and killed them if he could. This behavior would not seem to be a road toward domestication.

Another suggestion (Downs 1960) has been that wild social ungulates ("herd-animals") were driven into box-canyons or large corrals where food and water were available, and kept there for some days or even weeks as food on the hoof, one or more being killed as needed. Again, this close association between man and another kind of animal was somehow supposed to lead to domestication; actually, where archaeological evidence exists of fences or other devices associated with driving animals, the purpose is always to kill the animals at the end of the drive, not to preserve them alive. Furthermore, this type of drive, while highly efficient for animals living on the plains (equids, gazelles, bison, etc.) is useless in the type of rugged mountains in which goats live, and might well be only marginally effective for the hill country where sheep are found; particularly in the country of rough mountains and steep canyons at or around Zawi Chemi Shanidar where the earliest domestic sheep have been reported (Perkins 1964) such concentrations of animals could not have been achieved by driving.[5]

Prehistoric men, but not usually the women, for hundreds of thousands of years had hunted the wild, hoofed mammals which eventually became domesticated. Women, as they were available at the site of the kill, may have helped to cut up the game and carry the meat away; women could also have helped drive game (tending fires, waving branches, etc.), but the men were almost invariably the killers. Men, too, are conservative,

---

[5] I have elsewhere (Reed 1969) outlined reasons for the possibility, if not probability, of believing that such driving and penning of wild cattle (*Bos primigenius*), to have sacrificial bulls available as needed, may have led to domestication of cattle. Such domestication, however, occurred some two millennia after that of sheep and at least half a millennium later than that of goats and pigs. People were already accustomed to the keeping of animals.

changing the pattern of their actions only when shown and convinced that such change is beneficial; I cannot see any way that such male hunters would have initiated the domestication of animals. The simple fact remains that for hundreds of thousands of years they failed to do so. Only if several preliminary steps toward that domestication had been taken by other members of the community, would man the hunter come to realize the advantages of changing the pattern of his lifestyle toward keeping and protecting animals he had previously hunted to kill. Such other members of the community were women and children; I believe that the primary domestication — of sheep, goats, and pigs particularly — was a case of "a little child shall lead them."

Some years ago (Reed 1959) I discussed the possible role of pet-keeping as a path to domestication of animals. Certainly the keeping of young animals as pets leads to that close association between a human and a member of another species which most writers have stressed as a precondition for domestication. In that publication of 1959 I probably over-emphasized the role of imprinting as a precondition to the young of a wild animal becoming a tame member of the human community. We have learned since, as I have mentioned earlier in this article, that adult wild animals of many species — particularly those of many species which DID become domesticated — are tamable if only allowed to become familiar with humans. Thus the problem of the "flight-distance" — that distance, rather standard for each species, to which an animal will allow a possibly dangerous animal of another kind to approach before fleeing — is probably not of such importance in domestication as Hediger (1955) once thought, although the fact remains that eradication of the flight response is certainly easier in young, hand-reared animals than in wild, captured adults of the same species.

The "pet-keeping" theory of animal domestication has not been received with enthusiasm, but its critics have failed, in my opinion, to substitute any more acceptable suggestions. The major adverse criticism has been that many non-literate peoples have been observed to keep pets or tamed work-animals, but that in no such instance now known has such pet-keeping led to domestication. Such cases among hunting and gathering peoples would not be expected to lead to domestication, for at the time of breaking camp the young animal would be left behind unless the social bond was strong and the young animal or animals could keep up with "their" human family under their own power. Tamed wolf pups may have behaved thus. Some cases quoted against the concept of "pet-keeping" are those of the common practice in southeastern Asia of keeping young gibbons in captivity; as adults they become aggressive and then are released or killed. Another instance is that of macaques caught and trained to be work-animals. Such primates do not become domestic; perhaps primates are, in their own way, individually too clever to be satisfactory domestic animals.

Of the first four kinds of animals (dogs, sheep, goats, pigs) to become domesticated, all were and are social; if caught young and reared by humans, the social bond of the young animal is directed toward its human keeper. Of these four, two (dog and pig) are omnivores and the other two (sheep and goat) are ruminants, representatives of that group which has furnished most of our domestic animals (cattle *sensu lato*, reindeer, camelids), in which cellulose can be converted to usable carbohydrate and in which urea is physiologically recycled to compensate for diets low in proteins. Such animals can survive on diets on which other animals would starve; they are, as I have discussed at greater length elsewhere (Reed 1969), pre-adapted for domestication. Even so, they did not domesticate themselves. If hunters did not domesticate them, who did? If the sons of hunters, growing up and yearning to follow in their fathers' footsteps while practicing their bourgeoning skills on rats and lizards, sharpening their blood-lust, did not domesticate, who did? I suggest that the women and daughters did, with the latter being more important.

A pattern other than that of the hunter and the hunted must be sought for the establishment of the social bond between human and other animal, a bond which I believe was necessary for the success of early domestication. The animal becoming tamed — and taming was certainly a necessary prelude to domestication — must be dependent upon the human, and the human must furnish some necessities for the dependent. I regard this relationship — particularly during the period of the beginnings of domestication in the Near East with regard to sheep, goats, and pigs — as a relatively rare one-to-one relationship, not a mass conversion.

Little girls, increasingly as they grow, have estrogens coursing in their bloodstreams; little girls play with dolls, have maternal instincts. They are not yet, as their mothers may be, inured to killing and the necessities of killing; a little girl might well adopt, protect, and tend a weaned lamb, kid, or baby pig, thus establishing that one-to-one social relationship necessary for abolition of the flight reaction.

The survival of such a relationship between girl and adopted orphan must usually have been cut short by the death of the latter, due to natural causes, dogs, adult males, or a group of gleeful boys. In a hunting and gathering society the chance of successful rearing through a summer must have been minimal to nonexistent, but in a sedentary community the chance presumably would improve — not much perhaps, but some. (We must remember that, if the odds are 100 to 1 against an event happening, in 500 trials the odds are 5 to 1 that it will have happened.)

Men did not suddenly say: "We are going to be friends with sheep." No, the domestication of sheep was a secondary result of a change of attitude which at least allowed the keeping of lambs, even while adult sheep continued to be hunted for wool and skins. If the animal survived and grew, such a tamed lamb probably at first was killed for food by a frustrated hunter, unconcerned by the wails of his daughter, but eventually some "pets" must have been kept to reproductive age and produced young in the village. At that point, or even before, someone must have begun to think that having sheep in the village was an easier way to get meat and hides than lying in ambush for them in the hills.

The first of the food animals to be domesticated were all ungulates of medium size, and two of these were ruminants: sheep at Zawi Chemi Shanidar around 10,850 B.P. (Perkins 1964), goats from the Bus Mordeh Phase, Deh Luran, around 9000 B.P. or earlier (Hole, Flannery, and Neely 1969), and pigs at Çayönü around 8800 B.P. or earlier. The young of all of these animals are easily kept in captivity, tame readily, and can soon forage for themselves; under supervision of children they could be returned each night to the village. The behavior of these animals at the time of initial domestication was not in any way different than that of their ancestors had been for hundreds of thousands or perhaps millions of years. The behavior of the humans, and particularly I suggest that of the adult male humans, was what changed, and this change was initiated by a change in attitude.

We cannot find evidence for changes in attitude and flashes of prophetic thought in the archaeological searchings we do in ancient villages. We do find that domestic ungulates first appeared in the remains of those villages. Plant agriculture was not necessary to support domestic ungulates, but village life — even as simple a kind as presumably existed at Zawi Chemi Shanidar — was seemingly necessary.

What induced the change in attitude that came with village life and allowed the development of ungulate domestication? We may never know, but I suggest again that a little girl did lead them.

REFERENCES

ADAMSON, JOY
  1960   *Born free, a lioness of two worlds.* New York: Bantam Books.
BAKER, HERBERT G.
  1972   Human influences on plant evolution. *Economic Botany* 26:32–43.

BANKS, EDWIN M., DOUGLAS H. PIMLOTT, BENSON E. GINSBURG, *editors*
1967   Ecology and behavior of the wolf. *American Zoologist* 7:221–381.

BRAIDWOOD, ROBERT J., HALET ÇAMBEL, CHARLES L. REDMAN, PATTY JO WATSON
1971   Beginnings of village-farming communities in southeastern Turkey. *Proceedings of the National Academy of Sciences, U.S.A.* 68:1236–1240.

BRAIDWOOD, ROBERT J., HALET ÇAMBEL, BARBARA LAWRENCE, CHARLES L. REDMAN, ROBERT A. STEWART
1974   Beginnings of village-farming communities in southeastern Turkey — 1972. *Proceedings of the National Academy of Sciences, U.S.A.* 71: 568–572.

BRAIDWOOD, ROBERT J., BRUCE HOWE
1960   *Prehistoric investigations in Iraqi Kurdistan.* Studies in Ancient Oriental Civilization 31. Chicago: University of Chicago Press.

BRAIDWOOD, ROBERT J., CHARLES A. REED
1957   The achievement and early consequences of food-production: a consideration of the archeological and natural-historical evidence. *Cold Spring Harbor Symposia on Quantitative Biology* 22:19–31.

CARNEIRO, R. L., D. F. HILSE
1966   On determining the probable rate of population growth during the Neolithic. *American Anthropologist* 68:177–181.

DIVALE, WILLIAM T.
1972   Systemic population control in the Middle and Upper Paleolithic: inferences based on contemporary hunter-gatherers. *World Archaeology* 4:222–243.

DOWNS JAMES F.
1960   Domestications: an examination of the changing social relationships between man and animals. *Papers of the Kroeber Anthropological Society* 22:18–67.

FEIT, HARVEY, A.
1973   Twilight of the Cree hunting nation. *Natural History* 82(7):48–57, 72.

FOSSEY, DIAN
1970   Making friends with mountain gorillas. *National Geographic* 137:48-67.
1971   More years with mountain gorillas. *National Geographic* 140:574–585.

GEIST, VALERIUS
1971a   *Mountain sheep: a study in behavior and evolution.* Chicago: University of Chicago Press.
1971b   A behavioral approach to the management of wild ungulates. *Symposia of the British Ecological Society* 11:413–424.

HARLAN, JACK R.
1967   A wild wheat harvest in Turkey. *Archaeology* 20:197–201.

HARLAN, JACK R., DANIEL ZOHARY
1966   Distribution of wild wheats and barley. *Science* 153:1074–1080.

HASSAN, F. A.
1972   "Population growth and early food production in the Near East." Unpublished manuscript.

HAYDEN, BRIAN
1972   Population control among hunter-gatherers. *World Archaeology* 4: 205–221.

HEDIGER, H.
1955   *Studies of the psychology and behavior of captive animals in zoos and circuses*. London: Butterworth Scientific Publications.

HELBAEK, HANS
1966   Pre-pottery Neolithic farming at Beidha: a preliminary report. *Palestine Exploration Quarterly* (1966):61–66.

HELLMUTH, JEROME
1964   *A wolf in the family*. New York: A Signet Book, published by the New American Library.

HIGGS, E. S., C. VITA-FINZI
1972   "Prehistoric economies: a territorial approach," in *Papers in economic prehistory: studies by members and associates of the British Academy Major Research Project in the Early History of Agriculture*. Edited by E. S. Higgs, 27–36. Cambridge: Cambridge University Press.

HOLE, FRANK, KENT V. FLANNERY, JAMES A. NEELY
1969   *Prehistory and human ecology of the Deh Luran Plain: an early village sequence from Khuzistan, Iran*. Memoirs of the Museum of Anthropology, University of Michigan 1.

HOROWITZ, A.
1971   Climatic and vegetational developments in northeastern Israel during Upper Pleistocene-Holocene times. *Pollen et Spores* 13:255–278.

JARMAN, M. R., P. F. WILKINSON
1972   "Criteria of animal domestication," in *Papers in economic prehistory: studies by members and associates of the British Academy Major Research Project in the Early History of Agriculture*. Edited by E. S. Higgs, 83–96. Cambridge: Cambridge University Press.

KIRKBRIDE, DIANA
1966   Five seasons at the pre-pottery Neolithic village of Beidha in Jordan. *Palestine Exploration Quarterly* (1966): 8–61.

MARKS, A. E., C. R. FERRING, F. MUNDAY, P. JESCHOFNING, N. SINGLETON
1975   Prehistoric sites in near 'En-'Aqev, in the central Negev. *Israel Exploration Journal* 25:65–76.

PARKER, I. S. C., A. D. GRAHAM
1971   The ecological and economic basis for game ranching in Africa. *Symposia of the British Ecological Society* 11:393–404.

PERKINS, DEXTER, JR.
1964   Prehistoric fauna from Shanidar, Iraq. *Science* 144:1565–1566.
1966   The fauna from Madamagh and Beidha. *Palestine Exploration Quarterly* (1966):66–67.

PERROT, J.
1968a   La préhistoire palestinienne. *Supplément au dictionnaire de la Bible* 8:286–446.
1968b   Premiers villages de Syrie et de Palestine. *Académie des Inscriptions et Belles-Lettres, Comptes Rendus des Séances de l'Année 1968*, 161–177.

PHILLIPS, J., N. GOREN, O. BAR-YOSEF
i.p.   Epipaleolithic sites in northern Sinai: a preliminary report. *Israel Exploration Journal*.

REED, CHARLES A.
1959   Animal domestication in the prehistoric Near East. *Science* 130: 1629–1639.
1969   "The pattern of animal domestication in the prehistoric Near East," in *The domestication and exploitation of plants and animals*. Edited by Peter J. Ucko and G. W. Dimbleby, 361–380. London: Gerald Duckworth.

SOLECKI, RALPH S.
1955   Shanidar Cave, a Paleolithic site in northern Iraq. *Annual Report of the Smithsonian Institution for 1954*, 389–425.
1969   Survey in western Azerbaijan. *Iran* 7:189–190.

SOLECKI, ROSE L.
1969   "Milling tools and the epi-Paleolithic in the Near East," in *Études sur le Quaternaire dans le monde*. Edited by Mireille Ters, 989–994. VIIIe Congrès Union Internationale pour l'Etude du Quaternaire. Paris.

STEKELIS, M., O. BAR-YOSEF
1965   Un habitat du Paléolithique supérieur à Ein Guev (Israël). Note préliminaire. *L'Anthropologie* 69:176–183.

VAN LAWICK-GOODALL, JANE
1971   *In the shadow of man*. Boston: Houghton Mifflin.

VAN ZEIST, WILLEM
1969   "Reflections on prehistoric environments in the Near East," in *The domestication and exploitation of plants and animals*. Edited by Peter J. Ucko and G. W. Dimbleby, 35–46. London: Gerald Duckworth.

VAN ZEIST, WILLEM, H. E. WRIGHT, JR.
1963   Preliminary pollen studies at Lake Zeribar, Zagros Mountains, southwestern Iran. *Science* 140:65–67.

VITA-FINZI, C., E. S. HIGGS
1970   Prehistoric economy in the Mount Carmel area of Palestine: site catchment analysis. *Proceedings of the Prehistoric Society* 36:1–37.

WENDORF, FRED
1968   "Late Paleolithic sites in Egyptian Nubia," in *The prehistory of Nubia*. Edited by Fred Wendorf, 791–953. Dallas: Southern Methodist University Press.

WENDORF, FRED, ROMUALD SCHILD
1976   "The use of ground grain during the late Paleolithic of the lower Nile Valley, Egypt," in *Origins of African plant domestication*. Edited by Jack R. Harlan, Jan M. J. de Wet, and Ann B. L. Stemler, 269–288. World Anthropology. The Hague: Mouton.

WILKINSON, PAUL F.
1972a   "Current experimental domestication and its relevance to prehistory," in *Papers in economic prehistory: studies by members and associates of the British Academy Major Research Project in the Early History of Agriculture*. Edited by E. S. Higgs, 107–118. Cambridge: Cambridge University Press.
1972b   Oomingmak: a model for man-animal relationships in prehistory. *Current Anthropology* 13:23–44.

ZEUNER, FREDERICK E.
1963   *A history of domesticated animals*. London: Hutchinson.

Changing Economy in Ancient India

VISHNU-MITTRE

Archaeological research in India, supported by carbon-14 determinations, has brought out two important facts: one, the Neolithic and the highly advanced Harappan and other cultures were contemporaneous; and two, the Neolithic-Chalcolithic cultures did not commence in India prior to 4700 B.P. These two facts are the chief stumbling blocks in reconstructing the changing patterns of plant economy, particularly in evolutionary perspective. Together with these another significant consideration is our inability to trace not only the origins of various cultures but also their relationships within and outside India as evidenced by diverse opinions on this issue (Sankalia 1972). However, the various views fall into three categories: one, indigenous origin; two, foreign origin; and three, an indigenous origin with foreign cultural and economic contacts. For every category there are arguments for and against, and I must admit that the evidence in favor of any one is indeed weak.

There is no denying that agricultural beginnings did take place in ancient India. In view of their belated appearance around 4700 B.P. (or even if the date is stretched to 5000 B.P.) one would indeed be ill-advised to look for the origins of cultivated plants here, since work elsewhere has established that long before this time many of our cultivars had already

I have the pleasure of recording my thanks to Professor Jack R. Harlan, of the University of Illinois at Urbana-Champaign, for his examination of some remains of millets and for his comments on their identification.

On Maps 1–3, records of the remains of cultivated plants of the Indian subcontinent are presented. I am greatly indebted to Professor Sir Joseph Hutchinson for permission to reproduce these maps as well as Figure 1 from my article (Vishnu-Mittre 1974a) in *Evolutionary studies of world crops*, edited by Professor Hutchinson and published by the Cambridge University Press.

been domesticated and by about this time were on their way toward diffusion from the centers of their origin. Our knowledge of the origin of rice, however, is still far from complete. Was the Indian subcontinent the center of its origin? This is a question of prime importance that is still awaiting an answer.

Besides archaeology, there are two other sources which provide valuable information on the subject: one, literary sources; and two, cytogenetic and phytogeographic research. However rich the ancient literature of India may be, it is nevertheless steeped in chronological obscurity. The opinion that this literature could not predate the Iron Age in India is gaining ground (Vishnu-Mittre 1968; Allchin and Allchin 1968). Apart from that, the archaic language of the ancient literature is so difficult that interpretation of the names of cultivated plants mentioned there in terms of taxa known to us today is nearly impossible. However, attempts have been made.

Archaeological and cytogenetic studies have established the origin of cultivated wheat and barley in western Asia, of maize in Central America, and of several millets in Africa. However, southeastern Asia may prove to have been a center for the origin of rice. Our knowledge of the origins of several legumes, and of oil- and fiber-yielding plants is indeed not far advanced.

The material evidence of early agriculture as discussed here is restricted exclusively to remains of cultivated plants and their wild ancestors (see Plates 1–5). Hardly anything is known of implements used in cultivation or methods of cultivation, but the recent remarkable discovery of a Harappan furrowed field in Kalibangan in Rajasthan (Lal 1971) is indeed of much interest.

The description of the changing plant economy presented here is largely an elaboration of an earlier paper submitted to the International Archaeological Seminar held at Colombo in 1969 (Vishnu-Mittre i.p.). The present account, however, is based upon fresh discoveries and overall up-to-date comprehensive information on the history of cultivated plants in India (Vishnu-Mittre 1968, 1974a).

The problems concerning identification of materials, their archaeological provenance, and the role of carbon-14 and pollen analysis on elucidation of the facts concerning ancient plant economy have been discussed earlier in the papers referred to above.

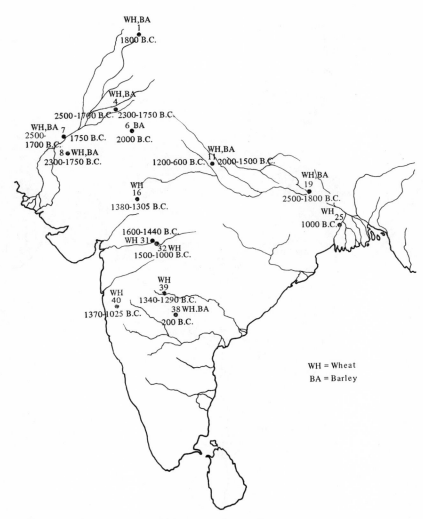

Map 1. Geographic distribution of records together with dates of wheat and barley in the Indian subcontinent

Sites plotted on Maps 1–3: 1. Burzahom; 2. Kangra; 3. Rupar; 4. Harappa; 5. Rangmahal; 6. Kalibangan; 7. Mohenjo-Daro; 8. Chanhu-Daro; 9. Khokrha Kot; 10. Hastinapur; 11. Atranji Khera; 12. Noh; 13. Ahar; 14. Nagda; 15. Garh Kalika, Ujjain; 16. Kayatha; 17. Kausambhi; 18. Rajghat; 19. Chirand; 20. Rajgir; 21. Pataliputra; 22. Oriyup; 23. Sonpur; 24. Mahesdal; 25. Pandu Rajar Dhibi; 26. Singhbhum; 27. Baidipur; 28. Ambri; 29. Lothal; 30. Rangpur; 31. Maheshwar; 32. Navdatoli; 33. Bhatkuli (Amraoti); 34. Kaundinyapur; 35. Pauni; 36. Paunar; 37. Nevasa; 38. Ter; 39. Sonegaon; 40. Inamgaon; 41. Kolhapur; 42. Hallur; 43. Kunnatur; 44. Periyapuram.

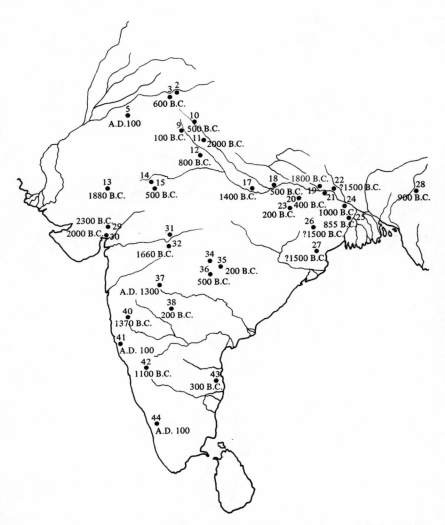

Map 2. Geographic distribution of records together with dates of rice in the Indian subcontinent

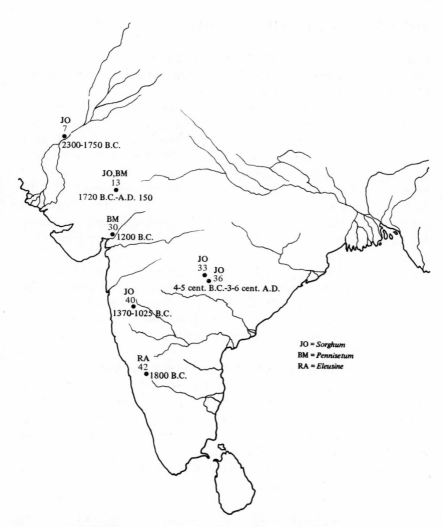

Map 3. Geographic distribution of records together with dates of millets in the Indian subcontinent

THE NEOLITHIC PLANT ECONOMY

Some information on the Neolithic plant economy is known from five sites in northern India and two sites from southern India. The economy of each area is vastly different (see Maps 1–3).

At Burzahom (4300 B.P.–3500 B.P.) in the Kashmir Valley, the presence of seeds of weeds or of forage plants such as *Lithospermum arvense*, *Medicago denticulata*, *Lotus corniculatus*, and *Ipomoea* sp. indirectly suggests cultivation of wheat and/or barley since these weeds are usually associated with wheat and barley (and also with millets). The kinds of bone tools, the pit dwellings, and the burying of dogs along with the bodies of their masters discovered at this site have been believed to suggest Chinese contacts (Allchin and Allchin 1968) although the ceramic industry does not compare with any Chinese Neolithic pottery. The perforated stone knife (a crop-cutting instrument) is distinctly of Chinese origin but this is post-Neolithic. The economy inferred for this site was based on hunting and gathering, and the evidence suggests affinities with the surviving hunting people of the peripheral regions north and northwest of China, and of central Asia. There is nothing to suggest contacts or relations with the Harappan cultures which coexisted in the Indus Valley and the Punjab.

The plant economy of the Neolithic peoples at Chirand in Bihar consisted of wheat (*Triticum sphaerococcum*), six-rowed barley both naked and hulled, rice (*Oryza sativa, Oryza* cf. *rufipogon*), together with *Pisum arvense*, lentil, and *Lathyrus sativus*. From the two other sites, Singhbhum and Oriyup in Bihar, only rice has been discovered. Wild rice, *Oryza perennis*, is known from Baidipur in Orissa.

The site of Chirand is dated to about 4000 B.P. (but many radiocarbon dates are erratic). My estimate of the lowest undated sediments (from the calculated rate of sedimentation), particularly of the layer which has yielded the above plant remains, may be between 4500–5500 B.P. (Vishnu-Mittre 1974b, i.p.). The other two sites (not yet radiocarbon dated) are believed to be subsequent to 3500–3400 B.P. A southeastern Asian influence is inferred at these sites (Sharma 1972a: 181), even though the basal early stage at Chirand and Singhbhum is not associated with metal or with shouldered quadrangular types of axes or adzes (the latter being typical of southeastern Asia), and the pottery traditions are distinctly Vindhyan and peninsular Neolithic (Sharma 1972b: 100).

The finds of rice at several of these sites in eastern India may be of interest, since the center for the origin of rice is believed to extend from eastern India to southeastern Asia (Vavilov 1951). There is evidence of wild rices too, particularly *Oryza perennis*, believed by cytogeneticists to be a progenitor of cultivated rice; in context of time it is not very old. Were its spikelets collected, intentionally or unintentionally, by the ancient people at Baidipur as those of wild rice are collected today by the aborigines in the State of Orissa? This wild rice still grows plentifully in Orissa and in Bihar too. By no means does rice seem to have been introduced here, and it must also have grown wild in the past. Did any independent domestication of rice take place in this part of the Indian subcontinent? This is a question for which we have no answer yet.

The finds of barley and wheat together with lentils at the Neolithic site of Chirand are indeed of much interest and there can hardly be any doubt that these elements, domesticated earlier in western Asia, were introduced here via the Harappans — a plausible possibility. The carbon-14 dates, even though erratic, do suggest a contemporaneity of the two cultures. However, no such indications exist from archaeological evidence.

In contrast, the Neolithic plant economy in southern India consisted of *Eleusine coracana*[1] at Hallur, dated to 3800 B.P., and the wild bean, *Dolichos biflorus* at Tekkalkota, dated to 3800–3500 B.P. Both sites are in Mysore State. To date, no record of rice exists from southern India. The plant economy of the famous cattle breeders in the Raichur-Bellary Doab is unknown as yet.

The gray burnished ware, the unburnt red ochre paint, and the stone-ax industry discovered at these southern Neolithic sites are reminiscent of the finds at Burzahom in the Kashmir Valley. A broad similarity of craft is observed between pottery here and at Hissar, Turang Tepe, and Shah Tepe in northeastern Iran.

Amazingly, the millet *E. coracana* is believed by cytogeneticists to have been domesticated in Africa although there is no archaeological evidence to support this belief.

THE HARAPPAN PLANT ECONOMY

In the north and northwest of the Indian subcontinent, almost coexisting

---

[1] A few grains of this and of millets from other sites have since been examined by Professor Jack R. Harlan, plant geneticist at the University of Illinois at Urbana-Champaign, Illinois, U.S.A. Whereas Professor Harlan (personal communication dated July 11, 1974) agreed with my identification of *Sorghum*, he considered the identification of *Setaria* doubtful and that of *Eleusine* incorrect. A reexamination of the bulk materials of millets from this and the other sites convinces me that *Eleusine* and *Setaria* as referred to in the text are correctly identified. The seeds of dicotyledons present in the material still remain unidentified.

with the Neolithic cultures elsewhere in India, there existed a very highly evolved culture, the Harappan, covering about half a million square miles. The "empire," as it has been called, extended from the Mekran coast in the west to Kutch towards the east of the Indus River, to Punjab in the north and to Alamgir beyond Delhi in the Ganga-Yamuna Doab in the northeast. Characterized by highly developed urbanization, common currency, trade, architecture, and elaborate town planning, the Harappan culture is dated by radiocarbon determinations from 4220 B.P. to 3540 B.P. (Agrawal, Guzder, and Kusumger 1973). A western Asian (Sumerian) origin for this culture can no longer be upheld in view of its strongly individual features, although inspiration (particularly for city life) from that direction cannot be overlooked (Wheeler 1960: 17). The investigation of skeletal remains reveals that the Harappans had biological similarities to the people living at present in various areas where the Harappan culture formerly occurred — the people of Sind, Punjab, and Gujarat (Ghosh 1965). This suggests an indigenous origin for this culture, with contacts with western Asia particularly in foreign trade.

The plant economy of the Harappans, both those living in the Punjab and in the Indus Valley, included wheat, barley, *Sorghum*, *Pisum arvense*, *Brassica*, *Sesamum*, and dates, known from the upper levels (late Harappan phase). Cotton was also known to them. The Harappans[2] living in Rajasthan (Kalibangan) consumed barley and chickpea (the material dated about 4000 B.P.). Rice, whether wild or cultivated, was known to the Rajasthan Harappans and those living in the area of Kutch-Gujarat (Lothal and Rangpur). It is remarkable that those living at Surkotada in Kutch used together seeds of several wild herbaceous plants such as *Scirpus supinus*, *Atriplex stocksii*, etc. for purposes best known to them. The only cereal known to them was perhaps the Italian millet, *Setaria italica*, to which species the several carbonized grains of *Setaria* found at this site are most similar (Vishnu-Mittre and Savithri i.p.).

Although the barley (*Hordeum vulgare*) used by the Harappans is the highly advanced form evolved in western Asia (found at Ali Kosh, Tell es Sawwan, and Mureybit) about 2,000–5,000 years prior to the Harappan culture, the Harappan wheat, the hexaploid *Triticum sphaerococcum*, is typically Indian and evolved here from either *Triticum compactum* or *Triticum aestivum*, each of which is also hexaploid. The earliest records of *T. aestivum*, dated from 7800 to 7600 B.P., are from Tell es Sawwan in western Asia (Helbaek 1966a). In no part of the Harappan Empire do the

---

[2]   The impressions in the terracotta cakes and *pai* from the Harappan site Kalibangan, Rajasthan, described as rice (Sharma 1972b) have since been identified as those of wheat (Vishnu-Mittre and Savithri 1975a).

Plate 1.   A. Husked barley from Ter. B. Husked and naked barley from Kalibangan.
C. Wheat from Ter

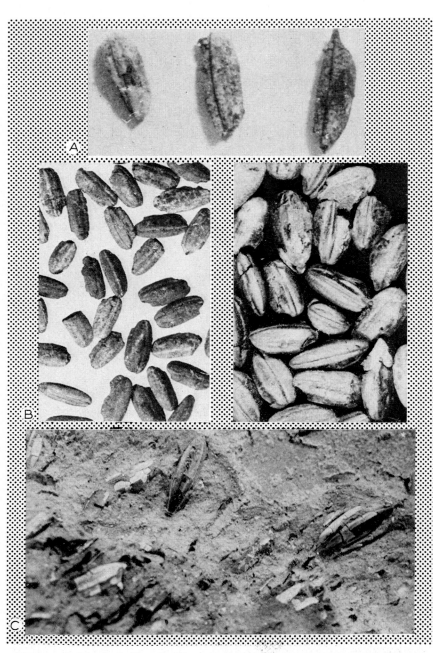

Plate 2. A. Rice husks from Baidipur. B. left, rice grains from Navdatoli-Maheshwar; right, rice spikelets from Ter. C. Impressions of rice spikelets on potsherd from Ahar

Plate 3. Top: left and middle, *Eleusine coracana* from Hallur; right, *Sorghum* from Amraoti. Bottom: left, *Paspalum scrobiculatum* from Ter; right, imprints of *Sorghum* on a potsherd from Ahar

Plate 4. Left, *Pisum arvense* from Ter; right, *Phaseolus aureus* from Paiyampalli

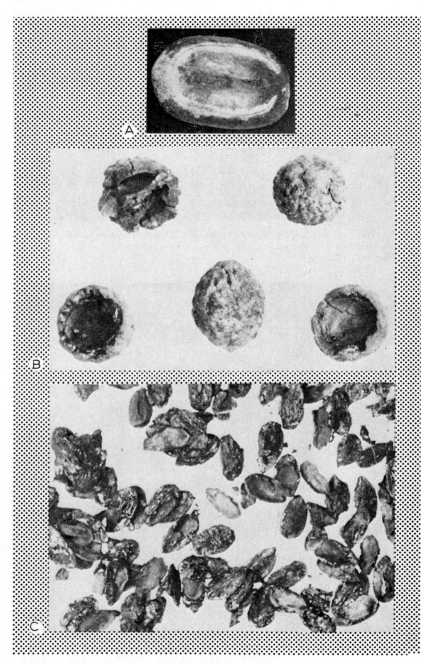

Plate 5.   A. *Ricinus communis* from Ter; B. stones of *Zizyphus nummularia* from
Navdatoli-Maheshwar; C. *Linum usitatissimum* from Navdatoli-Maheshwar

progenitors of *Hordeum vulgare* or *Triticum aestivum* occur, although *Aegilops tauschi* is known from the Kashmir Valley, Quetta, Wazirstan, and Hazara (Nasir and Ali 1972); wild emmer, the other ancestor, is not known at all in the Indian subcontinent. For *Sorghum* and *Eleusine coracana* the original home is Africa (Hutchinson 1971), although no archaeobotanical records are known from there.

Pisum arvense from Hacilar is of the same date (ca. 7800–7600 B.P.), whereas the earlier records of chickpea are found in Palestine (Helbaek 1966b). The diffusion from western Asia of several of these is apparent. We do not yet know whether the rice which has been found in Harappan sites was wild or cultivated. Wild rice grows even today in marshes in the Indus Valley (Nasir and Ali 1972).

According to Lambrick (1967), a minimum amount of skill was used by the Harappans in their agricultural operations, as is also true today in the Indus Valley. The spring crops (wheat and barley) were sown at the end of inundation and reaped in March–April. The autumn crops were sown at the beginning of inundation and reaped at the close of it.

THE POST-HARAPPAN PLANT ECONOMY PRIOR TO THE IRON AGE

During the period between the decline of the Harappan culture and the beginning of the Iron Age, i.e. between 3540 B.P. and 3000 B.P., there emerged several cultures in India characterized by copper technology (Chalcolithic culture). Their interrelationships and foreign contacts have recently been reviewed by Sankalia (1972), who believes that they were all the results of immigration from Iran and other parts of western Asia, followed by a gradual mixing of the newcomers with the local inhabitants, creating the various regional and subregional cultures. In addition to such theories of immigration from Iran, an alternate theory of movements of eastern Indian Aryans has also been suggested (Sankalia 1972).

Most sites in northern India were riverine. Rice is known at Mahisdal on the north bank of the Kopai River in the district of Birbhum, Bengal. Further west, at the Chalcolithic levels of Chirand in Bihar, rice is encountered again at the confluence of the Ganga, the Ghogra, and the Sarayu rivers. The dish-on-stand[3] with corrugated stem and a cream slipped ware, particularly in the design of a miniature sarcophagus painted

---

[3] The dish-on-stand is a ceramic design imported into Harappan sites from the west. It then became typical of Harappan sites and later was diffused to other parts of India along with other artifacts of the Harappan type.

with a bull and deer in dots in a cream pigment, are considered to be of foreign origin (Sankalia 1972). This copper-smelting site is believed to be the oldest in the valley of the Ganges.

Still further west at Kausambhi on the Tiveni in the Ganga-Yamuna Doab, rice is again the only cereal known. The bowl and dish-on-stand of foreign origin occur here too.

In the western parts of Uttar Pradesh and the eastern parts of the Punjab we come across a stratigraphic sequence beginning with the decadent late Harappan, in which occurs an ochre-colored pottery (OCP ware), and which was followed by the Iron Age. The stratum with the OCP ware, dated from 4000–3600 B.P. at Atranjikhera, Uttar Pradesh, has yielded remains of rice, barley, chickpea, and *Lathyrus* sp.; wheat was introduced here about 3200 B.P., and more or less at this time evidence of a fiber-yielding urticaceous plant, *Boehemeria*, is also obtained.

At Ahar in Rajasthan, the plant economy during 3885–3070 B.P. included rice and *Sorghum*, with perhaps pearl millet. At this site, rice was the only cereal until 3675 ± 110 B.P. when *Sorghum* was first introduced. Subsequently, until the beginning of the Iron Age, *Sorghum* and other millets assumed importance in the staple diet of the people at Ahar.

During 3100–3200 B.P., a few centuries prior to the commencement of the Iron Age, the plant economy at Noh near Bharatpur in Rajasthan was restricted to rice, *Dolichos biflorus*, and the bean *Phaseolus aureus*.

In central India, of the plant economy at Kayatha (3800–3550 B.P.) in Madhya Pradesh only wheat has been recovered, whereas at Navdatoli-Maheshwar (3660–3440 B.P.) the plants identified included wheat, rice, *Pisum arvense*, *Phaseolus mungos*, *P. aureus*, lentil, *Lathyrus sativus*, *Zizyphus nummularia*, linseed, and *Phyllanthus emblica*. The latter two were very likely the oil-yielding plants. An interesting feature noted at Navdatoli-Maheshwar is the introduction of rice in Phase II into an earlier wheat-based economy. Rice eventually became more popular than wheat. Evidence of flax fiber is known from Chandoli in Maharashtra and silk was known earlier at Nevasa in Maharashtra.

Among the other sites in Maharashtra, wheat is known from Sonegaon (3340–3200 B.P.) but at Inamgaon during 3660 B.P. to 3400 B.P. barley, lentil, *Phaseolus aureus*, *P. mungos*, *Dolichos biflorus*, *Pisum arvense*, *Lathyrus* spp., *Phoenix*, *Buchnania* and melon seeds comprised the plant economy, which continued until 1200 B.P. By about 3350 B.P. rice, sorghum, and wheat were introduced here (Vishnu-Mittre and Savithri 1975b).

Rice had indeed become a popular cereal during the Chalcolithic period; it was being used exclusively in eastern India but was used together with other cereals in northwestern and central India. Wheat, barley, linseed, etc. probably accompanied Harappan peoples who, after the decline of their culture, diffused into western Uttar Pradesh and from there into central India and from the western coast into Maharashtra. In some of these areas wheat and barley had been introduced earlier, perhaps through cultural contacts with the Harappans, although the various cultures continued to be independent entities. The only archaeological evidence, the dish-on-stand (indicating Harappan influence), seems to be supported by the archaeobotanical discoveries.

THE IRON AGE PLANT ECONOMY

The Iron Age in India began around 1000 B.P. and is characterized in northwestern India by a painted gray ware overlying a black and red ware whereas in southern India iron is associated directly with the black and red ware, both of which occur also at the megalithic sites, more widely spread in the south than in the north. Settlements of the Iron Age are widely spread in almost all parts of India. The origin of the northern Iron Age is believed to be from Asia Minor or the Caucasus through Indo-Iranian speaking peoples — an invading wave of the Aryans. Skirting around the northern boundary of the Indian desert, the western influence is believed to have penetrated along the rivers in Punjab into the Ganga-Yamuna Doab and then to have spread south and southeast through the flat arid region between the Indus and the Aravallis across the marshes of Kutch and the desert, radiating from there in several directions (northeast, east, and south). Iron Age burials in the south have provided evidence of its origins here, or of cultural contacts with central Asia, Iran, or the Caucasus, with the Levant and southern Arabia, Mesopotamia, the region of the Persian Gulf, and Yemen, in addition to local developments (Allchin and Allchin 1968). The Gulf of Oman as the original home of Indian megaliths has been recently suggested by Gupta (1970–1971). The new metal, iron, indeed equipped the ancient Indians of the Iron Age to fight against nature, to increase agriculture, and to fell forests, thus providing them with limitless potentialities for greater economic prosperity.

Surprisingly, the archaeobotanical record of the economy of the Iron Age is extremely poor; rice alone is known from Ahar (Rajasthan), Pandu Rajar Dhibi (Bengal), and Ambri (Assam). Rice and barley have been recovered at Atranjikhera in western Uttar Pradesh, and rice and *Paspalum scrobiculatum* at Hallur in Mysore State. The information, although

widely spread, is indeed very patchy. The ancient Indian literature however mentions in chronological order: barley, wheat, rice, cotton, saffron;
and barley, rice, wheat, beans (*Phaseolus aureus*, *P. mungos*), *Brassica*
(mustard), sesame, and millets (Vishnu-Mittre 1968).

THE EARLY HISTORICAL PERIOD

The end of the Iron Age is followed by the emergence of another more or
less uniform culture characterized by the northern black polished ware
(NBP ware). That culture extended from the lower Ganges to the Punjab
and is believed to correspond with the Mauryan period in Indian history.
The NBP ware replaced the painted gray ware (PG ware) or the black and
red ware around 2500 B.P. The origin of the settlers who left the pottery is
still unknown: the undocumented conjectures include ideas that they
came from the northern hills and forests, or from the west (Allchin and
Allchin 1968: 213). The technique of their pottery appears similar to that
of the Greek black ware. Among the various forms of pottery were the
shallow tray-bowl and a deeper carinated bowl, adoptions from the
preceding PG ware. Cities with ramparts characterized this period and this
feature extended to the area which is now the Northwest Frontier Province of Pakistan, where pottery (at Charsada) similar to that of Mundigak VII has been found. That this area was once a province of the
Achaemenid Empire of the Emperor Cyrus (who invaded this part of Asia
in about the sixth century B.C.) is highly suggestive of cultural influx from
Iran.

In central India at Somnath, sherds of imported NBP ware in Phase
III B are indicative of the Mauryan influence and a similar feature is
noted in coastal Gujarat (Broach, Nagal, and Nagara) and in other areas
of central India such as at Ujjain (Period II). The Mauryan influence
extended also into peninsular India: at Prakash in the Tapti Valley; at
Brahmagiri, Maski, and Piklihal; and on the eastern coast at Arikamedu
with Roman imports, the sherds of Arretine ware. The NBP ware seems
to have continued in use to the beginning of the Christian Era, almost
coinciding with the records known from history.

The plant economy during this period consisted exclusively of rice at
certain sites such as Sonepur, Rajgir, and Pataliputra (Bihar), Rajghat and
Hastinapur (Uttar Pradesh), Nagda-Ujjain and Garhkalia (Madhya
Pradesh), Khokhra Kot (Punjab), and Kunnatur (Madras). At Noh in
Rajasthan, in addition to rice, the bean *Phaseolus aureus* has recently
been discovered by Miss R. Savithri and myself.

At Kaundinyapur in Maharashtra (2500 B.P.–2200 B.P.) the plant economy consisted of rice, *Pisum arvense, Lathyrus sativus, Zizyphus nummularia,* and *Z. sphaericus.* More or less at this time (fourth to fifth century B.C. to third to sixth century A.D.) at Bhatkuli, another site in Maharashtra, the plant economy consisted of *Sorghum* and *Cicer arietinum,* and a yet another site (Paunar) of *Sorghum* and rice. At the latter site, *Sorghum* was more abundantly used than during the early and late Satavannah period (200 B.C.–250 A.D.) whereas the use of rice overtook that of wheat during the third of the eighth century A.D. (at the time of the rule of Venkataka and of Vishnukundin).

Around 200 B.C. to 400 A.D. at Ter in Maharashtra, the plant economy consisted of wheat, rice, barley, *Paspalum scrobiculatum, Dolichos biflorus, Pisum,* lentil, black gram, *Lathyrus sativus, Ricinus communis,* and *Zizyphus nummularia* (Vishnu-Mittre, Prakash, and Awasthi 1972). An interesting feature noted here is that during 200 B.C.–100 A.D. (the Satavannah period) wheat and rice were equally important cereals, but subsequently between 100 A.D.–250 A.D. (the late Satavannah period) wheat predominated over rice, and chickpea introduced at this time became an important article of the food economy during 250–400 A.D. (post-Satavannah period). Barley and *Paspalum scrobiculatum* were introduced during this period.

In Rajasthan at Ahar during 150 B.C.–50 A.D. the plant economy consisted of *Sorghum* and rice. Subsequently arachaeological evidence of the plant economy is restricted to rice as known from Rangmahal (Rajasthan), Kolhapur, and Nevasa (Maharashtra), and from Periyapuram (Kerala).

The discovery of maize from the pre-Columbian levels (early Muslim layers) at Kaundinyapur is a new addition to our plant economy. Pollen evidence dated to ca. 1400 A.D., from the Kashmir Valley has supported the above archaeobotanical evidence (Vishnu-Mittre and Gupta 1966).

The period of 50 A.D. to 500 A.D. was the time in Indian history when the Sakas and Kusanas entered India from central Asia (Sharma 1968). From Kusana levels at Noh in Rajasthan Miss R. Savithri and I have recently recovered carbonized barley.

CONCLUSION

The is no denying that we have built up interesting information concerning the plant economy of the various archaeological periods in India, and with the help of radiocarbon determinations we have been able to learn the past distribution of cultivars in both time and space. Based on this invaluable information, it is gradually becoming possible to understand the probable ancient routes along which the diffusion of cultivars has taken place within the Indian subcontinent.

The fact that primitive cultures appear to have been contemporaneous with highly advanced cultures, combined with lack of sufficient knowledge of their relationships within and outside the subcontinent, however baffling these may be, does conceal answers to several questions, particularly those relating to how and where agriculture first originated in this part of the world. The Neolithic peoples are usually given the credit for this great revolution but the lack of uniserial developmental phases in cultural development here seems to deny them such credit on the subcontinent. The question: "Did agriculture originate here with the Harappans and diffuse to the Neolithic peoples or *vice versa*?" is a moot point indeed. The meager archaeological information suggesting contacts between the Neolithic of Kashmir and that of southern India is not supported by the kind of plant economy known. The plant economy of Neolithic peoples at Chirand (Bihar) in northern India is akin to that of the contemporary Harappans. By stretching dates, Chirand might be placed much before the Harappan culture, thus according credit to Chirand for the first origin of agriculture in India; in that event, however, its derived plant economy, particularly from western Asia (wheat, barley, lentils, etc.) would be inexplicable. The slight southeastern Asian influence at this site (Sharma 1972b) is vaguely corroborated by the occurrence of rice. Are we really certain that rice was first domesticated in southeastern Asia? Strangely enough, the western Asian influence at Chirand is not supported by archaeology.

The millets in southern Indian Neolithic sites are believed to have been domesticated in Africa. Obviously, those millets must have been imported from there during the ancient history of India. Does not the meager evidence of similarity between the southern Indian Neolithic pottery headrests from the sites of Hallur and T. Narsipur (Nagaraja Rao 1971) with those from Egypt dated to 1400 B.C. suggest Neolithic Indo-African contacts?

In the Neolithic of the Kashmir Valley there is no archaeobotanical evidence to substantiate Chinese or central Asian influence. At Tekkalkota, a Neolithic site in southern India, the seeds of wild *Dolichos biflorus*, which grows in the south and elsewhere in India, are highly suggestive of food gathering, rather than of cultivation.

From the above it would appear that the plant economy of the Neolithic period in the Indian subcontinent was largely of the subsistence type, as witnessed today among various tribes in India. The occurrence of highly advanced cultivars at some primitive sites appears to have been due to contacts with highly advanced contemporary cultures, quite as happens today among the aborigines, who come in contact with highly advanced peoples at weekly or monthly temporary markets and at socioreligious gatherings. The tribal peoples bring their forest produce and coarse textiles with embroidery to these markets and exchange them for food grains, salt, oil, and textiles manufactured by the advanced urban folks. The contemporaneity of different cultures in the present context in India therefore implies interdependence between less and more highly advanced peoples and this must have also been the case in the past. The highly advanced Harappan culture indeed played a far more significant role in the diffusion of traits and cultivars among the nomadic Neolithic tribes than has been realized. But the strongly individualistic local nomadism remained the least influenced except for certain recognizable traits, cultivars, and pottery designs.

The plant economy of the Harappans on the whole appears to have been exotic, largely derived from Africa and western Asia via Iran. This would not be surprising, considering the extensive trade contacts this advanced culture had with western Asia. Besides trade by the land route, it had maritime trade with Iran and other parts of southwestern Asia through the seaport at Lothal in Gujarat, amply supporting the above contention. Rice, however, grew locally, and the Harappans made use of it rather than of any introduced rice from southeastern Asia. It is indeed amazing that these highly advanced peoples should have been food gatherers in the area of Kutch-Gujarat (at Surkotada and thereabouts). Surely they must have discovered some other economic use for the wild plants, or perhaps their seeds constituted special delicacies.

A fact of considerable significance that cannot be overlooked is that the carbonized grains of wheat at the Harappan sites reveal considerable variability and they seem to belong largely to shot-wheat, *Triticum sphaerococcum*, a species which is believed to have originated in the western part of the subcontinent. Its origin is believed to have been from *T. aestivum* or *T. compactum* as a result of adaptation to the aridity of climate then prevailing in the area. This species had obviously evolved naturally rather than as a result of the Harappans having had a hand in its evolution.

The plant economy of the post-Harappan period prior to the Iron Age is also largely of exotic origin; either the species of plants had been diffused as the Harappans migrated to other areas in India after the decline of the Harappan Empire or the plants were introduced afresh from or through Iran. However, we do not have much information to settle the issue in favor of either of these alternatives. The post-Harappan and pre-Iron Age cultures were, no doubt, indigenous, characterized as they were by hunting and farming traits and by an extremely poor building tradition very unlike that of the Harappans; however, foreign influences upon them cannot be ruled out, but no evidence has been found to support the "colonization theory," which attributes colonization to the first wave of the Aryans. I believe that the dish-on-stand found at several Chalcolithic sites ought to be taken a bit more seriously as evidence of Harappan cultural diffusion.

The plant economy of the Iron Age is too poorly known to throw adequate light on the problem of which peoples introduced iron. If, as believed by Gupta (1970–1971), the Gulf of Oman was indeed the original home of the megalithic cultures, the plant economy of the Iron Age should have been characterized by millets, since the area surrounding the gulf connects the northeastern part of Africa, well known as a center of origin for several millets, with India. This is contrary to the facts. This route could well have been used much earlier than the Iron Age but archaeological evidence for such use is lacking. There is hardly anything in the archaeobotanical records to compare with the information from ancient literature to support the view that the people using PG ware were those Aryans who entered India in a second wave.

A large gap occurs in our knowledge of the plant economy between Chalcolithic and late historical cultures because the Iron Age has not yielded much information. The present is not an opportune time to decide whether this gap is in any way real. If it is so, the reappearance of many cultivars in the early historical period could be assigned to foreign influences.

The ancient plant economy of the Indian subcontinent would appear, thus, to have been characterized largely by foreign influences from south-

---

Figure 1.   Distribution of cultivated plants in space and time in the Indian subcontinent

Key:

BA	Barley, *Hordeum*	MU	Mung, *Phaseolus*
BM	Bajra, *Pennisetum*	PE	Peas, *Pisum*
CA	Castor, *Ricinus*	PH	*Phyllanthus*
CO	Cotton, *Gossypium*	PS	*Paspalum scrobiculatum*
DP	Date palm, *Phoenix*	RA	Ragi, *Eleusine*
HG	Horse gram, *Dolichos*	RI	Rice, *Oryza*
JO	Jowar, *Sorghum*	SE	Sesame, *Sesamum*
LE	Lentils, *Lens*	WH	Wheat, *Triticum*
LI	Linseed, *Linum*	WD	Weeds
MA	Maize, *Zea*	ZI	*Zizyphus*
MS	Melon seeds, *Cucumis*		

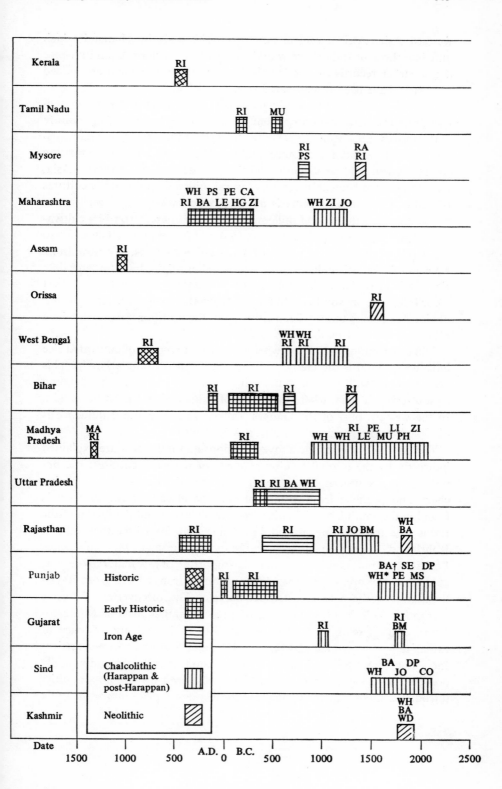

western Asia, Africa, central Asia, etc. The finds in Thailand which antedate those of Indian rice would suggest southeastern Asian influence if the earlier records of rice from that country or elsewhere are indeed proved to have been of cultivated rice.

From the above account and against the background of contemporaneity of cultures, it would appear that the earliest beginnings of agriculture in the Indian subcontinent were in the west (the Indus Valley and Baluchistan, as at Mundigak for instance) and that the plant economy comprising wheat, barley, field peas, lentil, and flax was derived from western Asia, where these had been domesticated several millennia prior to the cultures of India. The south of India is another region where early beginnings, dating to about the second millennium B.C., are characterized by cultivation of the millet ragi (*Eleusine coracana*) of African origin. There is also other, although meager, evidence of Afro-Indian contacts. In central India we again find exotic cultivars of western Asian origin, but at a later date rice tends to replace them. Of interest is the discovery that the earliest records of rice in southern India are from the Iron Age. Its diffusion obviously appears to have been either from the north or northeast, where older records are found.

The other important region where the earliest records of cultivated rice have been found is the Ganges Valley (the Ganga-Yamuna Doab). This area, together with eastern India, is indeed a part of the center extending to southeastern Asia, where the origin of cultivated rice must be sought. In the western part of the Ganges Valley, western cultural influence is observed by the presence of western Asian cultivars.

The how and why of the above diffusions and influences are explained indirectly by the mutual trading contacts of the early cultures: the importing into southern Neolithic sites of special rocks such as granite, chert, and pistacite from distant places; the glazed steatite disc beads found in the south but originating from Baluchistan and the region of the Indus; the transporting of nodules of fine flint from limestone hills at Rohri and Sukkur in western Pakistan to Harappa, Mohenjo-Daro, Lothal, Rangpur, and Kalibangan; the importing of raw materials such as gold from Mysore, silver from Afghanistan or Iran, copper from Rajasthan and southern and eastern India, etc. The discoveries of twelve Harappan seals in Mesopotamia, of Mesopotamian seals at Mohenjo-Daro, and of seals from the Persian Gulf at Lothal are evidence of extensive trading contacts by sea, by river, and overland between ancient India and its western neighbors. The diffusion of cultivars undoubtedly occurred at the same time, as the highly advanced trading communities introduced them into the contemporary less-developed cultures in India through meetings at weekly markets or socioreligious gatherings.

India's contributions to agricultural origins have obviously not been numerous, but at present we can say that *Sorghum, Eleusine*, pearl millet, *Dolichos biflorus, Paspalum scrobiculatum*, spp. of *Phaseolus, Brassica, Sesamum, Buchnania, Phoenix*, etc. were cultivated or consumed first in the Indian subcontinent. No earlier records of these have as yet been found elsewhere.

REFERENCES

AGRAWAL, D. P., S. GUZDER, S. KUSUMGER
  1973 "Radiocarbon chronology in Indian prehistoric archaeology," iı *Journal of Indian Prehistory, Golden Jubilee Volume*. Edited by T. K. Ravindran, 1–20. Trivandrum: Department of History, University of Kerala.
ALLCHIN, B., F. R. ALLCHIN
  1968 *The birth of Indian civilization: India and Pakistan before 500 B.C.* Harmondsworth: Penguin Books.
GHOSH, A.
  1965 The Indus civilization: its origins, authors, extent and chronology. *Indian Prehistory* 1964: 113–156.
GUPTA, S. P.
  1970–1971 "Gulf of Oman: the original home of Indian megaliths," in *Puratattva* (*Bulletin of the Indian Archaeological Society, V. D. Krishnaswami Commemoration Volume*). Edited by S. P. Gupta, 4–18. New Delhi: Indian Archaeological Society.
HELBAEK, H.
  1966a Commentary on the phylogenesis of *Triticum* and *Hordeum*. *Economic Botany* 20: 350–360.
  1966b Pre-pottery Neolithic farming at Beidha: a preliminary report. *Palestine Exploration Quarterly* 98: 61–66.
HUTCHINSON, JOSEPH
  1971 "A note on millets," in *Protohistoric cultures of the Tungbadhra valley*. Edited by M. S. Nagaraja Rao, 130–132. Dharwar. (Privately published.)
LAL, B. B.
  1971 "Perhaps the earliest ploughed field so far excavated anywhere in the world," in *Puratattva* (*Bulletin of the Indian Archaeological Society, V. D. Krishnaswami Commemoration Volume*). Edited by S. P. Gupta, 1–3. New Delhi: Indian Archaeological Society.
LAMBRICK, H. T.
  1967 The Indus flood plain and the "Indus" civilization. *Geographical Journal* 133: 483–495.
NAGARAJA RAO, M. S., *editor*
  1971 *Protohistoric cultures of the Tungbadhra valley*. Dhawar. (Privately published.)

NASIR, E., S. I. ALI
  1972   *Flora of West Pakistan. An annotated catalogue of the vascular plants of West Pakistan and Kashmir.* Rawalpindi. (Privately published.)

SANKALIA, H. D.
  1972   "The Chalcolithic cultures of India," in *Archaeological Congress and Seminar Papers.* Edited by S. B. Deo, 155–187. Nagpur: Nagpur University Press.

SHARMA, G. R.
  1968   *Kusana studies.* Allahabad: Allahabad University Press.

SHARMA, I. K.
  1972a Comments on "The Chalcolithic cultures of India" by H. D. Sankalia, in *Archaeological Congress and Seminar Papers.* Edited by S. B. Deo, 180–183. Nagpur: Nagpur University Press.
  1972b "Southeast Asia, India and west Asia," in *Archaeological Congress and Seminar Papers.* Edited by S. B. Deo, 95–112. Nagpur: Nagpur University Press.

VAVILOV, N. I.
  1951   The origin, variation, immunity and breeding of cultivated plants. *Chronica Botanica* 13:1–364.

VISHNU-MITTRE
  1968   Protohistoric records of agriculture in India. J. C. Bose Endowment Lecture. *Transactions of the Bose Research Institute* 31:86–106.
  1970   Biological concepts and agriculture in ancient India. *Indian Journal of the History of Science* 1: 144–161.
  1974a "The beginnings of agriculture: palaeobotanical evidence from India," in *Evolutionary studies on world crops: diversity and change in the Indian subcontinent.* Edited by Joseph Hutchinson, 3–33. Cambridge: Cambridge University Press.
  1974b Neolithic plant economy at Chirand. *Palaeobotanist* 21:18–21.
  i.p.   Ancient food economy in India with remarks on the Aryan hypothesis. *Proceedings of the Second International Conference on Archaeology Seminar, Colombo, 1969.*

VISHNU-MITTRE, H. P. GUPTA
  1966   Pollen morphological studies of the primitive varieties of maize (*Zea mays*) with remarks on the history of maize in India. *Palaeobotanist* 15: 176–184.

VISHNU-MITTRE, U. PRAKASH, N. AWASTHI
  1972   Ancient plant economy at Ter. *Geophytology* 1: 170–177.

VISHNU-MITTRE, R. SAVITHRI
  1975a Supposed remains of rice (*Oryza* sp.) in terarcotta cakes and pai at Kalibangan, Rajasthan. *Palaeobotanist* 22:124–126.
  1975b Ancient plant economy at Inamgaon *Puratattva* 8.
  i.p.   Ancient plant economy at Surkotada, Gujarat. Comment on "Excavations at Surkotada" by J. P. Joski, *Ancient India.*

WHEELER, R. E. M.
  1960   *The Indus civilization.* Cambridge: Cambridge University Press.

The Dynamics of Agricultural Origins in Palestine: A Theoretical Model

FEKRI A. HASSAN

The transition from hunting-gathering to agricultural production is undoubtedly one of the major events in human history, an event which has been indeed revolutionary, in the sense that it entailed radical changes in man's relationship with nature, others, and himself. Yet, despite many years of archaeological investigation culminating in an intensive period of research over the last fifteen years, the nature of the processes which led to agriculture remains unclear. The idea that climatic desiccation at the end of the Pleistocene was the major stimulus for the development of agriculture cannot be entertained any longer in view of lack of evidence for such desiccation in the Near East (Braidwood 1960; Butzer 1971; Binford 1968; and others). Environmental suitability of certain regions (viz. the hilly flanks) and cultural preadaptation, emphasized by Braidwood (1960, 1967), have been considered to be insufficient by themselves to give rise to agriculture (Binford 1968; Meyers 1971; Harris 1971).

Binford (1968), in a pioneer article which introduced demographic factors in archaeological explanations, argued that the origins of agriculture should be sought in a combination of factors related both to the changes in human adaptation following the end of the Pleistocene and to population pressure during the phase immediately preceding the origin of agriculture. According to Binford, the shift in human adaptation at the close of the Pleistocene was probably linked to worldwide changes in sea level. This shift, manifested by greater exploitation of fish and fowl, led to sedentariness and rapid population growth in those areas where food resources were most abundant. Excess population from these

I wish to thank Dr. A. E. Marks, Dr. R. Wetherinton, and Dr. J. Phillips, each of whom read an initial version of this paper and contributed useful remarks.

optimal areas was forced into less productive marginal habitats where agriculture was developed under the exigency of scarcity.

Although this model has won many favorable responses and two attempts were made to fit it to the data from the Near East (Flannery 1969; Wright 1971), the model suffers from some serious problems. On the theoretical level, the model fails to explain the link between environmental changes at the end of the Pleistocene and the development of new adaptive patterns during the Holocene. Specifically, how could the changes in the sea level have led to a greater dependence on fish and fowl? In addition, Binford's proposition of differential rapid population growth leading to dispersal of population into marginal habitats and consequent population pressure is contradictory to the prevalence of cultural checks on excessive population growth (Wagley 1951; Stott 1962; Benedict 1970; Katz 1972; and others). Hole (1971: 473) was therefore justified in stating, "Before one can posit an increase in population that forced man into marginal areas ..., one must offer a plausible explanation for this increase." On the empirical level, there is seemingly no evidence for an excessive increase of population in the Near East during the Epipaleolithic (Hole 1971: 473).

The settlement pattern during the Natufian seems to represent a re-orientation of settlement location in response to a new adaptive pattern rather than to an increase in population (Bar-Yosef 1970: 184–186; Henry 1973: 190–191; and below, Figure 1).

Regardless of these criticisms, Binford's model has awakened an interest in the role of demographic parameters in cultural change. Nonetheless, since Binford's model, as it has been recently described by one of its proponents (Flannery 1973: 284), is "still unproven and highly speculative," the need for alternative explanatory models is pressing. I should also hasten to add that even if a model is "validated" this does not mean that it has been proven, because some later alternative model may be as good or better (cf. Popper, in Platt 1966: 27).

This paper is not an attempt to provide a comprehensive model of agricultural origins everywhere. I believe in concurrence with Flannery (1973) that, at least so far, one model cannot explain the origins of agriculture on a worldwide basis. In addition, the present paper does not aim to expound the role of any single variable as the major cause for the emergence of agriculture. The model presented in this paper focuses on the cultural dynamics which are likely to have led to agriculture in Palestine. Within the framework of this model, agriculture is viewed not as a technological improvement induced simply by either environmental or demographic stress, but as a much more complex event which could

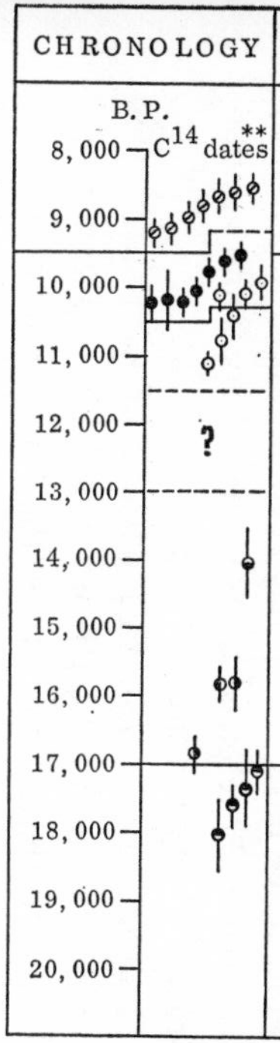

CHRONOLOGY	UNITS	SUBSISTENCE & ECONOMY	TECHNOLOGY	SETTLEMENT
B.P. C^{14} dates ** 8,000–9,000 (Neolithic)	PPNA	Cultivation of cereals, herding (goat, sheep), hunting, fishing, gathering (legumes and other plants, ? food exchange, trade.	Stone axes, sickle-blades, arrow heads (mostly tanged), some are pressure flaked), borers, querns, limestone bowls and plates.	Villages located on coastal plain & Jordan Valley, with permanent dwellings, hearths sub-floor burials.
10,000–12,000 (Epipalaeolithic)	Natufian	Intensive utilization of wild cereals, gathering (legumes and other plants), hunting (mainly gazelle), fishing, ? food exchange, trade. Initial steps toward domestication (hypothetical).	Blades and microlithic blades, scrapers; burins, borers, geometrics (lunates, trapezes, triangles), microburins. Bed rock and moveable mortars, sickle-blades, bone worked artifacts.	Sites located mostly in hilly regions. Many sites are large (100–1000 sq. m.) with permanent structures, hearths, storage pits, burials, and paved areas.
13,000–17,000 (Epipalaeolithic)	Kebaran Complex	Hunting (mainly deer and gazelle), gathering. The discovery of a few mortars suggests that acorns and/or cereals may have been gathered.	Geometric Kebaran B: Blades and microlithic blades, scrapers, burins, truncations, per forators, microburins, lunates and triangles. Geometric Kebaran A: Blades and microlithic blades, burins, trapezes, and rectangles. Non-Geometric Kebaran: Blades and microlithic blades scrapers, burins, truncations, notches/denticulates, obliquely truncated backed bladelets.	Small sites (50–500 sq. m.) located mostly on Coastal plain and lowlands.
18,000–20,000 (U. Palaeolithic)	Late Aurignacian	Hunting and gathering.	Blades, scrapers, burins, backed blades.	Small sites, located mostly in Mt. Carmel/Galilee and Judean Desert.

* A contemporaneous assemblage at El-Khiam, characterized by retouched points with concave bases and bilateral notches, is considered as a distinct unit-Khamian (Perrot 1952, Echegaray 1966, Bar-Yosef 1970, 1973). Another contemporaneous unit is the Harifian. This unit is represented in the Negev (Marks et al. 1972) and Sinai (Bar-Yosef 1973). Both units are believed to belong to hunter-gatherers (Bar-Yosef 1973).

** Date listings are provided by Bar-Yosef (1973) and Henry and Servello (in press). Questionable or unacceptable dates are not shown.

L. Aurignacian   G. Kebaran B   Pre-Pottery Neolithic A.
Kebaran   Natufian   Pre-Pottery Neolithic B.
G. Kebaran A   Harifian

Figure 1.   A chronology of settlement patterns during the Natufian

not have been possible without substantial changes in settlement, subsistence, demography, and social organization. These changes, in turn, were attuned to the macro- and microenvironmental conditions of the region where agriculture began. The emergence of agriculture was not a minor economic event which could have been easily accommodated by a slight readjustment of the sociocultural system. In addition, agriculture, at the level revealed in Neolithic settlements, is enmeshed in a complex pattern of production and exchange which can be hardly attributed to a sudden transformation under the pressure of any single short-term stimulus. Culture changes of this magnitude are more likely a result of cumulative changes in a large number of cultural variables over an extended period of time, which tend to reinforce certain trends that are liable to bring about, eventually, a perceptible alteration of the structural fabric of the cultural system.

The emergence of agriculture must ultimately be sought in the cultural changes and trends which became established by the end of the Epipaleolithic and in the success of agricultural practices in reinforcing these trends at a much lower social and economic cost than any other alternative innovation.

Agriculture based on the cultivation of cereals could not have begun without a subsistence pattern which included wild cereals as a major dietary component. The addition of cereals to the diet of the early Epipaleolithic hunter-gatherers in Palestine (ca. 17,000 B.P.) seems to be well documented by the presence of mortars, pestles, and storage pits (Bar-Yosef 1970; Ronen 1973). The addition of cereals to the diet was part of a more comprehensive change in the subsistence base. This change was marked by the exploitation of a wide variety of resources which were previously ignored or collected as nonessential dietary components. In addition to wild cereals, these resources included fish, fowl, and acorns. This subsistence base, which has been described in detail by Flannery (1969), is commonly referred to as a "broad-spectrum adaptation" after the phrase used by Flannery.

According to Flannery (1969: 78), this pattern of adaptation was initiated by an overflow of population from prime hunting zones into less favorable habitats. In these latter areas, the forced emigrants were compelled to utilize those resources that were ordinarily of minor interest in the prime hunting zones. Flannery's explanation, which parallels that of Binford (1968) on the shift from hunting-gathering to agriculture, suffers from the same theoretical weakness mentioned above with regard to Binford's model. Specifically, why should excessive population growth have taken place at the end of the Pleistocene and not any earlier?

Although excessive population increase might have been involved, its role must not be stressed, particularly since there is no substantial evidence for it. A more likely cause for the shift from specialized hunting-gathering to a broad subsistence base would have been the chronic climatic fluctuations which marked the global transition from the climatic regime of the Pleistocene to that of the Holocene. Microclimatic fluctuations are frequent at present in the Near East and were probably as or more frequent during the transition from the Pleistocene to the Holocene although the long-term annual average of precipitation and temperature, according to Butzer (1971), does not seem to have been significantly altered. A broad subsistence base would minimize the effect of fluctuations in the productivity of any particular animal or plant and would thus cushion the population against unpredictable short-term fluctuations from one year to another or from season to season. Although the data on climatic change in the Near East are not yet sufficiently detailed to permit a firm documentation of microclimatic fluctuations, climatic oscillations apparently were frequent during the period of the late Pleistocene-early Holocene, at least where palynological studies have been made (Neev and Emery 1967; Horowitz 1971). There is also evidence for one or more glacial readvances during the late Pleistocene and one or more stages of temporary readvance or reglaciation during the Holocene in the mountainous areas of Turkey and Iran (Butzer 1973). Regardless of the factors which might have led to a broad subsistence base, the incorporation of wild cereals in that base seems to have revolutionized the mode of life of the Epipaleolithic hunter-gatherers in Palestine. Man and cereals entered into a close and dynamic relationship: a relationship which was to lead, on the one hand, to a greater control by man over cereals, and on the other, to a reorientation of man's mode of existence around the cultivation of cereals. Intensive utilization of cereals was most likely encouraged by their high yield, storability, and high caloric content. Once the trend toward intensive utilization of cereals was established, changes in settlement, subsistence strategy, and social organization that were likely to reinforce this trend had a high probability of being adopted. These changes, which will be discussed below, would have converged to place a premium on further changes which might reinforce the trends set forth by the previous changes. Agriculture, which seems to have the potential for strengthening those trends, could thus have been a likely development.

First, let us consider the relationship of intensive utilization of cereals, which seem to have been established at ca. 12,000–11,500 B.P. as part of the Natufian subsistence regime, to settlement pattern, residential permanency, and size of local group.

In Palestine, the optimum environment for wild cereals is that of well-drained, loamy clay soils (Zohary 1969: 55–56) where the rainfall is between 400 and 1,000 millimeters. This restricts the distribution of good wild cereal fields to the hilly regions of Palestine. The concentration of most Natufian sites in these regions and the presence of mortars, pestles, sickle blades, and storage pits in these sites strongly suggest that most Natufian sites were located to take advantage of the best stands of wild cereals in the region (Henry 1973). The geographical pattern of Natufian sites is significant because it differs from that of the earlier sites of the Kebaran complex. Many Kebaran sites, for example, are located in the coastal region, where Natufian sites are exceedingly rare, as they are also less numerous in the Judean Desert and the Negev (Figure 2). In the

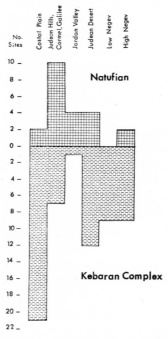

Figure 2.   Distribution of Natufian and Kebaran sites in the geographical zones of Palestine. Data from Bar-Yosef (1973)

Jordan Valley, recent surveys indicate that Natufian sites are located near the tops of the surrounding hills, whereas the Kebaran sites are generally located near the bases of the slopes (James Phillips, personal communication). Also noteworthy is the fact that Natufian sites are located at higher elevations in the south. This distribution seems to be an altitudinal adjustment to exploit an ecological zone similar to that present at lower elevations in the northern hills, where rainfall is more abundant (Henry 1973: 195–196).

The settlement pattern of the Natufian is also characterized by the presence of permanent structures. These are best shown at Eynan (Perrot 1966). Other open-air dwellings are known at Jericho, Beidha, El Wad, Nahal Oren (Bar-Yosef 1970: 178; Henry 1973), and Rosh Zin (Marks i.p.). Although permanent Natufian structures seem to suggest long-term residence, they do not necessarily indicate that those structures were occupied year-round. A distinction must be made between permanent structures and permanent residence. Many transhumant pastoralists do possess permanent structures, which are occupied only part of the year. Permanent structures seem to have an additional function, that of demarcating the territories surrounding them and to proclaim rights of ownership. At present, structures of this nature are likely to be located in the vicinity of scarce and valuable resources, such as springs and good pastures. In the case of the Natufian, one can postulate that such permanent structures were placed in the vicinity of those localities which supported the best stands of wild cereals. Within the hilly country in Palestine, the distribution of dense stands would have been extremely localized in those localities where hydrological, pedological, and microclimatic conditions were best (Flannery 1973: 280). It is certainly no accident that all Natufian sites are located on *terra rosa* and basaltic soils (Bar-Yosef 1970: 183; J. Phillips, personal communication), which are highly suitable for the growth of cereals.

Permanent structures, in addition, would have provided a place for storage and permanent or nontransportable processing facilities (e.g. bedrock mortars and grinding slabs). The storability of cereals and the high yield from fields of wild cereals, which sometimes extended more than two kilometers, must have made storage profitable. Storage in waterproof pits inside the houses would have protected the grain from sprouting (cf. Flannery 1973: 280).

The development of storage facilities which provided a source of food supply at one given place for a long time period must have encouraged long-term habitation and large residential units. The frequent presence of communal and individual burials in Natufian sites and the size of these sites suggests that this was the case. The Natufian sites are, in general, larger than the Kebaran sites (Bar-Yosef 1970; Henry 1973) and were probably inhabited by fifty to a hundred persons for extended periods of time.

Of importance is the fact that wild cereals disarticulate shortly upon maturation. In addition, in any given locality and for a given wild cereal, plants mature suddenly and simultaneously. Thus, within a week or two the maturing ears shed their grain and turn into dry, barren stalks (Zohary 1969: 57). Fields of wild cereals which extended over several acres would have required therefore a large working group to take advantage of the great yield within the short time in which it was available. Similarly, a large working group would have been required to process the large quantities of grain following the harvest.

So far, we have dealt only with the relationships between intensive utilization of wild cereals, group size, residential duration, and settlement patterns, which are illustrated schematically in Figure 3. Other resources were also utilized during the Epipaleolithic. These included fish, fowl, mussels, large and small mammals, and plants (primarily legumes and acorns). Probably these resources were exploited as they became available. Small groups from the cereals-oriented settlements could have been thus engaged in hunting and foraging expeditions. Indeed, the population might have dispersed after the reserve of grain was depleted, to reassemble at the time of the harvest. The Natufian settlements might have been thus characterized by stellar transitory camps to exploit the resources in the vicinity of the permanent architec-

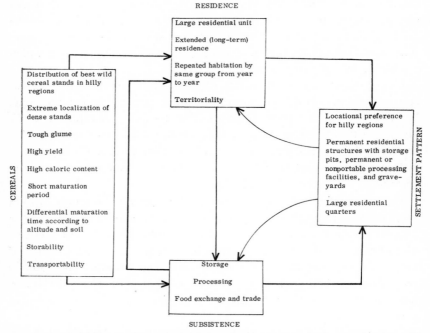

Figure 3.   A schematic chart showing interaction between variable sets related to wild cereals, residence, subsistence, and settlement

tural compound, as well as by seasonal camps. This settlement model reconciles the apparent conflict between those who believe that Natufian settlements were permanent (Perrot 1966; Binford 1968) and those who suggest that a seasonal subsistence pattern was practiced by the Natufian groups (Vita-Finzi and Higgs 1971). The Natufian sites show a bimodal distribution of area (Figure 4); Bar-Yosef (1970: 184) has suggested that the small sites might have represented transitory encampments. Natufian small sites, however, are almost exclusively in caves or on cave terraces, where the room for lateral expansion is severely restricted (Figure 5). Additional information therefore is required to corroborate the plausible assumption of seasonal and short-term (transitory) encampments. Such information can be obtained partially from the composition of the faunal, botanical, and/or artifactual remains at the sites. A step in this direction has been already undertaken by Henry (1973), who has suggested that the emphasis on scrapers in some of the small Natufian sites, e.g. Abu Usba and Jabrud III/2, may indicate that meat processing was the major activity at these sites. Possibly the Natufian populations did not share the same subsistence pattern. Study of dental attrition has suggested that the utilization of stone-ground foods (cereals or acorns) might not have been at the same level among different Natufian populations (Smith 1972). Legge (1972) has also suggested that animal resources might have supplied the bulk of the diet of the Natufian population at Nahal Oren. The probability that some Natufian settlements existed with a primary sub-sistence focus on hunting, probably in symbiotic relationship with other Natufian settlements with a primary focus on intensive utilization of cereals, must be entertained.

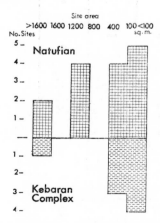

Figure 4.   Size distribution of Natufian and Kebaran sites of known size. Data from Bar-Yosef (1970) and Henry (1973)

The change in subsistence and the inauguration of permanent dwellings in the transition from the Upper Paleolithic and early Epipaleolithic (Kebaran) to the Natufian was most probably accompanied by concomitant changes in the pattern of social organization. A rudimentary or embryonic form of centralized organization probably emerged to ensure harmony within the relatively large population during the long-term residence in the permanent compounds, as well as to coordinate the management of the wide range of resources extracted from a wide range of biotopes at different parts of the year, and to coordinate economic and political relations with neighboring groups. The presence of some differences in mortuary practices seems to indicate some form of social hierarchy (Bar-Yosef and Goren 1973: 54), perhaps including a headman and individuals of high rank. Shells of *Dentalium* from the Red Sea are represented in many Natufian assemblages and were probably linked to a system of trade and exchange of resources. The difference in the time of maturation of wild cereals from one locality to another, depending on altitude and soil (Zohary 1969), and the transportability of grain could have prompted intergroup economic exchange. The interaction between subsistence, social organization, and both residential aggregation and duration (Figure 6) could have led to mutual reinforcement of certain

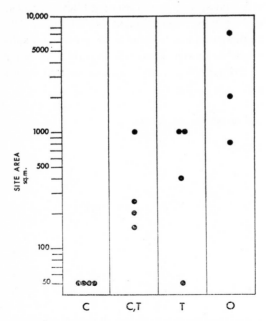

Figure 5.   Relation between site area and kind of site: C, cave; T, terrace; O, open air. Data from Henry (1973)

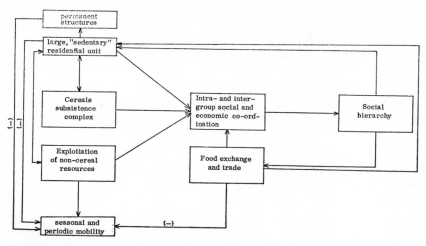

Figure 6. A schematic chart showing interaction between a subsistence regime based on intensive utilization of wild cereals and other components of the cultural system. The sign (—) indicates negative feedback: all other loops represent positive feedback. Note multiple negative feedbacks on mobility and multiple positive feedbacks on sedentariness and large group size

trends, such as sedentariness, large group size, managerial efficiency of economic exchange, and group cohesion. Feedback relations would have enhanced the development of these trends (Figure 6).

Agriculture does not seem to have been primarily adopted as a means to increase the yield of cereals. According to Zohary (1969) many fields of wild cereals are as productive as are varieties of durum and barley planted in ground prepared by a wooden plough. The transition to agriculture was more likely achieved by an accumulation of those innovations which enhanced year-round residence in one locality by relatively large groups, and by a selection of those practices which ensured a more reliable yield from year to year.

The shift to agriculture, as a major subsistence activity, could have been stimulated by a number of factors. First, as both the local group size and period of residency increased, it became progressively necessary to increase the catchment area from which additional resources (fish, meat, plants, etc.) were derived to meet the growing requirements of the population. This would have meant that a larger number of daughter groups would have had to engage in increasingly distant forays to secure the additional food. Obviously, a threshold would have been reached beyond which such mobility would have had to be curtailed. Excessive subsistence mobility is contradictory to the trend toward sedentariness, a trend which was linked to a wide range of cultural activities, e.g.

permanent structures, storage, food processing, and mortuary practices, to name only those which are explicitly manifest in the archaeological record. Mobility could not have increased, in addition, without weakening social integration and the cohesion of the group at the level required for the functioning of a large, proto-sedentary group.

Second, another stimulus would have hinged upon the vulnerability of large groups with limited mobility to the fluctuations of their environment. This is particulary aggravated if the environmental fluctuations are frequent and the resources are few.

Agriculture, then, could have emerged as a successful innovation by which the vulnerability of the population is reduced through expanding the area of cereal stands. Agriculture, thus, would have secured the survival of large groups over an extended time in the same locality. Nevertheless, agricultural communities with large size and permanent residency could not have been possible without other innovations, such as specifically "taming" or domestication of animals.

Hunting and exploitation of other sources of animal protein or vegetable substitutes, which involve a great deal of mobility, place certain limitations on the development of full-scale sedentary agriculture. Cereals are not sufficient by themselves to provide all nutritional requirements. During the Natufian, additional nutrients were obtained from other resources, collected probably through periodic or seasonal movements. One of the most important nutrients thus obtained must have been animal protein. For optimum utilization, eight essential amino acids are required in a proper ratio. Such ratio is present in milk, eggs, fish, and meat (Dubos 1971: 66). Cereals lack one or more of the essential amino acids and must therefore be supplemented by other sources of high quality protein (Cooper, et al. 1953: 40). The close relationship between the domestication of plants and animals can thus be explained in nutritional terms. Emphasis on the cultivation of plants yielding high quality protein such as leguminous plants during the Neolithic and the utilization of the pulses of wild legumes in the early phases of the Neolithic and the Natufian must have been nutritionally advantageous. Whether the domestication of cereals began before or after the domestication of other plants is a difficult problem, but this question seems to be a false issue, since "experimental" steps toward the domestication of either plants or animals could have been undertaken within a short span of time and could have been achieved at different times in different places. However, the domestication of animals, as well as of plants, seems to have been grounded in an economy favoring the exploitation of wild cereals. I wish to emphasize again that the domestication of animals and that of cereals are complementary from a nutritional viewpoint. Early agriculture would probably not have started independently of hunting and/or animal domestication, as well as of intensive gathering of seeds high in protein. On the other hand, full-time pastoralism is usually augmented by subsidiary cultivation or exchange of food with cultivators.

In the Natufian level at Beidha, *Capra* represented 76 percent of the total faunal assemblage. In the succeeding early Neolithic level, *Capra* represented 86 percent (Vita-Finzi and Higgs 1971: 32). In addition to the utilization of wild animals, goats were herded during the Neolithic at Beidha (Kirkbride 1968b: 267). Vegetable sources of high quality protein are represented in the Neolithic level at Beidha by field peas, two kinds of wild lentils, vetch, medick, cock's comb, and various other leguminous plants. At Jericho, gazelle, pig, and wild cattle are represented in the earlier level of the Pre-Pottery Neolithic A, but sheep/goat began to replace gazelle in the later level of Pre-Pottery Neolithic B (Clutton-Brock 1971). The emphasis on sheep/goat in the Neolithic level and the dominance of the domesticated varieties of these species at later Neolithic levels indicate a selectivity of these species over gazelle, probably because the former proved to be more successful domesticates or because they provided other benefits (such as wool or hair). The selection of sheep and goat could be, however, a result of some desirable behavioral traits or feeding habits. Legge (in Noy, Legge, and Higgs 1973: 91), for example, has suggested that goats were preferred over gazelles because of the latter's selective diet and restricted habitat.

In view of the basic need for animal resources, early Neolithic settlements would have been established not only where arable land was available but also where good grazing was accessible. In addition, since there was still a need at the early stages of the Neolithic for utilizing legumes and other wild plants, a location of the settlement where a variety of biotopes were within reasonable distance would have been highly advantageous. Large concentrations of people also require a permanent and abundant supply of water. For example, both Beidha and Jericho seem to satisfy these conditions. Beidha, which has been excavated and reported on by Kirkbride (1966, 1967, 1968a, 1968b) is located on the side of a valley with wooded steppe vegetation. The site is at the lower slope of a forested mountain ridge, which bounds the valley to the east. The site also overlooks a piedmont with a steppic vegetation. The piedmont, in turn, is traversed by the Wadi Araba, which would have supported a gallery forest along its channel. Permanent water could have been supplied from the spring of Dibadiba, some three miles away, and from rock pools in the immediate vicinity of the site. Jericho (Garstang and Garstang 1948; Kenyon 1957, 1960) is situated in the Jordan Valley, at or near the site of biblical Jericho. The site is close to the eastern base of the Judean hills and overlooks the plain traversed by the Jordan. A variety of resources were apparently available to the Neolithic inhabitants. Abundant skeletal remains of wild cattle and gazelles indicate access to good pasturage (Western 1971). The presence of skeletal remains of pigs and charcoals of riverine plants, e.g. *Salix* and *Populus*, suggests that riverine areas were available within the catchment territory. The appearance of *Tamarix*, which is now abundant along the banks of the Jordan and the Dead Sea (Western 1971), is a further indication that riverine or probably saline lacustrine flats, which could have also supported wild pig, were accessible.

The major attraction of Jericho, however, lies in a bountiful spring of water (1,000 gallons per minute; see Garstang and Garstang 1948: 22) with little seasonal variation. In addition to being a permanent source of drinking water, the spring feeds a large underground reservoir, which allows successful cultivation on the fertile alluvium of the Jordan Valley, even though local rainfall is insufficient to support stands of wild cereals.

One must note, however, that the early Neolithic stage in Palestine did not consist of a uniform adaptive pattern. Hunting and gathering continued, for example in association with the Khamian in the Judean Hills (Perrot 1952; Echegaray 1966; Bar-Yosef 1970, 1973) and the Harifian in the Negev and Sinai (Marks, et al. 1972; Bar-Yosef 1973). In some other localities, emphasis seems to have been placed in stock herding, as, for instance, during the period of the Pre-Pottery Neolithic A at Nahal Oren (Higgs, in Noy, Legge, and Higgs 1973).

It is most noteworthy that both Jericho and Beidha, and most other Pre-Pottery Neolithic sites (Phillips 1973), are located along the historic trade routes connecting the Nile delta, Sinai, Mesopotamia, and Anatolia. Obsidian, nephrite, and other greenstones from Anatolia, shells of *Dentalium* from the Red Sea, and turquoise from Sinai have been found at Jericho. Trade, which is manifest in the Natufian by the abundance of ornaments made of shells of *Dentalium*, could have also influenced the location of early Neolithic settlements.

The architectural features at Jericho — a massive tower and a thick wall erected in a wide rock-cut ditch — would seem to have required a level of social organization well beyond that of bands of hunting-gathering people.

The development of agriculture as the major subsistence activity is a very complex cultural process, which entails much more than planting. The potential for the domestication of plants and animals, as far as knowledge and initial requirements are involved, seems to have existed during the Epipaleolithic. This potential became functional only when certain societal and residential changes had taken place. These include, (1) a subsistence complex based partially on intensive utilization of wild cereals, (2) large local group concentrations, (3) long-term residence, (4) social hierarchy, and (5) trade and exchange of resources. Given these changes, the transition to agriculture was motivated by the need to control the production of cereals and to relocate settlements into areas of reliable and abundant water supply, good pasturage, a wide spectrum of biotopes, and centers for trade and exchange of food. Very likely these changes appeared separately at different places and the innovations diffused between contiguous groups. The great diversity of ecological zones and microenvironments in such a small area would have provided a rich repertory of experiences. Even at the slow rate of one kilometer per year (cf. Ammerman and Cavalli-Sfroza 1973) cultural innovations could have "rapidly" disseminated in such small areas. This could have been greatly aided by contact through trade or intergroup exchange of food.

I submit that agriculture became a major subsistence activity neither because a population discovered suddenly how to cultivate plants nor because they were forced to have recourse to agriculture under the exigencies of scarcity and deprivation. Agriculture was developed, in all probability, as a culmination of a series of concomitant and mutually interdependent changes in subsistence, settlement location, group size, temporal duration of residency, economic distribution, and social organization. It was adopted because it reinforced those changes which had become established during the Epipaleolithic (Figure 7), without exces-

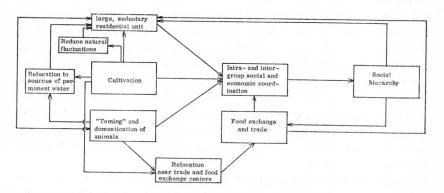

Figure 7. A schematic chart showing interaction between cultivation of cereals and other components of the cultural system. Note reinforcement of large, sedentary residential units, social hierarchy, and food exchange and trade as in Figure 6

sive social or economic cost. First, agriculture enhanced greater utilization of cereals, which were becoming a major component of the subsistence, with a host of related technological and perhaps ceremonial aspects. Second, agriculture secured a greater viability of the population against erratic microclimatic fluctuations in comparison to the lower viability of the population under an economy primarily dependent upon the gathering of wild cereals. Third, agriculture in combination with the exploitation of wild and/or domesticated animals, allowing relocation of settlements in areas with diverse resources and permanent sources of water, enabled a large group to reside in one locality all year round. This could have also been facilitated by increasing the volume of trade and intergroup food exchange. Fourth, the development of large-scale agriculture with the attendant development of permanent residence and the growth of local population, coupled with greater emphasis on trade and food exchange, could have enhanced the trend toward social hierarchy.

In summary, the emergence of agriculture in Palestine can be viewed as a culmination of certain adaptive trends which emerged during the Epipaleolithic. These trends were initiated by the transition from specialized hunting-gathering to a diversified subsistence base. The greater safety involved in a diversified subsistence base against periodic or seasonal shortage in any given resource could have rendered this mode of subsistence a successful alternative to specialized hunting-gathering if intensive microclimatic fluctuations occurred at the close of the Pleistocene. Field evidence usually focuses on macroclimatic changes, which tends to obscure seasonal and annual events which can directly affect any population that depends primarily on extracting natural resources. The inclusion of wild cereals among other resources that were previously either neglected or underutilized, was perhaps a major stimulus for further changes in the subsistence regime that led later to a mutual dependence between man and cereals. The inclusion of wild cereals could have been facilitated by their spread from their refuge areas after 14,000 B.P. (van Zeist 1969: 45). Once wild cereals were incorporated, a "positive feedback network" (cf. Flannery 1968) was established due to the great economic potential of cereals, which eventually led to a subsistence complex, a pattern of settlement and residence, and an intra- and intergroup organizational structure linked with intensive utilization of wild cereals (see Figures 3 and 6).

One of the major changes, in response to an increasing dependence on wild cereals, was the change toward sedentary habitation and larger size of the local group (Figure 3). This change in residential pattern was positively reinforced by the development of nontransportable facilities for processing and storage, and by permanent dwellings, social integration and cohesion, trade, and food exchange (Figure 6). The trend toward year-round sedentariness and large local population, however, was in conflict with two functional requirements. First, as the population continued to increase in size, either through ordinary growth or redistribution of population, and as the term of residency increased in response to improvements in processing, storage, harvesting, etc. the need to expand the catchment area from which additional resources were exploited had to grow correspondingly. Animals and legumes were particularly in demand to provide protein of high quality. The expansion of the catchment area implied greater seasonal and periodic mobility. But, higher mobility was in conflict with the trend toward sedentariness. The options, therefore were either: (1) to disband, which is incompatible with the already established trends; (2) to split into mobile hunters and sedentary gatherers of wild cereals, which is incompatible with the trend toward cohesive social units but less incompatible than (1); (3) to establish greater symbiotic relations with already existing hunters, who did not join in the cereals-oriented subsistence system; or (4) to relocate to areas with a greater diversity of biotopes and/or more yield in high-quality food per unit-area. The second functional requirement was the need for a permanent and sufficiently abundant source of drinking water to meet the demands of a large and sedentary population. This obviously could be only solved by relocating toward areas where perennial springs were available. The survival of a large and sedentary group, dependent upon wild plants, is more vulnerable than that of a small and mobile group. The vulnerability can be reduced by increasing the area of the cereal stands and/or relocating the cereals to those areas with underground water reservoirs (near bountiful springs or river deltas and fans). A high premium would have been thus placed upon relocating cereals to such areas, where perennial drinking water, good pasturage, and diverse resources were present. Agriculture would seem to have been thus the more likely alternative, that is, most compatible with the preexisting cultural trends. In addition, agriculture served to reinforce these trends (compare Figures 6 and 7).

The transition to agriculture, then, was grounded in a subsistence base heavily oriented toward the utilization of wild cereals and a settlement/residential pattern favoring large local group size and sedentary habitation. The transition occurred over a long span of time and involved a chain of mutual causal relationships between subsistence, settlement, group size, economy, and social organization.

The focus in this model is cultural dynamics. External variables, such as climate or independent growth of population, become meaningful

FEKRI A. HASSAN

only through their effect on the internal relations of the cultural system (cf. Faris 1975). The model is primarily a theoretical model. The fit between empirical data and the model has been attempted, but the present state of the data is insufficient for an adequate test of the model. Future systematic and culturally oriented investigation will provide the actual test of the model.

REFERENCES

AMMERMAN, A. J., L. L. CAVALLI-SFROZA
 1973   "A population model for the diffusion of early farming in Europe," in *The explanation of culture change*. Edited by Colin Renfrew, 343–357. London: Gerald Duckworth.
BAR-YOSEF, OFER
 1970   "The Epipalaeolithic cultures of Palestine." Unpublished doctoral dissertation. Hebrew University, Jerusalem.
 1975   "The Epipaleolithic in Palestine and Sinai," in *Problems in prehistory: North Africa and the Levant*. Edited by Fred Wendorf and Anthony E. Marks, 363–378. Dallas: Southern Methodist University Press.
BAR-YOSEF, OFER, N. GOREN
 1973   Natufian remains in Hayonim Cave. *Paleorient* 1:49–68.
BENEDICT, B.
 1970   "Population regulation in primitive societies," in *Population control*. Edited by A. Allison, 165–180. London: Penguin Books.
BINFORD, L.
 1968   "Post-Pleistocene adaptations," in *New perspectives in archeology*. Edited by S. R. and L. R. Binford, 313–341. Chicago: Aldine.
BRAIDWOOD, ROBERT J.
 1960   The agricultural revolution. *Scientific American* 203(3):130–148.
 1967   *Prehistoric men* (seventh edition). Glenview, Ill.: Scott, Foresman.
BUTZER, KARL W.
 1971   *Environment and archeology: an ecological approach to prehistory* (second edition). Chicago: Aldine.
 1975   "Patterns of environmental change in the Near East during late Pleistocene and early Holocene times," in *Problems in prehistory: North Africa and the Levant*. Edited by Fred Wendorf and Anthony E. Marks, 389–410. Dallas: Southern Methodist University Press.
CLUTTON-BROCK, JULIET
 1971   The primary food animals of the Jericho Tell from the Proto-Neolithic to the Byzantine period. *Levant* 3:41–55.
COOPER, L. F., E. M. BARBER, H. S. MITCHELL, H. J. RYNBERGEN
 1953   *Nutrition in health and disease* (twelfth edition). London: J. B. Lippincott.

DUBOS, RENE
1971 *Man adapting* (seventh edition). New Haven, Conn.: Yale University Press.

ECHEGARAY, JOAQUIN GONZALEZ
1964, 1966 *Excavaciones en la terraza de "el Khiam" (Jordania)*, two volumes. Biblioteca Praehistorica Hispana 5.

FARIS, JAMES C.
1975 "Social evolution, population, and production," in *Population, ecology, and social evolution*. Edited by Steven Polgar. World Anthropology. The Hague: Mouton.

FLANNERY, KENT, V.
1968 "Archeological systems theory and early Meso-America," in *Anthropological archeology in the Americas*. Edited by Betty J. Meggers, 67–87. Washington, D.C.: Anthropological Society of Washington.
1969 "Origins and ecological effects of early domestication in Iran and the Near East," in *The domestication and exploitation of plants and animals*. Edited by Peter J. Ucko and G. W. Dimbleby, 73–100. Chicago: Aldine.
1973 "The origins of agriculture," in *1973 Annual Review of Anthropology*. Edited by B. J. Beals, A. R. Beals, and S. A. Tyler, 271–310. Palo Alto, Calif.: Annual Reviews.

GARSTANG, J., J. B. E. GARSTANG
1948 *The story of Jericho*. London: Marshall, Morgan, and Scott.

HARRIS, J. C.
1971 Explanations in prehistory. *Proceedings of the Prehistoric Society* 37: 38–55.

HENRY, DON O.
1973 "The Natufian of Palestine: its culture and ecology." Unpublished doctoral dissertation. Southern Methodist University, Dallas.

HOLE, FRANK
1971 Comment on "Origins of food production in southwestern Asia: a survey of ideas," by Gary A. Wright. *Current Anthropology* 12:472–473.

HOROWITZ, A.
1971 Climatic and vegetational factors in northeastern Israel during the Upper Pleistocene-Holocene times. *Pollen et Spores* 13:255–278.

KATZ, SOLOMON
1972 "Biological factors in population control," in *Population growth: anthropological implications*. Edited by Brian Spooner, 351–369. Cambridge, Mass.: M.I.T. Press.

KENYON, KATHLEEN M.
1957 *Digging up Jericho*. New York: Praeger.
1960 *Archaeology in the Holy Land*. New York: Praeger.

KIRKBRIDE, DIANA
1966 Five seasons at the pre-pottery Neolithic village of Beidha in Jordan. *Palestine Exploration Quarterly* 98:8–61.
1967 Beidha 1965: an interim report. *Palestine Exploration Quarterly* 99: 5–13.
1968a Beidha 1967: an interim report. *Palestine Exploration Quarterly* 100: 91–96.

1968b Beidha: early Neolithic village life south of the Dead Sea. *Antiquity* 42: 263–274.

LEGGE, A. J.
1972 "Prehistoric exploitation of the gazelle in Palestine," in *Papers in economic prehistory: studies by members and associates of the British Academy Major Research Project in the Early History of Agriculture.* Edited by E. S. Higgs, 119–124. Cambridge: Cambridge University Press.

MARKS, A. E.
i.p. The Epipaleolithic of the central Negev: current status. *Eretz Israel* 13.

MARKS, A. E., H. CREW, R. FERRING, J. PHILLIPS
1972 Prehistoric sites near Har Harif. *Israel Exploration Journal* 22:73–85.

MEYERS, J. T.
1971 "The origins of agriculture: an evaluation of three hypotheses," in *Prehistoric agriculture.* Edited by Stuart Struever, 101–121. New York: The Natural History Press.

NEEV, D., K. O. EMERY
1967 The Dead Sea: depositional processes and environments of evaporites. *Bulletin of the Geological Survey of Israel* 41.

NOY, T., A. J. LEGGE, E. S. HIGGS
1973 Recent excavations at Nahal Oren, Israel. *Proceedings of the Prehistoric Society* 39:75–99.

PERROT, J.
1952 Têtes de flèches de Natoufien et de Tahunien (Palestine). *Bulletin de la Société Préhistorique Française* 49:439–449.
1966 Le gisement natoufien de Mallaha (Eynan), Israel. *L'Anthropologie* 70:437–484.

PHILLIPS, JAMES L.
1973 Comments on "The archaeology of Palestine from the Neolithic through the Middle Bronze Age," by G. Ernest Wright (*JAOS* 91 [1971]:276–293). *Journal of the American Oriental Society* 93:347–351.

PLATT, J. R.
1966 *The step to man.* New York: John Wiley and Sons.

RONEN, AVRAHAM
1973 "The Palaeolithic archaeology and chronology of Israel," in *Problems in prehistory: North Africa and the Levant.* Edited by Fred Wendorf and Anthony E. Marks, 229–248. Dallas: Southern Methodist University Press.

SMITH, PATRICIA
1972 Diet and attrition in the Natufians. *American Journal of Physical Anthropology* 37:233–238.

STEKELIS, M., T. YIZRAELY
1963 Excavations at Nahal Oren: preliminary report. *Israel Exploration Journal* 13:1–12.

STOTT, D. H.
1962 "Cultural and natural checks on population growth," in *Culture and the evolution of man.* Edited by M. F. Ashley Montagu, 355–376. Oxford: Oxford University Press.

VAN ZEIST, W.
  1969   "Reflections on prehistoric environments in the Near East," in *The domestication and exploitation of plants and animals*. Edited by Peter J. Ucko and G. W. Dimbleby, 35–46. Chicago: Aldine.

VITA-FINZI, C., E. S. HIGGS
  1971   Prehistoric economy in the Mount Carmel area of Palestine: site catchment analysis. *Proceedings of the Prehistoric Society* 36: 1–37.

WAGLEY, C.
  1951   Cultural influences on population: a comparison of two Tupi tribes. *Revista do Museu Paulista*, n.s. 5:95–104. (Reprinted 1969 in *Environment and cultural behavior*. Edited by Andrew P. Vayda. New York: The Natural History Press.)

WESTERN, A. CECILIA
  1971   The ecological interpretation of ancient charcoals from Jericho. *Levant* 3:31–40.

WRIGHT, GARY A.
  1971   Origins of food production in southwestern Asia: a survey of ideas. *Current Anthropology* 12:447–478, 570.

ZOHARY, D.
  1969   "The progenitors of wheat and barley in relation to domestication and agricultural dispersal in the Old World," in *The domestication and exploitation of plants and animals*. Edited by Peter J. Ucko and G. W. Dimbleby, 47–72. Chicago: Aldine.

Abstract: The Cultural Processes Leading to the Origins of Agriculture in the Ancient Near East

JEAN PERROT

Two parallel cultural processes may be observed in southwestern Asia leading to the origins of agriculture; they are related to different ecological systems and environment.

In the Zagros range (Kurdistan, Luristan), this process is related to an economy based on the exploitation of herds of wild goats and sheep moving up and down the wide transmontane valleys. Around 10,000 B.P., the pattern of settlement seems to have been characterized by summer camps on the Iranian plateau and winter settlements in the piedmont. A supplementary source of food was found in wild cereals. Emmer and barley, however, were not very abundant in this area, and man had to develop them through agriculture, paving the way to permanent settlements.

In Palestine, conditions in some ecological niches (e.g. Galilee, Carmel, the Upper Jordan Valley) made permanent settlements possible at an early date (Mallaha, ca. 12,000 B.P.). The economy was based on food collecting, mainly of cereals (emmer and barley). We do not know what started the movement toward sedentarization; however the consequences are clear. We observe major technological innovations: large circular stone shelters; clay-lined, bell-shaped silos; stone containers; heavy basalt implements (pestles, rubbing stones, etc.). An improvement is also apparent in the traditional technology of subsistence (bone and flint sickles, harpoons, gorgets, stones for fishing nets). The new conditions thus created may have created a better awareness of the potentialities of cereals; however we do not have archaeological evidence of agriculture — nor of the domestication of animals. The observable result is a fast growth of the population (Mallaha, ca. 12,000 B.P., had 200 inhabitants;

Jericho PPNA, ca. 10,000 B.P., had 2,000 inhabitants). When, under demographic pressure, human groups started to move toward and beyond the fringes of the cereals' natural habitat (Beidha, ca. 9000 B.P.), people felt the necessity and probably had the ability to start the cultivation of cereals.

SECTION FOUR

The Beginnings of Agriculture in the New World

The Origin of Zea mays

GEORGE W. BEADLE

In pre-Columbian times *Zea mays* — common name: corn or maize — was by far the most important human food crop in the western hemisphere. It still continues to be so in all of Latin America. On a world basis it is the third most important human food crop, with an annual production of some two hundred million metric tons.

At the time of Columbus, whose men found great fields of this strange new plant on the island of Cuba, essentially all major races of maize — some two to three hundred — were already in cultivation and had been disseminated from its place of origin, probably southern Mexico, to mid-Chile in the south and to the mouth of the St. Lawrence River in the north.

Centuries before Columbus the three great cultural, religious, and trading centers of Teotihuacan in the Valley of Mexico, Dzibilchaltun in

In the studies of teosinte-maize interrelations reported, the University of Chicago has generously provided laboratory, garden, greenhouse space, and technical assistance and time for experiments. The University of Illinois has provided space for growing hybrids as well as help in tending them. Space and help at the Botanic Garden of the Chicago Horticultural Society have been made available. The Rainbow Garden Association has provided plots for growing isolated hybrid populations. Facilities for growing hybrids plus help in harvesting and classifying have been provided by the International Maize and Wheat Improvement Center of Mexico, for my plantings there. Doctor Mario Gutiérrez has given me indispensable help in growing, harvesting, and classifying populations grown at the Center's El Batán Station. Professors Walton C. Galinat and H. Garrison Wilkes have helped in many ways. For help in collecting wild teosintes in Mexico and searching for mutant types among them the National Science Foundation has provided financial support.

Much of the substance of this account was presented as the Donald Forsha Jones Memorial Lecture at the Connecticut Agricultural Experiment Station on September 14, 1972.

Yucatán and Chan Chan in Peru supported populations of some 75,000 to 200,000 each. Obviously storable food was needed in great quantities. Maize and beans were among the most important of these.

Shortly before the conquest of the Aztecs by Cortez, Montezuma's tribute rolls indicate that the thirty-eight or so subdivisions of the empire were taxed an annual total of some 300,000 bushels of maize, an equal quantity of beans plus many other articles of food, clothing, ornamentation and other articles of value (Barlow 1949; Anderson and Barlow 1943).

Although modern plant breeders have greatly increased yields of maize through the development of new varieties and hybrid lines well adapted to various maize-growing regions and resistant to diseases and insect pests, this development of maize by the American Indian remains to this day man's most remarkable plant-breeding achievement (Kempton 1938).

CLOSEST RELATIVE OF MAIZE

For most cultivated plants, wild relatives are known from which they could reasonably have been derived. In fact, if one lists sixteen plant genera that include many of the world's most important food crops — maize, potatoes, sweet potatoes, beans, peanuts, manioc, cucurbits, and sunflower of New World origin, and wheat, rice, sugar cane, sugarbeets, barley, sorghum, soybeans, and oats of the Old World — for all except maize there are so many closely related wild species that it is difficult to determine just which one or more was ancestral to a given present-day crop plant. Bailey's *Manual of cultivated plants* (1949) lists for these sixteen crop-plant genera more than 500 species. Aside from the maize genus *Zea*, for which no wild species is recognized, not one of the other fifteen genera has less than six species assigned to it. It is thus no wonder that early plant explorers had great difficulty finding any wild relative that could conceivably have been the ancestor of maize. No other grass is known with a female inflorescence like that of an ear of modern maize. The reason is obvious, for this monstrous structure provides no effective means of seed dispersal, a must for any wild plant that depends on seeds for survival. If an ear of maize is left to its fate in nature, it will, under conditions favorable for germination, give rise to a group of seedlings so densely clustered that few are likely to produce mature "seeds." Thus all known living maize is dependent on man for survival.

Finally, however, early plant explorers found a candidate, a plant that grows in parts of Mexico, Guatemala, and Honduras, which natives in

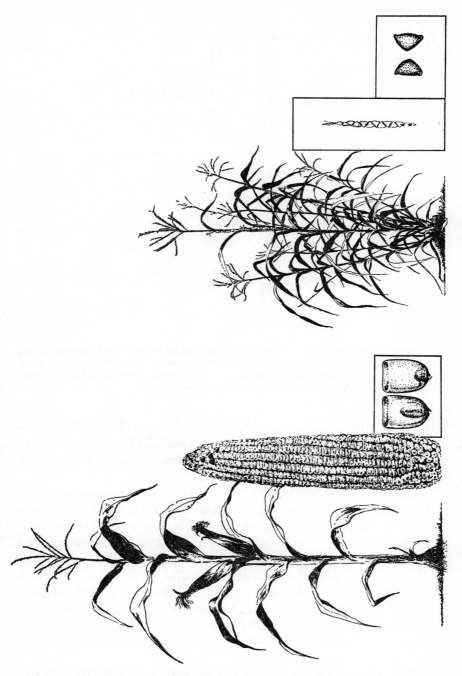

Figure 1. Comparison of maize and teosinte plants, female spikes and individual fruits ("seeds")

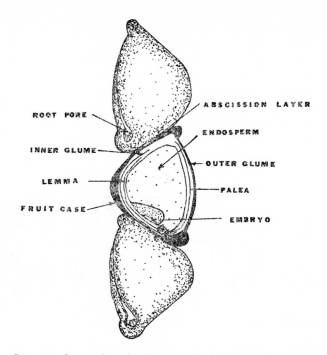

Figure 2.   Segment of normal teosinte female spike including a diagrammatic section through a modified rachis segment, called the cupule, which forms the major component of the fruitcase. The suppressed lower floret is not clearly indicated. The fruit-case consists of the rachis segment plus the outer glume

parts of Mexico called *teocentli*, or *teocintle*, from the Uto-Aztec language, meaning "God's corn." This is now anglicized to teosinte. Taxonomists assigned it to the new genus *Euchlaena* and gave it the specific name *mexicana*.

In 1790 teosinte was described by the botanist Hernández as a plant that "... looks like maize but its seed is triangular" (Wilkes 1967). Teosinte "seeds" (technically fruits) are arranged in a row, from five to ten, to form a somewhat flattened spike a few inches long and a quarter of an inch in width (Figure 1). This is teosinte's counterpart of an ear of maize. The triangularity of the individual fruits resides in the "fruitcases," which are dark, horny, cup-like segments of the rachis or axis of the spike closed on the outer long side by a lignified outer glume. On maturity the rachis segments fall apart through the development of abscission layers between adjacent fruits. Within each mature fruitcase is a single kernel much like that of maize (Figure 2).

In contrast to the one or a few ears produced by a modern plant of maize, a well-developed teosinte plant may produce a hundred or more ear equivalents, often many per node. As many as 9,000 "seeds" have been harvested from a single plant grown under cultivation in Mexico (Beadle and Gutiérrez, unpublished). Teosinte plants tend to be more highly tillered than most varieties of cultivated maize and each tiller produces female spikes at many nodes.

The most complete descriptions of races of teosinte are those of H. G. Wilkes (1967, 1972).

TEOSINTE AS AN ANCESTOR OF MAIZE

Is teosinte the ancestor of maize? A few botanists thought so. Vinson, for example, wrote in 1877, "Following the thinking of Darwin, teosinte is the ancestor of maize" (Wilkes 1967). But most of his contemporaries disagreed. The female inflorescences were so different they could not believe that one could have been transformed into the other in any plausible way.

Later a seemingly more likely candidate was found, a plant intermediate between teosinte and maize. Because of its small ear with partially exposed pointed kernels that resembled dogs' teeth, it was called *Zea canina*, dog maize or coyote maize. But this was soon found to be a naturally occurring hybrid between teosinte and maize, a hybrid that is easily made artificially and which is quite fertile. The fertility of this hybrid indicated that the genetic relation between teosinte and maize was much closer than previously assumed.

That was much the situation when the writer began graduate work at Cornell in 1927 with the late R. A. Emerson, who had shortly before demonstrated that teosinte is a so-called short-day plant, and that he could induce it to mature at the Cornell latitude by artificially shortening the summer day (Emerson 1924). This discovery made it practicable for him to use it in genetic studies. As a part-time graduate student-assistant, the writer was assigned to study the cytology and genetics of maize-teosinte hybrids.

We confirmed the fertility of the hybrids and showed that the ten chromosomes of the Mexican teosintes pair normally with those of maize at appropriate stages of meiosis (Beadle 1932), and further, that in the eight chromosomes for which we had suitable genetic markers, crossing-over in the hybrids was essentially the same as that in pure maize controls (Emerson and Beadle 1932).

Our conclusion, perhaps not stated in so many words, was that cytologically and genetically maize and the Mexican teosintes can reasonably be regarded as one species. Now, forty years later, this has been formally proposed on taxonomic grounds (Iltis 1972). The hypothesis that the wild form was the direct ancestor of its cultivated counterpart was thus entirely plausible in our way of thinking. We regarded the problem as essentially solved, that a relatively few major gene changes could and probably did convert the wild plant into a more useful cultivated one.

In discussions at this time Emerson pointed out that two mutants, a soft or reduced cupule and a non-shattering rachis, could make teosinte an easily usable food plant. It should be added that these postulated mutants are much the same as those that have played such significant roles in the evolution of the cultivated small grains of wheat, rye, barley, and oats, all of which are represented by varieties in which kernels can be threshed free of glumes, and in which the heads are non-shattering.

THE TRIPARTITE HYPOTHESIS

But there were skeptics. One was and still is, Professor Paul C. Mangelsdorf, formerly at Texas A. and M., then Harvard, and now at the University of North Carolina. In 1938 he and a colleague, R. G. Reeves, proposed that teosinte was not ancestral to maize, but instead was a relatively recent species resulting from hybridization of a wild maize, now extinct or undiscovered, and a species of the genus *Tripsacum* (Mangelsdorf and Reeves 1938, 1939; Mangelsdorf 1947). This hybrid is possible by special techniques. The evidence alleged to support this origin of teosinte was mainly that it is intermediate between the assumed parental species in many morphological traits.

Not everyone believed this evidence to justify the conclusion (Beadle 1939). The reasons were: first, that maize and *Tripsacum* have never been known to hybridize naturally, despite the fact that they grow in close proximity over millions of acres; second, that none of the eighteen chromosomes of *Tripsacum* pairs normally with any one of the ten chromosomes of maize; and third, that the hybrids produced artificially are completely male sterile. They produce offspring only in backcrosses in which the functional gametes of the hybrid carry the unreduced chromosome number, that is, ten from maize and eighteen from *Tripsacum*.

Nevertheless, this tripartite hypothesis has for a third of a century been supported by its proposers, with the result that it has thoroughly permeated genetic, botanical, plant-breeding, anthropological, and other literature. It is repeated in encyclopedias, in compendia, and in many textbooks, sometimes being transformed from an hypothesis to an established fact.

More recently Walton C. Galinat, a former associate of Mangelsdorf, has shown that the fruitcase of teosinte, which the tripartite hypothesis must assume to have been contributed from *Tripsacum* as a block of closely linked genes, could not have arisen in that way for the simple reason that no such group of genes can be demonstrated in *Tripsacum* (Galinat 1970). In contrast to teosinte, the fruitcase of *Tripsacum* appears to be specified by genes that are not closely linked.

DeWet and Harlan (1972) and deWet, Harlan, Lambert, and Engle (1972) of the University of Illinois, Urbana, have also argued against the tripartite hypothesis on the ground that, in their extensive studies of hybrids between maize and *Tripsacum*, they have never observed a segregant at all like teosinte.

It is of considerable importance to know that, contrary to the tripartite hypothesis assumption that teosinte is of relatively recent origin, teosinte has recently been reported to have existed some 7,000 years ago at a site about twenty miles southeast of Mexico City near the present town of Chalco. The two "seeds" recovered in an undisturbed pre-ceramic horizon are very much like the present most corn-like race of teosinte called Chalco (Lorenzo and González 1970). Could this race of teosinte have been the ancestor of maize? At this time one can do no more than speculate.

TEOSINTE AS A FOOD PLANT

One of the arguments against teosinte as an ancestor of maize has been that it is not obvious how its nut-like seeds with their heavy cases could have been used for food by primitive man. This view has persisted despite early Spanish evidence that teosinte seeds were indeed used as food. Wilkes (1967) referred to Vatican Codex 3738 in which it was said that in the tradition of the tribe "… in the old days [preconquest] they ate a wild plant called accentli [synonym of teosinte]." Young stalks of teosinte were undoubtedly chewed, as archaeological evidence indicates early maize was. Young spikes of teosinte can also be eaten before the cases become hardened.

In 1939, without knowledge of any documented use of teosinte as food, it occurred to me, as a boyhood lover of popcorn, that perhaps teosinte seeds would pop. A simple experiment demonstrated that they will. The popped kernels, exploded out of their cases, are indistinguishable from popped corn (Beadle 1939). That teosinte could have been used in this way in pre-ceramic times has been well documented by Anderson and Cutler (1950). Maize kernels placed in a fire, on glowing embers, on hot rocks, or heated sand, pop very well and either pop free of the fire or can be retrieved by simple wooden sticks or tongs. Teosinte would surely behave similarly.

More recently, as a result of a friendly disagreement with Professor Mangelsdorf on the edibility of ground whole teosinte seeds in which he expressed doubt as to whether one could tolerate ingesting the fifty percent or more roughage contributed by the cases, the question was posed to Professor Nevin Scrimshaw, a biochemist-nutritionist of MIT, whom we both know and who has worked in the tropics with teosinte. Scrimshaw proposed that I do the following experiment: Consume 75 grams of ground whole seeds of teosinte on each of two successive days. If no ill effects were experienced, increase the intake to 150 grams per day for two more days. If there were still no unpleasant consequences, the answer would be clear. There were no ill effects whatever.

Dry teosinte seeds have been ground with a pair of primitive grinding or pounding stones of a kind known to have been in use at least 8,000 years ago, with the conclusion that an energetic person inspired by extreme hunger could in one day, by a water flotation technique or in other ways, separate from the ground shell-kernel mixture enough shell-free meal of teosinte to feed a small family for one day or more (Beadle 1972). Whole, mature teosinte seeds can be eaten directly without great difficulty by first soaking them until they have been sufficiently softened to masticate. The shells can either be swallowed or selectively spit out.

RE-INVESTIGATION OF MAIZE-TEOSINTE HYBRIDS

Backing up a bit in the sequence of current interests in teosinte, shortly before I retired from academic administration I received a copy of Wilkes' monograph (1967), *Teosinte: the closest relative of maize*. It is by far the best and most useful document on the subject available and was read with great interest and admiration, qualified by a deeply felt reservation on noting in one passage his characterization of the maize-from-teosinte hypothesis as a "crude" attempt to explain the origin of maize, and in another as the "myth" that teosinte is maize's ancestor. Through correspondence the matter of the origin of maize was argued without coming to an agreement. The result, however, was that I decided to return to a study of the relation of teosinte to maize.

It should be added that Wilkes and I have become good friends, have collaborated in three teosinte-collecting trips in Mexico, and have influenced each other's thinking to some degree.

To supplement earlier small-scale studies indicating that near-equivalents to parental types could be recovered in second generation maize-teosinte hybrid populations, it was decided to grow large-scale populations of second generation and backcross populations in order better to estimate the magnitude of the genetic difference between the two.

As a first cross a primitive maize, the most teosinte-like that was clearly maize, and a maize-like teosinte that was unmistakably teosinte, were chosen as parents. These choices could be expected to reduce the differences to those that are most essential. On the advice of Dr. Edwin J. Wellhausen of the International Center for Maize and Wheat Improvement, headquartered in Mexico, Chapalote maize and Chalco teosinte were selected.

Mendel's laws say that in a second-generation segregating population with a one-gene difference, each parental type will be recovered with a statistical frequency of one in four; with two independently segregating gene pairs, one in sixteen; and so on for more genes. For ten, the recovery will be somewhat less than one in a million, and for twenty, which is possible with a segregating gene pair located near each of the twenty chromosome ends, the recovery of a particular parental type will be less than one in a trillion plants — which is close to the total number of plants grown per year in the entire world. Thus if teosinte and maize differed by a large number of significant and unlinked differentiating genes, even as few as ten or a dozen, good types of maize and teosinte would be so rare as to be unrecoverable in any population that could reasonably be grown and classified.

It was decided to grow up to 50,000 second generation plants if necessary, for this would give a reasonable chance of recovering parental types with as many as six or seven major independently segregating genetic units. With the 1973 plantings, just about that many will have been grown and classified.

Since teosinte plants will not mature at United States corn-belt latitudes, there was a problem of where to grow the segregating populations. Fortunately arrangements were made with Dr. Wellhausen to grow them at the International Maize and Wheat Improvement Center's El Batán station near Texcoco, Mexico. Doctor Mario Gutiérrez of the Center has collaborated in planting, growing, harvesting, and classifying the plants grown there. Professor Walton C. Galinat of the University of Massachusetts also collaborated in the classification of the first large second generation grown in Mexico.

What have been the results? In the second generation cross of Chapalote maize and Chalco teosinte good maize and teosinte types were recovered with a frequency of about one of each in 500 plants. These frequencies are intermediate between those expected with four and with five independently segregating genes. This does not, however, take into account that the recovered parental types are not likely to be homozygous for all differentiating genes, or that not all genetic units involved are likely to be segregating independently. Furthermore, it is unlikely that the significant segregating genetic units are single genes, for we know that in more or less comparable situations there is a selective advantage in having differentiating genes closely linked in a manner that favors the recovery of parental types. This is not in disagreement with the findings of Mangelsdorf and Reeves (1938) in isolating differentiating genetic units through repeated backcrosses of hybrids to an unbred line of maize.

Second generation and backcross populations have been grown involving other races of both maize and teosinte. They show that the frequency of recovered parental types may vary rather widely depending on the races involved.

In response to doubts expressed by Professor Mangelsdorf as to whether really "good" maize types were recovered a "cob quiz" was devised in which cobs from "pure" maize and those from hybrid populations were coded and presented separately to Professors Mangelsdorf and Galinat for classification. In both cases enough cobs of hybrids were judged to be those of good corn to confirm that "good" maize is indeed recovered in reasonable frequencies in second generation hybrids and in backcrosses of first generation hybrids to maize.

Despite the qualifications and reservations already mentioned, the genetic differences between maize and teosinte clearly cannot be so great as to render untenable the hypothesis of an ancestral relationship of teosinte to maize. When one considers that there are several hundred known genes for simple differing characters within varieties of maize in existence at the time of Columbus and almost surely as many or more for such qualitative ones as plant size, ear size and shape, number of ears, kernel size, response to day length, disease resistance, and other traits, it seems entirely reasonable to assume that pre-Columbian man could have discovered and preserved the far fewer mutants required to produce a useful plant from teosinte, that is, a primitive maize from which modern races of maize could subsequently have been selected. Two major differentiating traits, single versus double female spikelets and two-ranked versus four-ranked female spikes, are differentiated by single genetic units (Galinat 1971).

Archaeological Evidence

Beginning in the mid- to late forties many dry caves in southwestern United States and in Mexico have been explored by experienced archaeologists. Among the many recovered materials that reveal much about the lives of the peoples who occupied these sites are remains of maize, the most revealing of which are cobs. In zones of increasing depth and age in some caves, sequences of cobs are found that clearly indicate changes under domestication. The oldest cobs are found, on radioactive carbon dating, to have grown something like 7,000 years ago. Cobs of this age are very small, an inch in length, more or less, and are estimated by Mangelsdorf, MacNeish, and Galinat (1964), who have studied a great many of them in detail, to have each borne about fifty to sixty small kernels.

These cobs reveal a great deal about the evolution of cultivated maize over the past seven millennia. With respect to the origin of maize, Mangelsdorf and his associates allege the oldest of them to be the remains of a truly wild maize, this on the basis of the reported uniformity of the oldest cobs, plus the fact that they occur at earlier levels than other plant remains unmistakably known to have been cultivated. If there had been such a wild maize growing independently of teosinte, it is now extinct, or as yet undiscovered despite extensive searches for it. While it is logically impossible to prove that such maize never existed as a wild plant, one can seriously question whether the available evidence compels or even suggests such a conclusion.

Let us examine the alternative, and to some a more plausible interpretation, namely, that these oldest cobs represent stages in the transition of teosinte to maize through human selection.

First, early cobs are obviously much closer morphologically and genetically to teosinte than is modern maize, this for the very simple reason that cobs closely matching them are readily recovered in second and later generations of maize-teosinte hybrids, as Mangelsdorf (1958a) has shown and as has been abundantly demonstrated in the more recent hybrid populations.

Second, if the earliest archaeological types are indeed genetically closer to teosinte, as expected on the hypothesis that they were directly derived from teosinte, this should be evident in second and backcross generations of hybrids of recovered archaeological types with teosinte. Experiments now in progress indicate that the genetic differences are indeed reduced in number in this way.

Third, the earliest alleged wild maize is said to have fragile cobs. This is the equivalent of the fragile rachis of teosinte and could reasonably be expected to have persisted for some time after teosinte was deliberately cultivated.

Fourth, some of the earliest cobs are two-ranked, another teosinte trait.

Fifth, the earliest maize cobs are reported to have longer glumes than has modern maize, which Mangelsdorf suggested could well be the genetic equivalent of the tunicate character of modern maize. In fact, Mangelsdorf (1958b) has used tunicate types of modern maize in reconstructing a close approximation of the earliest archaeological specimens.

Elaborating on this suggested role of tunicate, there is reason to believe this character to have had a far more important bearing on the origin of maize than has previously been recognized, for it suggests how in a simple and plausible way teosinte could have been converted into a more useful food plant and a logical precursor of maize.

Professor Galinat has generously provided me with a number of lines of teosinte to which an intermediate allele of the dominant tunicate gene has been introduced from maize. With these many additional lines have been produced by further backcrossing to teosintes. These modified teosintes have just the characteristics Emerson postulated as the first steps in the transformation from teosinte to maize. The fruitcases of tunicate teosintes are reduced to shallow, less indurated cupules with enlarged but membranous outer glumes (Figures 3 and 4). In addition, as de Wet, et al. (1972) have pointed out, the abscission layers of the rachis are less well developed, with the result that there is much less tendency of the spikes to shatter upon ripening. Thus a single tunicate mutation can convert teosinte into a plant from which naked kernels can be threshed with ease. Furthermore, the yields of such plants can approximate those of wheat.

Had the tunicate mutant change been an early step in evolution of maize from teosinte, the presence of the tunicate trait in the archaeological maize would be accounted for. The plausibility of this interpretation would seem further increased by the fact that tunicate alleles are dominant and, in the heterozygous state, most useful for the purposes suggested. This means that if in early stages of cultivation a tunicate mutant of teosinte had been selected for planting, it would not have seemed to dis-

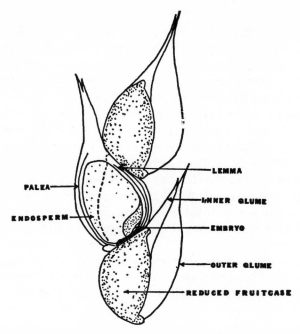

Figure 3. Segment of a tunicate teosinte spike corresponding to Figure 1, showing membranous outer glumes and moderate reduction of cupule. Kernels only partially enclosed in cupules

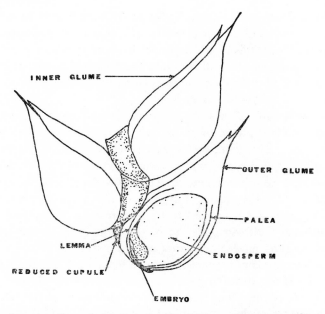

Figure 4. Segment of a tunicate teosinte spike corresponding to Figures 1 and 2, but with greater reduction in cupule such that kernels can be readily threshed free of smaller softer fruitcases and less indurated outer glumes

appear in the next generation through out-crossing, as would a recessive mutant. Furthermore, there would have been an advantage in getting rid of it in subsequent stages of evolution under domestication for exactly the same reasons that tunicate types of modern corn are less useful to man than their non-tunicate counterparts.

If the earliest archaeological specimens of maize were in fact wild maize, rather than a transitional form, it seems highly improbable that it and teosinte could have shared the same habitat, or overlapping ones, for teosinte, with its many attributes of a successful wild plant (well-protected kernels, an effective mechanism for seed dispersal, a built-in dormancy system that helps maximize the chance of germination under favorable circumstances, plus a remarkable ability to reproduce in the wild under a variety of circumstances), would surely have competitively replaced the wild maize.

If, on the other hand, teosinte and wild maize had occupied different habitats, as has been postulated, it is difficult to believe they could have remained as completely inter-fertile as the evidence shows they have been for thousands of years.

Pollen Evidence

Barghoorn, Wolfe, and Clisby (1954) have claimed to have established beyond reasonable doubt the existence of maize in the Americas prior to the arrival of man, this by the discovery of fossil pollen of maize in samples from a construction drill core taken at the Belles Artes site in Mexico City at a depth of more than 200 feet. This would indicate an age of from forty to eighty thousand years.

The identification of these pollen grains as maize was at first based on size, most modern pollen of maize being larger than modern pollen of teosinte. Kurtz, Liverman, and Tucker (1960) challenged this conclusion on the grounds that maize pollen varies markedly in size depending on environmental conditions and that therefore size alone is not clearly diagnostic, nor is the ratio of long axis of the grains to pore diameter, which character had been said to be a more reliable criterion. Galinat (1971) believes the fossil pollen to be too large for primitive maize and has suggested, as have others, that conditions of preservation of fossil pollen and methods of preparation may affect its size and thus invalidate this as a basis for identifying fossil pollen as maize or teosinte.

As a result of these uncertainties, a re-examination of the Belles Artes pollen was later made by Irwin and Barghoorn (1965). They concluded that the two pollens could be reliably distinguished by exine characteristics revealed by phase-contrast microscopy, and again judged the fossil pollen to be that of maize. But still more recently, Banerjee, a graduate student of Barghoorn, has used a superior method of electron microscopy which shows the two pollen exines to be indistinguishable (Banerjee and Barghoorn 1972). Grant (1972) confirms this.

Soil engineers experienced in drill-core sampling have expressed the opinion that without special precautions it is not possible, beyond reasonable doubt, to exclude contamination of core samples with material from higher levels, even in the interior of cores. It should be added that the upper horizons of the Belles Artes site contained modern maize pollen.

For these several reasons it seems clear that the fossil pollen evidence is at best inconclusive.

Linguistics

Such linguistic evidence as exists is consistent with the teosinte ancestry of maize. Why otherwise would teosinte be called "God's maize" or "God's grass"? As pointed out by Wilkes (1967), in the Nobogame area of Chihuahua teosinte is known as *madre de maíz* [mother of maize], presumably from an earlier native designation. Do these terms represent a kind of cultural memory? With many other existing native names for teosinte in the various parts of its range, this would appear to be a rewarding area for further linguistic study (Wilkes 1967).

Ecological Considerations

In addition to its highly successful mechanism of seed dispersal as compared with the apparently far less effective one of postulated wild maize, teosinte has other characteristics favorable to its survival in the wild.

Contrary to a statement by Wilkes (1967), teosinte "seeds" have a dormancy or mechanism of delayed germination which favors their germination in circumstances suitable for survival (Beadle, unpublished). In addition, the fruitcase of teosinte provides significant protection to the enclosed kernels, as compared with their naked or less well-protected counterparts in maize. Controlled experiments with mice, rats, squirrels, other rodents, and pigeons indicate this, for given a choice, maize kernels are strongly preferred to teosinte "seeds" by these animals (Beadle and Fox, unpublished materials).

The colors and patterns of the heavily indurated protective fruitcases of teosinte vary from grey to brown to black, often with mottling, spotting, or striping. In this and in shape they may very effectively mimic the pebbles and particles of the soil surface on which they fall. They are remarkably well camouflaged (Wilkes 1967).

Teosinte responds adaptively to the conditions under which it grows. In fertile soil with optimum moisture plants are large, well tillered and produce abundant "seed." Under adverse conditions, they respond by producing few or no tillers, restricting growth, and by producing no more "seed" than resources permit. In the extreme, this may be a single mature "seed." In contrast maize gambles on at least one whole ear and thus produces no "seed" at all if this fails.

Folklore

Regional folklore would seem also to contribute to further understanding of the role of teosinte in prehistoric times. The Wilkes monograph clearly indicates this. It records that Lumholz, who travelled extensively in Mexico at the turn of the century and reported his observations in considerable detail, noted that in the Nobogame area teosinte growing in or near fields of maize was said to be "good for the maize." It is easy to minimize the significance of such an assertion by assuming it to be an excuse for not making the effort to rogue the interloper out of the maize plantings. In fact, there is good evidence that teosinte can be "good for the maize" under primitive conditions of culture in which maize is grown in small areas, often relatively isolated from other maize. Under these conditions, with seed saved for successive generations, inbreeding is intensified. This we know reduces vigor and yields.

If teosinte grows adjacent to or in such isolated plots, hybrids between it and maize occur with a frequency that depends on a good many factors such as relative times of pollination and spatial relations (Wilkes 1972). When corn is pollinated by teosinte, the hybrid kernels are usually indistinguishable from pure corn and thus may be planted. The resulting first-generation hybrid plants exhibit marked hybrid vigor. Like those of *Zea canina*, however, their ears are small and undesirable and therefore will not be chosen in selecting seed for the succeeding crop.

These hybrid plants will, however, have previously shed abundant pollen which will be widely disseminated because of their tallness and vigor. Thus backcrosses to maize as the female parent will appear in the next generation. Some of these will be acceptable maize showing marked hybrid vigor. Second and later generation backcrosses to maize result in an even higher frequency of high-yielding good maize plants. In this way the maize will be rejuvenated according to the same principles used in producing modern high-yielding corn hybrids.

That such rejuvenation will indeed occur has been demonstrated in a well-controlled experiment by Lambert and Leng (1965) of the University of Illinois, Urbana. These investigators hybridized a well-adapted, high-yielding, inbred line of maize with four races of teosinte and made several successive backcrosses to the inbred maize parent. Yields in the second and third backcrosses were increased as much as 100 percent.

As both Mangelsdorf (1961) and Wilkes (1967) have shown, such hybridization is not infrequent in parts of Mexico where maize and teosinte grow in close proximity, thus creating sympatric populations in which genes of teosinte and maize are exchanged regularly at a rather low frequency. As has often been pointed out in more or less comparable situations, the selective advantage of getting back the parental types well adapted to the two habitats — maize fields and areas occupied by teosinte — will in time result in clustering of genes differentiating the two partners in the sympatric relation (Galinat 1971). That this has in fact taken place is indicated by several of the genetic studies previously mentioned.

Comparative Cytology

Another important line of evidence bearing on the maize-teosinte relationship comes from studies of supernumerary B-type chromosomes, an "abnormal" chromosome 10, and of heterochromatic knobs of varying sizes and positions that are found on both maize and teosinte chromosomes. These have been extensively studied by Longley and Kato (1965), and others (Galinat 1971). Most knobs in teosintes, as identified by position, are found in one or another of the many races of maize. Position, sizes, and frequencies of knobs also reveal much about centers of distribution and paths of dissemination of maize relative to teosinte. They confirm that the two species have had a close and long-continuing association and, insofar as the results are available, I judge them to be consistent with the view that maize is a direct descendant of teosinte. More extensive data, now in preparation for publication by McClintock, Kato, and Blumenschein, will undoubtedly add importantly to the total evidence bearing on this relation.

Biochemical Evidence

Seed storage proteins of maize and teosinte have been compared by a number of investigators. As an example, Waines (1972) and Gray, Grant, and deWet (1972) have shown by electrophoretic techniques that there is little or no qualitative difference in the two. Several enzyme systems have been investigated with no indication of significant differences in the two forms. Although the known sharing of a large gene pool by the two species would suggest few such differences, additional studies are clearly needed and are in fact under way or proposed in a number of laboratories.

THE TRIPARTITE HYPOTHESIS RECONSIDERED

At a conference held at Harvard in June 1972, Mangelsdorf conceded that the evidence against the tripartite hypothesis was substantial and persuasive. But consistent with his firm conviction that the earliest archaeological specimens of maize represent wild maize, he has since proposed an alternative hypothesis on maize and its relatives (1974). He kindly permitted me to see relevant excerpts in manuscript form. In his new proposal he assumes that maize, as represented by the earliest archaeological specimens, antedated the teosintes, which he now proposes were derived from wild maize by mutation. This indeed represents a reversal of position since he previously maintained that teosinte and maize were so different that teosinte could not have been ancestral to maize.

If maize could have given rise to teosinte, the reverse must also be both possible and far more probable, for teosinte is a highly successful wild plant and maize is not. Postulated wild maize, as represented in the earliest archaeological specimens, is assumed by Mangelsdorf, et al. to have dispersed its seeds in part by virtue of a fragile cob. In this there seems to be a curious inconsistency. If the earliest archaeological specimens were wild maize and had brittle cobs, how could they have survived harvesting, transportation to the caves, shelling of kernels, mixing with other debris on the cave floors, plus being tramped on prior to their being covered with protecting layers? If the cobs were fragile, this would indicate teosinte as an ancestor. If they were not fragile, it is difficult to believe they could have been wild maize, for how then would they have disseminated their seeds?

Regardless of how the question of the fragile cob is rationalized, the fruitcase-cupule relation seems overridingly persuasive as evidence that the direction of change was from teosinte to maize. How else can one account for the cupule of the corncob, clearly present in the earliest archaeological specimens? As Galinat (1970, 1971) has pointed out, the cupule indicates that corn must have evolved from an ancestor with a cupulate fruitcase. With *Tripsacum* excluded, teosinte remains the sole candidate. There is no other living or known extinct species that so logically satisfies all criteria.

REFERENCES

ANDERSON, E., R. H. BARLOW
  1943 The maize tribute of Montezuma's empire. *Annals of the Missouri Botanical Garden* 30:413–418.
ANDERSON, E., H. C. CUTLER
  1950 Methods of corn popping and their historical significance. *Southwestern Journal of Anthropology* 6:303–308.
BAILEY, L. H.
  1949 *Manual of cultivated plants.* New York: Macmillan.
BANERJEE, U. C., E. S. BARGHOORN
  1972 Fine structure of pollen grain ektexine of maize, teosinte and *Tripsacum. Thirtieth Annual Proceedings of the Electron Microscopy Society of America, Los Angeles, California* 226–227.
BARGHOORN, E. S., M. K. WOLFE, K. H. CLISBY
  1954 Fossil maize from the Valley of Mexico. *Botanical Museum Leaflets, Harvard University* 16:229–240.
BARLOW, R. H.
  1949 The extent of the empire of the cultura Mexica. *Ibero-Americana* 28:1–141.
BEADLE, G. W.
  1932 *Euchlaena* and its hybrids with *Zea*, I: Chromosome behavior in *E. mexicana* and its hybrids with *Zea mays. Zeitschrift für Abstammungs- und Vererbungslehre* 62:291–304.
  1939 Teosinte and the origin of maize. *The Journal of Heredity* 30:245–247.
  1972 The mystery of maize. *Field Museum of Natural History Bulletin* 43 (November): 2–11.
DE WET, J. M. J., J. R. HARLAN
  1972 Origin of maize: the tripartite hypothesis. *Euphytica* 21:271–279.
DE WET, J. M. J., J. R. HARLAN, R. J. LAMBERT, L. M. ENGLE
  1972 Introgression from *Tripsacum* into *Zea* and the origin of maize. *Caryologica* 1:25–31.
EMERSON, R. A.
  1924 The control of flowering in teosinte. *The Journal of Heredity* 15:41–48.

EMERSON, R. A., G. W. BEADLE
1932   Studies of *Euchlaena* and its hybrids with *Zea*, II: Crossing-over between the chromosomes of *Euchlaena* and those of *Zea*. *Zeitschrift für Abstammungs- und Vererbungslehre* 62:305–315.

GALINAT, W. C.
1970   *The cupule and its role in the origin and evolution of maize*. University of Massachusetts Bulletin 585.
1971   The origin of maize. *Annual Review of Genetics* 5:447–478.
1973   Preserve Guatemalan teosinte, a relict link in corn's evolution. *Science* 180:323.

GRANT, C. A.
1972   A scanning electron microscopy survey of some Maydeae pollen. *Grana* 12:177–184.

GRAY, J. R., C. A. GRANT, J. M. J. DE WET
1972   Protein electrophoresis as an indicator of relationship among maize, teosinte and *Tripsacum*. *Illinois State Academy of Science Newsletter* 4:5.

ILTIS, H.
1972   The taxonomy of *Zea mays* (Gramineae). *Phytologia* 23:248–249.

IRWIN, H., E. S. BARGHOORN
1965   Identification of the pollen of maize, teosinte and tripsacum by phase-contrast microscopy. *Botanical Museum Leaflets, Harvard University* 21:37–57.

KEMPTON, J. H.
1938   Maize — our heritage from the Indian. *Smithsonian Report for 1937*, 385–408.

KURTZ, E. B., J. L. LIVERMAN, H. TUCKER
1960   Some problems concerning fossil and modern corn pollen. *Torrey Botanical Club Bulletin* 87:85–94.

LAMBERT, R. J., E. R. LENG
1965   Backcross response of two mature plant traits for certain corn-teosinte hybrids. *Crop Science* 5:239–241.

LONGLEY, A. E., T. A. KATO
1965   Chromosome morphology of certain races of maize in Latin America. *International Center for Maize and Wheat Improvement Research Bulletin* 1:1–112.

LORENZO, J. L., L. GONZÁLEZ
1970   El más antiquo teosinte. *INAH Boletín* 42:41–43.

MANGELSDORF, P. C.
1947   The origin and evolution of maize. *Advances in Genetics* 1:161–207.
1958a   The mutagenic effect of hybridizing maize and teosinte. *Cold Spring Harbor Symposium on Quantitative Biology* 23:409–421.
1958b   Reconstructing the ancestor of corn. *Proceedings of the American Philosophical Society* 102:454–463.
1961   Evolution at a single locus in maize. *Science* 133:1366.
1974   *Corn, its origin, evolution and improvement*. Cambridge, Mass.: Harvard University Press.

MANGELSDORF, P. C., R. S. MAC NEISH, W. C. GALINAT
1964   Domestication of corn. *Science* 143:538–545.

MANGELSDORF, P. C., R. G. REEVES

  1938   The origin of maize. *Proceedings of the National Academy of Science* 24:303–312.
  1939   The origin of Indian corn and its relatives. *Texas Agricultural Experiment Station Bulletin* 574:1–315.

WAINES, J. G.

  1972   Protein electrophoretic patterns of maize, teosinte and *Tripsacum. Maize Genetics Cooperation News Letter* 46:164–165.

WILKES, H. G.

  1967   *Teosinte: the closest relative of maize.* Cambridge, Mass.: The Bussey Institution of Harvard University.
  1972   Maize and its wild relatives. *Science* 177:1071–1077.

Why Didn't the American Indians Domesticate Sheep?

CHRISTOPHER CARR

One of the striking differences between the Neolithic Revolutions in the Old and New Worlds is in the degree to which animal domestication occurred. While in western Eurasia, sheep, goats, cattle, pigs, and horses all played important roles in the change to Neolithic ways of life, in North and Middle America, the domesticated animals were apparently limited to the dog and turkey, both of which were secondary in importance to plant domestication in this life change. As wild sheep occur in both the New and Old World, the question arises, "Why didn't prehistoric man domesticate sheep in the New World?"

For several reasons, however, this innocent question is somewhat misleading. First, investigation of opportunities for DOMESTICATION is too narrow a perspective. When we talk of domestication, we are speaking of only the final stage of a process: a process of changing man-animal relationships. Domestication is commonly defined as that man-animal relationship in which animals are removed from their natural living area and breeding community, and are controlled in their breeding habits for profit (Bökönyi 1969). There are a number of man-animal relationships, however, which do not fit this definition, but which do achieve the same RESULTS for man: increased efficiency in the exploitation of animal resources. Wilkinson (1972: 112) has defined three ways by which man may increase his efficiency of animal exploitation, none of which necessarily involves domestication: (1) previously inaccessible resources may be exploited through the development of new man-animal relationships; (2) the productivity of the relationship with a pre-exploited resource may be increased by either reducing the energy involved in exploiting the resource, or by increasing the productivity of the resource; and (3) the development of new man-animal relationships may permit, on one hand, localization or concentration of the animal resource near the area of human settlement, or on the other hand, allow human occupation in previously marginal or uninhabitable localities. Zeuner (1963) has also described numerous man-animal relationships which do not fall within the range of the definition of domestication, but which do increase man's efficiency in animal exploitation.

A second reason for the misleading nature of the question, "Why didn't prehistoric man domesticate sheep in North America?" is its processual viewpoint. Many man-animal relationships need never develop into a relationship of animal domestication; they need not be part of a conscious PROCESS OF DOMESTICATION. Finally, the question is misleading because it implies the singularity of the process of domestication. As Zeuner (1963) has pointed out in detail, there may be numerous paths to domestication.

Therefore, it is perhaps somewhat misleading to take the viewpoint from the END OF A PROCESS and ask, "Why didn't prehistoric man domesticate sheep in North America?" Instead, the viewpoint of ORIGINS should be taken, and one may ask, "What prehistoric man-sheep relationships did exist in North America?"; "Did these relationships afford man the opportunity to domesticate sheep?"; and, finally, "If so, why didn't man take advantage of the opportunity?"

GENERALIZATIONS

It is the first question, "What prehistoric man-sheep relationships existed in the New World?" which is the most crucial. It is also the most difficult to answer because of the nature of existing archaeological data. In the first place, there are no cultural indicators, such as particular tool types, which might be used to suggest the type or intensity of management of sheep prior to domestication. While grinding stones, manos, and types and frequencies of metates are often used to reconstruct the presence, absence, or degree of use of maize agriculture in the New World, there are no tools which are specific to the development of sheep management and which might, equivalently, be used to indicate such relationships. Only the faunal evidence, the archaeological contexts, and the cultural complexes and continua as a whole are available for study. These, however, are not sensitive indicators of the type or intensity of the relationship. Osteological changes in the social ruminants, for instance, do not become apparent until well after domestication occurs. Prior to domestication, not even the quantity of sheep bones found in the refuse may be used to suggest the type of social relationship, for large quantities of bone from one animal resource may result from selective hunting (Zeuner 1963: 59).

The seriousness of the matter becomes very clear when we take a modern example of experimental man-animal relationships. Wilkinson (1972: 108) has described an experiment in which European elk (*Alces alces*) were "attached" to a particular location by teaching them to associate the area with food. The tamed animals were exploited for their milk, but allowed to interbreed with their wild counterparts. This was a particularly profitable and stable arrangement, as the tame elk drew the wild elk to the man-made feeding ground, providing a continuing renewal of the stock of elk. It would take a shrewd archaeologist to unravel such a circumstance from the archaeological evidence.

In view of this lack of sensitive indicators which might be used to discover prehistoric man-sheep relationships in the New World, I began this study with a broad comparison of the habits and distribution of sheep of the Old World and the New in light of the location of prehistoric centers of early sedentism and domestication of plants. By doing so, I hoped to discover some of the significant variables in man-sheep relationships and in the processes which did, in the Old World, lead to domestication of sheep. The working assumption which I made in this comparison, as well as in the remainder of this study, is that the processes leading toward domestication of sheep were most likely to have occurred in those areas in which man was sedentary. As Zeuner (1963: 62) has concluded:

The advanced state of domestication, in which movement [and thereby the breeding habits] of animals was completely controlled by man, was clearly impossible in pre-Neolithic times, ... [while] man was moving with the animals. ... But to proceed to the stage of confining animals to restricted spaces, man would have had to change his economic system, for the sake of an experiment the outcome of which would have been extremely uncertain. It is most unlikely ... [he] would have ever been willing to do this.

There are several important differences in the distribution and habits of sheep of the New World and Old World which are immediately apparent. In the Old World the centers of early sedentism, plant domestication, and sheep domestication all occur in the same general area — the foothills and inter-mountain valleys of the Zagros and Tauros Mountains — which lies within the geographic distribution of that population of wild sheep (*Ovis orientalis*) which archaeologic, genetic, and systematic evidence indicates was the ancestor of domestic sheep (Nadler, et al. 1973).

In the New World the situation differs; the distribution of wild sheep does not now reach and never has reached the Mexican centers of plant domestication and early sedentism. *Ovis canadensis*, the American bighorn sheep, ranges south only into central Sonora, Chihuahua, and Coahuila, the northernmost of the states of Mexico (Figure 1). In the most

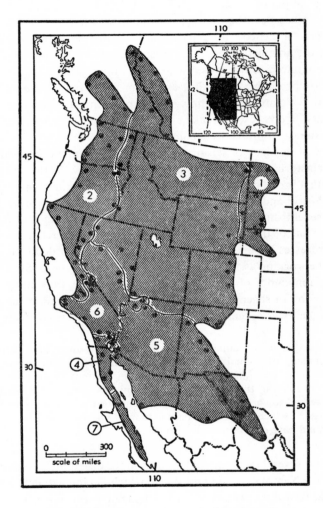

Guide to subspecies
1. *O. c. auduboni*
2. *O. c. californiana*
3. *O. c. canadensis*
4. *O. c. cremnobates*
5. *O. c. mexicana*
6. *O. c. nelsoni*
7. *O. c. weemsi*

Figure 1. Geographical distribution of the wild American bighorn sheep, *Ovis canadensis* (copied from Hall and Kelson 1959: 1031)

general terms, then, the possibility exists in the foothills and intermountain valleys in the Near East, where both hunting and gathering
were important subsistence activities in pre-agricultural and incipient
agricultural times, that the domestication of plants and sheep might have
developed, perhaps separately at first and then together, into a unified
economic system. In the New World, on the other hand, only sedentism
and plant domestication could develop together. Before the domestication of sheep became a possibility, plant domesticates, and the opportunity they offered for sedentary life, first had to diffuse northward, into the
home of the mountain sheep. But in pre-sedentary times the Cochise
lived in eastern Arizona, western New Mexico, and north-central Mexico
along the mountainous pathway by which plant domesticates diffused
northward. These Cochise were gatherers of plants and hunters of small
game, whose techno-economic system was pre-adapted only to the development of agriculture and not intensive social relationships with sheep.
The apparent lack of social relationships between the bighorn sheep and
those Cochise who found themselves in the pathway of the diffusing plant
domesticates made less likely the development of man-sheep relationships
which might have led to domestication.

Although this is a greatly over-simplified view of complex developmental processes involving diffusion and exchange of fragments of economic systems over discrete periods of time rather than diffusion and
exchange of economic systems as a whole, it does suggest the different
relationships between sedentism, plant domestication, and animal domestication in the Near East on the one hand, and in the New World on the
other. I will elaborate upon these processes and differences later.

While the American bighorn seems as SOCIABLE and is probably as tamable as the Asian sheep (Geist 1971: 41), there are differences in the
ECOLOGIC habits of the New and Old World sheep which suggest differing
opportunities for the development of social relationships between man
and sheep in the two continents. The sheep of southwestern Asia (Asiatic
mouflons) prefer open, rolling mountains and foothills. Within intermountain regions, they often follow the river valleys, not hesitating to
descend to the lower, rolling, open foothills to graze and drink (Clark
1964: 6). The American sheep, on the other hand, are generally (although
not always) found on higher, more precipitous mountains (Geist 1971: 4),
often above the timberline (Bailey 1931). One hypothesis (Geist 1971: 4)
for this difference is that in southwestern Asia, the goat (*Capra hircus
aegagrus*) occupies that ecologic niche of the more precipitous terrain.
Asiatic mouflons have seemingly specialized in the gentler terrain in the

face of this competitor. In North America, no serious competitors existed in the rocky zone when sheep entered the continent during the Pleistocene. They have, therefore, been able to exploit the niches equivalent to those of BOTH the goat and the sheep in the Old World. This difference in the ability of the Old World and New World sheep to use the more rugged mountainous zones may have resulted in a difference in the opportunities for the development of prehistoric man-sheep relationships on the two continents. In North America, when sheep were hunted, they could retreat into the more rugged country, just as they have in historic times, limiting man-sheep contact. In the Old World, however, sheep could not successfully withdraw into the more precipitous parts of the mountains as this niche was already filled by the goat. Relationships between sheep and hunters therefore had more opportunity to develop in the Old World. As economic dependence upon a hunted animal is one of the common bases from which more intensive social relationships are developed (Zeuner 1963: 15), this potential difference of opportunity must not be underestimated.

By the same line of reasoning, when human populations began to settle down and increase in number in the Near East, exploiting land and floral resources previously used by Asiatic mouflons, the sheep could not have withdrawn to the more rugged uplands. Sheep in the Near East, then, may have developed a symbiotic relationship with man, in which the browse of exhausted, fallow, and wintering fields was eaten by sheep, while man exploited them. In North America, however, sheep had the opportunity to retreat to the more rugged slopes.

Adaptation to different ecologic niches has other immediate consequences. The American sheep are superb jumpers and climbers (Geist 1971: 4). They are seldom found in areas where there is not, at least nearby, a cliff with broken face or talus slopes to provide a means of escape (Stone and Cram 1902: 63). When hunted, the American sheep run for precipitous terrain (Geist 1971: 4). In contrast, Asiatic sheep frequently wander away from the foothills into gentler country, and when hunted, will avoid the cliffs. This may have made New World sheep less desirable game for prehistoric man than other animals, such as deer and antelope, while in the Old World, sheep would have been more readily available. Again, the different potentials for the hunting of sheep in the New and Old World must be recognized as a significant difference in opportunities for the development of more intensive man-sheep social relationships.

The different ecological adaptations of sheep in the New and Old Worlds are also revealed in the different manners in which the New and Old World ewes bear their young. The ewes of Asiatic mouflons bear their lambs in open terrain or near rock piles in open landscape. They have multiple births (Geist 1971: 242). Under these conditions, the capture of a lamb is easy. In North America, ewes choose rugged cliffs as places to have their lambs, and normally bear only one lamb at a time (Geist 1971: 242), allowing less opportunity to capture the young. As it is the young, as opposed to adult, animals which are usually more easily tamed, these behavioral and biological differences further suggest the greater opportunity prehistoric man in the Old World had to develop social relationships with wild sheep.

While these differences in the ecologic behavior of the American bighorn and Asiatic mouflons do suggest differences in OPPORTUNITIES for the development of social relationships between man and sheep in the New and Old Worlds, they need not lead to a difference in the development of these relationships. Whether these ecologic variables are SIGNIFICANT FACTORS in the development of man-sheep social relationships depends on their systemic integration with a number of other ecologic and cultural variables. The desirability of a food resource for a man is weighed against the availability of all OTHER potential food resources IN HIS LOCAL ECOSYSTEM, rather than against the availability of that SAME food resource IN ANOTHER MAN'S ECOSYSTEM. Furthermore, differences in the orientation of cultural systems — toward hunting or gathering — may make the availability of plant or animal resources more or less significant. For instance, during pre-agricultural times in the Near East, where hunting as well as gathering was an important subsistence activity, animals were hunted in both rugged and gentle terrains (Perkins 1964; Braidwood, et al. 1971). In the drainage of the Upper Little Colorado River during pre-agricultural times however, the Cochise, whose economic system was oriented more toward gathering plants than hunting, do not seem to have exploited game resources in the more rugged uplands. The significance and the effect of the ecologic behavior of the New World sheep upon opportunities for the development of man-sheep social relationships, then, must be considered in the light of the ecology of local plant and animal communities and the orientation of particular cultural systems, rather than alone.

The idea should not be formed, moreover, that the niches occupied by sheep in North America and southwestern Asia do not overlap, for they do. The difference is simply that the range of the sheep in the New World extends to higher, more rugged terrain than does that of the Asiatic mouflons. Before the advent of the white hunter, mountain sheep in North America inhabited not only the higher, more rugged regions of many of the ranges of mountains in western North America (Hall and Kelson 1959: 1031) but were also found on the foothills or lower, where-ever some rugged terrain exists, such as in Death Valley, California (Welles and Welles 1961), or northwestern Nebraska (Jones 1951). In the 1880's, sheep were still plentiful in the Dakota badlands (Wister 1904: 167). Further west in the Wyoming badlands between the Yellowstone, Missouri, and Powder valleys, Lydekker (1898) reported that flocks of sheep:

... seek the prairie to feed at daylight, returning to the badlands at ten o'clock to rest until the afternoon, when they will again rise to feed among the badlands, often returning to the prairies in the evening and grazing until dark...

Wister (1904: 176) wrote of the sheep in Wyoming in the 1880's:

They had not taken to the peaks exclusively then; the great tableland was high enough for them. I very well recall a drive in July, 1885, when, from the wagon in which I sat, I saw a little band of them watching us pass in a country of sage brush and buttes so insignificant as not to figure as hills upon a map. That was between Medicine Bow and the Platte River.

In the more mountainous regions, such as Yellowstone, Wister has reported (1904: 199) that the bighorn once occupied the full altitudinal range, from the sage brush and cottonwood country, up through the pines and quaking aspen, onto the high, wet meadows and the willow brush country, and finally reaching above the timberline. Bighorn sheep are still found today on the low isolated mountain ranges of southwestern Arizona (Haury 1950: 27), where they are easily hunted (Bailey 1931: 18–20).

Today, at various times of the year, depending on local conditions of weather, terrain, and flora, bighorn sheep will come down from the more rugged heights into which they have fled in historic times. Most usually in winter and early spring, when browse becomes scarce in the upland pastures, either from over-grazing or from hardening of snows over the grasslands, the sheep may come down to the lower, evergreen-forested slopes, where snow is soft and they can dig for food. In these soft snows, however, the sheep are also defenseless against capture (Bailey 1931), just as are the newborn lambs of Asian ewes, out in the open terrain.

Bighorn sheep in the more mountainous regions of North America may also migrate down through the lower conifer-forested life zones in order to move from patches of grassland on the upslopes of one mountain to patches of grassland on the upslopes of the next. During the warmer and drier Altithermal, these high-elevation grassland habitats on the upslopes once formed a much more continuous belt between mountain peaks. When the climate became cooler and moister, however, brush and forests spread along the intermountain valleys and ascended the mountains, dividing the habitats of the sheep into smaller, isolated patches at the higher elevations. As this process occurred slowly, sheep continued their normal movements between mountains through the valleys, despite the fact that these latter were not a part of the bighorn's preferred habitat (Geist 1971: 125). These intermountain treks are predictable, and could have been utilized by prehistoric New World hunters.

There are not, then, any hard and fast generalizations that can be made concerning the different degrees of opportunity for the development of man-sheep relationships in the New and Old Worlds in terms of the ecology and behavior of the sheep. The degree to which the geographical distribution of sheep and prehistoric man overlapped in the New and Old World depended upon LOCAL CONDITIONS OF TERRAIN, WEATHER, AND FLORA. Furthermore, my generalizations of the differences in the geographic distribution of sheep in relation to the prehistoric centers of early sedentism, plant domestication, and animal domestication in the New and Old Worlds are only the most general of guides to the significant variables in LOCAL CULTURAL PROCESSES. To answer the question, "What prehistoric man-sheep relationships existed in the New World?" we must look for answers in terms of local ecological and cultural systems, not interregional, average situations which smooth out the significant variations in opportunities for the development of social relationships between man and sheep.

STRATEGY

As it was in the Greater Southwest that sedentary man and mountain sheep first had a chance to associate in North America, I have concentrated my survey of the different types of man-sheep relationships which might have existed in the New World in this smaller area. Even here, however, prehistoric man associated with sheep in a great variety of environments and at different times, during which numerous different cultural processes were at work (Haury 1950; Aikens 1970; Marwitt 1968; Lister 1966; Jennings 1966). Moreover, not only are the situations in which sedentary prehistoric man DID hunt or associate with sheep important, but also those situations in which he DID NOT. As all these different possibilities create multiple variables, it was important to design a research strategy which would narrow the survey to an examination of those local conditions in which the opportunities for the development of man-sheep relationships were the best, yet which also included a variety of cultural and environmental conditions.

If we are to answer the question, "Why didn't prehistoric man in the New World domesticate sheep if man-sheep relationships did exist in the New World?" a logical place to begin to look for man-sheep relationships which could have led to the domestication of sheep is in those areas in which a closed ecological system existed. Only in these areas could a system of positive feedback exist in which greater exploitation of resources would result in a continual decrease in resources, and increased demand for more intensive management of those resources or the seeking out of new resources.

The division of the Greater Southwest into those regions in which plant and animal ecosystems tend to be closed and those regions in which plant and animal ecosystems tend to be open somewhat parallels the basic geomorphic division of the region into the Colorado Plateau (eastern Utah, western Colorado, northern Arizona, northern New Mexico) and the Basin-and-Range Provinces (Nevada, western Utah, southern Arizona, southern New Mexico, northwestern Mexico). The Colorado Plateau is composed of a series of high mesas and plateaus with streams entrenched in canyons, as well as numerous mountain chains with intermountain valleys. Each canyon bottom, each high mesa surrounded by cliffs (often of slick rock), and each intermountain valley tends to form an individual closed system. Floral and faunal resources in each situation are limited in amount, making over-exploitation an ever-present possibility. As Jennings (1966: 18) has pointed out in reference to the region of Glen Canyon, had man subsisted mainly on the larger game in the canyon bottoms, the limited population of each canyon in the area would soon have become depleted or dispersed. The same would have applied to isolated high mesas and smaller intermountain valleys with closed ends.

The Basin-and-Range Provinces, on the other hand, are composed of a series of isolated, parallel, north-south mountain ranges, separated by desert basins. Each local region tends to constitute an open system, in which floral and faunal resources could have flowed into the area from adjacent locales as man drained them. The exception to this situation is the intermountain valleys in the more rugged terrains, such as those of east-central Arizona and west-central New Mexico.

In light of these differences in ecosystems in the Greater Southwest, and considering the different roles which man in the various regions of the Greater Southwest has played in the beginnings of agriculture and sedentism north of the nuclear Mexican region, I chose three areas in which to investigate man-sheep relationships: the intermountain valleys of the

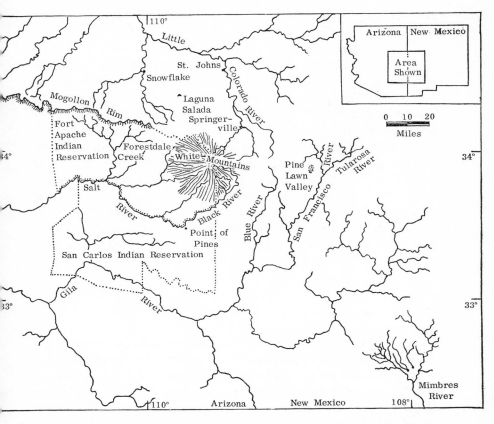

Figure 2.   East-central Arizona and west-central New Mexico (adapted from Haury 1940: 11)

northern portion of the Mogollon Culture Area, in east-central Arizona and west-central New Mexico (Figure 2); the canyon and plateau regions of the Anasazi Culture Area, in south-central Utah (Figure 6); and the intermountain valleys and canyon-and-mesa country of the Fremont Culture Area, in the northeastern two-thirds of Utah (Figure 6). These areas provide the opportunity to compare a number of different relationships between sedentism, agriculture, local environment, and the social relations between man and sheep.

EAST-CENTRAL ARIZONA AND WEST-CENTRAL
NEW MEXICO: THE TRANSITION TO SEDENTISM

One basic but important difference between the prehistory of man in the mountainous regions of the Mogollon Culture Area on the one hand, and in the Anasazi and Fremont Culture Areas on the other, is the role he played in the northward spread of agriculture and sedentism. North of the nuclear Mexican centers, agriculture and sedentism first appeared in the mountainous regions of the Mogollon area. These uplands, then, became a secondary center of dispersal of the new ways of life to those areas — the "frontier environments" of the Anasazi and the Fremont Culture Areas — which were environmentally unsuitable for incipient maize agriculture. As I shall reveal when the prehistories of the three areas are examined in terms of opportunities for the development of social relationships between prehistoric man and sheep, this distinction is crucial.

Environment

The environment of east-central Arizona and west-central New Mexico falls into two regions (Figure 2). To the north of the Mogollon is the Colorado Plateau, drained by the upper reaches of the Little Colorado River. To the south of the rim is a vast mountainous region dissected by the Black, Blue, San Francisco, and Tularosa Rivers, all of which flow into the Gila River.

In east-central Arizona and west-central New Mexico, I have chosen two areas in which to analyze the opportunities for the development of man-sheep relationships in terms of cultural history and local environment: (1) the region of Pine Lawn Valley of the San Francisco drainage, near Reserve, New Mexico, south of the Mogollon Rim; and (2) the canyon of the Upper Little Colorado River and the plateau to the west of it, in the region of Snowflake, Arizona, north of the Mogollon Rim. In both regions, Paul S. Martin and John B. Rinaldo have been the major contributors to archaeological research, with William A. Longacre also working on the project in the Upper Little Colorado River. For supplementary data, several reports are available on sites in the region of Point of Pines of the Black River drainage, on the San Carlos Apache Reservation (Wendorf 1950; Wheat 1954), and in Forestdale Valley, drained by a tributary of the Black River, on the Fort Apache Indian Reservation (Haury 1940; Haury and Sayles 1947). Dick's report (1965) on Bat Cave, near the plains of San Augustin, was also used. All of these secondary areas are south of the Mogollon Rim.

Pine Lawn Valley (Figure 2) is a valley, 4.8–6.4 kilometers wide and 16 kilometers long, between the San Francisco Mountains (to the west) which rise to an elevation of 2,740 meters above sea level, and the Saliz Mountains (to the east) which rise to 2,280 meters above sea level. The floor of Pine Lawn Valley, which ranges from 1,830 to 2,130 meters in elevation, is drained by a network of intermittent streams in deep, narrow canyons which flow into the San Francisco River, east of the Saliz Mountains. From the surrounding mountains, ridges extend onto the valley floor. In places, these extensions have precipitous cliffs, but otherwise descend more gently to the valley floor. At their bases, springs may be found. The San Francisco River, itself, has a floodplain — 1.2 to 1.6 kilometers in width — near Pine Lawn Valley, but becomes hemmed in by mountains to the south for 16.0 kilometers before reaching more open country. To the north of Pine Lawn Valley, the San Francisco River becomes entrenched in a deep canyon. Along the length of the San Francisco River, overlooking the valley floor, ridges and mesas 30 to 60 meters high extend from the surrounding mountains. Branching from the San Francisco River to the northeast of Pine Lawn Valley is the Tularosa River, which is entrenched in a canyon with fairly gently sloping walls.

While the region of Pine Lawn Valley is structurally composed of horizontal strata and is therefore classified as a part of the Colorado Plateau Province, its landforms are actually transitional between those of the Colorado Plateau and those of the Basin-and-Range Provinces. Both canyons and wider, inter-mountain valleys characterize the region.

Ecologically, the region of the Pine Lawn Valley falls into the Transitional Life Zone. On the valley floors of the San Francisco and Tularosa Rivers and their tributaries are found yucca, cholla, prickly pear, beeweed, sage, poppy, thistle, and numerous wild grasses. Cottonwoods occur along the more permanent streams. The tops of the mesas and ridges which extend into the valley are covered with low grasses and open forests of pinyon, juniper, and yellow pine. The pinyon and juniper may line the edges of the mesas and ridge tops which overlook the streams, while the yellow pines extend up the higher slopes of the mountains to their tops. Other, less frequent vegetation in the region includes currants, gooseberry, mesquite, and oak. The mammals found today in the Pine Lawn Valley region include mule deer, white-tailed deer, black bear, rabbit, tree squirrel, chipmunk, prairie dog, and woodrat; common game birds are wild turkey, quail, and dove. In addition, the remains of mountain sheep, wapiti, bison (probably obtained in the more open country to

the south), American antelope, lynx, coyote, fox, muskrat, ground squirrel, and skunk have been found in the archaeological sites in the area.
(The above description of the topography and environment is a compilation from Martin 1940, 1943, 1947; Martin, et al. 1949, 1950, 1952, 1956,
and the United States Geological Survey topographic maps of the area.)

While bighorn sheep are no longer found in the region of the Pine
Lawn Valley, they appear to have been plentiful during the mid-1800's.
When a beaver trapper, J. O. Pattie, made a trip down the San Francisco
River at that time, he wrote in his journal that the walls of the high and
rugged mountains surrounding the San Francisco River were occupied by
"multitudes of mountain sheep" (Pattie 1930). As the diet of mountain
sheep in the southern portion of their geographic range in North America
consists mostly of browse, and considering Pattie's remark, it is most
probable that the sheep which once inhabited the Pine Lawn Valley preferred the more open-forested, lower slopes of the mountains, the ridge
and mesa extensions into the valleys and canyons, and possibly the valleys and canyons themselves. As Clark (1964: xvi) remarked from a
hunter's viewpoint:

...the best places to look for the really big rams are in the hidden basins high
up in the mountains. These are usually in the form of an amphitheater surrounded by rock walls, ... through which a small stream drains the area ... Sheep are
often found resting right in the center of them.

Very similar to Pine Lawn Valley is Forestdale Valley, in the Fort
Apache Indian Reservation. Like Pine Lawn Valley, Forestdale Valley is
geomorphically transitional between the Colorado Plateau and the Basin-
and-Range Provinces. It is only 6.4 kilometers from the Mogollon Rim.
The valley, drained by the Forestdale Creek, a branch of the Black River
(Figure 2), is only about 300 meters wide, with near-vertical bluffs, 50
meters high, separating the floodplain from the uplands. Springs occur
along the base of the bluffs. With an elevation of some 1,980 meters,
Forestdale Valley, like Pine Lawn, falls within the Transitional Life Zone.
The valley floor is dotted with juniper and clumps of oak and walnut.
On the bluff tops are various grasses, live oak, pinyon, juniper, and dense
clumps of manzanita. On the hillslopes are found dense stands of yellow
pine, with some juniper and manzanita. The animals reported for Forestdale Valley include deer, wapiti, black bear, coyote, porcupine, rabbits,
and turkey (Haury 1940; Haury and Sayles 1947). I found no reports of
sheep explicitly within Forestdale Valley. The similarity of Forestdale
Valley to Pine Lawn Valley, however, suggests that probably at one time
sheep also inhabited this region.

Farther south from Pine Lawn and Forestdale Valleys, but still within the transitional zone between the Colorado Plateau and the Basin-and-Range Provinces, is Bat Cave (Figure 5). The cave is located in the cliffs of the Pelona Mountains, on the edge of the plains of San Augustin, a closed basin, 96 by 32 kilometers, surrounded by mountains. The elevation of the plains is approximately 2,140 meters, while the surrounding mountains rise another 300 to 610 meters. The basin bottom is covered with salt brush, while stickseed, stickleaf, paint brush, and mock penny-royal form a heavier cover on the lower mountain slopes around the basin. Shrubs grow on the rockier terraces, while in the canyons and arroyos which flow into the basin, other herbaceous plants are found. From 60 meters above the basin to the surrounding mountain tops, open forests of pinyon and juniper predominate. Grasses form a continuous groundcover in this microenvironment, with herbaceous plants and cacti occurring sporadically. The present fauna around Bat Cave is not reported by Dick (1965), but the remains of mammals recovered from the excavation of the cave included mountain sheep, bison, deer, antelope, wapiti, wolf (?), badger, porcupine, jack rabbit, cotton-tail rabbit, pocket gopher, and woodrat (Dick 1965: 90–91). All parts of the full altitudinal range in the area of Bat Cave could have been equally exploited by sheep, although the open-forested mountain slopes and canyons may have been preferred for their herbaceous plants.

In contrast to Pine Lawn and Forestdale Valleys is the region of Point of Pines (Figure 4), south of the Black River and Forestdale Valley, and the upper reaches of the Little Colorado, north of the Mogollon Rim. Point of Pines lies in the gently rolling prairie between the Nantack Plateau on the south, west, and north, and the Prieto Plateau on the north and east. The Nantack Plateau, a southward extension of the White Mountains, drops to the prairie in a fault scarp. To the northwest of the grassland is the entrenched Black River. A grassland (predominantly of blue grama), 16 by 19 kilometers, occupies the area between the plateaus and the canyons at an elevation of 1,890 meters; clumps of juniper, oak, and pine are scattered throughout the grassy flats. Interfingering with the prairie are ridges which extend from the Nantack Plateau and which rise to a general level of 2,140 meters. These ridges are heavily forested with juniper, pinyon, live oak, yellow pine, and isolated Douglas fir. In the canyon bottoms of the Black River are walnut and manzanita, while on the alluvial land along the bases of the ridges occur sumac, prickly pear and other cacti, thistle, poppy, and beeweed. The current fauna reported for the area include American antelope, deer, bear, peccary, rabbit, porcupine, badger, coyote, gopher, and turkey. Bison also occurred in the

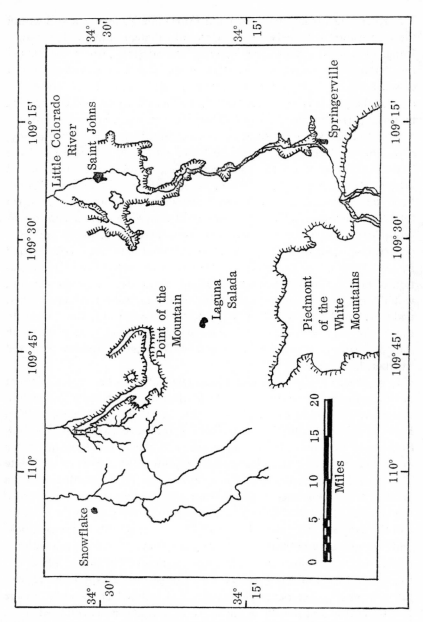

Figure 3.   Upper Little Colorado drainage, east-central Arizona (adapted from Martin, et al. 1964: 202)

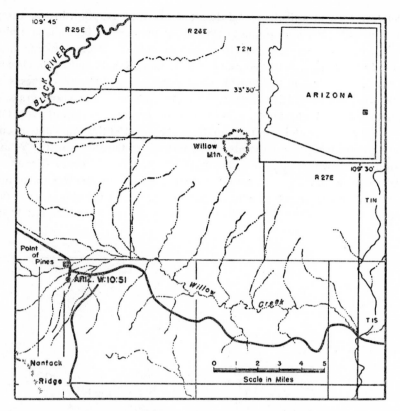

Figure 4. Region of Point of Pines, east-central Arizona (copied from Wendorf 1950: 13)

site refuse (Wendorf 1950; Wheat 1954). If sheep did occur in this region at one time, they most probably would have preferred the lower grasslands and alluvial terrain around the base of the plateaus, rather than the higher, heavily forested plateaus.

Similar to the region of Point of Pines, but north of the White Mountain Range, are the upper reaches of the Little Colorado, near Saint Johns, Arizona (Figure 3). This area is a gently rolling section of the Colorado Plateau, with the piedmont of the White Mountains to the south and southwest, the entrenched canyon of the Little Colorado to the east, and the "Point of the Mountain" mesa to the northwest. The region consists of four ecozones, only the highest of which falls within the Transitional Life Zone, the other three lying in the Upper Sonoran Life Zone. Along the edges of the entrenched Little Colorado River, which alternates between having broad alluvial valley bottoms and narrow bottoms between canyon walls, is found desert scrub, such as rabbit brush, along with prickly pear and grama grass. Above the canyon bottoms is a plateau which has been extensively eroded by now-dry stream systems into broad, flat valleys. A few lakes, such as Laguna Salada and Little Ortega Lake, are spotted on the plateau. On this plateau and the lower mesas in the area, between 1,530 and 1,830 meters altitude, are short grasses, chenopods, and amaranths, with junipers occurring only sporadically. On the higher mesas and lower mountain slopes around the grassland occur pinyon and juniper woodlands, while farther up the slopes of the White Mountains, which rise to 3,360 meters to the south, occur forests of yellow pine and Douglas fir. The present fauna for this region is not reported in the literature which I have read, but in the refuse from the excavated sites of the Upper Little Colorado area occurred deer, antelope,

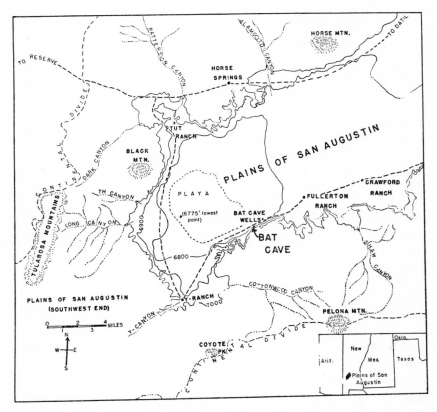

Figure 5. Topography around Bat Cave, southwestern New Mexico (copied from Dick 1965: 2)

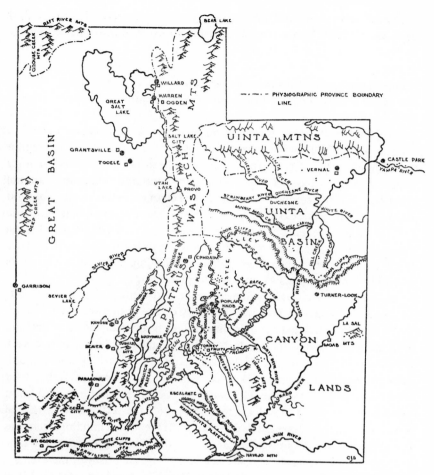

Figure 6. Topographic features in the region of Glen Canyon in the Anasazi Culture Area, and in the Fremont Culture Area (copied from Fowler 1963: xii)

rabbit, birds, and possibly mountain sheep (Martin, et al. 1962, 1964, 1967). Although there is no sure evidence that sheep inhabited this region in prehistory, the topography and vegetation are those characteristic of sheep country. Cockrum stated (1960) that in the past, wild sheep probably occurred throughout all of the mountainous regions of Arizona. If sheep did occupy the Upper Little Colorado area, their preferred habitats most likely would have been the lower mountain slopes and the rolling plateaus.

Having summarized the evironmental home of the sheep which once inhabited at least most of the above regions in east-central Arizona and west-central New Mexico, let us now introduce man into this setting.

Man, Sheep, and the Beginning of Sedentism and Agriculture in East-Central Arizona and West-Central New Mexico

After 9000 B.P. but before the spread of maize northward from Mexico, around 4000 B.P. (Mangelsdorf, et al. 1967: 4–5), the Mogollon region was inhabited by Desert Archaic food collectors, the Cochise (Haury 1962). These people exploited numerous, scattered, plant and animal resources, shifting camps with the seasonal changes in the location of food supplies. As it is the Cochise who, with the introduction of maize, made the transition to sedentism, and thereby developed the opportunity for the development of intensive man-sheep relationships, it is crucial that we know the extent to which these people relied upon sheep, and also more generally, upon animals as opposed to plants.

From present archaeological evidence in east-central Arizona and west-central New Mexico, we deduce that the Cochise in this area, both before and after the introduction of maize, relied heavily on plant collecting, with game animals — particularly upland game — playing only a very minor role in the economy. Of the large game animals which were hunted, deer, American antelope, and bison seem to have been preferred over sheep. Evidence of the orientation of the Cochise economy toward plant collecting is revealed in at least three ways: (1) the settlement pattern of the Cochise in the Upper Little Colorado; (2) the faunal and floral remains found in the Cochise sites of the area; and (3) the delay between the time of introduction of maize and the beginnings of sedentism in the area.

The results of the survey of Martin, Rinaldo, and Longacre (1962) in the drainage of the Upper Little Colorado have shown that Cochise camps in that area were scattered sporadically on the grassland plateau with NO evidence of camps in the forested piedmont of the White Mountains. Both shelters and open-camp sites were discovered. The open sites, which are three times as numerous as the shelters, are located on the shores of dry lakes on the plateau, on knolls in the valley systems which dissect the plateau, and on flat areas on the sides of the mesas, above the plateau. The shelters occur at the base of the mesas. Such a settlement pattern has suggested to Longacre (Martin, et al. 1962) that the open sites were temporary collecting camps used during the warmer months, while seasonal rounds were made between localized plant resources, and that the shelters were used during the winter.

Support for this hypothesis comes from the results of the excavation of two of the lakeside sites in the grasslands: Little Ortega Lake, and Laguna Salada; the latter has a radiocarbon determination of 5230 ± 60 B.P. (Martin and Rinaldo 1960). At both of these "beach sites," Martin and Rinaldo (1960) recovered manos and metates in large proportions compared to chipped stone debris. The faunal remains which were recovered from the beach sites were limited to one bone each of white-tailed deer, bison, and turkey; the bison would indicate the presence of some grassland habitats. The evidence derived from a palynological study at Laguna Salada (R. Hevly, in Martin, et al. 1964) indicates that this lake was surrounded by amaranths and chenopods, both of which produce easily gathered seed in large quantities; the easy availability of this and other foods may have attracted the Cochise to such lake shores (Martin, et al. 1964). That the resources around the lake were of importance to the Cochise in this area is shown by their continual reoccupation of the beach sites year after year (Martin, et al. 1962).

Culturally comparable to the beach sites at Laguna Salada and Little Ortega Lake is the Wet Leggett Site (radiocarbon determination 4506 ± 680 B.P., Martin, et al. 1952), a Cochise camp located on top of a ridge with arroyos on three sides, in Pine Lawn Valley. Here, too, large quantities of grinding stones were found, in proportions similar to the debris of chipped stone at the beach sites. From his analysis of the artifactual material at Wet Leggett, Martin concluded that during the Chiricahua horizon of the Cochise in Pine Lawn Valley, food gathering was probably the principal means of subsistence (Martin, et al. 1950a). No data on the Cochise settlement pattern in Pine Lawn Valley are available, however, to check this.

Faunal and floral evidence of the Cochise economy comes from three cave sites: Tularosa Cave, on the Tularosa branch of the San Francisco River; Cordova Cave, on the San Francisco River, 1.6 kilometers south of Pine Lawn Valley; and Bat Cave. The stratigraphic sequences for all three sites begin after the introduction of maize.

Tularosa Cave was occupied more or less continually from 2300 ± 200 B.P. (Martin, et al. 1952) to around 950 to 750 B.P., while Cordova Cave was occupied fairly continually from around 2250 to 1950 B.P., and intermittently after that, until around 1050 B.P. (Martin, et al. 1952). While no level-by-level report of the faunal and floral remains found in these caves is published, Martin, et al. (1956) have reported that for both sequences combined, a total of thirty-eight cubic cartons (each 35 centimeters on a side) of plant material were recovered, in comparison to only six such cartons of faunal remains. This flora-to-fauna ratio is probably signif-

Table 1.   Cultural sequence in the Mogollon culture area

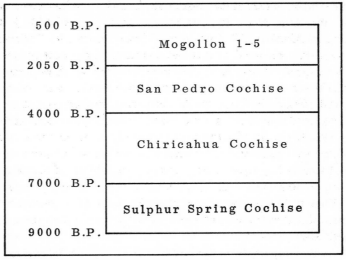

5 0 0 B.P.	
	Mogollon 1 - 5
2 0 5 0 B.P.	
	San Pedro Cochise
4 0 0 0 B.P.	
	Chiricahua Cochise
7 0 0 0 B.P.	
	Sulphur Spring Cochise
9 0 0 0 B.P.	

Adapted from Willey 1966:188.

icantly biased in favor of the faunal remains for the Cochise horizons, as, beginning around 1450 B.P., faunal remains occur more frequently. The high ratio of remains of plants as compared to those of animals found at Tularosa and Cordova Caves, despite their locations in a mountainous, game-filled environment, suggests the large degree to which the Cochise economy in east-central Arizona and west-central New Mexico was oriented toward the gathering of plant foods even when game was at hand.

The difference in the variety of remains of animals and plants at Tularosa and Cordova Caves also reveals this orientation. From the earliest levels of the caves, only the bones of deer, and apparently pronghorn antelope and muskrat, were recovered. Deer were by far the most common. This lack of variety in game, and the fact that the habitats of the deer and antelope occurred close to the cave entrances, suggests that only the easiest game at hand was hunted. Sheep are not among the faunal remains; this is not surprising in view of the greater difficulty involved in hunting sheep as compared to deer.

The floral remains, on the other hand, had great variety; no less than thirty-eight different species of wild plants were recovered from both caves. While over half of the bulk of the recovered floral remains from the pre-pottery levels of Tularosa and Cordova Caves were domesticates, including maize, kidney beans, squash (*Cucurbita pepo*), and bottle gourd, the wild plants came from a variety of ecozones, ranging from the canyon bottoms to the higher mountain slopes forested with yellow pine. The remains of wild plants included such foods as sunflower seeds, numerous pinyon nuts, a variety of grass seeds, walnuts, acorns, chenopods and amaranths, prickly pear, and the wild gourd. This range suggests that even though agriculture had been established, the plant-gathering economy of the earlier Cochise periods was still a major pattern of behavior of these people near the dawn of sedentism. Furthermore, the use of chenopods and amaranths at these caves strengthens the hypothesis that the Cochise at the "beach sites" were utilizing these grains.

The third site which yields evidence of orientation of the Cochise economy around plant collection is Bat Cave. The earliest levels of Bat Cave, in which domesticated maize, squash, and (slightly later) beans (*Phaseolus vulgaris*) are represented date to Chiricahua times. The people of the Cochise culture who used Bat Cave, like those who used Tularosa and Cordova Caves, were already relying upon agriculture to some degree, but continued to exploit a large variety of plants from a wide range of ecozones, extending from the bottom of the basin which the cave overlooks, through the pinyon and juniper forests. Fifty-eight species of plants were recovered, among which were edibles such as yucca, prickly pear, grass seeds, acorns, walnuts, juniper berries, and pinyon nuts. Amaranths and one species of *Chenopodium* were also found. Faunal remains occur only lightly throughout the Cochise levels of Bat Cave. In contrast to the great variety of plant resources utilized at the cave, the only large game animals represented are deer, antelope, and sheep. These only occur sporadically in the Cochise deposits, from late Chiricahua times onward. The distribution of the remains of the smaller animals over time is not reported (Dick 1965). In general, then, the faunal and floral remains from Bat Cave substantiate the indications of the strong orientations of the Cochise economy toward collecting of plant foods, indications which were suggested at Tularosa and Cordova Caves.

The third manner in which the heavy reliance of the Cochise economy upon collecting of plants is revealed is in the delay between the times of introduction of maize and the beginnings of sedentism in east-central Arizona and west-central New Mexico. For 2,000 years after the introduction of maize to the Cochise, no increase in the complexity of their culture or in the rate of cultural change occurred (Haury 1962; E. K. Reed 1964). Haury (1962: 115, 117) has explained this phenomenon by hypothesizing that before the introduction of maize to the Southwest, the Cochise may have practiced planting seeds of non-domesticated plants, such as chenopods and amaranths. Maize, then, would have been considered only one more plant added to the list of plants already cultivated. Whether or not the Cochise were actually cultivating before the introduction of maize, their economy must have been preadapted to an agricultural lifeway for the introduction of maize not to have stimulated cultural changes among them. This implies a considerable sophistication in utilization of plants by the Cochise, and their possession of a technology which was readily adaptable to the processing of introduced plant foods such as maize. The quantity and large proportions of ground stone artifacts among the assemblages found at the beach sites and Wet Leggett substantiate this viewpoint.

In sum, the present archaeological data on the settlement pattern of the Cochise, the faunal and floral remains they left behind, their stone technology, and the delay between the time of introduction of maize to the Cochise and their shift to sedentism, all suggest that the Cochise economy was heavily oriented toward the collecting of plants, not only for food but for other uses too. The large game animals which were hunted apparently were those that were more available and possibly more easily caught, particularly deer, as opposed to more evasive game such as sheep.

While sedentism affords the opportunity to intensify the management of animals, it is clear that in east-central Arizona and west-central New Mexico, the basis for such intensification was lacking: hunting did not constitute an important element in the economy of the pre-sedentary Cochise. From the Cochise plant-oriented economy, a sedentary way of life developed in which social relationships between man and animal — and particularly between man and sheep — continued to be, at best, of very minor importance. While the microenvironments utilized by man and sheep overlapped during the Cochise horizons and the initial periods of sedentism, man was busy gathering plants and hunting small game, rather than trying to catch sheep.

With a hypothesized increase in the yield of maize (Haury 1962), and the introduction of storage techniques and the idea of the pithouse (Martin, et al. 1964; E. K. Reed 1964: 178), farming villages began to develop at the end of the first millennium B.C. in the Greater Southwest. The earliest evidence of settled, village life is at Cave Creek (around 2250 B.P.), in the San Simon Mogollon Culture Area in southeastern Arizona (Willey 1966: 184). The earliest farming villages in east-central Arizona and west-central New Mexico date somewhat later: Crooked Ridge Village (Site Ariz, W:10:51, 1850? B.P.) in the region of Point of Pines (Wheat 1954), the Tumbleweed Canyon Site (around 1675 B.P.) in the drainage of the Upper Little Colorado (Martin, et al. 1962), the Bluff Site

(A.D. 287–318, dated by dendrochronology) in Forestdale Valley (Haury and Sayles 1947), and the SU Site (before 1450 B.P.) in Pine Lawn Valley (Martin 1940, 1943, 1947).

The continuity of the early village-farming economy with its Cochise base in east-central Arizona and west-central New Mexico is revealed by several kinds of evidence: (1) settlement pattern in the drainage of the Upper Little Colorado; (2) faunal and floral evidence from the excavated village sites mentioned above, and from Tularosa and Cordova Caves; and (3) artifactual data from these village and cave sites.

In the drainage of the Upper Little Colorado, clusters of two to four pithouses dating to the initial period of sedentism occur on the benches of mesa sides overlooking the grassland plateau, on knolls and ridges in the broad flat valleys dissecting the grassland plateau, and, to a lesser degree, on the bottomlands of the Little Colorado River and the edges of bluff-faced ridges extending into the valley (Martin, et al. 1962, 1964). While the bottoms of the Little Colorado provided good agricultural land for the early farmers in this region, the continued use of the possibly less well-watered lands of the rolling plateau suggests that the wild plant resources in this previously exploited microenvironment were still of importance. As during the Cochise horizons, the piedmont regions around the plateau do not yield any sites of camps or villages at this time or later. While agriculture was apparently gaining importance in the economy of these early farmers and beginning to replace, to some degree, the use of wild plant resources, exploitation of animal resources seems to have remained a minor activity.

This suggestion is substantiated by the faunal and floral remains recovered from Tularosa and Cordova Caves, and the excavated village sites. Until around 1450 B.P., the same large variety of wild plants from a wide range of ecozones is represented in the stratigraphy of Tularosa and Cordova Caves, while the quantity and variety of recovered game animals remain small, as in the Cochise horizons (Martin, et al. 1952). Despite the location of the twenty-three pithouses composing the Bluff Site in the heavily timbered environment of Forestdale Valley (which in later periods provided abundant game for pueblo peoples), very few non-human bones were found in the trash of this village. Most of the faunal remains were of deer, with a few antelope represented. The charred black walnuts recovered from the site suggest the continued exploitation of wild plants by these farmers (Haury and Sayles 1947). Similarly, at Crooked Ridge Village (Ariz W:10:51), located on one of the narrow, pine-forested ridges which extend from the Nantack Plateau and inter-finger with the adjacent rolling prairie, bone refuse was scarce. Only deer and turkey were represented in the remains, while walnuts and pinyon nuts and other unidentified seeds were present (Wheat 1954). Only at the SU Site in Pine Lawn Valley, located on one of the ridges which extend from the surrounding mountains onto the valley floor, were any variety of faunal remains recovered. Sheep, mule deer, white deer, lynx, coyote, domestic dog, turkey, jack rabbit, pocket gopher, rock squirrel and possibly sage hen were excavated from this site of 28 pithouses. The quantity of bone, however, is meager, with deer constituting most of the remains. Evidence of the continued use of wild plants in addition to agricultural activities is suggested by the charred hulls and seeds found in the refuse (Martin 1940, 1943, 1947).

The artifactual data from these early villages and caves also suggest the continuation of the Cochise technology, which was oriented toward the exploitation and processing of plants rather than animals. For example, at the SU Site (Martin 1940, 1943, 1947), most of the milling stones were of the type which are ethnographically known to be used for crushing and grinding wild seeds rather than processing maize. Mortars and pestles were also numerous. These tools, used primarily for crushing and milling seeds and nuts, greatly outnumbered all other tool types. The small number and heterogeneous, crude style of the projectile points indicated to Martin (1943) the lack of interest in hunting. Finally, out of a list of thirty-six traits for Cochise stone artifacts, thirty-five are represented at the SU Site. One-third of these traits occur at the beginning of the Cochise Culture. This retention of the Cochise technology is also documented at Tularosa and Cordova Caves.

In sum, the settlement pattern in the drainage of the Upper Little Colorado and the faunal, floral, and artifactual evidence from the early farming villages and Tularosa and Cordova Caves, all suggest a smooth economic transition in moving to a sedentary way of life in east-central Arizona and west-central New Mexico.

From the description of the microenvironments which the Cochise, and early village-farmers exploited in east-central Arizona and west-central New Mexico, and from a description and reconstruction of the microenvironments which the mountain sheep preferred in that region, it is apparent that the lack of the development of intensive man-sheep relationships once sedentism occurred was not the result of geographical factors such as non-overlapping habitats, but cultural factors instead. The Cochise and the succeeding early village-farmers did not take advantage of the opportunity to develop intensive man-sheep relationships once sedentism occurred because the cultural context in which sedentism arose was not oriented in a direction aimed at potential development of man-sheep relationships. Furthermore, the transition from a primarily plant-gathering economy to cultivation and finally sedentism was smooth, without pressures that might have caused the searching out of new resources. The sheep were at hand, and so were the opportunities to exploit them, but there was no need.

Possibly the behavior of the bighorn made them less easy to hunt than deer and antelope the few times that men did go hunting, as the bones of these latter game mammals occur in higher proportions in the sites of this time compared to those of sheep. With a sparse human population during the Cochise horizons and the periods of early sedentism, and in view of the small amount of hunting done at those times, probably the sheep would not have retreated permanently into the higher upland forests of this region, and abandoned the lower areas with browse, any more than they did before the late 1800's. Geographically, sheep must have wandered as close or closer to Cochise and early village sites than did the deer and antelope, which prefer irregular forests and open grasslands, respectively. Also the number of sheep which lived in east-central Arizona and west-central New Mexico during the Cochise horizons and the period of early sedentism was probably not significantly fewer than when Pattie traveled through the area in the mid 1800's. Sheep, then, may have been game which was less easily killed than were deer and antelope.

But while the preference of the Cochise and early village-farmers to HUNT deer and antelope over mountain sheep may be attributed, in part at least, to the relative ease of the catch, the lack of DEVELOPMENT OF MAN-SHEEP RELATIONSHIPS in east-central Arizona and west-central New Mexico cannot be so attributed. The fact remains that the economic orientation and cultural history of man at this time and this region of the New World did not provide either a fertile context from which man-sheep relationships might develop, or the pressure on man to search for new resources outside of that context.

Comparison to the Beginnings of Sedentism, Agriculture, and Domestication of Sheep in the Near East

In contrast to the man-sheep relationships and the processes which were involved in the beginnings of agriculture and sedentism within the geographical range of sheep in the New World are the processes of the domestication of sheep and the beginnings of agriculture and sedentism which occurred in the Near East. The difference between the prehistoric situation in the Mogollon Mountains and that on the flanks and in the intermountain valleys of the Zagros and Tauros Mountains seems to hinge on two or possibly three main factors: (1) the economic base from which sedentism arose; (2) the presence or lack of large, dense stands of gatherable food; and (3) possibly the presence or lack of pressure upon the economic system.

While the economy of the Cochise of eastern Arizona and western New Mexico was oriented toward the intensive use of plant resources with large game playing only a very minor role, in the hills around the Fertile Crescent both plants and animals — particularly the larger game mammals — were exploited just previous to the beginnings of agriculture and sedentism. The latest of the cultures of the Near Eastern Upper Paleolithic — Natufian, Zarzian, and others in the same period of time, that of the latest Pleistocene — had a strong economic dependence upon the hunting and use of all or many of the following: wild cattle, red deer, onager (half-ass), pig, gazelle, goats, and sheep (Reed and Braidwood 1960; Hole and Flannery 1967; Perrot 1968; Turnbull and Reed 1974). Of these the sheep, goats, pigs, and cattle were subsequently domesticated, and onagers were either semidomesticated or tamed for use. The gazelles, too, may for a time have entered into a closer association with man than that of merely being hunted (Legge 1972). The earliest record of domestic sheep — which is also the earliest record of a domestic ungulate — is at $10,750 \pm 300$ B.P. (barely post-Pleistocene) at Zawi Chemi Shanidar, northern Iraq, in one of the most rugged parts of the Zagros Mountains (Perkins 1964; Drew, Perkins, and Daly 1971); this open-air, semi-village site had a cultural overlap with the nearby Shanidar Cave, which had had a long history of peoples who depended upon the hunting of deer, pigs, goats, and sheep.

The prehistoric village of Çayönü in southeastern Turkey is probably the best illustration now known of the cultural transition from an earlier concentration upon the hunting of large mammals to dependence upon agriculture, the domestic animals being primarily sheep and goats (Braidwood, et al. 1971). The above survey could be extended, but all of the evidence indicates definitely that on the flanks and in the intermountain valleys of the Zagros and Tauros Mountains, man had already developed, prior to sedentism, a hunting relationship with large mammals, including sheep, which the Cochise never encouraged.

In addition to these two different economic contexts in the Near East and the Greater Southwest was a difference in the opportunities for settling down without the development of agriculture. Around the Fertile Crescent, massive dense stands of barley and almost pure stands of wild einkorn wheat provided large enough yields that it would have been possible, within approximately three weeks during the late spring or early summer, for a family to gather enough grain to provide staple food for a year (Harlan 1967). Dense stands of grains such as these do not occur in eastern Arizona and western New Mexico. For example, around Laguna Salada on the plateau west of the Upper Little Colorado River, grasslands are composed of wheat-grass (not a true wheat), grama, muhly, 3-awn, and galleta, interspersed with non-grasses such as sunflower, snakeweed, pinque, fleabane, goldenweed, zinnia, and aster. On the more sandy soils grow saltbush, sage, and Mormon tea, while shadscale and greaseweed are found on alkaline soils. Shallower soils are covered by Apache plum, diffrose, serviceberry, blackbrush, and squawbush. Only by the seeps and lakes do chenopods and amaranths grow (Martin, et al. 1964). While not all of the prairies in east-central Arizona and west-central New Mexico are this heterogeneous, large dense stands of plants with harvestable grains like those around the Fertile Crescent simply do not exist in the Mogollon Mountains. As a result, the people of the Cochise culture had to gather a number of less substantial, seasonal resources in different locales, and could not settle down until the introduction of high-yield domesticates.

The difference in the distribution of plant resources in the Mogollon Mountains and the Zagros and Tauros Mountains, along with the difference in the economic bases of the Cochise and the peoples around the Fertile Crescent, resulted in a difference in the order in which the processes of sedentism, plant domestication, and animal domestication could occur. In the Fertile Crescent, the existence and exploitation of dense stands of grains allowed sedentism to occur before the domestication of plants and animals. As both hunting and gathering were important in this region, it was possible, then, for the domestication of both plants and animals to develop at approximately the same times, although not always in the same places. Sheep were merely one, even if the first, of the ungulate domesticates. With this developmental sequence, the economic orientation toward both plant and animal resources was able to continue. In eastern Arizona and western New Mexico, however, sedentism occurred at least two thousand years after the introduction of plant domesticates. Not only was the economic basis of the pre-sedentary Cochise heavily oriented toward utilization of plant resources, but the long delay between the introduction of domesticated plants and the beginnings of sedentism allowed the integration of high-yield agriculture without offering the opportunity for the domestication of those few animals which were exploited.

A third factor which may have differed in the Fertile Crescent and the

Mogollon Mountains is pressure upon the economic system. Depending on whether Binford's, Flannery's, or Braidwood's hypothesis on the development of agriculture and the domestication of animals in the Near East (Meyers 1971) is correct, pressure on the economic systems of the peoples in the Fertile Crescent may or may not have spurred on the processes of domestication of plants and animals. It is apparent, however, that in eastern Arizona and western New Mexico, no pressure accompanied the development of agriculture. The transition between the gathering and collecting economy of the Cochise and the early village-farmers was slow and smooth. The Cochise were not forced to seek new resources outside of their heavily plant-oriented economic system, and as a result, were able to integrate high-yield agriculture into their pre-adapted economy without bothering with management of animal resources.

ECONOMIC PRESSURES IN EAST-CENTRAL ARIZONA AND WEST-CENTRAL NEW MEXICO

We must not overlook the fact that the manner of the transition between a moving and a sedentary lifeway which took place in east-central Arizona and west-central New Mexico, without the development of a man-sheep relationship, influenced the change in lifeways of peoples in other areas of the Greater Southwest. The early diffusion of maize northward from the Mexican highlands followed the higher elevations of the Cordilleran spine and found its lodging in eastern Arizona and western New Mexico (Mangelsdorf and Lister 1956; Haury 1962; Willey 1966: 183). At a later time squash, gourd, red kidney-bean and improved varieties of maize probably followed a path similar to the earliest maize and also found their way to eastern Arizona and western New Mexico. It was the peoples in the Mogollon Mountains, then, who dispersed these and other domesticated plants to the rest of the people of the Southwest (Willey 1966: 183). No intensive management of sheep or other animals ever developed in the Mogollon Mountains during the transition to sedentism; the idea of exploitation of animals was not among the elements which diffused to the Greater Southwest from the core dispersal center. In those areas which were occupied by peoples whose economic systems were oriented toward plant collecting and in which the people hunted sheep little or not at all, the process of the transition to sedentism which bypassed sheep domestication, in eastern Arizona and western New Mexico was continued with the introduction of domesticated plants.

After the beginnings of sedentism in the core area of the Mogollon then, the opportunities to domesticate sheep in the Greater Southwest were limited to: (1) those people who were hunting sheep when they received plant domesticates and settled down; and (2) those people who were already sedentary, including the Mogollon, but who found themselves in a situation in which the failure of some food resource to produce its normal yield or else a large increase in population resulted in pressure upon their economic system and the search for new resources outside of that economic system.

In the remainder of this paper, I shall focus on such possible pressures in three regions of the Greater Southwest: the Mogollon core area itself; the Anasazi canyonlands in south-central Utah; and the Fremont canyon-and-mesa lands and intermountain valleys.

In the midst of their smooth transition from plant collecting to agriculture, the Mogollon in east-central Arizona and west-central New Mexico were subjected to an economic pressure which could have led to more intensive social relationships with sheep or other, more frequently hunted animals, in the region. Beginning around 1450 B.P., as documented in Tularosa and Cordova Caves, the number of rows per ear of maize decreased from twelve to eight, with no corresponding change in size of cob or kernel being reported (Cutler 1952). The resulting decrease in maize yield would have put a fair amount of strain upon the Mogollon subsistence system, for at that time maize was an important component in their diet: one-half of all the floral remains at Tularosa and Cordova Caves from around 2250–1450 B.P. was maize (Martin, et al. 1952).

In response to this pressure on their economic system, the Mogollon shifted to more intensive use of these wild plants and animals which they had already been exploiting. At Tularosa and Cordova Caves, with the decrease in the number of rows per ear of maize, the proportion of wild plants compared to domesticates increased greatly. More intensive exploitation of a few wild plants from a single ecozone also occurred. Thistle, yucca, cacti, grasses, and wild gourds, all of which grew on the canyon floors below Tularosa and Cordova Caves, were the most numerous of the plants recovered at this time. The great variety of other wild plants from wide-ranging micro-environments were also exploited, however (Martin, et al. 1952).

The frequency of bones of hunted animals at Tularosa and Cordova Caves also increased in this period, with concentration remaining on the same few animals which had been exploited earlier: deer, and to a lesser degree, antelope (Martin, et al. 1952). In the refuse of villages, however, evidence shows that the variety of animals which were hunted was much larger. At Turkey Foot Ridge, located on a narrow ridge extending onto the floor of Pine Lawn Valley, bones were very abundant, and included in decreasing order of frequency, deer, jack rabbit, turkey, domestic dog, cotton-tail rabbit, pocket gopher, prairie dog, quail, elk, Canadian goose, bison, and woodrat. Bones of deer outnumbered those of all the other animals combined (Martin, et al. 1950b).

At Mogollon Village, located south of Pine Lawn Valley on a mesa top overlooking the San Francisco River, large numbers of bones were recovered from the refuse, including those from a variety of animals such as mule deer, antelope, bison, mountain lion, bobcat, coyote, gray fox, raccoon, badger, jack rabbit, cotton-tail, prairie dog, woodrat, pocket gopher, turkey, great horned owl, hawk, and mud turtle. Mule deer outnumbered all the other remains of animals by a proportion of three to one, while bison was represented by only one jaw (Haury 1940). At Harris Village, located on the floodplain of the Mimbres River (Figure 2), where ten-row maize was recovered, bones were abundant and included all of the animals found at Mogollon Village, and, in addition, the pocket gopher, dog, bear, and tortoise (Haury 1936).

While the decrease in the yield of maize in east-central Arizona and west-central New Mexico put pressure upon the subsistence system of the Mogollon culture and gave the Mogollon people the opportunity to develop more intensive management of animal resources, the response ran counter to the directions leading to animal management. Part of the pressure upon the Mogollon subsistence system was relieved by intensifying the use of a few wild plants in addition to collecting the large variety of other flora which had been exploited earlier. Pressure was also dissipated by intensifying the use of the previously exploited deer and by hunting a greater variety of small game. Thus the Mogollon were able to widen their economic base in addition to intensifying their use of previously exploited food resources, and consequently the intensive management of animal resources did not become a necessity. Without the over-exploitation and depletion of game resources in the relatively closed systems of Pine Lawn Valley, Forestdale Valley, the San Francisco Canyon, and similar regions, positive feedback mechanisms leading to management of game resources were never activated.

Why sheep were not hunted at this time is problematic. One of the striking features of the list of animals which were hunted immediately following the decrease in the yield of maize is the consistency of the species which were utilized, and the consistency with which sheep were not utilized. While the six site reports I mentioned above are the only ones which I studied from this specific time period and form only a small sample for such a large geographic area, the matter should not be over-looked. At Bat Cave (Dick 1965), where the Mogollon stratigraphy was not divided into fine units, mountain sheep occur sporadically from the San Pedro Cochise horizons to the surface (around 1000 B.P.). Mountain sheep were recovered from the SU Site, Pine Lawn Valley (Martin 1940, 1943, 1947), which dates to the period just preceding the shift in the Mogollon economy, and possibly at Carter Ranch (Martin, et al. 1964) in the Upper Little Colorado drainage, which dates to around 1000–800 B.P. As the remains of sheep are found in sites dating to periods of both low densities (before 1450 B.P.) and high densities of human population (after 1250 B.P.), retreat of sheep into higher, less convenient hunting grounds simply as a result of population increase can not explain this phenomenon. The one difference between the periods in which sheep do occur in site refuse and the period in which sheep do not is the intensity and range of Mogollon hunting. With the beginning of wide-range, more intensive hunting, sheep may temporarily have retreated to higher, more rugged ground, or dispersed to regions with fewer hunters. Only much more thorough analyses of remains of animals from Mogollon sites will reveal the exact circumstances.

In addition to the shift in the Mogollon economy, the decrease in the yield of maize also may have led to a greater dependence upon agriculture in the long run. In the drainage of the Upper Little Colorado between around 1450 and 1250 B.P., the locations of farming villages were changed from the benches of the sides of high mesas overlooking the grassland plateau to the well-watered floodplains of river valleys and locations near small streams. Occupation continued in the other areas having easy access to the stream bottoms, such as the knolls and ridges in the river valleys, and the edges of bluff-faced ridges extending into the valley (Martin, et al. 1964). In Pine Lawn Valley, the Mogollon people began to build their houses in locations closer to the bottom lands (Martin, et al. 1950a). These changes in site location were not the result of population pressures; seemingly only a slight increase in population occurred at this time (Martin, et al. 1964).

Possibly, however, with the decrease in the yield of maize at the beginning of this period, the Mogollon people of these regions, at least, may have tried to improve their techniques, land use, and the cultivation of maize in addition to shifting to more intensive use of the wild plants and animals. If this was the purpose of the change in settlement pattern in the Upper Little Colorado drainage and in Pine Lawn Valley, the experiment was apparently a success. Following around 1250 B.P., a rapid increase in population began in the drainage of the Upper Little Colorado. From the archaeological evidence, Martin has reasoned that there was, for the first time in this region, a shift in the social organization from kin-based bands to matrilineal clans having matrilocal residence and ownership of the increasingly important agricultural lands (Martin, et al. 1964). At Tularosa and Cordova Caves, the previously high frequencies of remains of animals and wild plants decreased to the level which had occurred before 1450 B.P. (Martin, et al. 1952). While some of the variety of animals and plants which the Mogollon had exploited in east-central Arizona and west-central New Mexico during the pressure period of around 1450–1250 B.P. continued to be utilized later, the amount of food which these resources provided was small compared to that provided by agriculture (Martin, et al. 1956, 1960, 1962; Bluhm 1957). In lieu of the decreased use of wild plants, there occurred a marked decrease in the frequencies of mortars and pestles, and an increase in the frequency of types of metates and manos more suitable to grinding maize (Martin, et al. 1950a, 1950b). The subsistence system of the Mogollon in east-central Arizona and west-central New Mexico was no longer under pressure, and the need for the development of intensive social relationships with sheep and other animals had been bypassed.

After around 950 B.P., the history of the Mogollon in east-central Arizona and west-central New Mexico is that of a complex system involving diffusion of cultural traits from the Anasazi of the north (Martin, et al. 1956), change in rainfall patterns (Schoenwetter 1962; Martin, et al. 1962), and the concentration of population into towns (Martin, et al. 1964). While it would be inappropriate to consider in detail the problems of such a complex time period within the context of this paper, a few points should be noted.

During the last few hundred years before the abandonment of east-central Arizona and west-central New Mexico, around 500 B.P. (Martin, et al. 1964; E. K. Reed 1964), the economic system of the Mogollon in this area was again under pressure. With the change of the pattern of rainfall from light summer rains to heavy summer "gully-washers" around 950 B.P., the agricultural system of the Mogollon apparently began to become unreliable. Beginning around 750 B.P., hunting increased slightly in the drainage of the Upper Little Colorado at sites such as Chilcott, Thode, Rim Valley Pueblo, and Hooper Ranch Pueblo. Maize, however, continued to remain the primary food source (Martin, et al. 1962), and the Mogollon clung to their agricultural lifeways, converging into larger towns on the few waterways left which still provided suitable land for agriculture. Why did the Mogollon not turn to wild animals and plants for food this time as they had earlier, around 1450 B.P.? Why did the Mogollon remain so committed to an agricultural system which was failing? Could it be that this time, the Mogollon relied upon the gods?

In conclusion, after the Mogollon in east-central Arizona and west-central New Mexico made the transition to sedentism, their economic system became stressed at least twice: once as a result of a genetically caused decrease in maize yield, and once as a result of an environmentally caused decrease in the yield of maize. These two circumstances provided a need for the Mogollon to seek outside of their prior, stable subsistence systems for new food resources. Among the options open to them was the development of intensive social relationships with sheep and other animals.

In the first situation, the Mogollon relieved the pressure from their economic system by intensifying the use of a few previously exploited wild plants and animals, by hunting animals not previously utilized, and possibly by changing their settlement pattern in order to exploit better their arable lands. For lack of archaeological indicators, the kind of social relationships which the Mogollon developed with their primary food animal, the deer, is unknown. The opportunity for the Mogollon to develop intensive social relationships with sheep at this time may have been restricted by the retreat or dispersal of the sheep from the more convenient hunting grounds.

In the second stressful situation, the Mogollon relieved a slight amount of the pressure on their subsistence system through an increase in hunting, at least. The Mogollon did not, however, relieve the greater portion of the pressure, for they clung to their prior, agriculturally based subsistence system. Intensive social relationships with sheep or other animals were not achieved. Because pressure upon their economic system continued to build, the Mogollon in east-central Arizona and west-central New Mexico were finally forced to abandon their homeland.

POSSIBLE ECONOMIC PRESSURES IN THE ANASAZI CANYONLANDS OF SOUTH-CENTRAL UTAH

Unlike the Mogollon region in its structural landforms, ecological systems, and prehistoric culture history is the plateau and canyon home of the Anasazi (Figure 6). The social relationships between the Anasazi and sheep, along with the possible stresses upon the economic system of the Anasazi, presented different opportunities for the development of intensive man-sheep relationships in the canyonlands than in the mountains of eastern Arizona and western New Mexico.

Environment

Within the greater canyonland region occupied by the Anasazi, the area of Glen Canyon in south-central Utah (Figure 7) has been chosen for analysis of the opportunities for the development of relationships between man and sheep.

The area of Glen Canyon is a section of the Colorado Plateau which is drained by the entrenched Colorado River and its tributaries. The region can be divided into three environmental zones: the riverine environment within the canyons, which lie below 1,070 meters in elevation; the slick-rock plateau beyond the canyon rim; and the higher, wooded plateaus, which lie between 1,370 and 2,140 meters above sea level. The bottoms of the canyons are covered with a wide variety of plants, including trees such as juniper, willow, oak, elm, hackberry, redbud, ash, and salt cedar; grasses such as grama, red top, cheat, salt, and bluestem; shrubs and herbs such as joint-fir, rushes, lilies, buckwheat, chenopods, poppets, jimson weed, legumes, cliff rose, and serviceberry; composites such as sage, rabbit brush, thistles, and sunflower; and cacti. The constitution of the flora varies between the wide main canyon of the Colorado River and its narrower tributaries. Mammals in the canyon bottoms include mountain sheep, mule deer, bison, bear, lynx, cougar, coyote, red fox, raccoon, ringtail cat, weasel, badger, and spotted skunk (Jennings 1966).

Above the canyon oases, little life is supported by the slick-rock plateau. The higher plateaus which catch heavier rainfall and which harbor springs, however, again provide a rich environment. The Kaiparowits Plateau (Figure 8) which lies just west of the Colorado River, provides a good example. Kaiparowits Plateau is eighteen miles long and lies mainly at an elevation of 2,220 meters, but rises at one point as high as 2,725 meters above sea level. The northern edge of the plateau is a sheer cliff which drops 790 meters to the Escalante River, a tributary of the Colorado River. Crosscutting the plateau are ten drainages which originate close to the sheer cliffs and downcut as they progress to the south. Covering the ridges between these canyons are open forests of pinyon and juniper interspersed with sage brush and rabbit brush. On the broader ridges and headwater basins of the canyons, only sage brush and rabbit brush grow. The floors of the canyons are covered with scrub oak, cacti, and yucca. In the wetter areas of the plateau, such as near the seeps and springs at

Figure 7. Topographic sketch of the region of Glen Canyon (copied from Gunnerson 1959: 3)

the heads of the canyons, aspen and yellow pine may be found (Fowler and Aikens 1963). Mammalian life on the upland plateaus such as the Kaiparowits is similar to but more numerous than that in the canyons and includes sheep (Jennings 1966).

The outstanding ecological feature of the region of Glen Canyon is its

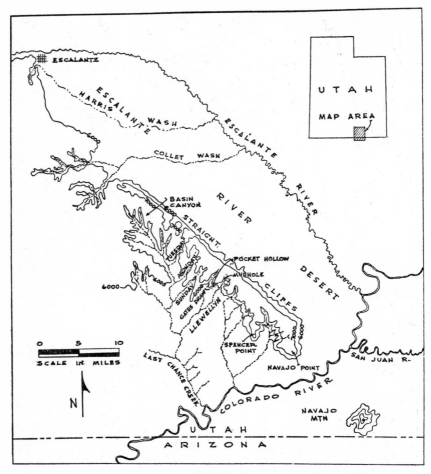

Figure 8.   Kaiparowits Plateau, in the region of Glen Canyon (copied from Fowler and Aikens 1963: viii)

division by the slick-rock plateaus into a number of isolated, closed ecosystems. Each canyon tends to remain a unit unto itself, and the canyons, in turn, tend to be separated from the higher, wooded plateaus. The only animals which venture across the slick-rock are birds, bats, and the large mammals, such as sheep and deer. The megafauna, however, in their seasonal migrations, travel between only specific canyons and mesas constituting their patchy range; they belong to a limited number of ecosystems rather than wandering freely between the oases. The environment in the region of Glen Canyon, then, is a rigid and fragile structure which could easily have been upset by prehistoric man's over-exploitation of particular resources (Jennings 1966), and therefore provided a mechanism which could have unleashed pressure upon the economic system of the inhabitants of the area.

Interpretations of Prehistoric Culture and Economic Pressures

The process of revealing pressures upon the economic system of the Anasazi in the region of Glen Canyon is deeply entangled in the interpretations of the prehistory of the greater Anasazi Culture Area. Since disagreements still exist over some basic issues in the prehistory of the greater Anasazi, and understanding of these disagreements is necessary for an evaluation of the economic system of the Anasazi in the region of Glen Canyon, I will first summarize the relevant data from the area without the overlay of interpretive frameworks which have been developed for the wider Anasazi Culture Area.

Prior to around 1050 B.P., occupancy of the region of Glen Canyon was spotty and discontinuous. During the culture periods Pueblo II and Pueblo III (around 1050–650 B.P.), however, numerous Anasazi from the Mesa Verde Culture Area to the east and Kayenta Culture Area to the south spread into and inhabited Glen Canyon and its tributary canyons (Figure 9). During their stay in Glen Canyon, the Anasazi farmed the canyon bottoms, locating their tiny gardens on the scattered patches of arable land. While domesticated maize, beans, and squash provided a major portion of their diet, the Anasazi also depended upon the numerous wild resources in the canyon. Wild amaranths, beeweed, sunflower, and prickly pear may have been cultivated, while other wild plants were gathered seasonally. A total of 110 species of plants (not all of which were edible) were recovered from the canyon sites (Jennings 1966). Wild animals also were utilized, including mountain sheep, deer, coyote, bobcat, ringtail cat, fox, beaver, badger, chipmunk, marmot, kangaroo-rat, woodrat, ground-squirrel, pocket gopher, birds, lizards, and fish (Lipe 1960; Sharrock, et al. 1961). The remains of the mountain sheep are most common, outnumbering deer, the second most common food animal, by a ratio of seven to one. While the quantity of non-human bones recovered from the canyon sites is small compared to the recovered floral remains, the relative importance of hunting to the economy of the Anasazi in the Glen Canyon region cannot be determined. Most of the canyon sites which were excavated were storage shelters for grain and were located above the canyon floor. Most of the dwelling sites in the canyon bottoms

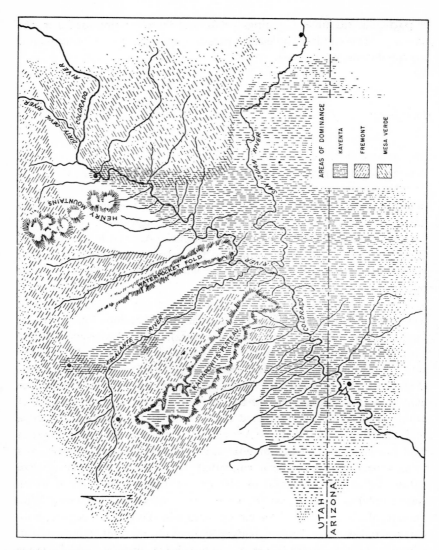

Figure 9.   Cultural divisions of the region of Glen Canyon, south-central Utah (copied from Jennings 1966: 37)

have been either buried or swept away by the aggrading and downcutting cycles of the Colorado River and its tributaries (Jennings 1966).

While the riverine environment zone of the area of Glen Canyon was occupied heavily throughout the period from around 1050 to 650 B.P., evidence of occupation of the high wooded plateaus does not begin until well after the Anasazi entry into the environmental complex of Glen

Canyon. Not until around 750 or 700 B.P. does Kaiparowits Plateau show any sign of occupation. Once habitation of the upland environments began, however, the population on the wooded plateaus reached and surpassed that in the canyons (Jennings 1966). On the Kaiparowits Plateau, more than 300 sites composed of architectural units, with one to five rooms, and located a kilometer to half a kilometer apart, have been found. All these sites are located in the sage-covered basins at the head of the canyons crosscutting the plateau, where seeps, springs, and arable land were available (Fowler and Aikens 1963).

While actual occupation of the high plateaus occurred late in comparison to the time of occupation of the canyon bottoms, the upland resources were tapped from the beginning of settlement in the area of Glen Canyon. Furthermore, travel between the high plateaus and canyon bottoms continued after the upland occupation. Evidence for these activities comes from several types of shrubs, such as mountain mahogany, which only occur in the uplands, but which have been found in the remains of sites in the canyon bottoms. Further indications of travel outside of the environment of the canyons are the numerous trails which lead beyond the canyon rim and onto the slick rock. Before the occupation of the uplands, the canyon dwellers may have hunted game on the high plateaus. The fauna was not only more numerous, but also less easily depleted on the larger, high plateaus than on the areally restricted canyon floor. "[The] canyons and the uplands were aboriginally a single ecosystem and... the aboriginal occupants of the area exploited the resources on this basis" (Jennings 1966: 30–31).

During the time of Pueblo II, a great increase in population occurred in the core region of Virgin, Kayenta, and Mesa Verde Anasazi. In the traditional interpretation, this increase in population was followed by an expansion of the Anasazi into marginal environments, such as Glen Canyon. From this viewpoint, the Anasazi who inhabited Glen Canyon were an overflow population pushed into agriculturally undesirable land from Mesa Verde and Kayenta (Jennings 1966: 35), and would have found themselves in an environment to which their agriculturally based subsistence system was not as well adapted, resulting in at least some pressure upon their economic system. As the economic system of the Anasazi in the Mesa Verde and Kayenta core areas previous to and during the expansion of Pueblo II had included hunting of game similar to that found in Glen Canyon, such as mountain sheep (E. K. Reed 1958; Lister 1964, 1966; Aikens 1966a), in addition to agriculture, these migrants could have supplemented their hypothetically less productive agricultural system with more intensive or varied use of wild resources. Among these resources were mountain sheep, the most common food animal found in the sites in the area of Glen Canyon. Here, then, is a situation in which a group of sedentary people, who already hunted and were familiar with mountain sheep, found their subsistence system under at least some stress. In circumstances such as this intensification of man-sheep relationships may occur.

While the pressure upon the economic system of the Anasazi in the areas of Glen Canyon and those adjoining could have been relieved initially through more hunting and gathering, such a solution may not have been a permanent one. With a fragile environmental structure in the area, and with more people moving into the canyons, over-exploitation of the ecosystems of the isolated canyons and plateaus may have resulted in new pressures upon the economy of the Anasazi which could not have been relieved only by more hunting and gathering. One way such a hypothetical pressure might have been dissipated was through farming of the uplands, which led to their occupancy late in the chronological sequence at Glen Canyon. The techniques necessary to farm the uplands need not have been different from some of those used in the canyons. On the Kaiparowits Plateau, for example, seeps and springs at the basin-heads of the canyons crosscutting the plateau provided water sources (Fowler and Aikens 1963) such as those which had long been used in the canyons (Jennings 1966). In this way, the need to develop more intensive man-sheep relationships may have been averted.

Whether such pressures did exist, however, is questionable. Jennings believed that:

... in Pueblo II time the Anasazi actually specialized in gardening in "marginal" areas, and ... by understanding water and its conservation and use [and the idiosyncracies of their crops], extended their domain into areas where neither then nor now is gardening truly feasible. This would leave the Glen Canyon dwellers not so much marginal as typical backwoods Anasazi — all of whom were working agricultural miracles in an environment which is today regarded as unfavorable for cultivation of crops without irrigation (Jennings 1966: 63).

From this viewpoint, the economic system of the Anasazi who entered the canyons was not under pressure, but blossoming. Why the Anasazi suddenly settled the upland plateaus 300 years after their entry into Glen Canyon, however, is left an unanswered question: "better climate, population pressure, colonizing zeal all are [reasons] variously invoked, but one cannot be sure" (Jennings 1966: 56).

The question of whether or not pressures did exist upon the economic system of the Anasazi who inhabited Glen Canyon will probably remain open until the pattern of the history of the larger Anasazi Culture can be untangled. Whether Pueblo II was actually a period of great population movements into previously unoccupied territories, or whether it was a period in which cultural traits were diffusing to populations which were increasing *in situ*, with only minor movements of populations by back-woods Anasazi, such as those who entered Glen Canyon, is not clear. The reasons for the late occupancy of the upland plateaus are also unclear. Opportunities for the development of intensive man-sheep relationships existed in the area of Glen Canyon; whether or not there was the need to choose between this and other options during times of economic stress, however, remains unsettled.

ECONOMIC PRESSURES IN THE FREMONT INTERMOUNTAIN VALLEYS AND CANYONLANDS

Inhabiting the northern two-thirds of Utah (Figure 6) and the adjacent portions of Colorado and Nevada between at least 1250 B.P. (Marwitt 1968) and 750 B.P. (Gunnerson 1969) were the Fremont; these people were horticulturalists who depended to a large degree on hunting as a secondary means of subsistence, plus considerable gathering (Aikens 1966b; Gunnerson 1969). The economic systems of these peoples differed from the Anasazi and Mogollon not only in the greater extent to which they relied upon game, but also in the precarious nature of their horti-culture in an environment which was a marginal habitat of maize. A setting such as this provides a fruitful context in which to look for pre-historic opportunities and needs for the development of intensive man-sheep relationships.

Environment

The Fremont Culture Area may be divided into three essential ecological regions: the mountains and intermountain valleys of the Wasatch Range and the fault-block ranges to the south, which run down the middle of Utah; the canyon-and-mesa country of the Colorado Plateau east of the Wasatch Range; and the Basin-and-Range Provinces, west of the Wasatch (Figure 6). Because the Basin-and-Range Province tends to be composed of open ecological systems, the Fremont in this environment will be excluded from this study.

The environment of the mountains and intermountain valleys of the

Fremont may be exemplified by Upper Round Valley, central Utah, in which the Fremont site of Pharo Village is located. Upper Round Valley is a basin, 5 × 11 kilometers, located within the Pavant Mountains, south of the Wasatch (Figure 6). The valley floor has an elevation of 1,830 meters while the surrounding mountains rise to more than 3,050 meters above sea level. Several perennial streams which flow from the surrounding mountains drain into a marsh in the basin. The valley is semiarid, with the western portion receiving more water than the eastern. On the western edge of the valley floor grows a mixed forest of willow, oak, and box elder. To the east, the vegetation grades into juniper and sage brush and then into sage brush with rabbit brush. The mountain slope on the east side of the valley is an almost vertical escarpment with meager vegetation, while the western mountain slopes are more gentle and have small clumps of scattered scrub oak. In the refuse of the site, the bones of mule deer, jack rabbit, cotton-tail rabbit, mountain sheep, coyote, pocket gopher, bison, marmot, rock squirrel, bobcat, bear, badger, prairie dog, beaver, striped skunk, red squirrel, porcupine, muskrat, and long-tailed weasel were found, in that order of frequency (Marwitt 1968).

The canyon-and-mesa region of the area of the Fremont Culture is drained by the entrenched Colorado River and its tributary canyons. Most of this area is either slick rock or covered with poorly stabilized sandy soils which separate the canyons and mesas into fairly isolated ecosystems. In the canyon bottoms, along the streams, grow cottonwood, willow, and a variety of herbaceous plants. Farther back from the rivers, shrubs such as salt brush, greasewood, rabbit brush, squaw brush, and yucca dominate. Shadscale and salt brush occur farthest from the streams. On the mesas and rolling hills above the canyons, pigmy forests of open pinyon and juniper interspersed with desert grasses prevail, while at higher, better-watered elevations, aspen and ponderosa pine occur. The fauna characteristic for the canyons and mesas include bighorn sheep, jack rabbit, cotton-tail rabbit, snowshoe hare, deer, wapiti, prairie dog, marmot, ground squirrel, pocket gopher, bison, woodrat, badger, coyote, beaver, and chipmunk, in that order of frequency as found in the Turner-Look, Old Woman, and Snake Rock sites combined (Gunnerson 1969).

In the intermountain valleys and the canyons and mesas of the Fremont Culture Area, maize horticulture is precarious today. The average annual growing season in the area is only 100 to 160 days. Of the 15–25 centimeters of precipitation which fall in the canyon-and-mesa country, and of the 37.5 centimeters, or less, of precipitation which fall in the higher intermountain valleys, only 65 percent falls within the growing season (Gunnerson 1969).

Fremont Economy and Economic Shift

The beginnings of agriculture and sedentism in the Fremont area are still obscured in the origins of the Fremont, who were the first sedentary horticultural people to occupy this environment. Prior to the time of Fremont occupation, the intermountain valleys and the canyons and mesas supported a scattered population of hunters and gatherers (Gunnerson 1969). Whether the Fremont Culture was a development *in situ* from these peoples (Jennings and Norbeck 1955), a manifestation of Virgin Anasazi who freely migrated north during the postulated expansion of Pueblo II (Gunnerson 1969), or, in part, a manifestation of the Great Plains Indians who migrated to the south and adopted many Southwestern elements (Aikens 1966b, 1970) is still unknown. Whatever its origin, the Fremont Culture had its roots in hunting-and-gathering peoples, and retained many of the characteristics of their economic systems.

"The Fremont never became irrevocably committed to horticulture as a means of subsistence" (Gunnerson 1969: 196); they always depended to a large extent upon the wild faunal and floral resources. While Fremont village sites in the intermountain valleys and canyon-and-mesa country hardly ever occur above 2,130 meters in elevation, at which point the growing season becomes too short for maize horticulture, throughout the Fremont area in the higher forests of pinyon and juniper occur numerous small hunting and gathering camps, of which the only evidence may often be a few flakes, a mano, or a metate. The Fremont exploited a number of animal resources (see above), of which mountain sheep and rabbits were the most common. Remains of animals occur abundantly in the horticultural village sites (Ambler 1966; Aikens 1967; Sharrock and Marwitt 1967; Marwitt 1968; Gunnerson 1969). West of the Wasatch Mountains around Great Salt Lake, the Fremont MAY have made seasonal rounds between their farmsteads (where they grew maize, beans, and squash) and hunting camps, where they subsisted upon migrating bison and waterfowl, along with chenopods, amaranths, and bulrushes (Aikens 1966b, 1967). Such seasonal sedentism may also have existed in the intermountain valleys and in the canyons and mesas (Gunnerson 1969: 136). Wild plants were also used by the Fremont to supplement their diet, although possibly not as much as were the animals. At Mantles Cave in the canyon-and-mesa country were found the seeds of Indian millet, pinyon nuts, lilies, wild sunflowers, chenopods, and juniper and the bulbs of lilies (Gunnerson 1969).

Agriculture may not have been a dependable means of subsistence for some of the Fremont in the higher intermountain valleys and in the area of the canyons and mesas. Evidence for this supposition comes not only from the abundant faunal remains found in the village sites, but also from the settlement patterns. Fremont villages and their associated farmlands at higher elevations nestled close to the mountain slopes where the air stays warmer at night and prevents frost, rather than occupying the valley bottoms, where the coldest air accumulates. By locating their farmlands in this manner, the Fremont may have been trying to extend their growing season a few extra, crucial weeks (Gunnerson 1969); presumably, a tight scheduling in horticulture was necessary to produce a fair yield at such higher elevations. During years of early winter, these Fremont may not have been able to produce their expected yields, and periodically may have had to exploit wild resources more heavily. The location of the higher Fremont villages in this manner cannot be attributed only to dependence upon mountain-slope runoff; at lower altitudes, where the growing season is longer, Fremont sites were not gathered by the edges of the valley bottoms but occurred along creeks in the valley bottoms (Sharrock and Marwitt 1967; Marwitt 1968; Gunnerson 1969).

While unexpected seasons of short growth were a continuing threat to the crops of the farmers at higher elevations, water supply was a critical environmental factor to the horticultural system of all the Fremont:

Throughout the Fremont area, there is relatively little land that would have received adequate natural subirrigation, and in most areas where Fremont sites are found, no such land is apparent. Thus, farming would have depended heavily upon some sort of irrigation or utilization of runoff (Gunnerson 1969: 134).

The use of ditch irrigation by the Fremont has been documented in widespread areas, from northeastern to central and south-central Utah.

In sum, the economy of the sedentary or semi-sedentary Fremont of the intermountain valleys and mesa-and-canyon country was approximately as dependent upon horticulture of maize, beans, and squash as it was upon hunting with some gathering (Gunnerson 1969: 136). The most commonly hunted game animal was the mountain sheep. Because of the marginal location of the Fremont in terms of length of growing season and water supply necessary for maize cultivation, the agricultural component of the Fremont economic system was fragile.

While their dependence upon sheep for food gave the Fremont the OPPORTUNITY to develop intensive man-sheep relationships throughout their history if they had so chosen, the NEED to develop intensive methods of exploiting animals such as sheep and also wild plants might not have come until late in Fremont history. Sporadically occurring short or dry summers may periodically have led to more extensive USE of wild animals and plants through increasing the frequency of hunting and gathering. "Since the Fremont area is precariously marginal as far as precipitation is concerned, it is reasonable to suppose that reductions in moisture so slight that they would not be obvious in the tree-ring record could [have affected] farming adversely" (Gunnerson 1969: 181). During such times of temporary stress, however, development of more intensive METHODS of using wild foods would not have been necessary. Long-term pressure upon the Fremont economic system which could have been relieved in one way by the development of more intensive methods of resource utilization did not occur until the end of the Fremont record. Between A.D. 1150 and 1166 and again between A.D. 1215 and 1299 (dated by dendrochronology), drought (Gunnerson 1969) or shifts in the rainfall pattern from winter-dominant rains with gentle summer rains to summer-dominant "gulley-washers" (Schoenwetter 1962; Jennings 1966) upset the delicately balanced horticultural system of the Fremont (Gunnerson 1969).

At the beginning of these climatic changes, the Fremont may have been able to respond to a decrease in the yield of maize as they may have done in other bad years, by hunting and gathering more frequently. As the conditions worsened and the length of time since the beginning of the climatic change increased, however, in the more heavily populated areas such as Ivie Creek (Figure 10a), Ferron Creek (Figure 10a), and Nine Mile Canyon (Figure 10b), more extensive hunting may have resulted in a depletion or dispersal of the game resources (Gunnerson 1969). Under these conditions, a simple increase in the frequency of hunting and gathering would not have relieved the pressure on the Fremont economic system. One of the options open to the Fremont in order to regain a stable subsistence system would have been to intensify the management of their game resources, the most commonly exploited of which was the mountain sheep.

Evidence for such pressures which could have led to more intensive social relationships between man and sheep comes from the Fremont's alternative solution to their problem. Unable to continue their farming, the Fremont apparently scattered out over the countryside (Gunnerson 1969: 182), exploiting environments which were less depleted of game.

The economic circumstances of the Fremont near the end of their way of life probably offered the most likely of all the situations which I have analyzed in this paper, in which intensive social relationships between man and sheep could have developed. Not only did the Fremont hunt

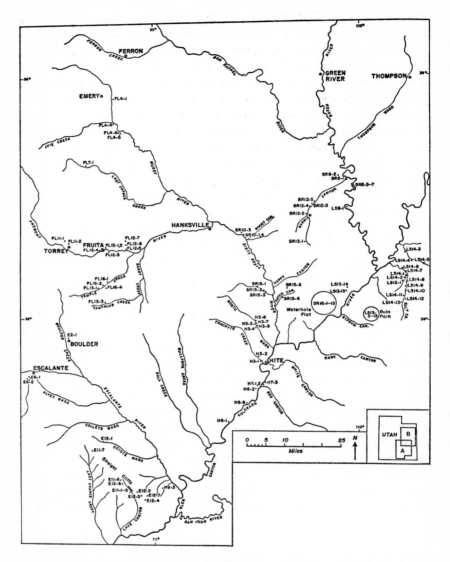

Figure 10a.   Location of Fremont sites in the canyon-and-mesa country, Utah (copied from Gunnerson 1969: 28)

mountain sheep extensively; they also were so little committed to their horticultural system that the solutions to their economic troubles, in the final analysis, could be found among their wild resources. While the Anasazi and Mogollon retreated southward during this period of climatic change to better-watered lands where they could continue to practice

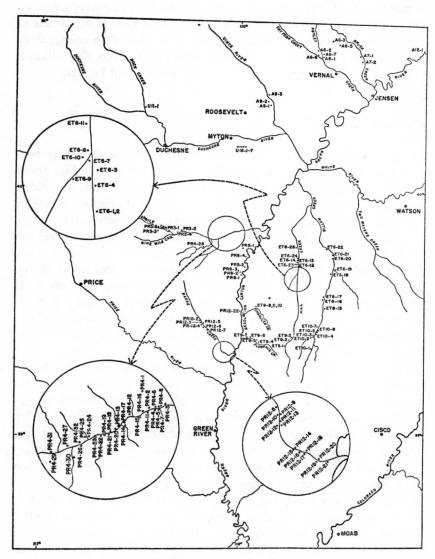

Figure 10b. Location of Fremont sites in the canyon-and-mesa country, Utah (copied from Gunnerson 1969: 29)

their agriculture (E. K. Reed 1964), the Fremont gave up their agriculture and turned to the resources of the wild animals and plants around them for help. Why the Fremont communities chose to break their social bonds and scatter over the countryside rather than look for new economic techniques to manage their game resources remains an unanswered question. Perhaps it was as simple a reason as a lack of the change of attitude of the Fremont towards the mountain sheep from that of an animal to be hunted to that of an animal to be managed (C. A. Reed, this volume). Perhaps they had never kept lambs as pets. One cannot be sure.

CONCLUSION

I began by asking three questions: (1) "What prehistoric man-sheep relationships existed in the New World?" (2) "Did these relationships afford man the opportunity to domesticate sheep?" and (3) "If so, why didn't man take advantage of the opportunity?" To the first question, it may be answered that in at least several areas of the Greater Southwest, sedentary agricultural peoples hunted sheep. The economic system of the Fremont even depended upon mountain sheep. In neither the Fremont nor the Anasazi nor the Mogollon Culture Areas, however, do I know of any archaeological evidence to demonstrate that sedentary peoples were doing anything more than hunting sheep. Not even a good case may be made for intensive, selective hunting of sheep, as would be indicated by large quantities of bones of sheep with few bones of other animals in these areas, let alone incipient management of sheep.

Prehistoric man in the Greater Southwest did have opportunities to develop intensive social relationships with mountain sheep which might have led to domestication. In the Mogollon Mountains from around 1450 to 1250 B.P. and from 750 to 500 B.P., possibly in the region of Glen Canyon of the Anasazi Culture Area around 1050 B.P. and again around 750 B.P., and in the Fremont Culture Area around 750 B.P., sedentary agriculturalists who were familiar with the habits of sheep found their economic systems under pressure. One of the options open to these peoples to relieve this pressure was to begin to manage more intensively those food resources, including sheep, which they had already exploited. Instead, in these particular situations, prehistoric man either widened the base of his economy to include previously unexploited wild resources, augmented the frequency with which he utilized previously exploited wild resources, moved to new environments where his previous economic system could again be stabilized, or scattered into smaller groups in order to live off the land.

Why didn't prehistoric man domesticate sheep in North America as he did in the Near East? In part, the answer may be found in the different ecological habits and biological processes of the Asiatic mouflon and the

American bighorn. In part, it may be found in the different geographical distributions of sheep in relationship to the areas of origins of agriculture and sedentism. In part, it may be found in the relative ease with which a shift to management of wild resources, as opposed to other options, could have been made in times of economic pressure. But it also should not be forgotten that we are dealing with men: men who may have had different attitudes toward their environment and how it was to be used, however similar were the resources around them and the pressures upon them.

REFERENCES

AIKENS, C. MELVIN
  1966a *Virgin-Kayenta cultural relationships.* University of Utah Anthropological Papers 79.
  1966b* *Fremont-Promontory-Plains relationships.* University of Utah Anthropological Papers 82.
  1967* *Excavations at Snake Rock Village and the Bear River No. 2 Site.* University of Utah Anthropological Papers 87.
  1970* *Hogup Cave.* University of Utah Anthropological Papers 93.
AMBLER, RICHARD J.
  1966* *Caldwell Village.* University of Utah Anthropological Papers 84.
BAILEY, VERNON
  1931 Mammals of New Mexico. *North American Fauna* 53:1–412.
BLUHM, ELAINE A.
  1957 The Sawmill site, a Reserve Phase village, Pine Lawn Valley, western New Mexico. *Fieldiana: Anthropology* 47:1–86.
BÖKÖNYI, S.
  1969 "Archaeological problems and methods of recognizing animal domestication," in *The domestication and exploitation of plants and animals.* Edited by P. J. Ucko and G. W. Dimbleby, 219–229. London: Duckworth.
BRAIDWOOD, ROBERT J., HALET ÇAMBEL, CHARLES L. REDMAN, PATTY JO WATSON
  1971 Beginnings of village-farming communities in southeastern Turkey. *Proceedings of the National Academy of Science USA* 68:1236–40.
CLARK, JAMES L.
  1964 *The great arc of the wild sheep.* Norman: University of Oklahoma Press.
COCKRUM, E. LENDELL
  1960 *The recent mammals of Arizona: their taxonomy and distribution.* Tucson: University of Arizona Press.
CUTLER, HUGH C.
  1952 A preliminary survey of plant remains of Tularosa Cave. *Fieldiana: Anthropology* 40:461–479.

* Indicates archaeological papers reporting the excavation of remains of wild sheep.

DICK, HERBERT W.
    1965* *Bat Cave.* School of American Research, Monograph 27.
DREW, ISABELLA M., DEXTER PERKINS, JR., PATRICIA DALY
    1971   Prehistoric domestication of animals: effects on bone structure.
           Science 171:280–282.
FOWLER, DON D., C. MELVIN AIKENS
    1963* *1961 excavations, Kaiparowits Plateau, Utah.* University of Utah
           Anthropological Papers 64.
GEIST, VALERIUS
    1971   *Mountain sheep.* Chicago: University of Chicago Press.
GRINNELL, JOSEPH
    1912   The bighorn of the Sierra Nevada. *University of California Publications
           in Zoology* 10:143–153.
GUNNERSON, JAMES H.
    1959* *1957 excavations, Glen Canyon area.* University of Utah Anthropo-
           logical Papers 43.
    1969* *The Fremont Culture: a study in culture dynamics on the northern
           Anasazi frontier.* Papers of the Peabody Museum of Archaeology and
           Ethnology, Harvard University 59(2).
HALL, EUGENE RAYMOND, KEITH R. KELSON
    1959   *The mammals of North America.* New York: Ronald Press.
HARLAN, J. R.
    1967   A wild wheat harvest in Turkey. *Archaeology* 20:197–201.
HAURY, EMIL W.
    1936   *The Mogollon Culture of southwestern New Mexico.* Medallion Papers
           20.
    1940   Excavations in the Forestdale Valley, east-central Arizona. *University
           of Arizona Bulletin* 11:1–147.
    1950* *The stratigraphy and archaeology of Ventana Cave, Arizona.* Tucson:
           University of Arizona Press.
    1962   "The Greater American Southwest," in *Courses toward urban life.*
           Edited by Robert J. Braidwood and Gordon R. Willey, 106–131.
           New York: Viking Press.
HAURY, EMIL W., E. B. SAYLES
    1947   An early pithouse village of the Mogollon Culture, Forestdale valley,
           Arizona. *University of Arizona Bulletin* 18:1–93.
HOLE, FRANK, KENT V. FLANNERY
    1967   The prehistory of southwestern Iran: a preliminary report. *Proceedings
           of the Prehistoric Society* 33:147–206.
JENNINGS, JESSE D.
    1966* *Glen Canyon: a summary.* University of Utah Anthropological Papers
           81.
JENNINGS, JESSE D., EDWARD NORBECK
    1955   Great Basin prehistory: a review. *American Antiquity* 21:1–11.
JONES, J. KNOX, JR.
    1951   Another record of a mountain sheep (*Ovis canadensis*) from Nebraska.
           Natural History Miscellanea 91:1.

LEGGE, A. J.
1972 "Prehistoric exploitation of the gazelle in Palestine," in *Papers in economic prehistory: studies by members and associates of the British Academy Major Research Project in the Early History of Agriculture*. Edited by E. S. Higgs, 119–124. Cambridge: Cambridge University Press.

LIPE, WILLIAM D.
1960* *1958 Excavations, Glen Canyon area*. University of Utah Anthropological Papers 44.

LIPE, WILLIAM D., FLOYD W. SHARROCK, DAVID S. DIBBLE, KEITH M. ANDERSON
1960* *1959 excavations, Glen Canyon area*. University of Utah Anthropological Papers 49.

LISTER, ROBERT H.
1958 *Archaeological excavations in the northern Sierra Madre Occidental, Chihuahua and Sonora, Mexico*. University of Colorado Studies Series in Anthropology 7.
1964* *Contributions to Mesa Verde archaeology: I, Site 499*. University of Colorado Studies Series in Anthropology 9.
1966* *Contributions to Mesa Verde archaeology: III, Site 866*. University of Colorado Studies Series in Anthropology 12.

LYDEKKER, R.
1898 *Wild oxen, sheep, and goats of all lands*. London: Rowland Ward.

MANGELSDORF, PAUL C., HERBERT W. DICK, JULIÁN CÁMERA-HERNÁNDEZ
1967 Bat Cave revisited. *Harvard University, Botanical Museum Leaflets* 22:1–31.

MANGELSDORF, PAUL C., ROBERT H. LISTER
1956 Archaeological evidence on the evolution of maize in northwestern Mexico. *Harvard University, Botanical Museum Leaflets* 17:151–178.

MARTIN, PAUL S.
1940* *The SU Site: excavations at a Mogollon village, western New Mexico, 1940*. Anthropological Series Field Museum of Natural History 32: 1–97.
1943* *The SU Site: Excavations at a Mogollon village, western New Mexico, 1941*. Anthropological Series Field Museum of Natural History 32: 98–271.
1947* *The SU Site: Excavations at a Mogollon village, western New Mexico, 1946*. Anthropological Series Field Museum of Natural History 32: 272–382.

MARTIN, PAUL S., WILLIAM A. LONGACRE, JAMES N. HILL
1967 Chapters in the prehistory of eastern Arizona, III. *Fieldiana: Anthropology* 57:1–178.

MARTIN, PAUL S., JOHN B. RINALDO
1950a Sites of the Reserve Phase, Pine Lawn Valley, western New Mexico. *Fieldiana: Anthropology* 38:397–577.
1950b Turkey Foot Ridge Site, a Mogollon village, Pine Lawn Valley, western New Mexico. *Fieldiana: Anthropology* 38:233–396.
1960 Excavations in the Upper Little Colorado drainage, eastern Arizona. *Fieldiana: Anthropology* 51:1–127.

MARTIN, PAUL S., JOHN B. RINALDO, ERNEST ANTEVS
1949 Cochise and Mogollon sites, Pine Lawn Valley, western New Mexico. *Fieldiana: Anthropology* 38:1–232.

MARTIN, PAUL S., JOHN B. RINALDO, ELAINE A. BLUHM, HUGH C. CUTLER
1956 Higgins Flat Pueblo, western New Mexico. *Fieldiana: Anthropology* 45:1–218.

MARTIN, PAUL S., JOHN B. RINALDO, ELAINE A. BLUHM, HUGH C. CUTLER, ROGER GRANGE, JR.
1952 Mogollon cultural continuity and change: the stratigraphic analysis of Tularosa and Cordova Caves. *Fieldiana: Anthropology* 40:1–528.

MARTIN, PAUL S., JOHN B. RINALDO, WILLIAM A. LONGACRE, CONSTANCE CRONIN, LESLIE G. FREEMAN, JR., JAMES SCHOENWETTER
1962 Chapters in the prehistory of central Arizona, I. *Fieldiana: Anthropology* 53: 1–244.

MARTIN, PAUL S., JOHN B. RINALDO, WILLIAM A. LONGACRE, LESLIE G. FREEMAN, JR., JAMES A. BROWN, RICHARD H. HEVLY, M. E. COOLEY
1964* Chapters in the prehistory of eastern Arizona, II. *Fieldiana: Anthropology* 55:1–261.

MARWITT, JOHN P.
1968* *Pharo Village.* University of Utah Anthropological Papers 91.

MEYERS, J. THOMAS
1971 "The Origins of agriculture: an evaluation of three hypotheses," in *Prehistoric agriculture.* Edited by Stuart Struever, 101–121. Garden City, N.Y.: Natural History Press.

NADLER, C. F., K. V. KOROBITSINA, R. S. HOFFMAN, N. N. VORONTSOV
1973 Cytogenetic differentiation, geographic distribution, and domestication in Palearctic sheep (*Ovis*). *Zeitschrift für Säugetierkunde* 38:109–125.

PATTIE, J. O.
1930 *The personal narrative of James O. Pattie, of Kentucky.* Edited by Timothy Flint. Chicago: R. R. Donnelley and Sons.

PERKINS, DEXTER
1964* The prehistoric fauna from Shanidar, Iraq. *Science* 144:1565–1566.

PERROT, J.
1968 La préhistoire palestinienne. *Supplément au Dictionnaire de la Bible* 8:286–446.

REED, CHARLES A., ROBERT J. BRAIDWOOD
1960 Toward the reconstruction of the environmental sequence of northeastern Iraq. *Studies in Ancient Oriental Civilization* 31:163–173.

REED, ERIK K.
1958* *Excavations in Mancos Canyon, Colorado.* University of Utah Anthropological Papers 35.
1964 "The Greater Southwest," in *Prehistoric man in the New World.* Edited by Jesse D. Jennings and Edward Norbeck, 175–191. Chicago: University of Chicago Press.

RINALDO, JOHN B.
1959 Foote Canyon Pueblo. *Fieldiana: Anthropology* 49:145–298.

SCHOENWETTER, JAMES
1962 The pollen analysis of eighteen archaeological sites in Arizona and New Mexico. *Fieldiana: Anthropology* 53:168–209.

SHARROCK, FLOYD W., KEITH M. ANDERSON, DON D. FOWLER, DAVID S. DIBBLE
  1961* *1960 excavations, Glen Canyon area.* University of Utah Anthropological Papers 52.
SHARROCK, FLOYD W., KENT C. DAY, DAVID S. DIBBLE
  1963* *1961 excavations, Glen Canyon area.* University of Utah Anthropological Papers 63.
SHARROCK, FLOYD W., JOHN P. MARWITT
  1967* *Excavations at Nephi, Utah, 1965–1966.* University of Utah Anthropological Papers 88.
SPICER, EDWARD H., LOUIS P. CAYWOOD
  1936 Two Pueblo ruins in west central Arizona. *University of Arizona Social Science Bulletin* 10:1–115.
STONE, WILMER, WILLIAM EVERETT CRAM
  1902 *American animals.* New York: Doubleday, Page.
TURNBULL, PRISCILLA F., CHARLES A. REED
  1974 The fauna of Palegawra, a late Pleistocene Zarzian site in northeastern Iraq. *Fieldiana: Anthropology* 63:81–146.
WELLES, RALPH E., FLORENCE B. WELLES
  1961 *The bighorn of Death Valley.* Fauna Series of the National Parks of the United States 6.
WENDORF, FRED
  1950 A report on the excavation of a small ruin near Point of Pines, east-central Arizona. *University of Arizona Social Science Bulletin* 19:1–150.
WHEAT, JOE BEN
  1954 Crooked Ridge Village. *University of Arizona Social Science Bulletin* 24:1–183.
  1955 *Mogollon culture prior to A.D. 1000.* American Anthropological Association Memoir 82.
WILKINSON, PAUL F.
  1972 "Current experimental domestication and its relevance to prehistory," in *Papers in economic prehistory.* Edited by E. S. Higgs, 107–118. Cambridge: Cambridge University Press.
WILLEY, GORDON R.
  1966 *An introduction to American archaeology,* volume one. Englewood Cliffs, N.J.: Prentice-Hall.
WISTER, OWEN
  1904 "The mountain sheep: his ways," in *Musk-ox, bison, sheep, and goat.* Edited by Caspar Whitney, 167–222. London: Macmillan.
ZEUNER, FREDERICK E.
  1963 *A history of domesticated animals.* New York: Harper and Row.

The Metate: An Early Grain-Grinding Implement in the New World

> Thou shalt not take the nether, nor the upper millstone to pledge; for he hath pledged his life to thee.
> Deuteronomy 24:6 (Douet version).

GEORGE F. CARTER

INTRODUCTION

The biblical reference to the millstone serves to illustrate both the importance of the grain-grinding implements to mankind and the confusion that exists concerning the earliest of these tools. Note this alternate version: "No man shall take a handstone or even an upper millstone in pledge for a debt; for that is to take life itself as a pledge." But the handstone WAS the upper millstone in the Near East in biblical times! What is reflected in this wording is the unfamiliarity of the translator with the milling equipment that preceded the invention of the rotary mill. This ignorance is typical of the reporting on what is one of man's more significant inventions for what it tells us about man's way of life and about his increasing interest in the hard-seeded grasses that were to become his staff of life.

Probably the grain-grinding tools are the first tangible evidence that we will ever have of man's shift of interest toward the hard-seeded grains as an important food supply. While the sickle has had more attention, the grinding tools may be earlier and perhaps even more informative. Clearly there was an immense period of time of specialized seed gathering that preceded the emergence of agriculture based on grass seeds, and we must look to the tools used in the harvesting and preparation of such materials for the first hints of this approaching revolutionary development.

Further, seed grinding along with pottery making led men to work with complex rotary-motion machines and thus foreshadowed the mechanical revolution — the harnessing of animal and then inanimate power. How odd, then, that the basic grinding tools are a center of confusion and lack of reporting.

Nomenclature

Some semblance of order in nomenclature is a first requirement. As an example of the utter confusion that can be found, consider the following statement by Lips (1956: 77):

Another important utilization of stone for household implements are the slabs and grinders on which primitive housewives all over the earth chop and mince their grains and vegetables. One large stone serves as a base, with a smaller, round stone as a pestle. From the harvesting tribes of North America to the agriculturists of Africa and the Pacific Islands, such slabs and mortars are common.

It would be difficult to write more confusingly or with greater mixture of descriptive terms for grinding and pounding equipment and processes. Lip's accompanying illustration shows a metate or saddle quern. Responsibility for such rampant confusion can in part be laid at the door of professionals, who have not yet developed a standard terminology.

As an example, without citation of the source (there is no point in singling out one from many), the following terms were used in one recent American publication. For the handstone (identity determined by either usage or illustrations): muller, mealing stone, pitted hammer stone, anvil stone, circular flat milling stone. For the nether stone: flat to slightly concave stone mortar, mortar with a deep concave surface. The last example shows a deeply troughed metate or saddle quern with a mano or muller resting in the depression. When professionals call the nether stone of the seed-grinding apparatus a mortar, confusion is nearing the ultimate. In Table 1 are assembled some of the terms in use. The list could be expanded but should be sufficient to illustrate the difficulty of proceeding without first establishing names for the things that we are to discuss.

The American names for the two parts of the apparatus on which grains were ground on a nether stone by a back-and-forth motion of a smaller stone held in the hand have long been metate and mano respectively. See, for instance, Kroeber's broad and casual usage of the first

Table 1. Names for grinding tools

Lower stone	Upper stone
New World	
metate	mano
milling stone	muller
grinding slab	handstone
mealing stone	pitted hammer stone
shallow mortar	mealing stone
Old World (British Empire)	
quern	muller
saddle quern	rider
dish quern	quern pounder
grindstone	grinder
mealing trough	mealing stone
stone bowls	crushers
plate-shaped mortar	rubber
flat mill	milling stone
dish mortar	pestle rubber

term: "Grains need threshing and then grinding into flour; this was done on saddle querns — what in Mexico and the southwestern United States are called metates — slabs on which a stone was pushed back and forth" (1948: 695), and "The grain was ground in a saddle quern or metate, with back and forth motion" (1948: 747).

In southern California, men who had Spanish-American backgrounds and firsthand knowledge of the Indians called all such implements metates and manos, adding descriptive adjectives for special shapes of metates such as troughed, basined, three-legged, and so forth. There is no English equivalent for metate except saddle quern, a confusing phrase, and no unequivocal name in English for the handstone, for muller can also mean a pounding implement such as a pestle.

The desire in some American quarters to change from the original term to grinding slab, mealing stone, milling stone, and so forth has caused confusion. Grinding slab is a descriptive but not distinctive name for the handstone. Grinding slab (or milling stone) and handstone are clumsy expressions, and only by definition can we know which word refers to the upper and which to the lower stone. The usual rule in taxonomy is to retain the old, established names. We have only two sets: saddle quern and muller, and metate and mano. As the table shows, saddle quern and muller are not consistently used in British publications, where there is apparently no generally used pair of terms. Further, saddle quern is a clumsy phrase and invites confusion with the rotary mill (quern). Americans once had such a pair of words — mano and metate — but seem now to be adrift in a sea of increasing confusion. I choose to use here these old, established terms: mano and metate. A discussion of the misconception of circular and back-and-forth motion in grinding grain on a metate is reserved for elsewhere. It will be shown that there is neither ethnological nor archaeological evidence for anything except a predominantly back-and-forth motion.

Earliest Use of the Mano and Metate: Seeds or Pigments?

Obviously, any device for grinding could be used to prepare various substances. Mankind has long been fascinated with colors, and pigments often need grinding in the process of preparation. Tough and stringy dried meats are improved by pounding and grinding. Any set of equipment for either pounding or grinding would probably be used for many things. The problem is to determine, if possible, the predominant earliest use, for ethnological studies show that metates are used primarily for preparing vegetable foods and secondarily for all other purposes; this is true among the seed gatherers as well as the agriculturists. If we were to judge the past by the present, we would have to conclude that metates were primarily for grinding seeds.

Currently, great emphasis is placed on the frequent occurrence of color stains on manos and metates from early sites, and the suggestion is advanced that the first use of these implements may have been for grinding pigments. Admittedly, man could have begun by preparing paints and later turned to grinding food, and the very ancient trait of painting the dead with red ocher indicates the great antiquity of the preparation of pigments, with implications of pounding or grinding. However, we should not be overly influenced by these color stains. Traces of pigments last. Traces of food, except under most unusual conditions, could not be expected to do so. Perhaps we should be looking for more subtle evidence of use. Grinding of grain tends to polish the stones. Grinding of clays formed by breakdown of granite scratches the stones because quartz crystals are commonly included in the clay. Pigment grinding should often scratch the stone and also leave a lasting stain. Scratching and staining would make lasting and obvious markings, and very probably, the minor uses that leave the most obvious evidence are excessively influencing our judgments.

Perhaps the matter can be approached through frequency studies. There would be relatively little need for grinding pigments in comparison with the need for grinding seeds, hence an abundance of well-worn grinding tools would suggest seed grinding more strongly than pigment grinding. Gabel (1963) reports that in the Lochinvar mound in South Africa, manos and metates were found in the bottom levels. Six metates were found and none showed ocher stain; thirty-eight manos were found and two showed ocher stain. Storck and Teague (1952) mention that some of the mortars and "rubbing stones" of the Magdalenian are stained with red ocher, "but many show no trace of color." These citations suggest that a minority of these tools are ocher stained. Because even an incidental use for grinding ocher might leave a lasting stain, while extensive use for grinding food would leave none, the data suggest a predominance of food grinding over ocher grinding. But the need for more data is obvious.

One reason for the belief that grinding tools were used first for pigments and only later for seeds seems to be the assumption that manos and metates cannot precede agriculture. In areas like the American West, this is obviously not true. For example, from at least 10,000 to 2000 B.P., and again after 650 B.P., in the North American Great Basin the metate was primarily used for grinding wild seeds, It is the seed gatherer's preeminent tool, and in that region, as well as in Australia and southermost Africa, it is totally unrelated to agriculture. Evidence will be presented below for metates in clearly preagricultural positions elsewhere. The whole subject of early grinding tools is filled with explicit or implicit assumptions about their function, age, distribution, and technique of use, and some of the assumptions can be shown to be wrong. I intend here to begin to clarify this situation.

Distribution: Age and Area

The mano and metate have, or had, a nearly worldwide distribution, being used at some time or another on all the continents, including Australia (Farmer 1959, 1960). As always with such a distribution, one is faced with the problem of multiple or single invention, and only extensive distributional studies that focus on space, time, and typology can supply the answer. Because of the lack of these studies, as well as the confused state of our nomenclature, the neglect in reporting these tools, and the assumptions about the recency of the tools, at this time only the sketchiest of outlines and most guarded conclusions can be presented.

The worldwide distribution of the metate suggests antiquity, and diffusion somewhat like that of the atlatl, the dog, or the use of fire. Further, the metate is often used by the simpler cultures of the world, such as the nonagricultural Australians and the nonagricultural tribes of the

Great Basin and southern California, suggesting that it is a part of some early way of life. These factors suggest that the mano and metate may have been part of man's early equipment and were carried with him as he spread over the earth. Because they are so important to the seed gatherers and continue to be important to seed cultivators, the implication is that the seed-gathering way of life is very early. Very probably, the metate-using seed gatherers evolved into the metate-using agriculturists in the Near East and in Mexico.

Multiple independent invention cannot be ruled out, but it is difficult to see just why the grinding of grains as opposed to other methods of preparing them should be invented early, or repeatedly, or at all. The claim that only three methods are available — pounding, rubbing, or rolling grains to reduce them to finer particles — is false. Grains can be soaked, sprouted, parched, popped, or boiled (especially if pottery is available), and these operations reduce or eliminate the need for mechanical reduction of the hard grains.

If grain is to be reduced mechanically, rolling would seem the least likely method. It involves the principle of the wheel, and for efficient use poses problems of a fixed handle with a free-turning roller. Perhaps significantly, it is rare in the world. Paris (1943) mentioned rollers for grinding grain among the Maya and the Chinese; Prakash (1961) mentioned rollers in use in India. In conversations with people back from Africa, I have learned that cylindrical manos are common in North Africa. They are used with a wrist action that gives at most a three-quarter turn. I know of no published descriptions of the equipment, the process, or the distribution of this complex, which may stretch from Indochina, through India, and across North Africa. This deficiency is typical of the present state of knowledge of grinding tools. In Mexico rollers continue in use to this day, and Indian women can be seen buying them in the marketplace in Oaxaca. That this is a transfer to America of a southeastern Asian mano that utilizes the principle of the wheel is a possibility that deserves investigation. The context of the roller mano is interesting: many similar parallels between southern Asia and America can be found (cf. Heine-Geldern's numerous papers) and a compelling case for the trans-Pacific diffusion of a specific tool (a specialized bark beater) from Celebes to Mexico can be made (Tolstoy 1963).

Pounding would seem to be a natural way to reduce a material. This would fit well with primitive man's shaping of stone by striking blows designed to remove flakes, and later by pecking it. Indeed, pounding of some foods on or with stones may antedate striking of stones to make tools. We often assume that earlier men were more impatient, more prone to quick methods than to slow ones (hence flaked stone before ground stone); if this argument were valid, we would expect that the technique of pounding grain might have preceded that of grinding grain. Our present information from studies of both distribution and chronology suggests, however, that for grains, the grinding method is the older throughout the world. With reservations because of the incompleteness of our knowledge, we can say that the choice of the metate suggests a traditional way of doing things, invented somewhere very early and diffused widely prior to the invention and spread of the pounding method. However, we need much more data before this conclusion can be considered as more than highly tentative.

We need to know with what group of lithic industries the metate is usually associated. In southern California the metate is not found with the early bifacially flaked core tools (handaxe-like) but is characteristic of the unifacially flaked tools (La Jollan culture) similar to the chopper traditions of southeastern Asia. If the associations were the same in Asia, the suggestion would seem to be that a complex of stone flaking and seed grinding was diffused, presumably from Asia to America. The metate is or was widely used in southeastern Asia, from India to China, and metates are found in the Hoabinhian culture, for which age estimates as high as 50,000 years have been made, although no one has specified just how far back the metate extends in this culture. If the metate has very great antiquity in Asia and is associated with unifacial core tools similar to those of the La Jollan culture of America, which also has metates, then this association may prove to be highly significant.

We obviously need much more information on the age of the metate in many areas. I can contribute most to this question by presenting data from the area of my own research.

THE MANO AND THE METATE IN THE NEW WORLD

Age of the Mano and the Metate in the New World

The age of the metate in America is generally thought to be post-Paleo-Indian, or at any rate, not more than 10,000 years. Krieger (1959: 31), in an acrimonious exchange with Carter, extended this worldwide:

A considerable amount of controlled and competent archeological work ... has shown rather definitely that food grinding tools first appeared between 9000 and 10,000 years ago. This estimate applies to the Old World as well.

This assessment of fifteen years ago is far from correct, as data presented below will make clear. Krieger, in this case, simply reflected the general view that the mano and metate appeared in the early Archaic, a view supported by such synthesizers of American archaeology as Gordon Willey (1966, 1971) and James Ford (1969). In his valuable survey of American archaeology, Ford has placed the metate as post-Paleo-Indian and characteristically appearing in the Archaic period. He recognizes the basined metate as an early form and notes the appearance of troughed metates about 6000 B.P. and metates with legs between 3000 and 2500 B.P. A review of the data from California will show that there is considerable reason to expect far older dates.

The metate is known to precede the mortar in much of California. In central California, Powers (cited in Holmes 1902) recorded that the historic tribes stated that in ancient times they had ground their acorns on a slightly hollowed stone "like a Mexican metate," a practice they had learned from Mouse. Later they learned from Coyote (the Uto-Aztecan trickster god) to pound their acorns in mortars. In the region of Santa Barbara, the early Oak Grove culture has the metate, the intermediate Hunting culture has both the metate and the mortar, and late Canalino culture used the mortar either exclusively or almost so. This pattern is also true of southern California and of Baja California, where the replacement was incomplete, for although mortars were well on the way to displacing the metate in southern California, they were still rare in northern Baja California and probably absent in southern Baja California. The data suggest an introduction of the mortar somewhere near central California and its slow gain of dominance over the metate in adjacent areas.

A hint concerning the time of these shifts in the area of San Diego comes from submarine archaeology (Minshall and Moriarty 1964). Small stone mortars have been recovered from beneath the sea, many of them from a drowned site. The amount of rise in sea level suggests an age ranging from about 9,000 years for the deepest to 5,000 years for the greatest accumulation. Metates have been found farther off snore, in still greater depths, suggesting an antiquity of 10,000 years or more. In California the most conservative authorities (Wallace 1962) will grant about 10,000 years for the age of the metate, and an assumption seems to be made that the later shift from the metate to the mortar accompanied either some ecological or some cultural shift from small wild seeds to acorns. No objective proof has been advanced for such a change due to ecological shifts.

Arnold (1957) found a series of occupations associated with an extinct lake (Lake Chapala) in the now-desert Baja California. The present rain-fall is between 12.5 and 25 centimeters, and a rainfall of 50 to 75 centi-meters would be required to restore a lake in the area. This condition indicates that full glacial-pluvial climatic changes are involved. A sequence of lakes, associated with weathering phenomena, and successive complexes of artifacts allow these conclusions: all of Wisconsin time is involved; metates are absent in the earliest lithic industry but present in the middle and later lithic assemblages (Arnold's conclusions). The lithic assemblage lacking the metate is marked by "ovate bifaces" (handaxes). The lithic assemblage associated with the metates includes scraper planes, flakes, and simple, leaf-shaped, bifacially flaked points (stemmed and notched points are rare). This latter assemblage seems to be a late phase of the ancient lithic industry of southern California that is characterized by a predominance of unifacial flaking and of the metate. That Arnold places this in Wisconsin time is most important.

The San Dieguito Culture (Table 2) represents the attenuated influence of the Paleo-Indian hunting cultures on the earliest simple gatherers of southern California. In the 1930's I assisted M. J. Rogers in fieldwork in southern California and spent hundreds of hours collecting artifacts from eroded sites of the San Dieguito Culture. We collected quantities of manos and metates and considered food-grinding equipment a normal part of the assemblage. This long-held view was reversed by Rogers when the cutting of a single trench through a deeply buried site produced no manos or metates. A later trench through this site also failed to produce any grinding tools (Warren and True 1961; Krieger 1964; Heizer 1964). Because the site is a quarry where felsite boulders in a stream bed were being worked, metates obviously could not be expected. As Heizer (1964) has aptly pointed out, one can easily draw an incorrect conclusion from the absence of a tool in situations where evidence of seed grinding would be much more expectable than at this site. In passing, we should note that, although this site is dated by radiocarbon at 9000 B.P., it is culturally a late San Dieguito site (Hayden 1966).

In the area of San Diego and elsewhere, the following sequence can be observed: those manos and metates of the protohistoric tribes made of granite are fresh, hard, and usually white in color; La Jollan manos are nearly fresh even when they have an age up to 9,000 years. Yellowed and weathered manos of granite are often found in the area and were fre-quently found on San Dieguito sites. They are more weathered than the historic and than the La Jollan, defined as post-San Dieguito (see Table 2). If they do not belong with the other lithic material on those sites, to what culture should they be assigned? The details of the weathering show that

Table 2.   Correlation of chronology and cultural sequences in southern and lower (Baja) California

General time-period	Area of Santa Barbara	Area of San Diego	Area of Lake Chapala, Baja California	Associated human remains
Late Recent (Bow and arrow)	Canalino	Diegueño*		
Mid-Recent Archaic	Hunting*	Late La Jollan*		
Early Recent	Oak Grove*	Late La Jollan*		
Late Wisconsin (Paleo-Indian)	Oak Grove*	San Dieguito*	Period II*	Burial in Imperial Valley
Early Wisconsin		Early La Jollan*	Period I	
Third Interglacial (= Riss-Wurm = ?Illinoisan-Wisconsin?)				
Late Third Interglacial, circa 80,000 B.P.				Frontal bone from La Jolla
Middle Third Interglacial circa 100,000 B.P.		Texas Street		
Early Third Interglacial				

Both sequences and times of cultural changes in southern and lower (Baja) California are questioned by various experts; the table above presents my judicious opinion. The general scale suggests the time intervals and the cultural sequences from flake and core tools to stone projectile points to the Archaic way of life, and finally — with the appearance of stone arrow points — to the Protohistoric way of life. Asterisks mark cultures where the metate is prominent.

The burial in the Imperial Valley, tentatively dated at 20,000 years, is being reported by Morlin Childers.

The human fossil frontal, dated at 80,000 years, is preserved in the San Diego Museum of Man and has been referred to previously by Carter (1957: 217). The date is inferred from the recent dating of the lowest terraces along the Pacific coast by U/Th ratios determined on molluscan shells.

they do not belong to any post-San Dieguito culture, but as at Lake Chapala, they belong at least to a mid-Wisconsin period (Arnold 1957). It is also noteworthy that mortars found in submarine locations and placeable at 5,000 to 9,000 years of age are never found on these San Dieguito sites and that mortars are later than metates in California.

At Lake Chapala the earlier metates and manos are weathered to such a degree that polished surfaces on both granite and basalt often have been destroyed wholly or in part. As geologists have often demonstrated, such weathering is not characteristic of the late Wisconsin but is normal for early Wisconsin and earlier time; this evidence would seem to indicate the age for the metates at Lake Chapala. Other data, outlined below, suggest much greater antiquity for the metate in southern California.

From Crown Point, a piece of land projecting into Mission Bay at San Diego (Figure 1), I have reported a series of particularly relevant finds

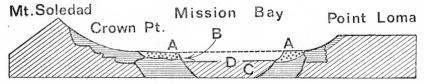

Figure 1.   Cross section from Mount Soledad to Point Loma along Crown Point·Mt. Soledad is a 900-foot-high block elaborately terraced. Point Loma is a 400-foot-high terraced block. The lowland between them is a river valley at times of lowered sea level and an embayment trapping sediments at times of high sea level. At A the Marina sands, a well-known Late Pleistocene sand deposit, is shown. This deposit formerly filled the embayment. Beneath it metates were found. Subsequent to the deposit of these sands, the San Diego River excavated the sands to far below present sea level. Subsequent rise of sea level to D in de-glacial time has led to the deposition of recent deposits C. If the sequence of cut and fill on this relatively stable San Diego block is the result of eustatic sea level fluctuations, as all present evidence suggests, then the age of the buried metates is last interglacial

(Carter 1957: 286–290). Crown Point represents a period of filling of Mission Bay with sand to a level well above the present sea level. Filling of the bays and lagoons along this coast is accepted as a phenomenon associated with a high sea level (Shumway, Hubbs, and Moriarty 1961; Hubbs, Bien, and Suess 1965). A fill associated with a sea level about ten feet above the present sea level would suggest a late last (third) interglacial age of about 80,000 years ago (Newell 1965). While there have been suggestions of minor sea-stands at slight elevations above the present within Recent time, the data assembled by Hubbs, Bien, and Suess (1965) tend to negate this theory, for they show a steady rise of sea level with no evidence for sea-stands significantly above the present at any time in the Recent. Furthermore, since the last filling of the area of Mission Bay most of the fill has been cut out far below present sea levels. This erosion clearly must be attributed to the lowered sea levels of last glacial time. Because the fill must precede its own erosion, the fill must date from the late last interglacial, unless we postulate a mid-Wisconsin sea-stand higher than the present one. If the sea-stand was about plus ten feet, which would be the absolute minimum required to create this fill (Carter [1957], for example, considered a twenty-five-foot sea-stand a more likely correlation, although a ten- or fifteen-foot sea-stand was mentioned as possible), then

Newell's date of about 80,000 years would seem appropriate. Dates from southern California archaeology, however, are being revolutionized. Bada, et al. (1974) report a human skeleton at 48,000. This implies man in America before the onset of Wisconsin I at $\pm 80,000$. There are now several unpublished dates for skeletal material in the 50,000 year range. Higher dates can be expected as more material is processed.

The first evidence for man near the base of the latest sand fill was the discovery of a group of large cobbles close together and strongly fire spalled. This assemblage, typical of temporary hearths commonly found in the area, was completely out of place in these coarse sands in its size, grouping, and evidence of fire. Four hundred yards to the north, a mano of very coarsely crystalline granite was found resting on the shell reef that underlies the sand deposit. The two flat sides of this cobble have been ground so strongly that the quartz crystals are cut off to form a gently curved surface typical of cobble manos in this area. Weathering of the granite since the planation of the quartz crystals leaves these surfaces raised because of the selective etching out of the softer minerals. Late glacial weathering of granites in California is less pronounced than this. The edges of the cobble show no wear. These characteristics identify manos, and such a pattern of wear is not found on stream cobbles.

At a depth of more than 6 meters in a sewer ditch cutting across Crown Point, engineers found two oval basined metates in a similar position: resting on a Pleistocene shell deposit at the base of the sand stratum that filled Mission Bay at a time when the sea stood about 7.5 meters above the present sea level.

No one has suggested any explanation of these data other than human habitation on the shores of Mission Bay prior to the last high sea-stand in this area. At one time the area was considered to be extremely unstable geologically, and the land-sea relationships were dismissed as attributable to local crustal movements. Detailed local studies by Carter (1957), Shumway, Hubbs, and Moriarty (1961), Hubbs, Bien, and Suess (1965), and others show that the raised beaches that had been assumed to be postglacial are interglacial, that the "Recent" alluvial covers are actually Wisconsin, and that the alleged evidence for great crustal instability is nonexistent (Allen, Silver, and Stehli 1960: Allen, et al. 1965).

There is a tendency to lose in the literature findings that at the time of publication were so out of step with the current knowledge as to be unbelievable, and then to fail to recover them when the growth of knowledge shows that they were possible, after all. Such a situation exists for the metate found in the region of Santa Barbara in the same relative position as the Mission Bay artifacts and reported by Rogers (1929);

a picture of the locality has been published by Carter (1959). The two metates and the mano at San Diego rested directly on a Pleistocene shell beach and were deeply buried by the alluvial fill of a subsequent high sea-stand. The most recent geochemical dating suggests a minimum age of 80,000 years for such marine transgressions (Mesolella, et al. 1969; Birkeland 1972). While the region of Santa Barbara is less stable than that of San Diego, Upson (1949) considered it to have been relatively stable since a mid-Pleistocene uplift and believed the lower terraces there to represent the effect of eustatic fluctuations of sea level. At the site where Rogers made his finds, a younger terrace has been truncated by a sea-stand higher than the present sea level, and the terrace cut by that sea-stand was dissected at a time of lower sea level than now (see Figure 2). If the lowest terrace represents the plus-ten-foot sea-stand of last inter-glacial time or of mid-Wisconsin time at the latest, then the mano and metates buried in a previous deposit must be still earlier and related to a time immediately following a twenty-five-foot sea-stand. If the area of Santa Barbara is regarded as somewhat less stable than that of San Diego, we might possibly fit these events into a somewhat later time, but one still well back into the last glacial period. The usual correlations with terraces suggest last interglacial time. The deep clay soil profiles on the lowest terrace and the strongly weathered soils on the higher terrace indicate

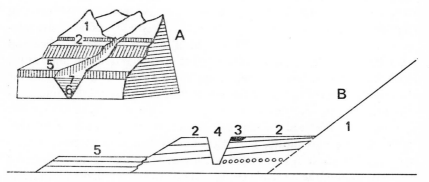

Figure 2.   Metates and geomorphology at Santa Barbara.   In A and B, 1 shows the mountainous background, 2 the higher of the two youngest terraces, and 5 the lower one. A surface midden of some 1,000's of years age is at 3, and the highway cut is designated by 4. The circles indicate the location of the marine beach formation. The metates were found on top of this. In A, 6 indicates the dissection of the valley below present sea levels, and 7 the current fill up to present sea level. The major criticism of Rogers's finds would be that a landslide might have carried manos and metates down to the beach level, and that even so experienced a field man as D. B. Rogers failed to detect this

weathering far beyond a 10,000-year scale. As at Crown Point, it seems improbable that these geomorphic features can be accounted for in Recent time; it is more probable that they fit late last interglacial events.

These findings also are supported by recent work on the coast of the area of Malibu, California (Birkeland 1972). Even in this area of obviously active crust, the eustatic analysis of terrace and valley fill is applicable. Evidence at Malibu suggests that the mid-Wisconsin sea level was about nine meters below modern sea levels, and that the last interglacial terrace cut and valley fill along the entire coast (Santa Cruz, Cayucos, Santa Monica Mountains, San Nicolas Island, Palos Verdes Hills) date from about 100,000 years ago. The dates from shell (open-system uranium series) for the lowest terrace range from 70,000 to 140,000, with a clustering about 100,000. Although a sea-stand higher than the present one in mid-Wisconsin time is possible, the weight of the evidence is against it. This study is of particular interest for its support of the work of W. M. Davis (1933) in the same area. My methodology at San Diego was like that of Davis. Birkeland's work with absolute dates confirms our conclusions and links San Diego and Santa Barbara. The drift of the evidence supports late interglacial dating of the metates and manos at Santa Barbara and San Diego.

In the chaotic state of reporting on metates, assumptions should not be allowed to override facts. While the situation at Santa Barbara, San Diego, and Lake Chapala seems out of step with the rest of America, where a 10,000-year limit is generally seen as probable, the finds in California form a coherent set supported by studies of geology, geomorphology, climate, and sea levels. Man in that part of America had specialized tools for grinding hard seeds from mid-Wisconsin time, at the latest, to late interglacial time, at the earliest. In the Great Basin the cultural descendants of these people continued to use these implements with little change and were so focused on their ancient way of life as to be epitomized as the Seed Gatherers. Most interestingly, not only did they fail to initiate agriculture, but also, despite millennia of contact with agriculturists, most of them were not stimulated either to undertake the domestication of their ancient seed plants or to borrow already domesticated plants from their neighbors.

Paleo-Indian Evidence

In the southeastern and midwestern part of the United States, the metate tended to disappear early in the Archaic. At Modoc Rock Shelter in

Missouri (Fowler 1959) the metate appeared only in the lowest levels. If a tool type is fading out toward the opening of a period, the notion that it may be a carry-over from an earlier period would seem worth investigation. The suggestion that the metate might belong in the Paleo-Indian lithic assemblage has both proponents and opponents (cf. Farmer 1960 and Krieger 1959). Actually, the question may be seen incorrectly. May the metate belong to a group earlier than the classic hunting cultures such as Folsom and Clovis? The Lively complex from Alabama (Josselyn 1966) clearly contains both ovate-biface-like materials, with which (on the basis of western American finds) the metate is not expectable, and unifacial tools of La Jollan type, with which the metate is expectable. Because the stratigraphy of the deep cave (Graham Cave) at Modoc Rock Shelter allows no room in the last 10,000 years or so for any complexes like these, the suggestion seems to be that a pre-Paleo-Indian people with seed-grinding tools preceded the Paleo-Indians in the eastern United States. This idea poses a flood of problems. Are manos in Paleo-Indian sites from a preceding culture? Are they the result of some cultural mixture? Is the Archaic a resurgence of the older foraging way of life enriched by the Paleo-Indian inventory? Just such a sequence seems apparent in southern California (Carter 1957), where a gathering culture emerged after enrichment by a hunting culture (San Dieguito) in the form of the La Jollan culture. The appearance in eastern North America of lithic complexes with preprojectile points comparable to those of the West is of broad significance for American cultural history, and knowledge of the presence or absence of the metate in these complexes will be of critical importance.

Problems intertwine. The problem of the antiquity of man in America cannot be separated from the question of the metate. Currently, we seem to be leaping from the long-held age estimate of 10,000 years to one of 20,000 or even 40,000. In January, 1973, a presentation at the University of California, Riverside, of Texas Street tools from the controversial interglacial site at San Diego (Carter 1957) resulted in complete acceptance of these disputed items as artifacts.

In the Colorado Desert of California, working with Morlin Childers of El Centro, California, I have seen a burial site at least 20,000 years old. This site is on the west side of the Imperial Valley, on a beach line about forty-six meters above sea level. Dates on the beach line are from shell and travertine; dates on the burial are from soil carbonates and are probably far too young. A more detailed description of the site is to be published by Childers.

Manos and metates of granite on old sites in different parts of the American West (Carter 1957, 1958) uniformly show degrees of weathering in keeping with pre-Wisconsin time on the granite-weathering scales normally used by geologists in this region. Excellent examples of this differential weathering can be seen in Childers's collection in El Centro, California. Many granite manos and metates found at the older sites were in such advanced states of decay that, were there still older sites with manos and metates, no record would exist.

Some years ago, Farmer (1960) reviewed the faint suggestions then available that the metate might be pre-Archaic as follows. Folsom sites east of the front range of the Rockies contain a few manos, and F. H. H. Roberts, Jr. found faceted pieces of sandstone at the Lindenmeir site in northern Colorado and noted that they suggested manos. The absence of metates perhaps has prevented these finds from attracting more attention, but the general assumption of a post-10,000-year dating for the metate is probably a more powerful force. Warnica (1966) reported the finding of a "stone used for grinding" in a stratum that yielded Clovis material, and referred to the finding of a small milling stone from a nearby Folsom site. The confusion in terminology is well exemplified by the fact that one must guess that Warnica meant a mano when he wrote "stone for grinding" and a metate when he wrote "milling stone." He did comment quite aptly that the presence of these stones suggested that the Paleo-Indian people were not entirely ignoring the vegetable resources around them.

Everyone recognizes that the Paleo-Indian evidence is very incomplete, for almost all our knowledge comes from butchering sites. That there is as much evidence suggesting seed usage as we actually possess is indeed highly significant.

Manos clearly appear in Paleo-Indian sites. Whether they were used as grinding stones (which seems probable), or were picked up on older sites and brought into camp, or were somehow accidental inclusions (which seems least likely) are problems that future work will solve. The data from San Diego establish the probability of pre-Paleo-Indian dates and should serve as a caution on theorizing that the metate was invented when the big game was exterminated and that under the compulsion of climatic change and the loss of big game as a means of subsistence men suddenly invented seed-grinding equipment and shortly thereafter a seed-based agriculture.

South America

In South America the mano and metate were reported at least as early as 1912 as associated with coastal midden cultures. Fifty years later (Lanning

1963) the metate was reported in early lithic industries in Peru and was associated with large, heavy, thick scrapers, bifacial disk choppers, large unretouched flakes, and rare projectile points. There is also clear evidence of climatic changes toward more humid conditions than now. Lanning thought that grinding tools were not exceptionally old in America and suggested that their occurrence here goes back only to the late Pleistocene. At El Jobo, Venezuela (Rouse and Cruxent 1957), the mano and metate appeared in early levels, and their presence at other early sites (such as the Ayampitin in Argentina) is reported and cross-dated by the Intihuasi site, which has a carbon-14 determination of $7,970 \pm 100$ years. Presumably, in South America as in North America, the mano and metate in early levels were certainly present before pottery and agriculture, and perhaps before projectile points. They are often associated with heavy flake-and-core lithic industries suggesting the La Jollan culture of North America, and this association tends to continue even after projectile points and pottery are added to the complex.

Krieger (1964) has presented a masterly summary of our knowledge of early man in America. We disagree on some points, especially concerning the metate (cf. Carter 1959 and Krieger 1959). Krieger (1964) considered the metate to mark the opening of the Proto-Archaic and, at most, to overlap the late Paleo-Indian period. His argument was environmentally deterministic: he viewed the metate as a mark of the shift toward dependence on vegetal foods in postglacial time due to the combination of associated climatic changes and extinctions of large animals. Krieger thought the metate appeared almost simultaneously — about 10,000 years ago — throughout the Americas, from Patagonia to Oregon. He tentatively suggested that the spread possibly occurred in 2,000 years. Bird (1965) placed manos (for pigment grinding) in Tierra del Fuego so close to 10,000 years ago as to call for nearly instantaneous spread. The total data would be more easily understood if more time were allowed.

Summary on Age of the Metate in the New World

The metate was nearly universal in America outside the sub-Arctic and surely extended back into the Paleo-Indian level. There is disputed evidence for the metate in sites with fluted points. This conflict pales beside the evidence from California, where several manos and metates have been found at the base of the alluvium overlying the last sea-stand that was significantly higher (ten feet higher) than the Recent level, with a probable minimum age of about 80,000 years. In the archaeological sequence in the United States, metates seem to be associated initially, not with bifacially flaked core tools, but with unifacially flaked tools (La Jolla, Early Milling Stone). In many areas metates persisted for long periods thereafter; in some areas they lasted into historic times. With growing recognition of the existence of pre-Paleo-Indian levels, we may be on the way to realization of the real antiquity of the earliest seed-grinding tools. Our progress has been blocked in part by the assumption that nowhere in the world is the metate older than 10,000 years. However, in the Old World, definite metates (grinding slabs) are known from 49,000 years ago at Florisbad, South Africa (see Kraybill, this conference), and, when archaeologists become more careful with their reporting, they probably will be found to have existed considerably earlier.

REFERENCES

ALLEN, C. R., LEON T. SILVER, F. G. STEHLI
   1960   Transverse structure of northern Baja California, Mexico. *Geological Society of America Bulletin* 71:457–482.
ALLEN, C. R., S. T. AMAND, C. F. RICHTER, J. M. NORDQUIST
   1965   Relationship between seismicity and geologic structure in the southern California region. *Bulletin of the Seismological Society of America* 55: 753–797.
ARNOLD, BRIGHAM A.
   1957   Late Pleistocene and Recent changes in land forms, climate, and archaeology in central Baja California. *University of California Publications in Geography* 10:201–318.
BADA, J. L., R. A. SCHROEDER, G. F. CARTER
   1974   New evidence for the antiquity of man in North America deduced from aspartic acid racemization. *Science* 184:791–793.
BIRD, J. B.
   1965   The concept of a "pre-projectile point" cultural stage in Chile and Peru. *American Antiquity* 31:262–270.
BIRKELAND, PETER W.
   1972   Late Quaternary eustatic sea-level changes along the Malibu coast, Los Angeles County, California. *Journal of Geology* 80:432–438.
CARTER, G. F.
   1957   *Pleistocene man at San Diego.* Baltimore: Johns Hopkins University Press.
   1958   Archaeology in the Reno area in relation to age of man and the culture sequence in America. *Proceedings of the American Philosophical Society* 102:174–192.
   1959   *Man, time and change in the Far West.* Annals of the Association of American Geography 49.

DAVIS, W. M.
1933 Glacial epochs of the Santa Monica Mountains, California. *Bulletin of the Geological Society of America* 44:1041–1133.

FARMER, M. F.
1959 "Some notes concerning grinding implements." Unpublished manuscript.
1960 A note on the distribution of the metate and muller. *Tebiwa, Journal of the Idaho State College Museum* 3:31–38.

FORD, J. A.
1969 *A comparison of Formative cultures in America.* Smithsonian Contributions to Anthropology 11.

FOWLER, M.
1959 Modoc Rock Shelter: an early Archaic site in southern Illinois. *American Antiquity* 24:257–270.

GABEL, CREIGHTON
1963 Lochinvar Mound: a later Stone Age camp-site in the Kafue Basin. *South African Archaeological Bulletin* 18:40–48.

HANSEN, G. H.
1934 The Utah Lake skull. *American Anthropologist* 36:135–147.

HAYDEN, J.
1966 Restoration of the San Dieguito type site to its proper place in the San Dieguito sequence. *American Antiquity* 31:439.

HEIZER, R. F.
1964 "The western coast of North America," in *Prehistoric man in the New World.* Edited by Jesse D. Jennings and Edward Norbeck, 117–148. Chicago: University of Chicago Press.

HOLMES, W. H.
1902 Anthropological studies in California. *Annual Report of the United States National Museum for 1900*, 161–187.

HRDLIČKA, ALEŠ
1912 Early man in South America. *Bureau of American Ethnology Bulletin* 52. Washington, D.C.

HUBBS, C. L., G. S. BIEN, H. E. SUESS
1965 La Jolla natural radiocarbon measurement, IV. *Radiocarbon* 7:66–117.

JOSSELYN, D. W.
1966 The Lively complex of Alabama. *Anthropological Journal of Canada* 4:24–31.

KRIEGER, A. D.
1959 Discussion. *Annals of the Association of American Geographers* 49:31.
1964 "Early man in the New World," in *Prehistoric man in the New World.* Edited by Jesse D. Jennings and Edward Norbeck, 23–81. Chicago: University of Chicago Press.

KROEBER, A. L.
1948 *Anthropology.* New York: Harcourt Brace.

LANNING, E. P.
1963 Pre-agricultural occupation on the central coast of Peru. *American Antiquity* 28:360-371.

LIPS, G. E.
1956 *The origin of things.* Harmondsworth: Penguin Books.

MESOLELLA, KENNETH J., R. K. MATTHEWS, WALLACE S. BROECKER, DAVID L.
THURBER
1969   The astronomical theory of climatic change: Barbados data. *Journal of Geology* 77:250–274.
MINSHALL, N. F., J. R. MORIARTY
1964   Principles of underwater archeology. *Pacific Discovery* 17:17–26.
NEWELL, N. D.
1965   Warm interstadial interval in Wisconsin stage of the Pleistocene. *Science* 148:1488.
PARIS, P.
1942   L'Amérique précolombienne et l'Asie méridionale, I. *Bulletin de la Société des Études Indochinoises* 17:35–70.
1943   L'Amérique précolombienne et l'Asie méridionale, II. *Bulletin de la Société des Études Indochinoises* 18:45–68.
PRAKASH, O. M.
1961   *Food and drink in ancient India.* Delhi: Munshi Ram Manohar Lal.
ROGERS, D. B.
1929   *Prehistoric man of the Santa Barbara coast.* Santa Barbara: Santa Barbara Natural History Museum.
ROUSE, I., J. M. CRUXENT
1957   Further comments on the finds at El Jobo, Venezuela. *American Antiquity* 22:412.
SHUMWAY, G., C. L. HUBBS, J. R. MORIARTY
1961   Scripps Estate site, San Diego, California: a La Jolla site dated 5460 to 7370 years before the present. *Annals of the New York Academy of Sciences* 93:37–132.
STORCK, J., W. D. TEAGUE
1952   *Flour for man's bread.* Minneapolis: University of Minnesota Press.
TOLSTOY, P.
1963   Cultural parallels between Southeast Asia and Mesoamerica in the manufacture of bark cloth. *Transactions, New York Academy of Science*, series two, 25:646–662.
UPSON, J. E.
1949   Former marine shore lines of the Gaviota Quadrangle, Santa Barbara County, California. *Journal of Geology* 59:415–446.
WALLACE, W. J.
1962   Prehistoric cultural development in the southern California deserts. *American Antiquity* 28:172–180.
WARNICA, JAMES M.
1966   New discoveries at the Clovis site. *American Antiquity* 31:345–357.
WARREN, CLAUDE N., D. L. TRUE
1961   The San Dieguito complex and its place in California prehistory. *Annual Report of the Archaeological Survey at the University of California at Los Angeles, 1960–1961*, 264–291.
WILLEY, GORDON
1966   *Archaeology of North America.* Englewood Cliffs, N.J.: Prentice-Hall.
1971   *Archaeology of South America.* Englewood Cliffs, N.J.: Prentice-Hall.

Our Father the Cayman, Our Mother the Gourd: Spinden Revisited, or a Unitary Model for the Emergence of Agriculture in the New World

DONALD W. LATHRAP

PREFACE

This paper has a life history very different from the rest of the essays here included. I had prepared no presentation for the Woodstock conference, but was stimulated by certain sections of the papers given advanced circulation by other participants. In particular, Bennet Bronson's discussion of the kind of plant with which man would first meddle, seemed to be a discussion of *Lagenaria siceraria* (Mol.) Standl, the white-flowered bottle gourd, even though Bronson (this volume) did not use the gourd as an example. Bronson thus confirmed my views on the importance of the gourd to an understanding of agricultural origins. Barbara Pickersgill and Charles B. Heiser, Jr. (this volume) also stressed the importance to early New World systems of crops yielding manufacturing materials and condiments, but perhaps most importantly I was encouraged by their concession that the remarkable distribution of the bottle gourd as witnessed by the archaeological record was in some sense a result of human activity.

Another energizing factor for these comments was an opinion expressed in the ORIGINAL version of one of the other papers in the symposium. The position was taken that early systems of proto-cultivation involving root crops tended not to be expansive, and that these systems shifted toward efficient, specialized root-crop cultivation only under the influence of expanding systems of seed-crop cultivation. There was the further implication that the archaeological record in South America was compatible with such an interpretation. In the course of this paper, I intend to turn such a position upside down and show that the appearance of civilization in the New World was triggered by the impingement of aggressively expansive, specialized vegecultural systems on localized seed-cropping systems of proto-cultivation.

The nucleus of this paper was in an extended series of comments which I gave on various occasions during the Woodstock conference. These were motivated by the issues just listed, and their form was considerably sharpened and focused under the severe cross-examination of various of the other members of the conference, in particular, Charles B. Heiser, Jr. I have repeatedly listened to the tapes of these exchanges, but they do not yield the exact text of what follows. In the four months since the conference at Woodstock, I have lectured on these issues to four classes at the University of Illinois, Urbana, most particularly in the Interdisciplinary Seminar on Agricultural Origins taught jointly with Charles S. Alexander and Theodore Hymowitz. The faculty seminar of the Agronomy Department of the University of Illinois, Urbana, granted me a forum in which I attempted to put all of these ideas together in a short, organized, and coherent structure. Finally, the Chicago Anthropological Society requested that I speak to them. That presentation of 7 December, 1973, approximated the present version.

Within the last few days I have seen a publication by Kent V. Flannery, "The Origins of Agriculture," which includes a systematic review of the remains of plants from archaeological contexts relevant to our understanding of the early agricultural systems of the New World (Flannery 1973). While Flannery's marshaling of the data shows his typical high level of scholarship, I do NOT regard his overview of these data as a balanced one. With no intention on my part, this paper developed into a kind of converse of Flannery's, almost a negative to his black-and-white print. We are aware of the same data, but in the words of William Blake:

Both read the Bible day & night,
But thou read'st black where I read white (Donne and Blake 1941: 609).

The final form of the manuscript was designed to heighten the contrast between Flannery's position and my own. We are, however, in total agreement that the emergence of agriculture was a process rather than an incident or discovery (Flannery 1973: 271).

In the period during which the manuscript was taking form, I received further written comment from Barbara Pickersgill and especially from David R. Harris, who translated some of my comments at Woodstock into a crisp systemic model with multiple feedback loops implied. The manuscript would not have been completed without the encouragement of George W. Beadle, and the continuous and ingenious pressures which Charles A. Reed brought to bear on me. The paper would never have been conceived had it not been for the Woodstock conference, which was in my opinion the best designed, best run, and most productive scholarly session which it has been my privilege to attend. As creator of the conference, Dr. Reed merits the deepest gratitude of all of the participants.

As always, my wife, Joan, performed multiple editorial services.

INTRODUCTION

This paper will attempt a large task. All I wish to do is overturn most of the current thinking about agricultural origins in the New World and about the kind of patterned human behavior involved in the very beginnings of agriculture. Immediately, it is absolutely essential to distinguish two very different points on the trajectory leading to that systematic distortion in human behavior we label agriculture. Fairly late on this trajectory we note a stage by which the cultivated plant is so modified from its wild ancestor that it can be consistently recognized as a cultigen by our trained archaeobotanists. We should never forget the importance of the warning reiterated by our botanical colleagues; by that point in time the plant, under human pampering, has usually become such a genetic misfit that it cannot survive without us. Constrained by the now frail constitution of his cultigen, man must schedule much more of his time for its perpetuation. Since the modifications away from a viable wild species are usually in a direction which will cause the plant to yield more calories per acre of land, these gross morphological changes in the cultivated plant ought to be accompanied by marked increases in the density of human populations, as the amount and dependability of food supply goes up (Flannery 1973: 299). I think it is the partially interlocking relationship between these three sets of data, which allows us to recognize a "Neolithic revolution": (1) gross genetic modification; (2) rescheduling of human activities; (3) patent demographic upsets. We tend to think that by this time man has fully domesticated the cultigen; but, as usual, it is later than we think. What has really happened by this time, is that the cultigen has fully domesticated man. The tyranny of the overbred cultigen over its human protector cannot be too much stressed, and is nowhere more obvious than in central Illinois today, where the farmer is in bondage to the insatiable appetite and immense vulnerability of his monstrous hybrid corn.

The other point, much earlier on the trajectory leading to intensified agricultural systems, is the initiation of any practice which increases the availability of a particularly useful species of plant. This *Anlage* can take several forms, but the transplanting of one or several individuals of a plant providing a key resource in the cleared area around a house is the form which I will emphasize. Since these instances of replanting and tending are often not even noticed by the ethnographer, their recognition in archaeological contexts is difficult. Typically the only evidence is the finding of remains of a particular plant in a site far outside the natural range of that species. I have already emphasized the tremendous regimentation which intensive agricultural systems place on man, but even the tending of a few individuals of a potentially rare plant imposes a certain discipline on human behavior, and it is a discipline which is likely to expand through time. Recent intensive research has increased the recognized time-depth for the "Neolithic revolution" to the range of 7000 to 10,000 B.P. It is my contention that if we are to examine the onset of Neolithic experimentation we must lower our sights to a minimum of 40,000 years of elapsed time.

A simple listing of other equally blasphemous statements is probably the best basis for proceeding. Carl Sauer's views (1952) on agricultural origins have always offered the best model for thought on this subject. Sauer was correct in focusing our attention on the alluvial flood plains of tropical rivers (1952: 23). He was probably correct in stating that all agricultural systems are historically related in deriving from a single localized pattern of Neolithic experimentation (1952), but he was probably wrong in localizing that pattern in southeastern Asia (1952). I vote for tropical Africa. Coursey's ideas concerning the time-depth for the cultivation of yams in tropical Africa are correct (Coursey 1972; Coursey and Coursey 1971) and he is probably correct when he claims that Sangoan and Lupemban are the oldest identifiable proto-Neolithic cultures in the world (Coursey 1976). His thoughts on the progression from yam "ceremonialism" to yam "cultivation" are pregnant with implications for the emergence of other agricultural systems. As Harlan has pointed out (statement during the conference), the evidence of the grain sorghums also demands that we consider Africa as a very early hearth of Neolithic experimentation. Turning to the New World, if all of the above statements are true, it must follow that all agricultural systems there derive from a single localized pattern of Neolithic experimentation. More importantly, there was a single "Neolithic revolution." Spinden (1917) was correct; all of the high civilizations of the New World rest on a single uniform "Neolithic," "Formative," or "Archaic" basement. And Kroeber, in the first edition of his *Anthropology* (1923: Figure 35), was correct in diagramming cultural development in the New World as a layer cake designed according to Spinden's specifications. Spinden and almost all who followed him have been wrong in assuming that it was maize which gave the initial impetus to the New World "Neolithic revolution." Only a few students of the problem, Sauer (1952: 43–5) and Bronson (1966), have been correct in implicating root crops and more specifically manioc.

The preceding series of bald assertions must sound particularly improbable in the light of MacNeish's work at Tehuacán and the claims concerning what this research has demonstrated (MacNeish 1967; Mangelsdorf, MacNeish, and Galinat 1967). If one examines the series of plant remains recovered by MacNeish and his coworkers rather than the claims, one must accept them as evidence that *no subsequently important cultivated plant was brought through the initial stages of domestication within the Tehuacán Basin!* What is surprising is the early date at which plants, already clearly marked as cultigens, start putting in their appearance. This is most spectacularly true of maize which, when it arrives at around 7000 B.P., is already beyond the genetic Rubicon which separates maize, the misfit, from its viable wild ancestor teosinte, *Zea mexicana* (see Beadle 1972, and this volume; cf. actual descriptions of early maize from Tehuacan [Mangelsdorf, MacNeish, and Galinat 1967: 179–80]).

The same general comment can be made for the picture emerging in the Highlands of the Central Andes, both at Guitarrero Cave (Kaplan, Lynch, and Smith 1973) and around Ayacucho (MacNeish 1969), and is irrefutably clear on the central coast of Peru, for which we have the most complete sequence of early plant remains in the New World (Cohen, this volume). Cultigens appear very early, but when they appear they are already fully differentiated as cultigens. On the basis of accomplished work, we can now specify that the Mexican Highlands, the central coast of Peru, the Callejón de Huaylas, and the Ayacucho Basin were areas where the initial experimentation with potential cultigens DID NOT TAKE PLACE (though Ayacucho may be close to the hearth of domestication for the guinea pig [Wing, this volume]).

I conclude that the single "Neolithic revolution" in the New World was an intensification of a system of cultivation of bitter manioc centered in the alluvial flood plains of Amazonia and northern South America which had attained high efficiency by 6000 to 7000 B.P., but to understand that stage, we must start much further back in time and look at a very different crop, *Lagenaria siceraria*, the white-flowered bottle gourd.

MAN AND THE BOTTLE GOURD

The bottle gourd is given little attention in most treatments of economic botany and is frequently slighted or omitted in discussions of agricultural origins. In our own culture its hard-shelled fruit may serve as a darning egg or as the proper house for inducing purple martins to nest (Audubon 1937: Plate 22). In more tropical areas of the New World it retains a larger importance in material culture. In the rural areas of Peru, even now, 3,800 years after the introduction of pottery, a wide range of shapes of bottle gourds remain as active cognate categories and significant technological materials (Jiménez Borja 1948: 50). For preceramic groups, or secondarily aceramic groups such as the Polynesians (Dodge 1943), the bottle gourd assumed a key role in material culture by functioning as cup, plate, bottle, net-float (Bird 1948: Figure 10), musical instrument, rattle, rasp, and a specialized container for materials such as ground lime. Picked slightly green, its fruit can even be used directly over the fire as a kind of nonreturnable cooking pot.

Its symbolic and ceremonial associations are curious. According to the Akawaio, a Carib-speaking group in Guyana:

A long time ago people living here fought among themselves until only one man was left alive. He had no wife and to remedy this he took a drinking gourd (*pötsaw*) and copulated with it, so making a woman of the gourd. With her he peopled the entire place. These people were called Pötsaugok the drinking cup people.... They make gurgling noises, like people drinking out of a *pötsaw*, because they originated in a drinking gourd (Butt Colson 1973: 42).

Reichel-Dolmatoff in his monumental ethnography of the Cogi, the Indians still inhabiting the Sierra Nevada de Santa Marta in Colombia, noted that the involuted religious life of these people is activated in times of economic hardship. During these periods of stress the men spend most of their time in the sacred house chanting along with the religious leaders. At such times the consumption of coca with lime increases tremendously, and the men are constantly fiddling with their lime containers, repeatedly sticking the spatula in and out. The lime container is, of course, a bottle gourd and the manipulation of the gourd and spatula is a conscious metaphor for copulation and a statement of sexual tension during periods of almost complete segregation of men and women (Reichel-Dolmatoff 1949–50, 1a: 78–9).

Reichel-Dolmatoff's observations are best compared with one curious aspect of the female transvestitism which Bateson has recorded as a standard part of the Naven ceremony of the Iatmul in northeastern New

Guinea. The role-reversing aspects of the Naven ceremony serve to bind across potential lines of fission in the society, and the women assume their male role with great gusto. As a part of the male attire, they wear and manipulate the lime container and spatula. (In New Guinea the lime container and spatula are part of the paraphernalia for the chewing of betel, not coca.) The Iatmul spatula is serrated so as to produce a rasping noise when inserted or extracted from the gourd container. The noise is a standard form of male-versus-male aggressive behavior. Men complain that the women rasp the spatulas so violently as to wear the serrations away (Bateson 1958: 15).

It is probably not unrelated conceptually that through much of Melanesia an appropriately shaped race of bottle gourd is grown to serve the specific function of a penis sheath (Heiser 1973b).

The African literature needs careful study with reference to the symbolic and ritual importance of gourds. In a popular summary of African mythology, I noticed repeated mention of a horizontally halved gourd as a symbol for the whole universe with the upper half representing the sky and the lower half the ocean (Parrinder 1967: 21–2, 42). The earth is then seen as a smaller gourd floating within the lower half. Gourds also tend to function as the containers for ritually potent materials such as the bones of deceased rulers (Parrinder 1967: 32).

By pooling these South American, Melanesian, and African fragments we may conclude that metaphorically the gourd is a womb, that it is the whole universe, or, stated more simply, the universal womb. The sensible way to treat this pan-tropical distribution of a peculiar set of beliefs about the bottle gourd would be to assume three historically independent developments. Certainly, the sexual symbolism involved here is rather obvious. I do not accept the sensible explanation, but am arguing that we are seeing little pieces of a single, historically valid, and extremely ancient cultural pattern. What is more, I am maintaining that the metaphors we have been examining have more than a grain of historical truth. The bottle gourd as a cultivated plant furnished the womb in which all more elaborate agricultural systems developed. Stated more precisely: the artificial propagation of the bottle gourd and certain other technologically significant crops such as cotton and fish poisons imposed particular disciplines on man and in the context of these behavioral patterns all of the other nutritionally significant agricultural systems arose.

THE ARCHAEOLOGICAL DISTRIBUTION OF THE BOTTLE GOURD

Let us turn to the botanical and distributional facts about the bottle gourd. *Lagenaria siceraria* is in the same botanical family as the diverse flock of New World cultigens in the genus *Cucurbita* which we call squashes and pumpkins, but the two genera are botanically quite distinct (Cutler and Whitaker 1961). Wild species in the genus *Lagenaria* are native to Africa (Whitaker 1971: 321–3). There is said to be a single species of wild *Lagenaria* in eastern Brazil, but it lacks the characteristics of a possible wild ancestor to cultivated *Lagenaria siceraria* (Heiser, personal communication 1973). In terms of the known range of feasible wild ancestors, *Lagenaria siceraria* must have been brought under cultivation in Africa. Though anciently a cultivated plant in southeastern Asia, in Oceania, and in the tropical New World, *Lagenaria* has not established itself in aggressive feral communities in any of these areas. Its maintenance outside Africa requires human intervention. Lehman (personal communication) has noted that the *Lagenaria* is among the first plants to disappear as a southeastern Asian swidden returns to bush. Its remarkable distribution in archaeological sites in the New World has led to repeated and intensive search for truly wild *Lagenaria* (Pickersgill, personal communications), but to date the search has been fruitless.

Even the evidence regarding the specialized insect pests on the plants in the Cucurbitaceae suggests, though it does not prove, that *Lagenaria siceraria* had a geologically recent introduction into the New World. The typical insect pests on the squashes and pumpkins avoid the bottle gourd, while the bottle gourd is most commonly afflicted with the melon aphid, an Old World insect (Wayne Howe, personal communication 1973; Howe and Rhodes 1973; Howe, Zdarkova, and Rhodes 1972).

To summarize, *Lagenaria siceraria* was brought under cultivation in Africa. Its survival outside Africa is dependent on human intervention, making it a classic example of an evolved cultigen.

One further point should be introduced here. Heiser, certainly the foremost practical student of the problem, has demonstrated that the New World bottle gourds are similar to the African bottle gourds and most dissimilar to the bottle gourds of eastern Asia (Heiser 1973a: 128). Africa stands at the center of the dispersal of the bottle gourd as a cultivar, contributing it directly to the New World. Trans-Pacific drift from southeastern Asia cannot account for the bottle gourds of the New World.

With the magnificent exception of Carl Sauer, thinking on the problem of agricultural origins has been dominated by strict inductivists. We are continually enjoined to accumulate more facts (preserved plant remains from secure archaeological context) as the road to God's truth. Here Paul Mangelsdorf (1953) and Richard MacNeish (1969: 3) must be identified as the high priests of the trend, but some of Harlan's recent writing also shows these tendencies (Harlan 1971; Harlan and de Wet 1973). Given this intellectual climate, the surprise is that so little attention has been given the archaeological distribution of irrefutable evidence for the presence of *Lagenaria siceraria*. An anticipatory summary of this distribution is: wherever one approaches a preserved archaeological record of man's initial altering of the availability of plants, the most likely datum to be encountered is irrefutable evidence of *Lagenaria siceraria*. Chester Gorman's excavations at Spirit Cave in Thailand have generated some unnecessarily acrimonious debate (see Flannery 1973: 285 for balanced comment), but at the very least they have demonstrated our first principle of evidence for Neolithic experimentation, the presence of a plant far outside the natural range of the species (Gorman, this volume). Here, between 10,000 and 8000 B.P., we find the bottle gourd as a cultigen (Gorman 1969). In the New World we find MacNeish's excavation in the Sierra Madre in Tamaulipas placing bottle gourd as present between 10,000 and 8000 B.P. (MacNeish 1958: 178, 192, 198). Similar datings are also recorded for Tehuacán and Oaxaca (Flannery 1973: 289).

If we turn to South America, the dated distribution of the bottle gourd is even more remarkable. On the far northern coast of Peru, Richardson has recovered several fragments of bottle gourd from a secure context in a Siches complex deposit, 8000–6000 B.P. (Richardson 1973).[1] Somewhat inland from Talara, Richardson has encountered other evidence

---

[1] A final reevaluation of the remains of gourds from the far northern coast of Peru was received after that section of this chapter was in final form (James B. Richardson, personal communication 1974): "On the basis of further work at the Siches Site PV 719 in 1972, 1973, we now know that this large site is a multicomponent preceramic midden ranging from Siches through Honda Phases. Test excavation No. 4, level 2, has resulted in the recovery of 13 further fragments of uncarbonized *Lagenaria* which are without doubt of the Honda Phase. Radiocarbon dates are currently being run on the level. However, the test made in 1967 has provided a radiocarbon date Gxo 996 4805±130 B.P. or 2855 B.C. which dates the *Lagenaria* fragment recovered in 1967. Thus the 6000 B.C. date for *Lagenaria* assumed to be in the Siches Phase (Richardson 1972: 267) should be corrected. The remains of *Lagenaria* are confined to the Honda Phase, dating to circa 3000 B.C. However, it should be noted that the absence of *Lagenaria* from the earlier Siches Phase levels of the site may be no more than an artifact of preservation. The Siches levels were deposited under conditions of higher rainfall, and no uncarbonized plant remains were recovered from these levels."

suggestive that agriculture may have become important by 6000 B.P., considerably earlier than on the better known central coast of Peru (Richardson 1972). For the central coast of Peru immediately north of Lima, Cohen has clear evidence of gourd in Arenal and Luz contexts, 8000–7000 B.P. some 2,500 years earlier than the next cultigen to appear in the area (Cohen, this volume). The real shocker is the occurrence of fragments of rinds from bottle gourds from levels at Pikimachay Cave in the Ayacucho Basin dating earlier than 13,000 B.P. The identification as *Lagenaria siceraria* is certain, made both by Pickersgill and Whitaker, with Whitaker tending to believe that the specimens were from a cultivated plant (Pickersgill, personal communication 1971). Flannery, on the basis of considerable knowledge of the excavations, is skeptical of the possibility that the fragments were intrusive (1973: 303) from the levels dated at 8000 B.P., where the next oldest preserved plant remains were encountered.

Flannery and I are generally aware of the same data. Only the information very recently presented by Richardson and Cohen is not included in his discussion (Flannery 1973). Yet we come to very different conclusions. In almost every part of nuclear America where there has been a successful search for very early plant remains, the bottle gourd appears at the very bottom of each sequence containing such plant-remains, usually between 10,000–7000 B.P., and in one instance as early as 13,000 B.P. Furthermore, there is its appearance in southeastern Asia in the range between 10,000–8000 B.P. Flannery explains away this whole record with reference to a pan-tropical distribution of a truly wild *Lagenaria siceraria*, which remains hypothetical both in the New World and in eastern Asia, in spite of the most intensive search. Flannery (1973: 292–4) makes merry over the gullibility of those who have given credence to the mysterious disappearance of the "wild" maize hypothesized by Mangelsdorf, yet he asks us to believe in an even more remarkable disappearing act on the part of his hypothetical "wild" *Lagenaria*. Conveniently available at 10,000 B.P. to the inhabitants of southeastern Asia and all of nuclear America, "wild" *Lagenaria* has since vanished from both areas. I find the set of data discussed far more compatible with the hypothesis that *Lagenaria* was introduced into both southeastern Asia and South America as a fully domesticated plant, and that it was brought under domestication in Africa at a very early time indeed.

If I have not overstated the importance of *Lagenaria* to an understanding of the emergence of agricultural systems, two criteria should be satisfied in the archaeological record: (1) *Lagenaria* should appear at the base of the record of man's utilization of plants; (2) *Lagenaria* should show a progressively greater importance to the technology, economy, and art of the people who cultivated it. The first criterion has already been supported in the previous discussion. Huaca Prieta, the best reported preceramic site on the coast of Peru, shows the diversification of uses of the bottle gourd required by the second criterion (Bird 1948). The importance of the gourd to the technology, art, and commerce of the Valdivia culture, on the coast of Ecuador, already provided with a competent ceramic technology, has been considered elsewhere (Lathrap 1973a: 176; 1974). That the most productive artistic medium was the carved gourd rather than the ceramic vessel, speaks well for the strength of my hypothesis.

As mentioned earlier, Coursey has presented the case for a very early pattern of root-crop agriculture in tropical western Africa (Coursey 1972, 1976; Coursey and Coursey 1971), and during the discussion at the Woodstock conference Harlan indicated that the data relevant to the spread of the cultivation of sorghum suggest that the cultivation of that crop started very early, somewhere in a belt extending across the southern Sudan in Africa. Speculation on the earliest instances of Neolithic experimentation in Africa should be the prerogative of scholars who have set foot on that continent. But, since I am arguing that the bottle gourd was brought under domestication in Africa early enough to have been spread as a cultigen to both southeastern Asia and nuclear America by 10,000 B.P. at the very latest, I should at least be forced to sketch my views on why we should look to the moist tropics of Africa as the earliest area in which man meddled with the natural availability of plants. In the first place I would agree with the position that Bronson takes in this volume, that man's first interest was to increase the supply of plants which were actually or potentially rare, rather than to increase the range of plants, such as the wild ancestors of wheat, which occur in large, nearly pure stands including thousands of individuals. This concern with increasing the availability of rare and widely dispersed species of plants is understandable in the moist tropics where MOST species are rare in the sense that individuals of each species are widely dispersed and few in number (Sternberg 1973; Janzen 1973: 1214). Any small unit of territory, specifically the unit of territory which can be conveniently exploited by a small human group, will have only a few individuals of each useful plant, a resource easily degraded.

If, as is now generally assumed, man evolved as a species on the savannahs of Africa, it is most likely that certain groups of man were first faced with the problem of adjusting to nonsavannah environments somewhere in Africa. On several occasions Thayer Scudder and I have had long discussions on the whys and hows of a human readjustment to the moist tropics of Africa. Groups exploiting the fantastically rich supply of animal protein available on the African grasslands would not willingly enter areas of continuous forest where the biomass of land mammals per unit of area was perhaps one fiftieth as great (Clark 1976: 88). Possibly the long-term effects of climatic shift must be invoked to get human groups into the moist tropics of Africa. Such groups would not have entered willingly. In times of increased aridity (the interglacials) the areas of continuous forest would have contracted considerably, greatly increasing the amount of savannah, with savannah penetrating the interfluvial zones between the various tributaries of the Congo system. Human populations would gradually expand to take advantage of the total areas of savannah. With the onset of more moist conditions, the area of continuous canopy forest would expand and eventually some groups would be pinned in the interfluve of the Congo drainage and engulfed in the encroaching forest (Clark 1959: 149–51). (We are, of course, viewing the process over millennia rather than decades.) Many such groups would become extinct, but those that survived would gravitate toward the river banks where there was a greater concentration of land mammals and semiaquatic animals, and where there was an abundant supply of animal protein in the form of fish and aquatic reptiles. Through time a culture more adapted to a systematic exploitation of the rich and reliable riverine resources would have evolved, correlated with a progressive neglect of the poorer and less dependable resources of the upland forests between the rivers. Eventually a systematic exploitation of riverine resources would permit communities to become sedentary. At this time we might also expect more emphasis on the digging of tubers (see Coursey 1976). As Lee and Binford, among others, have demonstrated beyond reasonable doubt (Lee 1972a; Harris, this volume) a shift from a way of life involving continuous wandering or an annual round of migration to a fully sedentary life (at least for women, children, and the aged) will cause an upward turn in the rate of growth of a population.

As fishing came to provide an ever greater part of the animal protein in the diet and even a significant part of the total caloric intake, cultural mechanisms would accumulate to increase the efficiency of that operation. Nets and net floats would be developed, and powerful fish poisons employed. It is in this context that a perceived scarcity of linted cotton as a source of fiber for nets, of bottle gourds as net-floats and containers, of particular leguminous vines in the genera *Lonchocarpus*, and *Tephrosia* as fish poisons, will arise. The principle of least effort may be an equally powerful explanation for a systematic localization of plant resources. The people involved would have increased the supply of these plants by transplanting and tending individual specimens in the yard surrounding their now permanent residences. It was also at this time that man began to modify the range of important plants, for each time population growth necessitated outward colonization, the daughter colony would replant the potentially scarce plant resources in house yards of the new community. This pattern of establishing new communities through a process of planned, outward colonization is conceptually, and in its results, very different from the free wandering on seasonal orbits typical of earlier human communities. The outward colonization may have occurred only every half-century or so, and served to extend the range of stable, non-migratory communities.

We have already noted at least two factors affecting our early riverine communities, sedentism and an abundant supply of fish which is basically nonseasonal in its availability. Both would be expected to increase rates of population growth and thus speed up the rate of outward colonization, as that process is viewed over a span of centuries or millennia.

Let us assume that under the regime sketched above the bottle gourd was brought under cultivation in Africa and eventually so modified and "improved" that it was no longer competitive in communities of wild plants. We must necessarily assume that this ennoblement took place sufficiently early to meet the timetable of its arrival in Thailand and Ayacucho. Given that constraint, I consider it not unlikely that the "Neolithic" experimentation sketched above started by 40,000 B.P. and was in part related to the rather broad cultural category, Sangoan.

I will leave to other scholars, and/or other papers, the problem of getting the cultivated bottle gourd out of Africa and into southeastern Asia by 10,000–9000 B.P. (Coursey 1973: 12–13). What I will attempt is a model relating to the events which brought *Lagenaria siceraria* to Ayacucho by 13,000 B.P., and to various points in Mesoamerica by 9000 B.P. This problem readily breaks down into two distinct segments: (1) getting cultivated *Lagenaria* from western Africa to eastern Brazil, across an appreciable stretch of open ocean; (2) getting the cultivar from the northeastern corner of Brazil to western South America and Mexico. We have already noted that Heiser's detailed studies (1973a) of variation in cultivated *Lagenaria* make it certain that cultivated *Lagenaria* was introduced from Africa to South America rather than from eastern Asia across the Pacific. If we assume an introduction into the New World from western Africa, then there is about one chance in a hundred that the introduction was elsewhere than northeastern Brazil, particularly the stretch of coast between Recife and the mouth of the Amazon. A glance at the map should be enough to convince one of this, and Schwerin (1970) has published an excellent discussion of the relevant winds and currents which facilitate a crossing at this point. The recent botanical expedition of the University of Reading was focused on the northeast of Brazil partially because of the proximity of this area to Africa (Bunting and Pickersgill 1971: 2–3). The question of the bottle gourd in the New World was of major interest to the participants. No truly wild gourds were found though an exceptionally wide range of distinct cultivars was encountered, including a strain deliberately maintained for its edible qualities (Pickersgill and Bunting 1972: 6). The diversity of cultivars of *Lagenaria siceraria* in northeastern Brazil is at least compatible with the hypothesis that its cultivation is particularly ancient in this part of the New World (Pickersgill and Bunting 1972: 6, Figure 5).

Since Schwerin (1970), Whitaker (1971), and Richardson (1972) have all discussed the various agencies which might have effected the trans-Atlantic crossing of *Lagenaria*, I will confine myself to a few brief observations. The one point on which everyone is now agreed is that a bottle gourd net-float, either embedded in its net or broken free, could have made the trip across the rather narrow strip of South Atlantic in a sufficiently short time to maintain the viability of its seeds. Carter's elegant experiment (Whitaker and Carter 1954) removed this particular point from the realm of controversy. I would argue that once bottle gourd net-floats came into use on the coast or even the lower courses of the rivers of western Africa such crossings would fall into the category of fairly common events. There is, however, a residual problem, as Whitaker has pointed out (1971: 324). While the gourd will reach the beaches of northeastern Brazil with its seeds still quite capable of terminating, the plant will not grow on the salt sands and some mechanism must get the seeds off the beach and into a more favorable environment. Man is the most likely mechanism. It seems to me that we are faced with three alternatives: (1) the net and its floats of bottle gourds was encountered on the beach by people who already had developed cultural practices concerning the replanting and tending of useful and potentially rare plants, and the obviously useful plant was incorporated into an already established pattern of Neolithic experimentation; (2) the net with its gourd floats reached the beach and was found by a group innocent of any tendencies toward Neolithic experimentation, but containing an Archimedes-like individual: upon contemplating the net, with fish still dangling in it, this genius shouted "Eureka" and proceeded to plant the gourd seeds so as to insure the supply of net-floats; (3) a boatload of fishermen made the crossing alive, joined small, already established communities, and introduced developed water craft, elaborate fishing techniques, and the bottle gourd as a cultivar to be cherished. Until recently the very existence of indigenous South American communities at 16,000 B.P. would have been questioned. Evidence for widespread and culturally diversified occupation of South America is now accumulating rapidly for this time period (Bryan 1973).

I tend to reject the first of these alternatives, mainly because it seems unlikely that patterns of Neolithic experimentation would have been maintained by groups filtered into the New World through the Bering land bridge.

The second alternative, the idea that one can achieve an extensive enlightenment from an encounter with an elaborate technological device washed up on the beach or embedded in a fish or sea mammal, I find unconvincing. It goes against everything I know, or think I know, about cultural process. Possibly my reaction is colored by the fact that Heizer (1944) has offered this kind of model as an explanation for the trans-Pacific transmission of technological complexes only slightly less elaborate.

These considerations leave me with a most reluctant acceptance of the third alternative as the most probable: that a viable group of fishermen made the canoe voyage from western Africa to eastern Brazil bringing with them not only the bottle gourd and the leguminous fish poisons (Quigley 1956), but also the African linted cotton, *Gossypium herbaceum* L., var. *africanum*. (Whatever the mechanism of dispersal, it is now clear that the Old World diploid parent to the New World amphidiploid cultivated cottons is of African rather than Asian origin [Stephens 1966: 200]). I suspect that the elaborate cultural patterns relating to technology, economy, and an adjustment to the spiritual world were of greater importance than the introduction of specific genetic material of particular varieties of plants. In general, I am not attracted by explanations resting on long sea voyages by small groups of fishermen (Lathrap 1967, 1973a), and am willing to examine the possibility only as a last resort. In this instance such a model does seem to have a higher probability than its alternatives.

This model of trans-Atlantic contact has been elaborated by Schwerin (1970). My only objection to his presentation is that his dating is far too conservative to handle the information now in hand. My provisional acceptance of at least one instance of early trans-Atlantic contact is caused as much by the pan-tropical parallels in technology and religion as by the evidence of the bottle gourd. Identities in the production of bark-cloth have been given considerable attention as evidence for pan-tropical contact. I find even more compelling the complex of long distance communication through the use of a two-toned, signal gong carved from a section of log. Perhaps most curious of all is the elaborate structure of male initiation ritual and the pattern of impersonating the collective male ancestors with a disguise consisting of a carved wooden face piece and a bark-cloth or grass garment. All of these strike me as too elaborate and arbitrary to be examples of the psychic unity of man and too deeply imbedded in the cultures of South America to be the result of one or more trans-Pacific contacts subsequent to 3000 B.P. (The existence of such relatively late trans-Pacific contacts does, however, seem to be at least partially supported by various lines of evidence [Estrada and Meggers 1961]).

I will entertain the conclusion that not just the bottle gourd but a small and viable group of people bringing an extensive set of cultural patterns was introduced from Africa to eastern South America. I am, however, willing to leave the question of trans-Atlantic transport open to further debate. What I am certain of is that, once in eastern Brazil, the bottle gourd did not float UP the Amazon and over the Andes to arrive at Pikimachay Cave, in the Ayacucho Basin, and in the Arenal context on the coast of Peru near Lima. Since the maintenance of the bottle gourd in the New World seems dependent on human intervention, the extension of its range must be linked to some form of human activity.

In view of Flannery's endorsement (1973: 272, 303) of Barbara Pickersgill as the most healthy skeptic among archaeobotanists, I find it encouraging that in her most recent statement, the paper of Pickersgill and Heiser in this volume, she goes along with the idea that at least in the New World the expansion of the range of *Lagenaria siceraria* was the result of human activities. Pickersgill and Heiser suggest that the mere fact of permanent or semipermanent human occupation considerably disturbs the immediate environment. The trash heaps within this cleared area will be exposed to the sun, of a loose structure, and have a high content of available nitrogen, a setting optimum for a number of actually or potentially useful plants. Such plants will flourish in considerable density on the trash heaps, and in this context the bottle gourd will be maintained. Pickersgill and Heiser go on to suggest that when an offshoot community colonizes a new location, a new trash heap will be initiated and the seeds of the bottle gourd will ACCIDENT-ALLY be reintroduced into the favorable trash heap environment, thus perpetuating the cultivar and extending its range. Heiser in the course of the conference further elaborated this hypothesis suggesting that the *shaman* of the group would bring along his rattle, and that in the course of further ceremonial activities in the daughter community, the rattle would get broken, with some of the seeds being conveniently introduced into the trash heap. In this elaboration of Anderson's trash heap model, the gourd functions, in the words of Pickersgill and Heiser, as a camp follower.

As a cultural anthropologist I must insist that the human activities responsible for the maintenance and spread of the bottle gourd in the New World were governed by cultural patterns specifically adequate to the task; or to put it more bluntly, the people knew what they were doing. I will further suggest that these patterns were inherently expandable to include other potential and actual cultigens, and that in their working out through time these patterns had a built-in push toward further cultural elaboration.

THE HOUSE GARDEN, A SYSTEM OF MODERATE INSTABILITY

What are the factors which prevent *Lagenaria siceraria* from flourishing as a wild or feral plant in the New World? No one seems to know precisely, but Heiser and I are in total agreement that further botanical and ethnobotanical research should be focused on just this point. If, however, we view the problem in terms of the maintenance and spread of the gourd in areas of tropical forest with a continuous canopy, we can hazard a couple of shrewd guesses. The plant will require far more light than is available on the floor of the tropical forest so that the forest canopy must be at least partially broken. The plant must be protected from the mass of low, dense vegetation which will immediately invade a cleared or partially cleared area, so that systematic and fairly finicky patterns of weeding must be instigated and maintained. These patterns would have been initiated most effectively in the immediate vicinity of the residence which by then had become a permanent structure. The earliest examples of the cleared and weeded areas would have contained at least the bottle gourd, cotton (*Gossypium caicoense* on the road to becoming both *G. barbadense* and *G. hirsutum*), and leguminous fish poisons of the genera *Lonchocarpus* and *Tephrosia*. To meet our assumed schedule, such patterns must have been extant on the coast of Brazil near the mouth of the Amazon 16,000 B.P. Pickersgill and Heiser (this volume), and Pickersgill and Bunting (1972) discuss *G. caicoense*, the "wild" linted, amphidiploid cotton found sporadically in north-eastern Brazil. Stephens in a letter (15 July 1972) admitted the possibility that *G. caicoense* or something very like it might be at the node between the two cultivated cottons of the New World, *G. barbadense* and *G. hir-sutum*, although he does not favor the idea: "The fact the *caicoense* looks like a 'central species' suggests the possibility that the common ancestor may have started out somewhere in eastern South America and that the differentiation of the two species may have begun in the same region — but that is just a speculation. (Perhaps I should add that I don't think one could consider *caicoense* as a possible ancestor of the kidney cottons — all forms of cultivated *barbadense* are much more akin to the wild *darwinii* of the Galapagos than to *caicoense*)." An understanding of the whole problem of New World cultivated cottons is made difficult by the ability of the New World amphidiploids to go feral and establish self-sustaining communities (Stephens 1965).

In the controlled environment around the house, too much sun may have been as undesirable as too little. Certain trees would intentionally have been left or replanted within the modified zone around the house. *Ceiba* is the classic tree to give a light to moderate shade in areas utilized by man, and it is, typically, left as the rest of the jungle is cleared. Its role as a sacred tree in Africa, as the "world tree" of the Maya, and as a sacred tree throughout South America probably stems from this function. Certain other trees would be left or transplanted because they provided industrial material such as thatch, high quality hardwood, and most particularly because they supplied edible fruit available at various times during the year. There should have been little lapse of time, on a scale calibrated to millennia rather than decades, between the instigation of practices necessary to maintain some plants crucial to efficient fishing and the achievement of that remarkable artifact, the house garden.

The following comments on the house garden as an institution derive almost entirely from my own observations and from the South American ethnographic literature. The importance of the phenomenon was driven home to me, when my wife in the course of her ethnographic work asked my Shipibo compadre, Catalino Agustín Cumapa, to identify and give the significance of all of the plants remaining in a section of his house garden which had been weeded the previous day. Exactly what transpired is an involved story with implications far beyond the scope of this paper, but the immense number of discrete botanical categories maintained, the care with which they were protected, and the conceptual complexity of the cultural patterns which governed the maintenance of the house garden all became abundantly clear. The subject also turned out to be a sensitive area on which to gather information. This account is intended as a kind of least common denominator for practices shared by cultures within the Tropical Forest Tradition of South America. It is my impression that the cultural attitudes are almost identical in tropical Africa and in the tropical parts of southeastern Asia and Oceania, although the full range of included plants may be very different. (My colleague, H. M. Ross, was immediately able to list all of the important trees and shrubs in the house gardens on Mailita in the Solomon Islands.)

The house garden, though it need not be fenced and usually is not, is conceptually sharply delimited from the surrounding forest (Reichel-Dolmatoff 1971: 107). The cleared area containing the house garden is conceived as safe, while the forest in general is considered dangerous with potentially malevolent spirits under almost every tree (Reichel-Dolmatoff 1971: 34). The Desana even conceive of the orderly space around the house as being guarded by monstrous, invisible harpy eagles (Reichel-Dolmatoff 1971: 108). In so far as the people keep the house garden in total order, it will be free from most malignant influences (Huxley 1957). There is no piece of vegetation permitted in the zone that is not left by intent or introduced for a specific culturally defined purpose. Thus each house or community is encased in, and protected by, a totally artificial, floral environment.

Man leaves the safety of the zone of the house garden only at a certain risk. The lakes and rivers, as the proper sphere of male activity, are relatively safe (Goldman 1963: 44–45, 50–51). The forest away from the rivers is more dangerous and its dangers increase manyfold at night (Goldman 1963: 44; Huxley 1957). Below a certain age children are strictly confined to the house garden. As a sanction to lock them within this secure playpen, they are occasionally terrorized by masked impersonators of the malevolent beings in the lake and forest. The masks of these spirits are, of course, of gourd. Likewise the malevolent spirit is far off base when he enters the orderly zone around the house and can be quickly routed by a whiff of smoke from the allopolyploid tobacco (Pickersgill 1972: 100) so carefully cultivated in the house garden.

There is, to my knowledge, no adequate, published inventory of the plants in a typical South American house garden. The orderly space around the house may contain 50 to 100 discrete botanical entities. A few of the more common should be mentioned. The calabash tree, *Crescentia cujete*, is valuable both for the moderate shade that it gives and for the hard-rinded fruit, which can be put to many of the functions of the bottle gourd, though the fruit of *Crescentia* has not been teased genetically into the wide variety of shapes available with the various cultivars of

Lagenaria. Few house gardens from southern Mesoamerica to the southern border of the Amazon Basin are without this tree, and it would be very difficult to guess what the original prehuman distribution was.

A variety of palms were left or transplanted to form a part of the house garden. The most significant of these is the peach palm, *Guilielma gasipaes,* whose wood is one of the valuable hardwoods designated by the term *chonta,* and whose fruit is abundant and of a particularly high nutritive value. The peach palm is a major factor in the caloric intake of the people and it reaches its maximum importance in southern Central America (Linares de Sapir and Ranere personal communication). Most of its range at the contact period, however, is an artifact. Almost certainly the peach palm is native only to the Upper Amazon, quite possibly being first introduced into the system on the central Ucayali or in eastern Ecuador (Yanguez-Bernal 1968). Other palms are maintained in the garden as sources of thatch, matting, wood, and fruit. The avocado *Persea* with its highly nutritious fruit is an ancient and typical member of the assemblage of the house garden. The leguminous tree, *Anadenanthera peregrina,* the source of the most powerful of the hallucinogenic snuffs, is typically planted in this context, and its range has been tremendously extended, especially out into the Antilles (Wassen 1965, 1967; Schultes 1972: 24–28). There is a bewildering array of other important trees planted or preserved for their edible fruit, ranging from *inga* and *guayava,* with the sweet fiber surrounding the seeds as the edible part, to *caimito* and *lucuma* producing large fleshy fruit.

Among the smaller trees or large bushes is cacao, *Theobroma.* The extension of plants of this genus into Mesoamerica is probably an artifact of the pattern of the house garden. Its typical use in the Amazon basin, where it was first added to the assemblage, is as a fresh fruit with the pulp surrounding the seeds being the part consumed. The use of the seed as a source of chocolate is more restricted, and possibly did not develop until the cultivar spread to coastal Ecuador or southern Mesoamerica (Marcos 1973; Cheesman 1944). Marañón, *Anacardium occidentale,* the cashew bush, is habitually included. The desired part was not the seed, the cashew nut of commerce, but the greatly enlarged pulpy stem which was eaten fresh or used as a source of a nonalcoholic beverage (Sauer 1950: 530). The two classic dye plants of the Amazon Basin, the blue-black *genipe (Genipa americana)* and the reddish-brown *achiote (Bixa orellana),* are almost invariably present. The perennial, kidney-seeded cotton of the Amazon *(Gossypium barbadense)* is also a tree-sized member of the assemblage of the house garden, as is the ancient and dietetically important papaya, *Carica papaya.*

Fairly low plants, tended as members of the assemblage in the house garden, are the most diverse segment of its population. A wide range of grasses and herbs is grown as a source of perfumes. Medicinal plants and plants used to increase specific skills and sensory acuities will run to twenty or thirty items in most gardens. The extremely important condiment, *aji, Capsicum* (Pickersgill 1969), is to be found here along with the species of *Solanum* cultivated for their fruit. Here also is the pineapple *Ananas sativus*. As mentioned earlier the fish poisons are typically present.

A wide array of minor food crops will be represented by small stands or a few individuals. For instance, I noted small patches of a cultivated tuberous *Oxalis* in house gardens in the Conibo community of Painaco. It is in the house garden that one will find small stands of the cultivated hybrid tobaccos, *Nicotiana tabacum* and *N. rustica*, first added to the assemblage someplace in the Upper Amazon (Pickersgill 1972; Goodspeed 1953).

The house garden functioned as an experimental plot. New species of plants brought in from the forest or received through contact with other ethnic groups would be introduced into the house garden in a conscious effort to evaluate their potential as useful cultigens. The composition of the house garden was dynamic; the species listed above were the bare minimum of what must be included, while the potential of other species was constantly being investigated. This process has gone on in post-Columbian times with the mango tree, various citrus fruits, and the cooking banana all achieving a crucial position in the assemblage. I would argue that the important food crops of Amazonia (the peanut, the sweet potato, the New World yam, the New World cultivated aroid [*Xanthasoma*], arrow root, and — most important of all — manioc, [*Manihot esculenta* Crantz]) were ennobled in the context of these experimental plots. I would argue that they were introduced into the house garden as minor additions to the available food supply. Under the artificial growing conditions and a degree of artificial selection, they were genetically modified so as to become the supremely efficient food producers of the tropical forest system at the time of the contact period. As genetic modifications accumulated, leading to larger and more nutritious edible parts, more individuals were planted, and larger areas were devoted to their cultivation. Eventually a pattern developed of dense stands of important food crops planted in clearings beyond the house garden.

Chacras, areas of the jungle cleared and burned strictly for use as agricultural land, were conceptually distinct from the house garden.

Whereas the house garden remained fixed for the duration of the settlement, the *chacra* moved, every three to five years, in response to soil
depletion and/or the incursion of weeds. While avoiding the extremes of
monocropping, so typical of the energy-demanding agricultural systems
of the temperate zone, the tropical forest *chacra* contained a large number
of individuals representing only two to five of the most efficient crops.
In this it contrasted sharply with the complexity of the community of
plants in the house garden. The *chacra* served as an efficient source
of bulk feed. While the house garden was safe, the spiritual position
of the *chacra* was ambiguously between the security of the house garden
and the peril of the continuous jungle. There was an aura of spiritual
disorder or at least potent sexuality about the *chacra* in which human
sex acts interact mutually and positively with the fecundity and productivity of the crops (Huxley 1957; Goldman 1963: 30).

David Harris in a recent letter to me gave further support to the essential cognitive distinction between the house garden and the *chacra*.
I had previously argued that the cultigens illustrated on the Chavín
monument, the Obelisk Tello, were dichotomized into gifts of the deity
of the sky and gifts of the deity of the underworld and water (Lathrap
1973b). The gifts of the great cayman of the sky are seed crops, while the
gifts of the great cayman of the water and the underworld are root crops
cultivated by cuttings from their underground organs. As Harris clarifies,
the gifts of the sky cayman, *aji* and the bottle gourd, are also classically of
the house garden, while the gifts of the great cayman of the water and
underworld, manioc and achira, are definitively crops of the *chacra*.

We can consider the gradual differentiation of the *chacra* as a good
example of cultural evolution leading to the cultural recognition of
two distinct categories of artificial floral environment. Harris has greatly
illuminated the general characteristics of this evolutionary trend (1972:
182–3). Under stress, the artificial but highly complex ecosystem of the
house garden shifts toward a larger, more efficient (in returns of calories
per acre), more expensive (in terms of the input of energy for preparation
and maintenance), and ecologically simpler artificial environment,
the *chacra*.

The aboriginal *chacras* studied by Harris (1971) off the Upper Orinoco
in Venezuela are only part way along this trend of intensification. For
reasons which have been discussed at length elsewhere (Lathrap 1968a,
1970), I suspect that the Waika *chacras* analyzed by Harris represent a
less intensive agricultural system than was typical of the large, complex
groups (Myers 1973) inhabiting the banks of the Amazon and its tributaries as of A.D. 1500 or of the intensive system of utilization of bitter

manioc appearing in the alluvial lands of northwestern Venezuela and northern Colombia by 7000 B.P.

The emergence and differentiation of cultural categories relating to various kinds of artificial environment, and the scheduling of sufficient time and energy for the maintenance of these artificial environments, is as important to an understanding of the evolution of agriculture as shifts in the genetic makeup of the cultigens.

The potential for change inherent within the house garden has two aspects which must be considered separately. The one was the shift from a fishing economy, with the house garden maintained as an adjunct to fishing efficiency, to an economy in which fishing retained its importance as a sorce of protein, but in which vegetable food raised in the *chacras* provided well over 50 percent of the total caloric intake. I would suggest the following sketch of the processes involved. Within the moist tropics the rivers provided a far more reliable source of animal protein than the forest in general, thus male activities tended to be concentrated on the rivers. As it became apparent that an adequate supply of food for the group could be derived from a small segment of the river, there was no necessity or even advantage in shifting the residence of the group during the course of the year. A fully sedentary mode of residence was thus initiated. As noted in the discussion of the beginnings of these trends in Africa, sedentism could be expected to lead to a marked upturn in the rate of population growth. Since men spent far less time wandering in the forest, collecting from the widely dispersed useful plants of the forest would become progressively less efficient. In response there would be an ever-increasing tendency to concentrate the previously dispersed plant resources in the vicinity of the house where they would be readily available. The scheduling of a progressively greater part of male working hours in fishing and hunting for aquatic resources offered the context for ongoing elaboration of watercraft. These efficient watercraft, typically dugout canoes, which I am assuming were first introduced from Africa, required an increasing expenditure of time and effort for their manufacture. This major investment was a further incentive to settlement stability at points where the canoe could be docked and cared for (Lathrap 1968b). All the edible plants transplanted into the vicinity of the settlement would have the tendency of increasing the amount of available food and of increasing the year-round stability of the food supply. The expansion of the total available food and the elimination of seasons of scarcity would give a further kick to the rate of population growth. The expanding population would have a progressively greater dependence on cultivated food sources. Eventually those plants, which through progressive modification under conditions of the house garden had achieved greatest efficiency in terms of calories per acre, and greatest reliability in terms of assuring year-round availability of food, would come to dominate the economy. The pattern of establishing a controlled environmental setting for important plants would gradually be extended beyond the limits of the house garden so that the clearing and planting of *chacras* eventually became the most significant pattern with reference to total caloric intake.

The other unstable aspect of the house garden as a system was its tendency to extend continuously in geographical range. We have already noted that the combination of intensive fishing and progressively greater dependence on progressively more efficient sources of vegetable food will favor population growth. As Bateson first observed, viable social groups must budget for institutions which will discharge the tensions and aggressive tendencies inevitable in group living. More specifically, ongoing interaction will progressively alienate subunits of the viable society from each other, unless appropriate ceremonial behavior is maintained. These institutions must become progressively more elaborate and expensive as group size goes up (Bateson 1958: 96–7). It was Bateson's belief, a position more recently also enunciated by Carneiro (1961, 1970, 1972), that as long as there is open territory to colonize, groups will fission rather than suffer an increase in the expense and complexity of their institutions. Lee has also isolated just this principle, noting that when the Bushmen of southwestern Africa are in larger than normal-sized groups, they rely on the adjudicating institutions of their more evolved Bantu neighbors rather than developing their own (Lee 1972b). When the group size greatly exceeds that which can be accommodated by the ceremonial institutions binding the society together, part of the group will move outward as a viable clone of the society.

I have discussed the working out of these tendencies in more detail elsewhere (Lathrap and Braun 1974). To oversimplify, let us return to our initial group of fishermen, with their tendency to house gardens, located near the mouth of the Amazon at 16,000 B.P. If their institutions were adequate to a normal group size of 50, the group would fission when population growth led to an aggregate of 80 or so. One part of the society would move off and colonize another stretch of riverbank while the other segment would retain its ancestral location. There would be no tendency to larger groups and more complex ceremonial and political institutions until all appropriate land in the immediate vicinity was settled. Given the conditions discussed above, we can expect that the process of outward colonization by groups of 40 or 50

Plate 1.   A typical house in the conservative Conibo community of Painaco, on the Lower Ucayali River in eastern Peru, Fall 1967. Note the well-weeded house garden with several species of carefully tended plants. The plants in the lower left function as perfumes

Plate 2. A small patch of a cultivated, tuberous *Oxalis* in a house garden in the Conibo community of Painaco, on the Lower Ucayali of eastern Peru, Fall 1967

Plate 3.   The largest house in the Conibo community of Painaco, with its well-weeded house garden including a patch of cultivated tobacco, *Nicotiana* sp.

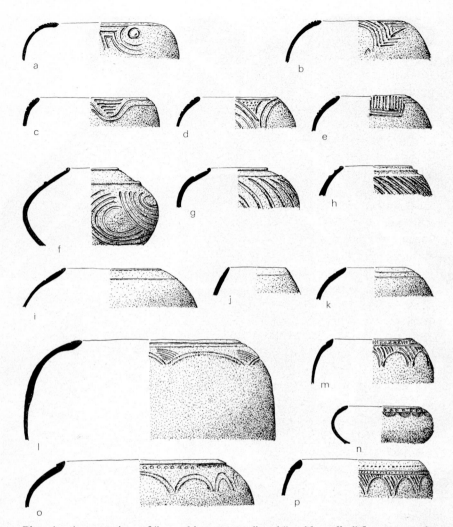

Plate 4. A comparison of "pumpkin tecomates" and "neckless ollas" from extremely early ceramic complexes of Nuclear America: a-e from the Canapote component of the Canapote site in northern Colombia, redrawn from notes furnished by Henning Bischof; f-h from the Barra component of the Altamira site in Chiapas, the earliest pottery in the lowlands of southern Mesoamerica, redrawn from Green and Lowe (1967: Figures 72–73); i-k from the Ocós component at the Izapa site in Chiapas, redrawn from Ekholm (1969: Figure 19); l-p from the Waira-jirca components at the sites of Kotosh and Shillacoto in the Huánuco Basin in the Central Highlands of Peru, the earliest pottery in the area, redrawn from Izumi and Sono (1963: Plate 139), Izumi and Terada (1972: Plates 124–125), and from Izumi, Cuculiza, and Kano (1972: Plate 51). All are drawn to the same scale; o is 42 centimeters in diameter

would have been relatively rapid. One can also specify quite precisely the directions which such colonization would take. Once the economic pattern of these people was committed to, and specialized for, intensive fishing as the mode of achieving adequate animal protein, the area appropriate to the total cultural system was greatly restricted, or "circumscribed" in Carneiro's terminology. Such groups could colonize successfully only along the active alluvial flood plains of major rivers, and along coasts with a significant potential for offshore fishing. Once such groups moved westward along the Brazilian coast into the Amazon system, the available resources of fish would be greater than those of the coast, leading to an even more efficient economic system and an accelerated upward spiraling of all of the processes we have been considering. This colonization would fill the inner flood plain of the Amazon and its larger tributaries with small groups of fishermen. Though the Amazon Basin is vast, the inner flood plain of the major rivers comprises much less than 5 percent of the total area. Moreover, the zone to be colonized was narrow, linear, and ran in an east-west direction so that the western front of the wave of colonization would proceed rapidly across the Amazon Basin bringing groups with their progressively more elaborate and more productive house gardens to the eastern foot of the Andes within a millennium or so. These processes are thus a sufficient explanation for the arrival of our efficient fishermen and house gardeners at the eastern feet of the Andes by 13,000 B.P. Given the general timetable necessitated by the dated distribution of the remains of *Lagenaria*, other non-cultural processes may also have operated to hasten the spread of these groups up the Amazon and to concentrate such populations in the western half of the Amazon Basin.

In his excellent discussion of the background of Neolithic experimentation in southeastern Asia, Chester Gorman in this volume notes that the rise in sea level of several hundred feet known to have occurred at the end of the Pleistocene would have tremendously reduced the amount of alluvial lowlands in southeastern Asia. The huge Sunda shelf, which in Pleistocene times connected the Indonesian Archipelago to the mainland, offered an area of tropical lowlands three or four times as great as what remained after 10,000 B.P. It was precisely the lower flood plains of the huge river systems eliminated by this massive inundation which would have been affected first. The inhabitants of these prime territories would have been pushed into the areas of remaining flood plains. An increased density of population on the remaining alluvial lands would be the probable result, and such an increase might be expected to produce further intensification of economic strategies, and an increase in group size requiring further elaboration of social institutions.

In northeastern Brazil and the lower Amazon Basin a far smaller area of land would have been affected by the rise of sea level at the end of the Pleistocene. There is a considerable area of coastal shelf extending to the north from the northeastern coast of Brazil and eastward from the mouth of the Amazon. The lower valleys of rivers crossing this shelf would have been lost to our hypothetical groups with a riverine orientation. The effect of the rise in sea level on the inner valley of the Lower Amazon would have been more drastic in terms of human utilization. Since the rise was dramatically rapid, at least in terms of the geological time scale, all of the lower valley would have been drowned with the elimination of all islands, natural levees, and point bar formations, the land forms typical of gradual alluvial aggradation. The destruction of those alluvial formations in the inner valley of the Lower Amazon would have greatly reduced the amount of land available for utilization by people with a riverine orientation, since these land forms are particularly suitable for settlement (Lathrap 1968a, 1968b, 1970). Given the range of elevations involved, the alluvial structures within the inner valley would have been submerged as far upstream as Manaos, and would only gradually have been reestablished in the following 10,000 years of alluvial aggradation (Sioli 1966: 385). Given the time span over which we are viewing these processes, the riverine communities would have appeared to have been flushed upstream by the rising ocean, and concentrated in the flood plains of the Upper Amazon and its tributaries. The concentration of our hypothetical fishing communities in the Upper Amazon would have had the same concomitants in terms of increased population density, intensification of economy, and acceleration of social evolution that Gorman has invoked for southeastern Asia.

Other lines of progressive colonization would move up the Rio Negro, across the Casiquiare Canal, down the Rio Orinoco, and out onto the Caribbean coast. Once on the Caribbean coast further colonization would involve the Maracaibo Basin and the major river systems of Colombia, the Magdalena-Cauca, Sinú, and Atrato. From here colonization would proceed northward on the Caribbean coast of Central America and penetrate along the alluvial lowlands flanking the major rivers entering the Caribbean. If we activate this model of outward colonization by 16,000 B.P. it should have covered all the tropical alluvial lowlands in nuclear America by 10,000 B.P. Clearly, each time one of these communities was established in a previously uncolonized area, it would establish the house garden, with its full complement of essential plants, as the protective zone in which the group flourished. I believe that this is the

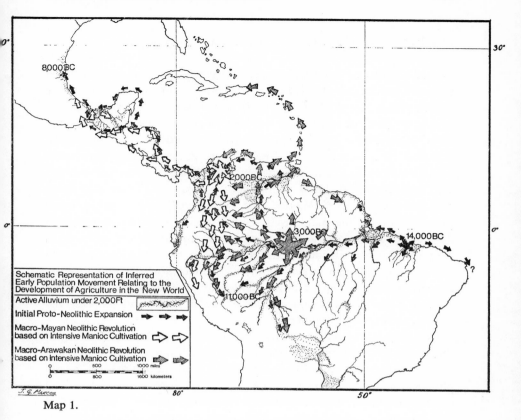

Map 1.

only model adequate to explain the movement of the bottle gourd from eastern Brazil to the eastern slope of the Andes by 13,000 B.P. and to the tropical lowlands of the Gulf Coast of Mexico, adjacent to the various higher and drier basins by 10,000 B.P.

As the pattern of house gardens was moved from one area of riverine tropical forest to another, it would have been exposed to differing zones of vegetation and thus to new potential cultigens to be integrated into the system. I would even suggest that there is a stratification of the food crops ennobled in this system. I suspect the sweet potato and the New World yam were very early absorbed into the system even before colonies moved beyond the lower Amazon. It would appear that manioc may have been introduced into the system relatively late in its history, possibly only after colonies had penetrated the Orinoco Basin and the northern lowlands of Colombia. Sauer (1952) presented a plausible argument for looking to this zone as the hearth of the cultivation of manioc. Certainly the earliest clear evidence of the effects of maximally intensified cultivation of manioc comes from Venezuela and Colombia. (See Map 1.)

MANIOC AND THE GREAT CAYMAN

Actual remains of the bottle gourd, *Lagenaria siceraria,* have formed the evidence which motivated the construction of my model of Neolithic experimentation in the New World. In spite of the importance of manioc in the agricultural systems of the New World, actual remains of the plant are extremely rare in the archaeological record. The major exception is on the arid coastal strip of Peru where it made its appearance as a fully developed and efficient cultigen by 3000 B.P. (Cohen, this volume). The intensive use of bitter manioc as the basis for the first Neolithic revolution in the New World must be inferred from evidence other than remains of the plant itself. Unlike maize with its extremely indurated cob, the avocado with its dense pit, or the various palm fruits with their highly silicious seeds, manioc has no hard parts likely to persist as identifiable structures after carbonization or partial decay. Luckily the processing of bitter manioc to produce unleavened bread or flour requires equipment with components which will be preserved in most archaeological contexts.

I am suggesting that the cultivation of manioc and the processing of this cultigen to a storable commodity had greatly intensified by 5000 B.P. In the tropical lowlands of Colombia and Venezuela by the third millennium B.C. we find the evidence of a legitimate Neolithic revolution with all of the criteria mentioned in the introduction to this paper. The evidence will here be presented in barest outline since most of the crucial points have been developed in other recent publications (Lathrap 1970, 1973a, 1973b, 1974, i.p.). The grater teeth and clay griddles specific to the production of manioc bread and flour are typical of the earliest sedentary settlements so far investigated in the alluvial lowlands of Colombia. This is best documented in the excavations of the Reichel-Dolmatoffs at the Momíl site on the Rio Sinú which conservatively extends into the third millennium B.C. (Reichel-Dolmatoff and Reichel-Dolmatoff 1956; Lathrap 1958; Foster and Lathrap 1973). The ceramics of the earliest component here are neither experimental nor crude and are a long way from the beginnings of a ceramic tradition. The same situation holds for the site of Rancho Peludo in the area of the Maracaibo Basin which may date to as early as 4600 B.P. (Rouse and Cruxent 1963: 48–9). I wish to emphasize that the use of bitter manioc as a basis for bread and flour production is indicative not of a subsistence agriculture but instead of an intensified agricultural economy in which appreciable amounts of the food produced are being fed into extended trade networks.

Contrary to the assumptions typically found in the literature, bitter manioc is the more evolved or ennobled cluster of cultivars among the maniocs. The selection process leading to the bitter group of maniocs has been in terms of higher starch yield and in terms of starch of a quality more appropriate for making bread and flour. The increase of glucoside in the tuber is an entailed side effect, rather than a characteristic selected for. Thus a concentration on bitter manioc as a staple is not a beginning step in the trajectory of its domestication, but the end point in the development of this fantastically efficient crop which outstrips almost every other cultivar in terms of calories produced per acre (Lathrap 1973a: 173–176; Schwerin 1971: 38, reaches the same conclusion after a particularly thorough examination of the ethnographic literature).

These conclusions of Schwerin and myself, reached independently, are opposed to those of some other investigators, and particularly, in the sphere of the contributors of this volume, to those of Harris, who has suggested (this volume) that cultural selection for bitter manioc was in response to its qualities of longer preservation while in natural storage below ground.

That this highly developed agricultural system had marked effects on demography, on group size, and on social complexity is indicated by a number of lines of evidence. Most obviously, the extent and density of the cultural deposit in sites such as Momíl indicate a level of size and community stability not achieved in highland Mesoamerica for another thousand years (Flannery 1973: 299).

Gordon Willey (1962) has most explicitly argued that all of the later civilizations in Mesoamerica seemed to derive their iconography, cosmology, and political systems from Olmec culture in the same way that all of the later civilizations of the Central Andes derived their iconography and organizational principles from Chavín culture. More recent work both in the Central Andes and in Mesoamerica has confirmed in detail Willey's position. He argued that the organizational principles offered by these complex iconographies and the cosmologies for which they stood were a major factor in permitting the development and articulation of large, tightly unified polities. Flannery, in one of his most recent essays (1972: 424), seems to adopt much the same position.

It is undeniable that the earliest and most typical setting of Olmec culture is on the alluvial flood plain of the Gulf Coast of southern Mexico. Although Chavín de Huántar is at a high elevation in the Andes, all of the elements of its iconography suggest a derivation from the tropical lowlands (Lathrap 1971). Most specifically there is direct evidence that the supreme being in the Chavín pantheon was a cayman, the typical crocodilian of the Amazon and Orinoco Basins, who was initially worshiped as the master of fish. This prime entity, who was in a real sense the whole universe, was transformed into a sky deity and a deity of the water and underworld. The Sky Cayman became the basic rain god and the Water and Underworld Cayman the source of fecundity. Both were celebrated as donors of the major cultivated plants and of these gifts the most important was manioc (Lathrap 1973b). In the most explicit exemplification of the Great Cayman as donor of plants, the Obelisk Tello, our friend the bottle gourd, *ají*, achira, and the peanut were also given honorable mention. Maize receives no notice!

It is easy to show that this supreme cayman deity of Chavín religion was the same entity as Itzamná, the supreme deity of Maya religion (Thompson 1970; Lathrap i.p.), who was also initially a cayman, and who in his first transformation becomes a cayman of the sky and a cayman of the water and the underworld. The importance of this concept can be fully identified in Classic Maya art. It is equally obvious in Olmec art, and is abundantly illustrated in Izapa style, the legitimate developmental link connecting Olmec to the later Classic and historic Maya (Lathrap i.p.). Most striking of all is the design on a vessel which Flannery and Schoenwetter illustrate as typical of the EARLIEST "Formative" culture appearing in the Valley of Oaxaca in the easternmost part of the Mexican Plateau. The design depicts the head of the Great Cayman of the Sky adorned with his crest of the harpy eagle (Flannery and Schoenwetter 1970: 149, upper of the two vessels).

The fact that the societies antecedent to Maya civilization and the cultural unit from which all of the later civilization of the Central Andes were derived all shared the same iconography and cosmology suggests that they were derived from a single more ancient ethnic unit.

A strong case has been made that the earliest tropical lowland agriculturalists in Mesoamerica, the first Mesoamerican groups to exhibit relatively large stable communities, were in fact manioc agriculturalists (Green and Lowe 1967: 59, 128). Flannery has explicitly rejected this argument (1973: 273), mainly, it would seem, because no remains of manioc were recovered from his excavations on the southern coast of Guatemala (Coe and Flannery 1967). Here among 50 identifiable plant remains, no fragments of manioc were recognized. If manioc tissue is 1000 times less likely to yield preservable fragments than either maize or the avocado (and I think this is a conservative statement of the case), its absence from a sample of 50 items is hardly surprising. Along with the strong inferential case developed by Gareth Lowe (Green and Lowe 1967), one must take into account the point emphasized by Bennet Bronson; the term for manioc is one of the ten words designating plants that can be reconstructed for Proto-Maya. Manioc as a concept was thus certainly present in the ethnic unit ancestral to all of the later Maya speech communities, at a time before the expansion and dispersal of these communities (Bronson 1966: 261). Interestingly, five more of these terms for plants refer to items noted in our discussion of the house garden: ceiba, avocado, chile, cacao, sweet potato.

If the people responsible for Chavín and Olmec were, in fact, derived from the same ethnic heritage there should be linguistic evidence linking key Mesoamerican speech communities to important speech communities in the area of Central Andean civilization. Recent work by Olsen (1964, 1965) on Uru-Chipaya and by Stark on Yunga (1968, i.p.), the language of the kingdom of Chimor, indicates that both of these converge to a single protolanguage, which in turn converges with Proto-Mayan at a node still earlier in time.

The model of Proto-Mayan expansion, to be proposed, centered on the flood plains of the major river systems of northern Colombia, and was given impetus by intensification of manioc agriculture. This model in no way conflicts with the one for the expansion of Macro-Arawakan which I presented earlier (Lathrap 1970), when I argued that the expansion of Macro-Arawakan was centered on the Central Amazon and was also impelled by an intensification of manioc cultivation. Indeed the two expansions were interactive. Each required the other, if we are to understand the final form which the two concurrent migrations took. In the absence of the Arawakan expansion the Macro-Mayan expansion would have dissipated most of its force in a spread throughout the flood plains of the Orinoco and Upper Amazon. Were it not for the Macro-Mayan populations, the Arawakan groups would have moved freely through the alluvial lowlands of Colombia and on up the eastern coast of Central America. Both ethnic groups were actively competing for the same ecological niche so that their colonization tended to be mutually exclusive.

Again, if there was an ethnic unity between the people bringing the earliest developed agriculture into Mesoamerica and those bringing Chavín culture into Peru, there should be identifiable archaeological evidence indicative of a unity of material culture. It has long been noted (Lathrap 1966) that the early Mesoamerican complexes characterized by a vessel form referred to as the "pumpkin tecomate" (MacNeish, Peterson, and Flannery 1970) are surprisingly similar to the earliest ceramics appearing on the northern and central coasts of Peru and in the northern highlands. These uniform, and rather drab, ceramics of Peru are dominated by a vessel form usually designated by Peruvianists as the "neckless olla," which is, in fact, physically identical to the "pumpkin tecomate." Until recently archaeologists have been puzzled by the lack of a connecting link. The ceramics excavated by Bischof at the Canapote site, in the northern lowlands of Colombia, form a very adequate ancestor both to the Barra ceramic complex, the earliest technologically sophisticated pottery in Mesoamerica (Green and Lowe 1967), and to the "neckless olla" tradition in the Peruvian highlands, especially as it appears in the Huánaco Basin at Kotosh (Izumi and Sono 1963). The parallels include not only the specific form of the vessel but also several characteristics of decoration (see Plate 4). The dating of the Canapote ceramics at around 4000 B.P. (Bischof 1966) presents no problems, since the "neckless olla" materials appear in Peru around 3800 B.P. (Izumi and Sono 1963) and the Barra ceramics need to date no earlier than 3500 B.P. (Green and Lowe 1967).

I suggest that all of the above lines of reasoning indicate the alluvial lowlands of northern Colombia as the hearth for the protocommunities ancestral both to Chavín and Olmec. I would further suggest that the almost explosive outward colonization was supported by, and necessitated by, a phenomenally efficient system of cultivation of bitter manioc achieved there. The total identity of the cosmology and iconography, which finds its earliest preserved expressions in the basalt monuments of San Lorenzo and La Venta and in the granite monuments of Chavín de Huántar, indicates that this cosmological structure and the complex and stratified society which it validated had fully developed before the two wings of this migration left their common home in the tropical lowlands of northern Colombia.

If we are correct in viewing the structured complexities of the cosmology which underlies both Olmec and Chavín art as a mirror of a society which was also both complex and stratified (Willey 1962; Flannery 1972), such advanced societies must have existed in northern South America by the third millennium B.C. If we view cultural evolution in terms of the working of population growth constrained within sharply restricted areas of economically suitable land, in this following the leads offered by Bateson (1958) and Carneiro (1970), we must assume that notable densities of population had been achieved on the restricted areas of flood plains of northern South America well before 5000 B.P. Here we must further investigate the first "Neolithic revolution" in the New World.

REFERENCES

AUDUBON, JOHN JAMES
1937   *The birds of America.* New York: Macmillan.
BATESON, GREGORY
1958   *Naven* (second edition). Stanford: Stanford University Press.
1972   *Steps to an ecology of mind.* New York: Ballantine Books.
BEADLE, GEORGE W.
1972   The mystery of maize. *Field Museum of Natural History Bulletin* 43 (10): 2–11.
BIRD, JUNIUS B.
1948   Preceramic cultures in Chicama and Virú. *Memoirs of the Society for American Archaeology* 4:21–28.
BISCHOF, HENNING
1966   Canapote, an early ceramic site in northern Colombia: preliminary report. *Actas y Memorias, XXXVI Congreso Internacional de Americanistas* 1:483–491.
BRONSON, BENNET
1966   Roots and the subsistence of the ancient Maya. *Southwestern Journal of Anthropology* 22:251–279.
BRYAN, ALAN L.
1973   Paleoenvironments and cultural diversity in Late Pleistocene South America. *Journal of Quaternary Research* 3:237–256.
BUNTING, A. H., BARBARA PICKERSGILL
1971   "A proposed plant exploration expedition to northeastern Brazil." Mimeographed manuscript, Department of Agricultural Botany, University of Reading.
BUTT COLSON, AUDREY
1973   Inter-tribal trade in the Guiana highlands. *Antropologica* 34.
CARNEIRO, ROBERT L.
1961   "Slash-and-burn cultivation among the Kuikuru and its implications for cultural development in the Amazon Basin," in *The evolution of horticultural systems in native South America, causes and consequences: a symposium.* Edited by Johannes Wilbert. *Antropologica,* supplemental publication 2:47–67.
1970   A theory of the origin of the state. *Science* 169:733–738.
1972   "From autonomous villages to the state, a numerical estimation," in *Population growth: anthropological implications.* Edited by Brian Spooner, 65–77. Cambridge, Mass.: M.I.T. Press.
CHEESMAN, E. F.
1944   Notes on the nomenclature, classification and possible relationships of cacao populations. *Tropical Agriculture* (BWI) 21:227–233.
CLARK, J. DESMOND
1959   *The prehistory of southern Africa.* Harmondsworth: Pelican Books.
1976   "Prehistoric populations and pressures favoring plant domestication in Africa," in *Origins of African plant domestication.* Edited by Jack A. Harlan, J. M. J. de Wet, and Ann B. C. Stemler, 67–106. World Anthropology. The Hague: Mouton.

COE, MICHAEL D., KENT V. FLANNERY
1967   *Early cultures and human ecology in south coast Guatemala.* Smithsonian Contributions to Anthropology 3.
COURSEY, D. G.
1972a The civilization of the yam: interrelationships of man and yams in Africa and the Indo-Pacific Region. *Archaeology and Physical Anthropology in Oceania* 7:215–233.
1973   "The comparative ethnobotany of African and Asian yam cultures." Paper prepared for the Third International Symposium on Tropical Root Crops, December 3–8.
1976   "The origins and domestication of yams in Africa," in *Origins of African plant domestication.* Edited by Jack A. Harlan, J. M. J. de Wet, and Ann B. C. Stemler, 338–408. World Anthropology. The Hague: Mouton.
COURSEY, D. G., CECILIA K. COURSEY
1971   The New Yam Festivals of West Africa. *Anthropos* 66:444–484.
CUTLER, HUGH C., THOMAS W. WHITAKER
1961   History and distribution of the cultivated cucurbits in the Americas. *American Antiquity* 26:469–485.
DODGE, ERNEST S.
1943   *Gourd growers of the South Seas.* The Gourd Society of America, Ethnological Series 2.
DONNE, JOHN, WILLIAM BLAKE
1941   *The complete poetry and selected prose of John Donne* and *The complete poetry of William Blake.* New York: Random House.
EKHOLM, SUSANNA M.
1969   *Mound 30a and the early preclassic ceramic sequence of Izapa, Chiapas, Mexico.* Papers of the New World Archaeological Foundation 25.
ESTRADA, EMILIO, BETTY J. MEGGERS
1961   A complex of traits of probable transpacific origin on the coast of Ecuador. *American Anthropologist* 63:913–939.
FLANNERY, KENT V.
1972   The cultural evolution of civilizations. *Annual Review of Ecology and Systematics* 3:399–426.
1973   The origins of agriculture. *Annual Review of Anthropology* 2:271–310.
FLANNERY, KENT V., JAMES SCHOENWETTER
1970   Climate and man in Formative Oaxaca. *Archaeology* 23:144–152.
FOSTER, DONALD W., DONALD W. LATHRAP
1973   Further evidence for a well-developed tropical forest culture on the north coast of Colombia during the first and second millennium B.C. *Journal of the Steward Anthropological Society* 4:160–199.
GOLDMAN, IRVING
1963   *The Cubeo, Indians of the northwest Amazon.* Illinois Studies in Anthropology 2.
GOODSPEED, T. H.
1953   Species, origins, and relationships in the genus *Nicotiana. University of California Publications in Botany* 26:391–400.

GORMAN, CHESTER F.
  1969   Hoabinhian: a pebble-tool complex with early plant associations in southeast Asia. *Science* 163:671–673.
GREEN, DEE F., GARETH W. LOWE
  1967   *Altamira and Padre Piedra, early Preclassic sites in Chiapas, Mexico.* Papers of the New World Archaeological Foundation 20.
HARLAN, JACK R.
  1971   Agricultural origins: centers and non-centers. *Science* 174:468–474.
HARLAN, JACK R., J. M. J. DE WET
  1973   On the quality of evidence for origin and dispersal of cultivated plants. *Current Anthropology* 14:51–55.
HARRIS, DAVID R.
  1971   The ecology of swidden cultivation in the Upper Orinoco rain forest, Venezuela. *The Geographical Review* 61:475–495.
  1972   The origins of agriculture in the tropics. *American Scientist* 60:180–193.
HEISER, CHARLES B., JR.
  1973a   "Variation in the bottle gourd," in *Tropical forest ecosystems in Africa and South America: a comparative review.* Edited by Betty J. Meggers, Edward S. Ayensu, and W. D. Duckworth, 121–128. Washington D.C.: Smithsonian Institution Press.
  1973b   The penis gourd of New Guinea. *Annals of the Association of American Geographers* 63:312–318.
HEIZER, ROBERT F.
  1944   Artifact transport by migratory animals and other means. *American Antiquity* 9:395–400.
HOWE, W. L., A. M. RHODES
  1973   Host relationships of the squash vine borer, *Melittia cucurbitae*, with species of *Cucurbita*. *Annals of the Entomological Society of America* 66(2):266–267.
HOWE, W. L., EVA ZDARKOVA, A. M. RHODES
  1972   Host preferences of *Acalymma vittatum* (Coleoptera: Chrysomelidae) among certain Cucurbitacae. *Annals of the Entomological Society of America* 65:372–374.
HURD, PAUL D., JR., GORTON LINSLEY, THOMAS W. WHITAKER
  1971   Squash and gourd bees (*Peponapis xenoglossa*) and the origin of the cultivated *Cucurbita*. *Evolution* 25:218–234.
HUXLEY, FRANCIS
  1957   *Affable savages.* New York: Viking Press.
IZUMI, SEIICHI, PEDRO J. CUCULIZA, CHIAKI KANO
  1972   *Excavations at Shillacoto, Huánuco, Peru.* The University Museum, The University of Tokyo, Bulletin 3.
IZUMI, SEIICHI, TOSHIHIKO SONO
  1963   *Andes 2: excavations at Kotosh, Peru, 1960.* Tokyo: Kadokawa.
IZUMI, SEIICHI, KAZUO TERADA, *editors*
  1972   *Andes 4: excavations at Kotosh, Peru 1963 and 1966.* Tokyo: University of Tokyo Press.
JANZEN, DANIEL H.
  1973   Tropical agroecosystems. *Science* 182:1212–1219.

JIMÉNEZ BORJA, ARTURO
  1948   *Mate Peruano*. Museo de la Cultura. Collección Arturo Jiménez Borja. Lima: Imprenta del Ministerio de Educación Pública.
KAPLAN, L., THOMAS F. LYNCH, C. E. SMITH, JR.
  1973   Early cultivated beans (*Phaseolus vulgaris*) from an intermontane Peruvian valley. *Science* 179:76–77.
KROEBER, ALFRED L.
  1923   *Anthropology*. New York: Harcourt, Brace.
LATHRAP, DONALD W.
  1958   Review of "Momíl: Excavaciones en el Sinú," by Gerardo and Alicia Reichel-Dolmatoff. *American Journal of Archaeology* 62:360–362.
  1966   Relationships between Mesoamerica and the Andean areas. *Handbook of Middle American Indians*, volume four: *Archaeological frontiers and external connections*. Edited by Gordon F. Ekholm and Gordon R. Willey, 265–275. Austin: University of Texas Press.
  1967   Review of "Early Formative Period of coastal Ecuador: the Valdivia and Machalilla Phases," by Betty J. Meggers, Clifford Evans, and Emilio Estrada. *American Anthropologist* 69:96–98.
  1968a "The 'hunting' economies of the tropical forest zone of South America: an attempt at historical perspective," in *Man the hunter*. Edited by Richard B. Lee and Irven DeVore, 23–29. Chicago: Aldine.
  1968b Aboriginal occupation and changes in river channel on the central Ucayali, Peru. *American Antiquity* 33:62–79.
  1970   *The Upper Amazon*. London: Thames and Hudson.
  1971   "The tropical forest and the cultural context of Chavín," in *Dumbarton Oaks Conference on Chavín*. Edited by Elizabeth Benson, 73–100. Washington, D.C.: Dumbarton Oaks Research Library and Collection.
  1973a The antiquity and importance of long-distance trade relationships in the moist tropics of pre-Columbian South America. *World Archaeology* 5:170–186.
  1973b "Gifts of the cayman: some thoughts on the subsistence basis of Chavín," in *Variation in anthropology*. Edited by Donald W. Lathrap and Jody Douglas, 91–105. Urbana, Ill.: Illinois Archaeological Survey.
  1974   "The moist tropics, the arid lands, and the appearance of great art styles in the New World," in *Art and environment in native America*. Edited by Idris Rhea Traylor and M. E. King. Lubbock: Texas Technological University Press.
  i.p.   "Complex iconographic features shared by Olmec and Chavín and some speculations on their possible significance," in *Primer Simposio de Correlaciones Antropológicas Andino-Mesoamericano*, July 25–31, 1971, Guayaquil.
LATHRAP, DONALD W., ROBERT BRAUN
  1974   "Under the double cayman: the emergence of civilization in the New World." Unpublished manuscript.
LEE, RICHARD B.
  1972a "Population growth and the beginnings of sedentary life among the !Kung Bushmen," in *Population growth: anthropological implications*.

Edited by Brian Spooner, 329–342. Cambridge, Mass.: M.I.T. Press.
1972b "The intensification of social life among the !Kung Bushmen," in *Population growth: anthropological implications*. Edited by Brian Spooner, 343–350. Cambridge, Mass.: M.I.T. Press.

MAC NEISH, RICHARD S.
1958 Preliminary archaeological investigations in the Sierra de Tamaulipas, Mexico. *Transactions of the American Philosophical Society* 48(6): 1–210.
1967 "A summary of the subsistence," in *The prehistory of the Tehuacán Valley*, volume one: *Environment and subsistence*. Edited by Douglas S. Beyers, 290–309. Austin: University of Texas Press.
1969 *First annual report of the Ayacucho Archaeological-Botanical Project*. Andover, Mass.: Phillips Academy.

MAC NEISH, RICHARD S., FREDERICK A. PETERSON, KENT V. FLANNERY
1970 *The prehistory of the Tehuacán Valley*, volume three: *Ceramics*. Edited by Douglas S. Byers. Austin: University of Texas Press.

MANGELSDORF, PAUL C.
1953 Review of "Agricultural origins and dispersals," by Carl O. Sauer. *American Antiquity* 19:86–90.

MANGELSDORF, PAUL C., RICHARD S. MAC NEISH, WALTON C. GALINAT
1967 "Prehistoric wild and cultivated maize," in *The prehistory of the Tehuacán Valley*, volume one: *Environment and subsistence*. Edited by Douglas S. Byers, 178–299. Austin: University of Texas Press.

MARCOS, JORGE G.
1973 "Cacao — a cultivar in moist tropics horticultural systems." Mimeographed manuscript prepared for Anthropology 429, University of Illinois, Urbana.

MYERS, THOMAS P.
1973 "Toward the reconstruction of prehistoric community patterns in the Amazon Basin," in *Variation in anthropology*. Edited by Donald W. Lathrap and Jody Douglas, 233–254. Urbana, Ill.: Illinois Archaeological Survey.

OLSEN, RONALD D.
1964 Mayan affinities with Chipaya of Bolivia, I: Correspondences. *International Journal of American Linguistics* 30:313–324.
1965 Mayan affinities with Chipaya of Bolivia, II: Cognates. *International Journal of American Linguistics* 31:29–38.

PARRINDER, GEOFFREY
1967 *African mythology*. London: Paul Hamlyn.

PICKERSGILL, BARBARA
1969 The archaeological record of chili peppers (*Capsicum* spp.) and the sequence of plant domestication in Peru. *American Antiquity* 34:54–61.
1972 Cultivated plants as evidence for cultural contact. *American Antiquity* 37:97–104.

PICKERSGILL, BARBARA, A. H. BUNTING
1972 "Reading University Plant Collecting Expedition to North-Eastern Brazil." Mimeographed manuscript, Department of Agricultural Botany, University of Reading, England.

QUIGLEY, CARROLL
1956 Aboriginal fish poisons and the diffusion problem. *American Anthropologist* 58:508–525.
REICHEL-DOLMATOFF, GERARDO
1949–1950 Los Kogi. *Revista del Instituto Etnológica Nacional* IV (1a and 2a).
1971 *Amazonian cosmos.* Chicago: The University of Chicago Press.
REICHEL-DOLMATOFF, GERARDO, ALICIA REICHEL-DOLMATOFF
1956 Momíl: excavacíones en el Sinú. *Revista Colombiana de Antropología* 5:109–333.
RICHARDSON, JAMES B., III
1972 The pre-Columbian distribution of the bottle gourd (*Lagenaria siceraria*): a re-evaluation. *Economic Botany* 26:265–273.
1973 "The preceramic sequence and the Pleistocene and Post-Pleistocene climate of northwest Peru," in *Variation in anthropology.* Edited by Donald W. Lathrap and Jody Douglas, 199–211. Urbana, Ill.: Illinois Archaeological Survey.
ROUSE, I., JOSÉ MARIA CRUXENT
1963 *Venezuelan archaeology.* New Haven, Conn.: Yale University Press.
SAUER, CARL O.
1950 "Cultivated plants of South and Central America," in *Handbook of South American Indians*, volume six: *Physical anthropology, linguistics and cultural geography of South American Indians.* Edited by Julian H. Steward, 487–542. Bureau of American Ethnology Bulletin 143.
1952 *Agricultural origins and dispersals.* New York: American Geographical Society.
SCHULTES, RICHARD EVANS
1972 "An overview of hallucinogens in the Western Hemisphere," in *Flesh of the gods.* Edited by Peter Furst, 3–54. New York: Praeger.
SCHWERIN, KARL H.
1970 *Winds across the Atlantic.* Mesoamerican Studies University Museum, Southern Illinois University 6.
1971 "The bitter and the sweet. Some implications of techniques for preparing manioc." Paper prepared for the 1971 Annual Meeting of the American Anthropological Association, New York.
SIOLI, H.
1966 "General features of the delta of the Amazon," in *Humid tropics research: scientific problems of the humid tropical zone deltas and their implications*, 381–390. Proceedings of the Dacca Symposium. Paris: UNESCO.
SPINDEN, H. J.
1917 The origin and distribution of agriculture in America. *Proceedings of the XIX International Congress of Americanists, Washington, D.C., 1915*, 269–276.
STARK, LOUISA R.
1968 "Mayan affinities with Yunga of Peru." Thesis for the Degree of Doctor of Philosophy, New York University.
i.p. Mayan-Yuanga-Uru-Chipayan: a new linguistic alignment. *Papers in Andean Linguistics*, first issue. Madison, Wisconsin.

STEPHENS, S. G.

1965 The effects of domestication on certain seed and fiber properties of perennial forms of cotton, *Gossypium hirsutum* L. *American Naturalist* 99:355–372.

1966 The potentiality for long range oceanic dispersal of cotton seeds. *American Naturalist* 100:199–210.

STERNBERG, HILGARD O'REILLY

1973 The need for new concepts in land evaluation. *International Union for Conservation of Nature and Natural Resources; 12th Technical Meeting, Banff, Canada; 12–15 September, 1972. Papers and Proceedings* 17: 237–257. Morges, Switzerland.

THOMPSON, J. ERIC S.

1970 *Maya history and religion.* Norman: University of Oklahoma Press.

WASSÉN, S. HENRY

1965 The use of some specific kinds of South American Indian snuff and related paraphernalia. *Etnologiska Studier* 28:1–116.

1967 "Anthropological survey of the use of South American snuffs," in *Ethnopharmacologic search for psycho-active drugs*, 233–289. Proceedings of a Symposium held in San Francisco, California, January 28–30, 1967. Workshop Series in Pharmacology, National Institute of Mental Health 2. Health Service Publication 1645. Washington, D.C.: U.S. Government Printing Office.

WHITAKER, THOMAS W.

1971 "Endemism and pre-Columbian migration of the bottle gourd, *Lagenaria siceraria* (Mol.) Standl," in *Man across the sea.* Edited by Carroll L. Riley, J. Charles Kelley, Campbell W. Pennington, and Robert L. Rands, 320–327. Austin: University of Texas Press.

WHITAKER, THOMAS W., GEORGE F. CARTER

1954 Oceanic drift of gourds: experimental observations. *American Journal of Botany* 41:697–700.

WILLEY, GORDON R.

1962 The early great styles and the rise of the pre-Columbian civilizations. *American Anthropologist* 64:1–14.

YANGUEZ-BERNAL, JUAN ANTONIO

1968 "The Pejbay or Chonta palm." Mimeographed manuscript, University of Illinois, Urbana.

The Beginning of Agriculture in Central Peru

RICHARD S. MacNEISH

An archaeological reconnaissance of highland Peru in 1966 revealed that the Ayacucho-Huanta Valley had considerable potential for yielding early artifacts in association with the remains of domesticated plants and animals (MacNeish 1969). Therefore, the R. S. Peabody Foundation for Archaeology undertook intensive interdisciplinary investigations in this region (see Figure 1) from 1969 through 1972 (MacNeish et al. 1970). The

I would like to acknowledge with thanks the scientists who have cooperated with our project. These were: in zoology, Drs. Elizabeth Wing of the Florida State Museum and Kent Flannery of the University of Michigan; in paleontology, Drs. Grayson Mead, then of the University of Calgary, and Bryan Patterson of Harvard University; in geology, Dr. Nathanial Rutter of the Geological Survey of Canada; in botany, Drs. Barbara Pickersgill of Reading University, Vaughan Bryant of Texas A. and M. University, Thomas Whitaker of the U.S. Department of Agriculture, and Walter Galinat and Lawrence Kaplan of the University of Massachusetts; in palynology, Dr. Charles Schweger of the University of Alberta.

I would like to express my particular thanks to Professor Angel Garcia Cook of the Instituto de Antropología y Historia of Mexico, who was in charge of both the archaeological survey and the excavation. In the reconnaissance he was aided by Wayne Wiersum of the University of Manitoba, Dennis Price from England, Augusto Cruzatt and Carlos Chahud from the University of Huancayo, as well as Hernando Carillo, Guillermo Cajardo, Ulpiano Quispe and Victor Cardenas of the University of Huamanga. While many of the excavations were undertaken by Angel Garcia, he was assisted by various supervisors in charge of specific excavations; these individuals were Urve Linnamae of the University of Saskatchewan, Dennis Price of England, and Hernando Carillo, Edmundo Pinto, Idilio Santillana and Carlos Chahud of the University of New Mexico.

The basic laboratory, in which many of the analyses were made, was under the direction of Antoinette Nelken-Terner of the CNRS of Paris, France; she was assisted by Robert Vierra, Carl Phagan and Ruthann Knudson, as well as a host of students from the Universities of Huamanga and of San Marcos.

Without Drs. Garcia Cook and Nelken-Terner this research project would never have been completed, and they are as much authors of this paper as I am. The project was generously supported by the National Science Foundation.

basic purpose of this reaearch was to gain some understanding of the beginnings of agriculture and animal domestication as well as the concomitant development of settled life for this region.

The Andean project bore many resemblances in both methods and problems to an earlier Peabody endeavor in the Tehuacán Valley of Mexico, the other center of New World agriculture (Byers 1967; MacNeish,

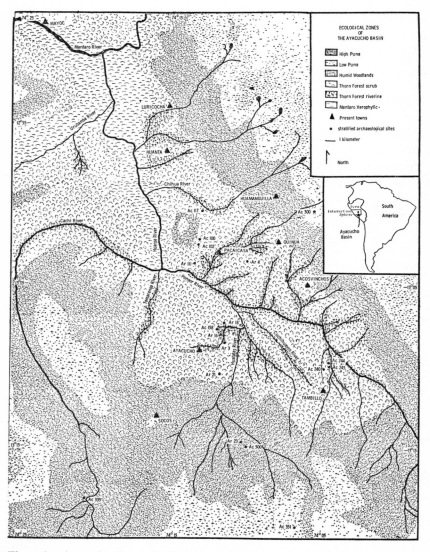

Figure 1.   Ayacucho-Huanta Valley with towns, sites, and ecological zones

Nelken-Temer, and Johnson 1967; MacNeish, Peterson, and Flannery 1970; Johnson 1972). Also, this highland Peruvian study gave us an excellent opportunity to test some of the hypotheses derived from the researches in Middle America concerning how and why agriculture began anywhere (MacNeish 1972).

Although the general problem of the beginnings of agriculture for both the Meso-American and Andean nuclear areas was very similar, there were some major differences. Although the two culture areas had some domesticates in common such as gourds, cotton, maize, guava, peanuts, and others that probably had spread from one continent to the other, most of the basic domesticates of each area had separate histories. Previous archaeological evidence (Byers 1967) has indicated that maize (*Zea mays*), pumpkins (*Cucurbita pepo*), squashes (*Cucurbita mixta* and *Cucurbita moschata*), amaranths, chili peppers (*Capsicum annuum*), white sapote (*Casimiroa edulis*), black sapote (*Diospyros digyna*), jack beans (*Canavalia* sp.), tepary beans (*Phaseolus acutifolius*), runner beans (*Phaseolus coccineus*), common beans (*Phaseolus vulgaris*), sieva beans (*Phaseolus lunatus*), avocados (*Persea americana*), ground tomatoes (*Physalis* sp.), prickly pear (*Opuntia* sp.) and agave (*Agave* sp.) were domesticated in the northern center of domestication in the New World, while in this article we shall demonstrate by archaeological evidence from central Peru that white potatoes (*Solanum tuberosum*), sweet potatoes (*Ipomoea batatas*), coca (*Erythroxylon coca*), peanuts (*Arachis hypogaea*), quinoa (*Chenopodium quinoa*), lucuma (*Lucuma bifera*), lima beans (*Phaseolus lunatus*), pacae (*Inga feuillei*), pepper (*Capsicum annuum*), guava (*Psidium guajava*), achira (*Canna* sp.), cotton (*Gossypium barbadense*), canavalia beans (*Canavalia* sp.), round common beans (*Phaseolus vulgaris*), and squash (*Cucurbita andreana*) were probably domesticated in the Andean center of domestication (Harlan 1971).

Further, unlike in Meso-America, in the Andean nuclear area domesticated animals (such as llama, alpaca, and guinea pig) were basic to the human pattern of subsistence.

A second difference between the two areas is the archaeological evidence from before 3000–4500 B.P., the crucial period of domestication of plants. Although botanists and archaeologists have long recognized that in Middle America there had been multiple origins of domesticated plants (MacNeish 1965) and that the interactions between sequence in a number of life zones or major environmental zones were of key importance in cultural and agricultural developments, we have had few pre-ceramic archaeological sequences. In fact, the only pre-ceramic sequences with pertinent remains of plants come from peripheral Tamaulipas in the northern desert

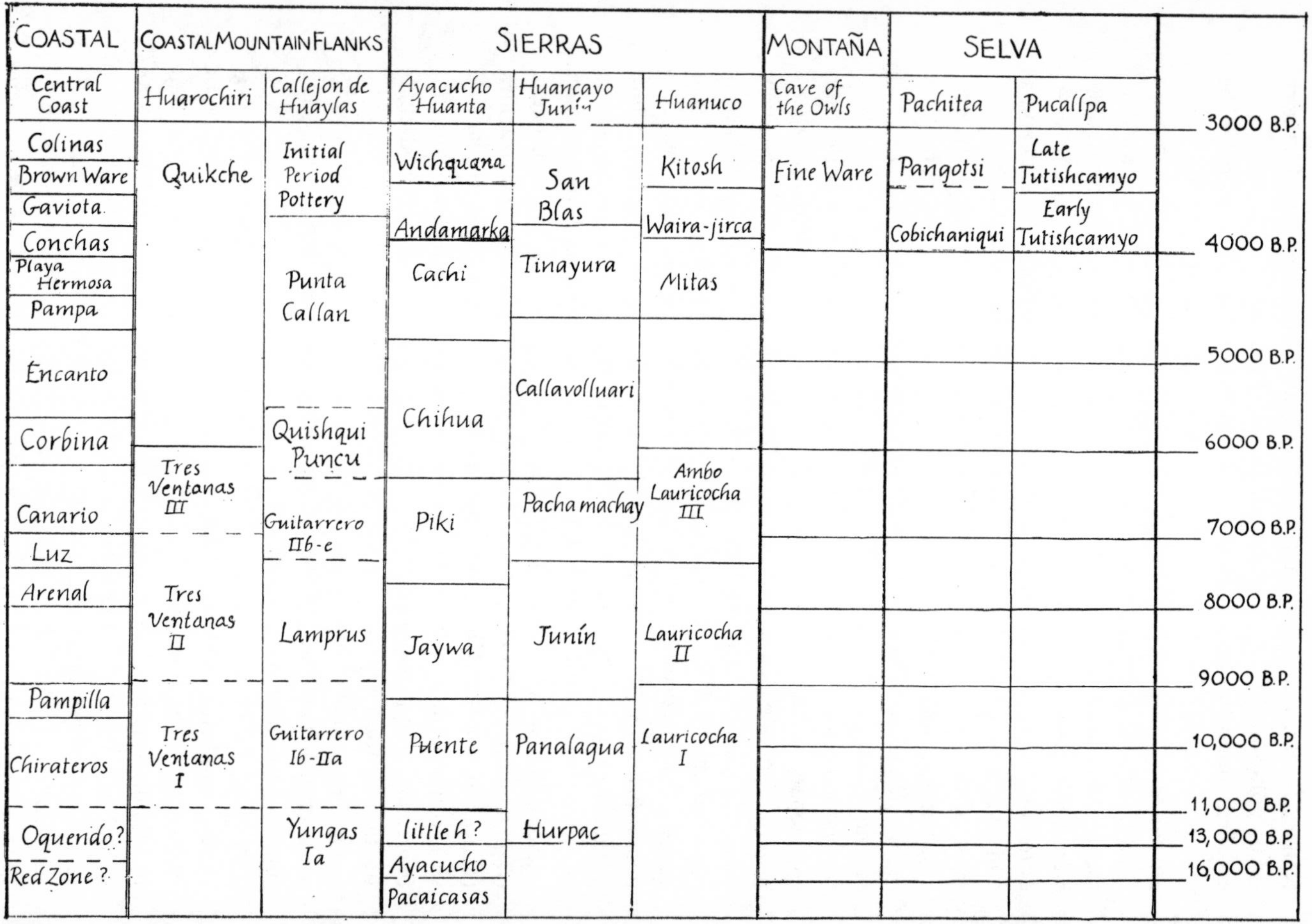

COASTAL	COASTAL/MOUNTAIN FLANKS		SIERRAS			MONTAÑA	SELVA		
Central Coast	Huarochiri	Callejon de Huaylas	Ayacucho Huanta	Huancayo Junín	Huanuco	Cave of the Owls	Pachitea	Pucallpa	B.P.
Colinas	Quikche	Initial Period Pottery	Wichqana	San Blas	Kitosh	Fine Ware	Pangotsi	Late Tutishcamyo	3000
Brown Ware									
Gaviota			Andamarka		Waira-jirca			Early Tutishcamyo	4000
Conchas / Playa Hermosa		Punta Callan	Cachi	Tinayura	Mitas		Cobichaniqui		
Pampa									5000
Encanto			Chihua	Callavolluari					
Corbina	Tres Ventanas III	Quishqui Puncu			Ambo / Lauricocha III				6000
Canario		Guitarrero IIb-c	Piki	Pachamachay					7000
Luz									
Arenal	Tres Ventanas II	Lamprus	Jaywa	Junín	Lauricocha II				8000
									9000
Pampilla	Tres Ventanas I	Guitarrero Ib-IIa	Puente	Panalagua	Lauricocha I				
Chivateros									10,000
		Yungas Ia	little h?	Hurpac					11,000
Oquendo?			Ayacucho						13,000
Red Zone?			Pacaicasas						16,000

Figure 2. Sequence of cultural phases in regions of life zones within the central Peruvian interaction sphere

area and the valleys of Tehuacán (Mangelsdorf, MacNeish, and Willey 1964) and Oaxaca (Flannery 1970) in the southern Mexican highlands. Most of the other subareas not only do not have pre-ceramic remains of plants, but most have no pre-ceramic sequences whatsoever. This situation contrasts with the central Andean interaction sphere where not only are there sequences earlier than 3000 B.P. in the coastal, Pacific Andean flanks, sierra and montane life zones (Lanning 1967), but there are even numerous pre-ceramic sequences from various regions within these larger life zones, many of which have remains of domesticates (see Figure 2).

Ecological studies along the coast from about the mouth of the Canete River to Las Haldas indicate there is a zone of relatively uniform environment that contains similar microenvironments (Patterson 1971). There is some suggestion that these have been exploited in somewhat the same manner during each of the early cultural periods. This coastal life zone has yielded the greatest amounts of preserved remains of plants and has been the scene of the greatest amount of archaeological activity in central Peru (Towle 1961). In our discussions of this area we shall use the periodization developed for the region of Ancón and Rimac even though more abundant artifactual and ecofactual materials (Patterson 1971) and more excavations occur in the region of Chilca.

Adjacent to the coastal zone is a transitional zone which has been termed the Pacific flanks of the Andes. Although this region has yielded longer stratigraphic sequences, many more chipped stone artifacts, and more mammalian bones than the coast, preserved remains of plants are very sparse, and only two regions have been intensively investigated. One of these is near Tres Ventanas Mountain overlooking the coastal Chilca and Lurín River Valleys to the south and has been called the Huarochiri region. Here two caves have been excavated, giving a long sequence from roughly 11,000 to 6,000 B.P. (Engel 1968), and some sites of later preceramic time have been found in survey (Patterson, personal communication). The other region in this flank zone is the Callejón de Huaylas and here the stratified Guitarrero Cave and an open site, Quishqui Puncu, have been excavated; two sites, Lampras and Conococha, have been tested and some survey has been undertaken (Lynch and Kennedy 1970). These excavations are the basis for a long sequence in the pertinent periods from 12,000 B.P. through the Initial Period to 3000 B.P. with many artifacts, bones, and some remains of plants. Although there has been some study of the microenvironments of the region and the importance of a transhumant way of life has been emphasized (Lynch 1971), actual investigations of how each of the various environmental zones was exploited in each phase have not been undertaken.

The research on the western flanks of the Andes contrasts with that of the coastal life zones and the eastern flanks. In actual fact, the only pre-ceramic and early ceramic remains we have for this large zone come from the Huánuco Valley, which is actually not in Montaña environs but adjacent to it. However, some of the pottery from the nearby Cave of the Owls, definitely in the Montaña, is related to that from Huánuco and suggests that the sequence of the Huánuco Valley does in fact pertain to at least part of the Montaña (Lathrap and Roys 1963). While a surface collection from Ambo yielded materials that typologically would seem to date to about 7000 B.P. (Ravines 1965), only the information from the magnificently described Mito, Waira-jirca, and Kotosh Phases seems to be pertinent to our problem of early agriculture and animal domestication in central Peru (Izumi and Tereda 1972). Unfortunately, the sequence is not very long and only a few remains of plants have been identified.

Linking these two flank areas of the Andes is the key life zone, the Sierras. One of the first long sequences of pre-ceramic remains was uncov-ered in the region of Lauricocha in the northern part of the central Peruvian interaction sphere (Cardich 1964). Although there is an excellent sequence of artifacts, the subsistence remains were not analyzed, nor have ecological studies been undertaken. Fortunately, this situation will be rectified by a new project starting just to the south in the nearby region of Junín-Huancayo.

Preliminary tests by Ramiro Matos, of San Marcos University, in a number of rock shelters have yielded artifacts that are a basis for a long sequence of pre-ceramic phases, and some of the many associated bones are being identified. Ecological studies have been begun by Kent Flannery of the University of Michigan, and it should be possible to correlate with them the information gained from the study of the many survey sites as well as excavated components. Geological surveys have been started, a long core for palynological studies has been taken by Herbert Wright of the University of Minnesota, and plans are under way to float excavated cultural layers in the expectation of obtaining remains of plants. Although we have some important information now, future endeavors should pro-vide much valuable information concerning the problem of the origin of agriculture in Peru. However, for the present the most pertinent data from the Sierras of central Peru come from the Ayacucho-Huanta Valley to the south.

From our investigations in Tehuacán, Mexico, we had learned that crucial to any archaeological program concerned with the process of domestication was an understanding of the relationship of man to his local environment. Therefore, almost from the outset of our investigations in Peru we made an attempt to define what were the local micro-environments or environmental zones. Interdisciplinary studies of soils, zoology, botany, palynology, climate, geology, and ethnology have allowed us to divide the region of the Ayacucho-Huanta Valley into a series of environmental zones that are: the high Puna, the low Puna, the Humid Woodlands, the Thorn Forest scrub, the Thorn Forest riverine, and the Xerophytic zones (see Figure 3 and Addenda).

In our archaeological reconnaissance in 1969 we made a conscious effort to find sites in each of these zones (the high Puna excepted, for originally we classified this zone with the low Puna). This effort was not just so we could have a distribution of sites in each zone, but to discover stratified sites in each zone that would give us complete archaeological sequences from 9000 B.P. to 3000 B.P. in each zone that then could be related to each other, thereby giving a relatively full understanding of the valley's total subsistence pattern. We were successful in obtaining such stratigraphic sequences for all zones, except for the Xerophytic zone and that of the high Puna, but even here we uncovered survey data representing most of our pre-ceramic phases (MacNeish et al. 1970).

Since these sequences are basic to our reconstruction of the ancient cultures with micro-evolving subsistence systems, which in turn are related to the broader problem of the origin and spread of agriculture in Peru, let me briefly summarize them. Our highest zone, the high Puna, above 4,500 meters in elevation, is characterized by frost all year, dry-season snowfall, Arctic brown soils that are poorly matured, short-tussock grass vegetation and the presence of vicuña, huemal deer, and rodents of the genus *Calomys*. This zone is now the locale where llama and alpaca are herded and frozen potatoes are processed seasonally, but there are few, if any, permanent habitations. Archaeologically, our earliest site from survey is in the period from 11,000 B.P. to 9100 B.P., when the environment may have been equally inhospitable. The other more recent pre-ceramic phases are represented by a single component each, and the initial ceramic period yielded only two sites, which have been interpreted as corrals. This relatively limited number of sites probably is a reflection of inadequate survey, not just small populations.

The next zone, the low Puna from about 3,900 to 4,500 meters above sea level, is very similar to the previous one in soils, vegetation, and in having frost all year. However, in addition to these environmental factors typical of the elevation, vicuña, huemal and white-tail deer, the rodent *Calomys*, and a small form of the rodent *Phyllotis* extend upward into this zone, and the snows of the dry season usually give way to uncomfortable cold frosts and rains. At present, this is the area of the greatest density of habitation. Herding is a way of life, but root crops (mainly potatoes) are grown. Here we excavated two rock shelters (Ae 300 [Boulder Cave] and Ac 351, [Owl Cave]), a sequence from 9000 B.P. to the present; ten surface components in the period from 9000 B.P. to 3000 B.P. were discovered, and pollen profiles from a nearby lake of an early wet period have been dated at 7065 ± 365 B.P. (I 6546) to 4675 ± 220 B.P. (I 6547). The pollen profiles suggest that an early wet period was followed by a dry one, then another wet period which merged into the present dry period.

Below the zone of the low Puna, from about 3,900 to 3,200 meters, is a radically different zone, the Humid Woodlands. It is characterized by brunisols, small scrubs, and some rather large trees, huemal and white-tail deer, wild guinea pig, guanaco, as well as rodents of the genera *Akodon* and *Phyllotis*, frosts in the dry season, and rains in the wet season (although occasional rains or fogs occur even in the dry season). This is a region where root crops are grown as well as quinoa, amaranths, oka, and now barley. Archaeologically, we excavated three sites, Jaywa Cave (Ac 335), Chupas Cave (Ac 500) and the Chupas ruin (Tr 23), and found fourteen pre-ceramic surface sites, giving an almost unbroken sequence from about 11,000 B.P. to 1550 B.P. The twelve stratified floors of Jaywa Cave were incredibly rich in artifacts, debitage, and osteological materials, and nine of them bear radio carbon determinations. The zone next to the oldest, J3, bears a date of $10,280 \pm 170$ B.P. (I 5699); Zone J2 is 9890 ± 310 B.P. (I 5683); Zone J1 is 9460 ± 145 B.P. (I 5275); Zone J bears an inconsistent date of 8645 ± 140 B.P. (I 5276); Zone I is 9560 ± 170 B.P. (I 5645); Zone H is 8980 ± 140 B.P. (I 5277); Zone F bears an inconsistent date of 7105 ± 130 B.P. (I 5278) and a consistent one of 8500 ± 125 B.P. (I 5686); Zone D is 8360 ± 125 B.P. (I 4501); and Zone C is 8250 ± 135 B.P. (I 4500). Zones F, E and D1 of Chupas Cave seemed to fall in the time range from 7450 B.P. to 4450 B.P., while the Zones A–D at Chupas ruin and pyramid run from about 3700 B.P. to 1550 B.P. One surface site was in the range from 9050 to 7750 B.P., one in the range of 7750 to 6450 B.P., four between 5050 and 3700 B.P., and one in the period from 3700 to 2950 B.P.

Our major archaeological effort, however, occurred in the Thorn Forest scrub zone from 3,200 meters to about 2,500 meters because here many caves had strata with preserved plant remains. Present-day soils in this zone are mainly chernosols and the vegetation is characterized by *Furcraea*, *Opuntia*, *Agave*, and trees of molle, acacia, and mesquite. Seasonally, white-tail deer, guanaco, rodents of the genus *Akodon*, and both big and little phyllotine rodents occur. There are well-defined wet and dry seasons and only occasionally do frosts occur. Considerable evidence

Environmental Zones	Xerophytic Zone	Thorn Forest: Riverine Sub-zone			Thorn Forest: Scrub Sub-zone								Humid Woodlands				Low Puna			High Puna	Before Present Dates
Sites	Surface Components	Excavated Sites		Surface Components	Excavated Sites							Surface Components	Excavated Sites			Surface Components	Excavated Sites		Surface Components	Surface Components	
		Ac 158	Ac 18		Ac 100 south room	Ac 100 central room	Ac 100 north room	Ac 102	Ac 244	Ac 117	Tc 240		Ac 335	Ac 300	Ar 23		Ac 300	Ac 351			
Wichquana Andamarka	Ar 52 Ar 406 Ar 421		Zone G H J K	Ar141 Ar143 As316 As349 Ar142 Ar243 As330 Ar241 Ar144 As121 As62 As34 Ar131 Ar331 As336							Zone G	Ar 337 As 223 As 308b Ar 234 As 320 As 303 Ar 444 As 319 As 306 As 221 As 235			Zone D1-D2 Zone D2-D3 Zone D4-D5 Zone D6	Ac 300b As 378b As 384b		Zone C	Ac 300D Ac 300C Ac 351c As 497b	As 501b As 504	3000
Cachi	As 400 As 395 As 401 As 393 As 411 As 390 As 417b Ar 108 As 420 Ar 109 As 422 As 40 As 423	Zone Ib Zone Ia Zone Ic Zone Id Zone Ie Zone If		Ar 338 As 147 As 194 As 195 As 313		Zone F Zone G Zone H	Zone VI		Zone E		Zone H	As 386 As 348 As 370 As 350 As 371b Ar 168 As 375 As 161 Ac 120 As 239 As 166 As 268 As 170 Ar 273 Ar 308a		Zone D1		As 267 As 284 As 360 As 380		Zone C1 Zone C2	Ac 300b As 497a	As 498	4000 5000
Chihua	Ar 404 Ar 427 As 401 As 422b As 418 As 420 As 417	Zone If1 Zone Ig Zone Ih1-2 Zone Ih Zone Ij Zone IIa0 Zone II		As 364 As 374 As 147 As 292		Zone X	Zone VII Zone VIII	Zone VI		Zone D		As 396 As 324 As 390b As 280 As 372 As 269 As 371a		Zone E		As 179 As 165 As 378 As 309 As 384	Zone C south		Ac 351b As 496	As 501a	6000
Piki	As 411 As 420 As 417 As 422 As 328	Zone III, Zone IIb, Zone IIa, IIa1 Zone VI, Zone V, Zone IV Zone VIIa, Zone VII, Zone VIa Zone VIII Zone IX Zone IXa Zone X		As 22 As 198	Zone f Zone f1	Zone K Zone U Zone V Zone W		Zone VII	Zone F			As 390a As 172 As 101 As 176 As 296 As 208 As 169 As 174		Zone F		Ac 371		Zone D	Ac 300a	As 502	7000
Jaywa	As 158a	Zone XI Zone XIa Zone XII Zone XIIa Zone XIII		As 2	Zone f2				Zone G			As 369 As 270 As 242 Ac 204a	Zone C Zone D Zone E Zone F Zone G Zone H			As 204	Zone C north		Ac 351a	As 499	8000 9000
Puente		Zone XIV						Zone VIII				As 306	Zone I Zone J Zone J1 Zone J2 Zone J3 Zone K								10,000
Biface					Zone h																12,000
Ayacucho					Zone h Zone h1																14,000
Pacaicasas					Zone i Zone i1 Zone j Zone k																18,000 22,000

Figure 3. Sequences of components in the environmental zones of Ayacucho-Huanta Valley

exists to suggest that the boundaries of this microenvironment as well as that of the Humid Woodlands have shifted through time because of periods of climatic fluctuation. The problem of the earlier levels of Pikimachay Cave in this zone that seem to be of the glacial period will be considered later. However, in later levels a number of soil profiles with pollen were studied and these show definite changes in vegetation. Buried soils in this zone are often brunisols and have arboreal pollen. Three of these have been carbon dated at 9066 B.P., 7255 B.P., and 4640 B.P. This combination suggests that following the period of glaciation the zone of the Humid Woodlands expanded over much of the zone that is now thorn scrub. Study of the pollen from excavated Zones F and VI of Pikimachay of about 4000 B.P. suggests that there was then a dry vegetation more like the present one, while a profile with pollen and buried soil dated at 1975 B.P. suggests that slightly wet conditions came next, only to be replaced by the present dry vegetation after 950 B.P. Much of this climatic information and data of changing environmental zones has not been completely analyzed (MacNeish et al. 1970), but our research on the archaeological stratigraphy is much more advanced.

In this zone, excavation in the three rooms (north, central, and south) in Pikimachay Cave gave us an almost complete sequence from about 22,000 B.P. to the present. While the earliest Zone k with human artifacts in the south room has not been dated, the zone above, j bears a date of $19,600 \pm 3000$ B.P. (UCLA 1653A), and a check on this date by another laboratory from materials just above the first samples at the junction of Zone j and i1 was dated as $20,200 \pm 1050$ B.P. (I 5851-A). Zone i1 was dated at $16,050 \pm 1200$ B.P. (UCLA 1653B), while Zone i bears a date of $14,700 \pm 1400$ B.P. (UCLA 1653C). Zone h1 above it is undated, but a bone from the overlying Zone h was dated at $14,150 \pm 180$ B.P. (UCLA 1464), while the overlying Zone ẖ is still undated. The overlying preceramic zones in this south room are undated, but analysis of the artifacts suggests Zone f2 is about 9000 B.P., Zone f1 is 7500 B.P., and Zone f is 7000 B.P. The sequence of this room was supplemented by that of the central room that saw Zones X, K, U, V, and W falling in the period from 7500 to 6500 B.P., while Zones H, G and F were between 4500 and 3900 B.P. with Zone F being dated at 3850 ± 120 B.P. (I 4154). This sequence in turn was supplemented by materials from the north room with Zones VIII and VII being between 5000 and 6000 B.P., Zone VI being about 4000 B.P., and Zone V being at about 3000 B.P.

Excavation in other small shelters in the scrub zone of the Thorn Forest supplement the later part of the sequence from Pikimachay Cave. Ayamachay Cave (Ac 102) had three pre-ceramic zones in it: Zone VIII at about

9350 B.P., Zone VII dated at 7560±140 B.P. (I 5694), and Zone VI at about 5700 B.P. Ac 244 near Huamangilla has a number of stratified zones, all with meager remains, that include Zone G between 9000 and 8000 B.P., Zone F between 8000 and 7000 B.P., Zone E between 5000 and 4000 B.P., and Zone D with ceramics of the Initial Period. The other two caves, Ac 117 and Tc 240 had few pre-ceramic layers, but no preservation of remains of plants; Zone D of Ac 117 (containing corn cobs) was dated at 5470±110 B.P. (I 5685) and 5250±105 B.P. (I 5688), while Cave Tc 240 had a single pre-ceramic layer, Zone H, at about 5000 B.P. and Zone G with Initial Period ceramics from 3750 to 3000 B.P. Also found in the survey were a number of open sites of different periods: one before 9100 B.P., four of the period from 9100 to 7800 B.P., eight of the period from 7800 to 6500 B.P., seven of the period from 6500 to 5100 B.P., fifteen (including three hamlets) from the period from 5100 to 3750 B.P., and eleven (including three hamlets with features indicating irrigation) from 3750 to 3000 B.P.

The next zone, the Thorn Forest riverine, is obviously closely related to the previous one and has many of its characteristics. It, however, does have permanent water from streams and some alluvial soils resulting in gallery forest at the rivers' edges. In terms of present day agricultural practices, this is where maize, lucuma, beans and many of the cash crops are grown. Although we found twenty-five early sites in this locality, only two sites were excavated, but they gave a well-documented sequence. The Puente site (Ac 158) had thirty-five stratified floors, and many of these were dated. Zone XIIa was dated 8860±125 B.P. (I 5057), Zone X was dated at 7420±125 B.P. (I 5056), Zone VIII was 7160±125 B.P. (I 5024), Zone VI was 6670±120 B.P. (I 5132), Zone IV was 6560±120 B.P. (I 5128), Zone IIb was 6615±120 B.P. (I 5129), Zone IIa was 6630±120 B.P. (I 5131), Zone II was 6360±110 B.P. (I 4502), Zone Ij was 6470±125 B.P. (I 5274), Zone Ih1 was 6036±120 B.P. (I 5273), and different parts of Zone Ic were dated at 3995±105 B.P. (I 5131) and 4040±105 B.P. (I 5055). Excavation in 1971 in the nearby Wichquana site Ar 18 revealed early ceramic remains in five stratified zones and a date on soil overlying them was 2650 B.P. Surface collections netted a single site between 9050 and 7750 B.P., two between 7750 and 6450 B.P., four between 6450 and 5050 B.P., five from 5050 to 3700 B.P. (including two that are hamlets), and fifteen from the period 3700 to 2950 B.P. Of this last group, six were hamlets and one of these had a pyramid on it.

As mentioned previously, no sites were excavated in the Xerophytic zone in the northern part of the valley at elevations under 2,500 meters. This lack of excavation was due to the fact that no caves with preserved remains of plants were discovered even though the area is extremely hot and dry and has desert vegetation including agave, cardon, and cactus as well as acacia, mesquite, and molle trees. We did, however, survey the area and found one site which was of the Jaywa Phase dated 9050 to 7750 B.P.; five were of the Piki Phase (7650 to 6450 B.P.); seven were of the Chihua Phase from 6450 to 5050 B.P. (two of these had architectural features suggesting they were hamlets); thirteen (two of which were hamlets) were of the Cachi Phase from 5050 to 3700 B.P.; and two hamlets and a pyramid site in the Initial Period dated between 3700 and 2950 B.P.

At the present time, much of the material from our excavations at Ayacucho is still unanalyzed.[1] The whole ceramic sequence after 3000 B.P., based upon tests in seven stratified ruins (twenty-two components) as well as the top levels of most caves (forty-eight components), and the later sites from survey (about 300 sites), is almost untouched, but this concerns another problem — the rise of civilization — and is another story that really occurred after the origin and spread of domesticates. Also, complete reconstruction of the way of life on each of our earlier ninety-three floors, our paleoethnographies, is just beginning. However, the basic typology of the 10,000 artifacts from these early components is complete and we do have a firm sequence of cultural phases, which sequence is buttressed by forty-six radiocarbon determinations. Further, the seasonality, settlement pattern, population, demographic, and subsistence aspects of these cultural phases have been studied and these are the data that must be used in a study of the origins and spread of early domesticates and concomitant rise of settled life.

Now let us consider this problem in light of not only our information from the region of Ayacucho-Huanta but with all the other relevant material of the central Peruvian interaction sphere. Our discussion will be phrased in terms of our periodization from the region of Ayacucho-Huanta.

The Pacaicasa Phase, from about 22,000 B.P. to about 15,500 B.P., obviously precedes any attempt at domestications, but it does represent not only the earliest evidence of human occupation in Ayacucho, but in all of South America (MacNeish 1971). It, therefore, behooves us to say a few words about this unique cultural manifestation. It is represented by seventy-one artifacts, about 100 flakes and cores, some of which are foreign to the cave, in association with ninety-six bones of extinct animals, some of which have been worked, in the four lowest cement-like strata,

[1] Dr. Luis Lumbreras, Director of the National Museum of Anthropology and History of Peru, and his students will be studying the ceramics they excavated in cooperation with our project.

Zones k, j, il, and i of Pikimachay Cave. The artifacts include four kinds, the most numerous being a sort of chopping tool. All but one are made of volcanic tufa, probably from the cave wall itself, and the majority of them (thirteen) are made from slabs. Two of these have straight, almost convex edges, while eight others are bifacial (chipped to a rough ellipsoidal form), and four of them have evidence of being used as hammers, and one of them is of basalt foreign to the cave. Also, made from large chunks of volcanic tufa are a series (nineteen) of unifacial tools with deep concave edges; of these, two have two deep concave edges that show evidence of retouching and use. These we have called spokeshaves, but they could very well have been used to scrape meat or bone rather than wood. The other major group (seventeen tools) are thinner unifaces with retouching and/or use along a straight to convex edge; of these seventeen, two of the thinner ones are pointed and could have served as projectile points, while one from the top Zone i has a blow on it. Of the other fourteen large artifacts, two are of material foreign to the cave; one of these is roughly plano-convex, and both have chipping along one of their narrow edges. Five have been chipped in such a way that there are a series (two to six) of spurs or denticulates on them. Wear patterns suggest they were used as choppers and scrapers.

The associated bones are mainly of unidentified species of ground sloths and include a jaw, a tooth, thirteen vertebrae, four scapular fragments (two of which have been cut), a radius, three ulnae, two metapodials, one carpal bone, one phalanx, two ribs, and four fragments of long bones, all of which had been shattered by chopping or hammering. However, one tooth from Zone il has been identified as *Scelidotherium tarijensis*, and parts of a jaw, sternum, humerus, and two metapodials, all but one from Zone i, belong to *Scelidotherium* sp. Nine bones (two fragments of jaws, three cannon bones, two femora, a carpal bone and a metapodial) are of horse, identified as *Equus andium*.

Also, from the same zone are three femora and a jaw of the rodent *Phyllotis* sp., and from Zone i is a vertebra and femur of a large carnivore. There also was a single femur of a deer from Zone j.

Although the sample of identified bones is small, there is a suggestion of climatic change during Pacaicasa times. Analysis of the soils of these deposits is not complete, but even preliminary chemical analyses from the various zones tend to confirm the climatic change by hypothesis, for Zones k and j are less acidic (pH of 6.7 to 7.7) than are i and il (pH of 7.85 to 8.15) and also have traces of organic matter, while Zone i has traces (.83 and .42) of carbonates.

The deer bone and the evidence of lower acidity and organic matter in the soils suggest Zone j was perhaps at a wet climatic period when there was a more woodland type of vegetation near the cave, while the bones of horse, rodent, and cat (?), plus the soils, suggest Zones i and i1 were at a drier period when the vegetation was of a more grassland type. What this means in terms of more general periods is difficult to determine on the basis of our present analysis, and the two opinions now given are dramatically opposed to each other. Our geologist suggests the earlier wet period, roughly from 22,000 to 17,000 B.P., of Zones j and k is a period of glacial advance and that the dry period represented by Zones i and i1, roughly from 17,000 to 15,500 B.P., is an interstadial, while I take the opposite view. Either interpretation has an obviously wider implication concerning glaciation in the Andes and South America, and much more study of this problem is needed.

These are, however, not the only general implications of these earliest materials, for they obviously have wide cultural ramifications. Although our sample of tools is small and there is some suggestion from the kinds of tools with the kinds of bones that we may have found that the occupation represents a butchering station that did not contain the full range of tools of their artifact assemblages, these are the earliest artifacts in South America, and obviously must have been derived from still earlier assemblages in North America, and ultimately northeastern Asia. Thus those earliest tools from Pacaicasa have a bearing on the whole problem of the peopling of the New World — a problem far from being understood.

Our second phase, Ayacucho, from roughly 15,500 B.P. to 13,000 B.P., as well as the seven artifacts from an UNNAMED COMPLEX, roughly in the period from 13,000 to 11,000 B.P. also, has more bearing on the problem of early man in America than it does on the early domestication of plants and animals. However, unlike most areas of the New World, there is sufficient material from a number of regions in central Peru even at this early period to furnish hints of interactions between various spheres of the area — a process that is of key importance in the understanding of the origin and spread of domesticates in later periods.

The largest amounts of materials and the most reliable still come from Pikimachay Cave, specifically from Zones h1 and h. These two zones have produced 209 artifacts, over 1,000 chips and cores (about 100 of which have been worked) in association with 517 nonhuman bones and a relatively large sample of pollen. Tools are a continuation of most of the older types, except slab choppers, but now almost as many of them were made of chalcedony pebbles, basalt, etc., all foreign to the cave, as from local material. New types of tools occur and include split-pebble scraper planes (five) and spokeshaves (six), pebble choppers (three), a series of flake side scrapers or knives (twenty-two), unifacial projectile points (nine), projectile points made from horse metapodials (two), a point from a sloth's rib, seven burins and a fluted wedge, two fleshing tools made from sloth ribs, an ulna awl, an antler punch, and an ornament cut from a camelid's phalanx. Distributions of bones and artifacts in Zone h show five concentrations, suggesting five forays into the cave when a number of activities were undertaken, although the initial purpose may have always been to beard the beast (sloth) in his den.

Bones include many (168) sloth bones from almost every part of the body, while two jaws and a humerus are of a large species of *Scelidotherium*, a tooth is of a small species of this genus, and a humerus, carpal, femur, and nine radii are of *Megatherium tarijense*.

Deer bones (twenty-five) occur, and there are six limb fragments and a tooth of *Equus andium*, twenty-seven bones of the rodent *Phyllotis*, three limb bones of a large cat, thirteen limb bones of a puma (*Felis concolor*), a skull and radius of *Dusicyon* sp., a jaw and vertebrae of *Conepatus*, limbs of *Lagidium peruanum* and six bones of llama, all the latter in doubtful contexts. It might be added that there is also a child's jaw with teeth, a radius, some phalanges and ribs — the oldest remains of man himself in South America.

The kinds of animals uncovered suggest a wet climate and more woodland environs around the cave, and this is confirmed by the pollen that includes *Alnus* (forty-seven grains), *Salix* (three), Compositae (fifteen), *Dodonaea* (twenty-eight), sedge (eleven), Gramineae (seventy-three), eight Chenopodiaceae, two *Ephedra*, two Caryophyllaceae, and two Amaryllidaceae.

This complex of pollen and other materials contrasts with that in the overlying Zone ẖ which contained a scraper plane, four flake side scrapers, a prismatic blade and a fragment of a lenticular point with a diamond shaped cross section associated with a horse metapodial, three llama bones and two bones of *Phyllotis*. The pollen contains mainly grass (127), some Compositae (twenty-six) and sedge (seventeen) and *Alnus* (nineteen), as well as *Dodonaea viscosa* (two), *Artemisia* (one), Rosaceae (three), Cruciferae (three), Ranunculaceae (three), Polemoniaceae (two), Alternanthera (five), Gentianaceae (one), and Bromeliaceae (two).

Again, there are different interpretations, with our geologist suggesting Zone h is of a glacial advance and Zone ẖ as the first postglacial phase, while I would be of the opinion that Zone h of 14,000 B.P. is of an interstadial, and Zone ẖ of 13,000 to 11,000 B.P. represents the final glacial advance. Again, more study is necessary.

There are, however, some comparable materials from the lower levels of Guitarrero Cave from the Callejón de Huaylas and these have been dated as 12,610 B.P. ± 360 years (GX1859) (Lynch and Kennedy 1970). Included in these materials are plano-convex scraper planes, one of which is denticulated, as well as flake choppers, large spokeshaves and a series of retouched flakes. All these artifacts can be duplicated in our Ayacucho assemblage and, as there, all the tools are unifacial. The two complexes seem related.

The other materials that possibly are of this time period come from the coast near Lima. One set of materials comes from the Red Zone at the Chivateros site on the banks of the Chillón River. These artifacts are so indeterminate that they are difficult to relate to anything (Lanning and Patterson 1967). The other materials that have been stated as being of this time are the surface collection made at the Oquendo site just south of the Chillón and the Tortugas site in the Lurín Valley. Both collections abound in blades, cores, and burin-like objects. From this standpoint, they bear some general resemblance to the materials from Zone ḥ as well as to the Ayacucho Phase; however, better contextual data from the coast are necessary before the significance of these relationships can be ascertained.

Thus, in this second period there is some evidence of a relationship within the central Peruvian interaction sphere — certainly between Ayacucho in the Sierras and Guitarrero on the Pacific Andean flanks. Obsidian, not native to the coast, occurs in the Oquendo complex and hints that even at this period there may have been trade linkages in this area.

However, not until the Puente Phase, 11,000 to 9100 B.P., do we really have enough data to discern the sort of relationships that might have existed within our Andean interaction sphere. In the Ayacucho region we have: six stratified components from Jaywa Cave in the Humid Woodlands; a single component, Zone VIII from Ayamachay, now in the Thorn Forest scrub (but pollen indicated it, too, was then in the Humid Woodlands); an excavated component, Zone XIV of the Puente site, in the Thorn Forest riverine zone; and a surface collection from the Thorn Forest scrub (see Figure 4).

Bones of mammals and birds found in these assemblages indicate that the Humid Woodlands zone was occupied during the dry season (April–September) while the dry quebradas (and perhaps the grassy plains) were exploited during the wet season. One of the main activities of the dry season, concentrated at the microband camps, was hunting deer and camelids, although there may have been some trapping and plant collecting.

In the camps of the wet seasons at lower elevations proportionately fewer deer and camelid bones were recovered, but many more bones of

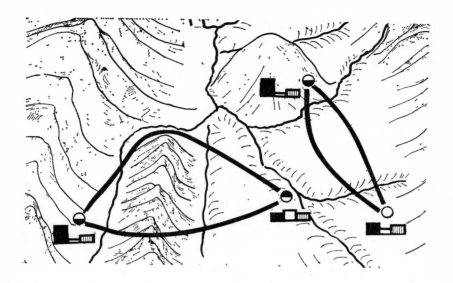

SETTLEMENT PATTERN

◐ Spring-Summer (October-March) Microband Camp

⊖ Fall-Winter (April-September) Microband Camp

SUBSISTENCE ACTIVITIES

▨ Hunting

☐ Trapping

▥ Plant Collecting

Figure 4.   A reconstruction of the settlement and subsistence patterns of the Puente Phase in the Ayacucho Valley

small mammals (including those of guinea pigs) were found. This suggests that trapping or animal collecting was perhaps a more important subsistence activity than hunting. Plant collecting might have occurred, but the only evidence we have of it are a few charred seeds of an unidentified plant at the Puente site. Although the evidence is not conclusive, it strongly suggests a seasonally scheduled subsistence system.

Our evidence from the other regions of the Sierra is not so precise, but there are hints that the way of life may have been much the same. The lower levels of Panalagua Cave near Junín contain numerous bones of large mammals, undoubtedly from successful hunting; the lithic technology and tool types show great similarities to those from Ayacucho. The assemblage from Panalagua, however, shows even more resemblance to that of Lauricocha I, which again contained many bones of large mammals. Whether these people also had a seasonally scheduled subsistence system remains to be seen (Cardich 1964).

In terms of artifact types, the two roughly contemporaneous components on the western slopes of the Andes are clearly related to those of the Sierras with Tres Ventanas I (Engel 1968) having a large number of projectile points, scraper types, and a burin in common with Puente of Ayacucho, while the more limited Guitarrero Ib complex (Lynch and Kennedy 1970) has some resemblance to that of Lauricocha I. Some bones of large mammals and many projectiles suggest that the people of Tres Ventanas had basically a hunting subsistence system and the many deer hunts from Guitarrero indicate it was similar. Also found in Tres Ventanas were grass seeds, jicama, and roots, indicating their diet was supplemented by plant collecting. Although both complexes have been mentioned as having transhumance or seasonally scheduled systems, the only evidence for such are a few coastal shells and leaves of opuntia (?) from Tres Ventanas.

The data from the coastal regions are even less adequate and come from the site at Chivateros quarry and the Pampilla sites in the Chillón Valley and the Conchitas complex from the Tablada de Lurín (of the Lower Lurín), both of the latter with very limited amounts of artifactual material. Information on subsistence is poor, but shells in the Conchitas site suggest that the inhabitants consumed marine shellfish from the coast and plant and animal foodstuffs from the lomas during the coastal wet season, but limited numbers of projectile points and few bones of mammals in all components hint that hunting was of minor importance. Whether more hunting was done in the valleys in the dry season as suggested by the location of the Pampilla site, or on the Andean western flanks as hinted at by the Tres Ventanas shells, is open to question.

In spite of the limited data from this period, there is some evidence of interactions between some of the life zones. Perhaps the best evidence for contact is that obsidian is found in all components from every region, hinting at a lively trade in this product and, of course, there are the shells and prickly pear leaves from Tres Ventanas I. On a slightly different level is the similarity of the flint technology throughout the whole area as well as many tool types in common between two or more of the regions, such as the leaf-shaped points, the incipient stemmed points, the keeled ovoid end scraper and the roughly semilunar side knives. These tools and the evidence from Ayacucho of a seasonally scheduled specialized hunting substistence hint at still another more basic type of interaction at this time.

As poorly as it is now understood, that interaction could have been of the sort that caused the ideas about specialized hunting techniques on a seasonal basis and the necessary techniques for making specialized tools to spread rapidly throughout the whole area, probably from a host of small centers, and this in turn would have made all the inhabitants better adapted to exploit their local environments more successfully.

The next period, 9100 to 7800 B.P., is more fully documented than the previous ones and has actual evidence of the use of domesticates. In the region of Ayacucho-Huanta, compounds of the Jaywa Phase occur in five of the six microenvironments. The excavated site of Jaywa Cave in the Humid Woodlands zone contained five floors that represent dry-season camps of microbands, judging by the numerous bones of birds and large mammals typical of the dry season, as well as the stem of a berry. Furthermore, there was one achiote seed on one of the floors and two or three human feces from which were recovered stems of berries, grass seeds and fibers of both monocotyledonous and dicotyledonous plants, in addition to traces of meat. Thus these dry-season big-game hunters were also collecting some plant foods. Pollen indicates that a surface site and Zone f2 of Pikimachay Cave were also in the Humid Woodlands in this period and numerous projectile points attest to the fact that hunting was important. Whether they were of the dry season could not be determined. The one excavated component and open site from the low Puna, as well as the single surface collection from the high Puna, reveal a similar picture.

This way of life contrasts with that found at lower elevations. In the Thorn Forest scrub the one excavated component (Zone VI of Ac 244) and two of the three surface sites contained limited numbers of projectile points, but had grinding stones. Since seeds for grinding do not appear until the wet season, this may indicate they were of this season, and it hints that plant collecting was an activity more important than hunting. The single surface site from the Thorn Forest riverine zone shows a similar tool assemblage and, also, might have been of the wet season and had a similar subsistence pattern. The other components from this zone are the five earliest floors from the Puente site, and our fuller data allow us to reconstruct a slightly different way of life. In these floors bones of small mammals and birds far outnumber those of deer and llama. The majority (over 200 individuals) of the bones of small mammals were those of *Cavia* and it is the opinion of one of our zoologists that many of them may have been tamed. This suggests that trapping or collecting animals was important; possibly a major subsistence activity was raising guinea pigs. All of these floors, also, had grinding tools, indicating plant collecting was undertaken. Further, this evidence and the faunal data indicate occupation during the wet season. A few bones of deer and llama appear, as do

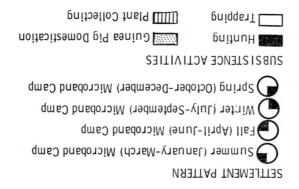

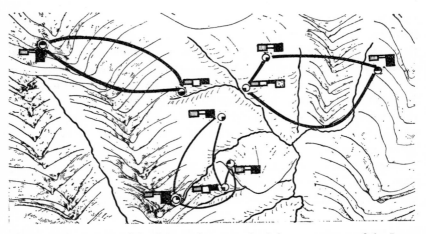

Figure 5.   A reconstruction of the settlement and subsistence patterns of the Jaywa Phase in the Ayacucho Valley

projectile points and butchering tools. This may be taken as evidence that some hunting was done. A detailed study of the technology involved in making these tools, and a study of sites at higher elevations, suggests another significant facet of the way of life of these Jaywa people. Apparently, the obsidian tools found in these life zones were almost exclusively manufactured in the Puna sites, while many of the specialized butchering tools of black basalt were made at lower elevations (often at the Puente site itself); both sets of tools were made by a single very specialized technique of flint knapping. This information taken in conjunction with the marked seasonality of sites at different elevations strongly suggests individuals were moving from one microenvironment to the next, and manufacturing certain tools seasonally, rather than the fact that tools were traded from one locale to the next by groups with different subsistence systems.

In summary then, the evidence from Ayacucho reveals that the slightly more numerous (twenty Jaywa components as against nine for Puente) populations of microbands moved from one microenvironment to another as the seasonal food resources became available. They exploited these resources with different subsistence techniques as well as undertaking slight subsidiary activities from one season to the next. Evidently the inhabitants were not only experimenting with and perfecting their limited techniques for acquiring both plant and animal foods, but were also gaining a much greater knowledge of the potential of their ecosystem as a whole (see Figure 5).

Our knowledge from the two adjacent Sierra regions (Huancayo-Junín and Lauricocha) is more limited, but the bones and tools suggest those people were still basically hunters, perhaps more skilled than in the previous period. Whether they were going through the same sort of development remains to be seen; unfortunately, no remains of this period of Lauricocha II have been uncovered in the Huánuco basin that might give us clues about transhumance or seasonal occupations (Cardich 1964).

Nothing has been reported from the Montaña at this period, but the achiote seeds from our Ayacucho component are native to that area or the Selva. This fact would not only indicate that there was trade from this zone, or to these zones, but that someone was living there who did some plant collecting.

The archaeological evidence from the coast at this time is only slightly better, but it is obvious that a new pattern was emerging (Lanning 1967). The Arenal complex, from near the end of the period in the Chillón and Ancón regions, occurs in both the lomas and floor of the Chillón Valley. The suggestion has been made that this group during the wet season utilized the abundant plant resources of the lomas, hunted game that grazed in the area, and supplemented these foods with marine shellfish, while during the dry season they utilized the plants and shellfish of the parts of the valley (deltas?) near the coast. Perhaps significant is the discovery that one lomas site contained a fragment of a gourd. One component with twined-woven mat at the Tablada de Lurín also contained many marine shells and fishbones, indicating the sea coast itself was also exploited from a base camp on the lomas. A surface site on a southern terrace of the upper reaches of the Chilca River also contained abundant flint materials including many leaf-shaped projectile points, suggesting a river-hunting camp. Its position directly below Tres Ventanas Cave, also with abundant flint tools of similar material, plus the fact that Tres Ventanas II also contains coastal shells, suggests that some groups may have been hunting and collecting in the highlands at certain seasons, and again in valleys at still another season (Engel 1968). In the region of Callejón de Huaylas, the well-stratified Guitarrero Cave does not seem to have been occupied during this period, but some of the materials in the Lampras region do seem related to those of Lauricocha time (Lynch and Kennedy 1970). Whether there was a relationship of transhumance to the coast is yet to be demonstrated.

Be that as it may, this is good evidence of a network of relationships between the various regions and zones. There is a widespread use of obsidian. Gourds were introduced to the coast from somewhere else and achiote seeds were brought to the region of Ayacucho and Huanta from their native habitats in the Selva or Montaña. Ground-stone tools occur in Ayacucho in this period but do not occur on the coast until the following period, while twined weaving occurred on the coast but did not spread into the highlands at Guitarrero and possibly Ayacucho until the next time level. There are some overlapping artifact types such as a few styles of projectile points (usually types with contracting stems) and scrapers (particularly the thumbnail variety) that occur in a number of different regions although the overall congeries are rather different. Although the evidence is meager, there are hints that certain useful and adaptive ideas or concepts from one region or even microenvironment began to spread to other ones. This in turn made for newer and better adaptations in these regions. Regional differentiation had begun as had crucial interstimulation between the various subspheres of central Peru, and the whole interaction sphere was on the threshold of fundamental changes.

This crucial period — 7800 to 6550 B.P. represented by the Piki Phase in the region of Ayacucho-Huanta — is better documented for all regions than any of the previous time periods. Our meager information from the higher elevations — materials from a surface site from the high Puna, and excavated and surface components from the low Puna — showed that the old system of dry-season hunting still persisted (see Figure 6).

Some components from the Humid Woodlands continued this pattern, but some adopted a new one. The lowest (F) floor of Chupas Cave, the two floors (f1 and f) of Pikimachay Cave, and Zone VII of Ayamachay Cave contain a large number of bones of cervids and camelids in associa-

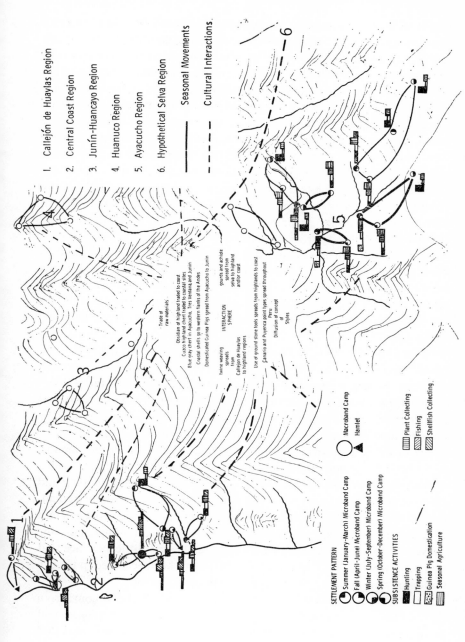

Figure 6. A reconstruction of the settlement and subsistence patterns in the central Peruvian interaction sphere during Piki times

tion with many projectile points; however, no grinding stones occurred. These camps all seem to have been for small bands hunting during the dry season, but a single rind of *Crescentia* from Ayamachay Cave attests to the fact that some plant collecting occurred. The other five excavated components from two of the same caves show an entirely different pattern. Zones K, U, V, and W of Pikimachay Cave have bones of rodents (including some of tame guinea pigs) and many birds, but only three bones of deer. Further, rinds of gourds and cucurbits, as well as other seeds, were recovered from Zone W. The floors seem to have been occupied in the wet season by groups who were trapping, plant collecting, keeping guinea pigs, planting or harvesting seed crops, and only rarely hunting. The other component, Zone E of Chupas Cave, was similar in that it had few bones or projectile points but many grinding stones, including a pebble-edge rocker mano.

Only one component (Zone E of Cave 244) was excavated in the then much diminished Thorn Forest scrub zone, but eight surface collections seem to come from components of this phase. The excavated floor yielded grinding stones and unidentified seeds, suggesting an occupation during the wet season with an emphasis on plant collecting and/or incipient agriculture.

More abundant remains come from the Thorn Forest riverine zone, thanks to the excavation of the site at Puente, although two surface sites occurred. Fifteen stratified floors were excavated; twelve of those floors show clear evidence of wet-season occupations, and all of them contained hundreds of bones of small mammals, including those of tamed or domesticated (?) guinea pigs, but only a few bones of camelids or deer. Many of them, also, yielded grinding stones, pebble-edge rocker manos, *majanas* or doughnut-shaped weights for digging sticks, and unidentified charred seeds. We believe their subsistence system included trapping and penning guinea pigs, with some plant collecting and/or incipient agriculture, and little if any hunting. The other three floors were more difficult to interpret, but except for one that was obviously a hunting camp, the subsistence pattern may have been the same. There is little evidence that they were wet-season camps and some may have been occupied in the dry season or during both the wet and dry seasons.

Our data from the Xerophytic zone are less abundant and come from the surface sites. Most of these had numerous scraper planes and grinding stones and few if any projectile points. Thus, there are hints that they were like those at the Thorn Forest riverine zone.

Summarizing our data from Ayacucho, one might say that there was a tendency for camps of the wet season to become slightly larger in size and longer in duration, perhaps for the simple reason that guinea pigs and storable plants played continuously growing roles in the pattern of consumption. However, we believe that more diagnostic of the period than this was the fact that as the options or alternatives for subsistence grew in number, new kinds of scheduling occurred that allowed for new subsistence strategies.

Certainly the old satisfying subsistence strategies of the previous periods probably continued to be used where the inhabitants hunted and collected in the uplands during the dry season while they trapped and raised guinea pigs at lower elevations. With such a system, yields were not large but were adequate, and risks of not obtaining the minimal necessary quantity of food were very low if one cared to work just a little, and particularly if lands still existed into which the slowly increasing population could expand. We believe, however, that during this period optimizing strategies began to be employed. Such strategies which utilized such scheduled options as agriculture in the wet season or animal domestication could give large amounts of food, storable or on the hoof, with minimal effort, but there was always the risk of natural disaster and the risk that the populations would increase to such a level that the system or subsistence options could not supply the basic foodstuffs.

This, of course, meant that there were continual pressures for improving the old food-producing options or inventing new and more efficient ones. In our opinion, the adoption of such an optimizing strategy — whether conscious or unconscious — was one of the crucial processes toward becoming agriculturists and that this was being done in Peru, at least in the central highlands, in this period.

We also believe that another crucial step toward an agricultural economy was that, while optimizing strategies were being adopted in one part of a nuclear area, a more efficient strategy was being adopted in other parts of this area and, more important, both were interacting.

We believe that such a more efficient strategy was being adopted in part on the central Peruvian coast in the Canario Period, and there is definite evidence it was interacting with other contemporaneous cultures in other zones (Lanning 1967). Basic to the adaptation of this new strategy was the location of some settlements in key spots where virtually all the areas of food resources were contiguous with each other so that regardless of the season the inhabitants never had to make more than a half-day journey in any direction to obtain their necessary foodstuffs. A site near the mouth of the Lurín on its south bank is an excellent example of this type of location (Patterson 1971). From this base one could exploit the nearby lomas to the south for plants and animals in the foggy months as well as obtain sea lions and fish from the rocky point on the nearby coast to the west in the dry summer months, while fish, marine shellfish, and some plants were easily available in the nearby river delta or sandy beaches at all times of the year, as were plants and game fish in the adjacent middle-river microenvironments. The site of Paloma, a round pithouse hamlet in the lomas at a permanent water source just north of the mid-section of Chilca River, occupied a similar strategic position for the local seasonal resources which could be supplemented with relatively little walking all year round by food collected from the delta of the Chilca River and the nearby slopes of the Andean mountains (Engel 1971). Another pithouse hamlet at the edge of the lomas near the coast just north of the Las Haldas River had a similar position.

In all of these examples, their special locations next to diverse micro-environments allowed people to have a good permanent year-round supply of food and a sedentary way of life without too much effort, and with little risk-taking by merely scheduling their limited subsistence options — fishing, collecting shellfish, hunting sea mammals or land mammals, or collecting plants. In fact, stable village life was possible without agriculture and the stage was set for great increases of population and diverse cultural advances.

Some evidence exists, however, that not all inhabitants took on this new way of life, for in the Chillón-Rimac-Ancón Valleys one still finds predominantly seasonal campsites, indicating the inhabitants moved to exploit the lomas in the wet seasons and went to other more coastal or riverine locations to secure the marine resources in the dry parts of the year. Also, the materials from the upper pre-ceramic levels from Tres Ventanas and Quikche Caves from the western slopes of the Andes, far above the Chilca and Lurín Rivers, contained not only many Canario-type artifacts, many bones, grass seeds, and Jicama remains, but also coastal shells (Engel 1968). These facts indicate that not only were these caves of this life zone being occupied seasonally but that they were related to the coastal occupations, perhaps in a transhumant manner.

On the basis of the present evidence, the subsistence pattern further north on the western Andean flanks in the Callejón de Huaylas is very different. In Guitarrero Cave IIb–IIe, were found many bones of deer and birds; some bones of camelids, *Sylvilagus*, *Marmosa*, *Conepatus*, and *Felis concolor* (puma) were found in association with fully domesticated common beans (*Phaseolus vulgaris*), as well as lima beans (Kaplan, Lynch, and Smith 1973). Whether these people with a subsistence system that included incipient agriculture had a local permanent settlement or transhumant connection to the coast is unknown.

However, the lithic types from the Callejón de Huaylas as well as those from Tres Ventanas show linkages to the Sierras with those from the Callejón de Huaylas and were more like those of the Pachamachay complex of the Junín-Huancayo region. In this latter region there are abundant surface sites and excavated materials from the upper levels of Pachamachay as well as the lower levels of Curimachay and Tilarnyoc Caves of this time period in a number of different microenvironments at high elevations. Some of these artifactually rich components contained large numbers of camelid bones with considerable variability, hinting that the llama may have been in the process of being domesticated in this sort of life zone. Also, in Curimachay, there were a few camelid bones, as well as grinding stones.

Incomplete as the data may be, there certainly are strong indications of some sort of seasonally scheduled subsistence system that was different from any of the previously mentioned regions.

What it was like in northern parts of the Sierra is difficult to determine, but we do have occupations at Lauricocha III and Ranchacancha in the Puna (Cardich 1964) and also very similar materials from Ambo in the Huánuco Valley next to the Montaña (Ravines 1965). Although these data are most inadequate, these facts hint at a seasonally scheduled subsistence system.

In spite of the very limited and incomplete information for this period, considerable evidence exists for interaction between the various regions, or spheres and subspheres. Obsidian occurred throughout the whole area; a distinctive dark blue-gray chert was utilized in Junín, Tres Ventanas and Ayacucho; and a brown chert, known only from Cuzco, occurred in some coastal sites.

Tree gourds and bottle gourds came into Ayacucho and the coast, perhaps from the eastern lowlands. Beans were being used in the Callejón de Huaylas and later were spread through the whole area. In the region of Junín, guinea pigs, possibly brought in from Ayacucho, were present. Ground-stone tools or the concept involved in making and using such types seemingly diffused from the highlands to the coast, while twined weaving was doing the opposite. Certain styles of artifacts such as a (Puyenca) rhomboid, (Chira) stemmed, and (Canario) leaf-shaped points were found throughout the whole area, as were certain lithic techniques, and must be considered evidence of widespread relationships. However, we must remember that in spite of the evidence of widespread contacts each of our regions was developing in rather different directions and that radically different subsistence strategies and economic orientations were beginning to appear. In fact, some of the various contacts that result in similarities of artifacts may have been in part the cause of differing developments and the optimizing subsistence strategies of the highlands may only have been feasible because they were buttressed by more efficient subsistence strategies elsewhere.

The trends that started in this period continued and developed further in the next period — 6550 to 5100 B.P. — represented by the Chihua Phase in the Ayacucho Basin. Again, we found relatively few sites at higher elevations, one in the high Puna and two surface sites and an excavated component in the low Puna. Artifacts and bones from the one in the high Puna suggest that major activities were knapping of flint and obsidian and hunting in the dry season. However, the finding of hoes with ground polish indicates that the older pattern may have changed significantly in that root crops had been added to the subsistence pattern of people at these high altitudes. In the present limits of the Humid Woodland only one component occurred, an excavated level at Chupas that temporally was very late, right at the transition from Chihua to Cachi. Rocker manos in the refuse suggest the grinding of springtime, wet-season seeds, either quinoa or unknown wild seeds. Pollen profiles, however, show that five surface sites as well as two excavated floors of Pikimachay Cave, and one floor of Ayamachay Cave, all now in the upper part of the Thorn Forest scrub, were then in the Humid Woodlands. Projectile points with deer bone from the latter floor indicate it was a dry-season hunting camp. The two floors of Pikimachay had preserved seeds and other plant remains and revealed a rather different picture (see Figure 7).

Seeds of *Berberis* (?) and fruits of *Solanum* indicate occupation at the late dry season, near the end of winter, while the presence of lucuma pits, beans (*Phaseolus vulgaris*), corn cobs, a cotton-twined textile in the refuse, perhaps peppers (*Capsicum* sp.), and fragments possibly of potato eyes and coca leaf in feces indicate a temporary camp by agriculturists. Similar to this camp was the lower floor, twice dated at about 5200 B.P., at Rosamachay Cave in the Thorn Forest scrub that contained cobs of the Ayacucho race of maize. This newly discovered race is the oldest maize in Peru and seems to be ancestral to the most primitive extant race, Confite Morocho, but more important it shows evidence of integration with teosinte and thus ultimately must have come from Meso-America. In addition to this site in the Thorn Forest scrub, seven more surface sites were discovered; some were very large in size (macroband camps?), and most of them had grinding stones. In the Thorn Forest riverine zone, four large sites were discovered and excavations at the Puente yielded eight more floors. While all contained some bones of guinea pigs, five have seed-grinding tools and suggestions of multiseason occupation, while the

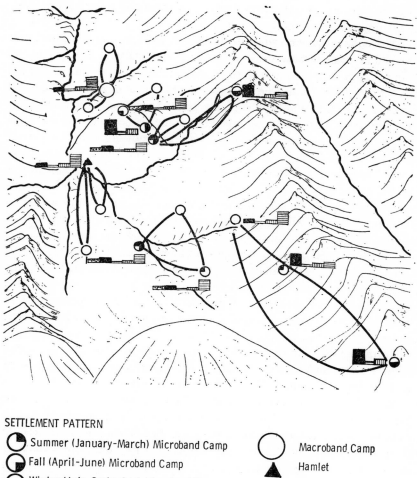

SETTLEMENT PATTERN

◔ Summer (January-March) Microband Camp

◑ Fall (April-June) Microband Camp

◒ Winter (July-September) Microband Camp

◕ Spring (October-December) Microband Camp

○ Macroband Camp

▲ Hamlet

SUBSISTENCE ACTIVITIES

▓ Hunting

□ Trapping

▥ Plant Collecting

▦ Guinea Pig Domestication

▤ Seasonal Agriculture

Figure 7. A reconstruction of the settlement and subsistence patterns of the Chihua Phase in the Ayacucho Valley

others seem to have been dry-season occupations for hunting or butchering. The seven surface sites in the Xerophytic zone are all large; four of them were along waterways and two of these had stone architecture, suggesting rather sedentary occupations.

All the above evidence suggests that the most important settlement unit at Chihua was the base camp at lower elevations with an agricultural complex that permitted groups to grow a limited food surplus during the wet season. These foods were supplemented by meat of game and domesticated guinea pigs, and by wild plants, but the surpluses were usually not large enough to last the inhabitants through the dry season, so at that time groups were forced to hunt, collect, or grow root crops in the Humid Woodlands and Puna zones, or occasionally to hunt and/or collect plants in the Thorn Forest scrub and even in the dry quebradas. A few groups may have collected plants or undertaken agriculture in the Humid Woodlands during the wet season and then gone elsewhere in the dry season.

Cultural phases of this period of time from the adjacent Sierra zone of Huancayo-Junín have not been well-defined, but the upper levels of Curimachay and Tilarnyoc do appear to have bones of possibly domesticated llamas while the Callavallauri site overlooking the broad flats of the Mantaro River contained grinding stones. In the light of these hints, plus the materials from adjacent Ayacucho, it would not be surprising to find that here was a subsistence system involving hunting or herding at high altitudes and agriculture at lower altitudes.

North of this region in the Sierra, no remains of this time have been reported. Although Lauricocha III is often stated as being such, we believe that in spite of the late C^{14} dates the types of projectile points as well as other tool types indicate that this manifestation more probably was of an earlier period. Again, adequate information is lacking for the Montaña, but tree gourds, achiote, lucuma, and coca, all lowlands domesticates, do occur in Ayacucho and in the next period such lowland domesticates as sweet potatoes and peanuts are present in coastal sites. All of the plants, as well as some mentioned from Ayacucho that later are present in the lowlands, may have been involved in some sort of tropical agricultural subsistence system that was basic to development in that region.

We can do little more than speculate about the subsistence system of the western Andean slopes for few cultural remains from this period have been found in adequate archaeological contexts. From the Huarochiri region we have but a few isolated Encanto-type projectile points, while from the Callejón de Huaylas there are some surface sites whose types of points suggest they are of this period.

Perhaps our most abundant data for the period come from the Corbina (6200–5750 B.P.) and Encanto (5750–4500 B.P.) Phases along the coast from Chancay to Canete and from the Lachay complex from the Rio Seco to Casma (Lanning 1967). In the southern part of this region there were hamlet sites placed in strategic spots adjacent to a number of different microenvironments so all could be exploited from a sedentary base. However, the strategic spot usually involved a riverine location, for well-watered fertile lands were needed to supplement the wild diet of fish, shellfish, and sea-mammals with such domesticates as gourds, two kinds of squash, and perhaps lima beans.

The hamlet called Chilca Monument I, in the delta of the Chilca River, is an excellent example of this type of site (Engel 1966). It, and others like it to the south are often surrounded with smaller sites which, although usually without architectural features, seem to have had very specific subsistence orientations. Some on the coast are obviously oriented to marine fishing and hunting of sea mammals by much improved techniques and to collecting shellfish. Other sites are in the lomas or are riverine. Whether these represent seasonal camps for forays by people with specialized subsistence techniques or whether they were of a more permanent nature inhabited by people who were subsistence specialists who had an exchange system with the hamlets is unknown, but we suspect both might have occurred.

In the Lurín, the former situation may have pertained for there is a hamlet with stone-slab pithouses in the Tablada de Lurín (lomas) surrounded by riverine and coastal camps oriented for exploiting maritime resources. Further north in the areas of Rimac, Chillón, and Ancón, where microenvironments are often not contiguous, the older system of seasonal camps may have continued even though some groups did practice agriculture, for squash was found (along with possible camelid bones) at one site and at Ancón there is evidence that besides being seasonal hunters and collectors of marine shellfish, the inhabitants were fishermen *par excellence.*

Further to the north our information is less precise, but there is evidence of hamlets, often surrounded by smaller sites, along the Rio Seco and Las Haldas Rivers. One suspects these people were practicing an economy not unlike that of the Chilca and Lurín locales.

As is obvious, the subsistence system of the coast was radically different from that of the highlands, but what is more, for the first time the lithic technology and lithic types (except for the resemblance of Piki ovoid to Encanto points) from these two general zones bear only general resemblances to each other. Obsidian and shells are, however, traded from one zone to another, but the major interactions seem to be in the spread of domesticates. Lima beans sometimes occurred on the coast and perhaps came from the high valleys on the western Andean slopes, while squashes and camelids (possibly tamed guanaco) probably spread down from the highlands. Guinea pigs spread through the highlands, perhaps out of the region of Ayacucho, while maize came into that region from the northern Sierra; potatoes and tamed guanaco or domesticated llamas may have entered it from the south. Lucuma and coca may have entered this same region from the Selva and/or the Montaña.

The full effect of the spread of these potentially food-producing items in terms of major increases in population or rapid cultural changes is, however, not apparent until the next period.

This next period is represented by the Cachi Phase (5100–3750 B.P.) in the Ayacucho basin. A major increase in population seems to have occurred, for we found fifty-five components, including seven hamlets, for this phase and only thirty-eight components in Chihua, the previous phase. However, as important as the increases of population are the indications of new economic orientations (see Figure 8).

One corral site occurred in the high Puna, and a corral site and an open site with two excavated components, all near ancient corrals, occurred in the low Puna. The sites are characterized by bones of camelids and deer, many fine projectile points, and a very specialized technique for knapping obsidian; additionally, the two low Puna sites had hoes. The four open sites in the Humid Woodlands are much like these; two of the open sites have many hoes as well as *majanas*, and the one excavated component, while having a possible fragment of a hoe, also has a rocker mano. No evidence has been found that the ground-stone tools or the hoes were made in these sites at high altitudes, but they look like imports from lower elevations where there is evidence that such tools were being made. The opposite seems true for the finely made obsidian tools, for while these occur at lower elevations, the chipping debitage which mainly is from an entirely different knapping technique gives no evidence of the making of fine obsidian tools. Thus, obsidian tools were being exchanged from occupations at higher elevations down to lower ones.

However, not only the technology is different between occupations at higher and lower elevations. In the Thorn Forest, which the palynological evidence indicates had expanded to present limits, fifteen large open sites were discovered, and three of these had architectural features on them suggesting they were hamlets. Also, the six excavated components from four caves seem to represent wet-season occupation by agricultural groups, for we uncovered maize, beans, lucuma, gourds, *Cucurbita moschata* and in poorer contexts *Cucurbita maxima*, pacae and cotton. Bones were not numerous, but included those of guinea pig and a proportionately significant increase of camelids. These camelids (as well as the

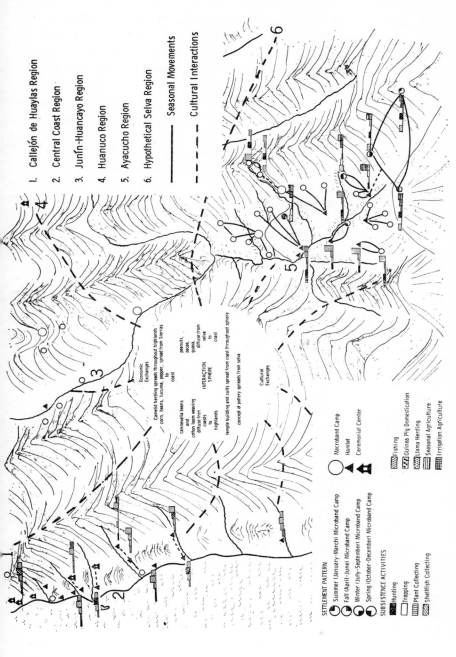

Figure 8. A reconstruction of the settlement and subsistence patterns in the central Peruvian interaction sphere during Cachi times

increased numbers from the Puente sites and the Mitos Phase at Huánuco) are not metrically different from the wild guanaco and stand out from the llama and alpaca from later levels. However, their marked increase and the occurrence of corrals make us suspect that camelid herding was undertaken, involving a wild or tamed, rather than a domesticated variety.

Components from the other lower environmental zones are much like this one. From the Thorn Forest riverine there were five large sites, two of which were hamlets, while in the Xerophytic zone thirteen sites were discovered, of which two also seem to have been hamlets. The only excavated components were six floors from the Puente site in the zone of the Thorn Forest riverine and each floor is slightly different from the others. However, most have grinding tools suggesting they were camps of agricultural people.

In summary, then, apparently at this time in the Ayacucho basin there was a minor system that included seasonal residence in different localities at high altitudes and subsistence activities based on dry-season herding and farming of wet-season root crops, as well as a major system that included permanent residence in hamlets with only occasional forays out from them. These subsistence activities were focused permanently on agriculture. The two systems appear to have been linked by an exchange network. Judging from modern ethnographic data, I would guess that this linkage survived through kinship and ritual ties that served economic functions. This pattern, often called vertical economy, persists to the present day in this region.

To the north, in the Junín-Huancayo region, large numbers of sites are assigned to the Tinyac Phase (4800–3500 B.P.). They include components from a series of high-altitude caves on the Puna: Pachamachay, Cuchimachay, Tilarnyoc, Pintadomachay, and Pachacutec, as well as at least two sites on or near the floor of the Mantaro Valley, the Ledig-Tschopik rock shelter 2 and San Pata near Huancayo and Jauja respectively. Although investigation in this region is just beginning, the locations of the sites suggest that some sort of vertical economy may be revealed here.

The limited information from further north in the Sierra hints at an even more intriguing problem concerned with the understanding of the beginning of still another type of settlement subsistence system or another type of vertical economy. At high elevations, near Cerro de Pasco, preliminary testing in the site of San Blas has revealed in its lower levels a large pre-ceramic hamlet or series of hamlets much involved with salt making as well as with llama herding. Further, the artifacts from the pre-ceramic levels, as well as the later ceramic levels, clearly show an intimate relationship with contemporaneous materials in the Huánuco Valley.

Specifically, the pre-ceramic materials from San Blas are closely related to those of the pre-ceramic Mito Phase from the bottom levels of the Kotosh site at the edge of the Montaña (Izumi and Tereda 1972). Preliminary reports of the excavation of Kotosh indicate that even at this time the site was more than a hamlet for there were ceremonial rooms and plazas or courtyards. Almost assuredly the subsistence was based on agriculture, but so far all that has been reported in this realm is that there were bones of llama and cuye (?) found in association with great quantities of carbonized plant remains, a few fragments of which might be maize. While there is no direct evidence of what the subsistence pattern was, the occurrence of such plants from the Montaña or Selva as lucuma, coca, guava, sweet potatoes, and peanuts in contemporaneous manifestation in central Peru and the occurrence of manihot (manioc) on the coast in the following period does hint at what sort of plants may have been utilized in the hypothetical subsistence pattern. One should note that no evidence has been found that manihot or other root crops were domesticated early in the Selva or Montaña, nor is there proof that the use of manihot or seed crops in the Selva or Montaña was in any way involved in the beginnings of agriculture, root or otherwise, in highland Peru. In fact, all the evidence now available shows quite the contrary.

Turning now in the opposite direction, the links from the Sierras to the Pacific Coast are generally absent for all we have are a few surface points and some possible corrals of later pre-ceramic time in the Huarochiri region and surface collections in the Callejón de Huaylas. The coastal materials from this period are abundant; in fact, they are downright overwhelming. The cultural sequence for the Ancón-Chillón sector has been divided into the Pampa Phase, Playa Hermosa Phase, Conchas Phase, and Gaviota Phase (Patterson 1971). Whether the first three phases occur from Canete to Casma on the coast cannot at present be determined, and classifying the materials from the southern Peruvian site of Asia as well as those to the north from Las Haldas and Culebras into the Gaviota Phase is open to question. However, in spite of the difficulties, we believe the Ancón-Chillón sequence is generally applicable.

During the early part of the period 4500–3900 B.P. (Pampa, Playa Hermosa, and Conchas Phases), the location of sites seems to have been governed by two factors, the presence of marine products and the availability of arable land in the lower parts of the valleys or on the deltas of their rivers.

At this time, large fishing hamlets were established in the immediate vicinity of rich fishing grounds and shellfish beds, often on a delta or a coastal rocky point. The sites at Ancón and Ventanilla near the Chillón definitely date to this period and probably many of the large deltaic and coastal shell mounds from the mouth of the Lomas, Mala, and Chilca just south of the Lurín do also; some large shell mounds near Chancay and Casma are more or less roughly contemporaneous with them. The other sites, often smaller in size, were also hamlets with either square or round pithouses and occur at deltaic or lower riverine or valley locations, with few if any occurring in the lomas or stretches of the upper rivers. Our most secure dated examples come from the Chillón, but similar sites abound in all central coastal valleys.

The presence of remains of large numbers of marine shellfish, mammals, and fish, along with occasional examples of such domesticates as canavalia beans, achira, pacae, guava, sweet potatoes, peppers, lima beans, lucuma, and even maize, does suggest that an exchange mechanism had been established whereby the fishermen sent marine protein from their permanent hamlets into the valley hamlets and received cultivated plant foods in return. Throughout this part of the period populations and agricultural produce seem to have been rapidly increasing and at about 3900 or 4000 B.P. a new efficient strategy of settlement subsistence came into being.

However, it is not the increased agricultural produce (that now includes cotton, peanuts, and coca, as well as guinea pigs and llamas) that really makes the strategy so different, for most groups are still heavily dependent on seasonal resources, but rather that people had moved from a system of equilibrium exchange for getting fishing products to farmers and farm products to fishermen to redistribution systems such that certain large villages or towns had a monopoly on certain food products, often marine, or a central dominant position in the exchange system, or both.

Examples of such centers, from north to south, would be Las Haldas on the Casma River, Culebras south of the Culebras River, Rio Seco on the north side of the Chancay Valley, Chuquitanta on the Chillón, Chira Villa on the Rimac River, and perhaps even Asia-like sites in the Chilca; Asia (Engel 1963) itself, in the Omas Valley, would be an example of such a center. Each is of different size, and has different architecture and relatively different kinds of associated numbers of administrative, ceremonial, living, and storage structures. All these centers seem to have been surrounded by fishing hamlets as well as by riverine-farming hamlets, some of which occurred in middle and almost upper positions along the river.

For this period, food remains again provide the most obvious evidence for interaction within the sphere. The use of llamas seems to have spread northward to Kotosh and presumably westward to Huarochiri. Guinea pigs were raised on the east side of the Andes at Kotosh as well as on the western coast at Culebras. Achira, lima beans, and cotton, along with the techniques for making twined cloth, had probably spread to the highland valleys, Maize, coca, chili peppers, and common beans had diffused to the coast from various highland regions. Perhaps they had also spread to the Montaña or Selva for during this period a number of domesticates (lima beans, lucuma, coca, sweet potatoes, and peanuts) with presumed origins in the tropical lowlands appeared on the coast.

Obsidian and other raw materials from the highlands still occurred on the coast, and shells for ornaments were traded to the highlands. There are hints, however, that agricultural products and raw materials were not the only commodities moving throughout the whole interaction sphere. My belief is that ideas about herding, wool, weaving, architecture, systems for control of water, and even ceremonial or religious practices were also becoming widespread. The whole tempo of exchange had speeded up considerably; most groups were relying on domesticated plants and animals, and populations were greatly increased. In fact, Peru had become a nuclear culture area and was only a step away from civilization itself.

This next period (3750–3000 B.P.) was one of the final spread of domesticates throughout the area of central Peruvian cultural interactions. After this period no further plants are domesticated and diffused out from this center of agriculture.

The ceramic styles of Andamarka (around 3750–3300 B.P.) and Wichquana (3300–2900 B.P.) occurred in the area of Ayacucho during this final period under discussion. The meager food remains associated with these ceramic styles suggest that the subsistence patterns were much the same as they were in the preceding period, with perhaps a little more emphasis on the growing of maize and the use of techniques for control of water.

Information from two surface components in the high Puna and four surface collections and an excavated floor in the low Puna indicates that the previous seminomadic seasonal settlement pattern, including herding and root-crop agriculture, remained relatively unchanged. Data from sites located at lower elevations indicate that there were new developments in this part of the region even though the basically agricultural subsistence pattern remained the same. The most obvious new developments occur in the settlement pattern. First, there are four sites with a number of new architectural features, including pyramids, made with a type of boulder-slab masonry. Two were excavated at Wichquana in the Thorn Scrub riverine zone and at Chupas in the Humid Woodlands, while one surface ceremonial site was in the Xerophytic zone and another in the Thorn Forest riverine zone. Secondly, the thirty-two surface sites at lower elevations cluster into five geographically distinct localities and in four of these there is a single site with a pyramid and other ceremonial features. I believe that the cluster of sites, eleven waterway hamlets, seventeen open camps and four cave components, was tied to these ceremonial centers or villages by kinship, ceremonial, and economic arrangements. Further, the larger proportion of bones of llamas in these villages with pyramids suggests that they were not only the nuclear centers for the surrounding farming communities, but were also the intermediaries between the agricultural groups at low elevations with the same agricultural plants of the previous phases, and the herders and root farmers at higher elevations.

In terms of interactions, the Ayacucho Valley seems to have been receiving ideas about pottery, architecture, and ceremonialism from the outside, but what was given in return is difficult to determine. Perhaps it was raw materials, lithic implements, hybridized Confite-Morocho maize, and ideas about water control.

To the north of Ayacucho in the regions of Mantaro and Huancayo, few if any ceramic sites of the Initial Period have been reported. Some of the many Puna sites with corrals and cave occupations may date to this period, but the best reported site is San Blas near Cerro de Pasco to the north. By this time, that site had grown into a huge village with a wide variety of architectural features, including ones connected with a highly specialized salt industry. The ceramics of this site clearly link it to the Kotosh site in the Huánuco Valley (see Figure 9).

At Kotosh the ceramic phases of Waira-Jirca and Kotosh-Kotosh pertain to this period, and during this time the site itself grew into a major town with a wide variety of architectural features. Although the final reports have not been published, little doubt exists that it was a major ceremonial and administrative center for a flourishing culture in an area that had a good solid agricultural base (Izumi and Tereda 1972).

In terms of interaction, the finding of Kotosh-like and perhaps some actual Kotosh-made pottery in the Cave of the Owls in the Montaña, indicates a linkage to the eastern lowlands (Lathrap and Roys 1963).

Turning now to the west, ceramics of Colinas-style brown-ware of the Initial Period occur in the upper levels of Quikche Cave in the region of Huarochiri. These ceramics bear some resemblance to the Andamarka pottery of the Ayacucho region. In fact, these materials might be cited as evidence that the earliest ceramics of Ayacucho spread into that region from the coast. Associated with the Quikche ceramics of the Initial Period were many bones of llamas, and these perhaps indicate that the area was the final link in a network of economic exchanges that extended down to the riverine systems leading to the coast.

To the north, on the western slopes of the Andes, is the Torril ceramic

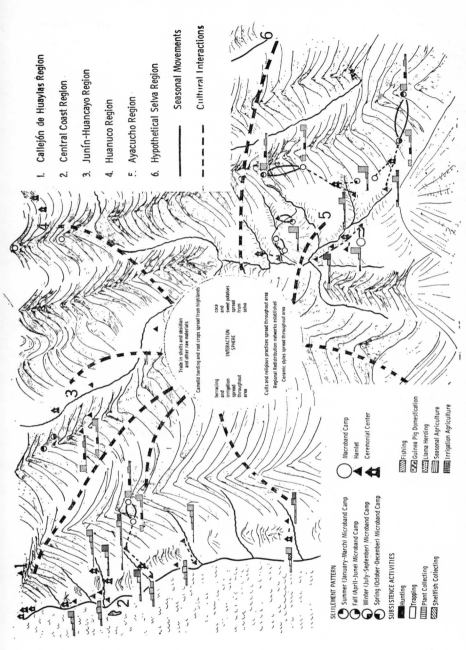

SETTLEMENT PATTERN

- Summer (January-March) Microband Camp
- Fall (April-June) Microband Camp
- Winter (July-September) Microband Camp
- Spring (October-December) Microband Camp

SUBSISTENCE ACTIVITIES

- Hunting
- Trapping
- Plant Collecting
- Shellfish Collecting

- ○ Macroband Camp
- ▲ Hamlet
- ⚑ Ceremonial Center

- Fishing
- Guinea Pig Domestication
- Llama Herding
- Seasonal Agriculture
- Irrigation Agriculture

1. Callejón de Huaylas Region
2. Central Coast Region
3. Junín-Huancayo Region
4. Huánuco Region
5. Ayacucho Region
6. Hypothetical Selva Region

— Seasonal Movements
--- Cultural Interactions

Trade in shells and obsidian and other raw materials

Camelid herding and root crops spread from highlands

coca and sweet potatoes spread from selva

terracing and irrigation spread throughout area

INTERACTION SPHERE

Cults and religious practices spread throughout area

Regional Redistribution networks established

Ceramic styles spread throughout area

Figure 9. A reconstruction of the settlement and subsistence patterns in the central Peruvian interaction sphere during the Initial Period

complex associated with pyramidal structures. These materials have never been adequately described, but presumably linked the coast with the Sierra (Kotosh).

The coast flourished at this time; a number of ceramic styles existed as well as a whole series of towns and/or ceremonial centers with monumental architecture such as Curayacu in the Lurín, La Florida in the Rimac, Ancón near the Chillón, and in the north Culebras, Las Haldas and Sechin. The latter, also, had monumental sculpture. Some like Las Culebras, Las Haldas and Ancón may have grown out of earlier towns, but some were entirely new. However, these were not only larger, and had more public monumental architecture than did those of the previous periods, but many were on new locations in the wide central portions of the river valleys. Further, many seem not to have had large residential sections, but instead were huge administrative and ceremonial centers occupied by full-time specialists and the upper ruling classes. Oriented to these redistribution centers, usually in the same drainage system, is a whole series of villages, towns, and hamlets that ranged from coastal locations specialized for procuring resources of the sea to villages on mountain flanks involved in herding and the growing of root crops. Some of the redistributive exchange systems may have even included a number of valleys and may be quite comparable to some sort of city-state.

In fact, all that seems missing to keep this from being called a true civilization is a social or governmental cohesive structure that united the technical, social, artistic, and intellectual achievements of the whole central Peruvian interaction sphere. This seemingly occurred in much of the area in the following period with the advent of the Chavín religion or style. However, this development was after the origin and spread of agriculture and village life and is outside the framework of our present discussion.

CONCLUSION

Having reviewed the details of the origin and spread of agriculture in central Peru and being well aware of the similar process in Meso-America, let me attempt to generalize about how and why it occurred initially in the New World. Perhaps these hypotheses may be relevant to understanding the process in the other original areas of development of agriculture in the Old World. Two sets of factors seemingly brought about the pristine origin of agriculture. First, there had to be certain prerequisites to allow it to happen and, secondly, there had to be other sets of processes that caused it to occur. These two sets of factors have often been termed necessary causes or conditions and sufficient causes or conditions. First, let us consider the prerequisites.

1.   In the New World, agriculture apparently originated in centers that have a definite set of characteristics. One obvious characteristic of these centers is that within them there are plants and animals that potentially can be domesticated. In the introduction to this article we mentioned some of these types of plants and animals for both the Andean and Meso-American areas. Specifically, in the Tehuacán Valley there seems to have been at least wild maize or a wild ancestor of maize (see Beadle, this volume) and a wild-type mixta squash that were potential domesticates, while in Ayacucho there were wild guinea pigs and wild quinoa with the same possibilities.

However, quite as important as this characteristic is another: that there be in these centers a series of life zones, usually with considerable micro-environmental and seasonal diversity, that range from one of relative uniformity where wild foods may be obtained with relative ease from one or more of its microenvirons, to life zones of relatively great diversity where foodstuffs can only be obtained by exploiting, often seasonally, and with considerably more difficulty, a wide range of microenvironments. In Meso-America, the environmental category named "Tropical Highlands and Extratropical Appendages," with its six natural regions and two subregions, would be an example of the diversified life zone dichotomy while "Tropical Lowlands," with its three natural regions and sixteen subregions, would represent the other end of the range. Coe and Flannery (1964), contrasting the microenvironments of the Tehuacán Valley with those of the Guatemala coast at Ocos, have illustrated the sort of range of life zones one expects in a center. In Peru, Tosi's thirty *Zonas de vida natural* (Tosi 1960) would be an example of the type of diversity one expects in a center. The Ayacucho Valley with its six microenvironments, described in this article and Patterson's description (1971) of the central coast between Ancón and the Lurín River with its microenvironments, would represent the sort of range that characterizes agricultural centers.

The final and equally important characteristic of these centers would be that these various life zones and even regional microenvironments are sufficiently accessible to each other so that they can form spheres of cultural interaction. I have indicated previously the sort of exchanges that took place between the regions in the "Peruvian Center," as here defined, and the literature on Meso-America has abundant examples of the systems of exchange that took place in that region.

2.   While the first prerequisite is vaguely ecological and geographical — and I hope no one considers this some sort of geographical determinism —

the second is developmental and/or temporal. The cultivation and/or domestication of plants and animals apparently occurs after a period of climatic and environmental change which upsets, perhaps very subtly, the relationship of man's established options for subsistence and the carrying capacity of the surrounding environs. Further, and seemingly of crucial importance, this disequilibrium occurred roughly contemporaneously with man's development of complex techniques for ecosubsistence so that a number of alternative options for subsistence were available, albeit previously rarely utilized. In both Tehuacán and Ayacucho the climatic and environmental change is at the end of the Pleistocene with its concomitant extinction of many animals. Previous to this time the preferred technique for subsistence had been hunting for the more numerous available fauna, but at the very end of the Pleistocene, at least in Tehuacán, other subsistence options such as collecting seeds, trapping, picking pods and fruits, and collecting leaves and stems in certain seasons in certain environments had been developed but little used. Now man could shift to using these alternatives when hunting became less profitable. Our early data from Ayacucho hint that such alternative options, for subsistence and perhaps ecological knowledge, may have been unknown at the time of earlier equally marked climatic shifts in the Pleistocene; thus crucial to a major cultural change was the coincidence, in the direction of developing agriculture, of climatic changes and changes in the ecosystem with the development of knowledge of ecosubsistence which included crucial alternative options for subsistence.

Our archaeological evidence from both the Andean and Meso-American centers would seem to indicate that necessary changes in the environmental subsistence relationships in these centers with their very specific characteristics resulted in the establishment of a new or alternative seasonally scheduled system of subsistence:

a.   Some of these seasonally scheduled subsistence systems in certain of the life zones of the centers became a sufficient cause for the development of husbandry or domestication of plants and animals. While our data are at present less precise from Peru, our information from Tehuacán in the well-documented El Riego Phase from 8000–7000 B.P. suggests how this process may have occurred. Here the evidence indicates that groups scheduled their movement from one microenvironment to another with changing seasons and practiced slightly different subsistence techniques in each environment with each season. In the spring they seem to have usually collected large amounts of grass seeds, including *Setaria* and wild maize (or teosinte?) in a few of those microenvironments, to which they often returned on an annual basis for centuries. This process we believe led to some enrichment and general improvement of these areas which then provided a new artificial environment for the seeds. This in turn in some instances may have led to various genetic changes in some seed plants such as maize, and eventual selection of some of the mutants, such as cobs with more kernels for planting, in that locale or another locale which they visited in calendar-round migration. The later planted mutants would have been domesticates while the seeds transferred to new microenvironments would have become cultivars. This process which occasionally resulted from a seasonally scheduled subsistence system in a center would not necessarily be the result of any great discovery or invention based upon experimentation, but rather was a gradual shift from using mainly one kind of plants (wild ones) to the more extensive use of very similar ones (domesticates or cultivars). My guess is that by such a process over a couple of millennia in a number of locales in centers, a number of plants might have become cultivated or domesticated. However, a few plants or animals domesticated in a few life zones do not necessarily lead to a settled agricultural way of life in villages.

b.   Such a settled agricultural way of life in villages may only be caused by a stimulating interaction between the different ways of life developed in the life zones at the center, and these may range from that of seasonal nomads with domesticates to that of settled villagers with economies based on natural resources. In Mexico, our understanding of how this process occurred is relatively vague because of the small numbers of finds from lush lowland regions, but our Peruvian data illustrate rather well how this process may have operated. As indicated previously, by Canario and Encanto times (7500–5500 B.P.), on the Peruvian central coast an efficient means for obtaining a stable supply of wild food had been developed that led to a more sedentary way of life with concomitant increasing populations. These sedentary populations, however, did not become village agriculturists until they received domesticates from other life zones with which they had been interacting. This situation contrasts with what seems to have happened in the Ayacucho where in the contemporaneous Piki and Chihua times there was a seasonally nomadic way of life, but one with a subsistence system which utilized a few domesticates or cultivars or tamed animals. Here exchanges and interactions with other areas which had domesticates gradually led to a more efficient means of food production, one concomitant with a more sedentary way of life and a rising population. Nevertheless, although the result was the same, neither one of the processes would have occurred without a stimulating interaction taking place between the life zones of the center.

After the establishment of the pristine village agricultural way of life, many other causal factors such as population pressure, new means of food production, and various other cultural phenomena set up a system of positive feedback that led to greater cultural changes and in some cases even to civilization. These processes are, however, beyond the scope of this paper for here we are only considering the origins of pristine agriculture.

In summary, I believe our investigations of the beginning of agriculture suggest the following general statement:

1. Necessary conditions — pristine agriculture may evolve (a) in centers with potential domesticates, considerable diversity of life zones, and possibilities of relatively easy interaction between those life zones; and (b) after environmental changes realign man's subsistence options which coincide with the development of knowledge of ecosubsistence allowing for a number of alternative options for ecosubsistence.

2. Sufficient conditions — and if one of the options for ecosubsistence selected is (a) a seasonally scheduled subsistence system, then the plants and/or animals will be domesticated or cultivated (tamed) in one or more parts of the life zones of that center; and (b) if there is a stimulating interaction between all or most of these life zones of that center, including those with domesticates or cultivars as well as those with efficient wild plant or animal subsistence strategies, then a village agricultural way of life will develop. This event, in turn, may become one of the necessary conditions for the rise of civilization.

In conclusion, I cannot help but wonder if these hypotheses are not worthy of consideration and testing by scientists investigating the problems of the origin of agriculture in Old World centers, such as the Near East and China.

REFERENCES

BYERS, D. S., *editor*
    1967   *The prehistory of the Tehuacan Valley*, volume one: *Environment and subsistence*. Austin: University of Texas Press.
CARDICH, A.
    1964   Lauricocha. *Centro Argentino de Estudios Prehistóricos* 3:1–171.
COE, M., K. V. FLANNERY
    1964   Microenvironments and Meso-American prehistory. *Science* 143: 650–654.
CUTLER, H. C., T. W. WHITAKER
    1967   "Cucurbits from the Tehuacan Caves," in *The prehistory of the Tehuacan Valley*, volume one: *Environment and subsistence*. Edited by D. S. Byers, 212–220. Austin: University of Texas Press.

ENGEL, F.
1963 A pre-ceramic settlement on the central coast of Peru: Asia, unit 1. *Transactions of the American Philosophical Society* 53(3):1–139.
1966 *Geografía humana prehistórica y agricultura precolombina de la quebrada de Chilca.* Lima: Universidad Agraria.
1968 "La grotte du *Mégathérium* à Chilca et les écologies du haut-holocène péruvien," in *Claude Lévi-Strauss memorial volume.* Edited by J. Pouillon and P. Maranda, 413–436. The Hague: Mouton.
1971 D'antival à huarangal. *L'Homme* 11(2):39–57.

FLANNERY, K. V., *editor*
1970 "Preliminary archaeological investigations in the valley of Oaxaca, Mexico." Mimeographed manuscript. Ann Arbor: University of Michigan Press.

HARLAN, J. R.
1971 Agricultural origins, centers and non-centers. *Science* 174:468–474.

IZUMI, S., K. TEREDA
1972 *Excavations at Kotosh, Peru, 1963 and 1966.* Tokyo: University of Tokyo Press.

JOHNSON, F., *editor*
1972 *The prehistory of the Tehuacan Valley,* volume four: *Chronology and irrigation.* Austin: University of Texas Press.

KAPLAN, L.
1967 "Archaeological *Phaseolus* from Tehuacan," in *The prehistory of the Tehuacan Valley,* volume one: *Environment and subsistence.* Edited by D. S. Byers, 201–212. Austin: University of Texas Press.

KAPLAN, L., T. F. LYNCH, C. E. SMITH
1973 Early cultivated beans (*Phaseolus vulgaris*) from an intermontane Peruvian valley. *Science* 179:76–77.

LANNING, E. P.
1967 *Peru before the Incas.* Englewood Cliffs: Prentice-Hall.

LANNING, E. P., T. C. PATTERSON
1967 Early man in South America. *Scientific American* 217(5):44–61.

LATHRAP, D. W., L. ROYS
1963 The archaeology of the Cave of the Owls in the upper Montaña of Peru. *American Antiquity* 29:27–38.

LYNCH, T. F.
1971 Pre-ceramic transhumance in the Callejon de Huaylas, Peru. *American Antiquity* 36:139–148.

LYNCH, T. F., K. A. R. KENNEDY
1970 Early human cultural and skeletal remains from Guitarrero Cave, northern Peru. *Science* 169:1307–1309.

MAC NEISH, R. S.
1965 The origins of American agriculture. *Antiquity* 39:87–94.
1967 "A summary of subsistence," in *The prehistory of the Tehuacan Valley,* volume one: *Environment and subsistence.* Edited by D. S. Byers, 290–310. Austin: University of Texas Press.
1969 *First annual report of the Ayacucho archaeological-botanical project.* Andover, Massachusetts: R. S. Peabody Foundation for Archaeology.
1971 Early man in the Andes. *Scientific American* 224(4):36–56.

1972   "The evolution of community patterns in the Tehuacan Valley of Mexico and speculations about the cultural processes," in *Man, settlement and urbanism.* Edited by Peter J. Ucko, Ruth Tringham, and G. W. Dimbleby, 67–93. London: Duckworth.

MAC NEISH, R. S., *editor*
1975   *The prehistory of the Tehuacan Valley,* volume five: *Excavations and reconnaissance.* Austin: University of Texas Press.

MAC NEISH, R. S., ANTIONETTE NELKEN-TERNER, ANGEL GARCIA COOK
1970   *Second annual report of the Ayacucho archaeological-botanical project.* Andover, Massachusetts: R. S. Peabody Foundation for Archaeology.

MAC NEISH, R. S., A. NELKEN-TERNER, I. W. JOHNSON
1967   *The prehistory of the Tehuacan Valley,* volume two: *The non-ceramic artifacts.* Austin: University of Texas Press.

MAC NEISH, R. S., F. A. PETERSON, K. V. FLANNERY
1970   *The prehistory of the Tehuacan Valley,* volume three: *Ceramics.* Austin: University of Texas Press.

MANGELSDORF, P. C., R. S. MAC NEISH, W. G. GALINAT
1967   "Prehistory of wild and cultivated maize," in *The prehistory of the Tehuacan Valley,* volume one: *Environment and subsistence.* Edited by D. S. Byers, 178–201. Austin: University of Texas Press.

MANGELSDORF, P. C., R. S. MAC NEISH, G. R. WILLEY
1964   "Origins of Middle American agriculture," in *Handbook of Middle American Indians,* volume one. Edited by R. J. Wauchope and R. C. West, 427–445. Austin: University of Texas Press.

PATTERSON, T. C.
1971   Central Peru: its population and economy. *Archaeology* 24:316–321.

RAVINES, R.
1965   Ambo: A new pre-ceramic site in Peru. *American Antiquity* 31:104–105.

SMITH, C. E.
1967   "Plant remains," in *The prehistory of the Tehuacan Valley,* volume one: *Environment and subsistence.* Edited by D. S. Byers, 220–256. Austin: University of Texas Press.

TOSI, J. A.
1960   *Zonas de vida natural en el Peru.* Lima: Instituto Interamericano de Ciencias Agrícolas de la OEA Zona Andina.

TOWLE, M. A.
1961   *The ethnobotany of pre-Columbian Peru.* Chicago: Aldine.

ADDENDUM 1*

Name of site	Number of site	Area	Environmental designation
Pikimachay Cave	Ac 100	Ayacucho-Huanta Valley	Thorn Forest, Scrub Zone
Jaywa Cave	Ac 335	Ayacucho-Huanta Valley	Humid Woodlands
Huamangilla Caves	Tc 240, Ac 44, 245	Ayacucho-Huanta Valley	Thorn Forest, Scrub Zone
Rosamachay Cave	Ac 117	Ayacucho-Huanta Valley	Thorn Forest, Scrub Zone
Guitarrero Cave		Callejón de Huaylas	
Quishqui Puncu		Callejón de Huaylas	
Lampras			
Conococha			
Cave of the Owls		Huánuco Valley	Montaña
Ambo		Huánuco Valley	
Boulder Cave	Ae 300	Ayacucho-Huanta Valley	Low Puna
Owl Cave (Tukumachay)	Ac 351	Ayacucho-Huanta Valley	Low Puna
Chupas Cave	Ac 500	Ayacucho-Huanta Valley	Humid Woodlands
Chupas ruin	Tr 23	Ayacucho-Huanta Valley	Humid Woodlands
Ayamachay Cave	Ac 102	Ayacucho-Huanta Valley	Thorn Forest, Scrub Zone
Puente site	Ac 158	Ayacucho-Huanta Valley	Thorn Forest, Riverine Zone
Wichquana site	Ar 18	Ayacucho-Huanta Valley	Thorn Forest, Riverine Zone
Chivateros site		Chillón Valley (Coast)	
Oquendo site		S. of Chillón River (Coast)	
Tortugas site		Lurín Valley (Coast)	
Panalagua Cave		Sierra (near Junin)	
Pampilla sites		Chillón Valley (Coast)	
Tablada de Lurín		Lower Lurín (Coast)	
Conchitas site		Lower Lurín (Coast)	
Tres Ventanas Cave		Huarochiri (Pacific Andean flank)	
Paloma site		Chilca River (Coast)	
Quikche Caves		Western slopes of Andes	
Pachamachay Cave		Junín-Huancayo (Sierra)	High Puna
Curimachay Cave		Junín-Huancayo (Sierra)	
Tilarnyoc Cave		Junín-Huancayo (Sierra)	High Puna
Lauricocha		Lauricocha region (Sierra)	Puna
Ranchacancha		Sierra	Puna
Callavallauri site		Huancayo-Junín (Sierra)	
Cuchimachay		Huancayo-Junín (Sierra)	High Puna
Pintadomachay		Huancayo-Junín (Sierra)	High Puna
Pachacutec		Huancayo-Junín (Sierra)	High Puna
Ledig-Tschopik rock shelter		Mantaro Valley (near Huancayo)	
San Pata		Mantaro Valley (near Jauja)	

* Addenda 1 and 2 have been provided by the editor.

Name of site	Number of site	Area	Environmental designation
San Blas		Sierra (North of Huancayo-Junín region)	
Kotosh site		Huánuco Valley	Edge of the Montaña
Ancón		Chillón Valley (Coast)	
Ventanilla		Chillón River Valley (Coast)	
Las Haldas		Casma River Valley (Coast)	
Culebras		S. of Culebras River (Coast)	
Río Seco		Chancay Valley (Coast)	
Chuquitanta		Chillón River Valley (Coast)	
Chira Villa		Rimac River Valley (Coast)	
Asia		Omas Valley (Coast)	
Quikche Cave		Huarochiri (Western flanks of Andes)	
Curayacu		Lurín River (Coast)	
La Florida		Rimac River (Coast)	
Sechin		Coast	

ADDENDUM 2

Major zones	Region or area	Sites
Pacific flanks of the Andes or Western flanks	1. Huarochiri	1a Tres Ventanas Cave 1b Quikche Cave
	2. Callejón de Huaylas	2a Guitarrero Cave 2b Quishqui Puncu 2c Lampras? 2d Conococha?
Eastern flanks of Andes	1. Huánuco Valley	1a Cave of the Owls 1b Ambo 1c Kotosh site
Sierras	1. Above Huánuco Valley	1a Lauricocha Cave 1b Ranchacancha
	2. Ayacucho-Huanta Valley	2a Pikimachay Cave 2b Jaywa Cave 2c Huamangilla Caves 2d Rosamachay Cave 2e Boulder Cave 2f Owl Cave (Tukumachay) 2g Chupas Cave 2h Chupas Ruin 2i Ayamachay Cave 2k Wichquana site

Major zones	Region or area	Sites
	3. Huancayo-Junín	3a Panalagua Cave
		3b Pachamachay Cave
		3c Curimachay Cave
		3d Tilarnyoc Cave
		3e Callavallauri site
		3f Cuchimachay
		3g Pintadomachay
		3h Pachacutec
		3i San Blas
	4. Mantaro Valley	4a Ledig-Tschopik rock shelter
		4b San Pata
Coastal valleys	1. Chillón River Valley	1a Chivateros site
		1b Oquendo site
		1c Pampilla sites
		1d Ancón
		1e Ventanilla
		1f Chuquitanta
	2. Lurín River Valley	2a Tortugas site
		2b Curayacu
	3. Lower Lurín	3a Tablada de Lurín
		3b Conchitas site
	4. Chilca River Valley	4a Paloma site
	5. Casma River Valley	5a Las Haldas
		5b Sechin
	6. Culebras River Valley	6a Culebras site
	7. Chancay Valley	7a Río Seco
	8. Rimac River Valley	8a Chira Villa site
		8b La Florida
	9. Omas Valley	9a Asia site

Origins and Distribution of Plants Domesticated in the New World Tropics

BARBARA PICKERSGILL and CHARLES B. HEISER, JR.

Over 100 species of plants were cultivated within the New World tropics at the time of European conquest. Vavilov (1950) allocated these to two centers of diversity, one in Mexico and one in South America; this latter he divided into Andean and Brazil-Paraguayan subcenters. He considered that agriculture had developed independently in the two centers. C. O. Sauer (1959) likewise noted considerable differences between the cultivated plants of Mesoamerica and those of South America, for which he accounted by postulating a long-standing difference in agricultural technology between the seed farmers of Mesoamerica who domesticated maize, beans, squash, amaranth, etc. and the root farmers of South America who grew principally crops propagated by vegetative means, such as manioc, sweet potato, achira (*Canna edulis*) and pineapple. Heiser (1965) concluded that the majority of the cultivated plants of the New World were domesticated in either Mesoamerica or South America, and that a surprisingly small number had been moved from one center to the other before the Spanish conquest. General agreement now exists that the differences between the cultivated plants of Mesoamerica and South America are real and considerable, and that these suggest that agriculture developed largely independently in the two centers. The question of whether two equally different and equally independent agricultural traditions arose within South America, in the Andes and the tropical lowlands respectively, is, however, still controversial.

C. O. Sauer (1952), in a general discussion of the origins of agriculture, considered that cultivation began among sedentary farmer-fishermen in a tropical forest environment; that man developed techniques of vegetative propagation before he learned to sow seeds; and that the first food crops cultivated were the starchy root crops. In the New World, Sauer (1959) contended that agriculture began in the tropical lowlands of northern South America and spread later both to the Andean area, where the emphasis on vegetatively propagated root crops was maintained, and to Mesoamerica, where seed crops were substituted for root crops. Sauer's ideas have been taken up by Lathrap, among others, and applied to the rise of the first civilizations of the New World. Lathrap (1974) suggested that a tropical lowland culture of farmer-fishermen, growing root crops as their staple food plants, spread from an original base in northern South America about 5000 B.P. and, by migration along the major river systems, reached Mesoamerica, where they became the fore-runners of the Olmec, and also reached the Peruvian Andes, where they developed the Chavín cult. Agriculture in both the Mexican highlands and the Andean area antedates 5000 B.P., so Lathrap did not claim that all New World agriculture began with tropical forest farmer-fishermen, but he did suggest a lowland agricultural tradition independent of highland agriculture and perhaps equally old.

Harlan (1971), on the other hand, considered that Mesoamerica was the only New World center in which agriculture originated. South America was to him a "non-center": a region in which many plants were domesticated in different places over a very wide area. Harlan did not maintain that diffuse domestication in a non-center resulted from spread of the idea of cultivation from a center followed by experimentation with locally available plants in different parts of the non-center, but this seems the simplest explanation of the general relationship he suggested between centers and their satellite non-centers.

In recent years a considerable amount of evidence bearing on origins and spread of agriculture in the New World has accrued from botanical work on some of the important cultigens and from increased archaeological interest in the subsistence of early cultures in both Mesoamerica and South America. In this paper, this evidence will be reviewed and then discussed in relation to the number of agricultural centers in the tropics of the New World and the relationships between these centers through time. Since the history under cultivation of over 100 species cannot be covered comprehensively in limited space, the works of C. O. Sauer (1950), Dressler (1953), Towle (1961), Mangelsdorf, MacNeish, and Willey (1964), and Heiser (1965) will be used as a foundation and we will confine ourselves to those crops for which there is significant new botanical and/or archaeological information. A map of the archaeological sites mentioned in the text is given in Figure 1.

Figure 1. Location of archaeological sites mentioned in the text

GRAIN CROPS

Maize (Zea mays)

The controversy surrounding the relationship between maize, teosinte and *Tripsacum* is the subject of a separate review at this symposium (Beadle, this volume). Excavations in the Tehuacán Valley of Mexico have shown that a primitive type of maize, possessing many of the attributes of a wild plant, was utilized and possibly cultivated about 7000 B.P. (Mangelsdorf, MacNeish, and Galinat 1967). The Tehuacán specimens have not, however, settled the question of whether "the ancestor of corn is corn" (Mangelsdorf, MacNeish, and Galinat 1964) or whether, as is currently being postulated (e.g. Beadle 1972; de Wet and Harlan 1972; Galinat 1971), teosinte is the missing ancestor of maize. All of the cobs from Tehuacán apparently showed the paired spikelets characteristic of maize (in teosinte, only one spikelet develops at each node) and the earliest cobs from Tehuacán were usually eight-rowed (i.e. four-ranked), though one or two were four-rowed (i.e. two-ranked) with the pairs of spikelets distichously arranged (similar to the two-ranked arrangement of teosinte female spikelets). The glumes and cupules of these early cobs were soft (corresponding structures in teosinte are indurated) but the rachises disarticulated more easily than those of modern maize (in teosinte, the rachis of the female spikelet disarticulates into single-seeded segments along definite abscission lines at maturity). If teosinte is indeed the ancestor of maize, then the early cobs from Tehuacán have already been considerably changed by human selection. Many of the characters that distinguish maize from teosinte are controlled by only one or two major genes (Langham 1940; Galinat 1971; Beadle 1972) and, given the occurrence of appropriate mutants, could be fixed fairly rapidly during domestication. However, the total absence of teosinte in the remains of plants from Tehuacán strongly suggests that these postulated changes occurred elsewhere, and the oldest cobs from Tehuacán must then be interpreted as coming from plants that were already domesticated.

Extant primitive races of maize in South America differ in a number of respects from corresponding primitive Mexican races, which was one factor used to support the suggestion that maize was also domesticated in a second center in South America (Mangelsdorf and Reeves 1939; Grobman, et al. 1961). The two great drawbacks to this suggestion are the lack of a suitable wild ancestor for cultivated maize in South America and the absence of any evidence for maize agriculture in South America as early as, or earlier than, maize agriculture in Mexico.

The only relative of maize native to South America is *Tripsacum australe*. The genus *Tripsacum* as a whole is, however, morphologically and cytogenetically much less similar to maize than is teosinte and is thus unlikely to be directly ancestral to cultivated maize. Teosinte is today confined to Mexico, Guatemala and Honduras (Wilkes 1967) and we know of no convincing evidence that its distribution was ever significantly more extensive; *Zea mays* does not occur wild anywhere at the present day. The wider the distribution postulated for an original wild *Zea mays*, the more difficult it becomes to explain its total extinction. Bartlett, Barghoorn, and Berger (1969) concluded that wild maize had once occurred in Panama on the basis of pollen grains which they identified specifically as those of maize, not teosinte or *Tripsacum*, at a depth of 43 feet in their core. Associated pollen grains provided no evidence for agriculture at this time. The 43-foot levels of nearby cores were radiocarbon dated between 6000 and 7500 B.P., but the 43-foot level of the core containing the maize pollen dated at only 3170 B.P. $\pm$ 60. Furthermore, only four maize grains were found in more than 12,000 pollen grains examined. The authors concluded that the 43-foot level of the core with the maize pollen had been contaminated with recent carbon, but that there was no evidence of any contamination with non-indigenous pollen. More convincing evidence than this is required to establish unequivocally the existence and preagricultural distribution of wild maize.

If maize was not domesticated independently in South America, then it must have been introduced from Mesoamerica. The precise dates for the earliest South American maize are by no means clear, but are so far not as early as the date of 7000 B.P. for maize in Tehuacán. On the Peruvian coast, maize was cultivated in the Culebras Complex of Preceramic Period VI, 4500 to 3800 B.P. (Lanning 1967). In the highlands, the earliest maize so far recovered comes from sites in the Ayacucho basin; MacNeish (personal communication) is of the opinion that this maize antedates maize on the coast by about 500 years. The cobs from Ayacucho are still being studied, but Galinat (personal communication) considers that the oldest belong to a race now extinct which he designates "Ayacucho" and which, in his opinion, is most closely related to the primitive Mexican race "Nal-Tel." Lathrap has suggested (Lathrap 1974, and personal communication) that the location of the inland sites of the Valdivia Phase in Ecuador, together with the low proportion of shell in Valdivia middens, indicates reliance on maize agriculture by 4700 to 3500 B.P. It should also be mentioned that the cores from Panama showed charcoal, some maize pollen, abundant weed pollen and near-absence of tree pollen at depths corresponding to approximately 3000–1750 B.P. (Bartlett, Barghoorn, and Berger 1969). This complex of changes suggests clearance of forest for cultivation. The archaeological data are thus compatible with the idea that maize agriculture spread gradually from Mesoamerica to South America by an overland route.

The most economical explanation of the observed differences between Peruvian and Mexican maize is that a Nal-Tel-like race spread from Mexico to Peru sometime between 7000 and 5000 B.P. After this, there was little exchange of maize between the two cultural centers except for a late spread of flour corn and sweet corn from South America to Mexico, perhaps about 1450 B.P. (see discussion in Pickersgill 1972). Over 3,000 years of evolution in isolation would, however, account for the distinctive features of South American maize.

Amaranths (*Amaranthus* spp.)

J. Sauer (1967) recognized three cultivated species of *Amaranthus* in the New World: *A. hypochondriacus* (syn. *A. leucocarpus*) in central and northern Mexico and the southwestern United States; *A. cruentus* in

Mexico and Guatemala and *A. caudatus* (within which he included *A. edulis*) in the Andes. These are in turn closely related to three wide-ranging weedy species; *A. powellii*, *A. hybridus*, and *A. quitensis* (though the latter two are morphologically similar and may be no more than geographic races of a single species; Coons n.d.). The usual interpretation of these data is that the three cultivated species were domesticated independently in different areas, though J. Sauer (1967) pointed out that his data would also fit the hypothesis of a single domestication, presumably in Mesoamerica, giving rise to *A. cruentus*, which then spread in cultivation and became modified by hybridization with local wild species in different parts of its range to produce cultivated *A. hypochondriacus* in the north and *A. caudatus* in the south.

Species of *Amaranthus* may have either 32 or 34 chromosomes. Chromosome number seems generally to be constant for any one species, but counts of both 2n = 32 and 2n = 34 have been reported for different collections of *A. caudatus* (León 1964). Among the other cultivated amaranths and their weedy relatives, 2n = 32 has been recorded for *A. hybridus*, *A. quitensis* and *A. hypochondriacus*, while 2n = 34 occurs in *A. powellii* and *A. cruentus* (Grant 1959; Khoshoo and Pal 1972). Khoshoo and Pal (1972) also reported considerable pollen sterility, combined with morphological abnormalities, in the F_1 hybrids *A. caudatus* (2n = 32) × *A. hypochondriacus* and *A. caudatus* (2n = 32) × *A. hybridus*, whereas hybrids between *A. hybridus* and *A. hypochondriacus* were reasonably fertile. These data fit suggestions of independent domestication for the three cultivated species, but do not give much support to hypotheses of a single domestication with subsequent spread and differentiation. Furthermore, the different cultivated species are known archaeologically only from the areas in which they are grown today, and there is no evidence that any one cultivated species spread from Middle to South America or vice versa. *A. cruentus* dates back to 5500–4300 B.P. in the Tehuacán Valley, Mexico (J. Sauer 1969); *A. hypochondriacus* occurs about 2200–1250 B.P. in Tehuacán (J. Sauer 1969); *A. caudatus* has recently been recorded from Gruta del Indio del Rincón del Atuel near San Rafael, Argentina, around 2000 B.P. (Hunziker and Planchuelo 1971). The hypothesis that the different cultivated species of *Amaranthus* were domesticated independently, in different areas and from different wild species, still best fits the known facts.

Chenopods (Chenopodium spp.)

Three species of *Chenopodium* are cultivated in the New World. Of these,

C. pallidicaule (cañihua) is little more than a semi-domesticate. It is grown above 3,600 meters in the Andes, where few other crops will survive, retains a strong tendency to volunteer, does not mature uniformly, has to be harvested before maturity since it has not yet lost its natural mechanisms of seed dispersal, and has the black seeds characteristic of wild species of *Chenopodium* (Gade 1970). Cañihua is a diploid, whereas the other two cultivated species are tetraploids (Simmonds 1965). *C. quinoa* (quinoa) is an important grain crop in the Andes, particularly above 3,000 meters. It is very variable, but cultivated forms always have pale seeds, in contrast to the black-seeded weedy forms which frequently grow in the same fields and belong to the same species (Heiser and Nelson 1974). *C. nuttalliae* (huahzontli) is grown in Mexico as a green vegetable, but is sometimes used as a grain crop (Nelson 1968). It is morphologically similar to *C. quinoa*, but separated by a considerable gap from the northern limit of the latter species (Simmonds 1965). The diploid ancestors of both species are unknown. Many species of *Chenopodium* are wide-ranging weeds, and possibly the two tetraploids originated independently, but from similar parentage, in Mexico and the Andes. This would explain the differences in usage and in common names for the species in the two areas. Another, admittedly tenuous, piece of evidence in favor of the independent domestication of *C. quinoa* and *C. nuttalliae* is Nelson's observation (1968) that the F_1 hybrid between pale-seeded forms of these two species had black seeds. This suggests that the change from black to pale seeds has been achieved by different mutations in the two species. It does not support suggestions of spread of one cultivated species followed by differentiation in a new area.

The only one of these species represented archaeologically is *C. quinoa*. It is recorded from about 1600 B.P. in the Andean highlands (house at Chiripa; Towle 1961); about 2000 B.P. in Argentina (Hunziker and Planchuelo 1971); and after 1000 B.P. on the coast of Peru (Ancón Necropolis; Towle 1961). Quinoa was almost certainly domesticated in the Andean highlands and the only surprising feature of its archaeologica l record is that it does not, as yet, extend back further in time.

LEGUMES

Beans (Phaseolus spp.)

Four different species of *Phaseolus* were domesticated in the New World. The species are clearly distinct morphologically, are genetically isolated from one another, and wild forms are known for each. It thus seems clear that each species was domesticated independently, rather than differentiating from a single cultivated species (Smartt 1969, 1970).

The tepary bean (*P. acutifolius* var. *latifolius*) today occurs wild and in cultivation in the dry areas of western Mexico and the American Southwest. However, the earliest archaeological record of this species is from Tehuacán, in central Mexico, 1,600 kilometers outside the present range of wild or cultivated tepary beans (Kaplan 1967). The tepary is clearly a Mesoamerican domesticate, but it is still not known precisely where and when it was domesticated.

The runner bean (*P. coccineus*) is another Mesoamerican domesticate. Both wild and cultivated forms grow best in cool, moist uplands. Characters of the pod indicate that the specimens of *P. coccineus* from sites in Tamaulipas, northeastern Mexico, dated 7500–9000 B.P., were wild beans (Kaplan 1967). The earliest cultivated *P. coccineus* comes from Tehuacán, about 2200 B.P. and Kaplan (1967) considered that it was probably domesticated outside the immediate area of Tehuacán.

There are even greater problems in determining where the common bean (*P. vulgaris*) was domesticated. Wild forms have been recorded from both Mesoamerica (Gentry 1969) and South America (Burkart and Brücher 1953, as *P. aborigineus*). According to Gentry (1969), cultivated *vulgaris* is closer to wild *vulgaris* than either is to *aborigineus*, but he stated too that the seeds of *aborigineus* suggest that it is an escape from early cultivated forms of *vulgaris*. Both Burkart and Brücher, and Gentry were insistent that their "wild" beans were truly wild and not escapes. Gentry went further and suggested that similarities in colors of seedcoats in cultivated and wild beans suggested multiple domestication within Mesoamerica, with one center in northwestern Mexico, another in central Mexico, and a third in Guatemala and southeastern Mexico. It is notoriously difficult to determine whether similarities between a crop and a wild plant occur because the crop was derived from the wild form, or because the wild plants represent escaped derivatives of the crop. Wild beans differ from cultivated beans in a number of characters, including seed size, seed permeability (which controls dormancy), pod dehiscence, and ability to survive in apparently undisturbed wild vegetation. These characters are probably controlled by a number of genes and, in general, it seems that once a plant has been modified by human selection to the extent outlined above it is unable to revert by itself to a form which could survive in the wild. The necessary "wild" characters may be introduced by hybridization with a related wild species, but in *Phaseolus* no wild species are known which form sufficiently fertile hybrids with *P. vulgaris* for such introgression to occur.

If primitively wild forms of *P. vulgaris* occur in both Middle and South America, then possibly the common bean was domesticated independently on the two continents. In Mexico, the common bean is known archaeologically from both Tamaulipas and Tehuacán from about 6000 B.P. onwards. In both areas, the oldest specimens represent domesticated beans, but beans did not become really abundant until agriculture replaced hunting and gathering as the major subsistence activity (Kaplan 1967). In South America, common beans have recently been recorded from sites in two parts of the Peruvian Andes. In the Callejón de Huaylas common beans were present in Stratum II of Guitarrero Cave (7680 B.P. ± 280; Kaplan, Lynch, and Smith 1973). In Ayacucho, common beans were also present but, because of disturbance in many of the plant-producing levels, it is difficult to be sure how early they were. However, they were certainly present by about 3000 B.P. (Kaplan, personal communication). In both Ayacucho and the Callejón de Huaylas the beans were clearly domesticated, not wild, types. Common beans may have been grown on the coast of Peru before 4500 B.P. (Lanning 1967), although the earliest well-authenticated record is 2900–2600 B.P. in the Ancón region (Cohen, this volume). They have long been considered a domesticate introduced from elsewhere; Lynch's excavations suggest that "elsewhere" may be the Andean highlands rather than Mexico.

P. lunatus includes both the large-seeded lima beans of South America and the small-seeded sieva beans of Mesoamerica. According to Kaplan (1967), these differences are reflected also in wild *P. lunatus*, which extends from Mexico to northern South America. This evidence suggests independent domestication of the lima and sieva beans. The archaeological record on the whole supports this: sieva beans are known only from Mesoamerica, where domesticated forms appear at about the same time (1850–1150 B.P., i.e. considerably later than other important crop plants) in Tamaulipas, Tehuacán and Dzibilchaltún (Yucatán Peninsula), leading Kaplan (1967) to conclude that domesticated sievas may have been introduced into Mexico via the Gulf Coast. Lima beans, on the other hand, are known only from Peru, and again only as domesticated forms: in the highlands from Stratum II of Guitarrero Cave (7680 B.P. ± 280; Kaplan, Lynch, and Smith 1973; lima beans were absent from the Ayacucho plant remains); on the coast from various sites of which the earliest is Chilca (5300 B.P.) but, in view of the controversies surrounding association of materials from this site with the various dated occupations, the oldest reliable record is perhaps better taken as at Huaca Prieta about 4500 B.P. (Towle 1961). Kaplan (1965) has suggested that lima beans may have been domesticated east of the Andes.

Jack Beans (Canavalia spp.*)*

Two species of *Canavalia* were cultivated in the Americas in pre-Columbian times. The archaeological record demonstrates that *C. plagiosperma* was restricted to South America, while *C. ensiformis* occurred in Mesoamerica and reached South America only in late prehistoric or early colonial times (J. Sauer and Kaplan 1969). Little is known of the ancestry of the two cultivated species. J. Sauer and Kaplan (1969) listed five wild species as possible progenitors, which together range virtually all through the New World tropics, and they pointed out that it is not known whether *C. plagiosperma* and *C. ensiformis* were domesticated independently or differentiated after a common origin in cultivation. Wild species of *Canavalia* are characteristic of moist lowland areas (seashore or river-banks) while the archaeological specimens almost all come from arid and/or highland areas and are from domesticated plants grown under irrigation. The exception is a cache of seeds from Dzibilchaltún (Yucatán Peninsula), dated about 2300 B.P., which included small seeds very similar to wild *C. brasiliensis*, which grows in the area, as well as large seeds which match modern *C. ensiformis* (J. Sauer and Kaplan 1969). This record is the earliest one for *C. ensiformis*. *C. plagiosperma*, on the other hand, goes back to at least 4000 B.P. at Huaca Prieta (J. Sauer and Kaplan 1969). None of the possible wild progenitors occurs in coastal Peru, though two are found in Ecuador and two in valleys on the eastern slope of the Peruvian Andes. Until more archaeological and biosystematic data accumulate it is thus uncertain whether jack beans were domesticated in Middle or South America, east or west of the Andes.

Peanut (Arachis hypogaea)

The cultivated peanut is a tetraploid which is not known in the wild. Its closest wild relative seems to be the annual tetraploid *A. monticola*, which is restricted to northwestern Argentina (Krapovickas and Rigoni 1957), though its limited range may represent only lack of collecting in this part of South America. *A. monticola* and *A. hypogaea* seem in turn to have a genome in common with the *villosa* group of perennial wild species which occur west of the Paraguay and Uruguay rivers (Krapovickas and Rigoni 1957). Krapovickas (1969) suggested that *A. hypogaea* originated in the foothills of the Bolivian Andes, since this is close to the area of its wild relatives and an area of considerable diversity in both morphology and uses of the cultivated peanut (though Krapovickas pointed out that the morphological diversity could result from hybridization between the two subspecies of *A. hypogaea* in this region). The peanut is a lowland crop, not grown above 2,000 meters. Remains of the pods are abundant in archaeological sites on the coast of Peru from the Initial Period (3800–2900 B.P.) onwards (Lanning 1967). They are thus not among the first crops cultivated on the Peruvian coast and they appear in the same period as a number of other crops of presumed humid lowland origin (Pickersgill 1969). In Mesoamerica, peanuts have been found only in the Tehuacán caves, where a single seed occurred in Palo Blanco levels (2200–1250 B.P.) and four more specimens in upper Venta Salada levels (1250 B.P.–1540 A.D.) (Smith 1967). Heiser's statement (1965) that the peanut was a late introduction which never became important in Mexico thus still stands.

CUCURBITS

Squashes and Gourds (Cucurbita spp.)

The pattern of domestication in *Cucurbita* is similar to that in *Phaseolus* in that different species (five in *Cucurbita*) have been domesticated independently in different areas and there has been little movement of species between Mesoamerica and South America. *C. pepo* and *C. mixta* had not spread south of Central America in pre-Conquest times, and *C. maxima* was limited to South America, but *C. moschata* and *C. ficifolia* occurred on both continents.

Although these five species are morphologically distinct, and have been for the last 5,000 years at least, their wild ancestors have not proved easy to identify. *C. pepo*, which is the northernmost cultivated species, is closely related to "wild" *C. texana* of central Texas; *C. mixta* is equally closely related to an unnamed "wild" species from southern Mexico (Whitaker and Bemis 1964). On the other hand, *C. pepo* and *C. mixta* can both be crossed with a number of other wild species from central and southern Mexico and Guatemala (Whitaker and Bemis 1964; Hurd, Linsley, and Whitaker 1971), although these hybrids are not as fertile as the hybrids of *C. pepo* × *C. texana* and *C. mixta* × its "wild" relative. The problem is deciding the status of *C. texana* and the unnamed species. Whitaker and Bemis (1964) thought that they were feral derivatives of their respective cultivated relatives, but conceded that they might possibly be ancestral to the cultigens. Although the cultivated species have been changed by human selection (see list of characters in Whitaker and Bemis 1964), these changes are not such as to prevent escaped forms from surviving in the wild, and feral escapes could thus establish more readily than in, say, beans.

The oldest archaeological specimens of *C. pepo* come from Guila Naquitz cave in the Oaxaca valley of southwestern Mexico (one seed from Zone D, 10,750–9840 B.P.; seeds and peduncles from Zone C, 9400–9200 B.P.; Whitaker and Cutler 1971). Wild species formed at least 50 percent of the total cucurbit specimens from both these zones, and the seeds of *C. pepo* were smaller than those of later levels. *C. mixta* was absent from the remains from Oaxaca but present in Tehuacán, possibly from the El Riego Phase (about 7000 B.P.), but certainly from the Abejas Phase (about 5000 B.P.) onwards (Cutler and Whitaker 1967). Oaxaca is a long way south of the known range of *C. texana*, so the fragmentary archaeological record thus far supports the suggestion that *C. pepo* and *C. mixta* both originated from the wild species of southern Mexico or Guatemala, and that *C. texana* is a feral derivative of cultivated *C. pepo*.

A similar problem arises in determining the relationship of South American *C. maxima* to the "wild" *C. andreana* of Argentina and Bolivia. An additional wild species, *C. ecuadorensis*, has recently been described from around Guayaquil, Ecuador (Cutler and Whitaker 1969). It has larger fruits and seeds than *C. andreana* and, unusual for a wild cucurbit, the fruits are not bitter. *C. ecuadorensis* will cross with *C. maxima*, but the hybrids are less fertile than those of *C. maxima* × *C. andreana*. It will also cross with *C. moschata*, but the fertility of these hybrids has not been reported. From a study of the pollinators of *Cucurbita*, the squash and gourd bees, Hurd, Linsley, and Whitaker (1971) concluded that there must have been at least two wild species of *Cucurbita* in South America before man arrived, one in Ecuador and one further south. *C. ecuadorensis* and *C. andreana* fit these distributions. Furthermore, both *C. ecuadorensis* and *C. andreana* have been identified archaeologically in coastal Peru, from Preceramic Period V (c. 5000 B.P.) at the Pampa site (Lanning 1967; Cutler and Whitaker 1969). If these identifications are correct, then both species are presumably primitively wild. However, they are unlikely to have been wild at Pampa since this site is located in the coastal desert and even the nearby Chillón Valley would not have provided a moisture regime comparable to the present habitats of these species. *C. maxima* appears late in the archaeological record (1350 B.P. on the coast of Peru, Towle 1961), which is surprising when one considers that its putative ancestor *C. andreana* was utilized so early.

Although *C. moschata* and *C. ficifolia* were grown in both Mesoamerica and South America before 1492 A.D. both species are without close wild ancestors. *C. ficifolia* is today grown fairly extensively in Mexico and

Central America, but the only archaeological record in this area consists of a single, rather tentatively identified seed from levels dated 1250 B.P. in Oaxaca (Whitaker and Cutler 1971). This contrasts with its occurrence in South America from 5000 B.P. until at least post-Cupisinique times (about 2500 B.P.) (Towle 1961). The archaeological record suggests that *C. ficifolia* is a southern species which spread north; on the other hand, pollinator and compatibility studies link *C. ficifolia* with both the South American *maxima* group and with a group of Mesoamerican wild species.

C. *moschata* is equally early in South America (4500–4300 B.P. in the region of Ancón; Cohen, this volume), but occurs also in prehistoric levels in Mexico and the southwestern United States. It was present in the Ocampo caves in Tamaulipas about 3400 B.P. and spread to the American Southwest around 1050 B.P. (Whitaker and Cutler 1965). Earlier records for *C. moschata* in Mexico are more doubtful. In Tehuacán, two seeds which were identified as *C. moschata* occurred in Coxcatlan levels (7000–5500 B.P.), two more seeds and a questionable peduncle in the Abejas Phase (5500–4300 B.P.), then a long gap until a single seed appeared in late Palo Blanco levels (2200–1250 B.P.). *C. moschata* only became really abundant in Tehuacán in Venta Salada times (1250 B.P.–1540 A.D.) (Cutler and Whitaker 1967). The lack of a clear wild ancestor for this species is an embarrassment in trying to explain its origin and wide early distribution. The hinge position which *C. moschata* occupies in relating the cultivated species of *Cucurbita* to each other and to the mesophytic wild species (Whitaker and Bemis 1964) suggests that it originated from the southern Mexican-Guatemalan complex of wild species and spread as a cultivated plant to South America sometime before 5000 B.P. Maize, on present evidence, spread south from Mexico around 5000 B.P., but if maize and squash spread as a complex, this association was broken in Peru, where *C. moschata* is considerably earlier than maize. Heiser (1965) suggested that the reported differentiation of *C. moschata* into a northern light-seeded race and a southern dark-seeded race might constitute tenuous evidence for two domestications of *C. moschata*, but Whitaker (1968) suggested that the reputed differences resulted from confusion between *C. moschata* and *C. mixta*.

Bottle Gourd (Lagenaria siceraria)

Bottle gourds are present in the earliest levels of many archaeological sites in the Americas: in Mexico by 9000 B.P. in Tamaulipas, 7500 B.P. in Tehuacán (Whitaker and Cutler 1965) and 9400–9200 B.P. in Oaxaca (Whitaker and Cutler 1971); in Peru by 7500 B.P. (and possibly earlier) in the highlands around Ayacucho (Whitaker, personal communication) and by 8000–6000 B.P. on the coast (Richardson 1972; Cohen, this volume). There are no well-authenticated reports of wild bottle gourds in the Americas, although in some parts of northeastern Brazil farmers say they never sow gourds because sufficient plants for their needs volunteer spontaneously, and volunteer plants occur in disturbed habitats such as roadside ditches and shingly lake margins. Early uses of gourds were probably diverse: containers, ladles, fish floats, rattles, and possibly as a food plant. The seeds are removed during manufacture of some gourd artifacts, but a few seeds might well cling to the papery interior of a gourd used for transporting dry materials, and gourd fish floats are made from the intact fruit. Gourds may thus have become widespread early in prehistory as camp-following weeds whose fruits were particularly useful to pre-agricultural, pre-pottery, semi-nomadic peoples. Intentional cultivation of gourds could then have developed independently in Mesoamerica and South America. The closest relatives of *L. siceraria* are African, and Heiser (1973) has found that Africa is the area of greatest variability in *L. siceraria*. However, he cautioned against the conclusion that *L. siceraria* is thus of greater age in Africa than elsewhere. Modern African and American gourds are placed by Heiser in *L. siceraria* ssp. *siceraria*, while Asiatic and Pacific gourds are included in ssp. *asiatica*. These data suggest that the bottle gourd spread from Africa to America but the gourd is present so early in the New World that its spread probably occurred prior to domestication.

ROOT CROPS

Manioc (Manihot esculenta)

The genus *Manihot* is a large one and few of the wild species are available in living collections, but the little work that has been done suggests that chromosome number is constant throughout most of the genus and that many apparently distinct species will form fertile hybrids when crossed artificially. *M. esculenta* will cross with two wild species from Surinam, *M. saxicola* and *M. melanobasis*, which it resembles morphologically (Jennings 1963). Other species morphologically similar to *M. esculenta* are *M. aesculifolia*, *M. pringlei* and *M. isoloba*, which all occur within the Maya area (Rogers 1965). Much more work is obviously necessary before we will be able to determine which wild species, South American or Central American, gave rise to *M. esculenta*.

M. esculenta is a lowland crop, and archaeobotanical records are particularly deficient for the lowland areas of the New World. Manioc was a staple on the coast of Peru, and tubers are found from the Initial Period of Early Horizon (probably about 3000–2800 B.P.) onwards (Towle 1961), but coastal Peru is one lowland area in which no possible wild ancestors of this crop occur (see map in Renvoize 1972), so it must have been domesticated elsewhere. In Mesoamerica, no authentic macroscopic remains of manioc have been found, but Callen (1967) claimed that "a starchy tissue that greatly resembles *Manihot*" was present in coprolites from the Santa Maria Phase (2900–2200 B.P.) onwards in Tehuacán, and that similar manioclike fibers and starch grains occurred in Tamaulipas. Tehuacán is too high for manioc to be grown in the immediate neighborhood, and until macroscopic remains are found we will retain some reservations about this identification. Pollen of *M. esculenta* has been reported from a core taken in Panama, at levels corresponding to an age of 1,800 years and in association with pollen of maize (Bartlett, Barghoorn, and Berger 1969), but we are not altogether clear how rigorously other wild Euphorbiaceae were considered and eliminated in making this identification. Evidence for prehistoric cultivation of manioc in lowland South America is entirely inferential. Flat pottery griddles of the type used today for toasting manioc flour occur from about 3000 B.P. onwards (Reichel-Dolmatoff 1965); but Sturtevant (1969) discussed a sixteenth-century account of starch extraction from a wild plant, which he identifies as the cycad *Zamia*, in Hispaniola which also involved the use of griddles to bake the starch. *Zamia*, and other wild sources of starch, occur in mainland South America, so one must obviously be careful in equating pottery griddles with cultivation of manioc. Lathrap (1973) identified manioc among the stylized plants represented on the Tello Obelisk at Chavín de Huántar. The date for appearance of manioc corresponds fairly well with the spread of the Chavín cult to coastal Peru, about 2900 B.P., but this simply links the problem of the origin of manioc with the equally problematic origin of Chavín. Lathrap (1971) has argued at length for an origin in the tropical forests; Lanning (1967) suggested the highlands of northern Peru and claimed that manioc reached the coast before the spread of the Chavín cult. Until more facts are available, the discrepancies between these hypotheses cannot be resolved.

Sweet Potato (Ipomoea batatas)

Speculation on the problem of how the sweet potato became an important crop on both sides of the Pacific before 1492 A.D. has tended to obscure the problems connected with its origin and pre-Columbian distribution within the Americas. The sweet potato is a hexaploid, with a chromosome number of 2n = 90, which presumably originated by chromosome doubling in a triploid (2n = 45) hybrid between tetraploid (2n = 60) and diploid (2n = 30) wild forms. Speciation in *Ipomoea* does not seem to have been accompanied by much change in chromosomal structure, and many of the potential wild ancestors of the hexaploid share the same genome. The morphology of the chromosomes of the hexaploid suggests that two of the three sets of chromosomes are more similar to each other than they are to the third (Magoon, Krishnan, and Vijaya Bai 1970). The sweet potato may thus have the genomic formula AAA'A'BB, and this reinforces the suggestion that at least two different wild species have been involved in its origin. Wild species of *Ipomoea* include both self-compatible and self-incompatible forms, and presumably at least one self-incompatible wild species was involved in the origin of the hexaploid in order to account for the self-incompatibility of the cultivated sweet potato. Nishiyama (1971) has suggested that the hexaploid arose from a cross between *I. leucantha* (2n = 30, self-incompatible) and *I. littoralis* (2n = 60, self-incompatible). Other species that have frequently been suggested as progenitors include the diploids *I. triloba* (self-compatible) and *I. trichocarpa* (sometimes reported self-compatible, sometimes incompatible), the tetraploid *I. gracilis* (self-incompatible), and *I. tiliacea*, for which both diploid and tetraploid counts have been recorded and which is reported to be self-incompatible (Nishiyama 1963, 1971). The reports in the literature are the more difficult to interpret because there is considerable taxonomic confusion in *Ipomoea* at present. Matuda (1963) considered *I. littoralis* a synonym of *I. gracilis*, for which he recorded a circumtropical distribution. He treated *I. leucantha* as a synonym of *I. triloba*, and gave its range as southern United States to Brazil.

Many of the putative wild ancestors of the sweet potato have wide distributions. Nishiyama (1971) concluded that the sweet potato originated in Mexico because it was in Mexico that he found a wild hexaploid (his clone K123, which he identified as *I. trifida*) morphologically similar to the sweet potato, capable of forming fertile hybrids with it, and possessing the same incompatibility alleles. Nishiyama thus considered K123 the wild ancestor of the sweet potato. Yen (1971) pointed out that similar weedy forms occurred in fields of sweet potato in Colombia, and suggested furthermore that K123 had been wrongly identified as *I. trifida*. He himself reported "true" *I. trifida* as a weed in sweet potato fields in the Colombian montaña, and recorded both diploid and tetraploid chromosome numbers for these plants. Wilson (1960) considered that *I. trifida* should be included in *I. trichocarpa*.

K123 is undoubtedly very closely related to the cultivated sweet potato, but this does not mean that it is the ancestor of the crop. Cultivated sweet potatoes may be capable of producing occasional non-tubering derivatives, like K123, which could escape and become established in the wild (Jones 1967). Alternatively, hybridization between the crop and weedy species such as Yen's *I. trifida* might introduce into *I. batatas* such "wild" characters as inedible roots and ability to survive without human interference, in the same way that hybridization between the cultivated radish and weedy *Raphanus raphanistrum* has produced derived weedy races of the cultivated species (Panetsos and Baker 1967).

Determining the status of K123 is likely to leave still unresolved the problem of whether the sweet potato originated in Mesoamerica or South America. Nishiyama (1971) favored Mexico; Yen (1971) the montaña of the eastern slopes of the Andes or the Amazon basin; O'Brien (1972), after a review of linguistic and archaeological evidence, was unable to decide between Central America and northwestern South America, though she slightly favored the latter. The archaeological record is actually of little help, because the sweet potato is another lowland crop. Numerous tubers have been recovered from coastal Peru, reputedly dating back to 4000 B.P. (Lanning 1967; Patterson 1971), which would make the sweet potato an earlier root crop than manioc in this area. No prehistoric specimens have been recorded from Mexico (not too surprisingly, since all the sites producing plant remains have been in the highlands), but the crop was presumably grown in Mesoamerica at the time of the Spanish Conquest. Furthermore, the Mexican name *camote* was quite different from the Andean name *apichu* (*kumara* now appears to be a Polynesian, not Quechuan, word probably not used in Peru until after the arrival of the Spanish) (Brand 1971). Bartlett, Barghoorn, and Berger (1969) recorded *Ipomoea* pollen from their core in Panama, associated with pollen identified as cultivated maize and cultivated manioc and about 1,800 years old, but as they themselves pointed out, this could have been pollen from one of the weedy species of *Ipomoea*, not the cultivated sweet potato.

At present, all that can be concluded with certainty is that the sweet potato was domesticated in the lowland tropics, probably before 4000 B.P. and certainly before 3000 B.P. The balance of the evidence at present favors a South American origin, with spread to Mexico at some unknown time before the Spanish Conquest, but this view may well change.

Achira (Canna edulis)

Achira is another starchy root crop which appears relatively early (about 4300 B.P.) in archaeological sites on the coast of Peru (Patterson 1971; Towle 1961). Very little botanical work has been done on this crop, and guesses on where it was domesticated must still start with Cardenas' report (1948) that achira was semi-spontaneous in the yungas of the eastern slopes of the Bolivian Andes, and León's opinion (1964) that the species could have originated in either the Caribbean area or the eastern slopes of the Andes. Achira may thus be another member of the tropical lowland complex of crops, though it can be grown at appreciably higher altitudes than either manioc or sweet potato.

Potato (Solanum spp.)

Although tuber-bearing species of wild potato occur in Mesoamerica, cultivated potatoes had not spread north of Colombia by the time of the Spanish conquest. In the Andean area, however, a number of different species were cultivated. The best known of these is the tetraploid S. tuberosum. This species probably originated in cultivation, from a hybrid between the cultivated diploid S. stenotomum and a diploid weed S. sparsipilum which grows in and around potato fields (Hawkes 1956, 1967; Howard 1973). Ugent (1970) suggested that S. sparsipilum is itself a species of hybrid origin which has arisen repeatedly from crosses between the cultivated diploid potatoes and one or more of the wild species, S. canasense, S. brevicaule, and S. raphanifolium. Both diploid and tetraploid cultivated potatoes are grown from Bolivia to Colombia. In the northern part of this range the diploids have non-dormant tubers and are grown at somewhat lower altitudes than the tetraploids, which have dormant tubers. In southern Peru and Bolivia, however, neither the Andean farmer nor the potato taxonomist can distinguish diploids from tetraploids, and variation in both is greater here than anywhere else. "Primitive" forms of S. stenotomum occur in the area of Lake Titicaca, and so do certain wild diploids morphologically similar to S. stenotomum. For these reasons, Hawkes (1967) considered that S. stenotomum, which he thought was ancestral to all the other cultivated potatoes, originated in this area. S. tuberosum probably also developed in the region of Lake Titicaca, but may have originated repeatedly wherever S. stenotomum and S. sparsipilum overlapped.

At higher altitudes in the Andes, both diploid and tetraploid cultivated potatoes have hybridized with the uncultivated *S. acaule*, which also grows as a weed in potato fields, to produce two more cultivated potatoes, triploid *S.* × *juzepczukii* and pentaploid *S.* × *curtilobum* (Hawkes 1962, 1967). These possess the frost resistance, but also the bitter tubers, of *S. acaule* and are thus used almost entirely for chuño manufacture (a process of freeze-drying the tubers which removes the bitter principle and converts the tubers to a light, dry, easily storable form).

Because of the scanty archaeobotanical record in the Andes, we do not yet know when potatoes were first domesticated. Tubers which may be potatoes were recovered from the highlands from a house at Chiripa (about 2400 B.P.), and on the coast from about 1000 B.P. onwards (Towle 1961; Hawkes 1967). Potatoes were also depicted on Mochica pottery (about 1950–1300 B.P.). Both chuño and unprocessed tubers are represented among the archaeological specimens. Most probably potatoes were grown in the highlands considerably earlier than this, but the only evidence is inferential. Around Ayacucho, stone hoes, which might have been used for cultivating root crops, first appear late in the Chihua Period (c. 5000–5800 B.P.), become abundant in the Cachi Period (4800–3700 B.P.), and thereafter are restricted to sites at higher altitudes. MacNeish (personal communication) suggested that these changes indicated the start of cultivation of root crops with subsequent differentiation into the farming of root crops at higher altitudes and the cultivation of maize-beans-squash at lower altitudes as occurs in the Andes today.

SPICES

Chili Peppers (*Capsicum* spp.)

As in *Amaranthus*, *Phaseolus* and *Cucurbita*, different species of *Capsicum* have been domesticated in different parts of the Americas. The genus as a whole appears to have originated in South America, where there are many more species than in Mesoamerica. Three South American species have been domesticated (*C. baccatum*, *C. chinense* and *C. pubescens*) and one Mesoamerican species (*C. annuum*). A number of wild species are still exploited for their pungent fruits.

C. baccatum is today the common cultivated chili pepper of the southern part of the Andean area. Cultivated forms seem to have been domesticated from wild, weedy forms of the same species which occur from southern Peru through Bolivia and Paraguay to southwestern Brazil

(Pickersgill 1971). Within this general area, more precise determination of where *C. baccatum* was domesticated is not yet possible, but the variability of cultivated forms is greatest in Bolivia, which may indicate ancient cultivation there. The earliest archaeological specimens of chili pepper from coastal Peru (Punta Grande and Huaca Prieta, about 4500 B.P.) almost certainly represent cultivated forms of this species (Pickersgill 1969).

   C. chinense, the cultivated chili pepper of lowland South America and the northern part of the Andean area, is probably a domesticated form of the very widespread *C. frutescens* (Pickersgill 1971). Again, the area of domestication of *C. chinense* is not known, but its variability is greatest in Peruvian Amazonia. It had certainly reached coastal Peru by the Early Intermediate Period (2220–1350 B.P.), because specimens from Pachacamac and the Nazca site of Estaquería are virtually identical to modern *C. chinense*. However, the specimens of *Capsicum* from Huaca Prieta show changes which suggest that a small-seeded, deciduous-fruited form very similar to *C. frutescens* reached the coast either just before or at about the same time as the introduction of pottery (Pickersgill 1969), i.e. at about the same time, and possibly from the same source, as manioc.

   C. pubescens is the only cultivated pepper without a related wild or weedy form. Its purple flowers and black seeds make it the most easily recognized of the cultivated species. Purple-flowered wild species which will form hybrids with *C. pubescens* occur in southern Peru and Bolivia; black seeds occur in some little-studied species from southern Brazil. The wild ancestor of *C. pubescens* may occur in one of these complexes. *C. pubescens* is the most cold tolerant of the cultivated chili peppers and occurs along the chain of the Andes from Bolivia to Colombia, reappearing in highland Mesoamerica. It may, however, be a post-Conquest introduction in this latter area. Among the Tzeltal-speaking Indians in the highlands of Chiapas, Mexico, *C. pubescens* is the only chili pepper with a name which includes Spanish roots, and Raven (personal communication) considers it definitely post-Conquest in this area. *C. pubescens* has not been identified archaeologically in either Mesoamerica or the Andean area, though the black seeds should be readily distinguishable from the straw-colored seeds of other cultivated chili peppers.

   C. annuum is the commonest cultivated chili pepper of Mexico and Central America and, like *C. baccatum*, seems to have been domesticated from wild forms which occur within this species (Pickersgill 1971). These wild forms have a wide distribution, from the southern United States to Colombia. The cultivated forms differ from most of the wild forms in the morphology of their chromosomes. All cultivated types have two pairs of short-armed chromosomes, whereas most wild races have only a single such pair. Wild races with two pairs of short-armed chromosomes, like the cultivated types, are common only in Mexico, where they range from coastal Sinaloa, in the northwest, through central Mexico, to the coast of Tabasco in the southeast. Probably *C. annuum* was domesticated somewhere within this area. The earliest archaeological specimens that we have seen come from El Riego levels (8500–7000 B.P.) of the Tehuacán caves and consist of seeds only. We cannot be certain that these are *C. annuum*, though later fruits and peduncles from Tehuacán and Oaxaca do correspond closely to *C. annuum*. Although the early specimens from Tehuacán have been claimed to be from cultivated plants, their seeds are well within the size range of modern wild *annuum*. There is a gap in the record for *Capsicum* in Tehuacán from about 4300–2900 B.P., and not until Santa Maria times (2900–2200 B.P.) do seeds occur of a size which unequivocally indicates domesticated peppers.

As in other genera in which different species were domesticated in Middle and South America, there seems to have been little exchange of species between the two continents in pre-European times. Smith and Heiser (1957) considered Middle American *C. annuum* to be a late, possibly post-Conquest, introduction as a cultivated plant in South America; South American *C. baccatum* and *C. chinense* are still uncommon in Mexico.

FIBERS

Cotton (Gossypium hirsutum and G. barbadense)

Both of the cultivated species of cotton in the New World are tetraploids, and studies of chromosomal morphology and pairing behavior indicate that they contain the A genome found in the cultivated species of the Old World and the D genome found in American wild diploid species. The tetraploids, like the cultivated cottons of the Old World, bear long spinnable lint hairs on the seeds, while the D diploids do not produce lint. At one time lint hairs were thought to occur only in cultivated cottons, because they would hamper seed dispersal in a wild species. "Wild" linted forms of the cultivated species were thus considered feral escapes, derived from the crop, not ancestral to it, and it followed that the AADD linted tetraploids must have originated from a cross between an Old World cultivated cotton, presumably introduced to the Americas by man, and an

American wild species. Now, however, at least one linted cotton, *G. herbaceum* race *africanum*, is accepted as truly wild (Hutchinson 1970). *G. herbaceum* is the species which most closely resembles the donor of the A genome to the New World tetraploids, and these findings suggest that, rather than originating in cultivation, the tetraploids may have arisen as wild plants, from a cross between a wild, linted, *herbaceum*-like diploid from the Old World which spread across the Atlantic by natural means, and a wild American diploid. "Wild" forms of both tetraploids, with sparse lint which does not seem to impede seed dispersal, are known: in *G. barbadense* from Ecuador, northern Peru and the Galapagos Islands; in *G. hirsutum* from the Caribbean (Hutchinson 1970; Stephens 1971; Stephens and Phillips 1972). There is also a third "wild" New World tetraploid, *G. caicoense* (which seems to be synonymous with *G. mustelinum*), intermediate between *G. hirsutum* and *G. barbadense* in some of its characters, and with a scattered distribution in the arid parts of northeast Brazil (Aranha, et al. 1969; Fryxell, personal communication) and possibly Colombia (Watt 1907; Hutchinson, personal communications). These "wild" tetraploids have been very little studied until recently, but Stephens and Phillips (1972) have suggested the scheme of relationships shown in Figure 2.

The archaeological record supports this scheme, in that no cultivated

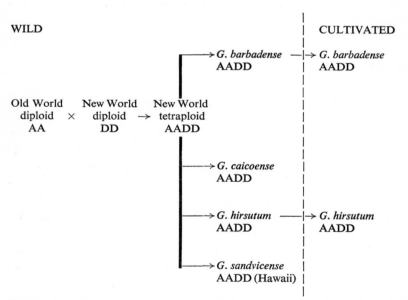

Figure 2.   Evolutionary relationships of the New World tetraploid cottons (data from Stephens and Phillips 1972)

Old World diploids have been found in any archaeological site in the Americas. Remains of cotton occur from about 5500 B.P. onwards in the Tehuacán Valley, Mexico and from about 4500 B.P. on the coast of Peru (Smith 1968); Lanning (1967) gave 5600 B.P. for the first appearance of cotton on the Peruvian coast — a date earlier than that for any cultivated plant except the bottle gourd. These specimens have not been critically identified as to species, and may be too incomplete for such identification to be possible, but it is usually assumed that the specimens from Tehuacán are *G. hirsutum* and the Peruvian specimens *G. barbadense* (Stephens 1970). Historical records suggest that the areas of the two species were on the whole different, with such overlap as did occur confined to the West Indies and Caribbean South America (see maps in Hutchinson, Silow, and Stephens 1947). As in other genera, there is no evidence for interchange of cottons between Mesoamerica and Andean South America.

DISCUSSION

The studies that have been carried out since the origins of New World cultivated plants were last reviewed (Heiser 1965) all reinforce the conclusion already reached by several workers: that there was considerable independence, at least in actual species domesticated, between Mesoamerica and South America. In Mesoamerica, the first crops cultivated were the squashes (*Cucurbita pepo* and *C. moschata*), bottle gourd, maize, amaranth (*Amaranthus cruentus*), common bean, and cotton, while avocado, chili pepper, and *Setaria* were utilized and possibly planted. Although cultivation seems to have started around 7000 B.P., it was at least 2,000 years before agricultural products supplied even 20 percent of the diet (MacNeish 1967). Meaningful comparisons with contemporaneous stages in South America are difficult to make, but there are tantalizing hints that plant cultivation in the Andean highlands may have begun at least as early as it did in Mexico (Kaplan, Lynch, and Smith 1973; MacNeish 1969; MacNeish, Nelken-Terner, and Garcia Cook 1970). Coastal Peru provides a more complete picture of the sequence of appearance of the different cultigens, but these sites are much later than early agricultural sites in Mexico — not surprisingly, because cultivation on any scale on the desert coast requires development and control of irrigation systems, which presupposes a period of prior development elsewhere, presumably in the highlands. The first crops cultivated on the Peruvian coast were gourds (*Lagenaria*), squash (*Cucurbita moschata, C. ficifolia,* possibly *C. andreana* and *C. ecuadorensis*), probably both common and lima beans, and possibly cotton, though this may have arrived later. Around 4500 B.P., chili peppers, achira, jack beans, and guava were added to this list. One might argue that, because *Lagenaria, Cucurbita moschata,* and common beans were among the first plants cultivated in both Mexico and Peru, there must have been some contact between the two areas. However, as we have attempted to show in our discussions of these species, independent domestication is equally possible, and further studies of these species are badly needed. The slowness with which agriculture took hold as a subsistence system in Mexico suggests that this new technique would not be immediately exported to or copied by adjacent peoples. In other words, the idea of cultivation is unlikely to spread until it has proved its worth as a system for producing plants for food or technology (cotton, gourds).

Whether the initial stimulus to the development of agriculture in Peru came from Mexico or not will be settled only by more excavations in highland Peru to establish precisely when the transition from hunting and gathering occurred. Subsequent exchanges of plants between these two centers were apparently limited to the spread of maize and possibly of *Cucurbita moschata* from Mexico to Peru about 5000 B.P., and a late spread (perhaps about 1950–1450 B.P.) of flour corn, sweet corn, peanuts, guava, and possibly pineapple, tobacco, and *Cucurbita ficifolia* from South America to Mexico. The differences in the species cultivated are the more remarkable because the dry highlands of Mexico and Peru are ecologically very similar, and crops have been readily exchanged between the two areas in historic times. The prehistoric contacts suggested by the botanical data do not fit very well with those deduced from other types of evidence. Willey (1955) postulated a north-to-south diffusion of maize agriculture, temple platform mounds and certain ceramic traits about 3000–2500 B.P., and a later south-to-north diffusion which spread metallurgy to Mexico. Temple platform mounds and maize agriculture are now known to have reached Peru earlier than Willey supposed, before pottery, and may perhaps have spread together. Metal working was early in Peru (gold and copper in the Early Horizon, about 2900 B.P.; bronze by the Middle Horizon [1350–1050 B.P.], Lanning 1967) but late in Mexico (after 1050 B.P., Coe 1962) and it is surprising that contacts which may have spread new types of maize, peanuts etc. about 1450 B.P. did not also spread metal artifacts as curiosities or trade pieces. Coe (1960, 1962) suggested direct sea trade between the Pacific coast of southern Mexico and Guatemala and southern Ecuador about 3500–2500 B.P., based on similarities in the pottery of the two areas (particularly the technique of iridescent painting) which he considered so striking that the traits could not have diffused through an overland series of filters. Lathrap (1966) agreed, rather hesitantly, that pottery and figurines of the Initial Period in Peru showed Mesoamerican influence lacking at that time in Colombia and Ecuador, again indicating contact by sea around 3000 B.P. Whatever the nature of these contacts, they left little mark on the subsistence of the two areas.

The question of when and where lowland root-crop agriculture developed is even more difficult. Tropical forests in which shifting cultivation of manioc, sweet potatoes, and other crops could be practiced occur from the Gulf Coast of Mexico south through Central America to the Orinoco and Amazon lowlands. As has been shown, we do not yet know whether manioc and sweet potatoes originated in South or Middle America. Archaeological preservation in the humid lowlands is so poor that even inferential evidence for the antiquity of root-crop cultivation is largely lacking on both continents. Uncertainties in the identification of archaeological tubers in areas such as coastal Peru, where they are preserved, make it difficult to determine when the major root crops reached this area. Various workers (Coe 1962; Willey 1955; Lathrap 1974) have suggested an intimate interrelationship between the cultures of Middle and South America about 3000–2000 B.P., apparently mainly on the basis of similarities between the more or less contemporaneous Olmec and Chavín cultures. Nothing is known of the subsistence base of the Olmec civilization, but the principal Olmec sites are located in the jungle lowlands of the Gulf Coast of Mexico. Lathrap (1971, 1973) has argued forcefully and persuasively for the tropical forest origins of the Chavín cult in Peru, although not all archaeologists agree with him (e.g. Lanning 1967). It is, however, striking that the oldest authenticated specimens of manioc and sweet potato correspond closely in time with the appearance of the Chavín art style on the coast. There is no archaeobotanical evidence to refute Lathrap's picture (1974) of diffusion of manioc cultivation throughout the lowlands of South and Central America before the rise of either the Chavín or the Olmec cultures.

Whether the development of lowland root-crop farming was stimulated by the start of cultivation in the highlands of Mexico and Peru is uncertain. In the Andean area, the dramatic relief means that extremely different ecological zones are separated by very short overland distances. There seem to have been frequent and well-established contacts between the Peruvian coast and the highland valleys throughout prehistory (Lynch 1971; Murra 1968). Despite the differences in altitude, there are ecological similarities between coast and highlands. Both are arid, with only scattered woody vegetation and an ephemeral annual ground cover, so that land could easily be cleared for planting. The tropical forest, on the other hand, is a very different environment. Problems of clearing land and control of weeds and water would differ considerably from those on the coast of Peru or in the highlands of Peru and Mexico. Jungle products such as monkeys, macaws, and coca leaf were traded with the Peruvian coast, but even the Incas never seriously attempted to colonize the tropical forests. In both Mexico and Peru the earliest crops preserved are seed crops and, on present evidence, it seems that humid lowland agriculture, with its rather different techniques, could well have been an independent invention.

However, C. O. Sauer's division (1959) of the New World into a Mesoamerican area of seed crops and a South American area of root crops now appears oversimplified. Both semi-arid regions, the Mexican highlands and Peru, developed an agriculture based largely on seed crops; lowland areas in both continents relied to a great extent on root crops. Admittedly in the Andean highlands a number of root crops (potato, oca [*Oxalis tuberosa*], ullucu [*Ullucus tuberosus*], mashua [*Tropaeolum tuberosum*], arracacha [*Arracacia xanthorrhiza*], maca [*Lepidium meyenii*], etc.) were added to a seed agriculture based on maize, beans, squash, quinoa, amaranth, and chocho (*Lupinus mutabilis*) while comparable root crops are lacking in Mexico even though starchy wild roots such as pochote (*Ceiba parvifolia*) were exploited in both pre- and post-agricultural periods (Smith 1967; Callen 1967). Although the time of origin of cultivation of root crops is unknown in the Andes, we doubt that the Andean tuber crops were domesticated as a consequence of development of root-crop agriculture in the lowlands. Rather, domestication of the Andean tubers probably resulted from attempts to exploit fully the known edible plant resources of the highland environment. The root crop, achira, which may have been domesticated on the eastern slopes of the Andes, spread to coastal Peru in association with a complex of seed-propagated crops well before the typical lowland tubers appeared.

Although we have archaeological sequences showing replacement of hunting and gathering by agriculture in both Mexico and Peru, these sequences do not demonstrate stages in the gradual domestication of the important crop plants. This situation is not surprising in Peru, where specialists generally concede that agriculture did not develop on the desert coast (which has so far provided the best archaeological sequences); it is surprising in Mexico. Nevertheless, in Tehuacán, common bean, amaranth, and maize appear in the earliest agricultural levels as fully fledged domesticates (assuming teosinte to be the wild ancestor of maize), with the important mutations distinguishing them from their wild ancestors already established. In the New World we have no data on the length of time required to convert a wild species into a cultigen, when the appropriate mutations occurred, or how fast they were fixed by human selection. We also have very little idea of the age of agriculture, at least in South America and, if Tehuacán indeed shows domesticates but not domestication, in Mesoamerica also. Any attempt to search for causal factors (climatic, ecological, or social) in the development of agriculture in the New World is premature until we know more accurately when this occurred.

Nor is it by any means self-evident that events in Mesoamerica and South America were sufficiently different to justify calling one a center of agricultural origin and the other a non-center as was done by Harlan (1971). Both areas have impressive lists of domesticated plants; the recent report of domesticated beans in Peru at about 8000 B.P. (Kaplan, Lynch, and Smith 1973) suggests that the hitherto apparently earlier development of agriculture in Mexico may well be an artifact resulting from accidents of archaeological preservation and archaeological interest; the apparently diffuse domestication of plants in South America reflects limited botanical work on the putative wild ancestors of South American crops and the confounding of two probably different centers of agricultural development in the Andean highlands and the humid lowlands. In both continents, although agriculture may have begun in semi-arid areas, crops characteristic of other, moister, ecological zones were later added, so that a picture of diffuse domestication could be built up for both "center" and "noncenter."

Finally, one contrast may be noted between the Old World and the New. In the Near East, remains of plants from early agricultural sites are of food plants exclusively (e.g. Hole and Flannery 1968). In the New World, "technological" plants such as bottle gourds and cotton were among the first plants cultivated in both Mexico and Peru. While the early Near Eastern farmer may have been eating bread in the sweat of his face, his New World counterpart had probably gone fishing.

REFERENCES

ARANHA, CONDORCET, HERMOGENES F. LEITÃO FILHO, IMRE LAJOS GRIDI-PAPP
  1969   Una nova espécie para o género *Gossypium* L. *Bragantia* 28:273–290.
BARTLETT, ALEXANDRA S., ELSO S. BARGHOORN, RAINER BERGER
  1969   Fossil maize from Panama. *Science* 165:389–390.
BEADLE, GEORGE W.
  1972   The mystery of maize. *Field Museum of Natural History Bulletin* 43 (November):2–11.
BRAND, DONALD D.
  1971   "The sweet potato: an exercise in methodology," in *Man across the sea.*

Edited by Carroll L. Riley, J. Charles Kelley, Campbell W. Pennington, and Robert L. Rands, 343–365. Austin: University of Texas Press.

BURKART, ARTURO, H. BRÜCHER

1953   *Phaseolus aborigineus* Burkart, die mutmassliche andine Stammform der Kulturbohne. *Züchter* 23:65–72.

CALLEN, ERIC O.

1967   "Analysis of the Tehuacán coprolites," in *The prehistory of the Tehuacán Valley*, volume one: *Environment and subsistence*. Edited by Douglas S. Byers, 261–289. Austin: University of Texas Press.

CARDENAS, MARTIN

1948   Plantas alimenticias nativas de los Andes de Bolivia. Introducción, I: Tubérculos, raíces y otros productos similares. *Folia Universitaria (Cochabamba)* 2:36–51.

COE, MICHAEL D.

1960   Archaeological linkages with North and South America at La Victoria, Guatemala. *American Anthropologist* 62:363–393.

1962   *Mexico*. New York: Frederick A. Praeger.

COONS, PATRICIA

n.d.   "The genus *Amaranthus* in Ecuador." Unpublished doctoral dissertation. Bloomington: Indiana University.

CUTLER, HUGH C., THOMAS W. WHITAKER

1967   "Cucurbits from the Tehuacán caves," in *The prehistory of the Tehuacán Valley*, volume one: *Environment and subsistence*. Edited by Douglas S. Byers, 212–219. Austin: University of Texas Press.

1969   A new species of *Cucurbita* from Ecuador. *Annals of the Missouri Botanical Garden* 55:392–396.

DE WET, J. M. J., J. R. HARLAN

1972   Origin of maize: the tripartite hypothesis. *Euphytica* 21:271–279.

DRESSLER, ROBERT L.

1953   The pre-Columbian cultivated plants of Mexico. *Harvard University Botanical Museum Leaflets* 16:115–172.

GADE, DANIEL W.

1970   Ethnobotany of cañihua (*Chenopodium pallidicaule*), rustic seed crop of the Altiplano. *Economic Botany* 24:55–61.

GALINAT, WALTON C.

1971   The origin of maize. *Annual Review of Genetics* 5:447–478.

GENTRY, HOWARD SCOTT

1969   Origin of the common bean, *Phaseolus vulgaris*. *Economic Botany* 23:55–69.

GRANT, WILLIAM F.

1959   Cytogenetic studies in *Amaranthus*, III: Chromosome numbers and phylogenetic aspects. *Canadian Journal of Genetics and Cytology* 1:313–328.

GROBMAN, ALEXANDER, WILFREDO SALHUANA, RICARDO SEVILLA, PAUL C. MANGELSDORF

1961   *Races of maize in Peru: their origins, evolution and classification*. National Academy of Sciences, National Research Council Publication 915. Washington, D.C.

HARLAN, JACK R.
1971   Agricultural origins: centers and non-centers. *Science* 174:468–474.
HAWKES, J. G.
1956   Taxonomic studies on the tuber-bearing Solanums, I: *Solanum tuberosum* and the tetraploid species complex. *Proceedings of the Linnaean Society of London* 166:97–144.
1962   The origin of *Solanum juzepczukii* Buk. and *S. curtilobum* Juz. et Buk. *Zeitschrift für Pflanzenzüchtung* 47:1–14.
1967   The history of the potato. *Journal of the Royal Horticultural Society* 92: 207–224, 249–262, 288–302, 364–365.
HEISER, CHARLES B., JR.
1965   Cultivated plants and cultural diffusion in nuclear America. *American Anthropologist* 67:930–949.
1973   "Variation in the bottle gourd," in *Tropical forest ecosystems in Africa and South America: a comparative review*. Edited by Betty J. Meggers, Edward S. Ayensu, and W. Donald Duckworth, 121–128. Washington: Smithsonian Institution Press.
HEISER, CHARLES B., JR., DAVID C. NELSON
1974   On the origin of cultivated chenopods (*Chenopodium*). *Genetics* 78: 503–505.
HOLE, FRANK, KENT V. FLANNERY
1968   The prehistory of southwestern Iran: a preliminary report. *Proceedings of the Prehistorical Society for 1967*, n.s. 33:147–206.
HOWARD, H. W.
1973   Calyx forms in dihaploids in relation to the origin of *Solanum tuberosum*. *Potato Research* 16:43–66.
HUNZIKER, ARMANDO T., ANA M. PLANCHUELO
1971   Sobre un nuevo hallazgo de *Amaranthus caudatus* en tumbas indígenas de Argentina. *Kurtziana* 6:63–67.
HURD, PAUL D., E. GORTON LINSLEY, THOMAS W. WHITAKER
1971   Squash and gourd bees *(Peponapis, Xenoglossa)* and the origin of the cultivated *Cucurbita*. *Evolution* 25:218–234.
HUTCHINSON, JOSEPH
1970   The genetics of evolutionary change. *Indian Journal of Genetics and Plant Breeding* 30:269–279.
HUTCHINSON, J. B., R. A. SILOW, S. G. STEPHENS
1947   *The evolution of* Gossypium. London: Oxford University Press.
JENNINGS, D. L.
1963   Variation in pollen and ovule fertility in varieties of cassava and the effect of interspecific crossing on fertility. *Euphytica* 12:69–76.
JONES, ALFRED
1967   Should Nishiyama's K123 *(Ipomoea trifida)* be designated *I. batatas?* *Economic Botany* 21:163–166.
KAPLAN, LAWRENCE
1965   Archaeology and domestication in American *Phaseolus* (beans). *Economic Botany* 19:358–368.
1967   "Archaeological *Phaseolus* from Tehuacán," in *The prehistory of the Tehuacán Valley*, volume one: *Environment and subsistence*. Edited by Douglas S. Byers, 201–211. Austin: University of Texas Press.

KAPLAN, LAWRENCE, THOMAS F. LYNCH, C. E. SMITH, JR.
1973   Early cultivated beans *(Phaseolus vulgaris)* from an intermontane Peruvian valley. *Science* 179:76–77.

KHOSHOO, T. N., MOHINDER PAL
1972   "Cytogenetic patterns in *Amaranthus*," in *Chromosomes today*, volume three. Edited by D. C. Darlington and K. R. Lewis, 259–267. London: Longman.

KRAPOVICKAS, A.
1969   "The origin, variability and spread of the groundnut *(Arachis hypogaea)*," in *The domestication and exploitation of plants and animals*. Edited by Peter J. Ucko and G. W. Dimbleby, 427–441. London: Gerald Duckworth.

KRAPOVICKAS, ANTONIO, VICTOR A. RIGONI
1957   Nuevas especies de *Arachis* vinculadas al problema del origen del maní. *Darwiniana* 11:431–455.

LANGHAM, D. J.
1940   The inheritance of intergeneric differences in *Zea-Euchlaena* hybrids. *Genetics* 25:88–107.

LANNING, EDWARD P.
1967   *Peru before the Incas*. Englewood Cliffs: Prentice-Hall.

LATHRAP, DONALD W.
1966   "Relationships between Mesoamerica and the Andean areas," in *Handbook of Middle American Indians*, volume four: *Archaeological frontiers and external connections*. Series edited by Robert Wauchope, volume four edited by Gordon F. Ekholm and Gordon R. Willey, 265–276. Austin: University of Texas Press.
1971   "The tropical forest and the cultural context of Chavín," in *Dumbarton Oaks Conference on Chavín*. Edited by Elizabeth Benson, 73–100. Washington: Dumbarton Oaks Research Library.
1973   "Gifts of the cayman: some thoughts on the subsistence basis of Chavín," in *Variation in anthropology*. Edited by Donald W. Lathrap and Jody Douglass, 91–105. Urbana: Illinois Archaeological Survey.
1974   "The moist tropics, the arid lands and the appearance of great art styles in the New World," in *Art and environment in native America*. Edited by Mary Elizabeth King and Idris R. Traylor, Jr., 115–158. The Museum, Texas Tech University, Special Publication no. 7. Lubbock: Texas Tech Press.

LEÓN, JORGE
1964   *Plantas alimenticias andinas*. Instituto Interamericano de Ciencias Agrícolas Zona Andina, Boletín technico 6. Lima.

LYNCH, THOMAS F.
1971   Preceramic transhumance in the Callejón de Huaylas, Peru. *American Antiquity* 36:139–148.

MAC NEISH, RICHARD S.
1967   "A summary of the subsistence," in *The prehistory of the Tehuacán Valley*, volume one: *Environment and subsistence*. Edited by Douglas S. Byers, 290–309. Austin: University of Texas Press.
1969   *First annual report of the Ayacucho archaeological-botanical project*. Andover: Robert S. Peabody Foundation for Archaeology.

MAC NEISH, RICHARD S., ANTOINETTE NELKEN-TERNER, ANGEL GARCIA COOK
1970   *Second annual report of the Ayacucho archaeological-botanical project.* Andover: Robert S. Peabody Foundation for Archaeology.

MAGOON, M. L., R. KRISHNAN, K. VIJAYA BAI
1970   Cytological evidence on the origin of sweet potato. *Theoretical and Applied Genetics* 40:360–366.

MANGELSDORF, PAUL C., RICHARD S. MAC NEISH, WALTON C. GALINAT
1964   Domestication of corn. *Science* 143:538–545.
1967   "Prehistoric wild and cultivated maize," in *The prehistory of the Tehuacán Valley*, volume one: *Environment and subsistence*. Edited by Douglas S. Byers, 178–200. Austin: University of Texas Press.

MANGELSDORF, PAUL C., RICHARD S. MAC NEISH, GORDON R. WILLEY
1964   "Origins of agriculture in Middle America," in *Handbook of Midule American Indians*, volume one: *Natural environment and early cultures.* Edited by Robert Wauchope, 427–445. Austin: University of Texas Press.

MANGELSDORF, PAUL C., ROBERT G. REEVES
1939   *The origin of Indian corn and its relatives.* Texas Agricultural Experiment Station Bulletin 574.

MATUDA, ELIZI
1963   El género *Ipomoea* en México. *Anales del Instituto de Biología de la Universidad Nacional de México* 34:84–145.

MURRA, JOHN V.
1968   An Aymara kingdom in 1567. *Ethnohistory* 15:115–151.

NELSON, DAVID C.
1968   Taxonomy and origins of *Chenopodium quinoa* and *Chenopodium nuttalliae*." Unpublished doctoral dissertation, Indiana University.

NISHIYAMA, ICHIZO
1963   "The origin of the sweet potato plant," in *Plants and the migrations of Pacific peoples*. Edited by Jacques Barrau, 119–128. Honolulu: Bishop Museum Press.
1971   Evolution and domestication of the sweet potato. *Botanical Magazine, Tokyo* 84:377–387.

O'BRIEN, PATRICIA J.
1972   The sweet potato: its origin and dispersal. *American Anthropologist* 74:342–365.

PANETSOS, C. A., H. G. BAKER
1967   The origin of variation in "wild" *Raphanus sativus* (Cruciferae) in California. *Genetica* 38:243–274.

PATTERSON, THOMAS C.
1971   Central Peru: its population and economy. *Archaeology* 24:316–321.

PICKERSGILL, BARBARA
1969   The archaeological record of chili peppers (*Capsicum* spp.) and the sequence of plant domestication in Peru. *American Antiquity* 34:54–61.
1971   Relationships between weedy and cultivated forms in some species of chili peppers (genus *Capsicum*). *Evolution* 25:683–691.
1972   Cultivated plants as evidence for cultural contacts. *American Antiquity* 37:97–104.

REICHEL-DOLMATOFF, G.
1965   *Colombia.* New York: Frederick A. Praeger.

RICHARDSON, JAMES B., III
1972   The pre-Columbian distribution of the bottle gourd *(Lagenaria sicera-ria):* a re-evaluation. *Economic Botany* 26:265–273.

RENVOIZE, BARBARA S.
1972   The area of origin of *Manihot esculenta* as a crop plant — a review of evidence. *Economic Botany* 26:352–360.

ROGERS, DAVID J.
1965   Some botanical and ethnological considerations of *Manihot esculenta.* *Economic Botany* 19:369–377.

SAUER, CARL O.
1950   "Cultivated plants of South and Central America," in *Handbook of South American Indians,* volume six. Edited by Julian H. Steward, 487–543. Smithsonian Institution Bureau of American Ethnology Bulletin 143. Washington, D.C.
1952   *Agricultural origins and dispersals.* New York: American Geographical Society.
1959   Age and area of American cultivated plants. *Actas del 33 Congreso Internacional de Americanistas* 1:215–229.

SAUER, JONATHAN D.
1967   The grain amaranths and their relatives: a revised taxonomic and geographic survey. *Annals of the Missouri Botanical Garden* 54:103–137.
1969   Identity of archaeologic grain amaranths from the valley of Tehuacán, Puebla, Mexico. *American Antiquity* 34:80–81.

SAUER, JONATHAN D., LAWRENCE KAPLAN
1969   *Canavalia* beans in American prehistory. *American Antiquity* 34: 417–424.

SIMMONDS, N. W.
1965   The grain chenopods of the tropical American highlands. *Economic Botany* 19:223–235.

SMARTT, J.
1969   "Evolution of American *Phaseolus* beans under domestication," in *The domestication and exploitation of plants and animals.* Edited by Peter J. Ucko and G. W. Dimbleby, 451–462. London: Gerald Duckworth.
1970   Interspecific hybridization between cultivated American species of the genus *Phaseolus. Euphytica* 19:480–489.

SMITH, C. EARLE, JR.
1967   "Plant remains," in *The prehistory of the Tehuacán Valley,* volume one: *Environment and subsistence.* Edited by Douglas S. Byers, 220–255. Austin: University of Texas Press.
1968   The New World centers of origin of cultivated plants and the archaeological evidence. *Economic Botany* 22:253–266.

SMITH, PAUL G., CHARLES B. HEISER, JR.
1957   Taxonomy of *Capsicum sinense* Jacq. and the geographic distribution of the cultivated *Capsicum* species. *Bulletin of the Torrey Botanical Club* 84: 413–420.

STEPHENS, S. G.
    1970   The botanical identification of archaeological cotton. *American Antiquity* 35:367–373.
    1971   "Some problems of interpreting transoceanic dispersal of the New World cottons," in *Man across the sea*. Edited by Carroll L. Riley, J. Charles Kelley, Campbell W. Pennington, and Robert L. Rands, 401–415. Austin: University of Texas Press.
STEPHENS, S. G., L. L. PHILLIPS
    1972   The history and geographical distribution of a polymorphic system in New World cottons. *Biotropica* 4:49–60.
STURTEVANT, WILLIAM O.
    1969   "History and ethnography of some West Indian starches," in *The domestication and exploitation of plants and animals*. Edited by Peter J. Ucko and G. W. Dimbleby, pp. 177–199. London: Gerald Duckworth.
TOWLE, MARGARET A.
    1961   *The ethnobotany of pre-Columbian Peru*. Chicago: Aldine.
UGENT, DONALD
    1970   The potato. *Science* 170:1161–1166.
VAVILOV, N. I.
    1950   The origin, variation, immunity and breeding of cultivated plants. Translated by K. Starr Chester. *Chronica Botanica* 13:1–364.
WATT, G.
    1907   *The wild and cultivated cotton plants of the world*. London: Longmans.
WHITAKER, THOMAS W.
    1968   Ecological aspects of the cultivated *Cucurbita*. *Horticultural Science* 3.
WHITAKER, THOMAS W., W. P. BEMIS
    1964   Evolution in the genus *Cucurbita*. *Evolution* 18:553–559.
WHITAKER, THOMAS W., HUGH C. CUTLER
    1965   Cucurbits and cultures in the Americas. *Economic Botany* 19:344–349.
    1971   Prehistoric cucurbits from the valley of Oaxaca. *Economic Botany* 25:123–127.
WILKES, H. GARRISON
    1967   *Teosinte: the closest relative of maize*. Cambridge, Massachusetts: Bussey Institution of Harvard University.
WILLEY, GORDON R.
    1955   The prehistoric civilizations of Nuclear America. *American Anthropologist* 57:571–593.
WILSON, KENNETH A.
    1960   The genera of Convolvulaceae in the southeastern United States. *Journal of the Arnold Arboretum* 41:298–317.
YEN, DOUGLAS E.
    1971   "Construction of the hypothesis for distribution of the sweet potato," in *Man across the sea*. Edited by Carroll L. Riley, J. Charles Kelley, Campbell W. Pennington, and Robert L. Rands, 328–342. Austin: University of Texas Press.

Animal Domestication in the Anaes

ELIZABETH S. WING

Animal domestication in the Western hemisphere is centered in the Andes. In comparison to the Near Eastern center of domestication, in the Andes this sequence of events is poorly known. In part this lack of knowledge may be due to the fact that the South American domesticates have not achieved the economic importance of animals from the Old World, and therefore study of their origin has been a less pressing problem. The Andean center of domestication is, however, an area in which this process of animal domestication can be studied and thereby offers an opportunity to gain greater understanding of the development of the closest relationship that exists between man and other animals, that of man and his domesticates.

The Andean domesticates include both native mammals, the llamas and guinea pig, and an introduced species, the dog. Dogs reached the Andean area, fully domesticated, in very early times, so early, in fact, that dogs may have accompanied the first human migration into South America. Our evidence indicates that the other domesticates were developed in the Andes, and for these we may hope to be able to document the progression of events from hunting and trapping their wild ancestors, to tending and taming, and finally to control of their genetics resulting in domestic animals.

I am much indebted to my many friends and colleagues who have entrusted to me for study faunal materials which they have excavated, and who have generously provided data. Thanks also go to Takeshi Ueno and Lynn Cunningham for their careful and painstaking work in helping to analyze these materials. The whole project would not have been possible without the generous support of the National Science Foundation through GS 3021 and GS 1954.

Various types of research have a bearing on this problem and must all be considered if we are to have a thorough understanding of these animals and how they became domestic. Basic taxonomic studies (Cabrera 1960; Hershkovitz 1969) and life-history studies (Pearson 1951; Koford 1957; Franklin 1973) are an essential background to studies of human utilization of animal resources and the development of domesticates. Specific studies of the physiology (Fernández Baca 1971) and biology (Herre 1952) of the domesticated species provide information about their innate characteristics. Ethnographic studies of present herding and animal-care practices (Flannery 1972) and documentation of past animal husbandry (Murra 1965) also provide important data about customs that have developed over long periods of time for the care of herd and house animals. In order to trace the sequence of events in the domestication of animals before the time of conquest we must rely on the archaeological record. For a more complete understanding of the origin of the South American domesticates we must, in fact, rely on a large series of sites which are distributed widely over western South America and were occupied for long and continuous periods. Through a combination of information about various aspects of the domesticated species we are beginning to gain a fuller understanding of animal domestication in the Andes (Herre 1952; Cardozo 1954; Gilmore 1950; Latcham 1922).

The data on which this report is based are faunal samples excavated by a number of different archaeologists in the Andean highlands. These sites extend from Lake Titicaca north to southern Ecuador (see Map 1) between 2,400 and 4,440 meters above sea level. The periods of occupation of each of these sites vary, of course, but the entire range of occupation is from about 11,000 B.P. to Inca times, in the late fifteenth century A.D.

The data which relate to time of occupation and location of each site, and summaries of the fauna represented in these sites are presented in Table 1. Each of the three domestic genera, *Lama*, *Cavia*, and *Canis*, is entered separately and all other species are combined in the category of wild game. A very high percentage of the wild game at each site consists of deer: *Hippocamelus* (huemal), *Odocoileus* (white-tailed deer), *Mazama* (brocket), and *Pudu* (pudu). Other, on the whole less important, game animals include viscacha (*Lagidium peruanum*), hog-nosed skunk (*Conepatus rex*), and a variety of birds among which the tinamou and the dove (*Zenaida auriculata*) are common. Rabbits (*Sylvilagus brasiliensis*) are also common in the northern sites. As indicated, the shift from hunted to tended and finally to fully domestic llamas and guinea pigs was a gradual one, and its early stages are not clearly reflected in the osteological material; therefore animals in the genera *Lama* and *Cavia* are listed separately (Table 1) from

Table 1. Summary of the fauna from Andean sites of Peru

Site	Location	Elevation in meters	Archaeologist	Time period	Lama spp. MNI	%	Cavia spp. MNI	%	Canis familiaris MNI	%	Wild game MNI	%	Total
Q'ellokaka	Pucara 7 km northwest	3930	Sergio Chavez	3400–3000 B.P.	5	28	3	17	1	6	9	49	18
Qaluyu	Pucara 4 km north	3930	Karen Mohr Chavez	3400–3000 B.P.	27	34	–	–	1	1	52	65	80
Pikicallepata	Sicuani	3410	Karen Mohr Chavez	3300–3100 B.P.	10	56	2	11	–	–	6	33	18
				3100–2900 B.P.	21	48	5	11	1	2	17	39	44
				2900–2650 B.P.	12	46	4	15	1	4	9	35	26
				2650–2200 B.P.	17	40	15	35	1	2	10	23	43
Minaspata PCz	Lucre Valley	3200	Edward Dwyer	3000–1600 B.P.	37	45	7	9	–	–	28	46	72
				1600–1300 B.P.	7	43	1	7	2	13	5	37	15
				1300–1500 A.D.	18	64	4	14	–	–	6	22	28
Marcavalle	Cuzco	3314	Karen Mohr Chavez	3000 B.P.	62	83	1	1	–	–	12	16	75
Puente Ac 158	Ayacucho Valley	2500–3000	Richard S. MacNeish	9100–7800 B.P.	5	2	201	85	–	–	32	13	238
				7800–7100 B.P.	2	2	83	72	–	–	30	26	115
				7100–6700 B.P.	2	3	32	40	–	–	47	57	81
				6700–6550 B.P.	3	10	5	17	–	–	22	73	30
				6550–6300 B.P.	4	8	10	21	–	–	34	71	48
Pikimachay Ac 100	Ayacucho Valley	2500–3000	Richard S. MacNeish	7800–6550 B.P.	1	3	14	41	–	–	19	56	34
				6550–5100 B.P.	6	26	4	17	–	–	13	57	23
				5100–3700 B.P.	9	32	4	14	–	–	15	54	28
				3000–2500 B.P.	7	19	8	22	1	3	21	56	37
				2500–2100 B.P.	8	57	–	–	1	7	5	36	14
				500–1500 A.D.	11	44	1	4	–	–	13	52	25
Wari	Ayacucho Valley	2500–3000	Richard S. MacNeish	1000 A.D.	56	66	20	24	4	5	5	5	85
Tarma	Tarma	4000	Harold Jensen	1400–1500 A.D.	53	70	1	1	–	–	22	29	76
Pachamachay	Junin	4000	Ramiro Matos	±4000 B.P.	250	82	6	2	1	0.3	48	16	305
Kotosh	Huánuco	2000	University of Tokyo Andean Expedition	5100–3700 B.P.	21	15	36	25	–	–	86	60	143
				3700–3400 B.P.	12	21	10	17	–	–	36	62	58
				3400–3000 B.P.	20	31	14	22	–	–	31	48	65
				3000–2700 B.P.	54	50	8	7	–	–	45	41	107
Guitarrero Cave	Callejón de Huaylas	2500	Thomas F. Lynch	12,610 B.P.	–	–	–	–	–	–	11	100	11
				10,600–7600 B.P.	6	10	–	–	–	–	53	90	59
				±7000 B.P.	3	17	–	–	–	–	15	83	18
				400 A.D.	16	13	3	2	1	1	105	84	125
12–51 (Pampa de Lampas)	Callejón de Huaylas	3970	Thomas F. Lynch	3000 B.P.	19	64	–	–	1	1	45	36	64
12–57 (Pampa de Lampas)	Callejón de Huaylas	4000	Thomas F. Lynch	3000 B.P.	35	80	–	–	1	2	8	18	44
Chobshi Cave	Ecuador-Sigsig	2400	Thomas F. Lynch	10,000–8000 B.P.	–	–	–	–	–	–	260	100	260

wild game, even though in some cases they were clearly wild, as I will try to point out.

No attempt has been made to apply species names to these genera except for *Canis familiaris*, which in the Andes was found fully domestic with no transitional stages between wild and domestic. However, the native domesticates which were developed from wild animals passed through transitional stages unlike either the wild ancestor or the domestic form as it is known today. Some of these transitional changes may involve characteristics of the animal not reflected in the skeleton, or at least not in the fragmentary remains excavated from prehistoric sites.

DOG *(Canis familiaris)*

Dogs in the Andes are kept primarily for protection. This is true today as it was in about 1844 when:

Tschudi describes the chief characteristics of this dog as treachery and mischievousness. Every Indian hut and shepherd of the Sierra and Puna had several. They seemed to show a special antipathy toward white people. A European traveller approaching an Indian hut on horseback would be beset by these dogs springing up against his horse to bite his legs. They are courageous, and fight an enemy with determination, dragging themselves to the attack even when mortally wounded (Allen 1920: 473).

As an extension of protection of their master and the home they also defend the herds, but are not known to guide the native herd animals to any great extent. Remains of dogs were not found in the sites at high elevation, suggesting that they were not used for herding in prehistoric times. Tschudi also said that the "Indians train them [dogs] to track and capture tinamous" (Allen 1920: 473). Training as hunting assistants is generally thought to be a recent development, although this role extends back at least to Mochica times (Early Intermediate Period) as evidenced by a ceramic depiction of a dog assisting in a deer hunt (Thomson 1971). Wherever they are found, dogs are scavengers around the home site, and there is no reason to suppose that they did not also fill this role in Peru. Garcilaso de la Vega speaks of the "immoderate passion" the Huancas had for dog's meat in at least the fifteenth and sixteenth centuries (Gheerbrant 1961: 200). The use of dogs for food may have been widespread in prehistoric times.

Six different native Peruvian types of dogs have been described (Allen 1920) (Table 2). All of these were seen or excavated from Inca sites along

Table 2. Comparative measurements of remains of dogs (in millimeters)

	Inca dog Ancón; 6 specimens (Allen 1920: 473)	Techichi Chicama and Coyungo; 2 specimens (Allen 1920: 489)	Short-nosed dog Ancón 1 specimen (Allen 1920: 499)	Peruvian pug-nosed dog Ancón and Pachacamac; 6 specimens (Allen 1920: 501)	Chilca specimen 1000–1400 A.D.	Rosamachay Ac 117 2400 B.P.	Wari 500 A.D.	Minaspata PC_z 700 A.D.
length of skull	165 (155–178)	142 (139–145)	141	137 (124–145)	168	134		
basal length	147 (139–159)	–	–	119 (104–125)	148	120		
palatal length	82 (79–86)	76 (74–78)	–	65 (60–67.5)	81.7	68.1		
orbit-premaxillary	69 (73–75)	61.5 (61–62)	55	51 (47–53)	68	55.5		
front C^1-back M^2, alveolar	68 (64–74)	64 (63–65)	59	55 (49–58)	68.5	57.5		
p^4 alveolar length	16.6 (16–17)	16.2 (16–16.3)	16	15 (14.5–16)	18.4	15.1	18	
M^{1+2} alveolar length	16.2 (15–17)	16	16.5	15.8 (14–17)	16.7	14.4		
zygomatic width	100 (92–108)	90	–	99 (91–109)	102.9	83.7		
occipital width	33 (32–35)	31.5 (31–32)	–	29 (27–31.5)	35.8	28.8		
nasal length	52.5 (48.5–56)	45	–	–	50.6	40.9		
ratio skull length/orbit-premax.	2.39 (2.37–2.42)	2.31 (2.28–2.34)	2.56	2.70 (2.64–2.82)	2.47	2.41		
humeral length			97			119	±140	122
4th metatarsal length						49.1	62.3	

the coast. The largest of these is the Inca dog, of which short- and long-haired types existed. The one dog's skull for which we have comparative measurements is of this type. It and a mummified puppy with long yellow fur, probably the so-called long-haired Inca dog, were excavated from the coastal site at Chilca by Dr. Jeffery Parsons, University of Michigan. Remains of dogs from the Wari site are not complete enough for many comparable measurements, but those available indicate animals of the size of Inca dogs. The other described types are all small and differ mainly in their snout length and leg length. Techichi, the small Indian dog, is smaller than the Inca dog but has similar proportions. Hairless dogs have been reported from the Peruvian lowlands, but no measurements are available for comparison. Finally, two short-snouted types existed: the "short-nosed dog," which also had very short legs, and the Peruvian "pug-nosed dog," which not only had an extremely short snout but also an undershot jaw. The mummified dog from a horizon which dates about 2400 B.P. at Rosamachay Cave in Ayacucho is in the same size range as the pug-nosed dog, but has a longer snout and narrower skull. The humerus from Minaspata may be from a similar small dog.

In summary, remains of dogs are scant but are present in most sites between 2,000 and 4,000 meters elevation. They are rarely found in sites above 4,000 meters. The four measurable specimens include two small types, and two similar in size to the Inca dog described from the coast.

GUINEA PIG *(Cavia* spp.*)*

Guinea pigs never achieved the worldwide popularity of dogs, even though both play the same basic roles as camp and household scavengers and are themselves a source of food. They still play a part in folk medicine and are offered as sacrifices to pagan spirits. Outside of South America, guinea pigs have not been successful as a socially acceptable food source (Gade 1967); they have, however, been used widely as experimental animals, and through this scientific use much has been learned about the biology of the domestic species *Cavia porcellus*. The wild ancestry of this species is, however, still poorly understood.

Cabrera (1960) recognized three major widespread species of the genus *Cavia: Cavia aperea*, ranging through southern Brazil and northern Argentina in southeastern South America; *Cavia tschudii*, ranging in the highland valleys of Peru, Bolivia, and northwestern Argentina; and *Cavia porcellus* (including the domestic species), which occurs in the wild state in Guyana, Venezuela, and Colombia. In addition to these, three species have been described from Argentina, Uruguay, Brazil, and Bolivia. Too little is known about these minor species to suggest how they might be related.

The three major species appear to be ecologically, geographically, and morphologically separate. For this reason I am following the classification proposed by Cabrera, rather than the synonymy proposed by Hüchinghaus (1961a), in which he placed these three major populations together into the single species *Cavia aperea*.

The domestic form *Cavia porcellus* has, through the agency of man, widely increased its range to include the entire area occupied by the genus *Cavia* and well beyond. The domestic *Cavia* is easily distinguishable, on the basis of a number of cranial and external characteristics, from *Cavia porcellus anolaimae* (Cabrera 1960). An explanation for the circumscribed distribution of *C. p. anolaimae* only near Bogotá, Colombia, is that this is a feral population (personal communication from Dr. Philip Hershkovitz). If true, the animals have diverged a great deal from the domesticated ancestor.

I will therefore discuss characteristics which are useful in separating domestic guinea pigs (Gilmore 1950) and which are found in the fragmentary remains of the skull, such as the conformation of the nasofrontal and fronto-parietal sutures, and presence or absence of the palatal spine (Table 3). A sample of *Cavia tschudii* (from Arequipa, Peru) is more similar to modern domestic (Peruvian) *C. porcellus* than is a sample *C. aperea* (from Argentina, Uruguay, Paraguay, and Brazil) in respect to the absence of a palatal spine. Such a spine is present in all *C. aperea* except the Brazilian specimen. Many of the remains of *Cavia* from the archaeological sites share more than the palatal characteristic with *C. tschudii*. Slightly less than half of the archaeological specimens also have the straight fronto-parietal suture and the M-shaped naso-frontal suture, as does *C. tschudii*. *Cavia tschudii* (*Cavia aperea tschudii* of Hüchinghaus 1961a, 1961b) does indeed seem to be closest to the ancestral form of the domestic guinea pig.

The development of domestic *Cavia* was by selection for genetic loss of wildness, for increased size, and for genes for particular colors. Only on rare occasions are the coat colors of the prehistoric guinea pigs preserved. A mummified guinea pig was found at Rosamachay Cave (Chupas Period), and has an agouti or "wild" coat color and otherwise cranial characteristics of domestic *C. porcellus*. Degree of tameness can only be surmised from archaeological remains by the relative abundance of one species. Of the domestic characteristics, size is the most easily measured in the skeletal remains, and changes resulting from selection for large size can be traced.

Table 3.   Summary of measurements and other characteristic found in *Cavia*, both modern and archaeological

	MANDIBLE Lower alveolar length					Height of jaw at diastema					SKULL Naso-frontal suture		Fronto-parietal suture		Palatal spine	
	Number	Range	Mean	Standard deviation	Coefficient of variation	Number	Range	Mean	Standard deviation	Coefficient of variation	Straight %	M-shaped %	Curved %	Straight %	Absent %	Present %
Cavia porcellus domestic	9	14.0–16.7	15.47	0.913	5.90	9	6.1–7.5	6.74	0.537	7.97	73	27	100	0	73	27
Cavia tschudii	40	11.2–14.5	12.93	0.934	7.22	40	4.2–6.5	5.30	0.561	10.58	36	64	26	74	68	32
Cavia porcellus anolaimae	15	13.0–16.2	14.75	0.792	5.37	15	4.7–6.2	5.41	0.494	9.13	7	93	23	77	0	100
Cavia aperea	9	12.4–15.4	13.94	0.997	7.15	9	5.0–6.9	5.94	0.576	9.70	0	100	12	88	33	67
Chilca A.D. 1000–1400	6	11.3–15.4	13.17	1.595	11.68	8	4.4–7.1	5.51	0.958	17.38	4	0	5	0	2	0
Kotosh 1800–2600 B.P.	12	10.4–14.6	13.27	1.287	9.70	16	3.8–6.9	5.61	0.857	15.27	4	0	4	2	1	0
Ac 158 Puente Piki-Jaywa 7000–8000 B.P.	21	12.4–15.1	13.74	0.767	5.58	253	3.6–6.5	5.20	0.485	9.33	3	3	7	5	2	0
Ac 117 Rosamachay 2400 B.P.	2	14.9–15	14.95	–	–	2	5.9–6.5	6.20	–	–	2	0	2	0	0	2
Eb4 Wari A.D. 800–1200	5	11.6–18.8	15.52	2.941	18.95	7	4.8–7.8	6.01	1.256	20.88	0	1	0	1	1	0
PCz Minaspata 3000 B.P.–A.D. 1500	47	11.8–18.6	13.58	1.091	8.03	54	4.4–7.9	5.40	0.704	13.03	1	1	4	3	2	0
Pikicallepata 2200–3400 B.P.	13	11.9–14.8	13.34	0.799	5.99	15	4.9–6.2	5.61	0.457	8.15	1	0	7	3	1	0

The most common part of the skull found is the symphyseal end of the dentary, and the best measurement that can be taken on this fragment is the height of the jaw in the middle of the diastema. Several size characteristics of *Cavia* are revealed by these measurements (Table 4). Two general trends are evident: in each area — Huánuco, Ayacucho, and Cuzco — the most recent samples available are the most variable; in two of these areas — Ayacucho and Cuzco — the mean of the diastemal measurement of the recent samples shows a large and significant increase in size over the older samples. This general increase in size and greater coefficient of variation, both clear evidences of the processes of domestication, occurred in the sample of A.D. 1300–1500 from Minaspata. This change is seen earlier in the Ayacucho Valley, probably by 3000 B.P., in the last sample from Pikimachay Cave. The samples from Kotosh do not appear to include the stages of initial size-increase. Very little difference is seen in diastemal size in the first two samples from Kotosh, which date from about 5000 to 3000 B.P. The decrease in size that follows, as seen in the sample from the last two phases (which date from about 2700 to 1500 B.P.), is attributable to the inclusion of more juveniles in the sample. An alternative explanation is that individual size in the native population of *Cavia* was larger than in other populations to the south, and we are seeing only a change in the use of more juveniles in the later periods. Only samples from earlier times in this area can solve this problem. Caution must be taken in comparing sizes of *Cavia* from different populations, even those represented in neighboring sites such as the sites of Puente and Pikimachay in the Ayacucho Valley, separated by only 10 kilometers. *Cavia* tend to form closely interbreeding population clusters which situation results in these differences between samples. These two sites had populations of *Cavia* that differed significantly in size, and this difference was consistent throughout the occupation of the sites of Puente and Pikimachay, with the exception of the sample from the most recent cultural period at Pikimachay, in which half the specimens are larger than any found previously in that site and the mean is almost 20 percent larger than the means of the earlier samples.

The presence and relative abundance of *Cavia* in the faunal samples (Table 1) reflect their use. They are exceedingly abundant in early cultural levels (those dating from almost 9000 B.P. to about 3000 B.P.) of central Peruvian sites located below 4,000 meters. They are absent, or virtually so, in sites above 4,000 meters and in preceramic sites of the Callejón de Huaylas and further north. In central Peru, in the three sites of Kotosh, Pikimachay, and Puente, for which we have faunal samples from long periods of occupation, we find close correspondence in abundance of

Table 4. *Cavia:* height of jaw taken from the middle of the diastema

	Number	Range	Mean±SE[a]	Standard deviation	Coefficient of variation
Kotosh Higueras and					
Sajarapatac	15	3.8–6.9	5.55±0.22	0.85	15.32
2700–1600 B.P.					
K. Chavín	5	5.0–6.2	5.84±0.215	0.48	8.22
3000–2700 B.P.					
K. Kotosh	10	5.3–6.9	6.14±0.18	0.56	9.12
3400–3000 B.P.					
K. Mito	22	5.3–7.5	6.17±0.119	0.56	9.08
5000–4000 B.P.					
Wari	7	5.1–7.8	6.22±0.51	1.24	19.94
500–800 A.D.					
Rosamachay	2	5.9–6.5	6.20		
2400 B.P.					
Pikimachay E5–E6	12	3.4–6.6	4.84±0.30	1.03	21.24
3000 B.P.					
G1–G2 4000 B.P.	2	4.1–4.4	4.25		
VIII 5000 B.P.	6	3.6–4.8	4.30±0.20	0.48	11.16
X 6500 B.P.	8	3.7–4.7	4.21±0.11	0.31	7.36
U 7000 B.P.	2	3.9–4.4	4.15		
Puente II–III	4	4.8–5.2	5.00±0.08	0.16	3.20
6500 B.P.					
V 6700 B.P.	7	4.8–5.5	5.16±0.10	0.26	5.04
VII 7100 B.P.	11	5.1–5.8	5.37±0.07	0.25	4.66
IX 7500 B.P.	31	4.2–5.9	5.15±0.07	0.41	7.96
XI 7800 B.P.	26	4.0–6.4	5.16±0.12	0.60	11.63
XIII 9100 B.P.	15	4.1–6.1	5.15±0.12	0.47	9.13
Minaspata					
1300–1500 A.D.	5	5.2–7.9	5.78±0.51	1.14	16.81
1900–1300 B.P.	13	4.4–5.8	5.11±0.13	0.46	9.00
3000–2200 B.P.	28	4.0–6.2	5.29±0.10	0.51	9.64
Pikicallepata	15	4.9–6.2	5.61±0.12	0.46	8.20
3400–2200 B.P.					
Chilca	10	4.4–7.1	5.54±0.27	0.85	15.34
1000–1400 A.D.					

[a] Mean±standard error.

guinea pigs. In occupations dating from 9100 to 6700 B.P. at Puente and Pikimachay, guinea pigs constitute 40 percent or more of the fauna. In the three thousand years that follow, only about a quarter of the fauna is composed of guinea pigs. After about 3000 B.P. the relative abundance of guinea pigs in faunas is still further reduced, in most cases to about 10 percent.

During this period (3000 B.P. to and including the time of the Spanish conquest), fully domestic guinea pigs were introduced to sites north of central Peru. Remains of *Cavia* are included in the mixed ceramic levels (Early Intermediate and some Late Early Horizon) at Guitarrero Cave in the Callejón de Huaylas, and in fact have been identified from sites as far north as the Lesser Antilles and the Dominican Republic (Wing, Hoffman, and Ray 1968). We do not have information on the extent of the spread of this animal southward.

The great relative abundance of guinea pigs in the Early Horizon is unique. A great preponderance of a single species occurs either when there is a dependence on a domesticated animal or when a highly specific method of hunting has been devised. As the guinea pigs of this period (9000–6000 B.P.) show no increase in size or greater variability in size, they cannot be considered fully domesticated. If, when more material is studied, the cranial characteristics used are found to be reliable in distinguishing domestic *C. porcellus* from its wild ancestor, then this early sample would seem to show some indications that selection for the ultimately domesticated guinea pigs had already begun. Although it is possible that hunting concentrated on capturing guinea pigs and excluded other small to medium-sized animals that live in the same habitat, it seems more likely that the initial taming stage of domestication had been achieved and that guinea pigs were being attracted to human occupation sites by food debris, warmth, and protection (Gade 1967).

LLAMAS AND ALPACAS *(Lama glama* and *Lama pacos)*

Very different associations are evident between man and the camelids. The Camelidae is the family which includes the vicuña (*Vicugna vicugna* or *Lama vicugna*) and guanaco (*Lama guanicoe*), both of which are wild, and the llama (*Lama glama*) and alpaca (*Lama pacos*), both of which are domestic. The vicuña is the most physically distinct of this group. It is the smallest, has continually growing incisors, and has never been domesticated. The lamoids other than vicuña form a highly variable group of animals. The guanaco is wild, and may be close to the wild ancestor of both domestic forms.

The two domestic animals have quite distinct though overlapping roles. The llama, the larger of the two, is basically a beast of burden, a task now increasingly shared by donkeys and motor vehicles. Llama wool is used for coarse fabrics, while the long fine fiber of the alpaca is of great value and may in fact prove to be this animal's salvation, as alpaca wool becomes an increasingly important commercial product. Both animals impart prestige and wealth to their owners, as well as providing meat and other byproducts such as hides, dung (used for fuel), and bone (a raw material for tools). The domestic camelids also produce bezoar stones which are reputed to have medicinal uses, and which also were important in Incan religious ceremonies.

Several breeds of the two domestic forms were developed. Breeds of the llama are consistently larger than those of the alpaca. At least two breeds of llama with vague characteristics can be distinguished — a large burden-bearing llama and the smaller common type. Two types of alpaca are distinguished by the characteristics of their wool — the Suri with long straight hair and the Huacaya with shorter curly hair. Crosses between llamas and alpacas are frequent and distinctive enough to be named: "huarizo" when the male parent is a llama and "misti" when the male is an alpaca. Hybridization between these two animals obviously adds to the problems in distinguishing between their fragmentary remains. I have used the size difference between the llamas and alpacas in attempting to trace the biological history of these two animals back to their wild ancestral form (Wing 1972). Other characteristics can be used to distinguish between these lamoids (Herre 1952), but these are rarely found on the very fragmentary remains excavated from the archaeological sites studied. A number of measurements have been taken on all major skeletal elements (Wing 1972); examples of these, the greatest width of the astragalus and greatest height of the calcaneum, are presented in Tables 5 and 6. Although these are the largest samples available at this time, they are still too small for as thorough an analysis as would be desirable. They do, however, illustrate certain size-related characteristics. One of the most obvious characteristics is the very high coefficient of variation for each of the total adult samples. These variations are in fact so high, ranging from 8.08 to 20.78, that the samples could not be considered single uniform interbreeding populations. When they are divided into small and large forms, according to the decision rules based on the results of a multivariate analysis of measurements of modern comparative skeletons (Wing 1972), this coefficient of variability is greatly reduced. All the samples from sites from 3000 B.P. to Inca times include both large and small lamoids. This increase in variability, as in the case of the guinea pigs, is an indication of selection which was undoubtedly controlled by man. I think we may assume that both large and small forms from the Formative Period and the periods that followed are primarily domestic, although the large forms may include guanaco and the small ones may not be alpaca as we now know them.

The earliest indications of domestic lamoids in valley sites is from the Chihua Period (6550–5100 B.P.) at Pikimachay Cave in the Ayacucho Valley, where we find a moderately great dependence on camelids. The few skeletal elements that are complete enough to measure include both large and small adult individuals. These two features, variable size and relative abundance, suggest a domesticated state, although larger samples from this time period must be studied to verify this.

Table 5. Measurements of the lamoid astragalus, greatest width (a), following 25.1 decision rule for distinguishing between large and small-sized groups

		Number	Range	Mean$\pm$SE[a]	Standard deviation	Coefficient of variation
Callejón de Huaylas						
PAn 12–58		4	21.0–32.5	26.65$\pm$2.36	4.71	17.67
	large	3	26.1–32.5	28.53$\pm$2.00	3.46	12.14
	small	1	21.0	21.0	–	–
PAn 3		9	22.5–31.0	27.31$\pm$1.17	3.51	12.85
	large	6	27.0–31.0	29.50$\pm$0.64	1.56	5.29
	small	3	22.5–23.3	22.93$\pm$0.23	0.40	1.74
Kotosh Huánuco						
Higueras		9	21.0–28.0	25.01$\pm$0.67	2.02	8.08
	large	5	25.2–28.0	26.32$\pm$0.49	1.09	4.14
	small	4	21.0–25.0	23.38$\pm$0.85	1.70	7.27
Sajarapatac		12	21.0–29.0	24.90$\pm$0.76	2.64	10.60
	large	6	25.3–29.0	27.18$\pm$0.53	1.30	4.78
	small	6	21.0–24.0	22.62$\pm$0.42	1.04	4.60
Chavín	large	6	27.3–30.8	28.43$\pm$0.58	1.41	4.96
Kotosh	large	1	30.0	30.0	–	–
Mito	large	1	27.3	27.3	–	–
Junín						
Tarma		12	20.1–31.0	25.38$\pm$0.996	3.45	13.59
	large	5	28.0–31.0	28.84$\pm$0.57	1.28	4.44
	small	7	20.1–25.0	22.91$\pm$0.72	1.92	8.38
Pachamachay						
	adult	24	19.8–31.4	24.29$\pm$0.08	0.38	15.52
	large	8	29.2–31.4	30.10$\pm$0.08	0.22	7.28
	small	17	19.8–24.0	22.16$\pm$0.03	0.14	6.23
Ayacucho						
Wari		32	22.1–31.5	26.99$\pm$0.76	4.30	15.93
	large	18	26.0–31.5	28.45$\pm$0.44	1.86	6.54
	small	13	22.1–24.8	23.61$\pm$0.25	0.91	3.85
Ac117	large	1	28.4	28.4	–	–
Cuzco						
Marcavalle		15	24.1–31.0	28.33$\pm$0.65	2.53	8.93
	large	13	26.2–31.0	28.92$\pm$0.60	2.15	7.43
	small	2	24.1–24.9	24.5	–	–
Minaspata		11	21.1–32.7	25.95$\pm$1.07	3.55	13.67
	large	6	25.2–32.7	28.27$\pm$1.26	3.10	10.96
	small	5	21.1–24.5	23.18$\pm$0.61	1.36	5.85
Pikicallepata		11	23.6–33.6	29.02$\pm$1.09	3.61	12.44
	large	8	27.1–33.6	30.74$\pm$0.87	2.47	8.04
	small	3	23.6–24.9	24.43$\pm$0.42	0.72	2.95
Qaluyu		6	23.5–31.6	27.03$\pm$1.53	3.74	13.84
	large	3	27.5–31.6	30.17$\pm$1.33	2.31	7.66
	small	3	23.5–24.2	23.90$\pm$0.21	0.36	1.51

[a] Mean$\pm$standard error.

Table 6. Measurements of the calcaneum, greatest height (a), following 37.6 decision rule

		Number	Range	Mean±SE[a]	Standard deviation	Coefficient of variation
Callejón de Huaylas						
8–126	large	2	42.2–43.3	42.75±0.55	–	–
PAn3		8	22.6–39.5	32.24±2.37	6.70	20.78
	large	3	38.5–39.5	39.00±0.29	0.50	1.28
	small	5	22.6–35.0	28.18±2.18	4.87	17.26
PAn 12–58		2	32.3–42.0	37.15±4.85	–	–
	large	1	42.0	42.0	–	–
	small	1	32.3	32.3	–	–
Chavín de Huántar						
PIRC		21	32.0–40.0	36.64±0.48	2.18	5.60
	large	8	37.1–40.0	38.75±0.35	0.99	2.55
	small	13	32.0–37.2	35.35±0.44	1.60	4.53
Kotosh Huánuco			32.0–43.0	37.78±0.65	3.09	8.19
Higueras		4	32.9–44.5	36.90±2.70	5.40	14.63
	large	1	44.5	44.5	–	–
	small	3	32.9–37.0	34.37±1.32	2.29	6.66
Sajarapatac	large	7	40.2–44.0	41.69±0.66	1.73	4.15
Waira-jirca	large	1	38.3	38.3	–	–
Mito	large	3	41.0–45.6	43.57±1.35	2.35	5.39
Junín		23				
Tarma						
	large	12	38.2–43.0	40.10±0.49	1.68	4.19
	small	11	32.0–38.0	35.25±0.63	2.10	5.96
Pachamachay						
	adult	12	32.5–44.9	35.15±01.12	3.90	11.09
	large	2	41.5–44.9	43.20±1.70	2.40	0.56
	small	10	32.5–35.2	33.55±0.27	0.86	2.56
Ayacucho						
Wari		5	33.1–40.3	36.86±1.46	3.27	8.87
	large	3	38.0–40.3	39.17±0.66	1.15	2.94
	small	2	33.1–33.7	33.40±0.30	–	–
Ac 100 (VIII)						
	small	1	35.7	35.7	–	–
Cuzco						
Marcavalle		19	29.2–47.4	40.83±1.02	4.45	10.90
	large	15	38.2–47.4	42.71±0.57	2.22	5.20
	small	4	29.2–36.9	33.75±1.68	3.56	10.55
Minaspata PC$_2$ 12–9						
	large	1	44.2	44.2	–	–
Pikicallepata		5	30.9–46.0	40.68±2.57	5.74	14.11
	large	4	41.5–46.0	43.13±1.01	2.02	4.68
	small	1	30.9	30.9	–	–

[a] Mean±standard error

If we are correct in the belief that a guanaco-like animal was the ancestor of llamas and alpacas, the earliest stage in domestication that could be detected on the basis of purely meristic data would be not before reduction in size to the size range of the alpaca. The distinction between guanaco and llama is extremely difficult to make. This may be explained in part by continual interbreeding between domestic and wild animals that occurred at least until Inca times. Early chronicles describe

... a hunt in the valley in 1534 by Manco Inca in honor of Pizarro, 11,000 heads of guanaco, vicuña, deer, and other animals were taken... some shorn of their fleece and released, some killed for the celebration, and some taken to tame and add to the domestic herds (Browman n.d.).

To pinpoint the earliest stages in domestication we may have to rely on patterns of use reflected in the faunal remains. An example of this is seen in the camelid remains from Pachamachay Cave, where a third to one half of the camelids are juveniles. The ages of these juveniles can be narrowed down to eighteen months, the age at which the first molar starts to erupt. This piece of information points to a precise butchering schedule in May through July, during the highland dry season. This time would be a good one to make charqui, the sun-dried meat.

Faunal samples from the early periods in valley sites do not include many camelids. Those for which we have measurements (from the earliest cultural periods at Kotosh, for example) are from large animals and are not highly variable. The sites located in the puna (4,000 meters or over) have far greater quantities of camelid remains, and these sites therefore hold the secrets of the initial stages of domestication.

The fauna of Lauricocha Cave is associated with cultural phases that span the period of camelid domestication (Cardich 1958, 1960). Lauricocha I, which dates from about 10,000 to 8000 B.P., contains a predominance of deer. Lauricocha II (8000 to 5000 B.P.) includes a few deer and smaller animals, but mainly has a predominance of camelids, both domestic and wild. Measurements of the camelid remains are not available for comparison with our data. Other early sites at high elevation in the Junín and Ayacucho areas are now being studied by Kent Flannery. Preliminary study of these faunas indicates that they too are composed largely of deer and camelids. Results of these studies will undoubtedly help to fill the gaps in our knowledge of the early stages of camelid domestication

A technique being developed by Isabella Drew (Drew, Perkins, and Daly 1971) for determination of domestication in animals by examination of thin sections of bone under polarized light, has been applied to camelid remains excavated in northern Chile (Pollard n.d.). By this technique, ten of eleven camelid specimens from the Vega Alta II Period (about 2500 to 2200 B.P.) were classified as domestic.

The northern and southern limits of the early domestication of llamas have not as yet been worked out. Both llamas and alpacas are distributed south of Peru, particularly in Bolivia, with the center of their ranges in the area of Lake Titicaca. At this time, however, we have no data on faunal samples from archaeological sites south of Lake Titicaca other than the site reported by Pollard. To the north, no camelid remains are found in the early faunal sample from Sigsig, Ecuador. Later sites in southern Ecuador may include introduced llamas.

Other data relating to the center of camelid domestication are the predominance of the small form in the northern part of Peru south to Tarma, and the predominance of the large form in the southern part of Peru north to Ayacucho. This suggests the earlier development of a small breed in the more northerly region of the Peruvian Andes, although again, more samples are needed to verify this.

INTERACTION BETWEEN MAN AND HIS DOMESTICATES

Man benefits in many ways from the domestication of animals. In exchange for rudimentary care, domestic animals provide a source of both goods (such as meat, bone, dung, and wool) and services (as, for example, companionship, protection, and transportation). With these goods and services available throughout the year, life is less precarious, and ultimately less energy needs to be expended for basic subsistence activities, thereby providing an energy surplus. The dynamics of this interaction between man and his animal resources may be summarized in an energy-flow diagram of the kind used by systems ecologists (Odum 1971). By this technique I have summarized in Figures 1 and 2 what appears to be the basic interaction between man and the domestic species. At this stage, the energy contributed by each domesticate and by wild plant and animal sources to human subsistence cannot be quantified. The energy-flow diagram does place man and his various environmental resources in a framework and points clearly to the types of data needed to clarify further these interrelationships. Although not directly equivalent to energy contribution, a measure of relative importance may be demonstrated by the percentage of each species in the faunal assemblages associated with each cultural period (see Table 1). By comparisons of the relative abundance of the domesticates and wild game in the faunal assemblages studied, three distinct patterns of use of animals are apparent. These differences in usage of animal resources correlate closely with the time period of the site and the life zone in which it is located.

Sites at high elevation, those over 4000 meters, are all hunting-and-herding camps (Figure 1b). Faunas excavated from sites located in the

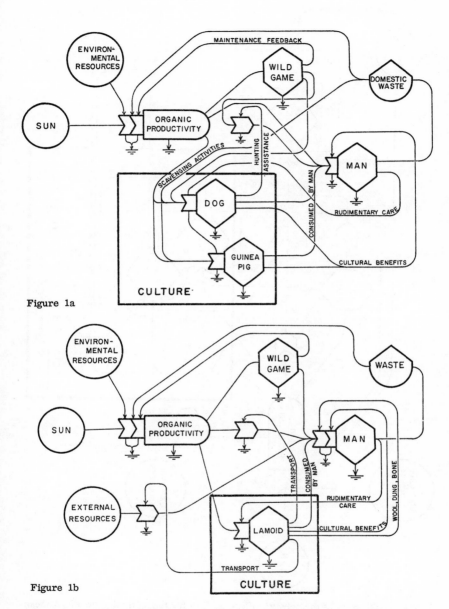

Figure 1. (a) Diagram of the energy flow for the cultural system in Andean valleys between 8000 and 5000 B.P.; (b) diagram of the energy flow for the cultural system at high altitudes (the puna) between 8000 and 5000 B.P. (Symbols are those used by Odun 1971)

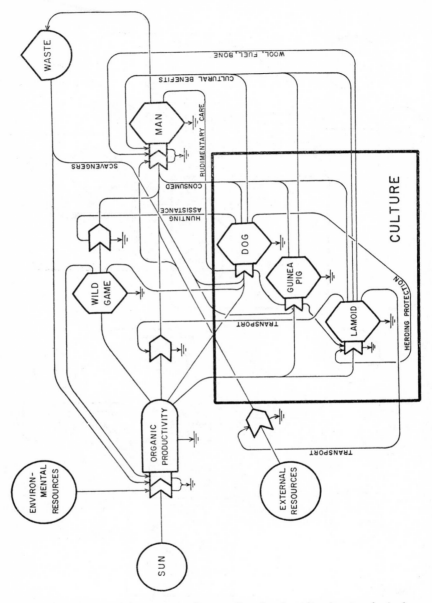

Figure 2.   Diagram of the network of energy flow for the cultural system in Andean valleys between about 3000 B.P. and A.D. 1500.

puna life zone (over 4,000 meters) consist almost entirely of remains of deer and camelids. The faunal assemblage reported by Cardich from the

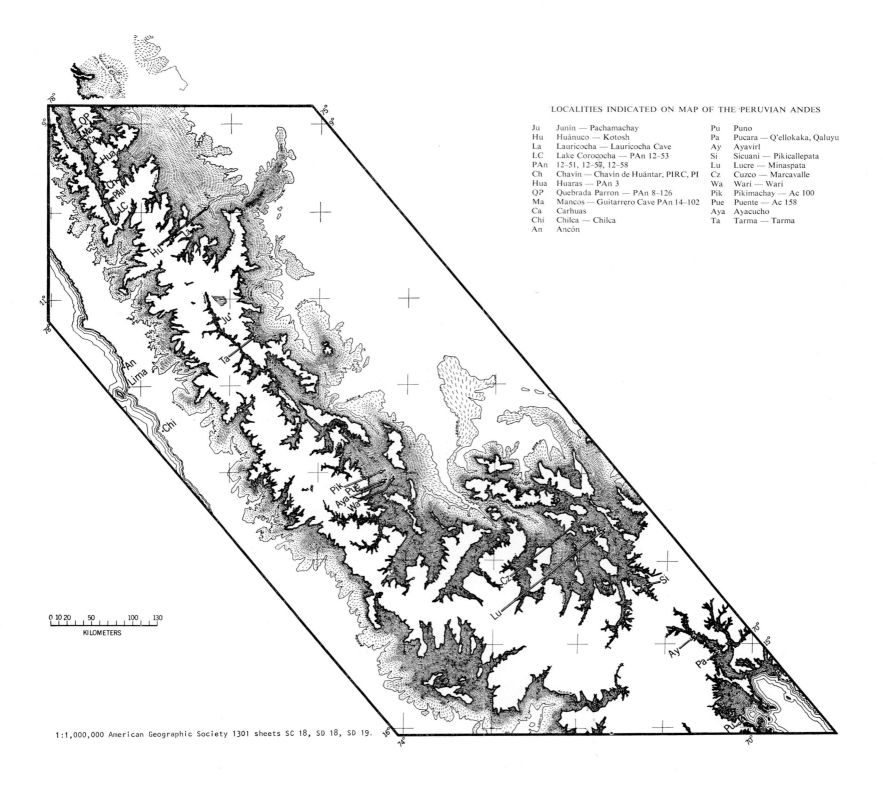

LOCALITIES INDICATED ON MAP OF THE PERUVIAN ANDES

Ju	Junín — Pachamachay	Pu	Puno
Hu	Huánuco — Kotosh	Pa	Pucara — Q'ellokaka, Qaluyu
La	Lauricocha — Lauricocha Cave	Ay	Ayavirl
LC	Lake Corococha — PAn 12–53	Si	Sicuani — Pikicallepata
PAn	12–51, 12–57, 12–58	Lu	Lucre — Minaspata
Ch	Chavín — Chavin de Huántar, PIRC, PI	Cz	Cuzco — Marcavalle
Hua	Huaras — PAn 3	Wa	Wari — Wari
QP	Quebrada Parron — PAn 8–126	Pik	Pikimachay — Ac 100
Ma	Mancos — Guitarrero Cave PAn 14–102	Pue	Puente — Ac 158
Ca	Carhuas	Aya	Ayacucho
Chi	Chilca — Chilca	Ta	Tarma — Tarma
An	Ancón		

0 10 20   50   100   130

KILOMETERS

1:1,000,000 American Geographic Society 1301 sheets SC 18, SD 18, SD 19.

Lauricocha caves reflects dependence on these two groups — deer and camelids. The faunal samples reported here from these high elevations are associated with the Inca site of Tarma and with three Formative sites, one in Junín and two near Lake Conococha in the upper Callejón de Huaylas Valley. In each of these four samples camelids predominate, constituting between 64 and 88 percent of the total faunal assemblage. The camelids are of various ages and adult sizes, indicating that they are principally domesticated.

Today, as in the past, the domestic social animals, both llamas and alpacas, provide numerous and varied benefits in exchange for their care. Man provides rudimentary care, primarily protection from predators, by corralling the animals at night and turning them out to graze in natural unfenced pasturage by day. The llamas, a component of the culture, provide a great variety of goods and services. They provide energy directly in the form of meat, reduce the expenditure of heat energy by providing wool and fuel, and also reduce expenditure of energy by transportation of goods. The transportation of goods in and out of the local environment obviously provides cultural benefits. The exchange of products with both the Amazonian lowlands and the coast, facilitated by the beast of burden, has and has had far-reaching consequences for broad interaction between different cultural groups. Other cultural benefits derived from herds are wealth and prestige to the owners, all of which add to the human sense of well-being.

During the earliest stage in taming these animals, as also earlier, while they were only hunted, they probably provided only meat and other byproducts such as skins, wool, and dung. Documentation of these stages in the history of animal use must come from faunal material excavated from early high-elevation sites such as those being studied by Kent Flannery.

During pre-Formative times, the use of animals in the highland valleys was quite different from that just described. From about 9000 B.P. until about 6000 B.P. guinea pigs were extremely abundant in the faunal assemblages. A few camelids were also present, as may be seen in the faunal summary for the first four periods at Puente and the first period at Pikimachay. We have no osteological evidence that either the guinea pigs or the camelids were domestic at this time period. The tremendous abundance of guinea pigs, however, does suggest that they were selectively caught, and this may have been possible if they were attracted to sites of human occupation by food debris and warmth. Guinea pigs scavenge human waste and are in turn consumed. When fully domesticated (Figure 1a), they also bestow a variety of cultural benefits such as protection and companionship. Guinea pigs have been used for divination, medicinal purposes, and sacrifice.

During the time period from 6000 B.P. to 3000 B.P., the process of domestication progressed to the point where control of the domesticates' genetics is reflected in their skeletons. This period is also one during which a relative abundance of these social mammals typical of high altitude becomes evident in valley sites (Figure 2). The increase in camelids is accompanied by a decrease in the number of guinea pigs. At high elevations a transformation from hunting camps to herding camps must have gradually taken place. This change would appear to reflect a shift from a predominance of wild game to a predominance of domestic herd animals, as evident from the relative abundance of each.

Much evidence is accumulating for a long history of transhumance in the Andes (Lynch 1971, n.d.; Browman n.d.). Specialized sets of tools for diverse activities and resource utilization at different elevations have been associated with preceramic sites. The differences in the associated faunal assemblages also point to periodic use of the resources of both valley and puna. When herding became established, the herds (animals perhaps initially used as beasts of burden) were introduced in larger numbers into the subsistence economy of the valleys.

The fullest development of herding at high elevation and valley-use of dogs and guinea pigs with introduced lamoids starts during the Formative Period, about 3000 B.P. and continues until the time of conquest in A.D. 1500. The diagram for energy flow (Figure 1b) for the high-elevation economy during this most recent period may be exemplified by faunas from such sites as Tarma, where lamoids constitute 70 percent of the fauna, and Pachamachay, where they constitute 82 percent of the fauna. At the same time, in the valleys at sites such as Wari, virtually the entire fauna (95 percent) is composed of domestic animals, with 66 percent lamoid, 24 percent guinea pig, and 5 percent dog.

SUMMARY AND CONCLUSIONS

1.   Dogs are represented in small numbers at most sites. They appear to include both a small and a large type of dog. They were introduced into the southern continent during early preceramic times, and since their introduction several distinctive breeds have been developed.

2.   Guinea pigs are present in great numbers, associated with early cultural materials from valley sites. This abundance suggests that they were attracted to the site of occupation or perhaps tamed and kept in

enclosures ready for use. The earliest osteological evidence of domestication, increased size, is seen in Formative times.

3. The South American camelids are adapted to life at high elevations in the Andes. It was in this life zone that they were first hunted and then tamed and domesticated. Great variability in size is our first and most dependable indication of domestication. Domestic camelids have been reported as early as 5000 B.P. from Lauricocha by Cardich. We also have evidence of domestic camelids from this period in the Ayacucho Valley, but we must look to faunal material from sites at high elevations for the earliest indications of camelid domestication.

4. Three stages can be recognized in the use of animals in the Andes. Between 9000 and 6000 B.P. there appears to have been a great dependence on guinea pigs (which may have been tamed) in valley sites, whereas in the puna sites subsistence was based on hunting deer and camelids. During the period 6000 to 3000 B.P. both guinea pigs and camelids were undergoing domestication. Valley sites indicate an increased use of camelids and continued use of guinea pigs and dogs. Sites at high elevations were probably undergoing transition from hunting to herding camps, although further study of these changes is needed to document the transition. From 3000 B.P. to the time of conquest there is an increased use of domestic animals as opposed to the hunting of wild game. Sites at high elevations were primarily herding camps. Valley sites show a diverse use of camelids, guinea pigs, and dogs.

REFERENCES

ALLEN, GLOVER M.
    1920   Dogs of the American aborigines. *Bulletin of the Museum of Comparative Zoology* 63: 431–517.
BROWMAN, DAVID L.
    n.d.   "Prehistoric pastoral nomadism of the Jauja-Huancayo Basin (central Peru)." Paper presented in 1972 at the Annual Meeting, Society of American Archaeology, Bal Harbour, Florida.
CABRERA, ÁNGEL
    1957–1961   Catálogo de los mamíferos de la América del Sur. *Revista del Museo Argentino de Ciencias Naturales "Bernardino Rivadaria" Ciencias Zoológicas* 4 (1, 2).
CARDICH, AUGUSTO
    1958   Los yacimientos de Lauricocha, nuevas interpretaciónes de la prehistoria peruana. *Studia Praehistorica* 1: 1–65.
    1960   "Investigaciònes prehistóricas en los Andes peruanos," in *Antiguo Perú: trabajos presentados a la semana de arqueología peruana*, 89–118.

CARDOZO, ARMANDO
1954   *Los arquenidos*. La Paz: Editorial Centenario.
DREW, ISABELLA, D. PERKINS, JR., P. DALY
1971   Prehistoric domestication of animals: effects on bone structure. *Science* 171:280–282.
FERNÁNDEZ BACA, SAUL
1971   *La alpaca, reproducción y crianza*. Centro de Investigación, Instituto Veterinario de Investigaciónes Tropicales y de Altura, Boletín 7.
FLANNERY, KENT V.
1972   "Herding communities." Paper presented at the Ayacucho-Huanta project meeting R. S. Peabody Foundation, Andover, Massachusetts.
FRANKLIN, WILLIAM L.
1973   High, wild world of the vicuña. *National Geographic* 143:77–91.
GADE, DANIEL W.
1967   The guinea pig in Andean folk culture. *The Geographical Review* 57: 213–224.
1969   The llama, alpaca and vicuña: fact vs. fiction. *Journal of Geography* 68:339–343.
GHEERBRANDT, ALAIN, *editor*
1961   *The Incas. The royal commentaries of the Incas* by Garcilaso de la Vega. Translated by Maria Jolas from the critical, annotated French edition. New York: Avon Library Books.
GILMORE, RAYMOND M.
1950   "Fauna and ethnozoology of South America," in *Handbook of South American Indians*, volume six, 345–464. Bureau of American Ethnology Bulletin 143.
HERRE, WOLF
1952   Studien über die wilden und domestizierten Tylopoden Südamerikas. *Zoologischer Garten* 19 (2–4):20–98.
HERSHKOVITZ, PHILLIP
1969   The evolution of mammals on southern continents VI. The recent mammals of the Neotropical Region: a zoogeographic and ecologic review. *Quarterly Review of Biology* 44:1–70.
HÜCHINGHAUS, FOLKHART
1961a   Zur Nomenklatur und Abstammung des Hausmeerschweinchens. *Zeitschrift für Säugetierkunde* 26(2): 65–128.
1961b   Vergleichende Untersuchungen über die Formenmannigfaltigkeit der Unterfamilie Caviidae Murray 1886. *Zeitschrift für Wissenschaftliche Zoologie* 166:1–98.
KOFORD, C. B.
1957   The vicuña and the puna. *Ecological Monographs* 27:153–219.
LATCHAM, RICARDO E.
1922   Los animales domésticos de la América pre-columbiana. *Publicaciónes del Museo de Etnología y Antropología* 3(1):1–199.
LYNCH, THOMAS F.
1967   *The nature of the central Andean preceramic*. Occasional papers of the Idaho State University Museum 21.
1971   Preceramic transhumance in the Callejón de Huaylas, Peru. *American Antiquity* 36(2):139–148.

n.d. "Seasonal transhumance and the preceramic occupation of the Callejón de Huaylas, Peru." Unpublished manuscript.

MURRA, JOHN V.
1965 "Herds and herders in the Inca state," in *Man, culture and animals: the role of animals in human ecological adjustment.* Edited by Anthony Leeds and Andrew P. Vayda, 185–215. Washington D.C.: American Association for the Advancement of Science.

ODUM, HOWARD T.
1971 *Environment, power, and society.* New York: Wiley-Interscience.

PEARSON, OLIVER P.
1951 Mammals in the highlands of southern Peru. *Bulletin of the Museum of Comparative Zoology* 106: 117–174.

POLLARD, GORDON C.
n.d. "Sedentism and desert adaptation in northern Chile." Paper presented in 1972 at the Annual Meeting, Society of American Archaeology, Bal Harbour, Florida.

THOMSON, CHARLOTTE
1971 *Ancient art of the Americas from New England Collections.* Boston: Museum of Fine Arts.

WING, ELIZABETH S.
1972 "Utilization of animal resources in the Peruvian Andes," in *Andes 4: excavations at Kotosh, Peru 1963 and 1966.* Edited by Seiichi Izumi and Kazuo Terada. Tokyo: University of Tokyo Press.

WING, ELIZABETH S., CHARLES A. HOFFMAN, CLAYTON E. RAY
1968 Vertebrate remains from Indian sites on Antigua, West Indies. *Caribbean Journal of Science* 8:123–139.

Native Plant Husbandry
North of Mexico

RICHARD A. YARNELL

Compared to the tropics, temperate North America played a small part in the initial development of cultigens. Maize was the basic crop wherever there was one north of Mexico during the last few hundred years before the arrival of Europeans. The common bean was secondary, and pepo squash was tertiary in dietary importance. Other widespread temperate North American crops included bottle gourd, tobacco, and sunflower. Sieva bean and moschata squash apparently did not reach eastern North America until early in the historic period. Other cultigens of the Southwest which were absent in the East include tepary bean, canavalia bean, mixta squash, cotton, two species of amaranth, and devil's claw. In the East, sumpweed (a marsh elder) apparently achieved the status of a cultigen but never spread west of the prairie area of the Mississippi drainage. *Nicotiana rustica* L. was cultivated in the East and in Mexico.

The evidence at our disposal indicates that only three cultigens were developed north of Mexico. Several other plants were cultivated, but only sunflower (*Helianthus annuus* L.), sumpweed (*Iva annua* L.), and devil's claw (*Proboscidea parviflora* Woot. and Standl.) evolved forms diverging significantly from naturally occurring conspecifics. We have only ethnographic data for devil's claw and sunflower as cultigens in the Southwest and only archaeological data for sumpweed as a cultigen in the East. The evidence of cultivation of the sunflower in eastern North America spans the past 3,000 years. Only sumpweed and sunflower show signs of domestication before the introduction of Mexican cultigens.

My interpretation is that the history of cultigens in the Eastern Woodlands started with the cultivation of a ruderal sunflower introduced by man from the West and a ruderal sumpweed native to the Mississippi drainage north and east to the Wabash Valley, Indiana. Ethnographic accounts report widespread utilization of wild sunflowers by Indians in western North America, but cultivation of sunflowers west of the Missouri Valley has been reported only in a zone through northern New Mexico and Arizona. Archaeology has produced evidence of utilization of wild sunflowers in the West but none for cultivation of them there. In the East, the archaeological, ethnographic, and ethnohistoric evidence appears to be relevant entirely to incipient or developed cultivation of sunflowers (see Table 1). There is no evidence of the utilization of wild sunflowers.

Table 1.   Dimensions of sunflower seeds and achenes (in millimeters)

Collection	Years ago	N	Carbonized seeds		Achenes (reconstructed)	
			Length, range	Mean, length × width	Length, range	Mean, length × width
Recent:						
cultigen		?			6.5–17	
ruderal		?			4.0–7.0	
wild		?			3.0–5.5	
Archaeological:						
Newt Kash Hollow	ca. 2,600	?				"ca. 7" × ?
Higgs	ca. 2,800	24	4.4–7.5	5.9 × 2.2	(5.7–9.8)	(7.6 × 3.1)
Salts Cave, fecal	2,300–2,700?	1,000			5.3–9.8	7.4 × 3.2
Salts Cave, vestibule	2,300–3,000?	45	4.5–7.4	5.7 × 2.3	(5.8–9.6)	(7.4 × 3.2)
Riverton	ca. 3,200	1		5.2 × 2.9		(6.8 × 4.0)

Current evidence indicates that developed cultivation of sunflower and sumpweed began about 3,000 years ago in the southern Midwest (Kentucky and Tennessee to Missouri). There may have been earlier cultivation in the central drainage of the Mississippi, but good collections of plant remains from Late Archaic sites are exceedingly rare.

A major exception is the Koster site in the lower Illinois Valley (Asch, Ford, and Asch 1972). Sunflower is lacking there, but twenty-three carbonized sumpweed seeds were recovered. My reconstruction of these seeds to the original size of achenes[1] yields an estimated mean of 3.0 × 2.1 millimeters. This compares with approximate modern mean dimensions of achenes of 3.0 × 2.2 millimeters (Yarnell 1972). Hence it appears that

[1]   The achene is a single fruit produced by a sunflower. Most people call the fruit a "seed." The true seed, however, is the soft edible piece inside with which one is rewarded when the hard, striped fruit-coat is cracked.

sumpweed was utilized at Koster during the Late Archaic Period and possibly was semicultivated but that domestication had not yet been inaugurated.

Late Archaic sunflower is represented by one carbonized sunflower seed measuring 5.2×2.9 millimeters from the Riverton site in the Wabash Valley, Crawford County, Illinois (Winters and Yarnell n.d.). Comparison of carbonized seeds to uncarbonized achenes from Salts Cave, Kentucky, indicates a mean length difference of 30 percent and a mean width difference of 40 percent. Using these figures, the reconstructed achene size for the Riverton seed would be 6.8×4.0 millimeters. Heiser (1954) has reported a range of achene length of 4.0 to 7.0 millimeters for the modern ruderal *Helianthus annuus* and 6.5 to 17.0 millimeters for the giant cultivated sunflower. This puts the Riverton seed in an intermediate status which can tentatively be considered early cultivated but not domesticated beyond an initial stage.

Recent excavation of the Higgs site (40 Lo 45) in the Tennessee Valley, Loudon County, Tennessee, has produced 110 carbonized sunflower seeds from a hearth associated with a structure of the Terminal Archaic Period. The radiocarbon determination for this feature is $2,850 \pm 85$ years (University of Georgia 517). A radiocarbon date for a pit in the floor of the structure is $2,730 \pm 220$ years (Case Western Reserve University 27). Twenty-four measurable sunflower seeds have a mean size of 5.9×2.2 millimeters and a reconstructed mean achene size of 7.6×3.1 millimeters, which is rather long and narrow (Andrea Brewer, personal communication; McCollough and Faulkner 1973).

The most abundant evidence of early domestication of plants in eastern North America is from Salts Cave, Kentucky. Fragments of achenes of sunflowers and sumpweeds are among the most prominent components observed in human fecal samples from the dry interior of the cave. Five dated feces range in age from 2,240 to 2,660 radiocarbon years (Watson 1969). More than 1,000 achenes and achene fragments of sunflower from the feces were measured. Mean size for the sample is 7.4×3.2 millimeters with a range of 5.3 to 9.8 millimeters $\times 2.2$ to 4.8 millimeters.

Excavation and recovery by flotation in the Salts Cave vestibule produced 218 carbonized sunflower seeds and achenes from the upper eight levels of about twenty levels of stratified deposit. Forty-five seeds with measurable length range from 4.5 to 7.4 millimeters with a mean of 5.7 millimeters. Twelve measurable achenes range from 5.0 to 7.5 millimeters long with a mean of 6.4 millimeters. Mean carbonized seed and achene length from the two highest levels are 5.8 and 6.7 millimeters respectively.

Five dates from the upper deposits of the vestibule range from 2660 to 3490 radiocarbon years (Watson 1974). The area of excavation is located between two slopes which rise above it on either side, so it is possible that the earlier dates are on redeposited materials; however, three of the dates are bracketed at 3,360 to 3,490 radiocarbon years. Hence some of the levels with sunflower and sumpweed could be as old as the Riverton occupation or no older than the Terminal Archaic of eastern Tennessee as manifested at the Higgs site.

Sumpweed is a rather inconspicuous member of the family Compositae (Asteraceae), tribe Heliantheae, subtribe Ambrosiinae, and not obviously similar to the conspicuous sunflowers of the same tribe. Yet, the seeds within the achenes of sumpweed and sunflower are quite similar in form, and both have a high content of oil which flows forth when the seeds begin to burn. Achenes of sumpweed are smaller and have a different shape, and the pericarps are thinner than are those of sunflower.

Two points of difference between sunflower and sumpweed are especially relevant. Sunflower is currently represented by large-seeded cultigen forms whereas sumpweed is not. Except for archaeological seeds and achenes, sumpweed is represented only by forms which grow in damp natural habitats and as weeds in ruderal habitats. Thus the argument in favor of aboriginal cultivation of sumpweed is dependent entirely upon the archaeological evidence (Jackson 1960; Black 1963; Yarnell 1972).

The second point is that sumpweed appears to have achieved the status of a cultigen near the northeastern limits of its natural range of distribution whereas domestication of sunflower in the Eastern Woodlands apparently took place well to the east of the range of its natural distribution. However, both species were cultivated aboriginally within and well to the east of their natural ranges, although the range of cultivated sumpweed was much more restricted than that of sunflower.

Sumpweed occurs naturally in somewhat hydric habitats and damp lowlands from south of Iowa and central Illinois in the Mississippi Valley, westward to the Plains, and south to the Gulf Coast of Mexico. There are occasional records of adventive sumpweed to the north and east of this region in artificially disturbed habitats. The range of archaeological recovery of sumpweed extends from Asheville, North Carolina, and eastern Kentucky westward to Kansas City and the Ozarks. Only the western half of this region overlaps the natural range of modern sumpweed.

Archaeological sumpweed was first reported by Gilmore (1931), who was impressed by the exceptionally large size of achenes from the Ozark bluff dwellers of northwestern Arkansas and southwestern Missouri, and

Table 2. Dimensions of sumpweed achenes: lengths and widths in millimeters (modified from Yarnell 1972)

Collection	N	Mean (mid-range)	Range
Modern			
S. F. Blake	?	(3.0 × 2.2)	2.3–3.8 × 1.8–2.6
Yarnell	60	2.9 × 2.5	2.3–3.8 × 1.7–3.2
Jackson	?		2–4.5 × ?
Ozark Bluff dweller			
S. F. Blake	?	(7.0 × 4.5)	4.8–9.3 × 3.2–5.7
Jackson	?		4.8–13 × 3.2–5.7
R. I. Ford	10	7.0 × 5.2	6–8 × 4.5–6
Mississippian			
Turner-Snodgrass[a]	33	7.3 × 4.5	6.0–8.7 × 3.6–5.3
McCollough[a]	19	7.0 × 4.5	5.5–8.8 × 3.9–5.3
Warren-Wilson[a]	6	5.9 × 4.3	4.7–6.6 × 3.9–4.8
Friend and Foe[a]	6	5.5 × 3.7	4.1–6.2 × 2.6–3.9
Middle Woodland to early Late Woodland			
Stillwell[a]	65	5.8 × 3.9	4.6–7.0 × 2.8–5.3
Apple Creek[a]	19	5.4 × 3.6	4.4–6.2 × 2.9–4.8
Macoupin[a]	193	4.8 × 3.3	2.8–8.5 × 1.7–5.4
Terminal Archaic to Early Woodland			
Newt Kash Hollow	10	5.6 × 4.6	5–6.5 × 3.5–5.5
Collins[a]	19	4.9 × 3.4	3.3–6.5 × 2.3–5.0
Salts Cave feces[b]	879	4.2 × 3.2	2.8–7.4 × 2.2–5.0
Salts Cave[a]	87	3.9 × 2.8	2.6–5.9 × 1.7–3.7
Late Archaic			
Koster[a]	20	3.0 × 2.1	2.4–3.6 × 1.7–2.5

[a] The dimensions are reconstructed from carbonized seeds and achenes.
[b] Means for achenes from individual feces range from 3.8 × 2.9 to 4.8 × 3.5 millimeters.

suggested that cultivation (meaning domestication) was responsible. These achenes, which are up to 13 millimeters long (Jackson 1960), are the largest ever found and presumably are 500 to 1,000 years old. They are rivaled in size only by the carbonized achenes of the Mississippian culture from southeastern Missouri, which had an original length up to about 9 millimeters, twice as long as the maximum reported for achenes of modern sumpweed (see Table 2). In volume, these achenes from southern Missouri and adjacent Arkansas averaged approximately ten times as large as modern achenes and those from the Koster site.

On the basis of data currently available, we can infer that the lengths of achenes of cultivated sumpweed averaged 3 to 4 millimeters during the early stages of domestication, 4 to 5 millimeters during the first millennium B.C., 5 to 6 millimeters during the first millennium A.D., and 6 to 7 millimeters thereafter. Thus it appears that selection (and perhaps polyploidy) resulted in an increase in achene length of about one millimeter per millennium. Presumably, this is an oversimplification of what actually happened.

Ample evidence exists that sumpweed was an important food plant in Kentucky during the first millennium B.C. Many human feces from Salts Cave, Mammoth Cave, and Newt Kash Hollow contain achenes of sumpweed as a major, and sometimes dominant, constituent. In later times, especially after the establishment of maize agriculture, sumpweed seeds may have been used mainly as an oil source. However, there are no fecal analyses reported for the later sites.

Analysis of 100 fecal samples collected from the dry interior of Salts Cave yielded the following estimates of relative quantity: 25 percent chenopod seed, 25 percent sunflower achenes, 14 percent sumpweed achenes, 16 percent hickory nutshell, 5 percent maygrass seeds (*Phalaris caroliniana* Walt.), 3 percent squash and gourd seeds, 2 percent other grain seeds, and 10 percent other materials (Yarnell 1974). Meticulous quantification of component weights was carried out by Robert B. Stewart on desiccated human feces from Mammoth Cave and Salts Cave (Watson 1974). His analyses yielded results which are similar to those of the earlier study. However, he found the proportion of maygrass and cheno-pod seeds to be somewhat greater and that of sunflower and sumpweed to be correspondingly lower in abundance. The seeds in the feces show some evidence of roasting or parching but no evidence of grinding or other preparation before eating. This is consistent with the surprising amount of "roughage" in the feces including sunflower and sumpweed hulls, small bones, fish scales, and large quantities of hickory nutshell.

Further confirmation of this premaize, prepottery pattern of subsistence comes from the quantified results of analysis of carbonized plant remains recovered by flotation from the vestibule of Salts Cave (Yarnell 1974). In addition to other excavations, one square meter was excavated for the express purpose of collecting plant remains. Thus far, materials from the uppermost ten levels containing midden deposits have been analyzed. Remains of squash and gourds were not recovered below the two highest levels, but sumpweed and sunflower and most of the other fecal components were recovered throughout the upper eight levels. Chenopod seeds were especially abundant, numbering nearly 20,000 in less than one cubic meter of earth fill and reaching a concentration of 179 seeds per gram of total remains of plant food in the highest level. Sumpweed, sunflower, and ruderal grain seeds all increase dramatically in number per gram of remains of plant food through the upper four levels of the midden. This indication of increased intensity of clearing and cultivation is reflected in the results of pollen analysis (Watson 1974).

The human feces from Newt Kash Hollow, Kentucky, are from a pre-maize, prepottery occupation dated about 2,600 radiocarbon years B.P. (Crane 1956). Sumpweed, maygrass, sunflower, hickory nut, and cheno-pod are the major components (Jones 1936). Carbonized sumpweed seeds have been recovered from the Collins site in Monroe County, Missouri, with an age of about 2,600 years (W. E. Klippel, personal communication). This extends the range of this early gardening complex to eastern Missouri. We can reasonably expect further extensions when more good collections of plant remains are recovered from sites in the central Mississippi drainage with an age of 2,500 to 3,500 years.

In Kentucky, at least, the cultivation of sunflower and sumpweed apparently preceded the introduction of squash and gourd, which in turn preceded the introduction of pottery and maize. Currently, the best estimate of the time of the introduction of cucurbits is around 2600 B.P. The dietary importance of the complex of chenopod-sunflower-sump-weed-maygrass had been increasing for several hundred years prior to that time, perhaps facilitating the introduction of cucurbits. Maize appears to have been introduced about 500 years later, preceding bean by as much as 1,000 years (see Table 3). This pattern of piecemeal introduction of cultigens is also characteristic for the American Southwest.

Table 3. Approximate archaeological chronology for central-eastern North America

Period	Years before present	Dates (B.C., A.D.)
Historic (no sumpweed)	400–0	A.D. 1550–1950
Mississippian (bean)	1100–300	A.D. 850–1650
Late Woodland	1500–300	A.D. 450–1650
Middle Woodland (maize)	2300–1400	350 B.C.–A.D. 550
Early Woodland (squash, gourd)	2700–2200	750–250 B.C.
Terminal Archaic (sunflower, sumpweed)	3000–2500	1050–550 B.C.
Late Archaic	5000–2500	3050–550 B.C.

The oldest secure evidence for each cultigen is early in the period to which it is assigned.

The earliest acceptable radiocarbon date for remains of cultigens from Bat Cave, New Mexico, is 2,862 years (Mangelsdorf, et al. 1967). This indicates that maize has been cultivated in the American Southwest for perhaps 3,000 years. There is a radiocarbon date of 4,840 years for a level of the Lo Daiska site near Denver, Colorado, in which maize was found

(Crane and Griffin 1962). However, maize probably was not present so far north at that time. In any case, there are no other sites in the American Southwest for which evidence of plant cultivation is reported to be as early as it is in the East. Noteworthy is the suggestion by Whitaker and Cutler (1965) that cucurbits were introduced into the Southwest at a date about 400 years later than our proposed time of introduction of cucurbits into the East. The possibility arises that plant husbandry in the East began as early as it did in the Southwest. The difference is that it began in the Southwest as a result of introduction from Mexico, whereas in the East the initiation of plant cultivation appears to have been an indigenous development. This independence lasted only during an initial period of development to a level of garden cultivation which, however, contributed substantially to subsistence, at least in central Kentucky.

The long standing question of the status of *Chenopodium* in the early eastern gardening complex is still unanswered. Chenopod seeds, and probably also greens, appear to have been the most important food of the American Indians who utilized Salts and Mammoth Caves. Abundant archaeological evidence exists for its importance throughout the central part of the Eastern Woodlands between 1,000 and 3,000 years ago. Large numbers of seeds have been recovered from Russell Cave, Alabama (Miller 1960), the Higgs site, Tennessee (Andrea Brewer, personal communication), the Cowan Creek Adena mound, Ohio (Goslin 1957), Ash Cave, Ohio (Andrews 1877), Snyders Hopewell site, Illinois (Struever 1962), the Apple Creek and Newbridge sites, Illinois (Struever, personal communication), and the Scovill site, Illinois (Munson, et al. 1971). Smaller numbers of chenopod seeds have been recovered from many other sites.

Currently there are no reports of large quantities of chenopod seed from sites with Mississippian culture. Perhaps the dramatic increase in production of maize eclipsed chenopod as a food source or the plant was utilized mainly at an immature stage for greens in the diet.

Many ethnographic references to chenopod exist. Taken together, they indicate widespread utilization of members of this genus as food. In addition, some problematical ethnohistoric evidence exists of cultivation of chenopod in eastern North America. Gilmore (1931) pointed out that "Species of *Chenopodium* were cultivated for food in South America, Central America and Mexico in pre-Columbian times, and still are at the present time." He called attention to the statement of Du Pratz regarding "the use and partial cultivation by the Natchez of a plant which he called '*belle-dame-sauvage*', [wild *belle-dame*]" and explained that *belle-dame* is the French name for European *Chenopodium*. Du Pratz indicated that the seeds were planted and that a large amount of grain was harvested in autumn (Gilmore 1931: 98). Du Pratz also referred to *choupichil* as a cultivated grain plant and called it a kind of millet which was hulled like wild rice (Gilmore 1931: 87). Since he apparently was referring to a grass, this would not be a *Chenopodium* but could be *Phalaris*.

W. C. Sturtevant (1965) has analyzed an early description by an eyewitness, Thomas Hariot, referring to the cultivation along coastal Carolina by the Algonkians of *melden* along with corn, beans, cucurbits, and sunflower. Both seeds and greens of *melden* were used as food. Sturtevant has suggested that this plant was either amaranth or chenopod. Hariot's comparison was to spinach and beets (Dutch *melden*) and to orage (orach, *Atriplex*) which are members of the family Chenopodiaceae. Orage does not particularly resemble amaranth in appearance but is similar to some species of *Chenopodium*.

One of the biggest problems we face in trying to determine the aboriginal relationship between man and chenopod in eastern North America is the lack of reliable identifications of archaeological seeds to species. This situation exists partly because of the close similarity of seeds of different species and partly because of incorrect identification of modern specimens. Almost all of the American archaeological seeds stated to belong to *Chenopodium album* probably are incorrectly identified. Identifications of *C. gigantospermum* Aellen (*C. hybridum* var. *gigantospermum* Rouleau) may be correct, but seed size seems to be the main criterion that was used. Most of the seeds of chenopod from Salts Cave are too large to be from any modern native species except *C. gigantospermum*, but this identification has not yet been confirmed by a qualified authority. Smaller chenopod seeds from many sites could be any of several species. Hence, we are speculating about the cultivation of a ruderal plant of uncertain or unknown identity and are left to consider the nature of the disturbed habitats which produced large quantities of chenopod 1,000 to 3,000 years ago. I suggest that the habitats were created by human activities which caused removal of vegetation and disturbance of soil, and that the activities were those required for preparation and maintenance of garden plots.

Devil's claw (*Proboscidea parviflora* Woot. and Standl.) is the only plant for which there is good evidence of native domestication in the American Southwest. The immature pods and mature seeds are edible, but the predominant use is for the decoration of baskets by the Pima and Papago. Black strips of epidermis peeled from mature pods are used for making the designs.

Castetter and Bell (1942) found that there is a cultivated form of devil's claw which differs from the wild-growing form in having longer pods and white seeds. Although the white-seeded variety was not found growing in the wild, it was often found as a volunteer in cultivated fields. Only the white-seeded devil's claw was planted by the Pima and Papago because the length, color, and texture of the pod epidermis were more appropriate for their use in basketry design than the pod of the wild form.

Castetter and Bell referred only to characteristics of the fruit and seeds of the cultivated devil's claw, but this should be enough to establish its status as a cultigen. Informants stated that devil's claw had been cultivated for a very long time, but Castetter and Bell suggested that cultivation is recent and that only wild plants were utilized aboriginally. Their suggestion seems unwarranted because the native assertion is supported by the distinct characteristics of the cultivated form: white versus black seeds (as in *Amaranthus*), longer pods, finer-grained pod epidermis, and deeper black pod epidermis. No way is known to estimate the amount of time required for artificial selection to develop these characteristics under native conditions, but several centuries is not an unreasonable estimate. Possibly early cultivation was undertaken because of the food value of the pods and seeds plus the drought-resistant qualities of devil's claw, and more recent cultivation may have been motivated by desire for basketry materials, as suggested by Castetter and Bell.

Various native plants, which are more clearly ruderal than cultigen in nature, were cultivated to a greater or lesser extent. In the West they include two or three species of tobacco, ground cherry (*Physalis* spp.), a wild potato (*Solanum jamesii* Torr.), and Rocky Mountain bee weed (*Cleome serrulata* Pursh.). All but *Cleome* are in the nightshade family (Solanaceae). Plants of this category in the East include two species of tobacco, Jerusalem artichoke (*Helianthus tuberosus* L.), apricot vine (*Passiflora incarnata* L.), and perhaps maygrass and others, including chenopod.

Besides the tobaccos, the plant most commonly referred to as cultivated is Jerusalem artichoke. However, there is no good evidence that it was ever domesticated or extensively cultivated aboriginally. It is a perennial and has all the characteristics of a ruderal species. One of its most useful qualities is that its tubers can be left in the soil until needed (Boswell 1959). Heiser, et al. (1969) have suggested that Jerusalem artichoke was spread by man prehistorically and that it is better adapted to the northern two-thirds of the United States than to the southern third. It was used mainly by Indians of the northern part of the eastern agricultural region (Yanovsky 1936). Its reputation as a cultivated plant seems to rest primarily on the Indian practice of utilizing the tubers of plants which appeared as volunteers in their fields.

In the Southeast there was a similar situation with regard to apricot vine. In this case there are archaeological records of the seeds, so there is evidence of some antiquity for a close relationship with man. This relationship is indicated by the strong association of apricot vine with habitats severely disturbed by man as well as by the ethnographic record. E. L. Sturtevant has related that this plant "has been cultivated by the Indians from early times. This is the *maracock* observed by Strachey on the James River...." (Hedrick 1919: 410). Swanton (1946) included it in his list of plants cultivated by the Chickasaw, the Creek, and Indians in Virginia.

The tobaccos are something of a special case. *Nicotiana rustica* was the only plant cultivated in Mexico and in the East for which we have no evidence of prehistoric cultivation in the Southwest. The area of its cultivation in the East extended from Florida and east Texas to southern Canada. *N. guadrivalvus* was cultivated by the Pawnee of Kansas and Nebraska, and northward to the Upper Missouri Valley, while *N. multivalvus* was cultivated by the Crow of Montana. Both of the latter species are closely related to *N. bigelovii*, which was cultivated by various groups in California and Oregon (Driver 1961).

Although *N. rustica* and *N. trigonophylla* were cultivated in the Southwest historically, the reliable archaeological records refer only to *N. attenuata*. Fewkes (1912) recovered a dish of this tobacco from one of the ruins at Casa Grande in southern Arizona. Cosgrove (1947) has reported this species from caves in the area of the Upper Gila, Arizona, and Cutler (1952) included it in his list of plants from Tularosa Cave, New Mexico. Jones and Morris (1960) reported *N. attenuata* from Basketmaker III cave occupations in northeastern Arizona; tree-ring dating indicates an age of about 1,300 years. Jones' identification of well-preserved tobacco from a pottery vessel was verified by T. H. Goodspeed. A large number of tobacco seeds were found inside a whole pottery vessel recovered from beneath the floor of a room of the Cedro Canyon site in Tijeras Canyon, east of Albuquerque, New Mexico. The estimated age is about 650 years. The species, as determined by Jones and Yarnell, is *N. attenuata*.

None of these records demonstrates that tobacco was cultivated pre-historically in the Southwest. However, as Wells (1959) has pointed out, *N. attenuata* occurs primarily in ruderal sites and is not well adjusted physiologically to the arid environments of the West. Furthermore, Wells has suggested that the tending of tobaccos by man has influenced their distribution in the West. Jones and Morris (1960) suggested, therefore, that *N. attenuata* was introduced from the South and dispersed by man. Not only does it not seem to be native, it does not even seem to be very well naturalized.

Although there is a cultigen form of *Amaranthus cruentus* L., this species is self-propagated in the Hopi irrigated gardens where it is cultivated. *Cleome serrulata* and *Solanum jamesii*, the latter a native ruderal potato, are self-propagating, cultivated, and harvested in Hopi cornfields (Whiting 1939). The Zuni cultivate ground cherries *(Physalis)*. They are not planted, but they are encouraged whenever they appear in the gardens (Bohrer 1960). These plants are ruderals which are cultivated but not propagated in the Southwest.

Some antiquity for this practice of "semicultivation" may be indicated by the striking association of these plants with Pueblo ruins in some localities (Yarnell 1965). This association is especially true of *Cleome*, the Rocky Mountain bee weed, which appears to have been the most important plant of the Pueblos after corn, beans, and squash. It was an important food plant which was collected in large quantities and made into hard cakes which could be stored for a long time. It was also the source of a black paint used on pottery over a wide area. Remains of *Cleome* were recovered from household debris at Pueblo Bonito in Chaco Canyon, New Mexico (Judd 1954). The seeds have rarely been reported from archaeological sites, but they are now being recovered in New Mexico and Arizona by the use of flotation (Vorsila Bohrer, personal communication).

Pollen analysis of midden deposits has contributed somewhat more impressive evidence of the prehistoric association of *Cleome* with man in the Southwest. Hill and Hevly (1968) found pollen of *Zea*, *Opuntia*, and *Cleome* each more abundant than the pollen of any other genus of economic plant at Broken K Pueblo in Arizona. Martin and Sharrock (1964) reported that *Cleome* is better represented by pollen than any other genus in some midden samples from Mesa Verde, southwestern Colorado, despite the fact that it is insect-pollinated. They also found pollen of *Cleome* to be abundant in human fecal samples from Glen Canyon, Utah, and compared it to corn, beans, and squash in dietary importance. Martin and Byers (1965) even suggested that it was cultivated at Mesa Verde. In view of these accounts, the suggestion of Kearney and Peebles (1951) that this plant gives the appearance of being introduced in Arizona is of interest.

In some respects, *Cleome serrulata* is the equivalent in the American

Southwest of *Chenopodium* in the East. Cultigen status cannot be attributed to either one, but both were of outstanding importance to agricultural peoples as food plants. Both seem to qualify as cultivated plants, but neither of them is known to have been intentionally propagated. Each, in its own region, was probably the most important of a number of plants which were locally cultivated but never truly domesticated and as such, they may be good examples of plants in an early stage of the special ecological relationship to man which is the subject of this inquiry.

REFERENCES

ANDREWS, E. B.
  1877   On exploration of Ash Cave in Benton Township, Hocking County, Ohio. *Peabody Museum of American Archaeology and Ethnology, Annual Report* 10:48–50.

ASCH, NANCY B., RICHARD I. FORD, DAVID L. ASCH
  1972   *Paleoethnobotany of the Koster site: the Archaic horizons.* Illinois State Museum, Reports of Investigations 24.

BLACK, MEREDITH
  1963   The distribution and archaeological significance of the marsh elder *Iva annua* L. *Papers of the Michigan Academy of Science, Arts and Letters* 48:541–547.

BOHRER, VORSILA L.
  1960   Zuni agriculture. *El Palacio* 67:181–202.

BOSWELL, VICTOR R.
  1959   *Growing the Jerusalem artichoke.* United States Department of Agriculture, Leaflet 116.

CASTETTER, E. F., W. H. BELL
  1942   *Pima and Papago Indian agriculture.* Albuquerque: University of New Mexico Press.

COSGROVE, C. B.
  1947   Caves of the upper Gila and Hueco areas in New Mexico and Texas. *Papers of the Peabody Museum of American Archaeology and Ethnology* 24(2).

CRANE, H. R.
  1956   University of Michigan radiocarbon dates, I. *Science* 124:664–672.

CRANE, H. R, JAMES B. GRIFFIN
  1962   University of Michigan radiocarbon dates, VII. *Radiocarbon* 4:183–203.

CUTLER, HUGH C.
  1952   A preliminary survey of plant remains of Tularosa Cave. *Fieldiana: Anthropology* 40: 461–479.

DRIVER, HAROLD E.
  1961   *Indians of North America.* Chicago: University of Chicago Press.

FEWKES, J. WALTER
  1912   Casa Grande, Arizona. *Smithsonian Institution, Bureau of American Ethnology, Annual Report* 28:25–179.

GILMORE, MELVIN R.
  1931   Vegetal remains of the Ozark bluff dweller culture, *Papers of the Michigan Academy of Science, Arts and Letters* 14:83–102.

GOSLIN, ROBERT M.
  1957   "Food of the Adena people," in *The Adena people*, volume two. Edited by W. S. Webb and R. S. Baby, 41–46. Columbus: The Ohio Historical Society.

HEDRICK, U. P., *editor*
  1919   *Sturtevant's notes on edible plants.* State of New York, Department of Agriculture, Annual Report 27(2).

HEISER, CHARLES, B., JR.
  1954   Variation and subspeciation in the common sunflower, *Helianthus annuus. American Midland Naturalist* 51:287–305.

HEISER, CHARLES B., DALE M. SMITH, SARAH B. CLEVENGER, WILLIAM C. MARTIN, JR.
  1969   *The North American sunflowers* (Helianthus). Memoirs of the Torrey Botanical Club 22(3).

HILL, JAMES N., RICHARD H. HEVLY
  1968   Pollen at Broken K Pueblo: some new interpretations. *American Antiquity* 33:200–210.

JACKSON, RAYMOND C.
  1960   A revision of the genus *Iva* L. *University of Kansas Science Bulletin* 41:793–876.

JONES, VOLNEY H.
  1936   "The vegetal remains of Newt Kash Hollow shelter," in *Rock shelters of Menifee County, Kentucky.* Edited by W. S. Webb and W. D. Funkhouser, 147–167. University of Kentucky Reports in Archaeology and Anthropology 3.

JONES, VOLNEY H., ELIZABETH ANN MORRIS
  1960   A seventh-century record of tobacco utilization in Arizona. *El Palacio* 67:115–117.

JUDD, NEIL M.
  1954   *The material culture of Pueblo Bonito.* Smithsonian Institution, Miscellaneous Collections 24.

KEARNEY, THOMAS H., ROBERT H. PEEBLES
  1951   *Arizona flora.* Berkeley and Los Angeles: University of California Press.

MANGELSDORF, PAUL C., HERBERT W. DICK., JULIÁN CÁMERA-HERNÁNDEZ
  1967   *Bat Cave revisited.* Harvard University, Botanical Museum Leaflets 22:1–31.

MARTIN, PAUL S., WILLIAM BYERS
  1965   "Pollen and archaeology at Wetherill Mesa," in *Contributions of the Wetherill Mesa archaeological project.* Assembled by D. Osborne, 122–135. Society for American Archaeology Memoirs 19.

MARTIN, PAUL S., FLOYD W. SHARROCK
  1964   Pollen analysis of prehistoric human feces: a new approach to ethnobotany. *American Antiquity* 30:168–180.

MC COLLOUGH. C. R., CHARLES H. FAULKNER
1973   *Excavation of the Higgs and Doughty Sites, I-75 Salvage Archaeology.*
Tennessee Archaeological Society, Miscellaneous Papers 12.

MILLER, CARL F.
1960   The use of *Chenopodium* seeds as a source of food by the early peoples
in Russell Cave, Alabama. *Southern Indian Studies* 12:31–32.

MUNSON, PATRICK J., PAUL W. PARMALEE, RICHARD A. YARNELL
1971   Subsistence ecology of Scovill, a Terminal Middle Woodland village.
American Antiquity 36:410–431.

STRUEVER, STUART
1962   Implications of vegetal remains from an Illinois Hopewell site.
American Antiquity 27:584–587.

STURTEVANT, WILLIAM C.
1965   Historic Carolina Algonkian cultivation of *Chenopodium* or *Amaranthus. Southeastern Archaeological Conference, Bulletin* 3:64–65.

SWANTON, JOHN R.
1946   *Indians of the southeastern United States.* Smithsonian Institution.
Bureau of American Ethnology, Bulletin 137.

WATSON, PATTY JO
1969   *The prehistory of Salts Cave, Kentucky.* Illinois State Museum, Reports
of Investigations 16.

WATSON, PATTY JO, *editor*
1974   *Archaeology of the Mammoth Cave area.* New York: Academic Press.

WELLS, PHILLIP V.
1959   An ecological investigation of two desert tobaccos. *Ecology* 40:626–
644.

WHITAKER, THOMAS W., HUGH C. CUTLER
1965   Cucurbits and cultures in the Americas. *Economic Botany* 19:344–349.

WHITING, ALFRED, F.
1939   *Ethnobotany of the Hopi.* Museum of Northern Arizona Bulletin 15.

WINTERS, HOWARD D., RICHARD A. YARNELL
n.d.   "Evidence of plants and their utilization at the Riverton site, Illinois."
Unpublished manuscript.

YANOVSKY, E.
1936   *Food plants of North American Indians.* United States Department of
Agriculture, Miscellaneous Publications 237.

YARNELL, RICHARD A.
1965   Implications of distinctive flora on Pueblo ruins. *American Anthropologist* 67:662–674.
1972   *Iva annua* var. *macrocarpa:* extinct American cultigen? *American
Anthropologist* 74:335–341.
1974   "Plant food and cultivation of the Salts Caverns," in *Archaeology of
the Mammoth Cave area.* Edited by P. J. Watson, 113–122. New York:
Academic Press.

SECTION FIVE

Conclusions

Origins of Agriculture:
Discussion and Some Conclusions

CHARLES A. REED

One major similarity between the civilizations of this world is that all depend directly or indirectly upon cereal grains — wheat, rice, maize, barley, oats, millets, sorghums, rye, and others less important — as food for their growing populations. This dependence is primary; without the seeds from these cultivated grasses, civilization as we know it seemingly would not have happened, in spite of all the root crops and other available vegetables. More fundamental, however, than the simple fact that several cereal grasses, independently in different areas at different times, were taken in hand by man and tended and cultivated is the essential fact that almost every plant in the normal state in nature had a seed head which at ripening developed a brittle rachis (central axis of the seed head), so that the head fell apart and the seeds scattered on the ground. However, the genotype was also capable, by changes in only a few genes (Harlan, de Wet, and Price 1973), of mutating to a form which did not allow the completion of the normal abscission layer across the rachis (see Beadle, this volume; Galinat 1974). This abscission layer normally becomes a plane of weakness across the node, but if the responsible gene or genes are not functioning the process is blocked, the plane of weakness does not develop at the time of ripening, and the internodes, each with its seed or seeds, do not separate.

The genetic character for a tough (nonshattering) rachis, so useful to man, is a pathological characteristic in the wild and is thus selected against. As long as humans only gather grain, they accentuate the selection against the gene causing the pathology, since a seed head with all of its seeds ripe and together, waving in the breeze, is a particular prize for the gatherer, who removes the pathological genes from the natural area of growth and eats them. That this pattern of unconscious selection does happen has been demonstrated in the gathering of wild teosinte (Galinat 1974: 33).

However, once man began planting, this unconscious selection, which results in the survival and thus the picking of nonshattering heads, provided a selective factor *for* the survival of what, in nature, were pathological genes; several other characteristics, similar in genetic principle to nonshattering, also occur in wild populations of grasses and other plants and have contributed to their success as domesticates (see Harlan, de Wet, and Price 1973 for elaborative detail). Flannery (1968) aptly termed this process one of positive feedback, in contrast to that of negative feedback when the seeds were merely gathered. Thus genes which were pathological and certainly semilethal in the wild not only allowed but channeled cereal agriculture into paths of "improvement" (from the human viewpoint), leading to the diversification of each kind of grain, to the spread of its cultivation beyond the normal range of the wild ancestor, and thus to the increase of its yield. On the crest of this golden flood of cereals, man has built his civilizations and increased his populations, has made the earth and the sunlight yield energy in excess of that needed by farmers so that others can write or paint or sculpt or hunt or build corporations and sell the stocks thereof, and has also produced the energy necessary to send men to the moon and photographic probes to Jupiter, and — via the technology of astronomy — to extend our sensitivities, our perceptions, to the edges of the universe.

We need a moment to pause and ponder: these pathological mutations were selected by man from the genomes of many grasses and utilized for his benefit, not theirs; are these mutations the same genetic aberrations, occurring successively over millions of years in the same genes by the same errors of replication of the same molecules of DNA in each of the phylogenetic lineages within the Gramineae since the ancestor of that family evolved in the Eocene? If so, and I suggest an affirmative answer to the question, this is a wonder of genetic diversity, that allows a multitude of metabolic disorders, each pathological, to appear constantly in all populations, only to be continuously eradicated — until a chance change of environment provides a niche in which the once pathological type can become successful. By his cultural patterns and experimentation — the experiments of multiple plantings — man provided those new environments many times for many kinds of plants, so that the once pathological genes were artificially selected and, often, then combined one by one with each other into single gene pools.

We can say, thus, that many species of grasses were preadapted to survive extremely successfully under those changed environmental conditions typical of primitive cultivation. We can easily detect this same principle of preadaptation in the behavior and physiology of several kinds of social mammals, particularly the Bovidae (cattle and their kin), as I have explained in greater detail elsewhere (Reed 1969).

The ruminating artiodactyls, of which the Bovidae are one of several families, have the ability to utilize cellulose — indirectly, true, through the symbiotic relationship of cellulose-producing bacteria living in the ruminant's stomach, but utilize it they do. The bacteria also produce most of the vitamins necessary for the animal's survival. By way of the circulatory system, bovids can also recycle urea from the urinary bladder back to the stomach, reutilizing nitrogen which most mammals excrete. Thus the members of the cattle family are preadapted to survive on woody foods low in nitrogen, the kind of diet the first domestic animals may often have been fed by early villagers. Additionally, most bovids are social animals, and all domestic ones were derived from such social groups.

The social Bovidae, thus, were preadapted by factors of physiology and behavior for survival in the changed environment of early villages. Dogs (domesticated from wolves) and pigs, although lacking the ruminant's four-chambered stomach, were likewise preadapted for domestication by their sociability and their omnivorous feeding behavior. In general, I believe that most of the animals domesticated early in the history of animal agriculture could have been as easily domesticated by the Late Miocene, if a human population capable of domesticating them had existed then, but dogs may well be an exception. Dogs are not really agricultural domesticates, of course, having been present during the latest Paleolithic in some areas as early as, or possibly earlier than, 12,000 B.P. (Turnbull and Reed 1974: 100–106), but the behavior of the pack perhaps did not evolve in wolves and other social canids until about five million years ago (Radinsky 1976). Without this preadaptation for sociability, domestic dogs would probably never have been.

We can thus assert with considerable expectation of truthfulness (even if not with actual knowledge) that by the Late Miocene at least, several kinds of animal and plant had acquired the genetic and behavioral characteristics which would have allowed them to become domesticated at that time if a proper hand directed by a proper brain had been present to do so. However, that hand as directed by that brain, and the two of them together conditioned by a particular, but unknown, level of culture, seemingly did not exist together in the proper combination until the end of the Pleistocene. These factors will be explored sometimes together, sometimes piece by piece, in this last chapter. No final answers will necessarily be forthcoming thereby; there are problems aplenty awaiting work and solution by those of you who have not been a part of the fun before.

CORRELATION BETWEEN ENVIRONMENTAL CHANGE AND THE ORIGIN OF AGRICULTURE

Several individuals, both in this volume and elsewhere, have written that environmental change, particularly that of the type occurring during or immediately following the end of a glacial period, could not be correlated with the origins of agriculture, since although such events (as many as 20 stadials? [Emiliani 1968]) have occurred during human history, no agriculture was associated with any of these prior end-of-stadial periods. In other words, the correlation between agricultural origins and the termination of such stadials was considered very low. Let us look at the evidence from another viewpoint:

  1.   No population prior to that of anatomically modern man (usually called *Homo sapiens sapiens*) is known to have had agriculture.

  2.   Anatomically modern man has existed for about 40,000 years (or possibly for 90,000 years in southern Africa [Beaumont and Vogel 1972; Protsch 1975]).

  3.   The last worldwide major glacial period began somewhat less than 40,000 years ago and had its maximum between 20,000 B.P. and 17,000 B.P.; definite increase in temperature was evident by 14,000 B.P., and by 11,000 B.P. the glaciers had melted back so far that we mark that date as the end of the Pleistocene[1] and the beginning of the Recent.

  4.   Anatomically modern man was present over the Eastern Hemisphere for some 30,000 years before the end of the Pleistocene but is not known to have had agriculture, even though many parts of the world were quite warm enough.

  5.   Agriculture began in several parts of the world during or immediately following that period of environmental change that was still continuing in the early Recent.

Conclusions:

[1]   My apologies to those geologists who believe, with considerable logic, that the Pleistocene has not yet ended, but continues with us yet (Flint 1971).

1.   The correlation between (a) the presence of anatomically modern man; (b) the end of the last glacial stadial; and (c) the beginnings of agriculture following relatively quickly during the period of end-of-stadial environmental change equals 1.0.

2.   The correlation between (a) the lack of agriculture during the first 30,000 years of the existence of anatomically modern man (except possibly in southern Africa) and (b) the lack of any period of end-of-glacial environmental change during that same time of 30,000 years also equals 1.0.

Correlations do not prove cause and effect, but I agree with Wright (this volume) that these particular correlations of 100 percent deserve full and careful consideration. Obviously, the factors listed above were not the only ones involved in agricultural origins (as I will discuss later), or agriculture would have emerged worldwide, but as Carter (this volume) has written, agriculture did pop up, like an epidemic of measles, in several parts of the world within a relatively short time.

Further conclusions which emerge (to me, at least) from consideration of the above facts and correlations are as follows:

1.   The hominid populations we call australopithecine, pithecanthropine (*Homo erectus*), and neanderthaloid[2] were seemingly not capable, for whatever cultural and/or intellectual reasons (we will probably never know) of any kind of plant tending or animal keeping which left discernible archaeological traces.

2.   The population we call anatomically modern man is, and probably from the time of its first emergence was, intellectually capable of practicing agriculture but did not do so for the first 30,000+ years of its existence, although the possibilities of Paleolithic and later herding and other types of close and continuing economic relationship between man and potentially domesticable animals prior to the time of known explicit domestication have indeed been suggested (Higgs and Jarman 1969; Jarman 1969, 1971, 1974). Of these suggestions, those for purposeful control by man of herds of red deer, particularly in southern Europe from the Late Paleolithic into the Neolithic (Jarman 1971, 1974) are the most interesting. If true, man was a controlling and conserving factor *re* red deer and perhaps other species of large game,

---

[2]   I am not one of those who downgrade the Neanderthals. They had large brains, cared for their sick and injured, and buried their dead with grave goods, so seemingly had a concept of an afterlife. To accomplish these and the other complexities of their lives within a social group, they must, I believe, have used a spoken language. We have no evidence, however, that they were gardeners or farmers or herders, nor any evidence whether they were or were not intellectually capable of these activities.

possibly for several thousands of years; but we have no direct evidence that such practices resulted in domestication, although the possibility that such control over reindeer in northern Eurasia led to domestication of that species has often been suggested (see Zeuner 1963: 124–128 for a summary).

3.   Some stimulus and/or stress in some populations of anatomically modern man during the first end-of-stadial period of environmental change experienced by that population resulted in the cultural shift from dependence on hunting/gathering to at least a partial dependence on gardening or other kinds of agriculture.

4.   Although direct archaeological evidence is as yet lacking that tropical gardening and/or slash-and-burn agriculture were being practiced prior to the beginning of the Recent, or even during the early Recent, indirect evidence suggests that such cultivation must have been occurring. For instance, domestic common beans, *Phaseolus vulgaris*, have been found in the Andean highlands as early as 7600 ± 280 B.P. (Kaplan, Lynch, and Smith 1973) but the natural habitat of the wild ancestral beans is at a lower altitude on the eastern side of the Andes; cultivation, presumably in a garden, must have proceeded for several hundred years, at least, before the fully domesticated form was achieved and acclimatized to the higher altitude of the Callejón de Huayla, where it was found. The same principle, that of primary but undocumented domestication of a plant at low elevations in the eastern foothills of the Andes with subsequent archaeological recovery in the Andean highlands, is also illustrated by the sweet potato, *Ipomoea batatas*, which has been recovered from an archaeological site in the Chilca Canyon (circa 80 kilometers north of Lima) at an altitude of 3,900 meters and dated by radiocarbon between 10,000 and 8000 B.P. (Yen 1974: 25); by contrast, the natural range of the wild ancestor is in the humid foothills of the eastern side of the Andes at an elevation of approximately 460 meters. This kind of evidence, of a shift of a domesticated plant from the humid tropics to a higher and/or drier environment, where remains of the plant can be recovered, identified, and carbon-dated, furnishes us at present with the best evidence for the antiquity of garden horticulture.

CULTURAL LEVEL AND ORIGINS OF AGRICULTURE: BASES FOR COMPARISONS

The determination of the minimum level of culture necessary for the inauguration of some sort of plant cultivation is a difficult problem, but one which should be analyzed more completely in the future. Interregional levels of culture are difficult to compare, given the difference in archaeological preservation between, for instance, the semixeric environment of the Near East and the humid tropics of either hemisphere. The kind of culture in which plant cultivation in the tropical forest could originate and be nurtured successfully would probably look simple and primitive to the person who, familiar with the Near Eastern Natufian, thinks automatically of that culture as the adaptive plateau (see the section "Near East" later in this article) necessary for any agricultural origin. I myself believe that something like the Natufian was probably a preadaptive necessity for the emergence of cereal agriculture, with its accompaniment of animal domestication, in the Near East, but obviously different standards prevailed elsewhere. Any attempt to rank such preagricultural adaptive plateaux from different parts of the world would be a basic error.

The concept of a particular cultural level being necessary as an adaptive plateau, without which level further cultural evolution involving plant cultivation could not have occurred in the particular pattern, has not been received kindly by some critics. I hope that my present presentation of this theme is clearer than were the previous ones; one has only to remember that in evolution, biological or cultural, one thing happens after another. (Thus airplanes did not get invented early in the Industrial Revolution for numerous reasons, one of which was that steam engines were too heavy; a century and more passed before a gasoline engine with a relatively high ratio of power to weight appeared. Such an engine had to have gasoline, and that meant oil wells; also, a spark had to be produced to ignite the gasoline. The story is a complex one, and so it was with agriculture; one thing could only happen after another.)

The idea of a certain kind and level of cultural complexity being a necessary prerequisite for the emergence of a particular kind of agriculture in a particular environment does not seem as illogical to me as some critics have suggested, and may suggest again, it sounds to them. The idea may have a longer history than I know, but, according to my memory, emerged from general discussions around the dining-tent table in the archaeological field camp at Jarmo in the spring of 1955. In the group we had there (Robert and Linda Braidwood, Hans Helbaek, Bruce Howe, Herbert Wright, Fred Matson, Vivian Broman, Patty Jo Watson, and myself) the origin of the idea is now impossible to allocate. We should, perhaps, have accepted a group responsibility for this concept of the importance of a particular complexity of cultural level necessarily preceding the appearance of agriculture; actually, of course, I had always thought the idea originally mine, but so might be the memory of each of the others. It was Robert Braidwood, however, who publicized the concept in several articles in the early 1960's, and it was he who bore the brunt of the criticism (Binford 1968); I thought the criticism unfair at that time, since by then we knew that our earlier ideas of relatively minor end-of-Pleistocene environmental change (Reed and Braidwood 1960) were quite erroneous, as shown by the emerging evidence of the palynological data (evidence summarized by H. Wright in this volume). The change in intellectual view necessitated by the accumulation of evidence on end-of-glacial environmental change had already shifted the emphasis away from that presented by Braidwood's earlier writings which Binford was criticizing.

I hope my present discussions of adaptive plateaux (see Figure 2 later in this article) will not be subject to misunderstanding. I hope, too, that my remarks, once I have explained that I believe that ongoing cultural evolution was influenced by prior events, will not be considered either orthogenetic or vitalistic; to the best of my knowledge no writing of mine has ever been so interpreted before, nor should it be now. For instance, to say that horses evolved a foot with one functional digit is a statement of fact; any subsequent attempt to analyze the complex relationships between successive gene pools, mutations, successive environments (including predators and competitors), and selection that occurred over tens of millions of years is — even if not utterly successful at every point in the story — a rational scientific exercise. However, the same sort of attempt involving man and cultural evolution may be liable to misinterpretation.

In the following sections of this chapter, I attempt to outline the cultural evolution leading to agriculture in each of several areas. However, for most of those areas I do not see the picture clearly enough to do an adequate job. I am confused by what I see in Mesoamerica: Lathrap (this volume) has presented a definite evolutionary pattern for South America, taking into consideration the evidence presently available, but I myself am not prepared to decide on the merits of Lathrap's proposals versus those of others. For southeastern Asia I have been forced to take an adverse view of many of the interpretations offered previously. Of northern China I can say little, since little evidence is available to me of previllage life. India, on the basis of present evidence, seems not to have been a region of innovation in the origin of agriculture. I am, thus, left with the Near East as offering the clearest picture of a history of continuing cultural change culminating in the cultivation of plants and the domestication of animals.

Since the Near East does emerge at present as having the clearest picture, we must guard against considering it a model against which to measure all other areas which were, or may have been, independent areas of agricultural origins. However, I believe firmly that each such area should be studied from the viewpoint of the sequence of environmental and cultural changes that preceded the initiation of agriculture in that region. What were the primary cultural adaptations, which the secondary, which the tertiary, etc.? What were the successive adaptive plateaux?

POPULATION AS A FACTOR IN THE ORIGINS OF AGRICULTURE

Students of human populations have generally, I believe, followed the Malthusian doctrine that the population of an area is limited by the amount of food which can be produced from that area, given the boundaries of the environment and the particular level of technology of the people. In this case, changes in technology, if and when they occur, constitute the independent variable; and the size, density, and rate of change of population, if any, is the dependent variable. Additionally, the potential rate of increase of the population is typically greater than the potential rate of increase of food production, so that there must automatically be a high death rate.

Darwin, as is well known, borrowed from Malthus the latter's formulations of populational growth and limitations thereof, plus the concept of selection in human populations, and applied these to the whole of the biological realm, past and present. To the biologist, "changes in technology" are evolutionary adaptations, but to the economist or anthropologist, "changes in technology" mean either improvements in simple physical technology (tools[3]), or changes in social systems, or increases in the efficiency of agricultural or commercial practices. In any case, following such an advance in technology, with the physical environment remaining constant, population supposedly would rise to the new limits allowed by the new level of the food supply, at which time the death rate would increase and the population would stabilize at the new level.

[3] Cultivated plants or domestic animals would in this sense be not only secondary energy traps but tools as well.

The agricultural economics and populations of prehistoric and/or wholly nonliterate peoples were not an important concern to Malthus, nor would he have had data on slash-and-burn agriculture or garden horticulture if he had been interested; but the general assumptions have been that the same principles would apply to such peoples as those formulated by consideration of the populations of Western Europe.

The alternative concept is that growth of a human agricultural population creates stresses in a society, which activate efforts ("challenge and response") to increase the food supply either by new inventions of a technological nature (improved or new tools) or by more efficient behavior and/or social organization. This model could apply only to those relatively few animals, including humans, which have a social organization and sufficient intelligence to transmit innovative patterns of behavior from one generation to another by imitative learning and/or purposeful teaching. Growth of population, thus, would be the primary factor and innovative behavior or new technology the dependent variable. A recent study of baboons in the Rift Valley of Kenya by Harding and Strum (1976) seems to illustrate that some primates other than *Homo* are capable, under conditions of austerity but with an increasing population, of increasing their food supply through innovative activity, predatory in this case, by individuals and groups of both sexes. For most animals, however, such culturally transmitted behavioral innovations are not possible.

I cannot believe that determinations of cause and effect in studies of growth of populations must invariably be answered in terms of Malthusian doctrine or its alternative, even though for most of biological evolution the Malthusian doctrine has undoubtedly been valid. However, with the addition of culture as a biological variable, escape — if only temporarily for a few millions of years — became a possibility for the hominids and some of their more intelligent kin. In the long run, Malthusian limitations on growth of population seem to be inevitable, if only because of lack of space and the constraints of the second law of thermodynamics (entropy and all that!).

With regard to agriculture, Malthusian concepts were challenged a decade ago by Boserup (1965), who saw the pressure of growing populations activating farmers to develop new techniques for increasing agricultural productivity, even if such techniques were no more than briefer and briefer fallowing of cultivated plots until finally intensive annual cultivation occurred, with resulting increased annual production but also correlated increase in the ratio between input of energy and output of food per unit area, i.e. with continued increase of input of energy (direct labor or otherwise) into a field, the production of food rises but the potential energy of the extra food produced does not increase in proportion to the extra energy required for the production of that food. Boserup did not, herself, apply her model to the problem of agricultural origins, and the question of such applicability remains. Mark Cohen, in a book in press written since our conference at Woodstock in 1973, believes indeed that growth of population has been the major factor in the independent initiation of agriculture in the several areas where he sees such beginnings (Cohen i.p.).

Boserup's book, although written by an economist, was in such general terms that it has generated some interest among anthropologists concerned with relations between size of population, growth of population, different types of agriculture, and correlated changes in agricultural practices over time. This interest has resulted in a book edited by Spooner (1972) and a series of articles in *Current Anthropology* (1972). Of the various articles in these two sources, almost all are concerned with populations already agricultural, and thus later than the time of our concern for the origins of agriculture. In Spooner's book, only the two papers by Lee (1972a, 1972b) and some remarks in the introduction to Durand's article deal with preagricultural peoples, and of the series in *Current Anthropology* only the one by Sussman is pertinent to the study of preagricultural populations. The material in these various articles has been woven into several chapters in this volume, often without exact bibliographic referencing; several such chapters are either directly or indirectly concerned with the possible role of population increase in agricultural origins, as the reader can discover or has discovered. Additionally, since those chapters were written, Mark Cohen (as mentioned above) has expanded his concepts *re* growth of population as he studied it on the Peruvian coast into a book with worldwide scope, and Cowgill (1975) has published a theoretical essay on the causes and consequences of ancient and modern changes in population.

Data on size or rate of change in preagricultural populations are few at best and usually almost entirely indirect (Cohen 1975); actual figures, as with my own suggestions for the population of Palestine before, during, and following the Natufian, presented in an earlier chapter in this volume, are admittedly guesses. The opinions of the individuals who have written about the relationship, if any, between agricultural origins and size and/or rate of increase of population differ widely, this disparity of concept being displayed at its widest within our own conference by Bronson, who is opposed to the idea of a necessary relationship, and Cohen, who believes that population pressure was the most important factor in initiating agricultural origins.

I have, in the line of duty for the preparation of this final chapter, read what I regard as the pertinent literature mentioned above, from Boserup on through. No consensus emerges, and, insofar as I can see, no general conclusion is possible at this time: in cultural anthropology this topic of the role of population seems to me to be one which will be discussed much more fully (and probably more heatedly, too) in the future than it has been in the past. From the existing literature I can only copy the words of a famous astronomer who, although writing of a different topic, expressed my thoughts well:

Myself when young did eagerly frequent
Doctor and Saint, and heard great argument
About it and about: but evermore
Came out by the same door where in I went.

OMAR KHAYYAM, *Rubaiyat* (as translated by Edward Fitzgerald)

My own idea is that an increase in population was one of the factors, even if not always at present detectable, preceding the initiation of agriculture. For the Near East, as outlined elsewhere in this book, I have expressed my belief that an increase in population was probably happening, although slowly, through the Kebaran and then proceeding, still slowly but at a somewhat faster rate, during the Natufian, where sedentarism occurred. My colleague James Phillips thinks that the Natufians were not more numerous than the Kebarans but were merely more concentrated into larger groups at fewer sites. I suspect that the present data do not allow the truth to emerge as yet, but I believe that my interpretation will prevail eventually. Whether he is or I am correct is perhaps unimportant; we agree (as does everyone, I believe) on the importance of the settling of Natufians into villages; in this case, the concentration and sedentarism of the populations are the key factors.

The pattern in northern China, although not yet as well authenticated for the preagricultural period, appears to me to resemble that of the Near East in major outline, although the evidence for preagricultural villages and either an increase in population or a condensation of population into these villages is not yet as clear as we expect it will be after further research.

We have no data on preagricultural populations as to size, growth, or local density in southeastern Asia. Gorman (this volume) has suggested that rising sea levels throughout the latter part of the late Pleistocene, continuing into the early Recent, would have forced people living on the Sunda Shelf to move slowly, generation by generation; due to the large size of the Sunda Shelf, this movement of peoples would have considerably increased the population of mainland southeastern Asia, producing a higher density of humans there than typical for the area before or typical of similar areas elsewhere. The resultant stress possibly may have activated people to try to increase their food supply by an increase in fishing, consumption of a wider variety of less-choice foods, and/or the initiation of gardening. Obviously, not all of the people displaced from the Sunda Shelf would have gone to mainland southeastern Asia; many would have increased the populations of Sumatra, Java, and Borneo, and many would have found themselves on low islands which eventually became covered with water. (One hopes that the stress of the increase in population density and final imminence of drowning led them to boatbuilding.)

Essentially, however, we have few facts concerning preagricultural populations in southeastern Asia, and in that near-vacuum of data, speculation would be useless.

In Mesoamerica, evidence for increase in population as a possible factor in the initiation of agriculture is scant; and, additionally, the pattern of preagricultural and early-agricultural cultural evolution is so different from that of the Near East that similarities are difficult to find. Planting and tending, as indicated by the evidence from Tamaulipas (MacNeish 1958, 1964a) and Tehuacán (MacNeish 1964b, 1967; Mangelsdorf, MacNeish, and Willey 1964) began at least as early as, and most probably a millennium earlier than, 7000 B.P., yet remained at such an incipient level that the annual cycle of hunting/gathering (with a correlated low density of population) continued for at least 3,000 years before people began to settle into the simplest of villages. So, at least, runs the story in the Tehuacán Valley, where the record is the best that has been both preserved and studied.

For the Tehuacán Valley, a semiarid area of some 2,400 square kilometers (circa 927 square miles) in southern Puebla and northern Oaxaca, MacNeish has offered two rather similar estimates (1964b, 1970) of size, growth, and density of population over a period of almost 9,000 years (Table 1). When we transform these estimates into a graph (Figure 1), several important factors become clearer:

1. Neither the density nor the pressure of population would seem to have been important in the introduction of agriculture into the Tehuacán Valley or its continuation there; by 7000 B.P. only a few more than a hundred people lived in the valley, and agriculture was

Table 1.   Outline of estimates of populations as correlated with chronological and cultural sequences for the Tehuacán Valley, in the highlands of southern Mexico, between the end of the Pleistocene and 450 B.P. (= 1500 A.D.). Data have been taken from Flannery (1966), Johnson and MacNeish (1972), and MacNeish (1964b,

Phase (= complex)	Time in radiocarbon years B.P.	Estimated mean population for the period stated	Estimated annual rate for population growth (percent)	Number of years to double population
Ajuereado	before 8750	(18) [9]	–	–
El Riego	8750–6950	(72) [54]	(0.09) [0.09]	(900) [850]
Coxcatlan	6950–5350	(180) [155]	(0.07) [0.08]	(1200) [1100]
Abejas a and Purron	5350–4250 4250–3450	(720) [329]	(0.09) [0.08]	(950) [1100]
Ajalpan St. Maria	3450–2750 2750–2100	[1023] (2200) [4029]	[0.10] (0.10) [0.20]	[450] (675) [350]
Palo Blanca	2100–1250	(18,000) [26,646]	– [0.20]	– [350]
Venta Salada	1250–450	(90,000) [87,338]	– [0.10]	– [500]

a   Both Richard MacNeish and Don Lathrap have informed me that the Abejas is the phase least represented and thus the most poorly defined in the above chronological sequence, and indeed a decrease in population may have occurred in the Tehuacán Valley at the time.

relatively unimportant there for the next 2,000 to 2,500 years.

2.   During this period between 7000 B.P. and 4500 B.P., the annual rate of increase of population did not change markedly, staying at or slightly below 0.09 percent.

3.   The total population even as late as 4000 B.P. had not reached 1,000.

4.   Seemingly, no permanent villages were established during a period of 2,500 or possibly even 3,000 years after the introduction of agriculture.

1967, 1970, and 1975), with necessary simplifications by myself to permit presentation as a table. I am indebted to Dr. Peter Klassen of the Department of Sociology, University of Illinois at Chicago Circle, for calculating the figures which appear in columns 4 and 5

	Percent of subsistence from		
Comments	Meat (mostly wild)	Wild plants	Cultivated plants
Annual cycle of hunting/gathering; communal drives of antelopes and jack-rabbits	–	–	–
Annual cycle of hunting/gathering; solitary hunting of deer; ?incipient agriculture? (?avocado and squash?)	54*	41*	55*
Annual cycle of hunting/gathering; but also beginning agriculture: chili pepper, avocado, squash, beans, sapote, primitive maize, ?amaranth?	34*	52*	14*
Full-time agriculture; semipermanent villages after 4000 B.P.	30* 31*	49* 34*	21* 35*
Temples in ceremonial centers with affiliated villages and seasonal camps; possibly some irrigation; addition of cotton, runner beans, and ?manioc?	29* 32	31* 23	40* 45
Full-time agriculture with irrigation; sacred cities or ceremonial centers with affiliated villages and camps	18	17	65
Full-time agriculture with commerce important; secular cities or towns with affiliated ceremonial centers, villages, and camps	17	8	75

Key: *   Estimates by MacNeish (1967) as based on evidence available; these figures are not definite.
     ( )   Figures in parentheses are based upon data in MacNeish 1964b.
     [ ]   Figures in brackets are based upon data in MacNeish 1970.

5.   A slight increase in rate of growth began as late as 3500 B.P., but the major increase in population in the valley seems to have been dependent upon the increasing development of irrigation and correlated clearing of new agricultural land in the valley's bottom.

The whole pattern of agricultural origins and early agricultural history as shown by the Tehuacán Valley is so totally different from that of the Near East that, aside from the near-equivalence of post-Pleistocene time and a cultural adaptation to a semiarid environment, common factors are difficult to find.. However, we must remember

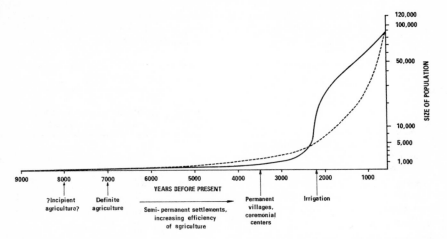

Figure 1. Estimates of growth of population in the Tehuacán Valley, Mexico, between 9000 B.P. and the end of the Aztec Empire. The dashed line represents the first estimates published by MacNeish (1964b); the solid line represents the estimates published by MacNeish in 1970. This graph should be correlated with Table 1

that, while the Tehuacán Valley has given us the best pre-urban archaeological record in Mesoamerica, the valley was seemingly never a major center of agricultural origins; indeed, teosinte has probably never grown in the valley and maize was introduced after an unknown period of incipient domestication and genetic manipulation in a place or places yet unknown.

Cohen (1975, and unpublished data) would argue against the above interpretation anent the low population density from the point of view that population stress varies with both cultural and physical environments and that conditions which may be stressful for one population may not be so for their descendants, who, although more numerous in the same area, have changed culturally to eat different foods, produce more food, or reduce the stress in other ways.

One of the more important cultural innovations related to increase in population growth is sedentarism. Such an automatic relationship may not be obvious to most readers but seemingly is present, unless of course the conditions of the more settled life are so extremely adverse (malnutrition, diseases, genocide, etc., as with a group newly settled by the superior force of a state, modern or ancient) that the population may dwindle toward extinction. However, under less destructive circumstances, a newly sedentary group of former hunters/gatherers will increase in numbers, and the !Kung Bushmen of southern Africa provide a living model (Lee 1972a).

Among the free-living !Kung, the women provide approximately two-thirds of the food by gathering; to accomplish this, each woman (except the very old, who may stay in camp) must, two or three times a week, walk five to twenty kilometers, carrying for a part of that distance seven to fifteen kilos of gathered nuts, berries, roots, and fruits. She must usually also carry any child younger than four years of age; if she has two such children, her life is thereby greater (not to mention increasingly complex). Lee has calculated the various possibilities of distance, weights of food, and numbers and weights of children in terms of kilograms per kilometer, but even without these data the selective value for births well spaced (four years or more) is obvious. Children born while a mother is still toting the previous child may simply be killed at birth and reported as having been born dead, but the more fundamental factor is that generally the women simply do not get pregnant again until about the fourth year after a previous birth. This absence of pregnancy, which is not due to absence of intercourse, has been attributed to the inhibitory effects of continued lactation, which usually lasts into the beginning of the fourth year of a child's life; but in other (and sedentary) societies, continued lactation is not necessarily protection against another pregnancy, as many a young mother has discovered to her surprise (sometimes within two months after delivery).

The physiology of the situation has only recently been elucidated (Kolate 1974; Frisch and McArthur 1974; Frisch 1975), and I will summarize these publications together: during nursing, 1,000 calories per day of a woman's energy are devoted to the production of milk; under the difficult conditions of gathering, as outlined above, the possibility of accumulation of fat by a nursing mother is usually reduced and often impossible. Stored fat is necessary for another pregnancy to occur, because a minimal relation exists between weight and height; below this ratio, menstruation will not be initiated (primary amenorrhea) or will cease if already initiated (secondary amenorrhea). Under conditions of amenorrhea, ovulation does not occur. The age of menarche is younger in females of well-fed populations, and the resumption of menstruation and ovulation after pregnancy but during continued lactation occurs sooner in comparison with poorly nourished lactating females. When the nomadic !Kung become sedentary, as is fast happening, members of both sexes become heavier, fatter, and taller, and the men become more socially dominant over the women. In the females, menarche occurs and the first child is born at a lower age, the period of nursing decreases, and the time between births de·

creases. The birthrate and the population increase, even though the people have afflictions, mainly infectious diseases, mostly unknown to their ancestors.

Near East

Of the various areas of the world considered in some detail by the participants at our conference, the emerging pattern of agricultural beginnings for the Near East seems to me to be clearer than is that for any other area. This viewpoint may be in part explained by my personal association with the area and its problems (I have given them more thought, certainly, over the last two decades than I have many other problems), but — the glow of local pride aside — I still think the picture, partial as it is, is clearer with regard to the beginnings of agriculture there than it is for other parts of the world. The reasons are fairly obvious: good preservation of bone and carbonized remains of plants even in open sites and a longer and more intensive history of participation of natural scientists with archaeological groups and thus a longer history of concentration on geological and biological evidence of past periods.

This section will borrow ideas and associations of ideas from many sources, not only from the contributors of other chapters to this book but also from others with whom I have worked in the field. I will not here try to give due credit to each person from whom I have borrowed, in part because I often cannot remember from whence an idea originally came, in part because I believe there is now at least quasi agreement on the major factors by people who have recently written on agricultural origins in the Near East. At least, having just finished re-reading the accounts of this topic in this volume by H. Wright, Redman, Harlan, and Hassan, and those by G. Wright (1971) and Flannery (1973), I think we agree on the major outline of the pattern. I am, however, particularly indebted to Redman (this volume) for the concept of "threshold level"; this I find to be a happy idea, and I borrow but change it in the borrowing to be part of a larger idea, that, by analogy with biology, of the "adaptive plateau" within the evolutionary pattern of an adaptive radiation.

For those who do not know about an adaptive radiation, I will explain. Starting with a primitive ancestral population, it is an evolutionary pattern of multiple divergent lineages, each becoming better adapted to a particular part of the total environment as time passes. The ancestral population must have had some particular set of characteristics which allowed subsequent evolution to occur in some direction but not in others. Consider, for instance, the ancestral placental mammals of the latter part of the mid-Cretaceous; they not only were small but were a minor folk in that Age of Reptiles. Their basic characteristics were, among others, those of being quadrupedal, pentadactyl, hairy, endothermic, viviparous; they cared for their young and nurtured them with milk, they had evolved placentae, and each probably already had a rudimentary cerebral cortex. From this population have evolved all living mammals as we know them, except the marsupials and egg layers. The important point here is that a population had reached a certain important "adaptive plateau" (Redman's "threshold level"), necessary for subsequent evolution of varied divergent lineages: elephants, primates, whales, rodents, ungulates, carnivores, bats, etc. Each of these lineages in turn had its beginnings from the level of the general adaptive plateau by the addition, acquired by multiple mutation and natural selection, of, usually, one additional basic adaptation, an adaptation which was often (or perhaps always) molded around a developing new behavioral activity: change in feeding, change in locomotion, etc. Each such new lineage then underwent its own, albeit lesser, adaptive radiation. Cultural evolution is analogous but of course more versatile, in that genetic cross-fertilization of adaptations between biological lineages cannot occur, but cross-fertilizations between cultural lineages can. However, during the Pleistocene, such cultural diffusion was undoubtedly slow and probably also rarer than in more recent periods. The concept of an adaptive plateau is the same, the concept of preadaptive possibilities and limitations to future change is similar, and the concept of new behavioral activities leading to the possibility (oft realized) of new adaptations is similar. Selection certainly is present; but in cultural evolution, changes in artifactual assemblages replace changes in genetic complexes; a new kind of artifact is similar to a mutation. (The whole evolutionary concept of adaptive radiation is dynamically Darwinian and should not in any way be misunderstood as being vitalistic, orthogenetic, or teleological.)

Additionally, within a major group of animals (such as mammals), convergent sets of similar adaptations can evolve from different lineages to produce recognizably similar adaptive patterns in relation to particular environments, such as aquatic, fossorial, arboreal, etc. In cultural evolution, we call this "independent invention," and, with regard to the origins of agriculture, Flannery (1972a: 272) has stated clearly his belief in such culturally independent evolutionary origins: "I do not believe that agriculture began the same way, or for the same

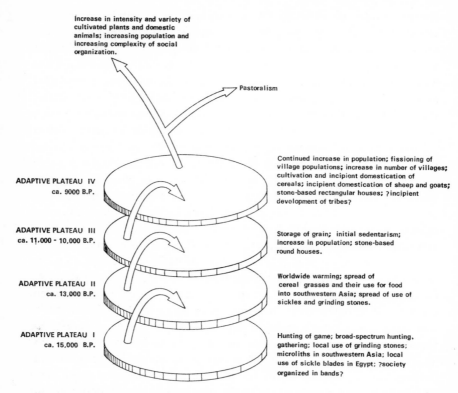

increase in intensity and variety of
cultivated plants and domestic
animals; increasing population and
increasing complexity of social
organization.

Pastoralism

ADAPTIVE PLATEAU IV
ca. 9000 B.P.

Continued increase in population; fissioning of
village populations; increase in number of villages;
cultivation and incipient domestication of
cereals; incipient domestication of sheep and goats;
stone-based rectangular houses; ?incipient
development of tribes?

ADAPTIVE PLATEAU III
ca. 11,000 - 10,000 B.P.

Storage of grain; initial sedentarism;
increase in population; stone-based
round houses.

ADAPTIVE PLATEAU II
ca. 13,000 B.P.

Worldwide warming; spread of
cereal grasses and their use for food
into southwestern Asia; spread of use of
sickles and grinding stones.

ADAPTIVE PLATEAU I
ca. 15,000 B.P.

Hunting of game; broad-spectrum hunting,
gathering; local use of grinding stones;
microliths in southwestern Asia; local
use of sickle blades in Egypt; ?society
organized in bands?

Figure 2.   Pattern of a series of adaptive cultural plateaux in Near Eastern prehistory, leading from hunting/gathering to beginning agriculture. The plateaux are
in part mental constructs, since cultural evolution is actually more continuous than
such a diagram might indicate. However, each level would have a different pattern
of flow of energy, and those successive differences are important in the totality
of the cultural evolution

reasons, in all . . . areas, nor do I believe one model can explain them
all."

In the Near East, for our present purposes, we can establish our
basic adaptive plateau in the late Pleistocene, at some 15,000 B.P. (see
Figure 2). The environmental situation was, at least for much of southwestern Asia, one of the dominance of sagebrush steppe, with probably
(in spite of Wright's opinion to the contrary elsewhere in this volume)
some local forests and grasslands around the southern fringes. The
behavioral complexes of the human groups included an emphasis on
the hunting of large and medium-sized game, but a major activity was
also that of widespread gathering and hunting of a broad spectrum of
plant products and smaller animals, both vertebrate and invertebrate.

Among the plants utilized for food, seemingly more intensively than in previous periods, were nuts and grass seeds (cereals). Of these, the latter eventually became the more important. The artifactual assemblage was richly varied; in southwestern Asia it was based on the blade-tool tradition but with microliths beginning to appear. Grinding stones were present locally. The preadaptive factor in this artifactual assemblage was the presence, at least locally in Egypt, of sickle blades (which are generally presumed to have been mounted to make a sickle).

From this adaptive plateau, this cultural threshold, a change in environment could, and undoubtedly did, shift the dynamic balance between culture and environment, offering in this case new opportunities for a particular cultural lineage to evolve toward a new adaptive plateau. The general worldwide warming was not in itself sufficient to change cultures toward what was eventually to become plant cultivation; only a particular adaptive plateau with particular preadaptive possibilities, joined by particular environmental changes (including certainly the spread of grasslands north into southwestern Asia), could lead to the particular changes that constituted a new adaptive plateau, which in turn formed a new cultural-environmental base from which the next step could evolve. As I try to impress upon my students, in evolution one thing can happen only after another; we do not find the Near Eastern pattern of original adaptive plateau, of particular preadaptive factors, and of particular end-of-Pleistocene environmental changes in the Maghreb, in Spain, in Arabia, or in India, nor do we find the first agricultural activities in the western part of the Eastern Hemisphere emerging in those areas either. Both in biological evolution and in a chain reaction in organic chemistry, one thing can only happen after another; under the conditions of band organization presumably existing worldwide during the Pleistocene (Flannery 1972a: 401), I do not find the pattern of cultural evolution to have been so different from that of biological evolution. (I realize that the general conclusions of Wagner's chapter in this volume on the topic of geographic and cultural determinism run counter to my conclusion in the last few sentences, but I find my prose more convincing than his.)

One of the environmental changes in parts of southwestern Asia at the end of the Pleistocene was an increase of grasslands. The response of the people living in, or moving into, the area was an increase in the use of the grass seeds for food, particularly those of barley and the wheats. This might have happened, and may have happened in part, without the sickle, but the sickle does seem to have had great adaptive value, as its use spread widely and quickly. A new cultural adaptive plateau was thereby achieved, with food-grinding tools and the sickle the essentials in the artifactual complex, although in the Natufian the basic pattern of hunting wild game and of gathering/hunting of the broad-spectrum type continued. With an expansion of a new (wheat and barley being then new to most parts of southwestern Asia) and nutritious source of food and the continuation of the old types, one would expect the resulting buffering against the environment to have resulted in an increase in population, and I strongly suspect that the population did increase somewhat, even without sedentarism.

The period of harvesting wild barley and the wheats in the Near East is limited to no more than three weeks, generally to no more than two weeks, and sometimes to only a few days, since the seed heads are self-shattering and will lose the seeds when ripe. The answer to this problem was, presumably, an all-out intensive effort during the brief period available for harvesting, followed by storage of the grain. Storage pits were certainly ancient in human prehistory and probably, for most of that period, were only rarely used for storage of food, since most food procured by hunters/gatherers spoils too quickly to be put into the ground for any extended period of time. However, the history of human culture has been in large part the modification of behavior to solve new problems and the modification of artifacts for new functions; for grain, one needs pits which are waterproof, for wet grain rots and damp grain, unless heated first, sprouts (when it can still be, and perhaps was, used for beer). The answer to this problem, at least in Natufian and later prepottery sites, seems to have been plaster-lined pits, often called "silos" in the professional literature. Massive storage of grain, so goes our evolutionary theory, provided the factor responsible for sedentarism (Flannery 1969; Taylor 1973). When a family or other group had gathered and stored a hundred kilograms or more of grain, upon which they planned to subsist in large part for the next year, they could not all depart and leave that treasure both uneaten and unprotected.

All of the interrelations between the working mother's child care, her nutrition, and her reproductive physiology (outlined in the section on "Population," this article) were undoubtedly also operative as the peoples of the Near East, in the latest part of the Pleistocene, began settling into villages, and, birthrate surpassing death rate, the population increased. The resulting stress, as the population of a village increased beyond the capacity of the local organization to keep order, led (so run my ideas) to fissioning, with a part of the population moving away to start a new settlement. The process continues; I saw one such new "village" in the High Zagros of northern Iraq — three houses, representing three families, on a shoulder of a mountain near the timberline, with new clearings and new fields scattered in the forest. Social contact was not lost thereby; the ties of kinship prevailed, and a new house was being built for a proper bride who, at the time of my visit more than twenty years ago, was to arrive by horseback within the week. Undoubtedly, the population of that new village increased quite as the population of the new and peripheral villages increased 10,000 and more years ago. Increasing population, I believe, caused stress, and the response was to begin the attempt to increase the yield of the cereal crops where they had grown but scantily before; indeed, the concept of the weed may have been born as the more successful natural vegetation was pulled and hacked out, the ground pried at with digging sticks, and seeds scattered and covered. In some areas such experiments must have worked and in some they obviously would not; the people in such latter parts may have gradually drifted back to a greater dependence on gathering/hunting, quite as did the people of the Fremont culture in parts of the drainage of the Colorado River, western North America (Carr, this volume).

Domestication of ruminants in the Near East did not occur, insofar as our evidence indicates, until sedentarism had become established. In my chapter earlier in this volume, I outline how I think such domestication might have happened. The Near East was blessed with a variety of wild ruminants: gazelles, deer (three kinds), goats and ibex, sheep, cattle, and dromedaries, plus pigs, all of which were hunted where they occurred. Of this group the deer, ibex, and gazelles were never domesticated except possibly as isolated experiments; sheep and goats were probably domesticated first, then pigs, then cattle, and dromedaries last. Cattle may have been domesticated independently in the southern Balkans, and indeed, independent domestication of any of the above groups may have happened. Sheep and goats may sometimes have been domesticated, or occurred as domesticates, prior to cultivation. Thus, while sedentarism was seemingly a precondition for domestication of these Caprini, plant agriculture was not. However, by the time (probably not earlier than 8500 B.P.) that cattle appeared as domesticates, plant agriculture was well established. The pig represents an intermediate situation; I think that possibly pigs could have been kept by villagers who did not cultivate, but pig keeping was undoubtedly easier for village farmers.

While the domestication of animals became of great importance in the Near East and allowed the cultural evolution of plowing, portage, milking, spinning, etc., domestic animals were not, in my opinion, a necessity for village agriculture and the subsequent evolution of towns, cities, and states. As Hassan (this volume) has discussed, people do need some essential amino acids not furnished by cereal grains; but this need is universal, and in other parts of the world farmers have met it with other plants, primarily legumes — and the people of the Near East also had legumes. I think those Near Easterners just liked meat; they had been successful hunters for hundreds of thousands of years and were accustomed to having meat in fair quantity. They also undoubtedly had invented many uses for skins, shaved hides, braided strips of leather, etc. They could have abandoned all this use of animals as they settled into a pattern of cultivation and as their population grew to such an extent that continued hunting depleted the supply of game, but, whether by cultural accident or otherwise, they domesticated ("took into the house") a surprising variety of hoofed mammals; and their history and ours has been the richer for those adoptions.

China

Professor Ho's chapter, with its title of "The indigenous origins of Chinese agriculture," points the accusing finger at the typical Western idea that an original Near Eastern agriculture (the foundation of Western civilization) had oasis-hopped across central Asia to find a new and fertile home in northern China. The original idea, expressed as a dogma in many texts, was based on two assumptions, I believe: (1) the Chinese were clever people, right enough, but they could not have done it all by themselves; and (2) the difference in time between the beginnings of agriculture in the Near East (now set at 9000 B.P.) and the beginnings of agriculture in northern China (now set at or soon after 6000 B.P.)[4] were sufficient to account for the spread of agriculture

---

[4]   Ho (1975:58) has quoted 5000 B.C. (circa 7000 B.P.) as the approximate time of first cultivation of millet, on the basis of several finds of jars filled with husks of *Setaria panicum* at Pan-p'o, in Shensi. An abundance of agricultural implements (not specified) and the complex pattern of the village testify to the presence of well-organized agriculture, possibly already centuries old. The discrepancy of a thousand years between Ho's date of 7000 B.P. and mine of 6000 B.P. is due to a difference of calculation of the radiocarbon dates and not to any difference in the actual time being specified; I am using a half-life for C^{14} of 5,570 years (as has uniformly been done throughout this volume), but Ho used a half-life of 5,730 years and then corrected the result by the bristle-cone pine factor (Table 1 in his article, this volume), to get nearly 5000 B.C. (or approximately 7000 B.P.). Both figures refer to exactly the same time; neither is incorrect. However, much confusion will undoubtedly occur in the minds of readers who are not aware of the present state of the terminology of radiocarbon dating.

from Mesopotamia to the Hwang Ho. As Ho points out in considerable detail, "It ain't necessarily so" (if I may borrow a phrase). This same conclusion has been reached independently by Chêng Tê-k'un (1973).

We know more now than we did early in this century, when the ideas of trans-Asian diffusion of Near Eastern agriculture to China were formulated. Not only is the distance great, but the geographic barriers are major, whether herders and farmers, slow mile by slow mile and generation after generation, took the high road across central Asia or the low road around the southern coasts. Of major importance now is the fact that considerable archaeological exploration in the areas supposedly traversed has failed to yield evidence of such early agricultural occupations. Another imposing argument, as Ho illustrates with evidence, is that when western imports of wheat, barley, and goats did finally arrive in China, they did so long after a thriving agriculture and civilization were already established. Since the earliest records for agriculture in China indicate that cultivation (of millets) and domestication (of pigs and dogs) involved only biologic forms native to the area, with no suggestion of foreign influence, Ho seems to have made his point. What influences, if any, from the southern half of China, or from farther south, may have been important in the origins of Chinese agriculture in the Wei valley, must remain unknown until more is learned of the late prehistory of the southern half of China, and of southeastern Asia as a whole. At present, any controversies based on regional patriotism as to whether this area or that area in eastern Asia was "first" with this or that innovation in the early history of agriculture can only be based on the happenstances of archaeological discovery, to be reversed perhaps with the next discovery.

At present, and until evidence is forthcoming to the contrary, I must agree with Professor Ho that northern China has all the appearances of having been an independent center of agricultural origin. The pattern there brings up some interesting parallels with the Near East, which is not to suggest any direct cultural comparison. However, agriculture in both began in an area which had long been and continued for some time to be dominated by an *Artemisia* steppe. In the Near East, we believe that a changing post-Pleistocene environment allowed invasion of parts of that open land by massive stands of different grasses; the evidence is not clear for northern China, but the possibility of a similar increase of wild millets under post-Pleistocene conditions is intriguing. Perhaps, due to the more northern latitude, the increase of such grasses occurred later in northern China than in the Near East, thus accounting, at least in part, for the lag in the origins of Chinese agriculture.

A major problem remains, however; whether it was similar to the pattern of agricultural development in the Near East or not, what were the cultural antecedents of that first agriculture in northern China? Should we expect to find late-Paleolithic camps with evidence of broad-spectrum hunting, gathering, and fishing? Should we expect to find later villages, settled communities lacking agriculture, comparable to those of a Natufian culture? Should we expect to find evidence for preagricultural increase in population? We certainly hope that some part of the present surge of activity in Chinese archaeology will be directed to answering these questions.

Rice was one of the most debated topics at the conference from which this book emerged, with Ho arguing on botanical, linguistic, and archaeological bases — as he had previously argued in print — for an early record of cultivated rice in eastern China, with a diffusion of the cultivation of rice outward from that area. Others argued for an early history in southeastern Asia. The final consensus of opinion was that wild rice occupied a wide area of southern and southeastern Asia (the latter including China south of the Yangtse), that the present state of archaeological work in southern China particularly, but in the remainder of southeastern Asia also, left vast areas unknown, and that the question simply should be deferred for the present — perhaps deferred considerably into the future — until sufficient evidence has accumulated to make a decision possible. Although at present the status of the claim for domesticated rice at or nearly at 6000 B.P. at Non Nok Tha in Thailand (see the next section of this article) must be held as "not proven," the continuing archaeological research of Drs. Pisit and Gorman at Ban Chiang (see the next section of this article) illustrates the kind of effort which, when duplicated at many sites over southeastern and eastern Asia, will provide a solution to this problem of the beginnings of the cultivation of rice, and to other problems too.

One problem yet remains, a problem of communication, in our understanding of the evolution of agriculture in northern China. We of the Occidental tradition in archaeology are all pleased that the Chinese have their own radiocarbon laboratory and are publishing dates on prehistoric sites (Ho, this volume; R. Pearson 1973). However, the barrier of language (our fault, not theirs) and the relative unavailability to most of us of the published reports of the excavations lead to continuing ignorance of the data. Thus at present we have dates on sites but little or no knowledge of the stratigraphy, artifacts, biotic remains. etc., or of the associations between these data within the sites. In some instances, where site reports have been available and translated (Chester

Gorman, personal communication), these necessary facts and correlations were not included, or were included only in such a general way that comparisons and evaluations desired by the Occidental archaeologist were not possible to make. As I stated at the beginning of this paragraph, the problem is one of communication and can be solved only by purposeful cooperation, preferably by exchange of personnel between laboratories and field excavations. Since one-fourth of the world's population speaks Chinese, the time would seem to have arrived for some of our students to begin to learn that language so that they can be the ones doing the communicating recommended here.

Southeastern Asia

Much of the present writing on early agriculture in southeastern Asia reminds me of similar articles on the Near East more than twenty years ago, when I, an innocent zoologist, was first thrust into the thicket of that literature. With regard to domestication of animals, with which I was involved at that time in that area, any bones which could be identified (even if only by the local workers on the excavation) as belonging to a presently domestic species were often identified in print as having come from domestic animals. After being thoroughly lost in that particular maze for some time, I set myself the job of clearing away the undocumented underbrush, which I accomplished in two articles (Reed 1959, 1960), thereby providing a firmer base upon which later research could build.

This task must obviously now be done for southeastern Asia. Wilhelm Solheim, an acknowledged archaeological expert in the area, has stated several times that domesticated plants were being grown about 14,000 years ago. I document some of his statements which began mildly but grew in the repeating: "I think it quite possible that as we recover more data from Mainland Southeast Asia we will find that the first domestication of plants in the world was achieved by the Hoabinhian peoples sometime around 10,000 B.C." (Solheim 1967: 898). Spirit Cave

... does ... have several domesticated plants, associated with the Hoabinhian stone industry. The plants identified from the site include pepper, areca nut, the bottle gourd, cucumber, and Chinese water chestnut, all either cultivated or tended in modern Southeast Asia, one and probably two different kinds of domesticated bean. ... This material comes from between and below two charcoal samples dated at 8550 ± 200 B.P. and 9180 ± 360 B.P. The Full Late Hoabinhian Culture would then be distinguished from Early

Hoabinhian Culture by the addition of edge-grinding of stone tools, the manufacture of cord-marked pottery, domesticated plants as above plus others, and slash-and-burn horticulture (Solheim 1969: 131).

The agricultural revolution, which was thought to have first occurred some 10,000 years ago among the emerging Neolithic societies of the Middle East, seems to have been achieved independently thousands of miles away in Southeast Asia. This separate agricultural revolution involved plants and animals for the most part unknown in the Middle East, and it may have begun as much as 5,000 years earlier (Solheim 1972: 34).

On the following pages Solheim struck a more conservative note; after listing the kinds of plants recovered from Spirit Cave, he wrote:

It seems probable that several of the plants were cultivated by the inhabitants of Spirit Cave. The relatively small number of specimens that Gorman recovered in 1966, however, does not make it possible to draw a clear-cut conclusion on this crucial point. [Additional specimens recovered in excavations of 1971 were being studied by Douglas Yen of the Bishop Museum.] Let us assume for the sake of argument that Yen's findings will be negative and the plants unearthed at Spirit Cave are merely wild species that have been gathered from the surrounding country-side to supplement the hunter's diet. What should we then conclude? Such a finding would be evidence of an advanced stage in the utilization of wild plants in Southeast Asia, a stage that in my opinion is at least as early as any equivalent stage known in the Middle East. On the other hand, what if Yen's finding is positive? This would be evidence that the inhabitants of Spirit Cave were engaging in horticulture at least 2,000 years before the date that has been suggested for the first domestication of plants in the Middle East (Solheim 1972: 36–37).

I suggest that what is called middle Hoabinhian was a culture or cultures whose adherents were experimenting with many different kinds of wild plants for many different reasons. At some point, probably about 13,000 B.C. somewhere in the northern reaches of Southeast Asia, such experiments culminated in the domestication of some of these plants and the consequent appearance of horticulture as a new means of food production. I suggest that it was the late Hoabinhian culture [as it is represented in the higher levels of Spirit Cave] that achieved the transformation from horticulture to generalized plant and animal domestication and that also achieved the invention of pottery. In different parts of the region different plants would have been selected for cultivation. The same was probably true of the animals involved: the pig, the chicken, and possibly even the dog .... When the lowest levels at Spirit Cave were being formed, about 10,000 B.C., the people there appear to have possessed such elements of late Hoabinhian Culture as an advanced knowledge of horticulture and perhaps domesticated pigs [On the accompanying chronological chart (Solheim 1972: 38), the period of "incipient horticulture" was indicated as beginning between

22,000 B.P. and 18,000 B.P., with "plant and animal domestication" beginning at or soon after 15,000 B.P.] (Solheim 1972: 38–39).

The most astonishing finds from Spirit Cave were the plant remains which indicate that somewhere in this general area domesticated and tended plants were being grown for use as food, and other purposes, from before 11,690 B.P. (Solheim 1973: 145).

... I now say that the late Hoabinhian was coming into existence here and there in Mainland Southeast Asia between 15,000 and 10,000 B.P. I would consider either of two cultural elements — the manufacture of cord-marked pottery or the domestication of one plant or animal — as diagnostic of the late Hoabinhian. During this time span a number of plants were cultivated and probably the dog and chicken were domesticated (Solheim 1973: 150).

[The cultural stage] *crystallitic* begins with the middle Hoabinhian at about 22,500 B.C., during which incipient horticulture was developing, and it ends with the late Hoabinhian.... During this period both plant and animal domestication took place (Solheim 1973).

On the basis of such extremely positive statements by Solheim, the general impression has developed in anthropological circles, and beyond, that definite agriculture in southeastern Asia has been proved for 12,000 B.P. or earlier (Hanks 1972: 20 is a typical example of such innocent error). The facts are quite different, as I shall indicate. Vishnu-Mittre and Guzder (1975) have, independently, agreed completely with my conclusions.

Chester Gorman, who excavated Spirit Cave in northwestern Thailand, has generally been more conservative in his statements about early horticulture and domestication in southeastern Asia than has his onetime professor, Solheim, but even so has sometimes extended his thoughts as to what could have been possible into definite statements of what actually was; after outlining the four cultural layers found at Spirit Cave, and naming, layer by layer, the kinds of plants found in each, he stated:

The use of the bottle gourd (*Lagenaria*) and *Cucumis*, a cucumber type, with the Chinese water chestnut (*Trapa*), the leguminous beans (*Phaseolus, Vicia*) and the possibility of pea (*Pisum*), however, form a group of food plants which suggest that at this early level the economy had already attained a development beyond simple food gathering. The beans in particular point to a very early use of domesticated plants (Gorman 1970: 357).

Most of the above quotation is properly cautious, but farther on, on the same page, he stated, "By about 7,000 B.C. (= 9,000 B.P.) associated plant remains indicate that plant domestication had already occurred in South-East Asia." The following year the excavator of Spirit Cave remained even more discreetly cautious about early domestication of plants at that site. After again listing the genera identified, he wrote:

Whether they are definitely early cultigens remains to be established. Clearly we need a better sample of these early plant populations. . . . Whether or not we are dealing with early domestication is, however, not the most important issue concerning these botanical remains. What is important, and what we can say definitely, is the remains indicate the early, quite sophisticated use of particular species which are still culturally important in Southeast Asia (Gorman 1971: 311).

In another paper, written earlier than the preceding but published later, Gorman was extremely conservative concerning possible cultivation of plants; a table of the identifications for each cultural layer, as made by Douglas Yen and his associates, was published, and Gorman stated:

The pattern of plant utilization . . . suggests the exploitation of wild or tended nuts for food, for example, the butternut (*Madhuca*), the *Canarium*, and *Terminalia*; for lighting and possibly consumption, the candlenut (*Aleurites*); the pepper (*Piper*) as a condiment; and the betel nut (*Areca*) as a stimulant. The bottle gourd (*Lagenaria*), the *Cucumis*, a cucumber type, the Chinese water chestnut (*Trapa*), and the leguminous beans, however, form a group of food plants suggesting a botanical orientation beyond simple food gathering. The leguminous plants are tentatively considered to represent early domesticated varieties[5] (Gorman 1973: 102).

Almost all statements about early cultivation or domestication of plants in southeastern Asia are based on the evidence (quoted above in some detail) from the deeper levels at Spirit Cave. Of the five layers, the deepest (number 5) is sterile; three radiocarbon determinations made on charcoal from layer 4 (the deepest of the occupied layers) plus one from a mixed sample at the boundary of layers 3 and 4 average out to a mean of 10,380 B.P.; if we calculate the range at 2 sigma of each of these four "dates" and take the extremes, the 2-sigma range for the four C[14] determinations mentioned above is between 12,470 and 8460 B.P. The tendency by Solheim and those who have copied him uncritically is to take the highest extreme of this range as the true time (circa 12,000 B.P.) for the original occupation of Spirit Cave. Using

[5]   Since Donald Lathrap (this volume) has argued that the bottle gourd (*Lagenaria siceraria*) was in Asia only because it had been carried by man from Africa as a tended or cultivated plant, its presence at Spirit Cave would seem to support Gorman's suggestion that a level "beyond simple food gathering" had been achieved. However, Charles Heiser (personal communication) has warned me that bottle gourds may have occurred naturally in southeastern Asia prior to the time of the human occupation of Spirit Cave, on the basis of the fact that the history of *Lagenaria* is so little known at present that we cannot state anything definite about its natural distribution at the end of the Pleistocene.

the same logic, I could claim the time of that earliest occupation to have been no more than around 8640 B.P.; I believe that the more often quoted figure of about 10,000 to 10,500 B.P. is probably more accurate. Part of the problem of course is that people sometimes use the "new" half-life for C^{14} of 5,730 radiocarbon years instead of the accepted standard (as used in this book) of 5,570 years; but the difference is only 3 percent, and that is not the major part of the problem.

Now that we have seen the evidence and gotten the dating of the earliest occupation at Spirit Cave settled, insofar as possible, let us consider the larger problem of the light shed upon the origins of agriculture in southeastern Asia. I see no light whatsoever; the cave was meticulously dug and well reported by Gorman, who deserves the greatest credit therefor. Remains of an interesting group of plants (Gorman 1973: Table 3) and of animals (Higham, this volume) were salvaged and indicate to me that the people who lived in the cave were highly proficient, broad-spectrum gatherers and hunters. To date, not a bit of evidence emerges from the public record which one can use to claim incipient horticulture or incipient cultivation or tending of any kind of plant, or slash-and-burn agriculture, or the domestication of any animal. Particularly in the deepest occupied layer (number 4) at Spirit Cave is the botanical record scant; only four pieces of plants were recovered: two fragments of the seedcase of a palm and two seeds, one bean and one pea. I find the evidence insufficient to provide the kind of foundation for priority of agriculture for southeastern Asia claimed by some and copied unwittingly by many others. The bones and shells of the animals present no evidence for domestication, and indeed, of the three animals (pig, dog, and chicken) recommended by Solheim in various articles for determining the status of early domestication in southeastern Asia, the dog and the chicken are entirely absent from Higham's list, not found in even the more recent layers.

Those who have argued for early (i.e. prior to 10,000 B.P.) cultivation of plants on the mainland of southeastern Asia have often bolstered their arguments with references to the palynological and archaeological record for the late Quaternary from Taiwan and the possible implications thereby for the origins of cultivation in southeastern Asia as a whole.

The data from Taiwan (Formosa) and the conclusions about those data emerge from the palynological study of a lake core which covered approximately the last 60,000 years (Tsukada 1966, 1967), and the study of several sites excavated by Kwang-chih Chang (Chang and Stuiver 1966; Chang 1967, 1968, 1969, 1970, 1973). The facts can be summarized as follows: (1) the climatic pattern of Taiwan for the last 60,000 years paralleled that of the remainder of the Northern Hemisphere rather closely, with a rise in temperature toward the end of the Pleistocene and an increase at that time (circa 12,000 to 11,000 B.P.) of subtropical and warm-temperate species of plants; (2) the Recent began (circa 11,000 B.P.) with a destruction of primeval forests, in part, at least presumably, by fire, since charcoal and pieces of burnt wood had been washed into the lake from whose bottom the core was taken; (3) an increase in pollen of grasses and chenopods occurred at 4200 B.P., coincident with the entrance of the Lungshanoid Culture from mainland China; prior to this time of 4200 B.P., a period of unknown length occurred during which no evidence of occupation was found in the archaeological record; (4) before that hiatus in the record, the island was continuously occupied, presumably for an extended though undetermined period of time, by a people with a corded-ware culture; (5) the only two C^{14} determinations on charcoal associated with corded-ware pottery produced dates of 19,670 ± 450 B.P. and 3080 ± 350 B.P.; the first is seemingly much too old for a culture with ceramics and the second much too young for corded-ware, since the corded-ware culture had supposedly disappeared prior to the time of 4200 B.P.; (6) very little evidence exists for any occupation of the island before that of the people with the corded-ware culture.

The conclusions which have generally been drawn from the above set of facts, particularly by Chang, are (1) the increase in the pollen of grasses and chenopods at or near 4200 B.P. indicates that the people who took the Lungshanoid culture to Taiwan were cultivating cereals, probably millet and rice; (2) the burning of the forests at the beginning of the Recent (circa 11,000 B.P.) occurred over too long a period (though the details were never specified) to believe that spontaneous forest fires could be responsible; (3) some other agency, presumably human, must have been responsible for the fires; (4) if man was burning the forest, he was probably doing it as part of a slash-and-burn pattern of primitive cultivation, perhaps associated with the growing of root crops; (5) if man was conducting slash-and-burn cultivation at about 11,000 B.P., the people must have been those of the corded-ware culture, since seemingly no other population was present prior to the Lungshanoid occupation of 4200 B.P.; (6) the lack of definitive agricultural implements is no deterrent to the above line of reasoning, since some peoples at present conduct slash-and-burn agriculture with no tools other than wooden digging sticks.

The argument, particularly when placed against the reconstruction by Carl Sauer (1952) of a hypothetical slow evolution of root-crop agriculture in tropical southwestern Asia, is most plausible, and Chang has presented it well (see particularly his publication of 1970 as a summary); he has always admitted the weaknesses and the gaps in knowledge, but has also always come back to the logic of his conclusions: man in Taiwan, a part of tropical southeastern Asia, was involved in slash-and-burn cultivation as early as 11,000 B.P. This conclusion was then placed, by both Chang and numerous others, against the chronological and archaeological sequence at Spirit Cave and correlated, too, with the established fact that the corded-ware culture was known to have been widespread over southeastern Asia and northern China prior to the appearance of Lungshanoid cultures. The weaknesses of the argument, of which Chang (even if not always others, seemingly) has been well aware, are that for Taiwan no acceptable radiocarbon dates are available for corded-ware levels, that the supposed association between pieces of burnt wood and charcoal in a lake core and the supposed causative pattern of slash-and-burn agriculture is certainly tenuous, and that nowhere else in all of eastern Asia does a date of 11,000 B.P. occur for corded ware.

Obviously, what we need are sequences of good dates from several sites, in different parts of southeastern Asia, all agreeing as to the chronological sequence and all thus supporting the same patterns of archaeological data and the same set of suppositions. Until we are able to achieve this level of agreement between dates and archaeological sequences, I must continue to render — concerning the problem of early post-Pleistocene cultivation in southeastern Asia — the Scottish verdict of "not proven."

Another agricultural "first" claimed for southeastern Asia is the cultivation of rice, as based on the evidence, primarily, from two sites: Spirit Cave and Non Nok Tha. Rice itself has not been identified from Spirit Cave; the evidence is artifactual and thus secondary. At about 8000 to 8500 B.P. (top of level 2) new artifacts were introduced into Spirit Cave which had no prior cultural history there; these are cord-marked pottery, quadrangular adzes, and small bifacially ground knives (Gorman 1971: 314). The knives are the important pieces here. Three fragments were found, nearly identical to the blades of rice-harvesting knives used at present in parts of Java and Celebes. Seemingly these knives are not today used on the mainland of southeastern Asia and cannot have been commonly used there in the past, as these knives from Spirit Cave are archaeologically unique for the mainland of southeastern Asia (Gorman 1971: 314). Gorman has stressed (1971: 324;

this volume) that the combination of adzes, pottery, and knives is typical of later sites with cultivated rice, and has suggested thereby that the people of Spirit Cave around 8500 B.P. may have been growing rice. The suggestion is a logical one, but no more. The knives are particularly intriguing, considering their precise use elsewhere for harvesting rice, but knives used for cutting stems of rice at present in the East Indies could have been used for cutting stems of various kinds of plants (perhaps including those of wild rice) eight millennia ago. The lesson of sickle blades from the Near East should not be lost upon us here; the presence in the archaeological record of Natufian sickle blades which were indubitably used for cutting stems of cereal grasses does not prove that those grasses were cultivated. I cannot accept the evidence from Spirit Cave as proof that rice was cultivated in that area at the time, so we must turn now to a site which had its beginning at least 4,000 years later than the time of deposition of the top of level 2 at Spirit Cave.

This site is Non Nok Tha, a village in north central Thailand which was occupied for several thousand years and on which crops and orchards are being grown at present (a circumstance which hampered the excavator, Donn Bayard).

Bayard has divided the strata of his excavation into three major periods: Early, Middle, and Late. Of these, only the Early Period is involved in our argument regarding the antiquity of cultivated rice in southeastern Asia. The two lower levels of this Early Period had pottery but no metal; level 3 had copper but no bronze. Beginning with the lowest level of the Middle Period, bronze replaced copper, and iron appeared at the beginning of the Upper Period. In the two main articles on Non Nok Tha (Bayard 1971, 1973), the main attention has been given to the metals (dates, chronology, technology of production, etc.), but we will focus instead on the published "dates" of the Early Period. Here, in some of the sherds, were found imprints of rice husks which had been used as temper when the original pots were made (Bayard 1973, Plate IV; Solheim 1973, Plate I).

No argument exists against the rice in the basal layer at Non Nok Tha being *Oryza sativa*; it is the earliest definite evidence of rice in southeastern Asia. The problems, however, are twofold: (1) the imprints of the rice husks do not allow identification as to wild or domestic (Vishnu-Mittre and Guzder 1975); and (2) the dating of the layers of that Early Period is uncertain.

The excavator's problems were considerable, since the site had been used throughout most of the period of its occupation for multiple graves as well as for a living site. The difficulty, thus, was in determining the exact boundaries between levels of occupation and the exact provenance of any sample taken for dating. Thirty-one such samples were taken: one collagen from bone, four sherds for thermoluminescent determinations, and twenty-six charcoal. The internal agreement between the layers and the dates is not good (Bayard 1971, Figure 8; 1973, Figure 5; the reader must use both articles and their figures and tables to follow the full story). As Bayard was concerned about the history of the metals he recovered, much of his discussion on chronology centered upon the validity of the arguments for an "early sequence" versus a "late sequence" for that history. Of Bayard's thirty-one "dates," he found eleven which line up on a chronostratigraphic table to make the "early sequence," and six which, with less certainty, form a "late sequence." Six of the charcoal samples, sent together to Florida State University for an age determination, possibly became contaminated en route and perhaps should not be used (although only two of them, dating into the future, seem to be discrepant, the other four tending to support the concept of a "late sequence"). The four thermoluminescent "dates" tend to support the "early sequence," but the single date on collagen is on the line of the "late sequence." Several of the C^{14} determinations on charcoal are too independently variable to offer support for either sequence. (When such variation exists, out of a total potentiality of 31 "dated" samples, one wonders if some part of the clustering which has been interpreted as "early sequence" or "late sequence" may not also be due to chance. One can also use such variability of "dates" from a single site as a lesson against placing too much trust in a single date from any site when only one or two dates are available.)

Bayard was concerned with his metallurgical sequences, but I have concentrated more on the nine "dates" from the Lower Period (Figure 3), which include three determined on the supposed contaminated samples of charcoal, but these are — at this level — no worse or better than any of the others, so I have left them in. The reader, if he desires, may mentally exclude them, but my argument is not affected thereby.

Since none of these "dates" cluster (Figure 3), and the earliest of them is from level 3 instead of the stratigraphically earlier levels 1 or 2, they seem to have been mostly ignored in determining the supposed time of the earliest occupation of the village, which has been estimated instead at or near 6000 B.P. (a date often quoted) by extending the chronostratigraphic line for the "early sequence" (based mostly on "dates" from the Middle Period) to level 1 of the Early Period (Bayard 1971, Figure 8; 1973, Figure 1).

Considering all of the variables, one can have little faith in either the "early sequence," the "late sequence," or any other possible sequence. Bayard, to his everlasting credit, carefully discussed the factors and possibilities involved, but then concluded that, for him, the "early sequence" was "preferable."

However, a few years later, Bayard (1975) again published the same chronological chart for Non Nok Tha, with six[6] additional C^{14} dates for the Early Period; this time, however, he suggested four, not two, possible sequences: LATEST, TRADITIONAL, INTERMEDIATE, and EARLY. The former "late sequence" became the TRADITIONAL; an even more recent sequence — bolstered by four of the additional radiocarbon dates (two apatite, two collagen) — became the LATEST; and the new INTERMEDIATE sequence was sandwiched between the TRADITIONAL and the EARLY (this latter sequence remained unchanged). This latest publication on Non Nok Tha, with six new radiocarbon dates (all later than 3000 B.P.) does not add anything but further confusion to our understanding of the chronology of the Early Period of that site; one can only say that if the "early sequence" is eventually shown to be correct (as may indeed happen, based on other sites), the victory will be one of thermoluminescent dates over radiocarbon.

In another, and very short, article, Bayard (1972) concentrated on the bronzes from Non Nok Tha, but he did not fail to outline the problem with the variable dates, and he also illustrated this problem with a chronological chart. Even so, this article has subsequently been quoted as the authoritative source for the statement, "twenty-four radiocarbon and four recent thermoluminescence dates now accurately date the first use of the site during the Early Period in the fourth millennium B.C. . . ." (Pietrusewsky 1975). Stories do get changed in the telling, and my conclusion is that in this way many people have managed to convince themselves and others that valid evidence exists to support the concept of very early agriculture in southeastern Asia.

This problem of cultivated rice at or near 6000 B.P. needs belaboring. In the first place, we have no evidence that the rice used in the Early Period was cultivated. More important to me, looking at all of these odd "dates" in the Early Period at Non Nok Tha (Figure 3), with only one of them (and that one in layer 3) close to 6000 B.P. but with four of them now (Bayard 1975) for counterbalance in the first millennium A.D., there are no preferences as to an EARLY SEQUENCE or a LATEST SEQUENCE or any other. (I am particularly, and adversely, impressed by

[6]   These dates came to my attention too late to be included in Figure 3.

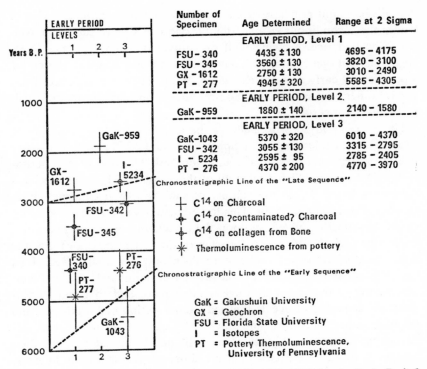

	Number of Specimen	Age Determined	Range at 2 Sigma
	EARLY PERIOD, Level 1		
	FSU – 340	4435 ± 130	4695 – 4175
	FSU – 345	3560 ± 130	3820 – 3100
	GX – 1612	2750 ± 130	3010 – 2490
	PT – 277	4945 ± 320	5585 – 4305
	EARLY PERIOD, Level 2.		
	GaK – 959	1860 ± 140	2140 – 1580
	EARLY PERIOD, Level 3		
	GaK – 1043	5370 ± 320	6010 – 4370
	FSU – 342	3055 ± 130	3315 – 2795
	I – 5234	2595 ± 95	2785 – 2405
	PT – 276	4370 ± 200	4770 – 3970

Chronostratigraphic Line of the "Late Sequence"

$+$ C^{14} on Charcoal

ϕ C^{14} on ?contaminated? Charcoal

ϕ C^{14} on collagen from Bone

$*$ Thermoluminescence from pottery

Chronostratigraphic Line of the "Early Sequence"

GaK = Gakushuin University
GX = Geochron
FSU = Florida State University
I = Isotopes
PT = Pottery Thermoluminescence,
       University of Pennsylvania

Figure 3. Nine dates published by Bayard (1971, 1972, 1973) for the Early Period at Non Nok Tha. The six dates shown by him on a later chart (Bayard 1975) are not here included

one erratic "date" on charcoal of 8100 ± 250 B.P. from the Middle Period, layer 2 [Bayard 1971, Figure 8], which "date" illustrates the extreme to which C^{14} irresponsibility[7] is possible for Non Nok Tha.)

The only conclusion I can reach with regard to the time of first occupation of Non Nok Tha (and the time of first evidence for rice in southeastern Asia) is that we do not know. Given the wide and erratic distribution of the fifteen "dates" in the Early Period (nine of Figure 3 plus six additional from Bayard 1975), and it is the Early Period with which we are involved, no one would use the figure of 6000 B.P. or any other figure for the time of that occupation. Indeed, if subsequent research shows that the LATEST SEQUENCE is more valid than any other,

---

[7] The phrase "C^{14} irresponsibility" was used by me in 1959 with regard to a scatter of dates for a site in the Near East. I was chided then for its use and additionally discovered that the phrase and my use of it had been picked up by fundamentalists in their efforts to discredit the technique of radiocarbon dating, so I never repeated the phrase. Now, however, I think that the time has come to do so.

the village would not have been first occupied until around 300 B.C. Under these conditions of uncertainty, one can simply state that Non Nok Tha had rice, growing wild or cultivated, from the time of its beginning, but one cannot with any validity make any strong claims for a particularly early date for rice there. We need firmer evidence, from several other sites in the early and middle Recent, and those sites will be found, I am certain.

Having done my best to evaluate the evidence for the possibility of early agriculture in general at Spirit Cave and on Taiwan, and early rice in particular at Spirit Cave and Non Nok Tha, the sites in southeastern Asia upon which almost all of the arguments for such earliness have been based, I find the validity of such supposed evidence either lacking or seriously in doubt. This last sentence is in no way to be construed as reflecting adversely upon the excavators of the various sites; I have the utmost admiration for each of them. I also believe that the archaeological trend in southeastern Asia now, as in the Near East twenty years ago, is toward a successful quest to untangle the problems of chronology that beset the investigators there and to begin to pinpoint the sequence of events that led from a period of broad-spectrum hunting/gathering toward and into early agriculture. Since these investigators work in a tropical area with heavy annual rainfall, their problems are more difficult than are those of archaeologists in many other parts of the world, but undoubtedly new techniques will be developed to overcome some of these difficulties.

In general, I see no theoretical objection to the expectation that earlier evidences of cultivated plants and domestic animals will be found in southeastern Asia than we now know. I am not objecting to a date of 6000 B.P. or any other for rice or domestic pigs or cattle at Non Nok Tha (Higham 1975) or any other site. All I am trying to say is that the evidence has to be firmer than that which has been presented.

However, I see no reason now to expect that the rather extravagant claims by some, for the greater antiquity of early agriculture in southeastern Asia than elsewhere in the world, will be realized. One should, I think, read Gorman's chapter in this volume with these admonitions in mind; his presumed sequence of cultural evolution in southeastern Asia may well prove to be the correct one, but I find no necessary basis for his suppositions that the incipient cultivation of rice, for instance (his Figure 2), would have started 12,000 to 14,000 years ago. It is going to be a difficult thing to prove, in any case.

(After writing the above critique on southeastern Asia, I became aware that Chester Gorman's continuing excavation in Thailand promises to clarify some of the probems outlined in the preceding pages. A published paragraph by Rainey [1975] and a short personal communication from Gorman himself, relative to excavations at the large, trilayered cemetery at Ban Chiang, in northeastern Thailand, indicate that objects of cast bronze were, indeed, being produced in Thailand as early as 5500 B.P. [dated by radiocarbon]. Pottery of uncertain horizon dated as early as 6550 B.P. by thermoluminescence may indicate that older strata, as yet unexcavated, exist. Most recently, an account in a weekly newsmagazine [*Time* 1976] repeated the above statements, with the additional information that the people of Ban Chiang grew rice and raised chickens and pigs. Published analysis of the evidence is most eagerly awaited. I believe that any people who were producing cast bronzes and burying their dead in large cemeteries must have been food producers. Perhaps the evidence from Ban Chiang will vindicate Bayard's personal preference for the validity of his "early sequence" at Non Nok Tha.)

India

On the basis of present knowledge, no evidence exists for the presence of agriculture in India before 5000 B.P. This date would be at least 4,000 years later, if not more, than the first-known agriculture in southwestern Asia and probably at least a millennium later than present evidence indicates early agriculture was present in southeastern Asia and northern China. Until the discovery of evidence to the contrary, thus, we must conclude that the practice of agriculture entered India from outside, although that part of India in the humid tropics may have been part of the southeastern Asiatic agricultural noncenter (Harlan 1971) and as such have had house gardens and root crops which left no archaeological evidence.

The late dates (after 5000 B.P.) of the evidence for the earliest agriculture in dry northwestern India, plus the appearance there of domesticates from the Near East (wheat, barley, sheep, goats, and possibly cattle and legumes), indicate introduction from the west. At the same time, further south in India, peoples with more primitive cultures were growing a variety of other crops (Vishnu-Mittre, this volume) which were probably of local origin.

In eastern India, rice could have been one of these local crops, but proof of early cultivation of rice is not definite as yet. Indeed, cultivated rice may have been a relatively late introduction into India; reports of the presence of rice during the Harappan period used to indicate early presence of rice in India were based upon misidentifications of impressions of wheat (Vishnu-Mittre and Savithri 1975).

India, at present, seems to have little to add to the solution of the problems of the worldwide ORIGINS of agriculture, although of course future archaeological discoveries could change this present opinion.

Sub-Saharan Africa

In addition to his article in this book, which includes study of the cereals of sub-Saharan Africa, Jack Harlan is also the editor of *Origins of African plant domestication*, a separate volume in the series *World Anthropology*. That book confirms my own overall impression that archaeological evidence for an independent center of agricultural origins in Africa is lacking. Much of sub-Saharan Africa lacks detailed archaeological research of the kind in which organic remains and ecological interpretations are sought, and over much of the area organic remains are rapidly decomposed and so destroyed. Thus direct archaeological evidence of agriculture prior to about 3500 B.P. is seemingly lacking, so that recourse must be had to a variety of indirect types of studies, from cytogenetics to linguistics.

Sub-Saharan Africa, as one of Harlan's agricultural noncenters, may have had a long history of garden cultivation with an emphasis on yams, which had an independent center of origin in western Africa as well as in Asia and America. The basic problem is the lack of chronology and a lack of knowledge of the time of the origins of yam cultivation in Africa as associated with other events, such as the diffusion (both cultural and by actual movement of cultigens) of agriculture from elsewhere. The elsewhere is generally thought to have been northeastern Africa (Egypt and environs), which in turn received several of its domesticates (at least wheat, barley, goats, sheep, and dogs) from southwestern Asia.

The basic question is, thus, did some type of cultivation exist in sub-Saharan Africa prior to the time that a form of Near Eastern agriculture reached the area, probably prior to the period of Saharan desiccation beginning at around 5000 B.P.? The classic opinion has been that sub-Saharan Africa, prior to such diffusion of agriculture up the Nile and across the Sahara, had no cultigens or domesticated animals, but that upon contact with cattle-keeping cereal growers along the margin between savannah and forest, the imitative natives of the forest were self-induced to plant yams. Another idea is that the same cereal growers, as they moved south into the forests of western Africa, substituted the forest-adapted root crop, yams, for the savannah-adapted grasses. The third idea, and one which seems to me to be as sensible as (if not more so than) either of the other two, is that the forest-dwelling hunters/gatherers may have already been tending — even if not actually cultivating — yams, particularly as yams are known to regenerate their tubers if the plants' roots are not disturbed by the gatherer.

So far as I can discover, no evidence exists for support of one concept over another, but yams certainly were cultivated prehistorically in tropical Asia and America; why not in tropical Africa also? Such a tending of root crops, leading to various degrees of cultivation, seems to have been a natural pattern of behavior of forest peoples in Harlan's agricultural noncenters (Harlan 1971).

I do not think that we should discount sub-Saharan Africa as a center of agricultural origin, but the problem is that, to date, we have so little evidence of what, agriculturally, was occurring there until relatively recently.

I hope that Harlan's *Origin of African plant domestication* will tell us more.

Mesoamerica

Our conference neglected Mesoamerica, although not intentionally. Two of the orginal members of our panel, Drs. Richard MacNeish and Kent Flannery, have devoted much time to the problems of agricultural origins in Mesoamerica and were expected to do so at our conference. However, MacNeish chose to write on highland Peru, while being unable to attend in person, and Flannery, due to the burden of other commitments, had to withdraw completely. We did have Herbert Wright's brief description of the environmental changes, as known, in Mesoamerica during the late Quaternary, and we had the botanical and genetic expertise of George Beadle, with his study of the prehistoric evolution of wild teosinte (*Zea mexicana*) to early maize (*Zea mays*) under conditions of primitive cultivation (Beadle, this volume). Jack Harlan, too, is knowledgeable about maize (Harlan, de Wet, Naik, and Lambert 1970; de Wet and Harlan 1972; Harlan, de Wet and Price 1973); he agrees with Beadle that teosinte, without introgression from any other source, was the ancestor of maize. No archaeologist in our group, however, could speak from personal experience as to agricultural origins in Mesoamerica, so at our conference we were forced to neglect this important area. However, at the time of our conference (August 1973) Flannery had in press (1973: 287–301) a succinct analysis of agricultural origins, including those in Mesoamerica, as correlated with environment and prehistoric cultures, and I have used this and other sources as a basis for my discussion in this section. (Lathrap, this volume, disagrees with Flannery and with most other investigators of the origins of Mesoamerican agriculture. He thinks that, far from being an independent center, Mesoamerica received the stimulus for its agricultural beginnings by colonization from the tropical lowlands of South America.)

Both botanical and cultural problems assail us when we approach Mesoamerica, and among these problems are the disagreements between the specialists who have worked there. Thus Whitaker and Cutler (1971) accepted as evidence of cultivation a single seed they identified as being from *Cucurbita pepo*[8] (summer squashes and pumpkins) from the deepest level (Zone D) of the Guila Naquitz Cave in the valley of Oaxaca, Mexico, dated at 10,700 to 9790 B.P. Of this seed they wrote, "This is probably among the oldest cultivated cucurbit seeds known from an archaeological site." Actually, if their identification is valid, that seed is not only evidence for the oldest known cultivated cucurbit but may also be the earliest record of any cultivated plant in the world. (After having written this last sentence, I trust reviewers and writers of texts or popular articles will take due note of the caution enjoined upon any such general sweeping statements by Harlan and de Wet [1973] and the doubts of Flannery [1973] concerning the validity of such claims for early cultivated squash.) Actually, Mexico MAY have the evidence for such early cultivation, since from a higher level of the same cave (Zone C) Whitaker and Cutler identified five seeds and peduncles as *C. pepo*, dated between 9300 and 9150 B.P., and nine more dated at about 8850 P.B. (Zone B). However, Flannery (1973: 288) has warned that most specimens of *pepo* recovered in Mexico from periods prior to 7000 B.P. look "wild"! Even so, 7000 P.B. is a respectable date for early evidence of cultivation, and by that date we can add maize, too, as already clearly distinguished from teosinte.[9] The reader is referred to Beadle (this volume) and to Flannery (1973) for further details.

[8]   The use of the specific name *pepo* automatically indicates cultivation, as this species, by definition, is not wild.
[9]   Mangelsdorf (1974:166–169) called this early maize "wild"; he does not believe, however, that maize evolved from teosinte under cultivation but thinks instead that

One important difference between the "seed" (really seed and fruit case) of teosinte and that of any other grass which has become a cultivated domesticate is that the former resists breaking by the teeth; if swallowed whole, the seeds of teosinte merely pass intact and physiologically undamaged through the gastrointestinal tract, and no nutrition is derived from them. Teosinte seeds can, however, be either popped or broken and then ground into a coarse flour, but they consist of more than 50 percent indigestible materials no matter what the form. Many other foods available in the valleys of the southern highlands of Mexico, where teosinte still grows and where its cultivation presumably first occurred, must have been preferred by the human inhabitants. The exact area of the original cultivation of teosinte will probably never be known, but, George Beadle (personal communication) has pointed out an area in the drainage of the Batas River, some thirty miles south of Chilpancingo, the capital of the Mexican state of Guerrero, with an elevation of approximately 1,225 meters (circa 4,000 feet) and higher, as an area where teosinte now grows well in its natural form and where it could logically have been cultivated early.

Teosinte may have been a poverty food more than 7,000 years ago, as it occasionally still is, but even so someone had to start growing and reseeding it, for mutations which would have been adverse to the survival of the wild plant were instead preserved and accumulated in a tended population. Actually, the earliest selection was undoubtedly not made by intent on the part of the prehistoric collectors, for "variants which have their spikes more tightly condensed into clusters in which the seeds remain within the confines of overlapping husks" will today be gathered by botanical collectors in excess of their number in the population, since the more normal "seeds" separate more readily and fall to the ground (Galinat 1974). As long as the early collectors did no more than gather, prepare, and eat, they merely removed the variant genes differentially from the general population of teosinte, but once they began to use their collected "seed" for planting, or even tossed some of it on a trash pile, they unconsciously began to accumulate genes for prevention of the disarticulation of the rachis (the central axis of the seed head) and thus began the process for the formation of an incipient cob.

The change from teosinte to maize appears to the nonbotanist to

---

a true wild maize existed from which the cultivated type was derived, after which the wild form became extinct. I have been convinced by Beadle that no "wild" maize ever occurred, but the judicious reader will want to read Mangelsdorf in detail to acquire a balanced picture.

have been a complex one, but we are told that the genetic differences are few. Essentially, the head of a single stalk of teosinte (as with all grasses) consists of a central rachis with a row of seeds, alternating in position, up each side. If this rachis is made nonshatterable (as with wheat or barley) and if several such units are fused together (unlike any other grass, wild or cultivated), the cob is achieved, with its paired rows of kernels. Another genetic change in the evolution from teosinte to maize was the exposure of the true seed in maize by the shrinkage of the hard fruit case (which encloses the seed in teosinte) to become only a supportive structure at the base of the seed. Lastly, mutations became incorporated which decreased the size of the protective glumes around each seed, and instead a number of husks came to surround the whole assemblage of seeds on a cob. Much of this genetic selection was undoubtedly unconscious, nor did it all happen at once or in one place; indeed, some of the actual history has been lost to us, but experimental geneticists have been able to reconstruct the story.

While teosinte is destroyed by overgrazing, in pre-Spanish times no such problem existed; and the plants must have grown wild in tremendous numbers, in places making dense stands (as they sometimes still do) where they could have been harvested with relative efficiency (Flannery and Ford 1972). Harvesting teosinte was presumably never an easy task, however; it grew naturally up small narrow mountain valleys and on rocky slopes; not only would many if not most of the seeds have been lost, but they are small (25,000 per kilogram), and half of each seed is indigestible roughage. Teosinte does have definite advantages, though, over most other foods: at its best the volume of yield per area equals that of wild wheat in the Near East; it grows well in disturbed areas (as in and around deserted campsites); the seeds are insect-resistant and birds choose other foods, which means that storage is relatively simple as compared to that of other cereals.

Certainly, wild teosinte would seem to have been the most unpromising of plants upon which to build the civilizations of two continents, nor did the Indians who began its cultivation probably have anything in mind beyond a possible source of food in an emergency. Actually, at the time of such incipient cultivation, more than 7,000 years ago, the Indians may have preferred *Setaria* (foxtail grass) as a domesticate (Callen 1967b), but it seemingly did not change under tending (if tended), whereas teosinte gradually evolved into early maize (called "wild maize" by Mangelsdorf and others) and, even with diminutive ears and few seeds per ear, became a much more productive crop and one, moreover, in which the seeds were retained on the plant for harvesting.

Neither teosinte nor its derivative, maize, nor both of these with the beans and squash which grew naturally with the teosinte in south central Mexico (Flannery and Ford 1972), nor all of these together plus a number of other staples collected by the Indians seem to have provided sufficient food on an annual basis for permanent camps to have developed, at least in the Tehuacán Valley. For centuries, thus, while being agriculturalists of a kind and preparing soil and planting seeds, the Indians of Mesoamerica remained essentially hunters/gatherers (mostly gatherers), moving in a fixed annual cycle in accordance with the known availability of several wild staples. The wonder is that maize, beans, and squash — the important nutritional triad of later periods — had any chance of selective improvement at all. But improved they were, although slowly, and finally maize began to produce crops which would, hectare by hectare, outyield some of the wild-gathered staples, particularly the seeds of the mesquite, a plant typical of the better soil of the valley bottoms. Only then did more intensive replacement of the native vegetation by maize occur, and only then did permanent villages of wattle-and-daub houses begin to appear (Flannery 1973). Time, meanwhile, had passed, several millennia in fact; at present the first definite villages in the southern Mexican highlands cannot be dated earlier than 3350 B.P., although the size and complexity of San José Magote, the largest such village of the period (Flannery 1972b: 44)[10] would indicate a prior history of a century or more of cultural evolution.

However, evidence of settlements "considerably older" is known from "the moist lowlands of southern and eastern Mesoamerica" (Don Lathrap, personal communication), which situation would be a logical deduction to make even lacking archaeological evidence, since by 3500 B.P. the incipient stages of the Olmec civilization must have begun; one suspects that much more was happening in the humid tropics of Mesoamerica than we have yet learned, since by about 3200 B.P. we have a fledgling civilization as represented by San Lorenzo.

(A review of the pattern of cultural changes *re* agriculture in Tehuacán, archaeologically the best known of the highland valleys of southern Mexico, in comparison with the early agricultural sequence in the Near East has already been presented by MacNeish [1971], and these comparisons [revised by myself] warrant attention.)

The pattern as expressed in Table 2 seems to me to be out of

---

[10] I have written this paragraph without having seen Kent Flannery's new book, *The early Mesoamerican village*, which obviously has much greater detail but will, I hope, follow the same outline.

Table 2. Comparison of the phases of cultural evolution of the Tehuacán Valley, Mexico, with those of the foothills of the Zagros Mountains, southwestern Asia, after MacNeish (1971)

Sequence in the foothills of the Zagros Mountains	Sequence in the Tehuacán Valley
1. Zarzi (17,000–11,000 B.P.)	Period of change from seasonal macro/microbands (Coxcatalan) to central-based bands (Abejas) (circa 5500–5300 B.P.)
2. Period from Zawi Chemi Shanidar and Karim Shahir to Jarmo (circa 11,000–8500 B.P.)	Period of change from central-based bands (Abejas and Purron) to semi-permanent hamlets (Ajalpan) (circa 5300–1800 B.P.)

sequence, with the Mexican series not culturally comparable and consequently much more recent than it should be. For instance, the Zarzian was a period of hunting of large herd mammals, but also with a tendency toward broad-spectrum gathering; MacNeish's supposed comparable stage in the highlands of southern Mexico is a time well past that of the hunting of herd ungulates, and indeed agriculture (even if not intensive) had already been practiced for at least 1,500 years. On the basis of these kinds of difference, I propose another model (Table 3).

In the original version of Table 3, I had a fourth column, "differences," but these proved to be too numerous and complex to be reduced to tabular form, and I will discuss them instead.

Table 3, Part I:

1. The large game available to hunters of the Ajuereado Phase in the valleys of the southern Mexican highlands was never, insofar as we know, as numerous as to species or as abundant as to biomass as was that of the foothills of the Zagros Mountains during the late Pleistocene (Turnbull and Reed 1974; Hole and Flannery 1967), when most of the meat eaten by Zarzians came from large to medium-sized wild mammals: onagers (the half-ass, an equid), red deer, cattle, sheep, goats, gazelles, and pigs. The people of Tehuacán during their comparable preagricultural period of hunting herd animals depended mostly upon American antelope (an ecological equivalent of the gazelle) and jackrabbits, with an occasional equid (usually loosely called "horse") (Flannery 1966, 1967). Other large mammals (mammoths, mastodons, camels, groundsloths, tapirs, peccaries) which one might expect to have been present around 10,000 B.P. were either absent from the valley or were so rarely hunted that their bones have not been recovered. The

Table 3. Comparison of the phases of cultural evolution in the Tehuacán Valley, Mexico, with those in the foothills of the Zagros Mountains, southwestern Asia, as considered by the present author

Sequence in the foothills of the Zagros Mountains	Sequence in the Tehuacán Valley	Similarities
1. Zarzian (13,000–11,500 B.P.)	Ajuereado (circa 10,000–8750 B.P.)	Hunting of herd ungulates ?Animal drives? No agriculture Broad-spectrum gathering
2. Phases typified by Zawi Chemi Shanidar or Karim Sharir or early Çayönü (11,500–9000 B.P.)	El Riego into Coxcatlan (8750–6000 B.P.)	Broad-spectrum gathering Earliest agriculture No pottery
3. Phase represented by Jarmo, Ali Kosh, PPNB at Jericho, and the later ("cell-type") houses at Çayönü (9000–8000 B.P.)	Late Coxcatlan and Abejas-Purron (6000–3450 B.P.)	Increasing dependence on agriculture Introduction of pottery (circa 8500 B.P. in southwestern Asia; circa 4000 B.P. in Mexico)

little cottontail rabbits, however, were hunted or snared in considerable numbers. One gets the impression of an area from which most of the larger mammals had, for reasons not known, disappeared and not been replaced by ecological equivalents.

Both the foothills of the Zagros and the highland valleys of southern Mexico were colder and drier than today, but the Zagros area was well provided with game, particularly by contrast with Tehuacán. The people of both areas, too, were undoubtedly indulging in broad-spectrum gathering, but the details are not clear, particularly for vegetable materials; the impressive variable was the greater availability of more kinds of large game animal in southwestern Asia, an availability that continued on through the prehistoric period into the present century, whereas by contrast open-country game ungulates, horses, and antelope (and even jack-rabbits) were gone from the Tehuacán Valley by 8700 B.P. or earlier, after which large amounts of meat derived from communal game drives were no longer available. The people were therefore automatically forced to rely more on intensive gathering, augmented by solitary hunting of white-tailed deer and trapping of small animals, as recounted by Flannery (1966, 1967).

2. One of the primary characteristics of the Zarzian and the Natufian is the wealth of microliths, which were undoubtedly used to

make numerous kinds of compound tool, but the Tehuacán Valley had no microliths (MacNeish, Nelken-Terner, and Johnson 1967), nor, seemingly, were sickles used. Whether this difference in prehistoric technology was or was not important in determining differences in the subsequent pattern of agricultural development is not known to me.

3.   If we extend our comparisons beyond the limited range of the foothills of the Zagros Mountains, the area originally specified by MacNeish (1971) for his comparisons, to the whole of the western part of southwestern Asia, a logical and indeed necessary extension, we find that the Natufians, even if not the Zarzians, were utilizing local wild grain, cutting it with sickles, probably storing it in quantity, and grinding or pounding it to make mush or flour. We have no artifactual evidence for such activities during the comparable phase in the life of the people of the Tehuacán Valley. They were probably utilizing grass seeds, but we know nothing of which were used or how these were gathered or prepared. One grass not used was teosinte; no trace of it has been found in the valley or in the feces of prehistoric inhabitants there (Callen 1967a).

4.   A fundamental difference, in at least one part of southwestern Asia, is that people were becoming sedentary prior to the end of the Pleistocene, whereas in Mesoamerica nothing similar happened, to our knowledge, until at least 7,000 years later.

Table 3, Part 2:

1.   By the end of this period (9000 B.P. in southwestern Asia, 6000 B.P. in the highlands of Mesoamerica), people in southwestern Asia were cultivating grain and/or herding domestic caprines: wheat and sheep, goats, and possibly pigs at Çayönü (Braidwood et al. 1974); goats at Ganj Dareh Tepe (Smith 1970); sheep at Zawi Chemi Shanidar (Perkins 1964); and two-rowed hulled barley and possibly emmer wheat in the Prepottery Neolithic A at Jericho (Hopf 1969). Meso-america never did acquire the domestic food animals (dogs and to a lesser degree turkeys were eaten later, true, but seemingly always as a minor part of the diet); but in the millennium between 7000 and 6000 B.P., the Mesoamericans had laid the foundation for the production of the basic foodstuffs upon which they were to build empires.

From the viewpoint of the Near East, the establishment of these cultivars (chili peppers, avocados, squash, beans, sapote, early maize, and possibly amaranths) was "premature," having been accomplished by people who were nonsedentary, still moving on their annual round of hunting/gathering, and still depending for more than half their food (if MacNeish's estimates are correct) on the gathering of wild plants.

One grass often claimed as a cultivar for this period (and sometimes earlier) is *Setaria* (foxtail millet). From the brief description in Callen (1967b), I am not convinced that *Setaria* was necessarily cultivated. Collected in quantities it certainly was, but no evidence is presented that such collections could not have been from wild plants. The case for cultivation is presented on the basis of some grains larger and fatter than normal, recovered from the Ocampo Caves, Tamaulipas, Mexico, and dated about 6000–5500 B.P. *Setaria* was recorded as a known food of the people of the Tehuacán Valley from about 7500 B.P. to and after the time of the Spanish conquest, but without any noticeable change in the size or shape of the grains. No evidence exists, thus, for its cultivation in the Tehuacán Valley even though the people were experimenting with the cultivation of several other plants and were importing additional cultivars into the valley. (Maize, for instance, was necessarily one such import, since teosinte does not grow there now nor is there archaeological or other evidence that it has grown there within the last 10,000 years.) I suggest the possibility that the larger and plumper kernels of *Setaria* from the Ocampo Caves may well fall within the natural range of variation of seeds of *Setaria* as it grew in that area at the time.

2. Throughout all of southwestern Asia, wild game remained an important part of the human diet, varying of course with local availability; thus at Jericho PPNA gazelles were the predominant wild animals procured, presumably by drives (Legge 1972). Where domestic animals were becoming important, the number of bones of wild animals decreases in the archaeological remains, but nevertheless hunting of large wild ungulates remained an important activity. None of the herd ungulates of southwestern Asia became extinct during this period or later, until elephants and wild cattle were exterminated during the Assyrian period (Reed 1970). In the Tehuacán Valley, by contrast, the people were dependent for meat (estimated to have furnished 34 percent of their food) upon white-tailed deer (which could be hunted most successfully alone, at certain times of the year), upon cottontail rabbits (probably snared), and upon numerous other small mammals and some birds, turtles, etc. (Flannery 1966, 1967). The problem of getting animal protein under these latter conditions must have been a major difficulty, and, as the population grew (Table 1), the deer particularly must have decreased, as indeed is shown by the archaeological record. Since no large supply of fish was available, the difference inevitably had to be made up by vegetable foods; and this factor may well

be a major one in the continuing attention given to cultivated plants by the people of Tehuacán and associated valleys of the highlands of southern Mexico.

Table 3, Part 3:

The major differences between the Near East and highland southern Mexico during these periods of increasing dependence upon agriculture were the following:

1.   much larger and more complex permanent villages or small towns in southwestern Asia but, insofar as we know, only the most rudimentary beginnings of villages late (circa 4000 B.P.) in the analogous sequence in Mexico;

2.   correlated higher density of population in the Near East (Braidwood and Reed 1957; Carneiro and Hilse 1966) as compared with that of the Tehuacán Valley (Table 1);

3.   correlated with differences in densities of population in the two areas, a greater complexity of social organization in the Near East (Carneiro 1967; Flannery 1972);

4.   major dependence of the people of the Near East upon domestic herd animals for protein, in contrast to the people of Tehuacán, whose need for protein was met increasingly by plant foods, with a probable emphasis on the seeds of legumes (beans and mesquite).

In summary, these comparisons show that analogous cultural patterns in the Near East generally preceded those of the Tehuacán Valley by 3,000 years or more. (In the case of the inauguration of permanent villages, the figure is nearer 7,000 years, with the more important difference that villages preceded agriculture in the Near East but occurred in the Tehuacán Valley only after 3,000 years of a history of cultivation.) These figures may well be changed, and generally reduced, if and when we learn more about the beginnings of agriculture in Mesoamerica, since I believe that the well-known archaeological sites in Tehuacán and Tamaulipas excavated by MacNeish and his colleagues yielded a wealth of specimens because of excellent preservation, not necessarily because those areas were centers of cultural evolution. Tehuacán certainly seems to have been receiving cultivars which had originally been cultivated elsewhere. We do not yet know where these areas of earlier cultivation may have been, but one suggestion is that of Lathrap (this volume) that colonizers from South America introduced the practice of growing tropical gardens, which in turn provided the stimulus that led to nontropical agriculture in Mesoamerica (see Lathrap's map, p. 739). If that suggestion is valid, the tropical forests of the lowlands will have to be explored in the search for Mesoamerica's earliest agriculture. If such "tropical forest agriculture," including both house gardens and the practice of slash-and-burn (creation of a *chacra*, in Lathrap's terminology), led directly to the Olmec culture and its ceremonial centers,[11] then such areas as Tehuacán and Tamaulipas were peripheral and backward, and comparisons of these outliers either with the Near East or with other areas of the world are useless.

Flannery (1973: 287) has said that much time will pass before we know WHY the people of Mesoamerica domesticated plants. That statement remains as true as when he published it; I have here added some of my own comments and questions but am not an iota closer to the solution of WHY agriculture began in Mesoamerica, except to suggest *à la* Lathrap that PERHAPS we have been looking in the wrong places. My own archaeological experiences have been xerophilic (eastern Oregon, Arizona, southwestern Asia, Egypt); if I had gone to Mexico I would have looked, as did MacNeish, Flannery, and others, for dry caves. If the real truth has instead long lain rotting in the jungle, archaeologists will have to search intensively for concentrations of different kinds of pollens and phytoliths; from these data they can then, we hope, deduce house plans, settlement patterns, and size of sites.

South America

Five articles (by Wing, MacNeish, Lathrap, Cohen, and Pickersgill and Heiser) in this book are concerned with problems of early agriculture in South America. Each author or pair of authors wrote independently, with no consultation with any other, with the result that these chapters may seem to have little in common at first glance, except that each necessarily has its place in the same chronology. Careful reading, however, shows that the five are related. Each intertwines with one or more of the others: Lathrap's concept of house gardens as an ancestral type of protocultivation in the Western Hemisphere is necessarily basic to all studies of later agriculture in the New World; MacNeish's essay traces archaeological prehistory and the patterns of human ecology in the southern Peruvian Andes from 18,000 B.P., or before, to and through the period of earliest agriculture (circa 7000 B.P.) in the

---

[11] I am aware of the interesting proposal (Meggers 1974) that the Olmec civilization received its major cultural stimulus from Shang China, but I believe that most Mesoamericanists discount this possibility.

area; Wing's chapter adds domestic animals to the history of changing ecology and the beginnings of agriculture in the Andes; Pickersgill and Heiser do the same for the major food plants; and Cohen shows in detail how coastal inhabitants of Peru, quite like those of the north-west coast of North America, utilized their total environment to produce permanent villages without agriculture and then resisted acquiring agriculture long after they were made aware of it through continuous trading with agricultural peoples inland.

Lathrap's chapter is the broadest in scope, covers the most time and territory, is the boldest and most imaginative, and offers to many readers a new view on the origins of agriculture in the Western Hemisphere, although parts of the general scheme have been expressed by Lathrap in previous papers in more technical literature.

Lathrap's thinking starts in sub-Saharan Africa 40,000 years ago, or earlier, where, contrary to the pattern in the rest of the Eastern Hemisphere, anatomically modern man may already have been established for fifty or sixty thousand years (Beaumont and Vogel 1972; Protsch 1975). Lathrap would put the earliest cultivation of bottle gourds (*Lagenaria siceraria*) in tropical Africa by 40,000 B.P., with house gardens developing from such beginnings, and has deduced that, from this beginning, the bottle gourd and the practice and/or the idea of the house garden were carried to other parts of the tropical world. Carter (this volume) has recommended a single-origin view of the beginnings of agriculture, but Lathrap has fleshed out his idea with a place of origin, a pattern of inauguration, and pathways of movement of a complex of human behavior and ideas. By so doing, he has strengthened the claims of those everywhere who believe in the primacy of tropical forest agriculture over supporters of the primacy of dry-land cereals, without of course having proved the matter.

The path of the bottle gourd and of the complex of practices and ideas that went with the men who carried the gourds is traced first to the tropical forests of western Africa, to an increasing population there resulting in adaptation to fishing from boats in rivers and then in the sea, and so, via fishermen lost and carried westward by the prevailing winds and currents, to the eastern bulge of South America, where they must have arrived by 16,000 B.P. (or, more probably, earlier). More than one such group of castaways must have been involved, to have made any impact on the culture of the area where they arrived. These fishermen, in Lathrap's opinion, also took to South America a complex of developed watercraft and fishing techniques, leguminous fish poisons, African linted cotton, communication over long distances by the use of a two-toned signal log, and various ethnic patterns of behavior.

Lathrap's discussion of the possibility of the introduction into South America from Africa of the basic practice of the house garden as the type of protocultivation from which all agriculture in the Western Hemisphere was derived is multifaceted and must be read to be appreciated; particularly important is his discussion of the developing role of manioc, of slash-and-burn agriculture, and of the expanding divinity — both in concept of role and areally — of the riverine alligator, the cayman of the basins of the Amazon and Orinoco. Where reliefs of the divine cayman are found far from the distribution of the actual animal, as is true in coastal Peru and Mesoamerica, diffusion of ideas and practices from the riverine lowlands must be assumed.

I find Lathrap's ideas both fascinating and enticing, as will others, and I expect that they will produce much comment, including some friction and perhaps fire. The important matter is that new ideas are added, for testing by future research and further thought, to our present set of hypotheses. For the present I wish only to point out (as others will certainly do if I do not) that Lathrap's dependence on *Lagenaria* as the original and main stem for the fruitful bush of fact and conjecture he has produced may not be well grounded and in any case seems not necessary to the health of the hypothesis.

The central pillar of Lathrap's reconstruction is the supposed absence of a known wild ancestor for *Lagenaria* in the Western Hemisphere and his belief that such an ancestor, with cultivated derivatives, has been present throughout the terminal 40,000 years of the Quaternary in tropical Africa. He has other evidence contributing to his theory that prehistoric man crossed the Atlantic between western Africa and the bulge of Brazil in the late Pleistocene, but the matter of the gourds, as he presents his hypothesis, is of primary importance.

Not all agree, however; Flannery (1973) did not, for one, and expressed the opinion that a wild ancestor of cultivated *Lagenaria* must have existed in the Western Hemisphere but become extinct after bottle gourds were taken into the garden. By this principle, early remains of gourds in archaeological sites in South America (as from Zone h,[12] Pikimachay Cave, Peru [MacNeish, Stockton, Nelken-Terner, and Cook 1970: 33]) or Mesoamerica (from the Infiernillo Phase, southwestern Tamaulipas, Mexico, dated between 9000 and 7500 B.P.

---

[12] The date for the occurrence of these pieces of gourd is usually quoted as being about 13,000 B.P. This date is seemingly a minimum one, since the only C^{14} determination I can find for Zone h is 14,000 $\pm$ 180 B.P. (MacNeish, Stockton, Nelken-Terner, and Cook 1970:15).

[Whitaker, Cutler, and MacNeish 1957]) could have been collected from wild plants. Lathrap (this volume) has likened this belief in an unknown hypothetical wild ancestral *Lagenaria* to the belief of Mangelsdorf and others in the supposed "wild" maize, never found. Since Flannery rejected the "wild" maize, he should, believes Lathrap, have also rejected a hypothetical ancestral wild *Lagenaria*, also never found.

The two situations are not the same, since a satisfactory ancestor exists for cultivated maize in the form of teosinte (Beadle, this volume), but no analogous population of wild ancestral bottle gourds is known with certainty (Charles Heiser, personal communication). However, the ancestral home of the bottle gourd is thought to have been more probably Africa than elsewhere (Heiser 1973a). Since I am not a botanist, the following discussion is based mostly upon Heiser (1969, 1973a, 1973b), Whitaker (1971), Richardson (1972), and personal communications from Charles Heiser.

While at least six species of *Lagenaria* occur, we are here concerned only with *L. siceraria* as a pantropical population. Although two subspecies (*L. s. siceraria = afrikana* and *L. s. asiatica*) and numerous varieties of *L. siceraria* exist, no wild ancestor has been determined with certainty. Additionally, weedy (feral) populations are found in favored localities along the banks of rivers and occasionally elsewhere. Charles Heiser (personal communication) and his students have seen such feral bottle gourds growing in Mexico and Ecuador, and herbarium specimens are available from other parts of tropical America. Considering the various possibilities concerning the place and time of origin of *L. siceraria*, its subsequent modes of distribution, and the ability to produce weedy plants (particularly along watercourses), we cannot know that *Lagenaria* was not native to the Western Hemisphere prior to the arrival of man; all we can say is that *L. siceraria* is a single pantropical population, distributed at present across the Americas, Africa, Asia, and the "Nesias" (Indo-, Mela-, Micro-, and Poly-). Our knowledge of the pattern of speciation in plants would lead us to the conclusion that this wide distribution of a single species had been accomplished relatively recently in the earth's history (Quaternary), and man would seem to be a logical, but not necessarily the only, distributive agency. The original center from which that distribution occurred was more probably Africa than elsewhere (Heiser 1969, 1973a; Whitaker 1971). One fact that seems valid is that the American varities, as shown by the character of the seeds and other structures, are similar to some populations found in Africa but dissimilar to Asiatic types (Whitaker, Cutler, and MacNeish 1957; Heiser 1973a).

Let us assume, for the sake of argument, that Africa had bottle gourds before South America did. The natural habitat of *L. siceraria* in a tropical jungle would seem to be sunlit stream banks. The gourds are adapted for dispersal by dropping into the water and floating downstream, to lodge during a period of high water in bankside thickets and grow a new generation. (Obviously, seeds of some gourds have to be planted upstream, and the agents here are probably seed-eating animals, mostly rodents.) Some of the floating gourds would continue out to sea, where they are natural long-distance dispersal agents for their enclosed seeds; the experiments of Whitaker and Carter (1954, 1961) have shown that bottle gourds can float in seawater for nearly a year and then be stored for another six years, after which some of the seeds are still viable. Since bottle gourds have been picked up on the coasts of Norway and Ireland, they seemingly floated there from South America or Mesoamerica or came from western Africa, in which case they must have crossed the Atlantic twice, first following the Atlantic South Equatorial Current and the Caribbean Current into the Gulf of Mexico, and then following the Gulf Stream to Europe. The trip to South America from Africa, thus, would seem to have been (and to be) an easy one for *Lagenaria*, and, indeed, gourds by the dozens may have floated across every decade for tens of thousands of years. Gourds do not, however, germinate on the seashore, as coconuts do, but if sufficient numbers over long periods made the trip successfully, I would assume that some would have lodged in shoreside thickets, where herbivorous or omnivorous animals (rodents and marsupials [13] come to mind) could have opened them and carried some of the seeds inland, or carried or dragged the gourd away from the shoreside to a spot where germination could have been successful. Indeed, Heiser (1973a) has recorded herbarium records of apparently volunteer plants growing on coastal sites in the Americas. A need for experiments is obvious.

Even gourds cast up on sandy beaches would, after human occupation of those coastal areas, be picked up occasionally by curious people or their more curious children, to be dropped later, possibly in a place where germination and growth of new plants would be successful. Under favorable circumstances, the numerous seeds in a single gourd would produce several plants which would set seeds, but a single plant would be sufficient to produce a new crop of seeds, for the flowers on the same plant can fertilize each other. Presto! a new plant would have

[13] The introduced opossum in California has been known to forage in the intertidal zone, chewing barnacles off the rocks. One should not discount the activities of our animal kin.

been added to the flora of the Western Hemisphere. Purposeful planting, as imagined by Lathrap and some others, would not be a necessity.

Once bottle gourds were established in an American environment, I suspect that any human population of hunters and gatherers would soon have utilized the fruits (gourds) as dippers and containers, perhaps as rattles, and thus, knowingly or unknowingly, spread the plants from one human group to another, since seeds cast upon trash piles will often grow.

I like Lathrap's concept of trans-Atlantic voyages by fishermen in dugout canoes from western Africa to eastern Brazil, and I suspect that if such men made such trips they may have carried gourds, but one does not have to postulate those trips to have *L. siceraria* in the Western Hemisphere because *Lagenaria* was perhaps native to the Western Hemisphere; if present in tropical western Africa, bottle gourds were seemingly well adapted to cross the Atlantic and become established on the coasts of the eastern Americas, anywhere, from Brazil to Mexico, without the necessity of human help. (Indeed, such successful trans-Atlantic invasions may still be occurring.)

The other side of the coin, with regard to my discussion of bottle gourds, is that remains of such gourds found in early cultural levels (as at Pikimachay Cave and in southwestern Tamaulipas) cannot automatically be assumed to have been cultivated, although my own thought is that the probability of some type of simple cultivation is high.

After this excursion into the nature and dispersion of *Lagenaria*, I return to Lathrap's main thesis that garden horticulture in the tropics of the Western Hemisphere had a long ancestral history antecedent to the time, around 9000 to 7000 B.P., when some type of cultivation of plants is typically thought to have had its beginning in the New World. Lathrap's hypothesis can stand on its several other points without the supposition that the bottle gourd was necessarily introduced across the Atlantic by man.

Provocative and logical as are Lathrap's ideas of a unified origin for American agriculture based on house gardens, these ideas, lacking foundation in archaeological data, serve at present as a stimulus for future thinking and future research. Unfortunately, the humid tropics are an adverse environment for preservation of organic materials, including bone. It is to be hoped that palynology, the detailed study of phytoliths, the application of "chemical archaeology," and the discovery and excavation of waterlogged sites will yield ranges of data not now available.

Lathrap's extension of his ideas is that the role and nature of the housegarden, with the growth of the root crops perhaps already being conducted separately to some degree in a *chacra* [a nearby clearing in the forest where the growth of bulk foods was concentrated], evolved into the practice of slash-and-burn agriculture in the New World. The nature of this combination of house garden plus *chacra* necessarily changed as its practice ascended the eastern slopes of the Andes or lapped around their northern end onto the Pacific Coast. Replacement of cultigens occurred, particularly at higher altitudes in the Andes (Sauer 1952: 50–51); of these replacements the most important (if not originally, certainly now) was the potato.

In contrast to this "new"[14] concept of Lathrap's, that agricultural man had his origins in the Amazonian tropics and moved from east to west in South America, the more standard idea is that the central Andean highlands were an original center of innovative agriculture, probably at first independent of influences from either the Amazonian lowlands or Mesoamerica. This concept is the one adopted automatically, and usually without explanation, by most authors writing on prehistory in South America, including most of those in this book. Actually, the two concepts can be merged, as Lathrap obviously means them to be, with the influence (as well as the cultigens, in part) moving into the highlands so slowly and unobtrusively that the slight archaeological evidence we get from such early appearances in the more xerophytic environments of the highlands appears to the excavators there to point to autochthonous origins. This difference in interpretation will undoubtedly continue for a considerable time.

An older idea, that South America owed to Mesoamerica the cultural stimulus (even if not at first the cultigens) for the initial phases of agriculture, has necessarily been abandoned as the radiocarbon dates have driven back the time for early cultivation in the Andes to periods as early as, and sometimes earlier than, the time for Mesoamerica. Actually, little botanical evidence exists showing any influence from Mesoamerica during the earlier period of agriculture in the Andes; indeed, if Lathrap is correct, cultural influence was flowing in the opposite direction, from south to north. Study of the cultigens discussed in this volume by Pickersgill and Heiser demonstrates that maize (first known from Rosamachay Cave, in the Ayacucho Basin, at circa 5200 B.P. [MacNeish, this volume]), may have been the first Mesoamerican cultigen to be transported south of the Isthmus of Panama. This maize,

---

[14] The idea is not really new, merely generally ignored for some decades after having been introduced by Nordenskiöld (1924). I have not, myself, seen this reference.

genetically, still had some characteristics traceable to teosinte, which has never been found growing south of Honduras. However, Lathrap (in Lathrap, Collier, and Chandra 1975: 21) has recently suggested that teosinte did once exist, and may yet be found, in the tropical lowlands of northern South America, which suggestion reopens the possibility (albeit a remote one, in my thinking) of an independent center for the origin of maize in South America.

However maize may have reached the northern part of west central South America, indirect evidence (Marcos, Lathrap, and Zeidler 1976) suggests that by about 4300 to 4200 B.P., and probably earlier, the plant was important in providing an agricultural base for the permanent settlement of Real Alto in lowland western Ecuador. If this is true of this one site, probably many others also existed upon the economic base of cultivated maize. The contrast with Mesoamerica, where to the best of our knowledge no such permanent, large, organized villages were occupied then or during the following millennium, is noteworthy.

Other than maize, Pickersgill and Heiser suggest from their list of important cultigens only two species of squashes, *Cucurbita moschata* and *C. ficifolia*, for introduction into South America from the north. Of these, the latter appeared almost 4,000 years earlier in South America and, additionally, is genetically linked by pollinator and compatibility studies with the wild *C. maxima* of South America, so that a southern origin, with later movement northward, should be considered. The earliest squash known from South America (circa 7750 to 7500 B.P.), that recovered from Zone W of Pikimachay Cave (MacNeish, this volume), was not necessarily cultivated, nor is any squash proved to have been cultivated that early in Mesoamerica (Flannery 1973: 288, 300–301).

The cultivation of the common bean (*Phaseolus vulgaris*) seems to have been initiated sooner (by 7680 ± 280 B.P., or possibly earlier) in South America (Kaplan, Lynch, and Smith 1973) than in Mesoamerica, where the earliest dated domestic beans were found at 6925 ± 200 B.P. (Kaplan 1965). Since the wild ancestor occurs in both areas, independent origins of cultivation may well have occurred.

While the Indians of the Western Hemisphere domesticated few animals in comparison to those of the Eastern (Zeuner 1963), the South Americans outdid the North Americans not only in numbers[15]

---

[15]   This estimate does not include the possibility, rather slight in my opinion, that the Indians of the Carolinas, in what is now the southeastern United States, had domestic white-tailed deer (*Odocoileus virginianus*) in the early sixteenth century A.D. (Swanton 1940).

of species domesticated but also in the economic and cultural importance of the domesticates. Both groups had domestic dogs, which could have been derived from North American wolves but were probably introduced as dogs from Asia via the Bering Bridge by the end of the Pleistocene; the oldest record of an American dog (although a record not accepted by everyone, see Herre and Röhrs, this volume) is from Jaguar Cave, Idaho, dated at no younger than 10,350 B.P. (Lawrence 1967, 1968). Domestic dogs, thus, had a respectable antiquity in the Americas and underwent considerable artificial selection during some ten millennia of pre-Columbian time.

The only other domesticated animal introduced from the Old World into the New in pre-Columbian times was a variety of chicken which lacked terminal caudal segments and laid blue eggs (Carter 1971). Although some prehistorians and historians continue to claim that no chickens existed in the New World prior to 1492, Carter's analysis of the data seems to me to tip the conclusion in favor of a pre-Columbian introduction by sea from southern or eastern Asia. Still lacking, however, is the confirming evidence of bones of chickens from known pre-Columbian archaeological strata.

The only animal known to have been domesticated in North America was the turkey (*Meleagris gallopavo*), which was reared in Mexico and Central America and introduced in pre-Columbian times into the northwestern part of South America (Gilmore 1950: 393), where it seemingly was never of great importance.

The two mammals domesticated in South America were and are found wild in the Andean highlands. Of these, the guinea pig (*Cavia porcellus*), discussed in this volume by Wing and by Herre and Röhrs, needs no further comment. The wild and domestic camelids of the genus *Lama*, however, present a more complicated situation. The use of different specific names for the domestic llama (*Lama glama*) and domestic alpaca (*L. pacos*) and another (*L. guanicoe*) for the wild ancestor, the guanaco, serves only to disguise the close relationships of these three populations and their distinctiveness from the vicuña (*L. vicugna*), which has been tamed on occasion but never yet truly domesticated. While statements have been made (O. P. Pearson 1951: 162; Zeuner 1963: 438) that hybridization between any two of the four kinds is possible, with production of fertile offspring in all cases, the situation is not so simple. I would expect that hybrids between guanacos and their domestic relatives, llamas, and alpacas, would be not uncommon, and also fertile when occurring, but, seemingly, crosses with vicuñas and the others are rare to absent in nature. Even though vicuñas have on occasion been observed mingling with other kinds of camelids (O. P. Pearson 1951: 162), they are more wary than the others and will typically move off if approached, even by a single alpaca or llama (Koford 1957: 211). Crosses of vicuñas and other camelids, usually with alpacas or with alpaca/llama hybrids, are not easy to produce; they are accomplished after rearing the young together. The degree of fertility of these hybrids of vicuñas seems not to have been determined as yet, but infertility is one variable often quoted as an adverse factor in attempts to breed such hybrids.

The wool of the vicuña, particularly that from the back, is the world's finest and was esteemed by the Incas even more than it is by their modern counterparts, the superwealthy. The Incas acquired the wool by organized drives; every three years, for each area of 100 to 150 kilometers (60 to 90 miles) in circumference within the natural range of vicuñas, some 20,000 to 30,000 Indians would drive all the animals possible (vicuñas, deer, guanaco, bears, and others) into a central area, where all but the younger vicuñas would be killed for wool, skins, and meat. These younger vicuñas, after shearing, would be released, to rebuild the population for the next drive three years later. The Spaniards, and others of European descent, have not been so conservative, and, until quite recently, vicuñas were slaughtered annually by the thousands, the meat for local consumption and the wool mostly for export.

Given the high value of the wool, and considering, too, the successful domestication of the guanaco, many people must have tried to raise young vicuñas with the thought of establishing a domestic herd. Perhaps the pre-Columbian Indians did so, but of this we have no record. The first such effort recorded was that of the Jesuits, who are reported to have had a herd of 600 vicuñas in Peru by 1767, when that religious order was expelled from all Spanish territories; further effort was abandoned at that time. Such attempts as occurred in the nineteenth century were failures, but more serious experiments began early in the twentieth century (Gilmore 1950: 453; Koford 1957: 215). Some of these efforts have been incipiently successful as experiments (Flowers 1969), but none has as yet succeeded financially.

The central problem with all such efforts at domestication of vicuñas has been the wildness of the males; though vicuñas of both sexes make interesting and docile pets while young, the males become increasingly dangerous with adulthood and try to acquire harems and establish territories. Under conditions of mild restraint, as in a corral or even a large pasture, adult males must be hobbled if females are present, or they will fight with each other and sometimes kill the females also.

Efforts to establish herds of vicuña/alpaca hybrids, often made, have not been particularly successful either, because of the incomplete fertility of the hybrids and their failure when bred together to establish a true-breeding phenotype in subsequent generations. However, more intensive efforts at domestication of the vicuña alone would seem to be a worthy endeavor; such experiments should be done at the national level, not by individuals, as hitherto attempted — by Peru, Bolivia, or Argentina, or all three together. Selective breeding for docility would seem to be a necessity, but in the meantime the wilder males of each generation might be castrated and kept as wool producers. Once herds of tamer animals have been achieved, selection for greater production of the high-quality wool, lacking guard hairs, could be begun. At present, for instance, each animal produces no more than about 120 grams of best-quality wool annually, and that only when young.

The other animal to have been domesticated in the New World was the muscovy duck, *Cairina moschata*, which is neither musky nor from Muscovy; indeed, the origin of the name is a mystery. This duck is not the typical domesticated mallard known to most Europeans and most Americans of European descent, but is a larger bird; the wild form is black with white wing patches and the male particularly has a bare face with knobby facial bumps (caruncles). As a domesticated duck, this bird is still common in South America and Mesoamerica, and during the last few centuries has also become popular in Africa and eastern Asia.

Most authors state simply that the muscovy duck was domesticated in South America; but Mexico has also been proposed as the place of domestication, on the basis that the range of *Cairina* extends into Mesoamerica far enough to overlap that of the wild turkey, and the people who domesticated the turkey could have done the same with the duck. The range of these wild ducks, true, does extend from northern Argentina through all of the lowland forests of South America (Meyer de Schauensee 1970: 56) and through all of central America into Mexico wherever forest-lined rivers and lakes occur at low altitudes. Wild muscovies thus are found up both coasts of Mexico, on the Pacific side north into Sinaloa and on the east into southeastern Nueva León and the southern half of Tamaulipas (Peterson and Chalif 1973; Sutton 1951; E. R. Blake, personal communication).

The range of the common wild turkey, *Meleagris gallopavo*, extended in former days southward through all of the forested highlands of Mexico into Oaxaca; in this state and also in some of the areas bordering the Gulf of Mexico the ranges of these two wild birds did overlap. This situation, however, is no evidence for any identity in area of original domestication; indeed the widespread prehistoric distribution of these domestic ducks throughout their natural range would indicate the possibility of multiple occurrences of domestication. Osteoarchaeological evidence for prehistoric domestic ducks in the New World has not come to my attention.

Cairina seems not to have reached Europe directly from the New World but instead to have been introduced indirectly from Africa, whence the original European names of "Guinea duck" and "Cairo duck"; indeed, the name *Cairina* is derived from "Cairo." Jeffreys (1956) uses this distributional and other historical evidence to suggest that these domestic ducks had reached Africa from America in late pre-Columbian times on trans-Atlantic ships of Arab traders, but no anserine osteoarchaeological evidence for this suggestion has yet been found in Africa.

The absence of more kinds of domesticated animal in the New World remains a mystery. Carr (this volume) has discussed the situation with regard to wild sheep in North America, but that is only one case. Particularly in pre-Columbian South America, the Indians had much experience in handling living animals; for that continent Gilmore (1950: 346–347) has presented an imposing list of thirteen species of birds and mammals which were tamed and kept for hunting, for food, or as sentinels. These, thus, were secondary energy traps for the humans, but none of them crossed the behavioral boundary of long-time breeding in captivity to become truly domesticated; another seven or eight species (including the vicuña, discussed above) were kept as pets, but none became domesticated.

Particularly mystifying is a situation in both South America and Mesoamerica, where the black-bellied tree duck (*Dendrocygna*, several species) is a resident and breeder throughout most of the area. The local people, well into the present century, collected either eggs or newborn ducklings; the eggs were hatched under hens. Reared by humans, these ducks were very docile and totally tame and stayed "at home" without confinement. Their eggs and meat were prized, and, like geese, they acted as alarms, whistling loudly if any stranger approached (Kortright 1943: 374–376). Why did they not breed under these conditions of freedom, thus entering upon the path to domestication?

Such situations as those in South America and Mesoamerica, where many pets were kept but few were domesticated, have led many students of domestication to disparage pet-keeping in general as a path toward domestication of animals. Rather than drawing such a blanket conclusion, I suggest that each case needs to be studied in as much depth as possible, to determine what factors — of human attitude, behavior, and culture, and of the pet's needs, behavior, psyche, and treatment — led to nondomestication, or, more rarely, to successful domestication.

CAPSULATED CONCLUSIONS

(These conclusions are not necessarily irrefutable.)

1. Probably most people knew enough about botany to understand the basic facts of reproduction by seeds and tuber cuttings long before the time of the beginnings of agriculture. This basic knowledge, a necessity for plant agriculture, was not by itself sufficient to induce gatherers to become planters.

2. The first postglacial period of environmental change following the evolution of anatomically modern man (*Homo sapiens sapiens*) was accompanied by, or followed shortly by, the appearance of agriculture in several areas on several continents. The several prior periods (possibly as many as twenty) of postglacial environmental change had not been followed by agriculture. The suggested conclusion is that only *H. s. sapiens* was mentally capable of the degree of complexity of annual planning necessary for the success of even the most primitive agriculture. However, multiple human cultural factors associated with postglacial environmental changes were also involved. These cultural factors were different in different parts of the world where agriculture began, but some necessary cultural and/or environmental factors were presumably absent in other parts of the world where agriculture did not begin.

3. The important cultivated food plants, both cereal grasses and root crops, were part of the earth's environment and were being used as food by many animals, including hominids, for millions of years before they were taken in hand and cultivated. The populations of those plants which became successful cultigens had several rare genetic characteristics, adverse under wild conditions, which were preadapted for success, and so had high rates of survival, under conditions of primitive cultivation.

4. Several millions of years before man tamed any animal, the important domestic food animals, which are mostly hoofed animals, had evolved the physiological and behavioral (particularly social) adapta-

tions which preadapted them for survival under conditions of early domestication. The important factor at the time of early domestication of animals was not an evolutionary change in the biology of the humans or the domesticates; it was instead a change in the ATTITUDE of the human male hunters, whereby they began to protect animals instead of killing them. The factors responsible for this change in attitude are not understood, but I suspect a feminine influence.

5.   If agriculture had only a single area of origin some 10,000 years ago, as Carter proposes in this volume, the mechanism of diffusion to the other regions of early agriculture has not yet been explained.

6.   Perhaps cultivation of house gardens in the humid tropics (the agricultural "noncenters" of Harlan 1971), with an emphasis on multiple cultigens (including possibly root crops), has an antiquity far older than the ten millennia B.P. (Before Present) otherwise here suggested for agricultural origins; but if this is so, the evidence has not been found as yet.

7.   Several recent studies of hunters/gatherers have shown that such people expend less energy per individual per unit of time at successful food-getting than do most agriculturalists. The density of population of such hunters/gatherers for most of the world must have remained relatively low for the continued success of that type of life, which WAS a successful type of life for millions of years.

8.   The low density of population of hunters/gatherers was maintained by widely-spaced births, frequent infanticides, and occasional episodes of local intensified death rates during droughts, floods, or particularly severe winters; this latter factor would obviously be of greater importance in regions away from the tropics.

9.   People in general did not seek to become agriculturalists, probably preferring hunting/gathering, but were forced eventually into agriculture by a series of events which they had not planned and the consequences of which they did not foresee.

10.   One factor possibly contributory to local increases in population may have been rising sea levels at the end of the Pleistocene (Binford 1968; Gorman, this volume) which slowly forced people to move, thus concentrating them locally along seashores; a correlated factor leading to such concentrations along shores was that the rising sea levels created numerous drowned valleys, where aquatic life (potential food) flourished.

11.   Where local resources were and are adequate, settled villages can develop, and have done so, without agriculture. Three such examples are the Natufian culture of the eastern Mediterranean, the coastal

peoples of northern Peru, and the peoples of the northwest coast of North America. Of these, the Natufians evolved an agriculture, the coastal Peruvians finally adopted agriculture about which they had known but which they had been avoiding for 1,000 years or longer (Cohen, this volume), and the people of the northwest coast retained their traditional life (until it was destroyed by European invaders) without recourse to agriculture.

12.   In such villages emphasis was placed upon preparation and storage of food.

13.   With the adoption of village life (sedentarism), population increased; women had more children because the age at first pregnancy was lowered, the time between births was lessened, and the tendency toward infanticide was reduced.

14.   Constrained within the limits of an environment which changed only slowly, if at all, the increasing populations of early villages would soon have suffered malnutrition and ultimately starvation unless people were constantly leaving, or something was done to increase the supply of food (by adopting or inventing new techniques), or both. The new techniques were cultural innovations, such as the building of better boats for hunting sea mammals on the oceans, or the planting, weeding, cultivation and/or irrigation of food plants, or the herding or domestication of food animals.

15.   The shift to agriculture by original innovators was not sudden, and it depended in large part upon the possession of preadaptive cultural artifacts and the practices of particular hunters/gatherers. Examples from the Natufians of the Near East are the gathering and storage in quantity of grains of wild grasses; sickles of chipped stone, set in handles, for reaping grain; grinding stones for preparing grain for cooking; and storage facilities.

16.   Probably at first such small areas of plants as were cultivated were considered minor additions to the major sources of food derived by hunting/gathering. With continued increases of population, however, the areas of cultivated plants increased and the time devoted to hunting/gathering decreased.

17.   Once a population had become so dependent upon its food crops, plant and/or animal, that it could not survive without them, it was trapped into continuing the annual agricultural cycle or suffering major losses in population. Only marginal agriculturalists, such as the people of the Fremont culture of western North America (Carr, this volume) could abandon agriculture and return successfully to full-time hunting/gathering.

18.   Two of the agricultural "centers" postulated by Harlan (1971), the Near East and northern China, remain valid in the context he proposed: discrete and relatively small geographical area of origin; relatively few domesticates; an energy base dependent primarily on cereal grains (grass seeds) from the beginning; relatively rapid cultural change from early villages to towns to incipient civilization.

19.   Two of the agricultural "noncenters" postulated by Harlan (1971), sub-Saharan Africa and the humid tropics of southeastern Asia and eastward, remain valid in the context he proposed: wide area with indistinct boundaries; many domesticates (mostly cultigens) developed at different times in different areas over a longer period of time than is true of "centers"; possible pre-Recent period of house gardens with some root crops; acquisition of cereals much later. (Harlan's original definitions have here been modified in part by myself.)

20.   In the New World, Harlan's "center" in Mesoamerica and his "noncenter" in South America do not appear at present to meet his requirements. Perhaps an original "noncenter" including the humid tropics of both South America and Mesoamerica provided an agricultural base of house gardens and slash-and-burn cultivation from which more discrete agricultural "centers" developed independently in the northern Andes and southern Mexico.

21.   Many unsolved problems remain.

REFERENCES

BAYARD, T. D.
  1971   Non Nok Tha: the 1968 excavation. Procedure, stratigraphy, and a summary of the evidence. *University of Otago Studies in Prehistoric Anthropology* 4:i-v, 1–76.
  1972   Early Thai bronze: analysis and new dates. *Science* 176:1411–1412.
  1973   Excavation at Non Nok Tha, northeastern Thailand, 1968: an interim report. *Asian Perspectives* 13:109–143.
  1975   On Chang's interpretation of Chinese radiocarbon dates. *Current Anthropology* 16:167-169.
BEAUMONT, PETER B., JOHN C. VOGEL
  1972   On a new radiocarbon chronology for Africa south of the equator. *African Studies Quarterly Journal* 31:65–89, 155–182.
BINFORD, LEWIS R.
  1968   "Post-Pleistocene adaptations," in *New perspectives in archeology.* Edited by Sally R. Binford and Lewis R. Binford, 313–341. Chicago: Aldine.

BOSERUP, ESTER
1965 *The conditions of agricultural growth: the economics of agrarian change under population pressure.* Chicago: Aldine.
BRAIDWOOD, ROBERT J., H. ÇAMBEL, B. LAWRENCE, C. L. REDMAN, R. B. STEWART
1974 Beginnings of village-farming communities in southeastern Turkey — 1972. *Proceedings of the National Academy of Sciences, USA* 71:568–572.
BRAIDWOOD, ROBERT J., CHARLES A. REED
1957 The achievement and early consequences of food-production: a consideration of the archeological and natural-historical evidence. *Cold Spring Harbor Symposia on Quantitative Biology* 22:19–31.
BYERS, DOUGLAS S.
1967 "The region and its people," in *The prehistory of the Tehuacán Valley*, volume one: *Environment and subsistence.* Edited by Douglas S. Byers, 34–47. Austin: University of Texas Press.
CALLEN, E. O.
1967a "Analysis of the Tehuacán coprolites," in *The prehistory of the Tehuacán Valley.* Volume one: *Environment and subsistence.* Edited by Douglas S. Byers, 169–185. Austin: University of Texas Press.
1967b The first New World cereal. *American Antiquity* 32:535–538.
1973 "Dietary patterns in Mexico between 6500 B.C. and 1580 A.D.," in *Man and his foods: studies in the ethnobotany of nutrition — contemporary, primitive, and prehistoric non-European diets.* Edited by C. Earle Smith, Jr., 29–49. University, Ala.: University of Alabama Press.
CARNEIRO, ROBERT L.
1967 On the relationship between size of population and complexity of social organization. *Southwestern Journal of Anthropology* 23: 234–243.
CARNEIRO, ROBERT L., DAISY F. HILSE
1966 On determining the probable rate of population growth during the Neolithic. *American Anthropologist* 68:177–181.
CARTER, GEORGE F.
1971 "Pre-Columbian chickens in America," in *Man across the sea: problems of pre-Columbian contacts.* Edited by Carroll L. Riley, J. Charles Kelley, Campbell W. Pennington, and Robert L. Rands, 178–218. Austin: University of Texas Press.
CHANG, KWANG-CHIH
1967 The Yale expedition to Taiwan and southeast Asian horticultural evolution. *Discovery, Yale Peabody Museum* 2(2):3–10.
1968 *The archaeology of ancient China* (revised edition). New Haven, Conn.: Yale University Press.
1969 *Fengpitou, Tapenkeng, and the prehistory of Taiwan.* Yale University Publications in Anthropology 73.
1970 The beginnings of agriculture in the Far East. *Antiquity* 44:175–185.
1973 Prehistoric archaeology of Taiwan. *Asian Perspectives* 13:59–77.

CHANG, KWANG-CHIH, MINZE STUIVER
1966   Recent advances in the prehistoric archaeology of Formosa. *Proceedings of the National Academy of Sciences USA* 55:539–543.

CHÊNG, TÊ-K'UN
1973   The beginnings of Chinese civilization. *Antiquity* 47:197–209.

COHEN, MARK N.
1975   Archaeological evidence for population pressure in pre-agricultural societies. *American Antiquity* 40:471–475.
i.p.   *Population pressure and the origins of agriculture.* New Haven, Connecticut: Yale University Press.

COWGILL, GEORGE L.
1975   On causes and consequences of ancient and modern population changes. *American Anthropologist* 77:505–525.

Current Anthropology
1972   Articles in *Current Anthropology* 13(2).

DE WET, J. M. J., J. R. HARLAN
1972   Origin of maize: the tripartite hypothesis. *Euphytica* 21:271–279.

DE WET, J. M. J., J. R. HARLAN, C. A. GRANT
1971   Origin and evolution of teosinte (*Zea mexicana* [Schrad.] Kuntze). *Euphytica* 20:255–265.

DURAND, JOHN D.
1972   "The viewpoint of historical demography," in *Population growth: anthropological implications.* Edited by Brian Spooner, 370–374. Cambridge, Mass.: M.I.T. Press.

EMILIANI, CESARE
1968   The Pleistocene epoch and the evolution of man. *Current Anthropology* 9:27–47.

FLANNERY, KENT V.
1966   The postglacial "readaptation" as viewed from Mesoamerica. *American Antiquity* 31:800–805.
1967   "Vertebrate fauna and hunting patterns," in *The prehistory of the Tehuacán Valley,* volume one: *Environment and subsistence.* Edited by Douglas S. Byers, 132–177. Austin: University of Texas Press.
1968   "Archeological systems theory and early Mesoamerica," in *Anthropological archeology in the Americas.* Edited by Betty J. Meggers, 67–87. Washington, D.C.: Anthropological Society of Washington.
1969   "Origins and ecological effects of early domestication in Iran and the Near East," in *The domestication and exploitation of plants and animals.* Edited by Peter J. Ucko and G. W. Dimbleby, 73–100. London: Gerald Duckworth.
1972a   The cultural evolution of civilization. *Annual Review of Ecology and Systematics* 3:399–426.
1972b   "The origins of the village as a settlement type in Mesoamerica and the Near East: a comparative study," in *Man, settlement and urbanism.* Edited by Peter J. Ucko, Ruth Tringham, and G. W. Dimbleby, 23–53. Cambridge, Massachusetts: Schenkman.

1973   The origins of agriculture. *Annual Review of Anthropology* 2: 271–310.

FLANNERY, KENT V., RICHARD I. FORD
1972   "A productivity study of teosinte (*Zea mexicana*)." Mimeographed manuscript. Ann Arbor: Museum of Anthropology, University of Michigan.

FLINT, RICHARD FOSTER
1971   *Glacial and Quaternary geology*. New York: John Wiley and Sons.

FLOWERS, NANCY
1969   The royal fleece of the Andes. *Natural History* 78(5):36–43.

FRISCH, ROSE E.
1975   Demographic implications of the biological determinants of female fecundity. *Social Biology* 22:17–22.

FRISCH, ROSE, JANET W. MC ARTHUR
1974   Menstrual cycles: fatness as a determinant of minimum weight for height necessary for their maintenance or onset. *Science* 185:949–951.

GALINAT, WALTON C.
1970   The cupule and its role in the origin and evolution of maize. *Bulletin of the Agricultural Station of the University of Massachusetts* 585:1–18.
1974   The domestication and genetic erosion of maize. *Economic Botany* 28:31–37.

GILMORE, RAYMOND M.
1950   Fauna and ethnozoology of South America. *Bulletin of the Bureau of American Ethnology* 143(6):345–464.

GORMAN, CHESTER
1970   Hoabinhian: a pebble-tool complex with early plant associations in South-East Asia. *Proceedings of the Prehistoric Society* 35: 355–358.
1971   The Hoabinhian and after: subsistence patterns in Southeast Asia during the late Pleistocene and early Recent periods. *World Archaeology* 2:300–320.
1973   Excavations at Spirit Cave, north Thailand: some interim interpretations. *Asian Perspectives* 13:79–107.

HANKS, LUCIEN M.
1972   *Rice and man: agricultural ecology in Southeast Asia*. Chicago: Aldine-Atherton.

HARDING, ROBERT S. O., SHIRLEY C. STRUM
1976   The predatory baboons of Kekopey. *Natural History* 85(3):46–53.

HARLAN, JACK R.
1971   Agricultural origins: centers and non-centers. *Science* 174:468–474.

HARLAN, JACK R., J. M. J. DE WET
1973   On the quality of evidence for origin and dispersal of cultivated plants. *Current Anthropology* 14:51–62.

HARLAN, JACK R., J. M. J. DE WET, E. GLEN PRICE
1973   Comparative evolution of cereals. *Evolution* 27:311–325.

HARLAN, JACK R., J. M. J. DE WET, S. M. NAIK, R. J. LAMBERT
  1970 Chromosome pairing within genomes in maize-*Tripsacum* hybrids. *Science* 167:1247–1248.
HEISER, CHARLES B., JR.
  1969 Systematics and the origin of cultivated plants. *Taxon* 18:36–45.
  1973a "Variation in the bottle gourd," in *Tropical forest ecosystems in Africa and South America: a comparative review*. Edited by Betty J. Meggers, Edward S. Ayensu, and W. Donald Duckworth, 121–128. Washington, D.C.: Smithsonian Institution Press.
  1973b The penis gourd of New Guinea. *Annals of the Association of American Geographers* 63:312–318.
HIGGS, E. S., M. R. JARMAN
  1969 The origins of agriculture: a reconsideration. *Antiquity* 43:31–41.
HIGHAM, CHARLES
  1975 Non Nok Tha: the faunal remains. *University of Otago: Studies in Prehistoric Anthropology* 7:1–187.
HO, PING-TI
  1975 *The cradle of the East*. Hong Kong and Chicago: Chinese University of Hong Kong Press and the University of Chicago Press.
HOLE, FRANK, KENT V. FLANNERY
  1967 The prehistory of southwestern Iran: a preliminary report. *Proceedings of the Prehistoric Society* 38:147–206.
HOPF, MARIA
  1969 "Plant remains and ealy farming in Jericho," in *The domestication and exploitation of plants and animals*. Edited by Peter J. Ucko and G. W. Dimbleby. London: Gerald Duckworth.
JARMAN, M. R.
  1969 The prehistory of Upper Pleistocene and Recent cattle. Part I: East Mediterranean, with reference to north-west Europe. *Proceedings of the Prehistoric Society* 35:236–266.
  1971 Culture and economy in the north Italian Neolithic. *World Archaeology* 2:255–265.
  1974 "European deer economies and the advent of the Neolithic," in *Papers in economic prehistory: studies by members and associates of the British Academy Major Research Project in the Early History of Agriculture*. Edited by E. S. Higgs, 125–147. Cambridge: Cambridge University Press.
JEFFREYS, M. D. W.
  1956 The muscovy duck. *Nigerian Field* 21:108–111.
JOHNSON, FREDERICK, RICHARD S. MAC NEISH
  1972 "Chronometric dating," in *The prehistory of the Tehuacán Valley*, volume four: *Chronology and irrigation*. Edited by Frederick Johnson, 3–55. Austin: University of Texas Press.
KAPLAN, L.
  1965 Archeology and domestication in American *Phaseolus* [beans]. *Economic Botany* 19:358–368.
KAPLAN, L., THOMAS F. LYNCH, C. E. SMITH, JR.
  1973 Early cultivated beans (*Phaseolus vulgaris*) from an intermontane Peruvian valley. *Science* 179:76–77.

KOFORD, CARL B.
1957   The vicuña and the puna. *Ecological Monographs* 27:153–219.

KOLATE, GINA BARI
1974   !Kung hunter-gatherers: feminism, diet, and birth control. *Science* 185:932–934.

KORTRIGHT, FRANCIS H.
1943   *The ducks, geese and swans of North America.* Washington, D.C.: American Wildlife Institute.

LADIZINSKY, G.
1975   Collection of wild cereals in the Upper Jordan Valley. *Economic Botany* 29:264–267.

LATHRAP, DONALD W.
1969   Review of *Peru before the Incas* by Edward P. Lanning. *American Antiquity* 34:341–345.

LATHRAP, DONALD W., DONALD COLLIER, HELEN CHANDRA
1975   *Ancient Ecuador.* Chicago: Field Museum of Natural History.

LAWRENCE, BARBARA
1967   Early domestic dogs. *Zeitschrift für Säugetierkunde* 32:44–59.

1968   Antiquity of large dogs in North America. *Tebiwa, Journal of the Idaho State University Museum* 11:43–49.

LEE, RICHARD B.
1972a   "Population growth and the beginnings of sedentary life among the !Kung bushmen," in *Population growth: anthropological implications.* Edited by Brian Spooner, 329–342. Cambridge, Mass.: M.I.T. Press.

1972b   "The intensification of social life among the !Kung bushmen," in *Population growth: anthropological implications.* Edited by Brian Spooner, 343–350. Cambridge, Mass.: M.I.T. Press.

LEGGE, A. J.
1972   "Prehistoric exploitation of the gazelle in Palestine," in *Papers in economic prehistory: studies by members and associates of the British Academy Major Research Project in the Early History of Agriculture.* Edited by E. S. Higgs, 119–124. Cambridge: Cambridge University Press.

MAC NEISH, RICHARD STOCKTON
1958   Preliminary archaeological investigations in the Sierra de Tamaulipas, Mexico. *Transactions of the American Philosophical Society,* n.s. 48(6):1–210.

1964a   "The food-gathering and incipient agriculture stage of prehistoric Middle America," in *Handbook of Middle American Indians,* volume one: *Natural environment and early cultures.* Edited by Robert C. West, 413–426. Austin: University of Texas Press.

1964b   Ancient Mesoamerican civilization. *Science* 143:531–537.

1967   "A summary of the subsistence," in *The prehistory of the Tehuacán Valley,* volume one: *Environment and subsistence.* Edited by Douglas S. Byers, 290–309. Austin: University of Texas Press.

1970   "Social implications of changes in population and settlement pattern of the 12,000 years of prehistory in the Tehuacán Valley of Mexico," in *Population and economics: proceedings of Section V* of the *International Economic History Association, 1968*. Edited by Paul Deprex, 215–249. Winnipeg: University of Manitoba Press.

1971   Speculation about how and why food production developed in the Tehuacán Valley, Mexico. *Archaeology* 24:307–314.

1975   "Summary of the cultural sequence and its implications in the Tehuacán Valley," in *The prehistory of the Tehuacán Valley*, volume five: *Excavations and reconnaissance*. Edited by Richard S. MacNeish, 496–506. Austin: University of Texas Press.

MAC NEISH, RICHARD STOCKTON, ANTOINETTE NELKEN-TERNER, ANGEL GARCIA COOK

1970   *Second annual report of the Ayacucho archaeological-botanical project*. Andover, Mass.: Robert S. Peabody Foundation.

MAC NEISH, RICHARD STOCKTON, ANTOINETTE NELKEN-TERNER, IRMGARD W. JOHNSON

1967   "Non-ceramic artifacts," in *The prehistory of the Tehuacán Valley*, volume two. Edited by Douglas S. Byers. Austin: University of Texas Press.

MANGELSDORF, PAUL C.

1974   *Corn: its origin, evolution and improvement*. Cambridge, Mass.: Belknap Press of Harvard University Press.

MANGELSDORF, PAUL C., RICHARD STOCKTON MAC NEISH, GORDON R. WILLEY

1964   "Origins of agriculture in Middle America," in *Handbook of Middle American Indians*, volume one: *Natural environment and early cultures*. Edited by Robert C. West, 427–445. Austin: University of Texas Press.

MARCOS, JORGE G., DONALD W. LATHRAP, JAMES A. ZEIDLER

1976   Ancient Ecuador revisited. *Field Museum of Natural History Bulletin* 47(6):3–8.

MEGGERS, BETTY J.

1974   The transpacific origin of Mesoamerican civilization: a preliminary review of the evidence and its theoretical implications. *American Anthropologist* 77:1–27.

MEYER DE SCHAUENSEE, RODOLPHE

1970   *A guide to the birds of South America*. Philadelphia: Academy of Natural Sciences.

MEYERS, J. THOMAS

1971   "The origins of agriculture: an evaluation of three hypotheses," in *Prehistoric agriculture*. Edited by Stuart Struever, 101–125. Garden City, N.Y.: Natural History Press.

NORDENSKIÖLD, ERLAND

1924   The ethnography of South America seen from Mojos in Bolivia. *Comparative Ethnographical Studies* 3.

PEARSON, OLIVER P.

1951   Mammals in the highlands of southern Peru. *Bulletin of the Museum of Comparative Zoology at Harvard College* 106:115–174.

PEARSON, RICHARD

1973   Radiocarbon dates from China. *Antiquity* 47:141–143.

PERKINS, DEXTER, JR.
1964   Prehistoric fauna from Shanidar, Iraq. *Science* 144:1565–1566.
PETERSON, ROGER TORY, EDWARD L. CHALIF
1973   *A field guide to Mexican birds.* Boston: Houghton Mifflin.
PIETRUSEWSKY, MICHAEL
1975   The palaeodemography of a prehistoric Thai population: Non Nok Tha. *Asian Perspectives* 17:125–140.
PROTSCH, REINER
1975   The absolute dating of Upper Pleistocene sub-Saharan fossil hominids and their place in human evolution. *Journal of Human Evolution* 4:297–322.
RADINSKY, LEONARD
1976   Cerebral clues. *Natural History* 85(5):54–59.
RAINEY, FROELICH
1975   "Archaeology," in *1976 yearbook of science and the future.* Edited by Dave Calhoun, 255–260. Chicago: Encyclopaedia Britannica.
REED, CHARLES A.
1959   Animal domestication in the prehistoric Near East. *Science* 130: 1629–1639.
1960   A review of the archeological evidence on animal domestication in the prehistoric Near East. *Studies in Ancient Oriental Civilization* 31:119–145.
1969   "The pattern of animal domestication in the prehistoric Near East," in *The domestication and exploitation of plants and animals.* Edited by Peter J. Ucko and G. W. Dimbleby, 361–380. London: Gerald Duckworth.
1970   Extinction of mammalian megafauna in the Old World late Quaternary. *BioScience* 20:284–288.
REED, CHARLES A., ROBERT J. BRAIDWOOD
1960   Toward the reconstruction of the environmental sequence of northeastern Iraq. *Studies in Ancient Oriental Civilization* 31: 163–173.
RICHARDSON, JAMES B., III
1972   The pre-Columbian distribution of the bottle gourd (*Lagenaria siceraria*): a re-evaluation. *Economic Botany* 26:265–273.
SAUER, CARL O.
1952   *Agricultural origins and dispersals.* New York: American Geographical Society.
SMITH, PHILIP E. L.
1970   Ganj Dareh Tepe. *Iran, Journal of Persian Studies* 8:174–176.
SOLHEIM, WILHELM G., II
1967   Southeast Asia and the West. *Science* 157:896–902.
1969   Reworking Southeast Asian prehistory. *Paideuma, Mitteilungen zur Kulturkunde* 15:125–139.
1972   An earlier agricultural revolution. *Scientific American* 226(4): 34–41.
1973   Northern Thailand, southern Asia, and world prehistory. *Asian Perspectives* 13:145–162.

SPOONER, BRIAN, *editor*
1972   *Population growth: anthropological implications.* Cambridge, Mass.: M.I.T. Press.

SUSSMAN, ROBERT W.
1972   Child transport, family size, and increase in human population during the Neolithic. *Current Anthropology* 13:258–259.

SUTTON, GEORGE MIKSCH
1951   *Mexican birds: first impressions, based on an ornithological expedition to Tamaulipas, Nuevo León, and Coahuila.* Norman: University of Oklahoma Press.

SWANTON, JOHN R.
1940   "The first description of an Indian tribe in the territory of the present United States," in *Studies for William A. Reed: a miscellany presented by some of his colleagues and friends.* Edited by Nathaniel M. Caffee and Thomas A. Kirby, 326–338. Baton Rouge: Louisiana State University Press.

TAYLOR, WALTER W.
1973   "Storage and the Neolithic revolution," in *Estudios dedicados al Professor Dr. Luis Pericot.* Edited by Edwardo Ropillo, 193–197. Barcelona: Instituto de Arqueología y Prehistoria, Universidad de Barcelona.

Time
1976   Article in *Time*, May 31, p. 48.

TSUKADA, MATSUO
1966   Late Pleistocene vegetation and climate in Taiwan (Formosa). *Proceedings of the National Academy of Sciences USA* 55:543–548.
1967   Vegetation in subtropical Formosa during the Pleistocene glaciations and the Holocene. *Palaeogeography, Palaeoclimatology, Palaeoecology* 3:48–64.

TURNBULL, PRISCILLA F., CHARLES A. REED
1974   The fauna from the terminal Pleistocene of Palegawra Cave, a Zarzian occupation site in northeastern Iraq. *Fieldiana: Anthropology* 63:81–146.

VISHNU-MITTRE, R. SAVITHRI
1975   Supposed remains of rice (*Oryza* sp.) in the terracotta cakes and *pai* at Kalibangan, Rajasthan. *Palaeobotanist* 22:124–126.

VISHNU-MITTRE, STATIRA GUZDER
1975   The early domestication of plants in South and Southeast Asia — a critical review. *Palaeobotanist* 22:83–88.

WHITAKER, THOMAS W.
1971   "Endemism and pre-Columbian migration of the bottle gourd, *Lagenaria siceraria* (Mol.) Standl.," in *Man across the sea: problems of pre-Columbian contacts.* Edited by Carroll L. Riley, J. Charles Kelley, Campbell W. Pennington, and Robert L. Rands, 320–327. Austin: University of Texas Press.

WHITAKER, THOMAS W., GEORGE F. CARTER
1954   Oceanic drift of gourds — experimental observations. *American Journal of Botany* 41:697–700.

1961   A note on the longevity of seed of *Lagenaria siceraria* (Mol.) Standl. after floating in sea water. *Bulletin of the Torrey Botanical Club* 88:104–106.

WHITAKER, THOMAS W., HUGH C. CUTLER
1971   Prehistoric cucurbits from the valley of Oaxaca. *Economic Botany* 25:123–127.

WHITAKER, THOMAS W., HUGH C. CUTLER, RICHARD S. MAC NEISH
1957   Cucurbit materials from three caves near Ocampo, Tamaulipas. *American Antiquity* 22:352–358.

WRIGHT, GARY A.
1971   Origins of food production in southwestern Asia: a survey of ideas. *Current Anthropology* 12:447–477.

YEN, D. E.
1974   *The sweet potato and Oceania: an essay in ethnobotany*. Bernice P. Bishop Museum Bulletin 236.

ZEUNER, FREDERICK E.
1963   *A history of domesticated animals*. London: Hutchinson.

ADDENDUM

My suggestion, borrowed from Lathrap, that earlier villages or towns than those described from southern Mexican highlands (p. 929) might be found in the lowland tropics has been verified by the announcement of Hammond (1977. *Scientific American* 236 (3):116–133) that the early occupation of the Mayan ceremonial site of Cuello, in northern Belize, has been dated at ca. 3930 B.P., with the possibility occurring of occupation more than 200 years earlier. The type of agriculture of the people who built the center has not yet been determined, but *milpa* (slash-and-burn) had not yet been adopted (Hammond, personal communication).

I have had an exchange of correspondence with Professor Wilhelm Solheim concerning my references (pp. 905–907) to his published remarks on early agriculture in Southeastern Asia. While my quotations are accurate, they cannot be as complete as the whole articles from which they were extracted, and Solheim believes that in each case the spirit of the article indicated that his remarks were meant to be considered as hypotheses, not finalities. He also has outlined to me the procedure whereby he determined the time of the first occupation of Spirit Cave to have been ca. 12,500 B.P.; this procedure (too complex to be outlined here) was different than that (pp. 908–909) I imagined he had used, and that suggestion of mine is thereby erroneous. Dr. Solheim has also informed me of some recent C^{14}-determinations and other data of which I had not been aware, but this new information cannot be listed or discussed here.

Considerable information concerning the archaeological site of Ban Chiang, not available to me at the time of writing (p. 917), is to be found in several articles in the journal *Expedition* (1976. vol. 18, no. 3). The accumulating evidence from this site particularly, but also from others similar to it in northeastern Thailand, indicates the strong probability that an advanced culture, including agriculture and bronze-smelting, existed in northeastern Thailand nearly 6,000 years ago.

SECTION SIX

Appendix

A Radiocarbon Chronology Relevant to the Origins of Agriculture

ADINA KABAKER

The following two tables include an extensive, but by no means total, listing of those radiocarbon determinations relevant to the points on the continuum of patterns of subsistence where agriculture began to be manifested; two charts which more graphically illustrate these points are also included. The attempt has been made to include some sites characterized by terminal hunting and gathering or intensive collecting, sites where one particular resource was so thoroughly exploited that sedentism occurred, sites illustrative of incipient cultivation, and finally sites characteristic of true village agriculture. All actual radiocarbon determinations cited in the various articles of this volume have also been charted.

Obviously, those stages mentioned above have all been found in the four or five major parts of the world where agriculture was ultimately found. However, no consistent timing is found in all areas. The exploitation of marine resources in coastal Peru began quite early and lasted for a longer time than elsewhere in the world where intensive agriculture had become developed, and the earliest village agriculture became established most firmly in the Near East. Some radiocarbon determinations in areas peripheral to early agricultural centers (northern Africa, the circum-Caspian, Greece, and the Balkans) have been cited to indicate the spread of village agriculture once it had begun in the nuclear areas of the Near East.

I am particularly grateful for advice concerning the dates to be included, and the sources where they could be located, to Robert Braidwood of the University of Chicago, and James Phillips and Charles Reed at the University of Illinois at Chicago Circle. The charts were drawn, under the direction of Ray Brod, in the Cartographic Laboratory of the Department of Geography at the University of Illinois, Chicago Circle. Without the kind help of these individuals, the difficult task of assembling and presenting the information in this section of this book would have been much more difficult.

The key to the column headed "subsistence" is as follows:
H and G — hunting and gathering
IC — intensive collecting
IER — intensive exploitation of a particular resource
IA — incipient agriculture
VA — village agriculture

In all of the manuscripts of this volume, as well as on the chronological charts of this section, we follow the practice of the journal *Radiocarbon* in using a half-life of 5,568 years for C-14 and consider the year A.D. 1950 as the "present," the time from which all C-14 determinations are calculated on the basis of Before Present (B.P.). By "years B.P." we mean "radiocarbon years," as reported in *Radiocarbon* or elsewhere, uncorrected for the "bristle-cone pine factor." Perhaps we should have used b.p. (instead of B.P.) for such uncorrected radiocarbon years (Antiquity 1973: 141), but at the time of the writing of the manuscripts none of us was aware of the increasing use of this particular convention.

Our use of uncorrected dates for years Before Present (i.e. before 1950) is not that followed by most archaeologists, who continue to use the symbols B.C. or A.D. for uncorrected radiocarbon determinations as if these were valid DATES calculated in calendar-years; actually, the difference between true dates (either those historically validated or those radiocarbon determinations corrected for the bristle-cone pine factor) and uncorrected radiocarbon determinations may be as much as 800 years, leading to errors in conclusions if the two kinds of "dates" are compared directly, on the assumption (too often made) that all dates designated B.C. must necessarily have been determined on the same standards.

In the chapters in this book, therefore, we consistently use B.P. for our "dates," in the sense as outlined above, except for historically validated dates or unless — as with some of the prehistoric radiocarbon determinations presented by Professor Ho — the proper corrective factor has been applied.

Table 1. Eastern Hemisphere

Site	Level or period	Date and laboratory number	Subsistence	Comments	Reference
I. Greece, Crete, Cyprus, and Bulgaria					
1. Elateia		8230±75 (GR-2933)	–	probably too early	(Watson 1965)
2. Nea Nikomedeia		8180±150 (Q-655)	VA		(Watson 1965)
3. Knossos		8050±180 (BM-124)	VA		(Watson 1965)
4. Knossos		7910±140 (BM-278)	VA	wooden stake with carbonized grain	(R. 11: 2, p. 280)
5. Knossos		7740±140 (BM-436)	VA	grain found with above	(R. 11: 2, p. 280)
6. Khirokitia		7710±160 (St-414)	VA		(R. 2: 1, p. 193)
7. Khirokitia		7600±150 (average of St-414, 415, 416)	VA	aceramic	(Watson 1965)
8. Knossos		7570±150 (BM-272)	VA	first brick house overlying earliest campsite	(R. 11: 2, p. 279)
9. Nea Nikomedeia	A4/3	7557±91 (P-1202)	VA	first building period	(R. 9: 1, p. 355)
10. Argissa Magula		7500±90 (GrN-4145)	VA	post from burnt ceramic house	(R. 9: 1, p. 129)
11. Khirokitia		7500±160 (St-416)	VA		(R. 2: 1, p. 193)
12. Elateia		7470±70 (GrN-2973)	–		(R. 5: 1, p. 182)
13. Elateia		7350±90 (GrN-3037)	–		(Watson 1965)
14. Nea Nikomedeia	B4/1	7281±74 (P-1203A)	VA	red on white painted pottery, microblades, antelope bones	(R. 9: 1, p. 360)
15. Elateia		7280±100 (GR-3041)	–		(Watson 1965)
16. Tell Azmak	Karanova I I/1	7158±150 (Bln-291)	VA		(R. 8: 1, p. 32)
17. Elateia		7030±130 (GR-3502)	–		(Watson 1965)
18. Knossos		7000±180 (BM-126)	VA		(Watson 1965)
19. Tell Azmak	Karanova I I/1	6878±100 (Bln-292)	VA	grain – *T. dicoccum* and *T. monococcum*	(R. 8: 1, p. 32)

Table 1 (continued)

Site	Level or period	Date and laboratory number	Subsistence	Comments	Reference
20. Tell Azmak	Karanova I 1/2	6720±100 (Bln-295)	VA	*T. dicoccum* and *T. aestivum*	(R. 8: 1, p. 33)
21. Tell Azmak	Karanova I 1/3	6675±100 (Bln-297)	VA	*T. dicoccum* and *T. aestivum*	(R. 8: 1, p. 33)
22. Tell Karanova	Karanova III	6360±100 (Bln-158)	VA	*H. vulgare, T. dicoccum,* and *T. monococcum*	(R. 8: 1, p. 37)
23. Tell Azmak	Karanova VI IV/1	5888±100 (Bln-149)	VA	*H. vulgare* and *H. polystichum*	(R. 8: 1, p. 34)
24. Tell Azmak	Karanova V III/2	5737±150 (Bln-143)	VA	*Vicia* cf. *angustivolia*	(R. 8: 1, p. 34)
25. Tell Azmak	Karanova V III/2	5630±150 (Bln-150)	VA	*H. vulgare, H. polystichum, T. monococcum,* and *Pisum elatium*	(R. 8: 1, p. 34)
II. Egypt and North Africa					
1. Kom Ombo	Microlithic area	15130±200 (Y-1376)	IC and H	handstones	(R. 11: 2, p. 642)
2. Kom Ombo	K/9 Sebilian	13560±120 (Y-1447)	IC and H	grinding-slabs and handstones	(R. 11: 2, p. 642)
3. Kom Ombo	J/11 Sebilian	13070±160 (Y-1375)	IC and H	grinding-slabs and handstones	(R. 11: 2, p. 642)
4. Haua Fteah		12300±350 (W-97)	H and G	Oranian evolved blades and burins	(Braidwood 1959)
5. Haua Fteah		10600±400 (W-104)	H and G	Oranian evolved blades and burins	(Braidwood 1959)
6. Guettara Wadi	DEG 2	10190±230 (Gif-882)	–	pre-Neolithic	(R. 14: 2, p. 291)
7. Ain Naga	ANG 2	9170±200 (Gif-1220)	–		(R. 14: 2, p. 292)
8. Amekni Tamanrasset		8670±150 (MC-212)	IC	possibly domestic cattle	(R. 11: 1, p. 126)
9. Hassi Mouillah		8600±150 (MC-150)	–	Epipaleolithic with Capsian Neolithic overlying	(R. 11: 1, p. 126)
10. Koudiat Kifen Lahda		8540±200 (Gif-879)	IC	Upper Capsian	(R. 14: 2, p. 293)
11. Medjez II	MJZII, 7	8480±300 (Gif-889)	IC	Setif facies of Capsian	(R. 14: 2, p. 292)
12. Medjez II	MJZII, 5	8270±185 (Gif-887)	IC		(R. 14: 2, p. 292)
13. Medjez II	MJZII, 4	7900±180 (Gif-886)	IC		(R. 14: 2, p. 292)
14. Medjez II	MJZII, 6	7780±180 (Gif-888)	IC		(R. 14: 2, p. 292)
15. Medjez II	MJZII, 3	7680±500 (Gif-885)	IC		(R. 14: 2, p. 292)
16. Hassi Mouillah		7650±170 (Gif-1195)	–	Neolithic of Capsian tradition	(R. 14: 2, p. 292)

				Date		Description	Reference
17.	Ain Naga	ANG 3		7500±220 (Gif-1221)	–	oldest date at this site — charcoal from hearth	(R. 14: 2, p. 292)
18.	Tassili-n-Ajer	No. 5		7400±300 (Gif-290)	IC		(R. 8: 1, p. 87)
19.	El Biod			7300±200 (MC-150)	–	ceramics scarcer than at Hassi Mouillah	(R. 11: 1, p. 126)
20.	Haua Fteah			7300±300 (W-89)	IC	evolved blade and microlithic	(Braidwood 1959)
21.	El Hadjar			7300±170 (Gif-880)	–	Iberomaurusian and Capsian	(R. 14: 2, p. 293)
22.	Catfish cave			7060±120 (Y-3467)	IER	barbed bone points	(R. 12: 1, p. 126)
23.	Safiet Bou Rhenan			6970±170 (Gif-884)	–	oldest Neolithic with ceramics	(R. 14: 2, p. 292)
24.	Haua Fteah			6800±350 (W-98)	IA	suspected domestication of sheep or goats	(Braidwood 1959)
25.	Amekni Tamanrasset	AMK 4		6800±220 (Gif-1222)	–	Sudanese Neolithic pottery and grindstones	(R. 14: 2, p. 293)
26.	El Kab			6400±160 (LV-393)	IC	grindstones	(J. Phillips, personal communication)
27.	Fayum	A		6391±180 (C-550-551)	VA		(Kantor 1965)
28.	Fayum	A		6095±250 (C-457)	VA		(Kantor 1965)
29.	Station de Méandre			5850±150 (Gif-883)	–	Capsian	(R. 14: 2, p. 292)
30.	Kom Ombo	GS2BI, 2		14390±200 (I-5180)	IC	Silsilian grinding-slabs and handstones	(Phillips and Butzer 1975)
31.	Tushka			14500±490 (WSU-315)	IC	? grinding-stones, lunates with sickle sheen	(Wendorf 1968)
32.	Esna	E71P5		11560±180 (I-3760)	IC	? grinding-stones, sickle sheen	(Wendorf and Schild i.p.)
III. Eastern Mediterranean: Maquis							
1.	Mersin	basal		7950±250 (W-617)	VA	lower Neolithic	(Watson 1965)
2.	Byblos	Level XLIII		7360±70 (GrN-1544)	VA		(R. 14: 1, p. 50)
3.	Byblos			7000±80 (GrN?)	VA	Eneolithic A	(Braidwood 1959)
4.	Byblos			6550±200 (W-627)	VA	Eneolithic A	(Braidwood 1959)
IV. Eastern Mediterranean: Mixed Woods and Grasslands							
1.	Ein Aqev			17890±600 (SMU-6)	H and G	a grinding-slab and a handstone	(Marks and Ferring i.p.)
2.	Ein Aqev			17500±290 (I-5495)	H and G		(R. 15: 2, p. 295)

Table 1 (continued)

Site	Level or period	Date and laboratory number	Subsistence	Comments	Reference
3. Ein Aqev		17390±560 (SMU-8)	H and G		(Marks and Ferring i.p.)
4. Ein Aqev		16900±250 (I-5494)	H and G		(R. 15: 2, p. 295)
5. Ein Gev (Ein Guev)		15700±415 (GrN-5576)	IC	Kebaran	(R. 14: 1, p. 49)
6. Kas Shamra		9030±400 (P-459/458)	VA		(R. 8: 1, p. 138)
7. Ras Shamra	VC	8364±101 (P-460)	VA	prepottery	(Watson 1965)
8. Munhata		8265±450 (av. of M-1792 and M-1793)	VA		(R. 12: 1, p. 178, 9)
9. Ramad I	0.50 meter	8210±50 (GrN-4426)	VA	PPN with plastered skulls	(R. 8: 1, p. 129)
10. Ramad I	5–10 meters	8200±80 (GrN-4428)	VA	PPN: einkorn, emmer, and barley	(R. 8: 1, p. 129)
11. Ras Shamra	VC	8142±100 (P-459)	VA	PPN	(Watson 1965)
12. Ramad I	1.45 meters	8090±50 (GrN-4821)	VA	PPN	(R. 8: 1, p. 129)
13. Ramad I	2.5 meters	7920±50 (GrN-4427)	VA	PPN	(R. 8: 1, p. 129)
14. Ramad II	1.80 meters	7900±50 (GrN-4422)	VA	PPN	(R. 8: 1, p. 129)
15. Ramad III		7880±55 (GrN-4823)	VA	PPN	(R. 8: 1, p. 129)
16. Ras Shamra	VB	7686±112 (P-458)	VA	pottery like Middle Neolithic of Byblos	(Watson 1965)
17. Ras Shamra	VA	7184±84 (P-457)	VA		(Watson 1965)
V. Eastern Mediterranean: Plains, Steppe					
1. Negev	E 22P 15/1	>37000 (TX-1119)	H and G	Levantine Mousterian	(R. 14: 1, p. 484)
2. Negev	E 22D 5/8A	15820±1730 (TX-1121)	IC	Kebaran	(R. 11: 2, p. 484)
3. Jericho		11166±107 (P-376)	IC	Natufian	(R. 5: 1, p. 84)
4. Jericho		10300±500 (BM-250)	IER	PPNA — *H. distichum, T. dicoccum* not necessarily cultivated; intensive exploitation of gazelle	(R. 11: 2, p. 290)
5. Jericho		10250±200 (BM-105)	IER	PPNA	(R. 5: 1, p. 107)
6. Jericho		10180±200 (BM-110)	IER	PPNA	(R. 5: 1, p. 107)
7. Jericho		9850±240 (F-69)	IER	PPNA	(Watson 1965)
8. Jericho		9800±240 (F-72)	IER	PPNA	(Watson 1965)
9. Jericho		9775±110 (P-378)	IER	PPNA	(Watson 1965)

	Site	Level	Date			Reference
10.	Jericho		9655±84 (P-379)	IER	PPNA	(Watson 1965)
11.	Jericho		9592±84 (P-377)	IER	PPNA	(R. 5: 1, p. 84)
12.	Jericho		9390±150 (BM-251)	IER	PPNA	(R. 11: 2, p. 290)
13.	Jericho		9320±150 (BM-252)	IER	PPNA	(R. 11: 2, p. 290)
14.	Jericho		9170±200 (BM-111)	VA	PPNB: barley	(Watson 1965)
15.	Beidha	Level II	9030±50 (GrN-5062)	VA	possibly out of sequence	(R. 14: 1, p. 50)
16.	Jericho		8956±103 (P-382)	VA	PPNB	(Watson 1965)
17.	Beidha	Level VI	8940±160 (K-1086)	VA		(R. 10: 2, p. 323)
18.	Jericho		8900±70 (GrN-942)	VA	PPNB	(Watson 1965)
19.	Beidha	Level VI	8860±50 (GrN-5063)	VA	PPNB	(R. 14: 1, p. 50)
20.	Beidha	Level IV	8810±50 (GrN-5136)	VA	PPNB	(R. 14: 1, p. 50)
21.	Jericho		8800±160 (F-39)	VA	PPNA	(Watson 1965)
22.	Jericho		8785±100 (GrN-963)	VA	plastered floor	(Braidwood 1959)
23.	Beidha	Level IV	8780±200 (BM-111)	VA		(R. 10: 1, p. 4)
24.	Beidha	Level IV	8730±160 (K-1084)	VA	goat, emmer	(R. 10: 2, p. 324)
25.	Jericho		8725±210 (F-40)	VA	hog-back brick	(Braidwood 1959)
26.	Beidha	Level VI	8710±160 (K-1082)	VA		(R. 10: 2, p. 324)
27.	Jericho		8710±150 (BM-253)	VA		(R. 11: 2, p. 29)
28.	Jericho		8658±101 (P-381)	VA		(Watson 1965)
29.	Beidha	Level V	8640±160 (K-1083)	VA	PPNB	(R. 10: 2, p.324)
30.	Jericho		8610±75 (P-380)	VA		(R. 5: 1, p. 84)
31.	Beidha	Level II	8550±160 (K-1085)	VA	PPNB	(R. 10: 2, p. 324)
32.	Jericho		8200±200 (GL-28)	VA	PPNB	(Watson 1965)
33.	Negev	E 22D 1/34	8170±180 (TX-1122)	IA	PPNB without sickles or grindstones	(R. 14: 1, p. 484)
34.	Jericho		7800±160 (F-38)	VA	PPNB	(Watson 1965)
35.	Jericho		7800±200 (GL-38)	VA	PPNB	(Watson 1965)
36.	Beersheba		7420±520 (C-919)	VA	Ghassulian	(Braidwood 1959)
VI. Anatolia						
1.	Haçilar	V	8700±180 (BM-127)	VA	aceramic; emmer, einkorn, and barley	(R. 5: 1, p. 108)
2.	Suberde	III	8520±140 (I-1867)	IER	aceramic; possible domestic grain; hunting village	(Bordaz 1973)
3.	Çatal Hüyük	IX	8436±102 (P-779)	VA	cattle, einkorn, emmer, barley	(Mellink 1965)

Table 1 (continued)

Site	Level or period	Date and laboratory number	Subsistence	Comments	Reference
4. Çatal Hüyük	X	8335±101 (P-782)	VA	cattle, einkorn, emmer, barley	(Mellink 1965)
5. Çatal Hüyük	IV	8279±99 (P-775)	VA	cattle, einkorn, emmer, barley	(Mellink 1965)
6. Çatal Hüyük	VI	8150±97 (P-770)	VA	cattle, einkorn, emmer, barley	(Mellink 1965)
7. Çatal Hüyük	VI	7936±94 (P-777)	VA	cattle, einkorn, emmer, barley	(Mellink 1965)
8. Çatal Hüyük	V	7870±94 (P-776)	VA	cattle, einkorn, emmer, barley	(Mellink 1965)
9. Çatal Hüyük	VI	7858±93 (P-797)	VA	cattle, einkorn, emmer, barley	(Mellink 1965)
10. Çatal Hüyük	VI	7800±94 (P-772)	VA	cattle, einkorn, emmer, barley	(Mellink 1965)
11. Haçilar	VII	7770±180 (BM-125)	VA	einkorn, emmer, barley	(R. 5: 1, p. 104)
12. Çatal Hüyük	VII	7765±92 (P-778)	VA		(Mellink 1965)
13. Çatal Hüyük	III	7757±94 (P-774)	VA		(Mellink 1965)
14. Haçilar	VI	7750±180 (BM-48)	VA		(Watson 1965)
15. Çatal Hüyük	VI	7750±93 (P-781)	VA		(Mellink 1965)
16. Çatal Hüyük	II	7747±79 (P-796)	VA		(Mellink 1965)
17. Çatal Hüyük	VI	7731±96 (P-769)	VA	grain	(Mellink 1965)
18. Erbaba		7730±120 (I-5151)	VA	domestic grain, pea, cattle, sheep, and goats	(Bordaz 1973)
19. Haçilar	VI	7570±79 (P-313A)	VA		(Mellink 1965)
20. Haçilar	IX	7564±92 (P-314)	VA		(Mellink 1965)
21. Haçilar	VI	7550±180 (BM-48)	VA		(R. 5: 1, p. 107)
22. Haçilar	II	7384±131 (P-316A)	VA		(Mellink 1965)
23. Haçilar	IX	7340±94 (P-314)	VA		(Watson 1965)
24. Haçilar	Ia	7197±119 (P-315)	VA		(Mellink 1965)
25. Haçilar	II	7170±134 (P-316)	VA		(R. 4: 1, p. 46)
26. Can Hasan	D	7033±89 (P-794)	VA		(R. 7: 1, p. 193)
27. Can Hasan	C	6670±76 (P-792)	VA		(R. 7: 1, p. 193)

VII. Euphrates, Tigris, Karun Drainage, Upper Euphrates: Plains, Steppe

#	Site	Date (lab)		Remarks	Reference
1.	Kote Berçem (Çayönü) K-12 T/2	9520±100 (GrN-4458)	VA		(R. Braidwood, personal communication)
2.	Çayönü	9320±55 (GrN-6243)	VA		(R. Braidwood, personal communication)
3.	Çayönü	9275±95 (GrN-6241)	VA		(R. Braidwood, personal communication)
4.	Kote Berçem (Çayönü) K-6/4-5	9200±60 (GrN-4459)	VA		(R. Braidwood, personal communication)
5.	Çayönü	8980±80 (GrN-6244)	VA	sheep (?), cattle	(R. Braidwood, personal communication)
6.	Çayönü	8795±50 (GrN-6242)	VA		(R. Braidwood, personal communication)
7.	Çayönü	8790±250 (M-1609)	VA	emmer, einkorn, lentil, pea, vetch, and flax	(R. Braidwood, personal communication)
8.	Çayönü	8570±250 (M-1610)	VA		(R. Braidwood, personal communication)
9.	Bouqras I top	8240±100 (GrN-4852)	VA	sheep, einkorn, emmer, and barley	(R. 9: 1, p. 128)
10.	Bouqras I bottom	8140±60 (GrN-4818)	VA	sheep, einkorn, emmer, and barley	(R. 9: 1, p. 128)
11.	Çayönü	8055±75 (GrN-5954)	VA		(R. Braidwood, personal communication)
12.	Bouqras II	7960±60 (GrN-4819)	VA		(R. 9: 1, p. 128)
13.	Bouqras III	7840±60 (GrN-4820)	VA		(R. 9: 1, p. 128)
14.	Halaf	7570±35 (GrN-2660)	VA		(R. 6: 1, p. 355)
15.	Girikihacyian	6950±45 (GrN-6245)	VA		(P. J. Watson, personal communication)

VIII. Tigris: Mixed Woods, Grasslands

1.	Banahilk	6660±70 (GrN-6355)	VA	Halafian	(R. 15: 2, p. 373)

IX. Upper Tigris: Plains, Steppe

1.	Pelegawra	13583±88 (average of GrN-6357, -6358, -6356)	H and G	Upper Paleolithic	(R. Braidwood, personal communication)
2.	Arpachiyah	8064±78 (P-585)	VA		(R. 7: 1, p. 188)

Table 1   (continued)

Site	Level or period	Date and laboratory number	Subsistence	Comments	Reference
3. Matarrah		7570±250 (W-623)	VA	possibly contaminated	(R. 2: 1, p. 183)
4. Hassuna		7040±200 (W-660)	VA		(R. 2: 1, p. 183)
5. Arpachiyah		7027±83 (P-584)	VA		(R. 7: 1, p. 188)
X. Tigris: Mixed Woods, Grasslands					
1. Shanidar	B	12000±400 (W-179)	H and G	Lower Zarzian	(Watson 1965)
2. Jarmo	PQ-14	11240±300 (W-657)	VA	probably contaminated	(Watson 1965)
3. Jarmo	N-18	11200±200 (W-665)	VA	probably contaminated	(Watson 1965)
4. Zawi Chemi (Shanidar)		10870±300 (W-681)	IC	Zarzian; ? dom. sheep	(Watson 1965)
5. Shanidar	B	10600±300 (?)		Zarzian	(Watson 1965)
6. Ganj-i-dareh		10400±150 (Gak-807)	IA		(R. 9: 1, p. 61)
7. Asiab		9755±85 (GrN-6413)	VA		(Protsch and Berger 1973)
8. Ganj-i-dareh		9239±196 (P-1485)	IA	goat	(R. 12: 1, p. 579)
9. Jarmo	PQ-14	9040±250 (W-607)	VA	goat, einkorn, emmer, and barley	(Watson 1965)
10. Ganj-i-dareh		8968±100 (P-1484)	IA		(R. 12: 1, p. 579)
11. Ganj-i-dareh		8888±98 (P-1486)	IA		(R. 12: 1, p. 579)
12. Jarmo		8830±200 (W-651)	VA		(Watson 1965)
13. Jarmo		8525±175 (H-551/491)	VA	goat, pig, einkorn, emmer, and barley	(Watson 1965)
14. Sarab	S, 5	7965±98 (P-466)	VA		(Watson 1965)
15. Jarmo		7950±200 (W-652)	VA		(Watson 1965)
16. Tepe Guran		7760±150 (K-?)	VA	ceramics present, floors of white gypsum	(Meldgaard, Mortensen, and Thrane 1964)
17. Jarmo		7750±250 (W-608)	VA		(Watson 1965)
18. Sarab	C, 1	7644±89 (P-467)	VA		(Watson 1965)
19. Sarab	S, 4	7605±96 (P-465)	VA		(Watson 1965)
20. Jarmo		6707±320 (C-113)	VA		(Watson 1965)
21. Jarmo		6695±360 (C-743)			(Watson 1965)
22. Jarmo		6106±330 (C-742)	VA		(Watson 1965)
XI. Karun Drainage: Semi-desert					
1. Ali Kosh		9900±200 (UCLA-750-D)	VA	Bus Mordeh; goat, emmer, and barley	(R. 7: 1, p. 355)

#	Site	Level/Depth	Date	Lab	Notes	Reference
2.	Darrä Kalon	III	9475±100 (R-274)	–	microblades, denticulates may be too old	(R. 9:1, p. 360)
3.	Tepe Sabz	1000–1020 cm. deep	9050±160 (UCLA 750-C)	VA		(R. 7:1, p. 355)
4.	Ali Kosh		8890±200 (SI-160)	VA	Mohammed Jaffir; goat, emmer, and barley	(R. 8:1, p. 419)
5.	Ali Kosh		8438±200 (DL-21 # 9)	VA		(Watson 1965)
6.	Ali Kosh		8415±180 (DL-21 # 9)	VA		(Watson 1965)
7.	Ali Kosh		8338±210 (DL-21 # 4)	VA		(Watson 1965)
8.	Ali Kosh		8240±175 (DL-21 # 9)	VA		(Watson 1965)
9.	Ghazir		7762±98 (P-930)	VA		(R. 8:1, p. 930)
10.	Ali Kosh		7760±330 (DL-21 # 4)	VA		(Watson 1965)
11.	Ali Kosh		7740±600 (SI-207)	VA	late phase	(R. 9:1, p. 379)
12.	Tepe Sabz	860 cm. deep	6925±200 (UCLA-750B)	VA	free threshing wheat; irrigation	(R. 7:1, p. 355)
13.	Tepe Sabz	270–280 cm. deep	6070±100 (UCLA-750A)	VA		(R. 7:1, p. 355)

XII. Iranian Plateau

#	Site	Level	Date	Lab	Notes	Reference
1.	Haji Firuz	D 15	7269±86 (P-455)	VA		(R. 5:1, p. 90)
2.	Zage	F XX	7147±91 (TUNC-12)	VA	possible source of both Sialk and Hissar	(R. 14:2, p. 459)
3.	Haji Firuz	V, 4	6895±83 (P-502)	VA		(R. 5:1, p. 90)
4.	Sagz-Abad		6083±84 (TUNC-11)	VA	similar to Sialk III and Hissar IB	(R. 14:2, p. 459)
5.	Dalma Tepe		5986±87 (P-87)	VA		(Watson 1965)

XIII. Col Hyr Basin

The following are some of the dates averaged by Carleton Coon in "Seven caves" and quoted by Braidwood (1959).

#	Site	Date	Lab	Notes
1.	Hotu	11860±840	H and G	"seal hunters"
2.	Belt	11480±550	H and G	"seal Mesolithic"
3.	Hotu	9200±580	H and G	"vole eaters"
4.	Belt	8570±380	H and G	"gazelle Mesolithic"
5.	Hotu	8070±500	IC	"sub-Neolithic"
6.	Belt	7790±330		"preceramic Neolithic"
7.	Belt	7280±260		"ceramic Neolithic"
8.	Hotu	6385±425		"software Neolithic"

XIV. Shiraz Ker Basin

#	Site	Level	Date	Lab	Notes	Reference
1.	Bakun	B	5990±81 (P-438)	VA	straw-tempered pottery	(R. 5:1, p. 90)

Table 1 (continued)

Site	Level or period	Date and Laboratory number	Subsistence	Comments	Reference
XV. Circum-Caspian					
1. Ak Tan'ga		8785±130 (LE-534)	VA	Hissar 6; early Neolithic	(R. 12: 1, p. 142)
2. Tutkaul	2nd horizon	8025±170 (LE-772)	VA		(R. 14: 1, p. 354)
3. Shomu Tepe		7510±70 (LE-631)	VA	Eneolithic	(R. 12: 1, p. 140)
4. Togolok Depe	2	7320±100 (Bln-719)	VA	Jeitun	(R. 12: 1, p. 418)
5. Tutkaul		7100±140 (LE-690)	VA	Hissar	(R. 12: 1, p. 143)
6. Chagylly Tepe		7000±110 (LE-592)	VA	Late Jeitun	(R. 12: 1, p. 141)
7. Togolok Depe	1	6890±100 (Bln-718)	VA	Jeitun	(R. 12: 1, p. 418)
8. Tutkaul	2nd horizon	6760±110 (LE-777)	VA		(R. 14: 1, p. 354)
9. Tel'Bin Tepe		6590±110 (RUL-159)	IA	early agriculture	(R. 7: 1, 226)
10. Djebel Cave	IV	6030±240 (RUL-1)	IC		(R. 7: 1, 226)
11. Ak Tan'ga		5950±380 (LE-474)	VA	Hissar 4	(R. 12: 1, p. 142)
12. Dyul' Tepe		5770±90 (LE-477)	VA	campsite	(R. 12: 1, p. 140)
XVI. China, Southeast Asia, and India					
1. Padah-lin	(Burma)	13400±200 (R-547/5B)	IC	earliest Hoabinhian	(Gorman, this volume)
2. Spirit Cave 3	(Thailand)	11350±280 (FSU-315)	IC	earliest Hoabinhian	(R. 13: 1, p. 24)
3. Tham Ongbah	XIIe	11180±180 (K-1366)	IC	earliest Hoabinhian	(R. 15: 1, p. 110)
4. Spirit Cave 5		10900±550 (FSU-316)	IC		(R. 13: 1, p. 24)
5. Tham Ongbah	XIa	10760±170 (K-1340)	IC	Hoabinhian implements	(R. 15: 1, p. 110)
6. Tham Ongbah	XIIb	10090±160 (K-1363)	IC	intensive collecting	(R. 15: 1, p. 110)
7. Tham Ongbah	XIIc	10010±150 (K-1364)	IC		(R. 15: 1, p. 110)
8. Tham Ongbah	XIId	9970±150 (K-1365)	IC		(R. 15: 1, p. 110)
9. Tham Ongbah	XIb	9750±150 (K-1341)	IC		(R. 15: 1, p. 110)
10. Tham Ongbah	XIIa	9350±140 (K-1362)	IC		(R. 15: 1, p. 110)
11. Spirit Cave	2a	8520±145 (FSU-318)	IC		(R. 13: 1, p. 24)
12. Spirit Cave	2	7905±195 (FSU-314)	IC		(R. 13: 1, p. 24)
13. Spirit Cave	2	7400±150 (FSU-317)	IC		(R. 13: 1, p. 24)
14. Huang-Shen-hsi	(Szechwan)	7273±130 (ZK-19)	IC(?)		(Ho, this volume)
15. P'an-po	(Shensi)	5894±110 (ZK-38)	VA	Yang Shao pottery, ground-stone	(Ho, this volume)
16. P'an-po	(Shensi)	5738±110 (ZK-121)	VA	spades, milling-stones	(Ho, this volume)
17. P'an-po	(Shensi)	5704±105 (ZK-122)	VA	milling-stones	(Ho, this volume)

No.	Site	Region	Date (Lab)	Code	Description	Reference
18.	P'an-po	(Shensi)	5427±105 (ZK-127)	VA	milling stones and hazel-nuts	(Ho, this volume)
19.	Hou-Kang	(Honan)	5330±105 (ZK-76)	VA	Yang Shao; *Setaria italica*	(Ho, this volume)
20.	Sung-tze	(Shanghai)	5194±105 (ZK-55)	VA	Ch'ing-lien-Kang; rice	(Ho, this volume)
21.	Miao-ti-kou	(Honan)	5257±100 (ZK-110)	VA	Yang Shao; pigs, dogs, and cattle	(Ho, this volume)
22.	Gua Kechel		4700±800 (?)	IC	end of Hoabinhian	(Gorman, this volume)
23.	Ch'ien-shan-yang	(Chekiang)	4567±100 (ZK-49)	VA	peach, melon, broad bean, groundnut, sesame, and Liang chu rice	(Ho, this volume)
24.	Ts'ao-chia-tsui	(Kansu)	4397±100 (ZK-108)	VA	Ma-chia-yao	(Ho, this volume)
25.	Navadatoli	(India)	4249±72 (P-476)	VA	earliest rice with scrub-burning	(Gorman, this volume)
26.	P'ao-ma-ling	(Kiangsu)	4164±95 (ZK-51)	VA	Neolithic; chicken bones; Lungshanoid	(Ho, this volume)
27.	Miao-ti-kou	(Honan)	4140±95 (ZK-111)	VA		(Ho, this volume)
28	Huang-lien-shu	(Honan)	4101±95 (ZK-91)	VA	Ma-chia-yao	(Ho, this volume)
29.	Ma'chia-wan-ts'un	(Kansu)	4018±95 (ZK-21)	VA	Ma-chia-yao	(Ho, this volume)
30.	Ch'ing-kang-ch'a	(Kansu)	3901±95 (ZK-25)	VA	Pan Shan	(Ho, this volume)
31.	Shuang-t'o-tsu	(Liaoning)	3897±95 (ZK-78)	VA	Lung-shan	(Ho, this volume)
32.	Wang-wan	(Honan)	3838±95 (ZK-126)	VA	Honan Lung-shan	(Ho, this volume)
33.	T'a-li-t'a-li-ha	(Chinghai)	3668±90 (ZK-61)	VA	?	(Ho, this volume)
34.	Ahar	(India)	3675±110 (?)	VA	Sorghum introduced	(Vishnu-Mittre, this volume)
35.	Navadatoli		3608±131 (P-202)	VA		(Gorman, this volume)
36.	Ta-ho-chuang	(Kansu)	3571±95 (ZK-15)	VA	Ch'i-chia	(Ho, this volume)
37.	Ta-ho-chuang	(Kansu)	3542±95 (ZK-23)	VA	Ch'i-chia	(Ho, this volume)

Table 2. Western Hemisphere

Site	Level or period	Date and laboratory number	Subsistence	Comments	Reference
I. Peruvian Highlands					
1. Pikimachay Cave	J/II juncture	20200±1050 (I-5851A)	H and G		(MacNeish, this volume)
2. Pikimachay Cave	above J	19600±3000 (UCLA-1653A)	H and G		(MacNeish, this volume)
3. Pikimachay Cave	II	16050±1200 (UCLA-1653B)	H and G		(MacNeish, this volume)
4. Pikimachay Cave	i	14700±1400 (UCLA-1653C)	H and G		(MacNeish, this volume)
5. Pikimachay Cave	overlying h	14150±180 (UCLA-1464)	H and G		(MacNeish, this volume)
6. Jaywa Cave	J3	10280±170 (I-5699)	H and G	seasonal, possible guinea pig domestication, grinding-stones	(MacNeish, this volume)
7. Jaywa Cave	J2	9890±310 (I-5683)	H and G		(MacNeish, this volume)
8. Jaywa Cave	I	9560±170 (I-5645)	H and G		(MacNeish, this volume)
9. Lauricocha Caves	deepest level L. 1	9525±250 (unpublished)	H and G		(R. 11: 2, p. 374)
10. Jaywa Cave	J1	9460±145 (I-5275)	H and G	seasonal, possible guinea pig domestication, grinding-tools	(MacNeish, this volume)
11. Akimachay Cave	no level	9066±(?) (?)	H and G		(MacNeish, this volume)
12. Jaywa Cave	H	8980±140 (I-5277)	H and G	seasonal, possible guinea pig domestication, grinding-tools	(MacNeish, this volume)
13. Guitarrero Cave	Stratum III	7680±280	IC	lima beans	(Pickersgill and Heiser, this volume)
14. Jaywa Cave	J	8645±140 (I-5276)	H and G	grinding-tools, inconsistent	(MacNeish, this volume)
15. Jaywa Cave	F	8500±125 (I-5686)	H and G	seasonal, possible guinea pig domestication, *Lagenaria siceraria* first at this level	(MacNeish, this volume)
16. Jaywa Cave	D	8360±125 (I-4501)	H and G	seasonal, possible guinea pig domestication, *Lagenaria siceraria* first at this level	(MacNeish, this volume)
17. Jaywa Cave	C	8280±135 (I-4500)	H and G	seasonal, possible guinea pig domestication,	(MacNeish, this volume)

	Site	Level	Date		*Lagenaria siceraria* first at this level	Reference
18.	Cave near Lauricocha	2	8140±150 (unpublished)			(R. 11: 2, p. 374)
19.	Puente site	XIIA	8860±125 (I-5057)	IC and IA	Piki complex — domestic gourd, quinoa, possible cucurbits — *C. ficifolia* and *C. moschata*	(MacNeish, this volume)
20.	Aymachay Cave		7650±140 (I-5694)	H and G		(MacNeish, this volume)
21.	Puente site	X	7420±125 (I-5056)	IC	Piki complex — intensive collecting — domestic gourd, quinoa, possible cucurbits	(MacNeish, this volume)
22.	Pikimachay Cave	no level	7255±(?) (?)	IC		(MacNeish, this volume)
23.	Puente site	VIII	7160±125 (I-5024)	IC	Piki complex (see above)	(MacNeish, this volume)
24.	Jaywa Cave	F	7105±130 (I-5278)	H and G	inconsistent	(MacNeish, this volume)
25.	Puente site	IIA	6730±120 (I-5131)	IC	Piki complex	(MacNeish, this volume)
26.	Puente site	IIB	6715±120 (I-5129)	IC	Piki complex	(MacNeish, this volume)
27.	Puente site	VI	6670±120 (I-5132)	IC	Piki complex	(MacNeish, this volume)
28.	Puente site	IV	6560±120 (I-5128)	IC	Piki complex	(MacNeish, this volume)
29.	Puente site	Ij	6470±125 (I-5274)	IC	Piki complex	(MacNeish, this volume)
30.	Puente site	II	6360±110 (I-4502)	IC	Piki complex	(MacNeish, this volume)
31.	Puente site	Ih1	6036±120 (I-5273)	IC	Piki complex	(MacNeish, this volume)
32.	Unnamed cave		5470±110 (I-5685)	IA	domesticated corncobs	(MacNeish, this volume)
33.	Unnamed cave		5250±105 (I-5688)	IA	domesticated corncobs	(MacNeish, this volume)
34.	Pikimachay Cave		4640±(?) (?)	IA	llama-herding, possibly potatoes	(MacNeish, this volume)
35.	Puente site	Ic	4040±105 (I-5055)	IA		(MacNeish, this volume)
36.	Puente site	Ic	3995±105 (I-5131)	IA		(MacNeish, this volume)

II. *Coastal Peru*

	Site	Level	Date		Description	Reference
1.	Chilca Cañon	V. 2475	9700±200 (Gif-864)	IER	oldest coastal village	(R. 13: 1, p. 224)
2.	Tequepala Cave		9580±160 (Y-1325)	IER	preceramic II	(R. 11: 2, p. 636)
3.	Tequepala Cave		9490±140 (Y-1372)	IER	preceramic II	(R. 11: 2, p. 636)
4.	Playa Chilca		8765±160 (Hv-1090)	IER	shell heap	(R. 9: 1, p. 636)
5.	Tres Ventanas	V. 2554	8140±130 (I-3127)	IER		(R. 11: 1, p. 103)
6.	Puyenca		8075±145 (Hv-1084)	IER	outlying coastal midden	(R. 9: 1, p. 209)

Table 2 (continued)

Site	Level or period	Date and laboratory number	Subsistence	Comments	Reference
7. Tres Ventanas	V. 2563	8030±130 (I-3108)	IER	midden	(R. 11: 1, p. 103)
8. Puyenca		7855±150 (Hv-1086)	IER		(R. 9: 1, p. 209)
9. Ancón	1	7380±160 (Y-1325)	IC	preceramic IV Luz complex	(R. 11: 2, p. 634)
10. Lurín	stratum 20	7270±125 (GX-264)	IER	carbonized body wrapping	(R. 9: 1, p. 196)
11. Chilca	Village 20-V. 1126	6970±300 (I-1192)	IER	"lomas settlers"	(R. 12: 1, p. 125)
12. Pampa of Haldas		6650±110 (I-3467)	IER		(R. 11: 2, p. 634)
13. Ancón	2	6520±120 (Y-1304)	IC	preceramic IV Luz complex	(R. 11: 1, p. 377)
14. Cerro Pucuyana	V. 2415	6265±55 (GrN-5545)	IER	aceramic village	(R. 12: 1, p. 126)
15. Ancón	V. 25	6150±120 (I-3560)	IC		(R. 12: 1, p. 225)
16. Chilca Cañon	V. 2415	6080±150 (I-3108)	IER		(R. 8: 1, p. 156)
17. Paracas	site 514	5890±145 (GX-218)	IER	end of prebean period	(R. 9: 1, p. 194)
18. Chilca Village 1	V. 794	5650±190 (I-813)	IA	pottery fragments	(R. 9: 1, p. 194)
19. Chilca Village 1	V. 806	5650±220 (I-835)	IA	precotton and preceramic	(R. 9: 1, p. 195)
20. Chilca Village 1	V. 829	5410±275 (I-892)	IER	deepest level	(R. 9: 1, p. 194)
21. Chilca Village 1	V. 800	5250±220 (I-811)	IER	some pottery — disturbed	(R. 9: 1. p. 194)
22. Chilca Village 1	V. 795	5250±220 (I-817)	IER	inconsistent	(R. 9: 1, p. 194)
23. Chilca	V. 1059	5130±110 (GrN-5547)	IER	charred plant remains — preagricultural village — some beans	(R. 11: 1, p. 377)
24. Chilca Village 1	V. 793	5025±200 (I-815)	IER	pottery fragments	(R. 9: 1, p. 194)
25. Chilca Village 1	V. 777	4975±160 (I-814)	IER	middle period	(R. 9: 1, p. 195)
26. Chilca Village 1	V. 796	4950±220 (I-814)	IER	middle period	(R. 9: 1, p. 195)
27. Chilca Village 1	V. 778	4850±170 (I-746)	IER	inconsistent	(R. 9: 1, p. 194)
28. Chavín de Huántar	V. 1654	4735±140 (Gif-77)	IER	preceramic with cotton	(R. 13: 1, p. 226)
29. Ancón (Encanto campsite)		4720±80 (UCLA-967)	IA	preceramic — cotton	(R. 8: 1, p. 476)
30. Chilca Village 1	V. 799	4525±220 (I-818)	IER	some pottery	(R. 9: 1, p. 194)
31. Chilca Village 1	V. 799	4500±190 (I-816)	IER	final precotton	(R. 9: 1, p. 195)
32. Chilca	V. 2486	4220±65 (GrN-5520)	IER	preagricultural	(R. 11: 1, p. 377)
33. Ancón (Tank site)		4200±80 (UCLA-968)	IA	twined textiles, shell fishhooks	(R. 8: 1, p. 476)
34. Chavín de Huántar	V. 2336	4120±200 (Gif-770)	IA	preceramic with cotton	(R. 11: 1, p. 226)

35.	Chilca Village 1	V. 1131	3623±200 (I-1229)	VA	pottery with corn, "Chavinoid"	(R. 9:1, p. 195)
36.	Chilca Village 6	V. 1176	3235±175 (I-1290)	IA	cotton — preceramic	(R. 9:1, p. 196)
III.	*Environs*					
1.	Quiani (Chile)	(1)	6170±220 (I-1348)	IER	shell fishhooks	(R. 11:1, p. 102)
2.	Quiani (Chile)	(2)	5630±134 (I-1349)	IER	no more fishhooks	(R. 11:1, p. 102)
3.	Puerto Hormiga (Colombia)	110 centimeters	5040±70 (SI-153)	IA	crude, fiber-tempered pottery	(R. 11:1, p. 102)
4.	Puerto Hormiga (Colombia)	75 centimeters	4970±70 (SI-152)	IA	(pre-Valdivia)	(R. 11:1, p. 102)
5.	Puerto Hormiga (Colombia)	80 centimeters	4820±100 (SI-151)	IA	(pre-Valdivia)	(R. 11:1, p. 102)
IV.	*Chiapas and Acapulco regions*					
1.	Santa Marta	(early)	8730±400 (M-980)	H and G		(MacNeish 1972)
2.	Santa Marta	(late)	7320±300 (M-979)	H and G		(MacNeish 1972)
3.	Puerto Marquez	Level 38	4900±130 (H-1263)	IC	preceramic	(MacNeish 1972)
4.	Puerto Marquez	Level 33	4400±140 (H-1258)	IC	pox pottery	(MacNeish 1972)
5.	Puerto Marquez	Level 35	4200±135 (H-1264)	IC	preceramic	(MacNeish 1972)
6.	Cotorra		3280±200 (M-978)	VA	agriculture	(MacNeish 1972)
7.	Chiapa de Corzo	(Cotorra)	3010±150 (GrN-774)	VA	agriculture	(MacNeish 1972)
8.	Cuadros		2928±105 (Y-1150)	VA	agriculture	(MacNeish 1972)
9.	Cuadros		2878±105 (Y-1154)	VA	agriculture	(MacNeish 1972)
10.	Cuadros		2764±90 (Y-1166)	VA	agriculture	(MacNeish 1972)
11.	Cuadros		2715±105 (CY-1151)	VA	agriculture	(MacNeish 1972)
V.	*Central Mexico*					
1.	Cueva Blanca	Zone E	11000±400 (M-2094)	H and G	preceramic	(Flannery 1969)
2.	Cueva Blanca	Zone E	10910±80 (SI-511)	H and G	preceramic	(Flannery 1969)
3.	Cueva Blanca	Zone E	10730±220 (SI-511R)	H and G	preceramic	(Flannery 1969)
4.	Guila Naquitz	Zone D	10700±350 (M-2099)	H and G	preceramic	(Flannery 1969)
5.	Cueva Blanca	Zone E	10050±350 (M-2093)	H and G	preceramic	(Flannery 1969)
6.	Guila Naquitz	Zone D	9790±240 (GX-0783)	H and G	preceramic	(Flannery 1969)
7.	Ixtapan		9670±400 (M-776)	H and G	associated with a mammoth	(MacNeish 1972)

Table 2 (continued)

Site	Level or period	Date and laboratory number	Subsistence	Comments	Reference
8. Cueva Blanca	Zone D	9470 ± 190 (SI-512)	H and G	Coxcatlan phase possibly too early	(Flannery 1969)
9. Guila Naquitz	Zone C	9400 ± 300 (M-2097)	H and G	preceramic	(Flannery 1969)
10. Ixtapan		9250 ± 250 (M-776)	H and G	date on the mammoth	(MacNeish 1972)
11. Guila Naquitz	Zone C	9230 ± 120 (GX-0783)	H and G	preceramic	(Flannery 1969)
12. Guila Naquitz	Zone B2	8860 ± 180 (GX-0784)	H and G	preceramic	(Flannery 1969)
13. Guila Naquitz	Zone B2	8620 ± 160 (SI-515)	IC	oldest beans so far, wild cucurbits	(R. 12: 1, p. 197)
14. El Riego		8463 ± 186 (I-461, 769)	IA	El Riego phase, some beans cultivated	(MacNeish 1972)
15. El Riego		8425 ± 250 (I-764)	IA	El Riego phase, some beans cultivated	(MacNeish 1972)
16. El Riego		7990 ± 300 (I-758)	IA	El Riego phase, some beans cultivated	(MacNeish 1972)
17. El Riego		7990 ± 225 (I-759)	IA	El Riego phase, some beans cultivated	(MacNeish 1972)
18. El Riego		7800 ± 174 (I-658, 765)	IA	El Riego phase	(MacNeish 1972)
19. Coxcatlan		7700 ± 250 (I-458)	IA	oldest squash seeds	(R. 11: 1, p. 89)
20. El Riego		7575 ± 195 (I-574, 675)	IA	El Riego phase	(MacNeish 1972)
21. Guila Naquitz	Zone E	7495 ± 90 (GX-0872)	IC	possibly too young, preceramic	(Flannery 1972)
22. Coxcatlan		7000 ± 220 (I-457)	IC	Coxcatlan phase, earliest wild corn	(MacNeish 1972)
23. El Riego		6737 ± 134 (I-651, 668)	IA	El Riego phase	(MacNeish 1972)
24. Coxcatlan		6350 ± 230 (I-761)	IA	Coxcatlan phase	(MacNeish 1972)
25. Coxcatlan		6100 ± 200 (I-573)	IA	Coxcatlan phase	(MacNeish 1973)
26. Coxcatlan		6071 ± 96 (I-459)	IA	Coxcatlan phase	(MacNeish 1973)
27. Coxcatlan		5847 ± 197 (I-768, 754)	IA	Coxcatlan phase	(MacNeish 1973)
28. Abejas		5250 ± 250 (I-569)	IA	Abejas phase, a mammoth	(MacNeish 1973)
29. Cueva Blanca		5245 ± 105 (GX-0783)	IA	Coxcatlan phase	(Flannery 1969)
30. Abejas		5311 ± 112 (I-766, 594, 652)	IA	Abejas phase	(MacNeish 1972)
31. Abejas		5025 ± 180 (I-654)	IA	Abejas phase	(MacNeish 1972)
32. Abejas		4960 ± 140 (I-593, 653)	IA	Abejas phase	(MacNeish 1972)

33.	Cueva de la Zona	Layer 3	4950±160 (Tx-235)	IA	Coxcatlan phase	(MacNeish 1972)
34.	Cueva de la Zona	Layer 21–22	4840±220 (Tx-150)	IA	Coxcatlan phase	(MacNeish 1972)
35.	Cueva de la Zona	Layer 2	4755±110 (Tx-237)	IA	Coxcatlan phase	(MacNeish 1972)
36.	Cueva Blanca	Zone D	4750±190 (M-2092)	IA	Coxcatlan phase	(Flannery 1969)
37.	Cueva de la Zona	Layer 1	4700±120 (Tx-236)	IA	Coxcatlan phase	(MacNeish 1972)
38.	Abejas		4700±136 (I-755, 572)	IA	Abejas phase	(MacNeish 1972)
39.	Purron		3875±131 (I-757, 762)	IA	Purron phase	(MacNeish 1972)
40.	Purron		3481±91 (I-753, 670, 666, 570)	IA	Purron phase	(MacNeish 1972)
41.	San Jose Mogote	Zone E	3280±180 (M-2330)	IA	Tierras Largas phase	(Flannery 1969)
42.	Ajalpan	(early)	3220±13 (I-929)	VA	agriculture	(MacNeish 1972)
43.	Ajalpan	(early)	3168±108 (I-901, 895)	VA	agriculture	(MacNeish 1972)
44.	San Jose Mogote	Zone G	3120±150 (M-2331)	VA	Tierras Largas phase	(Flannery 1969)
45.	San Jose Mogote	Zone C3	3120±120 (SI-464)	VA	San Jose phase	(Flannery 1969)
46.	Ajalpan	(early)	3100±140 (I-934)	VA	Early Ajalpan phase	(MacNeish 1972)
47.	Tierras Largas		3030±150 (M-2353)	VA		(Flannery 1969)
48.	Tierras Largas		3020±150 (M-2352)	VA		(Flannery 1969)
49.	San Jose Mogote	Zone D1	3000±120 (SI-466)	VA		(Flannery 1969)
50.	Ajalpan	(late)	2975±200 (I-566)	VA		(MacNeish 1972)
51.	Tierras Largas		2960±150 (M-2351)	VA	Tierras Largas phase	(Flannery 1969)
52.	Iglesia	(Valley of Mexico)	2940±250 (M-661)	VA	Late Ajalpan	(MacNeish 1972)
53.	Ajalpan	(late)	2930±157 (I-924, 927, 752)	VA	Late Ajalpan	(MacNeish 1972)
54.	San Jose Mogote	Zone C4	2930±120 (SI-465)	VA	San Jose Phase	(Flannery 1969)
55.	San Jose Mogote	Zone D1	2925±85 (GX-0785)	VA	San Jose Phase	(Flannery 1969)
56.	Ajalpan	(late)	2922±92 (I-923, 935)	VA	Late Ajalpan	(MacNeish 1972)
57.	San Jose Mogote	Zone C3	2880±95 (GX-0875)	VA	San Jose phase	(Flannery 1969)
58.	Ajalpan	(late)	2850±190 (I-767)	VA	Late Ajalpan	(MacNeish 1972)
59.	San Jose Mogote		2840±150 (M-2345)	VA	San Jose phase	(Flannery 1969)
60.	San Jose Mogote		2810±120 (SI-467)	VA	San Jose phase	(Flannery 1969)
61.	Barrio del Rosario	Zone F-3	2800±150 (M-2102)	VA	Terminal San Jose	(Flannery 1969)
62.	Ajalpan	(late)	2753±89 (I-931, 915)	VA	Late Ajalpan	(MacNeish 1972)
63.	Cueva Blanca	Zone C	2745±90 (GX-0874)	VA	Formative	(Flannery 1969)
64.	San Jose Mogote	Zone C2	2730±150 (SI-463)	VA	San Jose phase	(Flannery 1969)
65.	San Jose Mogote	Zone D3	2670±200 (M-2104)	VA	San Jose phase	(Flannery 1969)
66.	Ajalpan	(late)	2658±71 (I-916, 914, 908)	VA	Late Ajalpan	(MacNeish 1972)
67.	San Jose Mogote	Zone C1	2640±120 (SI-462)	VA	San Jose phase	(Flannery 1969)
68.	San Jose Mogote	Zone E	2610±150 (M-2355)	VA	San Jose phase	(Flannery 1969)

Table 2 (continued)

Site		Level or period	Date and laboratory number	Subsistence	Comments	Reference
69.	Barrio del Rosario	Zone D	2600 ± 110 (GX-1316)	VA	Guadalupe phase	(Flannery 1969)
70.	Barrio del Rosario		2510 ± 110 (GX-1315)	VA	Guadalupe phase	(Flannery 1969)
71.	Barrio del Rosario		2420 ± 80 (GX-1314)	VA	Guadalupe phase	(Flannery 1969)
VI.	*Northeast Mexico, Guatemala, and the Gulf area*					
1.	Lerma		9270 ± 500 (M-499)	H and G		(MacNeish 1972)
2.	Infiernillo		8540 ± 450 (M-500)	H and G		(MacNeish 1972)
3.	Infiernillo		8200 ± 450 (M-498)	H and G		(MacNeish 1972)
4.	Ocampo		5230 ± 350 (M-502)	IC		(MacNeish 1972)
5.	La Perra		4445 ± 280 (C-687)	IC		(MacNeish 1972)
6.	Flacco		3945 ± 334 (C-954)	IC		(MacNeish 1972)
7.	San Lorenzo		3100 ± 140 (Y-1798)	VA		(MacNeish 1972)
8.	San Lorenzo		3090 ± 80 (Y-1801)	VA		(MacNeish 1972)
9.	San Lorenzo		3050 ± 100 (Y-1800)	VA		(MacNeish 1972)
10.	San Lorenzo		3010 ± 80 (Y-1797)	VA		(MacNeish 1972)
11.	San Lorenzo		2930 ± 80 (UCLA-1267B)	VA		(MacNeish 1972)
12.	San Lorenzo		2870 ± 140 (Y-1802)	VA		(MacNeish 1972)
VII.	*United States*					
1.	Laguna Salada		5230 ± 60 (?)	H and G	preagricultural camp	(Carr, this volume)
2.	Lo Daiska		4840 ± (?) (?)	IA	cucurbits	(Yarnell, this volume)
3.	Wet Legett		4506 ± 680 (?)	H and G	preagricultural camp	(Carr, this volume)
4.	Bat Cave	(New Mexico)	2862 ± (?) (?)	IA	maize	(Yarnell, this volume)
5.	Higgs	(Tennessee)	2730 ± 220 (CWRU-27)	IC	sunflower	(Yarnell, this volume)
6.	Salts Cave		2660 ± 140 (M-1770)	IC or IA	gourd, squash, collecting and storing of marsh elder and lamb's quarter; also sunflower	(Struever and Vickery 1973)
7.	Apple Creek		2660 ± 130 (M-1408)	IA	squash, gourd, and nuts	(Struever and Vickery 1973)
8.	Stilwell		2650 ± 300 (M-31)	IA		(Struever and Vickery 1973)
9.	Stilwell		2600 ± 300 (?)	IA		(Struever and Vickery 1973)
10.	Salts Cave		2570 ± 140 (M-1574)	IC or IA		(Struever and Vickery 1973)
11.	Green Point		2480 ± 140 (M-1423)	IA	squash	(Struever and Vickery 1973)

12. Leimbach	2470±310 (OWU-185)	IA	Early Woodland, cultivated maize and squash	(Struever and Vickery 1973)
13. Leimbach	2460±260 (OWU-250)	IA		(Struever and Vickery 1973)
14. Mammoth Cave	2240±200 (M-1573)	IC or IA	squash, probably Early Woodland	(Struever and Vickery 1973)
15. Salts Cave	2350±140 (M-1577)	IC or IA	squash, sunflower, marsh elder, and lamb's quarter	(Struever and Vickery 1973)
16. Bridgewater	2310±130 (M-1998)	IA	squash rind	(Struever and Vickery 1973)
17. Tularosa Cave	2300±200 (?)	IA	early maize	(Carr, this volume)
18. Salts Cave	2240±200 (M-1573)	IC or IA		(Struever and Vickery 1973)
19. Salts Cave	2240±200 (M-1577)	IC or IA		(Struever and Vickery 1973)
20. Daines 2	2230±40 (M-2049)	IA	tropical flint maize	(Struever and Vickery 1973)
21. Mammoth Cave	2230±40 (?)	IC or IA	probable squash	(Struever and Vickery 1973)
22. Peisker	2180±130 (M-1403)	IA	Middle Woodland, maize	(Struever and Vickery 1973)
23. McGraw	2180±80 (UCLA-865)	IA	maize	(Struever and Vickery 1973)
24. Jasper Newman	2000±140 (M-1789)	IA	corn cobs	(Struever and Vickery 1973)
25. Renner	1938±250 (M-572)	IA	probable maize	(Struever and Vickery 1973)
26. Leimbach	1935±240 (OWU-251)	IA	squash	(Struever and Vickery 1973)
27. Macoupin	1900±140 (M-2243)	IA	maize	(Struever and Vickery 1973)
28. Snyders	1890±75 (M-1154)	IA	chenopods	(Struever and Vickery 1973)
29. Peisker	1880±120 (M-1570)	IA	maize	(Struever and Vickery 1973)
30. Snyders	1850±120 (M-1487)	IA		(Struever and Vickery 1973)
31. Peisker	1850±105 (O-2269)	IA		(Struever and Vickery 1973)
32. Renner	1850±200 (M-571)	IA	probable maize	(Struever and Vickery 1973)
33. McGraw	1810±80 (UCLA-679A)	IA	maize	(Struever and Vickery 1973)
34. Peisker	1770±130 (M-1405)	IA	maize	(Struever and Vickery 1973)
35. McGraw	1740±80 (UCLA-679B)	IA	maize	(Struever and Vickery 1973)
36. Macoupin	1730±130 (M-2245)	IA	maize	(Struever and Vickery 1973)
37. Snyders	1720±75 (M-1155)	IA	chenopods	(Struever and Vickery 1973)
38. Peisker	1700±120 (M-1569)	IA	maize	(Struever and Vickery 1973)
39. McGraw	1670±80 (UCLA-705)	IA	maize	(Struever and Vickery 1973)
40. St. Iwell	1550±120 (M-1263)	IA		(Struever and Vickery 1973)
41. Renner	1520±200 (M-573)	IA		(Struever and Vickery 1973)
42. McGraw	1515±166 (OWU-62)	IA	maize	(Struever and Vickery 1973)
43. McGraw	1510±80 (UCLA-679C)	IA	maize	(Struever and Vickery 1973)
44. Cowan Creek	1509±250 (C-214)	IA	*Cucurbita pepo*	(Struever and Vickery 1973)
45. McGraw	1469±65 (OWU-61)	IA	maize	(Struever and Vickery 1973)

Table 2 (continued)

Site	Level or period	Date and laboratory number	Subsistence	Comments	Reference
46. Goslin		1430±250 (C-874)	IA	Middle Woodland, squash	(Struever and Vickery 1973)
47. Stilwell		1330±120 (M-1262)	IA		(Struever and Vickery 1973)
48. Apple Creek		1310±110 (M-2001)	IA	squash and gourd	(Struever and Vickery 1973)
49. Newbridge		1290±130 (M-2000)	IA	squash rind	(Struever and Vickery 1973)
50. Renner		1270±250 (M-454)	IA		(Struever and Vickery 1973)
51. Apple Creek		1200±130 (M-2001)	IA		(Struever and Vickery 1973)
52. Apple Creek		1160±120 (M-1407)	IA	squash and gourd	(Struever and Vickery 1973)
53. Bridgewater		1050±200 (M-2002)	possible VA	squash rind	(Struever and Vickery 1973)
54. Apple Creek		1030±120 (M-1997)	possible VA		(Struever and Vickery 1973)
55. Renner		470±75 (M-1107)	possible VA	maize	(Struever and Vickery 1973)

REFERENCES

Antiquity
 1973 Editor's introductory note to "Radiocarbon dates from China" by R. Pearson. *Antiquity* 47:141.

BORDAZ, JACQUES
 1973 Current research in the Neolithic of south-central Turkey: Suberde, Erbaba and their chronological implications. *American Journal of Archaeology* 77:282–288.

BRAIDWOOD, ROBERT
 1959 Über die Anwendung der Radiokarbon-Chronologie für das Verständnis der ersten Dorfkultur-Gemeinschaften in Südwestasien. *Oesterreichische Akademie der Wissenschaften (philosophische-historische Klasse)* 19:249–259.

EHRICH, ROBERT, *editor*
 1965 *Chronologies in Old World archaeology* (second edition). Chicago: University of Chicago Press.

FLANNERY, KENT, *editor*
 1969 *Preliminary archaeological investigations in the valley of Oaxaca, Mexico.* Report to the National Science Foundation and the Instituto Nacional de Antropología e Historia.

KANTOR, HELENE
 1965 "The relative chronology of Egypt and its foreign correlations before the late Bronze Age," in *Chronologies in Old World archaeology.* Edited by R. Ehrich, 1–31. Chicago: University of Chicago Press.

MAC NEISH, RICHARD
 1972 *The prehistory of the Tehuacán Valley*, volume four. Austin: University of Texas Press.

MARKS, ANTHONY, R. FERRING
 i.p. Upper Paleolithic occupation of the central Negev, Israel: an interim report. *Eretz Israel* 13.

MELDGAARD, JØRGEN, P. MØRTENSEN, H. THRANE
 1964 Excavations at Tepe Guran, Luristan: preliminary report of the Danish Archaeological Expedition to Iran, 1963. *Acta Archaeologica* 34:97–133.

MELLINK, MACHTELD
 1965 "Anatolian chronology," in *Chronologies in Old World archaeology.* Edited by R. Ehrich, 101–127. Chicago: University of Chicago Press.

PHILLIPS, J. L., K. W. BUTZER
 1975 A "Silsilian" occupation site (GS-2B-II) of the Kom Ombo Plain, Upper Egypt: geology, archeology and paleo-ecology. *Quaternaria* 17:343–386.

PROTSCH, R., R. BERGER
 1973 Earliest radiocarbon dates for domesticated animals. *Science* 179:235–239.

STRUEVER, STUART, K. VICKERY
 1973 The beginnings of cultivation in the midwest-riverine area of the United States. *American Anthropologist* 75:1197–1220.

WATSON, PATTY JO
  1965 "The chronology of north Syria and north Mesopotamia from 10,000 B.C. to 2000 B.C.," in *Chronologies in Old World archaeology*. Edited by R. Ehrich, 61–90. Chicago: University of Chicago Press.
WENDORF, FRED
  1968 "Late Paleolithic sites in Egyptian Nubia," in *Prehistory of Nubia*, volume two. Edited by F. Wendorf, 791–953. Dallas, Texas: Southern Methodist University Press.
WENDORF, FRED, R. SCHILD
  1975 "The Paleolithic of the lower Nile Valley," in *Problems in prehistory: North Africa and the Levant*. Edited by Fred Wendorf and Anthony E. Marks, 127–169. Dallas, Texas: Southern Methodist University Press.

| TEAU PE | MIXED WOODLAND | PLATEAU STEPPE DESERT | COL. HYP. MARGIN | SHIRAZ-KER BASINS | CIRCUM CASPIAN | | SOUTHEAST CHINA INDIA | YEARS B.P. |

IRANIAN PLATEAU

1) 13400 ± 200

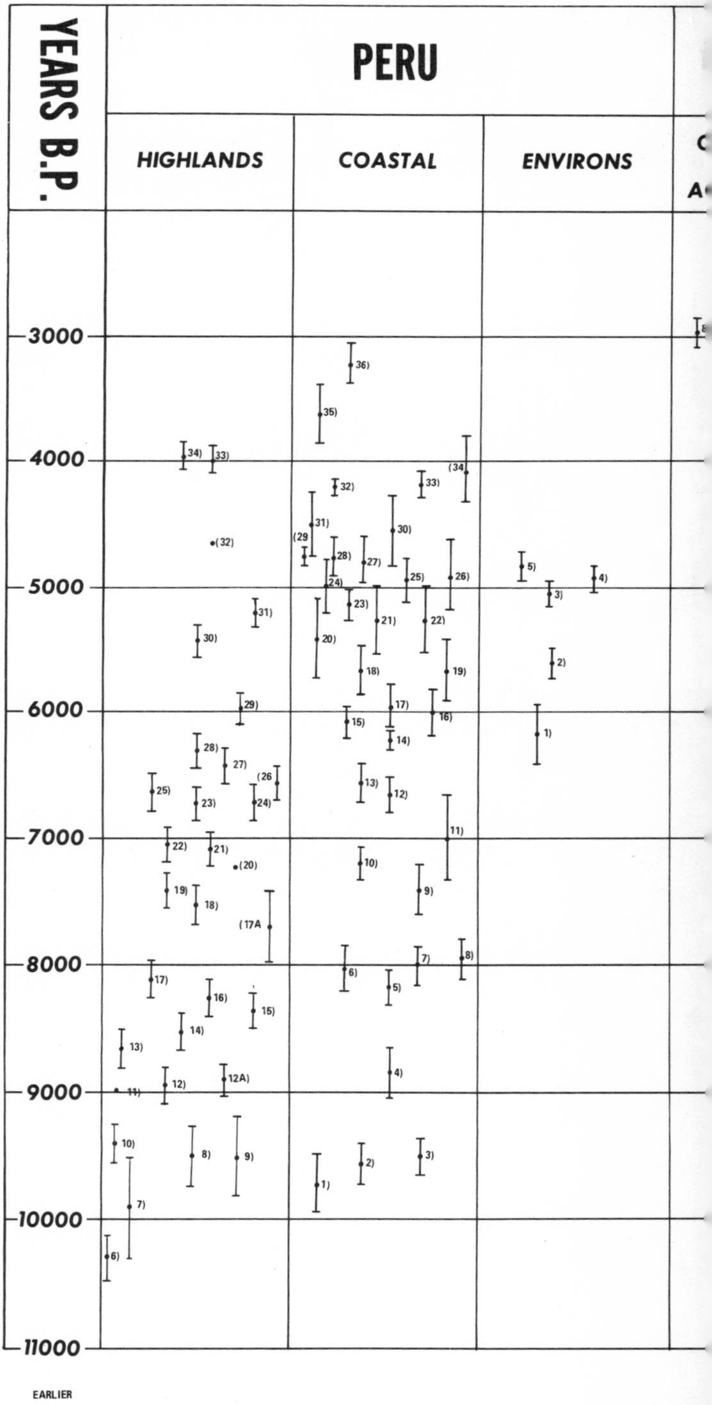

Chart 2. Western Hemisphere

EARLIER

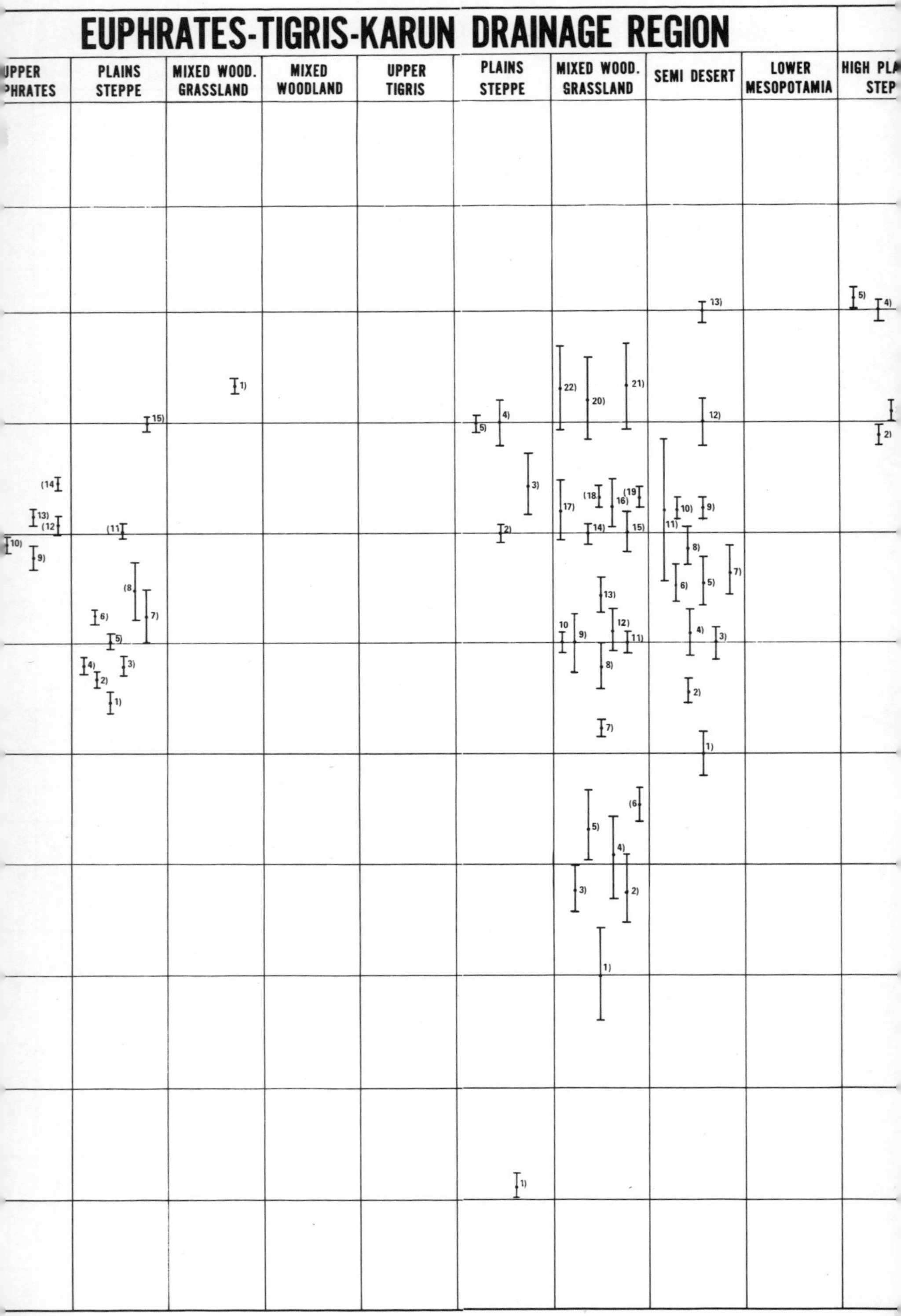

EUPHRATES-TIGRIS-KARUN DRAINAGE REGION

UPPER EUPHRATES	PLAINS STEPPE	MIXED WOOD. GRASSLAND	MIXED WOODLAND	UPPER TIGRIS	PLAINS STEPPE	MIXED WOOD. GRASSLAND	SEMI DESERT	LOWER MESOPOTAMIA	HIGH PLA STEP

Chart 1. Eastern Hemisphere

YEARS B.P.	GREECE CRETE BULGARIA	NORTH AFRICA EGYPT	EAST MEDITERRANEAN-ANATOLIA					
			MED. MAQUIS	MIXED WOOD GRASSLAND	PLAINS STEPPE	COM. MIST WOODLAND	HIGH PLATEAU STEPPE	E

1) 15310 ± 200

1) > 3700

2) 15820 ± 1370

* DATES WITH STARS ARE FROM ELSEWHERE IN THE U. S.
AND INCLUDED IN ARTICLES IN THIS VOLUME.

Biographical Notes

GEORGE W. BEADLE (1903) attended the University of Nebraska and Cornell University where his major studies were cytology, genetics, and biochemistry. His primary research interests have been centered on genes controlling meiosis in maize, genetics and development of eye-color in *Drosophila*, biochemical genetics of the bread-mold *Neurospora*, and the origin of maize. His research was accomplished at Cornell University, the California Institute of Technology, Harvard University, Stanford University, and the University of Chicago, while his botanical fieldwork, particularly *re* the origin of maize, has centered on Middle America. His publications include the following: *Genetical and cytological studies of Mendelian asynapsis in* Zea mays (1930, Cornell University Memoir 129); *A gene in maize for supernumerary cell divisions following meiosis* (1931, Cornell University Memoir 135); "Studies of *Euchlaena* and its hybrids with *Zea*, I: Chromosome behavior in *Euchlaena mexicana* and its hybrids with *Zea mays*; II: Crossing over between the chromosomes of *Euchlaena* and those of *Zea mays*" (1932, *Zeitschrift für Abstammungs- und Vererbungslehre* 62); "The differentiation of eye pigments in *Drosophila* as studied by transplantation" (with B. Ephrussi, 1936, *Genetics* 21); "The relation of inversions in the X-chromosome of *Drosophila melanogaster* to crossing-over and disjunction" (with A. H. Sturtevant, 1936, *Genetics* 21); "Teosinte and the origin of maize" (1939, *Journal of Heredity* 30); and "Genetic control of biochemical reactions in *Neurospora*" (with E. L. Tatum, 1941, *Proceedings of the National Academy of Sciences* 27). He is currently at the Department of Biology of the University of Chicago.

BENNET BRONSON (1938) was educated at Harvard University and the

University of Pennsylvania. His major fields of study are history and anthropology and his research interests are in early agriculture, ethnobotany, quantitative geography, economic archaeology, early urbanism, and the prehistory and early history of southeastern Asia. His archaeological fieldwork has been conducted in Guatemala, Thailand, Sri Lanka, and Indonesia. Among his publications are "Roots and the subsistence of the ancient Maya" (1966, *Southwestern Journal of Anthropology* 22); "A thermoluminescence series from Thailand" (with Mark Han, 1972, *Antiquity* 46); "Farm labor and agricultural evolution" (in *Population growth: anthropological implications*, edited by B. Spooner, 1972, Cambridge, Massachusetts: M.I.T. Press); and "Excavations at Chansen, Thailand, 1968 and 1969: a preliminary report" (1973, *Asian Perspectives* 15). He is currently at the Department of Anthropology, Field Museum of Natural History in Chicago.

JOSEPH RALSTON CALDWELL (1916–1973) was educated at the University of Chicago. His major field of study was anthropology with an emphasis on archaeology. His fieldwork was in prehistoric archaeology in Illinois, the southeastern part of the United States, and in Iraq and Iran. Some typical publications are *Trend and tradition in the prehistory of the eastern United States* (1958, Memoirs of the American Anthropological Association 88); "The new American archaeology" (1959, *Science* 129); "Eastern North America" (in *Courses toward urban life*, edited by Robert J. Braidwood and Gordon Willey, 1962, Viking Fund Publications in Anthropology 32); (editor) *New roads to yesterday: essays in archaeology* (1966, New York: Basic Books); (editor) *Investigations at Tal-i-Iblis* (with five chapters written by himself, 1967, Illinois State Museum Preliminary Reports 9); and "Pottery and cultural history on the Iranian Plateau" (1968, *Journal of Near Eastern Studies*).

Joe Caldwell, in addition to being a fine field archaeologist, was a humanist, a thinker and scholar, a gentleman, and my very good friend. His doctoral thesis, written early in the latter third of his life, was published as *Trend and tradition in the prehistory of the eastern United States*; it embodied concepts of changing cultural continuity which he had conceived while contemplating the origins of agriculture and civilization of two hemispheres. Although in need of revision now, almost twenty years after having been written, the monograph remains as an important factual and theoretical contribution to archaeology. His exploration of the site of Tal-i-Iblis, southeastern Iran, not only pushed back the history of the smelting of copper to earlier than 6000 B.P., but also illustrated the technological aspects of mining and smelting at this period of the history of metallurgy.

When he joined us in August 1973 for our conference, he came with a history of seven years of cardiac attacks which had left him thin and wasted. However, the resonant voice, the quiet humor, the smile, the genteel courtesy, the keen mind, and the ability to summarize clearly complex and diverse ideas were the same, and we all profited from his presence. When we parted in September 1973, I had the foreboding that I would not see my friend again; two days before Christmas that same year, he had his last massive cardiac attack. The world has his publications and his many friends have their memories of a man who was as near to being without flaw as any human can be. — CHARLES A. REED

CHRISTOPHER CARR (1952) was educated at the University of Illinois at Chicago Circle and the University of Michigan where his major area of study was anthropology. His research interests have been in North American prehistory and the development of electrical resistivity surveying methods for archaeology. He did archaeological fieldwork in Illinois for the Field Museum of Natural History, Illinois State Museum, Northwestern University, and the Foundation for Illinois Archaeology, and in Utah he did field research for the University of Utah. He is presently at the Department of Anthropology of the University of Michigan.

GEORGE F. CARTER (1912) was educated at the University of California in Berkeley. His major studies were geography and anthropology and his research interests have been primarily in the area of the antiquity of man in America, the origins of agriculture (particularly in the western hemisphere), and the evidence concerning pre-Columbian contacts with America by sea. Among his publications are *Plant geography and culture history in the American Southwest* (1945, Viking Fund Publications in Anthropology 5); "Plant evidence for early contacts with America" (1950, *Southwestern Journal of Anthropology* 6); *Plants across the Pacific* (1953, Memoirs of the Society of American Archaeology 9); *Pleistocene man at San Diego* (1957, Baltimore: Johns Hopkins University Press); "Archaeology in the Reno area in relation to the age of man and the culture sequence in America" (1958, *Proceedings of the American Philosophical Society* 102); "Movement of people and ideas across the Pacific" (in *Plants and the migrations of Pacific peoples: a symposium*, edited by Jacques Barrau, 1963, Honolulu: Bishop Museum Press); "Pre-Columbian chickens in America" (in *Man across the sea: problems of pre-Columbian contacts*, edited by C. L. Riley, J. C. Kelley, C. W. Pennington, and R. L. Rands, 1971, Austin: University of Texas Press); and "New evidence for the antiquity of man in America deducted from aspartic acid racemization" (with J. L. Bada and R. A. Schroeder, 1974, *Science* 184). He is currently at the Department of Geography, Texas A. and M. University.

MARK K. COHEN (1943) was educated at Harvard College and Columbia University where his major studies were in human ecology, paleoecology, and prehistory. His research interests have been concentrated on paleodemography and its relations to the origins of settled life and domestication in Africa and South America. His archaeological fieldwork has been conducted in both the eastern and western parts of the United States, at a Neolithic site in Greece, at Neolithic sites in the area of the East African Rift, and at several locations on the coasts of Peru and Chile. Among his publications are "A reassessment of the Stone Bowl Cultures of the Rift Valley, Kenya" (1970, *Azania* 5); "Two methods for estimating the Late Horizon population of the Rimac Province, Peru" (1974, *Journal of the Steward Anthropological Society* 5); "Some problems in the quantitative analysis of vegetable refuse illustrated by a Late Horizon site on the Peruvian coast" (1975, *Nawpa Pacha* 10/12); and "Archaeological evidence for population pressure in pre-agricultural societies" (1975, *American Antiquity* 40). He is presently at the Department of Anthropology, State University of New York at Plattsburg.

CHESTER F. GORMAN was educated at the University of Hawaii where his major field was anthropology with an emphasis on archaeology. His major interest is in the cultural evolution of Southeast Asia, particularly during the late Quaternary. His fieldwork has been conducted in Southeast Asia, primarily in Thailand. Some representative publications are "Archaeological salvage program; northeastern Thailand — first season" (with Wilhelm G. Solheim II, 1966, *Journal of the Siam Society* 54); "Excavations at Spirit Cave, north Thailand: some interim interpretations" (1970, *Asian Perspectives* 13); "Hoabinhian: a pebble-tool complex with early plant associations in Southeast Asia" (1970, *Proceedings of the Prehistoric Society* 35); and "The Hoabinhian and after: subsistence patterns in Southeast Asia during the late Pleistocene and early Recent periods" (1971, *World Archaeology* 2). He is currently with the South Asia Section of the University Museum, University of Pennsylvania.

JACK R. HARLAN (1917) attended George Washington University and the University of California at Berkeley. His major studies were botany and genetics and his major research interests have been in the genetics of grasses (experimental breeding and biosystematics), and in the origins, ecology, and distribution of cultivated plants. His fieldwork has been worldwide, much of it accomplished while collecting seeds of plants for the U. S. Department of Agriculture. His present research is focused on the origins of cultivated plants. Some pertinent publications, in addition to those cited in this volume, are "Anatomy of gene centers" (1951, *American Naturalist* 85); "Distribution and utilization of natural variability in cultivated plants" (1956, *Brookhaven Symposia in Biology* 9); *Theory and dynamics of grassland agriculture* (1956, Princeton, New Jersey: D. Van Nostrand); "Distribution of wild wheats and barley" (with Daniel Zohary, 1966, *Science* 153); "Barley: origin, botany, culture, winterhardiness, genetics, utilization, pests" (1968, *United States Department of Agriculture Handbook* 338); "Ethiopia: a center of diversity" (1969, *Economic Botany* 23); "The origin and domestication of *Sorghum bicolor*" (1971, *Economic Botany* 25); "Agricultural origins: centers and non-centers" (1971, *Science* 174); "Origin of maize: the tripartite hypothesis" (1972, *Euphytica* 21); "Comparative evolution of cereals" (with J. M. J. de Wet and E. G. Price, 1973, *Evolution* 27). He is currently at the Department of Agronomy of the University of Illinois.

DAVID R. HARRIS (1930) attended the University of Oxford and the University of California at Berkeley. His major fields of study were geography and ecology and his research interests have focused on human modification of terrestrial ecosystems in prehistoric and historic times, with particular reference to the tropics. He conducted his fieldwork primarily in the circum-Caribbean area and in northern South America, in the southwestern United States, in northern Africa and Greece, and in Papua, New Guinea, and the Cape York Peninsula, Australia. Some typical publications are *Plants, animals, and man in the outer Leeward Islands, West Indies: an ecological study of Antigua, Barbuda, and Anguilla* (1965, Berkeley and Los Angeles: University of California Press); "Recent plant invasions in the arid and semi-arid Southwest of the United States" (1966, *Annals of the Association of American Geographers* 56); "Ecosystems, agricultural systems and the origins of agriculture" (in *The domestication and exploitation of plants and animals*, edited by Peter J. Ucko and G. W. Dimbleby, 1969, London: Gerald Duckworth); "Swidden systems and settlement" (in *Man, settlement and urbanism*, edited by Peter J. Ucko, Ruth Tringham, and G. W. Dimbleby, 1972, London: Gerald Duckworth); "The origins of agriculture in the tropics" (1972, *American Scientist* 60); and "The prehistory of tropical agriculture: an ethnoecological model" (in *The explanation of culture change: models in prehistory*, edited by Colin Renfrew, 1973, London: Gerald Duckworth).

He is presently with the Department of Geography, University College, London.

FEKRI A. HASSAN (1943) was educated at the Faculty of Sciences, Ain Shams University, Cairo, and at Southern Methodist University in Dallas. His major studies were geology, anthropology, and chemistry and his research interests are North African and Near Eastern paleoanthropology, prehistoric demography, geoarchaeology, and the study of lithic artifacts with a special focus on the transition from hunting-gathering to food production in the Old World. His fieldwork in archaeology and Quaternary geology has been conducted in Egypt, Lebanon, Ethiopia, Algeria, and the United States. Among his recent publications are "On mechanisms of population growth during the Neolithic" (1973, *Current Anthropology* 14); "Population growth and cultural evolution" (1974, *Reviews in Anthropology* 1); "Mineralogical analysis of Sudanese Neolithic ceramics" (1974, *Archaeometry* 17); *The archaeology of Dishna Plain, Upper Egypt* (1974, Cairo: Papers of the Geological Survey of Egypt 59). He is presently at the Department of Anthropology of Washington State University.

CHARLES B. HEISER (1920) was educated at Washington University and the University of California. His research interests are in systematic and evolutionary botany and in the origin of domesticated plants. He has carried out fieldwork in Latin America, particularly in the Andes. In addition to scientific papers, he is the author of three books, *Nightshades: the paradoxical plants* (1969, San Francisco: Freeman); *Seed to civilization: the story of man's food* (1973, San Francisco: Freeman); and *The sunflower* (1976, Norman: University of Oklahoma Press). He is presently at the Department of Plant Sciences of Indiana University at Bloomington, Indiana.

WOLF HERRE (1909) was educated at the University of Halle-S. in Germany and the University of Graz in Austria. His major studies were zoology and paleontology and his research interests have been in vertebrate zoology, evolution, and experimental zoology (using domesticated animals as subjects). His fieldwork has been conducted in Lapland, Turkey, South America, Africa, the Soviet Union, Nepal, and Japan. Some typical publications are "Die Schwanzlurche der mitteleozänen Braunkohle des Geiseltales und die Phylogenie der Urodelen" (1935, *Zoologica* 87); *Das Ren als Haustier* (1955, Leipzig: Akademische Verlagsgesellschaft); *Die Haustiere von Haithabu* (1960, Neumünster: Wachholtz-Verlag);

"Über Ziele, Begriffe, Methoden und Aussagen der Haustierkunde" (1961, *Zeitschrift für Tierzüchtung und Züchtungsbiologie* 76); "The science and history of domestic animals" (in *Science in archaeology*, edited by D. R. Brothwell and E. Higgs, 1969, London: Thames and Hudson); "Domestikation und Stammesgeschichte" (in *Die Evolution der Organismen*, edited by Gerhard Heberer, 1971, Stuttgart: Gustav Fischer Verlag); and "Ergebnisse moderner zoologischer Domestikationsforschung" (with M. Röhrs, in *Domestikationsforschung und Geschichte der Haustiere*, edited by János Matolczi, 1973). He is presently at the Neue Universität in Kiel.

CHARLES F. W. HIGHAM (1939) was educated at St. Catharine's College, Cambridge University, and the Institute of Archaeology, London University. His major interest is prehistory, and his fieldwork began in northwestern Europe with an emphasis on the prehistory of animal husbandry but has since expanded to include research in Switzerland, Greece, Malta, Thailand, and Polynesia. He is presently concentrating, in cooperation with Pisit Charoenwongsa and Chester Gorman, on the archaeology of the Ban Chiang culture of southeastern Asia, with an emphasis on the assessment of hunting patterns and initiation of animal husbandry for the period 14,000 B.P.–1000 A.D. His publications include "Stock-rearing as a cultural factor in prehistoric Europe" (1968, *Proceedings of the Prehistoric Society* 33); "Trends in prehistoric European caprovine husbandry" (1969, *Man* 3); "Patterns of prehistoric economic exploitation in the Alpine foreland from the Neolithic to the end of the Bronze Age" (1969, *Vierteljahrsschrift der Naturforschenden Gesellschaft in Zürich* 113); "The assessment of a society's technique of bovine husbandry" (with M. A. Message, in *Science in archaeology*, edited by D. Brothwell and E. S. Higgs, 1969, London: Thames and Hudson); "The role of economic prehistory in interpreting the settlement of Oceania" (1970, *Studies of Oceanic culture history: Pacific Anthropological Records* 11); "The seasonal factor in prehistoric New Zealand" (1971, *World Archaeology* 2); and "Initial model formulation *in terra incognita*" (in *Models in archaeology*, edited by D. L. Clarke, 1973, London: Methuen). He is presently at the Department of Anthropology of the University of Otago, Dunedin, New Zealand.

PING-TI HO (1917) was educated at the National Tsing Hua University and Columbia University where his major field of study was and continues to be history with an emphasis on Chinese history. Among his publications are "The introduction of American food plants into China" (1955, *American Anthropologist* 57); *Studies on the population of China,*

1368–1953 (1959, Harvard East Asian Series 4); *The ladder of success in imperial China: aspects of social mobility, 1368–1911* (1962, New York: Columbia University Press); *History of Landsmannschaften in China* (in Chinese, 1966, Taipei: Hsüeh-sheng-shu-chü); "The loess and the origin of Chinese agriculture" (1969, *American Historical Review* 75); and *The cradle of the East: an inquiry into the indigenous origins of techniques and ideas of Neolithic and early historic China, 5000–1000* B.C. (1975, University of Chicago Press and the Chinese University of Hong Kong Press). He is presently at the Department of History of the University of Chicago.

ADINA R. KABAKER (1939) was educated at the University of Illinois at Urbana and University of Illinois at Chicago Circle. Her major studies were music, rhetoric, and anthropology and her research interests have been in the origins of agriculture and domestication, Near Eastern prehistory, tool typology, and poisons. She did her fieldwork in the Jordan Valley, Israel, with the Hebrew University. She is presently at the Department of Anthropology of the University of Illinois at Chicago Circle.

NANCY KRAYBILL (1932) was educated at the University of Illinois at Chicago Circle and the University of Kansas. Her major interests include the ecology of human nutrition in both contemporary and past populations and environmental stresses related to human nutrition and disease. Her research, done in metropolitan Chicago, was on the relationship of cultural practices surrounding the ingestion of milk and milk products with low levels of lactase-activity in people of Asian descent. She is currently at the Department of Anthropology of the University of Kansas.

DONALD W. LATHRAP (1927) was educated at the University of California at Berkeley and Harvard University. His major study was anthropology and his research interests have been in the emergence of civilization in nuclear America, in the study of tropical forest agricultural systems, and in primitive art. He did archaeological fieldwork in the western United States, Illinois, Peru, and Ecuador. Some typical publications are "Aboriginal occupation and changes in river channel on the Ucayali, Peru" (1968, *American Antiquity* 33); "The tropical forest and the cultural context of Chavín" (in *Dumbarton Oaks Conference on Chavín*, edited by E. P. Benson, 1971, Washington, D.C.: Dumbarton Oaks Research Library and Collection); *The Upper Amazon* (1970, London: Thames and Hudson); and "Gifts of the Cayman: some thoughts on the subsistence basis of Chavín" (in *Variation in anthropology*, edited by Donald W. Lathrap and J. Douglas, 1973, Urbana: Illinois Archaeological Survey). He is presently at the Department of Anthropology of the University of Illinois, Urbana.

RICHARD STOCKTON MACNEISH (1918) was educated at the University of Chicago where his major studies were paleontology and anthropology with an emphasis on archaeology. His research interests have been primarily in the western hemisphere: archaeology of North America and the highlands of Peru, and the origin of agriculture in Mexico and Peru, with fieldwork conducted in many parts of Canada, the U.S.A., Mexico, and Peru. Some typical publications are *Kincaid, a prehistoric Illinois metropolis* (with F. C. Cole, 1951, Chicago: University of Chicago Press); *Iroquois pottery types: a technique for the study of Iroquois prehistory* (1952, National Museum of Canada Bulletin 124); "An early archaeological site near Panuco, Vera Cruz" (1954, *Transactions of the American Philosophical Society* 44); "Preliminary archaeological investigations in the Sierra de Tamaulipas, Mexico" (1958, *Transactions of the American Philosophical Society* 48); *An introduction to the archaeology of southeastern Manitoba* (1958, National Museum of Canada Bulletin 157); and *Prehistory of the Tehuacán Valley* (editor, volumes 1–5, 1967–1974, Austin: University of Texas Press). He is presently at the R. S. Peabody Foundation for Archaeology, Andover, Massachusetts.

BARBARA PICKERSGILL (1940) was educated at the University of Reading, England, and Indiana University. Her major studies were botany, genetics, and archaeology and her research interests have been in the origins and evolution of cultivated plants, particularly in the tropics of the New World. Her fieldwork has been concentrated in the area of northern South America and adjacent areas. Some representative publications are "The archaeological record of chili peppers (*Capsicum* spp.) and the sequence of plant domestication in Peru" (1969, *American Antiquity* 34); "Cultivated plants and the Kon-Tiki theory" (with A. H. Bunting, 1969, *Nature* 222); "The domestication of chili peppers" (in *The domestication and exploitation of plants and animals,* edited by Peter J. Ucko and G. W. Dimbleby, 1969, London: Gerald Duckworth); "Relationships between weedy and cultivated forms in some species of chili peppers (genus *Capsicum*)" (1971, *Evolution* 25); and "Cultivated plants as evidence for cultural contacts" (1972, *American Antiquity* 37). She is presently at the Department of Agricultural Botany, Plant Science Laboratories of the University of Reading.

CHARLES L. REDMAN (1945) was educated at Harvard University and the University of Chicago. His major field is anthropology with an emphasis on archaeology and his research interests are in archaeological methods, origins of agriculture, beginnings of village life, and the development of urbanism. He has done fieldwork in New Mexico, Turkey, and Morocco. Among his publications are "Systematic, intensive surface collection" (1970, *American Antiquity* 35); *Explanation in archeology: an explicitly scientific approach* (with P. J. Watson and S. A. LeBlanc, 1971, New York: Columbia University Press); *Research and theory in current archeology* (1973, New York: John Wiley and Sons); *Multistage fieldwork and analytical techniques* (1973, An Addison-Wesley Module in Anthropology 55); and "Beginnings of village-farming communities in southeastern Turkey — 1972" (with R. J. Braidwood, H. Çambel, B. Lawrence, and R. B. Stewart, 1974, *Proceedings of the National Academy of Science, U.S.A.* 71). He is presently at the Department of Anthropology of the State University of New York, Binghamton.

CHARLES A. REED (1912) attended Whitman College, the University of Oregon, and the University of California, Berkeley, where his major studies were history and zoology. His research interests have been in comparative functional anatomy, mammalian paleontology, vertebrate zoology, and Near-Eastern prehistory. His fieldwork in vertebrate paleontology was conducted in the western United States; in archaeology in Oregon; and in zoology and prehistory in Iraq, Iran, Turkey, and Nubian Egypt. Some typical publications are "The achievement and early consequences of food production: a consideration of the archaeological and natural historical evidence (with R. J. Braidwood, 1957, *Cold Spring Harbor Symposia in Quantitative Biology* 22); "A review of the archaeological evidence on animal domestication in the prehistoric Near East" (1960, *Studies in Ancient Oriental Civilization* 31); "The mammalian genera *Arctoryctes* and *Cryptoryctes* from the Oligocene and Miocene of North America" (with W. D. Turnbull, 1965, *Fieldiana: Geology* 15); "The pattern of animal domestication in the prehistoric Near East" (in *The domestication and exploitation of plants and animals*, edited by Peter J. Ucko and G. W. Dimbleby, 1969, London: Gerald Duckworth); "The co-evolution of social behavior and cranial morphology in sheep and goats (Bovidae, Caprini)" (with W. M. Schaffer, 1972, *Fieldiana: Zoology* 71); and "The fauna from the terminal Pleistocene of Palegawra Cave, a Zarzian occupation site in northeastern Iraq" (with P. Turnbull, 1974, *Fieldiana: Anthropology* 63). He is presently at the Department of Anthropology of the University of Illinois at Chicago Circle.

MANFRED RÖHRS (1927) was educated at the University of Kiel where his major studies were zoology, botany, and microbiology. His research interests are vertebrate zoology, evolution, allometric growth, nervous systems, behavior, and animal domestication. He did fieldwork in Turkey, Scandinavia, Africa, and South America (including the Galapagos Islands). Among his publications are "Vergleichende Untersuchungen an Hirnen verschiedener Urodelen" (1955, *Zeitschrift für Wissenschaftliche Zoologie* 158); "Vergleichende Untersuchungen an Wild- und Hauskatzen" (1955, *Zoologischer Anzeiger* 155); "Allometrieforschung und biologische Formanalyse" (1961, *Zeitschrift für Morphologie und Anthropologie* 51); "Zur Frühentwicklung der Haustiere. Die Tierreste der neolithischen Siedlung Fikirtepe am kleinasiatischen Gestade des Bosporus" (with W. Herre, 1961, *Zeitschrift für Tierzüchtung und Züchtungsbiologie* 75); "Biologische Anschauungen über Begriff und Wesen der Domestikation" (1961, *Zeitschrift für Tierzüchtung und Züchtungsbiologie* 76); "Vergleichende Untersuchungen zur Evolution der Gehirne von Edentaten" (1966, *Zeitschrift für zoologische Systematik und Evolutionsforschung* 4); "Bemerkungen zur Bergmannschen Regel" (in *Evolution und Hominisation,* edited by G. Kurth, 1968, Stuttgart: Fischer); and *Haustiere – zoologisch gesehen* (1973, Stuttgart: Fischer). He is presently at the School of Veterinary Medicine in Hanover (BRD).

Vishnu-Mittre (1924) was educated at the University of Punjab, the University of Benares, the University of Lucknow, and Cambridge University. His major studies were paleobotany and palynology and his research interests have been in palynology, plant taxonomy, floral history and paleoclimates, environmental archaeology, origins of agriculture, and geomorphology. He conducted his fieldwork in several parts of India, and in Ceylon, Nepal, and the English Fenlands. Some typical publications are "Studies on the fossil flora of Nipania, Rajmahal Hills, Bihar" (1956–1959, *Palaeobotany* 2:75–84; 5:96–99; 6:31–46, 82–112; 7:47–66); "Some aspects of pollen analytical investigation in the Kashmir Valley" (1966, *Palaeobotany* 15); "Protohistoric records of agriculture in India" (1968, *Transactions of the Bose Research Institute* 31); *Evolution of life* (with M. S. Randhawa, Jagjit Singh, and A. K. Dey, 1969, New Delhi: Publication Directorate, CSIR); "Palaeobotany and environment of early man in India," (in *Archaeological Congress and Seminar Papers,* edited by S. B. Deo, 1972, Nagpur: Nagpur University Press); "Plant remains and climate from the late Harappan and other Chalcolithic cultures of India: a study in interrelationships" (1974, *Geophytology* 4); "The beginning of agriculture: palaeobotanical evidence from India" (in *Evolutionary studies in world crops. Diversity and change in the Indian subcontinent,* edited by Joseph Hutchinson, 1974, Cambridge University Press); "Environmental changes during the Quaternary" (in *Aspects and ap-*

praisal of Indian palaeobotany, edited by K. R. Surange, R. N. Lakhanpal, and D. C. Bharadwaj, 1974, Lucknow: Birbal Sahni Institute of Palaeobotany); and (editor) "Quaternary palynology and palaeobotany in India — an appraisement" (in *Late Quaternary vegetational developments in extra-European areas*, 1974, Lucknow: Birbal Sahni Institute of Palaeobotany). He is presently at the Birbal Sahni Institute of Palaeobotany, Lucknow.

PHILIP L. WAGNER (1921) attended the University of California at Berkeley where he studied geography and Slavic studies. He has done research in the cultural geography of Mexico and Central America and in the philosophical foundations of cultural geography, especially the relationships between comparatively advanced societies and their environments, as well as fieldwork in Mexico and Costa Rica. Some representative publications are "Nicoya; cultural geography of a Central American lowland community" (1958, *University of California Publications in Geography* 12); *The human uses of the earth* (1960, Glencoe, Illinois: The Free Press); *Readings in cultural geography* (edited with M. K. Mikesell, 1962, Chicago: University of Chicago Press); "Natural vegetation of Middle America" (in *Handbook of Middle American Indians. Volume I: The natural environment*, edited by Robert C. West, 1969, Austin: University of Texas Press); and *Environments and peoples* (1972, Englewood Cliffs, N.J.: Prentice-Hall). He is presently at the Department of Geography of Simon Fraser University, Burnaby, B.C., Canada.

ELIZABETH S. WING (1932) was educated at Mount Holyoke College and the University of Florida. Her major studies have been in zoology, botany, geology, and anthropology and her research interests are in the origin of the domestic animals of South America, in human adaptations to living on coasts, and in the study of human uses of animal resources (primarily in coastal and highland Peru and Ecuador and in the circum-Caribbean area). Some typical publications are "Vertebrates from the Jungerman and Goodman sites near the east coast of Florida" (1963, *Contributions to the Florida State Museum, Social Sciences* 10); "Vertebrate remains from Indian sites on Antigua, West Indies" (with C. E. Ray and C. A. Hoffman, Jr., 1962, *Caribbean Journal of Science* 8); "Utilization of animal resources in the Peruvian Andes" (1972, *University of Tokyo Andean Expedition, Andes Report* 4); and "Hunting and herding in the Peruvian Andes" (in *Archaeozoological studies*, edited by A. T. Clason, 1975, Amsterdam: North Holland). She is presently with the Florida State Museum, Gainesville.

HERBERT E. WRIGHT, JR. (1917) was educated at Harvard University where his major studies were geology and paleoecology. His research interests, in which he has done fieldwork in the specified areas, have been glacial and vegetational history of North America, the Peruvian highlands, and the Near East, and the geologic record of man's influence on the landscape. Among his publications are "Climate and prehistoric man in the eastern Mediterranean" (1960, *Studies in Ancient Oriental Civilization* 31); "Pleistocene glaciation in Kurdistan" (1961, *Eiszeitalter und Gegenwart* 12); "Preliminary pollen studies at Lake Zeribar, Zagros Mountains, southwestern Iran (with W. van Zeist, 1963, *Science* 140); "The natural environment of early food production north of Mesopotamia" (1968, *Science* 161); "The roles of pine and spruce in the forest history of Minnesota and adjacent areas" (1968, *Ecology* 49); "Late Quaternary vegetational history of North America" (in *Late Cenozoic glacial ages*, edited by K. K. Turekian, 1971, New Haven, Connecticut: Yale University Press); "Vegetation history" (in *The Minnesota Messinia Expedition: reconstructing a Bronze Age environment*, edited by W. J. McDonald and George Rapp, Jr., 1972, Minneapolis: University of Minnesota Press); and "The ecological role of fire in natural conifer forests of western and northern North America: introduction" (with M. L. Heinselman, 1974, *Quaternary Research* 3). He is currently with the Limnological Research Center at the University of Minnesota.

RICHARD A. YARNELL (1929) was educated at Duke University, the University of New Mexico, and the University of Michigan. His major studies were anthropology and botany and his research interests have concentrated on ethnobotany, domestication of plants, archaeology, cultural ecology, and identification and interpretation of archaeological botanical remains, primarily in relation to North American Indians. He has done fieldwork in various parts of the United States and in Quebec. Some representative publications are "Implications of distinctive flora in Pueblo ruins" (1965, *American Anthropologist* 67); "Paleoethnobotany in America" (in *Science in archaeology*, edited by Don Brothwell and Eric Higgs, 1969, London: Thames and Hudson); "*Iva annua* var. *macrocarpa*: extinct American cultigen?" (1972, *American Anthropologist* 74); and "Plant food and cultivation of the Salts Caverns" (in *Archaeology of the Mammoth Cave area*, edited by Patty Jo Watson, 1974, New York: Academic Press). He is presently at the Department of Anthropology of the University of North Carolina.

Index of Names

Index of Subjects

DATE DUE

~~NOV 1 2 1981~~		
SEP 2 8 1989		
OCT 9 1990		
DEC 9 1990		
DEC 1 8 1992		
DEC 1 7 1993		
DEC 1 2 1997		